American History through Literature
1870–1920

Editorial Board

American History through Literature
1870–1920

VOLUME **1** **ADDICTION** to **GHOST STORIES**

TOM QUIRK & GARY SCHARNHORST
Editors in Chief

CHARLES SCRIBNER'S SONS
An imprint of Thomson Gale, a part of The Thomson Corporation

THOMSON
™
GALE

Detroit • New York • San Francisco • San Diego • New Haven, Conn. • Waterville, Maine • London • Munich

American History through Literature, 1870–1920
Tom Quirk and Gary Scharnhorst, Editors in Chief

LIBRARY OF CONGRESS CATALOGING-IN-PUBLICATION DATA

American History through Literature, 1870–1920 / Tom Quirk and Gary Scharnhorst, editors-in-chief.
        p. cm.
    Includes bibliographical references and index.
    ISBN 0-684-31464-9 (set hardcover : alk. paper) — ISBN 0-684-31465-7
(v. 1 : alk. paper) — ISBN 0-684-31466-5 (v. 2 : alk. paper) — ISBN 0-684-31467-3
(v. 3 : alk. paper) — ISBN 0-684-31493-2 (e-book)
    1. American literature—19th century—Encyclopedias. 2. Literature and history—United States—History—19th century—Encyclopedias. 3. Literature and history—United States—History—20th century—Encyclopedias. 4. United States—History—19th century—Historiography—Encyclopedias. 5. United States—History—20th century—Historiography—Encyclopedias. 6. American literature—20th century—Encyclopedias. 7. History in literature—Encyclopedias. I. Quirk, Tom, 1946– II. Scharnhorst, Gary.

PS217.H57A843 2005
810.9'358'09034—dc22   2005023736

This title is also available as an e-book
ISBN 0-684-31493-2
And may be purchased with its companion set, *American History through Literature, 1820–1870*
ISBN 0-684-31468-1 (6-vol. print set)
Contact your Thomson Gale sales representative for ordering information

Printed in the United States of America
10 9 8 7 6 5 4 3 2 1

Contents

CONTENTS

Volume 3

T

U

V

W, Y

Acknowledgments

Acknowledgment is gratefully made to those publishers and individuals who have permitted the use of the following material in copyright. Every effort has been made to identify and secure permission to reprint copyrighted material.

Excerpts from Emily Dickinson, *The Poems of Emily Dickinson: Reading Edition*. Edited by Ralph W. Franklin. Cambridge, Mass.: The Belknap Press of Harvard University Press, 1999. Copyright © 1998, 1999 by the President and Fellows of Harvard College. Copyright © 1951, 1955, 1979, 1983 by the President and Fellows of Harvard College. All rights reserved. Reprinted by permission of the publishers and the Trustees of Amherst College. Excerpts from Hilda Doolittle, *Collected Poems of H.D., 1912–1944*. Boni and Liveright, 1925. Copyright © 1982 by The Estate of Hilda Doolittle. All rights reserved. Reprinted by permission of New Directions Publishing Corp. Reproduced in the British Commonwealth by permission of Carcanet Press Limited. Excerpts from T. S. Eliot, *The Complete Poems and Plays, 1909–1950*. Harcourt, Brace & World, 1952. Copyright © 1930, 1939, 1943, 1950 by T. S. Eliot. Copyright © 1934, 1935, 1936, 1952, by Harcourt, Brace and Company, Inc. Renewed 1980 by Esme Valerie Eliot. Reproduced by permission of Harcourt, Inc. In the British Commonwealth by permission of Faber and Faber Ltd. Sui Sin Far, unpublished letter to a publisher, 18 June 1896. Courtesy of the Autry National Center/Southwest Museum, Los Angeles, California. Reproduced by permission. Excerpts from Vachel Lindsay, "Bryan, Bryan, Bryan, Bryan," in *The Poetry of Vachel Lindsay: Complete & with Lindsay's Drawings*. Edited by Dennis Camp. Spoon River Poetry Press, 1984. Copyright © 1984 by Spoon River Poetry Press. Reproduced by permission. Edna St. Vincent Millay, "From Justice Denied in Massachusetts." Copyright © 1928 by Edna St. Vincent Millay. Renewed 1955 by Norma Millay Ellis. All rights reserved. Reproduced by permission of Elizabeth Barnett, Literary Executor of the Millay Society. Excerpts from *Island: Poetry and History of Chinese Immigrants on Angel Island, 1910–1940*. Hoc Doi, 1980. Reproduced by permission of the University of Washington Press.

Preface

The American poet Wallace Stevens once observed that a poem is the "cry of its occasion." The same might be said for all sorts of imaginative expression—novels, short stories, speeches, sermons, histories, plays, biographies and autobiographies; all are in some measure bulletins stemming from a deep-seated set of interests and convictions. The "cry" of such literary works is inevitably unique and inimitable, for it emanates from a single vantage point. Literary expression may be muted or gaudy, severe or antic, impassioned or ironic, but the "occasion" of the literary act, which is to say its context, is always in some measure historical. The purpose of these volumes is to present history and literature in tandem, to emphasize rather than to ignore the fact that, different as they may be, the two disciplines are natural allies. *American History through Literature, 1870–1920* is meant to address several kinds of readers at once— the high school or college student who wishes to acquire introductory information about a certain subject; library patrons who, out of desire to fill in some gap in their understanding, wish to peruse these volumes without premeditated purpose; the teacher of American literature, American history, or American studies who may consult these volumes in order to enrich his or her classes; the researcher who wishes to read an authoritative analysis or overview of a given subject and to be directed to other reliable sources of pertinent information on the subject; and finally, the so-called common reader, who, out of simple curiosity perhaps, wishes to learn more about the cultural ethos of America as it is reflected in history and literature. Each of these readers desires accurate, comprehensible, and readable essays on a great variety of subjects. We trust that this work answers those needs.

The study of literature and the study of history have always been mutually complementary endeavors, each discipline casting (to adapt a phrase of Herman Melville's) interesting "cross-lights" one upon the other. The fiction writer Edward Eggleston was one of the first presidents of the American Historical Association, after all, and the novelist and memoirist Henry Adams taught in the history department at Harvard. Literary works can make large and sometimes impersonal historical, political, and social forces vivid and palpable. History can make the small and otherwise incidental dramas of individual lives representative and comprehensible. Is such a novel as Upton Sinclair's *The Jungle* a literary text or a historical document? Or is an autobiographical account such as Booker T. Washington's *Up from Slavery* or Ulysses S. Grant's

Memoirs to be read only for "the story," what it tells us about an individual life, or for the broad sweeps of history it silhouettes? In all of these cases the literary significance of the works cannot be unraveled from their historical importance; they may consist of different weaves, but they form the same fabric. History is a movement, of course. Many in the latter half of the nineteenth century and the opening years of the twentieth were disposed to see that movement as "progressive," whether it was or not; others, local colorists and regionalist writers, for example, recorded the incursions of the modern upon the customs and language of the home place. History is a temporal movement, but it is also a texture, the crosshatched result of imaginative affirmations, displacements, counter-statements, resistances, even weary concessions to events. Other reference works offer an ample and authoritative charting of historical movements, but *American History through Literature, 1870–1920* is distinctive both in its emphasis upon the productive relations between historical and literary study and in its desire to render the texture of life as it was lived in this country during a half-century of turbulent and often bewildering change.

In order to convey the richness and diversity of American life during this period, the editors have cast a wide net. Over two hundred highly qualified literary scholars and historians have contributed to this effort. These volumes contain 247 essays (ranging in length from 1,500 to 6,000 words), many accompanied by sidebar items, each including a bibliography and cross-references to related topics. The articles are supplemented by over 200 illustrations, including some tables and maps. Broadly speaking, the articles are of several kinds:

Works. This category comprises analyses of individual titles, both literary and non-literary, that are revealing of the age. Where possible, each essay on a work describes the compositional history and reception of the work. Where appropriate, the essay also connects the text to the event or circumstances that may have motivated it, as for example the Wilmington, North Carolina, race riots of 1898 and Charles W. Chesnutt's 1901 novel *The Marrow of Tradition.* If the work's publication produced, perhaps accidentally, responses or social by-products, as with Sinclair's *The Jungle,* for example, those elements are part of the essay as well. The selection of individual titles is certainly a debatable issue, but our choices were not altogether arbitrary. We wished to give a comprehensive, not an exhaustive, sense of the era and the diverse artistic sensibilities that flourished, if only for a time, in the midst of eruptive and often perplexing cultural changes. Individual readers may be surprised that there is no entry on, say, Henry James's *The Bostonians;* others may be just as startled to find essays on Sidney Lanier's "The Marshes of Glynn" and Paul Laurence Dunbar's *Lyrics of Lowly Life.* There is no satisfactory answer to this imagined complaint. It is not enough to say that Lanier was reckoned among the finest poets of his day and that he rendered a finely cadenced view of the vanquished southerner, or to say that the African American Dunbar gave public readings of his vernacular poems that had as much to do with race relations as they did with poetic innovation. Nevertheless, both statements are true. More to the point, individual works were selected not only on the basis of artistic merit but also on their ability to contribute to the tissue of cross-connections these volumes seek to establish. Harold Frederic's *The Damnation of Theron Ware* may or may not be as fine a work as Mark Twain's *The Adventures of Tom Sawyer;* certainly it is less familiar. But Frederic's novel sheds intelligent light upon anti-Catholic feeling existing at the time and upon many other things as well, in ways that Twain's novel does not even attempt. We are pleased that Louis J. Budd of Duke University, the foremost Twain scholar for the past two generations and a former editor of *American Literature,* has contributed the entry on *Adventures of Huckleberry Finn.*

Ideas. Many essays describe the circulation and effects of certain ideas, such as anarchism or Darwinism, for example, and summarize the salient features of those ideas and the responses, both favorable and unfavorable, that they engendered. As with most of the essays, there are typically included some literary examples that both vivify and clarify how those ideas inspired or influenced imaginative literary treatment. The literary works cited may affirm those ideas (as in, say, Hamlin Garland's endorsement of Henry George's "single tax" economic theories in "Under the Lion's Paw") or contest them (as in Charlotte Perkins Gilman's treatment of S. Weir Mitchell's "rest-cure" for neurasthenic women in "The Yellow Wall-Paper"). We are delighted that the leading Gilman scholar in the world, Denise D. Knight, has contributed the entry on Gilman's story.

Genre or Genres. Essays that treat a genre (e.g., satire, burlesque, and parody; humor) usually enumerate the distinctive features of the genre, identify, where appropriate, the literary antecedents for the form, and describe the popularity of the genre. The social or cultural factors that prompted the creation and/or popularity of the genre are also described. Some of these genres, literary impressionism, for example, owe allegiances to the visual arts, particularly painting; others, such as photography and motion pictures, were the beneficiaries of developments in science and technology. The essays on realism and naturalism are particularly significant because they address and define the most comprehensive and important literary movements of the era. We are particularly pleased that Donald Pizer of Tulane University, the foremost scholar on American literary naturalism, has contributed the entry on this topic.

Aesthetics. Essays that deal with aesthetic movements or subjects (e.g., the arts and crafts movement or imagism) identify the principal characteristics of the subject; name persons, events, or titles that contributed to its formation or direction; and state the social or philosophic impulses that motivated it. In some instances it is as important to explain what the movement was reacting against (e.g., an anti-modernist or anti-industrial character) as to enumerate the artistic or social objectives of the aesthetic movement itself, and our contributors have succinctly addressed these dimensions with clarity and breadth.

Institutions or Events. Essays dealing with certain institutions (e.g., publishing or education) or particular events (the 1876 Centennial) trace, insofar as it is possible, the genesis and evolution of the subject matter and its social or political objectives or consequences (e.g., preparing students for citizenship or celebrating a national event). Often the contributor at least touches upon circumstantial elements that shaped the institution or the historical or symbolic significance of an event in the popular mind. Andrew Carnegie's endowment of public libraries, for example, is one sort of event; the Indian massacre at Wounded Knee in 1890 is quite another. Essays on these and other institutions and events tell us much about the national ethos.

Places. Essays dealing with particular places (e.g., New Orleans, Chicago, or New York) or whole regions (the New South) emphasize the literary life of the locale in terms that are both practical (e.g., as the site of major publishing houses) and cultural (e.g., as congenial to certain literary "schools" or groups). These essays are catholic in approach, identifying, for example, foreign-language newspapers and magazines, establishment of ethnic neighborhoods, significance of museums and libraries, or other cultural institutions or movements.

Society, Values, Culture, and/or Ethnicity. Essays that fall into one of these categories emphasize cultural, social, and perhaps political and legal elements, but they also may attempt to briefly define the atmospheric effects or the cultural ethos that a given subject (lynching, for example, or immigration) reflects or perhaps helps to engender. As with nearly all the entries in these volumes, there is typically some analysis of literary effects—how, for instance, the prevailing idea of success is dramatized in, say, an Edith Wharton or William Dean Howells or Horatio Alger novel, or how questions of acculturation are imaginatively rendered in Sui Sin Far or Abraham Cahan. We are pleased that Sanford E. Marovitz of Kent State University, one of the leading scholars in the field of Jewish American literature, has contributed the entry on

Cahan's *The Rise of David Levinsky,* and that Kenneth W. Warren of the University of Chicago, the leading scholar in the field of American realism and race, has contributed the entry on "race novels."

Publishing. Essays dealing with publishing include certain important journals or periodicals, publishers, editors, journalists, and so on. Depending on the particular subject, these essays identify the circulation or influence of the publishing institution, the effects individuals or periodicals had on shaping opinion or taste, the intended audience or readership, and the means of production and promotion. Special aspects or concerns of magazines or editors may also be emphasized. The *Century Magazine* ran an extended series on Civil War battles and leaders; for good or ill, *McClure's* was known for its muckraking journalism.

We wish to acknowledge the help and encouragement of all those involved in this project: Stephen Wasserstein, whose brainchild this project is; Alja Collar, who daily and dutifully, but always with good judgment and good cheer, kept the effort going; our editorial board (William L. Andrews, Louis J. Budd, Lawrence J. Buell, Susan K. Harris, Denise D. Knight, and William J. Scheick), who provided guidance and help all along the way; and the editors of the companion volumes, *American History through Literature, 1820–1870,* Janet Gabler-Hover and Robert Sattelmeyer, with whom we conferred often. Tom Quirk wishes to acknowledge the genial influence of his children: the older ones, without knowing it, reminded him to think historically; the younger one reminded him to think alphabetically. Gary Scharnhorst wishes to acknowledge his children, too: the older one reminded him to be pragmatic; the younger one reminded him to dream.

Tom Quirk
Gary Scharnhorst

ADDICTION

Addiction (chemical dependency) is caused by three substances: alcohol, narcotics, and tobacco (nicotine). In the period from 1870 to 1920, alcohol had a far greater impact on literary creativity than did narcotics or tobacco. The understanding of the nature of addiction—particularly addiction to alcohol—changed significantly from the Civil War period to the passage of the Eighteenth Amendment (Prohibition) to the Constitution in 1919. Throughout most of the nineteenth century, habitual drunkenness, for example, was judged, especially by temperance societies (which actually advocated abstinence or teetotalism) and by many Protestant clergy, to be a choice and a vice. The emerging opinion of many in the medical establishment and among liberal reformers, however, was that addiction to mood-altering substances was a treatable disease.

ALCOHOL

The three principal reform movements of the nineteenth century were abolition, woman suffrage, and temperance. The first reform was achieved by the Civil War, the latter two through constitutional amendments. These movements were linked by activists who were, in many instances, deeply involved in all three causes.

Whereas the moralists' uncompromising condemnation of habitual drunkenness largely prevailed in the popular literature of the nineteenth century, by the 1870s the medical (disease) model of the affliction began to gain a sympathetic audience. That alcoholism (a usage dating from 1849) was a treatable illness had a certain appeal not only for the medical establishment

but also for public officials because the attempts to cure the inebriate by simply eliminating the availability of liquor were not working. In spite of efforts by temperance advocates to ban or even physically destroy the saloon (e.g., Carry Nation's "hatchetation"), the statistics of alcohol consumption from 1870 to 1919 remained relatively stable, between 1.72 and 2.60 U.S. gallons of absolute alcohol a year per capita of the drinking-age population (the high for America was 7.10 gallons in 1830; the low, 0.90 in 1920, the first year of Prohibition) (Rorabaugh, p. 232; Lender and Martin, pp. 205–206). Because a large part of the population (especially women) did not drink, however, the consumption of spirits by those who did was heavy indeed.

The belief in the nineteenth century that alcoholism could be cured or at least treated and arrested achieved practical application primarily through two methods: self-help groups and the inebriate asylum. Self-help organizations such as the Washingtonian Temperance Society, started in Baltimore in 1840, were followed by similar societies leading ultimately to the founding of Alcoholics Anonymous in 1935. Most of these groups consisted of meetings of drunkards who had taken a pledge to stop drinking. They supported their sobriety by confessing to each other stories about their drunken behavior. The asylum movement aimed to establish treatment centers that would replace the more expensive hospitals and insane asylums. The first such center was the New York State Inebriate Asylum in Binghamton, an institution that existed from 1864 to 1879. The self-help groups were more successful in helping alcoholics maintain sobriety than

The philosopher and psychologist William James (1842–1910) explored the subject of addiction in depth. In The Principles of Psychology (1890) he dealt with the pathological aspects of addiction, and in The Varieties of Religious Experience (1902) he treated the spiritual and mystical effects of the use of alcohol and drugs. The following is from Varieties.

The sway of alcohol over mankind is unquestionably due to its power to stimulate the mystical faculties of human nature, usually crushed to earth by the cold facts and dry criticisms of the sober hour. Sobriety diminishes, discriminates, and says no; drunkenness expands, unites, and says yes. It is in fact the great exciter of the *Yes* function in man. It brings its votary from the chill periphery of things to the radiant core. It makes him for the moment one with truth. . . . The drunken consciousness is one bit of the mystic consciousness, and our total opinion of it must find its place in our opinion of that larger whole.

William James, *The Varieties of Religious Experience*, in *Writings 1902–1910* (New York: Library of America, 1987), pp. 348–349.

were the asylums, but in the nineteenth century neither lasted much past the original enthusiasm of their founders.

That African Americans had the strength to war against alcoholism and slavery at the same time is a testament to human endurance. A popular African American temperance pledge of the time was "Being mercifully redeemed from human slavery, we do pledge ourselves never to be brought into the slavery of the bottle" (Warner, p. 257). Frederick Douglass seemed at moments to be as concerned about the one as the other. Perhaps the most significant temperance novel of the period by an African American is *Sowing and Reaping: A Temperance Story* (1876–1877) by Frances E. W. Harper. Harper, like Douglass, devoted much of her long life to the abolition first of slavery and then of alcohol.

"Stories," says Edmund O'Reilly, in his analysis of recovery narratives, "may be the best means we have for comprehending alcoholism, since only stories can begin to contain alcoholism's bewildering, intractable, contradictory, protean nature" (Reynolds and Rosenthal,

p. 180). This conclusion is supported by the fact that almost all the major—and many of the minor—American writers from Edgar Allan Poe to Jack London recognized the narrative power of drinking behavior and included the theme of alcohol abuse in their work. Drinking was the subject matter in poems and plays as well as in stories, but with the notable exceptions of Walt Whitman and Emily Dickinson, the quality seldom rises above doggerel or preaching.

Regional literature, particularly humorous tales, is another matter. The yarns and satires of the Old Southwest and the West, for instance, document the reality that boozing and fighting were simply facts of life. But the drunk—like the prostitute—was almost always a stereotype, there to make a joke, not to make the case for sobriety or chastity. Mark Twain is an exception. Twain in fact took temperance—by which he meant moderation—very seriously, but in his stories drunkenness, not drinking, is the problem. Another exception is Owen Wister, whose *The Virginian: A Horseman of the Plains* (1902) depicts what was to become the classic western saloon scene: whiskey, cards, and guns. In a celebrated passage the Virginian, after Trampas the villain said, "Your bet, you son-of-a—," responded: "When you call me that, *smile*" (p. 23).

The theme of alcoholism as an often intractable problem that cannot be cured by willpower alone finds its most complex expression in the works of Harriet Beecher Stowe, William Dean Howells, Stephen Crane, and London. The long, rich career of Stowe (1811–1896) is a case in point. Nicholas O. Warner, in his analysis of drinking in Stowe's fiction, traces her characterization of drunkenness as a moral failing and a sin in her early work to her finally arriving at the conviction in the later work that uncontrolled drinking is a disease leading to the tragedy of alcoholism. By the time Stowe wrote about the alcoholic Bolton in *My Wife and I* (1871) and in *We and Our Neighbors* (1873), however, she had developed a character, sensitive if flawed, who is a victim of a compulsion beyond his will. Bolton desperately attempts to control his drinking but discovers that because of his nature this is impossible: fate displaces weakness, a situation his wife understands and accepts.

If Stowe's depiction of the alcoholic Bolton leans toward the sentimental, this cannot be said of Howells (1837–1920), that master of realism who chronicled through his voluminous writings the complexities of middle-class life. As John W. Crowley points out, from Hicks in *The Lady of the Aroostook* (1879), Bartley Hubbard in *A Modern Instance* (1882), and Berthold Lindau in *A Hazard of New Fortunes* (1890) to Alan Lynde in *The Landlord at Lion's Head*

(1897), alcoholism is (variously) characterized as moral decay or a disease of the will. The vulnerable individual is driven to drink by the vicissitudes and disorders of modern life. Howells takes a hard look at drunken behavior, but for all that he delineates his characters' failings with more nuance and understanding than Stowe. In the final analysis both authors combine the moral model of addiction with the medical model. They both knew that each model by itself would result merely in stock figures: the unredeemable, the wretch, the clown, the hopeless victim—in short, in types of little literary or moral seriousness.

Stowe's and Howells's worlds are those of the middle and upper-middle class: immoderate drinking and drunkenness were not to be displayed in public, embarrassment was privatized, and tragedy was familial. This was not the world of Crane, London, and Wister, a world in which the tavern and the saloon displayed public drinking at its worst and best. The saloon of the time could be the friendly tavern seen in Crane's (1871–1900) *George's Mother* ("a little glass-fronted saloon that blinked jovially at the crowds" [p. 216]), and then again it was described as an elegant or even a palatial establishment. Theodore Dreiser (1871–1945), in *Sister Carrie* (1900), describes Hurstwood's "resort," Fitzgerald and Moy's, as "a gorgeous saloon . . . ornamented with a blaze of incandescent lights, held in handsome chandeliers. . . . The long bar was a blaze of lights, polished wood-work and cut glassware, and many fancy bottles. It was a truly swell saloon" (p. 41). This was preeminently a man's world, the conviviality unconcealed.

Crane's grim view of drinking is illustrated in *Maggie, A Girl of the Streets: A Story of New York* (1893) and in *George's Mother* (1896). In *Maggie* he tells the story of the corruption of a naive woman by Pete, a bartender who presides over a saloon and who in the end becomes its best customer, arriving "at that stage of drunkenness where affection is felt for the universe" (p. 73). Crane's most powerful study of drinking, however, is *George's Mother* (1896). Crane's father, the Reverend Jonathan Townley Crane, author of *The Arts of Intoxication* (1870), and his mother were both well-known temperance workers, and Crane makes good use of this background in his novella. A famous print of the time, *The Drunkard's Progress* (1846), describes the nine steps of the downfall of the alcoholic from "a glass with a friend" through "a confirmed drunkard" to the last step, "death by suicide" (Monteiro, pp. 48–49). As George Monteiro argues, the nine stages roughly correspond to the rise and fall of George Kelcey, the alcoholic son in *George's Mother*. The stark realism of the destructive bickering between an evangelical mother and her aimless, boozing

John Barleycorn. Illustration by H. T. Dunn for Jack London's *John Barleycorn:* "I had the craving at last—and it was mastering me." SHAPIRO UNDERGRADUATE LIBRARY, UNIVERSITY OF MICHIGAN

son here is as painful to observe as is the witnessing of a pathologist's dissection. In his chilling story *George's Mother,* Crane creates a world where life seems scarcely worth living.

John Barleycorn (1913), London's (1876–1916) "alcoholic reminiscences," is in the tradition of addiction memoirs beginning with Thomas De Quincey's *Confessions of an English Opium Eater* (1822). London's memoir is perhaps the most powerful and the most important literary work about addiction published in this period. It is also a curious narrative that is almost perfectly ambivalent. London attempts to explain his temptation to drink and at the same time to warn his readers against the persuasions of John Barleycorn. Furthermore, he states that he supports both Prohibition and woman suffrage, the latter because women are far more likely to vote for the Prohibition Amendment than are men and must therefore be enfranchised. These declarations, though a minor part of the book, had much to do with making it a best-seller, as reformers sent copies of it to their huge membership.

The odd characteristic of *John Barleycorn* is that throughout his memoir London claims that he is not an alcoholic, yet his descriptions of his drinking, from his getting drunk at the age of five to his conclusion that "I survived . . . because I did not have the chemistry of a dipsomaniac" (p. 1107) reveal what clinicians would define as chronic physical alcohol dependence and denial of that dependence. London believed that he drank because he craved male companionship even though he detested the taste of liquor and did not especially care for the way it made him feel. Yet because he craved friendship he drank and drank—and drank. And he did so because his alter egos John Barleycorn and the White Logic compelled him. The former is the "friend" that leads him to drink in spite of himself, the latter the "philosopher" that rationalizes temptation. What distinguishes London's account from temperance novels and makes it such a powerful, sustained confession is his modern psychological insight and social awareness.

It is this modernity that signaled the fundamental change in the medical, the literary, and finally the public perception of the nature of alcoholic addiction. This change—that the substance was not so much the problem as was the abuse of it—eroded the moral power of the temperance movement: no longer could the inebriate be portrayed simply as weak and contemptible. In short, from Stowe to London's *John Barleycorn* the sympathetic ministrations of the psychologist began gradually to displace the puritanical thunder of Jeremiah.

NARCOTICS

Narcotics—opiates (opium, morphine, heroin, codeine, laudanum), cannabis (hemp, hashish, marijuana), and cocaine—were in widespread use in nineteenth-century America. Indeed, opium in one form or another was popular among all classes in Western society at least from the seventeenth century. David Musto, in his study of narcotics in America, points out that a rapid rise in the importation of raw opium and its derivative morphine began in the 1870s. Opiates were widely prescribed by physicians and were also included in many patent medicines. "The unregulated patent medicine craze in the United States hit its peak in the late nineteenth-century—a time when the opiate content of these medicines was probably also at its highest" (Musto, p. 3). A glance at the Sears Roebuck catalog for 1897 explains in part why. It offered laudanum, among other nostrums ("Directions on each bottle for old and young") at $3 for a dozen four-ounce bottles ("our goods go into every city, town and hamlet in every state").

There is some dispute regarding the extent of drug addiction in America at the turn of the century, but it appears that it peaked in 1900 at about 250,000 addicts. The Chinese were often blamed for the problem, yet it was in fact found among all groups—not least among women. Crane begins his "Opium's Varied Dreams," an 1896 article he published in the *New York Sun*, "Opium smoking in this country is believed to be more particularly a pastime of the Chinese, but in truth the greater number of the smokers are white men and white women," and he claimed that there were "25,000 opium-smokers in the city of New York alone" (p. 853). The increasingly widespread use of narcotics led to a series of reforms, beginning with the Pure Food and Drug Act of 1906 and the Harrison Act of 1914. The latter was designed not to prohibit the sale of drugs but to control them—a major difference from the attacks on alcohol—since opiates in particular had legitimate medical uses.

A word is needed about absinthe, a blend of 72 percent alcohol and herbals, including wormwood. Called La Fée Verte or the Green Fairy by nineteenth-century French artists, absinthe allegedly caused hallucinations, convulsions, and "brain-rot" (absinthism), though London, for one, was not impressed. "The trouble with [absinthe]," he writes in *John Barleycorn*, "was that I had to take such inordinate quantities in order to feel the slightest effect" (p. 1083). The drink gained a mythical status among the avant-garde: as with opium earlier, absinthe was thought to enhance the artistic imagination, and French artists and poets in particular consumed large quantities of it. Absinthe's perceived dangers, however, led to its banning in America in 1912 and in France in 1915. Though it frequently appeared in works of the European fin de siècle, it had little literary influence in America.

The drug that appears most prominently in the literature of this time is morphine, in large part because of its consumption by middle- and upper-class respectable women as an analgesic and as a treatment for neurasthenia, a popular affliction characterized by neurotic symptoms of fatigue and ennui. Just as the sensitive, world-weary male had his alcoholism, so the female had her morphinism, though the latter addiction was much easier to conceal than the former.

Although the use of drugs in America by the general population was at the time widespread, it had not yet significantly entered the literary or artistic imagination. London mentions his "adventures" in "Hasheesh Land" in *John Barleycorn* (p. 1092), but as with absinthe, narcotics for him were not part of the White Logic. The tales of Oscar Wilde, Robert Louis Stevenson, Sir Arthur Conan Doyle, and Sax Rohmer

The Old Absinthe House, New Orleans, Louisiana, c. 1915. This saloon became famous in the nineteeth century for its absinthe cocktails, which were made in large marble fountains. GETTY IMAGES

involving opium and cocaine were widely read, but not until Nelson Algren's *The Man with the Golden Arm* (1949) and William S. Burroughs's *Naked Lunch* (1959) do narcotics become a major subject for serious American writers.

TOBACCO

Drouet, in *Sister Carrie,* enjoyed dining at Rector's, where, amid a profusion of lights and in the company of actors and professional people, he had a splendid meal followed by liquor and a cigar. The experience would not have been complete without the cigar, and one is reminded that smoking has more than nicotine to recommend it. Nicotine, a stimulant like cocaine, is the addictive substance in tobacco, but the act of smoking is also habituating. This psychological-aesthetic experience, when integrated with the chemical substance, forms a powerful double hold on the user.

The population of the United States doubled between 1880 and 1910, and tobacco availability in all forms grew accordingly. Snuff and especially chewing tobacco were popular, and the spittoon (more elegantly, the cuspidor) was a fixture in most public buildings. Pipes, often beautifully designed, were marketed along with an array of tools for cigar smokers. Added to these attractions was the fact that tobacco products were remarkably cheap (cigarettes, for example, sold in 1876 for ninety-six cents per one thousand). The almost universal use of tobacco drew the critical attention of two powerful reformers, the Women's Christian Temperance Union (calling it "demon weed") and Theodore Roosevelt's trustbusters. The net result was that broken up, the tobacco companies became increasingly competitive largely by vastly expanding their advertising—as a child Jack London collected cigarette-card advertisements—and consumption accelerated.

Also, tobacco was thought to be a necessity. No less an authority than General John J. Pershing, the American commander in World War I, demanded tobacco for his troops, arguing that cigarettes were more necessary for them than food.

One notable genre where literature and tobacco merged was the verse anthology. These collections, filled with praise of the "divine weed," characterized the pipe in particular as a valued—and sometimes the only—friend. A representative volume is Joseph Knight's compilation *Pipe and Pouch: The Smoker's Own Book of Poetry* (1894), which went through many printings, including a leather-bound edition with its own pouch. The poems are the kind that would appeal more to J. Alfred Prufrock than to Prince Hamlet: sentimental, comforting, at times therapeutic. A verse letter by James Russell Lowell is included, thanking Charles Eliot Norton for a box of cigars ("Tobacco, sacred herb . . . Baffles old Time . . . And makes him turn his hour-glass slowly" [p. 34]). Ella Wheeler Wilcox, whose first published work was a volume of temperance poems, contributed:

> I like cigars
> Beneath the stars,
> Upon the waters blue.
> To laugh and float
> While rocks the boat
> Upon the waves,—Don't you?
>
> *(P. 121)*

In addition, the imagist poet Amy Lowell made a practice of smoking cigars in public.

Tobacco, then, as an addiction, a habit, and a pleasure was accepted by many—by men and increasingly by women—as a fact of life. Its health problems were by no means unknown, but such concerns at this time were defeated by the glamour and seduction that were beginning to come into play in advertising, popular songs, and film.

CONCLUSION

In the initial year of Prohibition, two novels were published that signified that social change was on the way: Sinclair Lewis's *Main Street* (1920) and F. Scott Fitzgerald's *This Side of Paradise* (1920). The revolt against the village and the rejection of social proprieties were modernist departures from the literary tradition that drew to a close as the First World War began. Both authors were enormously popular and much admired—and alcoholic. How relevant alcoholism was to their art is problematic, but an aspect of their celebrity was the defiance of decorum by their publicly drunken behavior that fifty years earlier would have doomed their careers as later it did their lives.

Chemical dependency or altered states of consciousness, those morally neutral terms that replaced the old, prescriptive labels for addiction, were becoming existential conditions for which a cure was not necessarily desired and of which the altered state was the reality consciously sought. It is profoundly ironic that at that moment when modernism announced the new sensibility, Prohibition went into effect.

See also Health and Medicine; Reform; Temperance

BIBLIOGRAPHY

Primary Works

Crane, Stephen. *Prose and Poetry*. New York: Library of America, 1984.

Crowley, John W., ed. *Drunkard's Progress: Narratives of Addiction, Despair, and Recovery*. Baltimore: Johns Hopkins University Press, 1999.

Dreiser, Theodore. *Sister Carrie; Jennie Gerhardt; Twelve Men*. New York: Library of America, 1987.

Knight, Joseph, ed. *Pipe and Pouch: The Smoker's Own Book of Poetry*. Boston: H. M. Caldwell, 1894.

London, Jack. *Novels and Social Writings*. New York: Library of America, 1982.

Wister, Owen. *The Virginian: A Horseman of the Plains*. 1902. Edited by Philip Durham. Boston: Houghton Mifflin, 1968.

Secondary Works

Conrad, Barnaby, III. *Absinthe: History in a Bottle*. San Francisco: Chronicle Books, 1988.

Courtwright, David T. *Dark Paradise: Opiate Addiction in America before 1940*. Cambridge, Mass.: Harvard University Press, 1982.

Crowley, John W. *The White Logic: Alcoholism and Gender in Modernist Fiction*. Amherst: University of Massachusetts Press, 1994.

Crowley, John W., and William L. White. *Drunkard's Refuge: The Lessons of the New York State Inebriate Asylum*. Amherst: University of Massachusetts Press, 2004.

Gilman, Sander L., and Zhou Xun, eds. *Smoke: A Global History of Smoking*. London: Reaktion, 2004.

Klein, Richard. *Cigarettes Are Sublime*. Durham, N.C.: Duke University Press, 1993.

Kluger, Richard. *Ashes to Ashes: America's Hundred-Year Cigarette War, the Public Health, and the Unabashed Triumph of Philip Morris*. New York: Knopf, 1996.

Lender, Mark Edward, and James Kirby Martin. *Drinking in America: A History*. Rev. and expanded ed. New York: Free Press, 1987.

McCrady, Barbara S., and Elizabeth E. Epstein, eds. *Addictions: A Comprehensive Guidebook*. New York: Oxford University Press, 1999.

Monteiro, George. *Stephen Crane's Blue Badge of Courage.* Baton Rouge: Louisiana State University Press, 2000.

Musto, David F. *The American Disease: Origins of Narcotic Control.* Expanded ed. New York: Oxford University Press, 1987.

O'Reilly, Edmund B. *Sobering Tales: Narratives of Alcoholism and Recovery.* Amherst: University of Massachusetts Press, 1997.

Reynolds, David S., and Debra J. Rosenthal, eds. *The Serpent in the Cup: Temperance in American Literature.* Amherst: University of Massachusetts Press, 1997.

Rorabaugh, W. J. *The Alcoholic Republic: An American Tradition.* New York: Oxford University Press, 1979.

Roth, Marty. *Drunk the Night Before: An Anatomy of Intoxication.* Minneapolis: University of Minnesota Press, 2005.

Vaillant, George E. *The Natural History of Alcoholism.* Cambridge, Mass.: Harvard University Press, 1983.

Warner, Nicholas O. *Spirits in America: Intoxication in Nineteenth-Century American Literature.* Norman: University of Oklahoma Press, 1997.

Roger Forseth

ADOLESCENCE

Although the term "adolescence" has existed for centuries to describe (in various and contradictory ways) a period of life between childhood and adulthood, the modern conception of adolescence—as a time of increasing freedom, rebellion, stress, change, confrontation, experimentation, and tempestuous emotions—began (at least for the middle class) in America shortly after the Civil War. In fact some historians have suggested that adolescence is essentially an American phenomenon, linked most clearly to the still-developing (and perhaps fundamentally adolescent) nation. Certainly economic and social changes in postbellum America led many in the reunited nation to think of themselves as struggling against conventions of the past and their own conflicting desires, as members of an adolescent country long out of the childhood of the new Republic, jaded by recent experiences and uncertain about the future.

After 1865 many young people began moving out of primarily agrarian family situations, where they worked alongside their parents and remained at home until they married and started their own families, and into school, where they began to associate for the first time with large numbers of their age group. Also, changing notions of success in America placed value on different qualities from those that were prized in the early part of the century. A relatively clear sense of entitlement or place in society was rapidly being replaced by an ethos of individual achievement, which was seen as being advanced through personal restraint and denial of impulse. Consequently adolescents who challenged the authority of their parents, teachers, or employers were seen as difficult and perhaps dangerous.

Perhaps more important, adolescents after the mid-nineteenth century had less of a role as productive (i.e., income generating) citizens. No longer working on the family farm and being replaced by waves of adult immigrants in manufacturing jobs, America's youth were becoming increasingly marginalized. Not surprisingly, as adolescents were needed less to fuel the economy, they were seen as more of a threat to society, a threat that must be managed. One response was social institutions, like the Boy Scouts and public high schools, which functioned to keep young people occupied and out of trouble. The result, however, of this benevolent isolation, at least for middle-class adolescents who did not need to contribute financially to their families, was that they became an increasingly alienated (and often idle) subgroup of society.

WORKING CLASS, IMMIGRANT, AFRICAN AMERICAN, AND NATIVE AMERICAN ADOLESCENTS

In many ways adolescence can be seen as a distinctly middle-class phenomenon, as the luxuries of extended schooling and relatively benign conflicts with authority were not routinely available to children of the working poor. Young people from the working and immigrant classes had little economic choice but to follow their parents into usually underpaid and dehumanizing factory jobs, which often put them at odds with the values and practices of their traditional families. These working children expected more freedom and demanded more respect than their traditional, authoritarian parents were willing to give them. The children of former slaves had to grow up with little practical support from their parents, who were struggling themselves to survive their new freedom, and Native American children were forced by economic and political necessity to assimilate into white, Christian culture.

For the working poor and immigrant families, where young adults were expected to work to help support the family, conflicts arose as previously more sheltered adolescents were exposed to behaviors and values in conflict with those of their families. For example, many young women at the turn of the century who consistently violated the standards of their homes—arguing with their parents, staying out late,

7

engaging in sexual activity—were reported to police and even committed to reformatories. In New York State in particular, an 1896 law resulted in "wayward girls" (most often accused of sexual indiscretions) being sent to correctional institutions like the New York State Reformatory for Women at Bedford Hills. The standard sentence was three years, and the results of such reformations were decidedly mixed, although the message to young women was quite clear—be good or be imprisoned.

Children of former slaves found that education and economics were often at odds, as families struggled to educate their children and still secure the necessary income from their work. The difficulties the Freedmen's Bureau (established in 1865) had with indentured child laborers is a case in point. The law provided that children could be indentured until the age of twenty-one if parents agreed, died, or could not support them. However, many white landowners took advantage of these desperate families and indentured even very young children (making them de facto slaves until their majority) without their parents' permission. When parents challenged the indentures, the courts wavered between supporting the often destitute parents and the often abusive white landowners.

As African American parents tried to secure the freedoms guaranteed by the Thirteenth and Fourteenth Amendments, faced lynching and other violence, and tried to make a living through factory work, domestic service, or sharecropping, their children began their education. One historian reports that while only a small number of blacks were literate at the end of the Civil War, the majority of all African Americans could read and write by the turn of the twentieth century. Booker T. Washington (1865–1915) recounts these all-too-common difficulties and his particular determination to overcome them in *Up from Slavery* (1901). Although he was born a slave, Washington worked to educate himself, attended Hampton Institute in Virginia, and in 1881 founded Tuskegee Institute, where students learned both academic and vocational skills. Other schools, such as the one for girls founded by Nannie Helen Burroughs in the District of Columbia in 1909, soon followed.

Native American children and adolescents struggled with survival after they were forcibly removed from their ancestral lands and struggled also with the loss of their identity as they were routed into Bureau of Indian Affairs schools. The first Indian school, and perhaps the best known and most representative, was the Carlisle Indian Industrial School (1879–1918), which was established in Carlisle, Pennsylvania, by the former U.S. Calvary officer Richard Henry Pratt to facilitate the assimilation of native children and train them for life as U.S. citizens. Pratt had been in charge of Cheyenne, Kiowa, Comanche, and Caddo warriors who had been relocated to a Florida prison camp, and he asked those men to send their children to his new school, which they eventually agreed to do.

Once at school, the process of assimilation began with cutting the students' hair, which frequently resulted in much unhappiness. Students wore uniforms (the boys) or Victorian dresses (the girls); all children wore shoes (not moccasins) and were forbidden to speak their native languages. As was the case at Tuskegee, students were trained in academic and vocational subjects, but they also studied art and music as well. In the thirty-nine years of its existence, more than ten thousand students were enrolled at Carlisle. Many found the process of being taken from their homes and immersed in white culture painful and confusing. For example, in *American Indian Stories* (1921), Zitkala-Ša (Gertrude Simmons Bonnin), later a teacher at Carlisle, poignantly and eloquently describes her experiences at an Indian school in Illinois. Zitkala-Ša tells of her homesickness and confusion with the unfamiliar language and customs, the cutting of her hair (which in her mind designated her as a coward), the beatings, and finally, her eventual alienation from her own culture. For these adolescents, taken from their homes and forced to adopt completely new and contradictory ways, adolescence was a particularly difficult and painful process of separation and loss.

INFLUENCE OF G. STANLEY HALL

G. Stanley Hall's *Adolescence: Its Psychology, and Its Relations to Physiology, Anthropology, Sociology, Sex, Crime, Religion, and Education* (1904) is justly credited with creating the twentieth century's image of the adolescent. This massive two-volume work (1,373 pages) used Darwinian and Lamarckian evolutionary theories to call attention to the importance of the adolescent period in the development of the human species. According to Hall, in adolescence ontogeny recapitulates phylogeny, with the history of the development of the species playing itself out in the development of the individual. Hall defined adolescence as a period of rebirth analogous to the development of the nation from a "primitive" beginning through a period of upheaval to a "civilized" adult nation. By influencing adolescent development, he said, civilization could be advanced.

In practice what this meant was that adolescence came to be treated as a period of psychological and intellectual stasis during which the individual prepares for adult life. Therefore more emphasis was placed on

Students in workshop at Tuskegee Institute, 1902. In order to address problems of unequal access to education, Booker T. Washington founded his school for black students in 1881. Courses included vocational training as well as academic studies. THE LIBRARY OF CONGRESS

physical and less on intellectual development, particularly the rote learning of childhood. In terms of moral development, parents and educators used this period to gently guide (and not force) adolescents to make moral choices, recognizing the growing complexity of the adolescent moral sense. (This approach has much in common with John Dewey's Progressivist, constructivist ideas about public education.)

Although much of the science behind Hall's theories of adolescent development has since been discredited, vestiges of his attention to adolescence remain. The contemporary sense of adolescence as an important stage of transition from the protected (and relatively simple) world of childhood to the responsibilities of adulthood has its origins in Hall's theories. Also, the concern about the relationship of youth culture

to the culture as a whole can be seen as an important part of Hall's legacy.

LITERARY REPRESENTATIONS OF ADOLESCENCE

The bildungsroman, or novel of adolescent moral education, has existed at least since Goethe's *Wilhelm Meister's Apprenticeship* (1796). American writers in the late nineteenth century and early twentieth century explored the genre as well, discussing not only education and acculturation but also social, psychological, and sexual development and the adventures and dangers of growing up. Written primarily for adults, although certainly read by adolescents, some works of this period treating white (usually male and middle-class) adolescence include Edward Eggleston's

The Hoosier Schoolmaster (1871), E. W. Howe's *The Story of a Country Town* (1883), Mark Twain's *The Adventures of Tom Sawyer* (1876) and *Adventures of Huckleberry Finn* (1885), Henry James's *Daisy Miller* (1879) and *What Maisie Knew* (1897), and Edith Wharton's *Summer* (1917).

Twain (1835–1910) sets the standard for the coming-of-age book in America. The artistry of his novel *The Adventures of Tom Sawyer* rises far above most other "bad boy" novels of the period. However, it too asserts, as do most novels of this sort, that middle-class white boys, while they may briefly behave in savage and sometimes even dangerous ways, will eventually (as Hall predicted) mature into productive and staid members of the community. Twain's short pieces on good and bad boys and girls, such as "The Christmas Fireside," "Advice for Good Little Girls / Boys," and "The Story of the Good Little Boy Who Did Not Prosper," continue this tradition of showing that youthful high jinks are a necessary part of childhood and may in fact be a prerequisite for later success.

Adventures of Huckleberry Finn offers an even more complex view of adolescence. In a story that has become familiar to most American schoolchildren, the novel takes Huck from being the abused son of a drunkard to a runaway to a free spirit who is willing to risk his soul and his freedom to help his friend Jim, a slave, escape captivity. Although the novel has been faulted for its racism, its sexism, and its problematic ending, as a provocative and entertaining story of male adolescent development it has had few rivals. Although the novel does provide a hero who may be more readily accepted and appreciated by young men than young women, *Huckleberry Finn* offers a model of adolescent self-determination that has influenced all subsequent adolescent fiction and probably many young adult lives.

James's (1843–1916) and Wharton's (1862–1937) novels focus on the awakening—both sexual and social—of female adolescents. Wharton's *Summer* features Charity Royall, a young woman who, after being "rescued" by a prominent local lawyer from a life of poverty and deprivation, dreams away her time working in a local library. Roused from her lethargy by Lucius Harney, Charity starts a romance with him and becomes pregnant. After Harney rejects her to marry someone of his social and intellectual class, Charity runs away from her lawyer guardian to try to find her parents. Eventually Charity decides to marry her guardian, who agrees to care for her and the baby. A story of sexual awakening and emotional development, *Summer* shows the consequences of one particular kind of adolescent rebellion and provides a morality tale for young women: stay within the bounds of approved sexuality or you may find yourself forced into a marriage of convenience.

Younger than Charity, Maisie in James's *What Maisie Knew* is the pawn in the struggle between her careless and selfish divorced parents. In this novel Maisie's parents trade her between them, threatening to withhold (or sometimes to send) her at inconvenient times. The parents both remarry (the father to Maisie's beloved governess), and the much younger stepparents dote on Maisie. Maisie's biological father and mother fight with each other, argue with their new spouses, and seek other lovers during their second marriages, while Maisie tries to figure out what in the world is going on. Eventually the two stepparents fall in love with each other, and Maisie, who thinks she has brought them together, is initially thrilled, because her surrogate parents are much nicer than her biological ones.

At the end of the novel, though, Maisie realizes that her stepparents (who have not yet divorced her natural parents) have put her in a troubling moral position, and she decides to reject them all and take up life with her new governess, a long-suffering widow. The child Maisie thus proves herself to be ultimately more insightful and moral than the adult characters, even if she is not always as quick as they are to notice the subtleties of relationships. James's position on the life of the developing adolescent appears to be that adults are frequently selfish and mysterious and their young charges are often at their mercy, even though the young can come to determine their own lives. Although she is unable to control much of what happens to her initially, finally Maisie is able to make morally correct choices, showing that she knows quite a great deal.

Daisy Miller (in James's novel of the same name), however, is another story. Trailed across Europe by her precocious younger brother and her completely ineffectual mother, Daisy seems unable (or perhaps unwilling) to acknowledge that there might need to be constraints on the behavior of a young, unmarried woman. In spite of the well-intentioned advice given her by Frederick Winterbourne (whose interest is likely more than avuncular) and sharper reprimands by others in the American expatriate community, Daisy continues to go about unchaperoned with various men, eventually settling on an Italian dandy of uncertain pedigree. Winterbourne, who at first champions Daisy, eventually turns his back on her; nevertheless, he is saddened by her death of "Roman fever," officially the result of a late evening in the Coliseum but metaphorically punishment for her rash behavior. In this novel, it appears, independence from social convention (at least for young women of the leisure classes) can lead only to death.

Louisa May Alcott's (1832–1888) *Little Women* (1868–1869) and Horatio Alger's (1832–1899) *Ragged Dick* (1868) represent other aspects of emerging American adolescent life and provide interesting commentary on gender stereotypes in the late nineteenth century. *Little Women* shows the various ways in which girls make the transformation into wives and mothers, whereas *Ragged Dick* forms the template for the adolescent American Dream. These novels, unlike those by James and Wharton, were directed toward a young readership and thus spoke more directly to their concerns.

Alger's novel, more entertaining than subsequent generations have given it credit for, features "Ragged Dick," who is transformed in the course of the novel from a bootblack living on the streets and sleeping in straw to Richard Hunter, Esquire, with a job in a counting room, a trusted friend, and prospects for the future. Dick achieves all of this through hard work, a cheerful countenance, and an inbred sense (coming from who knows where) of right and wrong. Dick is willing to lie, fight, smoke, and gamble, but he stubbornly refuses to steal and always keeps his promises. The message was satisfying to the emerging American middle class, which wanted to believe that urban children and youth were poor because of their own shiftlessness and dishonesty, but it also set a standard for (male) adolescent achievement. In Dick's world (and he is merely the first of many Alger novels in the same vein), success is possible with hard work, cheerful stoicism, frugality, and a little bit of luck.

Little Women, on the other hand, celebrates the virtues of home life and domesticity while at the same time offering a variety of possibilities for young women. Certainly marriage and children is one avenue open to the March girls, but at least for a time Jo manages to make her own living and support herself by her writing. The eventual marriages in the novel are various as well: from the moral domesticity (but long separations) of Marmee and Father, to the child-centered home of Meg, to the romantic marriage of Amy and Laurie, and finally to the working relationship of Jo and Professor Bhaer. Like *Ragged Dick, Little Women* praises hard work and sacrifice, but its emphasis on home and hearth provided young women with clearly domestic role models.

The experiences of working-class, immigrant, and African American adolescents are treated in several different ways in the literature of the period. Works of interest in this area include Stephen Crane's *Maggie, A Girl of the Streets* (1893), Paul Laurence Dunbar's *The Sport of the Gods* (1902), Willa Cather's *O Pioneers!* (1913) and *My Ántonia* (1918), and

Theodore Dreiser's "Old Rogaum and His Theresa" (1918).

Crane's (1871–1900) and Dreiser's (1871–1945) stories have much in common: both treat young women who run into conflicts with their families and are turned out of the house for what their parents consider to be their immoral behavior. The final outcome for each girl is very different, however. Maggie is thrown out by her drunken mother and takes up with a man who first "ruins" and then abandons her. She turns to prostitution and eventually dies, at which point her unrepentant mother finally agrees to "forgive" her. Theresa's traditional German immigrant father locks her out for violating his curfew, but he repents and frantically searches for her. Theresa is returned with virtue (and stubbornness) intact, but the reader recognizes just how close to disaster she was. Both stories accurately depict the reality of life for working-class women: without a secure home (and income) the only alternative is prostitution, followed quickly by illness and death. They also chronicle the in-between state of female adolescence, when girls are perched between adult independence (which in these cases may be dangerous) and childish subservience to the family.

Dunbar's (1872–1906) novel tells the story of the African American Hamilton family, the father of which is falsely accused of theft and imprisoned. The family moves to New York, where the daughter and son go astray—the daughter becoming a stage singer and the son a drunk, a womanizer, and eventually a murderer. The lesson of this novel seems to be that young people, especially those belonging to disfranchised minorities, are safer in the bucolic (if racist) South, carefully guarded by a watchful family. Much like the girls in Dreiser's and Crane's stories, Dunbar's young people go from being set loose in the city to disillusionment and immorality.

Cather (1873–1947) tells a more positive story of Nebraska's Norwegian and Bohemian immigrants, who succeed as a result of hard work and determination. The two young women in her novels, Alexandra Bergson in *O, Pioneers!* and Ántonia Shimerda in *My Ántonia,* grow from girls on the brink of financial ruin into independent women with families and prosperous farms, but their material achievements come at a price. Alexandra has to assume the financial and managerial role in the family after the death of her father, sacrificing a romantic life until late in the novel, and Ántonia, whose father also dies early in her life, works the family farm like a man, becoming (at least in the narrator Jim Burden's opinion) coarse and hardened in the process. For these two girls adolescent development is mostly a process of subduing individual desires to the necessities of the land. Still, these girls (and the women they become) are portrayed as compelling figures of power, energy, and self-determination. Clearly adolescence is less dangerous for young people on the frontier than it is for their urban counterparts.

During the last part of the nineteenth century a wide variety of books explicitly for adolescents began to be published which would continue into the twentieth century and contribute to the evolving definition of adolescence. Harry Castlemon's *Frank, the Young Naturalist* (1864), Martha Finley's *Elsie Dinsmore* (1867), Thomas Bailey Aldrich's *The Story of a Bad Boy* (1870), Susan Coolidge's *What Katy Did* (1872), and Oliver Optic's *The Boat Club* (1885) are some of the best known.

In two novels directed at young women, one can see divergent representations of female adolescence. The eponymous heroine of *Elsie Dinsmore,* a self-sacrificing adolescent girl like Eva in *Uncle Tom's Cabin* and countless other sentimental novels, was probably as well known at the time as Huckleberry Finn. Highly religious and endlessly persecuted by her unsympathetic family, Elsie exhibits an unyielding piety that finally wins over her father. *What Katy Did* gives readers perhaps one of the first glimpses of an independent, active young woman. Katy is funny and energetic, engaging in schoolhouse pranks and planning to do (not just be or have) something in her later life. An accident causes Katy to change from tomboy to invalid and the emotional center of the home, but her confidence and spirit resemble that of later twentieth-century heroines of young adult fiction, like those of Katherine Paterson, Judy Blume, Mildred Taylor, Cynthia Voigt, Karen Cushman, and Francesca Lia Block.

Adding to the field of young adult novels were the hundreds of books produced by the Stratemeyer Syndicate, a group of ghostwriters organized by the writer and publisher Edward Stratemeyer (1862–1930) around the turn of the century. These series books, mostly adventure and mystery, included Tom Swift (published from 1910 to 1941) and Ruth Fielding (1913 to 1934) and later the Hardy Boys (from 1926) and Nancy Drew (from 1930). At least 100 million copies of 600 titles have been published over the years. Sinclair Lewis even wrote a novel in this vein, although not for the syndicate, called *Hike and the Aeroplane* (1912). These series books tend to support stereotypes of boys as adventurers and primary actors, but both Nancy Drew and Ruth Fielding gave generations of girls characters who were brave, curious, and self-determined.

The message of much of the literature about adolescents at this time is that while young adults can make a stab at independence, ultimately they must succumb to adult authority. The books for young adults, however, offer a more hopeful picture. Ragged Dick rises by his own hand and with only a little adult intervention; Nancy Drew has only the most benign of parental influences in her widowed father; Hike can pilot an airplane back and forth across the continent, rescuing maidens, subduing rebels, and saving shipwreck victims, with the full support (but not the interference) of the adults in his life; and Katy can make plans to do something with her life. Not surprisingly, the adult novels about adolescence suggested the submission of adolescents to adult authority; the young adult novels for adolescents, on the other hand, hinted at something more subversive, and perhaps more modern.

See also Adventures of Huckleberry Finn; Children's Literature; *Daisy Miller; Maggie, A Girl of the Streets; My Ántonia*

BIBLIOGRAPHY
Primary Works

Alcott, Louisa May. *Little Women.* 1868–1869. Edited by Valerie Alderson. Oxford: Oxford University Press, 1994.

Aldrich, Thomas Bailey. *The Story of a Bad Boy.* 1870. Boston: Houghton Mifflin, 1927.

Alger, Horatio, Jr. *Ragged Dick; or, Street Life in New York.* 1868. New York: Signet, 1990.

Castlemon, Harry [Charles Austin Fosdick]. *Frank, the Young Naturalist.* 1864. Philadelphia: Henry T. Coates, 1892.

Cather, Willa. *My Ántonia.* 1918. Boston: Houghton Mifflin, 1988.

Cather, Willa. *O Pioneers!* 1913. Oxford: Oxford University Press, 1999.

Coolidge, Susan [Sarah Chauncy Woolsey]. *What Katy Did.* 1872. London: Collins, 1955.

Crane, Stephen. *Maggie, A Girl of the Streets (A Story of New York).* 1893. Edited by Kevin J. Hayes. New York: Bedford, 1999.

Dunbar, Paul Laurence. *The Sport of the Gods.* 1902. New York: Dodd, Mead, 1902.

Eggleston, Edward. *The Hoosier Schoolmaster.* 1871. New York: Hart, 1976.

Finley, Martha [Martha Farquharson]. *Elsie Dinsmore.* 1867. New York: Arno Press, 1974.

Howe, E. W. *The Story of a Country Town.* 1883. Edited by Claude M. Simpson. Cambridge, Mass.: Harvard University Press, 1961.

James, Henry. *Daisy Miller*. 1879. New York: Harper & Brothers, 1906.

James, Henry. *What Maisie Knew*. 1897. New York: Scribners, 1908.

Lewis, Sinclair. *Hike and the Aeroplane*. 1912. Hawley, Pa.: Yale Books, 1999.

Optic, Oliver [William Taylor Adams]. *The Boat Club*. 1855. Boston: Lee and Shepard, 1882.

Twain, Mark. *Adventures of Huckleberry Finn*. 1885. Edited by Gerald Graff and James Phelan. Boston: Bedford, 1995.

Twain, Mark. *The Adventures of Tom Sawyer*. 1876. New York: Harper & Brothers, 1903.

Washington, Booker T. *Up from Slavery: An Autobiography*. Garden City, N.Y.: Doubleday, 1901.

Zitkala-Ša [Gertrude Simmons Bonnin]. *American Indian Stories*. Washington, D.C.: Hayworth, 1921.

Secondary Works

African-American Odyssey: A Quest for Full Citizenship. Library of Congress exhibit. Available at http://memory.loc.gov/ammem/aaohtml/exhibit/aointro.html.

Alexander, Ruth M. "'The Only Thing I Wanted Was Freedom': Wayward Girls in New York, 1900–1930." In *Small Worlds: Children and Adolescents in America, 1850–1950*, edited by Paula Petrick and Elliott West, pp. 275–300. Lawrence: University of Kansas Press, 1992.

Ashford, Richard K. "Tomboys and Saints: Girls' Stories of the Late Nineteenth Century." *School Library Journal* 26 (January 1980): 23–28.

Donelson, Kenneth L., and Alleen Pace Nilsen. *Literature for Today's Young Adults*. 6th ed. New York: Longman, 2001.

Elliott, Glen R., and S. Shirley Feldman, eds. *At the Threshold: The Developing Adolescent*. Cambridge, U.K., and New York: Cambridge University Press, 1990.

Grinder, Robert E. "The Concept of Adolescence in the Genetic Psychology of G. Stanley Hall." *Child Development* 40 (1969): 355–369.

Hall, G. Stanley. *Adolescence: Its Psychology, and Its Relations to Physiology, Anthropology, Sociology, Sex, Crime, Religion, and Education*. 2 vols. New York: D. Appleton, 1904.

Handlin, Mary F., and Oscar Handlin. *Facing Life: Youth and the Family in American History*. Boston: Little, Brown, 1971.

Hawes, Joseph M., and N. Ray Hiner, eds. *Growing Up in America: Children in Historical Perspective*. Urbana: University of Illinois Press, 1985.

Goodman, Madeline, and John Modell. "Historical Perspectives." In *At the Threshold: The Developing Adolescent*, edited by Glen R. Elliott and S. Shirley Feldman, pp. 93–122. Cambridge, U.K., and New York: Cambridge University Press, 1990.

Kidd, Kenneth B. *Making American Boys: Boyology and the Feral Tale*. Minneapolis: University of Minnesota Press, 2004.

Riis, Jacob A. *The Children of the Poor*. New York: Scribners, 1892.

Sanger, William W. *The History of Prostitution: Its Extent, Causes, and Effects throughout the World*. New York: Harper, 1858.

Soderbergh, Peter A. "Birth of a Notion: Edward Stratemeyer and the Movies." *Midwest Quarterly* 14 (1972): 81–94.

Spacks, Patricia Meyer. *The Adolescent Idea*. New York: Basic, 1981.

White, Barbara. *Growing Up Female: Adolescent Girlhood in American Fiction*. Westport, Conn.: Greenwood, 1985.

Caren J. Town

ADVENTURES OF HUCKLEBERRY FINN

Under a composite scoring from comic books to literary criticism meant for a few hundred cultists, *Adventures of Huckleberry Finn*—originally published in England in 1884 as *The Adventures of Huckleberry Finn (Tom Sawyer's Comrade)*—is the American novel now best known at home and also in the world at large. Everybody wanting to pass as culturally knowledgeable will get around to reading it or means to. Those who do so may worry whether they are appreciating its qualities as a classic. If they first ponder the introduction to an advanced edition, they may experience the novel more cerebrally than emotionally. If they go on to the commentary their edition recommends, they may narrow *Huckleberry Finn* to some pattern. For a few it forms a virtual clubroom for exchanging a connoisseur's subtleties.

The book's popularity around the world, beyond the claims for *Huckleberry Finn* as the national epic or the quintessentially American novel, proves that it has universal appeal. It succeeds at some elemental level that sophisticates should respect. Yet if lured or required to cross-examine it, easy riders who floated along with Huck are intrigued by the subtle details that critics elicit from, for example, the contents of the drifting house in chapter 9 or from the paired episodes such as Huck's staged escape from Pap's cabin and Jim's "evasion" at the Phelpses. They may come to realize how expertly an agile narration and incandescence of detail disguise a shaky plot, how a tour de force of humor—in a gamut from irony (running its

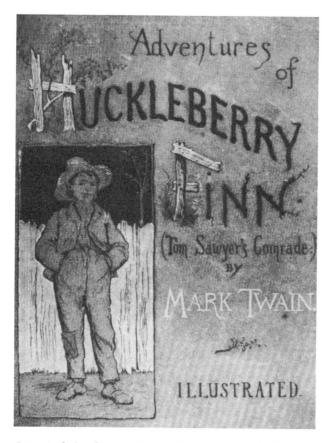

Cover of the first edition with illustrations by Edward W. Kemble. HULTON ARCHIVE/GETTY IMAGES

was rising to celebrity as an author, humorist, public speaker, and colorful personality. He had a model family and an impressive house in an impressive enclave of long-settled Hartford, Connecticut. During the months when agents were signing up buyers for his novel, he was criss-crossing the eastern half of the country, reading from his works. To an outsider, life was going great for Twain, who was still in vibrant health as he charged toward his fiftieth birthday. To say that he had no evident reason to write an anti-social book is to understate the obvious.

Still, *Huckleberry Finn* seductively describes breaking away from clocked routines and gliding downstream on a raft, seldom rowing, making do with whatever turns up, enjoying nature's sights and sounds. So biographers have underlined Twain's grumbles about keeping his large house (nineteen rooms, requiring as many as six servants), paying the bills, hosting short- and long-term guests, amusing or nursing or disciplining the children (three lively daughters eventually), and dealing with the swelling requests for professional advice, job referrals, and spot cash. Given these circumstances, Twain may have considered the novel's Jackson Island or even Pap's cabin as more bearable than his own home. As for the clear nights when Huck and Jim glide almost alone down the "big river" (as Huck calls it several times), it's easy to imagine Twain wishing himself on that same raft.

The escapist idyll makes the interrupting vignettes of cruelty, greed, selfishness, and gullibility all the sharper. They cut deeper, however, than the stresses of Twain's Hartford years alone can justify. Before he settled down into marriage, many experiences had lowered his opinion of human nature (the E. E. Cummings term "manunkind" seems to sum up Twain's attitude). These included his time in the raw river town of Hannibal in the 1840s, which was a stopover for rough types wandering westward. After coping with several big cities on his own and plying the Mississippi Valley between St. Louis and New Orleans, Twain encountered the sordid habits, hustles, and homicides in tumultuous Nevada and California, where he worked as a journalist. The dangers he had experienced in these locales are reflected in the many corpses that turn up in *Huckleberry Finn*. If readers add in the novel's other serious threats, they realize that Twain had learned to consider violence almost as natural as sunrises. Huck and Jim's practice of loafing or napping by day and rafting by night can be seen as safer, not just more pleasant, than getting involved with the many dangers on shore.

Critics like to explain Mark Twain's pen name as aptly chosen by a starkly divided personality. But

own gamut) to satire to burlesque—smooths over the improbability of a poor white boy and an African American adult teaming up to run south. Besides formal explications, academic enthusiasts keep discovering details about sociocultural sources, foreign editions, and popular merchandising. In addition, an impressive number of novelists have confirmed the novel's appeal both by explicit praise and by a character or voice that highlights Twain's distinctive achievement.

SELF-SUFFICIENT READERS

While inner-directed readers may try to ignore all coaching, they inescapably start with some notions about the author of a book, its country and date of origin, and its claim on their interest. However admirable their independence, they will better appreciate *Huckleberry Finn* by having some knowledge about the novel's author, who weaves his name into the first sentence. During the years when Mark Twain (the pen name of Samuel Langhorne Clemens, 1835–1910) wrote and revised *Huckleberry Finn*, he reasoning in a circle makes better sense about him. The violent or thieving white males who disrupted the idyllic night rides created tense yarns; adventures against humans sold better than struggling against fog. Twain was eager to earn big royalties and, having become his own publisher, big profits. Yet in the late nineteenth century, humor, if good enough, could outsell even adventures. So the Huck who holds on to his decency and instinctive dignity despite the invasive meanness he encounters can turn into a comic scamp who steals chickens or sneaks into the circus or hides butter under his hat. Twain saw no either-or problem here, felt no dilemma.

But Twain, steadily more analytic about his talent as a comic writer, was recognizing that the most enduring humor or humorist has a serious base. That suited both his Presbyterian upbringing and his ambitions. He read intently on the sources and sanctions for morality or ethics and particularly for conscience. By the 1870s he felt he was worth hearing on the debate between the utilitarian and intuitionist approaches. Also, increasingly, he took open positions on public issues, and nobody, except to counteract his popularity, questioned that staunch ideals made him a mugwump (a term for formerly Republican voters who backed the Democratic candidate Grover Cleveland in the presidential election of 1884). Yet he enjoyed romping with his daughters at their level, which must have helped shape Tom Sawyer's psychology, if not Huck's. Along with his accumulating seriousness he had stayed spontaneously playful. Many observers felt that he was at odds with the traditions of New England, where he settled in the 1880s, at least with its Puritan side. While *Huckleberry Finn* can throb with contempt for human failings, it can also suggest as much hope for benevolence and nobility as a born transcendentalist.

The book certainly draws on Twain's knowledge of the Mississippi Valley. As a steamboat pilot he became intimately familiar with the southern half of the river. He knew the towns on its banks, the "one-horse" farms behind them; his autobiographical musings boasted that *Huckleberry Finn* had simply moved his uncle's farm hundreds of miles south and that he had used his memories of one of his uncle's slaves in creating the character of Jim. He knew slaveholding ways, and, if we reason back to reality from fiction, he viscerally knew what life was like for a boy growing up beside the river. Huck, idealized, sits on the shoulders of a lowly Hannibal teenager. But nostalgia segued into pained memories; the shooting of Boggs was drawn from an event young Sam had witnessed in 1845. Taken selectively, *Huckleberry Finn* can be viewed as an antebellum version of Sinclair Lewis's *Main Street,* more humorous but also more condemnatory.

Even the most independent readers have to wonder about Huck's "comrade" Tom Sawyer, featured in the novel's subtitle and mentioned in Huck's opening sentence. Tom had originally been introduced to Twain's readers in *The Adventures of Tom Sawyer* (1876). In *Huckleberry Finn*, the early chapters, several admiring references in absentia, and the long climax keep Tom so prominent that many a memoir by readers fuses the two novels. *Tom Sawyer* certainly was the starting point for *Huckleberry Finn*. The earlier novel led Twain to "another boys' book" (*Adventures of Huckleberry Finn*, p. 678) that may have begun by reworking a discarded last chapter winding down Tom and Huck's hunt for treasure. As publisher, Twain seriously considered marketing the books together. Still, the insights to be gained from digging for *Huckleberry Finn*'s roots in *Tom Sawyer* dwindle before the differences in angle of narration, settings, timbre of humor, and underlying values. Likewise, Huck as used by Tom and Twain earlier is (to adapt a simile from Twain) like checkers compared to the chess of Huck as autobiographer.

Deeper insights can be found through other books Twain wrote before *Huckleberry Finn*, even—for deadpan humor—*The Celebrated Jumping Frog of Calaveras County and Other Sketches* (1867). His travel books showed his developing skill at (or was it his dependence on?) the "road" narrative, that is, at giving his improvisations a loose continuity by making them part of a journey. *Roughing It* (1872) showed, furthermore, Twain's growing deftness with the naive observer of bizarre events. Getting *Life on the Mississippi* (1883) together had revivified his knowledge of river culture; a few critics try to foresee Huck in the book's pre-sexual cub pilot. Earlier, *The Prince and the Pauper* (1881) had energized Twain's thinking about kings and commoners—and about their consciences. Though Huck had just learned to write, his book benefited from much professional expertise.

STUDIOUS READERS

Readers who want to understand the going consensus about *Huckleberry Finn* need to know more about how it was published, how it fit into literary history, how it reflected or ignored topical issues, and how well it expressed Twain's personal politics.

His breakout as a popular author had come through the channel known as subscription publishing. Though the endgame got complicated, agents first went door to door, wheedling advance orders with a prospectus—a bound sample of the book's contents—and earning a percentage on their completed sales. For the author, publishing that depended on bookstores was more prestigious but less profitable because only sizable cities could support them. Actually, Twain tried to move up to a "trade" approach with the three books that preceded *Huckleberry Finn*, but the leaner royalties drove him back to the marketing that had worked so richly for him starting with *The Innocents Abroad; or, The New Pilgrims' Progress* (1869). Still, long suspicious that publishers had been cheating him, he founded his own firm (Charles L. Webster and Co.) with his niece's husband as front man. It started out at a practiced pitch. Its circular trolling for agents promised them a "Mine of Humor," "A Book for the Young and Old, the Rich and the Poor" by the "Quickest Selling" author "in the World" (*Huckleberry Finn*, p. 661).

Twain never complained about his practical-minded clientele in the smaller towns who expected to be kept interested and amused while ending up edified. Since they wanted a hefty, showy book for their money, prospectuses promised many illustrations, which Twain soon considered worth his close attention. Now, as publisher, he chose the artist, deciding on a young cartoonist, E. W. Kemble. Whether he meant for Kemble to amplify the comedy of *Huckleberry Finn* or to soften the harsh undertones no known document can prove. But Kemble's caricatures, starting with cues that Twain had returned to the boy's-book genre, inescapably swayed any reader's responses. Reprints without his drawings make for a different experience; even more so do the editions illustrated by Norman Rockwell or Thomas Hart Benton. Illustration in the foreign editions can force American critics to rethink their emphasis on the novel's homespun appeal.

Embedding *Huckleberry Finn* in literary history gets trickier. Twain, insecure about his skimpy education, diligently filled in his knowledge of the classics, the books that the taste-setters of Western culture had canonized as the most important. Close analysts of his reading find *Huckleberry Finn* borrowing from—not parodying—Shakespeare or Thomas Carlyle or Charles Dickens, for instance. Distinct beyond doubt is the parallel between Don Quixote–Sancho Panza and Tom-Huck. Twain himself, in a private letter, gave the novel *Gil Blas* by French author Alain-René Lesage (1668–1747) as a template for his first-person narrator, though Huck just loosely rates as a picaro or near-criminal outcast. Following another genre that Twain's reading favored, his first working title was "Huck Finn's Autobiography." But the source-hunting ranges widely. Nor does it overlook the obvious such as the biblical parallels starting with the reference to Moses and the "bulrushers."

From 1879 to 1882 Twain paid a lot of attention to American humorists, helping to plan a one-volume "library" that his company published under his name in 1888. The humorists of the American Southwest, including Johnson J. Hooper and W. T. Thompson, may have suggested the episodes of the camp meeting and the circus-rider's hoax, though Twain could have based them on oral lore or even on direct experience. Listening to many a tall tale, particularly on the river and among western prospectors, he had also observed the effectiveness of a deadpan delivery, which may have, in fact, come by instinct before he honed it professionally. In *Huckleberry Finn*, he uses this technique with a great deal of finesse, softening toward understatement. This deadpan delivery was very forceful in an era of gushing domestic fiction and sentimental poetry. Western humor had also evolved toward the "literary comedians," with whom Twain was grouped in the 1870s. They particularly liked to satirize pretense and blind bookishness (as in the so-called Evasion chapters—the final sequence of the novel). Quality aside, in 1885 *Huckleberry Finn* came across as less unique than it seems now.

While local colorists usually patched in humor, their fiction centered on characters rooted in a rural locale with its distinctive dialect. For some critics, Twain's "Explanatory" note at the beginning of the novel already joined him to the local color genre, and his panorama of backcountry scenes fitted with local colorists' claim to documenting aspects of society that were fading away. Twain's notes show that he considered working in other typical events from his childhood years like a Fourth of July celebration. Apparently, *Huckleberry Finn* happens before the Mexican-American War and the Gold Rush—the title page presents it as taking place "forty to fifty years ago"—but it mentions no event or well-known controversy that would mark specific years.

Besides local color, Twain's alertness to literary history as he was living it included the "good bad-boy" subgenre. This writing convention developed as a reaction to Sunday-school fables that strained to give young readers an uplifting message. (The fables had, in turn, been an attempt to counteract the dime novels, which had encouraged dreams of derring-do rather than providing children with a message about fulfilling their duty.) Huck, who insisted on boarding the *Walter Scott*, will opt for "howling adventures amongst the Injuns." Having started early to burlesque uplifting tales for and about children, Twain was ready for the subgenre in which sound attitudes were incubating under coltish friskiness and the testing of limits. Evidently finding Thomas Bailey Aldrich's *The Story of a Bad Boy* (1865) tepid and George W. Peck's *Peck's Bad Boy and His Pa* (1883) superficial, Twain involved Huck in much riskier escapades. In chapter 31, he even let Huck decide to "go to hell" (p. 271). Yet Huck now collects far more praise for ethical nobility than does the American claimant in knee-pants of Frances Hodgson Burnett's *Little Lord Fauntleroy* (1886).

Literary historians have suggested other models for *Huckleberry Finn* such as the slave narrative, plausible only if Jim qualifies as the main character never out of the action for long. Twain's novel is suggestive of so many different models because his genius could absorb so many ideas and sources. Still, dissection of his borrowing can finally miss the depth of his originality. Classifying him under realism—exemplified in his times by the persuasion of William Dean Howells (1837–1920)—blurs how daringly Twain described Pap's drunken flailings in his cabin, the thieves' quarrel on the *Walter Scott,* the Royal Nonesuch scam, or the Bricksville loafers. The committee guarding the Concord (Massachusetts) Free Public Library saw that *Huckleberry Finn* presented sordid matters coldly or jeeringly or just lustily rather than piously, and they decided to ban the book.

Studious readers will find much commentary on the novel's political impact in 1885, a point that little interested reviewers at the time. A few historicists argue that any impact was irrelevant because the Civil War had ended chattel slavery. Others argue that the novel, like the later chapters of *Life on the Mississippi,* encouraged the rising New South by ridiculing an Old South whose resurgence no forward-thinking citizen could want. The main political approach argues, usually to defend the Evasion chapters, that the novel criticizes the Republican Party for backing down from Reconstruction and allowing whites to re-create a form of slavery through the sharecropping system and convict labor. The main years of the novel's composition did bracket crucial dates: in 1876 the presidential election led to federal troops withdrawing from the South, and in 1883 the Civil Rights Act of 1875 foundered as unconstitutional. Twain, who followed the daily news and was an insider at the *Hartford Courant,* had an opinion on all live issues.

The political debate comes down finally to racism—whether it is satirized, deploringly tolerated as a fact, or in effect supported, either by failure to confront it head on or by keeping Jim too close to the negative stereotype of blacks. Nobody has yet found significant African American response in 1885, though doubtless it would have confirmed the realism of Pap's poisonous tirade about a white-shirted "free nigger" (p. 35). Less certain is how it would have glossed the notorious exchange—"Anybody hurt?" "No'm. Killed a nigger."—now often sanitized as the run-up to satirizing Aunt Sally's "Well, it's lucky; because sometimes people do get hurt" (p. 279). Huck's using "nigger"

213 times is often excused as an authentic marker for his time, place, and status. But since the 1950s, African American parents—with white supporters—have periodically opposed making the novel a required text. The novel's defenders, rejecting the focus on the key epithet as a misreading, favorably infer Jim's private thoughts and especially his altruistic motives toward Huck and, from the other side, Huck's growing affection and respect for Jim.

Twain's own political history complicates an assessment of the antiracist force of *Huckleberry Finn.* Both early and late in his career he often claimed southern—rather than midwestern—roots, but by the 1870s he had settled in New England and married into a northern family that had supported the abolition of slavery. If only because the defeated white South had little to spend on books, he considered his public eastern, thinning out as subscription agents scoured westward. After *Life on the Mississippi* vented its nostalgia, the present-day chapters spoke to and for an industrializing, modernizing North. He took the attitude that the North's economy and culture set the national norm because the North had won the Civil War. Choosing George Washington Cable (1844–1925) as his co-performer in public appearances during 1884 and 1885 was apt. Cable, a Confederate veteran, had built his fiction on an exotic Deep South, but his essays militantly argued for the civil rights of former slaves; ostracized in the South, he would migrate to deepest New England. While touring with Cable, Twain negotiated to publish the memoirs of Ulysses S. Grant, idolizing him not as a president but as general of the victorious North. Yet Twain's priorities were economic. Between 1868 and 1883 he had voted for the Republican Party because it nurtured the entrepreneur, not because it sometimes pressed for the rights of freedpersons. His charities toward individuals had never expanded into making racial justice a political must. His support of Grover Cleveland in 1884 meant helping the Democratic Party, which aggressively supported white supremacy in the South.

As a novel about the United States rather than just the South, *Huckleberry Finn* looks still more cross-grained. Twain, while accepting people at all social levels generally, started out in the Whig Party, comfortable with its principle that the property-owning class, fittingly educated, could best guide a country teeming with immigrants and landless males vulnerable to quirky enthusiasms. The Gilded Age strengthened his sense that most of humankind by their nature followed self-interest or at least self-approval beneath any professed motives. In politics the masses hurrahed for the flattering demagogues and tolerated corruption, hoping to share the spoils. As wage earners, they listened to

Title page illustration by Edward W. Kemble for the 1932 edition. THE LIBRARY OF CONGRESS

radicals, even communists, hoping to expropriate the property earned by dogged enterprise. Twain was disgusted by the presidential election controversy involving candidates Rutherford B. Hayes and Samuel Tilden in 1876 but dismayed by the great strike of 1877. His private letters and several sketches, between 1876 and 1879 especially, rejected electoral democracy as based on the lazy and gullible commonalty displayed in *Huckleberry Finn*. To reassure the duke, the king declares: "Hain't we got all the fools in town on our side? and ain't that a big enough majority in any town?" (p. 228). The novel leaves us doubtful that even Huck will not grow up into another cadger of a "chaw," another poorly informed and gullible voter.

TEACHERS AND SCHOLARS

Though most of the intermediate typescripts and printer's proofs are lost, the missing first half of the holograph manuscript for *Huckleberry Finn* surfaced in 1990. Keen-minded editors, mostly working at the Mark Twain Project at the University of California, Berkeley, have reconstructed almost precisely both the course of the early drafts and the refining of the final text for printing. Now indisputably, the writing of the first draft broke into three phases: (1) between July and September 1876, Twain composed up to the middle of chapter 12 and from chapter 15 up into 18, breaking off when Buck Grangerford starts to explain feuds; (2) in 1879 and 1880 Twain went on from the feud through the shooting of Boggs; and (3) between June and September 1883, starting with the rush to lynch Colonel Sherburn, he wrote through to the ending and then composed a long insert from the middle of chapter 12 that also created chapters 13 and 14 (the *Walter Scott* adventure and the dialogues about King Solomon and the French language). Over the next seven months he revised, corrected most of the proofs, and fussed about marketing while, as usual, squandering energy on forgettable projects.

Such precise dating sharpens insight about the attitudes shaping *Huckleberry Finn*. Knowing that Sherburn's speech to the mob comes after a similar tirade was dropped cautiously from the travel book thickens analyses of Twain's judgments on the South he had revisited. Knowing that the *Walter Scott* episode and chapter 14 probably round off his inner image of Jim can readjust inferences about Jim's motives elsewhere. Matching the date of an essay Twain delivered at Hartford's Monday Evening Club to the time that specific chapters were conceived elicits the abstract ideas that may have driven them. Recognizing that Twain first composed the "Notice" that prefaces the novel in 1879 and 1880 and later added the disclaimer regarding the book's moral affects the more intricate theories about that section of the novel. Analyzing the many changes of a few words piles up evidence for Twain's craftsmanship. It also undercuts the charges of giving in to censors, whether himself or William Dean Howells or Olivia Clemens assisted by his daughters.

Clarified by the surrounding correspondence, other cruxes look simpler though not always resolvable. The definitive edition from the Mark Twain Project puts back the raftsmen vignette, lifted from the *Huckleberry Finn* manuscript to fill out *Life on the Mississippi*. Twain brought this section back to the novel, but then deleted it when his business manager almost casually persuaded him that the novel was too bulky. Another edition has restored, with a warning format, other passages that Twain cut from the holograph. Almost all reprints drop the heliotype (a sort of photograph) of a bust that a sculptor made of Twain in 1884. But, with debatable intentions and effect on the public, Twain had insisted on it for a second frontispiece. Still-finer analysis concludes that though Kemble composed the captions for his drawings, Twain often revised them and that his business manager composed the summaries in the table of contents, which Twain at least saw before they were set in type. While these details shape everybody's reactions vaguely, they interest an advanced critic in proportion to Twain's share in them, particularly where they reach for humor or indicate a state of mind.

The business side of *Huckleberry Finn*, like most matters that Twain was engaged with, is both tangled and interesting for scholars. Because "pirates," that is, publishers who paid no royalty, had preyed on several previous books, he took care to validate his copyright in the United Kingdom and Canada—issuing there in December 1884—before his company released the first American edition in February 1885. His irritation at falling short of the 40,000 subscribers he wanted before issuing at home softened as sales held up, reaching 51,000 by early May. With premium bindings at higher prices, the basic edition cost $2.75 bound in olive green or in blue for devotees wanting to match their copy of *Tom Sawyer*. (The earliest copies from the first printing have steadily increased in value. But many a prospector of flea markets has carried away the fool's gold of an edition in reset type and without the original drawings.) Always well known, never in need of discovery, *Huckleberry Finn* was running only slightly behind *The Innocents Abroad* and *Tom Sawyer* in sales when Twain died in 1910. Its popularity doubtless helped him to choose it more often as his favorite work above even *Personal Recollections of Joan of Arc* (1896).

Usually, magazines and newspapers ignored subscription books because their record for quality was poor and because their publishers did not buy advertising. Twain, changing tactics from book to book, had vacillated over sending out review copies. But his reputation, already near celebrity, got *Huckleberry Finn* noticed. So did its banning at the Concord Free Public Library, inclining the Boston and other New England newspapers to snipe at the book as indecorous. Reaching a far larger public, Joseph Pulitzer's New York *World* itemized its charges of "cheap and pernicious trash" and "careless hackwork." Still, many reviewers asserted positive, close to enthusiastic, opinions. More important, word-of-mouth praise, seconded here and there in print, increased yearly. By the 1890s a few Ivy League academics had joined in. Intriguingly, the still-thin African American press continued to ignore the book's relevance to the losing campaign for civil rights. Most British reviews admired the book, continuing the United Kingdom's enthusiasm for Twain's New World humor. Even sooner than in the United States, prestigious critics in Britain decided that *Huckleberry Finn* was a tour de force. So did many of Twain's British peers, including Robert Louis Stevenson and Rudyard Kipling.

As the novel's stature has risen, analysis has become more detailed. The commentary on the final two sentences alone would fill a book. Taken at their most simple level, those sentences pointed toward the sequel Twain already had in mind when he commented in July 1884 that "I mean to take Huck Finn out there," that is, "*among the Indians*" (Webster, p. 265). Less simply, to many though not all critics, it makes explicit the main point that Huck, as moral hero, must run away from society as conducted by the humankind he meets; a few insist that it confirms Huck as a child of nature, rejecting any kind of civilization.

Mounting praise for the narrative voice that Twain created for Huck has led to extensive rhetorical analysis of the book. This analysis has revealed an intricate artistry beyond the breakout that impressed

As Mark Twain's reputation grew in the 1890s, along with a new wave of nationalism in the United States, commentators began to make his character a model for being American. After Twain's death, emphasis gradually shifted toward his most distinctive, "native" books. After World War II the renewed wave of American self-confidence and self-awareness helped to focus admiration on Huckleberry Finn for both its attitudes and style. The accolades for it as quintessentially American have swelled until they compose their own exhibit of national self-definition.

All modern American literature comes from one book by Mark Twain called *Huckleberry Finn*. . . . All American writing comes from that. There was nothing before. There has been nothing as good since.

(Ernest Hemingway, Green Hills of Africa [New York: Charles Scribner's Sons, 1935], p. 22)

It is the nearest thing we have to a national epic. . . . Just as the Declaration of Independence (let us hope) contains in embryo our whole future history as a nation, so the language of *Huckleberry Finn* (another declaration of independence) expresses our popular character, our humor, our slant.

(Clifton Fadiman, "A Note on Huckleberry Finn," in Adventures of Huckleberry Finn [New York: Heritage Press, 1940], pp. 129–130)

If Mark Twain has seemed America's most "national" writer, Huckleberry Finn and his adventures have seemed so indigenous that to understand him and them is to understand Americans.

(Everett Carter, "The Modernist Ordeal of Huckleberry Finn," Studies in American Fiction 13 [1985]: 170)

In short, *Adventures of Huckleberry Finn* is as quintessentially American as is baseball or the voting booth; and those who do not understand the dreams and rhythms associated with each can never quite throw a mental grappling hook around America itself.

(Sanford Pinsker, "Huck Finn and Gerald Graff's 'Teaching the Conflicts,'" Academic Questions 12, no. 2 [1999]: 48)

T. S. Eliot: using colloquial speech for the narrator, not just those whom he quotes. Other admirers, without wading deep into definitions, have made "vernacular" the key term for Huck's prose, sometimes extending it into the catchword for a bundle of democratic-ethical values. More minute focus on technique has differentiated Huck into author, character, and comic mask besides narrator. That can raise new questions, such as whether his function as teller of the tale limits his inner growth, whether Twain's settling for a deadpan delivery stifles Huck's sense of humor, or whether Twain wanted to soften the moral and social lashings with a partly uncomprehending observer. Eventually, every interpreter of Huck has to ask whether he is a rounded, autonomous, and consistent character or more a clever, adjustable device.

That question applies more pressingly, and more politically, to Jim. First-rate critics and novelists have interpreted Jim as far smarter than a minstrel-show stereotype or a black happy to accept white dominance. This dignifying goes so far as to intuit a crafty, self-possessed Jim manipulating boys whom he needs to help him escape. Some critics maintain that Jim's down-home beliefs and spectral visions come from folk-wisdom. However, the case for Jim's inner stature has to stop with *Huckleberry Finn;* later manuscripts, published and unpublished, have him marching cheerfully under Tom's baton. Leslie Fiedler's theory that Jim formed a near-sexual bond with Huck has lost ground. Instead, enlarging Judith Loftus into a major character, feminists have contended that *Huckleberry Finn* overturns nineteenth-century stereotypes of gender; Jim does coach Huck on his disguise and later is made to cross-dress himself. But interpreting Jim as a motherly (or else fatherly) figure toward Huck is more defensible.

The most committed teachers and scholars push onward. The search for sources will never end. Twain insisted that all writers borrow, unknowingly if honest. In turn, literary historians have devoted a lot of time to analyzing the way that *Huckleberry Finn* influenced later authors. Several writers have admitted their direct debt to the book, including Sherwood Anderson, Ring Lardner, Ernest Hemingway, and James T. Farrell.

The same is true of African American writers such as Langston Hughes, Richard Wright, Ralph Ellison, and Toni Morrison. Progressive librarians and civil libertarians keep track of proposed bannings of the novel, including prominent instances in 1907 and the wave that started in the late 1950s. These can be seen as wry tributes to the novel's enduring appeal. Appropriate to Twain's ambitions, the book has become a part of mass culture, inspiring pop singles, movies, musical revues, and television programs. Strollers in the marketplace can spot Huck on ashtrays, bookends, board games, dolls, and other such bric-a-brac.

EXPLICATORS, PERSONAGES, AND PUNDITS

Close re-readers have sifted *Huckleberry Finn* for its finest gold dust or elevated it into the widest orbit of relevance. Contributing to both approaches, a masterly British critic holds: "The whole text . . . is layered like an archaeological mound. Every paragraph, every sentence presents a complex site of multiple, interpenetrating levels" (Beaver, p. 136).

Elaborate theories defy Twain's warning "Notice," which ironists take as in fact inviting the search for an authorial motive. Escape from society and its rules and regularities is the interpretation that has the most support. For several decades after the 1950s, the message tightened into a dichotomy between Huck-Jim's tiny paradise on the raft and dishonest, cruel doings on the shore, between "saints" and "sinners." In 1895, however, Twain had made the split internal, jotting that the novel had pitted Huck's "sound heart" against his "deformed conscience." Others see an agnostic pragmatism rejecting a Protestant rigidity that believed itself sanctified by the Bible. Civil religion, with the founding documents of the United States as its scripture, dignifies Huck into the pure democrat, so egalitarian as to team up with a runaway slave and so empathetic as to save the king and the duke from mobs and even to try again after they have turned in Jim as a runaway. Unfortunately for tidiness or profundity, exceptions undercut every theory. Some analysts emphasize instead the authorial heart and conscience that glow behind Huck's hypnotic voice, emitting a belief in—or at least a hope for—humankind's capacity to grow or simply for humane delight in experience.

An emphasis on personal identity has led explicators to build up Huck's symbolic rebirth as Tom. Redirected, that process deepens his psychic interplay with Pap, modernized into the abusive, alcoholic parent that family psychologists probe for. A brief vogue, blessed by Lionel Trilling and then T. S. Eliot, anointed Huck as acolyte to primal nature, to a "River God." Far more persuasive are sociocultural historians who align *Huckleberry Finn* with the daydream of resistance to feminizing decorum and fixity, a dream much indulged in by males of Twain's era, though certainly present in other eras as well. An exhaustive survey of other explications would get exhausting and dull, particularly when they block out the millions who have found *Huckleberry Finn* continually humorous, often comic, and sometimes hilarious. More critics should engage with the humor, if only to decide that it darkens from bland to satirical and ultimately to "sinister" effects, encapsulated when Aunt Sally first questions Huck.

The most heated analysis centers on the Evasion or final sequence. Hardly any reviewer complained about it. Twain, always alert to his audiences, kept it as a regular reading on his tour with Cable. Bernard DeVoto, while a lusty champion of Huck, was the first to insist that Twain's masterpiece made an "abrupt and chilling descent" in this section. Though Ernest Hemingway's complaint in 1935 of "cheating" the reader perhaps stirred up agreement with DeVoto, Leo Marx made the issue unavoidable with an emphatic, eloquent essay in 1953. He argued that the Evasion sequence was flat and fecklessly long and that its cruel capers violated the ethical dignity of both Huck and Jim as well as betraying the loyalty Twain had developed between them. More metacritically, Marx charged that the essays by Trilling (1948) and Eliot (1950) had praised the Evasion in behalf of formalist yet implicitly political values contradicting the novel's achieved progressivism.

Marx made his case so effectively that most of the commentary since then acknowledges its force. But the practical-minded suggest that Twain had hurried with the ending, impatient for royalties from his next bestseller, which was mainly a book for boys anyway. From a structural, adult viewpoint, defenders see Huck and Tom confirming the characters developed for them at the start. The social viewpoint sees the Evasion as capping the previous ridicule of the communal mind. Henry Nash Smith proposes that Twain wanted to end with an appropriately comic bravura that would not, however, drown out the cumulatively tragic overtones of the book. Smith believes that this approach reflected Twain's drive to sell, his pride as a craftsman, and his judgments on experience. Literary historians focus on the books that Tom keeps imitating and therefore discrediting—novels of romantic adventure from foreign authors. Arguments about the Evasion will persist and are ultimately based on a conflict between those who view Twain foremost as an artist and those who uphold the need for social justice and deplore lowering Jim's flight into a juvenile, pain-giving hoax.

Formalists, refusing to settle for Arnold Bennett's verdict of "divine amateur," play up many other triumphs of technique such as the range and nimbleness of Twain's satire through a minimalist observer. They find subtle pairings such as Boggs's drunken gallop and the faked-drunk rider at the circus or Jim's 'Lizabeth and the duke putting on "the deef en dumb" or the forty dollars from the slave-catchers and Tom's reward to Jim. Most formalists shrug off marvels such as Colonel Grangerford's hair changing from gray to black between chapters. Implicitly, they deny one critic's charge that "Huck's story as a novel is impossibility followed by implausibility and linked together by unlikelihood" (Quirk, p. 100). Trilling, for instance, declared it "in form and style . . . an almost perfect work" (Trilling, p. 110).

As the canonization of *Huckleberry Finn* has proceeded since World War II, its rarefied status makes the question of its racial impact all the more inescapable. Can a (arguably *the*) Great American Novel have a racist bias or a racist effect? While activists have kept that question newsworthy, opinion fractures into disagreements more complicated than black against white. Huck's taking risks for Jim leaves readers feeling exhilarated by the hope of human solidarity and incredulous at the verdict from John H. Wallace, an administrator in the secondary schools, that the novel "is the most grotesque example of racist trash ever written." Eager to accept the benefits of cultural diversity many readers approve when Shelley Fisher Fishkin asks "Was Huck Black?" though they may doubt that traces of African American speech in Huck's style override his whiteness. Many observers end up somewhere within what Jocelyn Chadwick-Joshua calls "The Jim Dilemma": how to establish Jim's generous, capable personhood within the distorting limits set by his color and predicament. For celebrants of *Huckleberry Finn* as the Great American Novel, innocent of racism, the grittiest challenge comes through Kemble's drawings. Approved by Twain, they fitted dismayingly well with the rising popularity of so-called coon caricatures of African Americans.

Many historians object that the slaves in Twain's St. Petersburg have unrealistic mobility. Free to move around locally, they could gather for a torchlight procession, Tom assumes. Though they endure a harsher routine than the devoted servants in Thomas Nelson Page's fiction, Twain may have aroused more sympathy for the owner-victimizers than for the victims like the Wilkses's slaves. Likewise, the book may have created more outrage at the complacency of whites like the Phelpses than concern for the pain of the slaves. Also, because Twain never takes the reader into Jim's private thinking, it may have engendered less pity for Jim's troubles than for Huck's struggles with his conscience. In 1996 novelist Jane Smiley attacked the canonizers and their supportive pundits head on. In her professional judgment, Twain and also Huck use Jim for their convenience. They keep him in the swamp at the Grangerfords until they need to get back on the raft. Then, soon, they make him tag along, at risk to himself and for no gain, as Huck meekly helps the king and the duke. Novel's end leaves racism as a private puzzle of Huck's feelings rather than a legalized injustice heading toward explosive events.

Nevertheless, *Huckleberry Finn* has continued rising toward what disturbs Jonathan Arac as "hypercanonization," toward being honored as the embodiment of its country's essence. Though four regions have been claiming Twain as their progeny, the novel now envelops and transcends them all. Not only academics but public figures declare it the finest expression of the American character; presidents are coached to proclaim their affection; no politician with nationwide sensitivity would admit to disliking it.

Twain's newly literate boy is now read worldwide. Sales have spilled over the normal channels for counting. The total is rising as unstoppably as the Mississippi in the spring, swelled by more than 700 editions in more than fifty languages. The responses of readers to come will vary with their niche on earth and their unique moment of time. But the long-increasing appeal of *Huckleberry Finn* ensures that readers will continue to enjoy it.

See also Adolescence; Blacks; Children's Literature; Humor; Reconstruction; Reform

BIBLIOGRAPHY
Primary Works

Twain, Mark. *Adventures of Huckleberry Finn*. Edited by Victor Fischer, Lin Salamo, and Walter Blair. Berkeley: University of California Press, 2003. A definitive, impeccably authoritative, and indispensable edition that includes facsimiles, annotations, a glossary, maps, and imaginative appendices. All quotations are from this edition.

Twain, Mark. *Adventures of Huckleberry Finn*. Edited by John H. Wallace. Falls Church, Va.: John H. Wallace and Sons, 1983. An "adapted" text that screens out racially offensive language.

Twain, Mark. *The Annotated Huckleberry Finn: Adventures of Huckleberry Finn (Tom Sawyer's Comrade)*. Edited by Michael Patrick Hearn. New York: Norton, 2001. Hearn copiously and knowledgeably weaves secondary materials into the text.

Secondary Works

Arac, Jonathan. *Huckleberry Finn as Idol and Target: The Functions of Criticism in Our Time.* Madison: University of Wisconsin Press, 1997.

Beaver, Harold. *Huckleberry Finn.* London: Allen & Unwin, 1987.

Blair, Walter. *Mark Twain & Huck Finn.* Berkeley: University of California Press, 1960.

Camfield, Gregg, ed. *The Oxford Companion to Mark Twain.* New York: Oxford University Press, 2003.

Carrington, George C., Jr. *The Dramatic Unity of "Huckleberry Finn."* Columbus: Ohio State University Press, 1976.

Chadwick-Joshua, Jocelyn. *The Jim Dilemma: Reading Race in Huckleberry Finn.* Jackson: University Press of Mississippi, 1998.

Champion, Laurie, ed. *The Critical Response to Mark Twain's Huckleberry Finn.* New York: Greenwood Press, 1991. Includes many of the most notable commentaries published about the novel between 1884 and 1990.

Cox, James M. *Mark Twain: The Fate of Humor.* Princeton, N.J.: Princeton University Press, 1966.

DeVoto, Bernard. *Mark Twain's America.* Boston: Little, Brown, 1932.

Doyno, Victor A. *Writing Huck Finn: Mark Twain's Creative Process.* Philadelphia: University of Pennsylvania Press, 1991.

Doyno, Victor A., ed. *"Huck Finn": The Complete Buffalo & Erie County Public County Library Manuscript—Teaching and Research Digital Edition.* Buffalo, N.Y.: Library Foundation of Buffalo & Erie County, 2003. CD-ROM that includes a facsimile of the manuscript, a transcription, an e-text of the first American edition, historical documents, thirteen books and over 300 relevant articles of secondary research and criticism, a gallery of foreign language editions, and a selected bibliography of criticism.

Egan, Michael. *Mark Twain's Huckleberry Finn: Race, Class and Society.* London: Sussex University Press, 1977.

Fischer, Victor. "Huck Finn Reviewed: The Reception of *Huckleberry Finn* in the United States, 1885–1897." *American Literary Realism* 16 (1983): 1–57.

Fishkin, Shelley Fisher. *Was Huck Black? Mark Twain and African-American Voices.* New York: Oxford University Press, 1993.

Haupt, Clyde V. *Huckleberry Finn on Film: Film and Television Adaptations of Mark Twain's Novel, 1920–1993.* Jefferson, N.C.: McFarland, 1994.

Inge, M. Thomas, ed. *Huck Finn among the Critics: A Centennial Selection.* Frederick, Md.: University Publications of America, 1985. Reprints the most-discussed reviews of the novel, the earliest from 1885; includes the well-known essays by Lionel Trilling, Leslie Fiedler, T. S. Eliot, and Leo Marx.

Leonard, James S., Thomas A. Tenney, and Thadious M. Davis, eds. *Satire or Evasion? Black Perspectives on Huckleberry Finn.* Durham, N.C.: Duke University Press, 1992.

Mensh, Elaine, and Harry Mensh. *Black, White, and Huckleberry Finn: Re-imagining the American Dream.* Tuscaloosa: University of Alabama Press, 2000.

Quirk, Tom. *Coming to Grips with Huckleberry Finn: Essays on a Book, a Boy, and a Man.* Columbia: University of Missouri Press, 1993.

Sattelmeyer, Robert, and J. Donald Crowley, eds. *One Hundred Years of Huckleberry Finn: The Boy, His Book, and American Culture.* Columbia: University of Missouri Press, 1985. Twenty-four essays from a well-balanced variety of approaches.

Seelye, John D. *The True Adventures of Huckleberry Finn.* Evanston, Ill.: Northwestern University Press, 1970.

Sloane, David E. E. *Adventures of Huckleberry Finn: American Comic Vision.* Boston: Twayne Publishers, 1988.

Smiley, Jane. "Say It Ain't So, Huck." *Harper's Magazine* 292 (January 1996): 61–67.

Smith, Henry Nash. *Mark Twain: The Development of a Writer.* Cambridge, Mass.: Belknap Press of Harvard University Press, 1962.

Trilling, Lionel. *The Liberal Imagination: Essays on Literature and Society.* Garden City, N.Y.: Doubleday, 1953.

Webster, Samuel C. *Mark Twain, Business Man.* Boston: Little, Brown, 1946.

Wieck, Carl F. *Refiguring Huckleberry Finn.* Athens: University of Georgia Press, 2000.

Louis J. Budd

AESTHETICISM

The term "aestheticism" is generally associated with artistic currents before and around the turn of the nineteenth century. It is especially prominent in the artistic, literary, and cultural discussion of late Victorianism and most particularly the 1890s, also referred to as the "mauve decade" (referring to the evasive, subversive, and aesthetic tendencies of the era), and largely congruent with ideas circulating in the current of decadence, *l'art pour l'art* (art for art's sake), and the fin de siècle (end of the century). The idea of exactly one mauve "decade" can be misleading, since the origins of aestheticist approaches to art go back far into the century, and its aftermath is visible into the 1920s and beyond in both European and American art. One of the most prominent and controversial figures of the era is certainly Oscar Wilde, but the group of aestheticist writers also comprises Walter Pater, Aubrey Beardsley, and many others as well as Donald Evans and Richard Le Gallienne, two aestheticists who later became known on the American scene. The movement influenced all literary genres and art forms from opera to the visual arts and design, where it was reflected in the arts and crafts movement. The discussions and controversies related to the movement had broad reverberations far beyond the turn of the century and extended from the realm of art to the social, political, and philosophical spheres.

DEFINITIONS

Aestheticism can be defined as the ideal of creating works of art that renounce any purpose or meaning other than their own refined beauty. This beauty is completely autonomous: it is free to abandon conventional ideas of social acceptance, economic value, or greater moral goal. Accordingly these works also abandon the ideal of representing nature and focus instead on the creation of an autonomous artistic creation. The values of the real are replaced by those that appeal to the beholder of beautiful creations. The ideal for fictional creations of this kind is to be elegant and eloquent, entertaining and playful, stunning and sharp. The use of the term "fin de siècle" is extended to anything seen as advanced, modern, or decadent at the end of the nineteenth century. "Decadence" itself is a term used since Roman antiquity to refer to phenomena of moral or cultural decay, deviance from the social norm, physical or moral laxity, perversion, or effeminate demeanor. The poets and artists ridiculed and exposed as decadents in the 1890s embraced the term and used it to distance themselves from the rigid cultural norms of Victorian Britain.

ORIGINS

The rise of aestheticism in the late nineteenth century originated in the art of the Pre-Raphaelites and the French symbolists. Poets, writers, and artists such as Charles Baudelaire, Joris-Karl Huysmans, and Pierre Loti created sceneries of indulgence and narcissism; their protagonists are mostly concerned with beauty and sensual matters. The artifacts show no or little concern for time and place and instead display an inwardness and self-consciousness that can best be seen in their predilection for a refined elegance of language and style, for decorative description, and for themes of reflection, dream, or oblivion. Gradually taking the shape of a movement, aestheticist thought spread from Paris throughout the Continent (notably to Barcelona, Vienna, Prague, Budapest) and to London. Aestheticism was an urban, intellectual, and cosmopolitan movement: since its subject matter was art itself, it relied on the education, taste, and wide reading of those interested in it. While it did not completely neglect political conflict and class struggle, the movement mostly used these issues as targets for bitter sarcasm and world-weary satire at best: social commitment was not the métier of the "decadents." However, their own self-fashioning as artists lent itself to confrontation with the governing moral, social, and political norms.

REACTION TO PROGRESS, IMPERIALISM, AND CAPITALISM

Aestheticism can indeed be understood as an attempt to counter the social and political developments of the era. In times marked by radical innovations and rapid urban and industrial growth—and, in Victorian England, an empire still evolving under the reign of a monarch who had been in power for over sixty years—there was a widespread consciousness at least among some intellectuals of a need for reflection and change. More people than ever before were literate and aware of the coming end of the century, of the vast technological progress and imperial conquests of the 1800s, and the industrial speed at which things were now advancing. Communications, business, and banking had increasingly pushed the limits of capitalism and imperialism, leaving little room for reasoning on the role, merit, and value of humans and their equality under these conditions. Darwinism appeared to provide the only valid explanation for this and was all too easily translated to the sphere of human existence. The movements of aestheticism, however, were more concerned with the marginal figures who had no place in the doctrine of Social Darwinism: vagabonds, artists, and all those who refused to adjust to the system of industrialized imperialism.

CHARACTERISTICS

Human beings in decadent art and writing are irretrievably flawed and live in a state of disruption both with themselves and with an equally flawed Nature. Since this is the case, humans can only overcome this imperfect melancholy state momentarily in acts of sin, disguise, or pretense. The "perverted" and unnatural is valued higher than any natural state, and anything that can provoke or prolong an unnatural state of things is welcome. Life is seen as play and performance without content or meaning, and it is inferior to any state of dreamy existence. Experience is artificially enhanced by drugs and absinthe, a strong and slightly toxic green alcohol. Exotic foreign travel is another means of indulging in aesthetic and sensuous spheres, making the Orient and the South Seas common destinations for decadent travelers. In most cases these destinations are sights that either stand for the futile grandeur of empires past (Grecian, Egyptian, or Byzantine ruins), primitivism, complete forlornness, or religious rituals. Images of the sacred in decadent works of art are abundant. The typical originator, protagonist, or agent in aestheticist works of art is the dandy or flaneur (casual passerby). The dandy displays a clear disdain for everything ordinary and quotidian, values elegance and taste, and has no regard for traditional gender roles and sexual norms. The impulse of the decadent movement aims more at evasion and escapism than at the actual confrontation with the real world, in which it takes little interest.

SOME LITERARY REPRESENTATIVES

Apart from the (in)famous Oscar Wilde (1854–1900), with his plays and *The Picture of Dorian Gray* (1891), a group of poets and writers in London gathered around *The Yellow Book,* a quarterly founded in 1894 by Aubrey Beardsley (1872–1898) and the American writer Henry Harland (1861–1905), who was the literary editor. The magazine soon became the central organ of the new aestheticist movement both in literature and the arts. Among other Americans involved with the development of the *Yellow Book* (which was named after the customary cover color of the scandalous French novels at the time) was the contributor Henry James, who was profoundly influenced by the London scene in his later descriptions of European sophistication (and corruption) and American naïveté (and innocence). Richard Le Gallienne (1866– 1947), an English writer and critic, also was a contributor and a close acquaintance of the English critic Max Beerbohm before moving to New York. Le Gallienne wrote poetry, fiction (*Quest of the Golden Girl,* 1896), and several volumes of essays, papers, and reminiscences of the 1890s. Le Gallienne's view of humans through the eyes of the decadent poet is among the most poignant of his times. He sees humans as mysterious beings behind masks, as beings that remain inexplicable, be they nostalgic or filled with bliss. The American poet Donald Evans (1884–1921) expressed similar views. Evans published several volumes of poetry, among them *Discords* (1912), and *Sonnets from the Patagonian* (1918). His love poems, such as "Resemblance" and "Loving Kindness," are filled with conflicts and

***The Yellow Book* advertisement, c. 1894.** Aubrey Beardsley's illustration for his *Yellow Book* is an example of aestheticist design. © SWIM INK 2, LLC/CORBIS

situations that defy normative visions of harmony and unmask the seductive appeal or cruelty of love. The themes, views, and aesthetics expressed in decadent writing outlasted their day and can be found in the works of writers such as Marcel Proust, Edith Wharton, and F. Scott Fitzgerald.

THE ARTS AND CRAFTS MOVEMENT: METHODS

If aestheticism and decadence have to be seen as subversive, the impulse of confrontation also drives the arts and crafts movement, a British initiative in the field of decorative arts and design whose influence was widely felt in both Europe and the United States. A group of artists, architects, and critics gathered under that name after the Arts and Crafts Exhibition Society had been founded in 1888 in London. Their aim was primarily to foster a broad understanding and acceptance not merely of art but of new methods and styles that relied on manual skill and aptitude, quality materials, plain methods of construction, and ample decorative surfaces. The focus of the craftsperson was to be on the production process and the materials used as well as on the use of the product and the function of its design. The idea was to restore the link between creative individuals and their work, the goal of this restoration being a renewed unity—lost with industrialization—of art and production, form and function. The shaping and making of objects should be returned to the hands of one individual and not be segmented into several steps that could be administered rationally and distributed among several workers.

SOCIAL AND POLITICAL GOALS

Beyond the spreading of artistic styles and methods of production, a broader social and political agenda was associated with the activities of the arts and crafts movement. The two chief proponents of this agenda were William Morris (1873–1932) and John Ruskin (1819–1900). Morris was a designer and skilled craftsman who also worked as a political essayist, writer, poet, and artist. Ruskin was an art historian and critic. Both worked toward a wider understanding of the procedures and actions involved in the making of design and artwork, referring to material arts (better, that is, more valuable, more lasting, and sometimes more prestigious materials, requiring more refined manual skills). The forms of art were not meant to be revolutionary, even though there was a greater potential for exhibiting art in public and propagating art in architecture (sculpture, furniture, frescoes). Ruskin took great interest in medieval traditions in the field of crafts and manufacturing, which he saw as a stage of individual

creativity in which human beings had not yet been alienated from their fabrications. He also favored agricultural and rural modes of production that allowed for a natural rhythm in work processes, a more human pace in production, and an ultimately holistic concept of work. Ruskin ultimately upheld the moral values and concepts of beauty inherent in craftwork and preferred them to those of industrial production. Both he and Morris saw the extensive use of machines as a central problem of human existence that enslaved humans in labor consisting of repetitive and senseless segments and destroying the sincere and meaningful work of individuals. Morris later became a committed socialist and communist who saw expansionist and imperialist Victorianism as a threat to human welfare. Another significant influence on the doctrine of the arts and crafts movement and its promotion was the English industrial designer Christopher Dresser, who had studied Japanese art and design, which he later taught in the United States, applying his knowledge mostly to the shaping of engines and industrial components.

ARTS AND CRAFTS, AESTHETICISM, ART NOUVEAU

While the arts and crafts movement worked toward a more detailed and profound arts appreciation and changes in the modes of production and reception or consumption, aestheticism lacked all political ambition and was eager to flee the pressures and restrictions of Victorian society. Both used the same models and ideals, dwelling on the ideas of an agrarian idyll and glorifications of the past, and both equally rejected the idea of progress, imperialism, capitalism, and pragmatism. After World War I the elements of both movements blended into art nouveau, which relied on organic models and exotic themes while it also favored geometrical simplicity and a focus on the effect of the artwork.

See also Art and Architecture; Arts and Crafts; Bohemians and Vagabondia; Foriegn Visitors; Genteel Tradition

BIBLIOGRAPHY

Primary Works

Baudelaire, Charles. *Les Fleurs du mal.* 1856. Paris: Imprimerie Nationale, 1978.

Evans, Donald. *Discords.* Philadelphia: N. L. Brown, 1912.

Evans, Donald. *Sonnets from the Patagonian.* Philadelphia: N. L. Brown, 1918.

Huysmans, Joris-Karl. *A rebours.* 1884. Paris: GF-Flammarion, 2001.

Le Gallienne, Richard. *Quest of the Golden Girl.* 1896. New York: John Lane, 1920.

Wilde, Oscar. *The Picture of Dorian Gray.* 1891. Oxford: Oxford University Press, 2005.

Secondary Works

Bell-Villada, Gene H. *Art for Art's Sake and Literary Life: How Politics and Markets Helped Shape the Ideology and Culture of Aestheticism, 1790–1990.* Lincoln: University of Nebraska Press, 1996.

Burns, Sarah. *Inventing the Modern Artist: Art and Culture in Gilded Age America.* New Haven, Conn.: Yale University Press, 1996.

Freedman, Jonathan. *Professions of Taste: Henry James, British Aestheticism, and Commodity Culture.* Stanford, Calif.: Stanford University Press, 1990.

Prettejohn, Elizabeth, ed. *After the Pre-Raphaelites: Art and Aestheticism in Victorian England.* New Brunswick, N.J.: Rutgers University Press, 1999.

Stokes, John. *In the Nineties.* Chicago: University of Chicago Press, 1989.

Weir, David. *Decadence and the Making of Modernism.* Amherst: University of Massachusetts Press, 1995.

Zorn, Christa. *Vernon Lee: Aesthetics, History, and the Victorian Female Intellectual.* Athens: Ohio University Press, 2003.

Christian Berkemeier

AFRICAN AMERICANS

See Blacks

AGING AND DEATH

Public attitudes regarding the end of human life changed dramatically between 1870 and 1920, and depictions in literature of aging and particularly ideas about death during this period reflect the changing social conceptions. The practices surrounding death moved from the domestic domain to the professional domain, from the public to the private, from the feminine to the masculine, and from the religious to the naturalistic.

ROMANTIC ATTITUDES

The influence of the Romantic period had left a funereal legacy in America that offered mourning survivors and the afflicted the conception that death represented a full and complete communion with nature.

Death was viewed as a natural phenomenon, and the focus was often not on the loss of the loved one, who was certainly grieved for, but on the good death as a demonstration of Christian values. James J. Farrell suggests that the sentimentality of the Romantics "established a style of funeral service that persisted throughout the nineteenth century" (p. 34), but it was the ideas behind the service—ideas that stressed the importance of the individual within the context of a continuum of history, especially a family history—that experienced the most profound change during the transition into the modern period.

During the Victorian era death was a family affair that involved all members of the household. The family gathered around to offer support in the last days of the dying person, who was tended to by the mother or another female representing the head of household. The individual was vitally important during this period, and the person's place within the family was contextualized through what Mary Louise Kete refers to as "sentimental collaborations." Such collaborations of sentiment, Kete suggests, represent an "exchange of sympathy which establishes the ground for participation in a common cultural or intellectual project" (pp. xv, xviii).

Sarah Orne Jewett (1849–1909) demonstrates the importance of communal bonds and exchange of sympathies in "Miss Tempy's Watchers" (1888), which finds two aging ladies standing watch over the corpse of their old and dear friend Miss Tempy. Jewett uses death as a plot device to bring together these two ladies, Miss Binson and Mrs. Crowe. The pair have grown apart socially over their lives and are divided by different domestic environments and financial standing and even align themselves with differing factions within their church. But watching over Miss Tempy provides them an opportunity to come closer together again as friends. More importantly, their shared duty, which is somewhat foreign to Mrs. Crowe, allows them to consider their own lives and habits in comparison with their friend. Particularly for Mrs. Crowe, it is a chance to ponder her own nature and the legacy she will be leaving to her community.

THE MODERNIST PERCEPTION

Edgar Lee Masters (1869–1950) established a modernist critique of the Victorian adoration of the small local community in his *Spoon River Anthology* (1915). In this collection of poems Masters offers readers a unique view of a local community by privileging the voices of its dead. Death was a powerful element in Masters's own life: as a young child he had been stricken with measles complicated by pneumonia, and the combination nearly claimed his life. Later he suffered the losses of several close friends and family members. John E. Hallwas sums up Masters's predicament by stating that he "sometimes felt at risk, terrified by the prospect of death, yet he was unable to achieve the comfort that Christianity provides" (p. 12). Masters was very intelligent and well read, however, and was exposed to freethinkers throughout his formative years. This exposure, combined with his distrust of religion, led him to a position of philosophical naturalism very like that of his literary contemporaries Stephen Crane, Frank Norris, and his good friend Theodore Dreiser. *Spoon River Anthology* addresses peoples' environment as the ultimate "rat trap" from which the only escape is death (Hallwas, p. 14). Masters differed from many of his contemporary naturalists both in focusing his work on poetry and also in analyzing "not just one individual who was trapped and defeated but a deeply interrelated community of people." Masters's genius was in demonstrating the "soul secrets" of "a whole community civically and ecologically related and intertwined" (Hallwas, p. 18).

A MECHANISTIC DEATH

The Social Darwinism of the naturalists seriously undermined the sense of individual autonomy and importance, leading to a perspective of people as cogs in a great machine, or animals, whose futures and fortunes were almost wholly beyond their own control. Farrell suggests that the naturalists essentially phased out God from their cosmology, replacing him with an impartial nature. Whereas the Romantics viewed nature as delicate, deity-driven, and beneficent, the naturalists regarded it as cold, impersonal, and indifferent to the plight of the individual. This conception of humanity as a species informs many books, such as *McTeague* (1899) by Frank Norris (1870–1902) and *The Call of the Wild* (1903) by Jack London (1876–1916).

London addresses the issues of individual death most directly in "The Law of Life" (1901), which centers on the death of an aged Native American in the frozen Klondike. Readers meet old Koskoosh in his final hours, blind and left behind by his tribe to die in the cold. His family has supplied him with furs for warmth and a supply of wood for the fire that burns before him, but they are packing up to move on and must leave him. His life will last only as long as his supply of wood. It is the way of the tribe, the law of life that the old and feeble must be separated from the pack and left to their fate, that same fate that awaits us all. Koskoosh understands himself only in relation to his tribe and describes himself as an "episode" in the greater entity of his people. For Koskoosh it is the tribe, the species, that is important and that enjoys longevity through the episodic engagement of individuals, who do their natural job of reproducing and later die. In "The Law of Life" London takes the Victorian conflict of death and gives it a naturalist twist; death comes inexorably for Koskoosh, but there remains the struggle. Gone is the omniscient and omnipotent God who will judge and deliver grace or wrath as the person merits it, but present are the wolves, who wait to consume the old man. He begins to fight for his remaining breaths but finally surrenders, knowing it is a fight he is destined to lose.

One social benefit of the newly mechanistic outlook on the body and its functions was that death was no longer considered a necessarily painful event. Doctors assured patients that death itself was quite natural (although it was now distinctly removed from the spiritual context it had formerly enjoyed) and compared the process to a machine simply wearing out or running down. No longer was the moment of death assumed to be a frightful struggle or a fearsome moment of judgment by God. The assurance that death is painless is evident in "Miss Tempy's Watchers," in which Miss Binson relates the local doctor's assurance that when the dying "come to the last, he'd never seen one but was willin', and most were glad, to go" (p. 687). This attitude of a death met smoothly and quietly is evidenced in many of Emily Dickinson's (1830–1886) poems. She was no stranger to death in her house, having tended to her own loved ones, and her poems reflect both the grief and the acceptance of a loved one's passing (Wolff, pp. 68–69). "I Heard a Fly Buzz—When I Died" illustrates a passing that appears as painless and smooth as the closing of a window blind, and "Elysium is as far" portrays death as being as close as the next room. In "Because I could not stop for Death," Dickinson offers a vision of death as a pleasant carriage ride into the sunset of eternity. This poem presents a view of death that involves no pain or suffering and little sense of loss. But loss is present in other poems, such as "The Bustle in the House" and "The last Night that She lived," which uses natural imagery to connect the dying to withering reeds but does not make light of the toll that death takes upon those left behind at the bedside.

The use of embalming, which had become increasingly popular during the Civil War, had helped to introduce the idea that medical science could control such natural processes as bodily decay. These factors were compounded by the burgeoning theory of disease as a bacteriological phenomenon; previously disease was thought to have followed familial lines, but science was demonstrating the existence of bacteria and its role in disease.

Mark Twain (1835–1910) addresses both embalming and the recent discovery of bacteriological forces in his *Life on the Mississippi* (1883). In his discussion of New Orleans he notes that people there bury their dead above ground, in vaults that follow architectural lines and are often quite elaborate. He finds many fresh flowers or, for the poorer residents, the "immortelle," which is a linen wreath or cross that is less expensive and requires less maintenance. The grounds are immaculately clean and neat, and he laments that the people of this region do not live as well as they die, for the neighborhoods of the living do not compare with those of the dead. In an authorial intrusion Twain stops himself, admitting that he has tried to make the graveyards appear serene and blissful and declaring that there is nothing "genuinely sentimental" about them (p. 319). In fact he asserts that the burial of the dead, while understandable in older times, must now be considered a public health hazard because the interred bodies spread disease. A corpse once buried will "glut the earth and the plant-roots and the air with disease" (p. 320), thus shortening the lives of many who live in the vicinity of the cemetery. He cites F. Julius Le Moyne, who stated that in time of epidemic, areas surrounding cemeteries experience much greater incidence of disease than those that do not share land with the dead. In its place Twain recommends cremation, which has two primary benefits: it eliminates the bacteriological threat of decaying corpses, and it does not tax the grieving so badly as burial. He cites a second doctor, Charles W. Purdy of the Chicago Medical Society, who stated that Americans spend more on burials than they do on elementary education. Cremations, on the other hand, may be done quite economically, or for those with greater means, it may still be made as "costly and ostentatious as a Hindu *suttee*" (p. 322). Twain ends his discussion of burial practices with an anecdote of his own, in which he meets an acquaintance who is making his fortune as an undertaker. The man confesses that the two chief moneymakers in his business are ice, which is used to preserve the body for viewing, and embalming. Neither would be required for cremation, and the undertaker states that times of epidemic are bad for business precisely because people are interred too quickly to take full advantage of their survivor's grief. The entire business is predicated on the manipulation of people's vulnerability in their grief.

The new conception of health as a mechanical, systemic model further connected it to economic factors during this period with the introduction of life insurance. The theory that individuals were at the mercy of economic forces helped lead to socialist literature such as Upton Sinclair's *The Jungle* (1906) and Frank Norris's *The Octopus* (1901) and *McTeague*. This theory touched poetry as well, as evidenced by

Edwin Arlington Robinson's (1869–1935) "The Mill" (1920), which provides a commentary on the tenuousness of life in an industrial age. The poem follows the wife of a miller who searches for her late husband, only to find he has hung himself from a rafter of the mill. The poem offers no explanation for his deed nor for his wife's response in seeking solace in the "black water" that will hide her demise from the world.

Perhaps the most common incidence of death in literature is what Alan Warren Friedman identifies in *Fictional Death and the Modernist Enterprise* as the "climactic death" (p. 31). Novels that end with death, such as Norris's *McTeague,* resolve the conflict in ways that are either unsatisfying or that present a dark editorial on the society they represent. *McTeague* is perhaps most effective at illustrating the impotence of the individual with its final scene, leaving McTeague cuffed to the dead body of Marcus, McTeague's close friend and rival for the affections of Trina, the love interest.

DEATH AS CRITICISM

Sometimes, as in Kate Chopin's (1851–1904) *The Awakening* (1899), the death may represent a reaffirmation of social rules. That death is Edna's only avenue of escape indicts the society that so impinges upon individual rights, yet the narrative also reifies the status quo by forbidding its protagonist any alternatives other than submission or death. Friedman states that in such plots the social "deviation is so great, or the world so disapproving, or both that the climax is death for the protagonist or the beloved. Death so represented precludes the possibility that a relationship, begun in violation, might be recast into a socially sanctioned form" (p. 45). Edna has violated social sanctions with her behaviors by failing to observe the customs of her class and by setting up housekeeping alone to pursue her artwork. Chopin offers readers a monolithic social structure in which the individual is offered only two alternatives: to take one's place in society or to remove oneself entirely with the self-destructive measures that Edna chooses.

In one of the earlier works of Henry James (1843–1916), *Daisy Miller* (1879), the young protagonist's death serves as a social critique of class and propriety and a lesson about maintaining and respecting the bonds and requirements of one's community. Daisy is a young American woman visiting Rome with her mother and brother. She is young and vibrant and has little time to concern herself with the small matters of social caste that her fellow Americans in Europe care so much about. In the end it is her affair with an

Italian of a lower caste that keeps her out late in the night air; she becomes ill and dies soon after.

The latter half of the century saw several of its most celebrated poets reaching their twilight years, and quite naturally, aging and the decline of life merged into their work. Ralph Waldo Emerson wrote "Terminus" in 1867, when he was sixty-three and was aware of his declining powers, and Walt Whitman (1819–1992) wrote several poems that appeared in editions of *Leaves of Grass* (1855) that cataloged his experience of growing older. These poems began many years before his death, starting with "Youth, Day, Old Age, and Night" in 1858 and "Song at Sunset" in 1860; then moving through such titles as "Now Finale to the Shore" (1871), "Queries to My Seventieth Year" (1888), and "Old Age's Lament" (1888); and finally concluding with "Old Age's Ship and Crafty Death's" in 1890, some thirty years later. In these poems Whitman examines his fluctuating attitudes about his own aging process, its trials, and its rewards. In one of his most famous poems, T. S. Eliot (1888–1965) examines the wealth that exists in a single moment of one's life. "The Love Song of J. Alfred Prufrock" (1917) touches on the odd juxtaposition of life as both transient and lasting. One's life may be measured out with coffee spoons, and yet Eliot is not deterred by the apparent mundanity and repetition of life, asserting instead that "In a minute there is time/For decisions and revisions which a minute will reverse" (p. 1421). Edwin Arlington Robinson, however, suggests a darker side to aging in "Miniver Cheevy" (1910). For Cheevy, who "sighed for what was not," life is a tedious journey that pales in comparison to the romantic tales of old (p. 1107). He fails to find comfort and joy in his own life and is frittering away his gift in regret and drink.

But Robinson is not so sour in his earlier "Isaac and Archibald" (1902). In this story two lifelong friends each confide in a young boy their fears for the other as they watch one another grow old and begin to falter. Old friends are reunited as well in Willa Cather's *My Ántonia* (1918), which suggests that perhaps life saves the best for last. In "A Mistaken Charity" (1887), Mary E. Wilkins Freeman offers readers two independent sisters who dare to rebel against the "mistaken charity" of local townspeople who try to place them in an old ladies' home for their own good. These stories suggest that while people may steadily lose their effectiveness as they age, they need not become dependent, nor should they surrender their livelihood and everyday activities.

In contrast to Freeman and her spry elders, Robert Frost (1874–1963) offers a more somber critique of aging and its economic hazards in his "The Death of the Hired Man" (1914). This poem finds a couple begrudgingly taking in an old and only sometimes reliable hired man who has come back to them to die. He has worked for them off and on for years, and although the husband does not wish to take him back, the wife understands that he has nowhere else to go. Although Frost's more famous poem "Stopping by Woods on a Snowy Evening" (1923) does not explicitly address aging, the speaker's description of his journey is widely considered to be a metaphor for the journey of life: he has traveled far enough to become weary but still, he says, has "miles to go before I sleep" (p. 1131).

See also The Awakening; Health and Medicine; "The Love Song of J. Alfred Prufrock"; *McTeague*

BIBLIOGRAPHY
Primary Works
Chopin, Kate. *The Awakening.* 1899. New York: Avon, 1972.

Eliot, T. S. "The Love Song of J. Alfred Prufrock." 1917. In *Norton Anthology of American Literature,* vol. D, 6th ed. New York: Norton, 2003.

Frost, Robert. "Stopping by Woods on a Snowy Evening." In *The Norton Anthology of Poetry,* 4th ed., edited by Margaret Ferguson, Mary Jo Salter, and Jon Stallworthy. New York: Norton, 1996.

Jewett, Sarah Orne. *Novels and Stories.* Edited by Michael Davitt Bell. New York: Literary Classics, 1994.

Masters, Edgar Lee. *Spoon River Anthology.* 1915. Edited by John E. Hallwas. Chicago: University of Illinois Press, 1992.

Robinson, E. A. "Miniver Cheevy." 1910. In *Norton Anthology of American Literature,* vol. D, 6th ed. New York: Norton, 2003.

Twain, Mark. *Life on the Mississippi.* 1883. New York: Harper & Brothers, 1917.

Secondary Works
Eastman, Richard M., and Robert E. Yahnke. *Aging in Literature: A Reader's Guide.* Chicago: American Library Association, 1990.

Farrell, James J. *Inventing the American Way of Death 1830–1920.* Philadelphia: Temple University Press, 1980.

Friedman, Alan Warren. *Fictional Death and the Modernist Enterprise.* Cambridge, U.K.: Cambridge University Press, 1995.

Hallwas, John E. Introduction to *Spoon River Anthology.* Chicago: University of Illinois Press, 1992.

Kete, Mary Louise. *Sentimental Collaboration: Mourning and Middle Class Identity in Nineteenth-Century America.* Durham, N.C.: Duke University Press, 2000.

Wolff, Cynthia Griffin. *Emily Dickinson.* New York: 1986.

Virgil Mathes

AGNOSTICISM AND ATHEISM

The philosophical ramifications of Charles Darwin's (1809–1882) *On the Origin of Species* (1859) were grasped in short order by both religious and nonreligious thinkers of the later nineteenth century. The theory of evolution represented, in the eyes of many philosophers and scientists, the final component in the fashioning of a purely secular conception of the universe, for it was believed to have destroyed the last remaining argument in support of a deity—the argument from design. The lingering belief that God had designed all entities—and specifically human and animal bodies—for maximum efficiency in the continuance of life now seemed headed for the intellectual dustbin, along with other theistic arguments such as the First Cause (rendered problematic by the work of David Hume), the "consensus of mankind" (an obviously untenable view in light of widespread and increasing skepticism), and the like. The notion of the First Cause rests upon the belief that, since all events in the universe are the results of some antecedent cause or causes, there must have been a First Cause (i.e., God) to get causation started. The "consensus of mankind" idea rests upon the notion that since belief in God is universal, it must be true (discounting the fact that such belief is now not universal and, even if it were, it could simply be the product of a universal error).

RELIGION AND SCIENCE

In the later nineteenth century, it was British and German thinkers who led the campaign for secularism, although few of them were courageous enough to declare themselves actual atheists. The mild-mannered Darwin himself avoided religious controversy as far as possible, admitting to his doubts about God only in his posthumously published autobiography; but "Darwin's bulldog," Thomas Henry Huxley (1825–1895), was not so shy. In America there was no parallel to the dramatic debates on evolution between Huxley and the Anglican bishop Samuel Wilberforce in 1860 or Huxley's later and even bitterer scourging of the aging William Ewart Gladstone in the 1890s over the veracity of the biblical book of Genesis; still less was there

anything similar to the years-long struggle of the atheist Charles Bradlaugh in the 1880s to take his seat in Parliament without swearing an oath on a Bible—a battle in which he at last prevailed. Huxley had coined the term "agnosticism" around 1868, and it was rapidly adopted by other thinkers such as Leslie Stephen ("An Agnostic's Apology," 1876), Herbert Spencer, and numerous other British thinkers. Their work, along with that of such Germans as Ernst Haeckel (1834–1919), was widely read in the United States. Haeckel's *Die Welträthsel* (1899) was quickly translated into English as *The Riddle of the Universe* (1900). Although this treatise's conclusions on the nature of the universe would be seriously vitiated by Einstein's theory of relativity early in the new century, it represented the pinnacle of that somewhat cocksure attitude of nineteenth-century scientists that they had indeed solved all the "riddles of the universe." Haeckel's formulation of God as a "gaseous vertebrate" (p. 288)—a cynical reference to the seemingly contradictory qualities attributed to the Judeo-Christian God—became a catchphrase. The influence of another atheist, Friedrich Nietzsche (1844–1900), was manifested only in the early twentieth century, as his works gradually began to be translated into English.

At the same time that biologists and physicists were providing naturalistic explanations of many phenomena previously assumed to have been the work of divine fiat, other scientists were doing their part in supplying a naturalistic explanation of the origin and continuance of religious belief. Although this work too had begun with the Enlightenment philosophers of France, along with such British offshoots as Hume (*Dialogues concerning Natural Religion,* 1779), the systematic work was done chiefly by British anthropologists ranging from Edward Burnett Tylor (*Primitive Culture,* 1871) to Sir John Lubbock (*Pre-Historic Times,* 1865) to Sir James George Frazer (*The Golden Bough,* 1890–1915). Their research established with overwhelming conclusiveness that the religious instinct was implanted in humanity at an extremely early stage of development, long before the development of the rational intellect. In the United States, the popular historian John Fiske (1842–1901) presented a summary of this work in *Myths and Myth-Makers: Old Tales and Superstitions Interpreted by Comparative Mythology* (1872). Although in many ways a somewhat simpleminded treatise, it proved tremendously popular and remained in print through the end of the century. In essence, Fiske maintained that primitive peoples were simply bad philosophers who had misconstrued natural phenomena and attributed them to the gods. The clear implication was that religion was a "primitive" trait that modern, civilized

THE PUZZLE OF EDEN

In Some Mistakes of Moses *(1879), Robert G. Ingersoll asks,*

Can any reason be given for not allowing man to eat of the fruit of the tree of knowledge? What kind of tree was that? If it is all an allegory, what truth is sought to be conveyed? Why should God object to that fruit being eaten by man? Why did he put it in the midst of the garden? There was certainly plenty of room outside. If he wished to keep man and this tree apart, why did he put them together? And why, after he had eaten, was he thrust out? The only answer that we have a right to give, is the one given in the Bible. "And the Lord God said, Behold the man has become as one of us to know good and evil; and now, lest he put forth his hand and take also of the tree of life, and eat, and live forever: Therefore the Lord God sent him forth from the Garden of Eden, to till the ground from whence he was taken."

Will some minister, some graduate of Andover, tell us what this means? Are we bound to believe it without knowing what the meaning is? If it is a revelation, what does it reveal? Did God object to education then, and does that account for the hostile attitude still assumed by theologians toward all scientific truth?

Robert Green Ingersoll, *The Works of Robert G. Ingersoll,* 12 vols. (New York: Ingersoll League, 1912–1929), 2:123–124.

and that it was a mundane document that had its own history just like any other sacred or secular text from antiquity.

The relatively new science of psychology played its role as well at the turn of the century. Although Sigmund Freud's (1856–1939) chief works on religion—*The Future of an Illusion* (1927) and *Moses and Monotheism* (1939)—were written only late in his career, his atheism had become a matter of public record decades earlier. Other psychologists also made advances in interpreting religious belief naturalistically as the product of indoctrination, wish fulfillment, and insecurity.

The result of all these movements in science and philosophy was a new conception of the course of European history, in which the influence of religion upon both human minds and human political and social institutions was seen to be diminishing—to the general advance of civilization. The British historian W. E. H. Lecky (1838–1903) emphasized these points in his two landmark works, *History of the Rise and Influence of Rationalism in Europe* (1865) and *History of European Morals from Augustus to Charlemagne* (1869). Some American historians addressed the issue of religion and science more directly, most notably John William Draper in *History of the Conflict between Religion and Science* (1874) and Andrew D. White in *A History of the Warfare of Science with Theology in Christendom* (1895). Both works were immensely popular and influential. Draper (1811–1882), who was born in England but immigrated to the United States in 1832, became a pioneering chemist and made important developments in photography. In the preface to his book, he made an important point: "The history of science is not a mere record of isolated discoveries; it is a narrative of the conflict of two contending powers, the expansive force of the human intellect on one side, and the compression arising from traditionary faith and human interests on the other" (p. vi). Although there is a suggestion of anti-Catholic bias in Draper's thinking, his treatise nevertheless suggested that the conflict of science and religion was really a struggle of two differing worldviews. White (1832–1918), the first president of Cornell University and an experienced diplomat, similarly maintained that science was destroying religious dogma in the realm of nature, and he perhaps unwittingly cast doubt upon the validity of Christian morals as well.

Even supporters of religion were compelled to speak in the language of science. Most notable among them was William James (1842–1910), who became the leading American philosopher of his day. His best-selling *Varieties of Religious Experience*

human beings should outgrow and were in fact in the process of outgrowing.

At the same time, philology was coming to the aid of secularism in the form of the "higher criticism," a movement in biblical criticism chiefly sponsored by German scholars of the later nineteenth century. The overall effect of the higher criticism was a conception of the Bible as a heterogeneous text written by many hands over the course of centuries or even millennia and a product of the social and political tendencies of the Jewish and early Christian society out of which it emerged. Without saying so, the higher critics suggested—in some cases unwittingly—that the divine inspiration of the Bible could not be upheld

(1902) purported to be an "empirical" study of religion from a psychological perspective, although his bias in favor of religion becomes quickly evident. James attempted to bolster the cause of religion by appealing to one of the last remaining arguments that had not yet been overthrown by critical scrutiny—the argument from "feelings." His exhaustive chronicle of a wide range of religious sentiments, visions, and hallucinations (almost all of them Christian, however) was manifestly designed to validate at least some of these phenomena as not explicable except by the postulation of an actual deity who had engendered them, although the deity James had in mind was a rather attenuated one. His nervousness in the wake of other scholars' expositions of the long history of religious error becomes evident when he writes: "It does not follow, because our ancestors made so many errors of fact and mixed them with their religion, that we should therefore leave off being religious at all" (p. 500).

THE INFLUENCE OF INGERSOLL

In spite of constitutional guarantees of freedom of religion (which only a few bold thinkers extended to cover freedom from religion), relatively few Americans emerged as full-fledged atheists, and those who did so were oftentimes dismissed as cranks. One such was Emma Goldman (1869–1940), whose championing of anarchism made her a prime bugaboo of the later nineteenth century and early twentieth century, whose very name could raise a shudder among the well-bred. Although she did not emphasize atheism in her thought, she was nonetheless convinced that it was an important component in her quest to secure individual freedom. She addressed the issue only rarely, as in the pamphlet "The Philosophy of Atheism and the Failure of Christianity" (1916). Similarly, Ambrose Bierce entertained himself and his readers by mercilessly ridiculing clerics of all stripes in the editorial pages of various San Francisco papers, including William Randolph Hearst's *Examiner,* but his words did not carry much influence except on the Pacific Coast.

The same could not, however, be said for Robert G. Ingersoll (1833–1899), a lawyer who became the most popular, and notorious, orator of the later nineteenth century. Although many of his speeches were political in nature (he was an important force in Republican politics following the Civil War, although he himself never held office; in 1876 he gave the nomination speech for James G. Blaine at the Republican National Convention), he attracted far greater attention for his fiery lectures against religion. It is not entirely clear whether Ingersoll was actually an atheist; he himself always maintained that he was only an agnostic, and numerous passages in his work suggest his hope that he could come upon a god very different from what he believed to be the vengeful and irrational god of the Jews and Christians. Ingersoll first came to prominence in 1872 with his lecture "The Gods" and followed it up with the treatise *Some Mistakes of Moses* (1879), itself a series of lectures. To some degree Ingersoll must have been influenced by the higher criticism in this scathing exposition of the contradictions and barbarities of the Pentateuch, although in many cases his arguments are ones that any skeptical reader of the Bible could have made. What sets Ingersoll apart is not the acuity of his thought—his credentials as a biblical scholar can easily be challenged—but his boldness in confronting the most sensitive points of Scripture and in the liveliness, even flamboyance, of his prose, laced as it is with rhetorical questions, thundering pronouncements (something that he may have picked up from his father, a Congregationalist minister), and a fervent passion for human freedom and dignity. It is this last feature that separates him from mere cynics like Bierce: Ingersoll could not be thought of as a mere scoffer and lampooner but as one who earnestly believed that freedom from the intellectual thrall of religion would lead to a healthier mind and a more wholesome society. A later lecture, "God in the Constitution" (1890), retains its value in the early twenty-first century in warning against attempts to breach the wall separating church and state.

Several nineteenth-century feminists also proclaimed their secularism and made it a central feature in their quest for women's rights. Although Susan B. Anthony wavered between the Quakerism of her youth and a vague Unitarianism, her thought was largely secular; Carrie Chapman Catt was more outspoken, seeing the Christian churches as chief havens of antifeminism. But the most daring of all was Elizabeth Cady Stanton, an avowed atheist who in the pamphlet *Bible and Church Degrade Woman* (1896) and other writings was unflinching in her hostility to the influence of Christianity in perpetuating political and legal injustices against women; she concluded that "the Church has done more to degrade woman than all other adverse influences put together" (p. 12).

Agnostic and atheistic writing achieved surprising popularity in the early twentieth century from an unusual source—the Little Blue Books published by Emanuel Haldeman-Julius (1889–1951), a Russian Jewish immigrant whose immensely popular publishing company sold millions of books, mostly reprints, for five or ten cents. Haldeman-Julius made no secret of his wish to convert the American masses to secularism. One of his most popular authors was the lawyer Clarence Darrow (1857–1938). Although Darrow's most significant works on the subject were written relatively late in life—among them *Infidels and Heretics: An Agnostic's Anthology* (1929) and the pamphlet *Is Religion Necessary?* (1931)—his atheistic credentials were of long standing. It was no accident that he leaped at the chance to defend John Thomas Scopes in the celebrated "monkey" trial of 1925. Nor is it surprising that H. L. Mencken (1880–1956) chose to write his acerbic reports of the trial for the *Baltimore Evening Sun*. Mencken, like Bierce, had been lampooning religion and the religious from his earliest newspaper days at the turn of the century, although his *Treatise on the Gods* (1930) is also a late work. In 1920 he translated Nietzsche's most unrestrained attack on Christianity, *Der Antichrist* (1888). Mencken was not actually an atheist, but his libertarian hostility to the influence of religion on society and politics (in the form of blue laws, prohibition—which he believed to have been engendered by a fanatical Methodist clergyman—and analogous infringements upon civil liberties) was relentless.

SOME LITERARY TREATMENTS

Given the extent to which agnosticism and atheism were vital issues during this period, affecting not merely abstract conceptions of the universe but the most intimate questions of individual and public morality, it is no surprise that these topics were treated in novels, stories, and even poems. Here again it might be said that the British were somewhat more forthright in facing these troubling matters, as evidenced by a succession of "loss of faith" novels from as early as James Anthony Froude's *The Nemesis of Faith* (1848) to the best-selling *Robert Elsmere* (1888) by Mrs. Humphry (Mary Augusta) Ward, a poignant portrayal of a young Anglican clergyman who finds himself unable to accept much of the supernaturalism of Christian doctrine (including the divinity of Jesus) and leaves the church for social work. The novel, widely read in the United States in numerous pirated editions, elicited volumes of commentary on both sides of the Atlantic.

It cannot be maintained that any American novel of the period had quite the impact of *Robert Elsmere*, although *The Inside of the Cup* (1913), by the popular novelist Winston Churchill, became the best-selling book of 1913. The novel is perhaps more an exposition of religious hypocrisy, especially by the wealthy, than it is a searching inquiry into the soundness of faith; and some readers felt that the easy victory of its protagonist, the conflicted Episcopal clergyman John Hodder, over the rich but unscrupulous Eldon Parr was a cop-out. Nevertheless, the novel sold widely and was made into a film in 1923. William Dean Howells's late novel *The Leatherwood God* (1916) is an unadventurous treatment of religious fanaticism.

Mark Twain (1835–1910) is a puzzling case. He deliberately withheld from publication many of the atheistic or anticlerical tracts he wrote over a lifetime, allowing only *What Is Man?* (1905)—a philosophical dialogue published anonymously that, although it does not address religion directly, is a searing attack on the principle of altruism and a systematic affirmation of determinism—to be issued in a limited edition. Such works as *The Mysterious Stranger* (1916) and *Letters from the Earth* (1962) appeared posthumously, and H. L. Mencken accused Twain of pusillanimity in not publishing these works in his lifetime; in the case of the latter work, however, it may not have been the religious content so much as the frank discussions of sex that impelled this self-censorship. What these later works reveal is Twain's disgust both at the paradoxes entailed by a literal reading of the Bible and at the notion that so selfish, hypocritical, and contemptible a race as human beings could imagine themselves made in the image of a benevolent God.

Perhaps the most prominent agnostic novelist of the period was Theodore Dreiser (1871–1945). His nonreligious, and occasionally antireligious, views are set forth obliquely in his informal treatise, *Hey Rub-a-Dub-Dub: A Book of the Mystery and Wonder and Terror of Life* (1920); and although none of his novels explicitly treats religious faith, they were widely recognized—and condemned—as exemplifying a mechanistic materialism that saw human beings as alone in a barren universe empty of God and salvation. The agnosticism of James Branch Cabell was somewhat more concealed under the baroque fantasy of his novels. Even poets like George Sterling got into the act: in his pungent sonnet "To Science" (*Sonnet*, July–August 1919) he could speak of a world "still haunted by the monstrous ghost of God" (1). The socialist Jack London, whose religious views were largely shaped by Nietzsche and Haeckel, could have added to the discussion if he had written the "Christ Novel" he had planned. He outlined its basic thrust as follows: "There is only one thing more wonderful than the reality of Christ, and that is, Christ never existing, that the imagination of man should have created him" (p. 259).

The fifty years from 1870 to 1920 effected a revolution in scientific—and, hence, religious—thinking, and religion would never again be regarded as the final arbiter of intellectual, political, social, or cultural issues. The hopes of certain agnostics and atheists of the period that religion was doomed to irrelevance may now seem like wishful thinking, but their forthright confrontation of religious obscurantism presented a challenge that no church or sect could ignore.

See also Christianity; Philosophy

BIBLIOGRAPHY

Primary Works

Draper, John William. *History of the Conflict between Religion and Science.* New York: D. Appleton & Company, 1874.

Haeckel, Ernst. *The Riddle of the Universe.* Translated by Joseph McCabe. New York: Harper & Brothers, 1900.

James, William. *The Varieties of Religious Experience.* London: Longmans, Green, 1902.

London, Jack. "Christ Novel (excerpt)." In *Critical Essays on Jack London,* edited by Jacqueline Tavernier-Courbin, pp. 259–263. Boston: G. K. Hall, 1983.

Stanton, Elizabeth Cady. *Bible and Church Degrade Woman.* Chicago: H. L. Green, 1896.

Sterling, George. "To Science." *Sonnet* 2, no. 5 (July–August 1919): 1.

Secondary Works

Buckley, Michael J. *At the Origins of Modern Atheism.* New Haven, Conn.: Yale University Press, 1987.

Gay, Peter. *A Godless Jew: Freud, Atheism, and the Making of Psychoanalysis.* New Haven, Conn.: Yale University Press, 1987.

Joshi, S. T., ed. *Atheism: A Reader.* Amherst, N.Y.: Prometheus Books, 2000.

Stein, Gordon. *God Pro and Con: A Bibliography of Atheism.* New York: Garland, 1990.

Stein, Gordon, ed. *An Encyclopedia of Unbelief.* Buffalo, N.Y.: Prometheus Books, 1985.

Turner, James. *Without God, without Creed: The Origins of Unbelief in America.* Baltimore: Johns Hopkins University Press, 1985.

Whitehead, Fred, and Verle Myhrer, ed. *Freethought on the American Frontier.* Buffalo, N.Y.: Prometheus Books, 1992.

S. T. Joshi

AGRICULTURE

See Farmers and Ranchers

ALCOHOLISM

See Addiction; Temperance

THE AMBASSADORS

If Henry James (1843–1916) ranks among America's greatest novelists due to the multiplicity of his writings with high artistic consistency, then *The Ambassadors* (1903) is his signature work. In the preface to the New York Edition of his revised novels and tales, James himself called this book "frankly, quite the best 'all round' of all my productions" (22:vii). Such high evaluation is still confirmed by scholars after many generations, although a good number of his other "productions" have been critically featured, rediscovered, and reemphasized for over a hundred years.

A LATE JAMES PLOT

The plot of *The Ambassadors,* like those of such classics as Sophocles' *Oedipus* or Jane Austen's *Emma,* is at once highly complex yet structured symmetrically with cascading reversals; it is also written in James's distinctive late style, featuring complicated syntax, conceptual diction, and subtly shaded nuance of perception. The protagonist, Lambert Strether, a New England widower with a literary sensibility, embarks on an ambassadorial mission to Europe to retrieve the wayward son of his almost affianced companion, Mrs. Abel Newsome, a widow and the matriarchal first citizen of Woollett, Massachusetts. She has demanded that Chadwick return to assume his domestic obligations and take his place within the family's imposing manufacturing business. Chad is allegedly in the clutches of some loose French female, and Strether understands that his own future with Mrs. Newsome, the benefactor of his *Literary Review,* depends upon successfully extricating Chad from the Parisian femme fatale. Strether first lands at Liverpool and makes friends with Maria Gostrey, an American expatriate who offers to serve as his guide to European culture, and they set off for Paris. Complications begin, however, when the fifty-five-year-old Strether arrives in the French capital and swiftly undergoes inner nostalgia tinged with regret: for he remembers vividly having come to Paris back in the 1860s as a newly married

Henry James in the garden of his home, Rye, New York, c. 1900. © BETTMANN/CORBIS

young man; he recalls especially a certain "vow of his youth" to dedicate himself to the "temple of taste that he had dreamed of raising up—a structure he had practically never carried further" (21:87). Strether's sense of his life's failure leads into his astonishment at finding a remarkably changed Chad, who has massively improved in character, taste, and sophistication in the wake of his European experience.

Strether dutifully though awkwardly announces to Chad his intention to fetch him home to Woollett, and yet the young man's entire demeanor and presence thoroughly disarm James's hero when Chad replies with mixed amusement and disgust that if Woollett really thinks "one's kept only by women," then "I must say you show a low mind!" (21:159). Strether's discomfiture with this transformed Chad is soon compounded by the discovery that Chad's female consort, Mme. de Vionnet, is the diametrical opposite of the "base, venal" woman (21:55) Strether

was supposed to encounter, especially when he is assured by his very favorite young person among Chad's European male friends that the "attachment" between the two is "virtuous" (21:180), which Strether's New England sensibility assumes means nonsexual. Indeed, when Strether himself sees more and more of the accomplished thirty-five-year-old Marie de Vionnet, whose defunct marriage to a reprobate precludes divorce in a Catholic society, he deeply believes her to be "one of the rare women he had so often heard of, read of, thought of, but never met" (21:252). Although Marie is about seven years older than Chad, Strether's allegiance shifts toward the young couple, and his letters to Mrs. Newsome attempt valiantly to expound the unexpectedly favorable nature of Mme. De Vionnet. However, when Mrs. Newsome's epistolary silence bespeaks her severe disapproval more eloquently than posted arguments might have done, Chad himself eventually re-surprises Strether by insinuating that, whenever Strether is ready to leave, he will go with him—although Strether by now has actually promised Marie de Vionnet to try to "save you if I can" (21:255).

At this juncture Mrs. Newsome deploys a second wave of ambassadors from her family to perform the task Strether has failed to do and possibly to retrieve the errant Strether himself. Arriving with her husband, Jim Pocock, Chad's older sister Sarah Pocock blisters Strether for insulting her mother by siding with Chad's disreputable tramp, whereas Strether's desperate hope that Sarah and the family will immediately perceive Chad's dramatic improvement from his connection with Marie does not come to pass. By now tired and demoralized by the whole series of encounters and with everything still thoroughly up in the air, Strether decides to retreat from his dilemma by taking a daylong excursion alone into the lovely French countryside somewhere—anywhere—outside Paris. In part he hopes to rekindle and fulfill a desire to visit the rural landscape reminiscent of a French canvas he long ago had desired to possess but had not the means to buy. He ends up at an intimate, picturesque inn called the Cheval Blanc (also the name of a rare wine), which fronts a small, meandering river.

By the sheerest chance on this occasion and moment—and in one of the more brilliantly rendered episodes in all of American fiction—Strether accidentally espies an idyllic Monet-like scene with a couple in a boat that turns out to be none other than Chad and Marie de Vionnet in a compromising attitude and context that indicate their full sexual intimacy. In deference to Strether's propriety, however, the two try to maintain the deception of being in the country only for the day by riding back with him to Paris on the

The following passage from The Ambassadors *is the heart of Lambert Strether's only defense after Sarah Pocock arrives from America and accuses him angrily of systematically betraying her mother's (Mrs. Newsome's) ambassadorial mission: to rescue Chad from a loose Parisian woman. What is noteworthy about Strether's reply is that, first, it captures his openness and tolerance of character and personality, and second, his explanation is highly evocative of William James's view of reality as ambulatory, in that the truest account of the world is one in which things are not to be easily distinguished where one cannot empirically divide them. In addition, notice the image subtly reminiscent of William James's concept of the stream of experience.*

I don't think there's anything I've done in any such calculated way as you describe. Everything has come as a sort of indistinguishable part of everything else. Your coming out belonged closely to my having come before you, and my having come was a result of our general state of mind. Our general state of mind had proceeded, on its side, from our queer ignorance, our queer misconceptions and confusions—from which, since then, an inexorable tide of light seems to have floated us into our perhaps queerer knowledge.

James, *The Ambassadors*, 22:200–201.

train, although it is obvious to him that they have even left behind their change of outfits for the night to keep up the pretense. Strether himself, whose entire allegiance had been founded on their attachment being virtuous in the sense of platonic and who cited so often to one and all Chad's "immense moral lift" from her goodness (21:284), is shocked both by his own naïveté and also the couple's "quantity of make-believe involved," which was what "most disagreed with his spiritual stomach" (22:265).

Disillusioned and acutely aware that Woollett, in the form of Mrs. Newsome and her daughter Sarah (both so much alike), had realized at least one element three thousand miles away that he had missed in front of his nose after four months abroad, Strether several days later receives an urgent request from Marie de Vionnet herself to visit her one more time. Chad, it seems, has left the country briefly, and Marie, sensing that he means to leave her, clings to Strether as the only

remaining ally. His intense admiration for Marie's character does not waver, and yet she does seem suddenly like "a maidservant crying for her young man" except that "she judged herself as the maidservant wouldn't" (22:286). Strether nevertheless promises once again to help her. When Chad returns after a few days, a truly exhausted Strether (who had felt mysteriously rejuvenated when he first landed at Liverpool in March) now climbs with difficulty to the young man's high rooms in the Boulevard Malesherbes and presses him in the strongest terms not to desert Marie: "You'll be a brute, you know—you'll be guilty of the last infamy" to forsake her. "You'd not only be, as I say, a brute, you'd be . . . a criminal of the deepest dye!" (22:308, 311). But Chad's extraordinary response is to announce enthusiastically his exciting new interest in "the great new force" of "advertisement," which to Strether he describes as "an art like another, and infinite like all the arts," that is, "in the hands, naturally, of a master" (22:315–316).

Fully certain that Chad now means to return to Woollett and take over the advertising segment of the manufacturing business, Strether ponders his abject failure as ambassador and prepares to return to America after he makes one final early July visit to his friend and best confidante, Maria Gostrey, who in the course of their time together has herself fallen romantically for Strether. When he informs Maria that, although he is sailing home, his relationship with Mrs. Newsome is obviously at an end, she asks him to stay abroad with the offer of a sunset love and her devoted service. But Strether declines, insisting that, no, he really "must go" in order, he finally decides, "to be right" and, like the puritan character he is, explains that "my only logic" is "not, out of the whole affair, to have got anything for myself" (22:326).

CRITICAL ESTEEM

This retelling of James's plot conveys only some droplets of the social and psychological intricacy any reader experiences with the late James. Why, however, is such a plot, even if composed in the author's complex later style, the soul (as Aristotle called plot) of a major classic novel? To begin with, James achieves great technical virtuosity by confining the narrative point of view within the mind and consciousness of his protagonist. This feature was emphasized as early as 1918 and 1921 by pioneering critics like Joseph Warren Beach and Percy Lubbock. One consequence of the technique is James's startlingly successful realization of someone like Mrs. Newsome, who never physically appears in any scene but is rendered vividly through Strether's reflections of and conversations about her. Another spin-off from this restricted point of view is the use of what James called "ficelles" (*Art of the Novel,* p. 322), or people who in dialogue with Strether enable him to relate crucial information that the reader would not have without an omniscient narrative. Maria Gostrey is a splendid example of a ficelle.

The Ambassadors also marks the return in James's large corpus to the international theme of America and Europe so prominent in his early period with such works as *The American* (1877), *The Portrait of a Lady* (1881), and the popular *Daisy Miller* (1879). His return to this subject after 1900 is marked by increased complexity, however, not only of the topic itself but also with his later prose idiom marked by longer periodic sentences, elliptical syntax, and capacious metaphor, all in the service of rendering the ongoing drama of human consciousness. A related idea is his unique treatment of a classic philosophical dilemma, freedom and determinism. James addresses this question by placing it at the exact center of Strether's speech that constitutes what James himself repeatedly called the initiating "germ" of his entire novel (*Art of the Novel,* p. 119): Strether laments to John Little Bilham, Chad's young friend, that he has failed to "live"; yet even if his "consciousness" was entirely predetermined, "one has the illusion of freedom; therefore don't be, like me, without the memory of that illusion" (21:218). This perspective, which mediates between determinism and free agency, is at one with the argument expounded by Henry's brother William James (1842–1910) in his pragmatistic philosophy and found in a series of writings Henry specifically endorsed and identified with his own fiction.

Another reason for the novel's landmark esteem is that it is a consummately executed work of art not just at the level of structural symmetry and ironic reversals but of figurative language. For all its psychological authority, its internationalism, its restricted point of view, and its philosophical resonance, *The Ambassadors* is surprisingly like a poem by dint of an intricate, interlocking system of metaphorical leitmotifs. It is sometimes easy to overlook this poetic feature because *The Ambassadors* is a long novel, not a lyric poem like a John Keats ode or a work with the patently elevated subject of a verse epic.

One other major reason for the abiding significance of *The Ambassadors* is that its artistry encases a deep structure or archetype of the fairy tale. That is, Strether, like the primordial knight, is sent on a quest by his monarch and patron, Mrs. Abel Newsome. If he performs his appointed task, that of bringing back to her a prodigal son from the snares of the evil temptress,

Strether's reward is her hand in marriage. James, however, performs brilliant reversals on this deep structure: the hero is not young but well into middle age; his damsel-monarch is both a rich bourgeois widow and "just a *moral* swell" (21:67). Most important, Strether does not merely fail in his mission, he inverts his entire stance and seeks to prevent it, causing the other "ambassadors" to arrive from Woollett and discredit him. As Sarah puts it at one point: "What is your conduct but an outrage to women like us?" (22:199), by which she means her mother and, in effect, all the decent American women of Woollett.

James's special genius in his later work is to transform situations from ordinary life—in the case of *The Ambassadors,* the "germ" of his hero's lament. This "germ" originated in a simple anecdote reported to him about his fellow writer and good friend William Dean Howells. While in the garden of the Paris home of James McNeill Whistler, the American painter, Howells was in a "Strether-like" regretful mood and expressed it to the young "Bilham-like" mutual friend, who later told James. The novelist's creative system, both here and in his other later fiction, is to invest such originating "germs" with imaginative complexity and with the late prose style convey an atmosphere replete with a major character's epistemological bewilderment. The reader, too, experiences the novelist's rendered world of affective flux, although that world somehow remains connected with ordinary life by the threads of traditional mimesis.

JAMES'S INTERNATIONALISM

James's international fiction can be thought of as a "second frontier" in American literary history in that when his fiction appeared in the late nineteenth century and early twentieth century, it seemed to parallel the completion of the national westward settlement, whereby the American psyche gravitated back toward its European "memory." In the early twenty-first century, however, an international vision comparable to James's in 1903 would probably need to expand into Hispanic, African American, and eastern European sources (not to mention Asia), since his Europe is western.

However it is defined, James's internationalism in earlier fiction like *Daisy Miller* or *An International Episode* (1879) came to transpose later into such thematic paradigms as innocence and experience, nature and art, the ethical and the aesthetic—with the first of each set of these dualities usually associated with America and the second with Europe. What ties Strether's American character to both Daisy Miller and, say, the more thoughtful yet highly imaginative Isabel Archer of *The Portrait of a Lady* is his quintessential innocence and predisposition to idealize others. In fact, what makes his character so very memorable to the reader is precisely his combination of New England puritan, imaginative idealist, and cultural innocent. Like Isabel Archer, Strether has no direct knowledge of the national financial life "downtown" within the bowels of corporate America. This ignorance bears directly on his innocence as well as on the calculating presence of certain others in the novel who do understand that world: Mrs. Newsome, her son-in-law Jim Pocock, and ultimately Chad himself. At the same time, Strether's favorable initiation at middle age into a permanent appreciation of European cultural values—embodied primarily in the person of Mme. De Vionnet, perhaps—makes *The Ambassadors* resemble at a distance James's spiritual autobiography. Early on, Strether's friend and compatriot Waymarsh tells him insightfully: "You're being used for a thing you ain't fit for. People don't take a fine-tooth comb to groom a horse" (21:109). Such "fineness" causes Strether to misread things, yet it is also the index to his best qualities, which invariably draw everyone to him that he meets abroad.

Maria Gostrey and Little Bilham are far more generous versions of a character type James deprecates in his earlier fiction, the Europeanized American. Both are warm confidants who deeply affirm Strether and wish him well. Bilham, the young American artist living abroad, is very close to him—the young man is both a surrogate son and a second self. One learns that Strether's own son died as a youngster from diphtheria. In fact, Strether's initial enthusiasm for the "transformed" Chad is really more applicable to little Bilham, whom Strether eventually wishes to make his heir, meager as such a bequeathal would be. The American figures other than Strether himself are represented by Mrs. Newsome, her daughter Sarah Pocock, Jim Pocock, Waymarsh, and by the end, Chad. Mrs. Newsome and Sarah are morally prescriptive and highly intolerant. Their fierce ethical fervor in 1900 is in a sense a cultural benchmark in that it is no longer attached to a great cause like abolition. Jim Pocock, by contrast, looks for a hot time in Paris while his wife, Sarah, takes care of her mother's serious business. Waymarsh from the very beginning is terribly anxious to get back to Woollett and later becomes Sarah's chief ally.

Marie de Vionnet is the prime representative of Europe in this novel, and in keeping with its theme of initiation and conversion, she is very favorably presented through the viewpoint character. Strether is struck at once by her extraordinary warmth and gracefulness combined with "common humanity" (21:213). That common humanity is most powerfully and ironically fulfilled at the conclusion by her poignant loss of Chad. But throughout the narrative she thoroughly captivates Strether in the same way Paris itself has done by its mystery and elusive charm: "She fell in at moments with the theory about her he most cherished, and she seemed at others to blow it into air. She spoke now as if her art were all an innocence, and then again as if her innocence were all an art" (22:15–116). Chad too will remain elusive, but not in the same way: Chad's momentous improvement through his relationship with Marie ignites Strether's dramatic about-face in his mission, but it is Chad's own about-face in favor of "advertisement" that leads Strether to his sense of abject failure. Chad's elusiveness, however, is also comparable to the Parisian aura that impinges upon Strether's ripe consciousness from early in the novel: "[Paris] hung before him this morning, the vast bright Babylon, like some huge iridescent object, a jewel brilliant and hard, in which parts were not to be discriminated nor differences comfortably marked. It twinkled and trembled and melted together, and what seemed all surface one moment seemed all depth the next" (21:89). Was Chad's new depth and transformation actually all surface after all? Could it even have been slick advertisement?

PHILOSOPHICAL UNDERPINNINGS AND WILLIAM JAMES

If Chad's transformation was indeed all surface, then such manipulation points to the theme of what one can call moral cannibalism—that is, the predisposition to use others exploitatively for one's gains or pleasures—while the passage itself just quoted expresses Strether's genuine epistemological bewilderment. The important concept for Henry James in this book is that an ethics of appreciation such as Strether's is deeply at odds with human cannibalism. His final renunciation at the close—"not to have got anything for myself" out of the whole affair—he calls his "only logic," but it is clearly an extension of his ethical consciousness. However, that same ethical sensibility is inevitably wedded to epistemological bewilderment in a perceptual world like that of the later James prose style, which never conveys just either-or. Mrs. Newsome and Sarah, by sharp contrast, both implicitly and explicitly would use others—the one Strether and the other Waymarsh—as means to their common end, and neither of them suffers an iota from epistemological bewilderment. Speaking with Maria Gostrey late in the book, Strether reluctantly declares: "That's just [Mrs. Newsome's] difficulty—that she doesn't admit surprises. It's a fact that, I think, describes and represents her; and it falls in with what I tell you—that she's all, as I've called it, fine cold thought" (22:239).

"Fine cold thought" residing within a prescriptive and absolutist mind is also the diametrical opposite philosophical opponent to the writings of William James. The deep connections between Henry James's creative work and his brother's pragmatistic thought is of course a complicated topic. Perhaps one additional proposition from William James's philosophy beyond the mediating stance between determinism and free agency expressed in Strether's "illusion of freedom" speech may be helpful. That concept is William's proposal in *Pragmatism* (1907), *The Meaning of Truth* (1909), and a number of essays that ideas themselves are inevitably transitional in nature and occur within an ongoing process of experience felt as the stream of consciousness. What this means is that ideas and concepts are constantly subject to modification and re-understanding in the light of their consequences in subsequent experience—both physical and mental experience—which always circumscribes them. To describe thinking in this way is also to designate the later method and prose of Henry James, a parallel the novelist himself certainly acknowledged more than once. Suppose one takes just one example from *The Ambassadors,* the term "virtuous" as in "virtuous attachment." Little Bilham declares to Strether that the attachment between Chad and Marie is virtuous, which Strether then gradually must learn to re-understand—nuance by nuance and episode by episode—to be an attachment that is not, as he originally assumed, without physical sexual intimacy. To Strether's credit as someone endowed naturally with a pragmatistic mind-set, his initial shock at the rural Cheval Blanc riverside notwithstanding, he strongly reaffirms the relationship and insists to Maria Gostrey that Little Bilham's terminology and characterization were accurate. To put this a bit more simply, Strether, unlike Mrs. Newsome, is open to "surprise" and therefore willing to redefine his moral concepts in the light of their ongoing consequences in experience. Mrs. Newsome, one could say, was "right" about the couple all along—provided one subscribes to William's absolutist opponents. The price for being open in Strether's way is bewilderment, but that condition is also the boon and honor of consciousness and imagination—perhaps as well the viewpoint of William's best-known essay title, "The Will to Believe."

ARCHITECTURE AND POETIC DESIGN

Apart from philosophical issues from William James, it is really the architecture and poetic design of *The Ambassadors* that remain its most compelling evidence as a masterpiece aside from point of view and the dramatization of consciousness. The symmetry of the plot is augmented, for example, by a sequence of balcony scenes (somewhat reminiscent of Nathaniel Hawthorne's *The Scarlet Letter*) that chart Strether's process of discovery and bewilderment. The first occurs when he walks to the Boulevard Malesherbes to meet Chad and sees emerging onto the balcony a young man whom he realizes after a brief moment is not Chad, although like Chad he suggests to Strether youth itself. This figure turns out to be Little Bilham, with whom Strether remains so close. At the other end of the book, a whipped, exhausted Strether comes to the same location to persuade Chad not to desert Mme. de Vionnet. He looks up, and the figure on the balcony this time is Chad. In other words, he no longer "sees" Chad in the likeness of Little Bilham.

In some ways, however, the most exceptional feature of James's poetry resides in his system of metaphors linking one segment of the novel to another. A relatively simple example is found when the same weary Strether, after looking up at Chad, discovers that the elevated "lift" to Chad's third-floor flat is broken; Strether, one recalls, had idealized the couple by expressively praising Chad's "moral lift" because of the relationship with Marie.

The best way to enter into James's virtuoso figurative system is to return to where the novel itself began, the great "germ" reported to James from which he later carefully composed Strether's poignant lament to Little Bilham. This speech, which James reiterated again and again was "the subject" that exhibited "the closeness with which the whole [of the novel] fits again into its germ" (*Art of the Novel*, pp. 307, 308) should be quoted fully enough to grasp James's poetic method. Strether declares:

> It's not too late for *you,* on any side, and you don't strike me as in danger of missing the train; besides which people can be in general pretty well trusted, of course—with the clock of their freedom ticking so loud as it seems to do here—to keep an eye on the fleeting hour. All the same don't forget that you're young—blessedly young; be glad of it on the contrary and live up to it. Live all you can; it's a mistake not to. It doesn't so much matter what you do in particular, so long as you have your life. If you haven't had that what *have* you had? This place and these impressions—mild as you may find them to wrap a man up so; all my impressions of Chad and of people I've seen at *his* place—well, have had their abundant message for me, have just dropped *that* into my mind. I see it now. I haven't done so enough before—and now I'm too old; too old at any rate for what I see. . . . And it's as if the train had fairly waited at the station for me without my having had the gumption to know it was there. Now I hear its faint receding whistle miles and miles down the line.

This passage begins the long and intricate perceptual realization by Strether in the rural French countryside of the couple in the boat who, by the sheerest of chance, turn out to be Chad and Marie de Vionnet. Strether's gradual discovery is actually being recalled in retrospection while he sits up alone late into the night meditating and contemplating his naïveté heretofore that the two (one of whom is married) have had a "virtuous" relationship with no sexual intimacy. The segment this passage opens is one of the finest in Henry James; it is important to remember that this citation is but the start of an extended, multipage dramatization of Strether's field of consciousness. Notice too that the boat "drifts wide," because Chad ("the oarsman") has just seen Strether looking out, though Strether does not know as yet at whom he looks. Once he does recognize them, he also perceives that it is entirely up to him to either acknowledge the surprised recognition or else pretend not to have seen them—in which case he knows they will go on past the dock and past the Cheval Blanc Inn, where dinner has been set for them.

What he saw was exactly the right thing—a boat advancing round the bend and containing a man who held the paddles and a lady, at the stern, with a pink parasol. It was suddenly as if these figures, or something like them, had been wanted in the picture, had been wanted more or less all day, and had now drifted into sight, with the slow current, on purpose to fill up the measure. They came slowly, floating down, evidently directed to the landing place near their spectator and presenting themselves to him not less clearly as the two persons for whom his hostess was already preparing a meal. For two very happy persons he found himself straightway taking them— a young man in shirt-sleeves, a young woman easy and fair, who had pulled pleasantly up from some other place and, being acquainted with the neighborhood, had known what this particular retreat could offer them. The air quite thickened, at their approach, with further intimations; the intimation that they were expert, familiar, frequent—that this wouldn't at all events be the first time. They knew how to do it, he vaguely felt—and it made them but the more idyllic, though at the very moment of the impression, as happened, their boat seemed to have begun to drift wide, the oarsman letting it go.

James, *The Ambassadors*, 22:256.

What one loses one loses; make no mistake about that. The affair—I mean the affair of life—couldn't, no doubt, have been different for me; for it's at the best a tin mould, either fluted or embossed, with ornamental excrescences, or else smooth and dreadfully plain, into which, a helpless jelly, one's consciousness is poured—so that one "takes" the form, as the great cook says, and is more or less compactly held by it: one lives in fine as one can. Still, one has the illusion of freedom; therefore don't be, like me, without the memory of that illusion. I was either, at the right time, too stupid or too intelligent to have it; I don't quite know which. . . . Of course I don't take you for a fool, or I shouldn't be addressing you thus awfully. Do what you like so long as you don't make *my* mistake. For it was a mistake. Live! (21:217–218)

Here it is James's interlacing of the rhetorical stages of the sonorous lament with figurative language that seems to bind this moment to the novel as a whole, thus corroborating his later belief in the New York preface that the germ stretches out from one end of the book to the other. For example, the train that Strether regrets to have missed even though it awaited him past departure time, so to speak, is finally "caught" by him much later ("selected almost at random" [22:245]) when he rides to the French countryside and eventually chances upon Chad and Mme. de Vionnet in the attitude that infers so clearly that they are sexual lovers. In other words, the train metaphor points directly across the canvas of the novel to a great recognition and meditation scene, which could well be described with James's own language about a different recognition scene in *The Portrait of a Lady*—"obviously the best thing in the book, but it is only a supreme illustration of the general plan" (*Art of the Novel*, p. 57). Similarly the imagery of the "great cook" and his "tin mould" for ornamental jellied dishes, although its immediate function is to represent the limitations of freedom, is another metaphor that stretches in both directions, establishing linkage with Strether's memorable series of special meals that act as benchmarks of his apprenticeship in Europe.

The "tin mould" metaphor functions as the principal signifier of consciousness and freedom or, more properly, as both the limitations and felt experiences of human freedom. James chooses the germ speech itself as the repository within the novel to embed the book's central philosophical question: whether or not we act as free agents. Strether is of course a character, not the author, yet a number of readers, not without some encouragement from James, tend to read this book as the sort of spiritual autobiography mentioned earlier. Then again, when Strether goes on to say, "don't be, like me, without the memory of that illusion," readers feel they are back with the character, with the fictive figure who originated, distantly, in William Dean Howells.

What James has done with the great germ speech is to take the all-too-human moment and weave his philosophical, thematic, and character studies into it through a poetics of metaphor and motif. Even the metaphor of the clock, whose loud ticking Strether associates with freedom, is implicitly a complex image consistent with these ideas above: for although the clock is rhetorically associated with the free European life, as opposed to New England constriction, the very same image is psychologically associated with the speaker's feeling that for him it really is "too late," which is precisely why the clock ticks so loudly. At the close of the novel, in conversation with Maria Gostrey, Strether whimsically compares himself and his adventure to one of the figures on a famous clock in Bern, Switzerland, that came out on one side, "jigged along their little course in the public eye, and went in on the other side" (22:322). Like the actual train rides compared to the metaphorical trains, the Bern clock diminishes the expectations of free autonomy otherwise proposed by the ticking metaphorical clock. For despite the early sense of new personal freedom he experienced after he disembarked from America, despite his fermenting declaration to live, despite his cultivation of an appetite for Europe, Lambert Strether cannot quite transcend his own temperament, even though his is fortunately one greatly embossed and not at all "dreadfully plain."

COMEDY OR TRAGICOMEDY?

The Ambassadors can present to all its readers a special challenge with respect to its specific genre: not the question of whether it is more a novel or a prose romance but whether it is primarily a comedy or else conveys a certain tragic resonance. At least James himself in this regard appears to understand exactly what he meant to say:

[Maria Gostrey] sighed it at last all comically, all tragically, away. "Then there we are!" said Strether. (22:327)

These are the last words of the novel, and as a textbook example of an open rather than a closed ending, they can trigger questions beyond the time and space of the tale itself, such as Strether's indeterminate future plans back home in Woollett without Mrs. Newsome or his lost editorship of the Woollett *Review*. Moreover, the open-ended world of the novel and its pragmatistic main character become most evident when one places side by side the opening words of the book, "Strether's first question," with its closing words: "Then there we are!" Together they point to a sort of horizontal mode of understanding and discovery by the protagonist—an idea, again, reminiscent of William James's thesis that, in all human knowing, concepts will arise from one's experience only to turn back again into the ongoing empirical stream that has given rise to them.

James's blending of "all comically" and "all tragically" are locutions that his narrator integrates into one semantic unit accompanied with a "sigh." The conceptual meaning here is suggestive of the earlier conceit of Paris as the jewel that is "all surface one moment . . . all depth the next" (21:89). Taken together with James's numerous statements to himself in the notebooks, these expressions tell one he had a strong sense of this book as tragicomedy. Most readers hopefully will respond to its beautifully mixed tonal mode, so that the novel—much like, say, *Don Quixote*—can evoke its "hard" and "soft" interpretations. To use still another analogy, *The Ambassadors*, like music, modulates from mourning and melancholia in the Freudian sense to a sharp comedy of manners tethered to miscalculation and misinterpretation somewhat in the style of a Molière play. The critic Daniel M. Fogel has explicated James's early success *Daisy Miller* as a "dark comedy of manners" (p. 97). In *The Ambassadors*, Strether does not die at the end, as does Daisy Miller, but neither is he as comic a character as Daisy for a very important reason: he possesses substantial interior powers of reflection and self-consciousness that often take a rueful cast and in the germ speech and occasionally elsewhere become verbalized to another person.

By the same token, he is a comic figure throughout much of this book, especially in his exchanges with Maria, Chad, Waymarsh, and some supporting figures, such as the brittle and indecorous expatriate Miss Barrace and the sculptor Gloriani. The high comedy of *The Ambassadors* is found in such disparate instances as Waymarsh's abrupt "bolt" away from Strether and Maria Gostrey in a "sacred rage" of irritation at their cosmopolitan talk (21:46). Another is in Strether's discombobulation at the sight of Chad's drastic change. Still another occurs later when Strether by accident encounters Mme. de Vionnet at Notre Dame Cathedral deep in prayer and opines that her relations with Chad must be "unassailably innocent," because "if it wasn't innocent, why did she haunt the churches?" (22:10). Apparently the Protestant New Englander fails to consider that Catholics, after all, may haunt churches when they feel sinful. In either case, Strether's own innocence and idealization of another's character remains consistent from James's pen.

In the end, however, if a reader still remains drawn to the non-comic side of this poetic and tragicomic novel, the reasons will always be found in the tone and poignancy of the central germ speech, or in the regret when Strether is newly arrived in Paris, or else in the all-night meditation following the boat encounter. The first of these central moments James insisted was deeply organic to the whole, much like an aria radiating throughout a musical composition. Such emphasis on organic wholeness not only comes from James's self-talk in the notebooks but is voiced emphatically six years after the publication of the book itself, when in the revised New York Edition preface James highlights Strether's outburst as "melancholy eloquence" (21:vi). It is the same preface—and the same place in the preface—in which he decides that *The Ambassadors* is his best novel.

See also Americans Abroad; *Daisy Miller; The Portrait of a Lady;* Realism

BIBLIOGRAPHY

Primary Works

James, Henry. *The Ambassadors.* In *The Novels and Tales of Henry James,* vols. 21–22. New York: Scribners, 1909. Comprises James's revised text.

James, Henry. *The Art of the Novel: Critical Prefaces by Henry James.* 1934. New York: Scribners, 1984.

James, Henry. *The Complete Notebooks of Henry James.* Edited by Leon Edel and Lyall H. Powers. New York: Oxford University Press, 1987.

James, William. *The Meaning of Truth: A Sequel to "Pragmatism."* New York: Longmans, Green, 1909.

James, William. *Pragmatism: A New Name for Some Old Ways of Thinking.* New York: Longmans, Green, 1907.

James, William. *The Will to Believe and Other Essays in Popular Philosophy.* New York: Dover, 1956.

Secondary Works

Armstrong, Paul B. "Reality and/or Interpretation in *The Ambassadors.*" In his *The Challenge of Bewilderment: Understanding and Representation in James, Conrad, and Ford,* pp. 63–106. Ithaca, N.Y.: Cornell University Press, 1987.

Beach, Joseph Warren. *The Method of Henry James.* New Haven, Conn.: Yale University Press, 1918.

Bellringer, Alan W. *The Ambassadors.* London: Allen & Unwin, 1984.

Fogel, Daniel M. *"Daisy Miller": A Dark Comedy of Manners.* Boston: Twayne, 1990.

Griffin, Susan M. "The Selfish Eye: Strether's Principles of Psychology." In her *The Historical Eye: The Texture of the Visual in Late James,* pp. 33–56. Boston: Northeastern University Press, 1991.

Hocks, Richard A. *"The Ambassadors": Consciousness, Culture, Poetry.* New York: Twayne Masterworks Series, 1997.

Hocks, Richard A. *Henry James and Pragmatistic Thought: A Study in the Relationship between the Philosophy of William James and the Literary Art of Henry James.* Chapel Hill: University of North Carolina Press, 1974.

Hocks, Richard A. "Multiple Germs, Metaphorical Systems, and Moral Fluctuation in *The Ambassadors.*" In *Enacting History in Henry James,* edited by Gert Buelens, pp. 40–60. Cambridge, U.K.: Cambridge University Press, 1997.

Hocks, Richard A. "The Multiple Versions of the Jamesian Germ for *The Ambassadors.*" In *Biographies of Books: The Compositional Histories of Notable American Writings,* edited by James Barbour and Tom Quirk, pp. 110–130. Columbia and London: University of Missouri Press, 1996.

Krook, Dorothea. *"The Ambassadors": A Critical Study.* New York: AMS Press, 1996.

Lubbock, Percy. *The Craft of Fiction.* New York: Scribners, 1921.

Wegelin, Christof. *The Image of Europe in Henry James.* Dallas: Southern Methodist University Press, 1958.

Richard A. Hocks

AMERICAN INDIAN STORIES

American Indian Stories, published in 1921 by Hayworth Publishing House, consists of works published previously in various magazines. These pieces were both autobiographical and fictional in character, and some saw slight revisions before being added to the collected work. Written by Zitkala-Ša (Sioux for "Red Bird"), the pen name for the mixed-blood Yankton Sioux writer and political activist Gertrude Bonnin (1876–1938), these well-written stories portray nostalgic reminiscence and fiery defense of the traditional ways of the writer's people. The stories included in the collection show the life of the Sioux at the transitional period at the end of the nineteenth century and the beginning of the twentieth. The message of the book concerns the humanity of the Sioux in the face of severe wrong and continuing dispossession. Zitkala-Ša's book appeared twenty-three years after she first began teaching at the famous Carlisle Indian School. The intervening years saw her engaged in activism and editing, and the experience gained in

Gertrude Bonnin (Zitkala-Ša). Photograph by Joseph T. Keiley, c. 1901. NATIONAL PORTRAIT GALLERY, SMITHSONIAN INSTITUTION/ ART RESOURCE, NY

both capacities is demonstrated in her pages. To fully appreciate the literary achievements of this writer, readers should consider how difficult it was for Native Americans, particularly women, to publish early in the twentieth century. Furthermore, this is especially true given the efforts of these writers to reach a white audience with the continuing viability of their traditional tribal cultures.

ABOUT THE AUTHOR

One of several Native American writers at work in this transitional period of literary production of those identifying as Indian, Zitkala-Ša writes to demonstrate continuing conflicts between tradition and assimilation. In doing so, her work also concerns conflicts between politics and literature as well as between traditional tribal religions and the various forms of Christianity that influenced Native Americans at the turn of the century. For instance, whereas Charles

Eastman's *Indian Boyhood* (1902) uses the word "superstition" for some Sioux traditions, to Zitkala-Ša it is Christianity that is made up of superstition. What some have seen to be sentimentalized and poetic language in her work is attributable to the popular journal style of the time, showing that like her predecessors in Native American literature, Zitkala-Ša comprehends the need to adopt the literary fashion of her time in order to reach her predominantly Euro-American audience.

Her first book, titled *Old Indian Legends*, was published in 1901. A collection of trickster tales, the book was illustrated by a colleague at Carlisle, a Winnebago teacher named Angel DeCora. This book's intention was to validate the continuing viability of Lakota culture. In the category of "retold tales," these stories are typical of many being written during this transitional period by other Sioux writers. Some of these stories were included in readers for schoolchildren on the East Coast.

Her autobiographical work and fictional pieces were published in the *Atlantic Monthly, Harper's Monthly Magazine*, and *Everybody's Magazine* between 1900 and 1902. These articles were later published in 1921 as the collection entitled *American Indian Stories*, which came to be the writer's most famous work. They suggest that her education caused a rift between Zitkala-Ša and her mother and the Sioux people and also demonstrated disagreement on many issues with Colonel Richard H. Pratt, her employer at the Carlisle Indian School. These disagreements show her pride in her heritage and culture as well as anger toward unjust treatment of Native American people. This is especially clear in the essay "The Great Spirit." While the stories can be read as separate pieces, having been previously published as magazine articles, they become particularly powerful when read together as a narrative. Starting with autobiographical depictions of the move from childhood to boarding school student and subsequently to being a teacher herself, the book leads to several stories concerned with a female protagonist. The final entry, "America's Indian Problem," evokes the political activist she had become over the course of her intense career.

AN INDIAN CHILDHOOD

The first section of *American Indian Stories* is subtitled "Impressions of an Indian Childhood" and begins with a chapter referencing the writer's mother, a significant gesture in a traditional culture with particular respect for matrilineal lines. Also significant is the fact that this first story opens with a reference to her mother's "wigwam of weather-stained canvas" (p. 68). The traditional dwelling of her people, of course, was made of buffalo hide, but in the state to which they had been reduced by the end of the nineteenth century, canvas was more easily obtained than buffalo. A primary part of her memory of her mother is of sorrow, initially associated with resentment toward "the palefaces," who caused the death of others in the woman's family. She insists that Dakotas were the only real men, and the white man is a sham. Of course, it should be noted here that the writer's father was a white man, although her mother notes that since the death of her uncle and sister, even her father is now buried on the hill. In this opening chapter Zitkala-Ša has the mother state that they were once very happy, before seeing their lands stolen by the white man (p. 69).

The second story in the collection describes the author's delight with the old legends of her people. She relates an occasion of inviting people from the village to share the evening meal and her childish impatience to hear their stories at that time. In the context of hearing the stories, she notes the distant howling of the wolves, as if to include the natural world in the telling of the stories.

In chapter 3 the memories of the girl's childhood reflect the children learning from their parents, beginning with her efforts to mimic her mother's skilled beadwork. The story also references the comforts of life in their tipi lodge. The beadwork leads to descriptions of imagined envy of her friends over imagined moccasins, then the story demonstrates the children reflecting the lives of their parents in generosity as they engage in playful gift giving.

Chapters 4 and 5 discuss particular incidents and personalities from the girl's tribe, again reflecting the generosity of spirit the child was raised to show. In the first case, a "crazy man" of whom the child was afraid is deserving of pity and is to be shown hospitality, despite her fear (p. 77). In the next case, a plum bush was to be left alone as its roots grew from the skeleton of a brave man who had been buried with the seeds that were used in a game the man had enjoyed playing during his life.

In the sixth chapter the girl remembers traditional ways of preparing preserved foods for the coming winter. The chapter is named for a chipmunk that stole bits of drying corn in his own efforts to lay food aside for the coming hard weather. Here one sees the people and the rodent engaged in a similar practice of preparation. It is in the context of winter that the writer then introduces the intrusion of missionaries, whose gift of glass marbles reminds the child of frozen river water. This chapter functions as a transition in the narrative inasmuch as the appearance of the missionaries reflects the girl's imminent departure from her traditional life.

After these several chapters of memoir, the author shifts to being lured away from home by the promise of apples, which is so powerful a symbol of temptation and regret that apples enter the titles of two chapters. The writer acknowledges that it is the apples that attract her, not yet the lure of learning letters (p. 84). The girl's mother wishes to prevent her from joining those who go with the missionaries to the boarding school, but she acknowledges that the changes that have resulted from the loss of the land will necessitate an education, and she sees that opportunity as belated payment for the theft of the land (p. 86).

SCHOOL DAYS

The second section of the collection is called "The School Days of an Indian Girl" and consists of several short chapters, the first of which describes her journey to "the land of red apples." Knowing no English, traveling far from home and made an object of derisive curiosity to the children of white travelers on the train, the little girl goes east to a boarding school with other Indian children. Regret soon follows in the depiction of the children's experience there, the loss of every aspect of their culture: language, religion, familiar scenery, and daily activity. This is especially represented by an unwanted haircut that completely ignores the victims' cultural context and leaves them with haircuts only cowards or mourners wore.

The white man's religion enters the text in the figure of the devil, who causes the child a bad dream concerned with what she calls an "evil divinity." After the dream she rubs a ragged hole into each eye of the picture of this devil from the "Stories of the Bible" book that first introduced him to her. The author's introduction into civilization is presented as an "iron machine" in which teachers' pencils moved "automatically" in marking absences. The next chapters show the writer's growing resistance to assimilation, and in the context of having met the white man's devil, she describes her own efforts both to rebel and excel as her own brand of deviltry.

Chapter 6 of this section shows the child returning home after three years of school and finding herself between worlds as a result. She describes herself as "neither a wild Indian nor a tame one" (p. 97). Others who had been to school are in a similar situation, and she notes that they were "no more young braves in blankets and eagle plumes" but rather "wore the white man's coat and trousers, with bright neckties" (p. 98). Sensing the child's uneasiness, her mother asks her to read from "the white man's papers," a Bible that missionaries had left with her years before. She accepts the book "for her [mother's] sake," but claims her "enraged spirit felt more like burning the book" as it "afforded me no help" (p. 99). The final chapter in this section describes her mother's displeasure at her deliberate disobedience in her return to the East. An outstanding example is winning an award for oratory when mean-spirited critics waved a large white flag bearing a dejected Indian girl and "words that ridiculed the college which was represented by a 'squaw'" (p. 103).

AN INDIAN TEACHER

Almost abruptly, with a new section in the text, the writer is teaching at the Carlisle Indian School. Sent west to recruit other students, she is reunited with her mother for a time. During this visit she is reminded again of her mother's resentment toward the white man, as seen in her indictment of the "paleface who offers in one palm the holy papers, and with the other gives a holy baptism of firewater." In this context she complains of still further encroachment of the white man as she notes the increasing number of homesteaders living in self-dug caves in the banks of the river (p. 110).

The final chapter of this section, "Retrospection," expresses the author's disgust with the hypocrisy of those who claim to be Christian yet continue to defraud her people. She laments having given up her "faith in the Great Spirit" in exchange for "the white man's papers." Firmly settled in the East, she bitterly decries "this semblance of civilization" in which she now lives (pp. 112–113). This is another transitional chapter because after declaring her loss of faith in her traditional spirituality and concluding this section of the collection, she reaffirms that faith in the subsequent essay.

FROM THE GREAT SPIRIT TO THE INDIAN PROBLEM

The final portion of the text is not subtitled and is not divided by chapters. The essay that originally saw publication as "Why I Am a Pagan" appeared under the title "The Great Spirit" in the collected version. Every aspect of the writer's description of that holy wonder is expressed in relation to the natural world of her homeland. Amidst this idyllic depiction of "pagan" spirituality, intrudes the converted Indian missionary. Dismissing his dogma, Zitkala-Ša reflects that she prefers to hear the voice of the Great Spirit in the birds, waters, and even the "sweet breathing of flowers" that ended the original version. To the version published in the collection she adds a paragraph that references "a fleeting quiet" in which she is "awakened by the fluttering robe of the Great Spirit," having "flowing fringes" consisting of the heavenly bodies of the universe (p. 117). Following this moving declaration of Native spirituality, the writer turns to fictional accounts of her transitional times, and the final essay is a manifesto declaring proposals to resolve "America's Indian Problem" and demonstrate the writer's life-long commitment to working for better treatment of indigenous people of all tribes.

See also Annexation and Expansion; Assimilation; Indians; Indian Wars

BIBLIOGRAPHY

Primary Work

Zitkala-Ša. *American Indian Stories, Legends, and Other Writings.* Edited by Cathy N. Davidson and Ada Norris. New York: Penguin, 2003.

Secondary Works

Allen, Paula Gunn. *The Sacred Hoop: Recovering the Feminine in American Indian Traditions.* Boston: Beacon, 1986.

Allen, Paula Gunn, ed. *Spider Woman's Granddaughters: Traditional Tales and Contemporary Writing by Native American Women.* Boston: Beacon, 1989.

Bell, Betty Louise. "'If This Is Paganism . . .': Zitkala-Ša and the Devil's Language." In *Native American Religious Identity: Unforgotten Gods,* edited by Jace Weaver, pp. 61–68. Maryknoll, N.Y.: Orbis, 1998.

Bernardin, Susan. "The Lessons of a Sentimental Education: Zitkala-Sa's Autobiographical Narratives." *Western American Literature* 32, no. 3 (1997): 212–238.

Fisher, Dexter. "The Transformation of Tradition: A Study of Zitkala-Sa and Mourning Dove, Two Transitional American Indian Writers." In *Critical Essays on Native American Literature,* edited by Andrew Wiget, pp. 202–211. Boston: Hall, 1985.

Hertzberg, Hazel W. *The Search for an American Indian Identity: Modern Pan-Indian Movements.* Syracuse, N.Y.: Syracuse University Press, 1971.

Willard, William, "Zitkala-Sa: A Woman Who Would Be Heard!" *Wicazo Sa Review* 1, no. 1 (1985): 11–16.

Young, Mary E. "Bonnin, Gertrude Simmons." In *Notable American Women, 1607–1950: A Biographical Dictionary,* vol. 1. Cambridge, Mass.: Belknap Press of Harvard University Press, 1971.

Rick Waters

THE AMERICAN LANGUAGE

The publication in 1919 of H. L. Mencken's *The American Language: A Preliminary Inquiry into the Development of English in the United States* established the English language in the United States as a subject worthy of study and repudiated a lingering colonial attitude that gave precedence to the forms and usages

H. L. Mencken. © CORBIS

of British English. Mencken's claim that the English language in America would soon develop into a separate language from that of the British Isles validated the sentiments of many Americans after World War I that the United States had finally attained cultural independence from England and had surpassed England as a world power. Mencken (1880–1956) knew that *The American Language* was actually the second major declaration of linguistic independence, consistent in spirit with Noah Webster's efforts following the American Revolution. In revitalizing the connection between language and nation in 1919, Mencken made accessible in a more comprehensive and appealing way one stream of purposeful language study that had been carried on mainly by amateurs throughout the nineteenth century in the United States (Andresen, pp. 208–209). Even observers of language who did not accept Mencken's thesis that American and British varieties of English were on the brink of becoming separate tongues were pleased by the distinctly American contributions to the language that Mencken recorded with much verve.

THE WORK

Mencken wrote his first article on American English in 1910 and returned to the topic intermittently in newspaper and magazine columns for several years, particularly during World War I, when publishers wanted Mencken to avoid topics that might appear unpatriotic. In the spring of 1918 he set to work on an entire volume on American English, and a year later *The American Language* appeared from Knopf. Published in a run of 1,500, it sold 1,373 copies in the first three months and within another year brought Mencken royalties totaling $609.20, the first of his books to make more than $500 (Mencken, *My Life,* p. 295).

The American Language is a curious piece to have been penned by H. L. Mencken, editor of the smugly named *Smart Set* and the upbraider of traditional middle-class, puritanical American values. The expected directness, clarity, and charm of style are there—and no doubt were a major reason for the book's success—but the cynicism, distrust, and pugnaciousness of his other writings are lacking. Mencken saw in American language an inherent liveliness and freedom as compared with British English and the American classroom models derived from British English. It is ironic that Mencken's chauvinism about American speechways became interpreted as linguistic patriotism, for during the most difficult times of Mencken's public life, it was precisely his patriotism that was questioned, caused by his deep love of things German. Mencken had grown up in an immigrant neighborhood in Baltimore, where German was the home language of many and where his family and their friends enjoyed German food, music, and literature. In the climate of wartime hostility during which Americans of German ancestry throughout the United States relinquished the language and cultural practices of their heritage, Mencken remained true to his. While submitting to the constraints that publishers placed on his writing for newspapers during the war years, he redirected his energy to writing *The American Language*. Its publication dispelled concerns about Mencken's patriotism and led to his becoming the most influential figure in establishing a distinctive American literary culture during the 1920s.

The Roaring Twenties suited Mencken's style. His gibes at every easy target were repeated and chuckled at across the nation. As coeditor first of the *Smart Set* and then of the *American Mercury,* he published fiction, poetry, and essays of cultural and literary criticism. The list of American writers who began their careers under Mencken's editorial tutelage is long and impressive and includes a number of African Americans. His daily correspondence with the famous and the unknown was prodigious. Behind the scenes, he had his hand in many projects, including the founding in 1925 of the journal *American Speech,* whose first editor was Louise Pound.

In the preface to *American Language,* Mencken wrote, "What I have tried to do here is to make a first sketch of the living speech of these States" (p. vii). Despite his record of poking fun at Ph.D.s and the academic establishment, *The American Language* of 1919 has all the identifying features of a scholarly book. The text has 321 pages divided into 9 chapters:

1. By Way of Introduction
2. The Beginnings of American
3. The Period of Growth
4. American and English Today
5. Tendencies in American
6. The Common Speech
7. Differences in Spelling
8. Proper Names in America
9. Miscellanea

In addition, it has a four-page preface, seventeen pages of bibliography, a twenty-eight-page list of "Words and Phrases," and a seven-page general index. The bibliography is full and includes a wide range of sources from newspaper articles to scholarly tomes. In the field of traditional history of the English language, it includes works by British authorities and seven titles by Henry Sweet and two by H. C. Wyld. In general philology, A. H. Sayce's two-volume *Introduction to the Science of Language* (1900) is listed as well as *The Life and Growth of Language* (1875) and *Language and the Study of Language* (1867) by William Dwight Whitney of Yale. George Phillip Krapp's *Modern English* (1910) is there, too. Mencken had also consulted every issue of *Dialect Notes,* the publication of the American Dialect Society begun in 1896.

No one had ever done anything like *The American Language.* Mencken had no models for organizing such a large amount of information about language and culture in America and almost no reference books on the subject. Leonard Bloomfield's foundational work in American descriptive linguistics was still more than a decade in the future, the *Oxford English Dictionary* was not yet completed, and the *Dictionary of American English* and the linguistic atlas projects for the United States were not yet begun. Despite the shortcomings that philologists were quick to point out, *The American Language* was a substantial contribution to scholarship. Furthermore, it challenged academicians to approach the speechways of American English with the same intensity and rigor that they had applied to the language of Chaucer and Shakespeare.

THE CRITICAL RECEPTION

By early-twenty-first-century standards, the contemporary reviews of *The American Language,* while mostly favorable, seem brief, superficial, and repetitious of each other. A letter to Mencken from the respected philologist Louise Pound (1872–1958) of the University of Nebraska dated 12 June 1919 mentions two of them. Pound writes:

> I have read so many reviews—some quite fatuous—which "miss" *The American Language* that I felt tempted to try a notice myself in some learned journal. . . . But now I come on two which seem good, one in *The New Republic* (if I remember rightly) and one in this month's number of *Current Opinion.* The latter is the most satisfying which I have seen. A thing which few seem to emphasize is the real value and soundness of the book as a contribution to scholarship! It's much broader and completer than if a professor had written it!

In a later paragraph in the same letter Pound modestly points Mencken to pertinent publications by herself and others. The swapping of bibliography between Pound and Mencken became a characteristic of their correspondence for the next three decades. Pound was one of several language scholars who took pains to help Mencken enlarge and update the facts of American English presented in subsequent editions of *The American Language.*

Two other Germanic philologists of note recorded their assessments of *The American Language* in scholarly journals within months of its publication—James R. Hulbert of the University of Chicago in *Modern Philology* (September 1919) and George O. Curme of Northwestern University in the *Journal of English and Germanic Philology* (July 1919). Hulbert's review is harsher, focusing on "the extraordinary faults that make it untrustworthy" (p. 119). Curme directly objects to Mencken's thesis, saying that "the materials submitted in this book do not indicate that there is such a thing as an American language" (p. 481). However, Curme forgives Mencken's lapses in facts: "The author, however, does not claim to be a philologist and is as modest as a man can be. He has a genuine interest in his native language and with the joy of an enthusiast has presented to the public useful material in a pleasing and entertaining style" (p. 483).

SUBSEQUENT EDITIONS AND THE BOOK'S LEGACY

Throughout the frenetic 1920s and into the 1930s and 1940s, when he was no longer in the national limelight, Mencken persisted in collecting materials for *The American Language.* The second and third editions followed quickly on the first, appearing in

1921 and 1923. The enlarged and rewritten fourth edition was published in 1936, followed by two hefty supplements in 1945 and 1948. The most usable version of *The American Language* is the abridgement with annotations and new material by Raven I. McDavid with the assistance of David Maurer, which Knopf issued in 1963; it remains available in subsequent paperback printings. In the 1960s, when the development of grammatical theory took over the field of linguistics, McDavid persisted in painstaking collection of regional pronunciations and vocabulary and in defending the contributions of Mencken to the story of American English, outlining the soundness of Mencken's scholarship in the preface to the abridgement and in the second annual Mencken Lecture (1966).

In the late twentieth century and early twenty-first century Mencken became an easy target for reproach. He is assuredly politically incorrect—for his fascist-Nazi leanings, his anti-Semitism, his sexism, his racism, and his blanket condemnation of the South. It is *The American Language* that will ensure Mencken a respectable place in American letters. No matter the shortcomings of the first and subsequent editions from the perspective of linguistic scholarship in the twenty-first century, *The American Language* of 1919 still bears scrutiny for its originality, scope, clarity, and ability to evoke appreciation for the vernacular forms of the language and for the speakers who are responsible for them.

Mark Harris, in the annual Mencken Lecture of 1987, speaks of two Menckens—the one of the stereotype and the one who authored and revised *The American Language:*

> If its author was a cynic or pessimist he remains concealed. Indeed, his years of devotion to *The American Language* undoubtedly went a long way toward deepening his affection for the varieties of life revealed to him by his studies of language, a long way toward sweetening his temper and improving his disposition. (P. 6)

The final sentence of the first edition shows that Mencken sensed the power of language to uplift from the beginning:

> In all human beings, if only understanding be brought to the business, dignity will be found, and that dignity cannot fail to reveal itself, soon or late, in the words and phrases with which they make known their high hopes and aspirations and cry out against the intolerable meaninglessness of life. (P. 321)

See also Slang, Dialect, and Other Types of Marked Language

BIBLIOGRAPHY
Primary Works
Mencken, H. L. *The American Language.* 4th ed. Edited by Raven I. McDavid with David Maurer. New York: Knopf, 1963.

Mencken, H. L. *The American Language: A Preliminary Inquiry into the Development of English in the United States.* New York: Knopf, 1919.

Mencken, H. L. *My Life as Author and Editor.* 1932. Edited by Jonathan Yardley. New York: Knopf, 1993.

Pound, Louise. Letter to H. L. Mencken, 12 June 1919. Pound Family Manuscripts. Nebraska State Historical Society, Lincoln, Nebraska.

Secondary Works
Andresen, Julie Tetel. *Linguistics in America 1769–1924: A Critical History.* London: Routledge, 1990.

Curme, George O. Review of *The American Language. Journal of English and Germanic Philology* 18 (July 1919): 480–483.

Harris, Mark. "The Two Menckens." *Menckeniana* 103 (fall 1987): 1–6.

Hobson, Fred. *Mencken: A Life.* New York: Random House, 1994.

Hulbert, James R. Review of *The American Language. Modern Philology* 17 (September 1919): 118–119, 302–303.

McDavid, Raven I. "The Impact of Mencken on American Linguistics." *Menckeniana* no. 17 (spring 1966): 1–7.

Connie Eble

AMERICAN LITERATURE

American literature, both in the way it was practiced and the way it was perceived, came of age in the period between 1870 and 1920. During these years American writing distinguished itself stylistically and thematically from the European tradition to which it had been dismissively compared for more than a century. American authors also increasingly gained respect as serious artists in the decades following the Civil War as literary critics inside and outside the academy began to appreciate the intrinsic merits of American poetry and prose.

EARLY CULTURAL CONTEXT
The cultural trauma of the Civil War produced a permanently altered sense of national consciousness among Americans who lived through it and beyond it. But the war between the states was only one of many

phenomena of the late nineteenth century that transformed the United States from a country fundamentally sectionalist in attitude (e.g., New England, South, Midwest, Far West) into a unified nation of the world that would come to consider its regional diversity a vital if mostly secondary trait.

The technological advances that followed the Civil War, particularly in the areas of American transportation and communication, also contributed mightily to the emergence of this new, more unified cultural awareness. In 1860, for example, fewer than thirty thousand miles of railroad existed in the United States, and major sections of the country remained essentially unconnected to each other. By May 1869, however, less than a decade later, as the last rail spike was being driven into the line linking the East and the West at Promontory Point, Utah, the number of miles of railroad crisscrossing the United States had almost tripled to nearly ninety thousand. The expansion of the railroads into every corner of the Union of course made travel throughout the country much easier (thus removing a major impediment to personal mobility that would tend to promote a regional—as opposed to a national—sensibility), but it also had the equally important effect of opening up commerce and communication between different geographical regions to a much larger degree.

Advances in publishing technology after the Civil War also worked to open contact between sections of the United States. Subscriptions to major newspapers and magazines skyrocketed in the 1870s and 1880s as Americans from all over the country grew hungrier for information from beyond their local borders. Already existing periodicals such as the *Atlantic Monthly* and *Harper's Monthly* widened their circulations dramatically in the last few decades of the nineteenth century as telegraph and transportation improvements made it possible for them to reach those more distant readers longing for access to these now more broadly focused national publications. Hoping to capitalize on newly opened markets and the increased readership among the American public, hundreds of new magazines appeared for the first time in the 1860s, 1870s, and 1880s, including *Galaxy, Overland Monthly, Scribner's Monthly,* and *Century Magazine,* to name a few of the most prominent.

Though late-nineteenth-century improvements in transportation and communication helped to foster a larger, more unified conception of an American culture, these advancements also had a simultaneous and somewhat paradoxical effect on the nation's consciousness. Ironically, as Americans seemed to be dismantling sectional boundaries in the 1870s and 1880s by traveling farther from home and by reading a wider variety of publications from across the United States, they were at the same time made newly aware of regional differences in speech and manners through contact with those people and places beyond their immediate milieus. This rediscovery of regional diversity in the context of a budding national culture would prove to have profound implications for the establishment of an indigenous American voice in literature in the decades following the Civil War.

THE RISE OF LITERARY REALISM

By 1870 a new generation of American authors, committed to the tenets of literary realism, had begun to emerge. The realist artistic vision, though expressed in a variety of ways by hundreds of writers in the late nineteenth century, was, at least in principle, relatively uncomplicated: portray people, places, and things as they actually appear in everyday life. Realism as an aesthetic movement was in large part a reaction against the idealizing (if universalizing) tendencies of literary romanticism, which had dominated literary expression in the United States since the early decades of the 1800s. The major novelists of the post–Civil War period, Mark Twain (1835–1910), William Dean Howells (1837–1920), and Henry James (1843–1916), self-avowed realists all, emphasized in their writing a fidelity to actual experience, particularly by focusing on the development of "common" characters confronting complex ethical issues.

Although Twain, Howells, and James as well as other American writers produced novels of the highest quality in the final decades of the nineteenth century, none of these works could be said to have truly achieved the status of the Great American Novel insofar as any of them alone represented the fullness of the American cultural experience. In fact, Howells himself famously argued that it would be impossible because of the regional diversity of the country for any one book to capture completely the American experience. American realist writers generally focused on the particular details of the geographical area of the country they knew best, recording the distinctive manners, colloquial speech patterns, and distinguishing traditions of its inhabitants. Of course the ways people talk and behave tend to be sectional in nature. And so the particular brand of realist literature produced by Americans in the late nineteenth century came to be known as regionalism.

Indeed, in many ways the last three decades of the nineteenth century constituted an age of regionalism in American literature. Coinciding with the growing interest among Americans in their country's sectional differences, regionalist writing flourished between

1870 and 1900. As the public appetite for stories with regional qualities increased, the proliferation of magazines following the Civil War provided an outlet particularly for the work of short-fiction writers whose work was distinguished by this quintessentially American brand of late-nineteenth-century literature. In the Far West, authors like Bret Harte and Dan De Quille as well as writers of Nevada's "Sagebrush School," Joseph Goodman and Rollin Daggett, to name just two, wrote accounts of outlaws, roughs, and prospectors. Midwestern writers such as Alice Cary, Joseph Kirkland, and Edward Eggleston chronicled the lives of prairie farmers and small-village folk. George Washington Cable, Joel Chandler Harris, and Grace Elizabeth King depicted the unique complexities of postwar life in the South. In New England, Harriet Beecher Stowe, Sarah Orne Jewett, and Mary Wilkins Freeman recorded the peculiar experiences of Yankees and spinsters. Taken together, these and other writers from the period produced a representation of American cultural experience that in both form and content matched the regional diversity of the United States.

AMERICAN LITERATURE AND THE EARLY AMERICAN ACADEMY

Although American authors enjoyed popular success among subscribers to national publications in the decades following the Civil War, American literature, generally speaking, had yet to achieve the status of serious art in the minds of those readers. Americans, still harboring lingering feelings of provincial inferiority a century after the signing of the Declaration of Independence, remained wary about maintaining that their own literary past could be ranked with the hallowed traditions of England and Europe. American literature was very young by comparison of course, and most of the reading public—including all but a handful of academic scholars—simply refused to believe that American literature could be as aesthetically elevated as the literature of the Old World. Universities throughout the United States did occasionally offer courses in designated types of American writers in the final decades of the nineteenth century, but for a student to announce an intention to study literature in the late nineteenth century invariably meant that the student would study English literature.

The slow growth of an academic curriculum in American literature seems lethargic indeed when contrasted to the maturation of other curricula of academic study in American universities at the time, such as American history. Less than 10 percent of the more than 150 universities in the United States had developed fledgling graduate programs in American literature by 1900, and only four Ph.D.s had emerged in the field. By contrast, scholars of American historical studies could report that nearly nine out of ten history dissertations written in American universities in the 1880s and 1890s dealt with native subjects. Moreover, by the 1890s most universities were offering equal selections of courses in ancient, European, and American history. Even within the relatively few colleges that were teaching American poetry and prose, English and other European literature received vastly more attention.

The civic pride generated in the 1870s by the national centennial celebration, along with the emerging post–Civil War conception of the United States as a national culture, helped to begin changing minds, both inside and outside the academy, about the stature of American literature. In the years leading up to the centennial, for example, publishers looking to cash in on enthusiasm for things American readily promoted the work of American writers, prompting many readers to consider for the first time their own authors, past and present. Furthermore, that the nation had reached such a significant milestone enabled many within the intellectual class to entertain seriously, perhaps for the first time, the notion that the United States might possess an aesthetic culture worthy of some consideration. These events clearly would have contributed to the search for and discovery of an American literary tradition.

Book-length collections of American literature marketed for the general public in the late nineteenth century also played a crucial role in shifting academic critical attitudes toward American writers. Although these large collections had been popular with American readers since the mid-1800s, colleges only gradually adopted this anthology format in the classroom. But once they did, competition among literature professors to produce an authoritative anthology specifically for use in the college classroom fostered an upsurge of academic interest in American literature. Scholars trace the first true college text of American literature back to John Seely Hart's (1810–1877) *Manual of American Literature,* published in 1872. Hart is likewise credited with offering, at Princeton, the first college course in American literature at an American university that same year. Hart's collection, like its contemporaries that were intended for a more general readership, was suggestive of a biographical dictionary or encyclopedia supplemented by small excerpts of poems and prose and representing the work of literally hundreds of American authors. Detailed attention to factual data and biography and the absence of historical and interpretive information characterized these first literary collections. But despite such limitations, Hart's anthology became a model for subsequent classroom texts.

Attempts by literary scholars to organize into professional associations during the 1880s further promoted the serious treatment of American literature in American college classrooms. In 1883, together with nearly forty language and literature specialists from universities around the country, A. Marshall Elliott founded the Modern Language Association of America, and one year later in 1884 that group published the first volume of the *Publications of the Modern Language Association of America,* which even in the early twenty-first century remains the flagship journal for academic literary scholarship. Also instrumental at about this same time was a national consciousness of the deaths of Ralph Waldo Emerson and Henry Wadsworth Longfellow in the 1880s and then of James Russell Lowell (1891), John Greenleaf Whittier (1892), Oliver Wendell Holmes (1894), and Harriet Beecher Stowe (1896), which deepened the sense that an era of American literary production had come to a close and could begin to be appraised.

Coinciding with the rising interest in American letters in the American academy during the 1880s, the next stage in the development of academic appreciation of American literature grew out of attempts by scholars to apply critical methodology to the study of literature. In November 1878 Moses Coit Tyler (1835–1900) published his renowned two-volume *History of American Literature, 1607–1765,* a work of great importance for having pioneered the art of literary historiography. Tyler's connective critical approach revolutionized American literature studies, and for at least the next half-century it became the dominant mode in academic literary scholarship. Moving the study of literature beyond mere biography and fact gathering, literary historiographers such as Tyler essentially approached the body of American letters as a portal to the American mind and spirit. According to them, American literature (which in concept at that time also included political and scientific documents) was the written record of the American cultural milieu and as such it reflected and preserved the nation's fundamental characteristics and thought. "There is but one thing more interesting than the intellectual history of a man," declared Tyler in his literary history of colonial America, "and that is the intellectual history of a nation" (1:5). As an archival repository of the American spirit, literature was at best considered only secondarily as a formidable artistic expression. For literary historiography the works of literature themselves became a means for study rather than the subject of study. Literary historians did make small gestures toward demonstrating aesthetic values in the literature, but their commentary (by modern standards) was vague and impressionistic. In spite of these shortcomings, the scholarship of Tyler and other literary historians

provided a long-deserved sense of critical legitimacy to American literature.

As a result of this progress, editors of classroom anthologies of American literature started adopting literary historiography into their formats. The first notable classroom anthology combining narrative literary history with selections of poetry and prose was Charles F. Richardson's (1851–1913) *American Literature, 1607–1885* (1887–1889). Though Richardson's text was divided into two volumes, separating the historical analysis from the actual literature itself, he unified the John Seely Hart–like collection of poetry and prose with the Tyler-like literary history handbook and treated for the first time the entire period of American literature up to his own day.

AMERICAN LITERATURE AT THE TURN OF THE CENTURY

During the 1890s a profound and noticeable shift began taking place in American literature. A hallmark feature of post–Civil War American literary realism had been plots that featured characters confronting complex ethical dilemmas. Thus a fundamental assumption that lay behind many realist texts was that the individual possesses the free will to decide between that which is right and wrong, moral and immoral, good and evil. By the end of the century American writers, influenced by the emerging trend in European literature called literary naturalism, were starting to question the broader notion of human freedom as they embraced aspects of scientific determinism, a system of thought that rejected the existence of free will as a way of accounting for everyday human behavior.

Conceptions of "determinism" were not completely unknown to Americans of the nineteenth century. For hundreds of years of course numerous interpretations of Christian theology had preached doctrines that denied human agency at most if not all levels of existence. But certain scientific developments in the early and mid-1800s began to assert arguments for more secular varieties of determinism. In 1859 Charles Darwin (1809–1882) published his groundbreaking study *On the Origin of Species,* and its subsequent effect on Western thinking, particularly in the latter decades of the nineteenth century, is nearly impossible to overstate. His theories of "natural selection" fundamentally undermined an ennobled vision of human life by intimating that human beings might be directly related to lower forms of animals. In addition to challenging centuries of foundational religious thinking, Darwin's hypotheses suggested that human behavior is largely governed by biologically determined forces that are beyond the individual's control.

Darwinian evolutionary theory quickly became the basis for any number of pessimistic late-century scientific hypotheses concerning human conduct. Most famously, perhaps, the Englishman Herbert Spencer (1820–1903) applied Darwin's observations to social models and in the 1870s coined the phrase "survival of the fittest" as he attempted to justify the social and economic inequities of the Gilded Age.

Darwin and Spencer as well as other revolutionary scientific thinkers of the nineteenth century incited a new generation of American writers to portray life as a battle in which human beings struggle against forces seemingly bent on their destruction. Stephen Crane, Kate Chopin, Theodore Dreiser, Frank Norris, Edith Wharton, and Jack London, to name a few of the most prominent figures, all produced fiction near the turn of the century that emphasized deterministic forces—social, biological, and environmental—exerting control over the lives of their characters. Crane's (1871–1900) *Maggie, A Girl of the Streets* (1893) is generally considered to be the first significant naturalistic novel by an American, and it showcases many of what would become the movement's hallmark features: a hostile setting, oppressed lower-class characters, images of despair, metaphors drawn from war and savagery, and profoundly tragic themes. The work of American naturalists that followed would likewise depict unflinchingly the bleakness of urban slums, arctic wildernesses, and impoverished rural environments; portray young women driven to prostitution, young men to brutality, and entire families to total annihilation; and explore the complex of overwhelming forces, external and interior, that compelled their characters toward seemingly inevitable fates. In the end, however, the despairing tone of literary naturalism was not without purpose. American naturalist authors generally wrote to transform the world around them, to bring to the attention of readers the effect of deterministic forces in their lives and to propose ways of coping with those forces. By doing so, these writers saw themselves as assisting in the improvement of society as a whole.

As turn-of-the-century American writers embraced literary naturalism, the American publishing scene proudly began to promote past American authors in ways that it had not before. Houghton, Mifflin, for example, introduced its Riverside Literature Series in the early 1890s, which featured the poetry and prose of America's most revered literary artists. Each volume in the series featured the work of a single writer, providing the public with affordable collections of American literature and providing American literary art with its long-deserved sense of cultural legitimacy. Sales were extraordinary right from the start, and second editions followed almost immediately. Also very popular among turn-of-the-century readers were illustrated omnibus collections of American literature. Donald G. Mitchell's *American Lands and Letters* (1897) is typical of the larger compilations of American writings that appealed to the general reader by providing hundreds of selections by multiple authors and large numbers of portraits and other images in a single volume. Additionally, the *Atlantic Monthly* and other highly respected magazines ran articles throughout the 1890s touting the merits of indigenous writers of the past while calling for a body of work from writers of the future worthy of the greatness of American culture. All said, as the country moved into the new century American literary art seemed finally to be receiving the kind of backing from the American print trade that had been so conspicuously absent in preceding decades.

Academic interest in American literary studies was also beginning to accelerate rapidly in the early years of the twentieth century. Forty-two doctoral dissertations, for example, were completed on American literary topics between 1900 and 1920 despite few graduate course offerings on exclusively American topics. To meet this expanding interest in American literature within universities, a number of literary histories and collections of poetry and prose virtually free of interpretive explication entered the market after 1900. Nevertheless, the earlier textbooks by Tyler and Richardson, along with Barrett Wendell's (1855–1921) *A Literary History of America* (1900), continued their hegemony as the trusted authorities until about 1915. Suggesting a more scholarly approach to American letters, Wendell's textbook was fashioned in the style of Tyler's and the first volume of Richardson's set but added to their format an extensive annotated bibliography of primary and secondary works. Neither Wendell's nor subsequent literary histories published during the next few decades advanced literary historiography beyond studies of language patterns and social science. Historical approaches to literature maintained their supremacy both in academic studies of American literature and in American literary textbooks long into the 1920s, as evidenced by the success of a second generation of influential and widely used literary histories, which included W. B. Cairns's *A History of American Literature* (1912) and *The Cambridge History of American Literature* (1917–1921).

AMERICAN LITERATURE AND THE MODERN ACADEMY: A CULMINATION

The transition of American literature studies into an age of modern sophistication began just after the end of World War I. In April 1921 the final two volumes of *The Cambridge History of American Literature* appeared, providing American literary studies with its long-sought sense of critical legitimacy. Later that same year scholars of American literature organized themselves and met for the first time as the American Literature Group at the Modern Language Association's annual meeting. Then in 1923 a section devoted exclusively to American literature was added to the *Publications of the Modern Language Association Bibliography* (previously confined to English, Germanic, and Romantic languages and literatures), with Norman Foerster becoming its first bibliographer. Thereafter activity in the field of academic American literary studies soared. The proliferation of scholarly attention to American authors consequently demanded that college English departments discuss standards and requirements pertaining to American literature, and by 1927 the American Literature Group was considering the possibility of setting up requirements for a Ph.D. degree in American literature. Finally in March 1929 the first scholarly journal entirely dedicated to American literary studies, *American Literature,* published its first volume under the editorship of Jay B. Hubbell.

The ferment of American literary scholarship during the 1920s inevitably began to exert influence on the production of American literary anthologies. In fact a clear difference between high school and college literature collections emerges only in the years following the end of World War I. Before then, anthology editors had intended that their textbooks be used as general guides to American literature for students of all levels, but by 1919 scholars were compiling collections specifically for yearlong college courses, interspersing historical background with the poetry and prose together in the now familiar same-volume format. Influenced by recent critical trends, scholar-editors began moving textbooks away from almost total emphasis on the historical backgrounds and biography, bringing about an expanded coverage of literature. In 1919 Fred Lewis Pattee published his first anthology of American literature designed for a yearlong survey. Norman Foerster's *American Poetry and Prose: A Book of Readings 1607–1916* (1925) became the first literary anthology designed for the college classroom that divided American literature under the conventional modern headings of "Colonial/Puritan Background," "Romanticism," and "Realism." Shortly afterward several other major literary textbooks appeared, one after another, ushering in the age of the modern anthology of American literature as well as inaugurating the proliferation of academic American literary studies that would by mid-century lead to the recognition of American authors and texts as major contributors to world literature.

See also Genteel Tradition; Naturalism; Professionalism; Realism; Regionalism and Local Color Fiction

BIBLIOGRAPHY
Primary Works

Boynton, Percy. *A History of American Literature.* Boston: Ginn, 1919.

Cairns, W. B. *A History of American Literature.* New York: Oxford University Press, 1912.

Crane, Stephen. *Maggie, A Girl of the Streets.* 1893. Edited by Thomas Gullason. New York: Norton, 1979.

Erskine, John, Stuart P. Sherman, William Peterfield Trent, and Carl Van Doren, eds. *The Cambridge History of American Literature.* 4 vols. New York: Putnam, 1917–1921.

Foerster, Norman, ed. *American Poetry and Prose.* 2 vols. Boston and New York: Houghton Mifflin, 1925.

Macy, John. *The Spirit of American Literature.* New York: Boni and Liveright, 1913.

Pattee, Fred Lewis, ed. *Century Readings for a Course in American Literature.* New York: Century, 1919.

Pattee, Fred Lewis, ed. *A History of American Literature since 1870*. New York: Century, 1915.

Tyler, Moses Coit. *A History of American Literature 1607–1765*. 2 vols. New York: Putnam, 1878.

Secondary Works

Csicsila, Joseph. *Canons by Consensus: Critical Trends and American Literature Anthologies.* Tuscaloosa: University of Alabama Press, 2004.

Graff, Gerald. *Professing Literature: An Institutional History.* Chicago: University of Chicago Press, 1987.

Vanderbilt, Kermit. *American Literature and the Academy: The Roots, Growth, and Maturity of a Profession.* Philadelphia: University of Pennsylvania Press, 1986.

Joseph Csicsila

AMERICANS ABROAD

The *Quaker City* excursion of 1867, the world's first luxury cruise, which took about seventy passengers from New York City to Europe and the Holy Land, was one of the most famous journeys of the nineteenth century. The undertaking and the work that grew out of it, Mark Twain's travel book *The Innocents Abroad; or, The New Pilgrims' Progress* (1869), exemplify the interest of Americans in European travel in the years following the Civil War. The contrast set up by Mark Twain between the Vatican Museum, which stores up all that is curious and beautiful in art, and the American Patent Office, which hoards all that is curious or useful in mechanics, is emblematic of the backward-looking orientation of Europe and the forward-looking orientation of the United States. Interest in the museums of Europe and the idea of Europe itself as a vast museum were largely responsible for the surge in transatlantic travel after the hiatus occasioned by the Civil War, with the Paris Universal Exhibition of 1867 serving as a further incentive. The estimates were that Americans would spend $75 million in gold in Paris, and that by the end of the year America would have sent considerably over a hundred thousand persons to Europe.

The renewed interest in European travel strained the capacity of ships and promoted the building of larger and more powerful vessels in the ensuing years. The *Quaker City,* built in 1854, was an early ocean paddle-wheel steamer, a hybrid relying on steam locomotion as well as on fully rigged masts both fore and aft. The ship that figures in William Dean Howells's novel *The Lady of the Aroostook* (1879) is still a regular sailing vessel, which in 1874 takes six weeks to accomplish the journey from Boston to Trieste, "a sail in the offing [winning] the discoverer envy . . . ; a steamer, celebrity" (p. 94) Soon, however, English shipyards started building steamships with screw propellers and iron hulls, an improvement that greatly reduced the time of passage across the Atlantic. Passenger trade now was taken over almost entirely by the English Cunard and White Star Lines and the German Hapag-Lloyd. Competition among these lines for the Blue Ribbon, the prestigious award for the fastest ship, promoted the building of ever faster steamers. The ill-fated *Titanic* was a competitor for the trophy, the equally ill-fated *Lusitania* a holder of it for many years. Both liners took many American tourists to their graves.

Americans went to Europe for many reasons: as students and scholars, as artists, as art lovers, and as simple tourists; as writers, diplomats and businessmen. They favored England, Italy, France, Spain, and Greece but also visited southern Germany and Austria. There were American colonies in major cities such as London, Paris, Rome, Florence, Madrid, Vienna, Berlin, Munich, Dresden, and in such smaller university towns as Göttingen and Heidelberg. Available statistical data demonstrate the extent of American expatriation during the period. Christof Wegelin in his careful analysis of the correlation between social and literary developments presents the following figures for U.S. citizens returning to major east coast ports from overseas, which document a steep rise in transatlantic travel in the second half of the nineteenth century: 19,387 in 1860; 25,202 in 1870; 36,097 in 1880; 81,092 in 1890; 108,068 in 1900; 144,112 in 1901 (Wegelin, p. 307). The records kept by the American colony of students at Göttingen indicate that during the period from 1870 to 1888 there were an average of twenty students enrolled per semester, with a high of thirty-five in the Michaelmas term of 1878 (Buchloh and Rix, pp. 51f.). In 1872 *Appleton's Journal* reported a total of sixty thousand Americans living in Europe. In 1874 the American colony in Paris numbered between three thousand and four thousand people. Toward the end of the century Rome had a colony of about two thousand permanent residents and could claim a yearly average of thirty thousand American tourists (Neuweiler, p. 16). In Bern, in September 1873, watching the Cook's tourists come and go as in "the march-past of an army," Henry James felt he had been given "a lively impression of the numbers of people now living, and above all now moving, at extreme ease in the world" (*Italian Hours,* p. 94). The age of mass tourism had begun, and there was nothing to disturb its steady growth until the First World War and the sinking of the *Lusitania.* The war years saw many American volunteers for various Ambulance Services and Red

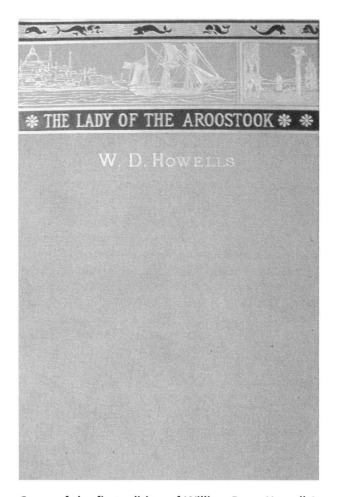

Cover of the first edition of William Dean Howells's *The Lady of the Aroostook*, 1879. The design features the skyline of Boston, an ocean-going vessel flying the Stars and Stripes, and the piazza San Marco (St. Mark's Square) in Venice, Italy—emblematically juxtaposing constituent elements of the international novel. SPECIAL COLLECTIONS LIBRARY, UNIVERSITY OF MICHIGAN

Cross units—as well as large numbers of servicemen of the American Expeditionary Force—arrive in Europe.

TRAVEL LITERATURE AND THE INTERNATIONAL NOVEL

The literature that grew out of the experience of Americans abroad in the period from 1870 to 1920—the so-called international novel as a distinct American genre and the so-called international theme as a distinct American subject matter—is linked to the experience of its authors as short-term tourists, medium-term holders of diplomatic assignments, and long-term expatriates. In addition to being influenced by their respective experiences in different places and different countries, their work is shaped and affected by a number of earlier works by American as well as British

authors that had attained the status of classics and had begun to be read by even the average tourist—in addition to the ubiquitous Baedeker—as guide books: Washington Irving's *The Sketch Book of Geoffrey Crayon, Gent.* (1820); Nathaniel Hawthorne's *The Marble Faun* (1860); the works of Byron as well as the travel sketches of Nathaniel Parker Willis and Bayard Taylor. More important than such influences were the mutual responses of the chief proponents of the international theme to the writings of each other; in its totality their work can be read as an implicit intertextual dialog about Americanness. Regardless of which of the chief constituent elements of the international novel the emphasis is made to fall on—the American traveler or expatriate, the foreign setting, the representative of a foreign culture—the conflict dramatized is one between different manners or mores and serves to demonstrate what it is to be an American.

Although *The Innocents Abroad* is a travel book rather than a novel, it is difficult to detach Mark Twain (1835–1910) from William Dean Howells (1837–1920) and Henry James (1843–1916), the two younger fellow-realists who devoted a large part of their fiction to discussing the European experience. While it may not have cut "the umbilical cord" with Europe, as the critic Van Wyck Brooks once suggested (p. 156), it did mark a departure from "the usual style of travel-writing" in that it set out "to suggest to the reader how *he* would be likely to see Europe and the East if he looked at them with his own eyes instead of the eyes of those who travelled in those countries before him," as Mark Twain put it in his preface (p. v). The author's deliberate rejection of the traditional attitude of veneration for European culture transformed the pervasive comparison between America and Europe into an implicit and explicit quest for the defining features of the American and his nation as a major theme of *The Innocents Abroad*, the very theme that was to dominate the international novel in the decades to come.

WILLIAM DEAN HOWELLS AND HENRY JAMES

Howells's favorable response to the work (in an anonymous review in the *Atlantic Monthly*) came from a man who had spent the years 1861 to 1864 as U.S. Consul in Venice and who on his part had warned the reader of his early travel sketches, *Venetian Life* (1866), that "he will hardly see the curtain rise upon just the Venice of his dreams—the Venice of Byron, of Rogers, and Cooper" (p. 11). With such experience and such response to the printed account of the experience of others, Howells was well prepared to write the earliest of his three international novels, *A Foregone Conclusion* (1874). In the first year of the Civil War, its protagonist,

Henry Ferris, the American consul at Venice ("one of my many predecessors in office," as Howells remarks in an authorial intrusion [p. 3]), receives a visit from Don Ippolito, an Italian priest. Though he refuses Don Ippolito a visa, Ferris takes pity on the priest and recommends him to the expatriate widow Mrs. Vervain as a tutor of Italian for her seventeen-year-old daughter Florida. Ferris is attracted to Florida, a beautiful blue-eyed blonde, but her "attitudes of shy hauteur," "a touch of defiant awkwardness," and the "effort of proud, helpless femininity" keep him from confessing his interest in her (p. 19), and his own cynicism helps to preserve the distance. Don Ippolito becomes infatuated with the girl. When eventually she rejects his advances, Ferris is a witness to the scene; Ferris misreads her gesture of compassion for an embrace, just as he had earlier misinterpreted her proud look, a "temporary expression," and turned it into the dominant feature of a sketch he made of her. The novel was to have ended with Florida's rejection of the priest, but Howells was prevailed upon by the editors of the *Atlantic Monthly* to add a happy ending. So the author has Ferris and Florida meet and marry in America, the Vervain fortune that had enabled mother and daughter to lead their extended expatriate life in Europe now serving as their income. But Howells was careful to undercut the sentimental novel's traditional happy ending: "People are never equal to the romance of their youth in after life, except by fits" (p. 259). Such undercutting is in line with his treatment of the opinions of Mrs. Vervain, a "gracious, silly woman" (p. 254), who in her very first speech is made to compare the "too light altogether" Italian hotel breakfasts to "our American breakfasts" and the supposed Venetian duplicity to "our American fairdealing and sincerity" (p. 21). From the very beginning she sees Venice through the eyes of those who have traveled there before her; she finds the gondolas "gloomy things" (p. 22) and tries to remember Byron's term for their protective tops. The answer—"a coffin clapped in a canoe" (p. 23)—is readily supplied by Ferris who, half in jest, will often take up the tourist's habit of praising his native country: "There is no land like America for true cheerfulness and light-heartedness. Think of our Fourth of Julys and our State Fairs" (p. 164).

The reputation of *A Foregone Conclusion* as an international novel, as well as that of *A Fearful Responsibility* (1881)—which grew out of the same autobiographical material—is generally overshadowed by other works. Henry James's unqualified praise for the genial book argues for a prominent place in the history of the genre, but traditionally his own novels— *The American* (1877), *The Europeans* (1878), *The Portrait of a Lady* (1881), and *The Ambassadors*

(1903), as well as his novella, *Daisy Miller* (1878)—take precedence in the canon.

The most famous of expatriate authors, James had begun to spend time in Europe even as a boy and visited Europe again in 1869 and 1872–1874. In late 1875 he settled in Paris; in 1876 he moved to London, becoming a British subject in 1915, a few months before his death in February 1916. *The American,* written in France and published in the *Atlantic Monthly* between June 1876 and May 1877, was long referred to as the first international novel and continues to be the best-known example of the genre. Although the author himself was to declare in hindsight that he had written a romance rather than the realistic novel he would have preferred to write, his use of the same kind of technique that Hawthorne had employed in *The Marble Faun*—aiming at what is typical rather than merely possible—is what accounts for its success with American readers. The novel dramatizes, in the author's own words, "the situation, in another country and an aristocratic society, of some robust and insidiously beguiled and betrayed, some cruelly wronged, compatriot: the point being in especial that he should suffer at the hands of persons pretending to represent the highest possible civilisation and to be of an order in every way superior to his own" (*Art of the Novel,* pp. 21f.) Writing *The American* thus was part of what James proclaimed to be one of the responsibilities of being an American: "fighting against a superstitious valuation of Europe" (*Letters* 1:274). Christopher Newman, the protagonist whose name points to his representative American identity, whose "sole aim in life had been to make money" (p. 533), has come to see Europe and to get the best out of it, including "a first-class wife . . . the best article in the market" (pp. 585, 549). A marriage is planned between him and Claire de Cintré, Newman's immense fortune gaining him acceptance by her aristocratic family. But finally the Bellegardes find that, however much they want his money, they cannot reconcile themselves to "a commercial person" (p. 758). Claire is put beyond his reach in a Carmelite convent, while Newman for a time savors the prospect of vengeance. Finally he vindicates himself by showing the "remarkable good nature" (p. 872) even his antagonists can discern in him: he burns the paper that contains the secret that he could have used to damn them. His magnanimity becomes "one of the large and easy impulses *generally* characteristic of his type" (*Art of the Novel,* p. 32)— James's own evaluation of the novel once more specifying Newman's archetypal Americanness, "the almost ideal completeness with which he filled out the national mould" (p. 516).

As with *A Foregone Conclusion,* the *Atlantic Monthly* (through Howells himself, now an editor)

> Long known as the "first international novel," Henry James's The American (1877), even in its first chapter, leaves no doubt that, though the novel is about the protagonist's experience of Europe, it is primarily about his identity as an American. The particular setting chosen for the opening scene, the Salon Carré in the Louvre in Paris, throws into relief salient points of his personality as he is sitting on the great circular divan staring at Murillo's beautiful moon-borne Madonna.

On a brilliant day in May, in the year 1868, a gentleman was reclining at his ease on the great circular divan which at the period occupied the centre of the Salon Carré, in the Museum of the Louvre. This commodious ottoman has since been removed, to the extreme regret of all weak-kneed lovers of the fine arts; but the gentleman in question had taken serene possession of its softest spot, and, with his head thrown back and his legs outstretched, was staring at Murillo's beautiful moon-borne Madonna in profound enjoyment of his posture. He had removed his hat, and flung down beside him a little red guide-book and an opera-glass. The day was warm; he was heated with walking, and he repeatedly passed his handkerchief over his forehead, with a somewhat wearied gesture. And yet he was evidently not a man to whom fatigue was familiar; long, lean, and muscular, he suggested the sort of vigor that is commonly known as "toughness." But his exertions on this particular day had been of an unwonted sort, and he had often performed great physical feats which left him less jaded than his tranquil stroll through the Louvre. He had looked out all the pictures to which an asterisk was affixed in those formidable pages of fine print in his Bädeker; his attention had been strained and his eyes dazzled, and he had sat down with an aesthetic headache. He had looked, moreover, not only at all the pictures, but at all the copies that were going forward around them, in the hands of those innumerable young women in irreproachable toilets who devote themselves, in France, to the propagation of masterpieces; and if the truth must be told, he had often admired the copy much more than the original. His physiognomy would have sufficiently indicated that he was a shrewd and capable fellow, and in truth he had often sat up all night over a bristling bundle of accounts, and heard the cock crow without a yawn. But Raphael and Titian and Rubens were a new kind of arithmetic, and they inspired our friend, for the first time in his life, with a vague self-mistrust.

An observer with anything of an eye for national types would have had no difficulty in determining the local origin of this undeveloped connoisseur, and indeed such an observer might have felt a certain humorous relish of the almost ideal completeness with which he filled out the national mould. The gentleman on the divan was a powerful specimen of an American.

James, *The American*, pp. 5f.

asked for a happy ending to *The American*. But James refused on the grounds of realism. Indeed, the romance contains sufficient realistic detail to temper its archetypes. On part of his traditional Grand Tour of Europe, for instance, Newman moves in the company of Benjamin Babcock, a Unitarian minister traveling on funds supplied by his New England congregation. Babcock's "high sense of responsibility" (p. 581) is used to offset Newman's easygoing, spontaneous enjoyment, while at the same time the attitude of this "saint" (Mark Twain's term for the reverent traveler) also throws into relief the basic naïveté of Newman's responses to the art and the mores of the Old World.

The same combination of innocence and naïveté— as it is perceived by the deracinated American expatriate Frederick Winterbourne—was to occupy James in *Daisy Miller*. The novella brought both its author and the "international theme" the highest possible degree of attention. Having been refused by *Lippincott's Magazine* in Philadelphia (a friend's speculation was that the editor might have found it "an outrage on American girlhood" [James, *Art of the Novel*, p. 268]), it appeared in England in the *Cornhill Magazine* for June and July 1878, was promptly pirated in Boston, and caused an extended debate. Howells remarked that James "waked up all the women with his Daisy Miller, the intention of which they misconceived. . . . The thing went so far that society almost divided itself in Daisy Millerites and anti-Daisy Millerites" (James, *Selected Letters* 2:230f.) James himself came to see the story as the fountainhead in a general assessment of the impact of the expatriate experience on his writing: "the international was easy to do, because, as one's wayside bloomed with it, one had but to put forth one's hand and pluck the frequent flower.

Add to this that the flower *was,* so often, quite positively a flower—that of the young American innocence transplanted to European air" (*Art of the Novel,* p. 133).

James's further experimentation with the theme was to produce such mature novels as *The Portrait of a Lady* and *The Ambassadors,* but he also attempted the reverse transplantation, though he remained skeptical as to its general success. In *The Europeans,* for instance, whose title places it in direct opposition to *The American,* he has two European-born and -educated protagonists visit their American relatives. With their traditional views and their formal manner the Wentworths, a New England Puritan family, provide the kind of codified behavior generally associated with European society, their very old big wooden house—a venerable mansion once slept in by General Washington—functioning as the counterpart of the ancestral home of European aristocracy, but striking the visitors merely "as if it had been built last night" (p. 902). The Wentworth kinsfolk, Eugenia, the Baroness of Münster, morganatically married to a German prince, and her brother Felix Young, an artist, bring to New England the very features that have always figured prominently in the American discourse on Europe. The reversal of roles and settings in themselves entail an aspect of parody, and James's care in making the necessary adjustments to the usual components of the international theme place an additional emphasis on the element of incongruity, the basis of a pervasive comedy. While the happy union of Felix and Gertrude Wentworth seems in keeping with the comic pastoral (in Buitenhuis's term), Eugenia's withdrawal from "this provincial continent" and her return to "the elder world" as her "natural field" reflect more closely James's lifelong conviction as to the incompatibility of the two worlds (p. 1037). As a reversal of the usual plot of the international novel, *The Europeans* examines the relative values and shortcomings of Europe as much as those of America. It fully belongs with the group of international novels, and along with these it exerted its influence, for instance on Edith Wharton. The Countess (Ellen) Olenska in *The Age of Innocence* (1920) performs the same function as Eugenia in *The Europeans; The Age of Innocence* also testifies to the heritage of the international theme in the field of the novel of manners at large, Wharton's *The Custom of the Country* (1913) serving as another example.

Howells's *The Lady of the Aroostook,* first published serially in the *Atlantic Monthly* in 1878–1879, has often been compared to *Daisy Miller* in its presentation of its protagonist as an archetype of American innocence. Lydia Blood, a nineteen-year-old schoolteacher from South Bradfield in Northern Massachusetts, spends six weeks aboard the *Aroostook* going from Boston to Trieste and on to Venice to join her aunt, the American expatriate Mrs. Erwin, and to receive training as a singer. The only woman aboard, she is the center of attention for passengers and crew. A love story develops; James Staniford, a wealthy and cultivated but cynical Bostonian, is slowly won over by Lydia's natural innocence and her unerring moral judgment. Her lack of social sophistication and his punctiliousness, along with minor plot complications, delay the happy ending for long enough to have the novel cover various aspects of transatlantic travel, the American expatriate experience, and the theme of American innocence. Most importantly, it is a companion piece to *Daisy Miller,* the novel and the novella agreeing in a surprising number of details. Both Daisy Miller and Lydia Blood are "cases of supernatural innocence," which (as Staniford puts it) "wouldn't occur among any other people in the world but ours" (p. 57). Both are provincial rather than city-bred, both are of the type of "the pretty girl of our nation" (p. 59), both demonstrate an unerring moral instinct in dangerously compromising situations. In each work there is a male counterpart whose approbation or love must be won, while the men must be brought to face up to their feelings. Staniford's admission, "my fault has been that I haven't made love to her openly, but have gone on fancying that I was studying her character" (p. 226), is a commentary on his attitude as well as on that of James's Winterbourne. In each work the heroine's disregard of social conventions is epitomized by her walking about unchaperoned, and in each work it is the American expatriate rather than the Italian who judges and censures the supposed transgressions of the heroine. Occasional humorous exaggeration notwithstanding, both works can also be read as cautionary tales regarding expatriation as a mode of life. Europe, in Staniford's words, "is the place for American irresolution" (p. 64); Mrs. Erwin, in the words of her English husband, is "cringing to the effete despotisms of the Old World, as your Fourth of July orators have it" (p. 292), and in the eyes of Staniford she has enslaved herself to her burdensome little world. Only when she joins the young couple in California does she regain her balance: "Cut loose from her European ties, Mrs. Erwin experienced an incomparable repose and comfort in the life of San Francisco" (p. 319).

James praised *The Lady of the Aroostook* but called it a romance and urged Howells to turn to American settings. When in the summer of 1882 Howells once more visited Europe to recover from the strain of finishing *A Modern Instance,* his plans as an author involved another return to the international theme, a novel intended to "contrast the nascent nationality of America and the dying nationality of Venice" (*Selected Letters* 3:20). But the original plan is barely perceptible in what was published as *Indian Summer* in

1885–1886. The novel tells the story of forty-one-year-old Theodore Colville, a newspaper editor from Des Vaches, Indiana, who returns to Florence—where twenty years earlier he had been jilted by a young American girl—in order to recapture his youth. He falls in love with Imogene Graham, a girl young enough to be his daughter. When both realize the mistake they are about to make by getting married, the engagement is dissolved, and Colville marries Evalina Bowen, a thirty-eight-year-old widow who had been a witness to the disappointed love of his youthful years. "It is largely a study of the feelings of middle-life in contrast with those of earlier years," the author remarked (*Selected Letters* 3:86). Accordingly, the emphasis is on the analysis of Colville's adjustment to middle age and the recognition that it is "the problems of the vast, tumultuous American life, which he had turned his back on, that really concerned him" (*Indian Summer*, p. 90). The setting is functional, and the novel thus incorporates analyses of the social structure of the American colony as well as its conventions and its everyday life. At one point it presents, as Colville's reflection, what amounts to Howells's own evaluation of the tendency of Americans to live abroad: "They seemed to see very little of Italian society, and to be shut out from practical knowledge of the local life by the terms upon which they had themselves insisted. Our race finds its simplified and cheapened London or New York in all its Continental resorts now" (p. 116). As a consequence, clashes of national mores such as had characterized *The American* and other early international novels are less frequent. In presenting this conclusion, *Indian Summer* all but questions the continued existence of an important premise of the international novel. At the same time, however, it deliberately invokes the history of the genre by explicit intertextual reference. One person remarks that he does not find his countrymen so aggressive and so loud "as our international novelists would make out," and Colville regrets not having met "any of their peculiar heroines as yet" (p. 37), before he is introduced to Imogene Graham from Buffalo, the novel's functional counterpart of Daisy Miller from Schenectady and Lydia Blood from South Bradfield. More specifically, there is a reference to Hawthorne's *The Marble Faun*, reduced to guidebook status by the addition of photographs, and finally there is an attempt on the part of Colville to interpret himself in relation to Imogene explicitly in terms of a novel by James or by Howells. This comparison involves an astute assessment of the differences in the way each author handles the international theme and its constituents: James favoring the great world, more dramatic incident, and the tragic rather than the happy ending.

Such intertextual referentiality indicates that the genre has been firmly established, and perhaps also that the international theme is beginning to cease to be a challenge to its foremost authors—or a matter of interest to the reading public. In 1885 Howells wrote that he had enjoyed writing the story, but concluded that "our people now don't want one on foreign ground, and I shall hardly venture abroad again in fiction" (*Selected Letters* 3:136). And even James, though in the course of his continued expatriate experience he returned to the international theme in *The Wings of the Dove* (1902), *The Ambassadors,* and *The Golden Bowl* (1904), had overcome what he called the "*emphasized internationalism*" (*Art of the Novel*, p. 199).

OUTLOOK

A different group of works grew out of the experiences of Americans on the European battlefields of the First World War. As war novels or antiwar novels they did not begin to get published until the 1920s, as part of the writings of the so-called Lost Generation. Their authors were a new generation of American expatriates who were discovering Europe as well as the international theme on their own terms and adapting it in their works to changing conditions in an increasingly internationalized world. Topical variations of the international theme throughout the twentieth century notwithstanding, however, its classic nineteenth-century examples have continued to be in high favor as defining documents of the American self, both as printed texts and as successful motion picture adaptations.

See also The Ambassadors; Daisy Miller; Tourism and Travel Writing

BIBLIOGRAPHY
Primary Works

Howells, William Dean. *A Foregone Conclusion*. Boston: J. R. Osgood, 1875.

Howells, William Dean. *Indian Summer*. Boston and New York: Houghton Mifflin, 1885.

Howells, William Dean. *The Lady of the Aroostook*. Boston: Houghton, Osgood, 1879.

Howells, William Dean. *Selected Letters of W. D. Howells: Volume 2 (1873–1881)*. Edited by George Arms and Christoph K. Lohmann. Boston: Twayne, 1979.

Howells, William Dean. *Selected Letters of W. D. Howells: Volume 3 (1882–1891)*. Edited by Robert C. Leitz III. Boston: Twayne, 1980.

Howells, William Dean. *Venetian Life*. New York: Hurd and Houghton, 1867.

James, Henry. *The American.* Boston: J. R. Osgood, 1877. Reprinted in *Novels 1871–1880,* edited by William T. Stafford, pp. 513–872. New York: Library of America, 1983.

James, Henry. *The Art of the Novel: Critical Prefaces.* Edited by Richard P. Blackmur. New York: Charles Scribner's Sons, 1934.

James, Henry. *The Europeans.* Boston: Houghton Mifflin, 1878. Reprinted in *Novels 1871–1880,* edited by William T. Stafford, pp. 873–1038. New York: Library of America, 1983.

James, Henry. *Italian Hours.* Boston: Houghton Mifflin, 1909.

James, Henry. *Letters: Volume 1 (1843–1875).* Edited by Leon Edel. London: Macmillan, 1974.

Twain, Mark. *The Innocents Abroad; or, The New Pilgrims' Progress.* Hartford, Conn.: American Publishing Company, 1869.

Secondary Works

Bradbury, Malcolm. *The Expatriate Tradition in American Literature.* BAAS Pamphlets on American Studies no. 9. Durham, U.K.: British Association for American Studies, 1982.

Brooks, Van Wyck. *The Dream of Arcadia: American Writers and Artists in Italy, 1760–1915.* New York: E. P. Dutton, 1958.

Buchloh, Paul G., and Walter T. Rix, eds. *American Colony of Göttingen: Historical and Other Data Collected Between the Years 1855 and 1880.* Göttingen, Germany: Vandenhoeck and Ruprecht, 1976.

Buitenhuis, Peter. "Comic Pastoral: Henry James's *The Europeans.*" *University of Toronto Quarterly* 31 (1961–1962): 152–163.

Cargill, Oscar. "The First International Novel." *Publications of the Modern Language Association of America* 73 (1958): 418–425.

Dulles, Foster Rhea. *Americans Abroad: Two Centuries of European Travel.* Ann Arbor: University of Michigan Press, 1964.

Earnest, Ernest. *Expatriates and Patriots: American Artists, Scholars, and Writers in Europe.* Durham, N.C.: Duke University Press, 1968.

Kar, Annette. "Archetypes of American Innocence: Lydia Blood and Daisy Miller." *American Quarterly* 5 (1953): 31–38.

Neuweiler, Siegfried. *Das "Internationale Thema" in Reiseberichten und Essays amerikanischer Zeitschriften (1865–1900).* Frankfurt am Main, Germany: Peter Lang, 1975.

Rahv, Philip, ed. *Discovery of Europe: The Story of American Experience in the Old World.* Boston: Houghton Mifflin, 1947.

Stowe, William W. *Going Abroad: European Travel in Nineteenth-Century American Culture.* Princeton, N.J.: Princeton University Press, 1994.

Strout, Cushing. *The American Image of the Old World.* New York: Harper and Row, 1963.

Wegelin, Christof. *The Image of Europe in Henry James.* Dallas, Tex.: Southern Methodist University Press, 1958.

Wegelin, Christof. "The Rise of the International Novel." *Publications of the Modern Language Association of America* 77 (1962): 305–310.

Horst Kruse

THE AMERICAN SCENE

At once impressionistic autobiography and documentary travelogue, personal reminiscence of his native land and cultural critique of American modernity, *The American Scene*'s idiosyncratic hybridity has led contemporary critics to consider it one of Henry James's (1843–1916) most important works. At the time of its initial publication in 1907 (which followed the serialization of many sections in *Harper's Monthly Magazine,* the *North American Review,* and the *Fortnightly Review*), the book's reception was rather tepid. The informal review that James's brother William James (1842–1910) wrote in a letter to him on 4 May 1907 indicates why, yet it also suggests the reason that *The American Scene* would later command so much interest. William James is impatient with his brother's "perverse" and "unheard-of method" of writing, whose difficulty and indirection require too much from readers in "this crowded and hurried reading age." As an "account of America," it is "supremely great," but it is "largely one of its omissions, silences, vacancies." It consequently produces "the illusion of a solid object, made (like the 'ghost' at the Polytechnic) wholly out of impalpable materials, air, and the prismatic interferences of light, ingeniously focused by mirrors upon empty space." The overall effect, according to William James, "is but perfume and simulacrum" (2:277–278, passim). While William James betrays his conventional genteel taste in literary style, his complaint points toward Henry's more innovative, modernist—perhaps even postmodernist—sensibility.

As *The American Scene* combines James's late style of indirection and "prismatic interferences" with his deeply engaged powers of observation and critique, it testifies to his capacity to convert the arguably humble genre of travel narrative into a highly complex drama of the making of modern subjectivity, indeed, of modernity itself. James was certainly a practiced travel

The lobby of the Waldorf-Astoria Hotel, photographed in 1902. James attributed the orderly serenity of the hotel to an "absolute presiding power" controlling an "army of puppets." © CORBIS

writer, having previously published such works as *A Little Tour in France* (1885) and many of the essays that comprise *Italian Hours* (1909). But *The American Scene* was occasioned by distinctly personal and particular circumstances, that is, by James's decision upon turning sixty in 1903 to make an extended trip to the United States, which he had not seen in twenty years. Publishing his impressions would help to finance the trip, as would lecture engagements which he later decided to accept. Having recently sent off to the publisher what was to be his last complete novel, *The Golden Bowl* (1904), James set sail in August 1904 and did not return to England until July 1905, staying several months longer than originally intended. His journeys took him up and down the northeastern and Mid-Atlantic states and southward to Richmond, Charleston, and Florida as well as westward to Chicago, Saint Louis, and California. The text covers only the eastern and southern portions of the trip; he had

planned to write a sequel treating the midwestern and western portions but never did.

CONTEXTS AND THEMES

As William James's comments indicate, American culture by the turn of the century, with its "crowded" and "hurried" ways, had undergone an urban transformation. Urban modernity's new and often disorienting features elicited journalistic, fictional, sociological, and philosophical attention—as seen, for instance, in Stephen Crane's New York sketches (1892–1896), Abraham Cahan's novella *Yekl: A Tale of the New York Ghetto* (1896), Theodore Dreiser's novel *Sister Carrie* (1900), the sociologist Robert Park's PhD dissertation "The Crowd and the Public" (1904), and the German philosopher Georg Simmel's influential essay "The Metropolis and Mental Life" (1903). Works such as these wrestle—sometimes with buoyant humor,

The open market on Delancey Street, New York City, 1905. In *The American Scene,* James described the crowding and endless activity of the city streets as "a welter of objects and sounds in which relief, detachment, dignity, meaning, perished utterly and lost all rights." GETTY IMAGES

sometimes with brooding seriousness—with the psychological and social effects of urbanization: immigration, wage labor, and poverty; hyperrationality, anonymity, and isolation; corporate capitalism, consumerism, and desire. *The American Scene* is best seen within this discursive context, for James dwells at length on urban modernity's manifestations, combining severe critique with extravagant relish. His willingness to plunge both psychologically and rhetorically into what instinctively troubles his genteel sensibility distinguishes him from more traditional analysts of American culture such as Henry Adams and E. L. Godkin.

From the outset James considers his decades-long absence from the country of his birth not a liability but, as he writes in the preface, a "great advantage . . . since if I had had time to become almost as 'fresh' as an inquiring stranger, I had not on the other hand had enough to cease to be, or at least to feel, as acute as an initiated native." Convinced that he would "under-stand" and "care" more yet also "vibrate with more curiosity" than other visitors (p. xxv), James alternately describes himself as, among other personae, "the restored absentee" (p. 118), "the repentant absentee" (p. 2), "the visionary tourist" (p. 106), "the shuddering pilgrim" (p. 94), "the hovering kindly critic" (p. 97), "the lone observer" (p. 465), and most notably "the restless analyst" (p. 7). He thus fashions himself as both intimately bound up with and impersonally detached from American culture. The mutual interference, to borrow his brother's term, of these modes of subjectivity heightens the text's sense of decentered restlessness, which James both records as American modernity's signature attribute and also himself embodies. In other words, James develops a persona who mimes American modernity, a persona whose intense observational and affective engagement with his subject matter imbues him with this subject's dynamic disequilibrium.

This dispositional elasticity is on display, for instance, in James's commentary on New York's "great religion of the Elevator" (p. 186). To his mind, "the packed and hoisted basket" required by the new architectural form, the skyscraper, is a loathsome mode of transportation, "an intolerable symbol of the herded and driven state and of that malady of preference for gregarious ways, of insistence on gregarious ways only" (p. 187). Despite such visceral contempt for the modern elevator's disciplinary order, James not only submits to it but does so in order also to experience an even more intense form of gregariousness. Having been hoisted to the "upper reaches" of one of New York's skyscrapers, James gains a view of the streets below that simultaneously triggers revulsion and "allure":

> The assault of the turbid air seemed all one with the look, the tramp, the whole quality and *allure,* the consummate monotonous commonness, of the pushing male crowd, moving in its dense mass—with the confusion carried to chaos for any intelligence, any perception; a welter of objects and sounds in which relief, detachment, dignity, meaning, perished utterly and lost all rights. It appeared, the muddy medium, all one with every other element and note as well, all the signs of the heaped industrial battle-field, all the sounds and silences, grim, pushing, trudging silences too, of the universal will to move—to move, move, move, as an end in itself, an appetite at any price. (Pp. 83–84)

With this Whitmanesque eroticization of the urban landscape, with this hyperbolic rush of interfering grammatical units, James's rhetorical excess discloses his willingness to abandon the constraints of the traditional genteel humanist. In unleashing a verbal "welter"—words being his "medium"—James mimes the very scene whose embattled and "heaped" "signs" disorient him.

James's return to the United States took place during the post-*Plessy* era in which much of the North had acquiesced to, if not outdone, the South's Jim Crow practices. But when he travels to the South, the alluring signs of the industrial battlefield give way to "lurid, fuliginous, vividly tragic" signs of the Confederate battlefield (p. 369). Richmond, in particular, "the Confederate capital," occasions his meditation on the region's "blood-drenched" past (p. 369). He voices bitter dismay over the South's seeming inability to shed its wartime "provinciality" (p. 374). He recalls the southern blacks he had encountered a few days earlier in the Washington, D.C., railway station, and he now protests their "ragged and rudimentary" conditions along with the South's denial of the black's "rights as a man" (p. 375). While declaring himself a "non-resident," hence unfit to moralize too harshly (p. 376), James suggests that the "haunting consciousness thus produced" by current racist ideology and practice "is the prison of the Southern spirit" (p. 375); it is what keeps both blacks and whites in a "blighted or stricken" state (p. 377). James may "tread . . . on tiptoe" (p. 376) around what was then so often called "the Negro problem," but his discerning honesty and social intelligence outstrip his reticence.

JAMES'S CULTURAL CRITIQUE

The political implications of James's dispositional elasticity become more visible when he turns to such sensitive topics as the immigrant alien, specifically, Jewish ones. As an urban flaneur bent on encountering new and disorienting social phenomena, James explores the Bowery, the Lower East Side, and even Ellis Island in search of what Jacob Riis some half-dozen years earlier dubbed "the other half." Some critics have considered these segments of *The American Scene* to be fraught with elitist condescension and anti-Semitism. But such views ignore James's animated engagement with social otherness and his empathetic treatment of the plight of immigrants. This orientation is on view when he recounts his visit to "terrible little Ellis Island, the first harbour of refuge and stage of patience for the million or so of immigrants annually knocking at our official door" (p. 84). James observes the depersonalizing, indeed alienating, effects of the "official" processing that immigrants undergo before being permitted to enter the country proper: "Before this door, which opens to them there only with a hundred forms and ceremonies, grindings and grumblings of the key, they stand appealing and waiting, marshalled, herded, divided, subdivided, sorted, sifted, searched, fumigated, for longer or shorter periods" (p. 84). To be sure, James is bewildered by the sight of such "ingurgitation" (p. 84) of immigrants and later by the "babel of tongues" (p. 118) the aliens create in Central Park as well as by the discovery of an Armenian laborer in the New Hampshire countryside (p. 119). Indeed James appears to find repugnant the Jews' fated mode of diasporic proliferation, comparing them to

> snakes or worms . . . who, when cut into pieces, wriggle away contentedly and live in the snippet as completely as in the whole. So the denizens of the New York Ghetto, heaped as thick as the splinters on the table of a glass-blower, had each, like the fine glass particle, his or her individual share of the whole hard glitter of Israel. (P. 132)

Moving from one conspicuously peculiar trope to another, he goes on apologetically to compare the ghetto Jews to "a long nocturnal street where every window in every house shows a maintained light" (p. 132), thus revealing his intense curiosity about and confusion by the new sociocultural realities of urban modernity. His shifting and prismatically interfering responses to this new order comprise James's representational method of conveying urban modernity's multiplicity, what he calls its "perpetually provisional" conditions (p. 408).

More pointedly made a target of James's critique than its immigration policies and processes is what he calls America's "hotel-spirit" (p. 441). If the officious and bureaucratic manhandling of the immigrant masses discomfits, what proves astonishing is the American propensity to transform so relatively modest a commercial enterprise as innkeeping into a massive managerial concern, one "of extraordinary complexity and brilliancy, operating—and with proportionate perfection—by laws of their own and expressing after their fashion a complete scheme of life" (p. 102). Dilating on the cultural and ideological significance of the "amazing hotel-world" (p. 102) exemplified by the Waldorf-Astoria, James observes how "the American genius for organization" and "consummate management" (p. 105) all too successfully and perfectly matches Americans' utilitarian impulse: the hotel, "blissfully exempt from any principle or possibility of disaccord with itself," is "so comprehensively collective—that it made so vividly, in the old phrase, for the greatest happiness of the greatest number" (p. 104). James likens this commercial order to an orchestra whose "colossal" conductor possesses "absolute presiding power, conscious of every note of every instrument, controlling and commanding the whole volume of sound, keeping the whole effect together" (pp. 106–107); the orchestra in turn is refigured as "an army of puppets" whose leader "has found means to make them think of themselves as delightfully free and easy" (p. 107). Without leveling the charge directly, James suggests how perilously near Americans are to surrendering themselves to plutocratic managerialism.

In staging this critique of American modernity's expansive utilitarian ideology, James can be seen to anticipate by several decades the sort of neo-Marxist analysis of the "culture industry" that Theodor W. Adorno and Max Horkheimer develop in *Dialectic of Enlightenment* (1944). But in an important sense James is unlike Adorno and Horkheimer: they are constrained as he is not by the imperative of consistency, which is legislated both by social philosophy's discursive conventions and, seemingly, by their intellectual disposition. They do not, as James does, follow up a withering critique with an account of "certain aimless strolls" that restore to New York its enduring, even endearing, attraction. Unlike them, James confesses the "secret" that despite New York's "ugliness" he is "willing at the lightest persuasion" to let go of the

critical orientation, impelled as he is by "one of those loyalties that are beyond any reason" (pp. 107–108). An American born and partly raised, James recognizes his embeddedness in, and even indebtedness to, American culture's contradictions:

> "It's all very well," the voice of the air seemed to say, if I may so take it up; "it's all very well to 'criticize,' but you distinctly take an interest and are the victim of your interest, be the grounds of your perversity what they will. You can't escape from it, and don't you see that this, precisely, is what *makes* an adventure for you . . . of almost any odd stroll, or waste half-hour, or other promiscuous passage, that results for you in an impression? . . . You *care* for the terrible town. (P. 108)

As indicated by his poetic license to transform the air into interlocutor, James insists on multiple and mutually interfering voices. He thus reveals how deeply inflected his discourse is by the American idiom. In this stagey talk one can almost hear Ralph Waldo Emerson's appeal to his many and contradictory moods or Walt Whitman's declaration that he is multitudinously large and therefore has leeway to contradict himself. Without perhaps such copious measures of plenary idealism, James in *The American Scene* registers, by way of his perambulatory and hybrid persona, the prismatically interfering conditions that constitute American modernity.

See also The Ambassadors; City Dwellers; Jews; New York; Tourism and Travel Writing

BIBLIOGRAPHY

Primary Works

James, Henry. *The American Scene.* 1907. Introduction and notes by Leon Edel. Bloomington: Indiana University Press, 1968.

James, William. *The Letters of William James.* Edited by Henry James, 2 vols. Boston: Atlantic Monthly Press, 1920. The editor is William James's son, not his brother the novelist.

Secondary Works

Agnew, Jean-Christophe. "The Consuming Vision of Henry James." In *The Culture of Consumption: Critical Essays in American History 1880–1980,* edited by Richard Wightman Fox and T. J. Jackson Lears, pp. 67–100. New York: Pantheon, 1983.

Cameron, Sharon. *Thinking in Henry James.* Chicago: University of Chicago Press, 1989.

Edel, Leon. *Henry James, the Master: 1901–1916.* Philadelphia: Lippincott, 1972.

Esteve, Mary. "Anerotic Excursions: Memory, Celibacy, and Desire in *The American Scene.*" In *Questioning the Master: Gender and Sexuality in Henry James's Writings,* edited by Peggy McCormack, pp. 196–216. Newark: University of Delaware Press, 2000.

Posnock, Ross. *The Trial of Curiosity: Henry James, William James, and the Challenge of Modernity.* New York: Oxford University Press, 1991.

Rowe, John Carlos. *Theoretical Dimensions of Henry James.* Madison: University of Wisconsin Press, 1984.

Taylor, Gordon O. "Chapters of Experience: Henry James." In his *Chapters of Experience: Studies in Modern American Autobiography.* New York: St. Martin's, 1983.

Trachtenberg, Alan. "The American Scene: Versions of the City." *Massachusetts Review* 8 (summer 1967): 281–295.

Mary Esteve

ANARCHISM

American anarchism has a paradoxical history. It is often treated as foreign—theorized in Russia by Michael Bakunin and Peter Kropotkin and enacted in the United States by the Irish Molly Maguires, Germans such as Johann Most, eastern European Jews such as Alexander Berkman and Emma Goldman, and Italians such as Nicola Sacco and Bartolomeo Vanzetti. Yet Ralph Waldo Emerson and Henry David Thoreau were anarchist heroes, William James was influenced by anarchism, and both the American artist and critic Robert Henri and the philosopher Will Durant carried the anarchist teachings of the modern school into the mainstream of American culture.

American developments in the modern arts and progressive education before 1920 were deeply influenced by anarchism. Its history seems discontinuous, marked only by eruptions of violence—Haymarket, the assassination of President William McKinley in 1901 by the Polish anarchist Leon Czolgosz, the riots accompanying Industrial Workers of the World (IWW) direct action—yet anarchism may provide the cultural logic that joins late-nineteenth-century realism to early-twentieth-century modernism. Immigration, labor, reformist social movements, the addition of western voices to the national debate, and science's challenges to religion interacted with anarchist thinking during this period to inaugurate new freedoms and a sense of social upheaval that eventually suffered from a severe counterreaction at the end of World War I.

The most newsworthy events of anarchism in the United States before the 1960s occurred between the 1870s and the 1920s, but sensationalism gave misleading prominence to the violence linked with anarchism. This period, in which millions of European immigrants came to the United States, also saw the publication of a flood of anarchist books and pamphlets and visits by anarchists both prominent and obscure—influences

---

The following is an extract from Emma Goldman's "Patriotism."

We Americans claim to be a peace-loving people. We hate bloodshed; we are opposed to violence. Yet we go into spasms of joy over the possibility of projecting dynamite bombs from flying machines upon helpless citizens. We are ready to hang, electrocute, or lynch anyone, who, from economic necessity, will risk his own life in the attempt upon that of some industrial magnate. Yet our hearts swell with pride at the thought that America is becoming the most powerful nation on earth, and that it will eventually plant her iron foot on the necks of all other nations.

Such is the logic of patriotism.

Emma Goldman, "Patriotism," in *Anarchism and Other Essays* (New York: Dover, 1969), p. 136. First published in 1917.

---

that found a welcoming tradition of individualistic and libertarian impulses already established in a country whose intellectual roots in the Enlightenment were based on similar utopian thinking and whose Revolution of 1776 stood as a historical exemplar of democracy and revolutionary action. The best-known American anarchist, Benjamin Tucker (1854–1939), published the American anarchist journal *Liberty* from 1881 to 1908. He was perhaps more individualistic than Bakunin or Kropotkin and their followers, but he welcomed them and translated and published their writings. Anarchism located the history of the United States in an international context.

ANARCHISM IN AMERICAN CULTURAL HISTORY

The impact of anarchism on American culture was both direct and indirect, and it was substantial. The native tradition, from Josiah Warren and Benjamin Tucker on, was individualistic. When radical advocates of "propaganda by the deed" seized the center stage with dynamite and bombs, newspapers sensationalized the threat of wild-eyed foreigners. Newspaper accounts often made no clear distinctions among the various revolutionary and progressive groups, so the anarchist support of workers or craftspeople could seem a vague and arbitrary terrorism.

The Molly Maguires, for example, were an Irish group in the complicated setting of Pennsylvania mining, where immigrants came with their own traditions of secret societies and where the Irish in particular were subject to discrimination that limited their opportunities for economic advancement. The first violence occurred during the Civil War: between 1862 and 1868 the Molly Maguires assassinated six mine owners and superintendents over issues of draft resistance and labor organizing. The second wave of violence between 1874 and 1875, with eight more assassinations, was in opposition to another labor union. Distinctions disappeared in subsequent representations, and the term "Molly Maguires" labeled first all Irish labor unions and then all workers as anarchist/terrorist organizations.

The Haymarket affair left a lasting impression on the public. The unfairness of the events and the subsequent trial also radicalized those who were supportive of labor. On 4 May 1886 a meeting was called by labor leaders (many German immigrants) to protest the deaths of two strikers killed by police at the McCormick Harvesting Machine Company in Chicago the day before. A bomb exploded, killing a policeman. When the police then opened fire, six more policemen and others in the crowd were killed. Eight anarchist leaders were tried, and in spite of widespread conviction that they were not guilty, four were hanged and one died by suicide. However, three others were pardoned after serving six years because Illinois governor John Peter Altgeld thought the trial had been unjust. Again, the rhetorical legacy of the event endured and outstripped the facts, resulting both in public outrage over the treatment of workers and in public outcry against the violent foreigners.

Alexander Berkman (1870–1936) and Emma Goldman (1869–1940) were among those who found Haymarket a turning point in their convictions. Berkman subsequently attempted to assassinate Andrew Carnegie's associate Henry Clay Frick and was imprisoned, while Goldman carried on alone. She had arrived in the United States in 1885 and was deported in 1919. In those thirty-four years she risked jail again and again, speaking in support of labor and birth control and, later, against the war. Her journal, *Mother Earth,* argued that artists, educators, and activists should join in a common purpose. Another important woman, Voltairine de Cleyre, also promoted anarchist politics, tracing historical continuities in *Anarchism and American Traditions* (1908).

In 1905 in Chicago, Big Bill Haywood gaveled into order the first convention of the Industrial Workers of the World or "Wobblies." Their belief in "direct action" and the general strike rather than

negotiation through leaders and contracts made them both feared and effective, even though smaller in number than other labor organizations. Their confrontations across the country left a legacy of struggle for free speech that endures, including Joe Hill's songs. Roger Baldwin founded the American Civil Liberties Union in 1920 as a response to violations of civil liberties he saw during Emma Goldman's speaking tour with the IWW.

The year 1920 also saw the sensational trial of the Italian anarchists Sacco and Vanzetti, accused of two murders during a robbery. After their conviction, a bomb in Wall Street killed more than thirty and injured hundreds. Many believed that they were possibly innocent because fear of anarchy biased the procedures and denied them justice. Worldwide protests followed, involving many artists and writers—among them Edna St. Vincent Millay, who subsequently wrote a poem in protest, "Justice Denied in Massachusetts."

Far from being rejected, the anarchist philosophy of free speech, individual responsibility, and mutual aid in a small-scale community entered the mainstream of cultural traditions in the United States. A rich anarchist counterculture grew up in a number of American regions, with social activities, lectures, newspapers (more than five hundred between 1870 and 1940), dramatic societies and theater groups, unions, clubs, cooperatives, mutual aid societies, picnics, concerts, and Ferrer schools. Francisco Ferrer established Modern Schools in Spain according to anarchist principles of a community-centered education. These inspired the creation of similar Modern School experiments in the United States. There were memorials of Haymarket and the Paris Commune held during the year. The Paris Commune arose in 1871, when the Prussians invaded and the working people of the city seized power and installed popular governance for a brief period.

ANARCHISM AND THE ARTS

Anarchism also influenced the history of American literature and the arts in the development of a modernist—revolutionary—aesthetic, joining American innovations to the British and Continental avant-garde. Americans such as James Whistler and the critic Sadakichi Hartman (Sidney Allan) were part of Stéphane Mallarmé's circle, who identified themselves with anarchist politics as well as aesthetics (Louise Michel, the anarchist heroine of the Paris Commune, was considered an ally; she thought herself a poet of violence). Events in the 1880s prompted literary responses, including a major novel, *The Princess Casamassima* by Henry James (1843–1916), which ambiguously joined the question of international anarchic politics and the question of the artist

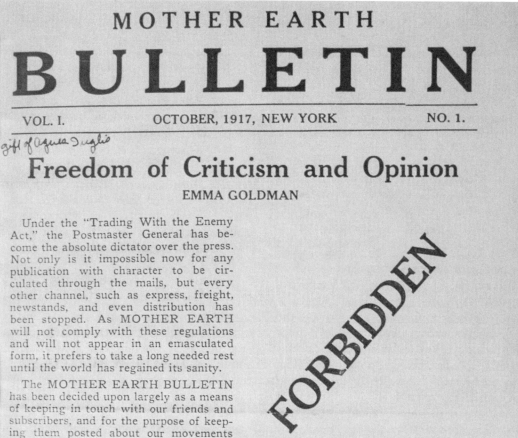

MOTHER EARTH
BULLETIN

VOL. I.   OCTOBER, 1917, NEW YORK   NO. 1.

gift of Agnes Inglis

Freedom of Criticism and Opinion
EMMA GOLDMAN

Under the "Trading With the Enemy Act," the Postmaster General has become the absolute dictator over the press. Not only is it impossible now for any publication with character to be circulated through the mails, but every other channel, such as express, freight, newstands, and even distribution has been stopped. As MOTHER EARTH will not comply with these regulations and will not appear in an emasculated form, it prefers to take a long needed rest until the world has regained its sanity.

The MOTHER EARTH BULLETIN has been decided upon largely as a means of keeping in touch with our friends and subscribers, and for the purpose of keeping them posted about our movements and activities.

FORBIDDEN

DEDICATION

This is the wee Babe of Mother Earth. It was conceived during the greatest human crisis—born into a tragic, disintegrating world. To give it life, Mother Earth had to choose death, yet out of Death must come Life again. The Babe is frail of body, but it comes with a heritage of strength, determination and idealism to be worthy of her who gave it birth.

To bring a child into the world these days is almost an unpardonable luxury. But the child of Mother Earth comes to you for a share of the beautiful love and devotion you gave its mother. Assured of that, it will make a brave effort to Live and to Do.—*E. G.*

EMMA GOLDMAN   -   -   -   -   -   Publisher and Editor

Office: 226 Lafayette Street, New York City

Telephone, Spring 8711

10c per copy $1.00 per year

Cover of *Mother Earth Bulletin*, October 1917. LABADIE COLLECTION, UNIVERSITY OF MICHIGAN LIBRARY as activist. William Dean Howells (1837–1920), like so many, found the Haymarket affair distressing, though he did not carry through with this idea in a particular work. Still, as Arthur Redding argues, perhaps the anarchist visions of August Spies or Johann Most influenced Howells's sympathetic portrayal of the socialist character Lindau in *A Hazard of New Fortunes* (1890). Howells printed Kropotkin's *Memoirs of a Revolutionist* in the *Atlantic Monthly*.

James's *The Princess Casamassima* (first published in 1885–1886 in the *Atlantic Monthly*) tells the story of an anarchist group in London and the tragic involvement of the talented bookbinder Hyacinth Robinson. Hyacinth's death by suicide seems to demonstrate that the artist should not try to practice "propaganda of the deed." However, James's book does not seem entirely unfriendly to the anarchists, who include the appealing (and foreign) bookbinder Poupin and the determined professional anarchist Paul Muniment. James shows aspects of class structure, including the interest of aristocrats such as the Princess Casamassima, whose sympathy for the underclasses is represented with irony. Appearing at a time when the *London Times* equated the violence of Irish acts and news of anarchist organizations from the Continent, promoting a widespread fear of underground terrorist activities, the novel conveyed to readers of the *Atlantic Monthly* the internationalism of anarchist themes and perhaps an individualist or psychological perspective that would have been consonant with American habits of mind.

In the 1890s and early 1900s, visits to the United States by Kropotkin himself as well as traveling troupes presenting the latest plays by Henrik Ibsen and other Continental dramatists, spread the ideas of anarchism and the challenge to tradition not only in New York but also in small towns across the country—reaching even to North Dakota, for example. The ideas from urban working-class and communal anarchism intermingled with American agrarian populism and the immigrant populations of the Great Plains. Little theater groups, many prompted by anarchist advocates of Ferrer Center practices such as Emma Goldman, sprang up in many locations, accompanying not only social work in the cities, such as that of Jane Addams in Chicago, but also western encounters with Native American and Spanish cultures, such as that of Mary Austin in Santa Fe, New Mexico.

William James (1842–1910) was early interested in anarchism and praised the anarchist Morrison Swift. The intellectual and theoretical influence of anarchism on William James's pragmatism is significant. In particular, his ideas of a radical empiricism seem to take up the anarchist reliance not on authority but on the discovery of truth through individual observation. William James influenced key figures in modern poetry (T. S. Eliot, Gertrude Stein, Robert Frost, and Wallace Stevens as well as the less-experimental Mary Austin) and in African American cultural history (W. E. B. Du Bois, Alain Locke, and Zora Neale Hurston).

Modernist circles in the United States in the years leading up to 1920 included a number of anarchists. Alfred Stieglitz's 291 circle and his journal *Camera Work* promoted the work of a number of anarchist artists. Man Ray created covers for Goldman's *Mother Earth*. John Weichsel and Robert Henri were teachers at the Ferrer Center, and Weichsel established the People's Art Guild to allow artists to sell their works outside the markets. The sculptor Adolf Wolff advocated formalism as the method of achieving freedom for the individual artist. Randolph Bourne's idea of the "beloved community" was anarchist. Bourne, one of the Young American Critics (with Van Wyck Brooks, Waldo Frank, and Lewis Mumford), envisioned a culture of democratic community rather than corporate individualism. Margaret Anderson, editor of the *Little Review*, supported Goldman in its pages.

Anarchist principles affected American modernist aesthetics, but the political lineage ranged from the right to the left. Ezra Pound (1885–1972) energetically imported a Max Stirner–influenced version of an anarchist-individualist libertarianism that had grown up in Great Britain in the movement associated with Wyndham Lewis's *Blast* (1914 and 1915), Dora Marsden's *Egoist* (1914–1919), and the *New Age* (1907–1922). The *Others* circle—Alfred Kreymborg, William Carlos Williams, Marcel Duchamp, Albert Gleizes, Mina Loy—all gathered at a Ridgefield, New Jersey, colony in 1915, and the journal was published by an anarchist printer. The anarchist *Revolt* group published its journal from January to March 1916; it included Hippolyte Havel, Neith Boyce, Margaret Sanger, Robert Minor, Hutchins Hapgood, and the artists Max Weber, Abraham Walkowitz, and Ben Benn. The next-to-last issue was censored by the post office for immorality and violence, and almost all the copies were confiscated.

There may be an analogy between the federalist structure of anarchist political organization and the disjunctive structures of modernist aesthetics, a resistance to authoritarian history, narrative, and form. Ezra Pound's interest in Chinese ideogram and juxtaposition as a formal principle is an example. However, many have argued that the political implications of anarchism itself are lost in moving from propaganda of the deed to poetic practice. Can poetic language be revolutionary? This is an enduring critical issue that accompanies the influence of anarchism.

See also Haymarket Square; Immigration; Jurisprudence; Law Enforcement; Socialism; Violence

BIBLIOGRAPHY

Primary Works

Baldwin, Roger, ed. *Kropotkin's Revolutionary Pamphlets: A Collection of Writings.* 1927. New York: Dover Publications, 1970.

Capouya, Emile, and Keitha Tompkins, eds. *The Essential Kropotkin.* New York: Liveright, 1975.

Dolgoff, Sam, ed. *Bakunin on Anarchy: Selected Works by the Activist-Founder of World Anarchism.* New York: Knopf, 1972. Printed as *Bakunin on Anarchism,* Montreal: Black Rose Books, 1980.

Woodcock, George, ed. *The Anarchist Reader.* Atlantic Highlands, N.J.: Humanities Press, 1977.

Secondary Works

Antliff, Allan. *Anarchist Modernism: Art, Politics, and the First American Avant-Garde.* Chicago: University of Chicago Press, 2001.

Avrich, Paul. *Anarchist Portraits.* Princeton, N.J.: Princeton University Press, 1988.

Avrich, Paul. *The Haymarket Tragedy.* Princeton, N.J.: Princeton University Press, 1984.

Blatt, Martin Henry. *Free Love and Anarchism: The Biography of Ezra Heywood.* Urbana and Chicago: University of Illinois Press, 1989.

Chicago Historical Society. "Evidence from the Haymarket Affair." Available at http://memory.loc.gov/cgi-bin/ammemrr.

Coughlin, Michael E., Charles H. Hamilton, and Mark A. Sullivan, eds. *Benjamin R. Tucker and the Champions of "Liberty": A Centenary Anthology.* St. Paul, Minn.: Michael E. Coughlin and Mark Sullivan, 1986.

Crowder, George. *Classical Anarchism: The Political Thought of Godwin, Proudhon, Bakunin, and Kropotkin.* Oxford: Oxford University Press, 1991.

DeLeon, David. *American as Anarchist.* Baltimore: Johns Hopkins University Press, 1978.

Joll, James. *The Anarchists.* 2nd ed. Cambridge, Mass.: Harvard University Press, 1980.

Kadlec, David. *Mosaic Modernism: Anarchism, Pragmatism, Culture.* Baltimore: Johns Hopkins University Press, 2000.

Kenny, Kevin. *Making Sense of the Molly Maguires.* New York and Oxford: Oxford University Press, 1998.

Marshall, Peter. *Demanding the Impossible: A History of Anarchism.* London: HarperCollins, 1992.

Miller, Martin A., ed. *Selected Writings on Anarchism and Revolution.* Cambridge, Mass.: MIT Press, 1970.

Nelson, Bruce C. *Beyond the Martyrs: A Social History of Chicago's Anarchists, 1870–1900.* New Brunswick, N.J.: Rutgers University Press, 1988.

Redding, Arthur F. *Raids on Human Consciousness: Writing, Anarchism, and Violence.* Columbia: University of South Carolina Press, 1998.

Roediger, Dave, and Franklin Rosemont, eds. *Haymarket Scrapbook.* Chicago: Charles H. Kerr, 1986.

Sonn, Richard D. *Anarchism.* New York: Twayne, 1992.

Tilley, W. H. *The Background of "The Princess Casamassima."* University of Florida Monograph 5. Gainesville: University of Florida Press, 1960.

Woodcock, George. *Anarchism: A History of Libertarian Ideas and Movements.* Cleveland, Ohio: World Publishing/Meridian, 1962.

Suzanne Clark

ANGLO-SAXONISM

Historians use the term "Anglo-Saxonism" to describe a loose assembly of cultural assumptions that influenced Anglo-American political and intellectual life in varying ways from the seventeenth century into the twentieth century. In its most general form, Anglo-Saxonism extolled the traditions of the English people before the Norman conquest, who were themselves usually understood to be the descendants of old Germanic tribes of northern Europe: a people superior to others by virtue of their cultural possession of ethical values, legal principles, and governmental structures founded on a bedrock of liberty and democracy. Early American Anglo-Saxonists (like Thomas Jefferson, an enthusiastic student of old English language and law) invoked the attractive figure of the sturdy preconquest English yeoman, and Anglo-Saxonism thus connected itself readily to seminally American, antiaristocratic ideals of political and juridical localism and of the rights of small landholders. An Anglo-Saxon heritage, then, was from very early on one important component of America's conceptualizing of a national character, often invoked as a kind of ruggedly homespun counterpoint to the high classical culture derived from Greece and Rome.

THE RISE OF ANGLO-SAXONISM IN THE LATE NINETEENTH CENTURY

In the late nineteenth century Anglo-Saxonism attained a particularly prominent place in public or popular discourses of nation, for several reasons.

First and perhaps most important, the century's proliferating racial theories in both Europe and the United States—generally taxonomic attempts at scientifically naturalizing the political histories of empire and slavery—shifted Anglo-Saxonism's terms, emphasizing the old English virtues as racial rather than localized in a cultural history. Seen through the lenses of Darwinian evolutionary thought and, in the early twentieth century, Mendelian genetics, these virtues seemed indisputably heritable as well; thus the moral characteristics of a people could perpetuate themselves in a bloodline—or dissipate through racial admixture.

Moreover, the tempting language of hierarchy and teleology entwined with Charles Darwin's evolutionary thought—a language of higher and lower, of success and failure—permitted the development, on both sides of the Atlantic, of a pervasive, powerful rhetoric of racial fitness and ultimate domination. This rhetoric in turn lent easy support to doctrines of imperial necessity in England, of Manifest Destiny in the United States. The Anglo-Saxons, in the popular terms of racial determinism, were naturally vigorous adventurers and leaders whose expansion over the face of the earth was a simple matter of biological inevitability. Such historical thinking, buttressed by an increasing fashionableness of "Teutonic" approaches to history in American universities, led by the 1880s to the vigorous apocalyptic language of the clergyman Josiah Strong, who wrote in his immensely popular *Our Country* (1885) of white Christendom's coming crisis: "the final competition of races, for which the Anglo-Saxon is being schooled. . . . And can any one doubt that the result of this competition will be 'survival of the fittest?'" (p. 214). Citing Darwin's *Descent of Man*, Strong noted that the uncivilized non-Aryans of the world "are now disappearing before the all-conquering Anglo-Saxons. . . . Whether the extinction of inferior races before the advancing Anglo-Saxon seems to the reader sad or otherwise, it certainly appears probable" (p. 215).

A few years later the young Theodore Roosevelt could write with similar extravagance (although without Strong's genocidal complacency) in the opening pages of *The Winning of the West* that "the day when the keels of the low Dutch sea-thieves first grated on the British coast was big with the doom of many nations. . . . The sons of the unknown Saxon, Anglian, and Friesic warriors now hold in their hands the fate of the coming years" (pp. 20–21). In his later political career, Roosevelt would come to see the hybrid American experience as an advance on the simple racial determinism implicit here, with "American-ness" itself—a political identification and allegiance rather than an immutable biological category—more telling than simpler racialized versions of Anglo-Saxonism. But in the 1880s, for Strong, Roosevelt, and others, the century's end seemed the fulfillment of humankind's greatest ethnic adventure, the flowering of racial strength and destiny that the American Sinophile and military writer Homer Lea would call, a generation later, simply "The Day of the Saxon."

Thinking of this kind, combining elements of white supremacy, optimistic progressivism, and a sense of impending crisis, had immediate psychic value for the historical circumstances of the United States in the years before and after the turn of the twentieth century. The new immigration of the 1890s created great (and unruly) "foreign" underclasses in the nation's major cities; the continental frontier "closed," in the historian Frederick Jackson Turner's famous formulation; the "Negro problem," unresolved by emancipation, haunted the exhausted agrarian South and the North's industrial centers. For all of these, the legend of a dominating, pioneering Anglo-Saxon race at the very core of the American experience provided a framing perspective that was also, for some anxious white Americans, a consolation. But the high-water mark of American Anglo-Saxonism coincided most clearly with the nation's own direct experiment in imperial expansion: the Spanish-American War of 1898, which also sealed the growing political rapprochement of Britain and the United States. In early 1899, in that war's aftermath, Rudyard Kipling issued his famous transatlantic poetic challenge (in the *New York Sun*, the *New York Tribune*, and *McClure's Magazine*) to a nation feeling its new international strength and the duties of its Anglo-Saxon heritage: "Take up the White Man's burden." The plea was at once both immediately political and deeply racial.

ANGLO-SAXONISM AND THE READING PUBLIC

For the American reading public, Anglo-Saxonism manifested itself in a number of ways, including a resurgent interest in Sir Walter Scott's chivalric romances and other medieval revivals, like Howard Pyle's illustrated children's fantasies. Kipling himself, England's self-aware literary spokesperson for Anglo-Saxonism and empire, married an American, lived in Vermont, and enjoyed remarkable American adulation in the 1890s and on into the new century. His famous poem "The White Man's Burden" provided the subtitle for the first of Thomas Dixon Jr.'s popular works, *The Leopard's Spots: A Romance of the White Man's Burden 1865–1900* (1902), an openly racist romance of the post–Civil War South (remembered mainly as one of the sources for D. W. Griffith's epic 1915 film *Birth of a Nation*). Like Kipling and others, Dixon

"THE WHITE MAN'S BURDEN"

Rudyard Kipling's "The White Man's Burden," shown here in its first American periodical appearance in February 1899, clearly aligned Anglo-Saxonist sentiments with modern imperialism.

Take up the White Man's burden—
Send forth the best ye breed—
Go, bind your sons to exile
To serve your captives' need;
To wait, in heavy harness,
On fluttered folk and wild—
Your new-caught sullen peoples,
Half devil and half child.

Take up the White Man's burden—
In patience to abide,
To veil the threat of terror
And check the show of pride;
By open speech and simple,
An hundred times made plain,
To seek another's profit
And work another's gain.

Take up the White Man's burden—
The savage wars of peace—
Fill full the mouth of Famine,
And bid the sickness cease;
And when your goal is nearest
(The end for others sought)
Watch sloth and heathen folly
Bring all your hope to nought.

Take up the White Man's burden—
No iron rule of kings,
But toil of serf and sweeper—
The tale of common things.

The ports ye shall not enter,
The roads ye shall not tread,
Go, make them with your living
And mark them with your dead.

Take up the White Man's burden,
And reap his old reward—
The blame of those ye better
The hate of those ye guard—
The cry of hosts ye humour
 (Ah, slowly!) toward the light: —
"Why brought ye us from bondage,
Our loved Egyptian night?"

Take up the White Man's burden—
Ye dare not stoop to less—
Nor call too loud on Freedom
To cloak your weariness.
By all ye will or whisper,
By all ye leave or do,
The silent sullen peoples
Shall weigh your God and you.

Take up the White Man's burden!
Have done with childish days—
The lightly-proffered laurel,
The easy ungrudged praise:
Comes now, to search your manhood
Through all the thankless years,
Cold, edged with dear-bought wisdom,
The judgment of your peers.

understood the late nineteenth century as a climactically decisive chapter in white racial history: "The future American must be an Anglo-Saxon or a Mulatto," says his senior protagonist, and "the future of the world depends on the future of this Republic" (p. 200). His novel's happy ending, a triumphal reassertion of racial separatism, is made possible by the Spanish-American War and a corresponding international rediscovery of Anglo-American race pride: "[The war's] sudden union of the English-speaking people in friendly alliance disturbed the equilibrium of the world, and confirmed the Anglo-Saxon in his title to the primacy of racial sway" (p. 412).

Other authors before and after the turn of the century deployed Anglo-Saxonism in various ways, although seldom with Dixon's single-minded enthusiasm. Frank Norris, for example, invoked racial destiny with a characteristically confusing mixture of irony and fervor at the end of *The Octopus* (1901), as the great wheat ship sails from California for India. "We'll carry our wheat into Asia yet," says the capitalist Cedarquist, "The Anglo-Saxon started from there at the beginning of everything and it's manifest destiny that he must circle the globe and fetch up where he began his march. . . . The irrepressible Yank is knocking at the doors" (p. 648). Some writers more or less openly satirized Anglo-Saxonism's simple nostalgia, like Mark Twain in *A Connecticut Yankee in King Arthur's Court* (1889). Finley Peter Dunne, the Chicago humorist and celebrant of a distinctly non-Anglo-Saxon immigrant world, mocked the naïveté of rallying the polycultural, polyethnic United States around a myth of racial homogeneity. "I tell ye," his persona Mr. Dooley observed dryly in 1898:

> whin th' Clan an' th' Sons iv Sweden an' th' Banana Club an' th' Circle Francaize an' th' Rooshian Sons of Dinnymite an' th' Benny Brith an' th' Coffee Clutch that Schwartzmeister r-runs an' th' Tur-rnd'ye-mind an' th' Holland society an' th' Afro-Americans an' th' other Anglo-Saxons begin f'r to raise their Anglo-Saxon battle-cry, it'll be all day with th' eight or nine people in th' wurruld that has th' misfortune iv not bein' brought up Anglo-Saxons. (P. 56)

JACK LONDON AND PROGRESSIVE RACISM

The American who came closest to rivaling Kipling as his nation's literary spokesperson for Anglo-Saxonism was his admirer Jack London, who famously peopled his work with masterful Nordic blonds enacting their violent destinies at the edges of the civilized world. London wrote vividly and explicitly about the non-Western challenges facing "our own great race adventure" in essays like his well-known 1904 piece on the Russo-Japanese War, "The Yellow Peril," and in stories like "The Unparalleled Invasion" (1907) and "The Inevitable White Man" (1908), whose aptly named protagonist Saxtorph murderously explores the proposition that "the white man's mission is to farm the world. . . . the white has to run the niggers whether he understands them or not. It's inevitable. It's fate" (p. 1558). In 1910 he vigorously led the openly racist call for Jim Jeffries, the "great white hope" of professional boxing, to take down Jack Johnson, the first black heavyweight champion.

London's case is instructive in its complexity, suggesting Anglo-Saxonism's protean functioning in the intellectual currents of his time. He saw himself as (and in most senses was) a politically progressive or radical thinker and an activist for human justice. Largely self-educated, he drew his politics from voracious reading in social theory and philosophy, from Darwin and Karl Marx to Friedrich Nietzsche but with special attention to Herbert Spencer, the father of Social Darwinism, who had wholeheartedly adapted evolutionism to social and historical analysis. London enthusiastically endorsed the utopian possibilities of modern "scientific" thought (as fantasies like "Goliah" and "The Unparalleled Invasion" attest) and aligned himself sympathetically with the culture of manly vigor espoused by imperialists like Roosevelt and Kipling, with the international eugenics movement, and with world socialism. By his mid-twenties he had also shipped as a sailor to Asia, hoboed across the United States, run as a Socialist-Labor candidate in the Oakland, California, municipal elections, joined the great Klondike gold rush, and explored urban industrial poverty in the slums of London. Thus London's version of Anglo-Saxonism, again something like Roosevelt's or Kipling's, is probably best understood as one expression of naively progressive, internationalist thinking—based in old ideas of Manifest Destiny, modernized by a simple "scientific" determinism, drawing its vocabulary from the racial discourse of the preceding fifty years, and made theatrical by an appeal to popular Orientalism. For London (as for Kipling and other great British imperialists) the brotherhood of man and the white man's burden, progressivism and racism, could and did coexist in a single political philosophy.

THE WANING OF ANGLO-SAXONISM IN THE MODERNIST WORLD

But even at the peak of Anglo-Saxonist optimism, such a philosophy seemed to many Americans willfully blind to its own brutal underpinnings. Along with its accolades, for example, "The White Man's Burden" elicited an immediate scattering of counterresponses in the United States, like William Walker's sardonic March 1899 *Life* cartoon, where brown and black bearers struggle beneath the imperial bulk of Uncle Sam and John Bull. And through the 1910s and 1920s, as the American racial, economic, and international experiences grew more complicated, the triumphant myth of the Anglo-Saxon available to Josiah Strong and Teddy Roosevelt in the 1880s seemed to most serious writers not only doomed to disappointment but in fact also comically inadequate to the modern world and its cultural ironies. By 1925 a social theorist like Lothrop Stoddard, whose *The Rising Tide of Color* (1920) gloomily announced the international triumph of black, yellow, red, and brown, could be satirically dismissed as a crank by F. Scott Fitzgerald in *The Great Gatsby* (1925); in 1929 William Faulkner (in *The Sound and the Fury*) similarly mocked Jason Compson's hayseed, all-American anti-Semitism. These high modernist white writers (and others like Ernest Hemingway, T. S. Eliot, Ezra Pound, and Willa Cather) were themselves hardly freer of their culture's deeply entrenched racial attitudes than had been their predecessors. It can be powerfully argued, in fact, that high modernism's nostalgic neoclassicism, its formalism, and its frequent appeals to myth carried forward in a subtler form the raw expression of white power that energized the

Anglo-Saxonism of the previous generation. But the innocent exuberance of Roosevelt, London, and the early Kipling, their simple confidence in Anglo-Saxon culture, virtue, and progress, disappeared almost without a trace into the complications of post–World War I America.

See also Immigration; Imperialism and Anti-Imperialism; Race Novels; Social Darwinism; Spanish-American War

BIBLIOGRAPHY

Primary Works

Dixon, Thomas, Jr. *The Leopard's Spots: A Romance of the White Man's Burden 1865–1900.* New York: Grosset and Dunlap, 1902.

Dunne, Finley Peter. "On the Anglo-Saxon." In his *Mr. Dooley in Peace and in War.* Boston: Small, Maynard, 1899.

Kipling, Rudyard. "The White Man's Burden." *McClure's Magazine,* February 1899.

London, Jack. *The Complete Short Stories of Jack London.* Edited by Earle Labor, Robert C. Leitz III, and I. Milo Shepard. Stanford, Calif.: Stanford University Press, 1993.

London, Jack. "The Yellow Peril." In his *Revolution and Other Essays.* New York: Macmillan, 1910.

Norris, Frank. *The Octopus.* New York: Doubleday, Page, 1901.

Roosevelt, Theodore. *The Winning of the West.* Vol. 1. New York: Putnam, 1889.

Strong, Josiah. *Our Country.* 1885. Edited by Jurgen Herbst. Cambridge, Mass.: Harvard University Press, 1963.

Secondary Works

Anderson, Stuart. *Race and Rapprochement: Anglo-Saxonism and Anglo-American Relations, 1895–1904.* East Brunswick, N.J.: Associated University Presses, 1981.

Horsman, Reginald. *Race and Manifest Destiny: The Origins of American Racial Anglo-Saxonism.* Cambridge, Mass.: Harvard University Press, 1981.

John N. Swift

ANNEXATION AND EXPANSION

After the Civil War, the United States' long-standing goal to expand westward assumed a new determination and efficiency. Although the territorial claims to the region had been purchased from France, Spain, and Britain years earlier, questions regarding slavery had prevented formal progress. With that debate eliminated, politicians and capitalists used their substantially increased military and industrial powers to control the land and the people that were located between the existing states and the Pacific coast. Eventually, their sights were set beyond the North American continent.

Control of continental western lands proceeded quickly. In the 1860s Nevada and Nebraska became states, and a U.S. claim to Alaska was purchased from Russia; in 1876 Colorado joined the Union; in the 1880s Montana, Washington, North Dakota, and South Dakota followed suit; by the 1890s Idaho, Wyoming, and Utah gained statehood, while a claim to Hawaii was established. In the early decades of the twentieth century, Oklahoma, Arizona, and New Mexico became states as well. Perhaps more important, the United States embarked upon an imperialistic program across seas with the Spanish-American War in Cuba as its centerpiece.

Historians often categorize American expansionism during the period between 1870 and 1920 into two sections: westward acquisition before 1898 and overseas conquest after 1898. However, the reasons for both were essentially the same: the control of more land and people meant, quite simply, additional resources, wealth, and power.

TAKING THE WEST FROM INDIGENOUS PEOPLES

Although initial interest in the western part of the continent centered upon fur and gold, enterprising individuals soon formed companies and political connections to exploit the seemingly unlimited potential for timber, minerals, fish, beef, and agricultural products. That these lands were already populated by indigenous peoples mattered very little to proponents of westward expansion. Increasingly, a philosophy of Social Darwinism was used to excuse the subjugation of others in the name of progress. Drawing upon *On the Origin of Species* (1859) by Charles Darwin (1809–1882), arguments for American hegemony tended to shift away from Manifest Destiny and toward natural selection. Insisting less often that U.S. imperialism was God's will, proponents contended instead that the fittest nation would survive the brutal competition for dominance. Ultimately this argument became dangerously linked to a belief in Anglo-Saxon racial superiority, which, in turn, gained support from many advocates of organized religion who sought to spread Christianity.

In fact, the existence of missionaries belied an enduring myth about the American West. Its lands were not open or unoccupied. Rather, a diverse number of

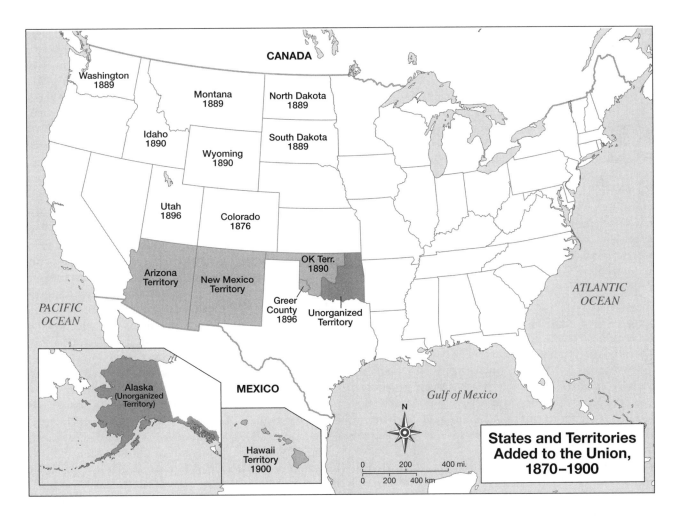

Native American cultures thrived on the plains, in the deserts, in the mountain, and along the coasts. These cultures were systematically destroyed and the people relocated to often unfamiliar and barren tracts of land unwanted by Euro-Americans. Native resistance was able to slow the advance temporarily. In 1876 Crazy Horse and Sitting Bull famously defeated the forces of George Armstrong Custer at the Battle of the Little Bighorn. Also in the 1870s Chief Joseph organized the Nez Percé rebellion in Oregon and Idaho, and in the 1880s Geronimo led the Apache wars in the Southwest. The United States, however, was determined to secure western lands, even while some citizens called for the fair treatment of Native Americans. During the so-called Indian Wars from 1865 to 1890, federal troops wore down Native American resistance with an unrelenting assault that made use of military advancements and winter campaigning (when Native Americans typically organized themselves into smaller groups).

Not only did indigenous Americans have little chance to defend themselves physically, but they were also under attack culturally. A nationwide system of boarding schools was established across the country, defined by the ideas of Richard Pratt, who said, "Kill the Indian in him, and save the man" (Pratt, p. 260). The goal was to remove Native American children from their parents and community, divest them of their cultural heritage, and teach them job skills that would allow them to assimilate into Euro-American culture. Unfortunately, the schools often left students unable to blend comfortably back into their indigenous communities or to gain acceptance within a racially divisive mainstream society. Drawing upon their experiences within this school system, Zitkala-Ša (also known as Gertrude Simmons Bonnin, 1876–1938) and Luther Standing Bear (also known as Ota Kte or Plenty Kill, c. 1868–c. 1939) exposed the dramatic changes forced upon American Indian children and their communities in, respectively, "The School Days of an Indian Girl" (1900) and *My People, the Sioux* (1928).

The onslaught against American Indians continued on other fronts as well. In 1887 the Dawes Severalty Act (also called the Allotment Act) further diminished

Native-controlled land by allotting parcels to individual American Indians. Although seemingly a generous effort to help Native Americans become yeoman farmers (each head of a household received 160 acres), it also allowed white settlers to purchase the remaining land, thus hugely diminishing reservation lands. Such outrages prompted many indigenous people to join the Ghost Dance religion begun by Wovoka, a Paiute who believed that the spirits of deceased Native Americans would return and that whites would be banished from the earth. The growing movement caused much anxiety among white settlers and federal agents. Laws were passed to criminalize its religious practices, and in 1890 approximately three hundred Ghost Dance followers were massacred at Wounded Knee, South Dakota. The slaughter has come to symbolize the end of Native resistance to Euro-American expansion.

NEW LANDS, NEW PROSPERITY, NEW WRITINGS

During this period of American Indian dislocation, Euro-Americans flooded into the newly available western lands. The United States actively promoted the cheapness, fertility, and accessibility of frontier land to the legions of foreign immigrants arriving in America during this time. The Homestead Act of 1862 provided 160 acres to any male willing to work the land for ten years, and the completion of the transcontinental railroad in 1869 allowed the transportation of people and goods to market with relative ease. Huge influxes of European immigrants were encouraged to farm the Great Plains, increasingly emptied of their Native American and bison populations. By 1890 the government had given titles to over forty-eight million acres.

The battle over land and its resources was one of the most fascinating, violent, and corrupt chapters in the nation's history, and many writers recognized its literary potential. Mark Twain (the pen name of Samuel Langhorne Clemens, 1835–1910) and Charles Dudley Warner (1829–1900) cowrote *The Gilded Age: A Tale of Today* (1873) to satirize the graft and greed of the time. Henry Adams (1838–1918) used his novel *Democracy: An American Novel* (1880) to expose Washington corruption, focusing particularly on Ulysses S. Grant's administration. Later, Frank Norris (1870–1902) produced *The Octopus: A Story of California* (1901), which investigated the conflict between the railroad conglomerates and the California farmers while also illustrating a fading Spanish culture. During the 1870s and 1880s, a veritable pack of writers began churning out dime novels that glorified the exploits of cowboys, ranchers, outlaws, prospectors, and prostitutes (those with hearts of gold anyway).

Most of this fiction was influenced by Bret Harte (1836–1902), who, writing in San Francisco, created a new western genre with short stories like "The Luck of Roaring Camp" (1868) and "The Outcasts of Poker Flat" (1869). Writing from Boston, Owen Wister (1860–1938) finalized the prototype with *The Virginian: A Horseman of the Plains* (1902), introducing the refined but rugged cowboy that would profoundly influence twentieth-century books, movies, and television programs. The iconic cowboy figured prominently in the fiction of the prolific Zane Grey (1872–1939), who won popular acclaim with *Riders of the Purple Sage* (1912) and *The U. P. Trail* (1918).

A new style of writing named realism emerged in the late nineteenth century. Responding to the swiftly changing cultural landscape, realists sought to capture the often-gritty truths of society as accurately as possible, avoiding the idealization associated with earlier Romantic writers. Twain was one of the most popular realists who capitalized upon the American West, developing an internationally recognized western persona in *The Innocents Abroad; or, The New Pilgrims' Progress* (1869), *Roughing It* (1872), and *Life on the Mississippi* (1883). A number of realists made serious literary topics of western homesteading. Hamlin Garland (1860–1940) focused on hardscrabble farming in Wisconsin, Iowa, and South Dakota in his collection *Main-Travelled Roads: Six Mississippi Valley Stories* (1891); Willa Cather (1873–1947) outlined the varied successes of immigrant women transplanted onto the Nebraska plains in *O Pioneers!* (1913) and *My Ántonia* (1918); and O. E. Rölvaag investigated the psychology of the initial Scandinavian pioneers in the upper Midwest in *Giants in the Earth* (1927). Looking farther west, Mary Austin (1868–1934) described the rhythms of life in the arid Southwest, most notably in *The Land of Little Rain* (1903) and *Lost Borders* (1909). Jack London (1876–1916) drew upon his experiences in Alaska (purchased from Russia in 1867, although not made a state until 1959) and the Yukon Territory during the Klondike gold rush of 1897 and 1898. The result was *The Call of the Wild* (1903), which illustrated London's ideas about survival of the fittest. He explored a similar theme in *The Sea-Wolf* (1904). Rex Ellingwood Beach (1877–1949) also wrote two novels about life in the far north during the gold rush: *The Spoilers* (1906) and *The Barrier* (1908).

Although writers (and filmmakers) would continue to recognize and exploit the cultural magnetism of the American West, many politicos and capitalists sought new conquests. In 1890 a census indicated that western lands were essentially filled by white settlers, and as a result the historian Frederick Jackson Turner famously declared the frontier closed. Having secured Native American territories, advocates of expansionism turned their attention overseas.

INTO THE CARIBBEAN AND OVER THE PACIFIC

Several factors enabled the United States to broaden its power beyond continental borders. In the 1880s and 1890s the navy increased its number of steel ships at the recommendation of Alfred Mahan's historical study of the importance of sea power to national ambition. The new fleet provided additional strength and authority on the oceans while simultaneously requiring additional bases throughout the world. Moreover, the expanded productivity of the plains and mountain states resulted in a glut of agricultural and industrial products with no market. The economic panic of 1893 and the deep recession throughout the 1890s prompted many capitalists to call for the opening of new markets, particularly in heavily populated Asia. The state-of-the-art U.S. Navy would facilitate this process.

Increasingly, Hawaii was viewed as a convenient stopping place for ships trading with Pacific-rim countries. In addition, the islands had long held a fabled place in America's eyes. Not only was it the location of Captain James Cook's ignominious end, but it was viewed as a sort of paradise beyond the strictures of civilization. Mark Twain had helped promote this view of Native Hawaiian life. After his four-month visit in 1866, he gained fame in the 1860s with his letters to the Sacramento *Union* (which he revamped for *Roughing It*). That his talks about the islands remained one of his most popular addresses on the lecture circuit attests to America's fascination with Hawaii. So when, in 1893, colonial sugar planters wrestled control of the islands from the monarch, Queen Liliuokalani, a serious debate began about annexing the islands into the United States.

The colonial planters who staged this coup lobbied hard to declare Hawaii a state in order to avoid import taxes and keep profits high. Their gambit was a reaction to their lost exemption from the U.S. tariff, a special arrangement that Congress eliminated to protect U.S. interests in the Cuban sugar industry. Rather than annex Hawaii outright, Democratic president Grover Cleveland commissioned a study to determine if annexation would appear too much like imperialism, of which he was apprehensive. Moreover, of the ninety thousand inhabitants, only a few thousand were of European descent. The majority were Native Hawaiians and Asians. This also gave pause, as xenophobia in the United States was high, particularly regarding Asians. The Chinese Exclusionary Act had been passed in

1882 and renewed in 1892, squelching immigration from China. Allowing Hawaii into the Union would make those Asians living in the islands U.S. citizens. Cleveland also learned that only a minority of Hawaiians desired annexation, and the coup was orchestrated by a small number of wealthy planters. He decided not to officially annex the islands, but in the 1898 elections Republicans gained the majority, and Hawaii was procured by congressional resolution.

More dangerous diplomatic games were being played in South and Central America. When Britain asserted its claim to Venezuela in an attempt to secure its newly discovered gold fields, Cleveland strongly resisted, arguing that the Monroe Doctrine reserved all the Americas for U.S. interests. Britain ultimately backed down, hoping to acquire the United States as an ally against an increasingly hostile Germany. The victory resulted in a growing sense of international influence for the United States.

THE SPANISH-AMERICAN WAR

A major test of the United States' bold new tactics occurred when Cubans rebelled against colonial Spanish rule in 1895. The Spanish responded by imprisoning thousands in camps, where many died in deplorable conditions. A great debate ensued in the United States over whether to act and why. Some argued for intervention to help Cuba fight for independence; some believed U.S. investments in Cuba must be safeguarded and expanded; some saw military involvement as a method to release domestic tension building over labor disputes and economic recession; others saw involvement as a selfish attempt to exert power over more people and land. Leading the charge for war were the Republicans Theodore Roosevelt and Henry Cabot Lodge, both outspoken nationalists and expansionists.

President Cleveland, however, opposed intervention, siding with those who believed that involvement would contradict the founding principles of the United States. His successor, William McKinley, who took office in 1897, shared this view initially, but eventually several factors changed his outlook. Roosevelt, assistant secretary of the navy, began redirecting forces to instigate war. Usurping his superior's powers, he even sent a telegram to a commander of the Asiatic squadron, telling him to prepare for "offensive operations in Philippine Islands" (Brands, p. 324), also controlled by Spain. In addition, contemporary newspapers drummed incessantly for war, printing sensationalistic and distorted news stories to agitate readers and increase circulation. A newspaper battle broke out between William Randolph Hearst, owner of the *San Francisco*

Examiner and the *New York Morning Journal* (later renamed the *American*), and Joseph Pulitzer of the *New York World*. Hearst, in particular, lobbied for war and flooded Cuba with correspondents; he reportedly cabled the illustrator Frederic Remington, "You furnish the pictures and I'll furnish the war" (Brands, p. 306).

Two specific incidents probably did more to facilitate U.S. involvement than any other. A private letter written by Spanish ambassador Enrique Dupuy de Lome was intercepted and publicized as an insult to McKinley, thus enraging many. Also, the U.S. battleship *Maine* was sunk in Havana Harbor (it was there as part of an early agreement between the United States and the warring factions in Cuba) in February 1898, killing 266 Americans. The press and Congress quickly blamed Spain. (While an 1898 study indicated that the explosion came from outside the ship, a 1976 study determined that it came from inside the boiler room, suggesting mechanical failure, not sabotage.)

The United States began its war with Spain in early 1898, and fighting ended in mid-August with Spanish forces defeated and the United States in control of Cuba. The episode raised serious questions about U.S. ambitions. Never did the United States extend diplomatic recognition to the Cuban rebels, and despite the fact that the war resolution expressly precluded annexation of Cuba, the United States still took control of the island. The Americans maintained their occupation until 1902, when the Republic of Cuba was established, but the Platt Amendment to the new Cuban constitution established the island as a protectorate of the United States. It did not stop there. The relatively easy victory and the inordinate success of the U.S. Navy prompted increased nationalism within the United States and created many additional supporters of expansionism.

With its victory over Spain, the United States assumed control of not only Cuba but also the Philippines, Puerto Rico, and Guam. Most historians agree that both imperialists and anti-imperialists were motivated by some level of racism. The imperialists felt no compunction about exploiting non-Europeans, and the anti-imperialists feared allowing nonwhites into a protracted alliance with the United States. Although the United States paid Spain $20 million in compensation, the people of the occupied nations received nothing but a new colonial ruler. The inhabitants of the Philippines immediately revolted against U.S. rule, particularly angry over McKinley's statements describing them as incapable of self-rule and announcing the intention to "uplift and civilize and Christianize them" (Brands, p. 330) (even though the majority were already Catholic). Filipinos employed guerrilla tactics, and the United States reacted by increasing its troop presence to seventy thousand. By 1902 the conflict was over, but 300,000 civilians had been placed in concentration camps, 5,000 U.S. soldiers and 220,000 Filipinos had died, and $160 million had been spent.

The Spanish-American War and its aftermath was managed in the interests of the United States, not the Cubans or Filipinos. The complacency engendered by the conflict was epitomized by the diplomat John Hay, who fatuously described the hostilities as "a splendid little war" (Dobson, p. 95). Roosevelt gained much fame for his bravado. His cavalry unit, dubbed the Rough Riders, stormed San Juan Hill amid flying bullets, a scene that Richard Harding Davis (1864–1916)—son of the novelist Rebecca Harding Davis—helped memorialize in *Notes of a War Correspondent* (1910). Some credit Davis's best-selling romance *Soldiers of Fortune* (1897) with helping to build support for economic and cultural imperialism. Stephen Crane also served as a war correspondent, as did Frank Norris. While Crane supported the administration and admired the Rough Riders' courage, he criticized Roosevelt's unit for carelessness. A collection of Crane's war stories set in Cuba was posthumously published as *Wounds in the Rain: War Stories* (1900), but it is considered inferior to most of his earlier works.

In fact, few great literary works are associated with the Spanish-American War. William Dean Howells believed that the war "can inspire nothing that is worthy in art or letters" (Foner, p. xiv), and yet many writers tried. Howells's own short story "Editha" (1905) takes a strong stand against the war. The poets William Vaughn Moody, Henry Blake Fuller, Ernest Howard Crosby, and William Lloyd Garrison published anti-imperialist poems. Crosby also wrote the humorous antimilitary novel *Captain Jinks, Hero* (1902). Raymond Bridgman penned the more solemnly didactic *Loyal Traitors* (1903), and Gertrude Atherton's *Senator North* (1900) criticized the decision for war. Satires by George Ade, Finley Peter Dunne, and Ambrose Bierce attacked U.S. involvement. Mark Twain was perhaps most scathing. Skeptical of U.S. intentions from the beginning, he wrote, "I bring you the stately matron named Christendom, returning bedraggled, besmirched and dishonored from pirate-raids in Kiao-Chow, Manchuria, South Africa and the Philippines, with her soul full of meanness, her pocket full of boodle, and her mouth full of pious hypocrisies" (Foner, p. xxxi). The poet Carl Sandburg (1878–1967), who served in Puerto Rico, described it as "a nightmare of blood, fever and blunders" (Niven, p. 43), although his published accounts in *Always the Young Strangers* (1953) are less dire. Edward Stratemeyer's *Fighting in the Cuban Waters* (1899) stands as one of the few novels that explicitly supported the war.

OLD DIRECTIONS FOR A NEW CENTURY

The year 1898 set the tone for twentieth-century actions around the globe. In 1900 the United States sent twenty-five hundred troops to China to put down the Boxer Rebellion, an uprising against foreign influence, and to gain a market foothold. In 1903 President Roosevelt orchestrated the expulsion of Britain and France from Colombian-controlled Panama, then fomented revolution within Panama. Quickly arranging a contract with the revolutionaries, the United States began constructing the Panama Canal and completed it in 1914. In 1905 the United States asserted control over the customs agency of the Dominican Republic, and from 1914 through 1924 U.S. Marines occupied the country. An occupation also began in Veracruz, Mexico, in 1914 and lasted six months. It came about because of a perceived slight to the American flag. In 1917 the United States paid Denmark for its claim to the Virgin Islands. If these incidents gained less attention than those earlier, it is perhaps because the imperialism of the United States was overshadowed by the European machinations that culminated in World War I. In addition, writers increasingly were experimenting with modernist forms and themes, distancing themselves from the realist tenet that artists could describe the exterior world objectively. As a result, less literary attention was paid to political and military subjects in the first two decades of the twentieth century.

See also Frontier; Imperialism and Anti-Imperialism; Indian Wars; Mexican Revolution; Migration; *My Ántonia;* Philippine-American War; Spanish-American War; The Western

BIBLIOGRAPHY

Secondary Works

Brands, H. W. *The Reckless Decade: America in the 1890s.* New York: St. Martin's Press, 1995.

Dobson, John. *Reticent Expansionism: The Foreign Policy of William McKinley.* Pittsburgh: Duquesne University Press, 1988.

Findling, John E., and Frank W. Thackeray, eds. *Events That Changed America in the Nineteenth Century.* Westport, Conn.: Greenwood Press, 1997.

Foner, Philip S., ed. *The Anti-Imperialist Reader: A Documentary History of Anti-Imperialism in the United States.* Vol. 2, *The Literary Anti-Imperialists.* New York: Holmes and Meier, 1984.

Healy, David. *U.S. Expansionism: The Imperialist Urge in the 1890s.* Madison: University of Wisconsin Press, 1970.

Kaplan, Amy. *The Anarchy of Empire in the Making of U.S. Culture.* Cambridge, Mass.: Harvard University Press, 2002.

Kaplan, Amy, and Donald E. Pease, eds. *Cultures of United States Imperialism.* Durham, N.C.: Duke University Press, 1993.

Niven, Penelope. *Carl Sandburg: A Biography.* New York: Scribner's, 1991.

Paolino, Ernest N. *The Foundations of the American Empire: William Henry Seward and U.S. Foreign Policy.* Ithaca, N.Y.: Cornell University Press, 1973.

Paterson, Thomas G., ed. *American Imperialism and Anti-Imperialism.* New York: Crowell, 1973.

Peyser, Thomas. *Utopia and Cosmopolis: Globalization in the Era of American Literary Realism.* Durham, N.C.: Duke University Press, 1998.

Pratt, Richard H. "The Advantages of Mingling Indians with Whites." In *Americanizing the American Indians: Writings by the "Friends of the Indian," 1880–1900,* compiled by Francis Paul Prucha, pp. 260–271. Cambridge, Mass.: Harvard University Press, 1973.

Welch, Richard E. *Imperialists vs. Anti-Imperialists: The Debate over Expansionism in the 1890s.* Itasca, Ill.: F. E. Peacock Publishers, 1972.

Western Literature Association, sponsor. *A Literary History of the American West.* Fort Worth: Texas Christian University Press, 1987.

Western Literature Association, sponsor. *Updating the Literary West.* Fort Worth: Texas Christian University Press, 1997.

Joseph L. Coulombe

ANTI-INTELLECTUALISM

The term "anti-intellectualism" refers to a perceived cultural bias in America against those dedicated to conceptual production and analysis rather than to pragmatic, practical industry. Much evidence suggests that this perception is an accurate one, even within institutions of higher learning—the oft-called "ivory towers"—when one looks simply at the appropriation of funds made within them. According to Richard Hofstadter (1916–1970), who authored *Anti-Intellectualism in American Life* (1963), one of the most important studies of this bias, the term itself was rarely heard before the 1950s, when McCarthyism made many people suspicious of thinkers and social critics. Despite the late usage of the term, however, the phenomenon itself goes back much further than the 1950s. Hofstadter is reluctant to define "anti-intellectualism," believing it a complicated phenomenon manifested in many forms; nevertheless, he writes: "The common strain that binds together the attitudes and ideas which I call anti-intellectual is a resentment and suspicion of the life of the mind and of those who are considered to represent it; and a disposition constantly to minimize the value of that life" (p. 7).

That this resentment and suspicion often went unnamed is perhaps accounted for by the relatively recent introduction of the word "intellectual." First coming into use in France in 1898, the term was soon used by William James (1842–1910) in an 1899 letter. James clearly sees the intellectual as one who stands in opposition to many social structures, an individual away from the herd. "We 'intellectuals' in America," writes James, "must all work to keep our precious birthright of individualism, and freedom from these institutions [church, army, aristocracy, royalty]. *Every* great institution is perforce a means of corruption—whatever good it may also do" (Hofstadter, p. 39). As Hofstadter notes, referring to oneself as one who stands outside the norms naturally leads to a backlash; those who accept traditional social structures view dimly those who stand outside and question or criticize those structures.

Though many historians of the 1960s and since have discounted Hofstadter's view of American intellectual history, arguing that he believed anti-intellectualism too pervasive in society, his study is still used in contemporary scholarship. Hofstadter provides a good basic framework with which to understand the roots and manifestations of anti-intellectualism in the United States. He clearly shows how it connects to American business, politics, religion, education, and, ironically, thought. Hofstadter writes that "anti-intellectualism is not the creation of people who are categorically hostile to ideas. . . . Few intellectuals are without moments of anti-intellectualism; few anti-intellectuals without single-minded intellectual passions" (p. 21). Hofstadter writes, for example, about the anti-intellectualism found in transcendentalism with its emphasis on feeling over reason, and of Benjamin Franklin's emphasis on practical success in the world, but he does not argue that the thinkers Ralph Waldo Emerson and Franklin are inherently anti-intellectual. Hofstadter states: "To be confronted with a simple and unqualified evil [anti-intellectualism] is no doubt a kind of luxury; but such is not the case here." Rather, Hofstadter argues that anti-intellectualism is "a broadly diffused quality in our

civilization" (p. 22), and he does a thorough job of demonstrating that point. The wide areas of his inquiry—business, politics, religion, and education—overlap in life and in literature and provide a useful framework to highlight works and events of the early twentieth century that exhibit anti-intellectualism.

THE ROOTS OF ANTI-INTELLECTUALISM

Following the notion of Van Wyck Brooks (1886–1963) that the prevailing influence on American culture is its Puritan origins, Hofstadter sees American anti-intellectualism as grounded in "the framework of our religious history" (p. 47). Hofstadter takes care, however, to note how important education was to a society that founded Harvard amidst the burdens of disease and war borne by the colonists, and that Harvard students studied not only theology but also the classics. One might assume that anti-intellectualism would stem from the Puritan values of practicality and industry, but Hofstadter sees it instead as a reaction to Puritanism. The initial appearance of anti-intellectualism coincided with the First Great Awakening, when American religion took a decided movement toward emotionalism and away from the self-restraint of Puritanism.

As is true of most social movements and forces, anti-intellectualism can be seen as a reaction to trains of thought that precede it. The nineteenth and early twentieth centuries brought Darwinism, Freudianism, and Marxism to the public eye, along with higher criticism (the study of sacred texts as literature) and a greater emphasis on scientific method. These ideas, associated with modernism, led to a psychological decentralization of humankind. If humanity was a product of evolution rather than special creation; if humanity was driven by unconscious instincts rather than guided by a benevolent creator; if human history was a product of class struggle, not the playing out of a divine comedy; if sacred texts were not inerrant and historically accurate—then large segments of humanity were left without the ways they had customarily thought of themselves. Thus, modernism was met with a reactionary zeal born out of psychological turmoil. In order to hang onto what they believed, many people found it necessary to fight new ideas with vehemence.

Hofstadter does not single out evangelicalism alone as the sustainer of anti-intellectualism: "If evangelicalism and primitivism helped to plant anti-intellectualism at the roots of American consciousness," writes Hofstadter, "a business society assured that it would remain in the foreground of American thinking" (p. 49). The quick-thinking and aggressive—these people were what spurred America forward, not the contemplative.

These traits became so pronounced in the American character that the standards of business influenced the professions, leading to a greater "egalitarian spirit . . . still more effective in politics and education" (p. 50). Similar ideas can be found in the writings of the historian Frederick Jackson Turner (1861–1932), whose "frontier hypothesis"—first voiced in "The Significance of the Frontier in American History" (1893)—emphasized the individualism and self-reliance of the American character rather than its intellectual exploits. Indeed, Hofstadter claims that the "first truly powerful and widespread impulse to anti-intellectualism in American politics was, in fact, given by the Jacksonian movement" (p. 155). Jacksonian democracy "is founded in the democratic institutions and egalitarian sentiments of this country," which leads to "the vulgarization of culture which that society constantly produces" (p. 407).

THE HIGHBROWS AND THE LOWBROWS

It was this kind of vulgarization that led Van Wyck Brooks to bemoan the "highbrow" and the "lowbrow" in American literature and culture in *America's Coming-of-Age* (1915). He was not alone in feeling this distinction. By the 1940s it had worked its way into popular culture via Cab Calloway's "Foo a Little Bally-Hoo," in which the singer optimistically intones that "the highbrows are swinging with the lowbrows." Frederick Lewis Allen (1890–1954), in *Only Yesterday: An Informal History of the Nineteen-Twenties* (1931), writes of what he calls "The Revolt of the Highbrows," a period in which a diverse group of intellectuals "rose in loud and bitter revolt" (p. 190). Allen says, "their revolt against the frock-coated respectability and decorous formality of American literature had been under way for several years; Theodore Dreiser, Willa Cather, Carl Sandburg, Edgar Lee Masters, Robert Frost, Vachel Lindsay, Amy Lowell, and the Imagists and exponents of free verse had been breaking new ground since before the War [World War I]" (p. 191).

In *Civilization in the United States* (1922), a collection compiled by American intellectuals, the consensus opinion was that "the most amusing and pathetic fact in the social life of America today is its emotional and aesthetic starvation" (Allen, p. 191). Though *Civilization in the United States* appeared later than 1920, the complaint existed prior to that date. One example of this "emotional and aesthetic starvation" is found in the 1905 short story "Paul's Case" by Willa Cather (1873–1947). It focuses on a Pittsburgh high school student who is afflicted with an educationally based torpor and a bleak existence at home. He is expelled from school, forbidden entrance to the the-

ater he dearly loves, and put to work. Shortly after entering the world of commerce, Paul absconds with a sum of money and travels to New York, leaving behind his father's dull apartment, where Paul's bedroom is decorated with portraits of George Washington and John Calvin. On the stolen money, Paul lives a brief life of luxury and excess, perhaps starved by earlier emotional deprivations. When he learns that his father is coming to New York to retrieve him, Paul jumps to his death in front of a locomotive, becoming a symbol of the individual constrained by society, the locomotive signifying the force and power of the society that accepts no variations.

Though "Paul's Case" can be read as a story of an aesthete confronting a barren society, the story also suggests that Paul is homosexual. In the context of anti-intellectualism, this is noteworthy because, as Hofstadter asserts, intellectuals have often been labeled as effeminate or homosexual within American society, perhaps suggesting to the homophobic mind that intellectualism is a perversion. This kind of charge is leveled at Wing Biddlebaum in *Winesburg, Ohio: A Group of Tales of Ohio Small Town Life* (1919) by Sherwood Anderson (1876–1941). Wing was a dedicated teacher who was lashed out of his town after a simple-minded schoolboy falsely accused him of sexual molestation. After later settling in Winesburg, Wing lives an isolated life, victimized by a public who believes the worst of one who seeks to enlighten its youth. Wing is not the only sufferer in Winesburg. The reader continually encounters characters suffering from a variety of emotional deprivations, living lives of quiet desperation unless they, like Winesburg's George Willard, somehow manage to escape from the tiny community to a place where they might be able to live fuller lives away from the stultifying effects of commerce, religion, and provincialism.

Though Frederick Lewis Allen's *Only Yesterday* concerns the decade of the 1920s, which is outside the scope of this volume, it is noteworthy that both he and Hofstadter identify the journalist H. L. Mencken and the novelist Sinclair Lewis as among the most important figures to speak out against the anti-intellectualism they saw in American society. In 1925 Mencken (1880–1956) covered the Scopes "Monkey Trial," perhaps one of the most famous twentieth-century instances of modernism colliding with religious fundamentalism. Mencken, however, had ample preparation prior to 1920 for covering that case, being known for his criticism of America and its "booboisie" as a writer for the *Baltimore Sun*.

In an essay first published in the *New York Evening Mail* (13 November 1917), Mencken took on what he saw as the intellectual poverty of the American South. His essay, "The Sahara of the Bozart," is not an example of eastern elitism; instead, it laments the loss of intellectual greatness that the South once presented: "The New England shopkeepers and theologians never really developed a civilization; all they ever developed was a government. They were, at their best, tawdry and tacky fellows, oafish in manner and devoid of imagination; one searches the books in vain for mention of a salient Yankee gentleman" (Mencken, "The Sahara of the Bozart," p. 159). Noting a few exceptions, such as James Branch Cabell, Mencken sees no artists, historians, sociologists, philosophers, theologians or scientists in the area between the "Potomac mud-flats and the Gulf." Mencken attributes this lack to a decline of southern aristocracy, a class that had the leisure to establish a culture, and to the "poor white trash" (Mencken, "The Sahara of the Bozart," p. 159) that came into power after the aristocracy faded. This less sophisticated group brought with it a lower-class philistinism and fundamentalism. Mencken thus outlines what Hofstadter identifies as an ironic product of democratization of society overall and, of course, the educational opportunities afforded by that society. Democracy, in one sense, leads to anti-intellectualism, simply because it elevates groups naturally antithetical to and suspicious of the intellectual. The effect of this is a strengthening of an anti-intellectual element within American culture and a further isolation of the intellectual. Such was the state of American culture and of the "booboisie" that defined it in popular terms.

SINCLAIR LEWIS AND *MAIN STREET*

Such was also the culture that Sinclair Lewis (1885–1951) dramatized in *Main Street* (1920), one of his many novels that anatomized American mainstream society. He did the same thing in *Babbitt* (1922), from which the words "Babbitt" and "Babbittry" entered the English language, signifying those who unthinkingly support an anti-intellectual status quo. *Main Street* tells the story of Carol Kennicott, an easterner who moves to Gopher Prairie, Minnesota, and futilely attempts to bring higher culture to the small midwestern town. Hofstadter has pointed out that anti-intellectuals are not necessarily stupid, as Carol learns when she discovers that "outside of tracts, conservatives do not tremble and find no answer when an iconoclast turns on them, but retort with agility and confusing statistics" (p. 276). Carol later wonders of her small-town companions, "when will they have me on the scaffold?" (p. 372), perhaps not only noting the pettiness of bourgeois society but also speculating on the fate, literal or figurative, of those who try to change it.

CONCLUSION

Anti-intellectualism is not a distinctly American phenomenon, nor did it come into existence suddenly and with a name. Nor did the revolt against it prior to and during the 1920s put an end to it. It did not go into remission when the term first came into common usage in the 1950s, nor did the use of that term check it. Anti-intellectualism still figures strongly in twenty-first-century America. One need look no further for evidence of the conflict than a daily newspaper or a cable news network, or to a situation comedy or "reality" show. Though people may disagree on who is the anti-intellectual, the phenomenon is characterized by doctrinaire thinking and by appealing to the lowest common denominators of the public taste. As H. L. Mencken famously said in his "Notes on Journalism," "No one in this world, so far as I know . . . has ever lost money by underestimating the intelligence of the great masses of the plain people."

See also Genteel Tradition; Literary Criticism; Pragmatism

BIBLIOGRAPHY
Primary Works
Anderson, Sherwood. *Winesburg, Ohio*. 1919. New York: Viking, 1960.

Brooks, Van Wyck. *America's Coming-of-Age*. 1915. Garden City, N.Y: Doubleday, 1958.

Cather, Willa. *The Troll Garden*. Edited by James Woodress. Lincoln: Published by the University of Nebraska Press for the Center for Great Plains Studies, University of Nebraska–Lincoln, 1983.

Lewis, Sinclair. *Main Street*. 1920. New York: Signet, 1961.

Mencken, H. L. "Notes on Journalism." *Chicago Tribune*, 19 September 1926.

Mencken, H. L. "The Sahara of the Bozart." In *The American Scene: A Reader*, edited by Huntington Cairns, pp. 157–168. New York: Knopf, 1977.

Secondary Works
Allen, Frederick Lewis. *Only Yesterday: An Informal History of the Nineteen-Twenties*. 1931. New York: Harper, 1957.

Hofstadter, Richard. *Anti-Intellectualism in American Life*. New York: Knopf, 1963.

Turner, Frederick Jackson. *Rereading Frederick Jackson Turner: The Significance of the Frontier in American History, and Other Essays*. Commentary by John Mack Faragher. New York: Holt, 1994.

Tim Sougstad

APPEAL TO REASON

The *Appeal to Reason* was the most important socialist weekly newspaper ever published in the United States. Its rise and fall—circulation peaked at about 760,000 readers in 1912 but declined after that—parallels the rise and fall of the socialist movement in America, which saw its greatest electoral victory in the 1912 presidential election, when the Socialist presidential candidate Eugene V. Debs received 6 percent of the popular vote. The *Appeal* is interesting to literary historians because of the various rhetorical and stylistic strategies its writers and editors used to convince its readers to support the socialist cause.

JULIUS AUGUSTUS WAYLAND

It is impossible to separate the history of the *Appeal* from the biography of its founder, Julius Augustus Wayland, who called himself the "One Hoss Editor." Wayland was born in 1854 into an Indiana family left nearly destitute by his father's death. He committed suicide in 1912, at the height of support for both the *Appeal* and the socialist movement but also in the midst of attempts by the government to suppress the paper. At the age of sixteen, Wayland became a printer's apprentice, eventually learning the business and operating his own shops, which published a weekly paper and printed other jobs.

During the early period of his newspaper career, Wayland developed several strategies that allowed him to prosper as a small-town newspaper editor. First, he demanded that subscribers pay in advance, which allowed him to meet initial costs, and he actively solicited new subscribers. In turn, he used the subscription numbers to solicit advertisers and to keep the rates for advertising high. Finally, he reinvested funds into the business, relying on the latest printing technology, which also helped to keep costs low. In short, Wayland was a businessman first. But as a newspaper editor, it was also inevitable that he would become involved in politics because most local papers received support from a specific political party. The first paper he purchased in 1873, the *Cass County Courier,* was staunchly Democratic, yet Wayland considered himself very much a Republican. Republican leaders supported his efforts to start a Republican newspaper, which he did in 1878, calling it the *Cass County News.* Wayland used this opportunity to become more vocal about Republican issues and to offer sharp criticism of the majority Democrats.

In 1882 Wayland moved to Pueblo, Colorado, where he not only built a prosperous printing business

Masthead for the 2 May 1914 edition of *The Appeal to Reason.* Reprinted in *"Yours for the Revolution": The Appeal to Reason, 1895–1922,* edited by John Graham and published by the University of Nebraska Press. LABADIE COLLECTION, UNIVERSITY OF MICHIGAN LIBRARY

but also managed to earn considerable wealth (about $80,000) by becoming almost inadvertently involved in real estate speculation as he began buying property to expand his printing business. Later, Wayland would declare that the "present system of private ownership is wrong" (p. 151), but at that time he saw real estate speculation as merely a more efficient way to make money. Toward the end of the decade, convinced that "another crisis was about to hit the country" (p. 24), Wayland began rapidly converting his real estate holdings to cash. During the time that he lived in Pueblo, probably around 1890, Wayland began studying the theories of socialism and eventually became both a convert to the movement and an agitator for it. In the introduction to *Leaves of Life,* a 1912 collection of his writing for the *Appeal,* Wayland himself describes this process. He began to have conversations with a local English shoemaker, William Bradfield, about railroad strikes, which he had almost certainly learned about through print jobs submitted to his shop. Bradfield gave him a pamphlet and then another. As a result of his study, Wayland notes, "I closed up my real estate business and devoted my whole energies to the work of trying to get my neighbors to see the truths I had learned" (p. 24). He became a kind of sidewalk advocate for socialist views, converting others through the force of his personality, but by the mid-1890s he had decided to return to the nation's heartland and to use his skills as a writer and newspaper editor to advance the movement.

Significantly, considering the way the *Appeal* would later serve as a quasi-official organ of the Socialist Labor Party, disseminating information about socialist theory and politics across the nation, Wayland came to socialism through works by John Ruskin and Edward Bellamy, whose approach to socialism was utopian, and not through Karl Marx, Friedrich Engels, or European writers, who focused more on the problems of labor and capital. Most historians now agree that the form of socialism advocated by the *Appeal* and its editors was a distinctly "American" form of the philosophy. Elliott Shore has identified four sources of Wayland's unique and sometimes even contradictory beliefs, which came to be known collectively as the "One-Hoss Philosophy": a faith in American democratic ideals, populism, the socialist views of Bellamy, and his own reading of Ruskin (*Talkin' Socialism,* p. 35). Wayland's philosophy was, as David Paul Nord describes it, "indigenous American socialism" (p. 78), and the *Appeal* "was a paper which served up its socialism on a plain earthenware platter seasoned to American tastes" (p. 88). Wayland firmly believed that social change could be effected through the ballot box, and he consistently favored all kinds of political

activism over the various kinds of labor activism that other socialists advocated. Quite simply, he felt that if enough people could be persuaded to vote for socialist candidates, the nation would change. But to persuade them to vote socialist, he had to first convince them that they were "slaves" to the ruling class, that the existing competitive economic system must be replaced with a cooperative one, and that this change could occur through radical political change.

In February 1893 Wayland left Pueblo and returned to Indiana, publishing the first edition of the *Coming Nation,* a precursor of the *Appeal to Reason.* But this publication was not just to be another publishing enterprise. Wayland envisioned the paper as part of a larger communal effort, which would, in effect, demonstrate the socialist principles that the paper espoused. To this end, Wayland moved the *Coming Nation* to Tennessee and founded the Ruskin Colony. But the communal lifestyle was difficult for Wayland, who resented giving over any control of the paper. As Mother Jones, who had been invited to join the colony but declined, notes in chapter 4 of her autobiography: "I visited the colony a year a later. I could see in that short time disrupting elements" (p. 28). In 1895 Wayland turned over the *Coming Nation* to the Ruskin Colony and returned to Kansas City, Missouri. There, Mother Jones found him "despondent" but urged him to start another paper, for which she agreed to solicit subscriptions. Thus, in August 1895 Wayland published the first issue of the *Appeal to Reason,* which he later relocated to the small town of Girard, Kansas, where it would be published until its demise in 1922.

CHARACTERISTICS OF THE *APPEAL TO REASON*

The *Appeal to Reason* consisted of short pieces by Wayland himself along with excerpts from writers like William Morris and Ruskin, letters from readers, and as the socialist movement grew, essays by staff writers and columnists as well as articles and essays by well-known socialist writers and politicians. It also published political cartoons, especially in the later period. Wayland's "paragraphs," short mediations about the meaning of socialism, were a distinct feature of the *Appeal* until his death in 1912. In a letter written in 1899 and quoted in *Leaves of Life,* Eugene V. Debs, the leader of the Socialist Party, tells Wayland: "You have a faculty of reaching the average man. More than anything else it is your pointed paragraphs that do the work" (p. 38).

In essence, Wayland invented a new genre of political discourse aimed at educating and persuading the masses. He relied on vivid analogies to show readers the disadvantages of the current system. In one paragraph he notes, "Debt is like morphine," and later in the same piece: "A people in debt is helpless. The usurers make the law and keep them in bondage" (p. 49). The idea of slavery was a particularly potent image for him. Several of his "paragraphs" draw analogies between black chattel slavery of the antebellum era and what he called "wage slavery": "The employer is the task master. He must get all he can out of his wage-slaves, just as did the chattel-slave master" (p. 147). Wayland often suggested that wage slavery was, in fact, even worse than chattel slavery and that those who perpetrate wage slavery "will do even viler things" (p. 151). He felt that the chattel slave had a more intrinsic value than individual wage slaves have under capitalism. In a 1907 paragraph, written in dialect, Wayland recounts a conversation between a slave and a master. When the master asks the slave to fix a leaky roof, the slave tells his master that if he falls off the roof, the master loses $500, the slave's value. The slave concludes: "Now if massah send up that Irishman whom massah is hiring for $1.50 a day, and he rolls off, and he falls down, and he breaks his neck, massah will lose nuffin" (Graham, p. 80). Through epigrams, parables, and fables, Wayland was able to teach socialist principles.

THE GROWING INFLUENCE OF THE *APPEAL TO REASON*

In 1901 Fred D. Warren joined the staff and in the next few years assumed from Wayland much of the responsibility for the paper's editorial content. Warren's political beliefs were similar to Wayland's; they shared the goal of effecting radical economic change through political action by an experienced, carefully educated electorate. And like Wayland, Warren accepted the contradictions inherent in advocating socialist views in a mass consumer society. For example, both agreed with the *Appeal*'s policy of accepting advertisements from the very capitalists they hoped to overthrow. In a 1913 article in the *Appeal* titled "What I Believe," Warren states, "I have no conscientious scruples against the use of any method, direct or indirect, that will secure to the working class possession of the machinery of production" (Graham, p. 87). Warren certainly took risks. The publication in 1906 of Debs's article "Arouse, Ye Slaves!" prompted none other than President Theodore Roosevelt to look for ways to stifle the *Appeal*. In 1907 Warren was arrested for threatening and defamatory language when the *Appeal* issued what purported to be a "reward" for the return of the former Kentucky governor to stand trial for conspiracy to commit murder. In 1911 he was charged by the federal government

with sending "obscenity" through the U.S. Post Office when the *Appeal* published a series of articles on abuse in Leavenworth prison. Despite all government effort to suppress the *Appeal* during the period before World War I, it was not until 1917 that the paper's second-class postage rights were denied under Title 12 of the Espionage Act.

Warren always stopped well short of advocating any kind of violence to achieve his ends, as he asserts in "What I Believe," "I think entirely too much of my head to risk butting it against a stone wall in the shape of a policeman's club wielded by a man who takes his orders from capitalist politicians" (Graham, p. 87). Warren, like Wayland himself, was not just a political activist but a journalist as well, maintaining a strong editorial hand. Under Warren's leadership the *Appeal* solicited not only essays but also poetry and fiction, publishing writers such as Charlotte Perkins Gilman and Stephen Crane. Upton Sinclair's *The Jungle* was serialized in the *Appeal*. In Nord's words, "It was a mixture of muckraking scandal, circulation hustle, and epigrammatic socialism that made the *Appeal* such a rip-roaring success" (p. 76). Its success was also boosted by advertising revenues and by an army of salespeople, numbering about eighty thousand by 1913, who sold subscriptions across the country. Although its influence began to decline, especially after Warren resigned in 1913, it remained until 1922 a significant voice for alternative political views.

See also Periodicals; Socialism

BIBLIOGRAPHY

Primary Work

Jones, Mary Harris. *The Autobiography of Mother Jones*. Edited by Mary Field Parton. Chicago: C. H. Kerr, 1925.

Wayland, J. A. *Leaves of Life: A Story of Twenty Years of Socialist Agitation*. 1912. Westport, Conn.: Hyperion Press, 1975.

Secondary Works

Graham, John, ed. *"Yours for the Revolution": The "Appeal to Reason" 1895–1922*. Lincoln: University of Nebraska Press, 1990.

Hume, Janice. "Lincoln Was a 'Red' and Washington a Bolshevik: Public Memory as Persuader in the *Appeal to Reason*." *Journalism History* 28, no. 4 (2003): 172–181.

Nord, David Paul. "The *Appeal to Reason* and American Socialism, 1901–1920." *Kansas History* 1, no. 2 (1978): 75–89.

Shore, Elliott. *Talkin' Socialism: J. A. Wayland and the Role of the Press in American Radicalism, 1890–1912*. Lawrence: University Press of Kansas, 1988.

Shore, Elliott. "The Walkout at the *Appeal* and the Dilemmas of American History." *History Workshop Journal* 22 (1986): 41–55.

Sterling, David L. "The Federal Government v. the *Appeal to Reason*." *Kansas History* 9, no. 1 (1986): 31–42.

Nancy Morrow

ART AND ARCHITECTURE

Scholarship in American art has largely followed that of literary studies, tending since the 1970s and with growing intensity since to recover neglected arts and artists and to emphasize the production of art in its social and cultural milieu. Students of art have broadly recognized that issues in aesthetics are closely related to the biographies of those who produce and use it and that therefore the history of American art is in fact an array of histories. As the roles of marginal groups have been more closely studied, histories such as Frances K. Pohl's *Framing America* (2002) and the volumes in the new *Oxford History of Art* (offering "a fresh look at art that moves away from traditional elitist approaches" [p. 1]), have made room for critical examinations of arts and issues barely addressed in traditional art histories. What has emerged is a considerably more complicated view of American art that challenges conservative ideologies of cultural uniformity. As a result, the canon of American art has been significantly expanded and thereby enriched—even though it has become considerably more difficult to conceptualize as a whole.

FROM ROMANTICISM TO MODERNISM

The post–Civil War period in American art and architecture is marked by the same kinds of energy that accompanied the rise of industrialization as found in literary realism and naturalism. From the Civil War to the First World War, from the Hudson River school to the Armory Show, from the nondescript pre–Civil War architecture to the skyscraper and the luxurious homes of the newly wealthy, the American vision went through remarkable transformations as it accommodated itself to new circumstances.

John Gast's allegory *American Progress* (1872) is emblematic of the national mood in the decade following the Civil War. At the center of the painting, a gigantic female figure representing the American spirit glides westward across the landscape, spreading light and power and nonchalantly stringing telegraph wire as she moves. At her feet are representative figures of the westward movement: frontiersmen, homesteaders, pony express and stagecoach riders; railroads follow her advance. To the west, in hasty retreat before these combined forces, are Native Americans and the bison that sustained them. Glimpsed to the far right are signs of settled civilization in the East: cities, ships, bridges. What the painting does not show is the boundless energy of urban and industrial growth and the tensions between immigrants and "Americans" and between the industrialists and the laborers who did the physical work. The final decades of the century were years of restless mercantile activity, and the captains of industry and the newly rich appeared complacent about the human costs of growth.

Despite the relief accompanying the end of the war, Lewis Mumford called these post–Civil War years "the Brown Decades"; he saw a civilization sobered by war and stripped of ideals. The national green bloom had faded, and American culture at large turned to darker hues to express its new sense of itself: brownstones, dark interiors and wallpapers, somber paintings. This is an exaggeration, but it has its core of truth—and against this truth the artists in the period struggled, supported by the examples of their forebears Ralph Waldo Emerson, Henry David Thoreau, and Walt Whitman. America had not yet fully given itself over to Emerson's demand for a specifically American art. Academic art, self-congratulatory and sentimental, looked often to the past for its models, repulsing serious artistic efforts to look at America through critical eyes. For the most part prestige lay in European, not American, art and so the struggle for a specifically American art was difficult and inharmonious.

After the Civil War and well into the 1930s, artists and writers turned to Europe, especially Paris, where artistic ferment was at its height. Many important American artists and architects studied in Europe—not only Paris but London and even Munich, as in the cases of Frank Duveneck and William Merritt Chase. A number of artists spent much of their lives, like their counterpart in literature Henry James, as expatriates in Europe, among them James McNeill Whistler, John Singer Sargent, Mary Cassatt, William Wetmore Story, and the Chippewa and African American sculptor Edmonia Lewis. Although few Americans were drawn to travel in Asia (John La Farge and Frank Lloyd Wright were important exceptions), Asian influences, especially Japanese, were important for artists as diverse as Cassatt, Whistler, and Chase. Many were encouraged by the example of the Boston Museum curator Ernest Fenollosa and, through him, the preeminent American collector of Asian art, Charles Lang Freer, whose collection became the core of the Smithsonian Gallery that bears his name.

American Progress, 1872. Chromolithograph by George Crofutt after the painting by John Gast. THE LIBRARY OF CONGRESS

American artists may have trekked to Europe for training, but equally as important was the transfer of European art to America to enter the growing American collections of Isabella Stewart Gardner, Duncan Phillips, Henry Clay Frick, Andrew Carnegie, Albert C. Barnes, Walter Arensberg, and Claribel and Etta Cone of Baltimore. And of course there was a need to house these collections, so American art museums sprang into existence: the Corcoran Museum in Washington in 1869, the Metropolitan Museum in New York, the Museum of Fine Arts in Boston in 1870, the Philadelphia Museum of Art in 1876, the Art Institute of Chicago in 1879, and though not until a half-century later, New York's Museum of Modern Art in 1929 and the Phillips Collection in Washington, D.C., in 1930.

Perhaps the two writers with the closest affinities with the arts other than literature were Henry James (1843–1916) and Theodore Dreiser (1871–1945). The cosmopolitan James is obviously of great importance, for he felt supremely at home with art objects and the artists who made them. His works, from *Roderick Hudson* (1876) to short stories such as "The Real Thing" and "The Jolly Corner," evince his abiding interest in the arts and the sometimes conflicted values associated with them and in the arts as cultural symbols that pitted James's America against "decadent" Europe. His *The American Scene* (1907) records his reactions to American cultural instability.

Of considerable interest are the many magazine pieces written by Theodore Dreiser as he surveyed his own American scene. Dreiser paid attention in print to many artists, some of whom have all but faded from historic consciousness, among them Bruce Crane, William Louis Sonntag, John Henry Dolph, Gilbert Gaul; in reviewing *America's Greatest Portrait Painters* in 1899, Dreiser spoke of Eastman Johnson, J. Alden Weir, and Childe Hassam but mentioned John Singer Sargent only in passing; Thomas Eakins is altogether absent. Dreiser lacked polish in artistic judgment, but his essays are energetic forays into the American scene in all its richness and motion, and he knew enough about the arts to make a sculptor the protagonist of his novel *The "Genius"* (1915).

Note should also be made of Henry Adams (1838–1918), historian, novelist, and art history theorist in works such as *Mont-Saint-Michel and Chartres* (1904) and "The Dynamo and the Virgin" from *The Education of Henry Adams* (1907). Adams's writings on art, along with his close friendships with John La Farge, Henry Hobson Richardson, and Augustus Saint-Gaudens, were extremely influential.

During this period there were many means by which Americans boasted of their achievements, but there were especially two remarkable opportunities to showcase the range of American art (as well as that of other nations): the Philadelphia Centennial in 1876 and the phenomenally successful World's Columbian Exposition in Chicago in 1893. The Philadelphia event was covered by William Dean Howells in "A Sennight of the Centennial" (*Atlantic Monthly,* July 1876). Howells admired the architecture, but in his enthusiasm for English art—and American machinery—he had little to say about American contributions to art.

ARCHITECTURE

After the Civil War, American architecture bloomed. Along with monuments to the fallen dead, courthouses and city halls proliferated. The growth of cities, westward expansion, and the needs of rapid industrialization required a responsive architecture to include handsome buildings intended for commercial purposes, and the astronomical increase in land value required the verticality that the skyscraper soon provided. At the same time, the nouveaux riches needed cultural proof of their ascendancy—the kind of proof that architecture could display in abundance.

Architectural advances are in great part related to accomplishments in engineering, and this was a period of dynamic American achievement: the transcontinental railroad, completed in 1869; the Brooklyn Bridge (begun by John Roebling in 1869, completed by his son Washington Roebling in 1883); the unveiling of Hugh Ferris's enormous wheel at the Chicago world's fair in 1893 (a direct response to the challenge of Alexandre-Gustave Eiffel's tower in 1889); the first flight at Kitty Hawk, North Carolina, in 1903; and the long-awaited opening of the Panama Canal in 1914. Of most immediate importance to architecture were the introduction of structural steel and the perfection of the passenger elevator.

As befitted an ambitious and aggressive culture, architects delighted in extravagance, resulting in a confusing hodgepodge of styles; the short-lived battle between Victorian gothic and French Second Empire styles contributed, according to Milton Brown, to "a common aggressively plastic picturesqueness

expressive of the brash adventurism of the period" (*American Art,* p. 249). The French Second Empire style was sometimes known as the "General Grant style" and sometimes was called the mansard style because of its most conspicuous feature, the curved or sloped roofs. Good examples include the building now housing the Smithsonian's Renwick Gallery in Washington, D.C. (1859–1861), designed by James Renwick, and the State, War, and Navy Building (1871–1875) by Alfred B. Mullett, an important figure in creating the architectural look of Washington, D.C. Competing with the Second Empire was gothic revival architecture, emphasizing flamboyant decorative possibilities and in its later phases influenced by John Ruskin. One of the most important examples is the Pennsylvania Academy of Fine Arts (1872–1876) designed by Frank Furness.

A more important development in American architecture was the Romanesque revival, sometimes called "Richardsonian" after Henry Hobson Richardson (1838–1886), its most important figure. The style is characterized by its massive look, employing heavy masonry and repetition of rounded arches for windows and doors. Its monumental seriousness lent itself to the demands of public buildings, churches, railroad terminals, and even university campuses. Richardson's work is found most remarkably in Trinity Church in Boston (1872–1877), the Allegheny County Buildings in Pittsburgh (1884–1888), and various libraries and railroad stations in Massachusetts.

In the cities, commercial structures responded to population growth, particularly in New York, Boston, Philadelphia, and newly emergent Chicago. Expensive land values required efficient use of space, and architecture responded with the skyscraper, which the architect Louis Sullivan (1856–1924), in an important 1896 essay, "The Tall Office Building Artistically Considered," declared should be "a proud and soaring thing." The skyscraper was made possible by the invention of the "safety" elevator designed by Elisha Graves Otis in 1852 (first installed in a New York department store in 1857) and the shift from heavy load-bearing masonry walls to skeletal steel structures. "Curtain" walls were hung on steel skeletons, thus saving space, allowing more light to reach the interior, and making possible greater height and elegance.

Chicago swiftly became the focus of this new dramatic architecture. The great fire of 1871 was catastrophic, but it opened up invigorating possibilities for new planning, leading to the birth of the "Chicago School," which emphasized functionality and rejected classical models. The most important figure in the Chicago School was Louis Sullivan, for Mumford "the

Whitman of American architecture" (and the man Frank Lloyd Wright continued to call "the master" long after Sullivan fired him). Sullivan designed influential structures such as the Carson Pirie Scott Building (1899) and, with his partner Dankmar Adler, the Auditorium Building on Michigan Avenue (1886–1890) and the Transportation Building for the Columbian Exposition—perhaps the only exposition building Sullivan did not despise (see Sullivan's *The Autobiography of an Idea*, 1924). Sullivan argued for a three-part building structure: a base (incorporating accessible retail spaces), a shaft (intermediate floors for offices), and a capital, usually decorative in appearance while hiding the building's elevator technology and utilities.

Another important figure in the Chicago School was Daniel Burnham (1846–1912), who with John Wellborn Root (the poet Harriet Monroe's brother-in-law) designed the Rookery (1885–1886) as well as the often-photographed Flatiron Building in New York (1902) and Union Station in Washington, D.C. (1907). Burnham's most momentous achievement was his role as "director of works" for the Columbian Exposition, leading a virtual who's who of architects and artists who put together the buildings and exhibits on 633 acres of Jackson Park in Chicago.

By far the largest building at the Columbian Exposition—indeed, it was claimed to be the largest building in the world—was the Manufactures and Liberal Arts Building, designed by George B. Post (1837–1913); it was nearly 1,700 by 790 feet (30 acres) and rose to a height of almost 250 feet. Post was the architect most closely associated with the skyscraper in New York; his Equitable Building (1868–1870) was apparently the first office building to employ elevators. Post's talents were broad: he designed the New York Stock Exchange (1901–1903), with its Roman temple front, and the campus of the City College of New York in the early 1900s as well as the Cornelius Vanderbilt Mansion on West Fifty-seventh Street (1879–1882, 1892–1894).

Other memorable buildings of the period include McKim, Mead, and White's Pennsylvania Station (1902–1911) and the Boston Public Library (1887), for which John Singer Sargent contributed important murals. Cass Gilbert's Woolworth Building (called "a cathedral of commerce"), upon its completion in 1913 the tallest building in the world, remains a remarkable contribution, its lobby a monument to early-twentieth-century commercial opulence.

The most important name in domestic architecture was Frank Lloyd Wright (1867–1959), whose chief contribution to a distinctively American culture was the organically structured prairie houses that attempted to retain the natural horizontal characteristics of their settings, with low pitched, cantilevered roofs. Perhaps the most famous example of this "Prairie School" architecture is his Robie House in Chicago (1909). Wright also influentially designed for public and commercial purposes, such as the Larkin Building in Buffalo, New York (1904), and the Unity Temple in Oak Park, Illinois (1905); he renovated Burnham and Root's Rookery lobby in 1905. By the end of World War I, Wright's fame was well established, even if many of his most famous works, such as "Fallingwater" (1936), the house built over a stream in the woods near Bear Run, Pennsylvania, were still far in the future.

Of necessity, Wright's clients were wealthy, but Wright did not design for ostentation, as did the builders of houses for the rich in Newport, Rhode Island—shells for "rituals of consumption and display" as Robert Hughes writes, with "opulence as an end in itself" (pp. 232–233). Chief among these architects was Richard Morris Hunt. His "Breakers" (1895), built for Cornelius Vanderbilt II, was a seventy-room takeoff on an Italian Renaissance palazzo—for Hughes "the archetype of Gilded Age excess" (p. 235). Even more extravagant was Hunt's "Biltmore" (1895) in North Carolina, a mansion of more than 250 rooms built for George Washington Vanderbilt III. The building was made of Indiana limestone, and its grounds included gardens laid out by Frederick Law Olmsted, famous for his work in designing Central Park and the landscape architecture at the Columbian Exposition.

John Singer Sargent visited the "Biltmore" early and did a portrait of its owner. Henry James visited it as well and disliked it, calling his room there "a glacial phantasy" and the building as a whole "a phenomenon of brute achievement" (Stern, p. 101). James was both fascinated with and critical of the Gilded Age mansions. He thought the rows of houses in Newport were "white elephants" that "look queer and conscious and lumpish—some of them, as with an air of the brandished proboscis, really grotesque—while their averted owners, roused from a witless dream, wonder what in the world is to be done with them" (*American Scene*, p. 224). He likewise thought Isabella Stewart Gardner gaudily materialistic and her "Fenway Court" in Boston little more than an ostentatious shell to house the art objects that she employed the art critic Bernard Berenson to collect for her.

Perhaps precisely because of its feel-good opulence, imaginative hotel architecture became exceedingly popular, such as the Royal Poinciana Hotel in

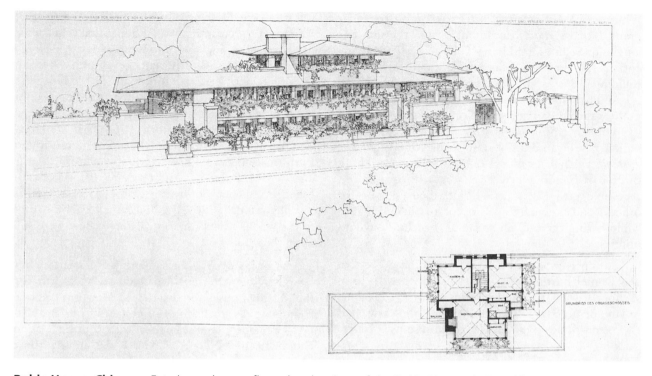

Robie House, Chicago. Exterior and upper-floor plan drawings of the Robie House, designed by Frank Lloyd Wright.
THE LIBRARY OF CONGRESS

Palm Beach, Florida (McDonald and McGuire, 1892–1894), a building so large, according to Gullible in Ring Lardner's *Gullible's Travels* (1917), that a telephone call from one end of the dining room to the other required a toll charge. The West was represented by James and Merritt Reid's Hotel Del Coronado (completed 1888) in San Diego, with its stunning Spanish-inspired red roof, large balconies, and huge ballroom; and Robert Reamer's extravagant "log cabin" hotel, the Old Faithful Inn (1904), in Yellowstone National Park. Other memorable western architecture included Bernard Maybeck's Roman-influenced Palace of Fine Arts built for the Panama-Pacific International Exposition of 1915 and the "castle" built by Julia Morgan (starting in 1919) for William Randolph Hearst in San Simeon, California—the Xanadu of Orson Welles's film *Citizen Kane* (1941). Also quite remarkable is the "Victorian Carson Mansion" (1884–1886) in Eureka, California, designed by Samuel and Joseph Newsom—described by G. E. Kidder Smith as "a spectacular example of gung-ho Queen Anne and nineteenth century eclecticism" (p. 271).

Two famous houses built for American cultural figures of the period are "Olana" (1870–1891), a "Persian" style mansion in Hudson, New York, designed primarily by its owner, the Hudson River school painter Frederic Edwin Church; and the elaborate Victorian house designed by Edward T. Potter for Mark Twain in Hartford, Connecticut (1874), where Twain was a neighbor to Harriet Beecher Stowe. Twain made the "curious house" his own in his verse "This Is the House That Mark Built" (Stern, p. 93).

The advances in American architecture in this period easily made it the most important and dynamic in the world—appropriately functional and extraordinary in appearance. Architecture had caught the American imagination so completely by the turn of the century that in 1905 the *Architectural Record* editor Herbert Croly noted the occurrence of architects as characters in American fiction of the time—in Edith Wharton's *Sanctuary* (1903), Robert Grant's *Unleavened Bread* (1900), and Robert Herrick's *The Common Lot* (1904).

SCULPTURE

Loosely related to developments in architecture is what Milton Brown calls "the national passion for monuments," especially in the years immediately after the Civil War. Much of the sculpture was commissioned to honor figures such as George Washington and Abraham Lincoln, and many mundane pieces commemorated the Civil War in the public squares of

The *Haymarket Martyrs Monument* by Albert Weinert, 1890. The monument pays tribute to the men who were executed for instigating the 1886 Haymarket Square Riot in Chicago, in which seven policemen and four other people were killed. The executions were controversial, with many believing that the men were executed for their pro-labor politics rather than for any criminal acts. The female figure standing over the fallen martyr represents outraged justice. PHOTOGRAPH BY DENAY WILDING. COPYRIGHT © DENAY WILDING. REPRODUCED BY PERMISSION.

American towns. The North's success in the Civil War and the defeat of slavery were common themes, such as Augustus Saint-Gaudens's *Memorial to Robert Gould Shaw* (1897), showing the white colonel on his horse riding beside marching black troopers, and Thomas Ball's *The Emancipation Group* (1874), depicting a crouched slave, wearing iron shackles, at the feet of Lincoln. As Barbara Groseclose writes, these pieces continue to question the dynamics of the relations between dominant white figures and subservient blacks. The antislavery movement honored its heroes, as in John Quincy Adams Ward's *Henry Ward Beecher* (1891) and made it possible for Edmonia Lewis to produce her *Death of Cleopatra* (1876).

Sculpture, subject to public taste and funding, was necessarily more cautious, less innovative than the other arts. Inspirational sculpture was to be found in abundance, the key figure being Daniel Chester French (1850–1931). His *The Minute Man* (1873–1874) in Concord is an early example, but his most important work remains his Lincoln Memorial in Washington, D.C. (1915–1919), with its imposing nineteen-foot-tall seated figure of Lincoln. French also produced a sculpture of Ralph Waldo Emerson (1879).

Perhaps in keeping with the period, many dramatically draped figures of grief appeared, such as in the *Adams Memorial* (1886–1891) by Saint-Gaudens and *The Angel of Death and the Sculptor* (1889–1893) and *Mourning Victory* (1906–1908) by French, the latter part of his Melvin Memorial in Concord's Sleepy Hollow Cemetery. The *Haymarket Martyrs Monument* (1890) by Albert Weinert created controversy because of polarized interpretations of the hooded female who stands defiantly in front of the body of one of the fallen.

Heroic sculpture was found in abundance at the Philadelphia Centennial and the Chicago Columbian Exposition, the latter including works by French, Saint-Gaudens, and Frederick MacMonnies, who created the massive Columbian Fountain in the Court of Honor, with a female Columbia on a barge surrounded by allegorical figures of Time and Fame and rowing figures representing science, industry, agriculture, and art. The tallest sculpture, at the opposite end of the court, was the work of French, a figure of a female *Republic* (nicknamed "Big Mary") towering sixty-five feet and holding aloft a globe upon which an eagle perched.

William Wetmore Story (1819–1895) has not maintained his reputation as a sculptor, despite Henry James's interest in him. James was most attracted to Story because of his expatriation to Italy, and he fascinated James enough to motivate the latter's two-volume work *William Wetmore Story and His Friends: From Letters, Diaries, and Recollections* (1903) as well as his novel *Roderick Hudson* (1876), which carries his young sculptor protagonist to Rome, where he is corrupted and destroyed. Nathaniel Hawthorne seems to have had Story in his mind in the writing of *The Marble Faun* (1860).

In the West, Frederic Remington (1861–1909) was the preeminent sculptor, with such memorable bronzes as *The Bronco Buster* (1895) and *Coming through the Rye* (1902). There were many lesser-known works of sculpture with western themes, especially focused on Indian life, as found in the work of Solon and John Borglum, and on animals, exemplified in the work of Edward Clark Potter. Potter often worked with French on sculptures requiring horses, and he created the famous lions in front of the New York Public Library (1910).

American sculpture was slow and cautious in entering the modern era, and many of the early-twentieth-century American sculptors came from Europe—Alexander Archipenko, Elie Nadelman, Jacques Lipchitz, and Gaston Lachaise among them. The stylized naturalism of Paul Manship is memorable, such as that found in *Dancer and Gazelles* (1916). The work for which he is best known, his gilded sculpture of Prometheus in Rockefeller Center Plaza, was still in the future (1934). Frances Pohl brings renewed attention to Abastenia St. Leger Eberle, a sculptor of "everyday life" and social consciousness; her *White Slave* (1913) is a dramatic protest against the kidnapping of young women into lives of prostitution.

PAINTING: LATE NINETEENTH CENTURY

Between 1870 and 1920 American painting underwent a dramatic series of transformations, from the romantic realism of the Hudson River school to the rough-hewn social realism of the Ashcan school and the full-blown modernism exemplified in the Armory Show of 1913. The predominant artistic works in the Civil War period were the Romantic landscapes of the Hudson River school and its followers, such as George Inness and Albert Bierstadt; the luminists John Kensett, FitzHugh Lane, and Martin Heade; and genre painters such as George Caleb Bingham and William Sydney Mount.

This was a period of considerable upheaval, as younger artists were forced to struggle against institutionalized American art. Two important institutions were the Pennsylvania Academy of Fine Arts, founded in 1802, and the National Academy of Design, started in 1826 by artists led by Samuel F. B. Morse. Both were predictably hostile to the kinds of innovations that led to modern art and resulted in a number of organizations within which young artists rebelled against staid artistic principles and methods, among them the Art Students League in New York (1875); the Society of American Artists, including La Farge, Inness, and Ryder (1877); and the Art Students League in Philadelphia, started by those who supported Eakins when he was dismissed from the Pennsylvania Academy in 1886.

For Lewis Mumford, the important artists who emerged shortly after the Civil War were grouped around Thomas Eakins on one side (including La Farge, Winslow Homer, and Mary Cassatt), roughly representing realism; and Albert Pinkham Ryder on the other, representing "moon-ridden" imagination. Between the two he placed James Abbott McNeill Whistler, not rich in imagination but a superb technician. Modern scholarship has vastly enlarged these categories and both clarified and questioned artistic intentions, but Mumford's instincts are helpful in surveying the field.

Thomas Eakins (1844–1916) is still considered an essential realist, perhaps best known for his intense psychological portraits, as, for example, his portraits of women—Maud Cook (1895), Edith Mahon (1904), and perhaps the finest, the pensive Amelia Van Buren (1891)—as well as his portraits of male professionals, such as that of Dr. Samuel David Gross in *The Gross Clinic* (1875) as he steps back from surgery, scalpel in hand, to lecture to the assembled audience. Eakins's friendship with Walt Whitman is commemorated in a memorable portrait (1888). As director of the Pennsylvania Academy of Fine Arts, Eakins encouraged nude study but went too far when he allowed women artists along with men in the room with the nude models; he was forced out in 1886. Among his students were Thomas Anshutz, whose *The Ironworkers' Noontime* (1880), displays working-class males on break in the factory yard; and the African American Henry Ossawa Tanner, whose *The Banjo Lesson* (1893) pictures a young black boy sitting on a black man's knee while the boy fingers the frets and experimentally strums the instrument. The intimacy of the two figures in the barren room and the man's attentiveness make this a portrait of generational bonding in conditions of poverty.

Winslow Homer (1836–1910), whose reputation has strengthened through time, started as an illustrator and became a prolific creator of Civil War scenes (many for *Harper's Weekly*) and later of powerful landscapes in watercolor and oil. He was important as well for his pictures of childhood innocence, as in *Snap the Whip* (1872), picturing boys at rough play in the schoolyard, and outdoor scenes of hunting and fishing. But Homer is perhaps most important for his sea pictures, of which *The Gulf Stream* (1899) is a superb, if puzzling, example, calling out for a narrative that is not available. The painting features a black man lying on the deck of a drifting fishing boat with a broken mast. The apparently hopeless man looks off into the distance as sharks swim in the foreground, while behind him, across the rough water, a ship is passing on the left and a typhoon is visible on the right. Peter Wood believes Homer intended the painting as commentary on the history of American slavery and colonialism.

Another important realist was Eastman Johnson (1824–1906), at one time called the "American

The Girl I Left behind Me, **1870–1875.** Painting by Eastman Johnson. © SMITHSONIAN
AMERICAN ART MUSEUM, WASHINGTON, DC/ART RESOURCE, NY

Rembrandt" because of his interest in portraits (and the fact that he studied at The Hague) but now perhaps best known as a painter of genre scenes, such as *The Cranberry Harvest on the Island of Nantucket* (1880). His *The Girl I Left behind Me* (1870–1875) is a captivating picture of a young girl, with braced feet and windblown hair, books in hand, looking out over a stormy romantic landscape.

The independent Mary Cassatt (1844–1926) is best known for her tender domestic scenes, of which *Mother and Child* (1905) is an excellent example, but she did other work as well, including the mural *Modern Woman* for the Woman's Building at the Columbian

Exposition (the building itself was designed by Sophia Hayden). Cassatt studied with the Impressionists Claude Monet and Edgar Degas in Paris and is linked to the "American Impressionists" Theodore Robinson, J. Alden Weir, John Twachtman, and Childe Hassam. The visual theories supporting Impressionism lend themselves to literary realism, as James Nagel's argument for Stephen Crane makes clear: Nagel believes *The Red Badge of Courage* (1895), with its epistemological and glimpsed vision, was considerably indebted to Impressionism.

At the opposite extreme from the realists are the poetic, lyrical "visionaries," the most important of whom is Albert Pinkham Ryder (1847–1917). His works are intense symbolic representations of states of consciousness, and he reworked them for years—indeed, it was said that a patron had waited so long for a painting Ryder had promised him that he planned to have his funeral procession stop by Ryder's house to pick it up. A good example is *The Race Track (Death on a Pale Horse)* (c. 1896), in Ryder's typical deep-brown and yellow colors, depicting a skeleton holding a scythe and riding a speeding horse around a fenced track. His *Jonah* (c. 1895) pictures the prophet struggling mightily in fiercely roiled brown waters, surrounded by odd shapes, one of which resembles a whale's snout; above the water is a representation of a bearded God. Ryder took many of his themes from literary sources, and he occasionally accompanied his paintings with poems of his own composition. Another important Romantic, influenced by Pre-Raphaelitism, is Elihu Vedder (1836–1923), whose illustrations for the *Rubáiyát of Omar Khayyám* (1884) achieved great success. His *Cup of Death* (1885), picturing a dark-winged angel with averted eyes holding a cup to the lips of a young woman, is akin to the sculpted figures of grief by Saint-Gaudens and French.

The expatriate James Abbott McNeill Whistler (1834–1903), much interested in art for art's sake, is most famous now for his portraits of his mother (*Arrangement in Gray and Black, No. 1*, 1871) and the English writer Thomas Carlyle (*Arrangement in Gray and Black, No. 2*, 1872–1873). He is also remembered for his lawsuit against John Ruskin when the critic accused Whistler of "flinging a pot of paint in the public's face" after viewing *Nocturne in Black and Gold: The Falling Rocket* (1875). Whistler published the memoir *The Gentle Art of Making Enemies* in 1890. Another expatriate and a close friend of Henry James, John Singer Sargent (1856–1925) is best known for his portraits, including the scandalous *Madame X* (1884), a full-length portrait of Amelie Gautreau, originally showing too much shoulder for proper Victorian audiences. Sargent also did the portraits *Isabella Stewart Gardner* (1888) and *Henry James* (1913); when it was shown at the Royal Academy, the James portrait was attacked by a suffragette—the James biographer Leon Edel claims she wielded a meat cleaver; the portrait suffered gashes to head and shoulder.

In the West, Albert Bierstadt (1830–1902) and Thomas Moran (1837–1926) often produced huge canvases celebrating sublime landscapes. Among their many works are Bierstadt's *Donner Lake from the Summit* (1873) and Moran's *Chasm of the Colorado* (1873–1874) and *Cliffs of the Upper Colorado River*

(1882). But perhaps the best-known western artist is Frederic Remington, who often painted and illustrated scenes of western adventure; his *A Dash for the Timber* (1889), for example, depicts a small group of rapidly retreating horsemen firing rifles back upon their Native American pursuers. Remington was also a minor novelist, publishing *John Ermine of the Yellowstone* in 1902 and *The Way of an Indian* (1906), concerning the decline of the northern Cheyenne. Together with Theodore Roosevelt and the novelist Owen Wister, Remington helped to create the mythology behind the West. Much later and only briefly (1915–1927), the Taos Society of Artists, an innovative cooperative, exerted some attraction in New Mexico. The founding members were Bert G. Phillips, Herbert Dunton, Joseph Henry Sharp, Oscar E. Berninghaus, E. Irving Couse, and Ernest L. Blumenschein, but over the years twenty-one artists were associated with it, including Robert Henri and John Sloan as "associate members."

Recent scholarship in American art has also given attention to forgotten and neglected artists from this period. Frances K. Pohl puts renewed focus on Cecilia Beaux, a friend of Sargent, whose *Sita and Sarita* (1894), a portrait of a woman in a white dress with one hand flat on her lap and the other caressing a black cat (with penetrating green eyes) on her shoulder. Pohl suggests the portrait's "sexual energy" is reminiscent of Édouard Manet's *Olympia* (1863). Pohl also notes the *Self-Portrait* of Ellen Day Hale (1885), an artist with connections to Nathan Hale and the Beechers. Another artist receiving renewed attention is Edward Bannister, a little-known African American artist who won the first-prize medal at the Philadelphia Centennial for his painting *Under the Oaks*.

Emphasis on the social and cultural history of American art has also examined such works as Robert Koehler's *The Strike* (1886), depicting a confrontation between owners and workers; at least one of the workers is picking up rocks to throw. And finally getting serious recognition is American Indian ledger art of the 1870s; works such as the Cheyenne artist Yellow Nose's dramatic *Drawing of the Battle of Little Big Horn* (c. 1885) provide intimate and detailed Indian perceptions of historical events normally reported quite differently for public consumption.

PAINTING: AMERICAN MODERNISM

Two broad paths led to the triumph of modernism in American art. The first was exclusively American, led by Robert Henri (1865–1929); it championed a new realism that relished Whitman's spirit of rebellion and used it as an argument for overcoming the tried and

***Hester Street*, 1905.** Painting by George Luks. © BROOKLYN MUSEUM OF ART, NEW YORK/THE BRIDGEMAN ART LIBRARY

true in American art. The second, more radical movement, was led initially by Alfred Stieglitz (1864–1946) and attached itself mainly to the European modernism exemplified in Pablo Picasso and Henri Matisse, the broad movement that fueled many innovations in European art in the early twentieth century, among them Cubism, Fauvism, futurism, Dadaism, and surrealism.

The movement led by Henri culminated in the most important rebellion against the conservatism of the traditional academy. Like their counterparts in literature, the younger artists wished to pursue the "democratic art" espoused by William Dean Howells; they were interested in painting realistic works depicting working-class characters and urban situations and themes. Henri's breakaway movement resulted in an exhibition at the Macbeth Gallery in New York in February 1908. The artists who exhibited there were dubbed the Eight (later the "Ashcan school")—including, besides Henri, William Glackens,

Everett Shinn, John Sloan (who from 1911 to 1916 edited the radical journal the *Masses*), George Luks, Maurice Prendergast, Arthur B. Davies, and Ernest Lawson. Henri had been a student of Thomas Anshutz and himself taught George Bellows, Edward Hopper, Stuart Davis, Rockwell Kent, and briefly the poet Vachel Lindsay; Henri's importance as a leader may be deduced from his book *The Art Spirit* (1923).

Although not all of the artists were drawn equally to "ashcan" subject matter, the best work of the Eight focused on urban American life and its swirling energies. In George Luks's *Hester Street* (1905), for example, the New York street is teeming with people walking, negotiating with street vendors, or just watching the rich variety of city activity. John Sloan's *Movies, 5 Cents* (1907) emphasizes the large and boisterous audience crowding the theater to take in this new cultural phenomenon. In *The "Genius"* (1915), Dreiser appears to have incorporated Sloan's *Six O'Clock, Winter* (1912) as a painting made by his protagonist, Eugene Witla (based on the artist Everett Shinn), depicting an elevated train platform with the train glimpsed against the cloudy twilight sky and the thronging crowd below seen in the garish light from the shop windows. Sloan's *McSorley's Ale House* (1912) pictures the establishment writer Joseph Mitchell called McSorley's Wonderful Saloon in his book of the same name (1943). Although he was not a member of the Eight, George Bellows also featured powerful urban scenes. His *New York* (1911) is full of activity: streets crowded with horse-drawn wagons, carriages and pedestrians, tall buildings in the background (with just a touch of sky at center top), all conveyed in rich browns, blacks, yellows, and greens; his *The Cliff Dwellers* (1913) emphasizes exuberance in the lives of the urban poor.

Alongside the struggle for American realism, another important force at work was the one exemplified by Alfred Stieglitz, who as early as 1906 had opened his 291 Gallery (at 291 Fifth Avenue in New York) for the exhibition of photography as art and the display of experimental European art. Milton Brown finds Stieglitz of the same degree of importance in bringing modern art to America as the avant-garde writer and collector Gertrude Stein. Broadly, the difference between the Eight and those who exhibited at 291 was the difference between the realists' pictorialism and the modernists' interest in abstract experimentation. Stieglitz gave opportunities to many experimental young American painters, including Arthur Dove, Georgia O'Keeffe, Max Weber, John Marin, Marsden Hartley, and Alfred Maurer.

This movement toward abstraction was the key to the International Exhibition of Modern Art, known as the Armory Show (held at the New York National Guard Armory), in February and March 1913, organized by the Association of American Painters and Sculptors. The Armory Show was an ambitious attempt to provide a general historical context for the innovative new art; it consisted of some thirteen hundred pieces of sculpture, paintings, and drawings, most of it American. Most of the Eight were represented, along with others including Maurer, Stuart Davis, Marsden Hartley, and early works by Charles Sheeler and Edward Hopper; John Marin presented watercolors of Cass Gilbert's newly completed Woolworth Building (1913). But the public hardly noticed the Americans in their outrage with the Frenchman Marcel Duchamp's *Nude Descending a Staircase, No. 2* (1912), which reduced the nude figure to cubist angles and planes. Because the protest was broad and severe enough to get into the newspapers, attempts were made to close the show on "moral" grounds, and the artists were described as madmen and anarchists. But the Armory Show succeeded in opening the door to the public's ultimate acceptance of modernism and made it easier for artists like Max Weber (*Rush Hour, New York,* 1915) and Joseph Stella (*Battle of Lights, Coney Island,* 1914, and *Brooklyn Bridge,* 1918) to incorporate abstract forms and shapes into their paintings with American settings.

The Armory Show also contributed substantially to several great modern collections, including that of Walter Arensberg, a lover of the arts who befriended many of the new visual artists and the poet William Carlos Williams. As case studies of influence across the arts, Williams and his friends are exemplary: always interested in new artistic possibilities, Williams wrote poems in response to the paintings of Charles Demuth, Marsden Hartley, and others; in turn Demuth illustrated literary works by Émile Zola, Edgar Allan Poe, and Henry James, including *The Turn of the Screw;* and Hartley befriended the playwright Eugene O'Neill. Imagism in American poetry was indebted as well to the new visual arts.

It is interesting to note, finally, that the Whitney Museum (1931) was organized largely around works from both the Ashcan realists and the more abstract contributors to the Armory Show, suggesting the crucial importance of both movements to the subsequent history of twentieth-century art. As a result of these artistic efforts, American art was emboldened, liberated from the constraints of tradition, and free to employ modernistic subject matter and methodologies as the artistic spirit moved—toward the regional realism of the 1930s or the abstract expressionism of the 1940s and 1950s.

See also Aestheticism; Arts and Crafts; Chicago; Impressionism; Museums; New York; Photography

BIBLIOGRAPHY
Primary Works
Dreiser, Theodore. *Art, Music, and Literature 1897–1902.* Edited by Yoshinobu Hakutani. Urbana: University of Illinois Press, 2001.

James, Henry. *The American Scene.* 1907. Edited by Leon Edel. Bloomington: University of Indiana Press, 1968.

James, Henry. *The Painter's Eye: Notes and Essays on the Pictorial Arts.* Edited by John L. Sweeney. Cambridge, Mass.: Harvard University Press, 1956.

Sullivan, Louis H. "The Tall Office Building Artistically Considered." *Lippincott's Magazine,* March 1986. Available at http://www.njit.edu/v2/Library/archlib/pub-domain/sullivan-1896-tall-bldg.html.

Secondary Works

Brown, Milton W. *American Painting from the Armory Show to the Depression*. Princeton, N.J.: Princeton University Press, 1955.

Brown, Milton W., et al. *American Art: Painting, Sculpture, Architecture, Decorative Arts, Photography*. New York: Abrams, 1979.

Condit, Carl W. *The Chicago School of Architecture: A History of Commercial and Public Building in the Chicago Area, 1875–1925*. Chicago: University of Chicago Press, 1964.

Croly, Herbert. "The Architect in Recent Fiction." In *The Origins of Modern Architecture: Selected Essays from "Architectural Record,"* edited by Eric Uhlfelder, pp. 281–283. Mineola, N.Y.: Dover, 1998.

Dijkstra, Bram. *Cubism, Stieglitz, and the Early Poetry of William Carlos Williams*. Princeton, N.J.: Princeton University Press, 1978.

Doezema, Marianne. *American Realism and the Industrial Age*. Cleveland, Ohio, and Bloomington: Cleveland Museum of Art and Indiana University Press, 1980.

Doezema, Marianne, and Elizabeth Milroy, eds. *Reading American Art*. New Haven, Conn.: Yale University Press, 1998.

Doss, Erika. *Twentieth-Century American Art*. New York: Oxford University Press, 2002.

Fried, Michael. *Realism, Writing, Disfiguration: On Thomas Eakins and Stephen Crane*. Chicago: University of Chicago Press, 1987.

Groseclose, Barbara. *Nineteenth-Century American Art*. New York: Oxford University Press, 2000.

Hughes, Robert. *American Visions: The Epic History of Art in America*. New York: Knopf, 1997.

Marling, William. *William Carlos Williams and the Painters, 1909–1923*. Athens: Ohio University Press, 1982.

Mumford, Lewis. *The Brown Decades: A Study of the Arts in America 1865–1895*. 1931. New York: Dover, 1955.

Nagel, James. *Stephen Crane and Literary Impressionism*. University Park: Pennsylvania State University Press, 1980.

Oxford University Press USA. *Oxford History of Art*. http://www.oup.com/us/collections/oha/series/?view=usa.

Perlman, Bennard B. *The Immortal Eight: American Painting from Eakins to the Armory Show, 1870–1913*. Westport, Conn.: North Light Publishers, 1979.

Pohl, Frances K. *Framing America: A Social History of American Art*. New York: Thames and Hudson, 2002.

Scheyer, Ernst. *The Circle of Henry Adams: Art and Artists*. Detroit: Wayne State University Press, 1970.

Smith, G. E. Kidder. *Source Book of American Architecture: 500 Notable Buildings from the 10th Century to the Present*. Princeton, N.J.: Princeton Architectural Press, 1996.

Stern, Robert A. M. *Pride of Place: Building the American Dream*. Boston: Houghton Mifflin; New York: American Heritage, 1986.

Uhlfelder, Eric, ed. *The Origins of Modern Architecture: Selected Essays from "Architectural Record."* Mineola, N.Y.: Dover, 1998.

Van Hook, Bailey. *Angels of Art: Women and Art in American Society, 1876–1914*. University Park: Pennsylvania University Press, 1996.

Winner, Viola Hopkins. *Henry James and the Visual Arts*. Charlottesville: University Press of Virginia, 1970.

Wood, Peter H. *Weathering the Storm: Inside Winslow Homer's Gulf Stream*. Athens: University of Georgia Press, 2004.

Joseph J. Wydeven

ARTS AND CRAFTS

The arts and crafts movement began in Britain in the 1850s as a reaction to what proponents saw as the consequences of rapid industrialization: worker alienation, upper-class extravagance, and artistic degradation. The movement's philosophical founder was John Ruskin (1819–1900), who argued in *The Stones of Venice* (1851) that working with machines alienated the worker from what he or she produced and, moreover, that the ability to mass produce objects had cheapened their value and cluttered the landscape. William Morris (1834–1896) seized on Ruskin's ideas about how art and technology impact society and translated them into a theory of design as a tool of social improvement.

Along with other reformers following Ruskin's lead, Morris sought to make the lives of artisans better by returning to a pre-industrial system where the individual artisan was both designer and manufacturer and where groups of artisans and craftspeople lived together in mutually beneficial societies. Second, Morris sought an antidote to what he saw as the ornamental excess and stylistic derivativeness of late Victorian art and design. The arts and crafts movement had several distinct goals: to create more satisfying working conditions, in part by democratizing the production of art; to develop a design style inspired by nature and in harmony with it, using materials native to a particular location; and to make the home itself a place of relief from the increasingly hectic industrial world. As Morris and other proponents of the movement's philosophy, such as Oscar Wilde, would argue, what is useful need not be distinguished from what is beautiful, if form and function are considered as an integral whole. In America the movement's ideals were disseminated in institutions such as the Cincinnati School of Design (1872), the

Massachusetts Normal Art School (1873), and the Rhode Island School of Design (1878) as well as in such events as the Philadelphia Centennial Exposition in 1876. The arts and crafts movement would take root in specially created artists' villages and colonies like the Craftsman organization founded by Gustave Stickley near Syracuse, New York; the Roycroft Society founded by Elbert Hubbard near Buffalo; and William L. Price's village at Rose Valley, Pennsylvania.

The philosophy of the arts and crafts movement would influence a number of different art forms. The movement was never so much a particular design "style" as it was a philosophy of producing and implementing design, which ultimately led to a unique and recognizable look in architecture, landscaping, interiors, furniture design, decorative arts, and even graphic design and bookmaking.

ARCHITECTURE AND COMMUNITY PLANNING

In the last quarter of the nineteenth century, American life changed dramatically from what it had been before the Civil War. The population grew rapidly with new waves of immigrants, and industrialization forced a movement from farm to city, where housing often proved inadequate both for families and individuals. As the industrial working classes grew, so too did the middle classes, who wanted to own their homes but who needed a style of home more modest and livable than the Victorian home had been. They wanted a home that required little maintenance and that could run smoothly without servants, and arts and crafts design principles seemed well suited to meet those needs.

Between 1901 and 1916 Gustave Stickley (1858–1942) published his magazine the *Craftsman,* which included articles about home building and offered plans for home and furniture designs generated in Stickley's studio. Many of Stickley's articles focused on what he called the "craftsman idea." He believed that "the influence of the home is of the first importance in the shaping of character" (p. 194). He argues, "We need to straighten out our standards and to get rid of a lot of rubbish that we have accumulated along with our wealth and commercial supremacy" (p. 195). He even believed that children raised in "large houses with many rooms elaborately decorated and furnished" might well grow up to be unhappy adults. The designs that Stickley and others shared with the American public through magazines and pattern books offered an alternative to this fate.

Arts and crafts architectural designs also often reflect an awareness of changes in American family life.

Fewer people were living with large, extended families, and more single people wished to have homes of their own. The tiniest bungalows, only about 600 to 800 square feet, were often referred to as "workman's bungalows" or "bachelor's bungalows" (University of Toledo, "Midwestern Architecture," p. 2). Stickley's designs reflect an awareness of variety of specific design needs. He offers a design for "two inexpensive but charming cottages [essentially a duplex] for women who want their own homes" (p. 72), which reflects growing opportunities for women as single professionals in the 1910s and 1920s. The *Craftsman* also offered "a Craftsman city house designed to accommodate two families" (p. 36), reflecting the fact that in the new urban environment it might not be desirable for two or more generations to live entirely under the same roof. Stickley also had plans for country homes, farmhouses, and cabins, reflecting not only his belief that more affluent city dwellers needed an escape to nature but also his belief that everyone would be better off if he or she considered abandoning the city for a country lifestyle that would allow him or her to raise his or her own food and poultry. In addition to Stickley's home plans, Americans were exposed to "Craftsman" designs in the *Ladies' Home Journal* and other magazines. Sears, Roebuck; Montgomery Ward; and the Aladdin Company of Bay City, Michigan, all offered complete house kits from about 1908 until as late as 1940. Aladdin's sales of home kits peaked in 1920 at $5 million (University of Toledo, "Midwestern Architecture," p. 3).

The arts and crafts movement also sought to change the ways houses were grouped together into neighborhoods. The "garden city" movement began in England as a way to counteract the grimness of factory towns. What the *New York Times* has called "the most successful and durable example" of this movement in America began in Queens, New York, in 1910 (Hellman, p. B1). In 1906 the financier Russell Sage left $70 million to his wife, Olivia, who decided to use part of her new fortune to build affordable housing. Mrs. Sage's lawyer, Robert de Forest, hired the landscape architect Frederick Law Olmsted and the architect Grosvenor Atterbury and encouraged them to illustrate in their design for a new community that "suburban development geared to modest wage earners need not be haphazard." De Forest also insisted, "I believe there's money in taste." But in keeping with arts and crafts principles, "a sense of visual modesty was to rule the design." Thus the garden city movement was an attempt not only to improve the lives of working and middle-class families but also to protect American communities from those who would, in Atterbury's words, "deck out our modest villages in

An arts and crafts–style living room. Drawing by Gustave Stickley, from the *Craftsman,* 1905. GRADUATE LIBRARY, UNIVERSITY OF MICHIGAN

Paris finery and ruin their complexions with architectural cosmetics" (Hellman, p. B30).

INTERIOR DESIGN
AND THE DECORATIVE ARTS

Interior design was an important aspect of building an arts and crafts home. The goal was to create a home that was open, spacious, and functionally flexible (in contrast to the Victorian home with its smaller, more numerous, and more specialized rooms). Advocates of the style also believed that a house should be furnished simply, with well-crafted pieces and well-chosen accessories, unified in style. Readers of the *Craftsman* and other periodicals would have plenty of ideas for everything from lighting fixtures to textiles to art pottery.

For Stickley the most important room in the house was the living room, which replaced the formal Victorian parlor. The new American family imagined by the arts and crafts movement would have little use for formal entertaining spaces and even less use for the myriad rooms described by Edith Wharton in her 1897 book *The Decoration of Houses:* ballrooms, salons, music rooms, and galleries (University of Toledo,

"Interior Design," p. 2). The fireplace was often the heart of the family-centered living room, with built-in bookcases and seating areas. Bookcases reflected a growing interest, even in the middle class, in owning and displaying books, and interior designs often included built-in bookcases (University of Toledo, "Interior Design," p. 2). Some of Stickley's designs for relatively modest homes even included a separate library room (p. 39). In short, interiors were designed to provide relief—perhaps especially for those in the middle classes—from urban and industrial society.

In the development of such decorative arts as pottery, glass, metalwork, furniture making, and textile design, artisans sought to create items that had an integrated sense of function and beauty. As Janet Kardon notes in *The Ideal Home,* "Objects created for the home were often vehicles for ideology" (p. 26). In contrast to the proliferation of objects both cheap and useless in the Victorian home, the arts and craft home contained objects that were handmade and that reflected local nature and culture. Many objects were influenced by Native American, African American, Asian American, and Hispanic American styles.

PRINTING AND GRAPHIC DESIGN

From 1890 until his death in 1896, one of William Morris's most ardent projects was the development of the Kelmscott Press. Toward the end of the nineteenth century more and more books were published but often in low-cost, cheaply made editions, which Morris and his followers abhorred. During this period the Kelmscott Press issued over fifty titles, all of which adhered to a clear philosophy of both content and design: "unity of design and manufacture, integrity of materials, and a reverence for historical idioms" (Wilson, p. 138). Morris hated "grayness" on the page and designed books made of handmade paper with beautiful illustrations and illuminations, along with small black type and wide margins (Naylor, p. 130). In America, Copeland and Day publishers of Boston were among the first to experiment with publishing books that conformed to these principles of design. Characteristics of these books included handmade, deckle-edged papers, black typeset (gothic was a popular choice), and text set in blocks with closely spaced lines (Wilson, p. 139). Two American periodicals, *American Printer,* published in New York, and *Inland Printer,* published in Chicago, helped to disseminate ideas about arts and crafts bookmaking.

The center of arts and crafts book publishing in America was the Roycroft Press, founded in East Aurora, New York, in 1895 by Elbert Hubbard (1856–1915) and later developed into a community of diverse craftspeople and artisans. At various times the community's workshops produced furniture, leatherwork, pottery, and metalwork as well as publishing limited-edition fine books. At its peak in 1910 the community had approximately five hundred workers. Hubbard had met Morris in England and sought to re-create the Kelmscott Press on American soil, and his press became both prolific and commercially successful. The success of the Roycrofters depended much on the charisma, energy, and political views of Hubbard himself, a Larkin Company soap salesman turned social activist who remained a shrewd businessman and marketing wizard. After 1915, when he and his wife were killed in the sinking of the *Lusitania,* the Roycroft community lost much of its focus and energy, even though the workshops stayed open under the guidance of Hubbard's son until 1938.

Between 1896 and 1915 the Roycroft Press issued anywhere from three to ten volumes per year, all characterized by chamois binding, imported handmade paper, old-style type, hand-illuminated initials, and bordered title pages. Hubbard discovered that his books could be sold to the masses by the strategy of mail order, bringing the pleasures of the well-made book into middle-class homes. Hubbard himself authored several of the books issued by the Roycroft Press, reaching nearly 40 million readers with his *Message to Garcia* (1899), an inspirational pamphlet that raised questions about the nature of work and individual responsibility. It became a minor classic. In the essay Hubbard tells the story of a young man, Rowan, who is asked to carry a message to the leader of the Cuban insurgents during the Spanish-American War and does so without questioning. Hubbard notes that "civilization is one long anxious search for" people like Rowan, noting that "the man who, when given a letter for Garcia, quietly takes the missive, without asking any idiotic questions, and with no lurking intention of chucking it into the nearest sewer, or of doing aught else but deliver it, never gets 'laid off,' nor has to go on a strike for higher wages" (p. 23). Hubbard cherished the ideal of the individual who works for community goals.

Along these lines, one of the main principles of the arts and crafts book was the idea that creating a book resulted from a meticulous collaboration among writer, designer, decorator, and printer. One of the most important designers in the Roycroft community was Dard Hunter (1883–1966), whose distinctive style helped to unify the various products created in the Roycroft community and give them a distinctive look. Between 1911 and 1915 Hunter mastered the art of making handmade papers and developed his own type styles in the Roycroft workshops. In 1919 Hunter moved to his childhood home of Chillicothe, Ohio, where he produced eight limited-edition books between 1923 and 1950 under the imprint of the Mountain House Press.

While the arts and crafts movement survived in the United States for only a few short decades, it has remained influential. Arts and crafts architecture and furniture design is still highly prized, and the principles underlying the practices have been widely studied. Even in publishing, the movement has had lasting influence. As Richard Guy Wilson notes, "The legacy of this brief but intense period survives to this day . . . in the vitality of small presses dedicated to fine printing" (p. 140).

See also Aestheticism; Art and Architecture; Book Publishing; Socialism

BIBLIOGRAPHY

Primary Works

Gwynn, Alfred E. *A Book of California Bungalows.* 3rd ed. Los Angeles: Alfred E. Gwynn, 1900.

Hubbard, Elbert. *A Message to Garcia and Other Essays.* 1899. New York: Thomas Y. Crowell, 1924.

Stickley, Gustave. *Craftsman Homes: Architecture and Furnishings of the American Arts and Crafts Movement.* New York: Dover, 1979.

Secondary Works

Bowman, Leslie Greene. *American Arts and Crafts: Virtue in Design*. Los Angeles: Los Angeles County Museum of Art, 1990. A catalog of the Palevsky/Evans and Related Works at the Los Angeles County Museum of Art.

Davey, Peter. *Arts and Crafts Architecture*. London: Phaidon Press, 1995.

Davey, Peter. *Arts and Crafts Architecture: The Search for Earthly Paradise*. London: Architectural Press, 1980.

Hellman, Peter. "In a Pocket of Queens, 'City' Meets 'Garden.'" *New York Times,* 15 August 2003, B1, B30.

Kardon, Janet, ed. *The Ideal Home, 1900–1920: The History of Twentieth-Century American Craft*. New York: Abrams, 1993.

Legler, Dixie. *Prairie Style*. New York: Archetype Press, 1999.

McAlester, Virginia, and Lee McAlester. *A Field Guide to American Houses*. New York: Knopf, 2002.

Makinson, Randell L. *Greene and Greene: Architecture as Fine Art*. Salt Lake City, Utah, and Santa Barbara, Calif.: Peregrine Smith, 1977.

Naylor, Gillian, et al. *The Encyclopedia of Arts and Crafts: The International Movement, 1850–1920*. New York: Dutton, 1989.

University of Toledo. "Midwestern Architecture" and "Interior Design." Catalogue of The Noble Craftsmen We Promote: The Arts and Crafts Movement in the American Midwest, University of Toledo, Canady Special Collections, 26 March to 30 June, 1999. www.cl.utoledo.edu/canaday/artsandcrafts.

Via, Marie, and Marjorie Searle, eds. *Head, Heart, and Hand: Elbert Hubbard and the Roycrofters*. Rochester, N.Y.: University of Rochester Press, 1994.

Wilson, Richard Guy. Introduction to *From Architecture to Object: Masterworks of the American Arts and Crafts Movement*. Edited by Sheila Schwarz. New York: Dutton, 1989.

Nancy Morrow

ASSIMILATION

According to the hero of Israel Zangwill's (1864–1926) 1909 British play *The Melting-Pot,* "America is God's crucible, the great Melting-Pot where all the races of Europe are melting and re-forming" (p. 33). Exemplifying the influence of this melting-pot ideal, the liberal Reform minister John Dietrich literally preached it to his Pittsburgh congregation in 1910, celebrating "people of every race, of every color, of every religion to be melted and tried, and out of which shall come a race superior to any the world has thus far

known" (p. 4). While assimilating immigrants in an American "melting pot" might suggest wondrous new combinations, it also could imply homogenizing all Americans. In 1915 the immigrant intellectual Horace M. Kallen (1882–1974) condemned the melting-pot concept as an attempt to make immigrants conform to "the qualities and ideals of the contemporary American of British ancestry" and offered "pluralism" (p. 193) as an alternative. Likewise, in his immigration history *From Many Lands* (1940), the Slovenian-American writer Louis Adamic (born Alojzij Adamic, 1899–1951) describes "melting pot," as "a poor phrase and concept" because it implies that "everybody is to be turned into something else with heat" (p. 301).

Despite its detractors, the melting-pot idea did help to counteract one major obstacle to immigration: the fear that different immigrant "races" were incompatible with America, even dangerous to its progress. Belief that newer immigrants could not assimilate fueled the anti-immigrant legislation that excluded most Chinese in 1882 as well as the laws that severely restricted eastern and southern Europeans from entering in the 1920s. As Matthew Frye Jacobson notes, passing these laws decreased the perceived immigration "risk" (p. 95). In addition, Jacobson points out that "cultural and environmental explanations" were "replacing biological understandings of race" overall (p. 99). There had initially been a widespread belief that intermarriage between the native born and the immigrant would cause degeneration of the "Anglo-Saxon race," but gradually the idea that such intermarriage might rather improve and help to assimilate immigrants gained ground. With racial and cultural "whiteness" a measure of qualification for citizenship, some immigrants assumed what Jacobson terms a "probationary white" status, gradually gaining acceptance in society (p. 103). As racial fears diminished, reformers focused on cultural assimilation of immigrants, often referred to as Americanization.

THE AMERICANIZATION MOVEMENT

Peaking in the 1920s, the Americanization movement aimed to assimilate immigrants through programs such as civics and English classes, employment training, and settlement-house activities. According to the historian Edward George Hartmann, unlike immigration restriction, Americanization "outlined a positive program of education and guidance" to produce "a patriotic, loyal, and intelligent supporter of the great body of principles and practices which the leaders of the movement chose to consider 'America's priceless heritage'" (p. 8). As Hartmann's synopsis indicates, the movement had somewhat vague and changeable goals, and the various

Anzia Yezierska. CULVER PICTURES, INC.

organizations developed different methods and priorities. The literary critic Priscilla Wald has characterized Americanization programs as combining "benevolence with bigotry" (p. 196). In a 1920 collection that provides guidelines for Americanization, Winthrop Talbot criticizes Americanizers who would homogenize all citizens; instead, he upholds a vision of a "glorious garden" where "cross fertilization and intensive cultivation develop large variety and wonderful fruitage" (p. 59). Yet in this same volume, Grover Huebner takes a more aggressive stance on neutralizing immigrant culture, remaining particularly apprehensive about Catholic immigrants. Despite these disparities, Royal Dixon (1885–1962), vice president of the League of Foreign-Born Citizens, praised Americanization's potential:

> For it is, indeed, every man's chance, if he will grasp it, to serve his country definitely and fruitfully, if he does no more than urge on the work of Americanization. If he takes an active hand, as he can readily do, he is assisting not merely this or the other foreigner to a higher level of understanding, but he is strengthening the nation as well. (P. 51)

Potential for such cross-fertilization existed in settlement houses, which promoted interaction between native-born residents and immigrants in classes, lectures, and social events at a neighborhood community center. In her autobiography *The Promised Land* (1912), the writer Mary Antin (1881–1949), who emigrated from the Jewish Pale region in Russia, describes a stimulating environment at Boston's Hale House settlement, where she joined a natural-history club that started her lifelong interest in science. However, as the historian Mina Carson notes, an element of "feudalism" infused the rhetoric and activities of settlement work. For instance, even Jane Addams (1860–1935), the founder of Chicago's Hull-House who aided immigrants while encouraging them to maintain some ethnic traditions, also articulates the settlement's paternalistic goals: "to develop whatever of social life its neighborhood may afford, to focus and give form to that life, to bring to bear upon it the results of cultivation and training" (p. 125) and "to preserve and keep whatever of value [immigrants'] past life contained and to bring them in contact with a better type of Americans" (pp. 231–232). While accepting immigrant cultural diversity, Addams asserts that "model" citizens must improve immigrants. To settlement workers and other Americanizers, immigrants presented unrefined, unformed clay to be molded.

The Polish immigrant writer Anzia Yezierska (c. 1885–1970) perceived the negative side of settlements and sharply criticizes them in her novel *Salome of the Tenements* (1923). As Gay Wilentz notes, in this novel, Yezierska "radically critiques the settlement education projects that aimed at Americanization through the melting pot theory" (p. ix). The immigrant protagonist, Sonya, quickly grows disillusioned with her husband's settlement house, where instructors teach immigrants to bake "milkless, butterless, eggless cake" (p. 134), instructing them to do without and effectively denying their right to a more comfortable lifestyle. For Sonya, it is evident that the settlement fails to acknowledge the full humanity of immigrants; even when it helps to meet their material needs, it neglects their dignity. She finds settlement employees manipulating attendance figures to please the founder. Sonya ultimately describes the settlement as "reason forced down the throats of the people! Hireling telling lies to hireling!" (p. 138). She witnesses the good intentions of the settlement gone awry through misguided programs and services. Yezierska suggests that statistics and formulas take precedence over people, and Americanization swerves from helping immigrants to become its own end.

IMMIGRANTS SEEKING ASSIMILATION

Independently of any Americanization agency or program, many immigrants felt a strong desire to assimilate, and they explored many means to accomplish this goal. In *Beyond Ethnicity: Consent and Descent in American Culture,* the literary critic Werner Sollors describes American ethnicity as a combination of "descent"—inheritance—and "consent"—active selection of one's identity. Arriving with a variety of descent identities, many American immigrants pursued the possibilities of consent almost immediately, exploring opportunities to redefine themselves.

In his autobiography, *A Far Journey* (1914), the Syrian immigrant Abraham Rihbany discusses the pros and cons of insulated immigrant "colonies" (p. 245) made up of new arrivals from the same country. While he finds his New York Syrian colony invaluable in establishing him in America, he becomes anxious since he speaks no English and encounters no new customs. Rihbany remarks, "I often asked myself, in those days, where and how do the real Americans live?" (p. 246). He determines that leaving the colony, and even the city, is necessary in order to mingle with other, non-Syrian, Americans and broaden his knowledge.

Overturning the stereotype of inassimilable Chinese, Sui Sin Far (the pen name of Edith Maude Eaton, 1865–1914) portrays Chinese families in an integrated suburb abandoning the tradition of arranged marriages in the title story of collection *Mrs. Spring Fragrance* (1912). In his 1923 autobiography *From Immigrant to Inventor,* the Serbian immigrant Michael Pupin (1858–1935), who became a successful engineering professor and inventor, relates his unique process of assimilation. He describes undergoing an "apprenticeship as greenhorn" (p. 126) while a new immigrant, with unavoidable misunderstandings and awkwardness. Through college at Columbia, he learns how to "play the game" (p. 115) of American life, balancing work, study, and entertainment while building a network of friends and mentors who aid his Americanization.

As an immediate step to assimilation, Mary Antin's father gives each family member a non-Russian name that is common in America. Antin herself praises the American public schools as instrumental in forming "good Americans" who will be "workers, thinkers, and leaders" (*Promised Land,* p. 175). Along with the settlement house and school, she embraced numerous opportunities through mentors, lectures, and libraries to gradually adjust herself to America. The writings of Antin, Rihbany, Sui Sin Far, and Pupin represent the experiences of immigrants who actively sought assimilation and found a variety of organizations and individuals to facilitate it.

The Russian immigrant Abraham Cahan (1860–1951) examines contrasting strategies of assimilation in his novella *Yekl: A Tale of the New York Ghetto*

Assimilation could create tension within immigrant families, especially when family members immigrated at different times. In Abraham Cahan's novella Yekl: A Tale of the New York Ghetto *(1896), the thoroughly Americanized Yekl feels alienated from his newly arrived wife:*

All the way to the island he had been in a flurry of joyous anticipation. The prospect of meeting his dear wife and child, and, incidentally, of showing off his swell attire to her, had thrown him into a fever of impatience. But on entering the big shed he had caught a glimpse of Gitl and Yosselé through the railing separating the detained immigrants from their visitors, and his heart had sunk at the sight of his wife's uncouth and un-American appearance.

Abraham Cahan, *Yekl: A Tale of the New York Ghetto,* in *Yekl and the Imported Bridegroom and Other Stories of the New York Ghetto,* pp. 33–34.

(1896). Yekl Americanizes his name to Jake and strives to assimilate by immersing himself in the American popular culture of baseball, boxing, and dance halls. After working hard to shed a "greenhorn" image, he cannot accept his traditional Jewish wife, Gitl, who follows him to America three years after his immigration. In contrast, Bernstein, a coworker who boards with Jake's family, approaches Americanization very differently, synthesizing Old World traditions with New World success. Like Antin, Bernstein focuses on education, painstakingly studying both the English language and Jewish holy books. Like Pupin, he achieves a balance of Old and New World priorities, retaining his religious practices, valuing family life, and pursuing business entrepreneurship. At the story's conclusion, Bernstein emerges triumphant to "a future bright with joy" (p. 89), marrying Gitl and opening a new grocery store. Meanwhile, Jake, who had been so determined to shed all vestiges of his European life, including his wife, faces an uncertain future. He will marry his more Americanized lover and open a dance school, but he feels like a "A Defeated Victor" whose future "loomed dark and impenetrable" (p. 89). Cahan affirms that immigrants make very conscious choices in directing their own assimilation, and he also suggests that immigrants who abandon all past associations experience discontent in America.

IMMIGRANTS CRITIQUING ASSIMILATION

Whether they explored assimilation on their own or through a formal Americanizing program, immigrants found need for caution. As Wald notes, many immigrants experienced ambivalence over assimilation. For instance, while Mary Antin celebrates American opportunity in *The Promised Land,* she also confronts the anti-Semitism that prevents her father from obtaining work. In her pro-immigration treatise *They Who Knock at Our Gates: A Complete Gospel of Immigration* (1914), Antin remarks, "a man has to have a country before he can prove himself a good citizen" (p. 38). Racism and other troubling features of the American cultural landscape caused immigrants to question whether they could assimilate or to what degree they wanted to assimilate. In his autobiography *The Soul of an Immigrant* (1921), the Italian immigrant Constantine M. Panunzio remembers that the greatest incentive to assimilate came from a desire to be accepted by an employer's family and by his school rather than from the "cruel" methods and "spirit of compulsion" he finds in "our so-called Americanization program" (p. 194). Even Americanization agencies that discounted racial differences often posed difficulties, proving so constrictive that immigrants resented or rebelled against them. Many immigrants who wished to assimilate wanted to do so on their own terms.

Louis Adamic warns of the dangers of uncritical or rushed assimilation in *Laughing in the Jungle: The Autobiography of an Immigrant in America* (1932), explaining that he "'played it safe,' as a sensible adventurer should do in a jungle" (p. 327). In *The Americanization of Edward Bok* (1920), Edward W. Bok (1863–1930), who became editor of the *Ladies Home Journal,* observes many unappealing aspects of America, complaining of wastefulness, low productivity, and inadequate English education for foreigners in the public schools. Most disturbing for Bok was that native-born citizens did not seem to value their voting rights. He argues that by avoiding these less-attractive characteristics, an immigrant can in some ways become more American than those born in the United States. The German immigrant Edward A. Steiner (1866–1956) encountered dangerous influences soon after his arrival. In his autobiography *From Alien to Citizen: The Story of My Life in America* (1914), he reports being mugged and then thrown into jail on his first day in Chicago. Steiner also discovered that saloons provide the most immediate influence over many immigrants, not only encouraging vices such as alcoholism and prostitution but also operating exploitative employment agencies. Many unscrupulous Americans, some of them immigrants themselves, waited to take advantage of those newly arrived in the United States. Yet Steiner admires

the work of more reputable Americanizing institutions such as the Young Men's Christian Association (YMCA) and the Immigrant Protective League, which shielded immigrants from victimization.

Unfortunately, even those who professed to aid and uplift the immigrant might also prove untrustworthy, as Anzia Yezierska often observes in her works. In her story "Wings" from the collection *Hungry Hearts* (1920), a young sociologist named John Barnes comes to live in the ghetto to study "Educational Problems of the Russian Jews" (*How I Found America,* p. 5). Shenah Pessah, the tenement's cleaning person, appears "a splendid type for his research" but one whose "lack of contact with Americanizing agencies appalled him" (pp. 5, 6). In an essay on Yezierska's work, JoAnn Pavletich comments that "as a scientist, [Barnes's] powerful, culturally authorized gaze fixes Pessah in the position of interesting, but ultimately inferior primitive object of study" (p. 90). Mary V. Dearborn likewise notes that what Yezierska "clearly hated most was being the subject of scientific study," as "Wings" and other stories show (p. 125). While Shenah envisions a romantic relationship developing with Barnes, he considers her merely an object to study and to reform. Yezierska demonstrates the dehumanizing condescension inherent in this type of study, as Barnes feels "the enthusiasm of the scientist for the specimen of his experimentation—of the sculptor for the clay that would take form under his touch" and marvels that "out of the thousands of needy, immigrant girls whom he might have befriended, this eager young being at his side was ordained by some peculiar providence to come under his personal protection" (pp. 6, 14). Approaching Shenah as a study object seems to encourage a cavalier attitude toward her feelings. After taking her to the library to introduce her to new books, Barnes kisses Shenah, throwing her into emotional turmoil. What he dubs a "passing moment of forgetfulness" (p. 15) means much more to Shenah, who experiences great distress when he leaves her. She remembers that he had characterized her as a "poor lonely little immigrant!" a label that later becomes a "cruel mockery" (p. 15). In this case, the Americanizer abuses his influence over the immigrant, confirming that he views her as inferior through both his impersonal scientific study and his disrespectful sexual imposition. Ironically, in this case, the immigrant survives despite the Americanizer's intervention rather than because of it.

IMMIGRANTS REDEFINING ASSIMILATION

In 1920 Julius Drachsler, a professor of economics and sociology at Smith College, argued that Americanization's "ethnic fusion" ideal usually amounted to a "radical fusion" that attempted to Anglicize new immigrants (p. 161). Anxious to assimilate successfully but wary of many Americanization techniques, immigrants also asserted a less-expected formula for assimilation: immigrants Americanizing the country's native-born inhabitants. Immigrant writers illustrate that Americanization could and should be more than a one-sided process and that they resisted such a "radical fusion."

Yezierska's story "America and I," from *Children of Loneliness* (1923), presents an immigrant gradually uncovering this part of the assimilation process. Constantly searching for her niche in her new country, the story's narrator finds that Americanizing agencies—her employer's "English class for foreigners," the "Women's Association," the "Vocational Guidance Center"—cannot bring satisfaction (*How I Found America*, pp. 149–150). The narrator believes that being American means being "a creator, a giver, a human being!" (p. 145). Working as servant and seamstress does not fulfill her, but there is also an overarching problem regarding America that the narrator finally recognizes: "I wanted to find it ready made" (p. 152). She has been expecting to assimilate herself into America as it is. However, this narrator experiences a "revelation" that America is "a world still in the making. I saw that it was the glory of America that it was not yet finished. And I, the last comer, had her share to give, small or great, to the making of America, like those Pilgrims who came in the *Mayflower*" (pp. 152–153). She decides to help build America by opening up "my life and the lives of my people" to other Americans, writing about the immigrant ghetto to form a "bridge of understanding" (p. 153). Rather than simply being assimilated, this immigrant helps to assimilate America to the culture of the immigrants and to become American by easing the intercultural tensions stimulated by immigration.

In his autobiography, Edward Bok expresses a similar sense that America itself needs "Americanization" through the immigrant (p. 445). He cites influential figures in the Americanization movement who pay only "lip-service" (p. 446) to American ideals, such as a speaker who emphasizes the importance of teaching immigrants to respect American institutions but in conversation condemns the president, the cabinet, and Congress. As Bok observes, "There are thousands of the American-born who need Americanization just as much as do the foreign-born" (p. 445). Immigrant perspectives, traditions, and appreciation for American liberties can help renew America, according to Bok.

Adopting this theme of immigrants influencing America rather than vice versa, the native-born intel-

lectual Randolph Bourne (1886–1918) introduced the idea of a "trans-national America" in 1916, remarking, "there is no distinctively American culture. It is apparently our lot rather to be a federation of cultures" (p. 91). Pointing out the limits of the melting-pot concept, Bourne instead proposes a "trans-nationality, a weaving back and forth, with the other lands, of many threads of all colors and sizes" (p. 96). For Bourne, immigration and its cultural infusion make America stronger, forming a multicultural, textured fabric and, thus, a multidirectional assimilation. Similarly, elaborating on his pluralism ideal, Horace Kallen envisions America as a symphony in which "each ethnic group is the natural instrument, its spirit and culture are its theme and melody, and the harmony and dissonances and discords of them all make the symphony of civilization" (p. 220). Written and played simultaneously, this symphony includes "nothing so fixed and inevitable" but ranges ever "wider and richer and more beautiful" (p. 220). More recently, the cultural critic Homi K. Bhabha has proposed the term "hybridity," which signifies "difference without an assumed hierarchy" (p. 3), a useful entrée into immigrant experience. Hybridity captures the different contributions immigrants may bring to America and also helps to describe their individual collections of traditions as they assimilate into America and assimilate America into themselves.

Werner Sollors has characterized the "double consciousness" of ethnic American writers. He describes these authors as "cultural producers" who "function as translators of ethnicity to ignorant, and sometimes hostile, outsiders and, at the same time, as mediators between 'America' and greenhorns" (p. 249). American immigrant writers demonstrated an awareness of their multiple roles as they struggled to express both the stresses and opportunities of assimilation. As they created literary translations of the immigrant experience, they also aimed to help "Americanize" their readers.

*See also American Indian Stories; Chicago; Chinese;
Immigration; Jews; Mrs. Spring Fragrance;
The Promised Land; The Rise of David Levinsky;
San Francisco*

BIBLIOGRAPHY

Primary Works

Adamic, Louis. *From Many Lands.* New York: Harper & Brothers, 1940.

Adamic, Louis. *Laughing in the Jungle: The Autobiography of an Immigrant in America.* 1932. New York: Arno, 1969.

Addams, Jane. *Twenty Years at Hull-House.* New York: Macmillan, 1910.

Antin, Mary. *The Promised Land.* 1912. Edited by Werner Sollors. New York: Penguin, 1997.

Antin, Mary. *They Who Knock at Our Gates: A Complete Gospel of Immigration.* Boston: Houghton Mifflin, 1914.

Bok, Edward William. *The Americanization of Edward Bok.* New York: Scribners, 1920.

Cahan, Abraham. 1896, 1898. *Yekl and the Imported Bridegroom and Other Stories of the New York Ghetto.* New York: Dover, 1970.

Dietrich, John. "'The Melting Pot': A Plea for the Unborn Children of America." St. Mark's Reformed Church, Pittsburgh, Pa., 8 May 1910.

Dixon, Royal. *Americanization.* New York: Macmillan, 1916.

Drachsler, Julius. *Democracy and Assimilation: The Blending of Immigrant Heritages in America.* New York: Macmillan, 1920.

Huebner, Grover. "The Americanization of the Immigrant." In *Americanization,* edited by Winthrop Talbot, pp. 174–184. New York: H. W. Wilson, 1920.

Panunzio, Constantine M. *The Soul of an Immigrant.* New York: Macmillan, 1921.

Pupin, Michael. *From Immigrant to Inventor.* New York: Scribners, 1923.

Rihbany, Abraham Mitrie. *A Far Journey.* Boston: Houghton Mifflin, 1914.

Steiner, Edward. *From Alien to Citizen: The Story of My Life in America.* New York: Revell, 1914.

Sui Sin Far. *Mrs. Spring Fragrance and Other Writings.* Edited by Amy Ling and Annette White-Parks. Urbana: University of Illinois Press, 1995.

Yezierska, Anzia. *How I Found America: Collected Stories of Anzia Yezierska.* Introduction by Vivian Gornick. New York: Persea, 1991.

Yezierska, Anzia. *Salome of the Tenements.* Urbana: University of Illinois Press, 1995.

Zangwill, Israel. *The Melting-Pot: Drama in Four Acts.* 1909. New York: Macmillan, 1914.

Secondary Works

Bhabha, Homi K. *The Location of Culture.* London: Routledge, 1994.

Bourne, Randolph. "Trans-National America." *Atlantic* 118 (1916): 86–97.

Carson, Mina. *Settlement Folk: Social Thought and the American Settlement Movement, 1885–1930.* Chicago: University of Chicago Press, 1990.

Dearborn, Mary V. *Love in the Promised Land: The Story of Anzia Yezierska and John Dewey.* New York: Free Press, 1988.

Jacobson, Matthew Frye. *Whiteness of a Different Color: European Immigrants and the Alchemy of Race.* Cambridge, Mass.: Harvard University Press, 1998.

Hartmann, Edward George. *The Movement to Americanize the Immigrant.* New York: Columbia University Press, 1948.

Kallen, Horace M. "Democracy versus the Melting-Pot: A Study of American Nationality." *Nation* 100, no. 2590 (18 February 1915): 190–194; 100, no. 2591 (25 February 1915): 217–220.

Pavletich, JoAnn. "Anzia Yezierska, Immigrant Authority, and the Uses of Affect." *Tulsa Studies in Women's Literature* 19 (2000): 81–104.

Sollors, Werner. *Beyond Ethnicity: Consent and Descent in American Culture.* New York: Oxford University Press, 1986.

Talbot, Winthrop. "The Faith That Is in Us." In *Americanization,* edited by Winthrop Talbot, pp. 56–62. New York: H. W. Wilson, 1920.

Wald, Priscilla. "Immigration and Assimilation in Nineteenth-Century U.S. Women's Writing." In *The Cambridge Companion to Nineteenth-Century American Women's Writing,* edited by Dale M. Bauer and Philip Gould, pp. 176–199. Cambridge, U.K.: Cambridge University Press, 2001.

Wilentz, Gay. Introduction to *Salome of the Tenements,* by Anzia Yezierska, pp. ix–xxvi. Urbana: University of Illinois Press, 1995.

Lori Jirousek

THE ATLANTIC MONTHLY

The *Atlantic Monthly* was founded in 1857 by a group that included its first editor, James Russell Lowell; Oliver Wendell Holmes Sr.; Ralph Waldo Emerson; the publisher Moses Phillips; and Phillip's assistant, Francis Underwood, who had initiated the idea. One of their goals in starting the journal was to provide additional income, readership, and publicity mainly for New England writers. But the *Atlantic* was founded also with a New England sense of moral and cultural mission. To mobilize regional writers in opposition to slavery was part of this mission. But Lowell, Emerson, and others also intended the magazine to establish a high standard for American literature and public intellectual discourse and to spread the cultural values of Yankee humanism in a relatively new and rapidly developing nation.

This sense of cultural mission was particularly acute following the American Civil War. Writers such as the U.S. senator Charles Sumner and the historian George Bancroft published sweeping visions of a great democratic nation freed from the moral blight of slavery and expanding to include the entire American continent. But Emerson, Thomas Wentworth Higginson, and others, while generally sharing a visionary optimism, warned that a nation preoccupied with geographical and economic expansion needed the moral and intellectual values of a liberal humanistic culture. The *Atlantic,* with a postwar national circulation around fifty thousand, intended to play a part.

In the 1870s William Dean Howells (1837–1920) made the *Atlantic* an influential vehicle for literary realism and liberal debate, although his readership was constantly eroded by new competition from New York's illustrated magazines. During the gradual waning of New England cultural influence over the next twenty-five years, the magazine became increasingly marginalized in a high-culture market niche. It retained much of its influence and excellence in literature but experienced some decline in circulation, range of views, and broader cultural impact. Beginning in the late 1890s, however, the editors Walter Hines Page, Bliss Perry, and Ellery Sedgwick, influenced by the progressive journalism of the era, gradually remade the *Atlantic* by reengaging it in contemporary issues, broadening its range of voices and ideas, and extending both circulation and influence.

HOWELLS AND REALISM

On 2 January 1871 William Dean Howells replaced the publisher James T. Fields as editor in chief of the *Atlantic,* and Fields sold his publishing interests, including the magazine, to James Osgood. Howells, who had been an assistant to Fields since 1866, was himself testimony to Fields's intention to expand the magazine's appeal beyond New England and include authors outside the old "*Atlantic* circle" whose reputations Fields had promoted so effectively. As a young midwesterner, Howells had been hired partly to identify and develop new authors, a job for which he showed genius. During his *Atlantic* editorship he solicited, published, advised, and supported a new, geographically diverse generation of American writers, most in the earliest, formative stages of their careers. These authors included fellow midwesterners like John and Sarah Piatt, Constance Fenimore Woolson, Ralph Keeler, W. H. Bishop, H. H. Boyesen, and Mark Twain; westerners such as Bret Harte and Charles Warren Stoddard; the southerners Paul Hamilton Hayne and Mary Noailles Murfree; the New Yorkers John William De Forest, Elizabeth Stuart Phelps (later known as Elizabeth Ward), Philander Deming, and Edith Wharton (who was Edith Jones when she first published in the *Atlantic*); and New Englanders as diverse as Sarah Orne Jewett, Celia Thaxter, John Boyle O'Reilly, and Henry James.

Howells's editorship of the *Atlantic* was a seminal event for American realism. Much of the movement's early development is reflected in his selection and editorial guidance of young authors as well as his prolific, supportive reviews of their work between 1866 and 1881. Those reviews articulated his concept of a socially engaged literature closely observing contemporary American life and examining its moral and social issues. His own development as a realist is also clear in his *Atlantic* publications. They evolved from imitative Romantic poetry to travel sketches to reportage on the current American scene to realistic novels such as *A Chance Acquaintance* (1873), which featured fully realized narratives, characters, and contemporary themes.

During his editorship, Howells clearly saw realism as an essential connection between literary culture, American democracy, and social reform. His own fiction began partly in nonfiction reportage, and he encouraged other writers such as Lillie Chase Wyman and J. B. Harrison to do investigative reporting on New England mill towns. He published their accounts and subsequently urged the authors to turn their journalistic works into realistic fiction.

Howells's *Atlantic,* like that of his successors Thomas Bailey Aldrich and Horace Elisha Scudder, was heavily literary. Fiction, literary articles, and reviews typically constituted about 50 percent of the journal, whereas political and social commentary comprised 10 to, at most, 20 percent. During the Civil War and the early Reconstruction era, the magazine had unequivocally supported the Republicans as "the party of righteousness" (*Atlantic Monthly,* January 1869, p. 124). But by the mid-1870s, despite Howells's personal friendship with the Republican presidents Rutherford B. Hayes and James A. Garfield, the journal voiced a tone of disillusion about the party. Over the next thirty years, the magazine reflected a sense that the juggernaut of economic development was outstripping the nation's moral and cultural vision and corrupting its values. Political and social commentary during this period ranged from reactionary to socialistic. A great many writers expressed alarm at the growing divisions between an expanding new socioeconomic elite led by wealthy industrialists; an increasingly foreign-born, urbanized, and aggressive labor force; and a liberally educated cultural elite with their Emersonian traditions of high culture and principled social responsibility. Most of the *Atlantic*'s readers belonged to this last group, and most of the journal's social and political commentators condemned the corruption of politics by both capital and labor, voiced their anxiety about potentially violent class conflict, and expressed a fear of cultural marginalization. In addition, the writers criticized the unprincipled power of plutocracy, advocated moderate regulatory reform, and noted the limits of laissez-faire economics. Howells's own sympathies were with

THE
ATLANTIC MONTHLY

DEVOTED TO

Literature, Science, Art, and Politics

VOLUME XLVIII.—NUMBER 289

NOVEMBER, 1881

CONTENTS

BOSTON
HOUGHTON, MIFFLIN AND COMPANY

NEW YORK: 11 EAST SEVENTEENTH STREET

The Riverside Press, Cambridge

Entered at the Post Office at Boston as second-class matter.

TERMS — SINGLE NUMBERS, 35 CENTS   YEARLY SUBSCRIPTION, $4.00

Cover of the *Atlantic Monthly,* November 1881. COURTESY OF THE ATLANTIC MONTHLY reform, and he ran articles advocating government regulation of railroads and equitable land distribution to homesteaders as well as one of the earliest muckraking articles, Henry Demarest Lloyd's exposé of Standard Oil, "The Story of a Great Monopoly" (1881).

Throughout his editorship, Howells struggled with a declining circulation, a frustration that dogged *Atlantic* editors for the rest of the century. Circulation had reached its nineteenth-century peak of fifty thousand in 1869, tumbled in 1870 after Howells published Harriet Beecher Stowe's exposé on Lord Byron's incest, and then drifted down to about twelve thousand by 1880. Howells experimented by adding new departments, including the popular "Contributors' Club," and several pages of brief, anonymous, often amusing pieces, but without effect. The major cause of the decline was the loss of readers and authors to what Henry James, in a letter to Howells, called "the New York picture books," meaning the illustrated monthlies, particularly *Harper's New Monthly, Scribner's,* and later *Century Magazine.* In addition to being richly illustrated, these publications had a somewhat lighter, more family-oriented, less bookishly intellectual mix of contents. By 1880 several had developed circulations exceeding 100,000.

In 1873 James Osgood had sold the *Atlantic* to Henry Oscar Houghton, whose various firms, eventually Houghton, Mifflin and Co., would own it until 1908. The risk-prone Osgood had considered adding illustrations to the *Atlantic,* but the financially conservative Houghton declined, as he declined also to compete with the per-page rate paid to popular authors by the New York monthlies. The development of new markets for good fiction, the decline of the old "courtesy of the trade" loyalty to one publisher or magazine, low circulation, and resulting low advertising revenues put the *Atlantic* at a distinct disadvantage. Houghton's response was generally to accept a high-culture market niche and to take the long view by valuing the magazine not for direct profit but for the prestige and the authors it brought to his publishing house. If he controlled expenses, he also allowed editors considerable freedom in shaping the magazine.

ALDRICH AND SCUDDER: HIGH VICTORIANISM

When Howells resigned in 1881, Houghton replaced him with Thomas Bailey Aldrich (1836–1907), who edited the magazine until 1890. Aldrich was a widely known author of both poetry and prose with considerable editorial experience. Like Howells, he had grown up in the provinces, started his literary career in New York, and come to Boston in 1866 to work for

Fields, then Osgood. Aldrich later edited Houghton's eclectic weekly *Every Saturday* while Howells edited the *Atlantic.* But both his literary and political ideologies had grown more conservative as Howells's grew more liberal. Aldrich's conservatism combined with the *Atlantic's* economic circumstances to define the magazine as a voice of high culture.

But Aldrich's ideas of the nature and purpose of high culture were quite different from those of the magazine's founders. Emersonian confidence that Yankee humanism could deeply influence the moral and social development of the nation had given way to a sense of political and cultural marginalization later expressed by the author Henry Adams. High culture became genteelly disengaged from mainstream American life and, at its narrowest, became an aesthetic refuge against a perceived rising tide of barbarism or a mark of Gilded Age status.

Aldrich's own professionalism and the *Atlantic's* tradition of liberal debate prevented him from reducing the magazine to the dimensions of his own philosophy. But there was more frequently a tone of pessimistic defensiveness and a failure to engage the new. Aldrich's editorial style was less generative than Howells's and more prescriptive. He developed few new writers but enforced rigorous standards of linguistic purity and aesthetic taste. In poetry he preferred a lapidary formalism, loathed populist dialect verse, ridiculed the poetry of personal pain, and considered Walt Whitman a freak of nature. In fiction, Aldrich mainly continued to publish the work of the magazine's established realists, including twenty stories by Sarah Orne Jewett and four major novels by Henry James. Aldrich repeatedly solicited serials from James at a time when the New York magazines had completely dropped his longer works. Thus the *Atlantic,* because of its high-culture niche, became the only American magazine that would publish the major novels of the most important fiction writer of the period.

In 1891 Horace Elisha Scudder (1838–1902), Houghton, Mifflin and Co.'s lead trade editor, who had patiently carried the *Atlantic* during Aldrich's annual three-month summer excursions, was appointed editor in chief. Scudder was a gentle, self-effacing, broad-minded Victorian with a prodigious capacity for work. He saw his editorship as an Arnoldian cultural mission to propagate the best that has been thought and said. He considered literature, past and present, the heart of the magazine and believed deeply that literature, without being didactic, was a powerful moral and educational force. He published probably the last commentaries on the

Greek and Roman authors written for a general audience. He eulogized and canonized members of the old *Atlantic* circle now dying and was instrumental in integrating their works into the public school curriculum. His aim in doing so was to develop American values and create a future readership for good literature. Influential as a critic and as an editor, he praised the ethical realism of Howells and Twain, solicited James for several stories that grew into short novels, persuaded Jewett to construct for the *Atlantic* a sequence of stories that became *The Country of the Pointed Firs* (1896), and published Kate Chopin's early sketches and first book.

PAGE, PERRY, AND SEDGWICK: PROGRESSIVE PUBLISHING

In 1895 Scudder, exhausted from editing both the *Atlantic* and Houghton, Mifflin and Co.'s trade publications, and George Mifflin (Henry Oscar Houghton's partner), eager to stem *Atlantic* losses, hired Walter Hines Page (1855–1910) as Scudder's assistant. Recommended by Woodrow Wilson, a frequent contributor to Scudder's *Atlantic*, Page at age forty had recently proved his abilities in the competitive world of New York journalism by resurrecting the *Forum*, a journal of current affairs. As he gradually transferred the reins, Scudder realized with a mixture of regret and resignation that Page would substantially change the *Atlantic* as he took it from the nineteenth to the twentieth century. The Victorian Scudder was attached to the culture of the past, believed in the moral power of literature, worked to educate public taste, sought to publish work of permanent worth, and saw the magazine partly as a monthly book. The dynamic Page represented a new, progressive magazine journalism influenced by the successes of Samuel Sidney McClure, founder of *McClure's Magazine*. Page emphasized current affairs rather than literature, worked to build circulation and advertising revenues by increasing debate on contemporary issues, sought social impact in the present, and believed a magazine had a shelf life of thirty days.

Page, with a progressive's contempt for high-culture aestheticism, pessimism, and alienation, worked to close the gap between literature and contemporary American life. He called literary criticism "mere talkee-talkee" (quoted in Sedgwick, *A History of the "Atlantic Monthly,"* p. 260) considered introspective literature neurotic, and believed no one with blood in his veins would read James. Instead, he published Jack London's first story for a national audience, popular swashbucklers like Mary Johnston's *To Have and to Hold* (1899), light serials by Kate Wiggin, social realism by Henry Blake Fuller and others, and a great deal of nonfiction sociological reportage. Believing that race and ethnicity

were critical issues in turn-of-the-twentieth-century America, Page contributed his own investigative reporting on race in the South and solicited important contributions from Booker T. Washington, W. E. B. Du Bois, Israel Zangwill, Abraham Cahan, and Jacob Riis. He was particularly supportive of his fellow North Carolinian Charles Waddell Chesnutt, publishing several of his stories of the color line that had been rejected in New York and persuading Houghton, Mifflin and Co. to publish three of Chesnutt's books.

Page not only reengaged the *Atlantic* in current affairs but sought controversy rather than avoiding it. When war was declared with Spain in 1898, he characteristically flew the American flag on the *Atlantic's* cover and ran prowar editorials that offended the anticolonialism of many readers, including his boss, Mifflin. In 1899, however, Page resigned suddenly to take over part of the bankrupt Harper empire at the invitation of Samuel Sidney McClure. His successor Bliss Perry (1860–1954) created an equal but opposite reaction by writing editorials and publishing articles denouncing U.S. colonialism in the Philippines and the Caribbean as a hypocritical betrayal of fundamental American values. To his credit, Mifflin intervened in neither case.

Unlike Page, Perry was not a professional editor but a professor of English, a job that he continued part-time during much of his editorship and returned to full-time in 1909. Perry was also unlike Page in that he was distinctly uncomfortable making cultural judgments in a commercial context. Like the tradition of Emersonian Yankee humanism from which both he and the *Atlantic* came, he favored liberal politics and liberal high culture and was sensitive to the influence of money on either. As editor, he generally followed his political instincts with no intervention from Mifflin; but under pressure to popularize the magazine, he made personally uncomfortable compromises on the cultural side. While continuing the *Atlantic* policy of broad debate, he published arguments for socialism by London and others, indictments of corporate capitalism, calls for government regulation, and a satire on Teddy Roosevelt that personally infuriated the president. He also initiated a major series on civil rights and race, including denunciations of racism by Paul Laurence Dunbar, Edward Wilson, and W. E. B. Du Bois, as well as his own editorial comparing the suppression of African American rights to colonial subjugation in the Philippines.

In literature, Perry restored large quantities of reviews, progressive literary criticism, and virtually the last nonacademic discussions of Western canonical authors. He was instrumental in not only publishing but also encouraging development of the earliest works of Mary Austin, the socialist Ernest Poole, and the Sioux writer Zitkala-Ša. But his cultural conscience bothered him when the business office pressured him into such compromises as declining work by Henry James and running light historical romances instead. When Mifflin decided to sell the *Atlantic* to Ellery Sedgwick in 1908, Perry had few regrets about returning to the less commercial culture of academe.

Ellery Sedgwick (1872–1960), by contrast, thrived at the crossroads of commerce and culture. He was both principal owner and editor of the *Atlantic* for nearly thirty years and by 1919 had expanded its readership from 20,000 to over 100,000. Like his mentor Page, he was a professional editor, shaped by apprenticeship in the progressive magazine journalism of New York in the muckraking era. Accordingly, he believed that a magazine must respond, sometimes controversially, to current issues and that the editor was responsible for proactively shaping each issue by identifying subjects of importance and soliciting analysis. His program for modifying the *Atlantic*'s high-culture tone and expanding circulation without alienating the old readership included limiting articles to a maximum of ten pages; substantially reducing literary reviews, criticism, poetry, and history; increasing coverage of current affairs and reportage; promoting debate; decreasing the quantity of fiction while increasing its popularity; and broadening the definition of literature to include narratives of personal experience.

Sedgwick's editorial strategy emphasized debate, controversy, and a pluralism of voices. His own inclinations at this time were moderately conservative in terms of culture and progressive in politics. Reflecting his values, the *Atlantic* generally advocated Wilsonian democracy and moderate economic reform, backed the League of Nations, and expressed British sympathies during World War I. But Sedgwick also solicited works from Max Eastman, Bertrand Russell, Sidney Webb, and others sympathetic to socialism and, as war neared, pointedly invited his friend H. L. Mencken to praise German political values. While personally attached to traditional poetic styles, he published early work by Amy Lowell, Carl Sandburg, and—in 1915— Robert Frost. In the generational culture wars during and after World War I, he published laments on the decline of manners and morals by the older, genteel idealists, but he also solicited nineteen articles by the iconoclastic Randolph S. Bourne to represent the younger generation aggressively.

In 1920 the *Atlantic* focused less on literature and more on current affairs and reached five times as many readers as in the 1870s. Editors, economics, and cultural change had modified the magazine, but much of

its essential character remained. No longer the dominant literary and cultural influence it had been, it was now one among many but still a distinct voice. Despite a brief period of narrowing, it had never been reduced, as some modernist critics suggested, to a retrospective, reactionary gentility. On the contrary, it had maintained and renewed its original Yankee humanist tradition of intellectual debate, social engagement, and challenge to conventional ideas, and it continued to publish a liberal-minded range of voices, values, and views.

See also Boston and Concord; *Century Magazine; Harper's New Monthly Magazine;* Houghton Mifflin; Periodicals; Realism; *Scribner's Magazine;* Short Story; Spanish-American War

BIBLIOGRAPHY

Primary Works

Howells, William Dean. *Selected Letters.* Edited by George Arms, et al. 6 vols. Boston: Twayne, 1979–1983.

Perry, Bliss. *And Gladly Teach: Reminiscences by Bliss Perry.* Boston: Houghton Mifflin, 1935.

Secondary Works

Ballou, Ellen B. *The Building of the House: Houghton Mifflin's Formative Years.* Boston: Houghton Mifflin, 1970.

Brodhead, Richard. "Literature and Culture." In *Columbia Literary History of the United States,* edited by Emory Elliott, pp. 467–481. New York: Columbia University Press, 1988.

Brooks, Van Wyck. *New England Indian Summer.* New York: E. P. Dutton, 1940.

Howe, M. A. De Wolfe. *The "Atlantic Monthly" and Its Makers.* Boston: Atlantic Monthly Press, 1919.

Mott, Frank Luther. *A History of American Magazines.* Vols. 2–4. Cambridge, Mass.: Harvard University Press, 1938.

Sedgwick, Ellery. *The Happy Profession.* Boston: Little, Brown, 1946.

Sedgwick, Ellery, III. *A History of the "Atlantic Monthly," 1857–1909: Yankee Humanism at High Tide and Ebb.* Amherst, Mass.: University of Massachusetts Press, 1994.

Wilson, Christopher P. *The Labor of Words: Literary Professionalism in the Progressive Era.* Athens: University of Georgia Press, 1985.

Ellery Sedgwick

AUTOBIOGRAPHY

The Civil War (1861–1865) marked the beginning of a transformation in American literary culture that culminated with the emergence of modernism around the time of World War I (1914–1918). In the largest sense, the Civil War—followed by a period of industrialization, technological innovation, urbanization, immigration, and imperial expansion—accelerated the decline of literary and artistic romanticism and the rise of realism. The new outlook was based on materialism, science (biology, economics, and geography), and determinism rather than on idealism, intuition, and individualism. These changes altered autobiography, and the notion of who was entitled to write one, and ultimately placed the possibility of textual self-understanding under suspicion, from which it has yet to emerge.

Nevertheless, the tradition of the self-made man, established by Benjamin Franklin (1706–1790), dominated the self-conceptions of many Americans of every race and ethnicity well into the twentieth century. African American writers, who produced slave narratives before the Civil War, now endeavored to make the most of their altered circumstances while struggling with the ongoing impediments to freedom during Reconstruction and the era of Jim Crow. During the Progressive Era near the turn of the twentieth century, the "New Woman" began to demand equality, opportunity, and political power. So did many immigrant writers, who by the end of the nineteenth century were arriving in unprecedented numbers, building businesses, and taking control of the cities. The struggles between capital and labor, coupled with new political movements such as anarchism, raised the specter of a new Civil War. Meanwhile, the final opening of the western states for settlement reinvigorated some elements in the American character (piety, acquisitiveness, and violence) while simultaneously calling these values into question, particularly as they were implicated in racism, imperialism, and environmental devastation. Amidst all this change, some of the heirs of the original European settler cultures wondered what had happened to *their* country. They sentimentalized the past and were uncertain about a future about to pass out of their exclusive control. All these struggles were reflected in American autobiography, which represented the reciprocal relationship between self and national identity in a period of rapid change.

SELF-MADE MEN

The exemplary American personality—practical, hardworking, and ambitious—presented in the *Autobiography of Benjamin Franklin* (1789) influenced the way Americans of all backgrounds presented themselves in their autobiographical writings, notwithstanding the burgeoning criticism of the Franklinian vision of the United States as an economic meritocracy. Franklin's memoir was surely the most widely disseminated American autobiography of the nineteenth century, and practically all would-be autobiog-

raphers, including women, African Americans, and recent immigrants, had to reckon with Franklin's model of the bourgeois American self (or a mediated version of it): someone born into poverty and obscurity who manages through hard work and moral virtue to rise to a position of wealth and fame. The spiritual journey also structured the success narrative, which often substituted economic success for the arrival in what John Bunyan in *Pilgrim's Progress* called the "Celestial City." In this case, wealth is a manifestation of moral virtue and is bestowed on people so that they might become benefactors to their society, a task that may well include the imperative to present themselves as moral exemplars. The self-made man tradition negotiates the tension between the material and the spiritual, the individual and the community, by asserting that self-interest coincides with the interests of society. The popularity of Horatio Alger Jr.'s *Ragged Dick* series (beginning in 1867), which invariably describes the ascent of poor but virtuous and hard-working boys, suggests how the self-made man tradition was useful both as a stimulus to capitalist economic development and as a means to invalidate the discontent of large numbers of oppressed and disadvantaged people by telling them: "You too could be rich, if only you had tried harder."

The Life of P. T. Barnum, Written by Himself—possibly the second-best-selling autobiography of the nineteenth century—reflects the influence of Franklin as well as an awareness of the limitations of his model of the American self. Barnum (1810–1981) originally had it published in 1855, but it was revised, expanded, condensed, and republished several times in many different editions until the end of the nineteenth century (most often with the title *Struggles and Triumphs,* first used in 1869). Like Franklin's *Autobiography,* Barnum's *Life* is the story of how a poor boy became a rich and famous man. From the beginning, however, Barnum emphasizes that he was born at a time that was substantially different from the eighteenth century. Image was already important for Franklin: by Barnum's time, however, image was everything in business, and Barnum became the founding father of American advertising. Nevertheless, to most of his readers, *Struggles and Triumphs* did not represent a rejection of Franklinian values; rather, the showman was a product of the go-getting marketplace these values encouraged. The tenet was: do what is necessary to succeed first then tend to the finer points of moral virtue and civic responsibility. Barnum's evolving autobiographies follow this pattern: as he becomes more prosperous, he cultivates the image of a benefactor of society, a purveyor of respectable, educational, and morally uplifting amusements rather than a hoaxer and humbug.

But even as he becomes an eminent Victorian, Barnum, like Franklin, continues to take pride in his humble origins and to wink at his readers, suggesting that even his public service is a form of personal opportunism, a means of access to the social and political power held by established elites.

CIVIL WAR MEMOIRS

A substantial proportion of Americans were directly involved in the Civil War and practically everyone was affected by it in some way. Two million men had served in the Union Army, and about 750,000 had fought for the Confederacy. Some 3.5 million slaves were liberated. Probably more than a million Americans were either killed or wounded in the war. It was undoubtedly the most traumatic event in American history, and it is not surprising that autobiographical writings of those who lived through that era would treat it as one of the formative experiences of their subjects' lives.

Louis Kaplan's *Bibliography of American Autobiographies* lists more than five hundred Civil War memoirs published before 1945. About seventy came out before 1870; fewer than twenty were published in the 1870s (though *Memoirs of Gen. William T. Sherman* appeared in 1875); but the rate of publication peaked in the next decade at nearly sixty, and such memoirs continued to be published in comparable numbers until about 1920, when Civil War veterans began to die out and the experiences of World War I assumed much greater prominence. The men who fought in the war, such as Warren Lee Goss, Thomas Wentworth Higginson, and Lewis Wallace, had a sense that they had made history, that they had important stories to tell, if not as individuals, then as representatives of the experiences of many Americans.

The most famous and influential of these autobiographical writings is Ulysses S. Grant's *Personal Memoirs.* Grant (1822–1885) wrote it under dramatic circumstances, while dying of throat cancer, and it sold more than 300,000 copies by subscription, becoming the best-selling title in the crowded genre of Civil War memoirs. It was, however, unlike many other works published in that era in that it was not an apologia for military blunders, a self-serving account of personal or regimental heroism, or a prelude to the pursuit of political office. Grant's spare prose, unlike the romantic style of some of his contemporaries, reflected and reinforced the image he had during the Civil War of a plainspoken, practical, resolute man. His memoirs are starkly descriptive, without vanity or remorse. He sometimes portrays his younger self as an object of mockery: for example,

his distaste for fancy uniforms was shaped by his judgment about the absurdity of his early admiration for them. And he corrects romanticized retellings of his activities, such as events surrounding the surrender of General Robert E. Lee at Appomattox. The commanding general of the Union, like his Confederate counterpart, tended to see himself as a tool in the hands of forces larger than himself. But, like Franklin, Grant portrays himself as a man trying to discover his talents and to find an elevated place in the world.

In addition to its historical importance as a documentary record of the activities of a major figure in American history, Grant's memoirs are an important document marking the shift in American literature from romanticism to realism; it moves away from idealism toward a desire for hard facts expressed in almost scientific terms. It attests to the ascendancy of the practical man rather than the sentimentalist, the man of action over the man of eloquence. It looks back to the Plain Style of Puritan writing, and it looks ahead to the clipped sentences of Ernest Hemingway. Both Gertrude Stein and Edmund Wilson praised it as a seminal work in American literature.

Equally remarkable is the transition in the writings of the poet Walt Whitman (1819–1892) from the flamboyant self-assertion of the first edition of *Leaves of Grass* (1855) to his wistful prose recollections of the Civil War era in *Specimen Days and Collect* (1882), which constitutes what might be considered a poet's workshop of images and memories of Whitman's activities in Washington, D.C., from 1862 to 1865, when Whitman worked as a government clerk and volunteer hospital aide. If *Specimen Days* is an autobiography, it is a highly experimental one. The sketches describe the aftermath of battles, hospital scenes, camp life, conversations with soldiers, and glimpses of Lincoln. Whitman serves as a mediating consciousness and sometimes as an actor in the events he describes. In this sense, *Specimen Days* supports the mythic vision of Whitman portrayed in his collection of Civil War poems, *Drum-Taps* (1865). *Specimen Days* also marks a shift in literary technique from notions of a fully integrated self that can look back with clarity: the diary format preserves the integrity of impressions of the moment. Whitman's use of that form also avoids any organizing plot, such as the ascent from poverty to wealth. Events follow chronologically but their meaning is not defined, emerging only from the narrative as a whole, where the hospital serves as a metaphor for America, with the poet as healer preparing for a reconciliation between North and South. Ultimately, *Specimen Days* tends toward a pastoralism that seems out of step with the urbanization and industrialization of the postwar years.

WALT WHITMAN'S "HOSPITAL SCENES AND PERSONS"

Whitman's Specimen Days *is an autobiography of the parallel development of the nation and the poet in the era of the Civil War. In particular, it reflects the shift in American literary culture away from romanticism toward realism. Whitman, like the photographer Mathew Brady, presents the painful aftermath of war in ugly detail rather than offering idealized portraits of military glory. Whitman and his America are redeemed by small acts of comradeship rather than by the capacity for violence.*

Letter Writing.—When eligible, I encourage the men to write, and myself, when called upon, write all sorts of letters for them, (including love letters, very tender ones.) Almost as I reel off these memoranda, I write for a new patient to his wife. M. de F., of the 17th Connecticut, company H, has just come up (February 17th) from Windmill point, and is received in ward H, Armory-square. He is an intelligent looking man, has a foreign accent, black-eyed and hair'd, a Hebraic appearance. Wants a telegraphic message sent to his wife, New Canaan, Conn. I agree to send the message—but to make things sure I also sit down and write the wife a letter, and despatch it to the post-office immediately, as he fears she will come on, and he does not wish her to, as he will surely get well.

Saturday, January 30th.—Afternoon, visited Campbell hospital. Scene of cleaning up the ward, and giving the men all clean clothes—through the ward (6) the patients dressing or being dress'd—the naked upper half of the bodies—the good-humor and fun—the shirts, drawers, sheets of beds, &c., and the general fixing up for Sunday. Gave J. L. 50 cents.

Wednesday, February 4th.—Visited Armory-square hospital, went pretty thoroughly through wards E and D. Supplied paper and envelopes to all who wish'd—as usual, found plenty of men who needed those articles. Wrote letters. Saw and talk'd with two or three members of the Brooklyn 14th regt. A poor fellow in ward D, with a fearful wound in a fearful condition, was having some loose splinters of bone taken from the neighborhood of the wound. The operation was long, and one of great pain—yet, after it was well commenced, the soldier bore it in silence. He

sat up, propp'd—was much wasted—had lain a long time quiet in one position (not for days only but weeks,) a bloodless, brown-skinn'd face, with eyes full of determination—belong'd to a New York regiment. There was an unusual cluster of surgeons, medical cadets, nurses, &c., around his bed—I thought the whole thing was done with tenderness, and done well. In one case, the wife sat by the side of her husband, his sickness typhoid fever, pretty bad. In another, by the side of her son, a mother—she told me she had seven children, and this was the youngest. (A fine, kind, healthy, gentle mother, good-looking, not very old, with a cap on her head, and dress'd like home—what a charm it gave to the whole ward.) I liked the woman nurse in ward E—I noticed how she sat a long time by a poor fellow who just had, that morning, in addition to his other sickness, bad hemorrhage—she gently assisted him, reliev'd him of the blood, holding a cloth to his mouth, as he coughed it up—he was so weak he could only just turn his head over on the pillow.

One young New York man, with a bright, handsome face, had been lying several months from a most disagreeable wound, receiv'd at Bull Run. A bullet had shot him right through the bladder, hitting him front, low in the belly, and coming out back. He had suffer'd much—the water came out of the wound, by slow but steady quantities, for many weeks—so that he lay almost constantly in a sort of puddle—and there were other disagreeable circumstances. He was of good heart, however. At present comparatively comfortable, had a bad throat, was delighted with a stick of horehound candy I gave him, with one or two other trifles.

Whitman, *Specimen Days*, in *Prose Works*, pp. 29–30.

Comparable to *Specimen Days* is the diary of Mary Boykin Chesnut (1823–1886) compiled during the Civil War, revised twenty years later, and finally published in 1905 as *A Diary from Dixie*. Chesnut was the wife of a southern senator and plantation owner, and her diary provides insights into Confederate politics and domestic life. In some cases, these are seen through the lens of the Reconstruction-era politics.

The Private Mary Chesnut: The Unpublished Civil War Diaries (1984) contains her defense of southern aristocratic womanhood set against the sexual immorality of slaveholders and female slaves, whom she regards unsympathetically as tempters who lure respectable men into adultery and miscegenation. Like Whitman, Chesnut does not provide an organizing narrative apart from the chronology of the war; the diary, however, does provide a consistent critique of the contradictions of southern culture, particularly with regard to slavery and gender roles.

AFRICAN AMERICAN AUTOBIOGRAPHY

At least a hundred autobiographies by African Americans were published after the Civil War and before the Harlem Renaissance of the 1920s and 1930s. Slave narratives—the most common form in the antebellum period—often participated in the Franklinian tradition of an interconnected spiritual and secular ascent culminating in manumission. *Narrative of the Life of Frederick Douglass, an American Slave, Written by Himself* (1845) is the most famous and influential example of the genre. Powerful as the *Narrative* is, Douglass (1818–1895) depicts himself less as an individual than as an iconic slave appealing to the sentiments of white readers: "Am I Not a Man and a Brother?"

The period after the abolition of slavery required a reconfiguration of the social and political aims of African Americans as a group. If antebellum slave narrative dramatized the quest for individual and collective freedom, postbellum autobiographies focused on the acquisition of political power, the building of institutions, and the achievement of economic independence within the dominant culture. In this sense, African American autobiography also reflects the cultural shift from Romantic individualism mingled with evangelical Christianity to a more secular, materialist outlook based on the emerging realist sciences of sociology and economics. Antebellum slave narrators struggled for freedom; postbellum autobiographers struggled to achieve a dignified, bourgeois way of life in the midst of ongoing racial discrimination. The evolution from Douglass's *Narrative* to his *My Bondage and My Freedom* (1855) and *The Life and Times of Frederick Douglass* (1882; rev. ed., 1892) reflects these larger patterns in African American autobiography. Douglass increasingly deals with his activities as a public figure—the "life and letters" mode—rather than dwelling on his experiences as a slave, from which he is increasingly detached (compare, for example, the succeeding versions of his battle with Covey, the slave breaker). As the century advanced, the image of Douglass as a slave—brutalized but intelligent, violent but pitiable—began to seem unsuitable as an exemplar on which to base the social advancement of African Americans.

Even as the Franklinian qualities of American autobiography were being questioned by writers such as Mark Twain (1835–1910), these same qualities were magnified in many African American autobiographies—particularly during the Jim Crow era—such as Henry Ossian Flipper's *The Colored Cadet at West Point* (1878), *Out of the Ditch: A True Story of an Ex-Slave* (1910) by Joseph Vance Lewis, William Holtzclaw's *Black Man's Burden* (1915), and *From Slavery to Affluence: Memoirs of Robert Anderson, Ex-Slave* (1927). These works avoid expressions of outrage against racial injustice and thus seem alien to moral sensibilities shaped by the civil rights movement of the late twentieth century. Flipper, for example, was subjected to dehumanizing cruelty and ostracism at West Point, but he does not criticize his classmates or the institutional support for racism; instead, he emphasizes his optimism about his future as a professional soldier (ironically, he would be unjustly court-martialed in 1881). Racism as a social pathology is not so much challenged by many African American autobiographers in this era as it is considered a surmountable hurdle on the road to success. These works encouraged African Americans to stifle their anger, demonstrate dignified moral superiority, and quietly build institutions.

The most influential African American autobiographer of this era was by far Booker T. Washington (1856–1915), the founder of Tuskegee Institute in 1881 and the author of *Up from Slavery: An Autobiography* (1901). Written in a clear, plain style comparable to Grant's, Washington's autobiography presents him as a successful man who never takes a moment's rest and who shows the way to economic independence for other African Americans. The work is written less for literary readers than for the upwardly mobile young man, the African American heir to Franklin and Douglass. Washington emphasized cleanliness, good manners, and industrial education rather than political resistance and access to elite institutions. Washington's views of education and support for racial separatism made him vulnerable to the claim that he was casting African Americans as a permanently menial class, a charge that would be made forcefully by W. E. B. Du Bois (1863–1963) in his semiautobiographical *The Souls of Black Folk: Essays and Sketches* (1903).

William Pickens's autobiography, *The Heir of Slaves* (1911), later revised under the title *Bursting Bonds* (1923), follows Du Bois rather than Washington, arguing that African Americans are being made to serve interests that are not their own. Like Washington, Pickens rose up from a slave family to become a professor at Talladega College in Alabama. But Pickens expresses his disillusionment with white control of ostensibly black institutions, and in fact left the academy to work for the newly formed National Association for the Advancement of Colored People. Pickens's book, along with Du Bois's, represents the transformation of African American autobiography from the Franklinian narratives of upward mobility (culminating in Washington's accomodationism) toward a more inward-looking and skeptical view of American culture—and a more militant opposition to white racism—during the Harlem Renaissance.

IMMIGRANT AUTOBIOGRAPHY

There are some affinities between African American autobiography and the life writings of the immigrants who came to the United States in unprecedented numbers in the late nineteenth and early twentieth centuries (at least 13 million between 1890 and 1910), often settling in major cities on the east coast. The autobiographies of immigrants during this era function partly as guides to survival and assimilation into a new culture, particularly a highly diverse, polyglot, urban culture. Just as Washington and Du Bois represented different outlooks on racism, recent immigrants presented a contrast between successful assimilation and group solidarity and political and economic exploitation.

The Danish immigrant Jacob Riis is best remembered for providing visceral, visual representation to accompany the many textual descriptions of the shame of the cities, where millions of recent immigrants lived in extreme poverty. His autobiography, *The Making of an American* (1901), describes the suffering he endured as a new arrival in America but also narrates the means by which Riis was able to elevate himself above drudgery, to marry well, and to become the personal friend of Theodore Roosevelt (who, incidentally, published his own autobiography in 1913). Over the course of his social ascent, Riis considers the complexity of his relationship to his former identity. He lost his Danish identity and became, for better or worse, "an American."

Mary Antin (1881–1949) describes a similar process of successful assimilation, though with less ambivalence, in *The Promised Land* (1912), originally serialized in the *Atlantic Monthly* in 1911. Antin depicts the sufferings of Jewish people in Polotsk, Russia: forced conscription, police persecution, and a prohibition on attending school. She embraces a new American identity given her by the public schools; she even changes her name from Maryashe. Antin develops an almost Emersonian view of universal human nature, though she can no longer think of herself as a Russian Jew, despite still feeling concern for the plight of her people.

There is often a note of loss in the accounts of assimilated immigrants. In *The Rise of David Levinsky* (1917), Abraham Cahan presents a fictional version of the successful immigrant's life and establishes a link between the novel and autobiography by alluding to Franklin's arrival in Philadelphia. Levinsky enters the city with only a few pennies and rises to become a millionaire in the clothing industry; ultimately, he is unhappy because he is alienated from the self he left behind to become an American. Just as the bourgeois African American suffers from a form of "double consciousness" and risks alienation from what seem to be more authentic origins (as in Charles Chesnutt's 1899 short story, "The Wife of His Youth"), Cahan's Jewish immigrant cannot integrate the wealthy person he has become with the poor child he once was. Levinksy's success is complicated by a sense of tragic loss.

Alexander Berkman's *Prison Memoirs of an Anarchist* (1912) is in most respects a refutation of the Franklinian dream of success for immigrants. Berkman is also a Russian Jewish immigrant, but, instead of pursuing business, he becomes an anarchist and a friend of Emma Goldman. Berkman is radicalized by his experiences of poverty and his disillusionment with the dream of American equality and opportunity. In 1892 he attempts to assassinate the Gilded Age industrialist Henry Clay Frick, but he fails and is sentenced to twenty years in prison. There he develops a fierce solidarity with his fellow prisoners, and ultimately devotes his life to them, becoming a kind of anti-success story, which paradoxically leads to Berkman's redemption through nonviolence and service to the oppressed.

WOMEN AND AUTOBIOGRAPHY

The traditions of spiritual self-examination, diary keeping, and private, introspective verse were kept alive throughout the nineteenth century largely by women, for example, in the poetry of Emily Dickinson and the diaries of Mary Boykin Chesnut. Although women were gaining ground at that time and into the Progressive Era, they still had fewer opportunities to enter the professions, assume positions of leadership, or otherwise gain the kind of public attention that most often led men to publish autobiographical works. There were notable exceptions, such as Laura Smith Haviland, a Quaker abolitionist whose *A Woman's Life-Work* (1881) was one of the most widely circulated American women's autobiographies before the twentieth century. Among several works by leaders of the early women's movement, Elizabeth Cady Stanton's *Eighty Years and More (1815–1897): Reminiscences of Elizabeth Cady Stanton* (1898) provides an authoritative personal history. There are also several memoirs of women's literary activities, such as Annie Fields's *Authors and Friends* (1896) and Julia Ward Howe's *Reminiscences 1819–1899* (1899).

In general, women who published autobiographical writings in the late nineteenth century tended to avoid exposing their private lives to the public gaze. The so-called New Women began to find professional opportunities in teaching, missionary work, social services, nursing, and journalism, but those who wrote tended to emphasize their public actions more than their private thoughts, possibly because they embraced realist objectivity and were turning away from a sentimentalist emphasis on emotions associated with Victorian womanhood. Jane Addams's *Twenty Years at Hull-House* (1910) begins with childhood impressions but is primarily an account of hands-on social activism (the building of "Settlement Houses" for immigrants in Chicago). Addams (1860–1936), like other reformers, does not probe the complexities of her unique personal development so much as consider her participation in larger social forces.

Possibly the most widely read autobiography ever written by an American woman is Helen Keller's *The Story of My Life* (1902). Keller (1880–1968) presents the story of how she prevailed over deafness and blindness brought on by a childhood illness and learned to read and speak through the intervention of a progressive teacher, Anne Sullivan, who overcame her own physical disabilities and abandonment by her parents. In many respects, Helen's education by Anne is an early feminist parable—resonating with African American and immigrant autobiographies—about the capacity of women to educate one another and overcome seemingly natural limitations. With her teacher, Keller goes on to become famous and to contribute toward building new social institutions, such as the American Federation for the Blind, for previously neglected groups.

Lucy Larcom's *A New England Girlhood: Outlined from Memory* (1889) is partly an elegy for the lost New England of her youth, which Larcom eventually left behind to become a missionary teacher in the American West. Before leaving, however, she worked as a spinning girl in the mill town of Lowell, Massachusetts, where she, along with many other young women, were for the first time paid for their work. They also attended lectures, produced newspapers and magazines, and participated in a kind of protofeminist community, which would vanish by the end of the century, as foreign immigrants replaced the more valued native-born

workers. Like other biographers in the era of realism, Larcom sees herself as representative of the societal forces of her time; her work, however, also expresses the sense of loss that comes with modernization and the desire, characteristic of the local color movement, to preserve some memory of what regional cultures were like before the industrialization and urbanization that followed the Civil War. This tendency, of course, was not exclusive to women writers.

MODERNITY, LOSS, AND THE FRAGMENTATION OF THE SELF

The period between the Civil War and World War I was characterized by a sense of disruption and loss greater than any earlier period in American history. Many autobiographers were stimulated by a desire to return to a lost past in American history, which was analogous to the desire to revisit the experiences of childhood innocence. This shift can be seen in the paintings of Winslow Homer, from Civil War scenes to images of childhood such as *Snap the Whip* (1872), as well as pastoral scenes of hunting and depictions of traditional seaboard culture. A similar impulse is demonstrated by the novelist William Dean Howells (1837–1920) in *A Boy's Town* (1890), *My Year in a Log Cabin* (1893), and *Years of My Youth* (1916), as well as in the autobiographical works of Henry James (1843–1916) such as *A Small Boy and Others* (1913), *Notes of a Son and Brother* (1914), and *The Middle Years* (1917). James lamented the shallowness of American culture, but he repeatedly sought some explanation for his identity by meditating on the years of his childhood, which he describes as if he were actually reliving the experiences with an intensity acquired through adult understanding. In a period of rapid change and dislocation, in which authors felt the loss of a grounded identity, autobiographies reflected a larger impulse in American culture—a sense of an infinitely regressing past that was somehow better than the present.

In some respects, the American West, which was opened to full-scale settlement after the Civil War, provided a means of national rejuvenation: the process of settlement could begin anew, and those who remained in the East could fantasize about the durability of American innocence. Western local colorists such as Bret Harte, Hamlin Garland, and Mark Twain epitomized and capitalized on this element of postbellum culture. Twain's semiautobiographical *The Adventures of Tom Sawyer* (1876), *Life on the Mississippi* (1883), and *Adventures of Huckleberry Finn* (1885) present an antebellum American culture—regional, folksy, adventuresome, irreverent—to which many back east longed

HELEN KELLER'S *THE STORY OF MY LIFE*

Helen Keller's The Story of My Life *is, possibly, the most influential autobiography written by an American woman, and it is a landmark work in disability studies. Blind and deaf from infancy, Keller describes how she learned to speak under the instruction of a progressive female teacher. In addition to its factual basis, Keller's account is an allegory of the circumstances of women achieving a public voice in the late nineteenth century.*

It was in the spring of 1890 that I learned to speak. The impulse to utter audible sounds had always been strong within me. I used to make noises, keeping one hand on my throat while the other hand felt the movements of my lips. I was pleased with anything that made a noise and liked to feel the cat purr and the dog bark. I also liked to keep my hand on a singer's throat, or on a piano when it was being played. . . .

[My teacher's] method was this: she passed my hand lightly over her face, and let me feel the position of her tongue and lips when she made a sound. I was eager to imitate every motion and in an hour had learned six elements of speech: M, P, A, S, T, I. Miss Fuller gave me eleven lessons in all. I shall never forget the surprise and delight I felt when I uttered my first connected sentence, "It is warm." True, they were broken and stammering syllables; but they were human speech. My soul, conscious of new strength, came out of bondage, and was reaching through those broken symbols of speech to all knowledge and all faith.

No deaf child who has earnestly tried to speak the words which he has never heard—to come out of the prison of silence, where no tone of love, no song of bird, no strain of music ever pierces the stillness—can forget the thrill of surprise, the joy of discovery which came over him when he uttered his first word. Only such a one can appreciate the eagerness with which I talked to my toys, to stones, trees, birds and dumb animals, or the delight I felt when at my call Mildred ran to me or my dogs obeyed my commands. It is an unspeakable boon to me to be able to speak in winged words that need no interpretation. As I talked, happy thoughts fluttered up out of my words that might perhaps have struggled in vain to escape my fingers. . . .

All teachers of the deaf . . . appreciate the peculiar difficulties with which I had to contend. In reading my teacher's lips I was wholly dependent on my fingers: I had to use the sense of touch in catching the vibrations of the throat, the movements of the mouth and the expression of the face; and often this sense was at fault. In such cases I was forced to repeat the words or sentences, sometimes for hours, until I felt the proper ring in my own voice. My work was practice, practice, practice. Discouragement and weariness cast me down frequently; but the next moment the thought that I should soon be at home and show my loved ones what I had accomplished, spurred me on, and I eagerly looked forward to their pleasure in my achievement.

"My little sister will understand me now," was a thought stronger than all obstacles. I used to repeat ecstatically, "I am not dumb now." I could not be despondent while I anticipated the delight of talking to my mother and reading her responses from her lips. . . .

When I had made speech my own, I could not wait to go home. . . . Almost before I knew it, the train stopped at the Tuscumbia station, and there on the platform stood the whole family. My eyes fill with tears now as I think how my mother pressed me close to her, speechless and trembling with delight, taking in every syllable that I spoke, while little Mildred seized my free hand and kissed it and danced, and my father expressed his pride and affection in a big silence. It was as if Isaiah's prophecy had been fulfilled in me, "The mountains and the hills shall break forth before you into singing, and all the trees of the field shall clap their hands!"

Keller, *The Story of My Life*, pp. 58–62.

to return, even if, as Twain abundantly shows, it was no better than the present (and might have been a good deal worse). Twain and other western regionalists created—and critiqued—an imagined national past in which time stood still and everyone had a deep-rooted sense of belonging in a place. That sense is reflected with less ambivalence in such autobiographical works as Mary Austin's *The Land of Little Rain* (1903) and John Muir's *My First Summer in the Sierra* (1911).

When Twain came to write his own autobiography, which was published posthumously in 1924, he acknowledged the artificiality of the process. There were many shameful incidents in his life that might make good stories, he said, but he could not bear to put them on paper. And for all his candor, Twain's fragmentary, episodic style suggests an unseen audience whose reactions he imagines and for whom he constructs himself as useful fiction. In some respects, Twain anticipates the modern suspicion surrounding autobiographical writing, with its reliance on a faulty memory and the manifold motivations—conscious and unconscious—for fabrication and concealment.

The Education of Henry Adams, written between 1905 and 1907 (privately circulated in 1907 but not published until 1918), is generally regarded as the end of the tradition of the self-made man and the beginning of modern autobiography. Adams (1838–1918) writes about himself in the third person, as if the present self had no connection to the past. *The Education* is an account of the author's intellectual development, though it is an education that leaves him ill equipped for life in the present. Although he came from a family in which it was almost assumed he would become president of the United States, historical forces relegated Adams to the sidelines of political power, making him merely an observer of the major events of his time. Perhaps the most complex experiment in American autobiography up to that time, *The Education* suggests that self-knowledge is impossible except through distance and detachment, and that as a result individuals are not free to choose their own destinies. One does not choose success; the self is a manikin constructed by historical forces such as the medieval conception of the Virgin or the dynamo of the machine age.

Although the Franklin model would remain the dominant form of self-representation throughout the twentieth century, intellectual writers—particularly as modernism replaced realism in the aftermath of World War I—could no longer believe in the possibility of self-determination and the heroic individualism that had characterized American autobiography for the previous century.

See also The Autobiography of an Ex-Colored Man; Biography; Civil War Memoirs; The Education of Henry Adams; The Personal Memoirs of U. S. Grant; The Promised Land; The Rise of David Levinsky; Success; Up from Slavery

BIBLIOGRAPHY

Primary Works

Adams, Henry. *The Education of Henry Adams: An Autobiography*. Boston: Houghton Mifflin, 1918.

Antin, Mary. *The Promised Land*. Boston: Houghton Mifflin, 1912.

Barnum, P. T. *Struggles and Triumphs; or, Forty Years' Recollections of P. T. Barnum, Written by Himself*. Hartford: J. B. Burr, 1869.

Berkman, Alexander. *Prison Memoirs of an Anarchist*. New York: Mother Earth, 1912.

Cahan, Abraham. *The Rise of David Levinsky: A Novel*. New York: Harper & Brothers, 1917.

Chesnut, Mary Boykin. *A Diary from Dixie*. New York: Appleton, 1905.

Douglass, Frederick. *The Life and Times of Frederick Douglass*. Hartford: Park, 1882.

Du Bois, W. E. B. *The Souls of Black Folk: Essays and Sketches*. Chicago: A. C. McClurg, 1903.

Grant, U. S. *Personal Memoirs of U. S. Grant*. New York: C. L. Webster and Company, 1885–1886.

Keller, Helen. *The Story of My Life*. New York: Doubleday, 1902.

Larcom, Lucy. *A New England Girlhood: Outlined from Memory*. Boston: Houghton Mifflin, 1889.

Pickens, William. *Bursting Bonds; Enlarged Edition, The Heir of Slaves*. Boston: Jordan and More Press, 1923.

Riis, Jacob. *The Making of an American*. New York: Macmillan, 1901.

Twain, Mark. *Mark Twain's Autobiography of Mark Twain*. New York; Harper & Brothers, 1924.

Washington, Booker T. *Up from Slavery: An Autobiography*. New York: Doubleday and Company, 1901.

Whitman, Walt. *Specimen Days and Collect*. Philadelphia: Rees Welsh, 1882. Reprinted in his *Prose Works*. Philadelphia: David McKay, 1892.

Secondary Works

Andrews, William L. "Forgotten Voices of Afro-American Autobiography, 1865–1930." *a/b: Auto/biography Studies* 2 (fall 1986): 21–27.

Boelhower, William. "The Making of Ethnic Autobiography in the United States." In *American Autobiography: Retrospect and Prospect*, edited by Paul John Eakin, pp. 123–141. Madison: University of Wisconsin Press, 1991.

Burr, Anna Robeson. *Autobiography, a Critical and Comparative Study*. Boston: Houghton Mifflin, 1909.

Cawelti, John G. *Apostles of the Self-Made Man: Changing Concepts of Success in America.* Chicago: University of Chicago Press, 1965.

Cooley, Thomas. *Educated Lives: The Rise of Modern Autobiography in America.* Columbus: Ohio State University Press, 1976.

Couser, G. Thomas. *Altered Egos: Authority in American Autobiography.* New York: Oxford University Press, 1989.

Couser, G. Thomas. *American Autobiography: The Prophetic Mode.* Amherst: University of Massachusetts Press, 1979.

Cox, James M. *Recovering Literature's Lost Ground: Essays in American Autobiography.* Baton Rouge: Louisiana State University Press, 1989.

Egan, Susanna. "'Self'-Conscious History: American Autobiography after the Civil War." In *American Autobiography: Retrospect and Prospect,* edited by Paul John Eakin, pp. 70–94. Madison: University of Wisconsin Press, 1991.

Holly, Carol. "Nineteenth-Century Autobiographies of Affiliation: The Case of Catherine Sedgwick and Lucy Larcom." In *American Autobiography: Retrospect and Prospect,* edited by Paul John Eakin, pp. 216–234. Madison: University of Wisconsin Press, 1991.

Howells, William Dean. "Editor's Easy Chair." *Harper's Monthly Magazine* 119 (1909): 796–798.

Jelinek, Estelle C. *The Tradition of Women's Autobiography from Antiquity to the Present.* New York: Twayne, 1986.

Kaplan, Louis. *A Bibliography of American Autobiographies.* Madison: University of Wisconsin Press, 1962.

Sayre, Robert F. *The Examined Self: Benjamin Franklin, Henry Adams, Henry James.* Madison: University of Wisconsin Press, 1964.

Sayre, Robert F., ed. *American Lives: An Anthology of Autobiographical Writing.* Madison: University of Wisconsin Press, 1994.

William Pannapacker

James Weldon Johnson. THE LIBRARY OF CONGRESS

THE AUTOBIOGRAPHY OF AN EX-COLORED MAN

James Weldon Johnson's only novel, *The Autobiography of an Ex-Colored Man,* charts the restless movement of a light-skinned man across boundaries of race, class, and region in turn-of-the-century America. Johnson (1871–1938) began writing what would be his most famous work in 1905, at a moment marked by his own restlessness. Only five years earlier, Johnson had joined his brother, J. Rosamond Johnson, in New York City to write song lyrics for musical theater, leaving behind his relatively settled life in Jacksonville, Florida, as a high school principal and newspaper editor who had recently passed the state bar and was engaged to be married. The Johnsons, along with their partner Bob Cole, quickly became the most successful African American songwriting team in musical theater. But while Johnson enjoyed this success, and the influence it brought, he soon found himself craving "escape" and "a little stillness of the spirit," as he put it in his memoir, *Along This Way: The Autobiography of James Weldon Johnson* (p. 223). He enrolled in literature classes at Columbia, began writing poetry and what would become his novel, and cultivated his connections in politics. With the help of Booker T. Washington, he was appointed U.S. consul in Venezuela (1906) and Nicaragua (1909–1913), and at the latter post, he wrote the bulk of *The Autobiography of an Ex-Colored Man* and saw it published, anonymously, by the small Boston house of Sherman, French and Company in 1912.

As its title suggests, *The Autobiography* is a first-person account of the life of a man who has disavowed his blackness, offering its readers a perspective on American race relations from one who has lived on

> *Johnson's narrator, a light-skinned African American who "passes" as white, never experiences race as a stable or fixed marker of his identity. He thus embodies a modernist departure from the tragic mulattoes of nineteenth-century fiction.*
>
> ---
>
> It is difficult for me to analyse [*sic*] my feelings concerning my present position in the world. Sometimes it seems to me that I have never really been a Negro, that I have been only a privileged spectator of their inner life; at other times I feel that I have been a coward, a deserter, and I am possessed by a strange longing for my mother's people.
>
> *The Autobiography of an Ex-Coloured Man*, p. 210.

both sides of the "color line." With its author's name withheld, the work's first reviewers generally took the claims of its preface, attributed to the publishers though probably written by Johnson himself, at face value: this was a work of sociological interest, offering the (presumed white) reader an authentic "view of the inner life of the Negro in America" (p. xl). Several black critics saw through its nonfictional guise (Jessie Fauset in *The Crisis,* for example, suggested it was fiction based on fact), and some southern white reviewers insisted it was fiction on the basis that a black man could never actually pass as white. Members of the black entertainment world in New York, however, variously attributed its authorship to light-skinned musicians known to be "passing" as white. Why Johnson withheld his name is not clear. Although he claims to have enjoyed the challenge of fooling his readers, he may also have chosen, along with his publishers, the genre of autobiography for its greater marketability, particularly given the degree to which his novel diverges from the more conventional realism being published by African Americans at the time.

Alfred A. Knopf reissued the novel at the height of the Harlem Renaissance in 1927, with Johnson's name finally attached, an introduction by Carl Van Vechten (1880–1964), and a book jacket illustrated by Aaron Douglass. By then, the novel's success was ensured by Johnson's reputation as a leader of the National Association for the Advancement of Colored People (NAACP), as the editor of *The Book of American Negro Poetry* (1922), and as coeditor (with

his brother) of *The Books of American Negro Spirituals* (1925–1926). He was also, by then, a recognized poet; *God's Trombones,* which would become his most famous book of poetry, was also published in 1927. While *The Autobiography* was now recognized as fictional, and indeed retrospectively hailed as the first major novel of the Negro Renaissance, it was still appreciated more for its sociological than literary value. Van Vechten's introduction, which made clear that Johnson and his narrator were not one and the same, remarks how it nonetheless "reads like a composite autobiography of the Negro in the United States in modern times" (p. xxxiv). While much of the narrative does read like an ethnographic essay covering many aspects of black American life, subsequent critics would be more interested in how the narrator's journey through and across the American racial landscape seems fraught with confusion, desire, regret, and bitterness. Indeed, the uneasy relationship between the unnamed narrator's detached perspective on and anxious investment in his own story makes this novel's point of view notably difficult to pin down and makes the novel a distinctly modern, and for some postmodern, narrative.

BRIEF SYNOPSIS

After introducing himself as someone with a "great secret," motivated by the impulse to confess as well as the perverse desire to "play with fire," the narrator begins quite conventionally with his origins (p. 3). Born in Georgia shortly after the Civil War, he recalls his white father only as an occasional, shadowy visitor to his mother's cottage, notable mainly for his shiny shoes and gold chain and watch. When his father becomes engaged to a southern white woman, the narrator and his mother are sent to live in Connecticut. To supplement the occasional checks she receives from her former lover, the narrator's mother works as a seamstress and raises her son without reference to his race. The narrator assumes he is white until a schoolteacher publicly identifies him otherwise during an informal school drill, a moment that introduces him to blackness as something mysterious and intangible, and leads him to a Du Boisian sense of "double consciousness."

As a teenager, the narrator seeks out books that can teach him about his "race," from *Uncle Tom's Cabin* (1852) to Frederick Douglass's slave narrative, while he also devotes himself to the study of classical piano, showing a musical talent that endears him to his father on his one and only visit to his secret family. A black classmate's graduation speech about Toussaint-Louverture awakens the narrator's ambition to become a "great coloured man, to reflect credit on the race and gain fame for myself" (p. 46), and this ambition leads him, after his mother's untimely death, back to the South to study at Atlanta University, eventually, one imagines, to embark on a career devoted to the "uplift" of the race.

The novel, however, frustrates this conventional narrative of "uplift," as it initiates the narrator's decidedly nonlinear journey into adulthood. When all of his money is stolen, the narrator abandons the idea of college and heads to Jacksonville (Johnson's home town) where he finds work in a cigar-making factory and begins to demonstrate a remarkable talent for adapting to different cultural environments. He quickly learns Spanish well enough to be hired as a "reader," keeping the Cuban cigar makers entertained with novels and newspapers, while he also gains his first real entry into what he calls "the freemasonry of the race" (p. 74) by giving piano lessons and going to church within the middle-class African American community.

When the cigar factory suddenly shuts down, however, the narrator abruptly returns north to seek work in New York, where he enters the emerging realm of "black Bohemia." Falling in with a crowd of gamblers, the narrator begins to spend time at the "Club," a gathering place for black entertainers and sports celebrities, and the place where he hears ragtime piano for the first time and thereby escapes the seduction of gambling. Impressed by the capacity of a "natural musician" (p. 101) without any formal training to produce such stirring and novel music, the narrator learns to produce his own ragtime performances of the classical repertoire. In so doing, he not only gives musical expression to his biracial identity, but he also distinguishes himself as the first to "rag the classics" and quickly becomes, he claims, "the best rag-time-player in New York" (p. 115). This section of the novel offers not only a detailed look at black Bohemia (which Johnson would echo in his cultural history, *Black Manhattan* [1930]), but also an early—and oft-cited—discussion of the significance of ragtime to American music.

The narrator's next move begins when a world-weary millionaire, one of the white "slummers" at the Club, finds himself so drawn to the narrator's ragtime playing that he hires him to play for his parties and, at times, for his own private enjoyment. The millionaire eventually whisks the narrator away to Europe as his paid companion, rescuing him from an entanglement with a rich white "widow" and her vengeful—and eventually murderous—black lover. After long, culturally enlightening stays in Paris, London, and Berlin, the narrator yet again dramatically changes his course, this time at his own instigation. After hearing a

German musician use one of his ragtime pieces as the basis for "classical" composition, he becomes determined to fulfill his childhood ambition to be a "great coloured man" by composing classical music based on black folk music (p. 46).

This desire takes him back to the American South, where he hopes to "catch the spirit of the Negro in his relatively primitive state" (p. 173) in the poorest and most rural communities. At a "big meeting" he experiences—and describes at length—the virtuosic performances of a black preacher and a song leader, which move him beyond expectation and, perhaps, beyond his capacity to "catch" with pen and paper. The last major turning point of the narrative soon follows: the narrator witnesses a black man being burned alive before a crowd of whites, many of them cheering at the spectacle, and feels such despair at its injustice, as well as "shame, unbearable shame" at belonging to so brutalized a people, that he completely abandons his ambitions and his "blackness." He moves back to New York to live as a white man, where he becomes in every way the image of modern American success, making his fortune in real estate and marrying a "lily white" woman with whom he has two children. He closes his narrative with the admission that, while he remains committed to keeping his children safely "white," and thus to passing, he lives with regret that he "has sold his birthright for a mess of pottage" (p. 211).

CRITICAL HISTORY

The scholarship on Johnson's novel, beginning in the late 1950s, shows a remarkable diversity of approaches and concerns, which register not only changing critical trends but also the text's central ambiguities. Three main concerns punctuate this critical history. First came the project of articulating an African American literary canon, and thus of situating Johnson's text in relation to those that preceded and succeeded it. Several early scholars focused on how the first-person narrative echoed or inverted slave narrative conventions, and they also saw it as anticipating postwar "protest" fiction such as Ralph Ellison's *Invisible Man* (1952). Much of this first wave of criticism was concerned with establishing *The Autobiography*'s canonical value as an important link between nineteenth- and twentieth-century traditions.

In the 1970s and 1980s, with its canonical status perhaps ensured, critics began to recognize and explore the novel's "irony," both within and toward the narrator's perspective. Discussion had already emerged about the reliability or unreliability of Johnson's narrator, but scholars now tended to emphasize the narrator's moments of blindness to his own prejudices and contradictions and to lament his "failure" to fully embrace his blackness. Some cast the narrator as an anti-hero who has betrayed his race, while others read him more tragically as trapped within a racist society and ideology. Several critics took issue that to emphasize Johnson's ironic detachment from his narrator ignores the degree to which the author sympathizes with his narrator and the more ambiguous relationship between irony and tragedy in this novel.

This concern with irony sowed the seeds for more recent critical interest in the politics of "passing" in the novel. Rather than lament the narrator's failure to claim his blackness, scholars since the 1990s tend to see the narrator's movement across the color line as a particularly rich illustration of the performativity of racial identity and, indeed, of identity in general. For these critics, the novel presents a postmodern critique of, rather than a modern search for, authentic selfhood.

Finally, it should be noted that Johnson's novel has long found a place in discussions of early-twentieth-century American music, from early histories of ragtime and African American composers to more recent work on the relationship between music and constructions of race.

See also Autobiography; Miscegnation; Race Novels; Success; Violence

BIBLIOGRAPHY
Primary Works
Johnson, James Weldon. *Along This Way: The Autobiography of James Weldon Johnson*. New York: Viking Press, 1933.

Johnson, James Weldon. 1912, 1927. *The Autobiography of an Ex-Coloured Man*. New York: Vintage Books, 1989. The "u" in "Coloured" was added after the first edition.

Johnson, James Weldon. *Black Manhattan*. New York: Knopf, 1930.

Secondary Works
Baker Jr., Houston. "A Forgotten Prototype: *The Autobiography of an Ex-Colored Man* and *Invisible Man*." In *Singers of Daybreak: Studies in Black American Literature*. Washington, D.C.: Howard University Press, 1974.

Bone, Robert. *The Negro Novel in America*. New Haven, Conn.: Yale University Press, 1965.

Fleming, Robert. "Irony as a Key to Johnson's *The Autobiography of an Ex-Coloured Man*." *American Literature* 43 (1971): 83–96.

Garrett, Marvin P. "Early Recollections and Structural Irony in *The Autobiography of an Ex-Colored Man*." *Critique* 13, no. 2 (1971): 5–14.

Goellnicht, Donald. "Passing as Autobiography: James Weldon Johnson's *The Autobiography of an Ex-Coloured Man*." *African American Review* 30 (1996): 17–33.

Kawash, Samira. "The Epistemology of Race: Knowledge, Visibility, and Passing." In *Dislocating the Color Line: Identity, Hybridity, and Singularity in African-American Narrative*. Stanford, Calif.: Stanford University Press, 1997.

Ruotolo, Cristina L. "James Weldon Johnson and the Autobiography of an Ex-Colored Musician." *American Literature* 72, no. 2 (2000): 249–274.

Skerrett, Joseph T., Jr. "Irony and Symbolic Action in James Weldon Johnson's *The Autobiography of an Ex-Coloured Man*." *American Quarterly* 32 (winter 1980): 540–558.

Stepto, Robert B. "Lost in a Quest: James Weldon Johnson's *The Autobiography of an Ex-Coloured Man*." In *From Behind the Veil: A Study in Afro-American Narrative*. 2nd ed. Urbana: University of Illinois Press, 1991.

Washington, Salim. "Of Black Bards, Known and Unknown: Music as Racial Metaphor in James Weldon Johnson's *The Autobiography of an Ex-Colored Man*." *Callaloo* 25, no. 1 (2002): 233–256.

Cristina L. Ruotolo

THE AWAKENING

By the time Kate Chopin (1851–1904) published her short novel *The Awakening* in April 1899, she had established a modest national reputation as the writer of two well-received volumes of local color short stories, *Bayou Folk* (1894) and *A Night in Acadie* (1897). Her novel was widely reviewed, and the initial buzz over her daring subject matter—female sexuality—produced $102 in royalties the first year. After this initial response, however, the book was quickly forgotten; Chopin received $40 in royalties in 1900 and only $3 in 1901, and despite being reprinted in 1906 by a different publisher, *The Awakening* seemed destined to join her undistinguished first novel, *At Fault* (1890), in oblivion. Later critics, including her first biographer, Daniel S. Rankin, whose study was published in 1932, followed her contemporaries in admiring her short stories, several of which had become well-known anthology pieces, but generally showed little interest in her novels. In the 1950s, however, *The Awakening* was rediscovered by Cyrille Arnavon and Kenneth Eble, who promoted the book in articles and brought it back into print. Arnavon's student Per Seyersted then single-handedly blazed Chopin's path to the American literary canon with two 1969 publications: *Kate Chopin: A Critical Biography* and the two volumes of *The Complete Works of Kate Chopin*. These books provided American

Kate Chopin. THE LIBRARY OF CONGRESS

academics with the tools necessary for the revival in Chopin studies that built in the 1970s and peaked in the 1980s with the publication of several book-length studies, culminating in Emily Toth's exhaustive 1990 biography. *The Awakening* is now one of the most frequently taught novels in college literature courses.

EDNA'S AWAKENINGS

Edna Pontellier experiences several literal awakenings in the course of the novel, but critics have disagreed about the nature of her metaphorical awakening. The first review, published a month before the novel, made the point presciently: "The author has shown herself an artist in the manipulation of a complex character, and faulty as the woman is, she has the magnetism which is essential to the charm of a novel. It is a quality hard to analyze, for it does not seem to be in what she says or does; it is rather, as in life, in what she is" (Monroe, p. 387). Edna has proven to be the sort of "round" character about whom sophisticated readers can completely disagree. While a few early critics interpreted the title as ironic, condemning Edna as an unredeemed and immoral monster, and a few modern critics enshrined her as a noble martyr to feminism, neither reading has proven conclusive. The narrator's occasional intrusions

demonstrate unmistakable sympathy and respect (though falling short of explicit endorsement) for Edna's struggle to achieve personal freedom, yet neither Edna nor Chopin exhibits overt interest in the stock issues of feminist politics. Chopin eschews simplistic melodrama: none of the major male characters is a villain, and even the generally insensitive Léonce visits Doctor Mandelet for "marriage counseling" and follows the good advice he gets from him. When Léonce sends gifts to his family, the ladies "all declared that Mr. Pontellier was the best husband in the world. Mrs. Pontellier was forced to admit that she knew of none better" (*Complete Works*, p. 887). The irony, while palpable, is directed at the cultural codes that distort and trivialize marriage, not at Léonce personally; he really is the best husband in the world of this novel.

Discussions now seldom see Edna in black and white but attempt instead to bring out more subtle patterns drawn in shades of gray. A fundamental open question remains the determination of precisely to what sort of "awakening" the title of the book refers. Indeed, even this apparently simple question is complicated: Chopin's original manuscript is titled "A Solitary Soul," opening the possibility that the decision to spotlight the theme of awakening was at least partly editorial and thus possibly a misleading emphasis. Readers have nevertheless agreed that Edna's awakening to passion and sexual desire constitutes a major theme; early critics were more likely to interpret this as negative and later critics to see it as positive. But most modern critics have seen her awakened sensuality as merely one sign of a larger awakening, variously characterized as aesthetic, cultural, economic, spiritual, philosophical, social, or defined by complex combinations of the above. The critical saga has been brought nearly full circle by several contemporary critics who have condemned Edna as a weak and selfish "adolescent" character who remains oblivious not only to the crucial socioeconomic issues of class, gender, and race but also to the biological imperative that mandates maternal responsibility. Ironically, these postmodern critics often seem to be mirroring the complaints of the moralistic early reviewers about the author's failure to produce a politically correct message for the edification of young readers.

EDNA'S FOILS: MOTHER-WOMEN AND ARTISTS

While the primary male characters in the novel have close antecedents in the works of Gustave Flaubert (1821–1880) and Guy de Maupassant (1850–1893), Chopin rounds out the characterization of her protagonist by juxtaposing her with minor characters, such as Mariequita and Mrs. Highcamp, who embody alternative cultural roles that Edna eventually rejects. As Barbara H. Solomon has noted, the two most obvious foils for Edna are Adèle Ratignolle and Mademoiselle Reisz, who represent the twin poles of Edna's experience. Adèle is the epitome of the respectable "mother-woman" who lives quietly within the conventions of society, selflessly devoted to her husband and children. Mademoiselle Reisz (the title declaring her independence from husband and children and invariably replacing her first name), a gifted musician, is the independent female, who sacrifices love and friendship for her art. Edna's development can be viewed in part as her movement away from the pole of the mother-woman and toward the pole of the artist, a movement enabled by two crucial influences that shape her experience: Reisz's music and the sea. Chopin explicitly links these two influences in describing Edna's response to Mademoiselle Reisz's music: "the very passions themselves were aroused within her soul, swaying it, lashing it, as the waves daily beat upon her splendid body" (*Complete Works,* p. 906). But Reisz's dedication to her art is shown to carry a heavy price—the artist, as she tells Edna, must be a solitary soul, and Reisz herself seems to lead a loveless existence. The difficulty of Edna's quest for a complete life, in which a woman could fulfill herself (serially if not simultaneously) as a wife, mother, artist, lover, and independent individual, is dramatized by the exemplification in Adèle and Reisz of the severely truncated roles available within their culture. Chopin similarly uses the male characters to exemplify the limiting cultural roles available to men: Léonce Pontellier as the husband, Alcée Arobin as the rake, and Robert Lebrun as the chivalric (and chaste) courtly lover combine to exhaust the acceptable possibilities.

THE ENDING

Edna's suicide has provided readers with a comparably durable interpretive problem. The ending exercised the first readers of the novel as much as it does those of the early twenty-first century, and several explicitly conceded that whether the ending would be read as positive or negative would depend largely upon the point of view of the reader. Many reviewers felt that the ending appropriately punishes Edna's behavior. Flaubert's *Madame Bovary* (1857) was defended from charges of immorality with the argument that Emma's suicide constitutes the author's implicit judgment on her, and by analogy Edna's suicide was read as the appropriate wages of her sin. Within this line of analysis, critical responses were divided between those who saw her suicide as a sign of her increasing moral blindness and weakness and those who saw it as a sign of her belated moral awakening and repentance.

Other reviewers, however, found in the ending not poetic justice but a serious artistic flaw. Unlike Flaubert's distanced and objective narrator, Chopin's narrator reveals considerable sympathy for the protagonist, occasionally speaking directly on her behalf in the "editorial" chapters. For many readers the ending betrays the narrative and thematic arc of the body of the novel and seems to have been imported from a sentimental romance in which the moral and social issues that the novel has raised are neutralized and dismissed by the heroine's death rather than squarely addressed and pursued to their conclusion. Emma Bovary's suicide rings true, as Flaubert depicts a weak and desperate person collapsing under great, and inexorably mounting, economic and psychological pressure. But Edna has plenty of money and friends, and she seems to have been steadily gaining strength and independence. In this view the plot provides insufficient realistic justification for Edna to commit suicide when she seems to have already overcome the primary cultural, moral, and material obstacles to her freedom. For many readers it is both inartistic and implausible that Edna, having developed gradually into a powerful and freethinking woman able to change her life and face the world on her own terms, should then kill herself on the last page, apparently because Robert Lebrun abandoned her.

Virtually every school of modern critical theory has been brought to bear on the problem. Cyrille Arnavon, calling the undermotivated suicide the main weakness of the novel, claims that the ending goes beyond Chopin's conscious intentions, and numerous critics have followed his lead in explaining the action as a reflection of Chopin's own deep ambivalence about her heroine's unconventional behavior (indeed Chopin's own "retraction" in *Book News* invites precisely this analysis). Arnavon's solution offers the first psychoanalytic reading, according to which Edna's flight from sexual experience triggers her suicide-escape. William Nelles has suggested that Edna's problem is fundamentally biological rather than psychological: Edna is pregnant by Arobin, a crisis sufficiently taboo, given the social and aesthetic mores of the time, as to provide both the implicit motive for her suicide and the reason that Chopin could not be more explicit about it in the novel. The most popular interpretive move made by critics to get the ending to fit the book, however, is to follow Per Seyersted in reading her suicide metaphorically rather than realistically: "It symbolizes a victory of self-knowledge and authenticity as she fully becomes herself" (p. 194). Several essays have extended Seyersted's approach by reading the novel as mythic rather than realistic: Sandra Gilbert, for example, explicates a feminist myth of Edna as Aphrodite as a matriarchal alternative to the patriarchal myth of Jesus; Rosemary Franklin reads Edna as a version of Psyche, whose obstacles and temptations construct a paradigm of female development (in Edna's case, thwarted development); and Lawrence Thornton adds the myth of Icarus to the list of parallels.

After more than a century of debate, the critical cruxes posed by Chopin's protagonist and her conclusion remain largely unresolved, suggesting that they are grounded in inherent ambiguities or ambivalence rather than merely reflecting the historical vicissitudes of popular or critical mores. The qualities of the novel that have kept it in perpetual interpretive play, along with its relative brevity and readability (not to mention the gender of its author and the timeliness of its revival), have made it one of the most widely taught novels in college literature courses and have ensured its high rank in the literary canon.

LITERARY INFLUENCES

Chopin may have been as widely read in, and as heavily influenced by, contemporary French literature as any American writer of her era. The similarity of the plot of *The Awakening* to that of Flaubert's *Madame Bovary* immediately led Willa Cather to dub it a "Creole *Bovary*." (In a telling shift, Cyrille Arnavon later emended Cather's formulation to an "American *Madame Bovary*" [p. 14] as he lobbied to get Chopin's novel into the canon and to remove the "local color" tag from her work.) The direct influence of Flaubert's plot on Chopin's is undeniable: an upper-class woman with a kind but obtuse husband has serial affairs and eventually commits suicide. Other early reviewers highlighted Chopin's naturalistic theme and refusal to condemn her protagonist as evidence of the influence of Émile Zola (1840–1902). Some later critics have looked beyond narrative sources to the influence of Impressionist painting or the poetry of Walt Whitman (1819–1892) on her style. Such comparisons have been instrumental in the gradual removal of the "local color" label from Chopin's work, and she is now just as likely to be compared to Theodore Dreiser and Stephen Crane as she is to Sarah Orne Jewett.

Chief among Chopin's literary influences, however, is the short fiction of Guy de Maupassant. Chopin herself discusses his impact on her artistic development in a manuscript fragment of her essay "Confidences" from 1896:

> It was at this period of my emerging from the vast solitude in which I had been making my own acquaintance, that I stumbled upon Maupassant. I read his stories and marvelled at them. Here was life, not fiction. . . . Here was a man who had escaped from tradition and authority, who had entered into

himself and looked out upon life through his own being and with his own eyes; and who, in a direct and simple way, told us what he saw. (*Complete Works,* pp. 700–701)

Chopin's admiration of Maupassant's style led her to translate eight of his stories from French into English (three were published, but her proposal for a book of translations was rejected). Maupassant's impact on *The Awakening* is pervasive: it begins with the title, which Seyersted believes was suggested by Maupassant's short story "Réveil" ("Awakening"). The plot of "Réveil," in which a married woman is sexually awakened by a younger man and then yields to the caresses of a playboy, may have helped Chopin to refine the template drawn from Flaubert with respect to her four main characters. Edna's marriage to Léonce is threatened first by her fantasies about Robert and then by her involvement with Alcée. In Maupassant's story, however, the woman awakens to the knowledge that she loves neither of the men, and the story concludes with her return to her husband. Edna's own more complex awakening includes the disillusionment about the lovers—"To-day it is Arobin; to-morrow it will be some one else. It makes no difference to me" (*Complete Works,* p. 999)—but precludes her reconciliation with married life, leading her instead to suicide. The figure of Doctor Mandelet parallels the observant physicians of many Maupassant tales, whose perspicuous judgment, reticence, and detached yet sympathetic perspective mirror that of the narrator and model an ideal reader's response.

THE EARLY RECEPTION OF *THE AWAKENING*

The tale told about the contemporary reception of *The Awakening* is almost as well known as the story told in the novel—and almost as much a fiction. While scholarship has debunked claims that the book was banned from libraries and that the author's career was prematurely ended by savage critical attacks, the myth of the book's martyrdom persists. The components of the myth began to come together shortly after Chopin's death in 1904, when Leonidas Rutledge Whipple wrote in an essay on Chopin for the *Library of Southern Literature* (1907) that the negative reviews of the novel killed Chopin's desire to write, so that she produced nothing in the last five years of her life. Rankin's 1932 biography of Chopin corrected Whipple's mistake, which had been repeated by several critics, noting that Chopin continued to write and publish in the years following the publication of *The Awakening*. But Rankin then put into circulation several fresh rumors. On the basis of interviews with Chopin's surviving children and acquaintances, Rankin asserted that because of harsh reviews the book was removed from the St. Louis Mercantile Library and that Chopin was denied admission to the St. Louis Fine Arts Club.

These claims were repeated in Seyersted's 1969 biography, with the added assertions that the book was also banned by the St. Louis Public Library and that the Wednesday Club, a women's literary group, excluded Chopin from their series on American prose writers in September of 1899 in what was possibly a further affront to her. Yet Seyersted also noted in his biography that Chopin was prominently featured in the Wednesday Club's special program on 29 November 1899 (three days after an adulatory full-page profile of her appeared in the *St. Louis Post-Dispatch*), at which she read a new story to the group. Despite ample evidence that Chopin was a widely admired literary celebrity, misinformation persists. In 1990 Emily Toth attempted to put the myth to rest with "The Alleged Banning of *The Awakening*" (an appendix to her biography of Chopin), in which she demonstrated that the "reminiscences" of Chopin's friends and family upon which much of the myth rests are entirely unsubstantiated, that both St. Louis libraries had bought multiple copies of the novel, and that there is no evidence of the alleged ban. Toth, however, concluded her appendix with a degree of resigned skepticism: "I suspect that most editors and reviewers will continue to proclaim that *The Awakening* was banned" because "Americans do enjoy book-banning stories" (p. 425).

The stories of Chopin's persecution depend largely on the belief that the novel was savagely attacked by critics. Rankin's biography emphasized the harshness and bitterness of the reviews, but many of these reviews can just as easily be seen as positive. The reviewer who quipped that "like most of [Chopin's] work, . . . 'The Awakening' is too strong drink for moral babes, and should be labeled 'poison'"—a blurb often quoted as evidence of the novel's negative reception—in the same article declared the novel "a work of genius." But the bulk of that review was devoted to praise of Chopin's "work of genius," and the reviewer's warning is a satirical jab at "moral babes" rather than an attack on the novel. Chopin's friend Charles L. Deyo had made much the same stipulation about the work's probable reception by immature readers: "No, the book is not for the young person, nor, indeed, for the old person who has no relish for unpleasant truths. For such there is much that is very improper in it, not to say positively unseemly." But taken in context the reviews are both favorable, and the characterization of them as harsh is largely a product of selective emphasis by partisan critics.

Chopin's own reaction to Deyo's review is unambiguous: she sent a copy of it to her publisher with a note commending it as "able and intelligent" (Seyersted, p. 175). Chopin's only public response to the reception of *The Awakening* is a four-sentence note in *Book News:*

> Having a group of people at my disposal, I thought it might be entertaining (to myself) to throw them together and see what would happen. I never dreamed of Mrs. Pontellier making such a mess of things and working out her own damnation as she did. If I had had the slightest intimation of such a thing I would have excluded her from the company. But when I found out what she was up to, the play was half over and it was then too late. ("Aims and Autographs," p. 612)

By the time the comment was published in July, more damning reviews had appeared, and critics have generally assumed that Chopin's comment reveals how stunned and bewildered the book's reception had left her. But Chopin had written the reply in May in response to an enthusiastic review in *Book News*—written by Lucy Monroe, an editor at Chopin's publishing house—that called the novel "remarkable," "subtle," and "brilliant." Chopin's response was written to the favorable early reviews and must be read as modestly self-deprecating humor.

Even the negative reviews typically praised Chopin's style and artistry; critics were divided, however, in their reaction to the controversial subject matter. Many critics emphasized how sympathetically Chopin treats Edna and remarked on the author's compassion for her weak character. But the claim that Chopin—or anyone knowledgeable about the literary marketplace in 1899—would have been astonished and devastated by such a mixed response is condescending. Chopin was far from naive, and she knew perfectly well she was writing controversial material, having had numerous stories rejected for their unconventional subject matter. The myth of Chopin's persecution by the public has frequently been recast as a story of her persecution by male reviewers and her resurrection by feminist critics, but the evidence is even less amenable to this version of the myth: male and female reviewers reacted similarly to the novel, and the rediscovery and republication of Chopin's novel in the 1950s and 1960s was almost entirely the work of influential male critics and editors.

See also Feminism; Naturalism; New Orleans; Realism; Regionalism and Local Color Fiction

BIBLIOGRAPHY

Primary Works

Chopin, Kate. "Aims and Autographs of Authors." *Book News* 17 (July 1899): 612.

Chopin, Kate. *The Awakening.* Chicago: H. S. Stone, 1899.

Chopin, Kate. *The Awakening: An Authoritative Text, Biographical and Historical Contexts, Criticism.* 2nd ed. Edited by Margo Culley. New York: Norton, 1994.

Chopin, Kate. *The Awakening: Complete, Authoritative Text with Biographical, Historical, and Cultural Contexts, Critical History, and Essays from Contemporary Critical Perspectives.* 2nd ed. Edited by Nancy A. Walker. Boston: Bedford/St. Martin's, 2000.

Chopin, Kate. *The Complete Works of Kate Chopin.* 2 vols. Edited by Per Seyersted. Baton Rouge: Louisiana State University Press, 1969.

Secondary Works

Arnavon, Cyrille. Introduction to *Edna,* by Kate Chopin. Paris: Club Bibliophile de France, 1953.

Bloom, Harold, ed. *Kate Chopin.* New York: Chelsea House, 1987.

Bloom, Harold, ed. *Kate Chopin's "The Awakening."* Broomall, Pa.: Chelsea House, 1998.

Boren, Lynda S., and Sara deSaussure Davis, eds. *Kate Chopin Reconsidered: Beyond the Bayou.* Baton Rouge: Louisiana State University Press, 1992.

Cather, Willa. Review of *The Awakening. Pittsburgh Leader,* 8 July 1899, p. 6.

Deyo, C. L. Review of *The Awakening.* In "The Newest Books," *St. Louis Post-Dispatch,* 20 May 1899, p. 4.

Dyer, Joyce. *The Awakening: A Novel of Beginnings.* New York: Twayne, 1993.

Eble, Kenneth. "A Forgotten Novel: Kate Chopin's *The Awakening.*" *Western Humanities Review* 10 (summer 1956): 261–269.

Ewell, Barbara C. *Kate Chopin.* New York: Ungar, 1986.

Franklin, Rosemary F. "*The Awakening* and the Failure of Psyche." *American Literature* 56, no. 4 (December 1984): 510–526.

Gilbert, Sandra M. "The Second Coming of Aphrodite: Kate Chopin's Fantasy of Desire." *Kenyon Review* 5, no. 3 (summer 1983): 42–66.

Koloski, Bernard, ed. *Approaches to Teaching Chopin's "The Awakening."* New York: Modern Language Association of America, 1988.

Martin, Wendy, ed. *New Essays on "The Awakening."* New York: Cambridge University Press, 1988.

Monroe, Lucy. Review of *The Awakening. Book News* 17 (March 1899): 387.

Nelles, William. "Edna Pontellier's Revolt against Nature." *American Literary Realism* 32, no. 1 (fall 1999): 43–50.

Porcher, Frances. "*The Awakening:* Kate Chopin's Novel." *Mirror* 9 (4 May 1899): 6. Review of *The Awakening.*

Rankin, Daniel S. *Kate Chopin and Her Creole Stories.* Philadelphia: University of Pennsylvania Press, 1932.

Seyersted, Per. *Kate Chopin: A Critical Biography.* 1969. Baton Rouge: Louisiana State University Press, 1980.

Skaggs, Peggy. *Kate Chopin.* Boston: Twayne, 1985.

Solomon, Barbara H. "Characters as Foils to Edna." In *Approaches to Teaching Chopin's "The Awakening,"* edited by Bernard Koloski, pp. 114–119. New York: Modern Language Association of America, 1988.

Thornton, Lawrence. "Edna as Icarus: A Mythic Issue." In *Approaches to Teaching Chopin's "The Awakening,"* edited by Bernard Koloski, pp. 138–143. New York: Modern Language Association of America, 1988.

Toth, Emily. *Kate Chopin.* New York: Morrow, 1990.

Whipple, Leonidas Rutledge. "Kate Chopin." In *Library of Southern Literature,* vol. 2, edited by Edwin Anderson Alderman and Joel Chandler Harris, pp. 863–866. Atlanta, Ga.: Martin and Hoyt, 1907.

William Nelles

BANKING AND FINANCE

From the time when the Mayflower landed at Plymouth Rock (1620) until the creation of the Federal Reserve System (1913), Americans exhibited a suspicion of banking and banking regulation. Before 1776 the colonies were agrarian and fiscally conservative. Almost all wealth was fixed in land, buildings, animals, crops, and slaves, as depicted in James Fenimore Cooper's Leatherstocking Tales, especially *The Pioneers* (1823). A few entrepreneurial colonists turned to England for credit, but most borrowed what they needed from family, friends, neighbors, local merchants, or business partners. They repaid these loans when crops were harvested or goods sold. In 1776 no bank existed in the colonies, so the United States sought armament loans from France and other enemies of England and the colonial army asked local merchants for supplies (food and clothing). In exchange for scarce goods, the local merchants received Continental notes (the earliest form of paper money in the United States), but these notes were little more than IOUs from a group of revolutionaries, IOUs that depreciated as soon as the merchants accepted them. After the Revolutionary War the United States chartered a central bank in 1791 and 1816, but the bank's charters expired, and free banking existed between 1837 and 1862, a period during which the United States experienced devastating bank failures (1837 and 1857). In the novel *Pudd'nhead Wilson* (1894), Mark Twain (1835–1910) returns to the America of his youth and briefly depicts the consequences of bank failures on poor Americans, such as Roxana, a former slave who loses her life savings, her entire retirement, when a New Orleans bank fails.

NATIONAL BANKING: BOOMS AND BUSTS, 1863–1912

The National Banking Acts of 1863 and 1864 allowed the federal government to charter banks, but these acts did not create a central bank, a single currency, or a means for regulating the money supply. The United States enacted these new banking regulations to fund the Civil War, not to regulate economic excesses, so despite the passing of these acts the nation experienced financial panics that grew both in length and severity: in 1873 the panic lasted fifty-nine days, in 1893 seventy-seven days, and in 1907 ninety-five days; the economic contractions that followed each panic lasted years. These insidious financial cycles occurred annually, but in the panic years credit became so scarce that banks were forced to suspend transactions, which resulted in bank failures. During the national banking period the United States continued to exhibit a suspicion of both bankers and banking regulation, which allowed a few ruthless financiers to profit even as the country suffered. In 1873 Charles Dudley Warner (1829–1900) and Mark Twain satirized the financial exploits of railroad speculators in their novel *The Gilded Age*, which gave a name to the entire period. Unlike a "golden age," the "gilded age" only appeared rich and prosperous—under the gilding existed financial speculation, corruption, and greed that ruined people's lives. In their novel Twain and Warner burlesque irrational

U.S. BANKING: 1860–1921

1860: More than 1,500 banks exist in the United States

1860–1878: Suspension of gold redemptions by the federal government

1863–1912: National Banking Era

1873: U.S. Coinage Act passes, undermining silver as a standard of evaluation

1873: Third major banking panic of the nineteenth century

1873: Mark Twain and Charles Dudley Warner publish *The Gilded Age*

1874: National Greenback Party formed to promote a liberal monetary policy

1875: U.S. Resumption Act passes, setting 1879 as the year to resume gold redemptions

1878: The Bland-Allison Act requires the U.S. Treasury to buy silver

1890: The Sherman Act requires the treasury to buy additional silver each month

1893: Fourth major banking crisis of the nineteenth century

1893: President Grover Cleveland repeals the silver purchase acts

1896: William Jennings Bryan runs for president on a free-silver platform but fails

1900: The Currency Act sets a rigid gold standard

1901: Frank Norris publishes *The Octopus*

1907: First major banking crisis of the twentieth century

1908: Upton Sinclair publishes *The Moneychangers*

1912: Theodore Dreiser publishes *The Financier*

1913: Federal Reserve System begins, creating a central banking system that still exists

1921: Almost 30,000 banks exist in the United States

---

railroad dealings that permit investors to sell railroad stock to purchase land, then borrow money against the land, then raise bond money from the towns along the new road, then sell portions of the land, and then, just before this financial pyramid collapses, borrow millions more from banks. In *The American Claimant* (1892), a sequel to *The Gilded Age,* Twain again dramatizes American financial excesses by following the exploits and speculations of Colonel Sellers.

On 1 October 1873, the same year Twain published *The Gilded Age,* Jay Cooke & Company of Philadelphia, one of the most prestigious banking firms in the United States, failed, triggering a suspension of banking that culminated in a depression. Although the 1873 panic, like most other panics, occurred in the fall, during a time when western banks required funds to cover grain purchases, railroad speculation, as depicted by Twain, contributed greatly to this economic collapse. Between 1860 and 1873 the miles of railroad track had doubled, so investors purchased railroad stocks at irrational prices, assuming that railroads would continue geometric expansion. But railroads had expanded too quickly, and when revenues from the roads failed to cover debt service, developers borrowed from banks and brokerage houses. These short-term loans worsened the railroads' circumstances, causing loan defaults. Jay Cooke's firm had foolishly invested $15 million in the Northern Pacific Railroad. But even as Cooke failed and the U.S. economy collapsed, a few financiers profited. In Theodore Dreiser's (1871–1945) novel *The Financier* (1912), the main character, Frank Algernon Cowperwood, who is a fictional representation of the financier Charles T. Yerkes (1837–1905), benefits from Cooke's failure: Cowperwood earns a fortune by selling stocks short, selling stocks that he did not own, then purchasing them at a lower price.

Dreiser's novel beautifully illustrates the financial excesses of the national banking period; in fact *The Financier* accurately chronicles most nineteenth-century banking practices and controversies. Cowperwood is born in Philadelphia the year after the Second Bank of the United States closed and free banking began. Cowperwood's father, as a banker in Philadelphia (the center of early American banking), knew Nicholas Biddle (1786–1844), the president of the Second Bank of the United States. In *The Financier,* Dreiser describes briefly the battle between President Andrew Jackson and Nicholas Biddle, characterizing it as one of the great controversies of the day, and later in the novel Dreiser dramatizes the national banking period, a time when laissez-faire banking practices precipitated economic chaos. Cowperwood, like Yerkes, loses a fortune in a relatively small panic caused by the Chicago fire (1871) due to excessive speculation, using his funds, his customer's funds, and Philadelphia tax revenues that were being held in a "sinking fund." These "sinking funds" were created by cities to manage bonds that would finance projects such as roads, utilities, or buildings. To assure investors that the bonds would be repaid, the city formed a "sinking fund" into which they placed taxes earmarked for the payment of interest and the repurchase of bonds. But the city treasurer selected a private financier, such as Yerkes (Cowperwood), to both sell the bonds and manage the sinking fund. Since the city did not expect to earn interest on the sinking fund, the private financier could invest the city's money and keep the profits—a practice that led to speculative investments in streetcar lines and railroads, placing the city's revenues at risk, and that lost or earned fortunes for a few well-connected financiers such as Cowperwood, who loses his and the city's money in the 1871 panic but who recovers his fortune in 1873 when others are losing everything.

The 1873 panic was both a banking and railroad crisis, but the panic of 1893 was more purely a banking crisis. As in the past, eastern banks distrusted western and southern banks and reluctantly loaned them money, so in August 1893, when the money supply tightened, New York banks severely cut currency transfers to rural banks, just as the western banks needed extra funds for harvests. Frank Norris (1870–1902) explores the connections between agriculture and high finance in *The Octopus* (1901) and *The Pit* (1903), the two volumes of his uncompleted Epic of Wheat trilogy. In the first volume, Norris investigates the production of wheat by California farmers whose lands and lives are controlled by the Pacific and Southwestern railroads. The "octopus" of the title is the railroad system that controls grain prices, shipping costs, interest rates, state legislation, and even local newspapers. The second volume, published posthumously, follows the wheat to the Chicago Board of Trade where futures are exchanged. In *The Pit* the main character is a wealthy speculator who is destroyed by an overproduction of wheat. In both novels Norris dramatizes the forces that controlled farmers, and in the projected third novel, Norris planned to follow American wheat to a famine in Europe.

During the panic of 1893, at the same time western banks were seeking credit for harvests, eastern bankers were fearing the "free-silver" movement.

A free-silver victory and subsequent monetary devaluation might have cost bankers a third of their wealth, so many chose not to loan money and placed assets in foreign markets, such as London. This flight of capital caused the federal treasury's gold reserve to fall below $100 million. In the United States, the history of gold as a store of wealth is complex and often misunderstood. Before 1900, the United States might be described as having had an unofficial bimetal standard (silver and gold), but gold backed most banknotes when gold was available. At times, to cover war debt, the federal government suspended gold redemptions, as occurred from 1860 to 1878. During the 1890s the free-silver movement, led by William Jennings Bryan, a populist running for president, called for an official bimetal standard, but Bryan lost his bid for the presidency. With the passage of the Currency Act (1900), the United States for the first time adopted a rigid gold standard, which regulated the money supply without regulating the economy or banks. Writing during this period, Henry Blake Fuller (1857–1929) focused his novels on the financial exploits of city dwellers, capturing fully the banking world of Chicago in *The Cliff-Dwellers* (1893) and *On the Stairs* (1918). In *The Cliff-Dwellers,* a bank teller embezzles money from the Underground National Bank, and in *On the Stairs,* Fuller details the rise of Johnny McComas at the Mid-Continent National Bank. Both novels explore how the greed of urban denizens caused financial instability in a banking system that lacked regulation.

After 1900, during the Progressive Era, the public and a few leading financiers became increasingly unhappy with the unstable, unregulated banking system, a discontent that was fueled by novelists who increasingly dramatized the world of high finance. Edwin Lefevre (1871–1943), originally educated as a mining engineer, published a collection of short stories titled *Wall Street Stories* (1901) and a series of novels—*The Golden Flood* (1905), *Sampson Rock of Wall Street* (1907), and *The Plunderers* (1916)— that accurately and critically depicted the financial markets. Other novelists from the early 1900s, such as David Graham Phillips (1867–1911), who wrote *The Deluge* (1905) and *The Cost* (1904), were labeled muckrakers, and they are known not only for novels but also for nonfiction articles that revealed the corruption of the day. Their novels often depict a hero who can either overcome or succumb to the immorality of business.

Another muckraker, Robert Herrick (1868–1938), wrote the novel *The Memoirs of an American Citizen* (1905), which tells the rags-to-riches story of Edward V. Harrington, who arrives in Chicago unemployed and is arrested for picking pockets. An intelligent young man, Harrington eventually succeeds in the meatpacking industry. After earning a fortune as a ruthless businessman, he turns to politics, using his business connections to become a U.S. senator. Early in life Harrington realizes that a hungry person can be arrested and jailed for stealing food, while a financier will be praised for embezzling millions. Throughout the novel the reader has sympathy for Harrington because he is pragmatic, not evil. He does what is necessary to survive and thrive, yet he will not send rotten meat to American troops as his competitors do, and his patriotic longings cause him to leave the business world and enter politics. Although Harrington "buys" his appointment to the Senate, the book ends with a sense that the government might do some good in regulating financial excesses. Other muckrakers wrote nonfiction articles that were as popular as novels. In a series of articles for *Everybody's Magazine*, Thomas W. Lawson (1857–1925), a Boston financier, attacked the robber barons by telling the story of Amalgamated Copper, and these articles were so popular that they were collected in a book, *Frenzied Finance* (1905). Lawson exposed both stock market and insurance abuses.

THE FEDERAL RESERVE SYSTEM, 1913

The financial crises of the nineteenth century and the muckrakers' exposés set the stage for banking reform, but before bankers and politicians chartered a new central bank, another devastating panic occurred in 1907, which began when several New York banks attempted and failed to corner the copper market. The New York Clearing House contained the crisis by extending credit to member banks; unfortunately customer panic spread to the trusts and brokerage houses that were not members of the New York Clearing House. J. P. Morgan, the wealthiest banker of the time, recognized that a collapse of the trusts would damage the entire economy and played a pivotal role in controlling the panic by pooling private money to support troubled companies. During this 1907 crisis the Bank of England, by raising interest rates, was able to minimize the economic damage to Great Britain. If the United States had had a central bank to distribute credit wisely, the 1907 panic and many nineteenth-century bank suspensions, panics, and failures could have been prevented. In response to the 1907 crisis, the best-known muckraker of the period, Upton Sinclair (1878–1968), published *The Moneychangers* (1908), a novel that attacked both the ethical and financial failures of the bankers and speculators whose actions precipitated and exacerbated the panic of 1907. And in 1912 Dreiser published *The Financier*, the first volume of his financial trilogy that would eventually include *The Titan* (1914) and *The Stoic*

(1947). In the final volume of Dreiser's trilogy, Frank Cowperwood dies, but the novel continues after Cowperwood's death, tracing the decline of his fortune during the 1907 panic.

The success of the Bank of England during this crisis of 1907, the plans of bankers such as J. P. Morgan, and the novels of writers such as Upton Sinclair and Theodore Dreiser all convinced politicians that federal banking regulations were needed; thus in 1913 the long American distrust of banks and banking regulation ended with a new banking system. Although President Woodrow Wilson was elected in 1912 as a Democrat who feared a strong central government, he signed into existence the Federal Reserve System, recognizing the need for a central banking system that could regulate the money supply and respond to future banking crises.

See also Muckrakers and Yellow Journalism; Presidential Elections; Wealth

BIBLIOGRAPHY

Primary Works

Dreiser, Theodore. *The Financier.* 1912. New York: Penguin, 1995.

Sinclair, Upton. *The Moneychangers.* 1908. Amherst, N.Y.: Prometheus, 2001.

Secondary Works

Chernow, Ron. *The House of Morgan.* New York: Grove, 1990.

Friedman, Milton, and Anna J. Schwartz. *A Monetary History of the United States, 1867–1960.* Princeton, N.J.: Princeton University Press, 1971.

Hammond, Bray. *Banks and Politics in America from the Revolution to the Civil War.* Princeton, N.J.: Princeton University Press, 1957.

Michaels, Walter Benn. *The Gold Standard and the Logic of Naturalism: American Literature at the Turn of the Century.* Berkeley: University of California Press, 1987.

Myers, Gustavus. *History of the Great American Fortunes.* 3 vols. Chicago: C. H. Kerr, 1910.

Oberholtzer, E. P. *Jay Cooke, Financier of the Civil War.* 2 vols. Philadelphia: G. W. Jacobs, 1907.

Rothbard, Murray. *A History of Money and Banking in the United States: The Colonial Era to World War II.* Auburn, Ala.: Ludwig Von Mises Institute, 2002.

Wicker, Elmus. *Banking Panics of the Gilded Age.* Cambridge, U.K., and New York: Cambridge University Press, 2000.

Roark Mulligan

BATTLE OF THE LITTLE BIGHORN

The basic facts of the Battle of the Little Bighorn are simple. On 25 June 1876 the Seventh Calvary regimental commander Lieutenant Colonel George Armstrong Custer and approximately 250 U.S. soldiers, scouts, and civilians were killed by what best estimates say were 2,000 Lakota, Hunkpapa, Cheyenne, and Arapaho warriors in the valley of the Little Bighorn River in what is now southeastern Montana. Beyond those sketchy details, however, the story becomes more complicated, in large part because no U.S. military personnel in Custer's party survived the battle and because the reports of those who observed from the margins were colored by various personal interests or linguistic and cultural differences. Almost immediately the story was transformed into an American myth.

Controversy has raged over the years about the major players: whether Custer was a "cavalier in buckskin," a foolhardy "glory hunter," or simply unable to adjust to the complicated war against the native inhabitants of the plains; whether Custer's subordinates, Major Marcus A. Reno and Captain Frederick W. Benteen, were guilty of negligence (or even cowardice) or were merely unable to follow orders in a confusing and life-threatening situation; whether the native combatants were vicious rebels or justified defenders of their homeland. As for the battle itself, there have been allegations of treachery, incompetence, drunkenness on duty, and conspiracies, but there have also been those who say that Custer and his forces were simply outnumbered and outmaneuvered by their foes and undone by their overconfidence.

What remains most interesting, perhaps, is not finding the definitive answer to why Custer was defeated at the Little Bighorn but exploring why so many generations of historians, battle buffs, artists, and writers have continued to care. After all, the number of dead is minuscule compared to the numbers that died in the Civil War (and in many other U.S. conflicts). While the defeat may have contributed to the eventual removal of Native Americans from their ancestral lands in the West, that program was certainly well under way at the time the battle took place, aided by the elimination of traditional hunting grounds and the decimation of the buffalo population. Nevertheless, since 1876 (when the first biography of Custer appeared) the speculation, analysis, revision, and outright fabrications about the battle have continued to grow.

BACKGROUND TO THE BATTLE
No accounting of this particularly complicated story can be completely free of bias, but some details about

George Armstrong Custer's life preceding the battle do remain (somewhat) free from debate. First, Custer was a brevet (honorary) major general in the Civil War, known for his bravery and skills as a tactician, although at times he was criticized for his foolhardiness and self-promotion. He was championed by General Ulysses S. Grant and by General Philip Henry Sheridan, and the term "Custer's luck" became well known throughout the army for his good fortune on and off the battlefield.

After the war, Custer survived various troubles (including being court-martialed for leaving his post without authorization and being drawn, or perhaps drawing himself, into one of the many scandals of Grant's presidential administration) but also added to his fame by serving in campaigns against the Native Americans on the western plains. He scored a decisive victory against the Cheyenne at the Washita River in present-day Oklahoma on 27 November 1868. However, this incident was not without controversy, as many of those killed were noncombatants and much of the Native Americans' food, shelter, and transportation was destroyed in the middle of winter. Some also speculate that Benteen's animosity toward Custer (which may have influenced his later behavior at the Little Bighorn) began during this engagement.

Custer was also plagued by allegations of cruelty toward deserters and insubordinate soldiers and too scrupulous attention to detail. The most charitable analysts say that Custer's temperament and leadership style were not suited to a peacetime army filled with resentful recruits and hapless volunteers. These may seem like irrelevant details in a discussion of the Battle of the Little Bighorn, but Custer scholars are united in thinking that they contributed to the eventual outcome of the engagement, even as they disagree about exactly how the events unfolded.

The string of events that culminated in the Battle of the Little Bighorn began when gold was discovered in the Black Hills of the Dakota Territories. In fact, the presence of gold in the Black Hills had been confirmed on an expedition Custer had led in 1874. Even though the U.S. government had made a treaty with area tribes promising them the Black Hills (which they considered sacred ground), the news of gold had already brought in prospectors and would-be settlers. Because of the potential for violence between Native Americans and Euro-Americans, the tribes in the area had been ordered to reservations, and the army was sent to round up (or destroy) those who remained outside. These included the warriors fighting alongside the Native American leaders Sitting Bull, Crazy Horse, and Gall.

THE BATTLE AND ITS SURROUNDING CHAOS

The U.S. forces dispatched on this mission included troops commanded by Generals Alfred Terry, George Crook, and John Gibbon in addition to Custer's regiment. The commanders planned to come at the renegades from several sides and surround them (although the exact location of the Native Americans and their numbers were not clear). Custer and his regiment were sent to the Little Bighorn from one direction, while the troops commanded by Terry and Gibbon would approach from another. Much ink has been spilled about the final instructions General Terry gave Custer, but the most recent consensus is that while Terry instructed Custer to wait for the other troops before he acted, he also told him to use his own judgment if he found the warriors. For most scholars, this indicates that Custer was later justified in taking the initiative and not waiting for Terry to arrive.

After receiving the somewhat ambiguous instructions from Terry, Custer took his regiment of men and divided them into three battalions, one led by Benteen, one by Reno, and one by Custer himself. (Custer had between 215 and 225 men with him.) Having no clear idea of the number of Native American fighters they would be facing, Custer gave instructions for Reno and Benteen to split off from his group. Custer expected that the three groups would join forces later, but this never happened.

When Reno's troops met the warriors outside of their encampment, the soldiers dismounted and created a skirmish line on foot, which some have seen as a mistake. From there, seriously outnumbered and hamstrung by what appears to have been a failure of nerve on the part of their commander, the troops moved toward the shelter of some trees. Then they made a reckless dash up the bluffs to what is now called, perhaps sarcastically, Reno Hill, with Reno leading the retreat (which is not what one expects of a commanding officer). There they stayed until joined later by Benteen.

Meanwhile, Custer and his men made their way to the valley of the Little Bighorn River, still uncertain about how many Native Americans they were going to encounter and whether or not the warriors would fight or retreat with the women and children encamped with them. The troops suspected that they had been sighted, however, as they saw Native Americans watching them along the trail, and their dust would have been hard to miss. They ended up on a ridge to the north of Reno Hill, known as Last Stand Hill, where they were surrounded by a large force of Native Americans. The battle there was relatively straightforward: outnumbering Custer's men

at least ten to one, the warriors (who were armed with bows and rifles) only had to circle Custer's men and pick them off one by one. The firing began in earnest around 4:30 P.M.; by 6:00 P.M. everyone in Custer's party was dead.

Benteen, for his part, seemed to be wandering in the wilderness, unable (he claimed) to see or hear Custer's troops. Even though Custer sent his now-famous message ordering Benteen to come quickly and to bring ammunition packs, Benteen claimed that he did not know how to find Custer. When Benteen arrived on Reno Hill, he was able to see Custer's predicament, but Reno (who was Benteen's superior officer) refused to allow any troops to follow Custer. (Captain Thomas B. Weir and his company did go without authority to Custer's aid, only to be turned back by large numbers of hostile forces.) The Native Americans laid siege to Reno Hill, and the fighting continued there through the evening. The U.S. troops were able to hang on, however, until the Native Americans left en masse the next day.

Custer and his men were discovered by Terry and Gibbon's scouting party, who had come too late to help. There was considerable mutilation of the bodies, but Custer's body was found undisturbed, except for having bullet holes in the chest and temple and being stripped naked. Of course, there has been speculation about whether the fatal blow to the head was self-inflicted, with much discussion of the lack of powder burns, the difficulty of shooting oneself in the left temple if one is right handed, the army's desire to protect Custer's wife Libbie from further distress caused by the accusation of a dishonorable suicide, and the often-stated intention of Custer to save the last bullet for himself. Whatever the means of his death, Custer was consistently reported to have looked peaceful.

THE AFTERMATH

The aftermath of Custer's death was certainly not peaceful. Reno and Benteen, anxious to clear their names of any suspicion, concocted a plot to draft a letter from their troops praising their bravery. (Many of the signatures on the letter were forged.) General Terry rewrote his last instructions to Custer to make his suggestions sound more like specific orders. Everyone, from generals to privates, from Native American scouts to hostile warriors, from alleged army survivors of the battle to Monday morning quarterbacks, weighed in on the subject. They talked of Custer's bravery, insubordination, or foolishness; of Reno's drunkenness, cowardice, inexperience, or prudent caution; and of Benteen's resentment, defiance of direct orders, confusion, or powerlessness to defy his superior officer.

***Custer's Last Fight,* 1884.** Detail of Cassilly Adams's famous, but probably inaccurate, painting. © BETTMANN/CORBIS

A court of inquiry that was convened in 1879 exonerated Reno, but it seemed to raise more questions than it answered and gave rise to the suspicion that the army had put pressure on the court to find in Reno's favor.

Even after all the participants died, the Battle of the Little Bighorn lingered in the popular imagination. Custer's wife Elizabeth (better known as Libbie) devoted the rest of her ninety years to celebrating the memory of her husband, writing hundreds of letters (by hand) to men under Custer's command, those claiming to be survivors, and anyone interested in Custer's story. Reno was court-martialed for drunken fighting and voyeurism. Benteen, who engaged in a life-long crusade to discredit Custer, was court-martialed for drunkenness and failure to perform his duties. He was later allowed to take an honorable discharge and retire for medical reasons and died ten years later, still criticizing Custer publicly and privately.

THE BATTLE IN POPULAR CULTURE

Perhaps the first to fictionalize (and profit from) the battle was William Frederick "Buffalo Bill" Cody, a scout for the U.S. Army during and after the Civil War and a friend of Custer. On 17 July 1876 Cody shot, stabbed, and then allegedly scalped the Cheyenne warrior Yellow Hand (who was rumored to have killed Custer). This event, part fact, part myth, was transformed into the melodrama *Buffalo Bill's First Scalp*

for Custer, which Cody produced and starred in that fall. In 1883 Cody created the stage show Buffalo Bill's Wild West, which, along with Pony Express rides, buffalo hunts, and a staged stagecoach attack, culminated in a presentation of "Custer's Last Stand," featuring Lakota who had actually fought in the battle.

The visual arts certainly have frequently depicted the Battle of the Little Bighorn (usually inaccurately). The most famous of these representations is probably the circa 1884 painting *Custer's Last Fight* by Cassilly Adams. The painting was bought by Anheuser-Busch beer magnate Adolphus Busch, who had Otto Becker design a print from it in 1896. Over the years, more than a million copies of the print have been distributed to bars and restaurants. Other paintings include *Custer's Last Charge* (1876) by Feodor Fuchs, possibly the earliest representation; John Mulvany's *Custer's Last Rally* (1881), said to be Walt Whitman's favorite painting; and the very accurate portrayals of the battle by the twentieth-century artist Nick Eggenhoffer.

Numerous poets have memorialized Custer's Last Stand, using it to further their personal, political, and aesthetic agendas. "From Far Dakota's Cañons" (1876), written by Walt Whitman (1819–1892) shortly after the news of the disaster filtered out, celebrates Custer's "tawny flowing hair in battle" (p. 593) and his heroic death. "The Revenge of Rain-in-the-Face" by Henry Wadsworth Longfellow (1807–1882) perpetuates the probably mythic account of the Hunkpapa

Sioux leader's murder of Custer's brother Tom, who was serving in the Seventh Calvary. Longfellow's version substitutes George Armstrong Custer in place of Tom Custer, however, for dramatic effect. "On the Big Horn" (1887) by John Greenleaf Whittier (1807–1892) is a later and more mournful plea for peace and unity between Native Americans and whites, while the epic "Custer" (1896) by Ella Wheeler Wilcox (1850–1919), which celebrates Custer's heroism and bravery, was written during what is probably America's most nationalistic and imperialistic period.

Critical studies of the Battle of Little Bighorn and Custer's life crowd the library shelves. Everyone from history professors to retired doctors has become obsessed with the story, attempting to clear Custer's name or at least resurrect—once again—the various controversies. Archaeological studies of the site have led to new information about the battle, and military strategists have carefully plotted and replotted the maneuvers. Studies have been done from the perspectives of Native Americans, women, and enlisted men. And, as always, there are many investigations that attempt to portray Custer as a hero or villain.

Why has this particular battle generated so much conversation over the many years since it happened? Many argue that it marked the last stand for native peoples in the American West as well as the last gasp for heroes of the Civil War. Also, it raises questions about the national myth of the United States: Is Custer an American hero who died bravely defending American interests, or is he an unwitting (or perhaps bloodthirsty and racist) villain setting out to destroy a people's legitimate right to their homeland? Even the name of the battlefield partakes of this conflict. First named a national cemetery on 29 January 1879, it became the Custer Battlefield National Monument on 22 March 1946. On 10 December 1991 Congress passed, at the insistence of the Colorado Republican congressperson Ben Nighthorse Campbell, legislation renaming it the Little Bighorn Battlefield National Monument. Thirteen years later, Campbell dedicated a statue that commemorates the Native American warriors and their struggles on Last Stand Hill.

Another way to read the continuing interest in the battle is to recognize the elements of tragedy in Custer's story, which seem as if they could have been created for a work of literature. These include his great early triumph, pride going before a fall, possible betrayal by subordinates, and human frailty. According to Vine Deloria, Custer died for our sins, and indeed he has become a sacrifice to the conflicted national position on native peoples and a scapegoat for the nation's guilt over power and strength as well as an enduring reminder of the gallantry and pathos of the human condition. Perhaps more cynically, the story of the Little Bighorn is, like all good stories, full of fascinating characters: a charismatic but overconfident leading man, the attractive and loyal woman who married him, reluctant and envious allies, heroic and menacing foes, a true-blue supporting cast—plus guns, horses, danger, and mystery. Most of all, though, it represents a 100-year-old nation struggling to reconcile Manifest Destiny with moral responsibility.

See also Indians; Indian Wars; Wounded Knee

BIBLIOGRAPHY

Primary Work

Whitman, Walt. "From Far Dakota's Cañons." 1876. In *Complete Poetry and Collected Prose,* pp. 592–593. New York: Library of America, 1982.

Secondary Works

Barnett, Louise. *Touched by Fire: The Life, Death, and Mythic Afterlife of George Armstrong Custer.* New York: Henry Holt, 1996.

Connell, Evan S. *Son of the Morning Star.* San Francisco: North Point Press, 1984.

Deloria, Vine, Jr. *Custer Died for Your Sins.* New York: Macmillan, 1969.

Frost, Lawrence A. *Custer Legends.* Bowling Green, Ohio: Bowling Green University Popular Press, 1981.

Gray, John S. *Custer's Last Campaign: Mitch Boyer and the Little Bighorn Reconstructed.* Lincoln: University of Nebraska Press, 1991.

Leckie, Shirley A. *Elizabeth Bacon Custer and the Making of a Myth.* Norman: University of Oklahoma Press, 1993.

Pearson, Roberta E.. "Custer Loses Again: The Contestation over Commodified Public Memory." In *Cultural Memory and the Construction of Identity,* edited by Dan Ben-Amos and Liliane Weissberg, pp. 176–201. Detroit: Wayne State University Press, 1999.

Sandoz, Mari. *The Battle of the Little Bighorn.* Philadelphia: Lippincott, 1966.

Sklenar, Larry: *To Hell with Honor: Custer and the Little Bighorn.* Norman: University of Oklahoma Press, 2000.

Utley, Robert M. *Cavalier in Buckskin: George Armstrong Custer and the Western Military Frontier.* Norman: University of Oklahoma Press, 1988.

Van de Water, Frederic F. *Glory-Hunter: A Life of General Custer.* New York: Bobbs-Merrill, 1934.

Wert, Jeffry D. *The Controversial Life of George Armstrong Custer.* New York: Simon and Schuster, 1996.

Whittaker, Frederick. *A Complete Life of Gen. George A. Custer: Major-General of Volunteers; Brevet Major-General, U.S. Army; and Lieutenant-Colonel, Seventh U.S. Cavalry.* New York: Sheldon and Company, 1976.

Caren J. Town

BEST-SELLERS

The years 1870 through 1920 saw the publication of numerous popular books and stories in the United States. Many of them lacked artistic complexity, adopted a predictable plot, and sugarcoated reality, offering little more than popular appeals. Other works—by Mark Twain, William Dean Howells, and Jack London, for example—have achieved a canonical status in American literature. Several forms of best-sellers are identified in American literature during this period: historical romance, stories of sentimental love or adventure (including westerns), local color fiction, sentimental novels for young readers, religious writing, and sociological fiction.

HISTORICAL ROMANCE

Historical romance was inhabited by stereotypical characters—either good or bad—and set in a distant time period. Writers typically borrowed their ideas from events in European and American history such as the French Revolution, American Revolution, and American Civil War, embellishing them for artistic appeal. Among the most important historical novelists were Lew (Lewis) Wallace (1827–1905), Silas Weir Mitchell (1829–1914), Francis Marion Crawford (1854–1909), Charles Major (1856–1913), Mary Johnston (1870–1936), and Winston Churchill (1871–1947). Wallace was a military leader and lawyer who earned fame as the author of the novel *Ben-Hur: A Tale of the Christ* (1880). It sold two million copies, was translated into many foreign languages, and was adapted into a movie twice, in 1925 and 1959. Classified also as a religious novel, *Ben-Hur* concerns the title character's triumph over his jealous rival Messala, the supernatural healing power of Jesus, and the rise of Christianity in the late Roman Empire. Wallace portrays how Ben-Hur is wrongly accused by Messala, escapes death, rescues his leprous mother and sister from imprisonment, and takes a just revenge against his enemy.

While *Ben-Hur* is set in biblical times, Mitchell's novels are based on events related to the French Revolution, American Revolution, and American Civil War. His most popular work was *Hugh Wynne, Free Quaker* (1896), which deals with adventures of the title character, a Quaker during the Revolutionary War. The story is narrated by Hugh Wynne himself, son of a Philadelphia merchant. During the Revolutionary War, he runs away from his strict Quaker father, becoming a "Free" Quaker and a military officer under George Washington. The rest of the novel deals with Wynne's romantic pursuit of—and winning the hand of—Darthea Peniston. Among other historical novels by Mitchell are *Roland Blake* (1886), *Circumstance* (1901), *Constance Trescot* (1905), and *The Red City* (1908).

Crawford was another widely popular historical romance writer of his time. He published forty-five novels, including the historical romances *Zoroaster* (1885), set in ancient Persia during the time of Cyrus; *Via Crucis* (1898), concerning an Englishman in the Second Crusade; *In the Palace of the King* (1900), the story of Spain under Philip II; *Marietta* (1901), about a glassworker in fifteenth-century Venice; and *Arethusa* (1907), the story of fourteenth-century Constantinople.

Major, also a lawyer and legislator, is remembered for his two best-selling historical novels, *When Knighthood Was in Flower* (1898) and *Dorothy Vernon of Haddon Hall* (1902). The former work, set in sixteenth-century England, is a love story between Queen Mary Tudor and Charles Brandon. In the latter work, set also in England, the title character is forced by her father to marry Sir Malcolm Vernon, whom she does not love. The novel chronicles how the strong-willed heroine seeks and marries the man of her heart, the son of the Earl of Rutland. Major's less-successful historical novels include *Forest Hearth: A Romance of Indiana in the Thirties* (1903) and *Little King: A Story of the Childhood of Louis XIV, King of France* (1910).

The author of twenty-two books mostly set in Virginia, Johnston achieved literary fame largely with her *To Have and to Hold* (1900). The most popular among her works and the number-one best-seller of the year, it tells of the journey of Jocelyn Leigh, a ward of King James, who refuses to marry an English nobleman. She flees to America under the name of Patience Worth and is sold as a bride to the valorous Captain Ralph Percy of the Virginia Colony. After a series of suspenseful events, the two fall in love and together return to England. The American Civil War forms the background of Johnston's next novel *The Long Roll* (1911) and its sequel, *Cease Firing* (1912). They are set in the South and based on thorough research of the war.

Churchill, frequently confused with the English statesman Sir Winston Leonard Spencer Churchill

(1874–1965), authored several best-selling historical novels with the American Revolution and the American Civil War as their backdrops: *Richard Carvel* (1899), *The Crisis* (1901), *The Crossing* (1904), *Coniston* (1906), and *Mr. Crewe's Career* (1908). Set in Revolutionary Maryland, *Richard Carvel* deals with Carvel's adventurous naval career as well as his romantic pursuit of Dorothy Manners. The novel sold almost one million copies. Richard Carvel's daughter, Virginia, appears as the heroine of *The Crisis*. Set in St. Louis of the Civil War era, this work focuses on the love relationship between this Southern lady and a Northerner, Stephen Brice. In *The Crossing,* Churchill uses such historical figures as George Rogers Clark and Daniel Boone to chronicle the settlement of Kentucky during the American Revolution. New England politics forms the background of *Coniston* and *Mr. Crewe's Career.* The former tells of the career of the corrupt and power-hungry Jethro Bass, modeled after the New Hampshire politician Ruel Durkee; the latter depicts the degree of political clout a railroad company exerts over the state government.

STORIES OF SENTIMENTAL LOVE OR ADVENTURE

Many popular writers during this period produced melodramatic love stories set in contemporary locations, both in and out of the United States. These stories emphasized action, depending upon predictable story lines, characters, and themes. Prominent among these writers were Helen Hunt Jackson (1830–1885), Richard Harding Davis (1864–1916), Francis Marion Crawford, Harold Bell Wright (1872–1944), and James Branch Cabell (1879–1958). Jackson, who sometimes wrote under the pen name Saxe Holm, was a dedicated defender of the rights of Native Americans. After a warm public reception of her *Bits of Travel* (1872), she wrote *A Century of Dishonor* (1881), a work of nonfiction in which she criticizes the U.S. government's unfair policy toward American Indians. Her best-selling novel *Ramona* (1884) was written to expose the prejudices against American Indians. It sold millions of copies mainly because of its love story of the half-Indian Ramona and the Indian Alessandro.

Davis, a highly successful reporter and romance writer, authored dozens of popular novels and plays set in the American West, England, Europe, and Latin America. Among his entertaining adventure stories were *Gallegher, and Other Stories* (1891), *Van Bibber, and Others* (1892), *Soldiers of Fortune* (1897), *Ranson's Folly* (1902), *In the Fog* (1901), and *The Dictator* (1904). He also wrote a number of commercially successful plays, including *Ranson's Folly* (1904; adapted from his 1902 title) and *"Miss Civilization"* (1905).

Crawford's sudden literary fame came with the publication of his first romantic novel, *Mr. Isaacs: A Tale of Modern India* (1883), a story of a diamond merchant. Italy provided the setting for the well-received novels *A Roman Singer* (1884), *To Leeward* (1884), *Marzio's Crucifix* (1887), *Saracinesca* (1887), *Sant' Ilario* (1889), *Don Orsino* (1892), *Corleone* (1896), *Pietro Ghisleri* (1893), *Casa Braccio* (1894), and *The White Sister* (1909). Among the works set in Germany were *Greifenstein* (1889), *A Cigarette-Maker's Romance* (1890), and *Doctor Claudius* (1883). The novels set in the United States include *An American Politician* (1884), *The Three Fates* (1892), *Katharine Lauderdale* (1894), and *The Ralstons* (1895).

Though scorned by critics, the clergyman-turned-novelist Wright was the most popularly read American writer in the early twentieth century. He authored a number of best-selling stories of sentimental love and adventure set in the Ozarks of Missouri and in the southwest United States. They were written to instill morals and to advocate living in nature. *The Shepherd of the Hills* (1907), his first commercial success, allowed him to retire from the ministry and to write full time. It was followed by such widely read works as *The Calling of Dan Matthews* (1909), *The Winning of Barbara Worth* (1911), *The Eyes of the World* (1914), and *When a Man's a Man* (1916). *The Winning of Barbara Worth* was his most successful work, selling over two million copies.

Among the most prominent adventure writers of this period were Mark Twain (1835–1910), George Wilbur Peck (1840–1916), and Jack London (1876–1916). Their works were produced mainly for popular consumption. The humorist Twain (Samuel Clemens), born in Missouri, achieved worldwide fame with such commercially successful adventure stories as *Innocents Abroad* (1869), a satirical and humorous travelogue based on the author's voyage to Europe, Egypt, and the Holy Land; *Roughing It* (1872), concerning Twain's adventures in the West and the Pacific Islands; and *The Adventures of Tom Sawyer* (1876), *Life on the Mississippi* (1883), *Adventures of Huckleberry Finn* (1885), set along the Mississippi River.

The Wisconsin humorist Peck won popularity with his humorous sketches of adventures. His first collection of such stories came out in 1871 with the title *Adventures of One Terence McGrant.* More successful was *Peck's Bad Boy and His Pa,* which was launched in 1883 and featured adventures of a mischievous boy. It was followed by such works as *Peck's*

Bad Boy and His Pa, No. 2 (1883), *Peck's Boss Book* (1884), *Peck's Irish Friend, Phelan Geoheagan* (1888), *Peck's Uncle Ike and the Red-Headed Boy* (1899), and *Peck's Bad Boy with the Cowboys* (1907). Thanks to his literary popularity, Peck also achieved political success, becoming mayor of Milwaukee (1890–1891) and governor of Wisconsin (1891–1895).

London's adventure stories are less humorous and more naturalistic than those by Twain and Peck. He first attracted the reading public's attention with the short story collection *The Son of the Wolf* (1900), which was compared to Rudyard Kipling's fiction. *The Cruise of the Snark* (1911) is an adventure story derived from his voyage to the South Pacific. London used his firsthand experience with the Klondike in writing his all-time best-seller *The Call of the Wild* (1903). His other celebrated works of adventure include *The Sea-Wolf* (1904), set in the sea and on a desert island, and *White Fang* (1906), a sequel to *The Call of the Wild* set in Alaska.

The late 1800s and early 1900s saw the wild popularity of westerns—adventure novels and short stories set in the trans-Mississippi West. A product of the American imagination during the westward expansion, these works used such staple characters as cowboys, ranchers, outlaws, saloon owners, town sheriffs, U.S. marshals, Indians, and scouts. Their story lines were predictable: good guys always beat bad guys. Many of these stories featured historical figures of the West such as Wild Bill Hickok, Wyatt Earp, Billy the Kid, Jesse James, Sitting Bull, and Geronimo and were later adapted into Hollywood movies with great commercial success. Some western stories first appeared in pulp magazines, including *Smith's Magazine* (founded 1905), *Western Story Magazine* (founded 1919), and *Ranch Romances* (founded 1924).

Among the most popular western writers were Owen Wister (1860–1938) and Zane Grey (1872–1939). Set in the Wyoming territory during the late 1870s and 1880s, Wister's *The Virginian: A Horseman of the Plains* (1902) set the pattern for the genre of western fiction, establishing the cowboy as a folk hero. The novel attained both critical and commercial success. A dentist turned author who eventually published over sixty books, Grey is the best-known writer of the life on western frontiers. Sales of his books reached more than fifteen million copies. His literary fame soared with the publication of his *Riders of the Purple Sage* (1912). Other well-known westerns by Grey include *The Last of the Plainsmen* (1908), *Desert Gold* (1913), *The Border Legion* (1916), and *The U. P. Trail* (1918).

Finally, in *Jurgen: A Comedy of Justice* (1919), James Branch Cabell mixes romantic and antiromantic elements. Set in medieval Poictesme, the protagonist—a middle-aged pawnbroker—travels through various places including heaven and hell before he comes back to his nagging wife. A fictional work of *succès de scandale* (success by scandal) it was banned under charges of obscenity.

LOCAL COLOR FICTION

As the United States expanded all over the continent, there appeared writers who set their stories in their own regions, featuring local customs, manners, and values. They used vernacular speech and local characters to mirror the lifestyle unique to their regions. Some writers offered humorous sketches of characters and experiences, while others described the provincialism of their respective regions through their works. Popularly successful local color writers included Bret Harte (1836–1902), Edward Eggleston (1837–1902), Edward Noyes Westcott (1847–1898), Joel Chandler Harris (1848–1908), and Zona Gale (1874–1938). Harte won worldwide fame with his stories of the American West, which were inhabited by romanticized characters, including miners and women of ill repute. *The Luck of Roaring Camp, and Other Sketches* (1870) helped to launch the local color movement in American literature.

A circuit preacher and schoolteacher turned writer, Eggleston is famous for his novel *The Hoosier Schoolmaster* (1871), which sold 500,000 copies. Based partly on the experiences of the author's brother, it tells of a first-year young schoolteacher in southeast Indiana and his amusing episodes in and out of school. The novel uses Hoosier dialect and offers a glimpse into backwoods life and culture in Indiana after the settlement of the region by whites.

Westcott became famous posthumously with his novel *David Harum: A Story of American Life* (1898), which tells of a clever, humorous small-town banker in upstate New York in the 1890s. David is an illiterate widower who is skillful in horse trading and enjoys dispensing words of wisdom. He kindly patches up the broken love relationship between John Lenox and Mary Blake, who thankfully name their child after him. *David Harum* sold over one million copies and was both dramatized and made into a movie.

Harris was a Georgia author who achieved fame as the creator of the black folk character Uncle Remus. In *Uncle Remus, His Songs and His Sayings* (1880), *Nights with Uncle Remus* (1883), and other collections, Uncle Remus tells a white boy a series of humorous fables in the Negro dialect. The animal characters in his stories include Brer Rabbit, Brer Fox, Brer Wolf, and Brer Bear, who exemplify useful morals for the reader.

The Wisconsin author Gale is known chiefly for her popular novella *Miss Lulu Bett* (1920) and other realistic stories about midwestern small-town life. *Miss Lulu Bett* studies the title character, whose emotional life is stifled by the drab midwestern village life. A thirty-four-year-old spinster, Lulu is the unpaid and unappreciated servant of her sister's family, but her life changes when she marries a new schoolteacher. The dramatized version of *Miss Lulu Bett* won the 1921 Pulitzer Prize.

SENTIMENTAL NOVELS FOR YOUNG READERS

Horatio Alger Jr. (1832–1899) and Frances Hodgson Burnett (1849–1924) are two of the most well-known authors of sentimental fiction for children, written both to instruct and to entertain. Alger popularized the genre of the American success story—the rags-to-riches story. In 102 juvenile books, including the *Ragged Dick* series (begun in 1867), the *Luck and Pluck* series (begun in 1869), and the *Tattered Tom* series (begun in 1871), he typically featured boys with humble beginnings who rise in society through hard work, integrity, and luck. His books claimed wide readership, and sales of his books reached over seventeen million copies.

The English-born American author Frances Hodgson Burnett is remembered for writing two hugely popular novels for children, *Little Lord Fauntleroy* (1886) and *The Secret Garden* (1911). The former focuses on a good American-born boy, Cedric, who inherits his grandfather's estate in England. The novel was later dramatized, receiving enormous commercial success. *The Secret Garden* features the ailing girl Mary Lennox, who moves from India to England to live with her rich uncle. A new environment improves Mary's health and temperament; she discovers a neglected garden on the grounds and transforms it into a charming place.

RELIGIOUS WRITING

This period saw the explosive popularity of religious novels, especially those on the failings of the church. Charles M. Sheldon (1857–1946) advocated the social gospel in his tremendously popular novel *In His Steps* (1896). A graduate of Brown University and Andover Theological Seminary and the pastor of the Central Congregational Church of Topeka, Kansas, Sheldon challenged Christians with the question of what Jesus would do in everyday life. Rather than squabbling over doctrinal differences, Sheldon maintained, Christians should focus on the two supreme commandments of Christ: loving God and loving neighbors. This novel of faith in action sold millions of copies and was translated into dozens of languages.

The New York journalist and author Harold Frederic (1856–1898) wrote several realistic and historical novels. His most popular work was *The Damnation of Theron Ware* (1896), set in upstate New York in the late 1880s and published as *Illumination* in the United Kingdom. It traces the spiritual journey of the title character, a Methodist clergyman. Ware is a young narrow-minded preacher who craves ecclesiastical power, fame, and money. The novel illustrates Ware's increasing awareness of his inadequacy as a pastor and of the problems with the church—sectarianism, anti-intellectualism, hostility toward culture, and religious hypocrisy. Finally, Ware resigns from his pastorate and starts a new life as a real estate agent in Seattle.

In the field of nonfiction, Mary Baker Eddy (1821–1910), the founder of Christian Science and the Church of Christ, published *Science and Health, with Key to the Scriptures* in 1875, which has sold millions of copies worldwide.

SOCIOLOGICAL FICTION

The Gilded Age (roughly the last quarter of the nineteenth century) and the succeeding decades revealed that unbridled capitalism and materialism can lead to moral corruption and plutocracy. Among the most notable writers who satirically portrayed the problems with American society was Edward Bellamy (1850–1898). Bellamy is best known for his highly popular utopian novel *Looking Backward* (1888), which envisions changes in the economic system of the United States. The hero of the novel falls into a hypnotic sleep that lasts from 1887 to 2000 and awakens to find the nation transformed into a socialist nation. The new society is marked by common ownership, equal opportunity, and happiness for all people.

CONCLUSION

Most commercially successful literary works in the period 1870–1920 offered simplistic and repetitive story lines, adopted stock characters, and were written in formulaic style. However, these works also met the needs of the American reading public, which wanted stories of an exalted past, exotic experience, moral teaching, and hope for a better future. Popular writers changed the literary landscape of the United States. They rejected the genteel literary tradition from the East, developing new writing materials—such as cowboys, ranchers, and adventurers—and often critiquing the mainstream American culture.

See also Book Publishing; Domestic and Sentimental Fiction; Historical Romance; Literary Marketplace; Regionalism and Local Color Fiction

BIBLIOGRAPHY
Secondary Works

Bold, Christine. *Selling the Wild West: Popular Western Fiction, 1860 to 1960.* Bloomington: Indiana University Press, 1987.

Cobbs, John L. *Owen Wister.* Boston: Twayne, 1984.

Coulombe, Joseph L. *Mark Twain and the American West.* Columbia: University of Missouri Press, 2003.

Dekker, George. *The American Historical Romance.* New York: Cambridge University Press, 1987.

Dickinson, A. T. *American Historical Fiction.* New York: Scarecrow Press, 1958.

Dinan, John A. *The Pulp Western: A Popular History of the Western Fiction Magazine in America.* San Bernardino, Calif.: Borgo Press, 1983.

Graulich, Melody, and Stephen Tatum, eds. *Reading "The Virginian" in the New West.* Lincoln: University of Nebraska Press, 2003.

Gutjahr, Paul C. *Popular American Literature of the Nineteenth Century.* New York: Oxford University Press, 2001.

Kimball, Arthur G. *Ace of Hearts: The Westerns of Zane Grey.* Forth Worth: Texas Christian University Press, 1993.

Korda, Michael. *Making the List: A Cultural History of the American Bestseller, 1900–1999.* New York: Barnes and Noble, 2001.

Leisy, Ernest E. *The American Historical Novel.* Norman: University of Oklahoma Press, 1950.

Scharnhorst, Gary. *Bret Harte: Opening the American Literary West.* Norman: University of Oklahoma Press, 2000.

Simonson, Harold P. *Beyond the Frontier: Writers, Western Regionalism, and a Sense of Place.* Forth Worth: Texas Christian University Press, 1989.

Smith, Herbert F. *The Popular American Novel, 1865–1920.* Boston: Twayne, 1980.

Walle, Alf H. *The Cowboy Hero and Its Audience: Popular Culture as Market Derived Art.* Bowling Green, Ohio: Bowling Green State University Popular Press, 2000.

Wright, Robert Glenn. *The Social Christian Novel.* New York: Greenwood Press, 1989.

John J. Han

THE BIBLE

The Bible, arguably *the* basic text of Euro-American civilization, has permeated American writing since its colonial beginnings. Biblical material, whether taken straight or approached with radical individualism, is perhaps the common ingredient in nineteenth-century American literature, contributing to a cohesive canon of works by Ralph Waldo Emerson, Nathaniel Hawthorne, Henry David Thoreau, Herman Melville, Walt Whitman, and Emily Dickinson. In the realism of post–Civil War America, the Bible remained such a basic source of creative reference that to enumerate its presence in the wealth of fiction between 1870 and 1920 would be nearly impossible. Edith Wharton took the title of her popular novel *The House of Mirth* (1905) from Ecclesiastes 7:4 to castigate the society of fools who kill her heroine; Stephen Crane clearly echoed the Crucifixion in the death scene of the tall soldier in *The Red Badge of Courage* (1895); and Willa Cather used imagery from both Genesis and Exodus to mythologize pioneering in *My Ántonia* (1918) and drew from the Nativity story in Matthew and Luke, as well as Revelation 12:1 and the Song of Solomon 4, to enshrine her heroine. In *The Rise of David Levinsky* (1917) Abraham Cahan's immigrant takes comfort in his Hebrew Book of Psalms, especially in Psalm 104, transformed for him en route to New York by his experience of the sea journey. While these few examples suggest the inclusive and varied literary uses of the Bible, consider also the creative effect achieved through biblical material. Three seminal works of this period may illustrate the point: *Adventures of Huckleberry Finn* (1885) by Mark Twain (1835–1910), *A Hazard of New Fortunes* (1890) by William Dean Howells (1837–1920), and *The Wings of the Dove* (1902) by Henry James (1843–1916). The novels are decidedly different from one another, and each employs biblical texts with unique creativity.

ADVENTURES OF HUCKLEBERRY FINN

In Twain's novel, Jim's diatribe against Solomon is an example of biblically based burlesque with a serious edge. It uses evidence from 1 Kings 11:3 that Solomon "had seven hundred wives, princesses, and three hundred concubines" to undermine the legendary basis of his wisdom—his judgment concerning the two harlots who claim to be mother of the same child (1 Kings 3:16–28). In listing the daily routine of kings, Huck includes "hang[ing] round the harem," noting that "Solomon had . . . about a million wives" (p. 65); Jim says a wise man would never tolerate the racket made by so many women and babies. When Huck defends Solomon's wisdom on the testimony of the Bible-reading Widow Douglas, Jim uses the incident of the harlots to disagree. Since the dispute was about a whole child and not a half child, the proposal to divide the living child with a sword indicates that the king did not "know enough to come in out'n de rain" (p. 66). Jim argues that Solomon devalued human life because he had "'bout five million chillen runn' roun' de house," but that "a man dat's got on'y one er two" would "know how to value em" (p. 66). The humor of the exchange turns poignant when one recalls that Jim has been separated from his two children and that when Huck first discovered him crouched on the raft he was moaning over them: "Po' little 'Lizabeth! Po little Johnny! Its mighty hard; I spec' I ain't ever gwyne to see you no mo', no mo'!" (p. 125).

While the Solomon discussion emphasizes social inequality and illuminates the plight—and the humanity—of the slave, it also introduces what will be a series of folksy misreadings and distortions of biblical texts, misreadings that elsewhere in the novel are used to justify activities diametrically opposed in spirit to both the Decalogue and the Beatitudes. For example, during the violent Grangerford-Shepherdson episode, Huck discovers in the Grangerford parlor, along with fake fruit and animals, turkey-wing fans, and the sentimental crayons of deceased daughter Emmeline, "a big family Bible, full of pictures" (p. 83). Like other family "treasures," this Bible embellishes a culture of purposeless blood feuding, and its presence foreshadows a similar violation of biblical tenets in the Boggs-Sherburn shootout in Bricksville. Colonel Sherburn, a cold-blooded killer, shoots harmless old Boggs merely because he disturbs the peace during his monthly drunks. The Bricksville yokels have tried to get Boggs out of harm's way, but once he is fatally wounded his painful staggering and clawing become theater for them. They elbow each other to get a look, and the event is acted out so perfectly by one yokel that "a dozen people got out their bottles and treated him" (p. 117). Twain introduces the Bible as chief prop in a bloody play exposing a society that delights in vicarious pain and specializes in nocturnal lynchings and double-crosses. When Boggs is taken into a store to die, "they laid him on the floor, and put one large Bible under his head, and opened another one and spread it on his breast—but they tore open his shirt first . . . where one of the bullets went in" (p. 116). It is as if the sacred text is expected to heal the wound by contact; the effect is chilling, yet Twain enhances the desecration: Boggs "made about a dozen long gasps, his breast lifting the Bible up when he drawed in his breath, and letting it down again when he breathed out—and after that he laid still; he was dead" (p. 116).

Title page from a circa 1870 American edition of the Bible. GETTY IMAGES

Such is salvation by superstition and osmosis—rather than by true faith and works!

Twain's biblical satire is subtler when the Bible is echoed rather than mentioned or discussed. To allow Jim to be left alone and unbound on the raft, and to hide his condition as a runaway slave while the frauds work hick towns along the Mississippi, the duke dresses him in "King Lear's oufit[,] . . . a long curtain-calico gown . . . and a horse-hair wig," colors his skin, and puts up a sign identifying him as "Sick Arab—but harmless when not out of his head" (p. 126). Readers familiar with gospel Passion texts will recognize Herod's "array[ing of Christ] in a gorgeous robe" in Luke 23:11; the wig may represent the thorns placed on Christ's head by soldiers, before they ridicule him as "King of the Jews!" (Matt. 27:29). In the duke's labeling of Jim, Twain's text is closest to John's account in

King James of the labeling of Christ: "And Pilate wrote a title, and put it on the cross. And the writing was, JESUS OF NAZARETH THE KING OF THE JEWS" (19:17). Jim's appearance as fool king immediately follows his heartbreaking confession about striking his deaf daughter; shortly afterward he is betrayed, and he gives up his chance to escape in order to protect wounded Tom Sawyer and help the doctor. As the biblical echoes multiply, Twain's purpose becomes clear: making Jim Christlike highlights his human depth and decency within a context of legalized slavery; his articulation of the golden rule gives Huck, the southern boy, insight enough to conclude that Jim "was white inside" (p. 216). Sold by the king for forty dollars, Jim becomes at once the "man of sorrows" of Isaiah's prophecy (53:3) and the Jesus betrayed by Judas for thirty pieces of silver (Matt. 27:3–9). Pilate's words to the crowd before the Crucifixion come to mind: "Behold the man!" (John 19:5).

A HAZARD OF NEW FORTUNES

In *A Hazard of New Fortunes*, Howells echoes the Bible to define as well as dignify and caricature the conflict between the self-made millionaire Jacob Dryfoos and his idealistic son, Conrad. The elder Dryfoos, a midwestern farmer turned oil speculator, has invaded New York, like his crude counterparts in Edith Wharton novels, for social opportunities. Committed above all things to increasing his fortune, Dryfoos exploits his labor force and has "undergone," as Howells's spokesman Basil March puts it, "a moral deterioration, an atrophy of the generous instincts" (p. 193). Conrad Dryfoos, however, is opposed to his father's business virtues; when his father forbids him to be a preacher he simply dedicates himself to the poor, whose condition the old man dismisses as the result of "laziness, and drink, and dishonesty, and foolishness" (p. 189). Their conflict climaxes during a transit strike when Dryfoos forces his son to admit sympathy for the workers and then strikes him over the eye. Conrad subsequently wanders into the strike zone as a peacemaker and is killed by a random bullet. When Mrs. Dryfoos notices the wound over her dead son's eye, her guilty husband breaks "into a low, wavering cry" (p. 372) and later confesses to March, "I wasn't very good to [my son] . . . I crossed him. . . . I ought to 'a let him been a preacher! O my son, my son!" (p. 390). This is an echo of David's lament in 2 Samuel 18:33 at Absalom's death: "O my son Absalom, my son, my son, Absalom! Would God I had died for thee, O Absalom, my son, my son!"

In the Bible the conflict between father and son has national significance, for Absalom has won over the people and forced David to flee Jerusalem: "The hearts of the men of Israel are after Absalom," a messenger informs David (2 Sam. 15:13). The conflict between old Dryfoos and his son also develops broad social consequences, for Howells's intention is to alert his readers to the effects of unregulated capitalism. March sees "accident and . . . exigency as 'the forces at work'" in America, "the play of energies . . . free and planless . . . persisting over . . . the destruction . . . of the weaker. The whole . . . seemed to him lawless, Godless," lacking "comprehensive purpose" (p. 160). Yet as Howells dignifies his realistic drama through biblical echo, he undercuts both it and its archetype. King David's scene of grief is almost parodied in the crude capitalist's "wavering cry," resembling "an animal's in terror" (p. 372), drowning in "a series of hoarse sounds like barks" (p. 390). Conrad's virtue and self-abnegation sharply contrast with Absalom's hubris and treachery, and Conrad's beauty, because it reflects his goodness, surpasses that of his counterpart. The biblical text prepares one for the words that cause old Dryfoos to break down: "From the sole of his foot even to the crown of his head there was no blemish in [Absalom]" (2 Sam. 14:25). Mrs. Dryfoos notices the blemish on Conrad caused by his father's ring: "Why, Jacob, what's that there by his pore eye?" (p. 372).

Howells attempts to resolve the complexities of *Hazard* by applying Christian principles to the volatile economic world surrounding his characters, and to do so he depends heavily on biblical texts. For example, Basil March cites Matthew 10:29 when accused by his wife of fatalism for speculating that Conrad's death might have been unalterable: "Then you think," he asks, "that a sparrow falls to the ground *without* the will of God?" But immediately he qualifies his heresy and surrenders to the mystery of chance and design: "I don't know what it all means, Isabel, though I believe it means good" (p. 423). Because March is troubled by her romantic idea that Conrad's death has essentially changed old Dryfoos, he attempts to distance the death from meaning. He cites Luke 16:29–31, from Christ's story of the rich man in hell pleading with Abraham to raise and send Lazarus to warn his rich brethren against neglecting the poor. Abraham explains that there is sufficient warning in the law: "If they hear not Moses and the prophets, neither will they be persuaded, though one rose from the dead" (p. 423). The story is apt for its disparity between rich and poor as well as for its larger lesson, which March articulates: "That if one rose from the dead it would not avail. And yet we are always looking for the miraculous!" (p. 423).

The peacemaking efforts of Conrad, when coupled with his death, however, ultimately have significance.

The idealistic society girl who inspired these efforts, Margaret Vance, identifies them as responses to Christ's promise, "Blessed are the peacemakers: for they shall be called the children of God" (Matt. 5:9). Conrad came on God's business, she argues, at the suggestion that peacekeeping should be left to the police: "But the blessing on the peacemakers is not for the policemen with their clubs" (p. 408). But March remains confused by the "economic chance world" that caused the catastrophe, that world of competition where "someone always has you by the throat, unless you have some one else in *your* grip" (p. 379), a world conditioned by a culture prizing "having and shining . . . as the chief good of life" (pp. 380–381). He wonders if such a culture could possibly represent "the kingdom of Heaven on earth . . . we pray for" (p. 379) and how it reflects not only the Lord's Prayer (Matt 6:9–10; Luke 11:2) but also related Gospel passages: Mark 10: 23–25, which makes poverty a condition for entering the kingdom of God; Luke 16:8–13, which distinguishes true riches from mammon and "children of this world" from "children of the light"; and Matthew 6:24, which equates love of money with despising God—"You cannot serve God and mammon." Jacob Dryfoos is identified as "a Mammon-worshipper, pure and simple" (p. 214), although this is the estimate of Angus Beaton, Howells's discredited artist, and must be qualified like much else in the text. Howells concludes with a biblical reflection: when the Marches meet Margaret Vance, now a religious sister, they detect in her eyes "the peace that passeth understanding" (p. 431), a phrase from Philippians 4:7 describing the reward for faith, charitable acts, moderation, and prayer. It is a fitting coda for *Hazard,* which grapples with what, like Paul's peace, seems insoluble.

THE WINGS OF THE DOVE

The process of distinguishing mammon from true riches is the burden of *The Wings of the Dove.* The transformation of worldly to spiritual fortune begins when one meets Milly Theale, an American heiress with a mysterious fatal disease, perched on a rock in the Swiss Alps and "looking down on the kingdoms of the earth" (p. 135), a reference to Christ being tempted on the mountaintop by worldly kingdoms (Matt. 4:8–9; Luke 4:5–6). In James's text the kingdoms of the earth represent human engagement, "taking full in the face the whole assault of life" (p. 136); Milly wants experience before she dies. Her companion, Susan Stringham, has a premonition that Milly's "passage" will be "complicated," imagining the kingdoms as "a mine of something precious" that "needed working and would certainly yield a treasure. She was not thinking, either, of Milly's gold" (p. 136).

That gold will occasion spiritual growth, for Milly will have used it trustworthily, as Luke 16:10–11 instructs.

Milly's descent to the worldly kingdoms becomes a journey into hell, entangling her in a network of mammon worshippers in London: Maud Lowder, Susan's wealthy friend, who wants Milly's fortune for her protégé Lord Mark; and Maud's niece, Kate Croy, who wishes to put off her wedding to her journalist fiancé, Merton Densher, until after Merton marries Milly and inherits her fortune. Kate weaves a plot so sinister that she hesitates to pronounce it and leaves that task to Merton. "What you want of me then is to make up to a sick girl" (p. 285), he soon concludes, much later grasping the full implication: "So that when her death has taken place I shall in the natural course have money?" (p. 394). The American girl is forewarned, yet in her innocence she is bedazzled rather than put on guard. Lord Mark tells her, "Nobody here . . . does anything for nothing" (p. 157), and Kate is even more explicit: "My honest advice to you would be . . . to drop us while you can" (p. 235). When Milly wonders why Kate says such things, Kate's reply returns the text to the anagogical level. "Because you're a dove," she says, and Milly considers the label an "accolade" (p. 236). Of course, James intends it to be one, complementing it with similarly suggestive figures: a "Christian maiden, in an arena," being "mildly . . . martyred" by "domestic animals" (p. 277), and "an angel with a thumping bank account" (p. 283). Like her bank account, Milly herself will be transfigured from gentle dove to divine power.

Milly Theale's situation and apotheosis follow the development of the biblical dove. James's title is taken from two psalms connecting the wings of the dove to captivity and deliverance. The singer in Psalm 55:6 seeks refuge from the betrayal of friends: "Oh that I had wings like a dove! For *then* would I fly away and be at rest." In celebrating rescue from attackers, Psalm 68:13 connects such wings with the spoils of war: Israel, the girl set free in the desert, "shall . . . be as the wings of a dove covered with silver, and her feathers with yellow gold." Combined, the psalms echo Milly's victimization and exploitation. As Kate's plot thickens in Venice, James embellishes with spoils the portrait of his "dove . . . undefiled," his "choice *one* . . . blessed . . . and . . . praised" (Song of Solomon 6:9). "She's a dove," exclaims Kate, "and one somehow doesn't think of doves as bejewelled. Yet [her pearls] suit her down to the ground" (p. 389). Merton Densher's estimate of Milly at this point reflects the divine power given the dove in Matthew 3:16, Mark 1:10, Luke 3:22, and John 1:32, where the Spirit of God descends like a dove, is like a dove, takes the shape of a dove. Merton realizes that Milly's dove-like qualities "applied to her spirit" and her wealth represents "a great power, . . . dove-like only so far as . . . doves have wings and wondrous flights . . . as well as tender tints and soft sounds. It even came to him dimly that such wings could . . . spread themselves for protection," gathering in all of them—"*he* in particular" (p. 389).

The nature of this protection is defined in James's resolution, after Milly is informed by Lord Mark of the plot against her and has, as Susan Stringham informs Merton, "turned her face to the wall" (p. 421), mimicking Hezekiah, who upon receiving his death sentence "turned his face toward the wall" and "did mourn as a dove" (Isa. 38:2, 14). Yet Milly summons Merton for a final interview, during which she releases him from the torture of waiting in Venice, and back in London at Christmas he receives word that she has left him a generous bequest, making possible his marriage to Kate. Guilt and the memory of Milly forbid him to accept the money, although Kate refuses to marry him without it and without his denial that he fell in love with the dove. While Kate claims that Milly "died . . . that [he] might understand her" and that now she herself understands "she did it for us" and "stretched out her wings" to "cover us" (p. 508), Kate never understands on the spiritual level Merton does. "We shall never be again as we were" (p. 509), she laments in departing, but these final words of the novel apply essentially to him. Kate remains as worldly as ever.

There are many more biblical references in these three novels than those explored here. In varying degrees, all three employ the Bible as a moral component. In each case, biblical texts provide these realists with opportunities for, as Flannery O'Connor puts it, "reading a small history in a universal light" (p. 58). Detecting and following up biblical references and echoes by consulting the Bible illuminates and significantly expands the texts that contain them.

See also Christianity; *The Damnation of Theron Ware;* Darwinism

BIBLIOGRAPHY
Primary Works
Cahan, Abraham. *The Rise of David Levinsky.* 1917. Edited by James Chametzky. New York: Penguin, 1993.

Cather, Willa. *My Ántonia.* 1918. Edited by John J. Murphy. New York: Penguin, 1994.

Crane, Stephen. *The Red Badge of Courage.* 1895. Edited by Sculley Bradley et al. New York: Norton, 1976.

Holy Bible . . . in the King James Version. Nashville, Tenn.: Nelson, 1984.

Howells, William Dean. *A Hazard of New Fortunes.* 1890. New York: Penguin Meridian, 1994.

James, Henry. *The Wings of the Dove.* 1902. Edited by John Bayley. New York: Penguin, 1986.

O'Connor, Flannery. *Mystery and Manners.* Edited by Sally and Robert Fitzgerald. New York: Farrar, Straus and Giroux, 1969.

Twain, Mark. *Adventures of Huckleberry Finn.* 1885. Edited by Sculley Bradley et al. New York: Norton, 1977.

Wharton, Edith. *The House of Mirth.* 1905. New York: Penguin, 1985.

Secondary Works
Anderson, Charles R. "For Love or Money: *The Wings of the Dove.*" In *Person, Place, and Thing in Henry James's Novels,* pp. 173–219. Durham, N.C.: Duke University Press, 1977.

Anderson, Quentin. *The American Henry James.* New Brunswick, N.J.: Rutgers University Press, 1957.

Baetzhold, Howard, and Joseph McCullough, eds. *The Bible according to Mark Twain.* Athens: University of Georgia Press, 1995.

Cady, Edwin H. *The Realist at War: The Mature Years, 1885–1920, of William Dean Howells.* Syracuse, N.Y.: Syracuse University Press, 1958.

Crews, Frederick C. *The Tragedy of Manners: Moral Drama in the Later Novels of Henry James.* 1957. Hamden, Conn.: Archon, 1971.

Ensor, Allison. *Mark Twain and the Bible.* Lexington: University of Kentucky Press, 1969.

Holland, Laurence B. *The Expense of Vision: Essays on the Craft of Henry James.* Princeton, N.J.: Princeton University Press, 1964.

Kirk, Clara, and Edward Kirk. "Howells and the Church of the Carpenter." *New England Quarterly* 32 (June 1959): 185–206.

Murphy, John J. "Biblical and Religious Dimensions of *My Ántonia.*" In *Approaches to Teaching Cather's "My Ántonia,"* edited by Susan J. Rosowski, pp. 77–82. New York: Modern Language Association of America, 1989.

Phipps, William E. *Mark Twain's Religion.* Macon, Ga.: Mercer University Press, 2003.

Singley, Carol J. *Edith Wharton: Matter of Mind and Spirit.* New York: Cambridge University Press, 1995.

Stuart, Christopher. "The Wings of the Dove: 'Across Wide Spaces and Bristling Barriers.'" *Literature and Belief* 23, no. 2 (2003): 1–24.

Vanderbilt, Kermit. *The Achievement of William Dean Howells: A Reinterpretation.* Princeton, N.J.: Princeton University Press, 1968.

John J. Murphy

BILLY BUDD

Unpublished and not even quite completed at Herman Melville's death in 1891, then reconstructed and retitled several times until the 1962 edition by Harrison Hayford and Merton M. Sealts Jr., *Billy Budd, Sailor (An Inside Narrative)* now reigns as the author's major achievement after *Moby-Dick* (1851). In 1958 Richard Harter Fogle thoughtfully called *Billy Budd* "Melville's nineteenth century version of classical tragedy, with old forms revivified by new issues" (p. 110), and in this one may liken it to *Moby-Dick*. Indeed, despite his constant revision of it from 1886 until his death at the age of seventy-two in 1891, the great short novel has mostly been taught to students as one of Melville's antebellum dark romances exhibiting "the power of blackness" (p. 91), a phrase Melville himself used in "Hawthorne and His Mosses" (1850) to discuss Nathaniel Hawthorne's writing. Yet the composition took place instead during the height and flowering of American postbellum realism thirty years or more after Melville had turned from fiction to writing mostly verse. Some might feel that his five-year struggle with the manuscript during the specific era of literary realism reflects the literary-historical moment (in Hippolyte Taine's sense) in which he was writing; others, perhaps that his older philosophical view of eternal questions and dilemmas was by now harder to convey in prose than in his verse. In either case, each reader simply must ponder the fact that what Hayford and Sealts call only "a semi-final draft" (Melville, *Billy Budd*, p. 1) after an extended and vexing process of composing still resulted in an enduring masterpiece. Given this surprising achievement, Melville's *Billy Budd* has attracted massive critical evaluation, although rarely incorporating analysis of Melville's compositional phases as specifically central to its theme or interpretation.

The tragic plot evolves as follows: Billy Budd, a surpassingly innocent and handsome young seaman, kills by a single blow John Claggart, a venomous petty officer (master-at-arms) who falsely and maliciously accuses him of mutiny. Billy's death blow is further complicated because he strikes only after he is unable to speak owing to his congenital stutter—an "organic hesitancy" (p. 53)—exacerbated by heightened emotion from Claggart's accusation borne of sheer envy and personal hatred. Nevertheless, naval law dictates hanging for the act, and the fact that the events occur in 1797 at sea on HMS *Bellipotent* in the aftermath of the major mutinies that rocked the British navy at Spithead and Nore in the spring of that year while England was at war with France seems to require strict adherence because of the threatening virus of anarchy

Herman Melville at age sixty-six, just a few years before his death. © BETTMANN/CORBIS

in the social order during wartime. At this juncture the third major actor in Melville's drama, Captain Edward Vere, although he understands fully Billy's innocence and his victimization by an invidious man, feels compelled to convince his subordinates to carry out the capital punishment. Vere even cries out that Claggart has been "struck dead by an angel of God! Yet the angel must hang!" (p. 101). And before he does hang, Billy declares in antiphonal counterpoint, so to speak, "God bless Captain Vere!" (p. 123)—with no taint from his usual stuttering. So the innocent comes to a tragic end.

With such a powerful sequential plot tied together and embedded within a rich linguistic texture and open-ended Melvillian diction and tone, it is not surprising that *Billy Budd* has prompted multiple readings. These range from the interpretation of Billy as a Christ figure and sacrificial lamb to the idea that the story is a philosophical parable that confirms Melville's mature reverence for true art as the analogue to a "victory of LAW"—as he expresses it in his poem "Dupont's Round Fight" (*Selected Poems*, p. 12). For many years after it was first published in 1924, *Billy Budd* was deemed, in the words of E. L. Grant Watson, a "testament of acceptance" (p. 319); that is, a work without the subversive elements found—in very different ways, to be sure—in Melville's fiction of the 1840s and 1850s. Gradually, however, criticism and interpretation began to turn, and by the 1950s academic readers under the influence of narrative point of view and the technique of unreliable narration revisited the novel and reinterpreted it ironically. This approach spawned a spate of critics who refused passively to accept Billy's slaughter and instead attacked Captain Vere as a misguided dogmatist and a destructive legalist.

Readings in this second wave have become known collectively by Phil Withim's term as Melville's "testament of resistance" (p. 115). Such opposing approaches, referred to sometimes as the "plain talkers" versus the "ironists," have constituted a critical controversy similar to that surrounding Henry James's *The Turn of the Screw* (actual ghosts versus a narrator's pathology). In such controversies each critical side claims that its opponents have not just missed a major dimension of a rich, multilayered text (such as overlooking multiple levels of meaning to the white whale) but also that the opposing side has misread by 180 degrees the entire foundation of the author's vision and purpose. The "resistance" approach, nevertheless, has often been bolstered by the presence of Melville's tonal references in the text to the ambiguous nature of various terms and lexicons; in fact, that dimension of his textuality can prompt phenomenological investigation of Melville's critique of language itself with dire implications for the legitimacy of law, civilization's otherwise reliable lexicon par excellence.

When Fogle denominated *Billy Budd* a "nineteenth century version of classical tragedy, with old forms revivified by new issues" (p. 110), he wished to remind the emerging ironists of "resistance" that long before the time of alleged pervasive narrative irony, there lay a vast tradition of dramatic irony and irony of fate in classical tragedy from Sophocles onward and including, of course, Melville's own favorite, William Shakespeare. Although neither wrote narrative fiction, Melville regarded them as mentors far more than he did such contemporary writers as Washington Irving; even his famous enthusiasm for Hawthorne was enunciated specifically by reference to Shakespeare. Perhaps today in the wake of *Billy Budd*'s complex critical history, it may help to reformulate Fogle's idea in the obverse: a nineteenth-century version of classical tragedy with *new forms* revivified by *old issues*.

Putting the emphasis on new forms can bring us back again to Melville's phases of composition. Hayford and Sealts in the introduction to their edition of *Billy Budd* explain that during the five or six years

In the opening to chapter 4, Melville alludes to his signature mode of composition and narration through indirection and apparent digression that is, however, typically pertinent to his theme. In this case, he goes on to explore the prevailing dominance of utilitarian thinking while yet deeming it to be ultimately fallacious, or at least at odds with epic or tragic grandeur.

In this matter of writing, resolve as one may to keep to the main road, some bypaths have an enticement not readily to be withstood. I am going to err into such a bypath. If the reader will keep me company I shall be glad. At the least, we can promise ourselves that pleasure which is wickedly said to be in sinning, for a literary sin the divergence will be.

Melville, *Billy Budd*, p. 56.

Melville struggled with the manuscript he underwent three such phases corresponding to his three major characters. Billy himself dominated the earliest phase, John Claggart the second, and Captain Vere (heretofore merely a background figure) the third. Suppose we try to reenact Melville's process of composition with the not unreasonable idea that he really did hope to compose, as earlier with *Moby-Dick*, some type of classical tragedy, though occasioned also by such contemporary events as the mutiny aboard the USS *Somers* in December 1842, with the ensuing executions and courts-martial, and the Haymarket Riot in May 1886. The figure of Billy Budd could not quite function as the plausible tragic hero in the traditional Greek or Shakespearean context, in part because Billy's extraordinary goodness and innocence seem to preclude the hamartia or "tragic flaw." Melville did seek to correct this problem when he introduced Billy's stutter in chapter 2 by attributing it specifically to the hand of Satan—"the envious marplot of Eden" (p. 53). Original sin, which Melville had called the source of "the power of blackness," was thus sutured onto an otherwise angelic Billy. But that solution could never quite sustain itself because Billy, however tainted by residual original sin, so to speak, is never in possession of any genuine self-consciousness: he has "about as much," Melville writes, "as we may reasonably impute to a dog of Saint Bernard's breed" (p. 52). Billy would thus remain the center of the novel's tragic

This hypothetical rumination by Melville's narrator from chapter 22 would seem to capture the idea that Captain Vere finds himself an unhappy participant in a necessary tragic action that goes against his own humanity; yet he must follow through with it. Ironist critics, however, would question both the reliability of this viewpoint and even the truth of the incident itself.

Captain Vere in end may have developed the passion sometimes latent under an exterior stoical or indifferent. He was old enough to have been Billy's father. The austere devotee of military duty, letting himself melt back into what remains primeval in our formalized humanity, may in end have caught Billy to his heart, even as Abraham may have caught young Isaac on the brink of resolutely offering him up in obedience to the exacting behest.

Melville, Billy Budd, p. 115.

movement, yet he could not function as the tragic hero in the traditional sense.

In the second phase of composition Melville developed John Claggart as the moral and spiritual bête noire to Billy, attempting to explore nothing less than the "mystery of iniquity" (pp. 76, 108). The narrator concedes that Claggart's "portrait I essay, but shall never hit" (p. 64). As the opposing parallel to Billy, Claggart, like the handsome, innocent sailor, exhibits entirely unknown human origins, a suggestion that promotes the idea that both figures symbolically lie outside of time, or at least outside human and social history. Since the eventual confrontation between them amounts to good versus evil, such out-of-time yet universal status may seem to us readers appropriate; indeed, the narrator also tries to explain the unexplainable Claggart by recourse to the Platonic—and later Christian—concept of "Natural Depravity: a depravity according to nature" (p. 75). With such basis for character delineation, it is not surprising that both emerge as far more type than character; and as types they can but eventually destroy each other—Claggart by Billy's single "angelic" blow, Billy by naval law.

Yet in one respect Claggart, at least, is not so atemporal or ahistorical, in that Melville associates his particular duplicity with a contemporary view opposed to the lexicon and insight derived from the mythical elements in Holy Scripture. This view is the biblical higher criticism of the later nineteenth century, one associated with the growth of scientific-positivistic thought and much allied with the newer realist movement that was in its prime while Melville tried to write Billy Budd. It is not, obviously, that Claggart is an advocate of the "higher criticism," rather that the disparity between his pleasant, rational, and highly discriminating veneer belies an interior volcanic "lunacy" and "riot" (p. 76) that the narrator associates with contemporary "higher criticism." For this reason the narrator invokes the "Hebrew prophets" over "Coke and Blackstone"—those monumental writers of British law—and even "admits" ironically that he must appeal to "some authority not liable to the charge of being tinctured with the biblical element" (p. 75). He concludes the analysis of Claggart with these words: "Dark sayings are these, some will say. But why? Is it because they somewhat savor of Holy Writ in its phrase 'mystery of iniquity'? If they do, such savor was far enough from being intended, for little will it commend these pages to many a reader of today" (p. 76).

Melville's third phase of composition he turned to Captain Vere in his search for the tragic hero. To begin with, he needed a character rather than a type as well as someone actually planted in time and history. So he introduces Vere to the reader as "Captain the Honorable Edward Fairfax Vere" (p. 60), thereby establishing him with a family prominent—and profoundly divided—at the time of the English Civil War, sharply contrasting with those of unknown origin and lineage, Billy and Claggart. Furthermore, in his development as a character we become privy to both his consciousness and his reading, reading that establishes the basis for his conservative political and philosophical viewpoint, which together with his scholarly demeanor earn him the ambiguous appellation "Starry Vere" (p. 61). What authorities such as Montaigne have refined in him is a deeply a priori cast of mind, yet one also thoughtful and "free from cant" (p. 62).

These features notwithstanding, the ironist school of Melville criticism perforce denies Vere the status of tragic hero in its condemnation of him as a duped and close-minded legalist. The plain-talking critic will find him exceptional but not subject to condemnation, even though the death of Billy betokens a tragic movement to the overall drama. How does one discern, then, a grand tragic flaw in Captain Vere without otherwise diminishing the character Melville brought forth from the background in his final phase of composition? One way is to emphasize the surprising fact that, in his speech condemning Billy to the drumhead court made up of his junior officers, Vere must eventually resort to the pragmatist's argument—the argument from immediate practical consequences—in order to convince them that anything less than full punishment will invite riot and anarchy among "the people" (the seamen; p. 112), especially in the climate of recent mutiny elsewhere. He turns to this pragmatic argument, however, only after first attempting—and utterly failing—to convince them by philosophical argument that exhibits his usual a priori cast of mind ("settled convictions . . . as a dike," p. 62). Still, why might such a change in Vere's mode of argument constitute hamartia?

The answer lies in the way Melville has already addressed the issue of utilitarian thinking—he calls such thinkers "Benthamites" (p. 57)—earlier in *Billy Budd*. He objects deeply to such thinking and explicitly opposes it to the grandeur undergirding the poetic "epics and dramas" (p. 58) of art, and he cites as an exemplar of that grand ritualistic style the legendary Lord Horatio Nelson. But Melville also knew only too well that in the course of the nineteenth century—the time frame between when *Billy Budd* is set in 1797 and when Melville wrote it nearly a century later—the utilitarian mindset had won out in philosophy, ethics, and culture, including its natural compatibility with the higher criticism and postbellum literary realism. In short, Captain Vere has been forced to employ the utilitarian argument in order to try to preserve from his perspective in 1797 a traditional and conservative worldview which, as Melville knew from his perspective in the 1890s, would run counter to the actual Benthamite direction of subsequent thinking and history in the course of the nineteenth century. Therefore Vere becomes in *Billy Budd* the most profound demonstration of the inevitable triumph of that history in the very attempt by which he hoped to implement and maintain the alternative history. In this respect Vere exhibits both hamartia and classical irony of fate. Melville thus manages, as he sought in the earlier "Benthamite" chapter, to "hold the Present at its worth without being inappreciative of the Past" (p. 57).

Melville's profound sense of that "Present" in *Billy Budd* is the signature of his creativity in late-nineteenth-century intellectual and cultural history. The mode of "indirection" he admits employing in this novel and the extended compositional process can answer to the method and practice of pragmatist minds and artists like William and Henry James, respectively, during the realist movement. "Truth uncompromisingly told will always have its ragged edges" (p. 128), he wrote, and although its primary reference is to the circumstances of Billy's death, the open-endedness of truth fits well into the newer paradigm of pragmatistic thought, while the novel he all but finished would engender a debate many compare with *The Turn of the Screw* (1898). Finally, Melville's achievement in *Billy Budd* may also be analogous to the work of the prolific Puritan writer Jonathan Edwards (1703–1758) in its honest attempt to convey a traditional viewpoint through a newer mode of presentation whose foundations tend to undermine that traditional view—a case, dramatically, of new forms revivified by old issues. It is an achievement Captain Vere would have welcomed historically and politically but must settle for in the artistic sphere.

See also The Bible; Jurisprudence; Philosophy

BIBLIOGRAPHY

Primary Works

Melville, Herman. *Billy Budd, Sailor (An Inside Narrative).* Edited by Harrison Hayford and Merton M. Sealts Jr. Chicago: University of Chicago Press, 1962.

Melville, Herman. "Hawthorne and His Mosses." *Literary World* 17 (17 and 24 August 1850). Reprinted in *American Literary Essays,* edited by Lewis Gaston Leary. New York: Crowell, 1960.

Melville, Herman. *Selected Poems of Herman Melville.* Edited by Hennig Cohen. New York: Fordham University Press, 1991.

Secondary Works

Brodtkorb, Paul, Jr. "The Definitive *Billy Budd:* 'But Aren't It All a Sham?'" *PMLA* 82, no. 7 (1967): 602–612.

Fogle, Richard Harter. "*Billy Budd*—Acceptance or Irony." *Tulane Studies in English* 8 (1958): 107–113. Reprinted in Stafford's *Melville's "Billy Budd" and the Critics.*

Hocks, Richard A. "Melville and 'The Rise of Realism': The Dilemma of History in *Billy Budd*." *American Literary Realism* 26, no. 2 (1994): 60–81.

Marovitz, Sanford E. "Melville among the Realists: W. D. Howells and the Writing of *Billy Budd*." *American Literary Realism* 34, no. 1 (2001): 29–46.

Parker, Hershel. *Reading "Billy Budd."* Evanston, Ill.: Northwestern University Press, 1990.

Stafford, William T., ed. *Melville's "Billy Budd" and the Critics.* Belmont, Calif.: Wadsworth, 1961. Reprints numerous critical essays including three cited in this article: Fogle, Watson, and Withim.

Watson, E. L. Grant. "Melville's Testament of Acceptance." *New England Quarterly* 6, no. 2 (1933): 319–327. Reprinted in Stafford's *Melville's "Billy Budd" and the Critics.*

Withim, Phil. "*Billy Budd:* Testament of Resistance." *Modern Language Quarterly* 20, no. 2 (1959): 115–132. Reprinted in Stafford's *Melville's "Billy Budd" and the Critics.*

Richard A. Hocks

BIOGRAPHY

Between 1870 and 1920, biography was an unstable genre, and many questions surrounded the practice of it. Who, for example, deserved to be the subject of a biography? Should biographers present their subjects as unique individuals or as representative of something larger? Should they consider only the public lives of their subjects or their private lives as well? Should they attempt to elevate their subjects or should they "debunk" them by revealing their unknown shortcomings? Must a biography present a complete, linear narrative of a subject's life? Or should a biographer distill the essence of a subject's "inner life" using a few telling anecdotes? Such questions reflect the development of biography as a genre, but also circumstances that were specific to the cultural context of the United States.

HAGIOGRAPHY AND BIOGRAPHY

In the broadest sense, modern biography reflects an abiding Western belief in the autonomy and importance of the individual. The genre emerged in part from the medieval Christian tradition of hagiography, that is, spiritual biography that presents the exemplary lives of saints so that believers might imitate them. Hagiography is not supposed to be strictly factual or objective; it presents idealized role models that help to construct and stabilize the values of the communities.

By the late eighteenth century, however, the values of the Enlightenment were encouraging greater objectivity in biographical writing. Secular biography sought to present factual, even scientific documentation of the actions of important figures in politics, exploration, science, and war in the emerging democratic nation-state. Secular biographies may have an exemplary character, but their importance to readers is presumed to lie less in the realm of faith than in their encouragement of civic progress. The main tendencies reflected in these two traditions—religious and secular, subjective and objective, idealistic and realistic, exemplary and individualized—were continually being renegotiated by communities of authors and audiences. The general development has been away from the religious traditions of hagiography. Nevertheless, both traditions supported a view that individual lives

were worth documenting for the instruction of future generations.

The circumstances of postcolonial cultural nationalism in the United States after the Revolution—coupled with the uneven spread of Enlightenment secularism to relatively isolated rural communities—meant that hagiographical writing persisted well into the nineteenth century, particularly in education and religious culture. After the Civil War, the assassinated Abraham Lincoln became the great exemplar of national virtues. Of course, there was a note of Northern triumphalism in this celebration of the Rail-splitter, but Lincoln was also a better model of the self-made man than the slave-owning George Washington, whom he replaced as a favorite subject of biography. Horatio Alger Jr. (1832–1899), author of the best-selling *Ragged Dick* series (beginning in 1868), applied the rags-to-riches template to *Abraham Lincoln, the Backwoods Boy; or, How a Young Rail-Splitter Became President* (1883). After President James Garfield was assassinated, Alger wrote a companion volume: *From Canal Boy to President; or, The Boyhood and Manhood of James A. Garfield* (1881). Similar popular volumes about Garfield as a self-made man and secular saint were written by James S. Brisbin, James Dabney McCabe, William R. Thayer, and many others. Of course, the somewhat priggish version of American presidents inflicted on generations of schoolchildren probably did much to encourage a complete rejection of the vestiges of the hagiographical tradition toward the end of the nineteenth century. These popular biographies would provide writers with a tradition to define themselves against, particularly in the so-called Gilded Age when the notion of a saintly politician seemed cloying and that of the self-made man a misguided justification of the excesses of capitalism.

MONUMENTAL BIOGRAPHY

While popular biographies reached large segments of the reading public by presenting simplified and idealized subjects, so-called monumental biographies were often unreadable compendiums of ill-digested letters and diaries presented chronologically within their historical context. With titles such as "Life and Times" or "Life and Letters," these biographies occupied several volumes and were ponderous in style as well as heft. If scrupulously edited, monumental biographies could be valuable repositories of primary documents. More often, these documents were selected, edited, and in some cases revised to suit the interests of the compiler-biographer. Readers were frequently left to extract their own interpretations from the mass of material and most had little interest in doing so.

Monumental biographies usually took many years to write because of the difficulty in gaining access to papers and permission to publish their contents. Unlike popular biographies, written on short notice to meet market demand, a monumental biography generally could not be produced until a generation or more had passed since the death of its subject. Most of the more reliable monumental biographies of revolutionary figures were not published until well into the nineteenth century. For example, William W. Henry published *Patrick Henry: Life, Correspondence, and Speeches* in three volumes in 1891. Toward the end of the nineteenth century, subjects' writings in such biographies increasingly tended to be presented in more complete form, particularly as close associates and relatives ceased to have control of the documents. Indeed, at that time an author's close association with the subject of a monumental biography was thought to undermine its claims to objectivity. This was particularly true when the biographer was a family member, friend, employee, or political associate.

Lincoln's secretaries, John G. Nicolay (1832–1901) and John Hay (1838–1905), collaborated for nearly fifteen years to write *Abraham Lincoln: A History* (10 vols., 1890). The biography was serialized in the popular *Century Magazine* (1886–1890), earning its authors the enormous sum of fifty thousand dollars. Nicolay and Hay were careful to avoid the shortcomings of *Herndon's Lincoln: The True Story of a Great Life* (1889), which considered Lincoln's religious unorthodoxy, his stormy marriage, and his youthful romances. Instead of personal anecdote, Nicolay and Hay relied as much as possible on documentary evidence, although many of Lincoln's papers were under the control of Robert Lincoln, who insisted on his right to dictate the interpretation of materials. Unlike William Henry Herndon (1818–1891), Nicolay and Hay spent little time on Lincoln's obscure youth; eight of the ten volumes focus on the Civil War. Their work was partisan, favoring the North and the Republican Party, and Lincoln was clearly presented as a heroic figure. Still, *Abraham Lincoln: A History,* although not monumental in scale, reflected an ongoing shift toward more interpretive forms of biographical writing.

Although the Nicolay and Hay biography was an important publication, monumental biographies for the most part were the literary equivalent of Grant's Tomb: structures so grandiose that one could scarcely remember who was buried inside. Of course, there was an economic incentive behind their size: subscriptions for two-volume biographies were more profitable than over-the-counter sales of single volumes. To judge from the many extant copies of monumental biographies with pristine pages, the vast majority of these works were never read by the owners who displayed them. Eminently respectable, they were biographies as furniture, signifiers of middle-class status. After World War I, monumental biographies would come to represent everything that was stodgy and hypocritical about the Victorian era.

In *Eminent Victorians* (1918), Lytton Strachey (1890–1932) complained of

> those two fat volumes, with which it is our custom to commemorate the dead—who does not know them, with their ill-digested masses of material, their slipshod style, their tone of tedious panegyric, the lamentable lack of selection, of detachment, of design? They are as familiar as the cortege of the undertaker, and wear the same air of slow, funereal barbarism. (Altick, p. 281)

Although they are often useful as scholarly resources, few monumental biographies could be regarded as literary, and, from the start, they coexisted with—and perhaps contributed to—the desire for shorter, more readable, and more analytic biographies by disinterested professional writers.

JAMES PARTON, PROFESSIONAL BIOGRAPHER

James Parton (1822–1891) was the first professional biographer in the United States; he invented the role as the market for biography was growing, but he also helped to create the market. He was not a hagiographer or a didactic nationalist, nor was he an associate of the famous or a specialist in a single figure like Nicolay and Hay. Parton attempted to capture the "inner life" of his subjects in deft strokes rather than overwhelming his readers with extensive documentation. Most of all, he wanted to elevate biography to a literary art, a hybrid of history and novel. Parton could adapt his style to the *North American Review* as well as to the *New York Ledger,* and the various forms his biographies took—multiple volumes, single volumes, shorter pieces for literary magazines, and popular articles for newspapers—catered to different kinds of readers.

Parton did not reduce the complexity of his subjects to suit a preconceived didactic purpose. He cited extensive printed sources and conducted interviews. His methods were historical, but his prose was journalistic, even literary, uncovering mysteries about his subjects. He used dramatic license such as invented dialogue and paced the narrative to maintain reader interest. In that sense, Parton pursued the connection between biography and the bildungsroman, a novel that describes a protagonist's moral or intellectual development. But Parton did not regard himself as a fiction writer, still less as a sensationalist. He refused to repeat unsubstantiated rumors, even on matters of substance, such as Aaron Burr's reputation as a womanizer.

For his subjects, Parton generally chose American figures who were already well known. His career began with *Horace Greeley* (1855), a biography that presented its subject as a virtuous, self-made man. It was remarkable in part because Greeley was still alive, but it rose above adulation by virtue of Parton's in-depth research. He followed *Horace Greeley* with *The Life and Times of Aaron Burr* (1858, enlarged to two volumes in 1864), which was also extensively researched and supplemented by interviews. In each case, Parton claimed he wanted to discover the complex inner man, not just present the public record. Burr, for example, is depicted as a morally flawed political visionary with many redeeming qualities. Parton's subsequent biographies—*The Life of Andrew Jackson* (3 vols., 1860–1861) and *The Life and Times of Benjamin Franklin* (2 vols., 1864)—were even more extensively supported with quotation and documentation, but they also demonstrated Parton's flair for storytelling. The success of these works made Parton the foremost American biographer in the 1860s. *Atlantic Monthly* praised him as a literary artist, and biography began to establish itself as a distinct genre, a mixture of history and literature.

In 1893, shortly after this pioneer's death, *McClure's Magazine* published "James Parton's Rules of Biography." In this essay, Parton explained his techniques: research your subjects thoroughly; do not eulogize them; keep events in perspective; and hold back nothing that the reader has a right to know. The biographer's job was not to provide moral instruction but to satisfy curiosity about the subject's life. "The great charm of all biography," according to Parton, "is the truth, told simply, directly, boldly, charitably" (p. 59). But Parton had a complex view of human behavior: "A human character is complicated. It is often inconsistent with itself, and it requires nice judgment to proportion it in such a way as to make the book correspond with the man" (p. 59). Such views mark Parton as an antecedent of biographers who sought to reveal the psychological complexity of their subjects, and his status would remain high in the late nineteenth century, when most biographies written by his generation were ridiculed.

LITERARY BIOGRAPHY

One of the factors influencing biographers such as Parton to explore the "inner life" of their subjects was the growth and spread of literary romanticism in the first half of the nineteenth century. Romanticism broadened who could be considered worthy of biography; it stressed the importance of individuals of "genius," who could be figures such as Washington or Napoleon but also writers and artists. In the American context, the exceptional individual was often seen as what Ralph Waldo Emerson called a "Representative Man," one who embodied the virtues of his time and place. Sainthood and the notion of the self-made man were reframed in the Romantic era as a quest for "character," a search for individuality. There was also a nationalistic quality to American literary biography, which sought to demonstrate that the United States could produce individuals of genius as well as successful practical men.

Literary biographies were frequently written in the monumental style by family members for a middle-class audience, and many of these are little more than letters strung together with brief transitions. Examples of this genre include Samuel Longfellow's *Life of Henry Wadsworth Longfellow with Extracts from His Journals and Correspondence* (3 vols., 1886) and Charles Edward Stowe's *Life of Harriet Beecher Stowe* (1899). One of the more notable examples is *Nathaniel Hawthorne and His Wife: A Biography* (2 vols., 1884), compiled by their son, Julian Hawthorne (1846–1934). Julian's avowed purpose was to shed light on his parents' celebrated marriage rather than to assert the literary merit of such works as *The Scarlet Letter* (1850). His method was to let the subjects "speak for themselves whenever possible," and Julian claims he did not "err on the side of reticence," though, he adds, "there was nothing to be hidden" (p. 1). He included long quotations from his father's unpublished letters, but he also edited the letters to suit the portrait he wished to present. The decision to depict a marriage was a remarkable endorsement in literary history of the value of private, romantic relationships, and, though the biography is generally positive, it also presents the psychological difficulty of being the child of a famous writer.

Biographies by the close friends and family members of authors were often highly flattering of subjects whose deaths the writers were still mourning. William Ellery Channing's recollections in *Thoreau, the Poet-Naturalist* (1873) presents the author of *Walden* (1854) as a modern-day Saint Francis. Such works were an invaluable resource for subsequent biographers, but the living guardians of an author's reputation were also an impediment to increasingly professionalized scholars seeking to write more objective biographies. In his novella *The Aspern Papers* (1888), Henry James (1843–1916) presents the heirs of a famous Romantic poet as hindering serious research rather than serving

Henry James's The Aspern Papers *(1888) describes the efforts of an American biographer to obtain a bundle of letters written by Jeffrey Aspern, a fictional romantic author based on Lord Byron. The letters are in the possession of an elderly former lover of the poet and guarded by her niece who, ultimately, will not surrender them to anyone besides the man who agrees to become her husband. The biographer is faced with a choice between his private happiness and his desire to document the life of his favorite author.*

The world, as I say, had recognized Jeffrey Aspern, but Cumnor and I had recognized him most. The multitude, today, flocked to his temple, but of that temple he and I regarded ourselves as the ministers. We held, justly, as I think, that we had done more for his memory than anyone else, and we had done it by opening lights into his life. He had nothing to fear from us because he had nothing to fear from the truth, which alone at such a distance of time we could be interested in establishing. His early death had been the only dark spot in his life, unless the papers in Miss Bordereau's hands should perversely bring out others. There had been an impression about 1825 that he had "treated her badly," just as there had been an impression that he had "served," as the London populace says, several other ladies in the same way. Each of these cases Cumnor and I had been able to investigate, and we had never failed to acquit him conscientiously of shabby behavior. I judged him perhaps more indulgently than my friend; certainly, at any rate, it appeared to me that no man could have walked straighter in the given circumstances. These were almost always awkward. Half the women of his time, to speak liberally, had flung themselves at his head, and out of this pernicious fashion many complications, some of them grave, had not failed to arise . . .

. . . Every one of Aspern's contemporaries had, according to our belief, passed away; we had not been able to look into a single pair of eyes into which his had looked or to feel a transmitted contact in any aged hand that his had touched. Most dead of all did poor Miss Bordereau appear, and yet she alone had survived. We exhausted in the course of months our wonder that we had not found her out sooner, and the substance of our explanation was that she had kept so quiet. The poor lady on the whole had had reason for doing so. But it was a revelation to us that it was possible to keep so quiet as that in the latter half of the nineteenth century—the age of newspapers and telegrams and photographs and interviewers. And she had taken no great trouble about it either: she had not hidden herself away in an undiscoverable hole; she had boldly settled down in a city of exhibition. The only secret of her safety that we could perceive was that Venice contained so many curiosities that were greater than she. And then accident had somehow favored her, as was shown for example in the fact that Mrs. Prest had never happened to mention her to me, though I had spent three weeks in Venice—under her nose, as it were—five years before. Mrs. Prest had not mentioned this much to anyone; she appeared almost to have forgotten she was there. Of course she had not the responsibilities of an editor. It was no explanation of the old woman's having eluded us to say that she lived abroad, for our researches had again and again taken us (not only by correspondence but by personal inquiry) to France, to Germany, to Italy, in which countries, not counting his important stay in England, so many of the too few years of Aspern's career were spent. We were glad to think at least that in all our publishings (some people consider I believe that we have overdone them), we had only touched in passing and in the most discreet manner on Miss Bordereau's connection. Oddly enough, even if we had had the material (and we often wondered what had become of it), it would have been the most difficult episode to handle.

Henry James, "The Aspern Papers," in *Complete Stories, 1884–1891* (New York: Library of America, 1999), pp. 230–232.

as useful collaborators. Relatives of biographical subjects might make access to their letters conditional on some distortion of the full truth; they might seek to sanitize the historical record or conceal crucial documents, which could surface later to the embarrassment of the biographer. As romanticism gave way to realism in the second half of the nineteenth century, there was a need for more disinterested, authoritative analyses of authors who could establish a national canon by reaching a wide audience.

Inspired by the *English Men of Letters* series (1878–1884), the *American Men of Letters* series was edited by Charles Dudley Warner (1829–1900). The series began with Warner's *Washington Irving* in 1881 and by 1904 twenty-two volumes in all had appeared. Published as a uniform series with the more successful *American Statesmen* series, they were a collectible pantheon of American authors such as N. P. Willis, Margaret Fuller, and Ralph Waldo Emerson. One of the more remarkable volumes in the series was George Woodberry's *Edgar Allan Poe* (1885). Woodberry (1855–1930) called himself a "documentary biographer" and regarded his research as almost scientific in its precision. He conducted research more thoroughly than any previous Poe biographer and corrected Rufus Griswold's defamatory portrait that had persisted since the 1840s. Woodberry's Poe was not a tragic Romantic figure so much as a talented writer ruined by moral shortcomings. Woodbury, along with several other writers in the *American Men of Letters* series, moved literary biography away from personal reminiscence and closer to modern research and criticism.

The success of the *American Statesmen* series and some volumes in the *American Men of Letters* inspired other series such as *American Crisis Biographies, American Worthies, American Men of Progress, Men of Achievement, Great Commanders,* and the short *Beacon Biographies* (31 vols., 1899–1910), edited by M. A. DeWolfe Howe. The *Beacon Biographies* were cheaply priced and pocket-size; they came with a portrait, a chronology, and a bibliography. They treated literary figures (James Fenimore Cooper, Emerson, Hawthorne), statesmen (Frederick Douglass, Thomas Jefferson, Lincoln), military leaders (Ulysses S. Grant, David Farragut, Robert E. Lee), and scientists (Louis Agassiz, John Audubon, Samuel Morse). The purpose of the series, according to Howe, was to provide brief, readable, and accurate accounts of important Americans in a variety of fields for a wide audience. The spread of such biographies reflected a convergence of conventions in a genre that had once been clearly divided between the hagiographic popular forms and the more documentary monumental forms.

GROUP BIOGRAPHIES, COLLECTIVE BIOGRAPHIES, AND "MUG BOOKS"

Even as biographies of a single subject began to establish some generic norms, new forms of biographical writing proliferated. Group biographies, for example, describe the interactions of a subject with other individuals. They may include anecdotes, remembered conversations, and exchanges of letters, among other elements. They are not comprehensive but instead re-create the web of relationships that defines an intellectual or social coterie.

Henry James's *William Wetmore Story and His Friends* (1903) describes a cluster of individuals who had dealings with the nineteenth-century American sculptor. James says the "subject is the *period*—it is the period that holds the elements together, rounds them off, makes them right" (Parke, p. 112). Other group biographies published near this time include *James Russell Lowell and His Friends* (1899), by Edward Everett Hale; *Literary Friends and Acquaintance* (1900), by William Dean Howells; and *Authors and Friends* (1896), by Annie Fields.

Collective biographies are usually arranged thematically or alphabetically. Following the British *Dictionary of National Biography* (1885–1901), edited by Leslie Stephen, *Appleton's National Cyclopaedia of American Biography* (1887–1889) aspired to be a comprehensive biographical dictionary, including founding fathers, patriots, and individuals of note up to the present time. The authoritative *Dictionary of American Biography* was first published in 1928 and continues to be updated. Directories such as *Who's Who in America* (1899–), founded by A. N. Marquis, began with 8,600 names and included only basic data (education, career, honors, memberships). *Who's Who* helped to define the regional, national, and professional elite. Indeed, having one's biographical sketch published in a reference work became so desirable that people sometimes paid for the privilege.

Local histories often included biographical volumes; in many cases, historical discourse proper was eliminated altogether in favor of biographical sketches of leading local citizens. These so-called mug books were a means for the rising middle-class to establish its legitimacy. The subscription agent was often the writer, and subjects paid a fee for the biographical sketches based on their length. These circumstances were never mentioned in the publication itself. Larger regional books such as Hubert Howe Bancroft's *Chronicles of the Builders of the Commonwealth* (1891) included only figures who had paid at least a thousand dollars to be included. Undoubtedly, mug books have value as regional histories, but their primary market was the subjects themselves, who regarded a printed biography as proof that they had "arrived." Mug books confirm there was an ongoing belief in the self-made man and in the importance of local communities.

During this period, however, novelists such as William Dean Howells (1837–1920) questioned the reality of the conventional rags-to-riches narrative that characterized nearly every American biography. Howells was a rags-to-riches story himself, but he came to see social mobility as a source of unhappiness and social disorder and as out of reach for most Americans. His novel *A Modern Instance* (1882) depicts the rise of a journalist from youthful poverty to professional success at the cost of his moral character and eventually his life. *The Rise of Silas Lapham* (1885) demonstrates the costs of rapid social mobility, showing how the behavior of the upper classes cannot simply be learned; even in America, the upwardly mobile individual is always an interloper. For Howells, the democratization of biography was one way that the illusion of the self-made man was perpetuated at the expense of social reforms.

THE "NEW BIOGRAPHY"

As the twentieth century approached, biographers began to respond to the ideas of Karl Marx, Charles Darwin, Friedrich Nietzsche, and Herbert Spencer. Less subject to the conditions of the immediate postcolonial period and its concern with nation-building, biographers in the Progressive Era began to question received wisdom about figures such as Washington and Lincoln. Although the "Great Man" approach remained popular in schools and among the general public, professional historians now tended to emphasize large-scale social forces over individuals. Literary realism also rejected the idea of heroism in favor of more accurate representations of human behavior based on the insights of science, economics, and psychology.

The True George Washington (1896) and *The Many-Sided Franklin* (1899), both by Paul Leicester Ford (1865–1902), were not comprehensive biographies arranged chronologically so much as a series of topical essays. The Franklin biography, for example, includes chapters titled "Physique: Theories and Appetites," "Relations with the Fair Sex," and "The Scientist." Other biographies reappraised national heroes such as Thomas Jefferson, William Penn, and Andrew Jackson. What were called "true" biographies sought to "humanize" their subjects by investigating themes absent in the more linear, comprehensive biographies By contrast, "real" biographies attempted to debunk their subjects, which they regarded as inflated and sanitized. Charles L. C. Minor's *The Real Lincoln* (1901) uses contemporary accounts to demonstrate that Lincoln invoked Christianity hypocritically and supported the abolition of slavery inconsistently for his own political advantage. Both the "true" and the "real" approaches encouraged the unauthorized publication of private letters, investigative reporting by muckraking journalists, and exposés by former employees and associates (who were well compensated for their information). Ida M. Tarbell (1857–1944), the author of *The Early Life of Abraham Lincoln* (1896), portrayed John D. Rockefeller as a corrupt monopolist in her *History of the Standard Oil Company* (1904). Tarbell showed how the ideal of the American self-made man embodied by Lincoln was out of reach for the average American in an age of unregulated capitalism and incipient class warfare.

The New Biography earned a bad name for itself among some readers, who regarded it as unpatriotic sensationalism at best. Owen Wister (1860–1938) attempted directly to refute the debunkers in adulatory biographies such as *The Seven Ages of Washington* (1907). M. A. DeWolfe Howe (1864–1960) drew on the monumental tradition, basing his lives on excerpts from letters, but, in works such as *Phillips Brooks* (1899), *Life and Letters of George Bancroft* (2 vols., 1908), *Letters of Charles Eliot Norton* (1913), *Memories of a Hostess* (1922), and *Barrett Wendell* (1924), his writing was more interpretive and more willing to explore sympathetically the complexities of his subjects. Similarly, biographies by William Roscoe Thayer (1859–1923) such as *The Life and Letters of John Hay* (1915) and *Theodore Roosevelt, An Intimate Biography* (1919) offered insight into the private lives of his subjects, but in doing so the author attempted to demonstrate the authenticity of the virtues displayed in their public lives. Roosevelt, he argued, was above all "pledged to Righteousness" (p. ix).

Thayer described his methods in a series of lectures called *The Art of Biography* (1920). He sought a compromise between idolatry and debunking, between hagiography and the New Biography. Thayer believed that everything about a subject's life should be open to investigation, but the results of this investigation should be interpreted in a novelistic manner. "The scientific method," he writes, "defeated its purpose by substituting material and mechanical standards for the spiritual. Science can vivisect bodies, but up to the present the soul of man eludes the microscope and the scalpel" (Novarr, p. 22). Thayer laments that the biographers of his era emphasized historical and natural forces above the unique qualities of the individual, which, according to him, it is the sole task of the biographer to describe. For Thayer, the biographer was ultimately an intuitive artist more than a historian, scientist, or political activist.

GAMALIEL BRADFORD AND "PSYCHOGRAPHY"

Gamaliel Bradford (1863–1932) was one of the most prominent and influential biographers of the early twentieth century. In addition to full-length biographies such as *Lee the American* (1912), he wrote more than a hundred substantial character sketches, which were collected in *Types of American Character* (1895), *Confederate Portraits* (1914), *Union Portraits* (1916),

By the mid-1880s, biographical sketches of leading citizens had fallen into a generic rut. Quick-sketch biographers, often compilers of mug books, had become a species of literary professional, though one of embarrassingly low rank for those with literary aspirations. Even the more naïve subjects of such mass-produced biographies—when not indulging their vanity—were self-conscious about the rigid conventions of the self-made man tradition.

When Bartley Hubbard went to interview Silas Lapham for the "Solid Men of Boston" series, which he undertook to finish up in "The Events," after he replaced their original projector on that newspaper, Lapham received him in his private office by previous appointment.

. . . "I don't know as I know just where you want me to begin," said Lapham.

"Might begin with your birth; that's where most of us begin," replied Bartley.

A gleam of humorous appreciation shot into Lapham's blue eyes.

"I didn't know whether you wanted me to go quite so far back as that," he said. "But there's no disgrace in having been born. . . . I was born on a farm, and—"

"Worked in the fields summers and went to school winters: regulation thing?" Bartley cut in.

"Regulation thing," said Lapham, accepting this irreverent version of his history somewhat dryly.

"Parents poor, of course," suggested the journalist. "Any barefoot business? Early deprivations of any kind, that would encourage the youthful reader to go and do likewise? Orphan myself, you know," said Bartley, with a smile of cynical good-comradery.

Lapham looked at him silently, and then said with quiet self-respect, "I guess if you see these things as a joke, my life won't interest you."

"Oh yes, it will," returned Bartley, unabashed. "You'll see; it'll come out all right." And in fact it did so, in the interview which Bartley printed.

"Mr. Lapham," he wrote, "passed rapidly over the story of his early life, its poverty and its hardships, sweetened, however, by the recollections of a devoted mother, and a father who, if somewhat her inferior in education, was no less ambitious for the advancement of his children. They were quiet, unpretentious people, religious, after the fashion of that time, and of sterling morality, and they taught their children the simple virtues of the Old Testament and Poor Richard's Almanac."

Bartley could not deny himself this gibe; but he trusted to Lapham's unliterary habit of mind for his security in making it, and most other people would consider it sincere reporter's rhetoric.

"You know," he explained to Lapham, "that we have to look at all these facts as material, and we get the habit of classifying them. Sometimes a leading question will draw out a whole line of facts that a man himself would never think of."

. . . "Yes, sir," said Lapham, in a strain which Bartley was careful not to interrupt again, "a man never sees all that his mother has been to him till it's too late to let her know that he sees it. Why, my mother—" he stopped. "It gives me a lump in the throat," he said apologetically, with an attempt at a laugh. Then he went on: "She was a little frail thing, not bigger than a good-sized intermediate school-girl; but she did the whole work of a family of boys, and boarded the hired men besides. She cooked, swept, washed, ironed, made and mended from daylight till dark—and from dark till daylight, I was going to say; for I don't know how she got any time for sleep. But I suppose she did. She got time to go to church, and to teach us to read the Bible, and to misunderstand it in the old way. She was *good*. But it ain't her on her knees in church that comes back to me so much like the sight of an angel as her on her knees before me at night, washing my poor, dirty little feet, that I'd run bare in all day, and making me decent for bed. There were six of us boys; it seems to me we were all of a size; and she was just so careful with all of us. I can feel her hands on my feet yet!"

. . . "We were patched all over; but we wa'n't ragged. I don't know how she got through it.

. . . Bartley hid a yawn over his note-book. . . . [He] had learned to practise a patience with his victims which he did not always feel, and to feign an interest in their digressions till he could bring them up with a round turn.

William Dean Howells, *The Rise of Silas Lapham*, in *Novels, 1875–1886: A Foregone Conclusion, A Modern Instance, Indian Summer, and The Rise of Silas Lapham* (New York: Library of America, 1982), pp. 861–864.

Portraits of Women (1916), *A Naturalist of Souls* (1917) *American Portraits, 1875–1900* (1922), and *Damaged Souls* (1923), his most popular work. Bradford called these sketches "psychographs" and they reflected the influence of Marx's materialist approach to history, Darwin's theory of natural selection, and, most of all, Freud's theories about the unconscious and the importance of childhood development. Bradford thought of psychography as a genre separate from biography. Psychography emphasized the inner self, the "soul" of the subject, which the author abstracted from the whirl of external events. Bradford was an exhaustive researcher but, like Parton and Thayer, he thought of himself as a literary artist informed by science. He too was wary of scientific or psychological generalizations that tended to reduce the uniqueness of individual human "character." Bradford was not interested in long sequences of facts; instead, he paid great attention to small but revealing details such as Freudian slips. "A careless word, spoken with no intention whatever," he writes, "may fling open a wide window into a man's inmost heart" (*Biography and the Human Heart*, p. 7).

In *Lee the American*, Bradford says that his aim was to "give a clear, consistent, sympathetic portrait of a great soul," and the focus is on the development of Lee's character rather than his accomplishments as a general (p. vii). Bradford gives notable attention to Lee's "Great Decision" to side with the Confederacy; he presents the conflicted inner man, not the marble statue of Lee, which is the "sort of thing that made Washington odious to the young and remote from the mature for generations," he writes (p. 25). Ultimately, Bradford's portrait of Lee is not iconoclastic; he presents Lee's life as a noble tragedy.

While some biographers were smashing the idols (Strachey) and others were trying to restore them unblemished (Wister), in works such as *Damaged Souls* Bradford attempted to rehabilitate figures with tarnished reputations: Benedict Arnold, Thomas Paine, Aaron Burr, John Brown, P. T. Barnum. According to Bradford, his purpose was to "bring out their real humanity and show that, after all, they have something of the same strength and weakness as all of us" (p. 4). His sketch of Barnum the showman and circus promoter, is deft, balanced, and largely positive. It is well researched, though not exhaustive or scholarly in tone, and, while Bradford praises Barnum as a purveyor of entertainment and a pioneer in advertising, he also shows his subject's lack of sensitivity toward the people he exhibited as freaks.

On the whole, Bradford's subjects emerged as complex human beings, but the author's psychoanalytic diagnoses were as much a reflection of the analyst's mind as of the subject's psychology. In that sense, "psychography," like the New Biography that preceded it, sought to be more objective without becoming ponderous, but ultimately it represented yet another negotiation between the ultimately unknowable reality of the subject and the organizing power of the biographer.

See also History; Success

BIBLIOGRAPHY
Primary Works
Bradford, Gamaliel. *Biography and the Human Heart.* Boston: Houghton Mifflin, 1932.

Bradford, Gamaliel. *Damaged Souls.* Boston: Houghton Mifflin, 1931.

Bradford, Gamaliel. *Lee the American.* Boston: Houghton Mifflin, 1912.

Hawthorne, Julian. *Nathaniel Hawthorne and His Wife.* Boston: Houghton Mifflin, 1892.

Parton, James. "James Parton's Rules of Biography." *McClure's Magazine* 1 (June 1893): 59–62.

Thayer, William Roscoe. *Theodore Roosevelt: An Intimate Biography.* New York: Grosset and Dunlap, 1919.

Secondary Works
Altick, Richard D. *Lives and Letters: A History of Literary Biography in England and America.* New York: Knopf, 1965.

Amigoni, David. *Victorian Biography: Intellectuals and the Ordering of Discourse.* New York: St. Martin's Press, 1993.

Casper, Scott E. *Constructing American Lives: Biography and Culture in Nineteenth-Century America.* Chapel Hill: University of North Carolina Press, 1999.

Cawelti, John G. *Apostles of the Self-Made Man: Changing Concepts of Success in America.* Chicago: University of Chicago Press, 1965.

Cockshut, A. O. J. *Truth to Life: The Art of Biography in the Nineteenth Century.* New York: Harcourt Brace Jovanovich, 1974.

Cunliffe, Marcus, ed. *The Life of Washington,* by Mason Locke Weems. Cambridge: Harvard University Press, 1962.

Dargan, Marion. *Guide to American Biography: Part II, 1815–1933.* Albuquerque: University of New Mexico Press, 1952.

Flower, Milton E. *James Parton, the Father of Modern Biography.* Durham, N.C.: Duke University Press, 1951.

Merrill, Dana Kinsman. *American Biography: Its Theory and Practice.* Portland, Maine: Bowker Press, 1957.

Nadel, Ira Bruce. *Biography: Fact, Fiction, and Form.* New York: St. Martin's Press, 1984.

Novarr, David. *The Lines of Life: Theories of Biography, 1880–1970.* West Lafayette, Ind.: Purdue University Press, 1986.

O'Neill, Edward H. *Biography by Americans, 1658–1936: A Subject Bibliography.* Philadelphia: University of Pennsylvania Press, 1939.

O'Neill, Edward H. *A History of American Biography, 1800–1935.* Philadelphia: University of Pennsylvania Press, 1935.

Parke, Catherine N. *Biography: Writing Lives.* New York: Twayne, 1996.

Peterson, Merrill D. *Lincoln in American Memory.* New York: Oxford University Press, 1994.

Wagenknecht, Edward. *Gamaliel Bradford.* Boston: Twayne, 1982.

William Pannapacker

THE BIRTH OF A NATION

The Birth of a Nation, directed by D. W. (David Wark) Griffith (1875–1948) in 1914 and released the following year, may be the most controversial feature film ever released in the United States. It is also one of the most seen and most influential of all films released anywhere in any period. Following the example of the historical novelists Sir Walter Scott and James Fenimore Cooper, it tells the story of the American Civil War and the Reconstruction period from the perspectives of two families, one southern and one northern. Its complexity, popularity, and political impact changed the opinions of film producers and viewers alike regarding the motion picture's role in the production of American identity—an identity that national antagonism over such issues as regionalism, immigration, labor relations, and the citizen status of African Americans made increasingly difficult to imagine as a singular and homogeneous entity.

GRIFFITH AND THE EARLY FILM INDUSTRY

When Griffith directed *The Birth of a Nation*, the film industry was roughly twenty years old, and Griffith had been part of it for only six. These years, however, had been the most transformative years in the film medium's already tumultuous history. During that time Griffith, more than any other individual filmmaker, helped to change the way both the audiences and the industry itself thought about cinema.

In 1908, when Griffith turned from stage and film acting to film directing for the American Biograph Company, films rarely exceeded two reels (approxi-

mately twenty-four minutes) in length and were shown on rotating programs with many other films. Story films had more or less dominated film production since 1905, but as plots became more intricate, critics complained that they were difficult for audiences to follow. The artisanal and disorganized nature of production at that time may bear partial responsibility for this problem; the position of the film director as it is known in the early twenty-first century—the manager of a film's production phase, considered primarily responsible for a film's quality—was not yet clearly defined. But Griffith's very first film, *The Adventures of Dollie* (1908), set attendance records in some movie houses, and critics for the *Moving Picture World* and the *New York Dramatic Mirror* took notice of its confident storytelling and deft production of suspense. By 1913 Griffith had made more than four hundred short films for Biograph, and audiences increasingly looked for the company's AB symbol as a sign of a film's quality.

The financial and critical success of his short films emboldened Griffith to quit his comfortable job at Biograph in a dispute over his promotion to a non-directing position. On 3 December 1913 he published a full-page advertisement in the *Mirror* touting himself as the heretofore uncredited director of Biograph's greatest successes. As scholars have noted, Griffith's purpose in buying this ad was not to seek work, for he had already secured a directing-producing contract with the Mutual Company. Rather, Griffith sought to shift Biograph's brand familiarity onto his own name and present himself as the undisputed master of the new medium.

Though Griffith certainly bought the ad to enhance his reputation, he also hoped to demonstrate, after a frustrating final sprint at Biograph, that film was a new and unique art form. Griffith had already begun to press Biograph to finance longer features before two Italian historical epics, Enrico Guazzani's nine-reel *Quo Vadis?* (1913) and Giovanni Pastrone's twelve-reel *Cabiria* (1914), came to the United States, thrilling American audiences with their spectacular production values. Griffith was furious that Biograph had not allowed him to chart the territory of the play-length feature himself. His attempt to replicate the success of *Quo Vadis?* with *Judith of Bethulia* (1913) met with scorn from the Biograph chiefs, who shelved the project immediately. (Once Griffith left, Biograph released the film in a four-reel version that was an immediate success.) But Griffith also saw that Pastrone and Guazzani had merely expanded the shocks and spectacles that had dominated film since its origins; they had not taken advantage of his own contributions to complex storytelling. In emulation of authors like Charles Dickens, Griffith appealed to a broad audience by utilizing complex plots, character identification, and a rigorous (and often puerile) sense of Victorian ethics. He claimed that film was a pictographic language that used reality itself to express ideas and that as such only film, among all the arts, could touch a universal audience. In an interview following the release of *The Birth of a Nation*, Griffith predicted that film would develop into a medium for teaching history to the masses; after consulting "a corps of recognized experts," a director could confidently film any past event with "no opinions expressed," and viewers everywhere would "merely be present at the making of history" (Geduld, p. 25).

GRIFFITH PLANS HIS EPIC

History—specifically a most contentious event in American history—was precisely the topic of *The Birth of a Nation*. Griffith had filmed the Civil War from a white southern perspective before in such films as *The Guerilla* (1908), *His Trust*, and *His Trust Fulfilled* (1911), but with *The Birth of a Nation*, Griffith took the position of a southern Lost Cause ideologue, advancing the myth that the heroic South fought the war in order to defend states' rights. The film was adapted from a 1905 novel and a 1909 play called *The Clansman*, written by the pastor, legislator, and white supremacist Thomas Dixon (1864–1964). Griffith and his co-scenarist Frank E. Woods revised the material to increase dramatic tension and humanize the characters, and they also included material from another Dixon novel, *The Leopard's Spots* (1902). To Dixon, the Reconstruction period added insult to the war's injury by showering undeserved rights (political equality, the vote) on the newly freed slave population and retracting the rights of southern whites. According to this widely held separatist view, the tide only turned with the rise of the Ku Klux Klan, an "invisible army" of hooded whites who lynched, mutilated, and terrorized blacks back into near-slavery levels of servitude. Dixon's works both reflected and fed the exacerbation of racial tensions at the turn of the century. The "separate but equal" ruling on *Plessy v. Ferguson* (1896) granted federal blessing to state segregation laws, and the ensuing national debate on segregation led to the establishment of the first major black political organization, the National Association for the Advancement of Colored People (NAACP), in 1909.

Griffith sought a subject of sufficient importance and sweep to match his artistic aspirations; he considered *The Clansman* a perfect candidate for the epic film he wanted desperately to produce. He had by this

Advertising poster for *The Birth of a Nation*, 1915.
GETTY IMAGES

time, in 1914, set up his own production company, the David W. Griffith Corporation, which would distribute its films through Mutual. Frank Woods secured the story rights from Dixon for an up-front fee and a percentage of the film's gross. Purchasing preexisting literary properties was already a standard industry practice, but nothing previously attempted could match the risks that Griffith was to take. Production companies had achieved some success with multireel features but were wary of financing mammoth productions like the one planned by Griffith; nor were many exhibitors convinced that longer films represented the future of the industry. In fact, because of the abnormal length projected for the picture (it was finally to run more than two and a half hours), no distribution company would handle it; Griffith and Mutual head Harry Aitken had to form yet another company, Epoch, to get the film to theaters, and they depended on individuals to book it regionally as a special "road show" event.

Griffith did nothing by halves. He spent Aitken's original budget of $40,000 just on the battle scenes, filmed in California's San Fernando Valley. Eventually he accumulated $110,000 in expenses and shot 150,000 feet of film; this was edited down to 13 reels, or about a tenth of that mass of raw footage. The number of extras for the battle scenes topped out at five hundred (Griffith's publicity campaign pumped this number up to eighteen thousand). The photography took about four months to complete at a time when salable films could be produced in a matter of days. Griffith rarely displayed doubt about the importance of the production or the inevitability of its completion. He continually borrowed money (even from his cinematographer Billy Bitzer), emptied his own salary from Mutual into the film's production, and oversold stock in the film to various speculators. The cast, not to mention their director, lived a hand-to-mouth existence as shooting continued, with the future film directors Raoul Walsh and Erich von Stroheim acting as assistant directors as well as extras. Perhaps most disconcerting to everyone but Griffith himself was the fact that he had no full shooting script, having effectively pre-edited the film in his head. Not even the actors knew how their performances would fit into the story—but with Griffith's constant reassurance, they did what he asked and put their faith in his vision.

GRIFFITH'S STORY OF THE WHITE SOUTH IN PERIL

The plot of *The Birth of a Nation,* which draws on conventional representations of the Civil War as a tragic tale of "brother against brother," is both melodramatically simple and formally complex. Dixon said privately that he hoped Griffith's film would stir a greater fear of black men among whites, particularly white women. By centering the viewers' identification on the two central families, both white, and relating in lurid detail their suffering at the hands of the freed slaves of South Carolina and the carpetbaggers (northern Reconstructionists) who encourage them, Griffith accomplished Dixon's agenda.

Part One begins with an intertitle demanding that the film receive the same right granted to the written word, to "show the dark side of wrong, that we may illuminate the bright side of virtue." It then introduces the Camerons, a southern plantation family, and the Stonemans, a northern family headed by U.S. congressman Austin Stoneman. Dixon based Stoneman on the Radical Republican and congressional leader Thaddeus Stevens but transformed him into a conventional melodramatic villain. Here Griffith follows suit, making Stoneman a flawed patriarch, marked as such by a crippled leg and a strongly implied sexual relationship with

his mulatto maid. This relationship, an intertitle states, will one day "blight a nation." Griffith contrasts Stoneman's decadence with the purity of his daughter, Elsie, and with the gentility of the Camerons, who pet their domestic animals, their children, and their kindly slaves in what one intertitle calls "a quaintly way that is to be no more." The two Stoneman sons go to Piedmont, South Carolina, to visit their friends the Camerons, and there Ben Cameron falls in love with Phil Stoneman's cameo photograph of his sister, Elsie. Tensions over the looming secession arise during the visit, while throughout the Piedmont scene the African American slaves appear as joyous, childlike people who suffer not at all from their lot.

Having established ties of affection between North and South as well as each side's loyalty to its cause, the film moves on to the war itself. Griffith recreates Sherman's march to the sea, replicates the iconic battlefield photographs of Mathew Brady's studio in all their pathos (the strewn bodies of young men who differ only in the color of their uniforms), and carefully pits Northern and Southern forces against each other through his editing; the two sides always attack from opposite sides of the screen, maintaining a sense of confrontation even when only one of the two armies appears in the frame. After much suffering on the battlefield and in the impoverished Cameron household, the war scenes climax with Ben, now known as the Little Colonel, eliciting cheers from Northern and Southern soldiers alike by stuffing a Confederate flag into a Union cannon, even as his battalion falls to Phil Stoneman's own. Robert E. Lee's surrender at Appomattox is reproduced, complete with historical footnotes on intertitles. Ben, hospitalized in the North but due to be tried as a terrorist, is visited by his mother, who, with the help of Elsie Stoneman, successfully pleads with Abraham Lincoln himself for Ben's release. The part ends with the assassination of Lincoln at Ford's Theater (accompanied by intertitle historical footnotes) before the eyes of Elsie and Phil. From the now-threadbare Cameron Hall, Ben's father reads of the murder of the "Great Heart," who promised to treat the South as children who had never left the fold. Old Dr. Cameron has the last word: "What will become of us now!"

Part Two shows the Reconstruction period as disastrous for the white South. Austin Stoneman, now the nation's most powerful political leader, sets up shop in Cameron Hall, determined, according to an intertitle, to "put the white south under the heel of the black south" (the words are Woodrow Wilson's). Stoneman oversees the election of black legislators to the South Carolina state house and sets up Silas Lynch, a mulatto, as lieutenant governor. The former slaves immediately abuse their new powers by disenfranchising the whites and publicly expressing their desire for white women. A famous scene in the South Carolina House sets the tone for the rest of the film by focusing squarely on this last issue, miscegenation. As a new law allowing interracial marriage is passed, the black legislators collectively look up to the gallery. This shot is followed by shots of the objects of their gaze, white women watching the proceedings, followed by closer shots of the legislators looking hungrily upward. The sequence ends with a long shot of the black men dancing in celebration, re-emphasizing the link Griffith has built between black political autonomy and sexual threat. This scene is footnoted like the earlier historical set pieces; however, the intertitle fails to mention that Griffith based the scene not on photographs or a historian's account but on a political cartoon.

The scandal of miscegenational desire is contrasted to the white romantic ties that symbolize a political remarriage between North and South. While Ben courts Elsie, Phil falls in love with Ben's sister Margaret. But thoughts of their brothers, killed by men who wore their new lovers' uniforms in battle, keep the women from accepting the men's proposals. Later, Ben watches some white children covering themselves with a white sheet to frighten black children and determines to use force to reverse the white South's humiliation. He employs his parents and sisters to harbor his secret plans and to sew costumes to disguise the members of his new guerrilla organization, the Ku Klux Klan.

Just as the Klan begins to terrorize its enemies, disasters strike. Elsie discovers Ben's Klan costume and rejects his love, though she promises not to reveal his secret. Then Gus, a cowardly and apelike freedman played, like all the principal black and mulatto characters, by a white actor in blackface, pursues Little Sister Flora Cameron through the woods in hopes of marrying her (though his relentless pursuit strongly implies attempted rape), and she throws herself from a cliff to protect her honor. Ben and his invisible army "try" Gus, kill him, attach a card marked KKK to his chest, and leave his body on Silas Lynch's doorstep as a warning. Lynch and his minions impose martial law and attempt to arrest Dr. Cameron, but two former Cameron slaves, who are described by intertitles as "faithful souls," run a diversion that allows the Camerons (aided by a "reformed" Phil Stoneman) to find refuge in a rural cabin inhabited by impoverished Union veterans. Meanwhile, Lynch kidnaps Elsie and announces to Stoneman that he has chosen to marry her. Stoneman, who seems, like many northern white spectators, to approve of racial equality in the abstract,

recoils in horror when it appears that his own family will be affected. Griffith uses crosscuts, concurrent shots of simultaneous events occurring in separate places, to show the black militia closing in on the Unionists' cottage while Elsie is assaulted and tied up by Lynch in "preparatio[n] for a forced marriage."

But just as Lynch is about to "marry" Elsie, the Klan breaks into Lynch's quarters to settle the score; and just as the militia corners the Camerons and the Union veterans who have joined forces to defend their shared honor as whites, Ben and the Klan arrive on horseback to defeat the attackers. The film concludes with all political and sexual crises resolved: the Klan scares black voters away from the polls at the next election, and the Camerons and Stonemans exchange brides and bridegrooms across the Mason-Dixon Line. As the newlyweds stare dreamily into the distance, a vision ambiguously attributed to Ben shows an allegorical war beast dissolving to reveal Christ, the "Prince of Peace," who promises what Griffith's Klan promises: "Liberty and union, one and inseparable, now and forever!" An additional scene, eliminated after the film's opening (and possibly apocryphal), portrayed "Lincoln's Solution" to the race problem: shipping African Americans back to Africa.

PUBLIC RECEPTION: PRAISE AND CONTROVERSY

The Birth of a Nation opened as *The Clansman* in Los Angeles on 8 February 1915. It ran an unprecedented seven months at Clune's Auditorium, a 2,500-seat theater normally reserved for live drama. It premiered in New York's Liberty Theater on 3 March 1915 as *The Birth of a Nation* (a title change taken from advertising copy for the film and suggested by Dixon) and ran there for an even more remarkable forty-eight weeks. Critics, ministers, and political leaders, including Chief Justice Edward D. White of the U.S. Supreme Court and President Woodrow Wilson (whose popular historical account of the United States the film cites in defense of its portrait of Reconstruction), recommended the film as a history lesson and a powerful work of art. Great showmanship went into its exhibition: ushers dressed as southern gentry; printed programs containing photographs of the cast and (often exaggerated) production details; a live orchestra playing the full score that Griffith had compiled with the composer Joseph Carl Breil; an intermission between "acts." Admission cost a whopping $2. Far from repelling viewers, the high price actually attracted middle- and upper-class patrons who might otherwise have avoided this film because of the cinema's reputation as a cheap amusement. Dixon boosted business by persuading his former college classmate, President Wilson, to screen the film at the White House; on 18 February 1915 it became the first film ever shown there, and Wilson endorsed it immediately. By 1920 it had grossed some $15 million, making Dixon, Aitken, and Griffith millionaires.

But if *The Birth of a Nation* was, in Wilson's words, "like writing history with Lightning," it also electrified the defenders of racial integration. Eight northern states banned it for fear of race riots and other repercussions, and indeed riots did accompany its opening in some cities. The *New York Globe,* the *Nation,* and other periodicals charged it with gross falsehoods. Jane Addams of Chicago's Hull House condemned its stereotypical representation of blacks and its promotion of race hatred—exactly the qualities that made it a faithful historical account in the eyes of separatists. The NAACP entered multiple lawsuits to restrict the film's release on grounds that it threatened public safety, forcing Griffith to edit out nearly two hundred shots; its protests helped the NAACP gain a truly national presence. Eventually President Wilson withdrew his support and publicly allowed that the film exaggerated events to achieve questionable ends. Professing to be shocked by the outcry, Dixon refused to abandon *Birth*'s supremacist message; he pressed his point by referring to the NAACP as the "Negro Intermarriage Society"—a preposterous claim that only made the NAACP's criticisms seem even more justified.

For his part, Griffith seemed more surprised than angered by the charges; while he fully believed in the myth of the Lost Cause, he did not share Dixon's fanatical desire to defend it. But Griffith's pride as an artist and historian was bruised, as his published rebuttal to the *Globe* attests: "This attack is an organized effort to suppress a production which was brought forth to reveal the beautiful possibilities of the art of motion pictures and to tell a story which is based upon truth in every vital detail" ("Reply to *The New York Globe*"). Less convinced of states' rights in their own case than where the South was concerned, Griffith and Aitken challenged the eight-state ban on First Amendment grounds before the Supreme Court (*Mutual v. Ohio,* 1915), but the Court upheld the states' jurisdiction, stating that moving pictures were not free speech but rather a "business pure and simple" (a ruling that remained in effect until the mid-1950s). The young film industry wished nothing to stand between it and its right to steer itself. Learning from Griffith's example, studios and distributors collectively developed rules governing film content that evolved into the modern MPAA ratings system.

Griffith's major responses to the controversy included a pamphlet, *The Rise and Fall of Free Speech in America,* and his follow-up film *Intolerance* (1916). In each case, however, he ignores the charges of *Birth*'s racism and simply defends "freedom" and "tolerance" in vague ways. *Intolerance* argues against religious and class intolerance by crosscutting among stories set in four different historical eras, and it bears at best a slippery relation to the legislative "intolerance" that punctured *The Birth of a Nation*'s success; one must not forget, too, that *Birth*'s separatist message appears, in fact, to be a plea for intolerance. But without making apologies for Dixon or Griffith, whose film has been faulted with reinvigorating the then-moribund Klan, it should be noted that the film's release and the subsequent debates made the deep racial hatred underlying the Lost Cause myth visible to many whites for the first time.

THE LEGACIES OF *THE BIRTH OF A NATION*

The film's impact on film history cannot be overstated. Its technical achievements were immediately recognized, praised, and emulated. The huge battles and historical re-creations attracted admiration for the way they were directed and for combining apparent accuracy with the pure spectacle audiences loved. The emotional impact of the most exciting and heartbreaking scenes of the film, particularly the Klan's climactic ride, were the most commented upon and admired.

But what, exactly, made the film such a breakthrough for the medium? Though the analysis is too crude, *The Birth of a Nation*'s major contributions to film form might be divided into three categories: framing, crosscutting, and associational editing. Framing refers to the distance of camera from subject as well as the composition of elements within the frame. Griffith knew better than any of his contemporaries how to punctuate shots that established settings and portrayed character interactions with close-up shots of reactions and significant objects. Though Griffith did not invent close-ups or point-of-view shots as he claimed in his 1913 advertisement, he intensified their narrative power in *The Birth of a Nation* by using them to invite spectator identification with the plights of characters, as when Flora and Elsie reach the heights of their distress.

Crosscutting, or what Griffith called "switchbacks" (after the switches that shuttled railroad engines from one track to another), alternates between shots of two or more simultaneous actions that depend on each other for dramatic tension. Griffith had used crosscutting to exacerbate tension in races to the rescue many times before, notably in domestic melodramas like *The Lonely Villa* (1909). But nothing yet filmed could compare, in suspenseful tension or emotional impact, to the double race to the rescue that concluded Griffith's epic.

But Griffith's most remarkable innovation was also his most subtle, less acknowledged (and less emulated) by the film industry than his framing or crosscutting techniques: associational (or parallel) editing, in which crosscuts produce conceptual parallels that in turn generate themes or develop characterizations. The introduction of the Camerons and the Stonemans in the opening scene, for example, implicitly compares them as representative families of the South and the North. But it also allows the viewer to view the children from both families as collectively sympathetic and loving figures, and it underscores the contrast between the stereotypical villainy of the northern father and the goodness of the kindly southern patriarch.

The film's undeniable dramatic power stems just as crucially from the identification with the protagonists that Griffith so carefully cultivates in his viewers. Critics universally hailed the subtle, emotional performances of the white principals, especially Mae Marsh as the Little Sister, Lillian Gish as Elsie, and Henry B. Walthall as Ben. While the performances may seem exaggerated and frenetic in the early twenty-first century, a comparison of their acting styles with those seen in most films of the time bears out the accolades. But it should not be forgotten that the very elements that made the film such an advanced example of storytelling and characterization worked as well to elicit tremendous sympathy for the Klan and its fictionalized plight, even among white spectators noncommittal on race relations. Critics in the early twenty-first century often attempt to apologize for the film's racism by claiming that Part One represents Griffith's "true" talent for complex, epic storytelling untainted by racism, and writing off Part Two as an unfortunate footnote to Griffith's genius. Other apologists distinguish between the film's form and its content and dismiss its content altogether, in order to praise its formal innovation for proving the artistic mettle of the motion picture. Ironically, each of these defenses slights Griffith's skill as a formalist who made every component of the film function dynamically within the whole. From the introduction of Stoneman's physical and sexual "weaknesses" and the subtle use of close-ups to parallel the white cotton plant with the face of a beautiful but distant white woman (Elsie) as objects to treasure and protect through Ben's anticlimactic fall in battle and the assassination of Lincoln, Part One's unresolved situations all turn on a sense of perpetual injustice done to the Cameron men and their "property," both material and sexual. Multiple viewings of the film make it difficult to imagine Griffith resolving these issues in any way but to punish, violently, his stock-melodrama villains for disempowering the Little Colonel—and then to restore to southern white men their antebellum mastery.

Griffith was, in fact, ahead of his time in technical achievement but squarely with the majority of filmmakers and audiences and indeed even a bit behind both in his sense of the exigencies of both drama and social progress. Not only does Griffith humanize separatism and racism, but he also makes baldly clear that in order to operate effectively, high melodrama must have its Other, a cartoonish enemy that embodies what film producers and the audiences they court profess to hate. Crosscutting, while colorblind in itself, caught white audiences up in Griffith and Dixon's race-baiting by taking their breath away, emphasizing narrative suspense, and dangling its resolution before rapt spectators—at the expense of logic, historical accuracy, or any concern over what might historically have motivated the Others so caricatured here to desire racial equality.

Those who would have been so concerned, of course, were primarily black viewers. While the film invites all white Americans to identify with an idealized nation that could only be unified by hatred for a mutual enemy, its message to black Americans was equally universal and equally clear: this thrilling experience of storytelling, this medium, indeed this nation, is not for you. At the very moment that film seemed to many to have fulfilled its potential as a populist entertainment, *The Birth of a Nation* actually underscored the cinema's exclusivity—the narrowness and privilege of the "universal" audience it defined for itself. Recognizing the importance of both Griffith and his epic in the history of American cinema means recognizing the mythological character of the Civil War in the national memory and indeed the ability of the cinema to produce national mythologies—to link viewers to otherwise repugnant ideologies through identification with both characters and other viewers in the same theater who also experience the mythology in the form of a pleasurable narrative. Rather than shy away from it or deny its importance or power, one might better return to *The Birth of a Nation* often, as a reminder of how the cinema has come to stand for "national memory" and of the ambiguous consequences of its position as such.

See also Ku Klux Klan; Motion Pictures; The New South; Reconstruction

BIBLIOGRAPHY

Primary Works

Griffith, D. W. "Five-Dollar 'Movies' Prophesied." *Editor,* 24 April 1915. Reprinted in Harry M. Geduld, ed., *Focus on D. W. Griffith,* p. 25. Englewood Cliffs, N.J.: Prentice-Hall, 1971.

Griffith, D. W. "Reply to *The New York Globe.*" *New York Globe,* 10 April 1915. Reprinted in Fred Silva, ed., *Focus on "The Birth of a Nation,"* pp. 77–79. Englewood Cliffs, N.J.: Prentice-Hall, 1971.

Griffith, D. W., director. *The Birth of a Nation.* Performers Henry Walthall, Mae Marsh, Lillian Gish, Ralph Lewis, and George Siegmann; director of photography G. W. "Billy" Bitzer; edited by D. W. Griffith with Joseph Henabery and Raoul Walsh. Epoch Producing Company, 1915.

Griffith, D. W., director. *His Trust/His Trust Fulfilled.* Performers Wilfred Lucas, Dell Henderson, Claire McDowell, Edith Haldeman, and Linda Arvidson. Biograph, 1911.

Secondary Works

Allen, Michael. *Family Secrets: The Feature Films of D. W. Griffith.* London: British Film Institute, 1999.

Barry, Iris, and Eileen Bowser. *D. W. Griffith: American Film Master.* New York and Garden City, N.Y.: Museum of Modern Art/Doubleday, 1965.

Cook, David A. *A History of Narrative Film.* 3rd ed. New York and London: Norton, 1996.

Geduld, Harry M., ed. *Focus on D. W. Griffith.* Englewood Cliffs, N.J.: Prentice-Hall, 1971.

Gunning, Tom. *D. W. Griffith and the Origins of American Narrative Film: The Early Years at Biograph.* Urbana and Chicago: University of Illinois Press, 1991.

Lang, Robert, ed. *"The Birth of a Nation," D. W. Griffith, Director.* New Brunswick, N.J.: Rutgers University Press, 1994.

Pearson, Roberta E. *Eloquent Gestures: The Transformation of Performance Style in the Griffith Biograph Films.* Berkeley: University of California Press, 1992.

Rogin, Michael. "'The Sword Became a Flashing Vision': D. W. Griffith's *The Birth of a Nation.*" In *"The Birth of a Nation," D. W. Griffith, Director,* edited by Robert Lang, pp. 250–293. New Brunswick, N.J.: Rutgers University Press, 1994.

Schickel, Richard. *D. W. Griffith: An American Life.* New York: Simon and Schuster, 1984.

Silva, Fred, ed. *Focus on "The Birth of a Nation."* Englewood Cliffs, N.J.: Prentice-Hall, 1971.

Paul Young

BLACKS

The years from 1870 to 1920 represent a turbulent era in the experience of blacks in America. The Thirteenth Amendment to the United States Constitution officially put an end to slavery in 1865, but then the nation was again challenged during the divisive Reconstruction era. The so-called Negro question—the problem of how to incorporate the former slaves into the American body politic, if at all—preoccupied both public debate and private conversation, and still remained unresolved in 1920.

W. E. B. DU BOIS

The man who would become the single most important figure in the development of the theoretical apparatus to understand and enrich the black American experience was just a toddler in 1870, but by 1920 was unrivaled in terms of his prominence as a political and sociocultural advocate for American blacks. William Edward Burghardt (W. E. B.) Du Bois (1868–1963) was born in the village of Great Barrington, Massachusetts, where the Burghardts, his mother's family, had lived as free black farmers since the seventeenth century. His intellectual gifts were evident from his youth; the valedictorian of his predominantly white high school class, he was sent to Fisk University in Nashville, Tennessee, to pursue a liberal arts college education. He was awarded a bachelor's degree from Fisk in 1888, then enrolled at Harvard University to continue his education. He earned his second bachelor's degree in 1890, a master's degree in 1891, and then became the first black man to be awarded a Ph.D. from Harvard in 1895.

Du Bois's dissertation, *The Suppression of the African Slave-Trade to the United States of America, 1638–1870,* was published as the first volume in Harvard University Press's Historical Series in 1896, and it remains the definitive inquiry into the efforts to eradicate slavery in the United States. Du Bois identifies three distinct modes of opposition—moral, political, and economic—to discredit the traffic in human bondage. Three years later Du Bois published *The Philadelphia Negro: A Social Study* (1899), a groundbreaking sociological research study completed under the auspices of a University of Pennsylvania postdoctoral fellowship. This analysis of the living conditions of blacks in Philadelphia's Seventh Ward was the first in-depth study of the social, political, and cultural forces that shaped the black American experience. Du Bois began teaching economics and history at Atlanta University in 1897, and for the next thirteen years published a number of essays on topics ranging from the family to entrepreneurship to religion to the arts.

These writings were developed from the Atlanta University Studies of the Negro Problem conference series.

Du Bois was the ideological opponent of Booker T. Washington (1856–1915), the president of Tuskegee Institute and proponent of the industrial education curriculum. Washington was arguably the most influential black man in America at the turn of the twentieth century, when he exerted unrivaled control over the progress of race relations in America. Powerful whites funneled virtually any decision affecting the black populace through Washington for endorsement—he had unofficial veto power over black political appointments, grant funding, policy decisions, and general initiatives affecting the black community. Critics such as Du Bois referred to this system as the Tuskegee Machine. Washington's autobiography, *Up from Slavery* (1901), sets forth his philosophy of humility, controlled ambition, and a conciliatory attitude toward whites in order to achieve peaceful and productive coexistence between the races. Du Bois, in contrast, promoted the concepts of the "talented tenth," double-consciousness, and life "within the veil." Discussed at length in his most famous work, *The Souls of Black Folk* (1903), Du Bois believed that every race possessed a naturally gifted elite who were destined to lead the masses, and he encouraged the upper 10 percent of black Americans to assume their responsibility for racial uplift. Double consciousness is his famous theory of the competing and irreconcilable identifications with race and nation intrinsic to the curious situation of being black in a country hostile to African ancestry. Living "within the veil" is Du Bois's prescient metaphor for what evolved into the concept of "invisibility" for Ralph Ellison in the 1940s—the partition concealing black individuality from the white majority but enabling blacks to be marginalized spectators of the world of white Americans. Through these ideas Du Bois advocated the more radical notions of higher education, professionalization, and cultural expression for African Americans in hopes of bringing dignity and parity to the black American experience.

Du Bois's politics began to change in the early 1900s, and he appeared to lose faith in the efficacy of rationality. This outlook is evident in his desperate appeal to a compassionate God in "A Litany of Atlanta," composed in the aftermath of the Atlanta Riot in the fall of 1906; the poem was anthologized by James Weldon Johnson in his 1922 collection *The Book of American Negro Poetry*. Du Bois's first novel, *The Quest of the Silver Fleece* (1911), is a curious and mythical fusion of romance, realism, and materialism. His historical study *The Negro* (1915)

traces the legacy of black culture from the continent of Africa. *Darkwater: Voices from Within the Veil* (1920) is a collection of essays and poetry. As editor in chief of *The Crisis,* the official magazine of the National Association for the Advancement of Colored People (NAACP), from 1910 to 1934, Du Bois penned editorials on a wide range of topics, including urban migration, lynching, the beauty of black women, and the plight of the black veteran. No other individual did more to reclaim, redefine, and recuperate the concept of American blackness from the repudiation of white supremacist conviction.

THE COLLAPSE OF THE FREEDMEN'S BUREAU

The year 1870 marked a significant transition in the lives of black people in America, with the dissolution of the War Department's Bureau of Refugees, Freedmen, and Abandoned Lands. Commonly called the Freedmen's Bureau, the agency was established by an Act of Congress on 3 March 1865 in an attempt to create a uniform infrastructure to manage the problem of millions of newly emancipated slaves rendered homeless and jobless by the collapse of the plantation economy that had been built upon their free labor. Essentially, former slaves became full wards of the state for approximately four years, as the Freedmen's Bureau had significant powers that were intended to protect the interests of America's newly recognized black citizenry.

Among the bureau's assorted functions were several that effectively heightened rather than assuaged racial tension in the postbellum South. One of these was the distribution to the freedmen of "abandoned" lands that had once belonged to the white masters who held them in captivity. Disputes naturally ensued when white families who had fled during the turmoil of war returned to reclaim their property only to discover it had been given away to their former chattel. In addition, because the black voice had been officially suppressed in southern courts of law, the bureau operated its own judicial system within which black people could bring lawsuits to defend their newly granted citizenship rights. In order to rectify the wrongs of the slave system, the Freedmen's Bureau courts invariably ruled in favor of black plaintiffs and awarded damages that only served to fuel southern white resentment of federal intervention. Most whites viewed this process as a punitive redistribution of wealth from white hands into black ones. The bureau also registered marriages, cosponsored American Missionary Association schools to teach literacy to adults and educate children, drafted and ratified employment contracts, maintained records of incidences of racially motivated violence, and distributed food, medicine, and apparel to the displaced and destitute former slaves.

In retrospect, one of the more controversial activities of the Bureau was the operation of the Freedmen's Bank, a well-intentioned but poorly managed savings and loan institution which actively encouraged former slaves to deposit their earnings for safekeeping and financial growth. When the bank folded in 1874, most of the fledgling investors lost not only the bulk of their painstakingly accumulated wealth, but also their confidence in the good faith of the government. The failure of the Freedmen's Bank undermined any belief former slaves may have developed in the American Dream of honest labor yielding prosperity.

THE COLORED ARISTOCRACY

Not all black Americans were directly affected by the financial collapse of the Freedmen's Bank, however, nor were they even serviced by the Freedmen's Bureau. At the other end of the black community's social spectrum from those who were liberated from slavery by the Emancipation Proclamation of 1863 was the so-called colored aristocracy. The members of this group were largely mulattoes, and they had either been born free or had been manumitted prior to 1863. Colored aristocrats, depicted most memorably by Charles Waddell Chesnutt (1858–1932) in his short story collection *The Wife of His Youth and Other Stories of the Color Line* (1899), lived in self-protected enclaves in most major metropolitan cities of the United States. Inclusion in the select group depended largely on the gentility evinced by a number of factors: the number of generations of free birth a person could claim, their level of education, the property they may have inherited from white progenitors, and their cultural refinement. Professional success was also a factor, and before the turn of the twentieth century, this usually was accomplished in service-oriented businesses developed from trades such as catering, livery, tailoring, and carpentry that blacks had also specialized in as slaves. Conflict within the race often ensued from the efforts of these colored aristocrats to maintain their distinction from those more lately released from the bonds of slavery and, thus, preserve their comparatively privileged social position.

Chesnutt's story "The Wife of His Youth" is often read as an allegory of the estrangement between those who had achieved their freedom during the Civil War and those who had sloughed off the brutalization of slavery over years of acculturation. Mr. Ryder represents the elite who have carefully distanced themselves from their origins in bondage through the cultivation of manners, taste, and intellectual development. In the story he meets a woman and initially fails to recognize her as his abandoned wife 'Liza Jane, a former slave. Ryder, or Sam Taylor, as 'Liza Jane knew him, worked for her owner although he had been born free. They met and married on the plantation before the Civil War despite their difference in status. 'Liza Jane had long ago helped him to escape being sold into bondage. The story ends with Mr. Ryder addressing his assembled guests at a society function, telling them that he intends to honor his commitment to 'Liza Jane rather than pursue a union with the beautiful young socialite whom he had intended to marry. Mr. Ryder's decision to respect his existing marriage, although he could legally repudiate the antebellum arrangement, demonstrates the conviction that the destinies of black people in America were inextricably intertwined. His actions suggest that the most polished and pedigreed descendants from black families that had been free for decades were perceived as indistinguishable from the most uncouth and uneducated rural folk from the Deep South. Nevertheless, black people who had established a measure of cordiality with and acceptance from the white community resented the influx of masses of relatively uneducated and uncultured black people who threatened their status and degraded their collective reputation by association. This was especially true during the so-called Great Migration, in which nearly one million southern black people moved to northern urban centers in the hopes of finding better employment opportunities and living conditions. It began in earnest in the 1890s, peaked between 1910 and 1930, and waned with the perpetuation of the Great Depression and the advent of World War II.

IMAGES OF BLACKS IN LITERATURE

Concerns about the race as a whole being judged according to the conduct of its least respectable members were well founded. The criminal element, the untutored, and the morally unexacting dominated the American psyche and dictated repressive social policies and practices. The news media inflamed public opinion against the black community by circulating reports of violent uprisings in the South in the wake of Reconstruction and fixating on sensationalized stories that purportedly illustrated the aberrant habits, inclinations, and activities of African Americans. These media reports suggested that undesirable behavior was biologically determined and located repulsive character traits firmly within a black racial identity.

The socially constructed nature of race was developed concomitantly by literature and film, which persisted in demonizing black men as relentless sexual predators and black women as promiscuously insatiable seductresses. Irrational fear of and revulsion toward black people were entrenched and perpetuated by authors such as Thomas Dixon (1864–1946) who wrote incendiary novels about race relations. Dixon's *The Leopard's Spots: A Romance of the White Man's Burden, 1865–1900* (1902) depicts black men, especially, as incorrigible fiends completely beyond redemption and white men as crusaders under a moral imperative to protect the virtue of white women and defend southern family values from the perceived threat of black antagonists. Dixon, a Baptist minister from North Carolina who abandoned his calling in order to reach a broader audience, embodies in vivid fashion the disconcerting collusion between religious conviction and white supremacy. The filmmaker D. W. Griffith based his groundbreaking, albeit overtly racist, silent drama *The Birth of a Nation* (1915) on Dixon's 1905 polemic *The Clansman: An Historical Romance of the Ku Klux Klan.* The final work in Dixon's trilogy, *The Traitor: The Story of the Fall of the Invisible Empire* (1907), completes the series by advocating a desire to maintain the social hierarchy existent under slavery in order to preserve a stable social order. The fear on the part of southern whites that there might be mass retaliation for the transgressions committed during slavery undoubtedly contributed to the appeal of Dixon's version of the origins of the Klan. A similar fear of slave uprisings had facilitated public approval for more repressive laws governing the management of slaves and restricting the mobility of free black people in the antebellum era.

The extant stereotypical images of black people were not all prone to excite alarm and perpetuate animosity between the races. The plantation tradition in literature romanticizes the antebellum South, entrenching notions of the benign and paternalistic nature of the so-called peculiar institution and painting black people as docile, childlike, and picturesque. An offshoot of the local color school of realism, the plantation tradition encompassed works by Joel Chandler Harris (1848–1908), Thomas Nelson Page (1853–1922), and George Washington Cable (1844–1925). Harris's *Uncle Remus, His Songs and His Sayings* (1880), Page's *In Ole Virginia; or, Marse Chan and Other Stories* (1887), and Cable's *Old Creole Days* (1879) and *The Grandissimes: A Story of Creole Life* (1880) all tended to evoke nostalgia for a patriarchal social order in which slaves served as unswervingly loyal and eternally grateful members of an idealized extended family unit. The success of these books drew upon the public fascination with stereotypical representations of black characters in blackface minstrel performances and traveling "Tom shows" and live dramatizations of selected scenes from the immensely popular novel *Uncle Tom's Cabin; or, Life among the Lowly* (1852) by Harriet Beecher Stowe (1811–1896). Part of the appeal of plantation literature to white Americans both North and South was that it facilitated a revisionist reconception of slavery with a benign aspect, assuaging the guilt associated with the prolonged subjection of so many millions of people to a brutal and dehumanizing institution.

Charles Chesnutt found a way to subversively appropriate the conventions associated with the plantation tradition. Whereas Joel Chandler Harris used the stock character type represented by Uncle Remus—an elderly former slave who interweaves fond reminiscences of the antebellum era in the series of folktales with which he indulges the children of his former master—Chesnutt created the supremely clever Uncle Julius. In his interactions with a northern couple planning to buy the plantation upon which he once worked, Julius crafts traditional tales that are calculated to further his own agenda. In "The Goophered Grapevine" (1887), a short story first published in the highly respected *Atlantic Monthly,* Chesnutt presents Uncle Julius as a trickster figure who invents an elaborate yarn to persuade the northern-born prospective buyers that the scuppernong vines on the property are enchanted in order to perpetuate his own access to the grapes. In addition, the author himself acts as a trickster figure in that he neglected to disclose his racial identity to the magazine's readership. In so doing, Chesnutt was able to reach and affect an audience largely inaccessible to most black writers. His literary accomplishment is all the more laudable in light of the subtlety with which he undermines the more overtly distorted representations of the slave experience and fashioned a central character who clearly adopts a palatable persona as a tool with which to placate and manipulate white people in a strategic fashion.

Charles Chesnutt was inspired to write in part by the example of Albion W. Tourgée (1838–1905), a white Union veteran from Ohio who relocated to Greensboro, North Carolina, in 1865. (This made him one of the so-called carpetbaggers who, like the white couple in Chesnutt's stories, moved to the South in the years following the Civil War.) Tourgée is best known for unsuccessfully representing Homer Plessy in the landmark case of *Plessy v. Ferguson,* which resulted in the 1896 Supreme Court decision that made segregation legally defensible through the social policy of "separate but equal" facilities for black and white people. Tourgée's novel *A Fool's Errand* (1879) traces the experiences of a white advocate for the interests of emancipated slaves during Reconstruction. The book became a best-seller, largely because it appealed to northern white readers through its depiction of race relations in the South and its glimpse into the unfamiliar sphere of black America. After reading Tourgée's work, Chesnutt reasoned that with his artistic skill, his racial identity, and his practical experience, he could fashion a more authentic and accurate portrait of the plight of the black community from the perspective of black characters. His first short story collection was published in 1899. Entitled *The Conjure Woman*, it includes "The Goophered Grapevine" along with six other tales (an expanded version of the collection was published in 1993 as *The Conjure Woman and Other Conjure Tales*). The stories are framed by the ongoing interaction between John and Annie, the couple from Ohio who purchase the old McAdoo plantation, and Uncle Julius McAdoo, who educates them concerning the history and lore attached to their recently acquired property in Patesville, North Carolina (a name John acknowledges he invents for the town in the interest of maintaining anonymity). *The Wife of His Youth and Other Stories of the Color Line*, Chesnutt's "Blue Vein" collection (a term that refers to the light skin color possessed by many of the elite African Americans), appeared a year later.

The novels that followed Chesnutt's story collections generally explore the way in which interracial prejudice and tension undermine racial solidarity and efforts to collectively combat legal barriers to equality. *The House behind the Cedars* (1900) focuses on the phenomenon of black people passing for white. *The Marrow of Tradition* (1901) is a fictionalized account of the Wilmington race riot of 1898. And *The Colonel's Dream* (1905) features a white would-be crusader who is thwarted in his efforts to bring social reform to a small southern town.

THE TRAGIC MULATTO

Although Chesnutt did not realize his own dream of fashioning a lucrative career out of his authorship, he was correct in his belief that American readers were fascinated by imaginative characterizations of black people. The extraordinarily influential literary figure William Dean Howells (1837–1920) wrote *An Imperative Duty* (1891), a novel that examines the nature of prejudice and explores attitudes toward race. Rhoda Aldgate, the novel's heroine, is raised by her white paternal aunt and uncle following the death of her parents but is never told that her birth mother had been an octoroon (a person of one-eighth black ancestry). When Rhoda is entertaining a marriage proposal, her aunt finally feels it incumbent upon her to reveal to Rhoda the secret of her origin, fearing the repercussions if it should come to light in some other fashion, particularly through a baby who could betray the bloodline through the unpredictability of genetic disposition. In the course of the narrative, Howells deals

***The Banjo Lesson*, 1893.** Painting by Henry Ossawa Tanner. A classically trained African American artist, Tanner was among the first to create sensitive yet realistic portraits of American blacks. In this painting, Tanner reworks the stereotype of the black musician. © HAMPTON UNIVERSITY MUSEUM, HAMPTON, VIRGINIA

with Rhoda's reaction to this revelation. Naturally, she is emotionally conflicted and fairly devastated; although she has no particular aversion to "colored" people, her attitude toward them is clearly condescending. In this way, Howells shows that the altruism and advocacy of the liberal Bostonians does not necessarily mean that they believed in complete social equality between the races. The fear pervading *An Imperative Duty* is the theoretical possibility of atavism—that despite even an overwhelming infusion of European blood, any African ancestry whatsoever could trigger irresistible reversion to a degraded and primitive condition. Howells focuses on the ability of Dr. Olney, Rhoda's white suitor, to overcome this fear and naturalized aversion as he ultimately persuades Rhoda to marry him against her fiercely articulated inclinations that issue from the intensity of her self-loathing once she learns of her connection to a formerly enslaved race. The same situation imagined from a black female perspective is handled very differently. *Iola Leroy; or, Shadows Uplifted* (1892) by Frances Ellen Watkins Harper (1825–1911) was published just one year after *An Imperative Duty*. In many ways it appears a conscious revisitation of the themes addressed in Howells's novel. Harper's title heroine, like Howells's Rhoda Aldgate, is the daughter of a white man who marries a woman he knows to be black. Whereas Rhoda's father is a northern man who falls in love with the illegitimate octoroon daughter of a slaveholder and his enslaved mistress, Iola's father is himself a southern slaveholder who marries one of his own slaves. Iola is raised within the culture of slavery as the young mistress of the plantation, never imagining for a moment that, by law, she should share the condition of the slaves. When her ancestry is revealed, Iola is certainly shocked by her sudden change in condition, but she does not experience the same intensity of self-loathing that Rhoda expresses, nor does she feel herself to be grossly inferior to all of her former associates, as Rhoda does. While Iola decides to consecrate herself to the noble purpose of racial uplift, she does not perceive this calling as a loathsome obligation that stems from her exclusion from decent society. While Iola also entertains an offer of marriage from a white physician, she rejects it; she does not locate her self-worth in the validation from a representative of the majority population who will disregard her ancestral "flaw," as Rhoda does.

The representational contrast between Howells and Harper is fairly indicative of the typical oppositional viewpoints of white and black American writers. Like Howells, Mark Twain (a pseudonym for Samuel Langhorne Clemens, 1835–1910) features a woman of one-sixteenth part African ancestry in his novel *Pudd'nhead Wilson* (1894). In despair after barely escaping her master's threat to sell her "down the river"—an invocation of the presumably harsher conditions of the plantation slavery of the Deep South—Roxy resolves to drown herself and her six-month-old son in the Mississippi to avert any future risk of what she perceives as a fate worse than death. In making preparations for her suicide/infanticide, she dresses herself in her finest attire and borrows clothing from Master Driscoll's son to outfit her baby so that his shroud will be equally magnificent. Only then does she register the remarkable likeness between her son and the Driscoll heir; born on the same day in the same house, the boys are practically twins. Since the master himself cannot tell the babies apart and his wife does not survive a week beyond childbirth, Roxy realizes that she can preserve her son from the perpetual risk of being sold without taking his life: after some measure of deliberation, she resolves to switch the babies, thereby elevating her slave child into her young master. Twain effectively demonstrates the socially constructed nature of domination and submission; when Roxy's son matures into a perfect tyrant, it

becomes clear that the doctrine of white supremacy has no biologically determined basis.

Though Twain's novel could certainly be enlisted to combat the facile acceptance of the purported inferiority of black people, its very ambiguity with respect to whether human development is predominantly a function of nature or nurture lends itself to being appropriated as further demonstration that people of African descent, and especially those "mongrelized" by an infusion of European ancestry, are depraved by nature. Certainly, white authors from the Reconstruction era through the turn of the twentieth century typically depicted the discovery of black heritage as a revelation precipitating a private catastrophe. In "Désirée's Baby" (1893) by Kate Chopin (1851–1904), a man of unparalleled social distinction develops an impetuous passion for and subsequently weds a young woman of unknown parentage. He is overjoyed at the birth of their first child, a son, until as the weeks progress the baby begins to exhibit incontrovertible evidence of pigmentation, thus illustrating the anxiety about atavism expressed in Howells's *An Imperative Duty*. When Désirée sees her baby attended by a quadroon slave, recognizes the similarity in complexion, and suddenly realizes the cause of her husband's complete withdrawal from her, she confronts him. He tells her that she is not a white woman, and, instead of returning to her foster mother, Désirée takes her baby and carries out Roxy's aborted resolution—she drowns the both of them in the river adjoining their plantation. The nameless young protagonist of "The Little Convent Girl" (1893) by Grace Elizabeth King (1852–1932) embraces the same fate. She leaves the cloistered company of nuns in Cincinnati and travels to New Orleans by riverboat in order to begin life anew with the mother she has never known. When it becomes apparent to her that the black woman onshore awaiting her disembarkation is indeed her mother, she decides to jump overboard rather than descend the gangplank and assume a black identity.

RACIAL CONFLICT

The virulently negative perception of a black racial identity encoded in the regionalist literature that attained such popularity between the close of the Civil War and the turn of the twentieth century simply reinforced the desire of many white Americans to maintain both physical and psychological distance from the unfortunate descendants of slaves. However, for others, especially in the South where many white people were resistant to the eradication of a strictly hierarchical social dynamic from which they profited, generalized distaste for blacks justified lynching and other acts of vigilantism as tools of social control through intimidation. The white supremacist perspective masked fear of retribution for the atrocities perpetrated by the slave system, with the oft-articulated belief that people of African descent were wild and lawless by nature. A racially motivated attack of this order seals the fate of the nameless protagonist of *The Autobiography of an Ex-Colored Man* (1912) by James Weldon Johnson (1871–1938). When, indistinguishable from the white mob due to his fair skin, he witnesses a lynching in a small southern town, he decides that he has no desire to claim membership in a race that could with impunity be treated worse than animals.

Racial violence was rampant, often escalating from mob assaults on targeted individuals to full-scale riots in which the black populace invariably suffered disproportionate casualties. What has been called the Wilmington Massacre of 1898 amounted to an armed suppression of black voters so that whites could regain political control of the region. While relatively few blacks were actually killed, hundreds were forced out of the city when their property was destroyed. During World War I, conflicts were often provoked by negative reactions to black veterans either wearing their uniforms in public or displaying resentment for being treated like second-class citizens in the country that they were risking their lives to defend. The violence became so widespread that the NAACP held a demonstration dubbed the Silent Protest Parade in Manhattan in 1917 to garner public attention to the disturbing trend. Nevertheless, in the year following the end of the war, racial antagonism erupted into bloodshed at such a high rate that the period is commonly referred to as the Red Summer of 1919.

Much of the interaction between blacks and whites from the Reconstruction era through 1920, then, was structured by the efforts to curtail the violence rooted in racial animosity and to establish a method of achieving peaceful and productive coexistence between the races. The black women's club movement, which reached its apex during the 1890s, evinced a demonstrated commitment to racial uplift and the unilateral improvement of the quality of the lives of black Americans. Drawing national attention to lynching, suffrage, and discrimination, among other issues, outspoken women activists such as Ida B. Wells-Barnett, Fannie Barrier Williams, Mary Church Terrell, and Mary McLeod Bethune were able to make a positive difference in the material circumstances in black communities. In addition, the Urban League and the NAACP, the two most prominent civil rights organizations in the United States, were both founded in the first decade of the twentieth century.

Black leaders, white philanthropists, religious organizations, and governmental agencies all agreed that emancipated bondsmen would most effectively accomplish a transition to productive citizenship through education. Several colleges were founded during Reconstruction with a specific mission to reach and refine the untutored black masses. Howard, Hampton, and Fisk Universities, Morehouse College, and Tuskegee Institute were all conceived as institutions to serve the emancipated population, whereas Ohio's Wilberforce University was actually established in the antebellum period to serve the children of wealthy white plantation owners and their slave concubines. As larger numbers of black people availed themselves of educational opportunities, more were able to enter the professions or establish businesses and achieve greater measures of economic independence. The fifty years spanning the end of Reconstruction to the brink of the Harlem Renaissance represent a major period of transition for blacks in America.

See also The Autobiography of an Ex-Colored Man; The Birth of a Nation; Civil Rights; *The Conjure Woman; Iola Leroy;* Jim Crow; Ku Klux Klan; Lynching; *The Marrow of Tradition;* Migration; Miscegenation; Race Novels; Racial Uplift; Reconstruction; *The Souls of Black Folk; Up from Slavery*

BIBLIOGRAPHY
Primary Works

Chesnutt, Charles W. *The Conjure Woman and Other Conjure Tales.* Durham, N.C.: Duke University Press, 1993.

Chesnutt, Charles Waddell. *The Wife of His Youth and Other Stories of the Color Line.* 1899. Ann Arbor: University of Michigan Press, 1968.

Cooper, Anna Julia. *A Voice from the South.* 1892. New York: Oxford University Press, 1988.

Du Bois, W. E. B. *The Quest of the Silver Fleece.* 1911. Philadelphia: Pine Street Books, 2004.

Du Bois, W. E. B. *The Souls of Black Folk.* 1903. New York: Penguin, 1989.

Hopkins, Pauline E. *Contending Forces: A Romance Illustrative of Negro Life North and South.* Boston: Colored Co-operative Publishing, 1900.

Johnson, James Weldon. *The Autobiography of an Ex-Coloured Man.* 1912. New York: Vintage, 1989.

Johnson, James Weldon. *Black Manhattan.* 1930. New York: Da Capo Press, 1991.

Terrell, Mary Church. *A Colored Woman in a White World.* 1940. New York: G. K. Hall, 1996.

Washington, Booker T. *Up from Slavery.* 1901. New York: Penguin, 1986.

Secondary Works

Carby, Hazel V. *Reconstructing Womanhood: The Emergence of the Afro-American Woman Novelist.* New York: Oxford University Press, 1987.

DuCille, Ann. *The Coupling Convention: Sex, Text, and Tradition in Black Women's Fiction.* New York: Oxford University Press, 1993.

Gatewood, Willard B. *Aristocrats of Color: The Black Elite, 1880–1920.* Bloomington: Indiana University Press, 1990.

Giddings, Paula. *When and Where I Enter: The Impact of Black Women on Race and Sex in America.* New York: Morrow, 1984.

Guy-Sheftall, Beverly. *Daughters of Sorrow: Attitudes Toward Black Women, 1880–1920.* Brooklyn, N.Y.: Carlson, 1990.

Horton, James Oliver. *Free People of Color: Inside the African American Community.* Washington, D.C.: Smithsonian Institution Press, 1993.

Lewis, David Levering. *W. E. B. Du Bois.* Vol. 1, *Biography of a Race, 1868–1919.* New York: H. Holt, 1993.

Lott, Eric. *Love and Theft: Blackface Minstrelsy and the American Working Class.* New York: Oxford University Press, 1993.

Morrison, Toni. *Playing in the Dark: Whiteness and the Literary Imagination.* New York: Vintage, 1993.

Ross, Marlon B. *Manning the Race: Reforming Black Men in the Jim Crow Era.* New York: New York University Press, 2004.

Samuels, Shirley, ed. *The Culture of Sentiment: Race, Gender, and Sentimentality in Nineteenth-Century America.* New York: Oxford University Press, 1992.

Sundquist, Eric J. *To Wake the Nations: Race in the Making of American Literature.* Cambridge, Mass.: Belknap Press of Harvard University Press, 1993.

Tate, Claudia. *Domestic Allegories of Political Desire: The Black Heroine's Text at the Turn of the Century.* New York: Oxford University Press, 1992.

Warren, Kenneth W. *Black and White Strangers: Race and American Literary Realism.* Chicago: University of Chicago Press, 1993.

Licia Morrow Calloway

BOHEMIANS AND VAGABONDIA

"Bohemians" and "Vagabondia": these terms represent a state of mind, a style of living, and an approach to writing. The two are closely related and overlap somewhat, but there is a crucial difference between them. One connotes stasis, whereas the other suggests movement. The phrase "bohemian quarters" refers to the artists' districts in major metropolitan areas and bohemians are the starving artists and authors who populate them. The term "Vagabondia," on the other hand, closely associates literature and the outdoors. Literary vagabonds are simply perambulatory bohemians. Both the stationary bohemians and the peripatetic litterateurs made important contributions to American literary and cultural history during the waning decades of the nineteenth century and the early ones of the twentieth.

PRECURSORS

To shape their personal outlook, turn-of-the-century bohemians in urban America found inspiration in earlier figures in American literary history as well as in British authors of more recent decades. Among their American precursors, none influenced these new bohemians more significantly than Edgar Allan Poe (1809–1849). Casting aspersions on Poe after his death, his detractors little realized that they were setting him up for veneration among subsequent American authors. Imagined as a derelict who indulged his baser instincts, flaunted social convention, and withstood poverty because he refused to compromise his aesthetic principles, Poe became an object of bohemian admiration.

Whereas Poe's life offered a general pattern for the bohemians to emulate, one particular work of the British author Edward FitzGerald (1809–1883) offered a specific philosophy of living. Perhaps no single work more greatly shaped bohemian attitudes of the late nineteenth century than FitzGerald's translation of the poetry of the twelfth-century astronomer-poet of Persia, *Rubáiyát of Omar Khayyám* (1859). Mocking traditional values, *Rubáiyát* emphasized the importance of enjoying and appreciating the sensual pleasures of the moment. In the world according to Omar Khayyám, the greatest desiderata were "a jug of wine, a loaf of bread—and thou." American readers were not quite ready for *Rubáiyát* when FitzGerald's translation first appeared, but the work became enormously popular starting in the 1880s and continuing into the twentieth century.

The numerous cheap, pocket-size editions of *Rubáiyát* let people tote the book with them and read it whenever and wherever they wished. Reading *Rubáiyát* thus became one of the pleasures of the moment the poem itself advocated. Carried in the pocket, the volume took on the quality of a talisman, allowing its possessors to assume the values it represented through a kind of contagious magic. The popularity of *Rubáiyát* extended well beyond the bohemian crowd. Also published in an expensive edition (1884)

Illustration by Rene Bull for a 1913 edition of *Rubáiyát*. BRITISH LIBRARY/BRIDGEMAN ART LIBRARY

handsomely illustrated by Elihu Vedder, the work could be found on the parlor tables of countless individuals in the 1880s. Herman Melville (1819–1891), for one, owned a gilt-edged copy of *Rubáiyát*. Though Melville had long since stopped trying to please the reading public, he was fascinated with the popularity of *Rubáiyát,* cut out multiple newspaper articles about it, and tipped them into his copy for safekeeping.

Other contemporary enthusiasts found different ways of honoring the work and its author. Omar Khayyám clubs were established in New York, Boston, and other cities across the United States. In 1898 John Hay (1838–1905), soon to be U.S. secretary of state, gave an address before the New York club titled, "In Praise of Omar." Hay's address was published separately in Portland, Maine, by Thomas B. Mosher (1852–1923) and also with editions of *Rubáiyát.* The writer and editor Elbert Hubbard (1856–1915), whose Roycroft complex at East Aurora, New York, was developing a reputation as a bohemian mecca, incorporated Hay's address as the introduction to an 1899 edition he published. Mosher and Hubbard, as editors and proprietors of important little magazines, represent another aspect of the bohemian movement.

Oscar Wilde (1854–1900) also influenced the outlook of the bohemians through both his writings and his personal presence. The American production of W. S. Gilbert and Arthur Sullivan's *Patience* in 1882 presented Wilde the opportunity to visit the United States: Wilde and one of the opera's characters, Bunthorne, became closely associated because of the "art for art's sake" aesthetic they shared, and the producers decided that bringing Wilde to America for a lecture tour would help promote *Patience* and could prove a lucrative venture in itself. Wilde reached New York on 2 January 1882. Upon his arrival, he purportedly told a customs official, "I have nothing to declare but my genius." The clever customs official purportedly responded, "That, sir, is a commodity which does not require protection in the United States." Wilde's initial lecture, "The English Renaissance," proved too weighty a subject for American audiences, so he greatly revised and abbreviated it into a lecture titled, "The Decorative Arts," which had much more popular appeal.

Wilde's lecture tour took him up and down the East Coast, across the North American continent, deep into the South, and through parts of Canada. In some places he spoke to huge crowds; in others to just a few. Everywhere he exemplified his personal aestheticism. Wilde saw himself as both spokesman and representative of the aesthetic movement, a man who, in terms of dress and mannerisms, emphasized the importance of cultivating beauty in an increasingly ugly and impersonal world. The mainstream American press ridiculed Wilde, yet he made many converts to the aesthetic movement among young, liberal, intelligent American men. Wilde inspired many new bohemians, who even copied his attire: roundabout jackets, their buttons filled with garish artificial sunflowers, became the fashion of the day.

The vagabond poets shared these same influences and had many others in addition. To those who enjoyed vigorous outdoor exercise, Walt Whitman (1819–1892) and Henry David Thoreau (1817–1862) may have been greater influences than the city-dwelling Poe. In a number of his poems, Whitman beckoned readers to follow the path he blazed, and many did. From its opening lines, "The Song of the Open Road," for example, celebrates the joy and freedom involved with tramping through forest and field:

> Afoot and light-hearted I take to the open road,
> Healthy, free, the world before me,

> The long brown path before me leading wherever
>   I choose
>
> (Poetry and Prose, *p. 297*)

Thoreau's *Walden* (1854) presented an alternative lifestyle eschewing social proprieties that readers began to admire in increasing numbers. A minor work that also let young litterateurs know that poverty was no obstacle to travel and pleasure was *Vagabond Adventures* (1870), by Ralph Keeler (1840–1873). Upon the publication of this autobiographical account of its author's low-budget travel adventures, America's great man of letters William Dean Howells (1837–1920) befriended Keeler and wrote in the *Atlantic Monthly* that he hoped *Vagabond Adventures* "would prove the germ of an American novel in the manner of *Gil Blas*, for writing which its author gave distinct promise" (p. 366). Sadly, Keeler died just a few years later and never fulfilled his literary promise. Nevertheless, *Vagabond Adventures* did exert a modest influence on subsequent travelers and writers. Mary Weatherbee, to cite one late-nineteenth-century American traveler, wrote, "For years I read delightedly all such vagabond adventures as those of young Ralph Keeler, of all the struggling authors and artists who, like myself, had counted privation and discomfort light in the balance against their desire to reach their Mecca" (p. 937). Whitman's encouraging words and the examples of Thoreau and Keeler provoked several young American authors to seek their own vagabond adventures.

LITERARY BOHEMIANISM

Though many authors and artists in late-nineteenth-century America can be termed bohemians, a bohemian movement per se never really coalesced in the United States as it had in Europe. Still, many high-minded creative types lived bohemian lives, meaning that they eschewed social conventions—habits, dress, even morals—and preferred to live a life dedicated to their art. Bohemians live in poverty because they refuse to compromise their art for the sake of commercial gain. The humorist George Ade (1866–1944) took literary bohemianism as his satiric target in his 1899 short story, "The Fable of the Bohemian Who Had Hard Luck." Of his title character, Ade writes, "After being turned down by numerous publishers, he had decided to write for posterity." The suggestion is that although bohemian authors might contend they cannot get published because they refuse to compromise their art, in fact (according to Ade) bohemians feign superiority as a way of masking their lack of talent.

Before establishing his reputation with *The Red Badge of Courage* (1895), Stephen Crane (1871–1900) lived the life of a bohemian, too. After privately publishing *Maggie, A Girl of the Streets* (1893), he moved into the Art Students' League Building in New York, where he found himself surrounded by young artists who exemplified the bohemian lifestyle. For his fourth novel, *The Third Violet* (1897), Crane made use of these personal experiences. After an excursion to the country, the novel's protagonist, Billie Hawker, returns to his New York studio, where he lives with numerous other artists. They often hide from their landlord because they cannot afford to pay the rent. They have virtually no food in their flat but, on one occasion, do manage to make coffee and eggs on a portable gas stove precariously balanced on a rickety chair. One character does pen-and-ink drawing for a sensational magazine, which has not paid him for three months. They are visited by a charming, attractive woman named Florinda O'Connor, a character inspired by George Du Maurier's *Trilby* (1894). Florinda works as an artists' model and holds unconventional views regarding the place of women in society. In conversation, they discuss how rotten the work of more successful artists is, as if to succeed the artist must throw away all his aesthetic principles.

Of all the writers active in late-nineteenth-century America, perhaps none more personally exemplified the bohemian spirit than Lafcadio Hearn (1850–1904). Born in the Greek Ionian Islands, Hearn attended school in France and England. Eventually his guardians withdrew him from school and sent him to America to fend for himself. He reached New York in 1869 and quickly made his way to Cincinnati, where he found work in the publishing industry, learning to set type and also doing some editing and proofreading. It was not until he started writing for the *Cincinnati Enquirer* in the 1870s that Hearn found his métier. He developed a reputation for crime reporting that showed his fascination with the seamier side of life. The lurid nature of the violence he reported contrasted sharply with his elegant style of writing and made his published accounts stand out all the more. In the mid-1870s, he coedited a literary weekly with Henry Farney entitled *Ye Giglampz*. In addition, he sidelined as a translator, publishing English versions of several stories by Théophile Gautier and also a translation of Gustave Flaubert's 1874 novel *La Tentation de Saint Antoine* (Temptation of Saint Anthony). An affair with a mulatto woman led to his dismissal from the *Enquirer* and eventually prompted Hearn to relocate to New Orleans in 1877.

Sickly and impoverished during his early months in New Orleans, Hearn was unable to find work until the middle of the following year, when he became assistant editor of the *New Orleans Item*, in which he published more translations of Gautier and other contemporary French authors, including Émile Zola. In 1881 Hearn obtained a much more prestigious position as literary editor for the *New Orleans Times-Democrat*, where he published numerous reviews and translations. He became intrigued with the diverse folk culture of New Orleans, which encouraged him to study folktales and legends from around the world. While living in New Orleans, Hearn finally gained acceptance within the national literary establishment and started publishing in some of the major magazines of the day, including *Harper's New Monthly Magazine* and *Lippincott's*. A commission with *Harper's* prompted him to move to the West Indies, where he lingered for two years. Returning to the United States in 1889, he split his time between New York and Philadelphia and continued writing at a furious pace. Upon contracting with *Harper's* to write a book-length work about Japan, he left America for Asia in March 1890, never to return.

Several aspects of Hearn's literary career in the United States exemplify the life of the bohemian: his bouts of hunger and poverty; his rescue from hunger and poverty by a chance newspaper or magazine assignment; his fascination with the dangerous classes, to use a term coined by Hearn's contemporary Charles Loring Brace; the miscellaneous nature of his writing activities; his desire to develop a voice of his own unfettered by the dictates of the literary establishment; his disregard of contemporary moral standards; his fascination with contemporary French literature, which many Americans considered morally bankrupt; his interest in many different cultures; his creativity in finagling assignments from magazines with deep pockets; and his restlessness. The bohemian quarters in cities across America during the late nineteenth century were filled with men and women exemplifying these qualities. Lacking Hearn's talent and perseverance, many of his fellow bohemians have been consigned to oblivion.

THE VAGABOND POETS

William Bliss Carman (1861–1929) is the foremost poet of Vagabondia. As a student at Harvard during the 1880s, he studied with Francis Child, the great authority on the traditional ballad, and such traditional verse significantly shaped Carman's writing style and his outlook on life. Combine this literary influence with his love of the outdoors and hiking and one has the form and subject matter of Carman's poetry. He was a prolific author, publishing numerous collections of essays, but his fame derives from his verse. One collection, *Songs from Vagabondia* (1894), which he cowrote with his fellow traveler and poet, Richard Hovey (1864–1900), gave the term "Vagabondia" its currency and gave subsequent nature-loving poets the inspiration to summon

> *The opening lines of William Bliss Carman and Richard Hovey's* Songs from Vagabondia *(1894) provide a good indication of the collection as a whole.*
>
> Off with the fetters
> That chafe and restrain!
> Off with the chain!
> Here Art and Letters,
> Music and wine,
> And Myrtle and Wanda,
> The winsome witches,
> Blithely combine.
>
> Carman and Hovey, *Songs from Vagabondia*, p. 1.

the call of the open road. Characterizing the general impetus of the poetry contained within this volume, a contributor to the *Atlantic Monthly* observed, "'Free' is the note struck at the outset, and the shaking off of conventional trammels is the constant theme of rejoicing." Carman and Hovey published two follow-up collections, *More Songs from Vagabondia* (1896) and *Last Songs from Vagabondia* (1900). Some years later Carman published a solo fourth collection, *Echoes from Vagabondia* (1912).

As a student at Dartmouth College, Richard Hovey established a reputation as an eccentric as he closely followed Oscar Wilde's aesthetic movement in terms of both dress and mannerisms. Once he and Carman became friends, they began to go on walking tours together. *Songs from Vagabondia* established Hovey's reputation, and the following Vagabondia books again gave his readers what they wanted, that is, verse exemplifying the bohemian lifestyle. Besides the cowritten Vagabondia collections, Hovey also published solo works, the most important being *Along the Trail: A Book of Lyrics* (1898).

The year Bliss Carman published the fourth and final volume in his Vagabondia collection, another sort of vagabond poet was making his way across the continent. Vachel Lindsay (1879–1931) devised an idealistic theory that it should be possible for a poet to convert the products of his or her work into sustenance. Before setting off on a lengthy tramp across the West, Lindsay had a collection of forty-four of his poems printed. He titled the pamphlet *Rhymes to Be Traded for Bread* (1912). An introductory paragraph presented his credo:

This book is to be used in exchange for the necessities of life on a tramp-journey from the author's home town, through the West and back, during which he will observe the following rules: (1) Keep away from the cities. (2) Keep away from the railroads. (3) Have nothing to do with money. Carry no baggage. (4) Ask for dinner about quarter after eleven. (5) Ask for supper, lodging and breakfast about quarter of five. (6) Travel alone. (7) Be neat, truthful, civil and on the square. (8) Preach the gospel of beauty.

A subsequent paragraph listed several exceptions to the rule of carrying no baggage.

Loaded with his pamphlets and the materials necessary to preach the gospel of beauty, Lindsay set off on foot from his hometown of Springfield, Illinois, on his way to Colorado, a journey he recounted in *Adventures while Preaching the Gospel of Beauty* (1914). The pamphlet met with mixed success. In Jefferson City, Missouri, Lindsay managed to trade two copies of his pamphlet for some doughnuts. At another stop, he traded *Rhymes* for some bread but no butter. In Kansas, he traded one woman a copy of *Rhymes* for dinner—providing he also spent an hour hoeing weeds in her orchard. In short, Lindsay learned that rhymes could be traded for bread—but they were no substitute for a strong back and arms.

By no means are the bohemians and literary vagabonds in American culture restricted to the few decades clustered around the turn of the century. As a state of mind, bohemia transcends time. Since 1920 perhaps no bohemian movement has more fully coalesced than the Beat movement, whose de facto leader, Jack Kerouac (1922–1969), delivered much the same message in *On the Road* (1957) as Ralph Keeler and Bliss Carman delivered before him. Having coined the phrase "the Beat movement," Kerouac was often asked when it started. He told one interviewer that it began in 1910. Choosing this particular date, Kerouac was being somewhat arbitrary, but the date does show his indebtedness to and continuity with the turn-of-the-century bohemians and vagabonds. The idea of living a life without compromise, of dedicating the self to one's aesthetic principles, of preferring poverty to prosperity as a way of safeguarding those principles transcends time.

See also Aestheticism; Genteel Tradition; Orientalism

BIBLIOGRAPHY
Primary Works
Carman, Bliss, and Richard Hovey. *Songs from Vagabondia.* Boston: Copeland and Day, 1894.

Crane, Stephen. *The Third Violet.* New York: D. Appleton, 1897.

Howells, William Dean. "Ralph Keeler." *Atlantic Monthly* 33 (March 1874): 366–367.

Keeler, Ralph. *Vagabond Adventures*. Boston: Fields, Osgood, 1870.

Lindsay, Vachel. *Rhymes to Be Traded for Bread*. Springfield, Ill.: Nicholas Vachel Lindsay, 1912.

"Major and Minor Bards." *Atlantic Monthly* 75 (March 1895): 407–411.

Weatherbee, Mary. "Europe on Nothing-Certain a Year." *Century Magazine* 32 (October 1886): 937–942.

Whitman, Walt. *Walt Whitman: Poetry and Prose*. Edited by Justin Kaplan. New York: Library of America, 1982.

Wilde, Oscar. *The Complete Letters of Oscar Wilde*. Edited by Merlin Holland and Rupert Hart-Davis. New York: Henry Holt, 2000.

Secondary Works

Cott, Jonathan. *Wandering Ghost: The Odyssey of Lafcadio Hearn*. New York: Knopf, 1991.

Hayes, Kevin J. *Stephen Crane*. Tavistock, U.K.: Northcote House, 2004.

Levin, Harry T. "The Discovery of Bohemia." In *Literary History of the United States,* edited by Robert E. Spiller, Willard Thorp, Thomas H. Johnson, and Henry Seidel Canby, pp. 1065–1079. New York: Macmillan, 1948.

Lewis, Lloyd, and Henry Justin Smith. *Oscar Wilde Discovers America, 1882*. New York: Harcourt, Brace, 1936.

Masters, Edgar Lee. *Vachel Lindsay: A Poet in America*. New York: Scribners, 1935.

Wallace, Mike. "Mike Wallace Asks Jack Kerouac: What Is the Beat Generation?" In *Conversations with Jack Kerouac,* edited by Kevin J. Hayes, pp. 3–6. Jackson: University Press of Mississippi, 2005.

Kevin J. Hayes

BOOK PUBLISHING

Early in the new twentieth century, the American publisher Henry Holt mourned the imminent death of the book. With cheap, flashy, and ever-changing magazines beckoning from every city street corner, he lamented, who would choose to read the relatively staid, cumbersome, and expensive book? Holt and others bemoaned the impending "massification" of print culture—ushered in by near-complete mechanization of production processes, unprecedented literacy levels, and a crowd of entrepreneurial publishers happy to hawk books like chewing gum or tinned tobacco, obliging the commonest of literary tastes. He feared that the book as he knew it, in a social and cultural as well as physical sense, could not survive the consequences.

The American publisher Henry Holt voiced concerns shared by many at the turn of the century when he lamented that profit-hungry authors and publishers threatened the future of good literature. The centuries-old tension between the cultural and the commercial aspects of book publishing intensified in the late nineteenth century, and it remains a perennial aspect of the modern industry.

The more authors seek publishers solely with reference to what they will pay in the day's market, the more publishers bid against one another as stock brokers do, and the more they market their wares as the soulless articles of ordinary commerce are marketed, the more books tend to become soulless things.

Henry Holt, "The Commercialization of Literature," *Atlantic Monthly,* November 1905, p. 578.

His worries were not entirely baseless. The years following the Civil War had been an era of unparalleled growth in reading, fueled in part by a strong national drive for basic popular education and literacy. In the 1870 census some 80 percent of white Americans over the age of ten declared themselves literate (although fewer than a quarter of nonwhite Americans could make the same claim). Despite the notorious difficulties in measuring literacy and its uses, it was clear to all that an unprecedented number of Americans not only could read but also, with great energy and enthusiasm, they often did. And as Holt so bitterly noted, most of that reading was readily found in newspapers and magazines, which enjoyed wide, even national, audiences for the first time in the nation's history.

But a vigorous growth in book publishing had also accompanied the push for universal literacy. Between 1880 and 1913, while the nation's population nearly tripled, the number of new titles published annually rose more than sixfold, from 2,076 to 13,470. Furthermore, those numbers generally reflect only trade titles, or books intended for purchase by "general readers," the sort of books sold in the early twenty-first century in a typical bookstore. Then as now trade publishing was dwarfed by other varieties of publishing, which distributed books to particular audiences through other channels. The textbook business alone was huge, swelled by a peculiarly American reliance on books for instruction, foreshadowing the vast markets for self-help and how-to books of the early twenty-first century. By 1860, for example, more textbooks were published each year in the United States than in all of Europe. Together with the robust activities of religious book publishers and those devoted to numerous ethnic communities, which also are rarely included in discussions of general publishing, the world of books and reading had grown vast indeed.

From the end of Reconstruction to the return of veterans from the Great War, then, as ever-growing numbers of readers presented new interests and new needs, publishers struggled both to satisfy and to shape those literary appetites. But theirs was neither a cohesive nor a coherent enterprise. Even in the sphere of general trade publishing alone, two fundamental types of publishing coexisted, sometimes in direct competition but more often operating in discrete arenas, serving different reading populations. Very roughly put, one addressed traditional audiences, typically educated readers for whom buying books was a familiar and well-regarded act; these readers were the primary audience for new works written by contemporary authors. The other vein of general publishing served less-sophisticated readers, many of whom were newly literate and unaccustomed to owning any book other than perhaps a family Bible. They were more likely to buy inexpensive reprint editions of older titles or simple formulaic fiction marketed by category more than by author.

This essay explores the activities of both strands of general publishing activity, which would gradually metamorphose into a more integrated, though no less complex, twentieth-century industry. The consolidation began soon after the Civil War, when the once largely regional nature of traditional American book publishing became solidly national, concentrated in three cities: Philadelphia, Boston, and especially New York. The mainstream industry was dominated by a dozen or so major houses, each governed by the literary, cultural, and business values of the men who ran them, men whose names continue to define the landscape of American publishing, even though none remain family-run businesses in the early twenty-first century. The Harper brothers in New York built the nineteenth century's largest publishing enterprise, and Charles Scribner, Henry Holt, G. P. Putnam, F. N. Doubleday, Henry Houghton, George Mifflin, and others all played important roles in shaping the nature of the maturing trade book business.

To understand publishers' roles in these heady decades of unprecedented demand for books and other reading material, one must trace the ways their methods of selecting, producing, marketing, and selling books are interwoven with the lively and sometimes volatile variety of those books' content. Because their markets were frequently different, traditional and popular publishers developed varying means of creating and distributing their wares.

EDITORS AND AUTHORS

Of the three fundamental components of the publishing process—editing, design and production, and marketing and sales—the last two were transformed more radically than the first between 1870 and 1920. Editorial practices also shifted dramatically, however, albeit with considerable grumbling and resistance. Before the 1890s or so, an unwritten but powerful code of "gentlemanly" conduct governed traditional publishers' dealings both with authors and with each other. This meant that an author was typically aligned with the same publisher throughout his or her career; publishers sought to develop and support their authors' careers, in tacit exchange for the authors' loyalty or promise to let them publish new works. An even stronger professional ethic discouraged one publisher from "stealing" another's authors. Charles Scribner particularly detested the commercial notion of bidding for a prized author's work, and he vilified any foolhardy writer or publisher who attempted to draw his house into the now commonplace practice.

In general, nineteenth-century traditional publisher-author relationships were both paternalistic and often mutually productive. Although they clearly needed each other and often enjoyed close personal friendships, many publishers and authors nurtured perennial grievances about the relationship. Most authors earned only modest royalties, and often they were paid nothing at all until a significant portion of the edition had sold and production costs had been covered. Furthermore, authors were commonly expected to bear the cost of manufacturing the stereoplates from which their books were printed. Publishers, on the other hand, perpetually complained (as many still do) about their precarious finances, lamenting that a chronic unprofitability of the majority of trade titles rendered theirs the "worst business in the world," as one mourned in 1906. In reality, both grievances were exaggerated. Although modest, authors generally earned more through royalties than through the earlier convention of a lump-sum payment, particularly on those fortunate titles that enjoyed strong sales. And publishers generally made respectable, though rarely lucrative, incomes from their livelihood.

Authors' most serious complaint was the lack of an international copyright law. Until the problem was remedied in 1890, American authors felt at an unfair disadvantage because publishers could issue pirated editions of foreign works, which could be sold more cheaply since no royalties were paid to the authors. This was far less common in traditional publishing than in popular, however. The low prices on which popular publishing depended were achieved by cutting costs as much in editorial as in manufacturing practices. Many popular titles were reprint editions of older, copyright-free "classics" as well as more recent works by such well-known British writers as Charles Dickens, despite their furious but futile objections. Most of these royalty-dodging pirated editions of British and French titles (primarily novels) were issued in one of the era's inexpensive, mass-produced series. Commonly known as "libraries," these sets of books with identically designed covers competed only indirectly with the standard clothbound editions in which American authors' new works were typically published. The popularity of such libraries was enormous. By the height of the craze in 1893, some ninety-four series vied for space on American families' bookshelves.

Popular publishers also issued a huge quantity of formulaic new fiction, commonly adventure stories, inspiring rags-to-riches tales, and sentimental domestic novels; these were often written on demand by hired writers for a set fee rather than royalties. A growing portion of the writers were women, who brought distinctive sensibilities to their fiction and kindled strong markets among women readers. Beginning with the huge success of dime novels in the 1860s, this phenomenon, known broadly as cheap fiction, frequently generated series of short novels featuring the same characters or settings. The partners Francis S. Smith and Francis Scott Street, for example, published several such series, including Frederic Dey's wildly popular Nick Carter books. When hot sales demanded publishing a new book each week and Dey naturally could not keep up, as many as five other writers were hired to produce the needed manuscripts. It was a small step from this and other instances of ghostwritten popular fiction to the "fiction factories" of the 1880s and 1890s. There a fleet of workers generated plot outlines by poring through newspapers for fiction-worthy accounts. These outlines were then sent out to writers on retainer with detailed specifications concerning the manuscript's length, deadlines, and payment fee.

While most authors writing for popular markets saw their artistic status diminish as they traded creative freedom for a reliable (and sometimes substantial) paycheck, conditions for authors writing for traditional markets slowly improved. Spurred in part by the changes wrought by the new copyright law, relationships between authors and traditional publishers grew more professional and businesslike in the 1890s.

Reading's popularity by the end of the century catapulted some authors to celebrity status, giving them more clout in their dealings with publishers. A new player, the literary agent, emerged to forcefully safeguard authors' interests. The presence of agents helped push toward such modern practices as offering formal standardized contracts, relieving authors of a share of production costs, and paying advances or a portion of expected royalties before the work is actually published.

PRODUCTION AND DESIGN

The great boom in reading could not have happened without the dramatic changes enabled by the shift to industrialized production methods. The new technology that enabled the increasingly mechanized production process made print more abundant, less expensive, and more timely than ever before. Four central ingredients of this mechanization were the development of steam-powered printing presses; mechanical, wood-based papermaking; stereotype plate making; and mechanical typesetting. The quantitative differences the new technology made are astounding. At the beginning of the nineteenth century a skilled printer working with a handpress could produce about two hundred impressions an hour; power-driven mechanized presses in the 1870s could spew out more than thirty thousand impressions an hour. By the 1880s an entire edition of a novel could be printed in only ten hours.

As with most technological breakthroughs, however, one advance is often stymied by bottlenecks in other areas. Even the new Fourdrinier papermaking machines could not generate enough sheets to keep up with the presses' capacity until the transition at mid-century from rag pulp to wood fiber pulp. Thanks to the cheaper and more plentiful supply of wood, the amount of paper produced in 1900 eclipsed by a hundredfold that made in 1800, and the price of even the higher grade book paper had dropped to a tenth of its earlier cost. Without this dramatic saving in paper costs, the explosion of magazines and cheap books, bound in paper covers, would not have been possible.

Type presented the last two, stubborn bottlenecks. Composed mainly of soft lead, type could not stand up to the heavy wear of industrial printing. This was solved with the invention of stereotype printing plates. By printing with steel plates made from a mold of the original hand-composed type, not only could many more impressions be printed but also the type could be promptly distributed and recomposed for other jobs. The final great advance came in the 1880s, when two methods of mechanical typesetting triumphed over the many others vying for adoption: Ottmar

Mergenthaler's Linotype system debuted in 1884, and Tolbert Lanston's Monotype machine appeared in 1887. Both methods substituted keyboard strokes for manual-type assembly, activating the mechanical casting of an entire line of type or of individual letters, and both systems produced fresh, sharp-edged type for each new composition at rates that far exceeded even the swiftest hand composition.

The commercial advantages of mechanized production were increasingly weighed against its aesthetic drawbacks, however. Machine-made paper was better suited for the high-speed printing process, for example, but it had little of the crisp durability of handmade. Similarly, when printers thinned their inks and printed with a light pressure to keep the presses running smoothly, many objected to the generally pale-looking pages that resulted. This only compounded complaints about the spindly, "weak" type styles that predominated in the era. By the 1890s, inspired by the arts and crafts movement and the revival of preindustrial book design values modeled by William Morris's Kelmscott Press in England, a handful of influential American publishers introduced a radical new look to their books.

Three firms in particular—Stone and Kimball (Chicago), Way and Williams (Chicago), and Copeland and Day (Boston)—led the way toward a dramatically new typographic style, one that emulated the darker, heavier letterforms and decorative woodcut borders and opening initials of medieval books and manuscripts. These pioneers helped to influence a profound shift in modern typography, away from the finely wrought, often ornately detailed Victorian style that showcased industrial achievement toward a new style rooted in the look of handcraft.

MARKETING AND SALES

Although technology had dramatically expanded the possibilities for print production, publishers realized they could not exploit them without effective ways to distribute and sell what was produced. This aggravated the perennial distaste many traditional book publishers felt toward publicity and marketing, stemming from their conviction that such activity sullied their gentlemanly demeanor. But theirs was a business, and promotional marketing was increasingly essential for success in the modern marketplace, even if one's wares included ideas and literature.

At mid-century, most traditional publishers depended on reviews for gaining attention for their books. Because they functioned primarily as publicity, reviews tended to be more like the early twenty-first century's "blurbs" in that writers, who were frequently paid to "puff" a work, served authors' and publishers'

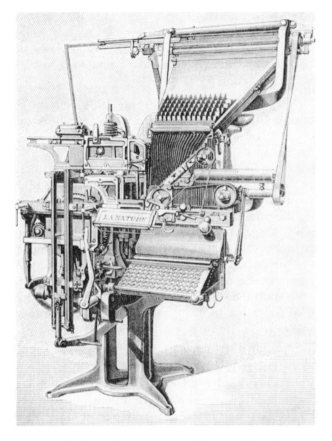

Mergenthaler's Linotype machine, 1885. Mergenthaler's typesetting machine substituted keyboard strokes for manual type assembly, greatly increasing the speed with which printed materials could be produced. © BETTMANN/CORBIS

interests more than readers'. Some authors had no scruples about reviewing their own books with extravagant praise.

Book advertising in the modern sense of printed circulars, display ads in magazines, and so on emerged—with lingering misgivings and reluctance—for good around the turn of the century. Saddled with few of the qualms felt by traditionalists, popular publishers led the way in marketing breakthroughs. One of the first to embrace advertising was the maverick Caro Clark, the only woman publisher in Boston at the time. Through tireless personal appearances and lavish billboard and newspaper ads, she sold more than 200,000 copies of *Quincy Adams Sawyer* (1900) by Charles Felton Pigdin. Defending her brash temerity, which mortified many other publishers, she candidly credited her advertising for the strong sales of the otherwise unremarkable novel. Clark pioneered the practice of developing a striking, unified graphic identity for each title, an image or scene duplicated in posters and ads that potential customers could not help but notice and remember. By 1910 publishers had shifted this promotional function to memorably designed book jackets, making them the cornerstone of a title's advertising effort.

Peaking between 1902 and 1904, efforts to "boom" books included an array of ingenious and audacious stunts. In 1898, for example, effusive full-page magazine ads for Charles Major's best-selling romance *When Knighthood Was in Flower* sparked phenomenal interest in the book. Likening the author to Shakespeare and Sir Walter Scott, but coyly withholding his name to further intrigue readers, these ads yielded not only huge sales but also a popular stage version of the novel, an early version of the media "tie-ins" that still delight publishers in the early twenty-first century. Later, to promote a new edition of the novel, the publisher hired a man dressed in faux medieval armor to ride through the astonished streets of Manhattan.

Traditional publishers' deep-seated ambivalence toward marketing had a practical as well as an ethical dimension: creating a demand for books was pointless without sufficient means of getting copies into buyers' hands. Distribution woes were often acute in the nineteenth century; only a tiny portion of U.S. counties had even a single bookstore. Many Americans, especially those living in rural areas beyond the East Coast, did not even know such stores existed. Furthermore, then as now, the number of trade titles published each year far exceeded the space available to display and stock them in any retail store. Competing for precious shelf space, publishers sent agents known as travelers to visit far-flung shops and pitch the season's new titles to store owners. Travelers were thus crucial to both marketing and distribution; the integrity or persuasiveness of their pitches usually made a huge difference for most mainstream titles' prospects.

Given this paucity of bookstores, publishers sought other means of reaching buyers. By far the most successful was an old but effective method, direct sales through agents traveling from door to door. Some 90 percent of all books purchased before World War I were bought in this way. Armies of agents canvassed urban neighborhoods and the rural countryside, as many as twenty thousand of them in 1894 in Chicago alone by one estimate. Popular publishers particularly relied on direct sales through agents, since so many of their potential customers otherwise seldom if ever bought books. Canvassing agent sales thus expanded the markets for books and reading dramatically by helping many ordinary people develop new habits of, or at least attitudes toward, owning books.

The closing decades of the nineteenth century were the heyday of subscription publishing or selling titles by taking orders for copies, often before they were printed. This method diminished publishers' financial risks, assuring them of the sales they needed before proceeding with particularly expensive ventures. For example, nearly a million copies of William Cullen Bryant's *Picturesque America* (1874) were sold in this way; the handsome parlor book filled with engravings was typical of one of the mainstays of subscription book sales—beautifully, even extravagantly produced volumes meant for display more than for reading.

Subscription selling, however, channeled much of the new appetite for books toward a narrow variety and relatively small number of available titles, which usually received intense marketing efforts followed by huge sales. In addition to lavish editions like *Picturesque America* usually purchased to impress visitors with one's gentility, subscription sellers had particular success with books about the recent Civil War, which appealed to people's still-stirred patriotism. Some contemporary fiction sold well in this way as well, as Mark Twain's great success demonstrated; nearly all of his novels were sold though door-to-door subscription sales.

With the great growth in ephemeral print—newspapers, magazines, flyers, and so on—publishers were able to get word of new titles and series to vast new audiences, who then ordered copies by mail. Most popular books were distributed through the mail, not through retail outlets. Accordingly, low postal rates were key to cheap books' success; fluctuations in postage rates and regulations often hastened the crest, or the collapse, of each boom market for cheap books throughout the 1870s and succeeding decades.

TASTES AND TRENDS

Cheap books and serialized fiction in magazines popularized recreational reading in America as never before. From 1890 to 1914 the demand was so insatiable that literary historians refer to the era as the great Fiction Boom. While popular publishers eagerly supplied inexpensive editions of older novels and seemingly inexhaustible quantities of formula fiction, traditional publishers enjoyed the boom as well, issuing record numbers of original works by the nation's most respected mainstream novelists. Some of them sold spectacularly well.

Paradoxically, the boom market troubled many traditional publishers, who struggled to balance their financial need to publish books Americans wanted to buy with their responsibility for nourishing the nation's cultural and intellectual development. These were not always conflicting conditions, of course. Even so, throughout the era publishers and other voices of the literary establishment fretted that literary merit and popular taste had precipitously diverged—a seemingly eternal complaint. Most publishers managed to pursue both objectives, however, by publishing a spectrum of titles.

Although its editor at Harper's did not consider General Lew Wallace's novel *Ben-Hur* "legitimate literature," for example, the firm recognized its potential popularity and published it in 1880. The book sold more than half a million copies in the following decade and became the first blockbuster best-selling trade novel in the modern era. It paved the way for hundreds of other new mainstream novels whose popularity would make literary history. In 1894 Anthony Hope's *The Prisoner of Zenda* helped launch a huge market for historical romance novels, and Kate Douglas Wiggin's 1903 novel *Rebecca of Sunnybrook Farm* similarly whetted the appetites of millions of readers for "home and Jesus" family novels.

On the other hand, although such popular titles clearly outsold serious ones, as they have always done, the era also sustained remarkably eager audiences for works recognized in the early twenty-first century as serious literary classics. The 1890s witnessed enthusiastic fan clubs for writers such as Robert Browning and Rudyard Kipling, and Shakespeare basked in near-cultlike reverence. Important nonfiction flourished as well. In the 1870s, the first university presses, at Cornell and Johns Hopkins universities, joined the publishing landscape. By 1919, thirty-eight university presses had been established, ensuring that important and provocative serious scholarship was disseminated throughout and beyond the nation's academic communities.

CENSORSHIP

With books and reading becoming more central than ever to American society by the late nineteenth century, new concerns arose about the nature and consequences of what was read. Most notoriously, Anthony Comstock (1844–1915) galvanized many Americans' worries when he proclaimed a new crusade to fight for "Morals, not Art or Literature." In 1872 the young Comstock persuaded the YMCA to sponsor his newly founded Society for the Suppression of Vice. The following year his tireless lobbying resulted in a congressional law outlawing the distribution of "obscene materials" and giving Comstock police powers to interpret and enforce it. For more than forty years Comstock terrorized booksellers and publishers, seizing hundreds of thousands of books whose morality he deemed suspect. He met little resistance until, in

1885, he began to attack the works of critically respected authors such as Honoré de Balzac, Émile Zola, and Leo Tolstoy. In 1905 George Bernard Shaw successfully defied Comstock's attempts to prosecute his works, but for the most part Comstock continued to exercise powerful control over American literary culture until his death. His work continued with unabated zeal into the 1930s under the leadership of his successor, John Sumner.

While some publishers stood firm in their defense of free literary expression, notably G. P. Putnam, Albert Boni, and Horace Liveright, most were fairly conservative themselves on moral issues. Houghton Mifflin of Boston refused to publish works of literary realism, for example, rejecting writers such as Theodore Dreiser and Upton Sinclair for the profanity and explicit violence in their work. And during World War I several New York publishers joined the efforts of a private group of writers known at the Vigilantes to ensure that only "patriotic," pro-British, and prowar sentiments were published. Others, however, recognized more shrewdly that attempts to suppress certain works usually only heighten their appeal. For every copy of a book confiscated by Comstock's forces, hundreds of others were avidly purchased, and works by controversial writers like Dreiser in fact enjoyed both critical success and substantial sales.

Although his 1905 prediction of the book's demise proved to be needlessly bleak, Henry Holt had astutely perceived that the nature of book publishing in America was fundamentally changing. By the end of the First World War, the traditional publishing world that he knew was poised to come of age as a modern industry. Despite his and others' anxious observations that traditional publishing was absorbing many aspects of more popular-minded publishing, time would quickly prove that it was largely energized—not suffocated—by the latter's commercial vigor. The strength of trade publishing in the 1920s and beyond was grounded in the legacies of both its popular and mainstream forebears.

See also Children's Literature; Copyright; Dime Novels; Editors; Harper & Brothers; Houghton Mifflin; Little Magazines and Small Presses

BIBLIOGRAPHY
Secondary Works
Boyer, Paul S. *Purity in Print: Book Censorship in America from the Gilded Age to the Computer Age.* 2nd ed. Madison: University of Wisconsin Press, 2002.

Brodhead, Richard H. *Cultures of Letters: Scenes of Reading and Writing in Nineteenth-Century America.* Chicago: University of Chicago Press, 1993.

Coultrap-McQuin, Susan. *Doing Literary Business: American Women Writers in the Nineteenth Century.* Chapel Hill: University of North Carolina Press, 1990.

Garvey, Ellen Gruber. *The Adman in the Parlor: Magazines and the Gendering of Consumer Culture, 1880s to 1910s.* New York: Oxford University Press, 1996.

Gaskell, Philip. *A New Introduction to Bibliography.* New York: Oxford University Press, 1972.

Hackenberg, Michael, ed. *Getting the Books Out: Papers of the Chicago Conference on the Book in Nineteenth-Century America.* Washington, D.C.: Center for the Book, 1987.

Hart, James D. *The Popular Book: A History of America's Literary Taste.* New York: Oxford University Press, 1950.

Hochman, Barbara. *Getting at the Author: Reimagining Books and Reading in the Age of American Realism.* Amherst and Boston: University of Massachusetts Press, 2001.

Kaestle, Carl F., et al. *Literacy in the United States: Readers and Reading since 1880.* New Haven, Conn.: Yale University Press, 1991.

Lehmann-Haupt, Helmut. *The Book in America: A History of the Making and Selling of Books in the United States.* 2nd ed. New York: Bowker, 1951.

Madison, Charles A. *Book Publishing in America.* New York: McGraw-Hill, 1966.

Tebbel, John. *Between Covers: The Rise and Transformation of Book Publishing in America.* New York: Oxford University Press, 1987.

Tebbel, John. *The Expansion of an Industry, 1865–1919.* Vol. 2 of *A History of Book Publishing in the United States.* New York: Bowker, 1981.

Thompson, Susan Otis. *American Book Design and William Morris.* New York: Bowker, 1977.

West, James L. W. *American Authors and the Literary Marketplace since 1900.* Philadelphia: University of Pennsylvania, 1988.

Megan Benton

BOSTON AND CONCORD

On 17 December 1877 Mark Twain attended a dinner in Boston honoring John Greenleaf Whittier on his seventieth birthday. The dinner was sponsored by the *Atlantic Monthly,* the most prestigious literary journal in America at the time. On this occasion Twain chose to tell a humorous tale that gently satirized three of New England's most distinguished literary figures: Henry Wadsworth Longfellow, Ralph Waldo Emerson, and Oliver Wendell Holmes. All three were present at the dinner. Twain thought the tale was inoffensive and well received, but his friend William Dean Howells

was horrified at this "bewildering blunder" and subsequently urged Twain to issue letters of apology to all three dignitaries. Twain, somewhat surprised and abashed by the whole thing, quickly followed his friend's advice. It was his first lesson in New England literary decorum (Emerson, p. 109). The episode was indicative of the significant changes that were reshaping the contours of the American literary landscape in the second half of the nineteenth century. The old romantic idealism, represented by Longfellow, Holmes, James Russell Lowell, Emerson, Whittier, Charles Eliot Norton, and others, was being challenged by a new, brash, realistic type of writing that was represented most prominently by Twain, Howells, and Henry James. Naturalism, an outgrowth of this realistic movement, would emerge in the last decade of the century as writers such as Stephen Crane, Frank Norris, Theodore Dreiser, and others arrived on the scene. Eventually the literary icons of the antebellum period would be displaced by these younger voices. Such a dramatic change could not occur without a struggle.

BOSTON

In the 1870s, Boston was still for the most part the hub of America's literary universe, as it had been for the previous two decades at least. Slowly, however, the center was beginning to shift to New York (Brooks, p. 1). One sign was the growing circulation of popular journals like *Harper's New Monthly Magazine* (founded in 1850) and *Century Magazine* (founded in 1870). These journals and others like them were aimed at a broader reading public than the more sophisticated *Atlantic Monthly.* They were part of a rapidly growing magazine-fed literary culture. As a result of this trend, Boston was slowly losing its ability to attract the younger generation of writers then emerging (Brooks, p. 377; Sedgwick, p. 77). Change was in the air. Even the venerable *North American Review,* Boston's oldest journal, moved to New York in 1878. The New York journals were filled with the writings of new authors like Twain, James, Howells, Hamlin Garland, Mary Wilkins Freeman, and others (Brodhead, p. 474). These "new realists" concerned themselves for the most part with everyday events in the lives of common people. They sought to tell their stories in a language that was immediate, unadorned, and simple. Often they incorporated the ungrammatical, accented diction of the common people. They also eschewed idealism. Howells (1837–1920), later summarized the essential theory of realism when he declared in *Criticism and Fiction* (1891), "let fiction cease to lie about life; let it portray men and women as they are, actuated by the motives and passions in the measure we all know, . . . let it not put on fine literary airs; let it speak the dialect, the language, that most Americans know—the language of unaffected people everywhere" (p. 51).

Many of the young writers who dared to speak this new language were, like Howells and Twain, from the American West. The Brahmin class of Boston viewed them as little more than invading Goths who threatened to destroy the edifice of American cultural sophistication and purity that they and their predecessors had labored so hard to build. Beginning in the late 1870s they would fight a holding action in defense of what became known as the "genteel tradition" in American literature. These individuals are described by Daniel Aaron as "men and women of culture and taste who did their best to mitigate the crudities of the Gilded Age" and who "glanced back nostalgically to the myth of unspoiled homogenous America, and shrank from the squalor, violence, and vulgarity of their own times." In their effort to preserve the past, they "closed ranks against naturalism, literary experimentation, and social heterodoxy, against any movement that might endanger . . . the 'spiritual rootage of art'" (pp. 734, 735). The struggle between the new and the old became especially intense in the 1880s as the realistic movement took hold of America's literary imagination. Charles Dudley Warner (1829–1900) offered a strong indictment of the movement in an article published in the *Atlantic Monthly* in April 1883. Robert Falk summarizes the sins of "modern fiction" noted by Warner as "overmuch photographic fidelity, a lack of idealization, a superabundance of analysis, an artistic indifference to nobility and virtue and justice, a preoccupation with the seamy side of life, a sad neglect of stories with happy endings, and a rejection of Sir Walter Scott" (p. 424). The latter was seen as projecting an ideal of chivalrous conduct and personal virtue that was most worthy of imitation. Warner himself made the source of his ire explicit.

> The characteristics which are prominent, when we think of our recent fiction, are a wholly unidealized view of human society, which has got the name of realism; a delight in representing the worst phases of social life; an extreme analysis of persons and motives; the sacrifice of action to psychological study; the substitution of studies of character for anything like a story . . . and a despondent tone about society, politics, and the whole drift of modern life. (Falk, p. 424)

Henry James responded to such criticisms in his essay "The Art of Fiction" (1884) by asserting that

> Art is essentially selection, but it is a selection whose main care is to be typical, to be inclusive. For many people art means rose-colored windowpanes, and selection means picking a bouquet for

Mrs. Grundy. They will tell you that artistic considerations have nothing to do with the disagreeable, with the ugly; they will rattle off shallow commonplaces about the province of art and the limits of art till you are moved to some wonder in return as to the province and the limits of ignorance. (P. 17)

Unfortunately Warner's views would carry the day for the time as Boston gradually became the center of literary conservatism rather than the vibrant hub of American literary life. The *Atlantic* became its fortress on a hill. There is a great irony in this. At the time of its founding, the *Atlantic Monthly* was a voice of liberalism and progress. In its first issue, which appeared in November of 1857 under the editorship of James Russell Lowell, the journal declared that "it will not rank itself with any sect of anties: but with that body of men which is in favor of Freedom, National Progress, and Honor, whether public or private" (Howe, p. 27). In the early years the journal routinely published the works of writers who were themselves the vanguard of America's most progressive thought in art, literature, and politics. These included Emerson, Longfellow, Norton, Holmes, Whittier, Harriet Beecher Stowe (1811–1896), Lowell, and many others (Howe, p. 24).

By 1881, however, when Thomas Bailey Aldrich assumed editorship, the *Atlantic Monthly* was, in the words of Willard Thorp, "bent on upholding the Ideal in literature," even though the vogue of idealism was largely a thing of the past for the new authors then emerging (p. 4). There were many reasons for this change. The horrors of the Civil War, the ruthless competitiveness of America's laissez-faire economy, the scientific harshness of Social Darwinism, the mighty and imposing figures of the new "captains of industry," a myriad of new scientific and technological developments, the exponential growth of industry and with it the factory system, as well as the rapid growth of cities with their imposing skyscrapers and depressing slums (inhabited mostly by recent immigrants) all combined to render idealism of any sort both quaint and largely irrelevant. As Henry Adams would later put it in his *Education* (1918), "the new American . . . was the child of steam and the brother of the dynamo" (p. 466). Such a gritty and scientifically conceived reality demanded a similarly gritty and scientific literary rendering. Eventually the new realism of the 1880s opened the way for the new naturalism of the 1890s, which sought to observe and record reality with almost scientific detachment (Pizer, pp. 108–110). This movement had its roots in Continental literature, especially the works of the French novelist Émile Zola. Not surprisingly, Aldrich "despised naturalism (an abominable Gaulish invention of Zola and Flaubert) and fought to

Bronson Alcott's Orchard House, c. 1900. The Concord School of Philosophy met in the small building on the left.
© LAKE COUNTY MUSEUM/CORBIS

keep American letters free from its taint." For Aldrich, literature—especially that published in the *Atlantic*—"could still be the preserver of the True and the Beautiful" (Thorp, p. 4).

Signs of this conservative entrenchment were everywhere. When Walt Whitman's (1819–1892) *Leaves of Grass* was published in Boston in its second edition in 1856 the reception was generally positive. Indeed, Gay Wilson Allen reports that "on the whole Boston and New England were actually more receptive to the book than was New York" (p. 174). Twenty-five years later Boston proved less receptive. When *Leaves of Grass* was issued in 1881 by Boston's James R. Osgood & Company, one of the country's most prestigious publishers, the defenders of public morality soon took notice. On 1 March 1882 the Boston district attorney informed Osgood & Company that its edition of *Leaves of Grass* violated the statutes banning "obscene literature" and demanded extensive excisions of offending materials. Whitman refused to make the changes specified, and the firm ceased publication of the work (Loving, p. 414). Episodes such as this had a telling effect over time on American writers. They looked elsewhere for a more open-minded literary and social culture. (Whitman subsequently took

his *Leaves* to Philadelphia, where it was published by Rees Welsh and Company.)

CONCORD

Even Concord, a center of liberal thought and literary creativity before the Civil War when it was home to Emerson, Henry David Thoreau, Bronson Alcott, and Nathaniel Hawthorne, was not immune from the Brahmin influence of nearby Boston. For a time the intellectual afterglow of the town's original brilliance was reflected somewhat in the activities of the Concord School of Philosophy. This was actually a series of summer lectures on various philosophical topics held at Bronson Alcott's (1799–1888) "Orchard House" home. The first session was in 1879. Alcott himself had never achieved much recognition beyond Concord. His reputation at this time was easily eclipsed by that of his famous daughter, Louisa May, whose *Little Women* (1868–1869) catapulted her to national fame. She followed this with a number of other successful works that appealed to the innocent sensibilities of many readers. She would remain a popular writer until her death.

A number of reasonably prominent people lectured in the School of Philosophy. Alcott offered one of the early presentations, a meditation on "The Powers of the Person in a Descending Scale." Benjamin Peirce lectured on "Ideality in Science," Thomas Wentworth Higginson on "The Birth of American Literature," and Emerson, now in his twilight years and suffering signs of Alzheimer's disease, lectured on the somewhat ironic topic of "Memory." The school lasted for ten years and was generally considered a success. Although some townsfolk at first reacted with trepidation to a project that "fill[ed] the village with long-haired men and short-haired women," as one historian put it, the school was eventually deemed acceptable because "What brings money to the town . . . is a success" (Scudder, pp. 282, 283).

Concord's toleration of the liberal element had its limits, however, as Mark Twain (1835–1910) discovered. When Twain's classic *Adventures of Huckleberry Finn* made its American appearance in February 1885 it was generally well received. One critic wrote of its "many pleasant episodes" and its "extraordinary power" in presenting living scenes of life along the Mississippi. A review in *Century Magazine* praised its strong moral sense, which was communicated deftly and realistically. "Life teaches its lessons by implication," noted the writer, "not by didactic preaching; and literature is at its best when it is an imitation of life, and not an excuse for instruction" (Emerson, p. 157). Concord, however, had a different opinion. In March the town's Library Committee voted to exclude the book. As reported in the Boston *Transcript* (17 March 1885), one member of the committee stated that he considered the book "as the veriest trash" while "the librarian and the other members of the committee entertain similar views, characterizing it as rough, coarse and inelegant, dealing with a series of experiences not elevating, the whole book being more suited to the slums than to intelligent, respectable people."

Despite such hostility to the new trends in literature, Concord became a popular destination for literary pilgrims from home and abroad, people who remembered its glorious past. Whitman made his last visit to Emerson in 1881 at the very time that the Boston controversy over *Leaves of Grass* was coming to the fore. Ignoring the matter for the time, Whitman reported spending a "long and blessed evening" with his old friend and loyal defender (Loving, p. 408). In less than a year, Emerson would be dead. His home eventually became a public memorial. The same would eventually be true for the Alcott's "Orchard House" and Hawthorne's "Wayside." The "Old Manse," Emerson's ancestral home and the Hawthornes' Concord abode for three years in the early 1840s, is also a popular pilgrimage site. It is located next to the Old North Bridge, which Emerson made famous as the place where "once the embattled farmers stood / And fired the shot heard round the world" at the beginning of the Revolutionary War. Perhaps the most sacred spot of all, however, is not a structure but Thoreau's precious Walden Pond, the site of his experiment in simple living made famous in the classic *Walden* (1854). Emerson deeded the property around the pond to the citizens of the state of Massachusetts at the time of his death in 1882. Since then thousands of pilgrims have made their way to "Thoreau's Cove" to place a stone on the cairn that memorializes his life and legacy (Harding, p. 144). Eventually all of Concord's literary giants would find their final resting places on Sleepy Hollow Cemetery's appropriately named "Authors' Ridge." Here, enjoying the same proximity in death as in life, lie the remains of Thoreau, Hawthorne, Emerson, Louisa May Alcott and her father, Bronson, and most of the authors' families.

WILLIAM DEAN HOWELLS

Among those drawn to Concord, even in the early years, was William Dean Howells, who was destined to become arguably the most important writer and critic of the post–Civil War period in terms of his influence on the literary trends of the time. When Howells, a self-described "passionate pilgrim from the West," first made his way to "the holy land at Boston" in 1860, he stopped at Concord. There he found Emerson, who was "shining a lambent star of poesy and prophesy at the zenith" (*Friends,* pp. 13, 10). In his conversation, however, Howells sensed that his literary tastes differed from those of the great philosopher. As he would recall their interview years later in *Literary Friends and Acquaintance* (1900), the young westerner felt that "Emerson had, in fact, a defective sense as to specific pieces of literature; he praised extravagantly, and in the wrong place, especially among the new things, and he failed to see the worth of much that was fine and precious" (p. 62). It was an early sign of the divergent literary views that would evolve in the balance of the century. Howells would eventually emerge as a leader among the new breed of writers that changed the face of American literature, but first he would complete an apprenticeship in Boston.

In 1860 Howells was welcomed by the Boston literary establishment as a fit successor to and a suitable defender of the genteel tradition. The young author from Ohio already had published some early work in the *Atlantic* (Lynn, pp. 79, 85). During this first visit, as he later recalled, he was thrilled when, while at a dinner party, Oliver Wendell Holmes looked from Howells to James T. Fields (head of Ticknor & Fields, publishers of the *Atlantic Monthly*), and remarked with a smile, "Well, James, this is something like the apostolic succession; this is the laying on of hands" (*Friends,* p. 37).

After serving for a time as an assistant, Howells eventually became editor of the *Atlantic Monthly* in 1871. As time passed, however, and his talent evolved, he became increasingly uncomfortable in the stuffy confines of Boston where the Brahmin caste, represented to him most immediately by Holmes, was a looming presence. As his biographer points out, during his tenure as editor, when Holmes submitted his literary work to the *Atlantic,* "Howells never failed to accept it. After Howells began to write novels in the early 1870s, Holmes not only read them, but also monitored them for social errors" (Lynn, p. 96). After leaving the *Atlantic* in 1881, Howells felt a new breath of freedom. He told a correspondent at the time that he was "reading everything of Zola's that I can get my hands on" (Lynn, p. 258). Following the trend of the time, Howells moved to New York in 1889 and took a position on the editorial board of *Harper's.* In his monthly "Editor's Study" column, he openly promoted the cause of realism and the realistic writings of Continental and British authors whose works, in some cases, he introduced to an American audience. These included such notables as Henrik Ibsen, Fyodor Dostoyevsky, and Leo Tolstoy (Gougeon, pp. 117–119). Meanwhile, Boston continued its reactionary ways. When Howells's *The Rise of Silas Lapham* (set in Boston and destined to become his most enduring work) was serialized in *Century Magazine* in 1885, it was condemned by one genteel critic as a work whose moral tone was "hopelessly bad" (Cady, p. 16). The following year, when Howells published *The Minister's Charge,* another exercise in the new realism, he incurred the severe disapproval and even hostility of a majority of Bostonians. Indeed, the criticism reached such an intensity that he had to warn his father not to believe what was being written about him in the newspapers (Lynn, p. 286). It was yet another sign of the times. Boston simply would not tolerate the "newness" that was coming to the fore in literature and in American culture generally. When Charlotte Perkins Gilman's powerful short story "The Yellow Wall-Paper" was recommended to Horace Scudder for publication in the *Atlantic* in 1890, he refused it. Scudder returned the manuscript to Gilman with a terse note that read: "Mr. Howells has handed me this story. I could not forgive myself if I made others as miserable as I have made myself!" (Gilman, p. 119).

TURN OF THE CENTURY AND AFTER

This attitude prevailed in the years following the turn of the century as Boston continued to censor itself.

Whereas before the Civil War, Boston had been recognized as the "chief center for the publication of literary works in the United States," due to the tireless efforts of ambitious and open-minded publishers like James T. Fields, it was now largely a cultural anachronism (Austin, p. 17). Progressivism was taking hold throughout America, but there was little that was progressive in Boston's literary outlook. Van Wyck Brooks points out that, in the years before the First World War, the "Watch and Ward Society" of Boston "prohibited sixty books that were generally accepted in the rest of the country." As a result "the phrase 'banned in Boston' [became] the novelist's dream of successful publicity, but Boston banned itself in excluding the world; and American writers generally now regarded it with a certain rancour as illiberal, sterile, indifferent, censorious and petty" (Brooks, p. 504).

There would be, however, occasional reminders of Boston's and Concord's liberal past. In August 1897 a brilliant young African American intellectual named W. E. B. Du Bois would make what his biographer considers his "national debut" in the *Atlantic Monthly* with an article titled "Strivings of the Negro People" (Lewis, p. 198). Boston and Concord, along with the rest of the country, would remember Emerson on the centenary of his birth. An elaborate memorial celebration was held in July 1903. Speakers at the event in Concord included the philosopher William James, the reformer Julia Ward Howe, and the future first president of the NAACP, Moorfield Storey. One of the last notable Boston publications of the period was Henry Adams's *The Education of Henry Adams,* issued by Houghton Mifflin in 1918. The following year the book was awarded the Pulitzer Prize. Ironically, it is a work that describes the virtual uselessness of the old values of Concord, Boston, and Harvard in dealing with the complexities of the modern age. Like his New England predecessors, Adams was a searcher, but unlike them, he discovered no truth that could bring unity and meaning to the world. Consequently he describes his autobiography as a story that "has no moral and little incident" (p. 4). Boston, once the hub of America's literary universe, had finally become a center that would no longer hold.

See also The Atlantic Monthly; Book Publishing; Genteel Tradition; Immigration; Libraries; Literary Friendships; Museums

BIBLIOGRAPHY
Primary Works
Adams, Henry. *The Education of Henry Adams.* 1918. Boston: Houghton Mifflin, 1973.

Gilman, Charlotte Perkins. *The Living of Charlotte Perkins Gilman: An Autobiography.* 1935. New York: Arno Press, 1972.

Howells, William Dean. "Criticism and Fiction." In *Criticism and Fiction and Other Essays,* edited by Clara Marburg Kirk and Rudolf Kirk, pp. 9–87. New York: New York University Press, 1959.

Howells, William Dean. *Literary Friends and Acquaintance.* New York: Harper & Brothers, 1900.

James, Henry. "The Art of Fiction." In *The Art of Fiction and Other Essays,* edited by Morris Roberts, pp. 3–23. New York: Oxford University Press, 1948.

Secondary Works

Aaron, Daniel. "Literary Scenes and Literary Movements." In *Columbia Literary History of the United States,* edited by Emory Elliott, pp. 733–757. New York: Columbia University Press, 1988.

Allen, Gay Wilson. *The Solitary Singer: A Critical Biography of Walt Whitman.* New York: Macmillan, 1955.

Austin, James C. *Fields of the Atlantic Monthly: Letters to an Editor, 1861–1870.* San Marino, Calif.: Huntington Library, 1953.

Brodhead, Richard. "Literature and Culture: 1865–1910." In *Columbia Literary History of the United States,* edited by Emory Elliott, pp. 467–481. New York: Columbia University Press, 1988.

Brooks, Van Wyck. *New England Indian Summer: 1865–1915.* New York: Dutton, 1940.

Cady, Edwin H. Introduction to *The Rise of Silas Lapham.* Edited by Edwin H. Cady, pp. v–xviii. Boston: Houghton Mifflin, 1957.

Emerson, Everett. *Mark Twain: A Literary Life.* Philadelphia: University of Pennsylvania Press, 2000.

Falk, Robert. "The Rise of Realism: 1871–1891." In *Transitions in American Literary History,* edited by Harry Hayden Clark, pp. 381–442. Durham, N.C.: Duke University Press, 1960.

Gougeon, Len. "Holmes' *Emerson* and the Conservative Critique of Realism." *South Atlantic Review* 59, no. 1 (1994): 107–125.

Harding, Walter, ed. *Henry David Thoreau: A Profile.* New York: Hill and Wang, 1971.

Howe, M. A. De Wolfe. *The Atlantic Monthly and Its Makers.* Boston: Atlantic Monthly Press, 1909.

Lewis, David Levering. *W. E. B. Du Bois.* Vol. 1, *Biography of a Race, 1868–1919.* New York: Holt, 1993.

Loving, Jerome. *Walt Whitman: The Song of Himself.* Berkeley: University of California Press, 1999.

Lynn, Kenneth S. *William Dean Howells: An American Life.* New York: Harcourt Brace Jovanovich, 1970.

Pizer, Donald. *Realism and Naturalism in Nineteenth-Century American Literature.* Rev. ed. Carbondale: Southern Illinois University Press, 1984.

Scudder, Townsend. *Concord: American Town.* Boston: Little, Brown, 1947.

Sedgwick, Ellery. *The Atlantic Monthly, 1857–1909: Yankee Humanism at High Tide and Ebb.* Amherst: University of Massachusetts Press, 1994.

Thorp, Willard. *American Writing in the Twentieth Century.* Cambridge, Mass.: Harvard University Press, 1960.

Len Gougeon

BOXING

From its origins as an illicit and disreputable pastime followed primarily by a small number of enthusiasts, the sport of boxing emerged as a significant cultural phenomenon throughout the United States by the turn of the twentieth century. First imported from Great Britain in the late colonial period, the spectacle of organized prizefights—often bloody, loosely regulated brawls fought with bare knuckles—catered to a curious assemblage of working-class participants, wealthy bachelors, and professional gamblers. Together, these so-called gentlemen of the fancy comprised a widespread, loosely organized network supporting occasional bouts and gloved sparring exhibitions as well as other athletic displays and contests. The evolution of professional boxing from the somewhat shadowy realm of the bare-knuckle prizefight resulted from the Progressive Era's extraordinary confluence of class and ethnic struggle, emergent consumer culture, a perceived crisis of masculinity among white, middle-class men, changes in newspaper publishing, and urban growth in the postbellum period. Furthermore, the appearance of dynamic figures from John L. Sullivan to Jack Johnson provided commanding personalities who helped define the role of the modern sports hero. While boxing as a subject suitable for literary endeavors would remain somewhat marginalized throughout much of the twentieth century, the emergence of literary naturalism and its embrace of atavism, brutality, and the urban milieu, as well as the increasing acceptance of boxing into the mainstream of American society in general, would contribute to the literary exploration of the boxing ring in this period, most famously in the work of Jack London.

THE RISE OF BOXING AS A PROFESSIONAL SPORT

Among the many dramatic consequences of the economic and demographic changes in the mid-nineteenth century were the growing popularity of amateur athletics and the establishment of professional athletics, most notably baseball, as a commercial enterprise. Growing numbers of both native-born and immigrant men helped create a "bachelor subculture" in large American cities, often based around the neighborhood saloon and enlivened by sporting contests, from billiards to cockfighting to boxing, in which men participated either as combatants or gamblers. Such semi-clandestine activities served as an urban, working-class counterpart to the more public athletic spectacles, such as baseball, collegiate football, or yachting. For Irish Americans, in particular, pugilism proved an attractive means by which to assimilate into the increasingly masculine culture of the American city. By the late nineteenth century, other ethnic communities, including Italians, Jews, and African Americans, would also seek to identify their own efforts at assimilation with success in the boxing ring, with varying results.

Although usually outlawed by local or state statutes, boxing matches gained a broader audience through the extended reach of specialized publications catering to the bachelor subculture. Newspapers, such as prizefight impresario Richard Kyle Fox's *Police Gazette* and the *New York Clipper,* often sold in corner saloons, featured sensationalized accounts of public scandals and lurid crimes as well as news from the worlds of theater and sports. Before the widespread adoption of the "sports page" in the newspapers of William Randolph Hearst and Joseph Pulitzer by the 1890s, more genteel, mainstream papers such as the *New York Herald* and the *New York Times,* which frequently editorialized against the inhumanity and indecency of boxing, offered detailed accounts of prominent prizefights, ostensibly published as crime news. In this way, both conventional and specialized journalism contributed to a growing public fascination with, if not acceptance of, boxing as both a profession and a form of entertainment.

JOHN L. SULLIVAN

The single most important figure in the evolution of boxing from illicit crime to legitimate entertainment was John Lawrence Sullivan (1858–1918), known as "the Boston Strong-Boy," a second-generation Irish American whose reign as heavyweight champion from 1882 to 1892 bridged distinct eras and served to popularize and institutionalize the sport. Beginning his career at a time when boxers and their managers negotiated over prize money, rules, and opponents on an almost entirely ad hoc basis, Sullivan retired after losing his crown to James John "Gentleman Jim" Corbett (1866–1933) in the first heavyweight title fight fought under the Marquess of Queensberry rules. These guidelines dictated strictly timed rounds

and the donning of padded gloves, and promoters and regulating bodies have continued to use similar regulations ever since.

In *John L. Sullivan and His America* (1988), biographer Michael T. Isenberg called Sullivan "the first significant mass cultural hero in American life" (p. 13). He served as a galvanizing icon for Irish Americans, working-class men, and a culture increasingly anxious about a supposed "feminization" of American society. Signaling the breadth of his significance as a cultural hero, Sullivan's name, and his legendary fight with Corbett, are invoked by Jake, the protagonist of *Yekl: A Tale of the New York Ghetto* (1896). The novel's author, Abraham Cahan (1860–1951), uses Jake's identification with Sullivan to show how his character assumes typically "Yankee" characteristics as he struggles with cultural assimilation and class friction.

BOXING IN LITERATURE

Within the broader category of sports literature, relatively few examples of boxing literature exist until the mid-twentieth century. Early representations of athletic themes and settings in literature are confined largely to the sporting subgenres of boys' books, dime novels, and pulp paperbacks that first appeared in the 1890s. Prominent among authors specializing in these types of heroic sports fiction were Ralph Henry Barbour, Albertus True Dudley, T. Truxton Hare, and Gilbert Patten (1866–1945). The latter, writing as Burt L. Standish, established the template for the college athletic hero with the Frank Merriwell series of novels (1896–1913), which celebrated an idealized combination of ingenuity, intelligence, cultivation, and athletic prowess in its Yale-educated protagonist. The dime novel formula, however, focused on sports such as baseball and football rather than boxing, which was rarely a part of collegiate athletics and was seldom practiced by the middle- and upper-class audiences for whom these stories were intended. Exceptions to this formula were provided by pulp biographies of prominent fighters, often more fictional than otherwise, such as those published by Street and Smith's *New York Five Cent Library* in the 1890s.

Literary naturalists, whose work reflected the growing influence of post-Darwinian scientific discourse and offered glimpses into the gritty, urban environment rarely depicted in polite literature, found in boxing a motif that suited both their thematic and contextual purposes. Frank Norris (1870–1902), for instance, extolled the virtues of prizefighting and other sports in his literary columns and published several athlete-hero stories in the San Francisco journal *The Wave,* including one about boxing titled "Shorty

Stack, Pugilist" (1897). As an important part of the urban landscape, boxing forms part of the backdrop for works such as *Maggie, A Girl of the Streets* (1893), written by Stephen Crane (1871–1900), in which small-time rounder Pete first meets Maggie when he and her brother Jimmie are on their way to watch a boxing match in Brooklyn. For characters caught in the crucible of the city, the prizefight and its surrounding culture offered a sense of identity in terms of gender, ethnicity, and nationality.

JACK LONDON

By far the most significant fictional use of boxing in this period can be found in the work of Jack London (1876–1916). His extensive knowledge of the sport and commitment to its place in American culture inspired several works of fiction focusing on the world of boxing, including two novels and a large body of journalistic writing. London's novels *The Game* (1905) and *The Abysmal Brute* (1913) both feature boxing protagonists and explore the workings of the professional prize ring. The former book tells the story of Joe Fleming and Genevieve Pritchard, two "working class aristocrats" (p. 45), and their ill-fated love affair, which unravels as Joe pursues his deep, almost spiritual, commitment to "the Game"—boxing. He is killed in the ring by a "swarthy" rival named John Ponta, a "beast with a streak for a forehead, with beady eyes under lowering and bushy brows, flat-nosed, thick-lipped, sullenmouthed" (pp. 117–118). With its clash between idealized, yet doomed, working-class Anglo-Saxons, both male and female, and the seductive and corrupt urban melting pot, embodied by the forbidding presence of Joe's nemesis in the boxing ring, *The Game* intermingles widespread cultural fears of immigration, unfettered capitalism, and the modern city.

In *Dreaming of Heroes: American Sports Fiction, 1868–1980* (1982), Michael Oriard claims that London "created the classic stereotype of the natural in sports literature" (p. 82) with *The Abysmal Brute*. The novel's hero, Pat Glendon, like *The Game*'s Joe Fleming, is an idealized figure, pure and incorruptible, who possesses instinctive skills as a fighter. Unlike Joe, however, Pat is a product of the wilderness of the American West, a displaced Leatherstocking in the corrupt world of San Francisco. Whereas Joe's tragic fate looms inevitably on the horizon, Pat draws upon his instinctive resources to win both the climactic boxing match and Maud Sangster, his pure female counterpart, before escaping the sinister city for a cleaner life in the unspoiled mountains.

Whereas London's boxing novels underscore the notion of the prizefight ring as an appropriate metaphor for the crucible of the modern city, his best-known short story involving the sport, "A Piece of Steak" (1909), is different. It employs pugilism in the pursuit of a theme often found in his Klondike tales—the inevitable and cyclical triumph of youth over old age. In this story, aging boxer Tom King, returns to the ring for a last fight with a young contender, only to be knocked out, a conclusion that affirms the irrevocable laws of nature.

JACK JOHNSON AND BOXING'S CULTURAL IMPACT

Among the events described in London's vast body of journalistic reporting, none proved more culturally significant than the heavyweight championship bout between Jack Johnson (born John Arthur Johnson, 1878–1946) and James Jackson Jeffries (1875–1953) on 4 July 1910. London himself had called on the retired champion Jeffries to return to the ring to defeat Johnson, the first African American to hold the title and a particularly controversial and polarizing figure in the history of American sport. Beginning with John L. Sullivan's firm declaration, "I will not fight a Negro. I never have and I never shall," an unofficial prohibition had been firmly established that barred black contenders from a title bout, most conspicuously the outstanding boxer Peter Jackson (1861–1901), who was born on the Caribbean island of St. Croix and later won championships in Australia and England. Subsequent champions, including Gentleman Jim Corbett, Robert Prometheus Fitzsimmons (1862–1917), and James Jeffries, maintained Sullivan's color line. Upon witnessing Johnson's assumption of the heavyweight crown in 1908 in a decisive victory over Jeffries's unimpressive Canadian successor, Tommy Burns, London himself insisted that "Jim Jeffries must emerge from his alfalfa farm and remove the golden smile from Jack Johnson's face" (*Jack London Reports,* p. 264).

When Johnson defeated an unprepared and humiliated Jeffries, touted as America's "Great White Hope," in Reno, Nevada, before an estimated crowd of up to twenty thousand, Johnson forced white Americans, including London, who viewed Jeffries as a prohibitive favorite, to confront their casual assumptions about athletic prowess and racial dominance. The towering Johnson, an imposing figure inside and outside the ring, not only assumed a public role reserved for white heroes but also flaunted racial conventions of Jim Crow America, dressing ostentatiously, driving expensive automobiles, and marrying a white woman. Johnson's transgressive attitude, as well as his consummate skills as a boxer, earned him a nearly legendary role within the African American community, and songs and stories quickly circulated that raised Johnson to the status of

Jack Johnson in the ring with James Jeffries, Reno, Nevada, 10 July 1910. © BETTMANN/CORBIS

folk hero alongside such mythical figures as Railroad Bill, John Henry, and Stack-o-lee. While members of the African American intelligentsia remained somewhat wary of Johnson's apparent confirmation of white racial fears of black men, his cultural impact ensured a place in subsequent literary texts. Among contemporary writers, author and political activist James Weldon Johnson (1871–1938), in particular, offered unapologetic praise for Johnson. In a piece published in *The Selected Writings of James Weldon Johnson* (1995), the author notes that Jack Johnson "not only looked the white man in the eye, but hit him in the eye" and concludes that "his pugilistic record is something of a racial asset" (p. 126). Jack Johnson would serve as a symbol of black pride and resistance throughout the twentieth century: among many examples across the cultural spectrum, his name is invoked prominently in the novel *Invisible Man* (1952) by Ralph Ellison; his life story serves as the basis for the play *The Great White Hope* (1967) by Howard Sackler; and his mythic resonance permeates the 1970

film soundtrack recording *A Tribute to Jack Johnson* by jazz trumpeter Miles Davis.

BROADER ACCEPTANCE

With the rise of Jack Dempsey (born William Harrison Dempsey, 1895–1983) to the heavyweight championship in 1919, boxing began a period of further commercialization and consolidation. Eager to avoid the perceived embarrassment of another African American at the top of the sport, promoters and regulatory commissions exerted tighter control over the prize ring, and Dempsey, known as the "Manassa Mauler," proved a popular white champion whom the boxing establishment could use to market boxing to a wider, more respectable audience.

As the sport entered the mainstream of American society, so did it gain legitimacy within the literary world. London's early advocacy of boxing in literature and his association of boxing with the cult of the masculine writer, as well as the growing body of literary texts about other sports, foresaw the plentiful examples of boxing-related texts later in the century. These included the short stories "The Battler" (1925) and "Fifty Grand" (1927) by Ernest Hemingway; *Never Come Morning* (1942) by Nelson Algren; *The Harder They Fall* (1947) by Budd Schulberg; and *Fat City* (1969) by Leonard Gardner. As a unique combination of ritualized combat and athletic display, boxing has continued to fascinate observers of American culture, and its rise during the Progressive Era epitomizes the volatile convergence of race, gender, and commerce that would help define this period in American history.

See also Maggie, A Girl of the Streets; Sports

BIBLIOGRAPHY

Primary Works

Johnson, James Weldon. *The Selected Writings of James Weldon Johnson.* Edited by Sondra Kathryn Wilson. Vol. 1. New York: Oxford University Press, 1995.

London, Jack. *The Game.* New York: Macmillan, 1905.

London, Jack. *Jack London Reports: War Correspondence, Sports Articles, and Miscellaneous Writings.* Edited by King Hendricks and Irving Shepard. Garden City, N.Y.: Doubleday, 1970.

Secondary Works

Betts, John Rickards. *America's Sporting Heritage: 1850–1950.* Reading, Mass.: Addison-Wesley, 1974.

Early, Gerald. *The Culture of Bruising: Essays on Prize-fighting, Literature, and Modern American Culture.* Hopewell, N.J.: Ecco Press, 1994.

Gorn, Elliot J. *The Manly Art: Bare-Knuckle Prize Fighting in America.* Ithaca, N.Y.: Cornell University Press, 1986.

Isenberg, Michael T. *John L. Sullivan and His America.* Urbana: University of Illinois Press, 1988.

Oriard, Michael. *Dreaming of Heroes: American Sports Fiction, 1868–1980.* Chicago: Nelson-Hall, 1982.

Riess, Steven A. *City Games: The Evolution of American Urban Society and the Rise of Sports.* Urbana: University of Illinois Press, 1989.

Roberts, Randy. *Papa Jack: Jack Johnson and the Era of White Hopes.* New York: Free Press, 1983.

Sammons, Jeffrey T. *Beyond the Ring: The Role of Boxing in American Society.* Urbana: University of Illinois Press, 1988.

John Dudley

BUSINESS AND INDUSTRY NOVELS

The American novel of business and industry came into its own immediately after the Civil War as a capacious form of cultural documentation. Unlike the western, the captivity narrative, or the sentimental romance, the business novel was not so much a genre as a type of alembic to which the elements of genre (the romantic subplot, moral regeneration, the villain) were submitted to be broken down, weighed, and revalued. Its men and woman descended directly from Herman Melville's (1819–1891) whalers and scriveners and generated George F. Babbitt and Jay Gatsby, but they navigated the new avenues of endeavor and experience offered by the Gilded Age with neither the certitudes of their ancestors nor the clarified expectations of those who followed in their footsteps.

To get some idea of the importance—both aesthetic and economic—of the novel of business and industry in these years, it is only necessary to note such typical trade-journal advertisements as the one placed in the 7 April 1906 edition of the *Literary Digest* by the J. A. Hill Company of New York for its "Wall Street Library," whose five volumes included *Stock Speculation* and *The A B C of Wall Street:*

> This is a subject which every intelligent American should understand, for the influence of this gigantic money-making machine extends to the furthest corner of the United States. . . . It shows how financial panics are caused, and how to anticipate them. It exposes Wall Street fakes. (*Literary Digest,* p. 546)

These notices ran alongside nearly identical advertisements for novels like Upton Sinclair's *The Moneychangers* (1908), John Charles Van Dyke's *The Money God* (1908), Henry M. Hyde's *Buccaneers: A Story of the Black Flag in Business* (1904), and Edwin Lefevre's collection of *Wall Street Stories* (1901). The juxtaposition is telling, as is the fact that Sinclair and Lefevre were journalists whose fictions were avowedly journalistic and that Van Dyke had published extensively on Renaissance and American painting but would one day edit *The Autobiography of Andrew Carnegie* (1920). The business novel developed coordinately with several other forms of writing. They included the muckraking journalistic exposé; works of economic sociology by Simon Newcomb and Thorstein Veblen; and the scholarly article of public conscience practiced by the likes of John Dewey and the brothers Charles Francis Adams Jr. and Henry Adams (the latter's novel *Democracy: An American Novel,* published in 1880, scandalously portrayed the business of politics). Also appearing at the same time were demotic screeds such as William H. Harvey's *Coin's Financial School* (1895) and narrative primers about such matters as monetary

Wall Street, photograph, c. 1911. As the financial center of the United States, Wall Street became a symbol of both the promise of wealth and the increasingly apparent negative effects of U.S. commerce. THE LIBRARY OF CONGRESS

policy and the tariff, curious books like the apocalyptic and proto-science fictional *Battle of Coney Island; or, Free Trade Overthrow* by "An Eye Witness," the likes of which poured forth from printing presses throughout the nation. Anxious to distinguish between the genuine article of American industriousness and the corrupting practices of Wall Street "fakes," novelists of widely varied political outlooks and aesthetic predispositions contributed their fictions (often based on real people and events) to what they hoped would be a cultural narrative of real value.

WHO'S WHO: THE BUSINESS OF SOCIETY AND THE SOCIETY OF BUSINESS

By 1870 the large and variegated enterprises taking shape with the help of economic theory and legal doctrine—especially the unanticipated applications of

the due process clause of the Fourteenth Amendment to the Constitution to corporate "personalities" that were both elusively fictional and redoubtably material—were unlikely to be "bossed" (a word with the disconcerting tendency to migrate from business to politics, potentially disarranging the cultural organization of authority) by the paternal tutors described by historian Paul E. Johnson in *A Shopkeeper's Millennium: Society and Revivals in Rochester, New York, 1815–1837,* or by Melville's Master of Chancery, that "eminently safe man" (Melville, p. 40) whose good intentions are underwritten by religious piety, political patronage, and legal precedent. There was no telling where the next tycoon would come from: he or she could be an inconspicuous Indianapolis pump worker like James Sheridan in Booth Tarkington's *Turmoil* (1914; also included in the author's *Growth* trilogy, published in full in 1927); nearly a Canadian, like the stalwart Vermont hero of William Dean Howells's *The Rise of Silas Lapham* (1885); or even a veteran of the inner-city criminal courts, in the manner of Van Harrington, who Robert Herrick would have us believe goes from bad to worse in the Chicago novel *Memoirs of an American Citizen* (1905). Likewise, fortunes lay imminent even in the most homely fields. Lapham publishes his name on the landscape in mineral paint, much to the chagrin of the Brahmins whose acceptance he grudgingly seeks. Henry Kitchell Webster cleverly played off the financial institutions against the trading pits in his novel *The Banker and the Bear* (1900), the subtitle of which—*The Story of a Corner in Lard*—speaks for itself. And Frank Norris (1870–1902) famously lent an epic sweep to the matter of wheat, first in the California valleys of *The Octopus: A Story of California* (1901) and then in the restricted compass of the Chicago mercantile market in *The Pit: A Story of Chicago* (1903). In a nation emerging from civil war and wracked by no less than three depressions and any number of panics during the next half century, it was a matter of some urgency to figure out just who these men and women were who were turning sows' ears into silk purses.

This is not to say that novelists viewed themselves as superintendents of the social register, though the efforts of the nouveau riche to gain entrée into traditionally forbidden (and often desiccated) corners of society is a notable aspect of the novel of business and industry. William Dean Howells (1837–1920), in particular, developed a redoubtable social vision. In *Annie Kilburn* (1888) he made the manufacturing village of Hatboro the scene of tension between the sources of tradition and new labor. Neither religion nor aesthetic drama (in the form of a misguided production of *Romeo and Juliet*) are able to allay the conflict. In *A Hazard of New Fortunes* (1890) he evoked the problems of labor and capital from the equally problematic relationship between cosmopolitanism and a precarious sense of national identity. Embodying the impetus of American industry as fully as his more run-of-the-mill quotidian counterparts in fiction, Christopher Newman, onetime manufacturer of leather goods and bathtubs in Henry James's *The American* (1877), falls victim to the nefarious Bellegardes largely because of the qualities of honesty and determination that made his fortune. For Harold Frederic (1856–1898) in his best-selling novel *The Market-Place* (1899), as for Howells and James, the problem of social acceptance is reflexive. It measures the rather restricted tolerances of the Lady Edith Cressages and Lord Plowdens of the world as well as the atrophied moral faculty of the ambitious and frantically industrious Joel Stormont Thorpe. To the credit of novelists

like Howells, James, Frederic, and Herrick, the cost of belonging is never equated with the depleted resources of tradition alone. The tycoons wanted their fair share of high society, and for better or worse, they were bound to get it.

As cautious as they often were in holding the line against social interlopers, the novelists of business and industry, particularly in the first years after the Civil War, interested themselves in character as much as situation in order to foster a sense of historical continuity between the recently concluded war and the new field of commercial conflict that was making the metaphor of war ever more pervasive and apt. Novels that locate a discontinuity, such as J. G. (Josiah Gilbert) Holland's *Sevenoaks: A Story of To-Day* (1875), "express," in the words of Henry Nash Smith in "The Search for a Capitalist Hero: Businessmen in American Fiction," "the basic revulsion of their authors against the emergent financial and industrial system of the post-Civil War period" (Smith, p. 78). Holland, better known for cofounding and editing *Scribner's Magazine* than for his forthrightly sentimental and sententious prose and verse, pits speculating and cosmopolitan village tyrant Robert Belcher against a vivid collection vernacular characters (several resembling James Fenimore Cooper's character Hawkeye), to the misfortune of the baronial capitalist.

Continuity, on the other hand, could serve either as a conservative vehicle for approbation or abhorrence. The well-known Washingtonian John Hay (1838–1905), following the example of his friend Henry Adams, published his first novel *The Bread-Winners: A Social Study* (1883) anonymously. His hero, Arthur Farnham, is a veteran Civil War commander who invests his inheritance in business (like Henry Adams's brother Charles Francis Adams Jr., also a former Union officer) and ends up marshaling the citizens of his native Buffland (a lakeside cross between Buffalo and Cleveland, as the name suggests) against benighted strikers led by the "oleaginous" "reformer" Sleeny, "the greasy apostle of labor" (p. 74).

John Barclay, protagonist of William Allen White's (1868–1944) sprawling *A Certain Rich Man* (1909), turns his war experience against his fellow citizens by gathering around him a cadre of sharp financial and political dealers from the first days of the Civil War. White was an eminent newspaperman from Emporia, Kansas, and his novel doubles as a fairly accurate record of early skirmishing on the Kansas-Missouri border and a melodramatic account of the way men like Barclay corrupted the heritage of abolition by directing its moral authority down the ramifying channels of commerce in pursuit of purely selfish ends.

(Barclay's father was an abolitionist preacher of New England stock who had been shot to death soon after arriving in Kansas.) Once Barclay experiences the obligatory epiphany and begins to work his own redemption, the civil and commercial wars justify themselves one to another with the decisiveness of a cracking blow struck to the skull of a cowardly striker by the firm hand of Barclay's counterpart in Hay's novel *Captain Farnham*, source of investment capital, civic order, and historical continuity.

THE NAPOLEONIC ASPIRATIONS OF THE NEW SOVEREIGNTY

Every army, even one whose campaigns are industrial or financial, needs a general to lead it, which perhaps accounts for the frequency with which the protagonists of business novels are likened to Napoleon. (Although this observation does not apply to the "Industrial Army" Edward Bellamy imagined in his 1888 novel *Looking Backward: 2000–1887*, the great "Trust" commanding it certainly qualifies as a revolutionary form of sovereignty.) Herrick's Van Harrington in *Memoirs of an American Citizen* is classed as a new kind of Napoleon, and Landry Court in Frank Norris's *The Pit* makes a similar comment about head honcho Curtis Jadwin's indomitable spirit: "I tell you he's Napoleonic" (Norris, p. 262). Elam Harnish, whose indicative nickname provided Jack London (1876–1916) with the title of his novel *Burning Daylight* (1910), descends from the Yukon a visionary land developer who strikes at trusts in California's Central Valley with "Napoleonic suddenness" (p. 156) before losing his bearings in drink and lethargic financial drudgery, only to regain his composure preparatory to a Silas-Lapham–like ascension. Such a formula bespeaks the worry widely shared at the time that the reins of government had passed into the hands of a new and unprincipled plutocracy bent on establishing a "feudalism" all the more onerous for its cynical and undisciplined modernity.

Whether it appeared as a sociopolitical combination exercising comprehensive cultural authority or a monolithic trust whose managerial unity disguised the diversity of its attributes, the plutocracy was feared as an insidious threat to the fragile brand of sovereignty peculiar to America. In *The Mammon of Unrighteousness* (1891), H. H. (Hjalmar Hjorth) Boyesen (1848–1895) related the manner in which brothers Aleck and Horace Larkin break from the influence of their adoptive father Obed, a landholder and university benefactor patterned upon Ezra Cornell, and become in their respective aesthetic and political triumphs the servants of an industrial order they neither endorse nor quite understand. Boyesen, like the more

sentimental Holland in *Sevenoaks*, perceived the seeds of corruption beginning to mature not in the new territories, but in the disconcertingly fertile ground of the old Northeast and its landed estates.

In several vigorous novels published in quick succession in the first decades of the new century, David Graham Phillips (1867–1911) dramatized the threat posed by the new and multiform plutocracy to traditional ways of conducting commercial and political business. Hampton Scarborough exposes the underhanded financial manipulations of John Dumont in *The Cost* (1904) and then accepts his party's nomination for president of the United States while taking apart Harvey Saylor's "Power Trust" in *The Plum Tree* (1905).

Superior to either of these novels is *The Deluge* (1905), perhaps because Phillips was following as he wrote the real-life example of maverick Boston financier Thomas W. Lawson, whose sensational exposé *Frenzied Finance* had begun its serial run the previous spring in *Everybody's Magazine*. Phillips's hero this time is Matt Blacklock, or "Black Matt," a publicist-financier—referred to condescendingly as the boss of a "bucket shop"—only slightly more scrupulous than the canting and sanctimonious "Seven," a group of capitalists he brings down in an eleventh-hour media blitz. Though Blacklock profits handsomely from his exposé, he rationalizes his lurid work as a public service. He then leaves the fray he created, having concluded that the people are responsible for fostering the Seven and thus "wear the yoke" of poverty and oppression "because they have not yet become intelligent and competent enough to be free" (p. 463). So much for popular sovereignty. A similarly pessimistic view is presented in *Memoirs of an American Citizen*, by Robert Herrick (1868–1938). Van Harrington is able to buy a seat in the U.S. Senate, where one is told he will shine forth a "sickening example" to his fellow citizens. These novels suggest that there is little chance that government institutions are adequate to control modern industry. (Such controls are referred to in Boyesen's *The Mammon of Unrighteousness*, when the character Horace Larkin pleads for their design.) Whether the novelists of business and industry in America thought they had designed adequate literary institutions remains very much in doubt.

FORMS OF REFORM

Novels of business and industry may have had their literary and intellectual shortcomings, but complacency was not among them. It was the rare work that did not outline some grievance or point out the need, if not the avenue, of reform. If the solution, such as it may have been, appeared to lie merely in some moonshine manner of individual sympathy, that was because most institutions were felt to be either outmoded or in collusion with the prevailing order. Howells made the obligatory gestures toward the clergy and the law in his books, but the basic (and indeed rather helpless) call for understanding undergirds Annie Kilburn's relationship with the laborers of Hatboro in *Annie Kilburn*. It also informs the reader's attitude toward J. Milton Northwick in *The Quality of Mercy* (1892), one of Hatboro's least sympathetic voices, who embezzles money from the insurance company he heads. In the wake of the Haymarket riot and influenced by Edward Bellamy's New Nationalism, Howells had by the time of *A Hazard of New Fortunes* turned toward a genteel variety of Christian Socialism. By contrast, an altogether more vigorous version of this same Christian Socialism benefits the impoverished and disenfranchised freedmen in Albion W. Tourgée's novels *Murvale Eastman, Christian Socialist* (1890) and *Pactolus Prime* (1890).

Elizabeth Stuart Phelps (1844–1911) embraced a muscular humanitarianism in *The Silent Partner* (1871). The pathos of Phelps's novel and its few mawkish moments hardly detract from the force inherent in the feminine alliance of the patrician Perley Kelso and the feisty and articulate mill girl Sip. More explicitly political were novels like T. Fulton Gantt's *Breaking the Chains: A Story of the Present Industrial Struggle* (1887) and Frederick Whittaker's *Larry Locke, Man of Iron; or, A Fight for Fortune: A Story of Labor and Capital* (1884), serialized fiction of a sentimental variety aimed at the working-class reader and advocating an immediate derailment of the capitalist gravy train.

The factor that threatened most directly the novelist's fictional arrangements seems to have been gender or, more precisely, the "sex relation," as Norris calls it in *The Pit* (p. 35), or the "mystery of sex" that flummoxes London's *Burning Daylight* (p. 335). There was something more at work here than the dulcet call of domesticity that the typical entrepreneur of fiction, even the most Napoleonic, heeded in the end. Seeking a force to offset the primal quality of multiplying assets in a faintly Darwinian atmosphere, and yet a force that comports with the economic imperative, novelists broached the topic of intercourse. J. G. Holland treated it as a folksy mystery, Jack London and Frank Norris as a countervailing pull. Theodore Dreiser (1871–1945), however, considers it as an integral aspect of doing business in his depiction of Frank Cowperwood in the powerful novels *The Financier* (1912) and *The Titan* (1914). In this respect, business novelists were bringing up to date Melville's observations in the "The Paradise of Bachelors and the

Tartarus of Maids" (1855) and exploring the territory Charlotte Perkins Gilman had lately opened up in *Women and Economics: A Study of the Economic Relation between Men and Women as a Factor in Social Evolution* (1898). These works suggest that there might be a force the institutions of the new sovereignty—literary and otherwise—could not manage.

BUSINESS FOR ART'S SAKE, OR ART FOR BUSINESS'S SAKE

The more successful novels of business and industry remain some of the most valuable achievements in the history of American literature. To understand why this should be so and why readers continue to approach Mark Twain's *A Connecticut Yankee in King Arthur's Court* (1889), Howells's *The Rise of Silas Lapham*, Henry James's *The American*, Norris's unfinished trilogy *The Epic of the Wheat*, and Dreiser's Cowperwood novels with such interest, it is necessary to perceive the relationship these writers and their cohorts in other disciplines—the Adams brothers in *Chapters of Erie and Other Essays* (1871), Gustavus Myers in *History of the Great American Fortunes* (1909–1910), and Charles Austin Beard in *An Economic Interpretation of the Constitution of the United States* (1913), to name a few—forged between modes of literary and business thinking. Like the seed-bearing narrator of Melville's "The Paradise of Bachelors and the Tartarus of Maids" and the tariff-encumbered Nathaniel Hawthorne in his essay "The Custom-House," these writers submitted their words to the industrial process and took note of the reciprocal exchange that resulted. This process is reflected in the title of Howells's famous essay "The Man of Letters as the Man of Business" (1891).

Material and ideational changes after the Civil War transformed industrial capitalism into finance capitalism. This transformation was described and aided by economists like Henry Carter Adams, David Ames Wells, Richard Theodore Ely, and John Bates Clark. Clark's essay "Capital and Its Earnings," which appeared in May 1888, was especially important. As a result of the transformation, the methods, means, and objectives of business underwent an attenuation. The alteration of the peripatetic salesman into the visionary organizer can be perceived in such close fictional cousins as Twain's Hank Morgan and Howells's Silas Lapham. In a world of floating assets and potential values, the methods of the financier bore an affinity to the methods of the artist, as the more thoughtful of Cowperwood's sexual conquests never fail to point out. Cultural changes in the arenas of production and political economy had made conceivable to Dreiser, Twain, and Howells a certain identity of endeavor between themselves and the subjects they wrote about that simply did not exist for Melville in the Chancery Offices on Wall Street or for Hawthorne in the Salem Custom House.

Chicago seemed to hold the key to an early understanding of the phenomena described above. With its stockyards casually yet uneasily rubbing shoulders with its trading pits, the city practically embodied the reciprocity of the material and the ideal—the base and the ephemeral—that was increasingly credited with the creation of economic value. One of the first novelists to recognize the promise of these materials was Chicago native Henry Blake Fuller (1857–1929), who would be singled out by Dreiser as the greatest influence on his own novels of business. Fuller was well equipped to point up the tensions between art and commerce, though he was temperamentally unfit to seize the opportunity for reconciliation his works indicated. An aesthete with a sensibility steeped in European romanticism, Fuller was put to work by his father tending the books and the plumbing of the family's real estate holdings in Chicago. Fuller's two business novels, *The Cliff-Dwellers* (1893) and *With the Procession* (1895), represent his best work. Wholesale marketer David Marshall and his son Truesdale in the latter volume are especially memorable characters; father and son, of divergent biases and aspirations, both try to preserve an experiential, even existential, integrity in an environment that undermines ethics in such a way as to jeopardize selfhood by offending something Fuller can only describe as good taste. Fuller must be credited in these novels with conserving the aesthetic impetus as a category within the pervasive (and increasingly protean and evasive) logic of business and industry. If his characters frequently are overwhelmed, their imaginations are never entirely deranged; balked and dissatisfied, Fuller's men and women rarely succumbed to alienation.

Following the suggestion of Fuller's work, novelists like Dreiser, Twain, and Norris (and James in *The American* before them) evoked aesthetically such essential novelistic concerns as the relationship of the individual to the wider community from within the imaginative environment informed increasingly by business and industry. When Dreiser in *The Financier* speaks of Cowperwood's pronounced sense of "financial individuality" (p. 182), he establishes a register of experience authoritative enough to comprehend finance and art, thus making his hero's rabid art collecting a viable pursuit rather than the egoistic excrescence some readers have criticized. Similarly, Hank Morgan is speaking Mark Twain's language, in more ways than one, when he tries to derive from the inferior materials of the sixth and the nineteenth centuries an institutional safeguard for the singularity of the

imaginative and technological "effects" he is always "getting up," as well as the broadly republican society in which both the effects and their singularity have meaning. These aspects of *The Financier* and *A Connecticut Yankee in King Arthur's Court* constitute rhetorical work carried on in dialogue with the intellectual and material resources of business and industry. The two novels are neither reactionary nor quite reformist. Dreiser had read too much H. L. Mencken to entertain such hopes, though Twain, for his part, voiced sympathy with organized labor and hostility toward politicians generally and bad writers in particular.

Twain and Dreiser may not speak in their fictions about business and industry with the clarity of Hawthorne or Melville, but that is because their words and those of their colleagues in the Gilded Age are generated, in effect, already from within the intricate contraption the narrator of the "The Paradise of Bachelors and the Tartarus of Maids" views from the outside as a coherent machine, forbidding perhaps, but comprehensible (even anthropomorphic) nonetheless. (Mark Twain's ill-fated and expensive dalliance with the failed Paige typesetter remains a convenient metaphor.) Like most of their readers, the writers of narratives of business and industry from 1870 to 1920 occupied the uncertain yet promising position of Laura Dearborn in *The Pit* as she contemplates the engrossing "solidity" of the Napoleonic speculator Curtis Jadwin. "She was intensely interested," Norris writes. "A whole new order of things was being disclosed, and for the first time in her life she looked into the working of political economy" (p. 130). An unlettered Van Harrington in Robert Herrick's *Memoirs of an American Citizen* follows a similar intuition and applies himself to a crash course in "history and politics and economics," featuring "old Mill . . . Darwin and Spencer, Stubbs and Lecky and a lot more hard nuts" (p. 52), with an eye to material success, if not moral improvement. Like Laura and Harrington, writers suspected that this inchoate "new order of things" was, to a certain yet definite degree, of their own making.

See also A Connecticut Yankee in King Arthur's Court; A Hazard of New Fortunes; The Jungle; Muckrakers and Yellow Journalism; Success; Wealth

BIBLIOGRAPHY

Primary Works

Anonymous. *The Battle of Coney Island; or, Free Trade Overthrown*. Philadelphia: J. A. Wagenseller, 1883.

Dreiser, Theodore. *The Financier.* 1912. New York: Meridian, 1995.

Gantt, T. Fulton. *Breaking the Chains: A Story of the Present Industrial Struggle.* 1887. In *The Knights in Fiction: Two Labor Novels of the 1880s,* edited by Mary C. Grimes. Urbana: University of Illinois Press, 1986.

Hay, John. *The Bread-Winners.* 1883. Ridgewood, N. J.: Gregg Press, 1967.

Herrick, Robert. *The Memoirs of An American Citizen.* 1905. Cambridge, Mass.: Harvard University Press, 1963.

Literary Digest 32 (7 April 1906): 546.

London, Jack. *Burning Daylight.* New York: Macmillan, 1910.

Melville, Herman. "Bartleby, the Scrivener." 1853. In *Great Short Works of Herman Melville,* edited by Warner Berthoff. New York: Harpers, 1969.

Norris, Frank. *The Pit.* 1903. Columbus, Ohio: Charles E. Merrill, 1970.

Phillips, David Graham. *The Deluge.* 1905. New York: Johnson Reprints, 1969.

Smith, Henry Nash. "The Search for a Capitalist Hero: Businessmen in American Fiction." In *The Business Establishment,* edited by Earl F. Cheit. New York: John Wiley, 1964.

Whittaker, Frederick. *Larry Locke, Man of Iron; or, A Fight for Fortune: A Story of Labor and Capital.* 1884. In *The Knights in Fiction: Two Labor Novels of the 1880s,* edited by Mary C. Grimes. Urbana: University of Illinois Press, 1986.

Secondary Works

Berthoff, Warner. *The Ferment of Realism: American Literature, 1884–1919.* New York: Free Press, 1965.

Fine, Sidney. *Laissez Faire and the General-Welfare State: A Study of Conflict in American Thought, 1865–1901.* Ann Arbor: University of Michigan Press, 1964.

Hendrick, Burton J. *The Age of Big Business: A Chronicle of the Captains of Industry.* New Haven, Conn.: Yale University Press, 1919.

Hicks, Granville. *The Great Tradition: An Interpretation of American Literature since the Civil War.* New York: Macmillan, 1935.

Horwitz, Howard. *By the Law of Nature: Form and Value in Nineteenth-Century America.* New York: Oxford University Press, 1991.

Howells, William Dean. "The Man of Letters as the Man of Business." In *Literature and Life: Studies,* pp. 1–34. New York: Harpers, 1902.

Johnson, Paul E. *A Shopkeeper's Millennium: Society and Revivals in Rochester, New York, 1815–1837.* New York: Hill and Wang, 1978.

Livingston, James. *Pragmatism and the Political Economy of Cultural Revolution, 1850–1940.* Chapel Hill: University of North Carolina Press, 1994.

Martin, Jay. *Harvests of Change: American Literature, 1865–1914.* Englewood Cliffs, N.J.: Prentice Hall, 1967.

Matthaei, Julie A. *An Economic History of Women in America: Women's Work, the Sexual Division of Labor, and the Development of Capitalism.* New York: Schocken Books, 1982.

Smith, Henry Nash. "The Search for a Capitalist Hero: Businessmen in American Fiction." In *The Business Establishment,* edited by Earl F. Cheit. New York: John Wiley, 1964.

Warren, Robert Penn. *Homage to Theodore Dreiser, August 27, 1871–December 28, 1945, on the Centennial of his Birth.* New York: Random House, 1971.

Ziff, Larzer. *The American 1890s: Life and Times of a Lost Generation.* New York: Viking, 1966.

Richard Adams

CAPITAL PUNISHMENT

Opposition to the death penalty in America had existed for more than a hundred years before 1870. Indeed, many of the same voices that spoke out against slavery also opposed the death penalty, finding inspiration in Quaker leaders, such as William Penn and Benjamin Rush. Opponents of capital punishment were also drawn to Enlightenment philosophers, such as the Italian economist and criminologist Cesare Beccaria (1738–1794), who argued that society should focus not on punishment but on crime prevention and the rehabilitation of those convicted of crimes. Beccaria's *Essay on Crimes and Punishments* (1764) was translated and read widely in colonial America, sparking reform in criminal justice even before the Constitution was written. Throughout American history, death penalty abolitionists not only claimed that the state lacks authority to exact punishment in this fashion but also noted the cruelty of the punishment as well as its finality. Gradually, imprisonment replaced execution for most crimes. Despite several attempts in the 1830s and 1840s to reform capital punishment, by the 1850s these efforts had been eclipsed by the intensity and urgency of the fight against slavery.

In the 1840s *New York Tribune* editor Horace Greeley (1811–1872) became a vocal and articulate opponent of the death penalty—as well as an abolitionist. Many of Greeley's arguments against the death penalty are reminiscent of the argument that Thomas Jefferson makes against slavery in *Notes on the State of Virginia* (1781) in the eighteenth century. Jefferson had noted that the practice of slavery weakened the morals of the slave-owning class. Similarly, Greeley in 1850 argued that the death penalty teaches revenge, weakens the natural horror of bloodshed, often ensures that the guilty will escape punishment, and may even make criminals more sympathetic to the general public (Vila and Morris, p. 64). In the early part of the nineteenth century several states considered abolishing the death penalty, whereas others sought merely to limit its use to only the most serious of crimes, such as murder or treason, or to restrict the procedures by which it might be implemented. Many states admitted to the Union in the second half of the nineteenth century prohibited, restricted, or limited the practice of capital punishment.

ORIGINS OF THE DEATH PENALTY REFORM MOVEMENT

Several factors contributed to renewed interest in death penalty reform during the period between the end of the Civil War and the beginning of World War I. For one thing, several high-profile criminal trials and executions, covered by an increasingly popular and sensationalist media, made the general population aware of the incompetence and unfairness with which the penalty was often carried out. Botched hangings, followed in later years by gruesome electrocutions, caused many to conclude that capital punishment amounted to torture. Granted, the Eighth Amendment specifically prohibited "cruel and unusual" punishments, but courts, including the Supreme Court, consistently failed to conclude that death per se qualified as such. In deciding *Wilkerson v. Utah* in 1879, the Supreme Court stated that the territorial statute prescribing death as the punishment for first-degree murder was constitutional and that the firing squad as a method of execution failed to qualify as cruel or unusual. Similarly, in 1890 the Court determined in *In re Kemmler* that electrocution was also an acceptable method of execution, even if, as was the situation in *Kemmler,* death was not instantaneous but required a second jolt of electricity. In both of these opinions, the Court ruled that punishments should be considered cruel only if they involve some kind of torture or lingering death. As the Court stated succinctly in *Kemmler,* the Eighth Amendment applied to "something more than the mere extinguishment of life." But courts continued to struggle with the question of what constituted cruel and unusual punishment. In *Weems v. United States* (1910), the Court concluded that any punishment might well violate the Eighth Amendment if it was disproportionate to the crime committed. While not a death penalty case (the defendant, a U.S. Coast Guard clerk in the Philippines, had been sentenced to hard labor for what amounted to embezzlement), the *Weems* decision was important to death penalty opponents because it broadened the scope of the Eighth Amendment's prohibition against cruel and unusual punishments (Vila and Morris, p. 71).

What was also clear to many observers by the 1870s was that immigrants and those of African American descent were far more likely than whites to receive a sentence of death, a situation that many people hoped that the Fourteenth Amendment, ratified in 1868, would change. But although most states did repeal laws requiring harsher penalties for blacks after the Fourteenth Amendment was ratified, the practice of unequal punishment persisted for more than a century (Vila and Morris, p. 65). Ironically, this situation sometimes actually helped death penalty opponents. The movement against capital punishment in Maine, for example, was fueled by the 1869 execution of Clifton Harris, a black man convicted of murdering two whites, and by the 1875 trial and execution of the Prussian immigrant Louis F. H. Wagner for the infamous Smutty Nose Island murders, described in Anita Shreve's 1998 novel *The Weight of Water.* Both of these cases involved claims of innocence, questionable evidence, apparent racial and ethnic bias, and botched executions. Maine's legislature abolished the death penalty in 1876 but reinstated it in 1883, when state officials noted a rise in the murder rate (Galliher et al., pp. 54–57).

Many of these concerns coalesced in the widely publicized and much debated Haymarket bombing incident of 1886–1887. In the wake of the assassination by an anarchist bomb of Russia's Tsar Alexander II in 1881, the fear of terrorism had been growing. Government officials around the globe felt that the need to suppress political dissent was a matter of survival. In the spring of 1886, labor unrest in Chicago had escalated sharply, until on 4 May a crowd of nearly two thousand people gathered at Haymarket Square. This protest was aimed specifically at the Chicago police, who had shot and killed two striking workers at the McCormick factory the day before. When the police arrived at the protest, someone tossed a bomb, killing a policeman and sparking another round of police shootings. The authorities were unable to determine who had thrown the bomb, so instead they rounded up all of those who had organized and supported the cause of the protesters, including Albert Parsons and August Spies, left-wing newspaper editors, and Samuel Fielden, who had been speaking at the rally. In the subsequent trial, the defendants were portrayed as foreign agitators, the judge clearly favored the prosecution, and newspapers like the *Chicago Tribune* lobbied unabashedly for the death penalty. The executions became a rallying point for Americans across the political spectrum. Emma Goldman later spoke of these events as her political awakening, and William Dean Howells risked public disfavor when he protested the executions. But for many Americans, the executions were viewed as essential to maintaining social order and political stability.

THEORETICAL UNDERPINNINGS OF THE DEATH PENALTY

Despite the many sensational cases, disparate punishment was almost certainly the result of not just local entrenched prejudices but also of widely accepted legal and sociological theories. By the end of the nineteenth century, the rationalist view of crime and punishment reflected in Beccaria and other writers of the Enlightenment was being replaced by theories of biological inheritance (criminality as genetic destiny) and environmental conditioning (criminality as the result of social circumstances). The publication of treatises such as Charles Loring Brace's *The Dangerous Classes of New York* in 1872 helped to fuel the perception that certain social classes were predisposed by nature or culture or both toward crime and thus somehow more deserving of the harshest penalties. Brace (1826–1890) offers his readers statistics showing that the vast majority of those incarcerated in New York prisons were either foreign-born or first-generation Americans. He explores in some detail the reasons why immigrants run afoul of the law. He presents both the causes of crime and solutions as well, and he emphasizes the importance of providing the children of the lower classes with education and preparation for a trade. The book is nevertheless rife with assertions such as, "Let but Law lift its hand from them

Postcard of a man awaiting electrocution, 1908.
Electrocution was first adopted as a means of capital punishment in New York State in 1888. The chair depicted here was developed by an electrician at Auburn Prison and was used in the first such execution on 6 August 1890. From the beginning, use of the electric chair was highly controversial, and grisly reports of botched executions circulated widely among a horrified yet curious public. © LAKE COUNTY MUSEUM/CORBIS

for a season . . . and we should see an explosion from this class which might leave this city in ashes and blood" (p. 29). Brace's theories could be used as easily by death penalty opponents to show the mitigating circumstances behind capital cases as by proponents to show the near impossibility of rehabilitating criminals.

Clearly, the widespread fear of crime, especially in urban areas, made lawmakers reluctant to repeal capital punishment; they were convinced that it served as a deterrent to crime. The idea of deterrence was not,

of course, a new idea but one firmly rooted in history, especially in the administration of criminal justice in early America. As Stuart Banner notes, in colonial America the death penalty was sometimes imposed without any intention of carrying it out, simply for its force as a tool of deterrence. Public executions were often halted at the last minute, and convicted criminals were sometimes subjected to mock hangings. According to Banner, such public rituals would have been absurd had officials not believed that such events "would have some salutary effect" on both the accused individual and the community (p. 54). But as early as the 1830s, executions were moved inside the penitentiary walls, and the processes of appeal, pardon, and clemency were becoming fraught with complexity and bureaucracy, making the kinds of dramatic gestures that Banner describes virtually impossible for the authorities to orchestrate. At the same time, in the post–Civil War era, lynching and vigilantism had become serious threats to the social order. The gallows had become a symbol whose evocative power over the community had been effectively usurped by those outside the established system. Ironically, the death penalty was, in some states, even promoted as a deterrent not to crime but to lynching. Iowa abolished the death penalty in 1872, only to reinstate it in 1878 in an effort to curb lynching, which had apparently flourished in remote areas with tacit approval of local authorities, who felt that they lacked the resources to maintain order. In time, the new social sciences were often used to refute the notion that the death penalty deterred crime—or at least to demand evidence that such was in fact true.

By the late 1880s, what many saw as a necessary deterrent others saw as mere vengeance on the state's part. For those who advocated capital punishment, of course, retribution was as good an argument as deterrence and perhaps even better, because it required no proof. Retribution, known in legal jargon as *lex talonis* (an eye for an eye), is a principle of justice originating in the eighteenth century B.C.E. in Babylonia and carried over into Judeo-Christian culture. But by the nineteenth century the *lex talonis* principle would be increasingly seen as absurd and irrational. Perhaps the most eloquent of the Progressive Era death penalty abolitionists was Clarence Darrow (1857–1938), a champion of labor unions, a criminal attorney, and in 1925 a founding member, along with Vivian Pierce and Lewis Lawes, of the American League to Abolish Capital Punishment. As early as 1902, with the publication of *Resist Not Evil*, Darrow argued vehemently against the notion that criminal punishments served a compensatory function.

With regard to the death penalty in particular, Darrow notes its futility: "By no method of reasoning can it be shown that the injustice of killing one man is retrieved by the execution of another" (p. 56). He argues that if deterrence were the real object of punishment, life in prison must be considered as efficacious as execution. Furthermore, the sentence of death would have to be administered in the most horrific and public way possible; yet as Darrow notes, public executions were abandoned when their deleterious effects were confirmed: "It is now everywhere admitted that the brutalizing effects of public executions are beyond dispute" (p. 66). Darrow argues that the effect of the execution on those who witness it is "to harden and brutalize the heart and conscience, to destroy the finer sensibilities, to cheapen human life, to breed cruelty and malice that will bear fruit in endless ways and unknown forms" (p. 70). In essence, Darrow argues that if capital punishment is not abolished because of its injustice to the criminal, it should be abolished because of the damage it does society as a whole. By the time Darrow published *Crime: Its Cause and Treatment* in 1922, he was also convinced that the possibility of erroneous convictions was a persuasive argument against the death penalty: "Doubtless more men have been executed for crimes they did not commit and could not commit than for any real wrong of which they were guilty" (p. 163).

THE DEATH PENALTY IN LITERATURE

Although the debate about capital punishment was quite ardent, it served relatively infrequently as the source of inspiration for imaginative literature before the 1920s, especially in comparison with its widespread use in novels, plays, and films since then. As David Guest puts it in the introduction to his study of what he calls "the execution novel": "The historical invisibility of the criminal justice system is especially noteworthy, given its conspicuous presence in contemporary culture. The military may dominate the history books, but the police hold sway in the media" (p. xx). It was, after all, military—not civil—justice that Melville explored in *Billy Budd,* considered by some to be the quintessential novel about law in American literature. Significantly, the novel was written between 1886 and 1891 but not published until 1924. The novel also describes not the legal codes of the late-nineteenth-century United States but the far more savage codes of Georgian England. Nevertheless, as H. Bruce Franklin notes, the novel reflects a clear understanding of the issues related to capital punishment in late-nineteenth-century society. The novel explores not only the question of whether any authority based on any code has the right to take a life but also the notion that a public execution serves to deter others who might be tempted to commit crimes. As Franklin explains:

> Like many of the arguments raised against the death penalty between the 1790s and the 1880s, Billy Budd strips away the illusions of justice and deterrence to reveal the essence of capital punishment: human sacrifice, a ritual of power in which the state and the ruling class demonstrate, sanctify, and celebrate their ultimate power. (P. 352)

As Captain Vere struggles with his duty to impose a military code that is not discretionary and with his clear knowledge that Billy had no criminal intent in the death of Claggart, the novel highlights a number of late-nineteenth-century concerns about the death penalty.

Military justice was also the setting of Ambrose Bierce's much anthologized story "An Occurrence at Owl Creek Bridge." Based loosely on Bierce's own Civil War experiences, the story was published on 13 July 1890 in the Sunday Supplement of the *San Francisco Examiner* and collected in *Tales of Soldiers and Civilians* in 1892. The story follows the experience of Peyton Farquhar, a Confederate sympathizer arrested by Union soldiers and summarily executed on the very bridge he had intended to sabotage. But the purpose of Bierce's story is not to question either the legality or the morality of the execution. Indeed, both Union and Confederate forces had to deal swiftly and unequivocally with the problem of sabotage, and the rules of war are always different from the rules of criminal justice. Farquhar's description of himself in the second section of the story as a "student of hanging" remains somewhat ambiguous, but clearly he was aware of the risks he took in an action that he undoubtedly considered military, not criminal. Rather, Bierce's purpose in the story is to use the execution to explore his own continuing fascination with what it meant to pass from life to death, and the circumstances of execution provided a unique glimpse of this "transitional phase." In the third section of the story, the reader follows Farquhar's delusion that the rope has broken and he has escaped into the woods, eluded Union forces, and returned home to his wife, only to learn in the last sentence that Farquhar has been swinging "gently from side to side beneath the timbers of the Owl Creek Bridge" (p. 312). Critics have debated whether the events that Farquhar imagines happened in a flash as he died or whether they happened over a longer period of time, say, fifteen minutes, as Donald T. Blume suggests in his 2004 study of the sketches included in *Tales of Soldiers and Civilians.* Assuming that Blume's reading of the story is accurate, it is easy to see how Bierce's story might give credence to claims of death penalty opponents that death by hanging is far from instantaneous and therefore a cruel form of punishment. Bierce's story also anticipates later journalistic and literary execution narratives.

The law and literature movement has revealed few other literary texts that explore the issue between 1870 and 1920. Theodore Dreiser may have been interested in the criminal mind and the consequences of criminal activity as early as *Sister Carrie* (1900), but it would be 1925 before he would publish his magnum opus on the death penalty, *An American Tragedy*. And Frank Norris's 1899 novel *McTeague* (one of Guest's "execution novels") ends not in the execution chamber but in Death Valley. Interestingly, these novels focus less on the questions of actual guilt (which is never really in question in these narratives) than on the causes of criminal behavior and whether it is reasonable for the criminal to pay for his or her crime with death. While the authors are concerned with the larger social and even biological forces that may lead the individual to crime, they seem much less interested in the possibility of mistaken criminal culpability, which would be an important theme in later twentieth-century film and literature.

See also Billy Budd; Haymarket Square; Jurisprudence; Law Enforcement; Lynching; *McTeague; Tales of Soldiers and Civilians*

BIBLIOGRAPHY

Primary Works

Bierce, Ambrose. "An Occurence at Owl Creek Bridge." 1890. In *The Complete Short Stories of Ambrose Bierce*, edited by Ernest Jerome Hopkins, pp. 305–312. Lincoln: University of Nebraska Press, 1985.

Brace, Charles Loring. *The Dangerous Classes of New York*. New York: Wynkoop and Hallenbeck, 1872.

Darrow, Clarence. *Crime: Its Cause and Treatment*. New York: Thomas Y. Crowell, 1922.

Darrow, Clarence. *Resist Not Evil*. London: Ernest Bell, 1904.

Melville, Herman. *Billy Budd*. New York: New American Library, 1961.

U.S. Supreme Court. *In Re Kimmler*. 136 U.S. 436, 1890.

U.S. Supreme Court. *Weems v. United States*. 217 U.S. 349, 1910.

U.S. Supreme Court. *Wilkerson v. Utah*. 99 U.S. 130, 1879.

Secondary Works

Banner, Stuart. *The Death Penalty: An American History*. Cambridge, Mass.: Harvard University Press, 2002.

Blume, Donald T. *Ambrose Bierce's Civilians and Soldiers in Context: A Critical Study*. Kent, Ohio: Kent State University Press, 2004.

Franklin, H. Bruce. "Billy Budd and Capital Punishment: A Tale of Three Centuries." *American Literature* 69, no. 2 (1997): 337–359.

Friedman, Lawrence M. *Crime and Punishment in American History*. New York: Basic Books, 1993.

Galliher, John F., Larry W. Koch, David Patrick Keys, and Teresa J. Guess. *America without the Death Penalty: State Leading the Way*. Boston: Northeastern University Press, 2002.

Gottfried, Ted. *Capital Punishment: The Death Penalty Debate*. Springfield, N.J.: Enslow, 1997.

Guest, David. *Sentenced to Death: The American Novel and Capital Punishment*. Jackson: University Press of Mississippi, 1997.

Moddelmog, William E. *Reconstituting Authority: American Fiction in the Province of the Law, 1880–1920*. Iowa City: University of Iowa Press, 2000.

Steelwater, Eliza. *The Hangman's Knot: Lynching, Legal Execution, and America's Struggle with the Death Penalty*. Boulder, Colo.: Westview Press, 2003.

Vila, Bryan, and Cynthia Morris, eds. *Capital Punishment in the United States: A Documentary History*. Westport, Conn.: Greenwood Press, 1997.

Nancy Morrow

CATHOLICS

By the mid-1800s the Roman Catholic Church had become the largest religious denomination in the United States. The Catholic population increased to three million in 1860 to over ten million in 1890 and to twelve million in 1900. The explosive growth of the Catholic population in the 1800s derived mostly from the large-scale immigration—first from western and northern European countries and later from southern, central, and eastern European countries. It is estimated that ten million Catholics came from Europe between 1820 and 1920. The growth of the Catholic population began to undermine the image of America as a Protestant nation. By 1850 America was a denominationally diverse country, as evidenced by the large number of Catholics in Maryland and Quakers in Pennsylvania.

ANTI-CATHOLICISM

The ever-growing presence of Catholics instilled fear in many Protestants in the United States, who wondered if the Anglo-Saxon culture would retain its

James Cardinal Gibbons. Gibbons was one of the central figures in American Catholicism during the late nineteenth and early twentieth centuries, helping to define the role of the Church in American society at a time of increasing opposition from other sectors. His apologetic, *Faith of Our Fathers,* published in 1876, is still regarded as one of the most eloquent expositions of Catholic doctrine. THE LIBRARY OF CONGRESS

dominance. They resented the regal pomposity and centralization of ecclesiastical power they saw in Catholicism. They were also suspicious that the large-scale immigration resulted from the Catholic Church's conspiracy to subjugate America to papal authority.

Many Catholics, especially first-generation immigrants, clung to their native languages, ethnic traditions, and values from Europe. Their reluctance to melt into the mainstream culture, especially in language and public education, compelled Protestants to believe that Catholics were un-American. Rome-based Catholicism appeared to be incompatible with America's Protestant values of individualism, equality, and freedom of conscience. Coupled with such Catholic doctrines as purgatory and transubstantiation, cultural differences caused continuous friction between Protestants and Catholics.

American anti-Catholicism was the strongest in the 1880s. The Haymarket Square Riot of 1886 in Chicago, which claimed the lives of more than a dozen police officers and civilians, erupted partly because of nativists' resentment against Catholics. The following year, the American Protective Association—a secretive anti-immigrant and anti-Catholic society—was founded. This organization offered addresses by priests turned Protestants, distributed anti-Catholic literature, and worked to prevent Catholics from being elected to public offices. The membership of the American Protective Association reached 2.5 million in 1896. Finally, the Immigration Restriction League, organized in 1894, demanded that immigrants be required to pass a literacy test; the league's goal was to limit the number of immigrants from southern and eastern Europe, whom they considered inferior and undesirable.

Besides numerous pamphlets and newspaper articles, a number of anti-Catholic books came out in the mid-1800s through early 1900s. Among the books hostile to Catholicism were George Henry Borrow's *Lavengro: The Scholar, the Gipsy, the Priest* (1851); Edith O'Gorman's *Trials and Persecutions of Miss Edith O'Gorman: Otherwise Sister Teresa de Chantal, of St. Joseph's Convent, Hudson City, N.J.* (1871); Father Charles Paschal Telesphore Chiniquy's *The Priest, the Woman, and the Confessional* (1880); Mark Twain's *A Connecticut Yankee in King Arthur's Court* (1889); Isaac J. Lansing's *Romanism and the Republic: A Discussion of the Purposes, Assumptions, Principles, and Methods of the Roman Catholic Hierarchy* (1890); Frank Norris's *McTeague* (1899); and George Perry Rutledge's *Center-Shots at Rome: A Series of Lectures on Catholicism* (1914). All of these works attacked Catholic doctrine, practices, and governance, both reflecting the ethos of the times and brewing religious bigotry in the American public. *A Connecticut Yankee,* for example, satirizes the Catholic Church as an oppressive, greedy, and superstitious institution unfit for the modern age. The protagonist, Hank Morgan, is a staunch Protestant who accuses Catholicism of bestializing the human soul and for interfering with secular affairs. Norris is not as vitriolic as Twain in his anti-Catholic sentiments, but through the character Marcus Schouler in *McTeague,* he still launches tirades against the church for attempting to gain control of the schools.

BUILDING CATHOLIC INSTITUTIONS: SCHOOLS AND FRATERNAL SOCIETIES

The Catholic Church affirmed its presence in the United States in part by establishing parochial grade schools and private institutions of higher learning. Parochial schools were designed to protect Catholic students from the Protestant idea of individual autonomy and to integrate Catholic doctrine and a secular curriculum. The first Catholic school was opened as early as 1782 at St. Mary's Church in Philadelphia.

In 1808 Elizabeth Ann Seton (1774–1821) established the first Catholic elementary school—the Paca Street School in Emmitsburg, Maryland. However, it was not until 1884 that church leaders decided to launch a comprehensive parochial school system to serve the needs of the ever-increasing Catholic population in the United States. That year, American bishops attending the Third Plenary Council of Baltimore determined to establish elementary schools in all local churches. Thereafter, hundreds of Catholic elementary and secondary schools were founded across the country.

In addition to private grade schools, over seventy Roman Catholic colleges, universities, and seminaries were established in the nineteenth century and the early twentieth century. By 1852 there were forty-seven male and one hundred female institutions. Between 1870 and 1920 more than seventy Catholic institutions of higher learning were added to those numbers; they included such diverse institutions as Loyola University of Chicago (1870), St. John's University (1870), Conception Seminary College (1883), St. John's Seminary (1883), John Carroll University (1886), Catholic University of America (1887), Gonzaga University (1887), Kenrick-Glennon Seminary (1893), DePaul University (1898), Ohio Dominican College (1911), College of Mount St. Joseph (1920), and College of St. Francis (1920).

Among the most influential Catholic organizations established in the late nineteenth century was the Knights of Columbus. A fraternal order of Catholic men age eighteen and above, this society was founded by Michael J. McGivney, a Connecticut priest, in 1882. Embracing the principles of charity, fraternity, unity, and patriotism, members provided social support to fellow Knights, engaged in various charitable activities, and propagated the Catholic faith. The Knights grew as a support for the institutional church and took strong stands against the Freemasons. On 14 April 1917 the organization, which had 400,000 members nationwide, pledged allegiance to President Woodrow Wilson. The following day participants in the annual Council of Archbishops meeting declared that all Catholics in the United States were bona fide Americans willing to fight for the country. A century after its founding, the Knights of Columbus grew to include over a million members with almost eight thousand local councils worldwide.

CATHOLIC PERIODICALS AND LITERATURE

A number of newspapers and magazines targeting Catholic readers were founded in the second half of the 1800s. Important Catholic newspapers included the *Morning Star* (1867), *Catholic Review* (1872),

and *Catholic Sun* (1892). Among the well-known Catholic magazines were *Ave Maria* (1865), *Catholic World* (1865), *Messenger of the Sacred Heart* (1866), and *American Catholic Quarterly Review* (1876). These periodicals—approximately two-thirds of which were published in European languages—offered a forum for creative writers, social commentators, and thinkers. By 1911 a total of 321 Catholic periodicals were published in the United States.

Representative Catholic writers in the period from 1870 to 1920 include Mary Anne Madden Sadlier, Mary Agnes Tincker, Joel Chandler Harris, Louise Imogen Guiney, and Rose Hawthorne Lathrop. Predominantly parochial in content and simplistic in style, their works are considered minor in American literary history. Sadlier (1820–1903) authored sixty volumes of popular fiction, plays, children's stories, religious writing, and translations of French literature. Her works portray the Irish famine and the lives of Catholic immigrants, propagate the Catholic faith, and critique the mainstream American culture. Her favorite genres ranged from domestic fiction to historical romance to Sunday school material. Among her most popular novels were *New Lights; or Life in Galway* (1853), *The Blakes and Flanagans: A Tale, Illustrative of Irish Life in the United States* (1855), *Bessy Conway; or, The Irish Girl in America* (1862), and *Purgatory: Doctrinal, Historical, and Political* (1886).

Tincker (1833–1907) began her career as a short story writer for the *Catholic World*, in which she also serialized her highly acclaimed Catholic novels, *The House of Yorke* (1871–1872), *Grapes and Thorns* (1873–1874), and *Six Sunny Months* (1876–1877). These were followed by such novels as *Signor Monaldini's Niece* (1879), *By the Tiber* (1881), *Aurora: A Novel* (1886), *The Two Coronets* (1889), and *San Salvador* (1892). Some of these works are not Catholic in religious orientation, but her last book, *Autumn Leaves: Verse and Story* (1898), distinctively represents the author's recovery of the Catholic faith.

A local color fiction writer, poet, and journalist, Harris (1848–1908) was one of the highly acclaimed authors in the late 1800s and early 1900s. His writing career spanned almost three decades—from 1879, when his first Uncle Remus story appeared in the *Atlanta Constitution*, until his death in 1908. His novels and collections of stories include *Uncle Remus, His Songs and His Sayings* (1880), *Mingo, and Other Sketches in Black and White* (1884), *Free Joe, and Other Georgian Sketches* (1887), *Daddy Jake the Runaway, and Short Stories Told after Dark* (1889), *Balaam and*

His Master, and Other Sketches and Stories (1891), and *Aaron in the Wildwoods* (1897). Interestingly, his fiction exhibits little trace of Catholicism in it although Harris practiced the Catholic faith for twenty years.

Born a daughter of an American Civil War veteran, Guiney (1861–1920) was a poet and nonfiction writer who was profoundly affected by the Catholic faith. Her poems were collected in *Songs at the Start* (1884), *The White Sail and Other Poems* (1887), *A Roadside Harp* (1893), *"England and Yesterday": A Book of Short Poems* (1898), *The Martyr's Idyl and Shorter Poems* (1899), and *Happy Ending* (1909; expanded 1927). She also published a number of articles on Catholic spirituality, English poetry, and saints in such periodicals as *Catholic World, Ave Maria,* and *American Catholic Quarterly Review.* Among her volumes of essays are *A Little English Gallery* (1894) and *Patrins* (1897).

Lathrop (1851–1926), the second daughter of Nathaniel and Sophia Hawthorne, is primarily known for her establishment of a refuge for cancer victims in New York City and for her cofounding (with Sister M. Rose) of the Dominican Congregation of St. Rose of Lima, later called the Servants of Relief for Incurable Cancer. She wrote the nonfiction books *Along the Shore* (1888), *A Story of Courage: Annals of the Georgetown Convent of the Visitation of the Blessed Virgin Mary* (written with her husband, 1894), and *Memories of Hawthorne* (1897; rev. 1923).

Not until the first half of the 1900s did Catholic writers begin to merge with mainstream American authors. Theodore Dreiser, Eugene O'Neill, and F. Scott Fitzgerald had Catholic backgrounds by birth or by conversion. Their aesthetics were informed by their religious faith in one way or another, although their philosophy was far from Catholic orthodoxy. Unlike nineteenth-century Catholic authors, whose main goal was to defend Catholic dogmas, they expressed their disillusionment with the Catholic Church as an organized religion. Dreiser (1871–1945)—author of such naturalistic novels as *Sister Carrie* (1900), *Jennie Gerhardt* (1911), and *An American Tragedy* (1925)—grew up in a strict Catholic home, struggled with the church's teachings, and became a harsh critic of the church.

O'Neill (1888–1953), recipient of the Nobel Prize for Literature in 1936, was born in an Irish-Catholic home and attended Catholic schools but renounced his faith as a teenager. Reading works by Schopenhauer, Nietzsche, and other anti-Christian writers played a significant role in the formation of O'Neill's religious skepticism. His works demonstrate both his affinity for and disillusionment with Catholicism. In the auto-biographical play *Long Day's Journey into Night* (1941), for example, loss of the Catholic faith is a major theme. O'Neill speaks through Edmund, who rebels against peasant Irish Catholicism as practiced by his father, Tyrone. Tyrone, who no longer attends Mass but prays regularly, expresses a concern for his two sons' lack of interest in the church; Edmund replies that he is no longer a Catholic and that he has become a follower of Nietzsche.

Born and raised in a Catholic home, Fitzgerald (1896–1940) was strongly affected by the faith. One of the main characters in Fitzgerald's best-selling novel *This Side of Paradise* (1920) is a Catholic priest, Monsignor Thayer Darcy. A paternal figure for Amory Blaine, Darcy is portrayed as a clergyman who is not only caring but also highly ritualistic, dramatic, and shrewd. He acts like a Stuart king in exile awaiting a call to rule his land, and his full purple regalia recalls a J. M. W. Turner sunset. Though Fitzgerald married Zelda Sayre in St. Patrick's Cathedral in New York in 1920, he had left the church for good a year earlier. He considered his Catholicism little more than a memory and was denied a Catholic burial after his death. However, Catholicism provided him with an outsider's perspective on contemporary American society.

Although anti-Catholicism has persisted in the United States, non-Catholic American writers have also been kind to Catholics in their works. In Harold Frederic's novel *The Damnation of Theron Ware* (1896), for example, Father Forbes and Celia Madden are represented as thoughtful and cultured Catholics. The title character, an initially shallow and sectarian Methodist minister, is impressed by open-mindedness and intellect.

CONCLUSION

Between 1870 and 1920 Catholics continued to merge into mainstream American society. They developed, expanded, and strengthened various institutions, including the churches, parochial schools, institutions of higher learning, charitable agencies, and hospitals. Hundreds of periodicals were published to disseminate the Catholic faith and to discuss issues facing believers. By 1920 American Catholics largely shed the image of foreigners without losing their religious identity; the blending of Catholicism and Americanism had taken place.

See also The Damnation of Theron Ware; Immigration; Irish

BIBLIOGRAPHY

Primary Works

Fitzgerald, F. Scott. *This Side of Paradise*. 1920. New York: Modern Library, 2001.

Frederic, Harold. *The Damnation of Theron Ware*. 1896. San Francisco: Rinehart Press, 1960.

Norris, Frank. *McTeague: A Story of San Francisco*. 1899. New York: Modern Library, 2002.

O'Neill, Eugene. *Long Day's Journey into Night*. 1955. New Haven, Conn.: Yale University Press, 2001.

Tincker, Mary Agnes. *Autumn Leaves: Verse and Story*. New York: William H. Young, 1898.

Twain, Mark. *A Connecticut Yankee in King Arthur's Court*. 1889. New York: Oxford University Press, 1996.

Secondary Works

Dolan, Jay P. *The American Catholic Experience: A History from Colonial Times to the Present*. Garden City, N.Y.: Doubleday, 1985.

Dolan, Jay P. *Catholic Revivalism: The American Experience, 1830–1900*. Notre Dame, Ind.: University of Notre Dame Press, 1978.

Dolan, Jay P. *In Search of an American Catholicism: A History of Religion and Culture in Tension*. New York: Oxford University Press, 2002.

Ellis, John Tracy. *American Catholicism*. 2nd ed. Chicago: University of Chicago Press, 1969.

Fanning, Charles. *The Irish Voice in America: 250 Years of Irish-American Fiction*. 2nd ed. Lexington: University Press of Kentucky, 2000.

Giles, Paul. *American Catholic Arts and Fictions: Culture, Ideology, Aesthetics*. New York: Cambridge University Press, 1992.

Glazier, Michael, and Thomas J. Shelley, eds. *The Encyclopedia of American Catholic History*. Collegeville, Minn.: Liturgical Press, 1997.

Greeley, Andrew M. *The American Catholic: A Social Portrait*. New York: Basic Books, 1977.

Handy, Robert T. *A History of the Churches in the United States and Canada*. New York: Oxford University Press, 1977.

Hennesey, James J. *American Catholics: A History of the Roman Catholic Community in the United States*. New York: Oxford University Press, 1981.

Herberg, Will. *Protestant, Catholic, Jew: An Essay in American Religious Sociology*. Rev. ed. Garden City, N.Y.: Anchor Books, 1960.

Jenkins, Philip. *The New Anti-Catholicism: The Last Acceptable Prejudice*. New York: Oxford University Press, 2003.

McAvoy, Thomas Timothy. *A History of the Catholic Church in the United States*. Notre Dame, Ind.: University of Notre Dame Press, 1969.

McGreevy, John T. *Catholicism and American Freedom: A History*. New York: Norton, 2003.

Marty, Martin E. *An Invitation to American Catholic History*. Chicago: Thomas More Press, 1986.

Messbarger, Paul R. *Fiction with a Parochial Purpose: Social Use of American Catholic Literature, 1884–1900*. Brookline, Mass.: Boston University Press, 1971.

Noll, Mark A. *A History of Christianity in the United States and Canada*. Grand Rapids, Mich.: Eerdmans, 1992.

Taves, Ann. *The Household of Faith: Roman Catholic Devotions in Mid-Nineteenth-Century America*. Notre Dame, Ind.: University of Notre Dame Press, 1986.

John J. Han

CENTENNIAL

In 1876 Philadelphia hosted an international exhibition dedicated to celebrating the centennial of America's independence from England. Attended by nine million visitors, the Centennial Exhibition became the primary site for launching the cultural reconstruction of the United States just when the period of political reconstruction that followed the Civil War was coming to an end.

Why did Philadelphia's cultural and political authorities determine to hold a world's fair to celebrate the centennial of American independence? The answer, ironically, is that they were inspired by British and European precedent. The world's fair movement began in London in 1851 when the British government, beset by fears of Chartism and the spread of socialism from the European revolutions of 1848, decided to organize the 1851 Great Exhibition of the Works of Industry of All Nations, better known as the Crystal Palace Exhibition. Backed by Queen Victoria's husband, Prince Albert, the Crystal Palace Exhibition provided an enormous stimulus to British nationalism, helped define Victorianism, and left little doubt among the middle classes about the essential rightness of British imperialism. In its wake, other European powers, especially France, set out to improve upon the English example, and a series of world's fairs swept European capitals, including Paris and Vienna. A small-scale exhibition took place in New York City in 1853 and 1854, but, with America already dividing for war, this fair stood little chance of success. After the Civil War, however, as Americans began thinking about rebuilding the republic, the apparent success of European fairs in stimulating feelings of nationalism proved an irresistible example to American business, political, and cultural elites. They viewed the exhibition as a means to

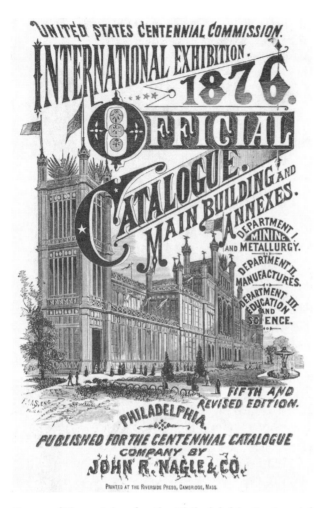

Cover of the catalog for the Philadelphia Centennial Exposition, 1876. © BETTMANN/CORBIS

the Paris Commune of 1871. In addition to these concerns, there were others: the ongoing insurgency in the American West as Native Americans battled miners, farmers, and the U.S. military; the debate over extending political rights to women; and the continuing racial conflicts that were fueled by disputes over the citizenship rights of African Americans. Any one of these issues could give pause for thought. Together, they added up to a profound sense of unease that the Centennial Exhibition was intended to alleviate.

To help assuage anxieties and counter the critics of America's rapid industrialization, exhibition authorities developed a strategy that sidestepped troubling discussions about the maldistribution of wealth that flowed from America's industrial and agricultural productivity. Instead, the fair embraced a vision of America's future national progress that defined progress in terms of industrial expansion and racial advance. The exhibition grounds, carved out of Philadelphia's Fairmount Park, were alive with exhibits dedicated to America's industrial prowess. The central icon of the fair was the 700-ton steam-driven engine built by George Henry Corliss (1817–1888) that supplied the power for driving hundreds of other machines on exhibit in Machinery Hall. Next door was the exhibition's Main Building, the largest building in the world, which contained exhibits from around the world. They were arranged according to a theory of racial hierarchy that gave the most "civilized" nations the most prominent display space and "other" nations less desirable space depending on their perceived backwardness. The racism that guided the fair's mental mapping resulted in the near exclusion of African American exhibits and in the representation of American Indians through ethnological collections from the Smithsonian Institution that suggested that Native Americans were best understood as anthropological specimens, not as human beings in their own right.

There was little doubt in the minds of contemporaries that the Centennial Exhibition was an important event. But what exactly was its significance? The answer was too crucial to leave entirely to the realm of chance opinion. From the beginning, exhibition planners sought to enlist leading literary figures from the North and South in opening-day ceremonies. It was hoped that these writers would attest to the importance of the fair and its attempt to renationalize the republic after the Civil War.

overcome bitter memories of the Civil War and the present reality of mounting violence between social classes. The idea of holding a fair in Philadelphia to commemorate the centennial of American independence began to develop as early as 1866. The United States Congress endorsed the proposition, and President Ulysses S. Grant, in the company of Emperor Dom Pedro II of Brazil, officially opened the fair on 10 May 1876.

The immediate historical context of the fair is worth noting. From the vantage point of Americans living in 1876, the future seemed uncertain at best. True, the Civil War had been over for eleven years, but a nationwide financial panic in 1873 had set nerves on edge. Furthermore, the gathering storm clouds of violence between capital and labor made many Americans wonder if post–Civil War America stood on the precipice of class warfare on a scale that had recently characterized

LITERARY NATIONALISM
Initially, exposition authorities turned to New England's Henry Wadsworth Longfellow to write an ode, Pennsylvania's Bayard Taylor to compose a hymn, and

The Corliss Engine. A much-lauded feature of the 1876 Philadephia Centennial Exposition, the gigantic Corliss Engine symbolized American enthusiasm for the benefits of technological progress at the end of the nineteenth century. THE LIBRARY OF CONGRESS

Georgia's Sidney Lanier to compose a cantata. Both Taylor and Lanier gladly accepted. Lanier (1842–1881) completed his composition in a matter of weeks and exulted: "I have tried to make it a genuine Song, at once full of fire and of large and artless simplicity befitting a young but already colossal land" (Lanier to Dudley Buck, 15 January 1876). Longfellow, however, declined to participate, leaving exposition planners in a dither about a literary representative from New England. They invited James Russell Lowell, William Cullen Bryant, and Oliver Wendell Holmes, but all pleaded a lack of time to do the occasion justice. With the help of Taylor (1825–1878), exposition authorities were able to prevail on the former abolitionist John Greenleaf Whittier (1807–1892) to fill the breach, but only by reaching an agreement with

Whittier that he would work on the hymn instead of the ode. To accommodate this change, Taylor switched his efforts toward composing the ode, and its debut was deferred until the Fourth of July. In retrospect, it seems somewhat surprising that Walt Whitman (1819–1892) was not asked to take part in the festivities. But exhibition officials, as well as many literary authorities of the late 1800s, regarded Whitman as idiosyncratic at best and disreputable at worst. He was never given serious consideration for a place on the official program.

By opening day, Whittier and Lanier had hammered together ringing paeans to the reborn American nation-state. In his "Centennial Hymn," Whittier seized the occasion to take dead aim at the contrast between Europe's fading glory and America's rising star. Invoking God's blessing, he intoned:

> Oh! make Thou us, through centuries long
> In peace secure, in justice strong:
> Around our gift of freedom draw
> The safeguards of Thy righteous law,
> And, cast in some diviner mold,
> Let the new cycle shame the old!

Not to be outdone, Lanier's "Centennial Cantata" stepped back to the voyage of the *Mayflower* and the founding of Jamestown and concluded "with a man's own song" touting a future where America's "fame shall glow."

Although he was not invited to participate in the opening ceremonies, Whitman, ever the democrat and nationalist, saw the fair as a wonderful opportunity to reflect on America's history and future and to promote his own reputation. For the occasion of the fair, he reissued "Song of the Exposition," written originally in 1871 for an industrial fair, and prepared a Centennial Edition of *Leaves of Grass*. To the extreme annoyance of Bayard Taylor, he also wrote "Walt Whitman's Actual American Position," an essay that seemed to blame his own poverty on the lack of attention from the American literary establishment.

Whitman was certainly captivated by the Centennial and in early July arrived on the fairgrounds in the company of another poet, Joaquin Miller (the penname of Cincinnatus Hiner Miller, 1839–1913), who was in the process of promoting himself as the bard of the American West. As Whitman approached the Corliss Engine, several reporters recognized him and asked him for his thoughts about the colossal machine. Whitman sat transfixed for a half-hour in absolute silence and then asked to be taken away. Whitman's companion, Miller, was less reticent to comment on the meaning of the fair and in "Song of the Centennial" exulted:

Oh, wondrous the wealth, prodigious the powers!
Unbounded the dominion, and matchless the
    love!
And this the inheritance! . . .
Then rise in your places. Rise up! Let us take a
    great
Oath together as we gather us here,
At the end and beginning of an hundred year,
For the love of Freedom, for Liberty's sake–
To hand the Republic on down, undefiled.
As we have received it, from father to child.

Miller would never receive the national acclaim of the other poets who participated in the exhibition, but his presence attested to another flaw in the configuration of opening day literary representatives, namely the failure to include anyone from the American West.

Poets, of course, were not the only writers who incorporated the fair into the literary imagination. William Dean Howells (1837–1920), the influential editor of the *Atlantic Monthly,* could not resist commenting on the fair's significance. In his essay "A Sennight of the Centennial," published in the *Atlantic Monthly,* Howells fell into line behind the opening-day poets and passed judgement on the "civilization" of the Old World as revealed in European and English art. English paintings, Howells observed, "were most delightful" (p. 94), while those from France were "horribly fascinating" (p. 95). German art he found "most disagreeable" (p. 93). All told, he concluded, the exhibit of European art "impressed one as that of pictures that had not succeeded at home" (p. 95). Seen in this light, American art came off rather well. "You felt that American art had made vast advances on the technical side," Howells declared, "but . . . that it was not poetical; that generally its subjects were seen, not deeply felt and thought; it wanted charm" (p. 95). Still, Howells assured his readers, "we had certainly no cause, considering all things, to be ashamed of the show of American paintings in comparison even with many of the English, and still less with those of other nations" (pp. 94–95). If art was the measure of civilization, America, it seemed, was on the right track.

AFFIRMATION AND DISSENT

At least that was the case as far as art was concerned. According to Howells, American women, another source of civilization in the eyes of American Victorians, had taken a decidedly wrong turn at the Centennial. The separate Women's Pavilion, Howells opined, left visitors "puzzled to know why the ladies wished to separate their work from that of the rest of the human race." One woman, suffrage leader Susan B.

Anthony, had an answer for him. In reciting the "Declaration of Rights for Women," delivered on the Fourth of July at a separate celebration from the fair's official Independence Day festivities, Anthony made clear that the Women's Pavilion was built on the assumption that women's issues deserved to be singled out for special notice. Women everywhere, she declared, still suffered the degradation of disfranchisement.

The author Marietta Holley (1836–1926) could not have agreed more, although she took a less serious tone in writing about the Centennial. Holley, who stood on the cusp of fame as "the female Mark Twain," found in the exhibition a perfect setting for telling a story about a rural family's visit to the fair and for expressing her strong support for women's rights. The result was her book *Josiah Allen's Wife as a P.A. and P.I.: Samantha at the Centennial* (1877). Before her death in 1926, Holley would sell about ten million books worldwide and gained a reputation as one of America's first female humorists. That the Centennial helped promote her career and that subsequent world's fairs helped sustain it underscores the centrality of these exhibitions to the history of American literature.

Among the women writers who traveled to the Centennial and incorporated its memories into their future work was Sarah Orne Jewett (1849–1909). In "The Flight of Betsey Lane," published in *Scribner's Magazine* in 1893, she had one of her characters recall:

> Nobody in these United States has ever felt half grateful enough to the promoters of the Centennial Exhibition at Philadelphia. It was the first great national occasion of general interest and opportunity for cultivation; as a people we were untravelled and unconvinced of many things until we were given this glimpse of the treasures and customs of the world. Without it we should never have been ready for the more advanced lessons of the great Columbian fair at Chicago. (P. 221)

In a version of this story included in *A Native of Winby, and Other Tales,* she was more explicit: "I call the Centennial somethin' like the day o' judgment" (p. 207).

Many other writers were only too happy to pass judgement on the Centennial. Herman Melville traveled to the fair and left with a positive impression. "You will be much impressed with it; it is immense— a sort of Vanity Fair" (2:756), he recorded in his log. The aspiring novelist and future historian Henry Adams (1838–1918), who would later travel to other fairs and write about them as liminal moments in human history, was less enraptured by the Centennial. "From my soul," he confided to his friend Charles Milnes Gaskell, "I hate and contemn these big shows—It is bigger, noisier, more crowded, and its contents more uniformly indifferent and vulgar than any of its predecessors" (Adams 2:292). Conceding that there were moments of pleasure to be found on the fairgrounds, he nonetheless confessed to having "registered an oath never to visit another of these vile displays" (p. 292). Mark Twain (1835–1910) was also drawn to the event. "I went there in July," he told his friend Howells, "and staid nearly a whole day; then I got discouraged and returned home. I became satisfied that it would take me two, or possibly three days to examine such an array of articles with anything like just care and deliberation."

Through their writings about the Centennial, American writers joined a distinguished group of European writers who also saw international expositions as profound reflections of their societies and roadmaps to the future. Literary reactions to world's fairs were mixed. Charles Dickens, for instance, endorsed the 1851 Crystal Palace Exhibition whereas Charles Baudelaire took aim at the 1867 Exposition Universelle in Paris, seeing it as an example of the Americanization of Europe. Hans Christian Andersen appreciated the fanciful side to the 1867 fair and wrote a fairy tale, "The Wood Nymph," about it. Leo Tolstoy, although he never attended the 1893 World's Columbian Exposition in Chicago, felt moved to condemn it as "a striking example of imprudence and hypocrisy" (Tolstoy 1:323). Well into the late-twentieth and early-twenty-first centuries, writers such as E. L. Doctorow and Erik Larson continue to look into the mirrors held up by world's fairs and find in them sources of identity formation and adventure. There is, in short, a literary dimension to world's fairs—one that provides insight into the fairs themselves as well as the broader cultures in which they take place.

See also Science and Technology; St. Louis World's Fair; Women's Suffrage; World's Columbian Exposition

BIBLIOGRAPHY

Primary Works

Adams, Henry. *Letters of Henry Adams*. Boston: Houghton Mifflin, 1930–1938.

Anthony, Susan B. "Declaration of Women's Rights." 4 July 1876. In *The Concise History of Woman Suffrage*, edited by Mari Jo Buhle and Paul Buhle, pp. 300–303. Urbana: University of Illinois Press, 1978.

Holley, Marietta. *Josiah Allen's Wife as a P.A. and P.I.: Samantha at the Centennial*. Hartford, Conn.: American Publishing Company, 1877.

Howells, William Dean. "A Sennight of the Centennial." *Atlantic Monthly* 38, no. 225 (1876): 92–107.

Jewett, Sarah Orne. "The Flight of Betsey Lane." *Scribner's Magazine* 14, no. 2 (1893): 213–226. Revised and reprinted in *A Native of Winby, and Other Tales*. Boston: Houghton Mifflin, 1894.

Lanier, Sidney. "Centennial Cantata." *Philadelphia Inquirer*, 11 May 1876.

Lanier, Sidney. Papers. Duke University.

Melville, Herman. *The Melville Log*. New York: Harcourt Brace, 1951.

Miller, Joaquin. "Song of the Centennial." In *Frank Leslie's Historical Register of the Centennial Exposition, 1876*. New York: Frank Leslie, 1877.

Tolstoy, Leo. *Tolstoy's Diaries*. Edited by R. F. Christian. New York: Scribners, 1985.

Whittier, John Greenleaf. "Centennial Hymn." In J. S. Ingram, *The Centennial Exposition Defined and Illustrated*. Philadelphia: Hubbard Bros., 1876.

Secondary Works

Brown, Dee. *The Year of the Century: 1876*. New York: Scribners, 1966.

Cordato, Mary. "Representing the Expansion of Woman's Sphere: Women's Work and Culture at the World's Fairs of 1876, 1893, and 1904." Ph.D. diss., New York University, 1989.

Giberti, Bruno. *Designing the Centennial: A History of the 1876 International Exhibition in Philadelphia*. Lexington: University Press of Kentucky, 2002.

Post, Robert, ed. *1876: A Centennial Exhibition*. Washington, D.C.: National Museum of History and Technology, Smithsonian Institution, 1976.

Rydell, Robert W. *All the World's a Fair: Visions of Empire at American International Expositions, 1876–1916*. Chicago: University of Chicago Press, 1984.

Robert W. Rydell

CENTURY MAGAZINE

Known primarily for its lavish wood engravings, extensive historical series, and innovative American fiction, *The Century Illustrated Monthly Magazine* was one of the most important periodicals during the late nineteenth century and early twentieth century.

Cover of *Century Magazine* based on a drawing by Elihu Vedder, May 1888. The Library of Congress

Often classified as a family house magazine because of its association with a reputable publishing firm, the *Century* may be compared favorably with other prominent magazines of the period, including the *Atlantic Monthly, Harper's New Monthly Magazine,* and *Scribner's Magazine.* Although not much evidence is available about the actual readers of the magazine, those who corresponded frequently with it included a high proportion of relatively well-educated (but not necessarily wealthy) people, particularly ministers, married women, teachers, newspaper editors, reformers, and public officials. *Century* readers were no doubt drawn to the magazine's moral and aesthetic elevation of taste, which the editors carried out by printing only those contributions that met their high standards of quality and respectability. Although the *Century*'s intended readership was primarily American,

the monthly was distributed in many other parts of the world, including Great Britain, France, and Canada. Readers and critics praised the monthly for both upholding journalistic standards and fostering a refined taste among readers.

INSTITUTIONAL HISTORY

The *Century*'s interest in cultivating American taste was rooted in its institutional history. Josiah Gilbert Holland, Roswell Smith, and Charles Scribner founded the magazine in 1870 as *Scribner's Monthly: An Illustrated Magazine for the People.* Rather than tying the magazine entirely to Charles Scribner's publishing firm, Smith, who became the business manager, and Holland, who became the first editor, set up a separate parent company—Scribner and Company—to run the magazine. In exchange for control of 40 percent of the company's stock, Charles Scribner lent his name to the project and the subscription list of his previous magazine, *Hours at Home;* Holland and Smith secured the remaining 60 percent. In addition to acquiring *Hours at Home, Scribner's* bought out the foundering *Putnam's Monthly.* These acquisitions provided *Scribner's* not only with subscription lists but also with the rosters of former contributors and some of their unprinted manuscripts. *Putnam's* had purposely printed the works of only American writers, and *Hours at Home* had an intensely American flavor as well.

The American emphasis of the earlier magazines must have appealed to Holland, who was intensely patriotic, because *Scribner's* quickly developed a rather American policy in both its editorial practices and its content. Although Holland attempted to secure some British and European writers for the magazine, he had little success because the other established American magazines—especially *Harper's Monthly*—had already secured most of the celebrated writers. As the periodical achieved greater influence, it began to seek out new writers from the South, most of whom did not have established ties to northern magazines. *Scribner's* also developed a reputation as particularly American because of its beautifully illustrated travel articles, historical series, and biographical essays, many of which focused on American subjects or discussed foreign locales or issues from an American perspective. By the mid-1870s Holland was using the editorial department "Topics of the Time" to address the nation about American concerns from a religious and moral standpoint. Around the same time, the magazine's assistant editor, Richard Watson Gilder, assumed more control of *Scribner's* because of Holland's failing health.

In 1881 Gilder became editor in chief of the magazine, which also took on a new name: the *Century.* Under Gilder, the periodical maintained the moral aspect of its enterprise while emphasizing more of an aesthetic dimension. The new name of the magazine signaled important changes in both its financial base and its cultural work. In the late 1870s, the magazine's parent company, Scribner and Company, had begun to clash with the book-publishing firm Charles Scribner's Sons, primarily because Scribner and Company had been publishing books with a separate imprint. When Charles Scribner's Sons objected to the use of the Scribner name to publish books the firm had not authorized, Roswell Smith consolidated Scribner and Company's stock and negotiated with Charles Scribner's Sons, eventually buying the shares that had represented Charles Scribner's control of the original magazine company. The agreement with the Scribner book company required that the magazine enterprise be renamed, and at Gilder's suggestion Smith renamed the enterprise after the Century Club, a prominent New York club for artists and writers located in the building next to Gilder's home on East Fifteenth Street. The magazine's parent company was thus called the Century Company, while the magazine became *The Century Illustrated Monthly Magazine,* and the entire operation moved to elaborate offices in a new building on Union Square. These institutional changes and Gilder's keen editorial guidance resulted in prosperity during the 1880s, when the *Century* expanded from a circulation of about 125,000 in 1881 to a peak of 250,000 by the middle of the decade. Although it failed to maintain that circulation when less-expensive weekly and monthly magazines emerged in the early 1890s, the *Century*'s circulation remained considerable, eventually subsiding to about 125,000 by 1900.

HISTORICAL SERIES AND PROJECTS OF REFORM

The magazine printed many nonfictional series that contributed significantly to readers' understanding of history, politics, and social reform. In the early years of the magazine, for example, Smith convinced Holland to commission the journalist Edward King to lead a $30,000 expedition into the South to learn about southern life. The result was King's fourteen-part series "The Great South" (1873–1874). Illustrated with more than 430 engravings originally sketched by J. Wells Champney, the series not only increased interest in the South and strengthened *Scribner's* southern readership, it also led to the discovery of southern writers of local color fiction, some of whom became important contributors. Other notable series followed, including

biographical articles such as Edward Schuyler's "Peter the Great" (1880–1881), John Hay and John Nicolay's "The Life of Lincoln" (1885–1890), and George Kennan's investigation of exiled revolutionaries in Russia in "Siberia and the Exile System" (1887–1891). In addition to series, the *Century* used editorials and essays to promote many other reform efforts, addressing issues such as international copyright, tenement housing, charity administration, and environmental conservation.

The magazine's most popular historical series, "Battles and Leaders of the Civil War," occupied about a third of every monthly issue from November 1884 through November 1887. Illustrated by Joseph Pennell and Winslow Homer, the series included not only contributions from seasoned veterans, such as Ulysses S. Grant and William Tecumseh Sherman, but also essays and letters by well-known literary figures, such as Mark Twain, Lew Wallace, John Greenleaf Whittier, and Brander Matthews. The series was especially popular with the *Century* readership because it included letters and supplementary materials from readers who had firsthand knowledge of the conflict. As they did with so many of their other projects, *Century* editors encouraged readers to use the Civil War series in both homes and local cultural clubs to elevate taste through reading, writing, and discussion activities.

AMERICAN LITERATURE AND TASTE

The elevation of taste was an especially crucial factor in the literature and literary criticism printed by the magazine. Although the magazine printed some poetry in nearly every monthly number, it was best known for its serialized fiction. Because of Holland's influence in the 1870s, most of the magazine's early fiction was sentimental and didactic. In her serialized novels such as *That Lass o' Lowries* (1876–1877) and *Haworth's* (1878–1879), for example, the English-born writer Frances Hodgson Burnett tugged at readers' heartstrings. Under the pseudonym "Saxe Holm," Helen Hunt Jackson contributed more than ten short stories to *Scribner's Monthly,* all composed in a sentimental mode. Holland himself contributed his popular didactic novels *Arthur Bonnicastle* (1872–1873), *The Story of Sevenoaks* (1874–1875), and *Nicholas Minturn* (1876–1877). In editorials, Holland typically made sure that readers understood that only fiction that served as "a royal vehicle for the progress of the moral" earned a novelist genuine aesthetic distinction (p. 735).

As Gilder gradually assumed more control of the enterprise in the mid-1870s, he shifted the emphasis away from a strict moral focus to more of an aesthetic aim. Gilder had keen editorial instincts, and his recruits quickly became some of the most noteworthy writers and artists to contribute to periodicals. His first recruits for *Scribner's Monthly* were writers of local color fiction, especially from the South. For example, one of the magazine's most important contributors, George Washington Cable, was discovered during King's southern expedition. Largely because of the magazine's influence and Gilder's skill as an editor, Cable's literary talent blossomed, resulting in stories published in book form as *Old Creole Days* (1879) and in his serialized novels *The Grandissimes* (1879–1880) and *Dr. Sevier* (1883–1884). Gilder mentored many other regional and local color writers, including Bret Harte, Edward Eggleston, Mary Hallock Foote, Frank R. Stockton, Hamlin Garland, Sarah Orne Jewett, Thomas Nelson Page, Mary Wilkins Freeman, and Joel Chandler Harris.

Given the overly moralistic bent of the magazine in the early 1870s and its reluctance to print groundbreaking fiction in the early twentieth century, modern critics and scholars tend to characterize the *Century's* cultural work as "staid" and "genteel." Although these labels certainly capture the conservative nature of the magazine and its persistent efforts to elevate taste, they fail to represent the innovative side of the *Century's* fictional offerings during its prime in the 1880s, when it printed a number of important new stories and novels by American realists. Unlike the didactic and sentimental novels that had been printed in *Scribner's Monthly*, realism tended to focus on ordinary, commonplace subjects and to represent them in direct, detailed description, often without providing explicit moral guidance for readers. Although Gilder and his editorial staff were careful about the novels and other contributions they chose to print, they also avoided direct censorship of authors. Gilder thus attempted to find literary works that would both challenge readers' desire for innovation and reinforce their regard for refined and moral conduct. During the 1880s Gilder and his staff worked with three writers whose serialized novels later became part of the literary canon: William Dean Howells's *A Modern Instance* was serialized in the magazine in 1881–1882 and *The Rise of Silas Lapham* in 1884–1885; excerpts from Mark Twain's *Adventures of Huckleberry Finn* (modified somewhat to make it more respectable) appeared in 1884–1885 and *A Connecticut Yankee in King Arthur's Court* in 1889; and Henry James's *The Bostonians* appeared in 1885–1886. Gilder also fostered writers whose realist novels in the early twenty-first century are neglected or even out of print, running serializations of Burnett's *Through One Administration*

(1881–1882), Howells's *A Woman's Reason* (1883), Hay's *The Bread-Winners* (1883–1884), and Robert Grant's *An Average Man* (1883–1884).

Sometimes the *Century's* fostering of a particular writer involved it in considerable controversy. For example, in the concluding number of Howells's novel *A Modern Instance* in October 1882, the magazine printed an editorial defending Howells's depiction of divorce, which, despite the claim of the editors, had been morally complex and ambiguous. The very next month the *Century* printed Howells's appreciative essay "Henry James, Jr.," in which he argued that he, James, and other American realist writers were at the forefront of literary innovation in English fiction. Because he had characterized Charles Dickens, William Makepeace Thackeray, and other prominent British writers as "writers of the past," both Howells and the *Century* came under fire in the British and the American press for tastelessly promoting Howells's literary efforts and for inappropriately providing readers with a story that portrayed the social problem of divorce. If anything, the controversy surrounding Howells spurred more interest in the magazine and, along with the popular Civil War series, led to a significant increase in circulation. Other realist novels from this period motivated actual readers to write indignant letters to the magazine, as they did when they protested what they believed was the unfair representation of the working class in the *Century's* anonymous serialization of Hay's antilabor novel *The Bread-Winners*. Instead of suppressing criticism, the magazine usually provided fair coverage to both sides of any controversy. The *Century* nevertheless always attempted to harness the responses of readers, critics, and the press to its larger agenda of elevating taste.

Although the *Century* continued to print American fiction in the early twentieth century, it refused to print literary naturalism and modernism, in part because Gilder and his staff believed those works were inappropriate for the magazine's refined readership. Like many other family house magazines of this period, the *Century* rejected work by Stephen Crane and Theodore Dreiser, choosing instead to print sentimental novels by Kate Douglas Wiggin and Elizabeth Stuart Phelps, historical romances by S. Weir Mitchell and Irving Bacheller, and more local color fiction by Garland, Cable, and Israel Zangwill, among others.

DECLINE AND LEGACY

After 1900 the magazine declined in its influence, especially following Gilder's death in 1909. Robert Underwood Johnson, who had served as associate editor, succeeded Gilder as editor in chief; he maintained the magazine's standards of elevated taste, even though circulation continued to drop. After Johnson resigned in 1913, the *Century* was subsequently edited by one editor after another, each with a different plan for the magazine: Robert Sterling Yard (1913–1914), Douglas Z. Doty (1914–1918), Thomas R. Smith (1919), W. Morgan Shuster (1920–1921), Glenn Frank (1921–1925), and Hewitt H. Howland (1925–1930), the last editor of the magazine until it was bought out by the *Forum* in 1930. Each of these editors tried various strategies for preventing the demise of the magazine, but none succeeded in reviving either the *Century*'s influence or its program of elevation. By 1929 the *Century*'s circulation had dropped below twenty thousand; Howland attempted to keep the magazine from declining further by issuing it as a quarterly, but his efforts failed.

The lasting contribution of the *Century* to American cultural life may be found in the imperative of elevation embodied in its many print artifacts that, through other forms and methods, still may be found in homes and classrooms—the modern-day versions of the novels, essays, historical series, and wood engravings that first appeared in the pages of the magazine. Although the magazine's project of elevation ultimately failed, the complexities of a taste that is both national and cosmopolitan, refined yet somewhat popular, and exclusive but intended for all readers make the story of the *Century* an important part of the history of American print culture. For without the *Century*'s participation in the advancement of an ideal of culture, late-nineteenth-century art, literature, and history would lack some of the finest examples of what was once regarded as genuine refinement.

See also Civil War Memoirs; Periodicals

BIBLIOGRAPHY

Primary Works

Gilder, Richard Watson. *Letters of Richard Watson Gilder.* Edited by Rosamond Gilder. Boston: Houghton Mifflin, 1916.

Holland, Josiah Gilbert. "Fiction." *Scribner's Monthly* 15, no. 5 (1878): 734–735.

Johnson, Robert Underwood. *Remembered Yesterdays.* Boston: Little, Brown, 1923.

Secondary Works

Bond, J[ames] Arthur. "'Applying the Standards of Intrinsic Excellence': Nationalism and Arnoldian Cultural Valuation in the *Century Magazine* during the 1880s." *American Periodicals* 9 (1999): 55–73.

Chew, Samuel C. "The Century Company." In *Fruit among the Leaves: An Anniversary Anthology,* edited by Samuel C. Chew, pp. 67–152. New York: Appleton-Century-Crofts, 1950.

Gabler-Hover, Janet. "The North-South Reconciliation Theme and the 'Shadow of the Negro' in *Century Illustrated Magazine.*" In *Periodical Literature in Nineteenth-Century America,* edited by Kenneth M. Price and Susan Belasco Smith, pp. 239–256. Charlottesville: University Press of Virginia, 1995.

John, Arthur. *The Best Years of the Century: Richard Watson Gilder, "Scribner's Monthly," and "Century Magazine," 1870–1909.* Urbana: University of Illinois Press, 1981.

Mott, Frank Luther. *A History of American Magazines.* Vol. 3. Cambridge, Mass.: Harvard University Press, 1938. See pp. 457–480.

Scholnick, Robert J. "*Scribner's Monthly* and the 'Pictorial Representation of Life and Truth' in Post–Civil War America." *American Periodicals* 1 (1991): 46–69.

Smith, Herbert F. *Richard Watson Gilder.* New York: Twayne, 1970.

James Arthur Bond

CHICAGO

The city of Chicago is in many ways a wonderful barometer of American history, progress, and culture between the years 1880 and 1920. Recovering from the devastation of a massive fire in 1871 that all but destroyed the foundations of the city, Chicago grew at a remarkable rate, spreading along the shores of Lake Michigan and, perhaps more significantly, reaching up into the sky. A combination of hard bedrock and architectural daring meant that Chicago became synonymous with the building of skyscrapers, pushing the limits of new building materials and new models for urban development.

The Home Insurance Company Building, designed by William Le Baron Jenney and completed in 1885, laid the groundwork for this building boom. Use of new methods of construction, specifically the employment of strong but relatively light steel beams for the structural framework, allowed architects to build higher and higher. The skyscrapers led to the image of "cliff dwellers" living in them, an idea at the center of some of the early novels written about Chicago as a major city and commercial center by writers such as Henry Blake Fuller. Rethinking the framework of a building allowed designers freedom in the use of elevators, wiring, and control of the interior climate.

While other cities, especially on the eastern seaboard, were still highly influenced by classical Greek and Roman styles, the architects in Chicago were reimagining what public buildings could be. Jenney was instrumental in training Daniel Burnham, William Holabird, Martin Roche, and Louis Sullivan, who went on to mentor Frank Lloyd Wright.

As a junction between East and West, Chicago flourished as railroad traffic increased through the city, and one of its major industries, beef, was a direct result. The enormous stockyards and slaughterhouses in Chicago became central to the meat industry of the nation. Chicago was immensely accessible to both people and industry thanks to improved transportation, including canals that linked the city to the Atlantic Ocean and to the Mississippi River. Blessed by its geographic position, the development of natural resources such as coal, lumber, and ore, and the pathways that met there, the population of the city grew from around 50 settlers in 1830 to 300,000 by the time of the fire in 1871, more than a million by 1890, and double that number by 1910. The World's Columbian Exposition in 1893 announced the arrival of Chicago as a modern city and as a key player on the national and international stage. As industry developed, immigrants from Europe, taking advantage of an unrestricted immigration policy, flooded into the city, choosing it as an alternative to New York. Inevitably the excess of cheap labor led to exploitation and unscrupulous profiteering, often at the expense of public health.

Upton Sinclair spent months talking to the immigrant workers of Packingtown and observing the conditions of meat preparation in the slaughterhouses and stockyards. He made contact with many of them through the settlement houses, and while completing his research, he tried (unsuccessfully) to convert Jane Addams to socialism. His novel *The Jungle,* published in 1906, led to institutional changes in the handling of meat, but it did not necessarily have much effect on the protection of workers. Sinclair's main purpose was to expose the exploitation of the employees, but as he famously said later: "I aimed at the public's heart, and by accident I hit it in the stomach." The furor caused by the novel eventually led to the creation of the Food and Drug Administration and, more immediately, to sweeping changes in the way meat was prepared and handled through the passing of the Pure Food and Drug Act and the Meat Inspection Act. Sinclair was one of the new breed of Chicago writers, but some of those associated with the Chicago Renaissance of the late nineteenth century were still very influential as the modern era dawned.

THE CHICAGO SCHOOL OR CHICAGO RENAISSANCE

Placed in the center of this rapid change were writers who were well positioned to document what they saw. Some of them, like Henry Blake Fuller, were descended from the old settlers of the city, while others, like Hamlin Garland, moved into the urban sprawl from rural areas. Chicago pulled writers into the modern world, forcing them to deal with issues like commerce, industry, immigration, technology, and rapid urban expansion. Apart from Fuller and Garland, other writers such as Theodore Dreiser, Frank Norris, Sherwood Anderson, Carl Sandburg, Upton Sinclair, and Edgar Lee Masters helped document Chicago as a place of "primary cultural consequence" (Smith, p. 3). Not all of the writing about the city was laudatory, however. Writers felt threatened by a city that seemed "inimical or, perhaps worse, indifferent to them," and they often reflect that Chicago "was a dispiriting place to live" (Smith, p. 7).

Literary society in Chicago grouped around a few significant meeting places. Lorado Taft's sculpture workshop on the Midway became a regular salon, and it was here that Hamlin Garland met his future wife, Taft's sister Zulime. Mrs. J. W. A. Young's summer home on Lake Michigan was opened up to artists, who could work or relax there, and older members of the literary circle could spend time mentoring the up-and-coming writers. This was known as the Top o' Dunes Club, and Fuller formed lasting friendships with some of the young people he met there, including the poet and dance critic Mark Turbyfill. The Little Room, an informal gathering of writers, artists, architects, and thinkers, met at least once a month, often at the studio of Anna Morgan in the Century Building on the lakeshore. It was inevitable that such a lively and eclectic literary scene developed its own outlets, including the influential literary review *The Dial, Chap-Book, Little Review,* and Harriet Monroe's *Poetry.*

Poetry, founded in 1912, began with the purpose of operating an open door policy. Any poet—published or unpublished, famous or undiscovered—was promised access to the editorial board for an honest review. As Monroe wrote in the inaugural issue, the magazine desired to publish "the best English verse which is being written today, regardless of where, by whom, or under what theory of art it is written." *Poetry* offered a forum for poets such as Ezra Pound, William Carlos Williams, Marianne Moore, and Wallace Stevens, and it provided the first U.S. publication of T. S. Eliot's "The Love Song of J. Alfred Prufrock." Monroe and the board of editors and advisers, including Fuller, also championed Carl Sandburg (1878–1967). Sandburg's

Chicago Poems captured the industrial and cultural changes of his city in free verse: the city he called the

Hog Butcher for the World,
Tool Maker, Stacker of Wheat,
Player with Railroads and the Nation's Freight
    Handler;
Stormy, husky, brawling,
City of the Big Shoulders.

(P. 4)

HENRY BLAKE FULLER

Henry Blake Fuller (1857–1929) was heavily influenced by the art, architecture, and literature of the Old World, but he saw a chance for the New World to define its own terms and conditions in aesthetic matters, and he worked toward this aim for the whole of his writing life. Fuller wrote two groundbreaking novels of urban and economic American realism, *The Cliff-Dwellers* (1893), and *With the Procession* (1895). Hailed by Theodore Dreiser and William Dean Howells (1837–1920) as one of America's leading and most important novelists of the era, alongside Henry James (1843–1916), Fuller was influential in Chicago literary circles but increasingly as a mentor and adviser rather than as a practitioner.

Fuller called *The Cliff-Dwellers* "my first essay in 'realism'" ("My Early Books"). He wrote the book, he says, "when the Columbian Exposition helped along a hearing for Chicago fiction" ("My Early Books"). Fuller captured the reality of Chicago as no one ever had, producing a city novel of accuracy and insight, not all of it pleasant or welcome to its subjects. William Dean Howells said of *The Cliff-Dwellers* and the later *With the Procession:* "I do not know how conscious Mr. Fuller may have been in his fealty to Chicago when he was writing his story, but it seems to me that I have never read a book more intensely localized, that is to say realized" (Howells, p. 214). Others, however, were outraged by the "warts and all" depiction of their beloved home city. Fuller focused on the conflict between material success and the price paid for it by family, friends, and conventional morality, the driving force of which was Chicago itself. In his obituary of Fuller, Robert Morss Lovett of the University of Chicago reflected that "it was a little disappointing to Fuller's backers that he should choose the World's Fair year for dwelling on the sordid side in *The Cliff-Dwellers,* but after all, realism was the coming thing" (p. 17). While the book was regarded outside the city as a huge success and Howells and others praised it as the first major work of midwestern realism, Chicagoans themselves were not so sure. It was the first step toward what would

In The Cliff-Dwellers *(1893), Henry Blake Fuller writes about the underside of Chicago life, showing the growing pains of the huge and expanding city:*

Each of these long canyons is closed in by a long frontage of towering cliffs, and these soaring walls of brick and limestone and granite rise higher and higher with each succeeding year, according as the work of erosion at their bases goes onward—the work of that seething flood of carts, carriages, omnibuses, cabs, cars, messengers, shoppers, clerks, and capitalists, which surges with increasing violence for every passing day. This erosion with a sort of fateful regularity has come to be a matter of constant and growing interest. . . .

So many miles of flimsy and shabby shanties and back views of sheds and stables; of grimy, cindered switch-yards, with the long flanks of freight houses and interminable strings of loaded or empty cars; of dingy viaducts and groggy viaducts and dilapidated fences whose scanty remains called to remembrance lotions and tonics that had long passed their vogue; of groups of Sunday loungers before saloons, and gangs of unclassified foreigners picking up bits of coal along the tracks; of muddy crossings over roads whose bordering ditches were filled with flocks of geese; of wide prairies cut up by endless tracks, dotted with pools of water, and rustling with the dead grasses of last summer; then suburbs new and old—some in the fresh promise of sidewalks and trees and nothing else, others unkempt, shabby, gone to seed; then a high passage over a marshy plain, a range of low wooded hills, emancipation from the dubious body known as the Cook County Commissioners.

Fuller, *The Cliff-Dwellers*, pp. 1, 175–176.

become a tempestuous relationship between the city and its first major writer.

Fuller's career shows many lengthy gaps in production sparked by aesthetic disillusion, when he restricted himself to book reviewing and literary articles. Despite praise from his peers, Fuller's name and reputation have been allowed to fade from canonical circles, and he has been wrongly ignored for many years. Part of the explanation lies in his unwillingness to stay with what worked for him. He quickly tired of the novel of realism and tried (among other genres) the short story about Americans abroad, the one-act play, free verse in the style of Edgar Lee Masters, and the shorter modern novel. He effectively committed professional and economic suicide in 1919, when he published *Bertram Cope's Year*, an openly gay novel, at his own expense. Ironically it is the only book of Fuller's that is still in print. He confined himself to writing periodic book reviews for the next nine years before a final spurt of creativity produced two novels—*Gardens of This World* and *Not on the Screen*—in just over six months. The second of these appeared after Fuller's death in July 1929, when he succumbed to heart failure in the middle of a Chicago heat wave.

ROBERT HERRICK

Fuller's friend Robert Herrick (1868–1938) was born in Cambridge, Massachusetts, and was educated at the Massachusetts Institute of Technology (MIT); he moved to Chicago in 1893 to take up a post at the University of Chicago. His major theme, the conflict between personal values and the moral ambiguities of capitalistic success, was close to Fuller's concern in his realist works. Although Herrick complained about the teaching duties that consumed much of his time, he still managed to write thirteen novels between 1893 and 1923, when he resigned his position. His major novels include *The Common Lot* (1904), a thinly veiled account of his own battle to build a house on University Avenue, and *Chimes* (1926), which depicts the university as a creation of new wealth and a president who is uncultured but enthusiastic. *The Web of Life* (1900) takes the destruction of the world's fair site as a backdrop to a key scene. Herrick was not a very content man, but he found a niche for himself at the end of his life when his administrative skills earned him the post of governor of the Virgin Islands.

JANE ADDAMS AND HULL-HOUSE

Jane Addams (1860–1935) was one of the most prominent female social activists of her era. In 1889, with Ellen Gates Starr, she founded the social settlement Hull-House on Chicago's Near West Side, a home for the disadvantaged that provided child care, education, language and arts classes, help in finding employment, a meeting place for trade union groups, and facilities for single working girls. As the population of Chicago grew and became more diverse, Addams became aware that support services were needed by the underprivileged. In a time of great racial and ethnic discrimination, Hull-House supported Italian, German,

The aftermath of the World's Columbian Exposition in 1893 brought problems to Chicago. Being a city on the world stage brought an influx of immigrants who were now, more than ever, aware of the city of Chicago, its reputation, and the lure of its promise. Once the fair had passed, so did much of the welcome outstretched to the peoples of the world. The pressures of the city confines, the need for accommodation, and the quest for decent, regular work squeezed the resources of the city and led to economic and social tensions. Robert Herrick set his novel The Web of Life *(1900) in and around the ruins of the fair's White City. In the novel he looks back to the days following the closure of the fair and reflects on it in this way:*

These days there were many people on the streets, but few were busy. The large department stores were empty; at the doors stood idle floor-walkers and clerks. It was too warm for the rich to buy, and the poor had no money. The poor had come lean and hungry out of the terrible winter that followed the World's Fair. In that beautiful enterprise the prodigal city had put forth her utmost strength, and, having shown the world the supreme flower of her energy, had collapsed. There was gloom, not only in LaSalle Street where people failed, but throughout the city, where the engine of play had exhausted the forces of all. . . . Tens of thousands of human beings, lured to the festive city by abnormal wages, had been left stranded, without food, or a right to shelter in its tenantless buildings. . . . The laborer starved, and the employer sulked.

Herrick, *The Web of Life*, pp. 135–136.

Russian, and Irish immigrants. By the 1920s the area around Hull-House was populated by Mexicans and African Americans who had chosen to settle there, and they joined the cultural mix. As the demand on Hull-House grew, the complex expanded until there were thirteen buildings, including a Labor Museum and the Jane Club for young women.

The experience of working at Hull-House motivated Addams and her supporters to begin a program of political social activism. They saw intrinsic discrimination on a racial and class basis and developed programs to fight this through legislation. In 1893 the Illinois legislature passed a bill protecting the rights of women and children. The Federal Children's Bureau, created in 1912, and the federal child labor laws from 1916 reflected the local efforts of Addams and her fellow reformers. Addams also was directly responsible for the projects that resulted in the Immigrants' Protective League, Juvenile Psychopathic Clinic, and Juvenile Protective Association. She continued to spread her message of social reform through her writing, including *Twenty Years at Hull-House* (1910), and speaking engagements.

The list of organizations that Jane Addams either created or served with is impressive and extensive. These include the National Federation of Settlement and Neighborhood Centers, National Conference of Charities and Corrections, National Consumers League, Camp Fire Girls, and National Playground Association. She was an active supporter for the founding of the National Association for the Advancement of Colored People (1909) and the American Civil Liberties Union (1920), and she was heavily involved in the campaign for woman suffrage. It seems natural and appropriate that Addams would become a key figure in the international peace movement at the beginning of the twentieth century. In 1915, during the First World War, she and women from both neutral and involved nations met to try and stop the war. She remained a pacifist as the United States entered the war in 1917, and she founded the Women's Peace Party (WPP) to protest the conflict. The WPP became the Women's International League for Peace and Freedom in 1919, and in recognition of her work, Addams was awarded the Nobel Peace Prize in 1931. When she died on 21 May 1935 she was buried in Cedarville, Illinois, her hometown.

FOUNDING OF UNIVERSITY OF CHICAGO

The American Baptist Education Society and the oil baron John D. Rockefeller founded the University of Chicago in 1890. The university was nondenominational from the beginning and gained a reputation for admitting minorities and women when other major institutions would not. The campus was developed in Hyde Park, a recently annexed suburb of the city, on land donated by the department store magnate Marshall Field. The architecture of the campus copied the English gothic of Oxford and Cambridge, with cloisters, towers, and gargoyles. Under its first president, William Rainey Harper, the university developed a program that combined the undergraduate liberal arts college with graduate study and research after the German model. Classes ran all year, an innovation for the time, allowing students to graduate when they finished the requirements

of the degree. By 1910 the university had adopted a Latin motto, *Crescat scientia, vita excolatur* (Let knowledge increase so that life may be enriched) and a coat of arms bearing a phoenix emerging from the flames.

See also The Jungle; Poetry: A Magazine of Verse; Sister Carrie; World's Columbian Exposition

BIBLIOGRAPHY
Primary Works
Addams, Jane. *Twenty Years at Hull-House.* 1910. New York: Signet Classic, 1961.

Fuller, Henry Blake. *The Cliff-Dwellers.* 1893. Ridgewood, N.J.: Gregg Press, 1968.

Fuller, Henry Blake. "My Early Books." Henry Blake Fuller Papers, Midwest Manuscript Collection, The Newberry Library, Chicago.

Fuller, Henry Blake. *With the Procession.* 1895. Chicago: University of Chicago Press, 1965.

Herrick, Robert. *The Web of Life.* New York: Macmillan, 1900.

Howells, William Dean. *Selected Literary Criticism.* Vol. 2, *1886–1897,* edited by Donald Pizer. Bloomington: Indiana University Press, 1993.

Lovett, Robert Morss. "Fuller of Chicago." *New Republic,* 21 August 1929, pp. 16–18.

Sandburg, Carl. *Chicago Poems.* New York: Henry Holt, 1916.

Secondary Works
Duffey, Bernard I. *The Chicago Renaissance in American Letters: A Critical History.* Westport, Conn.: Greenwood Press, 1954.

Miller, Donald L. *City of the Century: The Epic of Chicago and the Making of America.* New York: Simon and Schuster, 1996.

Pilkington, John. *Henry Blake Fuller.* New York: Twayne, 1970.

Scambray, Kenneth. *A Varied Harvest: The Life and Works of Henry Blake Fuller.* Pittsburgh: University of Pittsburgh Press, 1987.

Smith, Carl S. *Chicago and the American Literary Imagination, 1880–1920.* Chicago: University of Chicago Press, 1984.

Williams, Kenny J. *In the City of Men: Another Story of Chicago.* Nashville, Tenn.: Townsend Press, 1974.

Keith Gumery

CHICAGO WORLD'S FAIR

See World's Columbian Exposition

CHILDREN'S LITERATURE

Samuel Osgood, writing in the *Atlantic Monthly* in 1865, stated, "Fruitful as America has been and is in children's books, we have not yet apparently added a single one to the first rank of juvenile classics." During the next five decades, this gap was decisively filled, with works such as Louisa May Alcott's *Little Women* (1868–1869), Mark Twain's *Adventures of Tom Sawyer* (1876), L. Frank Baum's *The Wonderful Wizard of Oz* (1900), and Frances Hodgson Burnett's *Little Lord Fauntleroy* (1886) and *The Secret Garden* (1911), books that had a wide readership on both sides of the Atlantic. In this period of national expansion, industrial and economic growth, and increasing cultural confidence following the Civil War, literature for children and young people in America underwent an unprecedented transformation from didacticism to literary ambition and achievement. Responding to and helping to create an increasingly affluent and well-read audience, writers, editors, and illustrators of works for young people generated a broad range of stories and images that rejected or altered the moralistic approach of antebellum literature for children and presented instead a vital, energetic, and diverse spectrum of books for juvenile readers.

Earlier American writers for children, such as Samuel Griswold Goodrich, writing under the pseudonym Peter Parley, and Jacob Abbott, sought to teach religious and social morals, with varying degrees of severity. A characteristic story by Peter Parley, "The Pleasure Boat; or, The Broken Promise" (1843), concludes as follows: "The father knelt down, and they all knelt with him, and they thanked God that the life of the little boy had been saved, and prayed that the erring boys and girls might be kept from further disobedience" (Goodrich, p. 214).

NEW DEPARTURES

Newly dominant themes after the Civil War were self-advancement, patriotism, domestic life, and humor. Horatio Alger Jr. (1832–1899) wrote over seventy books featuring boys advancing their fortunes through hard work, honesty, and finding the right patron—the "rags-to-riches" formula that has become synonymous with his name. Beginning with *Ragged Dick* (1867), Alger developed his pattern of following a poor boy, in this case a bootblack (frequently a newsboy in later books), who, through shrewdness and

determination, rises to the position of accounting clerk, a meteoric ascent narrated in wooden prose. Alger glorified a personality type that had been excoriated as grasping and selfish by Frances Trollope in her *Domestic Manners of the Americans* (1832), an unsympathetic account of American mores. In contrast, Thomas March Clark, in his humorous *John Whopper the Newsboy* (1871), gives a favorable account of American boys, as does William Taylor Adams (aka Oliver Optic, 1822–1897), Alger's main competitor, in his nautical adventure series, which Louisa May Alcott (1832–1888) attacked as "optical delusions" in her novel *Eight Cousins* (1875):

> Now, I put it to you, boys, is it natural for lads from fifteen to eighteen to command ships, defeat pirates, outwit smugglers, and so cover themselves with glory, that Admiral Farragut invites them to dinner, saying, "Noble boy, you are an honor to your country!" . . . Even if the hero is an honest boy trying to get his living, he is not permitted to do so in a natural way, by hard work and years of patient effort, but is suddenly adopted by a millionaire whose pocket-book he has returned; or a rich uncle appears from the sea just in the nick of time; or the remarkable boy earns a few dollars, speculates in pea-nuts or neckties, and grows rich so rapidly that Sinbad in the diamond valley is a pauper compared to him. (P. 150)

The criticism was ironic, in that the plots Alcott ridiculed were not much different from her own covert writings and from Jo March's literary effusions. Her masterpiece of domestic life, *Little Women* (1868–1869), was, in Elizabeth Keyser's words, "a transitional book" that had predecessors such as Harriet Beecher Stowe's *Uncle Tom's Cabin* (1851–1852), Maria S. Cummins's *The Lamplighter* (1854), and Susan Warner's *The Wide, Wide World* (1850) but unlike those works addressed itself specifically to children. Writing in the tradition of religious and rational moralism, Alcott transformed autobiography into fiction in a lively portrait of family life with such winning warmth and realism that the March family, sometimes regarded by critics as an American matriarchy, has won the hearts of generations of readers and of viewers of the film adaptations based upon it. Although her novel was moralistic and didactic—Alcott herself referred to it in a letter as "moral pap for the young"—she attenuated the religious teaching of the novel in the direction of universalism, and her characters were drawn with humor and verve, enlivening the often drab tradition of didacticism. Her immensely popular stories enabled her to sustain herself as a writer of children's books, a new departure for writers in America, and she engaged a broad audience of readers who made demands on her that she was sometimes unwilling to meet, as in her insistence on not marrying Jo to the popular Laurie but instead to the more sedate and fatherly Professor Bhaer.

Another writer who practiced the art of the domestic story was Lucretia Hale, whose humorous tales recorded in *The Peterkin Papers* (beginning in 1868) concerned an obtuse and accident-prone family incapable of using common sense. Her stories appeared first in *Our Young Folks* and then in *St. Nicholas*.

Samuel Clemens (1835–1910), writing as Mark Twain, fundamentally changed American children's literature by elevating regional experience—stories of riverfront boyhood on the Mississippi, in a region that was at that time "the West," into national and international significance. Mark Twain despised the moralistic tradition of previous children's books, and satirized it in "The Story of a Good Little Boy" (1870) and "The Story of the Bad Little Boy" (1875). He turned that tradition upside down, with great vigor and humor, by elevating the "good bad boy" to heroic status in *The Adventures of Tom Sawyer* (1876) and by criticizing the values of southern society through the naive voice of the child, cast in Huck's inimitable frontier dialect, in *Adventures of Huckleberry Finn* (1885). Clemens also wrote in the more conventional genre of historical fiction in *The Prince and the Pauper* (1882), which some of his genteel critics and supporters praised as his finest work.

POPULAR CHILDREN'S PERIODICALS

In 1867 William Taylor Adams founded a magazine for children, *Oliver Optic's Magazine: Our Boys and Girls*. It was one of a flood of periodicals addressing themselves to young readers in the post–Civil War era, supplying the demands of an increasingly literate audience and publishing many of the most distinguished writers of the time. Alcott herself published much of her writing for young people, including *Eight Cousins*, in periodicals. The most influential and highest quality children's periodical of the era was *St. Nicholas Magazine*. Founded in 1873 as an offspring of *Scribner's Monthly*, it was edited for thirty-two years by the extraordinarily capable Mary Mapes Dodge. She had established a national reputation with her novel of Dutch life, *Hans Brinker; or, The Silver Skates* (1858). Her editorial philosophy emphasized the need for clear and firm but implicit moral messages:

> Doubtless a great deal of instruction and moral teaching may be inculcated in the pages of a magazine; but it must be by hints dropped incidentally here and there; by a few brisk hearty statements of the difference between right and wrong; a sharp, clean thrust at falsehood, a sunny recognition of

truth, a gracious application of politeness, an unwilling glimpse of the odious doings of the uncharitable and base. (Dodge, p. 354)

As R. Gordon Kelly has described in *Mother Was a Lady*, Dodge edited her magazine with an awareness of the processes of urbanization and industrialization in the nineteenth century, and she sought to prepare her readers, through high-quality fiction, for the world as the American upper and middle classes thought it ought to be, and through nonfiction, for the world as it actually was. She engaged some of the most prominent writers of her day to publish in the pages of *St. Nicholas*, including Mark Twain, Jack London, Noah Brooks, Laura Richards, Susan Coolidge, Kate Douglas Wiggin, Frances Hodgson Burnett, Rudyard Kipling, and Robert Louis Stevenson. When Kipling, allegedly rather condescendingly, asked whether he should write for *St. Nicholas*, she is reported to have retorted, "If you think you're capable of it!" She also knew how to nurture and sustain the interest of generations of readers through devices such as the St. Nicholas League, a department in which readers published their stories, poems, and sketches. Contributors who won awards in this department as young writers included Eudora Welty, Edna St. Vincent Millay, and Stephen Vincent Benét. The historian Henry Steele Commager has described how, as a child, he eagerly awaited the arrival of *St. Nicholas Magazine* on his front stoop and how the older children snatched it away from the younger ones to read it first.

Other important children's periodicals of this era include the sensational *Frank Leslie's Boy's and Girl's Weekly* (1866–1884), which featured brutal and violent stories and lurid illustrations and was immensely popular. There were scores of Sunday school publications, among them *Youth's Temperance Banner, Young Evangelist, Young Christian Soldier,* and the long-lived *Youth's Companion* (1827–1929), which was intended by its founder, Nathaniel Willis, to help young readers learn stern moral values of "piety, morality, brother love" but which gradually became secularized. As David L. Greene has written: "Throughout most of its long career, *The Youth's Companion* was unequaled in reflecting current fashions and trends in children's literature" (Kelly, *Children's Periodicals of the United States*, p. 513). *Demorest's Young America* (1866–1875) strove to oppose the "low and demoralizing class of literature, prepared expressly to gratify that love of the marvelous, the absurd, and the unnatural that is fostered in the young" (*Demorest's Young America*, August 1873, p. 255), and like many periodicals of its time, it passionately advocated the temperance cause. *Riverside Magazine for Young People*

(1867–1870), published in New York, was short-lived but set a standard of excellence seldom surpassed in the genre.

REGIONALISM AND DIALECT STORIES

Edward Eggleston (1837–1902) made a name for himself with *The Hoosier School-Master* (1871), first serialized in a periodical, and continued his success as an author of Indiana stories with *The Hoosier School-Boy* (1883). His use of authentic regional speech patterns is mirrored in other writers of the period, such as Mark Twain, Charles Chesnutt, and Kate Chopin. In his Uncle Remus stories, Joel Chandler Harris (1845–1908) retells dialect tales from African American oral storytellers about Brer Rabbit, Brer Fox, and the creatures of the Briar Patch. His first collection, *Uncle Remus, His Songs and His Sayings,* was published in 1881. Further collections included *Nights with Uncle Remus* (1883), *Uncle Remus and His Friends* (1892), and *Uncle Remus and the Little Boy* (1910).

Alice Hegan Rice's (1870–1942) *Mrs. Wiggs of the Cabbage Patch* (1901) describes life in a shanty-town in a former cabbage patch in South Louisville, Kentucky, using dialect for comic effect. Despised by Jack London for its "pernicious preachment" and by Upton Sinclair, who referred to it as "sugar-coated sentimentality," it was nonetheless tremendously popular and appeared in multiple stage and film versions, including a 1934 movie with W. C. Fields and Zasu Pitts.

Gene Stratton-Porter (1863–1924), also accused of sentimentality by critics, won a wide audience with her novels *Freckles* (1904) and *Girl of the Limberlost* (1909), which features explorations of nature in the Limberlost swamp of northeast Indiana. In *Girl of the Limberlost,* Elnora Comstock collects rare moths to raise funds to put herself through high school. She is a sweet, compassionate girl who alleviates her embittered mother's ill temper. Stratton-Porter can be regarded as an early environmentalist whose concern for the protection of the natural world influenced generations of young readers.

Ernest Thompson Seton (1860–1946) was born in South Shields, England, but immigrated to Canada at the age of six and eventually settled in the United States. In 1910 he founded, with Lord Baden Powell, the Boy Scouts of America. He published about forty collections of stories about animals, nature study, and working with wood. Among his most influential books is *Wild Animals I Have Known* (1898), which, like many of his other works, is based upon close observation of wildlife.

SERIES BOOKS

Edward Stratemeyer (1862–1930), the son of a German immigrant, founded an empire of juvenile series books, including the Rover Boys, Tom Swift, and the Motor Boys. Stratemeyer's first paid story appeared in 1888, and he soon was writing regularly for publication in boys' magazines. He became a prolific and phenomenally productive writer of adventure stories, the success of which led to his founding of the Stratemeyer Literary Syndicate in New York City in 1905. He employed a group of writers and provided them with pseudonyms, plot outlines, and characters. His enterprise grew into the largest juvenile fiction publishing enterprise in the country.

Emulating Oliver Optic, Stratemeyer created such well-known series as the Hardy Boys, the Bobbsey Twins, and many others. Using a variety of pseudonyms as well as his own name, Stratemeyer himself is estimated to have written 160 books and to have outlined stories for about 800 more. Stratemeyer completed unfinished works by Oliver Optic (William Taylor Adams) and Horatio Alger after the deaths of these authors. In 1929 Stratemeyer hired Mildred Wirt Benson to ghostwrite stories about the girl sleuth Nancy Drew. Though Harriet Stratemeyer Adams was long credited as the author of the "Carolyn Keene" books, "a lawsuit in 1980 . . . established conclusively [Benson's] claim to original authorship," Nancy Tillman Romalov writes (p. vi). In its summary of his life, *Fortune Magazine* stated: "As oil had its Rockefeller, literature had its Stratemeyer."

Gilbert Patten (1866–1945), using the pen name Burt L. Standish, was the author of another phenomenally popular series character, Frank Merriwell, a brainy and brawny Yale-educated star athlete whose adventures often involved close calls. In the words of Mark Alden Branch in a *Yale Alumni Magazine* article, "The Ten Greatest Yalies That Never Were": "In the days when the phrase 'Yale man' conjured up an image of a solid, athletic fellow who played fair and came from a good family, Frank Merriwell was an ideal for many American boys—an unequivocal paragon of virtue who had, as one reviewer put it, 'a body like Tarzan's and a head like Einstein's'" (Branch). He was always impeccably polite and well mannered. It was a generally understood compliment to call someone "a regular Frank Merriwell."

Though L. Frank Baum (1856–1919) is best known for *The Wonderful Wizard of Oz* (1900), in large part due to the influence of the famous film adaptation, he was a prolific writer who responded to the popularity of Oz by producing seventeen Oz titles, including *The Marvelous Land of Oz* (1904), *Ozma of*

" You ought to be ashamed of yourself." Illustration by W. W. Denslow for the first edition of *The Wizard of Oz.*
THE LIBRARY OF CONGRESS

Oz (1907), *Tik-Tok of Oz* (1914), and *The Magic of Oz* (1919), and who experimented with various other excursions into fantasy. The Library of Congress has touted *The Wonderful Wizard of Oz* as "the first totally American fantasy for children," though Baum's claim to be writing a completely new kind of fantasy needs to be regarded with some skepticism. Mainly he claimed to wish to avoid the violence and brutality of the European folktales, a desire he shared with earlier American writers, such as Nathaniel Hawthorne and Palmer Cox. Before he invented Oz, Baum tried his hand at *Mother Goose in Prose* (1897), illustrated by Maxfield Parrish, gentle stories he first told to his sons.

ROMANTICISM

Eleanor Porter (1868–1920) was the author of *Pollyanna* (1913), a missionary of optimism, whose positive attitude converts all the melancholy or despairing members of her small-town community to cheerfulness. Pollyanna is still popular with the conservative Right and in several Slavic countries, including Russia.

Though Frances Hodgson Burnett (1849–1924) was born in England and is claimed by both English and American literary historians, she spent a significant portion of her life in the United States and wrote about American themes, particularly in *Little Lord Fauntleroy* (1886). Cedric Errol (Little Lord Fauntleroy) is the son of an American father and a British mother. He has grown up with American egalitarian attitudes and is friends with the corner grocer and likes "the milkman and the baker and the apple-woman" (p. 8). When his aristocratic English relatives invite him to travel to England, they assume his mother is an opportunist, seeking the family fortune, but they are charmed by the straightforward Cedric, who wins friends with his honesty and bravery.

Ironically the illustrations of the novel, emphasizing Cedric's long locks and frilly clothing, eclipsed the book's portrayal of a bold and "manly" little boy, and the popularity of Fauntleroy fashions was a blight upon a generation of middle-class and upper-middle-class boys in the late 1880s and early 1890s.

In her masterpiece, *The Secret Garden* (1911), Burnett displays a typically American faith in science (influenced in part by her affiliation with Christian Science, an American religious movement founded by Mary Baker Eddy). Mary Lennox, a sickly, selfish orphan who returns from colonial India to her relatives' mansion in Yorkshire, is gradually healed by exposure to the healthy moor air, a wholesome diet, exercise, and the brusque, honest speech of the Yorkshire working class. Her cousin Colin Craven, who experiences a parallel transformation, believes in the "Magic" of science with unreserved naïveté. As the narrator says:

> In each century since the beginning of the world wonderful things have been discovered. In the last century more amazing things were found out than in any century before. In this new century hundreds of things still more astounding will be brought to light. At first people refuse to believe that a strange new thing can be done, then they begin to hope it can be done, then they see it can be done—then it is done and all the world wonders why it was not done centuries ago. (P. 353)

This unalloyed optimism was swept away by the Great War (1914–1918), with its machine guns, poison gas, trench warfare, and the slaughter of a generation of young men. Burnett's romanticism about the healing power of nature also reflects the nostalgic yearning, characteristic of her time, for a preindustrial contact with nature in the age of industrialization.

Alice Jane Chandler Webster ("Jean Webster," 1876–1916), in her popular novel *Daddy-Long-Legs* (1912), which led to many film versions, promoted a

"'Are you the Earl?' said Cedric. 'I'm your grandson. I'm Lord Fauntleroy.'" Frontispiece by Reginald B. Birch for the 1899 edition of *Little Lord Fauntleroy* by Frances Hodgson Burnett. SPECIAL COLLECTIONS LIBRARY, UNIVERSITY OF MICHIGAN

different kind of romanticism. As Gillian Avery has pointed out in her influential history of American children's books, *Behold the Child* (1994), Judy, the orphan at the center of her tale, is naturally self-assured "in spite of her disadvantaged background" (p. 181) and wins the hearts of readers just as she wins the heart and hand of her wealthy patron, a trustee at her orphanage, who offers to pay for her college education if she will write him a letter each month describing her progress.

LOOKING FORWARD
In 1919 W. E. B. Du Bois (1868–1963) announced the arrival of a children's magazine "for 'The True Brownies.'" It was called *The Brownies' Book,* and though it was only published for two years (1920–1921), it prophetically heralded a new racial self-awareness, promising a "little magazine" "designed especially for the Children of the Sun" and setting a high standard for children's fiction with multiracial consciousness. It reflected the long journey of American children's books from unquestioned racism to the socially critical and multiform children's literature of the new century.

See also Adventures of Huckleberry Finn; Adolescence; *Uncle Remus, His Songs and His Sayings*

BIBLIOGRAPHY
Primary Works

Alcott, Louisa May. *Eight Cousins; or, The Aunt-Hill.* Boston: Roberts Brothers, 1875.

Alcott, Louisa May. *Little Women.* Boston: Roberts Brothers, 1868–1869.

Baum, L. Frank. *The Wonderful Wizard of Oz.* Chicago and New York: G. M. Hill, 1900.

Burnett, Frances Hodgson. *Little Lord Fauntleroy.* New York: Charles Scribner's Sons, 1886.

Burnett, Frances Hodgson. *The Secret Garden.* New York: Grosset and Dunlop, 1911.

Clemens, Samuel (Mark Twain). *Adventures of Huckleberry Finn.* New York: Charles L. Webster, 1885.

Clemens, Samuel (Mark Twain). *The Adventures of Tom Sawyer.* Hartford, Conn.: American Publishing Company, 1876.

Demers, Patricia, ed. *A Garland from the Golden Age: An Anthology of Children's Literature from 1850–1900.* Toronto: Oxford University Press, 1983.

Dodge, Mary Mapes. "Children's Magazines." *Scribner's Monthly*, July 1873, pp. 352–354.

Goodrich, Samuel Grisewold (Peter Parley). "The Pleasure Boat; or, The Broken Promise." In *From Instruction to Delight: An Anthology of Children's Literature to 1850*, edited by Patricia Demers and Gordo Moyles. Toronto: Oxford University Press, 2003.

Harris, Joel Chandler. *Uncle Remus, His Songs and His Sayings: The Folklore of the Old Plantation*. New York: D. Appleton & Company, 1881.

Secondary Works

Avery, Gillian. *Behold the Child: American Children and Their Books 1621–1922*. London: Bodley Head, 1994.

Bixler, Phyllis. *Frances Hodgson Burnett*. Boston: Twayne, 1984.

Branch, Mark Alden. "The Ten Greatest Yalies That Never Were." Yale Alumni Magazine, February 2003. Available at http://www.yalealumnimagazine.com/issues/03_0/fictional.html.

Griswold, Jerry. *Audacious Kids: Coming of Age in America's Classic Children's Books*. New York: Oxford University Press, 1992.

Kelly, R. Gordon. *Children's Periodicals of the United States*. Westport, Conn.: Greenwood Press, 1984.

Kelly, R. Gordon. *Mother Was a Lady: Self and Society in Selected American Children's Periodicals, 1865–1890*. Westport, Conn.: Greenwood Press, 1974.

Keyser, Elizabeth Lennox. *Little Women: A Family Romance*. Athens and London: University of Georgia Press, 1999.

Keyser, Elizabeth Lennox. *Whispers in the Dark: The Fiction of Louisa May Alcott*. Knoxville: University of Tennessee Press, 1993.

MacLeod, Anne Scott. *American Childhood: Essays on Children's Literature of the Nineteenth and Twentieth Centuries*. Athens and London: University of Georgia Press, 1994.

Regan, Robert. *Unpromising Heroes: Mark Twain and His Characters*. Berkeley: University of California Press, 1966.

Romalov, Nancy Tillman. "Editor's Note." Special Issue on Nancy Drew. *The Lion and the Unicorn: A Critical Journal of Children's Literature* 18, no. 1 (June 1994): v–xi.

Stone, Albert E. *The Innocent Eye: Childhood in Mark Twain's Imagination*. New Haven, Conn.: Yale University Press, 1961.

Thwaite, Ann. *Waiting for the Party: The Life of Frances Hodgson Burnett*. New York: Scribners, 1974.

J. D. Stahl

CHINESE

In 1885, three years after Congress passed the Chinese Exclusion Act, the *American Missionary*'s October issue included a letter from Saum Song Bo in response to a flyer requesting donations to build a pedestal for the Statue of Liberty. Emma Lazarus (1849–1887), with whom Ralph Waldo Emerson corresponded, wrote her famous poem, "The New Colossus" (1883) to help raise money for the pedestal's construction. While the poem's final five lines have become indelibly linked with the statue—"Give me your tired, your poor, / your huddled masses yearning to breathe free" (p. 27)—they also highlight America's duplicity made visible by Saum. He writes:

> I consider it as an insult to us Chinese to call on us to contribute toward building in this land a pedestal for a statue of liberty. That statue represents liberty holding a torch which lights the passage of those of all nations who come into this country. But are the Chinese allowed to come? As for the Chinese who are here, are they allowed to enjoy liberty as men of all other nationalities enjoy it?

Saum's letter alludes to Chinese exclusion whose restrictions and their aftermath have figured largely in Chinese American literature.

IMMIGRATION AND POPULATION STATISTICS

Poor peasants from China's Pearl River Delta initially migrated to the United States in search of better opportunities for themselves and their families. In 1846, when America raised its flag in California's San Francisco's Portsmouth Square, Chinese entrepreneurs opened businesses and laid the groundwork for what would become Chinatown. After the Civil War, southern states recruited Chinese laborers to replace slave labor. It was the 1848 discovery of gold in California, however, that brought Chinese immigrants to the United States in greater numbers. Between 1850 and 1880 their population jumped from 7,520 to 105,465, with 77 percent living in California (see table). Their increasing numbers intensified Americans' anti-Chinese bias as evidenced in a series of race-based laws that specifically targeted the Chinese. Initially welcomed as a cheap labor source, the United States moved closer to exclusion as the nation fell into an economic depression in the late 1800s. Although Chinese immigrants played a significant role in the economic development of the American West, they also roused strongly nativistic feelings among many white Americans.

Chinese population in the United States, 1870–1920

Year	U.S. population	Chinese population	Percentage of total
1870	39,818,449	63,199	.16
1880	50,155,783	105,465	.21
1890	62,947,714	107,488	.17
1900	75,994,575	89,863	.12
1910	91,972,266	71,531	.08
1920	105,710,620	61,639	.06

SOURCE: U.S. Bureau of the Census.

U.S. census statistics reveal how exclusion laws affected the Chinese population count in the United States.

FROM THE GOLD RUSH TO THE GOLDEN SPIKE

News of the California gold rush fueled Chinese immigration to Gam Saan, or Gold Mountain as the Chinese called America. Yuanzhu Chen's *A Collection of Taishan Folk Rhymes* (1929) and Zhaozhong Hu's *A Collection of Popular Cantonese Folk Rhymes in America* (1970) provide a glimpse of the impoverished conditions in China that encouraged immigration. Additionally, the collections' rhymes also reflect the pain of leaving home and the repeated dreams of and hopes for success in America. These stories evolved out of the Chinese oral tradition whose tales have also influenced contemporary writers. They are evidence that Chinese immigrants came for gold but found Americans' antipathy toward foreigners instead.

Mark Twain's (1835–1910) work presented more sympathetic portrayals of the Chinese than what typically appeared in the media. His "John Chinaman in New York" (1870), written for the *Galaxy*, expresses compassion toward a Chinese man berated by passersby. Twain followed up this piece with a series of letters under the general title "Goldsmith's Friend Abroad Again" (1871). A San Francisco Chinese immigrant shocked by Americans' mistreatment of the Chinese purportedly wrote the letters. The invented Chinese writer came to America, believing the nation practiced its ideals of equality. Once he arrived, he became the victim of a violent attack, was thrown in jail, and was convicted of a crime without witnesses. He was not allowed to testify against the Irish Americans who physically assailed him. Employing his typical sarcastic wit in "Letter 7," Twain critiques the California Supreme Court's decision that banned Chinese individuals from testifying against whites in court cases. He wrote, "In this country white men can testify against Chinamen all they want to, but Chinamen ain't allowed to testify against white men!" (p. 73). Twain's letters display the indignation he felt at the injustices against the Chinese.

Not all of his writing about the Chinese was vitriolic. *Roughing It* (1872) provides a witty account of Twain's travels through Nevada and northern California. Several chapters lavish praise on Chinese immigrants and express a measure of indignation at anti-Chinese discrimination. He describes Chinese immigrants in Virginia City and Chinese laborers who helped build the transcontinental railroad; in the chapter titled "The Gentle, Inoffensive Chinese," Twain describes the Chinese as harmless, in contrast with the descriptions of harm brought against them by Americans.

Chinese immigrants who came for gold recognized the danger to their lives inherent in this quest, so they gradually moved into agriculture, fishing, and manufacturing. They also worked as cooks, gardeners, and launderers. In 1870 three-fourths of California's agricultural workers were Chinese, and they played a significant role in the development of California's agricultural industry. Chinese fishermen also transformed Monterey into one of California's most successful fishing ports by being the first to fish commercially for shrimp, abalone, cod, halibut, flounder, and shark. They worked in the sardine factories and played a major role in the development of Monterey and the Cannery Row area that John Steinbeck featured in his novel *Cannery Row*.

ECONOMIC DEPRESSION AND CHINESE RESTRICTIONS

No matter where they settled, the Chinese established social and civic organizations similar to those in China. In 1849 San Francisco's groups merged into one organization, the Chinese Consolidated Benevolent Association, or the Chinese Six Companies. They served the community by assisting immigrants and meeting community needs. As the most powerful organization in Chinatown, the Six Companies transformed their wealth into political power and challenged laws discriminatory to the Chinese.

With the demise of the railroad and mining industries, the economy fell into a slump, and competition for jobs intensified anti-Chinese sentiment. Americans initially welcomed Chinese workers to the United States as a cheap labor source but later blamed them for lower wages, lost jobs, and poor working conditions. Organized labor and individuals began demanding that the United States place restrictions on the Chinese. Labor activists organized anti-Chinese clubs.

a white mob lynched fifteen Chinese people in Los Angeles's Chinatown in 1871. In response, the Six Companies wrote President Ulysses S. Grant a protest letter demanding greater civil rights and protections for the Chinese but to no avail. Local and state governments in western states attracted national attention with anti-Chinese legislation, which influenced Congress to pass similar federal laws.

The writer Bret Harte (1836–1902) included Chinese characters in over twenty of his works, including a play entitled *Two Men of Sandy Bar* (1876), which featured Hop Sing, a Chinese laundryman. Harte spoke out against the injustices the Chinese suffered; yet anti-immigrationists adopted his seemingly negative portrayals of the Chinese to support their cause. For example, Harte had intended his poem "Plain Language from Truthful James" (1870) to ridicule those who harbored anti-Chinese sentiments, but it produced the opposite effect. Rather than deride Truthful James and Bill Nye, who had intended to cheat the Chinese character Ah Sin during a card game, Harte's readers disparaged Ah Sin for turning the tables and beating the Irish at their own game. Readers misinterpreted "The Heathen Chinee," as the poem came to be called, when they read Ah Sin as dishonest, deceptive, and sly, an image that fueled white fear and paranoia about Chinese labor undermining white labor. Harte eventually criticized his poem when he saw its unintended effects.

In spite of the response his poem received, Harte continued to portray the Chinese as "dark," "pagan," "superstitious," and "threatening" in two short stories—"Wan Lee, the Pagan" (1874) and "See Yup" (1898). Harte's Chinese characters fulfilled white expectations. In "See Yup," for instance, a group of Chinese miners become rich by selling a worthless mine to some white miners. In 1876 Harte and Twain collaborated on a play based on and named after Harte's character, Ah Sin. Although the play also addressed "the Yellow Peril," a term used to describe Asian countries' perceived threat to Western civilization, Ah Sin's character was written to be a wily, gibberish-speaking, unredeemable Chinese laundryman. The play was a disaster and was short-lived, yet their characterization of Ah Sin became the model that new writers adopted to fashion their own Chinese characters.

Although Harte and Twain had set out to vindicate the Chinese, other playwrights created productions that betrayed Americans' fear of the Chinese presence in the United States. Henry Grimm's *The Chinese Must Go* (1870) and Joseph Jarrow's *The Queen of Chinatown* (1899) expressed white anxieties

Chinese Immigrants at the San Francisco Custom House. Woodcut from the cover of *Harper's Weekly,* 3 February 1877. Increasing alarm at the numbers of Chinese immigrants led to the passage of the Chinese Exclusion Act in 1882. THE LIBRARY OF CONGRESS

Labor union leader Denis Kearney, head of the Workingmen's Party of California, urged lawmakers to stop the flow of Asians into the United States. Newspapers also fueled nativist tendencies.

In response, politicians passed over six hundred ordinances and laws restricting Chinese people's activities. Their fishing declined between 1875 and 1900, when white fishermen pressured the California legislature to pass laws that restricted the Chinese from fishing, processing, or selling their catch. Additionally, after a suspicious fire destroyed the Chinese quarter, the state quickly established regulations that prohibited the Chinese from rebuilding the China Point fishing community. Violence erupted, and in one incident,

The following excerpt is from a poem by a Chinese immigrant detained on Angel Island on San Francisco's coast.

A thousand sorrows and a hatred ten-thousand-
        fold
burns between my brows.
Hoping to step ashore the American continent is
        the
most difficult of difficulties.
The barbarians imprison me in this place.
Even a martyr or a hero would change
        countenance.

Lai, Lim, and Yung, eds., *Island: Poetry and History of Chinese Immigrants on Angel Island, 1910–1940*, p. 162.

over the presumed threat that Chinese men posed to white male dominance in the labor market and to white women. Both portrayed the Chinese as opium peddlers and enslavers of white women. Such presentations justified and rationalized federal laws restricting the Chinese that had been passed earlier.

CREATING BACHELOR SOCIETIES AND CHINESE-FREE COMMUNITIES

Anti-Chinese laws shaped the development of Chinese communities, because many prevented the formation of families. In 1834 the first Chinese woman arrived in New York City. Three decades later, there were only 1,784, and many were prostitutes. To prohibit the importation of prostitutes, the federal government passed the Page Law (1875), which also discouraged other Chinese women from immigrating. Antimiscegenation laws prevented intermarriage between white women and Chinese men. Consequently, legislation created a lack of marriageable women, transforming Chinese communities into bachelor societies.

The Chinese Exclusion Act (1882) was the first law to prohibit immigration based on race. Initially aimed at Chinese laborers, Congress broadened the law in 1888 to include "all persons of the Chinese race." The act also prohibited Chinese immigrants currently in the United States from claiming citizenship with exemptions for diplomats, merchants, and students. Exclusion was to last ten years, but the Geary

Act (1892) extended them another ten. The law did allow one to return to China, but a return required a certificate of residence as proof of one's right to be in the country. Those caught without the necessary papers were imprisoned or deported. *Fong Yue Ting v. United States* (1893) challenged the Geary Act, but the Supreme Court upheld it. Passage of the Immigration Act (1904) made Chinese exclusion permanent. The push to rid the United States of the Chinese is played out on a global scale in Jack London's (1876–1916) short story "The Unparalleled Invasion" (1913), a tale that pushes the practice of westward expansion and United States imperialism beyond the Pacific Ocean. This science fiction piece describes the United States annihilation of the Chinese in their homeland, a move that, in the story, opens China up for European settlement.

THE EFFECTS OF EXCLUSION

Exclusion and anti-Chinese bias resulted in racial self-hatred among many Chinese immigrants who had made the United States their home. The biracial writer Winnifred Eaton (1875–1954) denied her Chinese heritage and assumed a Japanese identity, naming herself Onoto Watanna. Americans popularized the sentimental novels she set in Japan, depicting romantic relationships between Japanese women and American men. Her novel *Me, a Book of Remembrance* (1915) is a thinly disguised autobiography that partially depicts her attempt to hide her true heritage. Unlike Watanna, her sister, Edith Maude Eaton (1865–1914), embraced her Chinese heritage as reflected in her pen name, Sui Sin Far. Sin Far was the first short story writer of Chinese ancestry to defy stereotypes, humanize her subjects, and champion the Chinese. Her stories in *Mrs. Spring Fragrance* (1912) grapple with complex issues, such as forced assimilation, racism, biculturalism, and interracial marriage. One such story, "In the Land of the Free," critiques unjust immigration restrictions by recounting a family's anguish after the state seizes their infant son, whom it holds for ten months until the family is able to provide the necessary documents proving he is their child. The numerous articles and stories she wrote sorted out issues of acculturation and cultural conflict at a time when most Americans only knew the Chinese through popular stereotypes, depicting them as perpetually foreign.

Many Chinese immigrants found ways to circumvent the kind of immigration restrictions depicted in Sui Sin Far's short story. In *United States v. Wong Kim Ark* (1898), the Supreme Court ruled that the Fourteenth Amendment's guarantee of citizenship to those born in the United States also applied to Chinese immigrants' children. In addition to the opportunities that *Wong Kim Ark* created was the 1906 San Francisco earthquake and fire, which destroyed all birth and immigration records. Despite the prohibitions against Chinese immigration, there were loopholes in laws that allowed Chinese Americans in the United States prior to 1882 to return home, marry, and return with their sons, whom United States law declared as citizens. In order to reenter, however, the federal government required certain documents proving their children's identities. This requirement created the phenomena known as "paper sons." Those without the necessary family ties fabricated paper documents or bought the documents required by the United States, which helped them to assume new identities. "Paper sons" made up the largest population of Chinese immigrants from 1910 to 1940 and enabled the Chinese community to develop a second generation and survive the exclusion years.

The government's discovery of this ploy led to harsher interrogations and the creation of an immigration station on Angel Island on San Francisco's coast in 1910. More of a detention center, Angel Island held Chinese immigrants sometimes for weeks or months, until their immigration papers and medical examinations returned with favorable results. Isolated and alone, detainees revealed their experiences and emotions through poems carved in walls. These writings have been compiled in two collections, *Island: Poetry and History of Chinese Immigrants on Angel Island, 1910–1940* (1991) and *Songs of Gold Mountain* (1992). Both collections are significant because they form the foundation of a mostly silenced Chinese American experience from the late nineteenth century and early twentieth century. The writing reveals the authors' felt despair and anguish after coming to America only to have their dreams crushed by a presumably open and democratic nation. Their detention contradicted the reality they faced when the United States denied them the promises of liberty and freedom guaranteed to all. Detainees' writing also expressed resentment when other immigrants realized the promises offered in Lazarus's poem inscribed on the Statue of Liberty's pedestal.

See also Assimilation; Civil Rights; *Mrs. Spring Fragrance*; "Plain Language from Truthful James"; San Francisco

BIBLIOGRAPHY

Primary Works

Eaton, Edith Maude. *Mrs. Spring Fragrance and Other Writings.* 1912. Edited by Amy Ling and Annette White-Parks. Urbana: University of Illinois Press, 1995.

Eaton, Winnifred. *Me, a Book of Remembrance.* 1915. Jackson: University Press of Mississippi, 1997.

Grimm, Henry. *The Chinese Must Go.* 1870. In *The Chinese Other, 1850–1925: An Anthology of Plays,* edited by Dave Williams. Lanham, Md.: Rowman and Littlefield, 1997.

Harte, Bret. "Plain Language from Truthful James." 1870. In *Yale Book of American Verse,* edited by Thomas R. Lounsbury. New Haven, Conn.: Yale University Press, 1912. Available at www.bartleby.com/102/.

Harte, Bret. "See Yup." 1898. In *Stories in Light and Shadow.* Available at http://www.gutenberg.org/catalog/world/readfile?pageno=40&fk_files=2316.

Harte, Bret. *Two Men of Sandy Bar.* 1876. In *California Gold-rush Plays,* edited by Glenn Loney. New York: Performing Arts Journal Publications, 1983.

Harte, Bret. "Wan Lee, the Pagan." 1874. In *The Luck of Roaring Camp and Other Writings.* New York: Penguin Books, 2001.

Harte, Bret, and Mark Twain. *Ah Sin.* 1876. In *The Chinese Other, 1850–1925: An Anthology of Plays,* edited by Dave Williams. Lanham, Md.: Rowman and Littlefield, 1997.

Jarrow, Joseph. *The Queen of Chinatown.* 1899. In *The Chinese Other, 1850–1925: An Anthology of Plays,* edited by Dave Williams. Lanham, Md.: Rowman and Littlefield, 1997.

Lai, Him Mark, Genny Lim, and Judy Yung, eds. *Island: Poetry and History of Chinese Immigrants on Angel Island, 1910–1940.* Seattle: University of Washington Press, 1991.

Lazarus, Emma. "The New Colossus." 1883. In *The Heath Anthology of American Literature,* vol. 2, edited by Paul Lauter et al., 4th ed. Boston: Houghton Mifflin, 2002.

London, Jack. "The Unparalleled Invasion." 1913. In *The Strength of the Strong.* Available at http://sunsite.berkeley.edu/London/Writings/StrengthStrong/.

Saum Song Bo. "A Protest against the Statue of Liberty." 1885. University of Houston Digital History. Available at http://www.digitalhistory.uh.edu/asian_voices/voices_display.cfm?id=29.

Twain, Mark. "Goldsmith's Friend Abroad Again, Letter 7." 1871. In *The Heath Anthology of American Literature,* vol. 2, edited by Paul Lauter et al., 4th ed. Boston: Houghton Mifflin, 2002.

Twain, Mark. "John Chinaman in New York." 1870. In *Collected Tales, Sketches, Speeches, and Essays: Mark Twain.* New York: Library of America, 1992.

Twain, Mark. *Mark Twain: "The Innocents Abroad," "Roughing It."* 1872. New York: Library of America, 1984.

Secondary Works

Andrew, Gyory. *Closing the Gate: Race, Politics, and the Chinese Exclusion Act.* Chapel Hill: University of North Carolina Press, 1998.

Chan, Sucheng, ed. *Entry Denied: Exclusion and the Chinese Community in America, 1882–*. Philadelphia: Temple University Press, 1991.

Hom, Marlon K. *Songs of Gold Mountain: Cantonese Rhymes from San Francisco Chinatown.* Los Angeles: University of California Press, 1992.

Hyung-Chan, Kim, ed. *Asian-Americans and the Supreme Court: A Documentary History.* Westport, Conn.: Greenwood, 1992.

Lee, Josephine. *Performing Asian America: Race and Ethnicity on the Contemporary Stage.* Philadelphia: Temple University Press, 1997.

Lee, Josephine, Imogene L. Lim, and Yuko Matsukawa, eds. *Re/collecting Early Asian America: Essays in Cultural History.* Philadelphia: Temple University Press, 2002.

Moy, James. *Marginal Sights: Staging the Chinese in America.* Iowa City: University of Iowa Press, 1993.

Salyer, Lucy E. *Laws Harsh as Tigers: Chinese Immigrants and the Shaping of Modern Immigration Law.* Chapel Hill: University of North Carolina Press, 1995.

Sandmeyer, Elmer Clarence. *The Anti-Chinese Movement in California.* Urbana: University of Illinois Press, 1991.

Takaki, Ronald. *Strangers from a Different Shore: A History of Asian Americans.* Boston: Little, Brown, 1989.

Wong, K. Scott, and Sucheng Chan, eds. *Claiming America: Constructing Chinese American Identities during the Exclusion Era.* Philadelphia: Temple University Press, 1998.

Yung, Judy. *Unbound Feet: A Social History of Chinese Women in San Francisco.* Berkeley: University of California Press, 1995.

Elizabeth Archuleta

CHRISTIANITY

As social, economic, and intellectual changes occurred in the United States from 1870 to 1920, reactions from religious communities ranged from those who welcomed and embraced the changes to those who saw in those same changes dire threats not only to religion but to the nation's future as well. The fracturing of denominations within Protestantism and a profound diversification of Roman Catholicism and non-Christian religions further complicated the spiritual landscape. The diminution of the place and prestige of religion in society, as Henry Steele Commager has noted, amounted to one of the essential differences between the nineteenth- and twentieth-century mind-sets.

The nation's effort to recover from the Civil War experience marked the beginning of this transition. Denominations divided during the struggle between the North and the South (principally Baptists, Methodists, and Presbyterians) considered how and even whether they should reunite after the war. Congregations and denominations of black worshippers emerged to provide leaders and direction for their people. Newly arriving immigrants brought with them sometimes quite different religious practices and beliefs. Revivalism became a prominent, if stereotyped, outlet for periodic religious fervor. Earnest desires to improve literacy yielded an impulse not only for public education but also for the establishment of Sunday schools. The rapid expansion of the Roman Catholic population gave clerics stronger voices while also presenting problems of diversity, sometimes addressed by founding parochial schools. It was a time of opportunity but also a time when the culture's values and beliefs were challenged on almost every level. That challenge could only be fully addressed by a broad-based reconsideration of the religious paradigm.

FOUR FORCES

Typically, historians of the period from 1870 to 1920 identify at least four forces shaping intellectual and religious life: industrialization-urbanization, immigration, Darwinism, and European thought, particularly biblical criticism. The political, social, and economic manifestations of these forces can be elaborated in the stories of burgeoning cities and factories, semicompetent presidents, corrupt politicians, populism, progressivism, nativism, trade unionism, and three wars (the Indian wars, the Spanish-American War, and World War I). As a result, the nation looked quite different in 1920 than it had in 1870. It was an urban nation, one of the most powerful in the world, and had shed its "innocence."

In the fifty years between 1870 and 1920, dozens of cities in the United States tripled, quadrupled, and even quintupled in population. Individuals and families from rural communities and immigrants from abroad flooded into towns, transforming them into cities teeming with diverse peoples. They pursued fabled opportunities to prosper in the emerging industrial economy. Relocation often entailed a bitter adjustment not only to the physical environment but also to the emotional landscape of the cities. For one familiar with patterns of rural life, being surrounded by cluttered buildings and incessant noise alienated the individual from "nature's" God and God's nature. The sermons of a country parson or parish priest, reflecting on the wonders of creation evident in a field of hay or on the truths of many parables rooted in agrarian lifestyles, seemed irrelevant amid the jostle of urban survival. Village churches gave way to storefronts, and uniform congregations became confusing conglomerates.

At least among many Protestant churches, a well-chronicled "work ethic" seemed to predispose members to active participation in the Industrial Revolution. On closer examination, however, many of the values of industrialization contradicted traditional teachings of Protestantism. Martin Luther and John Calvin had indeed opened the door to the possibility that all vocations might be considered sacred. They, however, operated primarily in a commercial agricultural context. Industrialization, as it developed in Europe well after the Protestant Reformation and eventually exploded in the United States after the Civil War, encouraged and rewarded unbridled competition, emphasized profit, and exploited labor as a means to a capitalist end. Religious leaders who spoke against the abusive nature and contrary values of the new economy sometimes found themselves challenged either to moderate their positions or to reinterpret scripture in light of the realities of modern life. Catholics could take some solace from the position of Pope Leo XIII in *Rerum Novarum* that soundly defended private property as well as the rights of labor to organize and agitate for social change.

A new wave of immigration added to the growth of the cities. Between 1865 and 1920, 25 million immigrants poured through the gates of opportunity into American society, increasing the population by 80 percent. The unplanned increase in demands for housing, basic services, and jobs both taxed the social resources of American cities and provided a cheap labor pool for industry. This new period of immigration brought people from eastern and southern Europe and from Asia rather than from western and northern Europe. The new immigrants were Roman Catholic and Orthodox Christians, Jews, Muslims, and Buddhists rather than Protestant Christians. As they settled into neighborhoods in large cities or secluded themselves in the countryside, many of the immigrants struggled to maintain homeland traditions while adjusting to the demands of their new environments. The new immigrants formed parochial school systems, settled in strictly defined neighborhoods, built their own churches, synagogues, mosques, or temples, and sometimes identified with a single segment of the economy. The paradox of engagement and isolation often created tension with people who

touted longer histories in the United States. A vigorous nativist movement reemerged in the country, questioning the desirability of so much immigration and intimating dire consequences from the unchecked mixing of diverse populations. Henry Adams brooded over the decline of America in his autobiography, *The Education of Henry Adams* (1918), while Jacob Riis in *The Making of an American* (1901) and Mary Antin in *The Promised Land* (1912) chronicled the triumph of their Americanization.

The dark foreboding that centered on immigration came not only from workers being displaced by cheaper laborers but also from a variation of Darwinian thought. First, the formal works of Charles Darwin were debated in the universities, and then religious leaders began to tease out the theological implications. Some rejected the theory of evolution. For example, Charles Hodge, Princeton Seminary professor and leading conservative theologian, labeled Darwinism "atheism" in a famous 1874 publication. Others embraced evolution; James McCosh, president of Princeton University, found no incongruities between faith in a God with unlimited creative capacity and the mechanisms, even evolution, through which that creativity might be manifested. Eventually, the use of the theory of natural selection took an ominous turn when Herbert Spencer, William Graham Sumner (an ordained minister as well as a sociologist), and later Francis Galton argued that public social policy should be shaped by assumptions about "survival of the fittest" and the elimination of "defective" gene strains from the human pool.

The impulse to examine critically the sacred texts, generally labeled "higher biblical criticism," spread across the Atlantic primarily from German universities and English scholars. Appropriation of techniques from linguistics, history, anthropology, and archaeology to the examination of the text, rather than relying on church doctrine and a literal reading, challenged standard interpretations of authorship, meaning, and application of Christian scriptures. Generally labeled as an element of liberal Protestantism, higher biblical criticism served the interests of those searching to understand the context of the ancient writings as well as to extend their application to the modern environment.

Many other historical factors, such as westward expansion, entailing conflict with Native American peoples and spirituality, influenced the course of religious thought and behavior in the late nineteenth century and early twentieth century. None, however, carried the weight of the four noted above. Similarly, these four points of social cleavage—industrialization-urbanization, immigration, Darwinism, and European thought, especially biblical criticism—formed the most significant framework for a consideration of literature with religious themes. On many levels, the culture felt its religious moorings slipped by the necessity to reject or accommodate new ideas and practices. Oliver Wendell Holmes Jr. may have expressed the thoughts of thousands when, while convalescing from Civil War wounds, he concluded that he was done with religion and would henceforth seek meaning and comfort in other sources of belief. Many of the intellectual elites of his generation no longer felt obliged to acknowledge theological or doctrinal roots of their thoughts and theories. The experiences of war, followed by the assassination of Abraham Lincoln and the chaos of Reconstruction, were dark clouds at the dawning of a new era. Gradually and in diverse ways, literary figures, politicians, artists, and ministers responded to the challenges.

REJECTIONS OF "MODERN" LIFE

The nation struggled with the implications of building a modern society. Whether due to the failure of "cultural authority" or as the culmination of a "crisis of belief and values," social critics rejected what they considered the negative implications of modern life. Some turned away from the rigors of modern life and encouraged a resurgence of Romantic ideals. The comforts and conveniences of the modern age eroded sensitivity to sin and induced an "abandonment of moral responsibility," they argued (Lears, p. 300). The postwar "Holiness movement" encouraged its followers to adopt traditional dress, behavior, and thought in order to resist corruption by modern ways. At the other extreme in the rejection of modernity lay an effort to meet head-on the forces that threatened to pull the nation along the path of modernity. Reform movements motivated by an effort to prevent the abuses of industrialization resulted. Henry Adams (1838–1918) and William Dean Howells (1837–1920) were representatives of these branches of antimodernism. Adams's "religious quest," prompted by the deaths of his wife and sister, was a metaphor for the quest many experienced after the cultural death experience of the Civil War. Inspired by religious architecture such as the abbey of Mont-Saint-Michel and the Cathedral of Notre Dame of Chartres, Adams wrote that the modern scene lacked an ability to conceive of and execute such monuments to God and to beauty. His critique of contemporary America embraced the old virtues and beliefs and mourned their degradation. In a letter to a friend, Adams lamented: "Hell is all there was to make life worth living. Since it was abolished, there is no standard of value" (p. 285).

A variation of Adams's Victorian antimodernism may be found in the work of William Dean Howells. Howells's novels and public expressions displayed the confrontation with each of the threatening forces evident on the late-nineteenth-century scene, including capitalist individualism, Social Darwinism, and scientific positivism. In *The Leatherwood God* (1916) and *The Undiscovered Country* (1880), he examined the flaws of hyperemotional spirituality and the threat of spiritual manipulation. Howells saw not only rampant industrialization but also the quasi-scientific efforts of the Progressive Era reforms as elements of social policy that threatened to overturn the virtues of collective identity. In one historian's analysis, Howells came to "espouse Marxian socialism" but one that was firmly rooted in Christianity (Parrington 2:245). In *The Rise of Silas Lapham* (1884) and *A Hazard of New Fortunes* (1890), Howells examined the personal and spiritual costs of participation in the aggressive capitalist order. *Through the Eye of the Needle* (1907) even more pointedly infused Howells's critique of modern culture while offering his utopian solution. *A New Moral World* (1885) by James Casey, *Garden of Eden, U.S.A.* (1895) by W. H. Bishop, and *Paradise on Earth* (1913) by Jeff Hayes—all promoted optimistic visions of social change predicated on goodwill and cooperation, whereas Abraham Cahan's *The Rise of David Levinsky* (1917) presented a dark picture of Jewish assimilation.

LIBERAL PROTESTANTISM

Howells recognized the need for a religious response to modernity that used arguments and ideas not entirely dredged up from the past. He supported an approach known as "liberal Protestantism," headed by Lyman Abbott and Henry Ward Beecher, which argued that biblical higher criticism and Darwinian thought, rather than contradicting Christian belief, provided deeper understandings of the marvels of God's creative ability. In addition, it confronted the doctrines of original sin and eternal punishment as faulty readings of the text. Ministers such as Charles Sheldon, William Ware, and E. P. Roe produced novels that placed moral messages in a nineteenth- and twentieth-century American context. Sheldon (1867–1928) used the simple question "What would Jesus do?" (again in vogue in the early twenty-first century) to suggest that the truths of the New Testament could be appropriated for an ethic in modern times. Sheldon introduced the question in *In His Steps* (1898). Edward Bellamy's (1850–1898) *Looking Backward* (1888) advanced his hero into the future in order to comment on the state of contemporary society. Bellamy's utopia was a profoundly Christian critique of his own age, encouraging a revival of faith in order to redeem all of society. Similarly, Howells's *A Traveler from Altruria* (1894) cast his version of a utopia based on true Christian principles. On another track, Abbott and others argued for a kind of "Christian evolution," whereby believers might become more and more perfect through the practice of Christ-like behavior. Washington Gladden's *Who Wrote the Bible?* (1891) contributed to what came to be called the "New Theology" school that welcomed biblical criticism and comparative religion as tools to deepen spiritual sensitivities. Liberal Protestantism also opened the door for even more unorthodox expressions. Francis Ellingwood Abbot drafted "Fifty Affirmations" for the Free Religious Association. Its essence promoted a universal affiliation of believers, without the need for denominations, creeds, or specific views of divinity. The association eventually merged with the much older Unitarian Fellowship. Felix Adler founded the Society for Ethical Culture, and Mary Baker Eddy established the Christian Science Church.

Industrialists such as Andrew Carnegie and John D. Rockefeller provided still other options for reconciliation with modern life. Carnegie defended the accumulation of wealth as a worthy goal in life by touting a "Gospel of Wealth" based on the "sacred" principles of free enterprise. He argued, and demonstrated in his own life, that the duty of the rich was to spend their money on projects improving society. As far as he was concerned, "the man who dies rich dies disgraced" (Mathisen, p. 216). John D. Rockefeller taught Sunday school nearly all his life, helped found the University of Chicago as a Baptist institution (but which later originated the New Theology), and funded an inquiry into the effectiveness of missions that became a model for many organizations. Carnegie, Rockefeller, and others thus testified to a link between the industrial elite and the religious ethos of the nation. Certainly the novels of the Unitarian-educated Horatio Alger elevated the image of the decent young man achieving respectability by the exercise of good character. Even more popular was the minister Russell Conwell's "sermon," *Acres of Diamonds,* in which he defended the accumulation of wealth as a natural process and the rich as models of character.

CYNICISM AND PRAGMATISM

On the opposite end of the spectrum from liberal Protestantism lay a pervasive cynicism regarding religious practice and its positive influences on culture. When Beecher became embroiled in a sensational morals trial (he was accused of having an illicit affair with one of his parishioners), caustic commentators

intimated that a "modern" view of the doctrine of eternal punishment had produced the "loosening" of standards of behavior. Mark Twain (1835–1910) employed religious themes and subjects in many of his works and consistently challenged hypocrisy and intolerance. To him, the standard beliefs and practices of American Christianity defied logic and smelled of pomposity. In a series of articles in the *North American Review* (1902–1903), Clemens ridiculed the Christian Science Church. Especially in *The Diary of Adam and Eve* and *Letters from the Earth,* Clemens revealed that he knew a great deal about the Bible but also that a serious subject could be handled well with humor. Going one step further, Robert Ingersoll (1833–1899) came to be known as "the notorious infidel" for his aggressive promotion of atheism. Ingersoll traveled the country debating ministers, giving public lectures, and challenging the religious elite to think beyond their prescribed boundaries.

William James (1842–1910), a leading figure in the development of pragmatism, posed still another set of responses to the forces confronting religion at the end of the nineteenth century. James's work, especially his landmark *The Varieties of Religious Experience* (1902), focused not only on the psychological dimensions of belief but also on the social impact of expressed faith. He argued that pragmatism offered a reorientation of the focus of religious life, resembling the Protestant Reformation and on the same order as the campaign against established churches and toward voluntary associations that had begun at the time of the American Revolution. Furthermore, as a "theistic evolutionist," he found much to admire in evolutionary theory, especially as it might apply to the social sphere. James saw nothing incongruent between his Protestantism and a deterministic description of society. But his admiration of religion was limited to his particular brand. James discounted Catholic contributions and bordered on anti-Semitism.

THEOLOGY

A theological analysis of the religious trends of the period reveals a decidedly mixed bag. Within its boundaries, arguments for a "social" gospel, fundamentalism, and even atheism made their cases. In the process, public figures and private citizens struggled to discern their own paths and the purpose of their religious institutions. Perhaps the most compelling evidence of this struggle appeared in Harold Frederic's *The Damnation of Theron Ware* (1896). The novel serves as an object lesson for understanding the personal toll of the theological battles raging as a simple upstate New York minister struggles to understand

and to contend with the modern world. Ware steps into the fray when he decides to write a book. In collecting materials, he finds his long-accepted religious beliefs challenged, and he moves inexorably toward doubt. Exposure to biblical criticism, comparative religions, and scientific rationalism leads to risky behaviors and nearly personal disaster. The message is that one option for addressing the modern world is to embrace it, but at great personal hazard. This message, embedded within a popular novel, demonstrated that the popular press had become the chief agent for engaging rather sophisticated religious debate and was much more persuasive in informing the masses than the traditional pulpit.

Though the Social Gospel movement did not entail a highly developed theology, it nonetheless posed theological arguments that deserve attention. Not content to await God's judgment of society nor to condemn "the world" in a detached manner, Social Gospelers sought ways to enlist liberal Protestantism in political, social, and economic battles. Primarily through the work of Washington Gladden, George Herron, W. D. P. Bliss, and Walter Rauschenbusch (1861–1918), the Social Gospel centered on providing social services through urban churches. Criticized for its thin emphasis on sin and salvation, the movement replied, in effect, that it was difficult to hear the Gospel message when one's stomach was growling. The Social Gospel movement supported reform measures designed to improve housing, food distribution, medical services, and general living conditions of the urban poor, often invoking the Golden Rule as their justification. Social Gospelers were often associated with worker organizations, publicizing their plight and motivating church support. Rauschenbusch's *A Theology for the Social Gospel* (1917) attempted to capture both the need for and the justification of an ecumenical approach to social ills. Gone was the antebellum confidence that reform might happen one person at a time. The church, social agencies, and even government itself must be organized and focused on the amelioration of misery and injustice.

One final theological impulse emerged around the resistance to biblical criticism and Darwinian evolution. When some seminaries and ministers tried to incorporate elements of these new views into the curriculum or sermons, cries of heresy arose and several trials ensued. Methodist, Lutheran, and Presbyterian seminaries, and several ministers, stood trial for their expressions of unorthodox belief, particularly on the inerrancy of Scripture and the literal reading of the stories contained therein. "Holiness" movements in the late nineteenth century emphasized personal purity through adherence to a strict behavioral code

and a conservative view of Scripture. Ostensibly rooted in Methodism and tied to antebellum "perfectionism," the postwar movements attracted rural followers who intuitively believed that the challenges to biblical authority sprang not from scholarship but from a spiritual crisis. D. L. Moody (1837–1899) championed the more urban wing of the revivals that invariably accompanied the expression of spiritual angst. Moody skillfully combined marketing techniques usually used to promote consumer goods with traditional messages of sin and salvation to forge an international revival organization. Edward Eggleston in *The Faith Doctor* (1891) subjected "faith healers" to ridicule for their hyperemotionalism.

FUNDAMENTALISM

Moody stood in the gap between the holiness groups attempting to address the evils of society by providing a positive alternative and the more Calvinistic rejection of society as a whole. Late in the nineteenth century, pastors and denominational leaders began to form discussion groups and Bible schools to explore the implications of the "dispensationalist" writings of J. N. Darby (1800–1882). At first loosely organized, "fundamentalism" took center stage in the spiritual wars brewing in the late nineteenth century and early twentieth century. Drawing on fears within society, the fundamentalists spotlighted the most obvious religious threats of the day. No one was more visible in this struggle than Billy Sunday (1862–1935), the man who, one historian contends, "stands at the center of the cultural confusion of the years 1890–1920" (McLoughlin, p. 146). Capitalizing on his popularity as a professional baseball player, Sunday crafted an influential series of campaigns as a traveling evangelist. His message was traditional though his methods matched those of the finest marketing firms of the day. Sunday was a consummate entertainer, playing on the emotions and sentiments of his audience. He preached against the evils of the day (including the liberal Protestants) and of the necessity to "hit the sawdust trail" (many of his revivals were held in large tents with aisles covered in sawdust). Sunday focused his social reform enthusiasm on Prohibition and "cleaning up" the cities in which his revivals took place.

Sunday's popularity illustrated the swing in theological temperament and general religious sentiment. Antebellum America's optimism, expressed in reform impulses and exuberant expansion, rested on an anticipation of the literal return of Christ to the earth, known as postmillennialism. In this view, society's improvement was a precursor to the fulfillment of prophecies regarding the Messiah. After the Civil War the Seventh-Day Adventist Church and the Witnesses (later Jehovah's Witnesses) built significant followings based on their message anticipating the imminent return of Christ to the earth. The Witnesses went so far as to target 1914, ironically the year of the beginning of the Great War, as the time when the Kingdom of God would be fully established. Premillennialism, the expectation that a time of trials and testing of the faithful would precede the Second Coming, became the more compelling popular view following the culturally devastating effects of the Civil War and in light of the nation's declining moral character into the twentieth century. Woven together with dispensationalism from England and enlivened by revivals such as Sunday's—particularly the Pentecostal Azusa Street revival of 1906—fundamentalism both reflected and fed popular apprehensions about society. Pentecostalism eventually yielded to the pressures for greater organization, gathering together in the Church of God in Christ, the Church of God (Cleveland, Tennessee), the Assemblies of God, and the Foursquare Church.

THE END OF AMERICAN "INNOCENCE"

It is fitting to end with a comment about Henry James (1843–1916), brother of the psychologist and pragmatist William James. Henry James reflected the double-mindedness of Americans about their newfound state of being. At once proud and insecure, the characters in his novels fumbled into the modern world expectantly and afraid, just as the nation did in reality. In the midst of the paradox of renunciation and confident engagement, the period immediately after the Great War witnessed what Henry May called the "end of American innocence." By that turn of phrase May meant that America came fully to grips with the implications of the period of industrialization, urbanization, immigration, expansion, education, philosophy, and intellectual challenges. One segment of society, the liberal Protestants in the case of religion, adopted the values of efficiency and professionalism and applied them across the board. Another segment—the fundamentalists, holiness advocates, antimoderns, and cynics—found ways of resisting and subverting the forces of modernity. With new technologies allowing wider distribution of their works, literary figures described and elaborated on Americans' attempts to maintain their moral and spiritual footing.

See also The Bible; Catholics; *Christianity and the Social Crisis;* Christian Science; *The Damnation of Theron Ware;* Jews; Mormons

BIBLIOGRAPHY
Primary Work
Adams, Henry. Henry Adams to Elizabeth Cameron, 16 April 1900. In *Letters of Henry Adams,* 3 vols., edited by Worthington Chauncey Ford, 2:285. Boston: Houghton, Mifflin, 1930–1938.

Secondary Works
Baetzhold, Howard G., and Joseph B. McCullough, eds. *The Bible according to Mark Twain: Writings on Heaven, Eden, and the Flood.* Athens: University of Georgia Press, 1995.

Carter, Paul A. *The Spiritual Crisis of the Gilded Age.* DeKalb: University of Northern Illinois Press, 1971.

Davies, W. E. "Religious Issues in Late Nineteenth-Century Novels." *Bulletin of the John Rylands Library* (Manchester) 41 (1958–1959): 328–359.

Engeman, Thomas S. "Religion and Politics the American Way: The Exemplary William Dean Howells." *Review of Politics* 63, no. 1 (2001): 107–128.

Handy, Robert T., ed. *The Social Gospel in America, 1870–1920.* New York: Oxford University Press, 1966.

Henderson, Harry B., III. *Versions of the Past: The Historical Imagination in American Fiction.* New York: Oxford University Press, 1974.

Hutner, Gordon. *American Literature, American Culture.* New York: Oxford University Press, 1999.

Kazin, Alfred. *God and the American Writer.* New York: Knopf, 1997.

Lears, T. J. Jackson. *No Place of Grace: Antimodernism and the Transformation of American Culture, 1880–1920.* New York: Pantheon Books, 1981.

McLoughlin, William G. *Revivals, Awakenings, and Reform: An Essay of Religion and Social Change in America, 1607–1977.* Chicago: University of Chicago Press, 1978.

Marsden, George. *Fundamentalism and American Culture: The Shaping of Twentieth-Century Evangelicalism, 1870–1925.* New York: Oxford University Press, 1980.

Martin, Jay. *Harvests of Change: American Literature, 1865–1914.* Englewood Cliffs, N.J.: Prentice Hall, 1967.

Mathisen, Robert R., ed. *The Role of Religion in American Life.* Washington, D.C.: University Press of America, 1982.

May, Henry F. *The End of American Innocence: A Study of the First Years of Our Time, 1912–1917.* New York: Knopf, 1959.

O'Connor, Leo F. *Religion in the American Novel: The Search for Belief, 1860–1920.* Lanham, Md.: University Press of America, 1984.

Parrington, Vernon Louis. *Main Currents in American Thought: An Interpretation of American Literature from the Beginnings to 1920.* 3 vols. New York: Harcourt, Brace, 1927–1930.

Reynolds, David S. *Faith in Fiction: The Emergence of Religious Literature in America.* Cambridge, Mass.: Harvard University Press, 1981.

Reynolds, David S. "Shifting Interpretations of American Protestantism, 1870–1900." *Journal of Popular Culture* 9 (winter 1975): 593–603.

Cole P. Dawson

CHRISTIANITY AND THE SOCIAL CRISIS

Christianity and the Social Crisis (1907) appealed to American Protestants at a time when men and women of conscience were struggling to understand their Christian responsibilities; rapid industrial development had created both unprecedented wealth and unimaginable poverty and had made paupers and petty criminals of hard-working people. Its author, Walter Rauschenbusch (1861–1918), a Baptist theologian and church historian, was not the first churchman to propose a Christian response to the social upheavals of the late nineteenth century. Josiah Strong published *The New Era* in 1893, the same year as George Davis Herron's *The New Redemption,* and Washington Gladden's *Social Salvation* appeared in 1902. All spoke of the need to conceive of salvation in social rather than individual terms. Their writings and organizations formed the kernel of what would be known as the Social Gospel at the turn of the twentieth century. But *Christianity and the Social Crisis* offered the most compelling historical analysis, locating the essence of Christian teaching in community and linking the prophets of the Old Testament to the teachings of Jesus of Nazareth. Rauschenbusch insisted that responding to the social crises of industrialism would restore true Christianity, which, over the centuries, had been hampered by institutional concerns, ascetic suspicion of the wider world, and a false confidence in personal piety that blinded Christians to the needs of others.

The originality and force of Rauschenbusch's analysis lay in his ability to draw out the lives and history of early Christians from New Testament sources. Instead of plucking quotable passages out of context, Rauschenbusch used the Gospels and Epistles to present modern readers with a picture of how the early followers of Jesus had sought to live according to his principles. One example after another demonstrated their commitment to communal care, to meeting the needs of fellow seekers without demanding complete equality of material condition. That history, he argued, provided a powerful lesson for modern Christians. Neither retreating from modern industrial life nor calling for a radical Christian communism, Rauschenbusch invited readers simply to respond to the needs of others with love, compassion, generosity, and faith—to live in community as Jesus had taught.

Although Rauschenbusch was a learned and meticulous scholar, he adopted a plain style of writing and made *Christianity and the Social Crisis* both accessible and compelling to a nonscholarly audience. He employed earthy analogies to appeal to readers, suggesting, for example, that a nation's wealth was like manure on a farm. "If the farmer spreads it evenly over the soil, it will enrich the whole. If he should leave it in heaps, the land would be impoverished and under the rich heaps the vegetation would be killed" (p. 281). Similarly, he relied on his gift as a storyteller to narrate New Testament episodes in ways that made Jesus, his disciples, his audiences, and his message come alive to the modern reader. Thus, Jesus' call for human brotherhood was no mere bromide but a message that spoke to a world divided between Jews and Gentiles and that reminded Christians that their Hebrew ancestors had relied on and attended to the needs of Gentiles. For example, Elijah had found refuge in the home of a Phoenician, and Elisha had healed a Syrian leper. With his simple, direct prose and informed historical perspective, Rauschenbusch inspired a generation of American Protestants, who in turn coalesced around the Social Gospel reform agenda.

THE HEYDAY OF THE SOCIAL GOSPEL

Shortly after *Christianity and the Social Crisis* appeared in print, Rauschenbusch left the United States for a year of study abroad. When he returned, he was both stunned and gratified to learn that the book had enjoyed a wide readership and had exerted a great influence. Readers inspired by his work looked to him for guidance in implementing his ideas. In the early years of the twentieth century, Americans could not escape the widespread problems arising from industrialism, urban growth, and profound social tensions. Upton Sinclair's *The Jungle* (1906) exposed the social evils that accompanied large-scale food processing, which exploited immigrant workers and resulted in contaminated products. Lincoln Steffens exposed the political corruption that prevailed in many municipalities, calling it "the shame of the cities." Novelists such as Hamlin Garland, Frank Norris, and Elizabeth Stuart Phelps and journalists such as Stephen Crane and Ray

Stannard Baker described in vivid detail the travails of farmers and wageworkers as they toiled without relief yet sank deeper into debt and despair. Labor uprisings in the 1890s, followed by violent suppression, threatened to embroil the nation in class warfare. The depression of 1893 and the panic of 1907, set off by plummeting stock market prices, made it all too clear that market forces and capitalist speculation could ruin anyone—even those in the professional middle class. In addition, the social makeup of the nation included people who spoke languages other than English, wore clothing that reflected foreign traditions, and seemed utterly alien, which made them objects of fear, prejudice, and violence. Moreover, since the end of the Civil War, African Americans had become part of the nation's citizenry, but the Thirteenth, Fourteenth, and Fifteenth Amendments to the Constitution did little to protect them from lynching, disfranchisement, dispossession, poverty, and discrimination. After reading *Christianity and the Social Crisis,* many American Protestants—laypersons and clergy alike—recognized their obligations as Christians to scale this mountain of social ills. They turned to Rauschenbusch and others to find out specifically what to do.

In the years between Rauschenbusch's first book and his second, *Christianizing the Social Order* (1912), a flood of new reform initiatives swept the nation. The Social Gospel movement was rooted in late-nineteenth-century efforts, such as the rise of "institutional churches," which catered to material as well as spiritual needs seven days a week. It also had its roots in the efforts of Charles Stelzle, wageworker turned Presbyterian minister, to reach workers in noontime services and in spontaneous local efforts to supply food, clothing, fuel, and shelter to families hit hardest by the depressed conditions of the 1890s. The early-twentieth-century movement spawned more systematic efforts to combat the social crisis. Rauschenbusch's clarion call had arisen from his experience as a pastor in New York City's "Hell's Kitchen," where in the 1880s he had personally ministered to the suffering of working people struggling with poverty, disease, and squalor, which he attributed to low wages and overcrowded conditions. By the time he wrote *Christianizing the Social Order,* Rauschenbusch could point to the social interests of the Religious Education Association (established in 1903), the founding of the Presbyterians' Labor Temple in New York City (1910), and the Men and Religion Forward Movement (1911–1912) as examples of the concerted efforts he had earlier imagined necessary for those who sought to live in the modern age according to Christian principles.

In 1908 delegates to the Federal Council of Churches, representing more than seventeen million American Protestants, endorsed the Social Creed of the Churches, committing themselves to support labor unions, protective legislation, and active involvement in social amelioration. Over the next few years, Protestants under the sway of the Social Gospel collaborated with reform-oriented governments to push for state intervention on behalf of workers, immigrants, rural communities, and families whose lives had been irrevocably altered by factory labor, urban existence, and the pervasive impact of market exchange. Some members of the clergy ran for public office, hoping to bring Christian principles to city hall or the statehouse. Others served as arbitrators in labor disputes. Settlement houses and institutional churches expanded their programs to help working-class families bridge the gap between low wages and the high cost of living. They provided free or inexpensive meals and wholesome family entertainment, classes in industrial training and domestic science to improve the life chances of young people, and visiting nurses and day care centers. Some initiatives—notably, the Men and Religion Forward Movement and the Social Service agencies of the Methodist Church—targeted black communities but unfortunately failed to bring an end to violence and discrimination against African Americans. Nevertheless, social activism generated by *Christianity and the Social Crisis* contributed significantly to the flowering of the age of social reform known as the Progressive Era. Social Gospelers sought government regulation to introduce a measure of justice into modern social relations.

LEGACY

The world war that began in 1914 dampened enthusiasm for the Social Gospel, but it did not extinguish the movement. Rauschenbusch, deeply troubled by the advent of war, which pitted loved ones in the United States and Germany against one another, did not survive the conflict. Many Social Gospel programs adopted a business orientation in the 1920s and beyond, making use of advertising, mass media, and celebrities to appeal to Christians and measuring success in terms of social efficiency. In the Great Depression of the 1930s and during World War II, the Social Gospel faced stiff criticism because of its purported unrealistic optimism and its underestimation of humankind's capacity for evil. But *Christianity and the Social Crisis* found new life after the war in the work of Martin Luther King Jr., who credited it with shaping his Christian message in the African American struggle for civil rights.

See also Christianity

BIBLIOGRAPHY

Primary Works

Rauschenbusch, Walter. *Christianity and the Social Crisis.* New York: Macmillan, 1907.

Rauschenbusch, Walter. *Christianizing the Social Order.* New York: Macmillan, 1912.

Secondary Works

Crunden, Robert M. *Ministers of Reform: The Progressives' Achievement in American Civilization, 1889–1920.* New York: Basic Books, 1982.

Curtis, Susan. *A Consuming Faith: The Social Gospel and Modern American Culture.* Columbia: University of Missouri Press, 2001.

Evans, Christopher H. *The Kingdom Is Always But Coming: A Life of Walter Rauschenbusch.* Grand Rapids, Mich.: Eerdmans, 2004.

Evans, Christopher H., ed. *Perspectives on the Social Gospel.* Lewiston, N.Y.: Edwin Mellen, 1999.

Gorrell, Donald K. *The Age of Social Responsibility: The Social Gospel in the Progressive Era, 1900–1920.* Macon, Ga.: Mercer University Press, 1988.

White, Ronald C., Jr., and C. Howard Hopkins, eds. *The Social Gospel: Religion and Reform in Changing America.* Philadelphia: Temple University Press, 1976.

Susan Curtis

CHRISTIAN SCIENCE

In the late 1860s Mary Baker Eddy (1821–1910) founded a movement that became a new religion—Christian Science. Drawing on secular practices of mesmerism and mental healing, Eddy organized a church based on the actions of Jesus Christ. For example, Christian Scientists emphasize biblical passages such as Matthew 10:1, which proclaims that Jesus gave his disciples "authority over unclean spirits, to cast them out, and to heal every disease and every infirmity." Christian Science unites medicine and religion in a practice of healing as an act of belief. As the new religion evolved, Scientists came to believe that they could bring Christianity to its final stage, in which Eddy would figure as divine mother, successor to Christ. Christian Science grew in both membership and influence through Reconstruction and the Progressive Era. The church has endured into the twenty-first century and, with Mormonism, is one of the two most influential religions founded in the United States in the nineteenth century.

Christian Science reflects the popularized idealism of the nineteenth century. Essential to its faith is the understanding that illness results from error. Material reality is mere appearance, arising from sinful thought and condition. The body is illusion and there is no death. The erroneous claims of illness should thus be met, to use the terminology of Christian Science, by demonstrations of faith through prayer. While Christian faith healing has been practiced for many centuries, Eddy made the case for a new revelation and built a powerful medico-religious organization on her assertion.

BIOGRAPHY IN CULTURAL CONTEXT

Throughout her life Eddy displayed symptoms that doctors in the nineteenth century would have diagnosed as hysteria or neurasthenia—nervous disorders that disrupted sleep and digestion and that caused prostration and tantrums. Even as an adult, Eddy had to be carried to bed and rocked to sleep. As Willa Cather (1873–1947) documents in *The Life of Mary Baker G. Eddy and the History of Christian Science* (1909), a collection of articles that Cather ghostwrote for a journalist from Rochester, New York, named Georgine Milmine, disruption was a constant feature of Eddy's life. Eddy tried many of the nineteenth-century's popular therapeutic practices: phrenology, spiritualism, mesmerism, Sylvester Graham's diet, homeopathy, and hydropathy. She became a patient and student of the influential mental healer Phineas Parkhurst Quimby (1802–1866) and worked often with his manuscripts. Quimby understood mental healing to be a science and, in his writings, connected the practice to Christianity. In 1866, shortly after Quimby's death, Eddy injured herself by falling on an icy sidewalk in Lynn, Massachusetts. For comfort she read the Bible and discovered that she felt better. She later claimed the experience as a miracle. The moment was also fortunately timed. Eddy's second husband, Daniel Patterson, soon deserted her, and she needed to earn a living. Later, when she was accused of plagiarizing from Quimby, Eddy insisted on her moment of revelation. By 1870 she had written *The Science of Man, by Which the Sick Are Healed; or, Questions and Answers in Moral Science* and had developed a business: she trained students to be religious healers, charging them for their instruction and also claiming a percentage of their earnings.

The religion, its church, and the business of education and publishing grew rapidly. Brilliant in business, Eddy understood management, public relations, and legal strategy. The enterprise of Christian Science enjoyed visible success in a period of financial empire building; Eddy became a prominent and controversial self-made woman. As her organization grew, Eddy controlled it through a highly centralized

DEMONSTRATIONS OF FAITH

The following letter from October 1887 was selected by Cather as one of the "demonstrations" reported in the Journal of Christian Science. *The account raises the question of the dog's consciousness, implying that the dog imagined the snakebite. The notice also describes what Christian Scientists would call a right use of faith, the opposite of malicious animal magnetism or mesmerism.*

Dog and Rattlesnake

DEAR JOURNAL: Our dog was bitten by a rattlesnake on the tongue a short time ago, and the verdict, as is usual in such cases, was death; but through the understanding of God's promise that we shall handle serpents and not be harmed, if we but believe, I was able to demonstrate over the belief in four days. The dog is now as well as ever.

MRS. M. E. DARNELL

Cather and Milmine, *The Life of Mary Baker G. Eddy and the History of Christian Science,* p. 320.

command structure, with particular attention paid to the language of church communications, the education and certification of healers, and the management of information.

Successful as she was, to the end of her life Eddy was obsessed by the threat of mesmerism. If one could heal through prayer, one could also torment. In *Science and Health, with Key to the Scriptures* (1875), the primary text of Christian Science, a chapter entitled "Animal Magnetism Unmasked" explains the distinction: "Christian Science goes to the bottom of mental action, and reveals the theodicy which indicates the rightness of all divine action, as the emanation of divine Mind, and the consequent wrongness of the opposite so-called action, —evil, occultism, necromancy, mesmerism, animal magnetism, hypnotism" (Eddy, p. 104). Certain that she was pursued by mesmerists, Eddy moved frequently and finally went into seclusion. Her flock, numbering thousands, continued to revere and worship her as the church continued to grow.

The phenomenal growth of the church can be seen as a complex reaction to modernization. Having been organized at the moment when medicine was itself professionalizing, as modern science entered a period of expansion alongside industrial capitalism, Christian Science moved to the center of cultural debate. Since its founding, the church has prompted controversy regarding its relationship with modern medicine and medical ethics, freedom of religion, the power of mind, and the separation of church and state. As concerns about public hygiene grew through the Progressive Era, Christian Science became a target of litigation over healthcare, particularly of children. Whenever children died through absent treatment or failure to vaccinate, Christian Scientists were taken to court. The new religion also drew large numbers of women in a period when women of the middle class began to move in increasing numbers into the paid workforce. Many women made a living by their practice as healers at a time when medical schools largely excluded them.

CHRISTIAN SCIENCE IN PRINT

In 1875 Eddy published the first edition of *Science and Health, with Key to the Scriptures,* a book that had sold more than nine million copies by the time the 1994 edition appeared. In 1879 she established the church that became the Church of Christ, Scientist. In 1883 the monthly *Journal of Christian Science* began publication. Each number opened with a "crashing editorial," including accounts of "demonstrations," or successful healings (Cather and Milmine, p. 318). In 1908 the *Christian Science Monitor* became the international journal of the church. In a century of publication, the *Monitor* has earned a reputation for the quality and independence of its reporting. As Eddy founded it, the *Monitor* was devoted to self-defense and propaganda. Yet by the 1950s its style had changed. In the opinion of Charles S. Braden in *Christian Science Today: Power, Policy, Practice* (1958), the *Monitor* became "the greatest contribution the Scientists have made to modern American life" (Braden, p. 70). This achievement demands a heavy subsidy. The church *Manual* requires all Scientists to subscribe to the *Monitor* and to seek other subscribers and member advertisers. Just as the rejection of modern medicine has been advantageous to the church in many respects, the rejection of commercial advertising has preserved the independence and thereby improved the reputation of the *Monitor.*

LITERARY RESPONSES

Among responses of professional writers to Christian Science, three examples of durable literary interest— Mark Twain's, Willa Cather's, and Harold Frederic's— may suggest a broader general opinion. Commentators outside the church tend to be skeptical of the effects

Christian Science Church, Boston, c. 1900–1920. Construction of the Mother Church gave Christian Science the status of an established religion. Mark Twain noted the structural irony of the church edifice, given the fundamental belief of Christian Science that the material world exists only as erroneous thought. THE LIBRARY OF CONGRESS

and the profit motive of Christian Science, even as they may question the claims of professional medicine. The fact that Scientists, many of them women, earned money while denying the effect of material medicine and the very existence of the material world—notwithstanding the wealth of the church and the opulence of its buildings—struck many observers as blatant hypocrisy. The diatribe by Mark Twain (Samuel Langhorne Clemens, 1835–1910) is the best known of anti–Christian Science writings, typical in its argument but exceptional, like other works of protest by Twain, for its comedy. Originally written as journalism pieces for *Cosmopolitan* in 1899 and *North American Review* in 1902 and 1903, Twain's writings on the religion were later collected in *Christian Science* (1907): "Its god," Twain wrote of Christian Science, "is Mrs. Eddy first, then the Dollar. Not a spiritual Dollar, but a real one. From end to end of the Christian-Science literature

not a single (material) thing in the world is conceded to be real, except the Dollar" (p. 68). Moreover, Twain argued, Christian Science posed a threat to modern democracy and the Christian world. Antidemocratic, anti-intellectual, and widely popular, it was a movement as powerful as what he called Mohammedanism, a cult Twain thought was destroying the ancient intellectual traditions of the East.

Twain's *Christian Science* opens with a tale of calamity, a fall from a cliff in the Alps. With broken arms and legs and "one thing or another" (p. 3) Twain suffers under care of a bony and grim healer from Boston. Declaiming on the illusion of pain, the healer accidentally steps on the cat. The cat yowls. The ensuing conversation exploits the illogic: the cat must have imagined the pain but cannot imagine pain, having no imagination. The healer denies it all: "Peace!" she cries at last. "The cat feels nothing, the Christian feels nothing" (p. 11). In the end, Twain is cured by a horse doctor.

Turning to Eddy's "verbal chaos" (p. 116), Twain argues that Eddy could not have written *Science and Health, with Key to the Scriptures.* The English is simply too good. Juxtaposing passages from *Science and Health* with Eddy's poetry and other "offenses against third-class English," Twain's aim is to "pierce through the cloud" (p. 238) of Eddy's language. From her autobiography, for example, Twain makes fun of Eddy's ambiguous prose: "Many pale cripples went into the Church leaning on crutches who came out carrying them on their shoulders" (p. 119). Twain also raises the issue of plagiarism—that Eddy lifted her more accomplished prose from others. While such allegations had circulated since the early days of the movement, in Twain's hands the argument was both influential and funny. Among those who reacted was Eddy herself. Twain reproduces her remarks in the book as "a friend's duty to straighten such things out" (p. 331).

"*Environment,*" Twain argues, "is the chief thing to be considered when one is proposing to predict the future of Christian Science" (p. 93). Cather seems to have largely agreed. She approached her subject through investigative journalism and psychobiography. Both writers present Eddy's notorious illogic as a key to her success, Twain using satire and Cather epigram: "Only one idea had ever come very close to Mrs. Glover [Eddy]," Cather wrote, "and neither things present nor things to come could separate her from it. . . . Others of his pupils lost themselves in Quimby's philosophy, but Mrs. Glover lost Quimby in herself" (p. 133).

Cather never publicly acknowledged authorship of *The Life of Mary Baker G. Eddy and the History of Christian Science.* Letters discovered after her death confirmed her association with the book and the articles that preceded it in *McClure's* (January 1907–June 1908). Her first extended work, *The Life of Mary Baker G. Eddy* documents Cather's early technique. From the patchy structure—pieces of interviews and extracts of depositions held loosely by narrative and analysis—emerges a portrait of a vindictive, charismatic self-promoter:

> To-day some of these who have long been accounted as enemies by Mrs. Eddy, and whom she has anathematised in print and discredited on the witness-stand, still declare that what they got from her was beyond equivalent in gold or silver. . . . One of the students who was closest to [Eddy] at

that time says that to him the world outside her little circle seemed like a madhouse. (Pp. 155–156)

Insightful and arresting, these character sketches predict Cather's later work. Equally arresting is her sympathetic reading of Christian Science.

Cather presents Eddy's biography through a report on the appeal of the new religion to people at the edges of the modernizing world. As westward movement and urbanization reduced the population of her native New England, Eddy "gave people the feeling that a great deal was happening" (p. 123). She attracted followers by her affected speech and behavior, "an interesting figure in a humdrum New England village" (p. 122). Cather also followed the movement of Christian Science on the frontier. She read widely in the *Christian Science Journal* from the 1880s. How, she asked, could a loving mother in Pierre, North Dakota, watch her baby die as a healer treated him for animal magnetism? "The sufferings of the baby," Cather writes, "and the terrible fortitude of the mother sound like a passage from the earlier and harsher chapters of religious history, which so often make us wonder whether there is anything else in the world that can be quite so cruel as the service of an ideal" (p. 324). Yet these were "not ignorant or colourless people. . . . they loved each other and their children" (p. 326). Cather found that Christian Science gave people an ideal they could grasp in a world otherwise transitory and impoverished. It was, Cather maintained—as source after source proved to her—an ignorant and entirely understandable "revolt from orthodoxy" (p. 337). Eddy's obsession with malicious animal magnetism found its way through the journal into the "conduct and affections" of people around the country and abroad (p. 322). Her "teachings brought the promise of material benefits to a practical people, and the appeal of seeming newness to a people whose mental recreation was a feverish pursuit of novelty" (p. 375). Demanding conditions in the western United States increased the popularity of Christian Science: "This religion had a message of cheer for the rugged materialist as well as for the morbid invalid. It exalted health and self-satisfaction and material prosperity high among the moral virtues—indeed, they were the evidences of right living, the manifestations of a man's 'at-oneness' with God" (p. 375).

To Christian Scientists, the book was incendiary. The church took extraordinary steps to stop its publication. Failing that, they bought and destroyed large numbers of copies and, according to story, succeeded in keeping reviews out of the press. The book all but disappeared until 1993, when the University of Nebraska Press republished it.

Cather had no illusions about orthodox allopathic medicine. Like Twain, she could cite the failings of doctors. Patients did not always respond to medical treatment, and many died under medical care. The emotional value and effect of belief on physical well-being was likewise undeniable. Though neither Twain nor Cather refers to the work of William James (1846–1910) or Sigmund Freud (1856–1939), an awareness of the new field of psychology, as the mind cure of the nineteenth century evolved into the psychoanalysis of the twentieth, is implicit in both studies.

Rational skeptics who distrusted doctors might find an alternative in Christian Science. In the literary world, the best-known exemplar of such a view was the novelist and *New York Times* correspondent Harold Frederic (1856–1898), author of *The Damnation of Theron Ware* (1896). Frederic served as exemplar not through his writing but through the example of his life. In 1898, following a stroke, Frederic died in London while under care of Christian Scientists. He had long been an informed critic of modern medicine and modernization itself. There is no evidence that Frederic believed in Christian Science. Rather, he appears to have chosen the treatment as an act of self-determination. Frederic's death was a transatlantic sensation, resembling a witch hunt. This happened in part because Frederic was a popular writer and journalist and in part because the press discovered he had led a double life, with wife and children in one household and mistress and children in another. While the manslaughter case against his mistress, Kate Lyon, and the healer never went to trial, the international coverage following Frederic's death was, in Cather's opinion, a boon to Christian Science. The news "brought the new cult to the attention of thousands of people for the first time" (p. 447). For her part, Eddy thought the death of Harold Frederic had severely damaged the church. According to Ernest Sutherland Bates and John V. Dittemore in *Mary Baker Eddy: The Truth and the Tradition* (1932), she told her healers to stay away from such dubious cases in the future.

Professional medicine would strenuously disagree with the alternative that Frederic chose. As William Lloyd Garrison, son of the renowned abolitionist, wrote in a letter in 1908, the opposition mounted by physicians against Christian Science on grounds that Scientists were not doctors and should not be paid for their services was selfish and hypocritical: "The medical faculty is very jealous and narrow towards all not of their fellowship" (Albertine, p. 63). The highly publicized Frederic case was but one of several that arrayed the forces of modernization and professional medicine against both skeptics and Christian Scientists. Controversy over Christian Science recurred episodically throughout the twentieth century, centering often on high-profile trials. With the New Age movement and the rise of interest in spiritual healing, the debate over Christian Science and alternative approaches to health has extended into the twenty-first century.

See also The Damnation of Theron Ware

BIBLIOGRAPHY
Primary Works
Cather, Willa, and Georgine Milmine. *The Life of Mary Baker G. Eddy and the History of Christian Science.* 1909. Lincoln: University of Nebraska Press, 1993.

Eddy, Mary Baker. *Science and Health, with Key to the Scriptures.* 1875. Boston: First Church of Christ, Scientist, 1994.

Twain, Mark. *Christian Science.* 1907. New York: Oxford University Press, 1996.

Secondary Works
Albertine, Susan. "'With Their Tongues Doom Men to Death': Christian Science and the Case of Harold Frederic." *American Literary Realism 1870–1910* 21, no. 3 (Spring 1989): 52–66.

Bates, Ernest Sutherland, and John V. Dittemore. *Mary Baker Eddy: The Truth and the Tradition.* New York: Knopf, 1932.

Braden, Charles S. *Christian Science Today: Power, Policy, Practice.* Dallas, Tex.: Southern Methodist University Press, 1958.

Schoepflin, Rennie B. *Christian Science on Trial: Religious Healing in America.* Baltimore: Johns Hopkins University Press, 2003.

Susan Albertine

CIRCUSES

At a time when most communities had little in the way of entertainment, the traveling circus, under its canvas pavilion, brought thrills, spectacle, and wonderment to a longing public. Isolated audiences knew little about natural history and the circus introduced them to the zoo and the museum, animals and oddities. At its best, the circus brought momentary joy to millions of people. Circuses began in the late eighteenth century and continued until competing amusements and advancing technology made their mode of operation obsolete. Circus history is interwoven with the evolution of waterways, roadways, and railways from crude channels, paths, and tracks to complicated networks. As circuses moved from travel in a single wagon to rail transportation in multiple train cars, from one-ring to three-ring spectacles, and from fifty-foot "round-tops" to huge tent cities, they reflected the burgeoning of American industry and commerce.

THE CIRCUS AND LITERATURE
Some western circuses traveled the Mississippi and its tributaries by riverboat prior to the Civil War. One such circus was included by Mark Twain (1835–1910) in *Adventures of Huckleberry Finn,* first published in 1885. In chapter 22 Huck expresses his awe and wonder at attending a circus. He considers the grand entry, the customary parade around the ring to introduce the troupe, a delightful sight, and laughs at the interplay between the ringmaster and the clown. One passage describes in detail what was called, among other things, "Metamorphosis" or the "Pete Jenkins act." The sketch, a circus classic, in this case involves a drunken man who comes out of the audience. After bantering with the ringmaster and being encouraged by the unsuspecting spectators, he mounts a bareback horse his clumsy riding causing a round of laughter from the audience. Eventually he strips off his clothing layer by layer, transforming himself into a slim and handsome professional equestrian.

The color and romance connected with the circus were the inspiration for other writers of novels, short stories, and nonfiction. Children's books, dime novels, and both pulp and slick magazines presented factual or fanciful circus narratives. Such notables as Horatio Alger Jr., Eugene Field, and Jack London included circus themes in their works.

HORSES AND WESTERN THEMES
The introduction of a hippodrome track within the circus arena occurred in 1872, when P. T. Barnum's Great Traveling World's Fair increased the space between the ring and the audience by using a larger canvas pavilion designed to accommodate an extended seating area. With such a track, horses could move at a faster pace and more performers could be involved in a single event, making it possible for greater spectacle and expansive storytelling on horseback. The following year a second ring was added and by the end of the decade the three-ring circus came into being.

The major circuses used cowboy and Indian themes during much of the 1870s, but with Buffalo Bill Cody's Wild West Show in 1883, their hippodrome acts took on more frontier color. For example, in 1886 W. W. Cole's circus advertised thirty minutes of Wild West entertainment featuring Dr. William F. Carver, champion shot of the world, and one hundred Indians, cowboys, and scouts. Half the program consisted of hippodrome and Wild West performances—a pony express demonstration, an Indian attack on the Overland Mail Coach, and Mexican vaqueros and Texas cowboys on bucking broncos.

P. T. BARNUM AND THE BIRTH OF THE MODERN CIRCUS
The beginning of the modern circus came in 1871, when W. C. Coup and Dan Castello talked P. T. Barnum (1810–1891) into forming a show with them. Barnum, already an international celebrity, had created such cultural icons as Jenny Lind and Tom Thumb, and would within a few years add the elephant Jumbo to the list. The size and expense of this first-year circus company was far beyond anything that had existed in the past—three large exhibition tents separating the menagerie, the museum, and the arena; between five and eight horse tents holding about thirty head of "baggage stock" (horses that pulled the wagons) each; a total spread of canvas covering nearly three acres. Daily expenditures amounted to as much as twenty-five hundred dollars. P. T. Barnum's Great Traveling Museum, Menagerie, Caravan, and Hippodrome established a new set of standards, which were soon adopted by the entire industry.

During this time gamblers, pickpockets, short-change artists, and fakers traveled with the shows; in return for money paid to the owners, they were left undisturbed to prey on the crowd that flocked to the showground. This practice was most prevalent in the 1860s and 1870s, particularly in the new territories of the south and west. Local newspapers frequently warned their readers in advance to be cautious at the circus. When the Barnum circus was founded, the proprietors hired detectives as part of the troupe to protect the public and advertised the fact. Shortly, other shows followed and major grift, as it was called, was gradually eliminated.

As the greatest promoter and advertiser of his day, Barnum developed many devices that became established practice. A major contribution was his invention of the *Advance Courier,* a throwaway newspaper of sorts numbering some twenty or more pages that was distributed by the millions ahead of the show to extol its wonders. During the winter layoff period, Barnum wrote much of the bill himself and attentively supervised others' writing.

Famous for his living curiosities, he was the first to do ethnic exhibitions in the circus ring. In 1872 he imported from Fiji what were purported to be cannibals and brought a band of "Digger" Indians from the American West; in 1880 he exhibited a group of Zulu warriors.

The greatest achievement resulting from Barnum's skills as a promoter was to puff up his own image. No other man whose contribution to the nation was so unimportant has received such attention and adoration from the American press and the American public. He contrived his own celebrity and bathed in it. His autobiography is an example of pure self-service and self-righteousness. Copies of the book, which cost him nine cents apiece and retailed for $1.50, were sold by the tens of thousands from a circus "high-box" (outdoor ticket-selling box) and in other public places, further magnifying the self-made myth. Throughout his career, the print media were awed by his persona and capitalized on his fame. During the 1870s, P. T. Barnum's Greatest Show on Earth was a true reflection of the image P. T. Barnum had invented for himself.

THE RISE OF RAILROAD TRANSPORTATION

When travel became feasible and improved roads allowed shows to move heavily loaded wagons with some regularity, enterprising showmen left the cities and their equestrian companies trouped along the eastern seaboard and then inland, following the expanding frontier. The growth of the American circus could not have continued without the establishment of a complex railroad system throughout the country. It was not until 1872, however, the second season of P. T. Barnum's Great Traveling Exposition and World's Fair, that a serious commitment to traveling by rail was made. One of the proprietors, William C. Coup (1837–1895), can be given credit for innovations in the design of flatcars and for developing special techniques for loading and unloading them and intricate train schedules that allowed shows to make longer jumps between towns and to carry more equipment and personnel. That year the show toured sixteen states, all by rail, venturing as far west as Kansas.

With the transition to permanent rail travel, the American circus entered its golden age, featuring mammoth street parades, three rings of continuous performance, huge spreads of canvas, and a company made up of literally hundreds of performers and workingmen. This was also an age of brutal competition, paralleling that in American industry and banking. Huge sums were spent on advertising, with billing crews covering the surrounding towns and countryside for a fifty-mile radius.

ADVERTISING

The use of large lithographs for advertising purposes began in the mid-nineteenth century, pioneered by the American circus. These lithos, which used splashes of color to depict the exciting events on the circus program—horsemanship, trapeze flying, animals, and so on—were daubed on the sides of buildings, fences, or any flat surface within public view. Each "stand" included as much litho paper as the space allowed. A so-called one-sheet measured 28 by 42 inches. It was not uncommon to see as much as a hundred-sheet spread on the side of a large building.

By the latter part of the nineteenth century, there was a sizable bill-posting industry, enough to encourage the creation of a trade paper, *Billboard*, founded in 1893. Because many of the readers were people connected with outdoor amusements, by 1900 the paper was running news items relating to circuses, carnivals, fairs, and so on. Within ten years from its origin, *Billboard* had changed its emphasis to become a show business weekly.

The circus parade announcing the events in the large white tents also served as a dynamic advertisement. In earliest times, the "mud shows" made a grand entry into town, after members of the circus had stopped on the outskirts to wash the wagons, don parade costumes, and bedeck the horses and equipment with fancy trappings. But when shows were finally able to transport enormous quantities of paraphernalia by flatcar and stock car, the parade evolved into an immense processional of elaborately carved pageant and bandwagons adorned with mythological or biblical scenes and accompanied by elephants, camels, elegantly caparisoned horses with plumed and bejeweled harnesses and performers on foot in glittering costumes, all designed to enhance the moral and educational image of the circus. The parade, a moving pageant along the main streets of America, became a show in itself, always proportionate to the attractions inside the tents. When the modern circus eliminated it from the daily schedule, an important part of the touring tradition was buried once and for all.

With newspapers operating on a continuing basis in almost every community, the industrious age of advertising began and the circus was in the forefront, extolling its attractions in word and picture. The press corps was a colorful breed. It was their duty to spread the myth of prosperity, to bolster coffers sagging as a result of public apathy, to produce sprightly and star-spangled printed matter, indelibly marking the circus's greatness. The successful agent was endowed with a lively imagination, generating a constant flow of ideas to keep his client before the public. His mind was

The Greatest Show on Earth. Lithographs such as this one were popular advertising for the traveling circus.
© BETTMANN/CORBIS

replete with superlatives and his principles allowed him freely to advance unlimited, unsubstantiated claims. And, yes, he was a writer of some ability.

Exuberance of language was his tool. With it, he created a unique style of writing. Such phrases as "a congestion of amusement" and "a resonant tantara of merriment" appeared often. The climate of competition between the big shows led to a war of words, as claims about the stupendous wonders under the big top were made and countered.

With the merging of the two behemoths of the industry into the combined Ringling Brothers and Barnum & Bailey Circus in 1907, the need for big catchwords disappeared. The "big show" really was big, a "scintillating, kaleidoscopic, unparalleled, heterogeneous, aggregation of multiplied wonders." The press agent's tool, his hyperbole, was rendered impotent by real wonders more colossal than words can describe.

The circus is an institution of surprising longevity. Its promotional gimmickry has been flamboyantly perverse. Its exploitation of caged or otherwise confined animals has been callous. Its petty swindling of its patrons is sadly legendary. Its managerial greed has led to brutal competitive wars of self-destruction. Yet the blare, the pomp, the daring, the tinsel and glitter—yes, even the smell—of the ring spectacle has gulled us all into childish fantasy.

See also Theater; Wild West Shows

BIBLIOGRAPHY
Primary Works
Barnum, P. T. *The Life of P. T. Barnum, Written by Himself.* 1855. Urbana: University of Illinois Press, 2000.

Twain, Mark. *Adventures of Huckleberry Finn.* 1885. Edited by Victor Fischer, Lin Salamo, and Walter Blair. Berkeley: University of California Press, 2003.

Secondary Works
Hensley, Donald L. "The Circus and the American Short Story." *Bandwagon* 18, no. 4 (1974): 14–15.

Saxon, A. H. *Enter Foot and Horse: A History of Hippodrama in England and France.* New Haven, Conn.: Yale University Press, 1968.

Saxon, A. H. *P. T. Barnum: The Legend and the Man.* New York: Columbia University Press, 1989.

Slout, William L., and Stuart Thayer. *Grand Entrée: The Birth of the Greatest Show on Earth, 1870–1875.* San Bernardino, Calif.: Borgo Press, 1998.

Thayer, Stuart. *Annals of the American Circus, 1793–1860.* 3 vols. Seattle: self-published, 1976–1993.

William L. Slout

CITY DWELLERS

The late-nineteenth century emergence of the city as a dominant American space revolutionized the national culture. Largely spontaneous and unplanned, the urban explosion of the last half of the 1800s irrevocably changed the economic, social, and cultural dynamics of life in the United States. Census figures cited in the *World Almanac and Book of Facts 2002* (*World Almanac,* pp. 382–383) provide dramatic evidence of the astonishing growth of urban America: between 1850 and 1900 the population of New York City rose from approximately 700,000 to almost 3.5 million; Philadelphia from 120,000 to almost 1.3 million; Boston from a little over 136,000 to 560,000; Cleveland from 17,000 to almost 382,000; and Chicago from under 30,000 to almost 1.7 million. In *Form and History in American Literary Naturalism,* June Howard writes that "in 1870, 26 percent of Americans lived in urban areas, and there were fourteen cities with populations greater than 100,000; in 1900, 40 percent lived in urban areas, and thirty-eight cities had populations greater than 100,000" (p. 33). Urban migration accelerated throughout the twentieth century until its culmination in the post–World War II emergence of the suburb.

NEW YORK CITY

Because a great deal of this urban growth occurred in the northern part of the nation, and especially in the Northeast and the Midwest, the tensions between North and South that had previously brought about the Civil War remained strong. In the last three decades of the nineteenth century and into the twentieth, the hegemonic control that the urban North had begun to establish over the rest of the nation intensified, inevitably producing regional resentments. New York City became the embodiment of the northern city and inspired intense emotions, both positive and negative.

Seemingly in the process of an unending expansion, New York supplanted Boston as the cultural center of the United States. In *The Bostonians* (1886), Henry James (1843–1916) sees the ascendance of upstart New York over the Massachusetts home of transcendentalism and the abolition movement as the triumph of a new, superficial, market-driven culture over a more cerebral and idealist national past. In this and in other writings, James also expresses misgivings about the implications of the kind of ethnic and racial diversity increasingly visible in New York City, the very diversity that Walt Whitman (1819–1892) would be inspired by and proclaim as the defining and redemptive characteristic of the American nation.

Population in select U.S. cities, 1870–1920

City	1870	1880	1890	1900	1910	1920
Baltimore	267,354	332,313	434,439	508,957	558,485	733,826
Boston	250,526	362,839	448,477	560,892	670,585	748,060
Chicago	298,977	503,185	1,099,850	1,698,575	2,185,283	2,701,705
Detroit	79,577	116,340	205,876	285,704	465,766	993,078
Cleveland	92,829	160,146	261,353	381,768	560,663	796,841
New Orleans	191,418	216,090	242,039	287,104	339,075	387,219
New York	942,292	1,206,299	1,515,301	3,437,202	4,766,883	5,620,048
Philadelphia	674,022	847,170	1,046,964	1,293,697	1,549,008	1,823,779
St. Louis	310,864	350,518	451,770	575,238	687,029	772,897
San Francisco	149,473	233,959	298,997	342,782	416,912	506,676
Total U.S. population	39,818,449	50,155,783	62,947,714	75,994,575	91,972,266	105,710,620

Note: In 1898 Brooklyn, the Bronx, Queens, and Staten Island were united with Manhattan to create the City of Greater New York.

SOURCE: U.S. Bureau of the Census.

William Dean Howells (1837–1920) was also loyal to Boston and ambivalent about New York City as a cultural force. In *A Hazard of New Fortunes* (1889), he explored the moral implications of the political, economic, and social power centered in New York, employing his unique cultural perspective, which was a mixture of his small-town Ohio upbringing and his lengthy adult residence in Boston. The sheer ambivalence of his resulting conclusions in *A Hazard of New Fortunes* produced a cultural breakthrough according to Sidney H. Bremer in *Urban Intersections: Meetings of Life and Literature in United States Cities*. Bremer writes that "here the city is, for the first time, the subject rather than the setting of a U.S. novel" (p. 53). Howells, though, was too much a traditionalist to develop an appropriately cinematic method for recording the diverse and ever-shifting New York life; that would be left to John Dos Passos (1896–1970) in *Manhattan Transfer* (1925). *Manhattan Transfer,* in fact, is evidence that the literary high modernists of the 1920s and 1930s would emerge as the authentic voices of American urbanism. Their experiments with narrative innovation, especially fragmentation, were often inspired by, and designed to reproduce, the nonlinear nature of urban life.

In the context of James and Howells, it should be said that it was not only middle-class white novelists in whom the cultural revolution represented by New York City and the northern city in general evoked an ambivalent response. Paul Laurence Dunbar (1872–1906) in *The Sport of the Gods* (1902), one of the earliest novels set partially in Harlem, dramatized the near destruction of a black family from the rural South by the hedonistic life of the city. For Dunbar, the ragtime music inspired by Scott Joplin, with its emphasis upon playful spontaneity, serves as an inclusive metaphor for the immorality of Harlem life. Dunbar's fictional family is saved only by a retreat to the rural South. Abraham Cahan (1860–1951) focused his 1917 novel *The Rise of David Levinsky* around the tensions and conflicts inevitably faced by Jewish immigrants, especially those from eastern Europe, in the pressure to assimilate into American culture. For Cahan, assimilation meant material success and economic prosperity, but only at the price of spiritual emptiness and the compromise of a rich cultural legacy. Cahan's concerns would be taken up again by Anzia Yezierska, Michael Gold, and Henry Roth among others.

Immigration was perhaps the central factor in the unplanned explosion of urban America, and especially of New York City. In fact, the diversity of the new urban America was as dramatic as its sudden growth. June Howard points out that "in 1880, 80 percent of the population of New York was foreign-born or born

of immigrants; in Chicago the figure was 87 percent; in Detroit, 84 percent; in St. Louis and San Francisco, 78 percent" (p. 33). Thus, New York's Ellis Island, the federal facility through which immigrants to the East Coast were processed, can be said to have given birth to a vibrant new American culture.

Unfortunately, cynical politicians and opportunistic political parties quickly sensed the advantages to be gained by exploiting the new immigrant population. In New York, the Democratic political machine known popularly as Tammany Hall successfully manipulated tensions between nativist Americans, Irish immigrants, and the more recent arrivals from eastern Europe, the American South, and Asia. Controlled by William M. "Boss" Tweed and others, Tammany ruled city politics for more than seventy years.

Newly arrived immigrants in New York were predominantly housed on the city's East Side in overcrowded and poorly sanitized tenement districts. The tenement, in fact, became an emblematic new space in the middle-class American mind, a space connoting extreme poverty and ominous exoticism. Thus "established" Americans, whose more remote immigrant forebears were primarily English, Scottish, or at least western European, were simultaneously repelled by and attracted to the tenements. The ghetto, or inner city, that was emerging at the turn of the twentieth century, inspired emotions that bordered on the hysterical in such nativist writers as Frank Norris and Jack London. In sharp contrast, Stephen Crane (1871–1900) in 1893 privately published the early ghetto classic *Maggie, A Girl of the Streets (A Story of New York),* set in the infamous Bowery neighborhood of the city. Crane concisely expressed the dominant middle-class perspective of the inner city when describing his idealized, if not particularly intelligent, heroine, Maggie Johnson, as having "blossomed in a mud puddle" into "a rare and wonderful production of a tenement district, a pretty girl" (p. 24). Crane then dramatizes her descent into prostitution and her subsequent physical and spiritual destruction.

But it was a journalist rather than a novelist who most memorably depicted the tenement life of New York's East Side. In 1890 Jacob Riis (1849–1914), a first-generation immigrant from Denmark who came to America at the age of twenty-one and had firsthand experience of the East Side, published *How the Other Half Lives,* a pioneering work of photojournalism. Virtually a self-taught photographer, Riis recorded in brutally honest pictures the desperation and degradation of tenement life. His accompanying text, also honest and at times eloquent, inspired the city to institute some badly needed reforms of tenement living conditions. Unfortunately, Riis, in separate chapters devoted to various immigrant groups, propagates a number of demeaning racial and ethnic stereotypes—for example, Chinese Americans as secretive and unnaturally obsessed with cleanliness, Irish Americans as plagued by alcohol and senseless brawling, Italian Americans as prone to criminal activity. Despite this truly unfortunate aspect of his book, Riis's contribution to the school of muckraking journalism that emerged at the turn of the twentieth century was significant. (The term "muckraker" was rather loosely attached to a group of journalists devoted to exposing various forms of corruption in American society.)

An increase in criminal activity and the beginnings of organized crime in America were inevitable consequences of the extreme poverty and bitter ethnic tensions in New York City. The Five Points, or Mulberry Bend, section quickly became synonymous with urban crime and violence. In 1928 Herbert Asbury (1891–1963) published *The Gangs of New York,* a rather remarkable text (part history, part sociology, part fiction, and part folklore) that managed to simultaneously condemn the Five Points phenomenon, while evoking its exotic appeal. According to Asbury, Five Points "by 1840 . . . had become the most dismal slum section in America. In the opinion of contemporary writers it was worse than the Seven Dials and Whitechapel districts of London" (p. 29). Asbury proceeds to write an account of the rise of gang crime in the Five Points area that is at times preposterous and unbelievable but that serves nevertheless as one of the earlier evocations of the criminal as mythic urban antihero. He is, moreover, just as guilty as Riis of perpetuating ethnic stereotypes. Still, he is undeniably correct in pointing out that New York City gangs were often exploited by the city's political power structure, especially Tammany Hall, and that they fed on ethnic conflict.

Beginning even before the Civil War, African Americans became a kind of "domestic" immigrant group in New York. Freed slaves sought refuge in the Five Points neighborhood where they were, at best, tolerated by the Irish and other European immigrants and, at worst, greeted with outright hostility. The resulting tensions exploded in the 1863 Draft Riots inspired by the expansion of Civil War conscription. During the riots African Americans were tortured and lynched by roving white urban gangs. Nevertheless, as Dunbar foresaw, albeit with misgivings, Harlem by the 1920s had become the center of a vibrant African American community and culture. Jazz clubs imported talent from New Orleans, and an important group of black writers and artists worked out of Harlem. Thus, when Alain Locke in 1925 published his anthology of contemporary African American literary and artistic expression, he chose *The New Negro: An Interpretation* as his title. A group of New York–based African American writers that included Langston Hughes, Zora Neale Hurston, Claude McKay, Jean Toomer, Countee Cullen, Jessie Redmon Fauset, Nella Larsen, and Wallace Thurman were central to what would become known as "the Harlem Renaissance." All of these writers except Larsen and Thurman were included in Locke's *The New Negro.*

Jacob Riis was not the only significant muckraking journalist from New York. In 1904 Lincoln Steffens (1866–1936), an admirer of Theodore Roosevelt and sometime associate of Riis, collected seven previously published magazine articles about major American cities under the general title *The Shame of the Cities.* Writing specifically about St. Louis, Minneapolis, Pittsburgh, Philadelphia, Chicago, and New York, Steffens delineates the degree to which these six urban governments were controlled and corrupted by the dominant merchant class while condemning the complicity of city dwellers in the hegemonic power of laissez-faire capitalism. Rather remarkably, Steffens finds New York City and Chicago to have the least corrupt and the most responsible governments of the six urban centers.

CHICAGO

Next to New York City's emergence as America's preeminent city, the meteoric rise of Chicago was the most dramatic urban story of the last half of the nineteenth century. Originally a railroad and trading center and literally built on a swamp, Chicago, through the single-minded energy and vision of a group of determined entrepreneurs, rapidly established economic and cultural hegemony over much of the Midwest. The city parlayed its origins as a frontier trading hub into a national and even international center of commerce. The rise of Chicago was hardly pretty: in the stockyards district the assembly-line transformation of cattle into meat and related products was carried out with little concern for the health and safety of the workers or for city sanitation. The stockyards quickly became a magnet for European immigrants and newly freed slaves escaping the racial violence of the South. Upton Sinclair (1878–1968) intended his 1906 novel *The Jungle* to be a muckraking exposé of the exploitation of immigrant labor in the stockyards; and *The Jungle* possesses sufficient power, especially in its detailed accounts of the abuse of immigrant workers in the stockyards, to remain a central text in the Chicago school of literary naturalism that emerged in

Gotham Court Tenement, Cherry Street, New York City, c. 1890. Photograph from *How the Other Half Lives* by Jacob Riis. GETTY IMAGES

the early 1900s. *The Jungle* is, moreover, one of the few American novels that can categorically be said to have inspired governmental reforms; they were limited, however, to federal regulations of the meatpacking industry, which primarily affected the middle and upper classes, who as consumers of beef and pork were invested in governmental regulation of the meatpacking industry. The novel produced little, if any, improvement in the working and living conditions of Chicago's immigrant population.

Theodore Dreiser (1871–1945), Henry Blake Fuller (1857–1929), and Frank Norris (1870–1902) were other leading Chicago realists and naturalists. It has been said that the fiction of Dreiser, and especially *Sister Carrie* (1900), marked the emergence of the immigrant voice in American fiction; and, whether that is true or not, *Sister Carrie* is a still-unsurpassed study of urban consumerist culture. The novel's heroine, Carrie Meeber, originally from a Wisconsin village, is so thoroughly seduced by the luxury items advertised and, for that matter, sanctified in downtown Chicago store windows that, before the novel is over, she has come to personify the very spirit of consumerism. Dreiser focuses on Carrie's desire, and she desires material possessions most of all, with sex representing one means of obtaining them. It is more than a little appropriate that the novel takes place in both Chicago and New York City, the dominant shrines of the American consumerist culture.

Henry Blake Fuller made a Chicago skyscraper both the setting and the cumulative central character of his 1893 novel, *The Cliff-Dwellers*. Along with such architects of the "Chicago school" as Louis Sullivan, Fuller thus valorizes the skyscraper as a vertical space of limitless possibility. Most obviously in New York City and Chicago, the skyscraper came to symbolize the new American capitalism. In two volumes of a planned "wheat trilogy," Frank Norris dramatized the potential for Chicago, as a centrally located urban and trade center, to assume control of American agriculture in the American West and Midwest. In fact, *The Octopus: A Story of California* (1901) and *The Pit: A Story of Chicago* (1903) envision the Chicago-based railroad industry and the Board of Trade as destroying the wheat ranchers of California and threatening to control the productive capacity of nature itself.

Social protest is a central ingredient in the fiction of Sinclair and Norris, who were both associated with the muckrakers. The rapid rise of Chicago to economic hegemony evoked concern in both of them, as well as in other writers. As in New York City, poverty and overcrowding assumed desperate and even tragic proportions in Chicago. Nevertheless, as Steffens notes,

the political structure of turn-of-the-twentieth-century Chicago was not as flamboyantly corrupt as those that dominated other flourishing midwestern urban centers, especially St. Louis and minneapolis. This happened in part because Chicago was governed by an inner circle of merchant princes ambitious for the city's economic and cultural future. As a result, they were conscious of its reputation among the post–Civil War national and international business elite.

The single-minded determination of such leaders as Marshall Field and Potter Palmer enabled Chicago to rise phoenix-like from a devastating 1871 fire that caused $100 million in property damage, approximately a third of the city's property valuation. The city leadership simply used the fire as an opportunity to encourage eastern financiers and businessmen to see in the challenge of rebuilding Chicago a unique opportunity for profitable investment, and they were phenomenally successful in pitching this idea. At the time of the fire, the city's population had reached approximately 330,000, making it the fourth largest city in America. Not long after its revitalization began, it had become the "second city" to New York in population, economic power, and cultural influence. To celebrate its power and influence, the city staged a legendary world's fair, the World's Columbian Exposition, in 1893. In addition to some famous and infamous sideshow entertainment, it offered dramatic exhibits of the city's architectural and related cultural innovations.

ST. LOUIS

For a considerable time into the twentieth century, St. Louis, which also began as a frontier trading post and soon became a special magnet for Irish and German immigrants, rivaled Chicago as a midwestern economic and cultural center. Not surprisingly, its civic leadership was not going to be outdone without a fight, and, eleven years after the World's Columbian Exposition in Chicago, St. Louis sponsored its own world's fair, the Louisiana Purchase Exhibition of 1904. In terms of sheer space, it was even larger than the earlier Chicago extravaganza. Like the Chicago fair, the Louisiana Purchase Exhibition was a strange mix of local boosterism, national and international cultural exhibits (the more exotic the better), and architectural and cultural innovation. Also, as in Chicago eleven years earlier, evidence of economic oppression, political corruption, and racial bigotry, was, at least as far as possible, denied and disguised. In fact, there seems to have been a great deal to hide. The tone of Steffens's essay on St. Louis, contained in *The Shame of the Cities,* is set in its opening words: "St. Louis, the fourth city in size in the United States, is making two announcements to the world: one that it is the worst-governed city in the land; the other that it wishes all men to come there (for the World's Fair) and see it" (p. 18). Steffens, in fact, evokes the name that personified New York's urban corruption in the title of his essay about St. Louis, "Tweed Days in St. Louis" (p. 18).

SAN FRANCISCO

Urbanization reached the West Coast as well. After the 1848 discovery of gold in California, the "Gold Rush" to the West began. San Francisco, with its ideal location on San Francisco Bay and the Pacific Ocean, exploded from a village of a few hundred people in the 1840s to a city of almost 150,000 by 1870. By 1900 its population had reached almost 300,000. By the turn of the twentieth century it had started to develop the special identity that would characterize the city in the future. Part frontier boom town and part cosmopolitan cultural center, it epitomized West Coast culture until the emergence of Los Angeles later in the twentieth century.

Like Chicago, San Francisco survived a disaster that would have meant the end of most urban centers. In 1906 an earthquake, followed by a series of deadly fires, destroyed 490 city blocks and 250,000 buildings in San Francisco and caused property damage of approximately $350 million. But also like Chicago, the city quickly rebuilt and reassumed its position as the cultural capital of the West Coast. Like its midwestern counterpart, San Francisco became the home of an important group of literary naturalists, including Frank Norris (who was born in Chicago but who grew up in San Francisco) and Jack London (1876–1916). In contrast to Dreiser, Riis, Cahan, and other significant New York and Chicago literary realists and naturalists with recent immigrant experience, Norris, London, and other leading members of the San Francisco naturalist school wrote from a distinctly nativist Anglo perspective. Norris's groundbreaking naturalist novel *McTeague: A Story of San Francisco* (1899) is, on one level, a kind of allegory of the disintegration of the allegedly pure Anglo frontiersman trapped in a distinctly "foreign" urban immigrant culture. Similarly, London's *The Valley of the Moon* (1913) recounts a search for non-urban space where Anglo-Saxon purity can be rediscovered.

Nevertheless, San Francisco became the primary West Coast home of Chinese Americans who were initially recruited to do the physical labor of constructing railroads in the United States and subsequently exploited and subjugated both economically and legally. Inspired by the attempts of individual states to control immigration, the federal government passed two laws in 1882 that virtually prohibited further Chinese immigration. Ultimately, all immigration from Asia would be restricted. Angel Island was established in 1910 as a clearinghouse and detention center for what little Asian immigration remained (primarily relatives of earlier immigrants). Still, there was already a considerable Chinese American population on the West Coast, and San Francisco's Chinatown became its urban center. Nativist fears of a "yellow peril" impeded the assimilation of Asian Americans into mainstream culture, thus ironically guaranteeing preservation of many Chinese cultural traditions. Like Abraham Cahan for New York Jewish immigrants, Edith Maude Eaton (1865–1914) explored the possibilities and the tensions inherent in the assimilation of Chinese Americans into mainstream American culture. Born in England to a Chinese mother and an English father, Eaton wrote under the pen name Sui Sin Far. Her collection of short stories *Mrs. Spring Fragrance* was published in 1912.

From coast to coast, the United States, in the last half of the nineteenth century, was transformed from a culture of agrarian farms and small towns into an urban nation with undisguised imperialist ambitions. With most of the world already controlled by Europe, the United States, with a few exceptions, had to settle for internal exotic colonies—the ghettoes of the new American city. Whatever the concerns about or even opposition to such a dramatic cultural change, the push toward a city-dominated economy and culture was irresistible. During the twentieth century, that push would only intensify. Cultural diversity, and thus a new understanding of what the nation was and what its legitimate aspirations should be, was the major gain from this crucial national transformation. Such benefits did not come without extensive suffering, scandal, and oppression, but they were ultimately realized.

See also Assimilation; Chicago; Immigration; *The Jungle; Maggie, A Girl of the Streets;* Migration; Muckrakers and Yellow Journalism; New York; Poverty; *The Rise of David Levinsky; Sister Carrie*

BIBLIOGRAPHY
Primary Works

Asbury, Herbert. *The Gangs of New York: An Informal History of the Underworld.* 1928. Reprint, n.p.: Wheeler Publishing, 2003.

Crane, Stephen. *Stephen Crane: Prose and Poetry.* Edited by J. C. Levinson. New York: Library of America, 1984.

Steffens, Lincoln. *The Shame of the Cities.* New York: Hill and Wang, 1960.

Secondary Works

Bremer, Sidney H. *Urban Intersections: Meetings of Life and Literature in United States Cities.* Urbana: University of Illinois Press, 1992.

Howard, June. *Form and History in American Literary Naturalism.* Chapel Hill: University of North Carolina Press, 1985.

World Almanac and Book of Facts 2002. New York: World Almanac Books, 2002.

James R. Giles

CIVIL RIGHTS

The black experience in America can be largely defined in terms of the struggle to secure civil rights—the liberties inherent in legal, social, and institutional equity in the American body politic. Though 1870 opened with the promising ratification of the Fifteenth Amendment that granted suffrage to black men, the fifty-year period that followed saw African Americans subjected to the cruel irony of the post-emancipation barrage of exclusionary restrictions designed to maintain the racial hierarchy that had existed under slavery. Freedom from slavery represented a nominal condition as white supremacy in the United States was perpetuated by the increasingly repressive laws dubbed "Jim Crow" for a minstrel stereotype of blackness appropriated by a white stage performer in the 1820s. Disfranchisement, restricted access to public facilities, discriminatory hiring practices, delegitimation of court testimony, and exclusion from private establishments were all sanctioned by Jim Crow statutes, which varied in intensity from state to state. Though the North is typically considered to have been more tolerant of the black presence, the first Jim Crow laws were enacted in Northern states during the antebellum era in order to exert control over the free black population. Jim Crow gained currency in the Southern states in 1870 as part of the backlash against Reconstruction that was fueled by the disintegration of the Freedmen's Bureau, the governmental infrastructure that had provided legal protection and assistance to the millions of emancipated slaves since the end of the Civil War.

BLACK CODES AND RECONSTRUCTED RIGHTS

Although the Confederate effort to secede from the Union ended with the surrender at Appomattox, the effort to maintain the way of life the Southerners had fought to defend continued despite the dictate of the Emancipation Proclamation: the thwarted secessionists did not expect race relations to deviate from the established order of white supremacist repression. While blacks relished the liberties they hoped to enjoy once released from the shackles of chattel slavery, many whites labored to make their newly acquired freedom nominal, at best. Surprisingly, those who favored white supremacy found their cause aided by the successor to the assassinated Abraham Lincoln, President Andrew Johnson (1808–1875). Though virulently opposed to the institution of slavery, Johnson believed as strongly in the natural superiority of the white race as any of the staunchest Southern separatists. Though he did not block the creation of the Freedmen's Bureau, Johnson opted to make it an agency of the military rather than one of the government, and, except for rescinding General William Tecumseh Sherman's 1865 order to distribute abandoned lands to former slaves along the coast of South Carolina and Georgia, did little to involve himself in the Bureau's efforts to facilitate the transition of Southern blacks from slaves to free American citizens. Johnson's inaction tacitly sanctioned the rampant incidents of violence and injustice committed against blacks by the vanquished white Southerners; his policy was to allow the individual states to reconcile the relations between the races without significant federal intervention.

Codification of the unwritten rules that governed the hierarchical interaction between blacks and whites resulted in state regulation of the working conditions and mobility of black citizens. White planters were granted the sole discretion to determine the hours of and compensation for labor, and blacks were confined to agricultural and domestic labor unless they were able to secure a special permit. African Americans were also subject to a strict curfew, and the unemployed could be imprisoned, fined, or forced to work for whomever would pay the fine. There was no provision for the public funding of African American education, and blacks were prohibited from voting. Essentially, the legislation was designed to compel blacks to return to their former slave occupations, where they would be under the control of and economically dependent upon their former owners. Until 1870 the Freedmen's Bureau effectively overruled these so-called Black Codes, but the fact that the Southern states attempted to establish them represents the desire to implement a government-controlled caste system virtually indistinguishable from the so-called peculiar institution.

Reconstruction—the effort to bring the South in alignment with the Union—was fraught by a clash of ideologies between President Johnson, who favored federal inaction in consideration of the primacy of states' rights and appointed white supremacist provisional governors to the Southern states, and the Radical Republicans, a powerful group of senators and representatives who advocated black civil rights and racial equality. In 1866, despite Johnson's opposition, the Radical Republicans were able to muster enough votes to override presidential vetoes of the Civil Rights Act and the bill extending the operations of the Freedmen's Bureau, which had been created the previous year. The Radical Republicans were also able to determine the conditions for readmission of the former Confederate states to the Union. They mandated that the Southern states ratify the Fourteenth Amendment, which guarantees full citizenship rights to any person born on American soil, and they required the states to restrict the political participation of former Confederates. On the heels of a successful congressional election that secured their majority control, the Radical Republicans pushed through the Reconstruction Acts beginning in 1867. These laws instituted the presence of federal troops in the Southern states until they complied with the stipulations for rejoining the Union, including amending their state constitutions to incorporate blacks as citizens entitled to equal protection under the law and full civil rights.

While Reconstruction reigned, blacks in the South made great strides toward achieving a political voice and representation in the government. They held their own political conventions before the 1867 elections so they could choose candidates to endorse and platforms to support. Many blacks sought and held public office during the 1870s, including the United States Senators Hiram Rhoades Revels and Blanche K. Bruce of Mississippi. P. B. S. Pinchback was elected to the Senate as well as the House of Representatives from Louisiana, but was not permitted to take his seat in either congressional body due to challenges against the legitimacy of the election processes. He did serve as Lieutenant Governor of Louisiana, and for a brief period was the acting governor of the state. There were also twenty black members of the House of Representatives during Reconstruction, among them Joseph Hayne Rainey and Robert Smalls of South Carolina, Benjamin S. Turner of Alabama, and John R. Lynch of Mississippi.

Reconstruction officially ended in 1877 after the controversial election of Rutherford B. Hayes as president in the 1876 election. Hayes lost the popular vote but made the concession of promising to remove federal troops from the South in return for the disputed electoral votes of Florida, Louisiana, and South Carolina. The withdrawal of the military presence from the South meant the resumption of state self-government and the consequent resurgence of the Southern Democrats, who acted quickly to reverse the measures taken under Reconstruction to secure social and political equality for blacks. One of the final triumphs of Reconstruction was the passage of the Civil Rights Act of 1875, which mandated nondiscriminatory access to theaters, hotels, and railroad cars for blacks as well as whites. This act, however, did not survive a judicial challenge—it was declared unconstitutional by the United States Supreme Court in 1883.

THE IMPACT OF FREDERICK DOUGLASS

Frederick Douglass spoke at a rally after the court's decision on the Civil Rights Act of 1875, and opined that the strict constitutionality of the legislation should have been subordinated to the nobility of its purpose: to secure justice on the behalf of all American citizens, regardless of the ancestry of their forebears or the color of their skins. Douglass emerged as the principal spokesperson and leader for the race from the antebellum period until his death in 1895. Born a slave in Talbot County, Maryland, in 1818, Douglass escaped to the North at the age of twenty and began speaking as a fugitive slave on the abolitionist circuit three years later. In 1845 the first version of his most famous publication appeared, *Narrative of the Life of Frederick Douglass, An American Slave, Written by Himself,* which is widely considered the slave narrative that defines the genre. Several subsequent installments of Douglass's autobiographical writings chronicled his subsequent experiences. These included *My Bondage and My Freedom* (1855) and *Life and Times of Frederick Douglass* (1881). Both Charles Waddell Chesnutt (1858–1932) and Booker T. Washington (1856–1915) wrote biographies of Douglass, published in 1899 and 1907, respectively, a testament to his significance as a pioneering race leader even among the most eminent black men of the era.

Douglass was a vociferous opponent of the Jim Crow segregation that gathered momentum in the wake of the 1883 repudiation of the Civil Rights Act of 1875. In the six years that followed the official demise of Reconstruction in 1877, blacks had been ousted from most of the political offices they had occupied during the era and lost much of the ground they had gained, principally through legislative mandate, toward true equality with whites. During the years from 1866 to 1877 blacks had constituted the majority in the South Carolina House of Representatives, but that numerical surplus evaporated once the Republicans lost political control of the South. Although the Fifteenth Amendment prohibited the restriction of voting rights on the basis of "race, color, or previous condition of servitude," it did not explicitly prohibit states from using other means to effectively bar blacks from voting. This was accomplished through the use of poll taxes and literacy tests and by holding segregated primaries to determine the candidates who would run for office. Disfranchising laws were bolstered by the tried-and-true method of intimidation: Sarah Ann Pringle, a white woman who resided in Texas during Reconstruction, recalled in a memoir that white men who had been disallowed by federal mandate from voting in the gubernatorial election of 1873 due to their active support of the Confederacy used force to defend their access to the ballot. They armed themselves, prepared to shoot anyone who attempted to bar them from the polls, and frightened off the would-be black voters with a volley of gunshots.

Such revolutions in miniature happened throughout the South. Charles Waddell Chesnutt's *The Marrow of Tradition* (1901) is a memorable literary account of politically motivated violence. It is based on the massacre and subsequent mass exodus of blacks from Wilmington, North Carolina, in 1898 following an effort by white men to regain Democratic control of the city by inflaming public opinion against what they called Negro domination.

Many of the stories in Chesnutt's collection *The Wife of His Youth and Other Stories of the Color Line* (1899) trace the black experience throughout Reconstruction to its aftermath—a climate of racial hostility. "The Web of Circumstance," the last of the book's nine stories, centers on Ben Davis, a former slave who becomes a moderately successful blacksmith and chides his fellow blacks for squandering their earnings on travel and elaborate churches instead of investing in property. Wiser financial management, he suggests, would have resulted more swiftly in collective black prosperity. Davis's advice, however, is systematically undercut by the unfortunate series of events that plagues him when he is accused of stealing an ornately decorated whip belonging to one of his white clients. The blacksmith is prosecuted and sentenced to five years in the penitentiary without even so much as being able to testify in his own defense. During the term of his incarceration his property is confiscated for taxes and legal expenses, his wife runs off with his former assistant, his daughter becomes an alcoholic and accidentally drowns herself, and his son is lynched after killing a white man. Ben Davis himself, after resolving revenge against the man whose whip he is wrongfully accused of stealing, finally decides against retribution, but is killed by the man nevertheless because he misconstrues Davis's retreat as a threatened assault on his young daughter.

Chesnutt's tale constitutes a many-layered critique of the aborted promise of civil rights under Reconstruction. Ben Davis's advocacy of translating the fruits of independent labor into property acquisition loses much of its force in isolation—his lack of education and reliance upon being in favor with local whites make him vulnerable to the judicial persecution he suffers. In the court of law his reputation for honesty and integrity cannot combat the general prejudice against blacks bolstered by the chain of circumstantial evidence that indicates his guilt. His views on the unrealized potential for racial uplift are twisted by the prosecuting attorney into radical propaganda castigating whites for their continued oppression of former slaves, and Davis can understand none of the rhetoric being attributed to him. Because he has all but ostracized himself from the black community, Davis has no one besides his family to support him. In addition, his previous behavior may have inspired sufficient resentment among other blacks that they are happy to see his ruin and may even have even helped to bring it about. Through the figure of Ben Davis, Chesnutt shows that without political and civil rights, including full participation in the electoral process, legal influence, and access to education, the accumulation of land and ownership of property mean nothing to racial progress because they are insecure holdings.

The insecurity of property became abundantly clear to Frederick Douglass. In 1874 he was named president of the Freedmen's Bank, an institution dedicated to protecting the deposits of emancipated slaves. The bank collapsed that same year despite Douglass's attempts to save it by contributing $10,000 of his personal funds. The bank's failure was caused by ill-advised financial speculation long before Douglass was named president, but he bore much of the criticism for the collapse. The direction of the bank was one of several federal appointments Douglass held under the administrations of Ulysses S. Grant, Rutherford B. Hayes, and James A. Garfield; the other positions included federal marshal to the District of Columbia from 1877 to 1881, recorder of deeds from 1881 to 1886, and U.S. Minister to Haiti from 1889 to 1891.

In his final years Douglass became active in the national anti-lynching campaign led by Ida B. Wells-Barnett (1862–1931). The last speech he wrote, "The Lesson of the Hour: Why Is the Negro Lynched?" was delivered in January of 1894 at the Metropolitan A.M.E. Church in Washington, D.C., and later published under the title *Why Is the Negro Lynched?* (1895). In the speech he indicted the false perception of Southern black men as ruthless sexual predators, which had been disseminated by such champions of moral purity as Frances Willard of the Women's Christian Temperance Union. Douglass noted that this idea had contributed to the practice and toleration of lynching. Public sentiment, as Douglass was well aware, exerted an immeasurable influence on the advancement of civil rights for blacks in America.

ATLANTA COMPROMISE AND *PLESSY V. FERGUSON*

Public sentiment was swayed once again, and again to the detriment of the black American populace, when Booker T. Washington was invited to deliver the opening address at the 1895 Cotton States and International Exposition held in Atlanta, Georgia. Perhaps, had he not succumbed to a heart attack in February of that year, Frederick Douglass might have been entreated to deliver the speech that the Southern organizers hoped would signal to Northern white industrialists that race relations were improving. Instead, Booker T. Washington, the Hampton Institute–educated founder and president of the labor-intensive Tuskegee Institute, was asked to give a public address. Though it pleased the vast majority of Americans who heard or read it and propelled Washington to the national stage as the new voice of black America, the speech may have done more to facilitate the entrenchment of Jim Crow than any deliberate effort to galvanize support for segregation.

The speech commonly known as the Atlanta Exposition was Washington's attempt to conciliate post-Reconstruction resentment between the races and convince Southern whites that blacks shared their commitment to Southern progress and were their best allies in rebuilding the region. In trying to forestall potential white interest in replacing their forfeited slave labor with an influx of immigrant workers, Washington may have overdone his effort to depict Southern blacks as docile, tractable, industrious, forgiving, and altogether willing to subordinate any desire for greater civil rights to the need to work alongside whites in restoring the South to its antebellum glory. The lines that white America fixated upon and interpreted as the black endorsement of Jim Crow segregation used the human hand as an analogy for race relations with respect to leisure and labor: Washington said that while the races could be as divided as the fingers socially, "in all things essential to mutual progress" (Washington, *Up from Slavery*, p. 230) they could work with the united power of the hand.

The key to appreciating the import of Washington's pronouncement is determining what "social" really means. If it signifies, as it came to in the law and custom of white supremacist ideology, that blacks and whites were not to meet on terms of equality in any place where sociability might result, then strict segregationist policies were certainly in order. The races could not share the same public facilities or privileges and expect to maintain social separation, and working relationships had to be governed by a strict hierarchy in order to remain professional and not bleed over into the nebulous "social" category. In this way, many blacks felt as if Booker T. Washington had indeed compromised their interests and thwarted their advancement in order to cater to the sensibilities of proud white Southerners not yet able to stomach the notion of racial equality. This sentiment gathered momentum after the decision rendered by the Supreme Court in the case of *Plessy v. Ferguson,* handed down the next year, which sanctioned the "separate but equal" doctrine that prevailed until the ruling of *Brown v. Board of Education* in 1954.

Homer Plessy, a Louisiana octoroon (a person of one-eighth black ancestry), violated the state's Separate Car Act of 1890 by refusing to leave a whites-only railroad car on 7 June 1892. The train was stopped and Plessy was taken into custody, thus embarking upon a judicial journey that would end unsuccessfully four years later at the United States Supreme Court and was a precursor to the twentieth-century Rosa Parks incident. The arrest was orchestrated by the *Comité des Citoyens,* a group composed largely of mixed-race descendants from the celebrated *gens du coleur* society of free blacks that flourished in the French Quarter of antebellum New Orleans. The organization was formed in 1891 expressly to challenge the Separate Car Act as a step toward dismantling all statutes that violated the civil rights of Americans of African descent. Complicit in the effort were railroad workers who resented being compelled to police the color line by ejecting blacks from the cars reserved for whites and the detective who was compensated for his arrest of Plessy—the *Comité des Citoyens* did not want to surrender their compatriot to the unpredictability of the treatment he might have received at the hands of just any law enforcement officer.

Plessy's situation is reminiscent of a scene from the fictionalized memoir *The Autobiography of an Ex-Colored Man* published anonymously by James Weldon Johnson (1871–1938) in 1912. The unnamed narrator describes a conversation concerning the "Negro question" that he has with four white men representing four different American constituencies—an unreconstructed Texas cotton planter, a Union veteran, a Northern intellectual recently transplanted to a Deep

South state college, and a Jew. What enables him to be privy to their uncensored viewpoints is that, masked by his ambiguously fair skin, he is riding unmolested on a whites-only railroad car through the segregated South. Like Plessy and the men of the organization he represented, the protagonist of Johnson's novel is not interested so much in establishing proximity to whites but in enjoying the luxuries restricted to whites alone. The discrimination that forced blacks of all classes to share the same grossly inferior accommodations violated the spirit of the so-called separate-but-equal facilities policy. The grassroots movement to unseat Jim Crow that originated in Louisiana was a noble struggle that enlisted the courageous efforts of Louis Martinet, the black lawyer and publisher of the *New Orleans Crusader,* the black daily that served as the official organ of the *Comité,* and Albion W. Tourgée (1838–1905), a white lawyer and author of the semi-autobiographical novel *A Fool's Errand* (1879), who argued Plessy's case before the Supreme Court. Nonetheless, public opinion did not favor the eradication of segregation. The popularity of Booker T. Washington's recommendation that the considerations of cooperative labor take precedence over the demands for social recognition made it all the more unlikely that the nation would be receptive to challenges against Jim Crow laws.

Washington's views were also criticized on other grounds. Paul Laurence Dunbar (1872–1906), perhaps best known as a dialect poet of the 1890s, registered concerns that a unidimensional focus on politics would inhibit racial uplift. An erudite young man from Dayton, Ohio (he died of tuberculosis at age thirty-three), Dunbar excoriated the black press for its scant attention to grammatical correctness and its overemphasis on exhaustively cataloging the wrongs perpetrated against the race. He exhorted the multifaceted development of black America in the areas of science, art, and literature, a perspective later articulated most persuasively by W. E. B. Du Bois. Like Du Bois, Dunbar was skeptical of the industrial education solution advocated by Booker T. Washington and worried that white America would use Washington's rhetoric to forestall black ambition. In an article entitled "Our New Madness," which appeared in *The Independent* on 16 September 1897, Dunbar expresses his concern that, despite his "honesty of purpose," Washington is "not doing either himself or his race full justice" in his public addresses (p. 182). Dunbar felt that Washington's speeches resulted in decontextualized quotes that whites used to corroborate their desire to limit blacks to domestic, agricultural, and trade labor.

BOOKER T. WASHINGTON AND W. E. B. DU BOIS

Booker T. Washington's approach to the problem of amalgamation—uniting the races into a single body politic—is often labeled "accommodationist": he opted to accept and work around white opposition to black advancement rather than openly defy it. He championed the efficacy of industrial education, which focused on practical training and the intrinsic dignity of labor, in order to avoid unnerving whites who worried about blacks seeking to elevate themselves from their "proper places." After the overwhelming success of his Atlanta Compromise speech in 1895, influential whites both North and South viewed Washington as the undisputed leader of the race, especially since Frederick Douglass's passing earlier in the same year. Virtually every issue pertinent to the welfare of black Americans was funneled through Washington for endorsement. He approved political appointments, lent support to proposed legislation, proposed individuals for jobs, and solicited funds from his wealthy contacts. For a black person with ambition he was an invaluable friend to have and a formidable enemy. Critics labeled Washington's formalized system of influence the "Tuskegee Machine."

On the other end of the ideological spectrum from Washington was the Harvard-educated William Edward Burghardt (W. E. B.) Du Bois (1868–1963), a member of the intellectual and cultural elite. Du Bois believed in his theory of the "talented tenth"—that every race had its best and brightest, and this ten percent would be the vanguard to lead the community into collective advancement. Unlike Washington, Du Bois felt that liberal arts education would be the means by which blacks could gain access to the upper echelons of society, echoing Charles Chesnutt's sentiment that educational exclusion would be the demise of the black community, however prosperous it became through manual labor. Du Bois most famously articulated his opposition to Washington in the third chapter of his magnum opus, *The Souls of Black Folk* (1903), "Of Mr. Booker T. Washington and Others." Du Bois points out that Washington's advocacy of postponing the effort to secure political power, civil rights, and access to higher education in the interest of preserving harmonious labor relations resulted in the elimination of black voting rights, legally enforced second-class citizenship, and the reduction of public funds for advanced education for blacks. What is not demanded will not be supplied, Du Bois argued.

In 1903 a close friend of Du Bois, William Monroe Trotter (1872–1934), publicly opposed Washington at a rally in Boston. Believing the Tuskegee Machine to be responsible for having Trotter arrested following the denunciation, Du Bois issued a call to black men committed to the cause of civil justice and the abolition of caste distinctions. In July 1905 twenty-nine men responded to the call, and the group was dubbed the Niagara Movement after the site of the first meeting—the Canada side of the falls, where they convened after being refused accommodation on the American side of the border. The Niagara Movement became racially integrated and gender inclusive when it evolved into the National Association for the Advancement of Colored People (NAACP) in 1909, at the height of Washington's national prominence. Du Bois founded *The Crisis,* the magazine of the NAACP, and served as its editor for the next twenty-five years. In his *Crisis* editorials, as well as the Atlanta University Studies of the Negro Problem conference series, which predated his activity with the NAACP, Du Bois identified a plethora of issues facing the black community that required legislative address and reform. *The Crisis* also featured the literary work of up-and-coming black writers, many of whom flourished during the Harlem Renaissance, resulting in the "civil rights by copyright" initiative that pushed the cultural achievements of blacks in order to shape public perception and achieve parity with whites in America. Although segregation and legally sanctioned discrimination would essentially withstand opposition until the advent of the nonviolent protest movement led by Martin Luther King Jr. in the 1960s, the legacy of resistance left by men and women such as Douglass, Plessy, Du Bois, Wells, and Dunbar set precedents for action and inspired the continuation of the struggle for civil rights.

See also The Autobiography of an Ex-Colored Man; Blacks; Jim Crow; Ku Klux Klan; Lynching; *The Marrow of Tradition; Plessy v. Ferguson;* Racial Uplift; *The Souls of Black Folk; Up from Slavery*

BIBLIOGRAPHY

Primary Works

Chesnutt, Charles. *Frederick Douglass.* 1899. Mineola, N.Y.: Dover Publications, 2002.

Chesnutt, Charles W. *The Marrow of Tradition.* 1901. New York: Penguin, 1993.

Chesnutt, Charles Waddell. *The Wife of His Youth and Other Stories of the Color Line.* 1899. Ann Arbor: University of Michigan Press, 1968.

Douglass, Frederick. *Frederick Douglass: New Literary and Historical Essays.* Edited by Eric J. Sundquist. Cambridge, U.K.: Cambridge University Press, 1990.

Douglass, Frederick. *The Life and Times of Frederick Douglass: His Early Life as a Slave, His Escape from Bondage, and His Complete History.* 1881. Mineola, N.Y.: Dover Publications, 2003.

Douglass, Frederick. *Why Is the Negro Lynched?* Bridgwater, n.p.: J. Whitby and Sons, 1895.

Du Bois, W. E. B. *The Souls of Black Folk.* 1903. New York: Penguin, 1989.

Dunbar, Paul Laurence. *In His Own Voice: The Dramatic and Other Uncollected Works of Paul Laurence Dunbar.* Athens: Ohio University Press, 2002.

Johnson, James Weldon. *The Autobiography of an Ex-Colored Man.* 1912. New York: Vintage, 1989.

Washington, Booker T. *Frederick Douglass.* 1907. New York: Argosy-Antiquarian, 1969.

Washington, Booker T. *Up from Slavery.* 1901. New York: Penguin, 1986.

Wells-Barnett, Ida B. *Crusade for Justice: The Autobiography of Ida B. Wells.* Chicago: University of Chicago Press, 1970.

Wells-Barnett, Ida B. *Southern Horrors and Other Writings: The Anti-Lynching Campaign of Ida B. Wells, 1892–1900.* Edited by Jacqueline Jones Royster. Boston: Bedford, 1997.

Wells, Ida B., et al. *The Reason Why the Colored American Is not in the World's Columbian Exposition: The Afro-American's Contribution to Columbian Literature.* 1893. Urbana: University of Illinois Press, 1999.

Secondary Works

Foner, Eric. *Reconstruction: America's Unfinished Revolution, 1863–1877.* New York: Harper and Row, 1988.

Lewis, David Levering. *W. E. B. Du Bois.* Vol. 1, *Biography of a Race, 1868–1919.* New York: Holt, 1993.

Medley, Keith Weldon. *We as Freemen:* Plessy v. Ferguson. Gretna, La.: Pelican, 2003.

Meier, August. *Negro Thought in America, 1880–1915: Racial Ideologies in the Age of Booker T. Washington.* Ann Arbor: University of Michigan Press, 1963.

Mieder, Wolfgang. *"No Struggle, No Progress": Frederick Douglass and His Proverbial Rhetoric for Civil Rights.* New York: Peter Lang, 2001.

Moore, Jacqueline M. *Booker T. Washington, W. E. B. Du Bois, and the Struggle for Racial Uplift.* Wilmington, Del.: SR Books, 2003.

Wintz, Cary D., ed. *African-American Political Thought, 1890–1930: Washington, Du Bois, Garvey, and Randolph.* Armonk, N.Y.: M. E. Sharpe, 1996.

Wormser, Richard. *The Rise and Fall of Jim Crow.* New York: St. Martin's, 2003.

Licia Morrow Calloway

CIVIL WAR MEMOIRS

Remembering the American Civil War is something of a national pastime. From films, documentaries, and reenactments of battles to merchandise, monuments, and historical sites that memorialize the "Great Conflict," no event in U.S. history has received more attention than the Civil War. One reason why the war retains its hold on so many imaginations is that the meaning of the conflict remains a subject for debate. Was the war a crusade to abolish slavery or a fight about states' rights? What were the decisions and factors leading to victory and defeat? Most pressing for many Americans living in the decades after the war were questions about the possibilities of closure. Or in the words of Abraham Lincoln's Second Inaugural Address (1864), how could recently reunited Americans "bind up the nation's wounds" (p. 289)?

Between 1870 and 1920 one response was to read and write about the war. Some texts, like Stephen Crane's *The Red Badge of Courage* (1895), describe the lives of soldiers in battle. Others, like John William De Forest's *The Bloody Chasm* (1881), Frances E. W. Harper's *Iola Leroy* (1892), and Thomas Dixon's *The Clansman* (1905), explore the challenges of reconciliation in the aftermath of the war. Though Edmund Wilson and Daniel Aaron have argued that few literary masterpieces came out of the Civil War, much fiction, poetry, and drama took up the war as a literary topic. The conflict even gave rise to its own subgenre, the Civil War memoir.

THE MEMOIR

Combining autobiography and history, the memoir was one of the most popular forms of Civil War literature. Generally presented as nonfiction and relating experiences in a first-person voice, the form reached its peak in the 1880s, when hundreds of Civil War memoirs appeared before an insatiable public. Some memoirs, typically those of war heroes, came out immediately as books. Others were published as newspaper or magazine articles, some of which were later collected. In 1877 the *Philadelphia Weekly Times* ran a series of memoirs that became *Annals of the War* (1879). In *Battles and Leaders of the Civil War* (1887–1888)—a four-volume set expanded to five in 2002—*Century Magazine* gathered the many memoirs it began publishing in 1884. The popularity of such Civil War narratives lived on through the twentieth century, attesting to the enduring interest that Americans took in the national conflict. Indeed, first-hand accounts of the Civil War continue to be published, even if they are often reconstructed by editors from correspondence, diaries, and journals.

Civil War memoirs drew variously on existing literary traditions. Like Puritan conversion narratives, they often trace a series of setbacks and triumphs ordained by a guiding Providence. Like Benjamin Franklin's *Autobiography* (1771–1790) and Horatio Alger's post–Civil War novels, memoirs often tell stories of lessons learned and challenges overcome through a combination of character, faith, application, and luck. Civil War memoirs also attracted readers long enamored with military histories and myths—from Greek and Roman narratives to the legends of King Arthur to accounts of modern military heroes such as George Washington and Napoleon Bonaparte. Some memoirs drew on sentimental tropes of self-sacrifice and emotional suffering, and like the romances of Sir Walter Scott and James Fenimore Cooper, many report feats of courage and skill against long odds. Finally, some memoirs can be read as examples of literary realism and naturalism insofar as individuals seem to be buffeted by unrelenting institutional and cosmological forces as the brutal physical realities of the war threaten to overwhelm humanitarian ideals.

Taken as a whole, Civil War memoirs form a recognizable but diverse body of work. Many narratives were written from memory decades after the war. Other writers relied on letters, journals, maps, and newspaper accounts. Some focused on facts and material details, while others offered more impressionistic responses. The motives for writing were also wide-ranging—vindication from criticism, monetary gain, the desire to set the record "straight," the urge to define one's role in history, howsoever exalted or modest. Though most Civil War memoirs were written by people directly involved in the fighting, recollections came from various perspectives—famous generals and common soldiers, combatants and civilians, blacks and whites, men and women, Southerners and Northerners. What is most interesting about many memoirs is their writers' efforts to make sense of the war, to bring political, religious, and psychological order to a chaotic and often traumatic event in which a country broke apart and violently came back together. Also central to the genre is the challenge of reconstructing the past and negotiating what Michael Kammen calls "the problematic relationships between myth and memory, tradition and history" (p. 17).

THE GENERALS

The best-selling Civil War memoirs were those of prominent generals, who tended to focus on organizational difficulties, military tactics, and battle descriptions, often to justify their decisions and bring retrospective order to the war. Memoirs from Union generals include George B. McClellan's *McClellan's Own*

Story (1887), P. H. Sheridan's *Personal Memoirs* (1888), and John Pope's 1886 articles (collected in *The Military Memoirs of John Pope*, 1998). The most famous of such accounts is Ulysses S. Grant's (1822–1885) *Personal Memoirs* (1885). Grant's book sold over 300,000 copies by subscription alone—not only because Grant was a war hero largely credited with the Union's victory, and not only because he served two terms as president of the United States (1868–1876) but also because his memoirs were written under extraordinary circumstances. In 1884 Grant went bankrupt after being defrauded by a business partner. To add to his woes he was diagnosed with inoperable cancer of the throat. Grant had resisted writing his history, but he now had little choice. Racing against his impending death and watched by a sympathetic public, Grant wrote (and dictated) a lengthy memoir remarkable for the clarity of its prose and the expansive scope of its vision. Grant primarily sticks to the facts, but he offers opinions on major figures such as Lincoln, Jefferson Davis, and Robert E. Lee. He discusses the causes of the war (slavery and Southern "Demagogues" [p. 117]), the lesson of the conflict ("the necessity of avoiding wars in the future" [p. 635]), and the wisest course for postwar America (guarantee political rights for blacks and work toward national harmony). Grant's memoirs, like his military labors, proved to be a hard-won success. He died three weeks after completing his book, but with the help of his publisher, Mark Twain, he made enough money to pay off his creditors and ensure the comfort of his family.

If Grant's book tends toward reconciliation and closure, William Tecumseh Sherman's (1820–1891) *Memoirs* (1875, revised 1886) never quite give up the fight. At the end of the war Sherman was the second most prominent Union general, yet he remained a villain in the South, mainly because of his March to the Sea, a destructive campaign designed to destroy the Confederacy's infrastructure and morale. Sherman's *Memoirs* sold ten thousand copies within its first month. It also, despite its author's claims, was more contentious than conciliatory. Sherman blames the war and its casualties on the South and defends his March to the Sea. He "waves the bloody shirt" by recalling Confederate atrocities at Fort Pillow and Andersonville prison. Sherman even angered some Northern readers, who felt that he claimed too much credit for himself by slighting fellow generals, including Grant. In his revised *Memoirs* of 1886, which stretch over one thousand pages, Sherman answers many of his critics, providing copious memoranda, correspondence, and charts while reprinting objections from his opponents and offering precious few retractions. In its passionate attention to detail and refusal to let go of past animosi-

---

The following excerpt is from William Tecumsch Sherman's Civil War memoirs:

In this free country every man is at perfect liberty to publish his own thoughts and impressions, and any witness who may differ from me should publish his own version of facts in the truthful narration of which he is interested. I am publishing my own memoirs, not *theirs,* and we all know that no three honest witnesses of a simple brawl can agree on all the details. How much more likely will be the difference in a great battle covering a vast space of broken ground, when each division, brigade, regiment, and even company, naturally and honestly believes that it was the focus of the whole affair! Each of them won the battle. None ever lost.

Sherman, *Memoirs*, p. 5.

---

ties, Sherman's *Memoirs* show how the war continued to be fought in books long after Appomattox, as numerous parties with divergent interests struggled to shape America's memory of the conflict.

The two most celebrated Confederate generals never wrote their memoirs. Thomas Jonathan "Stonewall" Jackson was killed during the war. Lee chose not to write his recollections, adding to his reputation as a private, self-sacrificing man. James Longstreet recorded his war experiences in *From Manassas to Appomattox* (1896), as did Colonel John S. Mosby in *Mosby's War Reminiscences and Stuart's Cavalry Campaigns* (1887), while G. T. Beauregard and Joseph E. Johnston wrote articles for *Century Magazine.* Jefferson Davis, president of the Confederacy, wrote *The Rise and Fall of the Confederate Government* (1881), though the work may be more accurately called a history than a memoir. One Southern general widely read is Edward Porter Alexander (1835–1910), whose *Military Memoirs of a Confederate* (1907) is augmented by more personal recollections in *Fighting for the Confederacy* (written between 1897 and 1907, published in 1989). In many ways *Fighting for the Confederacy* participates in the myth of the Lost Cause, a view that lauds the heroic, doomed efforts of the South against a powerful but blundering invader. Alexander names states' rights, not slavery, as the cause of secession. He blames the Union for instigating the war and laments the lost opportunities for Confederate victory. Contented slaves appear in the narrative, as do tragic accounts of Southern bravery.

Yet *Fighting for the Confederacy* is not an entirely one-sided memoir. The leadership of both Grant and Jackson comes in for praise and censure. Even Lee, Alexander's beloved commander, is held accountable for mistakes, particularly in Alexander's stirring recollection of Pickett's Charge at Gettysburg. Rich in personal anecdote and military detail, *Fighting for the Confederacy* provides an immediate sense of the war, though it also offers reflection and judgment.

COMMON SOLDIERS

In the nineteenth century American histories for the most part focused on powerful men. Many Civil War memoirs fit this "top-down" model of history, though rank-and-file soldiers also recorded their wartime recollections. A wealth of their diaries, journals, and letters is available in modern print editions, many of which are listed in Garold L. Cole's *Civil War Eyewitnesses* (1988–2000), an annotated bibliography. As might be expected, these documents tend to show a different side of the war. Though the Virginian Robert Catlett Cave insisted that "privates did not concede to their generals a monopoly of military judgment" (p. 14), common soldiers wrote less about large-scale strategies and more about their own immediate experiences—the hardships and joys of camp life, individual actions in battle, the less conspicuous but important roles played in national events.

Along with John Esten Cooke's *Wearing of the Gray; Being Personal Portraits, Scenes and Adventures of the War* (1867), one of the best-known Civil War memoirs from the ranks is George Cary Eggleston's (1839–1911) *A Rebel's Recollections* (1875), a book first serialized in the *Atlantic Monthly* and one that went through four editions by 1905. Eggleston was raised in Indiana but moved to Virginia as a teenager. He voted against Virginia's secession but eventually fought on the Confederate side. Having lived in both the North and South, Eggleston understandably wrote his memoir to foster sympathy between sections. In deference to the South, Eggleston retains some features of the Lost Cause narrative. The Confederacy fights for honor, not slavery. Southern generals are depicted as heroes. Slaves are well treated in Eggleston's book, until they are freed and become "desperados" (p. 181). At the same time, Eggleston also appeals to a Northern readership. He admits the utter defeat of the South and looks forward to peaceful race relations. Like other Northern writers, he lays much blame not on the South as a whole but on Jefferson Davis. Unrepentant about secession and yet respectful to the Union, *A Rebel's Recollections* works toward reconciliation, even as it overlooks more brutal and contentious aspects of the war.

Ambrose Bierce was critical of the Civil War in his memoirs:

One would think war horrible enough without the monstrous exaggerations that seem inseparable from the story of it. Nothing is more common than to hear and read about "mowing down" the enemy or being mown down by them, projectiles cutting "wide gaps" through charging columns, "heaps of slain" that clog the cannon wheels, "rivers of blood" and the rest of it. All this is absurd: nothing of the kind occurs—nothing, rather, of the degree. These are phenomena of the campfire, the hearthstone, the "rostrum" and the writing-desk. They are subjective—deeds of memory in a frame of mind. They have a fine literary effect when skillfully employed, and in purely literary work are allowable in landscape painting to aggrandize the mountains. Outside of literature their use is to humbug the civilian, frighten the children and grapple the women's hearts with hooks of steel—all tending to the magnification of the narrator.

Bierce, "Prattle," p. 61.

Like Eggleston, other common soldiers found opportunities to publish their memoirs. Privates and sergeants received occasional space in *Battles and Leaders of the Civil War*. Others published pieces in newspapers and magazines, including James P. Sullivan, whose reminiscences are gathered in *An Irishman in the Iron Brigade* (1993), and the novelist John William De Forest, whose war nonfiction is collected in *A Volunteer's Adventures* (1946). Some of the war's most evocative and most critical depictions came from Ambrose Bierce, who reprinted many of his war memoirs in his *Collected Works* (1909; also in *A Sole Survivor: Bits of Autobiography*, 1998). Bierce entered the Union army as a private and left as a first lieutenant. He witnessed some of the war's most furious fighting and later wrote such classic short stories as "Chickamauga" (1889) and "An Occurrence at Owl Creek Bridge" (1890). Like his fiction, Bierce's memoirs are polished performances that yet reveal the horrors of the war—eviscerations, burned corpses, brain fragments, even pigs feeding on the faces of the dead. Ironic and caustic, Bierce understands how the war is romanticized and sanitized by memory, even as he sometimes falls prey (and knows he falls prey) to the cheerful temptations of nostalgia.

Yet for all the common soldiers who wrote about the war for family, self, and posterity, relatively few published their memoirs between 1870 and 1920. One explanation for this is that prominent generals commanded larger audiences and had more access to publishers. Only in the twentieth century did many "bottom-up" recollections appear in their entirety. Among these posthumously published memoirs are Cave's *Raw Pork and Hardtack* (published 1996), David Holt's *A Mississippi Rebel in the Army of Northern Virginia* (written in the early 1920s, published in 1995), and Henry Kyd Douglas's *I Rode with Stonewall* (completed in 1899, published in 1940). A Virginian on Stonewall Jackson's staff, Douglas (1838–1903) disapproved of slavery but fought for the Confederacy. His memoirs paint a complex picture of Jackson—capable of great tenderness and violence, fearless as well as God-fearing. Another interesting memoir, this time from a Yankee, is Alfred Bellard's (d. 1891) *Gone for a Soldier* (written in the late 1880s, published in 1975). The New Jersey–born Bellard enlisted as a private in the Army of the Potomac, and his memoirs (including rough sketches and drawings) focus on his day-to-day life as a soldier—marches, weather, work details, food, accommodations, and battles. Reflecting the boredom, complaints, and cynicism that could mark the life of a soldier, Bellard's memoirs give an unromantic, revealing picture of the war.

BLACK SOLDIERS

Another perspective on the war focuses on African American soldiers. Not allowed in the Union military until 1863, almost 200,000 black troops enlisted in the Union cause (while a lesser number served or were conscripted on the Confederate side). As David W. Blight has shown, the presence of blacks in the Civil War was often "whitewashed" away in the decades that followed, in part because conflicts over racial equality remained an obstacle to national reunion. But if many postwar Americans sought intersectional harmony at the expense of black rights, others memorialized African American contributions during the war.

One such figure was the white abolitionist Thomas Wentworth Higginson (1823–1911), whose *Army Life in a Black Regiment* (1870) details his experiences commanding African American military units. Higginson's regiment was composed of ex-slaves freed by Union forces. At a time when Northerners debated whether blacks should be allowed in the military, Higginson's First South Carolina Volunteers vindicated the abilities of black soldiers. In *Army Life in a Black Regiment,* Higginson describes his men as disciplined, intelligent, honest, and—most important—courageous. Like most white Americans of the time, abolitionists included, Higginson engages in some racial stereotyping. But while he often depicts his men as naturally musical and childlike, he also attends to the cultural conditions that shaped their lives under slavery. Higginson's memoirs insist upon the potential of African Americans as citizens. By looking back on the Civil War, he fights for black rights in the postwar period.

The same is true of other war accounts written by African Americans. Refusing to forget black achievements, William Wells Brown's *The Negro in the American Rebellion* (1867), George Washington Williams's *A History of the Negro Troops in the War of the Rebellion, 1861–1865* (1888), and Joseph T. Wilson's *The Black Phalanx* (1888) all recall black Civil War soldiers from a historian's perspective. Of particular interest was the renowned Massachusetts Fifty-fourth, a black regiment that suffered massive casualties in its assault on Fort Wagner, thus demonstrating to the nation and world the mettle of African American soldiers.

Though not precisely a soldier, Susie King Taylor (b. 1848), in her *Reminiscences of My Life in Camp with the 33d United States Colored Troops* (1902), describes her work as a laundress, nurse, and teacher in a black regiment. Taylor was stationed in South Carolina near Higginson, who wrote an introduction to her book. Her narrative is sparse but also remarkable, detailing her escape from slavery into Union lines, her dedication to her "boys," her learning to shoot, and her resourcefulness in caring for the wounded and hungry. Taylor ends her memoirs with a chapter titled "Thoughts on Present Conditions," making explicit her call for racial equality and assailing those Americans who refused to fulfill the egalitarian promises of the war. The broader cultural desire to ignore black rights, coupled with educational and economic disadvantages, can help to explain the relative dearth of Civil War memoirs published by African Americans between 1870 and 1920. However, many primary documents are now available in print collections, such as *On the Altar of Freedom: A Black Soldier's Letters from the Front* (1991), *A Grand Army of Black Men: Letters from African-American Soldiers in the Union Army* (1993), *Voices of the 55th* (1996), *A Voice of Thunder: The Civil War Letters of George E. Stevens* (1997), and *Freedom's Soldiers: The Black Military Experience in the Civil War* (1998).

THE HOME FRONT

The Civil War is traditionally associated with military forces. But as scholars such as Elizabeth Young, Kathleen Diffley, and Drew Faust have shown, the experiences of women and men on the home front are no less compelling. For Americans not directly involved in the fighting, the war affected family members, domestic arrangements, and entire worldviews. Noncombatants provided material support and ideological direction to various war efforts. Civic unrest and the return of the wounded brought the war home to many Americans. With battles raging on native soil and with news spread quickly by voice, print, and image, the war changed the lives of many civilians, some of whom wrote their memoirs.

From a Southern perspective, Kate Stone's *Brokenburn: The Journal of Kate Stone, 1861–1868* (1900) reprints her writings from the war and its aftermath, revealing the anger, anxieties, and privations Stone (1841–1907) endured on her family's Louisiana plantation before fleeing into Texas to escape the Union army. Stone's narrative traces a dramatic arc—from initial optimism, to utter despair, to a homecoming and a final acceptance of defeat. Along the way Stone describes such traumatic events as the deaths of two brothers, an uprising of slaves, and the destruction of her childhood world. Most famously, Mary Boykin Chesnut's (1823–1886) memoirs show the war as seen—and reconstructed—by a South Carolina woman married to a prominent Southern politician. Chesnut kept journals of her wartime experiences (later published as *The Private Mary Chesnut*, 1984). Her memoirs first appeared as *A Diary from Dixie* (1905), a text presented as a day-to-day diary but one that Chesnut wrote in the early 1880s by revising her earlier journals. The complicated composition history of *A Diary from Dixie* shows how memories of the war are under constant revision. Chesnut's book is also a fascinating portrait of a witty, willful, and complex woman who disliked slavery but supported the Confederacy, was simultaneously inspired and disabled by the war, and found both a solace and a burden in the writing of her wartime experiences.

Like Chesnut's texts, Elizabeth Keckley's *Behind the Scenes; or, Thirty Years a Slave, and Four Years in the White House* (1868) describes the domestic contexts in which Civil War struggles took place. Keckley (c. 1818–1907), a freed slave, became the dressmaker for Mary Todd Lincoln, the president's wife. Her book is part slave narrative and part memoir, mixing fiction with historical fact while gossiping about famous war figures and, more intimately, their wives. Showing the cruelty and generosity of both Northern and Southern whites, *Behind the Scenes* is an antislavery book that yet appeals to national reconciliation. Keckley's careful use of symbol and voice also suggests that while blacks and women were often forced behind the scenes, they nonetheless played powerful roles in the war, a point made more explicitly in Frederick Douglass's autobiography, *Life and Times of Frederick Douglass* (1881, expanded 1892).

The most notable memoir from a noncombatant may be Walt Whitman's *Specimen Days* (1882), an autobiography that recounts (among other things) his work in Union hospitals. Like many of his generation, Whitman (1819–1892) calls the Civil War "the distinguishing event of my time" (p. 689). He describes the horrors of the hospital—groans and blood, despairing deaths, wagons full with amputated limbs. Yet as in his book of Civil War poems, *Drum-Taps* (1865), Whitman finds heroism and wholeness in the war without denying its destructive effects. Based on Whitman's wartime journals, *Specimen Days* is a visionary but also grounded effort to find in the grim realities of the war a vindication of America's indestructible potential for unity, freedom, and compassion, all represented, Whitman suggests, in his own personal largesse.

Finally, another major literary figure who looks back on the war is Mark Twain (1835–1920), whose "Private History of a Campaign That Failed" (1885) simultaneously satirizes and participates in the genre of Civil War memoirs. Published in *Century Magazine* during the heyday of its memoir series and appearing after Twain was criticized for profiting from the dead Grant's *Personal Memoirs,* Twain's "Private History" begins by noting the rage for Civil War heroes only to present his own wartime experience as someone who "didn't do anything" (p. 417). In his fictionalized story, Twain and his teenage friends are swayed by romantic views of the war, but their laughable efforts to form a military company show that they lack the skill and will to take part in the conflict. It is only after they ostensibly kill an innocent stranger that they learn the true magnitude of the Civil War. That tragedy erupts in the comic plot indicates how hard it was in the postwar period to romanticize the war. And that Twain and his Missouri company barely dodge, allegedly, an engagement with the young Grant shows how close the war came to many Americans, even those who lived through it as a private affair.

See also Autobiography; *Century Magazine;*
   Civil War Memorials and Monuments; *Personal*
   Memoirs of U.S. Grant; Reconstruction

BIBLIOGRAPHY

Primary Works

Bierce, Ambrose. *Collected Works*. New York: Neale, 1909.

Cave, Robert Catlett. *Raw Pork and Hardtack: A Civil War Memoir from Manassas to Appomattox*. Edited by Walbrook Swank. Shippensburg, Pa.: Burd Street Press, 1996.

Eggleston, George Cary. *A Rebel's Recollections*. 1875. Bloomington: Indiana University Press, 1959.

Grant, Ulysses S. *Personal Memoirs of U. S. Grant*. 1885, 1886. New York: Penguin Books, 1999.

Lincoln, Abraham. *Speeches and Letters*. Edited by Peter Parish. London: Everyman's Library, 1993.

Sherman, William Tecumseh. *Memoirs of General W. T. Sherman*. 1875, rev. 1886. New York: Library of America, 1990.

Twain, Mark (Samuel Clemens). "The Private History of a Campaign That Failed." In *The Portable Mark Twain*, edited by Tom Quirk, pp. 417–437. New York: Penguin Books, 2004.

Whitman, Walt. *Complete Poetry and Collected Prose*. New York: Literary Classics of the United States, 1982.

Secondary Works

Aaron, Daniel. *The Unwritten War: American Writers and the Civil War*. New York: Knopf, 1973.

Ayers, Edward. "Worrying about the Civil War." In *Moral Problems in American Life: New Perspectives on Cultural History*, edited by Karen Halttunen and Lewis Perry, pp. 145–166. Ithaca, N.Y., and London: Cornell University Press, 1998.

Berlin, Ira, Joseph P. Reidy, and Leslie S. Rowland, eds. *Freedom's Soldiers: The Black Military Experience*. Cambridge, U.K., and New York: Cambridge University Press, 1998.

Blight, David W. *Race and Reunion: The Civil War in American Memory*. Cambridge, Mass., and London: Harvard University Press, 2001.

Cole, Garold L. *Civil War Eyewitnesses: An Annotated Bibliography of Books and Articles, 1955–1986*. Columbia: University of South Carolina Press, 1988.

Cole, Garold L. *Civil War Eyewitnesses: An Annotated Bibliography of Books and Articles, 1986–1996*. Columbia: University of South Carolina Press, 2000.

Diffley, Kathleen, ed. *To Live and Die: Collected Stories of the Civil War, 1861–1876*. Durham, N.C., and London: Duke University Press, 2002.

Faust, Drew Gilpin. *Mothers of Invention: Women of the Slaveholding South in the American Civil War*. Chapel Hill: University of North Carolina Press, 1996.

Kammen, Michael. *Mystic Chords of Memory: The Transformation of Tradition in American Culture*. New York: Vintage, 1991.

Wilson, Edmund. *Patriotic Gore: Studies in the Literature of the Civil War*. New York: Farrar, Straus and Giroux, 1962.

Young, Elizabeth. *Disarming the Nation: Women's Writing and the Civil War*. Chicago: University of Chicago Press, 1999.

Maurice S. Lee

CIVIL WAR MEMORIALS AND MONUMENTS

Hundreds of monuments were erected in the decades following the American Civil War, 1861–1865. They stand in small county seats and rural cemeteries across the eastern United States as well as on New York's Fifth Avenue, Richmond's Monument Avenue, the Boston Common, and Arlington National Cemetery. Their complexity and variety are testimony to a conflict whose causes and meaning still defy conclusive analysis. Some broad contours of development can be traced in the elegies and monuments erected by local communities, however. In the fifty-year span 1870–1920, the emphasis shifted from mourning and bereavement to reconciliation and celebration.

BEREAVEMENT AND FUNEREAL ERA, 1866–1889

The practical necessity of retrieving, identifying, and burying the dead occasioned memorials in the first three decades after the war. The monuments, usually erected in cemeteries, promulgated defiance and pathos, using the customary mourning symbols of the Victorian era—wreaths, scrollwork, and inscriptions of poetry. The scale and degree of ornamentation varied, but the most common statue was an obelisk, a tapered, four-sided stone shaft with a pyramidal peak. Sculptures of ordinary soldiers were erected beginning in the 1870s. The representative soldier was neither aloof nor abstract and "hardly seemed suited for a war memorial," Foster observes, standing "at ease, with his rifle resting on the ground and his arms resting on it. He seemed anything but a dashing, daring knight and, in fact, hardly seemed martial at all" (p. 129). The result was a relaxed iconoclasm—an enormous effort to create an appearance of indifference—a soldier who was un-martial, sometimes slouching, usually at parade rest. This was utterly appropriate as an American memorial to endurance and confidence. Defeat, even death, was not final: personified as the soldier, "he" was still comfortably present. Memories would fade and arguments over interpretations of the war would continue, but these stone or metal evocations achieved the aim of their sponsors and designers by preserving the illusion that the past was not dead.

The Confederate battle flag was a common symbol in the South, but religious symbolism often took precedence. The Judeo-Christian narrative of life, death, and resurrection informed perceptions of the history of the Confederacy and of the service and deaths of so many Confederate soldiers. It seems it provided sufficient rationale to southerners as they endured what the Buchanan, Virginia, monument calls the "Dark Reconstruction" period and took solace in the prospect that God would ultimately administer justice. *Deo Vindice* (God Is Our Protector), the national motto for the Confederacy established in 1862, also served as a rallying cry and credo. In time, the phrase was inscribed on thousands of monuments and tombstones.

The rhetorical challenge of northern monuments was simpler. The military results of the war were beyond dispute, while its justification was readily captured in succinct abstractions that balanced achievement and mourning. Typical was the Mifflin, Pennsylvania, courthouse elegy erected in 1870, which declares "Victory" but announces that it stands "In Memory of the Soldiers from Juniata County Pa. who Died in the War of the Great Rebellion." Equally taciturn is the White Plains, New York, monument of 1872 to its soldiers "Who Died in the Service of Their Country in the Civil War."

Solemn, restrained texts were common on both sides. The North Carolina obelisk at Winchester, Virginia's Stonewall Confederate Cemetery was erected with a two-initial, two-word inscription: "-N-C-Confederate Dead." The omissions are notable: three sides of the monument are blank, North Carolina is not spelled out, and no sentiments, tributes, or apologetics are expressed. The 1874 monument to the Union soldier on the Antietam battlefield at Sharpsburg, Maryland, is immense. The presiding cemetery monument, sculpted in bronze and granite, weighs 250 tons, with a base surmounted by a prototypical soldier over twenty-one feet tall standing at parade rest. The inscription, in contrast, is strikingly taciturn: "Not for Themselves But for Their Country— September 17, 1862."

As early as the 1870s, the withdrawal of federal troops from the South and the centennial of the American Revolution gave rise to a semblance of reconciliation between North and South. In the South, that reconciliation was qualified with—ironically— patriotic justifications for the war of secession. The eulogists of the Confederate monument in Harrisonburg,

Virginia, declared that the southern lives sacrificed "vindicated the principles of 1776." The accompanying inscriptions—"Success is not Patriotism. Defeat is not Rebellion"— affirmed the faith of a shadow community of defiance and dissent. The South's defeat could not be reversed by an act of rhetoric, but in these texts the war was justified as a veritable second American Revolution. That stance—that the war was a lost but righteous cause—gradually gained favor. The former Confederate general Wade Hampton was unabashed in a dedication address at the Warrenton, Virginia, Confederate monument on 12 June 1877:

> Why should we admit we are in the wrong? . . . If the principles which justified the first revolution were true in 1776, they were no less true in that of 1861. . . . If Washington was a patriot, Lee cannot have been a rebel; if the grand enunciation of the truths of the Declaration of Independence made Jefferson immortal, the observance of them cannot make Davis a traitor. (Warman, p. 68)

In general, however, it is the memory of those who fought that remains prominent in northern and southern monuments. Elaborations are few, justifications terse. The 1876 monument in Cortland County, New York, for example, is simply a "Centennial Offering" in "Memory of Those Who Fought in Defense of the Union." The Grand Army of the Republic memorial in Woodlawn Cemetery (1885) south of Syracuse is simply declared to be "In Memory of Our Dead Comrades." The Canton, New York, monument in the town square merely states, "In Memoriam 1861–1865."

RECONCILIATION OR CELEBRATION ERA, 1890–1920

The peak of monument development occurred in the reconciliation or celebration era. By 1914, Charles Reagan Wilson notes, "over a thousand monuments existed in the South," and "many battlefields had been set aside as pilgrimage sites containing holy shrines" (p. 178). The Gettysburg battlefield would have nearly thirteen hundred monuments erected by 1920, most of them northern. The semicentennial of the war took place in the years 1911–1915 and served as an impetus; so too were the nationalist fervor aroused during the Spanish-American War and World War I and the aging or passing of the first generation of descendants. County seats, urban centers, city parks, and battlefields were chosen as sites more often than cemeteries. Political motives superseded religious paeans. Many monuments were funded by state legislatures; some even had federal support. Women's groups such as the South's Ladies Memorial Association or the United Daughters of the Confederacy had already sponsored many of the earlier monuments, but by the turn of the century they were more frequently the primary organizers.

The manufacture of the monuments was also distinctive. The inscriptionists drew from the cultures of ancient Greece and Rome for their tributes and elegies; the scale and design of the monuments attest to the influence of Egyptian revivalism. Some were handcrafted by local artisans; other designers, for example, F. William Sievers and Edward Valentine, had national or international reputations. With time, the erection of monuments became an industry. Soderberg writes that before the war "only four companies made statuary in the U.S.[;] by 1915 there were sixty-three" (p. xxv). Still, community distinctions are preserved. "Far from being produced on an assembly line, those statues were individually made, usually using a standard model, which could be changed to suit the [sponsoring] organization's committee"

(p. xxiv). The Tappahannock, Virginia, courthouse monument is inscribed with a roster of 772 names; that at Hanover with 1,078 names; while the Charlottesville university cemetery lists 1,096 soldiers. Opulence was often the order of the day. Gilded Age satisfaction is no more evident in northern elegies than in the gold-clad equestrian monument to the Union general William T. Sherman, designed by Augustus Saint-Gaudens and located on Fifth Avenue in New York City. The 1903 statue epitomized northern sentiments of "glorious contentment," to quote Stuart McConnell's title. A beaux arts extravagance marked the enormous domed Pennsylvania monument at Gettysburg. The elegy, dedicated in 1910, is sixty-nine feet tall, surmounted by the bronze goddess Victory, and adorned with four bas-reliefs and eight bronze statues. At the base, 86 bronze tablets list 34,530 names: Pennsylvania's "Sons Who Fought for the Preservation of the Union."

The Robert Gould Shaw memorial, Boston. Bas-relief sculpture by Augustus Saint-Gaudens, 1897.

Many of the monuments erected during the semi-centennial of the war were celebratory. Apologetics and nationalist aims had less standing; sentiment and grandeur prevailed. The Front Royal, Virginia, monument, dedicated 4 July 1911, is lavish in its visual adornment and textual tributes to its Confederate soldiers: "To those Who Gave Much and those Who Gave All." The trend toward sentimentalism and wistfulness would continue. The courthouse memorial at Monterey, Virginia, was dedicated 4 July 1919 as a "Loving Tribute to the Past, the Present, and the Future." The paean was inscribed beneath a statue of a young Confederate soldier facing north, a hand shading his eyes as he gazes into the distance, as if to guard against any further threats of incursion from that direction. The Confederate monument at Arlington National Cemetery in northern Virginia is the most lavish elegy of its kind. Reconciliation was deemed the central theme of the Moses Ezekiel design. President Woodrow Wilson delivered a conciliatory address at the dedication ceremonies on 4 June 1914, and Union and Confederate veterans placed wreaths on the graves. There is no intimation on the monument, however, that the claims behind secession or the "Lost Cause" were not legitimate. The seal of the Confederacy was prominently inscribed; so too was a bas-relief of Minerva, goddess of war, and a shield bearing the word "Constitution." The overall stance in the rhetoric of northern and southern monuments—grudging reconciliation by the South, the solace of victory in the North—might be inscribed for the ages, but postwar monuments marked continued conflict. The Union was preserved and a status quo ante of peace was restored, but the issue of rights—state and civil—was not destined to be resolved.

Race played its part. The Robert Gould Shaw Memorial on Boston Common, an Augustus Saint-Gaudens design, was erected in 1897 in honor of the colonel of the Fifty-fourth Massachusetts Infantry, the first all-black regiment recruited in the North. Shaw was killed in action on 18 July 1863, one of 256 casualties the Fifty-fourth incurred that day in an attack on Fort Wagner, South Carolina. The assault was repulsed, but the virtues of black troops—which were doubted by factions on both the Union and the Confederate sides—were proven beyond doubt. The war had "but one meaning in the eye of history," William James concluded at the dedication ceremonies: the abolition of slavery, and "nowhere was that meaning better symbolised and embodied than in the constitution of this first Northern negro regiment" (James).

Slavery and its abolition are never explicitly cited in southern monuments. ("States rights" is arguably an oblique reference.) Nevertheless, the facade of Virginia's postwar unity in devotion to the Lost Cause was subverted at the West Point Cemetery of Elmwood Cemetery, Norfolk. A monument to Union soldiers in this black cemetery was completed in 1920. It was the only Union monument erected by southerners in Virginia and the only monument to black Civil War troops in that state. It was not the only claim to a legacy in the community: three Confederate monuments stand in the adjacent Elmwood Cemetery, and a fourth—to "Our Confederate Dead"—was erected in downtown Norfolk in 1907. The defiance implicit in the claims of southern monuments that the "Patriotism . . . of Confederate Soldiers" was committed to a "Just and Holy Cause," as espoused at the Oxford, Mississippi, courthouse, for example, did not go unchallenged.

See also Art and Architecture

BIBLIOGRAPHY

Primary Work

James, William. "Dedication Speech: Oration at the Exercises in the Boston Music Hall, May 31, 1987 [*sic*], upon the Unveiling of the Shaw Monument." Department of English, College of the Holy Cross. Available at http://www.holycross.edu/departments/english/sluria/wjspeech.htm.

Secondary Works

Craven, Wayne. *The Sculptures at Gettysburg.* New York: Eastern Acorn Press, 1982.

Foster, Gaines M. *Ghosts of the Confederacy: Defeat, the Lost Cause, and the Emergence of the New South, 1865 to 1913.* New York: Oxford University Press, 1987.

Jacob, Kathryn Allamong. *Testament to Union: Civil War Monuments in Washington, D.C.* Baltimore: Johns Hopkins University Press, 1998.

McConnell, Stuart. *Glorious Contentment: The Grand Army of the Republic, 1865–1900.* Chapel Hill: University of North Carolina Press, 1992.

Soderberg, Susan Cooke. *Lest We Forget: A Guide to Civil War Monuments in Maryland.* Shippensburg, Pa.: White Mane Publishing, 1995.

Sparrow, John. *Visible Words: A Study of Inscriptions in and as Books and Works of Art.* Cambridge, U.K.: Cambridge University Press, 1969.

Warman, Joanne Browning, ed. *The Memorial Wall to Name the Fallen: Warrenton, Virginia, Cemetery.* Warrenton, Va.: Black Horse Chapter, No. 9, United Daughters of the Confederacy, 1998.

Wilson, Charles Reagan. *Baptized in Blood: The Religion of the Lost Cause, 1865–1920.* Athens: University of Georgia Press, 1980.

Timothy S. Sedore

CLUBS AND SALONS

Writing in 1835, Alexis de Tocqueville noted that "Americans of all ages, all conditions, and all dispositions constantly form associations" (vol. 2, bk. 2, chap. 5, p. 106). Tocqueville rightly identified America as a nation of joiners. Key figures throughout American history have been club members, from George Washington and Benjamin Franklin, who were Masons, to Richard Nixon, Ronald Reagan, and George H. W. Bush, who have been members of San Francisco's secretive and elite Bohemian Club. Writers, artists, and their patrons have also formed private clubs, breaking the romantic notion of the starving artist as social outsider, isolated and misunderstood.

As Tocqueville forecast, club popularity expanded throughout the nineteenth century, and by 1910 about one-third of all adult males belonged to at least one club. Many joined for the life insurance policies clubs offered their members, but the need to join went beyond insurance benefits. Clubs, most of which excluded women, offered their members a refuge from the melting pot of American culture; they were (and remain) places where people of similar social and economic backgrounds could enjoy the security of brotherhood. Like-mindedness, however, can sometimes become narrow-mindedness, as Sinclair Lewis shows in *Main Street* (1920) and *Babbitt* (1922), novels satirizing the overly earnest, backslapping mentality then part of businessmen's clubs, such as Rotary (1905), Kiwanis (1915), and Lions (1917). In spite of outsiders' suspicions, clubs endured as centers for political, economic, intellectual, and artistic leaders to gather, share ideas, and form alliances, thus helping shape the American political and cultural landscape.

INTELLECTUAL CLUBS

An important intellectual club during this period was the Radical Club of Boston, which began meeting in 1867. In keeping with the earlier Transcendental Club (1836) started by Ralph Waldo Emerson (1803–1882), the Radical Club invited women as well as men to join the group. The group's chronicler, Mrs. John T. Sargent, notes that there were thirty "persons" who attended the first meeting that spring. Emerson, himself a member of no less than five clubs, gave what was presumably the inaugural talk, "Religion." The Radical Club continued meeting at its Chestnut Street, Boston, home until 1880, covering issues ranging from Darwinism to Don Quixote, and women were among the presenters. Julia Ward Howe (1819–1910), for example, famous for "The Battle Hymn of the Republic," spoke on "Limitations," stressing the importance of personal restraint. Other important

Radical Club members included Henry Wadsworth Longfellow, Oliver Wendell Holmes, and Henry James Sr. Radical Club meetings provided Emerson and other members what good clubs give all their members: a sustaining blend of easy relaxation and mental stimulation among friends.

ELITE CLUBS

As wealth accumulated and centralized in the nineteenth century, so did memberships in elite social clubs. The most venerable of these is New York's Union Club, founded in 1836. The image of the mustachioed clubman seated on a leather wingback chair, smoking expensive cigars, drinking imported liquor, and boasting and laughing among his friends can be traced to the Union and other exclusive clubs that began in the nineteenth century. Membership was limited to around a thousand men, which proved too restrictive toward the end of the century as New York's population of wealthy people ballooned. The Union began capriciously blackballing applicants, an act that "murders a man, socially" (Fairfield, p. 58). One such applicant was the railroad baron John King, a self-made millionaire who allegedly offended Union Club members because he ate his food off his knife. King's sponsor, however, was J. P. Morgan, and King's rejection sent a clear message about how the club's old guard felt about the newly rich, including Morgan himself. Fed up with this and other insults, Morgan started a new club, famously (and perhaps apocryphally) telling his architect, "Build a Club fit for gentlemen. Damn the expense" (Porzelt, p. 9). The result became the Metropolitan Club, a dramatic, $2 million marble and gilded iron response to the Union Club's snub. The clubhouse's interior remains one of the most opulent in New York.

The Harvard Club, another of New York's prestigious social organizations, had only sixteen members in 1865 but grew to more than five hundred by 1888 as Harvard graduates headed to the city for work. The club built its headquarters at 11 West Twenty-second Street, in a neighborhood soon to house the New York Yacht, Century, and Yale Clubs. Like other clubs at the time, the Harvard Club became a kind of surrogate home by accommodating most its members' daily needs. The clubhouse expanded to include a bar and formal dining room, two floors of bedrooms, squash courts, and high on the top floor of the seven-story building, a swimming pool nicknamed the "Plunge."

Gender discrimination would have prohibited the writer Edith Wharton (1862–1937) from clubs such as the Union, Metropolitan, and Harvard, but that did not stop her from imagining the experience in her

The library of the Metropolitan Club, New York City, c. 1895. Designed by renowned architect Stanford White and financed by J. P. Morgan, the Metropolitan Club was intended to demonstrate the wealth and reinforce the social status of its members. THE LIBRARY OF CONGRESS

short novel *The Touchstone* (1900). In it, the main character Stephen Glennard decides to publish two volumes worth of very private letters from a famous woman author who once loved him but who has died. The story begins inside a club where men look out windows cursing the "difficulty of there being no place to take one's yacht to in winter but that other played-out hole, the Riviera" (p. 6). The club, its members, and their moneyed society become catalysts for Glennard's morally questionable decision to anonymously publish the letters. Doing so allows him to marry and lead a comfortable life, but the ethics of what he has done wrack him with guilt that leads to

crisis. As Wharton characterizes them, clubs were just another place for those of privilege to gather while they exploited and corrupted the aspirations of the lesser classes, and particularly those people grasping at the fringes of high society.

While high society people on the East Coast gathered at the Union, Metropolitan, Harvard, and other exclusive clubs, San Francisco's elite joined the Bohemian Club. It was started in 1872 by a handful of friends from the *San Francisco Examiner,* and early members included the writers Ambrose Bierce (1842–1914) and Joaquin Miller. Mark Twain (1835–1910) and Bret Harte (1836–1902) were made honorary members; Jack London (1876–1910) and Frank Norris (1870–1902) later joined the club as well. By 1878, when the group held its first campout in the redwood forest, a two-hour drive north of San Francisco, membership among the artists, writers, and musicians of the club had become coveted by businessmen and politicians, who soon came to dominate its ranks. By the time the English author Rudyard Kipling (1865–1936) published *American Notes* (1899), he would write, judging from the San Francisco clubhouse's grandeur, "It was hard to realize that even twenty years ago you could see a man hanged [in San Francisco] with great pomp" (p. 26). Despite his instinctual sense of cultural superiority, Kipling was impressed by the four-foot statue of an owl, the club's mascot, perched on the banister of the club's staircase and by the soft carpets, the smell of expensive cigars, and the fine paintings, many of which were done by club members. He was highly entertained by the stories he heard (some of which he retells) and by the "dinner the memory of which [would] descend with [him] into the hungry grave" (p. 43).

The Bohemian Club became famous for its annual campout, where more than two thousand members and their guests stayed in one of the 129 "camps" along the Russian River. The camps themselves appear as if they were constructed by wealthy Boy Scouts under the tutelage of Disneyland's design team. Members began holding a ritualistic Cremation of Care ceremony in which robed "priests" set fire to an effigy symbolizing worldly cares. The ceremony takes place beneath a twenty-foot statue of an owl and signals the official opening of the encampment. Bacchanalian revelry ensues as friends move from camp to camp in a continuous party where no one has to drive home. The club maintains its literary roots partly by staging two commissioned plays, one an intellectual drama called the "high jinks" and the other a comedy called the "low jinks." The performances take place on two outdoor stages and include set designs on par with those seen on Broadway. In a nod to Shakespearean custom and because the club traditionally did not allow women, male actors play the roles of both men and women, often to great comic effect in the low jinks performance. Professional actors play the lead roles, while club members fill in as extras.

One of the early members involved in the productions was Frank Norris, who used the Bohemian Club as the backdrop for his somewhat autobiographical early novel *Blix* (1899). In it, the narrator describes Conde Rivers (Norris) as "one of the younger members, but [who] was popular and well liked, and [who]

on more than one occasion had materially contributed to the fun of the club's 'low jinks'" (p. 127). The novel has the Norris character using the Bohemian Club's library as a place to work on his writing, but the attraction of the card room, where smoke from expensive cigars fills the air and the poker games last past four in the morning, entices him away.

The Bohemians Jack London and Ambrose Bierce also used the Bohemian Club in their writing, although not extensively. In a lone paragraph of his travel narrative *The Cruise of the* Snark (1911), London mentions "crack sailors" who were part of the Bohemian Club. But London, an adventurer and "man's man" who grappled early with poverty, was always a little scornful of high society people who had never known real work or the common struggles of lower classes. As the Bohemian Club grew and became known more for its wealthy power brokers than for its artists and writers, London must have questioned some aspects of his membership. In *The Cruise of the* Snark, members of the club haughtily dismiss the *Snark*'s construction, believing the boat will be too slow. Then London writes, "Well, I wish I'd only had those crack sailors of the Bohemian Club on board the *Snark* the other night for them to see for themselves their one, vital, unanimous judgment absolutely reversed" (p. 27). It is an old story: poor underdog triumphs over wealthy aristocrats. In his tone here, however, London conveniently overlooks the fact that this "triumph" involves the rich man's sport of yacht racing and that he was himself a member of the rich man's club.

Such attitudes are even more difficult to define in Ambrose Bierce's mystery story, "The Realm of the Unreal" (1893), which tells of a Bohemian Club member being cuckolded and otherwise abused by the "disagreeably engaging" Professor Valentine Dorrimore, a hypnotist from Calcutta (p. 107). The two are introduced among several men in the Bohemian Club's library, and when the protagonist calls hypnotists "pretenders," Dorrimore makes him the fool and beats him up in the process. Bierce's disposition toward the club is more playfully ambiguous than London's *Snark* in part because of the narrative point of view. In both cases a club member or members are proved wrong, but because readers tend naturally to sympathize with the narrator, the tone in "The Realm of the Unreal" seems less antagonistic; with its happy resolution (the narrator gets married), the story may even be considered comic. It would be easy to imagine Bohemian Club members reading the story in their library—or even having Bierce reading it to them—and enjoying it with impunity.

Not unexpectedly, discussing almost all issues in addition to literature was commonplace at the Bohemian Club, but one topic remained surprisingly off-limits. As with most exclusive clubs, the Bohemian began a policy against talking business on club grounds, going so far as to post the line from *A Midsummer Night's Dream,* "Weaving spiders come not here," on several redwood trees in their Bohemian Grove retreat as a reminder. Members took the admonition seriously, loudly and teasingly pointing out "weaving spiders" on the rare occasions when they heard a conversation drift toward business. Like most types of clubs, elite clubs cherish their members' friendships—the deals that are undoubtedly made as a result of those friendships can only take place outside the clubs' well-guarded gates.

CLUBS FOR ARTISTS AND THEIR PATRONS

Among the elite clubs at the turn of the century, some were devoted to bringing together artists and wealthy benefactors. The Century Association was founded in 1846 by the poet and editor William Cullen Bryant (1794–1878) as a club for artists and, unlike the Bohemian Club, remained true to that intent. In 1891 the club moved into its West Forty-third Street clubhouse, a building designed for them by Stanford White, who had designed some of the most elite clubs in New York, including the Metropolitan. The group held regular meetings and dinners, hosted presentations and discussions, and had a library and reading room. The club also had an art gallery where it displayed works of its members, which included some of the most important nineteenth-century painters, Albert Bierstadt most famously.

Less exclusive but therefore generally more accessible to younger, more progressive men in the arts, the Lotos Club began in 1870 when six New York newspaper men decided to form a club "to promote social intercourse among journalists, literary men, artists, and members of the theatrical profession" (Fairfield, p. 217). By starting their own club, the journalists were likely reacting to the social stigma against their profession, one strong enough to prevent their inclusion in more elite clubs. In the eyes of high society, journalists were working class and hence not "clubbable" men.

This elitism extended to the Authors Club, a group started in 1882 by the poet and *Century Magazine* editor Richard Watson Gilder. According to club policy, only "the author of a published book proper to literature" was allowed to join; newspaper reporters and authors of "technical books and journalism as such" were specifically told they were not

eligible (Osborne, p. 5). Andrew Carnegie, himself an author of at least three books on political and social issues by the time he joined in 1886, endowed the club with $10,000 to be used to help starving writers and their families. The club seems to have stretched its own definition of literary authorship to make Carnegie a member, but his support allowed it to resist the kind of wealthy patron that came to "dilute" the ranks of other artistic clubs, like the Bohemian and Lotos, as their popularity increased.

For dramatists, there was the Players Club, begun in 1888 by the actor (and brother of Abraham Lincoln's assassin) Edwin Booth (1833–1893). With redesign work by Stanford White, Booth made his home at 16 Gramercy Park into the clubhouse. The club's reputation as the East Coast headquarters for actors continued to grow as notables like Mark Twain and Sir Laurence Olivier became members. In addition to the socializing that took place under John Sargent's portrait of Edwin Booth, club members produced and acted in charity performances of classic plays.

Not to be outdone by New York, Boston had its own coterie of artistic clubs, including a chapter of the Authors Club, presided over by Julia Ward Howe, who had also been a Radical Club member. For painters and sculptors, there were several choices, including the Boston Art Club, the Paint and Clay Club, and the St. Botolph Club, which takes its name from the city's patron saint. Formed in 1879, the St. Botolph Club had 450 members by 1890 and became famous for organizing early exhibits by Claude Monet and American impressionists. The club was not limited to the visual arts, playing host to Walt Whitman in the spring of 1881, where he was received by the founding member William Dean Howells (1837–1920). Other founding members include the politician and author Henry Cabot Lodge and the publishers Henry Houghton and George Mifflin.

Howells, like other men of his social class at the time, was involved in several clubs, helping to found not only St. Botolph but also the Tavern Club. It began as many clubs then did with a group of men who regularly got together for dinner. A now legendary story describes the group's disgust when some of P. T. Barnum's traveling circus performers came into the restaurant where future Tavern Club members were already seated. One of the troupe, who was armless, ate with his toes. As the story goes, the fellow who then suggested a private club was himself not invited to become a member, thus quickly cementing the club's reputation for exclusivity (De Wolfe Howe, p. 4). The first election committee met in August 1884, and Howells became club president, serving until 1888.

In the early days, the Tavern Club hosted monthly dinners for an invited guest. Several dinners were given for important actors, such as Henry Irving, but in March 1885 the club also hosted Howells's good friend Mark Twain. Twain was a regular on the club lecture circuit, giving talks at the Lotos, Savage, and Authors Clubs, among others. (Some of these talks were collected in *Mark Twain's Speeches* [1910].) In January 1901 Twain returned to the Tavern Club for another dinner in his honor. One of the club's members dressed as a Twain impersonator and greeted the author as he entered the dining room. Playing on his dual personas as Mark Twain and Samuel Clemens, the author is reported to have said, "All my troubles in life—and I have had many—have been caused by that man!" The happy evening that followed is "secure in its place among the best moments in the life of the Club" (De Wolfe Howe, p. 119).

A man of great diplomacy who was highly praised by Tavern Club members for his early presidency, Howells wrote less about club life than his very active participation might suggest. He mentions clubs only briefly in *A Hazard of New Fortunes* (1890) when a club jokester "feigned to drop dead from his chair" (p. 197) as an enthusiastic manager of a new magazine begins promoting his publication yet again and once more a little later when the magazine becomes "the talk of the clubs" (p. 221). The fictitious Saratoga Club makes a short appearance in chapter five of *The Day of Their Wedding* (1895): "In fact, with its discreetly drawn curtains, its careful keeping of grass and flowers, the club-house looked in the bright morning sun like the demure dwelling of some rich man who did not care to flaunt his riches" (p. 57). Here and elsewhere in his work, Howells emphasizes understated displays of old-money society.

Of his novels, Howells's most revealing use of clubs is found in *The Rise of Silas Lapham* (1885), the story of the newly rich Lapham family's encounter with Boston's elite. Early in the novel Silas Lapham says in disgust:

> I like to see a man *act* like a man. I don't like to see him taken care of like a young lady. Now, I suppose that fellow [Corey, his daughter's suitor] belongs to two or three clubs, and hangs around 'em all day, lookin' out the window,—I've seen 'em,—instead of tryin' to hunt up something to do for an honest livin. (P. 58)

Lapham's perspective is that of the outsider, a person who has only seen clubmen as they stand behind glass, observing Lapham and the rest of the masses as they pass by uninvited and unwelcome. Quickly in the next chapter Howells contrasts this view with that of a club insider: "'It's astonishing what a hardy breed the young club-men are,' observed his [Corey's] father. 'All summer through, in weather that sends the sturdiest female flying to the sea-shore, you find the clubs filled with young men, who don't seem to mind the heat at all'" (p. 63). Howells writes that these two conversations take place almost "at the same moment" (p. 62), as if to emphasize the difference in worldviews brought by social status. In none of these descriptions does Howells, ever discreet, take readers inside a club with any detail; this area remained "for members only," even in fiction.

WOMEN'S CLUBS AND LITERARY SALONS

Women's clubs also increased in numbers in the nineteenth century, and by 1880 there were roughly nine hundred such clubs across the nation (Charles, p. 25). While many groups were religiously based, a significant number were secular, focusing on social issues, such as education, public health, and suffrage. Edith Wharton reveals the social snobbery and petty one-upmanship some clubs experienced in her satiric short story "Xingu" (1911), which describes a women's lunch club and its efforts to entertain an arrogant author. However, many women's clubs engaged in important philanthropic work, and such efforts yielded vital social improvements, including establishing libraries, reforming New York's filthy slaughterhouses, and helping all women earn, in 1920, the right to vote.

In Europe women had been hosting clublike gatherings, or soirees, since the eighteenth century. In France, Madam de Staël's intellectual "salon" became such a threat to Napoleon that he forced her into exile. In Henry James's short story "Brooksmith" (1891), about an especially adept servant who subtly ensures guests' happiness at his employer's salon, the narrator wistfully describes the salon experience: "We never were a crowd, never either too many or too few, always the right people WITH the right people—there must really have been no wrong people at all—always coming and going, never sticking fast nor overstaying, yet never popping in or out with an indecorous familiarity" (p. 761). A good salon was an almost impossibly perfect combination of painters, writers, and intellectuals regularly gathering for cocktails, hors d'oeuvres, and (most important) conversation in the home of an artistically inclined socialite. In America, however, James complained that "our women have not the skill to cultivate it [the salon]—the art to direct through a smiling land, between suggestive shores, a sinuous stream of talk" (p. 760).

Despite James's misgivings, America has had successful salons, beginning in 1845, when Anne Lynch

Botta (1815–1891) arrived in New York, hosting the likes of Ralph Waldo Emerson, Margaret Fuller, William Cullen Bryant, Herman Melville, and Edgar Allan Poe in her home. Botta opened her doors to her artistic and bohemian friends—and almost any interesting people they cared to bring along. Sometimes there would be formal topics and presentations, such as the evening in 1879 when two members of the Ponca Indian tribe delivered a talk. Botta was a master of both bringing creative people together and keeping the conversation from stagnating.

Botta was one of the first people consulted in 1868 about founding a club exclusively for women. The then-radical idea began when women writers were excluded from a dinner for Charles Dickens, who was completing a reading tour, hosted by the New York Press Club. The new group eventually chose the name "Sorosis," a botanical term describing fruits that are formed by the merging of many flowers. The pineapple became the club's emblem. However, despite the avant-garde nature of the Botta salon, Botta's husband opposed her collaboration with the all-women group. Notwithstanding Botta's absence, the Sorosis Club quickly expanded in members and stature by working, according to their constitution, "to establish a kind of freemasonry among women" and "to exert an important influence on the future of women and the welfare of society" (Croly, pp. 8–9).

In mock homage to the slight involving Charles Dickens, the Sorosis Club hosted an annual dinner to which men and women were invited, signaling the progress made between the sexes. Such meetings were not on the agenda of the Heterodoxy Club, a notably more feminist organization. From 1912 to the 1940s, this group of "unorthodox women," as the member and New York socialite Mabel Dodge Luhan (1879–1962) fondly described it in her memoirs, met in Greenwich Village. Their founder, Marie Jenney Howe, had read Charlotte Perkins Gilman's book *Women and Economics* (1899) and recruited Gilman (1860–1935) as a charter member. The ranks were filled with educated women, many of whom had careers as well as families and children, divorced single mothers, and women who were openly involved in lesbian relationships. In addition to Gilman, there were several writers among them, including Mary Austin and Susan Glaspell, whose work was shaped in part by their membership in Heterodoxy.

In late January 1913, at about the same time she joined the Heterodoxy Club, Mabel Dodge began hosting regular "evenings" among her artist and intellectual friends. During the next two years, her Greenwich Village living room became one of the most important intellectual salons in twentieth-century America. "Mabel," as she was known, played a behind-the-scenes role in the winter of 1912 helping to prepare the 17 February opening of the Armory Show, the modern art exhibit highlighting European Impressionists that transformed the art world. When she began her salon, Mabel seemed to know all of New York's bohemian intelligentsia. The group debated avant-garde ideas about art and literature, the philosophies of Nietzsche and Henri-Louis Bergson, the merits of socialism and Marx's communism. Sex was a regular topic, as was psychoanalysis. The journalist Lincoln Steffens, upon whose suggestion Mabel began her salon, later claimed that it was in her home that he first heard Freud's and Jung's theories discussed.

Mabel Dodge's salon began to wind down as World War I began. When the Fourteenth Amendment passed in 1922, women's clubs celebrated, but the victory removed an important common cause and recruiting tool, and memberships declined. Memberships in clubs of all kinds suffered during the Great Depression and World War II, when many clubs collapsed. These events helped to end the boom years for American clubs, which reached their zenith at the turn of the century.

See also Literary Colonies; Literary Friendships

BIBLIOGRAPHY

Primary Works

Bierce, Ambrose. *The Complete Short Stories of Ambrose Bierce*. Edited by Ernest Jerome Hopkins. Lincoln: University of Nebraska Press, 1984.

Howells, William Dean. *The Day of Their Wedding*. 1895. New York: Harper & Brothers, 1896.

Howells, William Dean. *A Hazard of New Fortunes*. 1890. New York: Modern Library, 2002.

Howells, William Dean. *The Rise of Silas Lapham*. 1885. New York: Penguin, 1986.

James, Henry. "Brooksmith." In his *Complete Stories 1884–1891*. New York: Library of America, 1999.

Kipling, Rudyard. *American Notes: Rudyard Kipling's West*. 1899. Edited by Arrell Morgan Gibson. Norman: University of Oklahoma Press, 1981.

London, Jack. *The Cruise of the* Snark. 1911. New York: Penguin, 2004.

Norris, Frank. *Blix*. 1899. In *A Novelist in the Making: A Collection of Student Themes and the Novels "Blix" and "Vandover and the Brute,"* edited by James D. Hart. Cambridge, Mass.: Harvard University Press, 1970.

Wharton, Edith. *The Touchstone*. 1900. London: Hesperus Press, 2003.

Secondary Works

Beckert, Sven. *The Monied Metropolis: New York City and the Consolidation of the American Bourgeoisie, 1850–1896.* New York: Cambridge University Press, 2001.

Bender, Thomas. *New York Intellect: A History of Intellectual Life in New York City, from 1750 to the Beginnings of Our Own Time.* New York: Knopf, 1987.

Birmingham, Doris A. "Boston's St. Botolph Club: Home of the Impressionists." *Archives of American Art Journal* 31, no. 3 (1991): 26–34.

Charles, Jeffrey A. *Service Clubs in American Society: Rotary, Kiwanis, and Lions.* Urbana: University of Illinois Press, 1993.

Croly, Jane C. *Sorosis: Its Origin and History.* 1886. In *The Leisure Class in America*, edited by Leon Stein. New York: Arno Press, 1975.

De Wolfe Howe, Mark A. *A Partial (and Not Impartial) Semi-Centennial History of the Tavern Club, 1884–1934.* Boston: Tavern Club, 1934.

Fairfield, Francis Gerry. *The Clubs of New York.* 1873. In *The Leisure Class in America*, edited by Leon Stein. New York: Arno Press, 1975.

Ferguson, Charles. *Fifty Million Brothers: A Panorama of American Lodges and Clubs.* New York: Farrar and Rinehart, 1937.

Lombard, Charles. "An Old New York Salon-French Style." *New-York Historical Society Quarterly* 55, no. 1 (1971): 38–51.

Osborne, Duffield. *The Authors Club: An Historical Sketch.* New York: Knickerbocker Press, 1913.

Porzelt, Paul. *The Metropolitan Club of New York.* New York: Rizzoli, 1982.

Quennell, Peter, ed. *Affairs of the Mind: The Salon in Europe and America from the 18th to the 20th Century.* Washington, D.C.: New Republic Books, 1980.

Schwarz, Judith. *The Radical Feminists of Heterodoxy: Greenwich Village, 1914–1940.* Lebanon, N.H.: New Victoria, 1982.

Williams, Alexander. *A Social History of the Greater Boston Clubs.* Barre, Mass.: Barre Publishers, 1970.

Michael Smedshammer

THE CONJURE WOMAN

It is a curious fact of literary history that the collection of stories for which Charles Waddell Chesnutt (1858–1932) will be remembered as a major American author is one he never envisioned himself. *The Conjure Woman* (1899) is by any measure a seminal text in the African American literary tradition and a premier achievement of the late-nineteenth-century local color movement. Indeed, Chesnutt's slim volume deserves to be included with Sherwood Anderson's *Winesburg, Ohio* (1919), Ernest Hemingway's *In Our Time* (1924), and other classic titles on a short list of America's finest story collections. Unlike Anderson's and Hemingway's intensely personal and carefully integrated works, however, *The Conjure Woman* came into existence almost as an afterthought, and the book's formal construction might be said to reflect the vision of its editor more fully than that of its author. Chesnutt was proud of the critical success accorded to his collection of dialect tales, but he understood himself as a different sort of writer, and he remained throughout his career deeply ambivalent about his own work in the local color mode.

LOCAL COLOR FICTION

To appreciate Chesnutt's odd relationship to his masterpiece, it is necessary to consider the popularity of local color writing in late-nineteenth-century America and to review some details of the book's composition history. With dramatic improvements in transportation and communication systems after the Civil War, America entered an era of rapid centralization. Traditional political and cultural practices dividing various regions of the country were challenged and in many cases overrun by Union conquest of the South and national expansion in the West. New corporate entities, such as Standard Oil and the Union Pacific Railroad, facilitated the movement of large populations into formerly remote areas and made shareholders rich by extending commerce to untapped markets. As an ironic but unsurprising consequence of the frantic process of centralization, many citizens became nostalgic about what they perceived to be the lost Eden of rural America, and a school of backward-looking fiction developed in response to the prevailing mood. The publishers of flashy new literary journals such as *Scribner's Magazine* and *Century Magazine* (themselves, of course, both products and instruments of the emerging mass market) helped perpetuate the trend. The major monthlies were flooded with local color stories featuring the dialect, folkways, and idiosyncrasies of tightly knit communities in Maine, Georgia, Wisconsin, California, and other regions.

Some of America's finest writers emerged in this climate of public opinion and built national reputations by recovering the local. Mark Twain, Bret Harte, Sarah Orne Jewett, Mary Noailles Murfree, Hamlin Garland, and Edward Eggleston, to name only a few of the most notable, all became literary celebrities

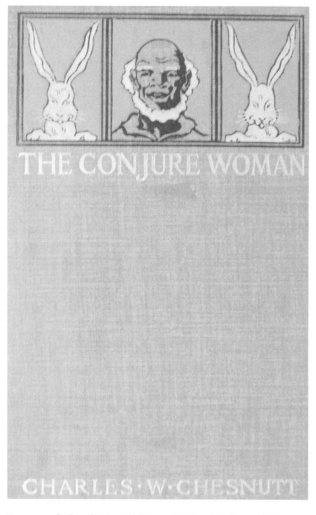

Cover of the first edition of *The Conjure Woman*.
SPECIAL COLLECTIONS LIBRARY, UNIVERSITY OF MICHIGAN

loyal black retainers who long for the days before emancipation, when duty, honor, and self-sacrifice purportedly characterized the obligations of both races toward one another. This reactionary formula was unquestionably designed to forestall the postwar aspirations of African Americans by suggesting that blacks themselves preferred life under the old system to the responsibilities of democracy and the degradations of modern consumer capitalism.

CHARLES W. CHESNUTT

As a young southerner with dreams of a literary career, Chesnutt witnessed the success of writers such as Harris and Page, and he understood that a large audience existed for stories about the people and places of his North Carolina youth. He was born the son of free black parents in Cleveland, Ohio, and his family moved shortly after the Civil War to Fayetteville, North Carolina, where he spent his childhood in the turbulent decade of Reconstruction. A phenomenally gifted student, he found time to teach himself French, German, and Latin while taking full advantage of the unprecedented educational opportunities offered by the State Colored Normal School. His teenage summers were spent in the hinterlands of North and South Carolina, where Chesnutt traveled as an itinerant teacher, instructing former slaves and their families in basic literacy and mathematics. After finishing school in 1880, he served as principal of his former academy before moving his family to Cleveland, where he studied law and eventually opened a lucrative court stenography business. He remained a resident of Ohio for the last fifty years of his life, dividing his time and remarkable energies between family, business, writing, and civic affairs.

Although concentrated within a relatively brief period, Chesnutt's southern years had been full of the sorts of characters and experiences that sold magazines, and he knew it. For an African American man with literary aspirations, however, the decision to exploit this market by adopting the conventions of southern local color fiction was by no means a simple one. As a teenager Chesnutt had toyed with the idea of writing humorous sketches about the outlandish spiritual practices of his black neighbors, and he carefully noted in his journal that northern readers were inclined to favor sketches of rural folklife among the former slaves. But he understood as well as any of his contemporaries that Americans of African descent had nothing to gain and everything to lose from a form of fiction that shored up stereotypes of the childlike freedman who regrets his political, social, and economic liberties. Writing in 1890 to his friend and mentor, the southern author George Washington

during this period by claiming some culturally and geographically distinctive region as their own. For most of these writers the re-creation of a village or agrarian past was a harmless fantasy, a glance at a simpler world, but for southerners writing in the immediate aftermath of war and Reconstruction, nostalgia for the good old days of slavery involved a politically charged message. Indeed, quaint stories of plantation life before the war, such as Joel Chandler Harris's Uncle Remus tales, implicitly endorsed the national decision to abandon Reconstruction in 1876. This move returned political control of the former slave states to southern white Democrats and thus effectively disenfranchised African Americans throughout the South. Thomas Nelson Page (1853–1922) and other southern local colorists—all of them educated white men and women—specialized in portraying

UNCLE JULIUS ON SCUPPERNONG GRAPES

Julius deals heavily in stereotypes of African American character and behavior as he tries to discourage John and Annie from buying the local vineyard. His depiction of black cravings for "watermillyums," "possum, en chick'n" is thoroughly demeaning of himself and his neighbors, and yet Julius flatters the prejudices of his northern listeners in order to win crucial leverage in the ensuing negotiation over who will actually control the coveted grape vines.

Now, ef dey's an'thing a nigger lub, nex' ter 'possum, en chick'n, en watermillyums, it's scuppernon's. Dey ain' nuffin dat kin stan' up side'n de scuppernon' fer sweetness; sugar ain't a suckumstance ter scuppernon'. W'en de season is nigh 'bout ober, en de grapes begin ter swivel up des a little wid de wrinkles er ole age,—w'en de skin git sof' en brown,—den de scuppernon' make you smack yo' lip en roll yo' eye en wush fer mo'; so I reckon it ain' very 'stonishin' dat niggers lub scuppernon'.

Chesnutt, "The Goophered Grapevine," in *The Conjure Woman and Other Conjure Tales*, pp. 35–36.

Cable, Chesnutt complained about popular representations of African Americans in magazines of the day and vowed to resist the dominant trend:

> I notice that all of the many Negroes . . . whose virtues have been given to the world in the magazine press recently, have been blacks, full-blooded, and their chief virtues have been their dog-like fidelity to their old master, for whom they have been willing to sacrifice almost life itself. Such characters exist. . . . But I can't write about those people, or rather I won't write about them. (*To Be an Author*, p. 65)

Chesnutt wished to place his work in the major literary periodicals, of course, and so his promise to defy convention called for an intricate compromise: he would have to entertain readers by providing most of what they expected from a story of rural southern life, full of reminiscences about "slab'ry times," but in such a way that no one could wish a return to the relations of authority that had pertained under slavery, relations that were, in fact, reappearing with frightening uniformity across the post-Reconstruction South (*The Conjure Woman*, p. 36). Ironically, Harris, Page, and other local colorists had pointed the way toward such a compromise, for although their black characters epitomized a "dog-like fidelity to their old master," Uncle Remus and figures like him had at least addressed readers with imagination and eloquence in an idiom that was nominally their own. Indeed, for all their interest in making black political participation appear unnecessary, southern local colorists had actually given extended speaking parts to black vernacular characters for the first time in mainstream American fiction. Chesnutt would capitalize on this slender opportunity by investing his black vernacular storyteller, Uncle Julius, with linguistic resources that confound the usual politics of southern local color writing.

COMPOSITION HISTORY

Julius made his debut in 1887, when a story entitled "The Goophered Grapevine" appeared in the prestigious *Atlantic Monthly*, one of several literary magazines that specialized in bringing folksy southern tales before a national readership. The story is introduced by John, an educated white businessperson from the Midwest who has come to the war-ravaged South with his ailing wife, Annie, in search of investment opportunities. In the pastoral setting of a decaying old plantation, they encounter an aged black storyteller, Uncle Julius, who appears to have stepped out of Harris's and Page's fictional world of simple harmonies, where former slaves recall the good old days of honest toil under a benevolent white master. Chesnutt is careful to hit all the conventional notes: Julius politely offers to give his seat to the white couple, declares his love of watermelon, smacks his lips at the mere mention of chicken, and drifts off into a nostalgic reverie when his auditors convince him to tell a story about old times on the plantation. John explains that Julius "seemed to lose sight of his auditors, and to be living over again in monologue his life on the old plantation" (*The Conjure Woman*, p. 35).

With this most formulaic introduction, Julius proceeds to illuminate an antebellum world full of mystery and suffering, where acquisitive masters destroy their own property in a mad search for profit and enslaved human beings become magically indistinguishable from the crops they must raise but are forbidden to taste. Without deviating from the basic patterns of local color writing, indeed without raising his voice even in mild protest, Chesnutt makes it clear that Julius has no reason to relish his antebellum past, except insofar as his stories may help him to negotiate some control over his environment in the presence of a new threat, suggested by the financial designs of his northern listeners. As the elaborate narrative frame of "The Goophered Grapevine" makes clear, John and Annie have ventured south to invest in a region where "labor was cheap, and land could be bought for a mere song" (*The Conjure Woman*, p. 31). Julius's cautionary tales thus operate as a form of currency in the unequal transaction with his new landlord and employer. Much like Chesnutt himself, Julius adopts a narrative persona that flatters the expectations of his audience, yet his performance in that highly conventional role is designed as much to instruct them about social relations in the present as it is to entertain them with a tale from the plantation past. This is local color fiction with a decisive twist, for the storyteller's dreamy descent into southern history and legend serves to allegorize a future he is determined to prevent.

Julius, John, and Annie returned to the *Atlantic Monthly* a year later in "Po' Sandy" (1888), another weirdly tragic tale of witchcraft and suffering on the McAdoo plantation before the war, and a third story featuring the same cast, "The Conjurer's Revenge," appeared in the *Overland Monthly* in 1889. Although pleased with his success and eager to keep his work in front of a large reading public, Chesnutt felt constrained by the tight formula and restricted subject matter of the conjure stories, and he began to experiment with other characters and narrative situations. In "Dave's Neckliss" (1889), his third contribution to the *Atlantic Monthly*, he retained Uncle Julius as the dialect storyteller but dropped the element of conjure from the tale, focusing instead on a more psychological account of the degradations of slavery. With its striking characterization of a fully literate black cultural leader, "Dave's Neckliss" begins to reflect Chesnutt's desire to move beyond the narrow expectations of his magazine audience—to move, as he wrote to Albion Tourgée, "out of the realm of superstition [and] into the realm of feeling and passion" ("To Be an Author," p. 44). Black dialect itself seemed an obstacle to this movement, and after 1889 Chesnutt decided to drop "the old Negro who serves as mouthpiece . . . as well as much of the dialect" ("To Be an Author," p. 44). Julius may have turned the conventions of local color fiction to his own subversive purposes, but he remained an imaginative product and an unmistakable echo of racial attitudes Chesnutt wanted to critique more directly. Thus, having written just three conjure stories and a small handful of other tales in Julius's broken idiom, Chesnutt abandoned dialect fiction entirely and devoted the next ten years of his creative life to writing stories and novels in standard English.

The fruit of this decade-long effort was substantial—"The Sheriff's Children," "The Wife of His Youth," "Her Virginia Mammy," "The Passing of Grandison," and most of the novel manuscript for *The House behind the Cedars* (1900) all came from this period—but by 1897 Chesnutt could look back upon ten years of continuous literary production since his first appearance in a major periodical, and he still had no book to show for it. In the hope that a selection of his best stories might combine to make a book, he sent everything he had written to Walter Hines Page of Houghton, Mifflin, and Company, parent company of the *Atlantic Monthly*, and asked for the firm's consideration. Page wrote back in March 1898 with the devastating opinion that the stories were simply too miscellaneous to be effectively marketed in a single volume. He did offer one slim hope, however: "All the readers who have read your stories agree on this—that 'The Goophered Grapevine' and 'Po' Sandy,' and the one or two others that have the same original quality that these show, are stories that are sure to live—in fact, I know of nothing so good of their kind anywhere" (Helen Chesnutt, pp. 91–92). Page went on to speculate that if Chesnutt could provide five or six more conjure stories, Houghton, Mifflin, and Company would probably agree to publish the entire set as a book.

In one sense this was welcome news, and Chesnutt immediately complied with Page's request, churning out six new conjure stories during the next six weeks. On the other hand, he had been offered book publication at a steep price, for Chesnutt had deliberately dropped the conjure formula and dialect fiction altogether in order to explore the possibilities of a more realistic and more socially progressive form of protest fiction. Page's flattering assessment that "The Goophered Grapevine" and "Po' Sandy" were the best things "of their kind" suggested that Chesnutt's conjure stories belonged to a well-defined tradition—a tradition of southern local color writing, not of social protest. His insistence on the conjure element implied that certain protocols, or stock motifs, were a condition of successful publication in that mode. Chesnutt was willing to go along with all of this as long as he could get a book into print, but his negotiations with Page raise a troubling question about whose book it really was. In May 1898 he sent the six new conjure tales to Houghton, Mifflin, and Company, and Page made the decision to include four of them—"The Gray Wolf's Ha'nt," "Mars Jeems's Nightmare," "Sis' Becky's Pickaninny," and "Hot-Foot Hannibal." Finally, Page devised a title, *The Conjure Woman*, organized the sequence of tales, and supervised the cover design, which featured an oddly irrelevant rabbit. Alert readers will notice that this is the only rabbit in Chesnutt's book, and some may even speculate that Page's design intends to evoke Joel Chandler Harris's famous Brer Rabbit as one more way of fitting *The Conjure Woman* into a recognizable mold.

RECEPTION AND ASSESSMENT

Critics liked *The Conjure Woman,* and Chesnutt initially received a number of favorable reviews. In fact, his literary reputation peaked in 1900, when America's most influential critic, William Dean Howells, published the laudatory essay "Mr. Charles W. Chesnutt's Stories" in the *Atlantic Monthly.* Subsequent generations of critics, including leading black intellectuals of the Harlem Renaissance era, were put off by the plantation setting of the tales and by Chesnutt's apparently demeaning characterizations of postwar African Americans. This attitude prevailed throughout the 1940s and 1950s, when Chesnutt was largely dismissed as a "transitional figure" linking early African American writers, such as Frederick Douglass and William Wells Brown, with their modernist descendants (Redding, p. 68). Yet Chesnutt and *The Conjure Woman,* in particular, have made a stunning comeback since the early 1980s, and some of the most influential American critics are once again reading him seriously. Books by William L. Andrews, Houston A. Baker, Eric Sundquist, Charles Duncan, and Dean McWilliams have restored Chesnutt to center stage in American literary studies by refining the understanding of the rhetorical shell games that occur throughout the conjure stories, games in which there are no clear winners and losers but rather a tragic stalemate that captures the mood of an era.

In his extremely useful introduction to the 1993 edition of *The Conjure Woman and Other Conjure Tales,* Richard H. Brodhead points out that while no book moves seamlessly from its writer's mind into its reader's hands, Chesnutt's masterful collection was produced with an unusual degree of editorial control. This might be a reason for preferring one of his later books, such as *The Wife of His Youth and Other Stories of the Color Line* (1899) or *The Marrow of Tradition* (1901). Indeed, readers will find that Chesnutt speaks more directly to the social and political realities of the post-Reconstruction period in these non-dialect works. But the stories of *The Conjure Woman* are deftly engaged with precisely the same questions of discipline and control that shaped its publication, and this uncanny symmetry makes the book's compositional history into just another way of approaching the complexity of Chesnutt's art. *The Conjure Woman* may not be Charles W. Chesnutt's book in the way one normally assumes that a work of art originates within the mind of a creative individual. It is his masterpiece, however, for its artful manipulation of the obstacles barring African American expression in both Julius's antebellum world and in Chesnutt's own.

See also Blacks; Humor; The New South; Reconstruction; Regionalism and Local Color Fiction

BIBLIOGRAPHY
Primary Works

Chesnutt, Charles W. *The Conjure Woman and Other Conjure Tales.* 1899. Edited by Richard H. Brodhead. Durham, N.C.: Duke University Press, 1993.

Chesnutt, Charles W. *The Short Fiction of Charles W. Chesnutt.* Edited by Sylvia Lyons Render. Washington, D.C.: Howard University Press, 1974.

Chesnutt, Charles W. *"To Be an Author": Letters of Charles W. Chesnutt, 1889–1905.* Edited by Joseph R. McElrath and Robert Leitz III. Princeton, N.J.: Princeton University Press, 1997.

Secondary Works

Andrews, William L. *The Literary Career of Charles W. Chesnutt.* Baton Rouge: Louisiana State University Press, 1980.

Baker, Houston A. *Modernism and the Harlem Renaissance.* Chicago: University of Chicago Press, 1987.

Chesnutt, Helen M. *Charles Waddell Chesnutt: Pioneer of the Color Line.* Chapel Hill: University of North Carolina Press, 1952.

Duncan, Charles. *The Absent Man: The Narrative Craft of Charles W. Chesnutt.* Athens: Ohio University Press, 1998.

Keller, Frances Richardson. *An American Crusade: The Life of Charles Waddell Chesnutt.* Provo, Utah: Brigham Young University Press, 1978.

McWilliams, Dean. *Charles W. Chesnutt and the Fictions of Race.* Athens: University of Georgia Press, 2002.

Redding, J. Saunders. *To Make a Poet Black.* Chapel Hill: University of North Carolina Press, 1939.

Render, Sylvia Lyons. *Charles W. Chesnutt.* Boston: Twayne, 1980.

Sollors, Werner. *Beyond Ethnicity: Consent and Descent in American Culture.* New York: Oxford University Press, 1986.

Sundquist, Eric J. *To Wake the Nations: Race in the Making of American Literature.* Cambridge, Mass.: Belknap Press of Harvard University Press, 1993.

Wonham, Henry B. *Charles W. Chesnutt: A Study of the Short Fiction.* New York: Twayne, 1998.

Henry B. Wonham

A CONNECTICUT YANKEE IN KING ARTHUR'S COURT

Mark Twain's *A Connecticut Yankee in King Arthur's Court* (1889) remains one of the author's best-loved and most controversial novels. The fantastic tale of Twain's time-traveling protagonist Hank Morgan has been adapted for several film versions, including one starring Will Rogers and another Bing Crosby; has been pitched to the younger crowd with Disney's *A Kid in King Arthur's Court* (1995); and has been transformed into a memorably zany Bugs Bunny cartoon. The novel is in some sense Twain's most popular work, having so captured the public imagination that the plot has attained nearly the status of folklore rather than literary creation.

The novel is likewise one of the richest of Twain's works for scholars, for even the genre of the work provokes discussion. Is the work a historical novel? A burlesque historical novel? Science fiction? Fantasy? Comedy? Satire? Most scholars agree that the book contains some elements of all of these genres but are even more divided about what the ultimate import of the work might be. By having a Yankee mechanic travel back into the Arthurian age, Twain seems to poke fun at historical England as well as contemporary Britain and America. The novel's complex themes (history, culture, democracy, progress, imperialism, religion, and art) guarantee that no consensus will coalesce in the years to come.

TWAIN DREAMS OF A NOVEL

Of the many stories told about how Twain (1835–1910) came to write his many books, perhaps none is as picturesque as that told about the genesis of *Connecticut Yankee*. Twain was traveling with the Louisiana writer George Washington Cable on the lecture circuit when he and his companion were forced by a sudden rainstorm into a Rochester, New York, bookshop. There Cable handed Twain a copy of Sir Thomas Malory's fifteenth-century *Morte d'Arthur*, and Twain, so the story goes, was immediately smitten by the archaic language. In short order Twain and Cable, both of whom had perfected the art of writing dialect, began speaking in archaic language gleaned from Malory and commenced referring to each other as "Sir Mark" and "Sir George." Twain's journal from this time records a "dream of being a knight errant in armor in the middle ages" (*Mark Twain's Notebooks and Journals*, 3:78). Whether the dream was experienced by Twain or inscribed in the notebook as an idea for a novel is unclear, but it is true that Twain began, as he said,

"to make notes in my head for a book" (p. 79), the novel that became *A Connecticut Yankee in King Arthur's Court*. To do so he read a variety of historical works during the entire period of composition, from 1885 to 1889.

Twain's dream, with Malory's help, did contribute to the novel. Indeed Twain includes in *Connecticut Yankee* whole pages lifted more or less intact from Malory's work. One can, however, argue that *Morte d'Arthur* was not the most significant of Twain's sources. In addition to Malory, Twain consulted such works as W. E. H. Lecky's *History of the Rise and Influence of the Spirit of Rationalism* (1884), *History of European Morals from Augustus to Charlemagne* (1874), and *A History of England in the Eighteenth Century* (1887); Thomas Babington Macaulay's *The History of England from the Accession of James II* (1849–1861); Thomas Carlyle's *The French Revolution* (1837); George Standring's *The People's History of the English Aristocracy* (1886); Charles Ball's *Slavery in the United States* (1836); Hippolyte Taine's *The Ancient Régime* (1876); and articles on the penal system in czarist Russia by George Kennan (*Century Magazine*, 1887–1888). Twain left a record of many of these sources in his writing notebooks, in letters to colleagues, and especially in the marginalia he indelibly impressed in many of the volumes themselves.

Many of the sources Twain consulted seem to suggest that while he intended to target England specifically, he planned to include monarchies and hierarchical societies in general as part of his attack. Some scholars have identified Matthew Arnold as one of Twain's targets by virtue of his criticism of the United States, first in his review of Ulysses S. Grant's *Memoirs* in 1887 and later in his "Civilisation in the United States" (1888). Both articles hit close to home not only because Twain was Grant's publisher and public defender but also because Arnold in his later piece derided America's lamentable devotion to "the funny man": as America's preeminent "funny man," Twain took umbrage at such criticism. Moreover, Arnold represented elements of Victorian England Twain detested, in particular its devotion to romantic legends of knights, lords and ladies, and King Arthur. What is clear is that Twain was not relying primarily on Malory's work and that his research involved historical works of the eighteenth and nineteenth centuries that chronicled both English and colonial American history. Those sources support the arguments of scholars who have maintained that Twain's book is a satire of both British and American societies.

The Slave Driver. Illustration by Daniel Carter Beard from the first edition of *A Connecticut Yankee in King Arthur's Court.* THE LIBRARY OF CONGRESS

CONNECTICUT YANKEE
AND THE SATIRICAL FORM

Twain often employed the device of switched or paired characters in his novels as vehicles for satire. In *The Prince and the Pauper* (1881), for example, Edward Tudor and Tom Canty are indistinguishable apart from their clothing and their speech. Twain uses the two to comment on issues of social justice and education as the two trade places and each begins to experience an unfamiliar stratum of English society. Twain also employs the device in *Adventures of Huckleberry Finn* (1885), *The Tragedy of Pudd'nhead Wilson* (1894), and other works to comment on such issues as injustice based on class and race. In *Connecticut Yankee,* Twain creates a similar kind of situation, but Hank Morgan himself refers to it as a "transposition of epochs—and bodies" (p. 48). By sending his Yankee mechanic back in time, Twain instigates a discussion of different value systems espoused by sixth-

century England and nineteenth-century America, allowing the author to "defamiliarize" or "make strange," as the Russian formalist Victor Shklovsky would say, both ages for his readers. Twain thereby draws his readers' attention to rules, laws, and moral codes that cannot be viewed as stable but as contingent products of historical development. Implicitly the "transposition" creates a dialogue between the two systems, for the American system is carried in Hank Morgan's head and Camelot is the setting in which he lands. In his early sketch "The 'Tournament' in A.D. 1870," Twain had written that it is "hard to tell which is the most startling," the idea of a telegraph in the Garden of Eden or a "knightly tournament" in Brooklyn (p. 418). Just as both are made to appear ridiculous in the sketch, Twain creates a form in *Connecticut Yankee* that allows him the opportunity to satirize two ages at once, the feudalism of Arthurian England and the industrialism of Jay Gould and Andrew Carnegie.

POP CULTURE IN CAMELOT

Arthurian legend was highly popular during the Victorian Age, both in England and America. The poems that make up Alfred, Lord Tennyson's *Idylls of the King* appeared from 1859 through 1885 and achieved wide currency as symbols of a high-minded Victorian idealism. Twain was not immune to the fascination, and the formal contrast allowed him to glory in the dialects and relics of the Arthurian age even as his realism undermined the idealistic depictions of Malory and Tennyson. Twain's return to the past is in part a strategy undertaken to attack the present's use of the past; the return to the past would therefore seem to be an implicit critique of both ages.

Indeed Twain directs his criticism of the Arthurian age at cognate institutions in his own era. Thus his critique of the "Established Roman Catholic Church" (p. 129) is one of the novel's many anachronisms but speaks to Twain's criticism of currents in contemporary religion. Many scholars have noted the anti-Catholicism of *Connecticut Yankee,* elements that resulted in poor reviews in Catholic publications and even in some secular publications. Still, mainstream American culture at the time was anti-Catholic. For conservative Protestant denominations and churches, the Catholic Church remained a symbol of oppression, and preachers like Lyman Beecher became famous for speaking out against the dangers of Catholic political domination. Political machines such as the Irish-dominated Tammany Hall, against which Twain had railed in "The Revised Catechism" (1871), added fuel to the fire. Fear of Catholicism was not restricted to traditional Protestant churches, however. Even Protestant denominations that were part of the liberalization and democratization of American religion during the nineteenth century viewed the Catholic Church as at the very least symbolic of a pre-Enlightenment sensibility. Twain's opposition to Catholicism can be explained by appealing to these two seemingly contradictory currents in American culture, for many conservative and liberal leaders of American religion feared Catholic political domination even though they agreed on little else. Twain's anti-Catholicism is similarly ubiquitous in *Connecticut Yankee.*

Hank Morgan directly condemns the Catholic Church at many points, citing it as the only power superior to his own, but Twain also develops his novel in ways that implicitly criticize the church in slightly more subtle ways. When Hank is in imminent danger of being burned at the stake, a monk chants in Latin as the flame is to be started. Later, in Morgan Le Fay's dungeon, a man is tortured on the rack and attended by a priest. In both circumstances the presence of church authorities might be warranted by the imminent necessity of the last rites, but Twain depicts the Roman Catholic Church as guilty by association, using its power to consecrate abuses by the aristocracy. At several points too Twain specifically refers to the "Curse of Rome," by which either an individual or an entire country might be temporarily or permanently separated from the church. In chapter 29, "The Small-Pox Hut," Twain gives readers an example of an individual suffering under "the Church's curse" who is then shunned by all and ultimately dies alone (p. 332). In chapter 41, "The Interdict," Twain provides an example of the entire country suffering such a curse. While it is true that Twain did strike some of the negative characterizations from his manuscript and softened the anti-Catholic tone somewhat, overall the work partakes of the Protestant triumphalism of its age, with Hank Morgan proposing to solve most of Camelot's ills by introducing "a complete variety of Protestant congregations" (p. 127).

The institution of slavery is likewise criticized as it relates to the American experience but through the agency of English history. The writer's descriptions of Camelot owe much to Twain's experiences growing up in Hannibal, Missouri, a slaveholding region before the Civil War. In chapter 30, "The Tragedy of the Manor House," Hank asserts that one of the poor inhabitants of Camelot who yet maintains the aristocratic system is "just the twin of the southern 'poor white' of the far future" (p. 343). Twain's own memories certainly did assist him in the construction of his novel, but so too did his research: Charles Ball's *Slavery in the United States,* the descriptions of prisoners

in Carlyle's *French Revolution,* and George Kennan's articles all bring the slavery issue into the near past as opposed to the sixth century. Some of the sources also comment directly on American slavery—not only Ball's work but Lecky's as well. In chapter 21 of *Connecticut Yankee,* Hank Morgan and King Arthur happen across a band of pilgrims as well as a group of slaves chained to one another. In composing the scene, Twain drew on many sources, but they are again roughly contemporaneous to Twain's own era, consisting of eighteenth- and nineteenth-century history and contemporary accounts of Russia. For Twain slavery in a variety of forms is the direct result of monarchical government and hierarchical, established churches, specifically Roman Catholicism. Twain dismisses established religion as "an established slave-pen" (pp. 185–186), commenting on the mental slavery that accompanies real slavery. Consequently Hank directs his efforts at destroying both monarchical government and the established church. Dan Beard's illustration of the slave driver of chapter 34 as the American robber baron Jay Gould connects the slave drivers of the past with the entrepreneurial slave drivers of Twain's present, a connection explicitly made in the novel. This contrast of civilizations is truly a criticism of both the past and present English and American (and continental) civilizations, and Twain's novel achieves a universality that allows him to comment on human history more generally.

Twain also introduces elements that connect the oppressive hierarchies of religion and politics in the Arthurian age to genocide and the Indian wars. Twain's attitudes toward Native Americans have been the subject of some debate, and many critics have commented negatively on his depictions of the "Goshoot Indians" in *Roughing It* (1872). In *Connecticut Yankee,* Twain's conception is perhaps more enlightened as he reveals the chauvinism of his narrator Hank Morgan: it is the protagonist, not the author, who derisively refers to the inhabitants of Camelot as "white Indians" (p. 66). Hank conceives of himself as an agent of civilization who brings its benefits to the natives. It is known that Twain had read such works as Elizabeth Custer's *Tenting on the Plains* (1887), George Armstrong Custer's *My Life on the Plains* (1874), and Francis Parkman's *The California and Oregon Trail* (1849) and *The Jesuits in North America in the Seventeenth Century* (1867). Twain's conception of the imperialistic relationship between Hank Morgan and the "natives" of Camelot, however, owes more to Lecky's *History of England in the Eighteenth Century* than to any other single source, for he saw the Scottish system of "chiefs" and "clans" as clear analogues to Native American society. Twain even noted in one copy of

Lecky's history that the Scots were like "Iroquois." Twain draws upon Lecky's description of English attempts to civilize the Highlands of Scotland in his own descriptions of Hank's attempt to civilize Camelot. As in Lecky's work, a great deal of blood is shed in Twain's fictional account.

Hank Morgan's actions suggest too a brotherhood between thieving English knights in Arthurian England and the captains of industry in his own world. Many have noted that Twain probably intended his protagonist's name to suggest that paragon of Gilded Age acquisitiveness, J. P. Morgan. Hank tellingly describes Camelot as "a corporation where nine hundred and ninety-four of the members furnished all of the money and did all the work, and the other six elected themselves a permanent board of direction and took all the dividends" (p. 160). Twain had expressed sympathy for the motives and actions of the Knights of Labor in the 1880s, and after his book was published, he even considered offering it on discount to such labor organizations. It should be no surprise, then, that chapter 33, subtitled "Sixth-Century Political Economy," owes much to contemporary debates over taxation and trade. Twain's Hank speaks with all the enthusiasm of a convert to the free trade position, and in this he resembles his creator. Twain came over to the free trade position during the initial stages of composition of *Connecticut Yankee,* supporting Grover Cleveland's free trade positions in the 1884 and 1888 presidential campaigns. Twain was also influenced by Dugald Stewart's *Lectures on Political Economy* (1855), though possibly only through secondary discussions of the Scots economist's work in Lecky's *A History of England in the Eighteenth Century.* Hank's attempts to educate the inhabitants of Camelot about free trade and so better their lives follow a predictable pattern, one that Twain gleaned from numerous historical examples. As Hank attempts to explain his new ideas, he meets with incomprehension, derision, and rejection. Time and again Hank responds violently, and one should note that his official title in Camelot, "The Boss," allies him not with labor but with management. In chapter 33, Hank attempts to explain free trade, but the people only understand that protection keeps their wages higher, not that their buying power is thereby reduced. Stultified, Hank purposefully lures them into admissions that would land them in the pillory but then realizes he "had overdone the thing" (p. 379) and frightened them nearly to death. Twain makes the most of the contrast between civilizations, heightening the comic effect through Hank's Yankee dialect. Hank's victory over Dowley, for example, is a "smasher" (p. 379). In another scene, Hank's description of knight errantry as "a most chuckle-headed trade" and really "just a corner in pork, that's all" (p. 223) brilliantly evokes the absurdity of both worlds, English past and American present.

INVENTING THE NINETEENTH CENTURY

One of the most obvious of the "contrasts" between civilizations is in the level of civilization as measured by inventions and labor-saving devices. Hank's improvements abound in the novel but particularly in chapter 10, "The Beginnings of Civilization." Here he enumerates the many improvements he has created and instituted in just four years. "I was just another Robinson Crusoe cast away on an uninhabited island" (p. 100), he opines, and like his literary ancestor he brings civilization to his own island, England. He introduces telephone lines, telegraphs, newspapers, soap factories, "teacher factories," and electricity. Twain uses the inventions for comic effect: King Arthur and Hank are saved from hanging by the last-minute arrival of Launcelot and a battalion of knights on bicycles. Hank introduces baseball as a substitute for jousting and harnesses the repetitive movements of St. Stylite, a holy man who prays by bowing incessantly while perched atop a pillar, using the energy to operate a loom to manufacture cloth. Both developments support Hank's attempts to democratize society by decreasing the reverence with which the aristocratic and church hierarchies are held. The newspaper is perhaps the most obvious of such developments, for Hank contends that a free press is necessary in a free country. Education that would free people from their "training," as Hank terms it, is likewise essential (p. 208). Even Hank's personal life provides a comedic contrast of the two ages when Sandy names their daughter "Hello-Central" after hearing him muttering the phrase in his sleep: "Hello Central" was the salutation with which one greeted a "Hello Girl," an early telephone operator.

WAGING WAR ON THE PAST

Other inventions from the nineteenth century have less-pacific uses, for while Hank hopes for a "complete revolution without bloodshed" (p. 67), he finally realizes the impossibility of his plan. He uses blasting powder quite early in the novel, when he destroys Merlin's tower in chapter 7, but he manages to restrain what he calls the "circus-side of my nature" (p. 160) that desires an all-out, violent revolution. During a joust Hank first uses a lariat, but when Merlin steals it he relies on his revolver, killing Sir Sagramour and many other knights. Traveling incognito with King Arthur, Hank uses dynamite to save them from some knights they had angered. Throughout the novel, then, Hank relies on a variety of weapons typical of the nineteenth century to extricate himself from tight situations. The most controversial example by far is chapter 43, "The Battle of the Sand-Belt," in which Hank exhorts his men that their struggle against chivalry has only one possible conclusion: "We will kill them all" (p. 479). To accomplish this task Twain's protagonist relies on all the skills Hank had learned working at the Colt Firearms Factory in nineteenth-century Connecticut. Although many critics complain that the ending is so brutal and shocking that it must have been provoked by the multiple disasters of Twain's personal life during this time, particularly the failure of the Paige typesetter and the imminent bankruptcy of the Charles L. Webster Publishing Company, in both of which Twain had invested heavily, one should note that Twain's journal entries prove that he had planned for this ending from the very earliest stages of the novel's composition. In this final battle Hank employs dynamite, Gatling guns, and electric fences to kill twenty-five thousand knights. Hank has been compared to Hitler, Mussolini, and Stalin, though one should note that his motives, if not his methods, were superior to those of such real-life mass murderers. Twain's primary models for these last chapters were Carlyle's descriptions of the Terror during the French Revolution and Lecky's description of the Master of Stair, mastermind of the English genocide in the Scots Highlands, in *A History of England in the Eighteenth Century.*

CONTINUING DEBATE

Debate over Twain's view of history and progress in the novel is nearly as intense as discussion of Twain's attitudes toward race in *Adventures of Huckleberry Finn.* In both novels the concluding chapters have served as the focal points for discussion. If the "Evasion" ending of *Adventures of Huckleberry Finn* leads some critics to suggest that Twain was really not an "ablishionist," in Huck's term, after all, "The Battle of the Sand-Belt" has led some critics to question whether Twain really believed human progress was possible and whether all the nineteenth-century advances instituted in Camelot really held utopian possibilities at all. Perhaps even in such an imaginative work the author felt that the past could not be "changed," and so Hank's plans for Camelot were foredoomed. Indeed, from the beginning, Twain planned to end his novel with an impressive display of nineteenth-century war machines, seeming to suggest that human nature remains violent even while capable of great innovation. The novel predicts no utopian technocracy but rather suggests the likelihood of dystopia.

Ironically, even as technology wins "The Battle of the Sand-Belt," magic wins the war itself: Merlin sends Hank Morgan back into the future, and the Yankee's technological advances actually destroy his attempt to engraft democratic values on an aristocratic society. Likewise, in *Connecticut Yankee*'s last chapter, "Final P.S. by M. T.," nothing but death can broach the gulf of time separating Hank Morgan from his wife, Sandy, and their child, Hello-Central. The conclusion of the novel features a one-ended telephone conversation, with Hank deliriously "calling" the past but connecting with only "unreplying vacancies" (p. 453). Other advances of the nineteenth century are depicted as useful but also as at least potentially dangerous. The failure of technology in the end of the novel seems to suggest that technological advances hold the potential for great good but they also allow for a more advanced barbarism capable of mass slaughter at the push of a button.

See also Humor; Reform; Satire, Burlesque, and Parody; Science and Technology

BIBLIOGRAPHY

Primary Works

Malory, Sir Thomas. *Morte d'Arthur.* Globe edition. Edited by Sir Edward Strachey, Bart. New York: McMillan, 1871.

Twain, Mark. *A Connecticut Yankee in King Arthur's Court.* Edited by Bernard L. Stein. Berkeley: University of California Press, 1979.

Twain, Mark. "General Grant's Grammar." In *Mark Twain's Speeches,* pp. 135–137. New York: Babriel Wells, 1923.

Twain, Mark. *Mark Twain's Notebooks and Journals.* Vol. 3, *1883–1891.* Edited by Robert Pack Browning, Michael Frank, and Lin Salamo. Berkeley: University of California Press, 1979.

Twain, Mark. "The Revised Catechism." In *Collected Tales, Sketches, Speeches, and Essays 1852–1890,* pp. 539–540. New York: Library of America, 1992.

Twain, Mark. "The 'Tournament' in A.D. 1870." In *Mark Twain: Collected Tales, Sketches, Speeches, and Essays 1852–1890,* pp. 418–420. New York: Library of America, 1992.

Secondary Works

Baetzhold, Howard G. *Mark Twain and John Bull: The British Connection.* Bloomington: Indiana University Press, 1970.

Baetzhold, Howard G. "'Well, My Book Is Written—Let It Go . . .' The Making of *A Connecticut Yankee in King Arthur's Court.*" In *Biographies of Books: The Compositional Histories of Notable American Writings,* edited by James Barbour and Tom Quirk, pp. 41–77. Columbia: University of Missouri Press, 1996.

Budd, Louis J. *Mark Twain: Social Philosopher.* Bloomington: Indiana University Press, 1962.

Carter, Everett. "The Meaning of *A Connecticut Yankee*." *American Literature* 50 (1978): 418–440.

Fulton, Joe B. *Mark Twain in the Margins: "The Quarry Farm Marginalia" and "A Connecticut Yankee in King Arthur's Court."* Tuscaloosa: University of Alabama Press, 2000.

Fulton, Joe B. *Mark Twain's Ethical Realism: The Aesthetics of Race, Class, and Gender.* Columbia: University of Missouri Press, 1997.

Gardiner, Jane. "'A More Splendid Necromancy': Mark Twain's *Connecticut Yankee* and the Electrical Revolution." *Studies in the Novel* 19 (1987): 448–458.

Gribben, Alan. *Mark Twain's Library: A Reconstruction.* 2 vols. Boston: G. K. Hall, 1980.

Johnson, Ronald M. "Future as Past, Past as Future: Edward Bellamy, Mark Twain, and the Crisis of the 1880s." *American Studies in Scandinavia* 22 (1990): 73–79.

Michaels, Walter Benn. "An American Tragedy; or, The Promise of American Life: Classes and Individuals." *Representations* 25 (1989): 71–98.

Rowe, John Carlos. "How the Boss Played the Game: Twain's Critique of Imperialism in *A Connecticut Yankee in King Arthur's Court.*" In *The Cambridge Companion to Mark Twain,* edited by Forrest G. Robinson, pp. 175–192. New York: Cambridge University Press, 1995.

Sewell, David R. "Hank Morgan and the Colonization of Utopia." *American Transcendental Quarterly,* n.s. 3 (1989): 27–44.

Slotkin, Richard. *The Fatal Environment: The Myth of the Frontier in the Age of Industrialization, 1800–1890.* Middletown, Conn.: Wesleyan University Press, 1985.

Smith, Henry Nash. Introduction to *A Connecticut Yankee in King Arthur's Court.* Edited by Bernard L. Stein, pp. 1–30. Berkeley: University of California Press, 1979.

Williams, James D. "Revision and Intention in Mark Twain's *A Connecticut Yankee.*" *American Literature* 36 (1964): 288–297.

Williams, James D. "The Uses of History in Mark Twain's *A Connecticut Yankee.*" *PMLA* 80 (1965): 102–110.

Joe B. Fulton

COPYRIGHT

Copyright has been a source of contention in the United States nearly from the moment the first law went into effect in 1791. One of the primary sources for this ongoing debate is the constitutional amend-ment authorizing the law. The framers called for copyright "to promote the Progress of Science and the useful Arts, by securing for limited Times, to Authors and Inventors, the exclusive Right to their respective Writings and Discoveries" (Leaffer, p. 6). The language appears to grant primacy to the public welfare, "the Progress of Science and the useful Arts," over the rights of the individual creator. This has led to an ongoing struggle between those who champion the literary property rights of the individual and proponents of the "public good" who call for a more narrowly defined law of shorter duration.

Subsequent legislation and jurisprudence have addressed numerous questions emerging from the expansion of print culture in the United States, including the precise length of the "limited Times" of copyrights, the exact nature of the works that are protected, and whether or not the law should extend to cover the works of creators from other nations. While arguments regarding different facets of copyright continue in the early twenty-first century, public debate and activism were particularly prominent in the late nineteenth century as authors, printers, publishers, and readers struggled over the creation of an "international copyright law," a law that would protect the works of writers from abroad. Proponents of such a law argued that it was both a matter of justice and of encouraging the profession of authorship in the United States by leveling the playing field. This could only happen, they argued, if publishers were discouraged from reprinting popular foreign novels without payment or permission. Opponents claimed that it would limit poor readers' access to inexpensive texts and hurt American book manufacturing, all to serve the financial interests of coddled British writers.

AFTER THE WAR: THE REEMERGENCE OF THE COPYRIGHT BATTLE

Various pieces of copyright legislation had been debated and enacted in Congress or sent to an early grave in committee throughout the first half of the nineteenth century, but the issue largely disappeared as the nation grappled with the upheaval of the Civil War. Not long after the conclusion of the war, however, copyright once again emerged as a topic of debate. A number of senators presented petitions and called for the consideration of the subject. The rhetoric of the public debate turned heated with the publication of a second edition of an influential tract, *Letters on International Copyright* (1868). Its author, a prominent publisher named Henry C. Carey (1793–1879), took aim at legislation granting rights to foreign writers while simultaneously criticizing American writers' pursuit of stronger laws for their own works. In his new preface, Carey described the matter as a conflict between the monopolistic desires of a few authors and the democratic interests of the American public: "On the one side, there will be found a few thousand persons interested in maintaining the monopolies that had been granted to authors and publishers, foreign and domestic. On the other, sixty or eighty millions, tired of taxation and determined that books shall be more cheaply furnished" (p. 14). Carey seems to have rereleased his book in order to turn the tide against international copyright once again, for that same year the Committee on the Library in the House of Representatives produced a report favoring the creation of such a law. While the report claimed that it would be "an act of national justice and honor" (U.S. Congress, U.S. House, Committee on the Library, p. 1), Congress took no action.

Despite this setback, authors did gain a victory in 1870 with the passage of a bill granting them copyrights for translations of their work and for dramatic adaptations. As such a law would suggest, the exact nature of literary property was still a source of contention. Authors and their advocates tried to argue that texts were like any other piece of property. In a response to Carey's *Letters*, Stevenson Archer, a representative from Maryland, published a speech he gave on international copyright in 1872. As he stated, "The simple truth is, the author has a right, an absolute right, in his books, precisely such as he has in his house or his land" (p. 9). While proponents of copyright had made similar arguments for many years, they never gained much traction during the nineteenth century. Indeed, in spite of its supporters' best efforts, the international copyright bill proposed in 1872 fared no better than the earlier measures, this time even receiving an unfavorable report from the Joint Committee on the Library in 1873. In the years following the Civil War, the battle over copyright would continue to preoccupy Congress and the nation's writers and publishers.

"PIRATES"

If authors were considered either victims or greedy monopolists, then the publishers who took advantage of the gaps in American copyright law were either the heroes of the underprivileged reading class or the immoral "pirates" of the book trade, seizing property that belonged to others. Throughout the nineteenth century, American writers bemoaned the fact that they were forced to compete with cheap reprints of well-known British authors. First Sir Walter Scott and then Charles Dickens became emblematic of the flood of foreign novels barring the progress of American literature. As the century progressed, the "piracy" of texts—reprinting them without permission

from or compensation for the authors—was taking place on both sides of the Atlantic. While this began with works by James Fenimore Cooper and greatly accelerated with the success of Harriet Beecher Stowe's *Uncle Tom's Cabin* (1852), it was a considerable trade by the 1880s, and readers in England were enjoying inexpensive editions of popular American works. Unlike the United States, Great Britain did allow foreign authors to secure copyright, but it required that authors be on British soil when the work was first published in the country. While authors such as Mark Twain (1835–1910) and Harriet Beecher Stowe (1811–1896) spent time traveling to Canada to meet this requirement, it posed a considerable financial and logistical burden. As many authors pointed out, it also made it nearly impossible for an unknown writer to secure copyright for a first work. As difficult as this hurdle was, British authors had no available option in the United States, and there were several American publishers willing to take advantage of this fact.

Of course, whether or not this constituted any sort of "piracy" depended on where one stood. In testimony before Congress in 1886, one publisher who reprinted the *Encyclopaedia Britannica* proudly declared of his firm, "We are what these gentlemen call 'pirates,' and I have got the black flag up now" (U.S. Congress, U.S. Senate, Committee on Patents, p. 82). In his eyes, the push for international copyright was "the clamor of two hundred authors against the interests of fifty-five millions of people" (p. 74). This pitting of the minority against the majority was a common feature of opposition to stronger copyright laws. When Congress refused to consider international copyright in 1873, the Joint Committee on the Library concluded that it would be "not only an unquestionable and permanent injury to the manufacturing interests in producing books, but a hinderance to the diffusion of knowledge among the people and to the cause of universal education" (Morrill, p. 8). Far from pirates, those publishers who reprinted foreign works without compensating their authors presumed to serve democratic ideals and to aid national industry.

Authors were inclined to take a different view of the matter. William Cullen Bryant declared, "[The author] enters the great forest of ideas, which is common ground, hews down trees, shapes them into articles of furniture, or builds a house with them, and he who takes from him that furniture is a thief, and he who breaks into that house is a burglar" (*International Copyright*, p. 14). It was common for authors to equate unauthorized reprinting as theft, but even the strongest supporter had to concede that in many cases there was nothing strictly illegal about "piracy." In his article "American Authors and British Pirates"

(1887), the author Brander Matthews—one of the founders of the influential American Copyright League—conceded: "At bottom, the publishers, good or bad, are not to blame; it is the condition of the law which is at fault. While men are legally permitted to make money by seizing the literary property of others, some will yield to temptation, and take what is not theirs to take" (p. 212). Pirates were a legal part of the nineteenth-century book trade.

THE AMERICAN COPYRIGHT LEAGUE

Given the nature of the debate, it is not surprising that throughout the efforts to strengthen copyright laws, authors and like-minded publishers banded together to show their support for change. Such a process had begun with a memorial signed by prominent writers and delivered to Congress by Henry Clay in 1837 and was given more formal shape in the 1840s with the American Copyright Club, an organization headed by William Cullen Bryant (1794–1878). This later became the International Copyright Association in 1868. By far the most energetic iteration of these groups, and ultimately the most successful, was the American Copyright League. Begun in 1883, it was headed by James Russell Lowell (1819–1891), who penned this motto:

> In vain we call old notions fudge,
> And bend our conscience to our dealing;
> The ten commandments will not budge
> And stealing will continue stealing.
> *(Matthews,* These Many Years, *p. 225)*

Its secretary was publisher George Haven Putnam (1844–1930), who picked up the torch carried by his father, the prominent publisher and magazine editor George Palmer Putnam. Putnam was one of the few publishers to support the cause from its early days. The league was active in lobbying the American people as well as the government. It produced a number of publications, including even a sermon written by the member and clergyman Henry Van Dyke in 1888, *The National Sin of Literary Piracy.* The organization counted among its members Henry James, William Dean Howells (1837–1920), and nearly every other prominent living author. A pamphlet published by the league included statements from Louisa May Alcott, Rebecca Harding Davis, and Frederick Douglass. Authors gave public readings of their works to raise awareness and to raise funds to support their efforts throughout the 1880s.

Of course, some of the league's most important work was done before Congress. It threw its support behind a bill presented by Senator Joseph Hawley of Connecticut in 1885 that called for establishing reciprocal copyrights: foreign authors would receive the same copyright protections provided American citizens if their nations extended the same rights its citizens enjoyed to American authors. In November, Twain and two other members of the league met with President Grover Cleveland; Twain wrote in his notebook on 19 November, "I ventured to urge him to make I.C. the child of his administration, & nurse it & raise it" (p. 211). The president evidently paid some attention, for he included a call for action on international copyright in his address to Congress in December 1885 (Solberg, p. 24).

In 1886, as the Senate Committee on Patents turned to consider the Hawley bill, it also had another measure to consider. The Chace bill, supported by a number of publishers, printers, and typesetters, allowed for copyright protection of foreign works provided they were printed and manufactured in the United States; in other words, it forced authors to make arrangements for American publication, and it barred the importation of foreign works. This "manufacturing clause," as it became known, was a major source of contention for the American Copyright League, who feared that it ensnared a measure designed to protect authorial rights in a debate on protectionism.

Supporters of both bills, as well as opponents of any new measure, appeared before the Senate committee in 1886, and the league sent some of its most prominent members, including Mark Twain and James Russell Lowell. Their case was a difficult one, given the competing bills, and it was complicated further by Twain's surprising remarks. After first acknowledging that he was hesitant to speak in opposition to the league, he went on to say:

> I should like to see a copyright bill passed here which shall do no harm to anybody concerned in this matter, and a great many more people are concerned in it than merely the authors. In fact I suppose, if the truth is confessed, the authors are rather less concerned pecuniarily in any copyright measure than many other people—publishers, printers, binders, and so on. The authors have one part in this matter, but theirs is the larger part. (U.S. Congress, U.S. Senate, Committee on Patents, pp. 15–16)

Twain's comments not only parted from the consistent message of the league but seemed to minimize copyright's importance to authors. Subsequent speakers for the bill attempted to address Twain's remarks and to argue in favor of the law, but they were unsuccessful, and supporters were forced to wait yet again.

"INTERNATIONAL COPYRIGHT" AT LAST: THE ACT OF 1891

The "manufacturing clause" eventually proved to be the secret to producing a bill that Congress would accept. When Putnam testified before the House Committee on the Judiciary in 1890, he announced that the American Copyright League now included not only authors but also members of those trades that had once opposed it:

> The league . . . now comprises in addition to the authors . . . nearly all the publishing firms in the country, representatives of the typographers, who are authorized to speak for the National Typographical Union, representatives of the Typothetae, authorized to speak for the National Union of Employing Printers, representatives of the National Association of Librarians, representatives of the press syndicates, and a large number of representatives of the general public, whose co-operation in the attempt to secure adequate recognition for literary property is entirely unconnected with any direct interest in the business of writing, making, or selling books. (U.S. Congress, U.S. House, Committee on the Judiciary, pp. 28–29)

Although some smaller publishers and trade groups continued to protest, they were no match for the unified effort, and Congress passed the bill on 3 March 1891. Foreign authors were finally granted the same rights as American authors in the United States, provided they manufactured their books in the country and so long as their own nations provided reciprocal rights. These were no small obstacles for some writers, and the publication requirement served to keep the issue of establishing a copyright that was truly international in more than name a pressing concern. Over the next few years, there was continued agitation for the United States to revise its laws in this regard. The United States did join the Buenos Aires Convention in 1914, allowing for reciprocal copyrights with several Latin American countries, but efforts to go beyond this failed for many years.

The bill was a moment of triumph after a long struggle, however. When it passed, Walt Whitman remarked to a friend: "We have our international copyright at last—the bill is signed today. The United States, which should have been the first to pass the thing, is the last. Now all civilized nations have it. It is a question of honesty—of morals—of a literature, in fact" (Traubel, pp. 54–55). For American writers, the bill had always been tied to the idea of a national literature, and its passage meant that they could now compete on an even footing in the marketplace. This was not the end of their efforts, of course. There were still other issues to address, particularly the matter of duration of copyrights and new forms of recording

and transmitting works, but the Copyright Act of 1891 was an important milestone in American literary history.

BACK TO THE DRAWING BOARD: THE COPYRIGHT ACT OF 1909

In 1831 Congress amended the copyright law to extend copyright from fourteen to twenty-eight years, with the possibility for renewal for another fourteen years at the conclusion of the first term. For authors who felt that literary property should be treated the same as real estate or any other product of labor, this limitation was unacceptable. As Howells noted:

> If property in houses or lands—which a man may get by dishonest trickery, or usury, or hard rapacity—were in danger of ceasing after forty-two years, the whole virtuous community would rouse itself to perpetuate the author's right to the product of his brain, and no griping bidder at tax-sales but would demand the protection of literature by indefinite copyright. (Budd, p. 151)

Throughout most of the nineteenth century, the issue of international copyright had occupied advocates of stronger literary property rights, but with that issue at least partially addressed, the question of duration came to the forefront. The 1909 revision of the copyright law extended the term of the renewal to twenty-eight years, allowing for the possibility of a fifty-six-year copyright: the "limited times" set forth in the Constitution were growing less limited, a trend that would continue throughout the twentieth century.

There was one other major aspect of the revision that, in retrospect, seems a harbinger for things to come. The law for the first time allowed for recording and mechanical reproduction rights, reflecting the emerging audio and visual technologies. The provision itself was aimed primarily at protecting the rights of composers whose scores were being copied onto piano rolls, but it represented one of the first clear indications of how copyright law would have to be continually modified to adapt to new modes of reproducing and transmitting texts. Along with the extension of the length of protection, these two changes in the laws of literary property signaled the new era of copyright struggles that continues in the early twenty-first century.

See also Book Publishing; Literary Marketplace

BIBLIOGRAPHY
Primary Works
Archer, Stevenson. *International Copyright. Speech of Hon. Stevenson Archer, of Maryland, Delivered in the House of Representatives, March 23, 1872.* Washington, D.C.: F. and J. Rives and Geo. A. Bailey, 1872.

Carey, H. C. *Letters on International Copyright*. 2nd ed. New York: Hurd and Houghton, 1868.

International Copyright. Meeting of Authors and Publishers, at the Rooms of the New York Historical Society, April 9, 1868, and Organization of the International Copyright Association. New York: International Copyright Association, 1868.

Matthews, Brander. "American Authors and British Pirates." *New Princeton Review* 4, no. 5 (1887): 201–212.

Matthews, Brander. *These Many Years: Recollections of a New Yorker*. New York: Scribners, 1917.

Morrill, Lot Myrick. *International Copyright*. U.S. 42nd Cong., 3rd sess. S. Rept. 409. Washington, D.C.: Government Printing Office, 1873.

Traubel, Horace, ed. *With Walt Whitman in Camden*. Vol. 8. Edited by Jeanne Chapman and Robert MacIsaac. Oregon House, Calif.: Bentley, 1996.

Twain, Mark. *Mark Twain's Notebooks and Journals*. Vol. 3, *1883–1891*. Edited by Robert Pack Browning, Michael B. Frank, and Lin Salamo. Berkeley: University of California Press, 1979.

U.S. Congress. U.S. House, Committee on the Library. Report [To accompany bill H. R. No. 779]. 40th Cong., 2nd sess. Rept. 16. Washington, D.C.: Government Printing Office, 1868.

U.S. Congress. U.S. Senate, Committee on Patents. International Copyright. 49th Cong., 1st sess. S. no. 161. Washington, D.C.: Government Printing Office, 1886.

U.S. Congress. U.S. House, Committee on the Judiciary. *Testimony before the House Committee on the Judiciary on International Copyright*. Washington, D.C.: Government Printing Office, 1890.

Van Dyke, Henry. *The National Sin of Literary Piracy: A Sermon Preached by Henry Van Dyke, D.D.* New York: Scribners, 1888.

Secondary Works

Budd, Louis J. *Mark Twain: The Contemporary Reviews*. American Critical Archives 11. Cambridge, U.K.: Cambridge University Press, 1999.

Leaffer, Marshall. *Understanding Copyright Law*. New York: Matthew Bender, 1999.

Solberg, Thorvald. "International Copyright in Congress, 1837–1886." In *Copyright Miscellany*. Boston: John W. Luce, 1939.

U.S. Congress. *Copyright Law Revision*. Washington, D.C.: Government Printing Office, 1960.

Martin T. Buinicki

THE COUNTRY OF THE POINTED FIRS

Sarah Orne Jewett's sketches of an anonymous writer's summer on the Maine coast appeared in the *Atlantic Monthly* in four installments during 1896. They were collected later that year, along with two related sketches, in *The Country of the Pointed Firs*. During a time of rapid change and social turbulence precipitated by financial panic, labor agitation, anti-immigration legislation, and racist violence, Jewett's delicately nuanced stories of country people persevering and even thriving despite poverty and harsh conditions—vigorous as the region's pointed firs—struck a chord with readers. Although Jewett was already well known as a writer of New England stories and novels, her strangely unclassifiable text (was it a novel or a collection of stories?) won high praise from readers such as Henry James, Rudyard Kipling, and the fellow New Englander Mary Wilkins Freeman. Years later Willa Cather, who benefited from Jewett's artistic guidance, wrote that this book would face the future serenely: it was an American classic assured of a long life able to stand alongside Nathaniel Hawthorne's *Scarlet Letter* (1850) or Mark Twain's *Adventures of Huckleberry Finn* (1885). Its future was not to be so serene, however. Rather, *The Country of the Pointed Firs* almost immediately became a literary test case, one that elicited responses ranging from adulatory appreciation to patronizing dismissal and outright rejection.

At stake was the work's representation of the region in relation to the nation and later, to the empire the nation was aspiring to become. Also at issue was its portrayal of the bonds between women and the nature of gender as well as the connections between highbrow urban tourists and their rural working-class hosts. Then there was the possible racism and ethnocentrism of a text that so explicitly celebrated the northern European roots of New England families and folkways. Finally, there was Jewett's own authorship: her motivation and her place in American literary culture. Was she a minor or a major author? Was she motivated to write by the ambition to belong to a professional elite or by concern, as Harriet Beecher Stowe once wrote, to make her readers "feel right" or, in Jewett's case, "see right"? Over the years, these debates prompted more refined, complex, and far-reaching readings of a book that met at least one test required of an American classic: although it did not face time serenely, it offered readers a text that was rich, layered, and a challenge to interpret, much like the period in which it was written.

THE AUTHOR

Sarah Orne Jewett was born on 3 September 1849 in South Berwick, Maine, into a moderately wealthy family

***Shepherdess Guarding Her Flock,* 1862–1864.** Painting by Jean François Millet. Introducing the character of Esther Hight in "A Dunnet Shepherdess," Jewett writes, "I found myself possessed of a surprising interest in the shepherdess, who stood far away in the hill pasture with her great flock, like a figure of Millet's, high against the sky." © ARCHIVO ICONOGRAFICO, S.A./CORBIS

with a long history in Maine and New Hampshire. Jewett's paternal grandfather had been a shipowner and trader; her father was a respected country doctor and obstetrician. Her mother's family was perhaps even more distinguished; the Gilmans counted one New Hampshire governor among them. Not a large town and not on the coast, South Berwick had once thrived by selling lumber and masts for the shipping trade. Along with that of the entire region, its economy suffered during the embargo of 1807 and the War of 1812. It further declined with the rest of rural New England after the Civil War, as jobs disappeared and ambitious young people left farms for the city and the

West. While tourism offered towns on the coast new sources of revenue, inland villages such as South Berwick had fewer resources. Textile mills like the one in Salmon Falls, New Hampshire, just blocks from the grand white Georgian house occupied by the Jewetts, struggled, as did the often-maligned Irish and French Canadian immigrants who worked in them.

Because she suffered from rheumatoid arthritis, Jewett was frequently taken out of school and accompanied her father on his rounds in the countryside. Well-educated and cosmopolitan, Theodore Jewett encouraged his daughter to respect the lives of his rural patients and later to realize her hopes of becoming a writer. Her first stylistic mentor, he introduced her to writers such as Laurence Sterne and Cervantes. Less is known about Jewett's mother, Caroline, but she too influenced her daughter's literary taste by giving her Jane Austen and George Eliot to read. One of the most important of Jewett's early feminine influences was Harriet Beecher Stowe, whose *Pearl of Orr's Island* (1862) opened her eyes to the artistic possibilities of her own region. Later Jewett came to admire Gustave Flaubert and to emulate his spare, elegant style. Other influences included the visionary philosophy of Emanuel Swedenborg and the pastoral Romanticism of William and Dorothy Wordsworth.

Jewett's early stories were accepted by William Dean Howells (1837–1920), then an editor at the *Atlantic Monthly*. Her first success was *Deephaven* (1877), a book that anticipates *Pointed Firs* both in its form—linked sketches—and its subject matter—two genteel young women spending the summer in a decayed seacoast town. As her reputation grew, Jewett tried a variety of genres, including children's stories such as *Play Days* (1878) and more conventionally plotted novels such as *A Country Doctor* (1884), which traced the development of a young woman who forgoes marriage to become a doctor. Jewett's 1901 novel *The Tory Lover* was a less-successful attempt to write in the popular historical romance genre. Finally, there was her history for young readers, *The Story of the Normans* (1887), which drew on current theories of racial traits to extol the achievements of the Normans and their descendants, some of whom included the Jewetts themselves.

Shortly before Theodore Jewett's death in 1878, Jewett, now established on the Boston literary scene, became acquainted with Annie Fields (1834–1915), widow of the influential publisher James T. Fields. A celebrated literary hostess and author in her own right, Annie Fields became Jewett's companion in what historians call a "Boston marriage." Modern terms such as "lesbian" seem anachronistic when applied to this relationship, but there is no doubting the two women's devotion to each other. Jewett spent a part of each year with Fields, traveling abroad or staying at her homes in Boston and Manchester-by-the-Sea. Their letters, which contained everything from passionate terms of endearment to literary commentary, reveal the diverse roles the women played in each other's lives. The two also participated in a large network of artistic women, including, among others, Celia Thaxter and Sarah Wyman Whitman. Just as Jewett's writing sheds light on rural women's lives and friendships, her life opens a window on the new professionalism of women artists.

THE BOOK

The Country of the Pointed Firs was originally inspired by visits Jewett made to Maine's Penobscot Bay in 1889 and 1895. After a stay with Lilian and Thomas Bailey Aldrich in Tenant's Harbor the summer of 1895, Jewett and Fields rented a cottage for September in nearby Martinsville. There they came to know Rosilla Bachelder and Dan Butland, local residents who, according to Jewett's biographer Paula Blanchard, were the models for Almira Todd and Elijah Tilley, major characters in *Pointed Firs*. After the first four installments of the book appeared in 1896, Jewett revisited the area to refresh her memory before writing "Along Shore" and "The Backward View," the last two sketches in the collection, which was published in November by Houghton Mifflin. Later, she returned imaginatively to the fictional world of Dunnet Landing several times. "A Dunnet Shepherdess" and "The Queen's Twin" were collected in *The Queen's Twin and Other Stories* in 1899. "The Foreigner" appeared in the *Atlantic* in 1900, and "William's Wedding" was published in 1910, after Jewett died in 1909 of a stroke, possibly the result of lingering injuries from a carriage accident in 1902.

Although these sketches portray discrete episodes in the anonymous narrator's stay in Dunnet Landing, they are subtly linked to show her growing insight into the local community and her increasing acceptance by it. A turn-of-the-century urbanite suffering from "modern nervousness," she arrives seeking psychic renewal and the peace to get her writing done. Over the summer, she comes to know her landlady, Mrs. Todd, a big-bodied herb gatherer and wisdom dispenser, along with Mrs. Todd's mother, Mrs. Blackett, and her brother, William. The sketches show her gaining her hosts' trust as she listens to their tales of the past and tries to see the world through their eyes. In one episode, she attends the annual reunion of Mrs. Todd's maternal family, the Bowdens, and feels almost "an adopted Bowden" (p. 459) herself. Ultimately, she travels beyond Mrs. Todd's mentorship by cementing a friendship with Elijah Tilley, an aging fisherman who confides his grief for his dead wife. When the summer ends, she leaves on the "unpunctual" steamer and watches as the village and all its surroundings disappear from sight.

Later stories about Dunnet Landing were carefully situated within the narrator's original visit, except for "William's Wedding," set during the narrator's return the following spring. Unfortunately, later editions of *Pointed Firs* often interpolated these later stories, with the exception of "The Foreigner," into the 1896 narrative. As a result, the careful chronology of the sketches was destroyed, and the expository material necessary to

This passage, taken from the chapter "The Bowden Reunion," describes the procession of the Bowden family to the grove above the family homestead. Some critics have argued that Jewett's narrator represents the Bowden family, with its French descent, as the epitome of an American national identity defined as both white and northern European. Other critics have noted Jewett's "romantic racialism" but have argued that, while she believed in the existence of racial traits, she never advocated discrimination or exclusion based on race or ethnicity. Critics are thus divided over whether the narrator invests this family procession with narrowly racial or broadly universal implications.

There was a wide path mowed for us across the field and, as we moved along, the birds flew up out of the thick second crop of clover, and the bees hummed as if it still were June. There was a flashing of white gulls over the water where the fleet of boats rode the low waves together in the cove, swaying their small masts as if they kept time to our steps. The plash of the water could be heard faintly, yet still be heard; we might have been a company of ancient Greeks going to celebrate a victory, or to worship the god of harvest in the grove above. It was strangely moving to see this and to make part of it. The sky, the sea, have watched poor humanity at its rites so long; we were no more a New England family celebrating its own existence and simple progress; we carried the tokens of all such households from which this descended, and were only the latest of our line. We possessed the instincts of a far, forgotten childhood; I found myself thinking that we ought to be carrying green branches and singing as we went.

Jewett, *The Country of the Pointed Firs,* in *Novels and Stories,* pp. 460–461.

the later stand-alone stories disrupted the subtle flow of the narration. Critics reading these versions, the only ones available for many years, might be excused for thinking *Pointed Firs* more a collection of miscellaneous pieces than a progression of linked stories. With the restoration of the original edition, however, that progress is revealed. The central thread is the narrator's growing understanding of this place and people. Thus episodes typically move from the narrator's meeting a new character to a dialogue that results in her learning an important piece of personal or local history. The suc-

cessful completion of these social negotiations is often a moment of intimacy marked by a significant silence. To the imaginative reader, these silences can be full of shared emotion. But Jewett's stories can also give the reader a sense that "nothing happens." Jewett's subject here is a psychological event, a concern shared with her contemporary and friend Henry James (1843–1916), who often focused on interior "adventures" in his own tales.

Jewett's choice to withhold her narrator's name and history also reveals her affinities with modernist writers such as Ernest Hemingway, who argued that much of a good story should be submerged, like the hidden seven-eighths of an iceberg. Virtually all one learns of Jewett's narrator comes from how she sees. Her education, her cosmopolitanism, her empathy are unaccounted for, though visible in her interpretive power and descriptive skills. Many critics have also noted the "poetic realism" of Jewett's style and narrative strategies. With its attention to affective bonds as well as its self-conscious craftsmanship and appeals to the reader's imagination, *Pointed Firs* can be seen as a hybrid modernist text forged from the two novelistic traditions that inspired it: the sentimental ethos of Stowe and the artistic restraint of Flaubert.

RECEPTION

Critical valuations of *The Country of the Pointed Firs* fluctuated dramatically according to the context within which it was read. Initially praised by Howells and other realists as the epitome of the then-dominant regionalist or local color genre, Jewett's work soon met with opposition from naturalist writers eager to break free from a tradition they perceived as overly genteel, feminized, and repressive. In contrast to the ambitious "national" narratives of Frank Norris, Jack London, and Theodore Dreiser, Jewett's Maine stories seemed minor, belonging to a marginal genre concerned with a marginal region. With the advent of feminist theory and women's history in the 1970s and 1980s, however, scholars such as Josephine Donovan, Marjorie Pryse, Sandra Zagarell, Elizabeth Ammons, and Sarah Way Sherman approached *Pointed Firs* with new tools. Now the context was domestic women's lives, previously unstudied but recovered through archival materials such as diaries and letters. From this perspective, the work of Jewett and her fellow regionalists Mary Wilkins Freeman and Rose Terry Cooke exemplified ways of seeing and writing distinctive to women. These critics, praising how the regionalists' characters, many of them older and working-class women, overcame a cultural bias toward heterosexual romance and golden-haired heroines, revealed how gender and class had shaped a genre whose central concerns and artistic power had previously gone unrecognized. Buoyed by these new readings, *Pointed Firs* seemed at last to meet the requirements of a major literary work.

Yet this scholarship generally did not address the significance of race and ethnicity to regionalist texts, a question that became the focus of scholarship in the following decade, as once more *Pointed Firs* became a test case. In *Cultures of Letters* (1993), for example, Richard Brodhead assessed Jewett's career within the context of a developing "tourist economy" and the related consolidation of elite white culture as typified by the periodicals, such as the *Atlantic,* in which her best-known work appeared. He noted how her regional stories were frequently flanked by travel narratives describing "exotic" locales and argued that both genres appealed to the imperialist gaze of an emergent ruling class. Amy Kaplan's influential essay "Nation, Region, and Empire" (1991) took a similar approach, portraying the regional story as a nostalgic return to an imagined preindustrial past, a return complicit in the construction of a national identity purged of racial and ethnic complexity. Kaplan's argument that Jewett's work appealed to readers' nativist, racist, and xenophobic sentiments was seconded by essays in June Howard's *New Essays on "The Country of the Pointed Firs"* (1994). For example, Sandra Zagarell and Elizabeth Ammons read the book against the background of legislation passed in 1882, 1888, and 1891 restricting Chinese immigration and in terms of the 1896 Supreme Court decision legalizing segregation. Zagarell linked Jewett's affirmation of Norman achievement and her narrator's praise of the Bowdens' long-ago French, possibly Huguenot, descent (a heritage persisting alongside their Yankee Protestantism) to the period's racial theories, particularly of the superiority of the "Nordic" race. Ammons, focusing on the Bowden reunion scene, saw anticipations of fascism in the family's processional march. In these interpretations, the narrator's comment that "clannishness is an instinct of the heart" (p. 469) resonated in a disturbing way with the contemporary rise of the Ku Klux Klan.

Although these scholars framed important questions about Jewett's work and its historical context, their conclusions were soon complicated by new readings. Charles Johanningsmeier, for example, demonstrated in 1997 that Jewett wrote for a more diverse audience than had been recognized, publishing not just in elite periodicals but also in mass-circulation newspapers and popular magazines. June Howard's 1996 article noted that these lesser-known stories also evidenced broader literary interests than critics had realized. For example, Sarah Way Sherman's 2002 analysis of Jewett's story "The Gray Mills of Farley" (1898) showed how, rather than erasing New England's industrial history, Jewett's fictionalized portrayal of the nearby Salmon Falls mills condemned the treatment of Irish and French Canadian workers by absentee corporate owners. Similarly, in their 1996 collection, *The Irish Stories of Sarah Orne Jewett,* Louisa Renza and Jack Morgan explored Jewett's perceptive treatment of Irish immigrants in stories that had rarely been studied by scholars. Finally, Mark Sammons and Valerie Cunningham's history *Black Portsmouth* (2004) explained that by the 1920s the Ku Klux Klan in Jewett's region was targeting French Canadian immigrants as well as African Americans. Along with Jews, the Catholic French Canadians were considered a threat to white Anglo-Protestant dominance. Jewett's sensitivity to this prejudice informs "The Foreigner," a late Dunnet Landing story that sympathetically portrays a lonely French-speaking woman from the Caribbean whose foreign ways and Catholic faith "set some narrow minds against her" (p. 544). Seen from this angle, Jewett's appreciation of French culture hardly seems xenophobic.

Perhaps the most vigorous case for Jewett as a critic rather than an advocate of racism and nativism came from Marjorie Pryse and Judith Fetterley's 2003 study of regionalism and American literary culture, *Writing out of Place.* Drawing on earlier feminist approaches as well as recent work in queer theory, Pryse and Fetterley distinguished between local color and regionalism, genres usually conflated by literary scholars. They argued that local color, as illustrated by writers such as Bret Harte, was a more masculine tradition whose stories did turn an objectifying "tourist's gaze" on rural subjects. By contrast, they described regionalism, written primarily by women, as opposing the patriarchal and racist power of the dominant culture. In their reading, *Pointed Firs,* again a test case, is a resistant, not a complicit text. Its empathetic narrator, far from exploiting her Dunnet Landing characters, now models the regionalist practice of empowering marginalized people by seeing with them rather than looking at them. It is worth pointing out, however, that despite the narrator's friendship with Mrs. Todd in "The Foreigner," a friendship that results in her learning the displaced Frenchwoman's story, Jewett leaves that story's deepest conflicts unresolved. Acknowledging the boundaries of Dunnet Landing's community, "The Foreigner" poignantly reveals the difficulty that even warmhearted Mrs. Todd had "neighboring" with someone so different from herself. Jewett offers no easy answers here.

See also Realism; Regionalism and Local Color Fiction

BIBLIOGRAPHY

Primary Work

Jewett, Sarah Orne. *Novels and Stories*. Edited by Michael Davitt Bell. New York: Library of America, 1994.

Secondary Works

Ammons, Elizabeth. *Conflicting Stories: American Women Writers at the Turn into the Twentieth Century*. New York: Oxford University Press, 1991.

Bell, Michael Davitt. *The Problem of American Realism: Studies in the Cultural History of a Literary Idea*. Chicago: University of Chicago Press, 1993.

Blanchard, Paula. *Sarah Orne Jewett: Her World and Her Work*. Reading, Mass.: Addison-Wesley, 1994.

Brodhead, Richard H. *Cultures of Letters: Scenes of Reading and Writing in Nineteenth-Century America*. Chicago: University of Chicago Press, 1993.

Campbell, Donna. *Resisting Regionalism: Gender and Naturalism in American Fiction, 1885–1915*. Athens: Ohio University Press, 1997.

Cary, Richard, ed. *Appreciation of Sarah Orne Jewett: Twenty-Nine Interpretive Essays*. Waterville, Maine: Colby College Press, 1973.

Cather, Willa. "Preface." In *The Country of the Pointed Firs and Other Stories*, by Sarah Orne Jewett, pp. 6–11. Garden City, N.Y.: Doubleday, 1956.

Donovan, Josephine. "Jewett on Race, Class, Ethnicity, and Imperialism: A Reply to Her Critics." *Colby Quarterly* 38, no. 4 (2002): 403–416.

Donovan, Josephine. *New England Local Color Literature: A Woman's Tradition*. New York: Frederick Ungar, 1983.

Fetterley, Judith, and Marjorie Pryse. *Writing out of Place: Regionalism, Women, and American Literature Culture*. Urbana: University of Illinois Press, 2003.

Foote, Stephanie. *Regional Fictions: Culture and Identity in Nineteenth-Century American Literature*. Madison: University of Wisconsin Press, 2001.

Howard, June. "Unraveling Regions, Unsettling Periods: Sarah Orne Jewett and American Literary History." *American Literature* 68, no. 2 (June 1996): 365–384.

Howard, June, ed. *New Essays on "The Country of the Pointed Firs."* New York: Cambridge University Press, 1994.

Inness, Sherrie, and Diana Royer, eds. *Breaking Boundaries: New Perspectives on Women's Regional Writing*. Iowa City: University of Iowa Press, 1997.

Johanningsmeier, Charles. "Sarah Orne Jewett and Mary E. Wilkins (Freeman): Two Shrewd Businesswomen in Search of New Markets." *New England Quarterly* 70, no. 1 (1997): 57–82.

Kaplan, Amy. "Nation, Region, and Empire." In *The Columbia History of the American Novel*, edited by Emory Elliott, pp. 240–266. New York: Columbia University Press, 1991.

Kilcup, Karen L., and Thomas S. Edwards, eds. *Jewett and Her Contemporaries: Reshaping the Canon*. Gainesville: University Press of Florida, 1999.

McCullough, Kate. *Regions of Identity: The Construction of America in Women's Fiction, 1885–1914*. Stanford, Calif.: Stanford University Press, 1999.

Mobley, Marilyn Sanders. *Folk Roots and Mythic Wings in Sarah Orne Jewett and Toni Morrison: The Cultural Function of Narrative*. Baton Rouge: Louisiana State University Press, 1991.

Morgan, Jack, and Louis Renza, eds. *The Irish Stories of Sarah Orne Jewett*. Carbondale: University of Southern Illinois Press, 1996.

Nagel, Gwen L., ed. *Critical Essays on Sarah Orne Jewett*. Boston: G. K. Hall, 1984.

Renza, Louis. *"A White Heron" and the Question of Minor Literature*. Madison: University of Wisconsin Press, 1984.

Roman, Margaret. *Sarah Orne Jewett: Reconstructing Gender*. Tuscaloosa: University of Alabama Press, 1992.

Sammons, Mark J., and Valerie Cunningham. *Black Portsmouth: Three Centuries of African-American Heritage*. Durham: University of New Hampshire Press, 2004.

Sherman, Sarah Way. "Jewett and the Incorporation of New England: 'The Gray Mills of Farley.'" *American Literary Realism* 34, no. 3 (spring 2002): 190–216.

Sherman, Sarah Way. *Sarah Orne Jewett, an American Persephone*. Hanover, N.H.: University Press of New England, 1989.

Sarah Way Sherman

COURTSHIP, MARRIAGE, AND DIVORCE

The enormous cultural changes—urbanization, commercialization, secularism, feminism, and expansionism—that occurred in the years between the end of the Civil War and the end of World War I transformed the American culture of marriage. These years saw the culmination of Victorian idealization of domesticity as well as its rapid decline. The literature of the period not only reflects these changes but is at times also implicated in them, particularly in the rising importance of romantic love as the bedrock of marriage. The increasing emphasis on romantic love has been credited and blamed for changes in courtship and marital expectations as well as, perhaps most infamously, the rapidly ascending divorce rate.

Critics, such as Jane Tompkins, and historians, such as Glenda Riley, note themes common to both literature and culture: the cult of domesticity, heightened gender differentiation, the separation of the public and private spheres, and the shifting meanings of romantic love. An increasingly literate middle class was reading more than ever; consequently newspapers and magazines such as *Peterson's Magazine* and the *Ladies' Home Journal* experienced enormous growth in circulation. In addition to magazines, book sales also rose. The trials of marriage, from courtship to divorce court, were popular subjects in news reports and gossip columns as well as short stories, plays, and novels. Many of the writers treat these phases of marriage simultaneously, juxtaposing the passions of youthful courtship with placid marital stability and the destructive forces of divorce. By doing so, these authors demonstrate the dramatic shifts occurring between generations in their ideals of marriage.

FROM VICTORIAN COURTSHIP TO MODERN DATING

By the nineteenth century the popular Puritan belief that love bloomed after marriage had given way to the idea that romantic love was a prerequisite for marriage. Courtship, then, was not a matter of confirming compatibility but of allowing love to reveal itself. Marriage became the affirmation of true love. In her study of Victorian courtship letters, Karen Lystra writes that the letters share a concept of love as "anchored in [the] ideal of an essential self which could be communicated" (p. 7). Love struck when these selves met. Fortunately for literature's sake, the course of true love rarely runs smoothly, and the obstacles to true love—social barriers, parental interference, and miscommunication—provided infinite plot twists appealing to audiences.

From its inception the United States encouraged autonomy in the selection of marriage partners, though family and one's social world clearly had some influence. However, with such an emphasis on the essential self, marriage became an ever more personal matter, yet another facet of American individualism. This tension between social and parental pressure and individual choice in spousal selection was a popular trope in much of the drama and literature of the period. One of the ways authors demonstrated this tension was to depict the contrast between older, and usually non-American, systems of arranged marriage and American free choice. In "The Imported Bridegroom" (1898), Abraham Cahan (1860–1951) tells the story of Asriel, a Jewish immigrant who has found great financial success in the United States but who, as he nears the end of his life, regrets his secular American lifestyle for fear of his soul. Asriel arranges a marriage

for his daughter, Flora, to a Talmudic prodigy who, Asriel is sure, will make up for his years of secularism. Flora, however, wishes to marry a doctor. In the end Asriel and Flora both get what they want—almost. Flora does marry the imported bridegroom but only after she has persuaded him to study secretly to become a doctor; the groom becomes more interested in his newfound circle of intellectuals than he is in his bride. Sui Sin Far (Edith Maude Eaton, 1865–1914) also contrasts arranged marriages with those of free choice. For example, in "Mrs. Spring Fragrance" (1912) she describes how thoroughly "Americanized" the title character has become by demonstrating her orchestration of a plot to extricate the American-born daughter of a Chinese neighbor from an arranged marriage, though she is happy in her own arranged marriage. Her husband misunderstands her machinations, thinking she is having an affair herself. Concerned, Mr. Spring Fragrance queries his other neighbor, the youthful Anglo-American Mr. Carman, about whether love can bloom in an arranged marriage, and he answers no, "love, in this country, must be free, or it is not love at all" (p. 24). Mr. Spring Fragrance is relieved when he finally hears of his wife's plot regarding the neighbor's daughter, realizing his wife, who does love him, is perhaps not so "Americanized" after all.

While less specifically confining than arranged marriages, another pressure circumscribing spousal choice was social advancement. In many popular plays such social pressure was used for comedic effect, as in Edgar Fawcett's (1847–1904) *Our First Families* (1880), in which the wealthy Mrs. Van Rensellaer Manhattan wants her daughter, Eva, to marry into the suitably wealthy and aristocratic Knickerbocker family. Similarly, Geoffrey Knickerbocker is pressured to marry Eva by his uncle's threat of disinheritance. However, Eva is in love with Leonardo Tompkins, and Hebe Joscelyn is in love with Geoffrey. So Hebe helps Eva and Leonardo elope, freeing Geoffrey to marry her. Writers also explore the tragic elements of the pressure to marry for social advancement, as in Edith Wharton's (1862–1937) *The House of Mirth* (1905). The orphan Lily Bart has inherited little but her father's name and her mother's beauty. Realizing that she has little choice but to marry if she is to remain in her parents' social circle, Lily is torn between her pragmatic desire to marry Percy Gryce or Simon Rosedale for money and her romantic desire to marry Lawrence Seldon for love. Her ambivalence leads her to ruin chance after chance at marriage, though her offers move ever farther down the social scale. Tragically, Seldon does not realize he wants to marry Lily until it is too late. Alone and impoverished, Lily has overdosed on sleeping pills when he arrives to propose. Using courtship for social climbing and financial motivation is also a central concern of Henry James, as is evident in such novels as *Washington Square* (1881).

Ethnic background also limited the selection of one's spouse, as in Charles W. Chesnutt's (1858–1932) 1900 novel *The House behind the Cedars* (1900). With light skin, good looks, and good educations, the siblings John and Rena Warwick can easily "pass" as white; however, while John does so successfully for years, Rena's ethnicity is exposed during her courtship with the wealthy, white George Tryon. Like Seldon in *The House of Mirth*, Tryon does not acknowledge his true feelings until it is too late and Rena, brokenhearted, has died from fever. However, not all such tales had to be tragic. In *Iola Leroy; or, Shadows Uplifted* (1892), Frances E. W. Harper (1825–1911) celebrates African American identity by creating a heroine who, once her African American ancestry is revealed to her, refuses to pass and refuses to marry Dr. Gresham, a white man who loves her. Eventually Iola does marry, but she marries Dr. Latimer, who shares her ethnic background. The pressures of ethnicity also provided theater with powerful dramatic conflict. In Edward Sheldon's (1886–1946) play *The Nigger* (1909), a wealthy southern gentleman, Philip Morrow, who is poised for governorship, removes himself from his candidacy and breaks off his engagement to a white woman when a letter reveals that his grandmother was an African American slave. Morrow then dedicates himself to improving the lot of fellow blacks. Similarly, the conflicts of interracial courtship for Native Americans is dramatized in William C. de Mille's (1878–1955) play *Strongheart* (1905). At first Strongheart, a Native American student at Columbia and a valued member of the football team, gets along very well with his classmates, particularly Frank and Dick. However, when Strongheart's intention to propose to Frank's sister Dorothy is revealed, Frank and Dick accuse him of betraying his race. Furthermore, when Black Eagle comes from Strongheart's tribe to tell him his father has died and he must assume his chiefdom, Black Eagle claims that the tribe will never accept his marriage to a white girl.

In addition to exploring racial and class tensions in courtship, some literature began to examine changing ideas about sexuality. In the nineteenth century women were expected to control not only their own sexual passions but also those of men; however, by the end of the century women were overcoming the Victorian view that they were passionless. Popular interpretations (and perhaps misinterpretations) of the work of Freud and of sexologists such as Havelock Ellis aided in changing the perceptions of women's sexuality. By 1920 women were acknowledged to enjoy sex as well as men. In fact, sex became increasingly intertwined with the notion of romantic love, so that there was yet another shift in this romantic ideal. While love was considered the height of self-revelation in the late nineteenth century, in the early twentieth century love became contingent upon sexual pleasure. Ellen Rothman cites one editor who noted in 1913 that "sex o'clock" had struck in America. While many writers still avoided explicit sexuality, many naturalist and early modernist writers were more direct in their treatment of sexuality in courtship. In Theodore Dreiser's (1871–1945) *Sister Carrie* (1900) and *Jennie Gerhardt* (1911), the author does not shy away from portraying premarriage sexual relations, though he still reveals the anxiety of sexuality as well as the continuing censure of premarital sexuality. For both Carrie and Jennie, their class status initially compromises their chastity but offers them a means of financial though not moral advance. Once outside the conventions of traditional sexual morality, which approves of sex only within the confines of marriage, they find it impossible to work their way back in. Neither one becomes legally married. Similarly and even more brutally, in Stephen Crane's (1871–1900) *Maggie, A Girl of the Streets* (1893), the morals of chastity seem a luxury for poverty-stricken Maggie and her family. Sherwood Anderson's (1876–1941) series of stories *Winesburg, Ohio* (1919) also explores the tragedy of sexual frustration and repression, revealing sexual repression to be one of the key issues in his "book of grotesques." Some women writers also noted a double standard regarding premarriage sexuality. Most concisely, perhaps, is Frances E. W. Harper's (1825–1911) poem "A Double Standard" (1895), in which she speaks from the point of view of a "fallen" woman who laments,

> Crime has no sex and yet to-day
> I wear the brand of shame;
> Whilst he amid the gay and proud
> Still bears an honored name.
>
> (P. 176)

Not all depictions of courtship ended pessimistically, however. In fact, many popular stage melodramas presented true love in marriage as salve not just for personal pain but national trauma. Set against the backdrop of the Civil War, Bronson Howard's (1842–1908) successful play *Shenandoah* (1889) overlooks the more troubling aspects of the war, such as the high number of casualties, slavery, and racism, and focuses on the love affairs between Northerners and Southerners. The New Yorker Kerchival West and the Virginian Robert Ellington became best friends while at West Point, each falling in love with the other's sister. The Civil War, however, forces them to take opposing sides both from each other and from the woman each loves. In the end all is forgiven and they meet, symbolically,

Before and After; or, Sunshine and Rain. Late-nineteenth-century wood engraving depicting the disillionment of marriage. The engraver ironically reverses the old saying that love can comfort distress like sunshine after rain. THE GRANGER COLLECTION, NEW YORK

in Washington, D.C., demonstrating, as Gary A. Richardson argues, melodrama's ability "to reunite the nation emotionally" (p. 130) and the political potential of sentimentalism as defined by Joanne Dobson: that it "celebrates human connection, both personal and communal" (p. 266).

Nonetheless, many writers and critics, such as the influential William Dean Howells (1837–1920), thought that these popular stories of courtship fueled dangerous fires of idealism. Like popular novels and chivalric tales, many courtships shared a plot structure based on "tests," usually of the man's love for the woman. In his short story "Editha" (1907), Howells demonstrates that these tests could be quite serious. Editha sends her fiancé off to fight in a war in which he does not believe. He dies in the first battle, but the tragedy is lost on Editha. Although briefly affected by a confrontation with her fiancé's mother, who demands that she remove her clothes of mourning, Editha

elevates her suffering to heroic status, preferring "to live again in the ideal" (p. 444). Rather than understanding the real dangers of war, Editha willfully remains the sort Howells describes in *Criticism and Fiction* (1891): "nurtured in the superstition of the romance, the bizarre, the heroic, the distinguished, as the things alone worthy of painting or carving or writing" (p. 67). Howells's criticism of Editha's romanticized view of her fiancé's sacrifice reflects a growing realism in some depictions of courtship in the twentieth century that countered some romantic idealism of the nineteenth.

"THE MARRIAGE PROBLEM"

As both pragmatic social contract and romantic bond, marriage often created conflicting ideals. Lystra describes Victorian marriage as the transforming of "an essentially voluntary and volatile romantic bond to the involuntary obligations and duty-bound roles of husband and wife" (p. 192). Not only is such passion in marriage hard to maintain but, to use Elaine Tyler May's terms, the "great expectations" of fulfillment in marriage often led to disappointment. In addition to providing social status and economic security, marriage was also to provide spiritual, emotional, and sexual satisfaction—a tall order. In short, marriage became a central image of the American dream. The plots of Steele MacKaye's (1842–1894) play *Won at Last* (1877) and David Belasco (1853–1931) and Henry C. de Mille's (1850–1893) play *The Wife* (1887) dramatize marriages that achieve this dream, though both marriages start out on false grounds. In *Won at Last*, Grace Loring has married for love but soon after the wedding discovers that her husband, Fleming, has married her only because it was his father's dying wish that he take a wife. Grace then has an affair, and Fleming attempts suicide, but in the end they are reunited, realizing that they are in love and will live a happy life together. Similarly, in *The Wife*, Helen Truman marries John Rutherford, though she is in love with Robert Gray. His understanding after she confesses her love for another man makes her realize that it is Rutherford she really loves. These couples have achieved an ideal balance, as have those Howells portrays in the novels *The Rise of Silas Lapham* (1884), *Their Wedding Journey* (1871), and *A Hazard of New Fortunes* (1890).

Yet perhaps the most outstanding feature of the portrayal of marriage during this time in both the high literature and the popular media was its critique. While the ideal of marriage was high, rarely was its ideal portrayed. The "marriage problem" was a popular topic in magazines such as the *Ladies' Home Journal* and *Godey's Lady's Book*. Stories of unhappy marriages were everywhere, perhaps fueling couples' dissatisfaction with their own marriages but also indicative of the dangers of setting such high expectations for marriage.

As is evident from the discussion of courtship, marriage was often portrayed as confining and repressive for both men and women and as a battleground between individual desire and expression and social duty. In Wharton's 1920 novel *The Age of Innocence* she evokes the plot of self-sacrifice nostalgically and sympathetically in Newland Archer's decision to marry May Welland and give up Ellen Olenska. Rather than only highlighting or condemning Newland's sacrifice, Wharton demonstrates the benefits of his life with May, however boring at times, and ends the novel with Newland realizing that a life with Ellen was better as a romantic ideal than it would have been as reality.

The tension between individualism and social expectation is also a theme in Henry James's *The Portrait of a Lady* (1881). Having rejected proposals of marriage from both the American Casper Goodwood and the British Lord Warburton, Isabel Archer asserts her independence. Freed from financial concerns for marriage because of a generous inheritance arranged by her cousin Ralph Touchett, Isabel marries Gilbert Osmond, apparently not seeing that he is marrying her for her money. Although the marriage is unhappy and she is given another chance to return to America with Casper Goodwood, whom she realizes that she does love, Isabel decidedly stays with Osmond, in order to fulfill her own sense of morality and duty and perhaps realizing that with Osmond she is, ironically, freer than she would be with the possessive Goodwood.

Sometimes marriage is portrayed not only as repressing sexual desire but also dulling artistic and individual expression; in contrast, adultery gives vent to both. In the semiautobiographical novel *The "Genius"* (1915), Dreiser correlates his hero Eugene Witla's artistic temperament with his sexual prowess. Witla has numerous affairs, but the tension caused by trying to restrain his sexual and artistic energy lead him to a nervous breakdown. In Kate Chopin's (1851–1904) novella *The Awakening* (1899), Edna Pontellier has become bored with her marriage and "awakens" to an artistic and romantic world through her attraction to Robert Lebrun. When he breaks off their friendship, she walks naked into the ocean, suicidally giving herself completely to sensuality. The other side of the story is told by such plays as James A. Herne's (1839–1901) *Margaret Fleming* (1913), which celebrates the moral strength of a woman by contrasting her behavior to that of her adulterous husband.

For many of these authors, as well as for many critics, one feature of depictions of marriage is their feminist critique. Both male and female authors tell stories of stunted and restricted female lives. One of the most ironic is Chopin's "The Story of an Hour" (1894), in which a wife goes into mourning upon hearing of the death of her husband but soon realizes she is now free to do what she wants. When he walks through the door an hour later—the report of his death has been a mistake—she dies suddenly from her heart condition, "of joy that kills" (p. 538). Another outstanding example is that of Charlotte Perkins Gilman's (1860–1935) "The Yellow Wall-Paper" (1892), in which the heroine goes "insane" as she is forced to undergo a rest cure after the birth of her child. Given nothing else to do, the protagonist identifies with the woman she sees trapped behind the wallpaper, a woman symbolic of all those oppressed by patriarchal traditions of marriage. Much of Rose Terry Cooke's (1827–1902) short fiction also illustrates a feminist critique. For example, in "How Celia Changed Her Mind" (1891), Cooke tells the story of a spinster who, as the story opens, feels stigmatized by her status. Celia helps her neighbor's daughter Rosabel elope, and when she is confronted by the girl's father, she believes that he only talks down to her because she is not married. Thus, when Deacon Everts proposes, she accepts, knowing this is not a marriage of love or even friendship. Not only is Rosabel's marriage horrible—she dies in poverty, worn out from illness and bearing children—but so is Celia's. Thus when Deacon Everts finally dies, Celia rejoices in her widowhood, inviting all the town's "old maids" to Thanksgiving dinner.

Other writers painted more brutal depictions of marriage. In "Fantasie Printanière" (1897), an early sketch of characters for his novel *McTeague* (1899) the naturalist writer Frank Norris (1870–1902) contrasts two marriages, those of the McTeagues and their next-door neighbors the Ryers. McTeague and Ryer hate each other, though they have much in common: both of them brutally beat their wives. When sober, Ryer beats his wife with a piece of rubber hose filled with gravel, and when drunk, McTeague beats his wife with his bare hands. The women are good friends, though they do not discuss their mutual suffering until one day when they begin to compare bruises and scars. Yet rather than commiserate, the women fight, arguing about whose husband beats her the worst, or best, as the case may be, eventually coming to blows themselves. The husbands find this amusing, putting aside their own differences and becoming the best of friends. Alice Dunbar-Nelson (1875–1935) also exposes the cruelty of domestic abuse in "Tony's Wife"(1895), which recounts the powerlessness of the "wife," who is never named, as if to emphasize her own lack of identity. Tony spends his life beating his "wife" and then, when he is on his deathbed, gloats that they are not even really married, so she will not receive any inheritance. The story ends with Tony's "wife" homeless, nameless, and penniless. While these dismal portraits of marriage may be extreme, the institution of marriage and the changes it was undergoing were being thoroughly examined in the literature of the period.

THE SOARING DIVORCE RATE

Between 1867 and 1929 the divorce rate increased 2,000 percent, and as the rate rose, divorce became an increasingly popular subject in magazines, newspapers, popular fiction (such as M. V. Dahlgren's 1887 novel *Divorced*), and even film (such as the 1900 comedy *Why Mrs. Jones Got a Divorce*). As Norma Basch illustrates, there were even pamphlets recounting the trials of famous divorce cases. Numerous factors contributed to this dramatic increase: the women's movement, western expansion, urbanization, secularization, and changing expectations of marriage top the list. Marriage had been viewed as a secular contract in America since

the time of the Puritans, but the decreasing emphasis on religion weakened the moral restrictions on divorce while increasing emphasis on worldly satisfaction. Thus when marriage did not satisfy, divorce, though possibly socially stigmatizing, was not soul imperiling. The lower incidence of divorce among immigrant Catholic populations, whose religious beliefs prohibited divorce, also suggests that secularization among the wider population attributed to the divorce rate.

The "loose" moral life made possible by the modern city—with its mobility, anonymity, alienation, dense population, coed workplace, and apartment living—was thought by some to be the cause of many divorces. In many divorce novels, such as Wharton's *The Custom of the Country* (1913) and Howells's *A Modern Instance* (1882), the city provides a backdrop for fragile marriages. Wharton and Howells both portray the urban emphasis on rental property and hotel living as reflective of, if not the cause of, marital discord. Also, in comedic plays such as Langdon Mitchell's (1862–1935) *The New York Idea* (1906), the fashionable world of New York frames the cavorting of a set of couples, many of whom have been divorced and are seeking new marriages and remarriages. In the end the hero and heroine rekindle their love and discover that due to a technicality they were really never divorced at all.

Nineteenth-century western expansion is also thought to have increased divorce. After the Civil War, eastern states in general saw a tightening of grounds for divorce in an effort to curb the rising divorce rate, though to little effect. However, western states had more lenient divorce laws. Some cities, such as Sioux City, South Dakota, and later Reno, Nevada, became notorious divorce colonies because with low residency requirements they were thought to encourage migratory divorces (a divorce in which a person seeking divorce would move to another state in order to claim residency and divorce by that state's laws). The literature of divorce reinforces the association of the West with divorce. Many characters who divorce, such as Wharton's Undine Spragg and Robert Grant's (1852–1940) Selma White in *Unleavened Bread* (1900), are from the West; in addition, divorce cases in these novels are often tried in the West. The literary conflation of divorce and the West emphasizes not only the historical and geographical association but also the mythic association of the West with American individualism and entrepreneurship.

Expounding on this connection between the entrepreneurial spirit of the West and divorce, in her study of women and American divorce novels Debra Ann MacComb has shown how marriage came to be another

In Edith Wharton's The Custom of the Country *(1913), the author's parody of newspapers' society columns illustrates many of the changing mores around courtship, marriage, divorce, and remarriage in America at the turn of the twentieth century. In addition to invoking the courtship language of the "boy and girl romance," Wharton emphasizes the consumerist elements of the marriage market, ironically illustrating the shift from European feudal aristocracy to American capitalist aristocracy. Mimicking the press's blunt writing style, Wharton also lampoons the press's lascivious exposure of private domestic life, its attention to clothing and jewels, and the law's complicity in the rising divorce rate, especially Western law. Finally, by juxtaposing Paul's confusion about his mother's marriages and divorces with Mrs. Heeny's inarticulate admiration, Wharton deftly and subtly intimates the sad consequences a culture of divorce may have on its children.*

"Why is mother married to Mr. Moffatt now?"

"Why, you must know that much, Paul." Mrs. Heeny again looked warm and worried. "She's married to him because she got a divorce—that's why." And suddenly she had another inspiration. "Didn't she ever send you over any of those splendid clippings that came out the time they were married? Why, I declare, that's a shame; but I must have some of 'em right here."

She dived again, shuffled, sorted, and pulled out a long discolored strip. "I've carried this around with me ever since, and so many's wanted to read it, it's all torn." She smoothed out the paper and began:

"'Divorce and remarriage of Mrs. Undine Spragg-de Chelles. American Marquise renounces ancient French title to wed Railroad King. Quick work untying and tying. Boy and girl romance renewed.

"'Reno, November 23d. The Marquise de Chelles, of Paris, France, formerly Mrs. Undine Spragg Marvell, of Apex City and New York, got a decree of divorce at a special session of the Court last night, and was remarried fifteen minutes later to Mr. Elmer Moffatt, the billionaire Railroad King, who was the Marquise's first husband.

"'No case has ever been railroaded through the divorce courts of this State at a higher rate of speed: as Mr. Moffatt said last night, before he and his bride jumped onto their east-bound special, every record has been broken. It was just six months ago yesterday that the present Mrs. Moffatt came to Reno to look for her divorce. Owing to a delayed train, her counsel was late yesterday in receiving some necessary papers, and it was feared the decision would have to be held over; but Judge Toomey, who is a personal friend of Mr. Moffatt's, held a night session and rushed it through so that the happy couple could have the knot tied and board their special in time for Mrs. Moffatt to spend Thanksgiving in New York with her aged parents. The hearing was set at seven ten P.M. and at eight o'clock the bridal couple were steaming out of the station.

"'At the trial Mrs. Spragg-de Chelles, who wore copper velvet and sables, gave evidence as to the brutality of her French husband, but she had to talk fast as time pressed, and Judge Toomey wrote the entry at top speed, and then jumped into a motor with the happy couple and drove to the Justice of the Peace, where he acted as best man to the bridegroom. The latter is said to be one of the six wealthiest men east of the Rockies. His gifts to the bride are a necklace and tiara of pigeon-blood rubies belonging to Queen Marie Antoinette, a million dollar cheque and a house in New York. The happy pair will pass the honeymoon in Mrs. Moffatt's new home, 5009 Fifth Avenue, which is an exact copy of the Pitti Palace, Florence. They plan to spend their springs in France.'"

Mrs. Heeny drew a long breath, folded the paper and took off her spectacles. "There," she said, with a benignant smile and a tap on Paul's cheek, "now you see how it all happened . . ."

Paul was not sure he did; but he made no answer.

Edith Wharton, *The Custom of the Country* (New York: Scribners, 1913), pp. 584–586.

consumer product. In *Unleavened Bread*, Robert Grant tells the story of Selma White, who wants to escape the provinciality of her hometown. Increasingly callous, she marries, divorces, and remarries in order to move up socially and financially, ending up as the politically active wife of a senator. Similarly, Wharton's Undine Spragg in *The Custom of the Country* views marriage as, in Elizabeth Ammons's terms, "woman's business in life" (p. 100). As in *The House of Mirth* and many short stories, such as "The Other Two" (1904), Wharton in

The Custom of the Country illustrates the cutthroat nature of the marriage market for women. Undine, like her father, is a master of the market, placing money, prestige, and upward mobility above everything else, including love and her child. As MacComb illustrates, Undine becomes a symbol of what happens when capitalism consumes all, including marriage. In "The Other Two," Wharton also tells the story of a woman, Alice, who moves up the social ladder by divorcing and remarrying.

By changing women's prospects and expectations in life and giving them an avenue through which to express discontent, the women's movement was often blamed by both men and women for the rising divorce rate. In some ways, critics were right. William O'Neill surmises that the expanding variety of options the women's movement made available, such as higher education, a wider range of careers, and some economic independence, most likely increased women's expectations in life and strengthened their ability to demand satisfaction, to leave not just abusive but also unhappy, unsatisfying marriages. In fact, feminists such as Elizabeth Cady Stanton championed divorce as a means of liberation from the bonds of marriage for many women. Edna Ferber's (1887–1968) *Roast Beef, Medium* (1913) offers one glimpse of the woman "freed" from marriage. A top-notch salesperson for a petticoat company, Emma McChesney occasionally fantasizes about cooking in a well-used kitchen and cleaning house but always rallies to the challenges of the market. However, more often than not, the divorced woman is at fault, as in Wharton's *The Custom of the Country* and Robert Grant's *Unleavened Bread*.

While the feminist critique was a prominent element in fictional depictions of divorce, ethnic identity was also a factor. Abraham Cahan's short story "Yekl, a Tale of the New York Ghetto" (1896) is illustrative. Having established himself in New York long before he is able to pay for the passage of his wife and son, Yekl, who now goes by Jake, has become accustomed to American dance halls and his freedom to flirt and dance with whomever he chooses. In fact, he does not tell anyone he has a wife, so when Gitl arrives, everyone is surprised. For Jake, Gitl is not exactly what he remembers. She refuses to put aside European Jewish customs, such as wearing a wig or scarf, and Jake, who refers to himself as a "yankee," is embarrassed by her and misses Mamie, an Americanized woman with whom he often danced. In the end Jake divorces Gitl, who then marries Mr. Bernstein, a man who seems to appreciate Jewish tradition. The story ends with Jake, now engaged to Mamie, regretfully heading toward the mayor's office for the wedding, fantasizing about rushing into Gitl's apartment to reclaim his authority as husband and father, torn between his Yankee desire for freedom and his ethnic heritage.

Perhaps the primary causes of the rising divorce rate, in both fiction and history, were high expectations of marriage. The ideal wife was expected to strike a balance between being a paragon of chastity and being a sex kitten. She also expected to gain everything from spiritual and emotional fulfillment to financial stability from her marriage. Men were expected to be both understanding and tough, and they were expected to provide not just financial stability but to keep up with the Joneses. Dissatisfaction with husbands is what propels Undine Spragg and Selma White. Howells tackles these impossible expectations in *A Modern Instance,* faulting both Marcia Hubbard's excitable passions and Bartley Hubbard's scandalmongering journalism, which is also implicated in their bad marriage and divorce. Similarly, Augustin Daly's (1838–1899) play *Divorce* (1884) illustrates many of the tensions surrounding the emphasis on romantic love. Wanting the best for her daughters, Mrs. Ten Eyck persuades them to marry for money, not love. One daughter marries for love and one for money; each has her troubles, the former suffering from a too-passionate husband and the latter from one not passionate enough. It is only when the couples are confronted with actual divorces, encouraged by unscrupulous lawyers, that they find a balance between passion and a sense of social duty, leading to happy marriages.

THE REMARRIED AND THE UNMARRIED

One would think that with the rising divorce rate and criticism of marriage in the press, marriage rates would have declined in this period. However, as May illustrates, the opposite occurred. While the population increased 300 percent between 1867 and 1929, the number of marriages increased 400 percent. Thus people were getting married at slightly higher rates and divorcing at even higher rates, suggesting that people were not rejecting marriage but rather that they expected more out of it than ever before, and when marriage failed to fulfill these expectations it was becoming easier and easier to divorce. Often divorce occurred not just because husbands or wives wanted their freedom, as in Ferber's *Roast Beef, Medium,* but also because they wanted to move on to the next marriage, as in Wharton's *The Custom of the Country.* Nonetheless, remarriage continued to be treated very conservatively by many writers. One common trope was the death of one of the divorced spouses. Often it is only when one spouse dies that the other is truly free to marry, regardless of the law. Not until the death of Bartley Hubbard in Howells's *A Modern Instance* can Ben Halleck even begin to consider asking for Marcia Hubbard's hand, and even then it is the moral dilemma of remarriage, rather than divorce, that leaves Atherton, a lawyer and the most moral figure in the novel, at a loss for words: the novel ends, "I don't know. I don't know!" Similarly Ralph Marvell, seemingly Undine's first husband in Wharton's *The Custom of the Country,* kills himself, allowing Undine to marry the French aristocrat Raymond de Chelles. Finally Undine ends up married to Elmer Moffatt, the husband of her youth. Thus the first marriage, and perhaps the institution of marriage, is saved in the end, though Undine is already beginning to feel again dissatisfied. In some ways the issue of remarriage is almost more telling than those of courtship, marriage, and divorce because it encapsulates all three. Those authors who entertain remarriage in their novels, such as Howells, Wharton, and Daly, also embrace marriage, even with all of its problems.

Lastly many authors explore this marriage cycle, from courtship and marriage to divorce and remarriage, from the point of view of those who remain outside marriage. The bachelor who observes and criticizes marriage mores from the outside became practically a stock character in many novels of manners. James's Ralph Touchett in *The Portrait of a Lady* and Lambert Strether in *The Ambassadors* (1903) and Wharton's Lawrence Seldon in *The House of Mirth* are prime examples. While bachelor characters are often pulled out of their protective shells during the course of many novels, spinsters often serve to criticize patriarchal traditions of marriage. In Mary Wilkins Freeman's "A New England Nun" (1891), Louisa Ellis, long engaged to Joe Dagget, releases him to marry Lily Dyer, thankful not to have her orderly life disturbed by marriage. In *Three Lives* (1909), Gertrude Stein (1874–1946) tells the stories of two women, the "good Anna" and Melanctha, who avoid marriage. Melanctha, a mulatto, wanders among men and intimate friendships with women, never confining herself to marriage and frustrating other characters' (and readers') attempts to confine her to any traditional role. Nonetheless, even these characters who reject marriage can hardly escape confronting it, for although ideas about courtship, marriage, and divorce changed significantly between 1870 and 1920, getting married was—and remains—a key measure of normalcy.

See also The Awakening; Domestic and Sentimental Fiction; *A Hazard of New Fortunes; The House of Mirth; Iola Leroy; Maggie, A Girl of the Streets; Mrs. Spring Fragrance;* Sex Education; *Sister Carrie;* "The Yellow Wall-Paper"

BIBLIOGRAPHY
Primary Works

Chopin, Kate. "The Story of an Hour." In *The Heath Anthology of American Literature,* 2 vols., edited by Paul Lauter, 2:536–537. Boston: Houghton Mifflin, 1998.

Harper, Frances E. W. "A Double Standard." In *Complete Poems of Frances E. W. Harper,* edited by Maryemma Graham, pp. 176–177. Oxford: Oxford University Press, 1988.

Howells, William Dean. *Criticism and Fiction.* 1891. Edited by Clara Marburg Kirk and Rudolf Kirk. New York: New York University Press, 1959.

Howells, William Dean. "Editha." In *The Heath Anthology of American Literature,* 2 vols., edited by Paul Lauter, 2:434. Boston: Houghton Mifflin, 1998.

Sui Sin Far. *Mrs. Spring Fragrance and Other Writings.* Edited by Amy Ling and Annette White-Parks. Urbana: University of Illinois Press. 1995.

Secondary Works

Ammons, Elizabeth. *Edith Wharton's Argument with America.* Athens: University of Georgia Press, 1980.

Bailey, Beth. *From Front Porch to Backseat: Courtship in Twentieth-Century America.* Baltimore: Johns Hopkins University Press, 1988.

Barnett, James. *Divorce and the American Divorce Novel 1858–1937: A Study in Literary Reflections of Social Influences.* New York: Russell and Russell, 1939.

Basch, Norma. *Framing American Divorce: From the Revolutionary Generation to the Victorians.* Berkeley: University of California Press, 1999.

Bennett, Bridget, ed. *Ripples of Dissent: Women's Stories of Marriage from the 1890s.* London: J. M. Dent, 1996.

Boone, Joseph Allen. *Tradition Counter Tradition: Love and the Form of Fiction.* Chicago: University of Chicago Press, 1987.

Bordman, Gerald. *American Theatre: A Chronicle of Comedy and Drama, 1869–1914.* New York: Oxford University Press, 1994.

Cherlin, Andrew J. *Marriage, Divorce, Remarriage.* Rev. ed. Cambridge, Mass.: Harvard University Press, 1992.

Dobson, Joanne. "Reclaiming Sentimental Literature." *American Literature* 69, no. 2 (1997): 263–288.

Freeman, Kimberly A. *Love American Style: Divorce and the American Novel 1881–1976.* New York: Routledge, 2003.

Lystra, Karen. *Searching the Heart: Women, Men, and Romantic Love in Nineteenth-Century America.* Oxford: Oxford University Press, 1989.

MacComb, Debra Ann. *Tales of Liberation, Strategies of Containment: Divorce and the Representation of Womanhood in American Fiction, 1880–1920.* New York: Taylor and Francis, 2000.

May, Elaine Tyler. *Great Expectations: Marriage and Divorce in Post-Victorian America.* Chicago: University of Chicago Press, 1980.

O'Neill, William L. *Divorce in the Progressive Era.* New Haven, Conn.: Yale University Press, 1967.

Richardson, Gary A. *American Drama: From the Colonial Period through World War I.* New York: Twayne, 1993.

Riley, Glenda. *Divorce: An American Tradition.* Oxford: Oxford University Press, 1991.

Rothman, Ellen. *Hands and Hearts: A History of Courtship in America.* New York: Basic Books, 1984.

Stein, Allen F. *After the Vows Were Spoken: Marriage in American Literary Realism.* Columbus: Ohio State University Press, 1984.

Tanner, Tony. *Adultery in the Novel: Contract and Transgressions.* Baltimore: Johns Hopkins University Press, 1979.

Tracy, Karen. *Plots and Proposals: American Women's Fiction, 1850–90.* Chicago: University of Chicago Press, 2000.

Kimberly A. Freeman

CROSS-DRESSING

Though cross-dressing in literature can, and occasionally does, conform to the generally understood concept of transvestitism, more often the donning of the opposite gender's clothes serves other purposes. Cross-dressing in a broader sense includes appearing as a member of a gender, class, or race group other than the one(s) normally inhabited. Because these roles were more strictly enforced in the nineteenth century than in the twentieth, cross-dressing then was literally easier to accomplish and also more politically charged. Stringent gender roles, racial anxiety, and an exclusive pants or skirt dress code set clear boundaries that, when crossed by women in breeches or men in skirts, left no room for doubt that the crossings were deliberate.

Not surprisingly, these crossings found their way into the fictions published during the nineteenth century. Literary uses of cross-dressing here served one or more narrative purposes: (1) concealment, (2) tricksterism, and (3) augmentation to characterization. Alone, each of these categories may explain the narrative function of an event of cross-dressing, or two or more categories may be involved in the event. Secondarily though still importantly, literature, as a product in a dynamic relationship with the culture in which it is produced, also contains a political element, and thus the political implications of cross-dressing also

creep into literature. Regardless of the motivation for or political impact of the donning of unconventional dress, however, each category relies upon an ingrained understanding, both in the wearer and in the observer, of gender-specific garb and behavior. Moreover, usually both author and reader are in on the secret of who is masquerading. This secrecy and the eventual revelation, always present in cross-dressing events, are used in historically specific ways. But clues are time- and culture-bound and can go unnoticed, especially by readers from later time periods. Thus narrative and political uses to which cross-dressing is put and evidence posed for a cross-dressing event can reveal as much about the reader as the writer.

A CULTURAL AND HISTORICAL UNDERSTANDING OF CROSS-DRESSING

In the United States race exerts a significant influence upon the culture, and beginning early in the history of the North American colonies fears of race mixing resulted in the ratification of many antimiscegenation laws. Interracial marriage between Europeans and others, primarily Africans and American Indians, was first outlawed in Virginia in 1667, and by the Civil War five states had antimiscegenation laws in their codes. These laws not only mandated severe fines for interracial marriage but also imposed long terms of indentured servitude or lifetime slavery upon the white partner and children of the marriage. Other evidence of race-mixing anxiety appears in the commonly accepted "one-drop rule." This rule stipulates that any person with a single black ancestor, regardless of distance removed, is black. In marking any person with questioned heritage as unequivocally black—and therefore of a lower social status in the nineteenth-century United States—the rule also reveals the anxiety invoked by the idea of "black" people passing as "white." And while the term "passing" commonly refers to a light-skinned person presenting himself or herself as "white," the word clearly conveys an idea similar to cross-dressing.

"Passing," either by women or African Americans, entails the adoption of the clothes, manners, and speech of the mimicked group, and only where the distinction between genders, classes, or races is deep-seated, rigid, and based on exclusivity is passing possible. If a society or culture does not designate specific clothing appropriate for, and only for, one gender, class, or race, then imitation is not possible, as all clothing is acceptable on all members of the society. But where clothing is designated as unsuitable for one group, imitation can occur, and almost inevitably distinctions between groups reflect a hierarchy of importance and influence. Furthermore, where persons are not socially equal, dress is an easily modified and highly visual "cue" that reflects that condition of inequality. But these visual cues are not static. For example, in the early twenty-first century in the United States male infants are dressed in blue, while female infants are dressed in pink. Too often this scheme of gender marking is thought to be "natural"; yet until the widespread availability of indoor plumbing and colorfast fabrics at the beginning of the twentieth century, both boys and girls wore white. Shortly after these conveniences became routine and when the color coding of infants became common, boys were dressed in pink—considered to be a more "manly" color— while girls were dressed in blue (Bullough, p. viii). Yet in the early twenty-first century boys and men who wear pink often become the butt of jokes and are openly harassed because pink is considered an effeminate color.

These precise connotations of sex and gender with color and style are recent, however. Before the eighteenth century male homosexuality as an intrinsic characteristic did not exist. Males might engage in homosexual acts, but the male's position in society and his privileges as a male were not threatened by his homosexual activities. Females too might be emotionally close to other females, relationships that often masked lesbian activities. But these relationships, often called "Boston marriages," and activities were less troubling than women's sexual encounters with men due primarily to a widespread belief in women's lack of a libidinal drive. And only after the homosexual was invented could behaviors and styles, including clothing, be attached to his or her person.

CROSS-DRESSING IN POPULAR CULTURE AND LITERATURE

As homosexuality became a character trait rather than an incident, cross-dressing became stigmatized as a symptom of that character. Other "symptoms" also clung to the stigma of homosexuality: hypersexuality, criminal inclinations, and racial perceptions. Cross-dressing thus became associated with disreputable people and behavior. Unsavory professions such as the theater and traveling shows provide some of the most common examples of women who donned masculine clothing. "Wearing the breeches," as the practice of female cross-dressing came to be known, appeared first in Europe but quickly crossed the Atlantic. By the first half of the nineteenth century many of the noted actresses in the United States had tried the breeches at least once, and many made a career of playing male roles. Charlotte Cushman (1816–1876) is the best known of the breeches actresses and the one most often mentioned, but her experience is not typical and should not be thought of as representative. Cushman's acting career, unlike many female actresses who occa-

sionally "donned the breeches," included many male roles. She was the first and, to date, only woman to play Cardinal Wolsey in Shakespeare's *Henry VIII* (Mullenix, p. 61). Furthermore, Cushman was an outspoken woman who served as a mentor and sponsor for other women.

Another form of the "breeches" performance occurred in the demanding environment of the American West, where survival was less certain than in the civilized East. Women who went west usually did so with their husbands or as brides and housekeepers. Once there, however, the difficult conditions and subsequent mortality rate left not a few of these women alone and responsible for their own welfare if not also for a homestead and children. Solitary women cared for themselves—and often those people in need around them—through a variety of professions: prospector, mail coach and freight hauler, cabin boy, and outlaw. Lillie Hitchcock Coit (1842–1929), belle of San Francisco; Mary Fields, born a slave in Tennessee and past the age of fifty when she arrived in Montana in 1884; and Nellie Cashman, an Irish immigrant who arrived in the United States as a teenager in the late 1860s, all donned pants and jackets as they pursued their adventures and professions. And while many of these "passing" women were known to be female, many others, including Charley Parkhurst (b. Charlotte Parkhurst or Pankhurst c. 1812, d. 1879) and Little Joe Monaghan (1848–1904) lived as men until their deaths. Though their existences were undoubtedly lonely and were unquestionably unconventional, the women chose their secretive lifestyle because it offered freedoms then unavailable to women, such as voting and moving unimpeded by gender in social and business settings.

Yet not all cross-dressing was done quietly. Like female thespians, some men openly adopted women's apparel—at least for a night. Cross-dressing balls were popular in both Europe and the United States in the nineteenth century (Bullough, p. 191). C. H. Hughes, tellingly a specialist in nervous and mental diseases, penned one of the earliest accounts of a cross-dressing ball. Held in lower-class, black neighborhoods because they were some of the few venues unfettered by the social constraints of white society, these balls reinforced whites' perception of blacks as less evolved than Europeans and therefore more prone than whites to primal and hedonistic urges. Hughes writes: "I am credibly informed that there is, in the city of Washington, D.C., an annual convocation of negro men called the drag dance. . . . In this sable performance of sexual perversion, all of these men are lasciviously dressed in womanly attire, short sleeve, low-necked dresses, garters, frills, flowers, ruffles, etc., and deport themselves as women" (Bullough, p. 191). Here Hughes reveals an understanding of two characteristics of transvestitism that become important in the occurrence of cross-dressing in literature. First, the very act of donning the clothes of the other gender often marks the wearer as a person of low character, questionable morals, and sexually deviant behavior. Second, cross-dressing is implicitly understood as a performance. In the satirical *The Tragedy of Pudd'nhead Wilson* (1894), Mark Twain combines both of these understandings: that is, the cross-dresser is a person of low character and she or he performs a gender.

Twain's representations of cross-dressing stem from swapped identities. While still infants Thomas Driscoll, the son of a plantation owner, and Valet de Chambre, the son of a slave, are switched. The charade works because the infant slave possesses only 1/32 African heritage and is born the same day as the rightful heir. The substituted infant is raised as heir to the plantation, while the genuine heir, Thomas, is raised as a slave. Distinguishable only by class-identifying clothes, Thomas and Valet de Chambre effectively cross-dress for the duration of the novel. Belying any notion that blackness or whiteness is inherent, no one but the nurse who switched them knows one boy from the other. Years later, deeply in debt due to gambling and only recently made aware of his parentage, the false heir wears a woman's dress and practices feminine mannerisms as he prepares to burglarize homes in the small town of Dawson's Landing. Here cross-dressing is shown to be more than clothes: the successful impersonator must act the part. Furthermore, the motivation for the false heir's disguise is also significant: he dresses as a woman to unobtrusively slip into his victims' homes. Thus though Tom's goals are not sexual, they are immoral and, in accordance with popular opinion, reveal the cross-dresser's "low character."

Twain often employs the ruse of men in drag, and his uses display the multiple narrative purposes cross-dressing serves. In *Adventures of Huckleberry Finn* (1885), his title character dons a dress to conceal his identity while collecting information. The boy's primary motive is concealment, but he is given away by his inability to act the part of a girl. In contrast, Finn's fellow river traveler, the Dauphin, more successfully cross-dresses when wearing a gown to portray Shakespeare's Juliet. The Dauphin's aspirations do not lie in the limelight, however. The performance is merely part of a confidence game that he and his partner practice in towns along the river. Thus, as Juliet, the Dauphin occupies dual categories: he is a trickster, and as he masquerades as Juliet he develops a character, and his characterization as immoral is also enhanced.

Dr. Mary Walker. A champion of women's rights, Walker advocated the wearing of men's attire and often did so while lecturing. She served as the model for Dr. Prance in Henry James's novel *The Bostonians*. © BETTMANN/CORBIS

Yet perhaps the most successful literary cross-dresser is the one who is never confirmed. In the purest sense, writers employ the trickster cross-dresser when they tease readers with leading descriptions. Henry James, one of the most skilled writers in either the U.S. or the European canon, presents such a trickster in *The Bostonians* (1886). Sharing some parallels with the real-life Dr. Mary Walker (1832–1919), James's Dr. Prance raises questions regarding her gender. Walker, who wore pants and a coat at a time when women wore only dresses, challenged gender perceptions. James, however, relies on nuance to make his case for a cross-dressing Dr. Prance: he never mentions her attire but instead merely describes her as looking like a boy, as sparse and "dry" with cropped hair. Only through his visible distaste for the early women's movement and a "masculine" tendency toward laconic speech is Prance's ill-fitting gender revealed. Ultimately though, her maleness or femaleness, like her gender, remains unconfirmed: Is Prance a male living as a woman or a female with a masculine bent? James quietly declines to confirm either suspicion.

Clearly Prance crosses a definite boundary, though the precise character of that boundary remains undefined. This case is unusual; such ambiguity rarely extends beyond the last page of the book because cross-dressing in literature usually has a purpose tightly bound to the revelation of the deception. Once the deception is revealed, the central mystery dissolves, but if the cross-dressing character is never revealed, the deception, extending even to the reader, is complete. And as with any social construction, if no one knows the difference, there is no difference to know.

See also Same-Sex Love

BIBLIOGRAPHY
Primary Works
James, Henry. *The Bostonians*. 1886. Middlesex, Eng.: Penguin, 1986.

Twain, Mark. *Adventures of Huckleberry Finn*. 1885. New York: Bantam, 1993.

Twain, Mark. *Pudd'nhead Wilson and Those Extraordinary Twins*. New York: Harper, 1894. Available at http://etext.lib.virginia.edu.

Secondary Works
Bullough, Vern L., and Bonnie Bullough. *Cross-Dressing, Sex, and Gender*. Philadelphia: University of Pennsylvania Press, 1993.

Cruz, Bárbara C., and Michael J. Berson. "On Teaching: The American Melting Pot? Miscegenation Laws in the United States." *OAH Magazine of History* 15, no. 4 (summer 2001). Available at www.oah.org/pubs/magazine/family/cruz-berson.html.

Duberman, Martin, Martha Vicinus, and George Chauncey Jr., eds. *Hidden from History: Reclaiming the Gay and Lesbian Past*. New York: Meridian, 1990.

Foster, Jeannette H. *Sex Variant Women in Literature*. Tallahassee, Fla.: Naiad Press, 1985.

Garber, Marjorie. *Vested Interests: Cross-Dressing and Cultural Anxiety*. New York: Routledge, 1992.

Gillman, Susan. *Dark Twins: Imposture and Identity in Mark Twain's America*. Chicago: University of Chicago Press, 1989.

Mullenix, Elizabeth Reitz. *Wearing the Breeches: Gender on the Antebellum Stage*. New York: St. Martin's, 2000.

Reiter, Joan Swallow. *The Old West: The Women*. Alexandria, Va.: Time-Life, 1979.

Senelick, Laurence. "Boys and Girls Together: Subcultural Origins of Glamour Drag and Male Impersonation of the Nineteenth-Century Stage." In *Crossing the Stage: Controversies on Cross-Dressing*, edited by Lesley Ferris. London: Routledge, 1993.

Slezak, Richard. "Lillie Hitchcock Coit." 2000. Available at http://members.aol.com/minotaur64/coit.htm.

Mary P. Anderson

DAISY MILLER

Henry James's novella *Daisy Miller* (1878) ranks as his first notable success, achieving a popularity—even a notoriety—surpassing anything he had written up to that point in his career. Its vogue helped to usher in the figure of the "American Girl" as a mainstay of national literature in the United States in the late nineteenth century. The story brings into sharp relief the contrast of European and American manners, around which most of James's later work revolves. The success of *Daisy Miller* further opened the door for the author to explore the ramifications of the "international theme" and to assert a kind of proprietary right to it. The tale solidly established a benchmark and a type for which James would always be remembered.

The author based the narrative of his infamous heroine—who exhibits "an inscrutable combination of audacity and innocence"—upon a morsel of gossip he had picked up the year before from a friend in Rome. She told him about a young woman from home ("a child of nature and of freedom") who had managed to pick up a "good-looking Roman, of vague identity" but whose social career was soon checked by others in the American expatriate community who disapproved of her apparently loose behavior (James, Preface, p. 1269). It was all James needed. "Dramatize, dramatize!" he commanded himself, and the result was a minor masterpiece of social and moral inquiry.

"A GREAT HIT"

If plagiarism is the last refuge of an undergraduate scoundrel, literary piracy is the first resort of a pub-lishing opportunist. *Daisy Miller* was not the first work of James's to receive this dubious compliment (an unauthorized British edition of his 1877 novel *The American* immediately showed up in London book-stalls), but the unexpected appearance of this rather unassuming tale in (not one but) two American peri-odicals aroused much greater interest in an author who was then still relatively unknown beyond the modest subscription list of the *Atlantic Monthly*. For Henry James, *Daisy Miller* was the *succès de scandale* that every writer secretly dreams of—a work that transforms the author's name (or, at least, that of his title character) into a household word.

This outcome was surely not what James would have expected after the editor of *Lippincott's* swiftly returned his manuscript "with an absence of com-ment" that struck the author at the time "as rather grim"—a rejection that prompted him to give *Daisy Miller* instead to a British periodical (James, Preface, p. 1269). Without delay, Leslie Stephen published James's novella in two numbers of his magazine, the *Cornhill* (June and July 1878), and soon this story of an innocently forward girl from Schenectady was making reverberations on both sides of the Atlantic. From London, the writer told his family in America that, much to his satisfaction, the tale was showing every sign of having made "a great hit." "Every one is talking about it," James boasted, "and it has been much noticed in the papers. Its success has encour-aged me as regards the faculty of appreciation of the English public; for the thing is sufficiently subtle, yet people appear to have comprehended it. It has given me a capital start" (James, *Letters* 2:179). In short

Frontispiece by Harry W. McVickar for the 1892 edition of *Daisy Miller*. SPECIAL COLLECTIONS LIBRARY, UNIVERSITY OF MICHIGAN

order, it was also giving him a run for the money. Whatever reasons the reticent editor in Philadelphia had for spurning *Daisy Miller,* they were not shared by the men in charge of Boston's *Living Age* or New York's *Home Journal,* in the pages of which James's pirated text began to circulate stateside that summer. In America, however, James's tale struck readers not so much a "hit" as a slap in the face. Within months, the *New York Times* reported that "many ladies . . . feel very indignant with Mr. James for his portrait of Daisy Miller, and declare that it is shameful to give foreigners so untrue a portrait of an American girl" (Volpe, pp. 57–58). Even the venerable *North American Review* feared that *Daisy Miller* would become "the *sobriquet* in European journalism" to describe the typical American young woman, "irredeemably vulgar in her talk and her conduct" (White, pp. 106, 105).

Even if these contemporaneous interpretations resulted from a fundamental misreading of James's story (the writer later told another correspondent that Daisy—as the floral allusion suggests—was "above all

things *innocent*"), their impact was immediate and widespread (James, *Letters* 2:303). William Dean Howells went so far as to declare that society almost divided itself into warring factions of Daisy Millerites and anti–Daisy Millerites; and, as editor of the prestigious *Atlantic,* he was in a good place to know. Civil war was averted, of course, but the literary firestorm gave James his first real taste of popular success. Hoping to cash in on the story's immediate vogue, Harper & Brothers published *Daisy Miller* in the cheapest possible format (twenty cents in paper wrappers, thirty-five cents in cloth), and twenty thousand copies flew off the shelves within weeks. As James later observed (and lamented), *Daisy Miller* was to be the most prosperous child of his invention, foremost among the very few of his titles that continued measurably to sell years after its first appearance. Its publication was a defining moment in his literary life.

The opposing views held by the reading public about Daisy Miller's moral character essentially reflect the internal drama of the story, which hinges upon just that problem of interpretation. Because we see Daisy largely through the judgmental eyes of Winterbourne, a more cosmopolitan American expatriate, discerning the true motivation for her outwardly immodest behavior becomes problematic. The deliberate absence of an omniscient narrator complicates and intensifies our experience of the story, especially if we leave ourselves open to the possibility that Winterbourne's chill assessment of Daisy may be compromised, psychologically, by his own moral failings. James himself remarked upon the subtlety of his narrative mode (which owes much to Hawthorne, in fact), knowing all the while that the flatness of his treatment would encourage a certain kind of misreading.

James appended two words to his title, calling his novella *Daisy Miller: A Study,* as if to suggest something trifling about his chosen subject. However slight the story might seem, it would be a mistake nonetheless to think of it merely as a provisional sketch, a modest prelude to the ampler treatment of, say, *The Portrait of a Lady* (1881). Daisy Miller becomes a "study" only through the act of clinical observation, and to be "studied" in James (as in Hawthorne before him) is, typically, to be violated. Before the story even begins, then, James intends to give his provincial heroine the benefit of the doubt—knowing that no one else (particularly Winterbourne) will be so generously inclined. After Daisy's inevitable demise (the Protestant cemetery is her final resting place), we learn in the story's final paragraph that Winterbourne has abandoned Rome for Geneva, from whence reports come that "he is 'studying' hard—an intimation that he is much interested in a very clever foreign lady." James's use of inverted commas signals the prurient implication of his subtitle, further coloring the reliability of Winterbourne's interpretation of Daisy's besmirched character.

VERSIONS AND REVISIONS

In the story's next incarnation—as a play—surprisingly enough, Daisy Miller does not get carried off either by Roman fever (her fate in the novella) or a broken heart. Instead, she happily marries Winterbourne and the cheerful couple safely returns (like Hawthorne's Kenyon and Hilda before them) from the malarial precincts of Italy to the snug shores of America. James was sure that to revamp *Daisy Miller* for the stage, he would have to supply the de rigueur happy ending; but even with that, *Daisy Miller: A Comedy* (1883) got few laughs. The theater managers for whom the author mutilated his masterpiece eventually spurned it, and almost in desperation James was obliged to vend his dramatic wares in the mute pages of the *Atlantic*. James's not-quite-profitless act of revision starkly reminds us of his willingness to tamper with his own prose. Consequently, it is imperative that readers of *Daisy Miller* know with some precision from which text they are drawing inferences or forming critical judgments.

James frequently revised his work when it first made the transition between magazine and book publication. Since he did not always have the benefit of seeing serial proofs, intervention at this stage allowed him to correct misprints and, occasionally, to introduce new wordings or to restore material omitted by squeamish editors. Toward the end of his career, James had a more significant occasion and aesthetic rationale for revisiting his early texts. In collecting his work for the definitive New York Edition, published by Scribners (1907–1909), he elaborately revamped much of its selective contents to reflect the more rococo stylistic preferences of his later manner. For the purposes of this edition, James introduced hundreds of new variants into the text of *Daisy Miller*. Even a small sampling will convey a material sense of difference between these two versions of his tale.

[1879] Poor Winterbourne was amused, perplexed, and decidedly charmed. He had never yet heard a young girl express herself in just this fashion; never, at least, save in cases where to say such things seemed a kind of demonstrative evidence of a certain laxity of deportment. And yet was he to accuse Miss Daisy Miller of actual or potential *inconduite*, as they said at Geneva? He felt that he had lived at Geneva so long that he had lost a good deal; he had become dishabituated to the American tone.

[1909] Poor Winterbourne was amused and perplexed—above all he was charmed. He had never yet heard a young girl express herself in just this fashion; never at least save in cases where to say such things was to have at the same time some rather complicated consciousness about them. And yet was he to accuse Miss Daisy Miller of an actual or a potential *arrière-pensée*, as they said at Geneva? He felt he had lived at Geneva so long as to have got morally muddled; he had lost the right sense for the young American tone.

[1879] Winterbourne wondered how she felt about all the cold shoulders that were turned toward her, and sometimes it annoyed him to suspect that she did not feel at all. He said to himself that she was too light and childish, too uncultivated and unreasoning, too provincial, to have reflected upon her ostracism or even to have perceived it.

[1909] Winterbourne wondered how she felt about all the cold shoulders that were turned upon her, and sometimes found himself suspecting with impatience that she simply didn't feel and didn't know. He set her down as hopelessly childish and shallow, as such mere giddiness and ignorance incarnate as was powerless either to heed or to suffer.

[1879] Daisy, lovely in the flattering moonlight, looked at him a moment.

[1909] Daisy, lovely in the sinister silver radiance, appraised him a moment, roughness and all.

Though his phrasings are more baroque, their cumulative effect is really to make the story less subtle, to make the reader more aware of the potentially distorting intervention of Winterbourne's observing consciousness. As the critic Philip Horne observed, it is almost as if James wanted "to prevent a repetition of the misunderstandings which had controversially attended the first appearance of the tale" (p. 248). In retrospect, perhaps, James was trying to make the public more clearly see what Howells had felt all along: "that never was any civilization offered a more precious tribute than that which a great artist paid ours in the character of Daisy Miller" (p. ix).

See also Americans Abroad; Feminism; Realism

BIBLIOGRAPHY

Primary Works

Howells, William Dean. Introduction to the Modern Library edition of *Daisy Miller* and *An International Episode*, pp. i–ix. New York: Boni & Liveright, 1918.

James, Henry. *The Complete Plays of Henry James.* Edited by Leon Edel. New York: Oxford University Press, 1990. Reprints the text of *Daisy Miller: A Comedy* (1883).

James, Henry. *Complete Stories, 1874–1884.* Edited by Edward W. Said. New York: Library of America, 1999. Reprints the text of the first English edition of *Daisy Miller* (1879).

James, Henry. *Henry James Letters.* 4 vols. Edited by Leon Edel. Cambridge, Mass.: Belknap Press of Harvard University Press, 1974–1984.

James, Henry. Preface to vol. 18 of the New York Edition. In *Literary Criticism*, vol. 2, *European Writers and Prefaces to the New York Edition*, edited by Leon Edel, pp. 1269–1286. New York: Library of America, 1984. In the twenty-four–volume New York Edition, published by Scribners in 1907–1909, James collected and revised his most important works to that time.

Stafford, William T., comp. *James's Daisy Miller: The Story, the Play, the Critics.* New York: Scribner, 1963.

Secondary Works

Anesko, Michael. *"Friction with the Market": Henry James and the Profession of Authorship.* New York: Oxford University Press, 1986.

Edel, Leon. *Henry James.* 5 vols. Philadelphia: Lippincott, 1953–1972.

Gard, Roger, ed. *Henry James: The Critical Heritage.* London: Routledge and Kegan Paul, 1968.

Hocks, Richard A. *Henry James: A Study of the Short Fiction.* Boston: Twayne, 1990.

Horne, Philip. *Henry James and Revision: The New York Edition.* Oxford: Clarendon Press, 1990.

McWhirter, David, ed. *Henry James's New York Edition: The Construction of Authorship.* Stanford: Stanford University Press, 1995.

Reeve, Neil H., ed. *Henry James: The Shorter Fiction—Reassessments.* New York: Macmillan, 1997.

Vaid, Krishna Baldev. *Technique in the Tales of Henry James.* Cambridge, Mass.: Harvard University Press, 1964.

Volpe, Edmond L. "The Reception of *Daisy Miller.*" *Boston Public Library Quarterly* 10 (1958): 55–59.

White, Richard Grant. "Recent Fiction." Review of *The Europeans* and *Daisy Miller. North American Review* 128 (January 1879): 97–110.

Michael Anesko

THE DAMNATION OF THERON WARE

"The sole courageous or truthful novel ever written by an American on the subject of religion" (Beer, p. 150). Thus Thomas Beer, a novelist and critic, wrote in 1923 of *The Damnation of Theron Ware; or, Illumination* by Harold Frederic (1856–1898). Published in 1896, Frederic's novel depicts the loss of faith of a young Methodist minister influenced by a series of modernist figures in an upstate New York town, Octavius. The modernists include a Catholic priest, Father Forbes, influenced by the historical and demythologizing Higher Criticism of the Bible; Dr. Ledsmar, a nonpracticing physician who is both a Darwinian scientist and an expert in comparative religion; and Celia Madden, a young Irishwoman who, though nominally Catholic, pays her devotion to the Greek spirit of beauty and freedom from moral restraint. Theron begins the novel as a happily married man though one somewhat disappointed by being assigned to the stingy congregation of Octavius. After a powerful scene in which he witnesses Father Forbes administer the last rites to a young Irishman dying from a fall, he becomes acquainted with Forbes, Ledsmar, and Miss Madden. As his "illumination" under their influence proceeds, he becomes alienated from his now seemingly ignorant parishioners and his wife, Alice. Allured by Celia, he displays increasing prurience in his determination to understand the nature of her relationship to Forbes. Imagining himself accepted by Celia, he follows Forbes and her to a hotel room in New York, where she rejects him decisively as a "bore." He then attempts a drunken spree and contemplates suicide but is rescued by Sister Soulsby and her husband (or lover), pragmatist debt-raisers who have earlier orchestrated a campaign to bring solvency to Ware's church. The end of the novel finds Alice and Ware reconciled, Ware out of the ministry, and the couple heading for Seattle, where he thinks he might yet be able to turn his talent for oratory into success in politics.

BACKGROUND AND INFLUENCES

Robert Myers has suggested situating *Theron* historically by linking Frederic's social concerns to T. J. Jackson Lears's "concept of 'antimodernism'" (p. 119).

Advertising poster for *The Damnation of Theron Ware*, 1896. THE LIBRARY OF CONGRESS

The novel reflects anxieties of late-nineteenth-century cultural elites caused by "rapid social transformation" (p. 119) and exacerbated by the decline of religious authority—undermined, as the novel stresses, by the Higher Criticism of the Bible. Frederic's notes for *Theron* suggest his deep concern "that America had become overcivilized and that the homogenous American spirit was being torn apart" by "class unrest" and "conflict between the sexes" (p. 119). Thus Frederic "seems to privilege the Roman Catholic Church as an alternative" (p. 119) to modern overcivilization and fragmentation. Whether Frederic does privilege an antimodern Catholic Church is debatable: many critics have stressed the difficulty of finding any privileged center or authority in the novel. Myers argues further, following Lears, that antimodernism

gave rise to a "self-focused pursuit of 'authentic experience'" that helped "ease the adjustment to a culture of consumption" (p. 119). The application to *Theron* is again fascinating to consider, for clearly Ware is "self-focused" (p. 119) and in search of authenticity. Yet ultimately he seems only an example of the empty other-directedness of consumerism. Perhaps this is Frederic's way of suggesting the hopelessness of the quest for authenticity in a culture lacking meaningful standards or authority.

The influence of the Higher Criticism is repeatedly evident in *Theron,* never more clearly than when the theologically innocent Reverend Ware consults Forbes and Ledsmar regarding a planned study of Abraham. When Ware mentions the "complexities and contradictions" of Abraham's "character," Forbes responds, "I fear that you are taking our friend Abraham too literally, Mr. Ware. . . . Modern research, you know, quite wipes him out of existence as an individual. The word 'Abram' is merely an eponym—it means 'exalted father'" (p. 60). The notes Frederic took in preparation for writing *Theron*—now at the Library of Congress—have led Stanton Garner and others to identify four works as the primary sources of Frederic's knowledge of comparative religion: William Edward Hartpole Lecky's *History of European Morals from Augustus to Charlemagne* (1869), John William Draper's *History of the Conflict between Religion and Science* (1874), Ernest Renan's *Recollections of My Youth* (translated into English in 1883), and Arthur Schopenhauer's *Religion: A Dialogue and Other Essays* (English translation 1889). As Myers has argued, several of these sources reflect an ambivalence about the decline of traditional faith that is not unlike Frederic's own: "Over the years Frederic's own attitude toward religion had altered between contempt for religious superstition and a recognition of the social value of religion" (p. 121). Both these attitudes are present in the novel. Frederic criticizes the self-serving hypocrisy and anti-Irish, anti-Catholic prejudice of the conservative Methodists and of Theron himself, who recognizes that his image of the Irish has been largely formed by the vicious cartoons of Thomas Nast and Joseph Keppler. He also satirizes the concern for status and money of the progressive Methodists. Particularly prescient on the whole matter of biblical authority is a remark from Frederic's notes, quoted by Myers, suggesting his insight into the way scientism and religious fundamentalism breed and sustain one another—a development Americans continue to experience. Frederic complains of the "ridiculous" modern situation, "where agnostics by loudly insisting [that] Religion [is] not Pure Truth force zealots to foolishly insist that it is" (pp. 121–122).

Garner points to the influence on Frederic's book of several nineteenth-century novels involving ministers: Oliver Wendell Holmes's *Elsie Venner* (1861), Mark Rutherford's (William Hale White) *The Autobiography of Mark Rutherford, Dissenting Minister* (1881) and *The Revolution in Tanner's Lane* (1887), and Mrs. Humphry Ward's *Robert Elsmere* (1888), in which Elsmere, like Ware, comes under the influence of modern biblical scholarship. Frederic's novel was in turn an important influence on Sinclair Lewis's *Elmer Gantry* (1927). An important and acknowledged literary influence on Frederic was Nathaniel Hawthorne, and critics have related features of *Theron Ware* to such works as "Young Goodman Brown," "Rappaccini's Daughter," *The Scarlet Letter* (1850), and *The Blithedale Romance* (1852). Other aspects of the novel are rooted in Frederic's own experience. Octavius is based on Utica, New York, where Frederic was born and reared. Many of the novel's specific settings and characters have their roots in Utica. The original inspiration for Father Forbes seems to have been Frederic's friend Father Edward Aloysius Terry, a theological liberal born in Ireland and the pastor of St. John's in Utica. Frederic and Terry became friends in the late 1870s, and Frederic witnessed Terry's painful transfer by his bishop from St. John's to a parish in Albany—a transfer apparently forced, according to Bridget Bennett, by complaints from other local priests "envious of his personal popularity and angry with his liberalism" (p. 37). Frederic's friendship with Terry was also instrumental in educating Frederic about the intensity of anti-Irish and anti-Catholic feeling among local Protestants. A friend of both men, Patrick Mullany, is quoted in Frederic's papers as having remarked that, while in school near Utica, he learned that "many of his fellow citizens thought that it was a disgrace to be Irish and a crime to be Catholic" (Bennett, p. 36).

Other features of the novel may also be rooted in Frederic's experience. Frederic's father-in-law, David Williams, may have supplied a model for the conservative trustees of Ware's church. Frederic himself had attended Methodist Sunday school in Utica. His own interests in a variety of the arts closely match those of Celia Madden, and he did at least some experimenting with plants along the lines of Dr. Ledsmar. Theron's dissatisfaction with his marriage to Alice and his attraction to Celia reflect Frederic's marital situation. The novel was written in the early 1890s in London, where Frederic was working as a correspondent for the *New York Times*. During this period he was living in two households—during the week with his mistress Kate Lyon and their children, eventually three, and on the weekends with the legal Mrs. Frederic, the former Grace Williams of Utica, and their four children.

INTERPRETIVE QUESTIONS

One of the difficulties facing the reader of *Theron* is suggested by remarks of Father Forbes on the church. Forbes insists "there must always be a church" to serve as a "police force" and a form of "social machinery." Theology is at best a "sort of intellectual diversion, like the ritual of a benevolent organization" (p. 243). Clearly Forbes speaks to some extent for Frederic here, yet the priest's account of the church and of faith seems decidedly pale in comparison to the real effects of faith Frederic shows elsewhere. Frederic clearly admires the "venerable Fathers in Israel" (p. 243), the oldest generation of Methodist preachers at the opening conference. He presents Jeremiah Madden with great respect, stressing how his losses have led to a quiet faith and a strong connection to his people. He powerfully displays the suffering of poor people as they gather around the dying Irishman MacEvoy. For these people the Latin phrases of extreme unction are words of life, not simply part of an aesthetically pleasing performance supplied by an important agency of social order.

Also difficult to evaluate is Frederic's attitude toward the pragmatism of Sister Soulsby. Her religious creed is simple: "The sheep and the goats are to be separated on Judgment Day, but not a minute sooner" (p. 336). She urges on Ware the need for "*sabe,*—common sense" (p. 142) and believes that "everything in this world is produced by machinery—by organization" (p. 171). She recognizes quite acutely that a church must have "authority of some sort" and that the "general state of excitement" she and Soulsby orchestrate functions temporarily as "the authority, the motive power . . . by which things are done" (p. 174). Yet Luther Luedtke sees Sister Soulsby as a satanic figure, pointing to her wheedling Ware into betraying Levi Gorringe, the one trustee who has treated him well. Other critics have treated her in a more balanced way or identified Frederic with her pragmatism. Fritz Oehlschlaeger's view is that Frederic recognizes the necessity of her pragmatic emphasis on common sense and organization and yet shows her philosophy to be inadequate as a response to human helplessness and tragic suffering. Nor is there adequate recognition in the sister's pragmatism of the absurdity of the human ego, as manifested in one like Theron Ware. The Soulsbys salvage Ware at the novel's end, but they leave him as absurdly self-infatuated as he has been throughout the book.

DAMNATION OR ILLUMINATION?

Perhaps the most difficult question of the novel regards how to read Theron's "illumination" or "damnation." Should he be read primarily as an innocent taken in by a series of irresponsible modernists who seek to undermine his faith and identity? Or is he a thoroughly unattractive figure who gravitates toward Celia, Forbes, and Ledsmar out of sexual prurience and the need to feel superior to the people from whom he comes? Perhaps he is best understood as a characteristically American figure who combines a lack of self-knowledge with an intense belief in his own potential for self-improvement. He is remarkably centerless, despite his purported Methodist faith, and lacks any real standards by which to judge his learning or ability. As he discovers how little he knows of Abraham and the Chaldeans, he can—in the course of a page—go from condemning himself as "an extremely ignorant and rudely untrained young man" to exalting himself as one greatly superior to his colleagues in the conference who "were doomed by native incapacity to go on all their lives without ever finding" out how "clownishly ignorant" they were (p. 59). Ultimately Theron's sense of himself is aesthetic. His primary concern is for the impression he makes upon others.

Theron's need for self-confirmation is evident in his attraction to the novel's maternal figures: Sister Soulsby, Celia Madden, the Catholic Church. His "illumination" charts simultaneously a regression from something approaching a mature sexual relationship with Alice to adolescent prurience focused on the confused maternal and sexual image of Celia. On his way to Celia's one night, he recognizes his need for "some restful, soothing human contact, which should exact nothing from him in return, but just take charge of him" (p. 184). Later, in the forest scene, Theron feels as if he "were a boy again—a good, pure-minded, fond little child," and Celia appears as "the mother that [he] idolized" (p. 259). Theron may have become a boy again, but he is anything but a "pure-minded" one. He voyeuristically seeks to understand Celia's relationship to Forbes while simultaneously entertaining the idea that Alice is unfaithful to him—at least in spirit—with Gorringe. His pursuit of Celia leads to the New York hotel where she administers the most appropriate of rejections for one whose narcissistic sense of himself depends so fully on the mirror others provide. "It is all in a single word, Mr. Ware," she tells him. "I speak for others as well as myself, mind you—we find that you are a bore" (p. 321). No longer will he be able to mingle with the "really educated people" whose acceptance he needs—in the absence of any real personal distinction—to feel superior to the simple people with whom his lot has otherwise been cast. Celia's rejection nearly undoes Ware, but he is rebuilt by the Soulsbys and closes the novel as self-infatuated and other-directed, in the negative sense, as ever. He relinquishes the ministry, but as he and Alice prepare to leave for Seattle, politics seems a new possibility. There rises "before his fancy" a vision of a "great concourse of uplifted countenances" all "looking at *him*" (p. 344).

See also The Bible; Catholics; Irish; Oratory; Realism

BIBLIOGRAPHY
Primary Work
Frederic, Harold. *The Damnation of Theron Ware; or, Illumination.* 1896. Text established by Charlyne Dodge. Lincoln and London: University of Nebraska Press, 1985. Page citations of the novel refer to this text.

Secondary Works
Beer, Thomas. *Stephen Crane: A Study in American Letters.* New York: Knopf, 1923.

Bennett, Bridget. *The Damnation of Harold Frederic: His Lives and Works.* Syracuse, N.Y.: Syracuse University Press, 1997.

Briggs, Austin, Jr. *The Novels of Harold Frederic.* Ithaca, N.Y.: Cornell University Press, 1969.

Dooley, Patrick K. "Fakes and Good Frauds: Pragmatic Religion in *The Damnation of Theron Ware.*" *American Literary Realism* 15 (1982): 74–85.

Garner, Stanton. "History of the Text." In *The Damnation of Theron Ware; or, Illumination,* pp. 353–415. Text established by Charlyne Dodge. Lincoln and London: University of Nebraska Press, 1985.

Luedtke, Luther S. "Harold Frederic's Satanic Soulsby: Interpretation and Sources." *Nineteenth-Century Fiction* 30 (1975): 82–104.

Myers, Robert M. *Reluctant Expatriate: The Life of Harold Frederic.* Westport, Conn.: Greenwood, 1995.

Oehlschlaeger, Fritz. "Passion, Authority, and Faith in *The Damnation of Theron Ware.*" *American Literature* 58 (1986): 238–255.

Fritz Oehlschlaeger

DANCE

In the late nineteenth and early twentieth centuries, America was fertile ground for innovations in dance that had a pronounced influence on the form itself and contributed to the formation of national identity. The experimentation of female dancers initiated the modernist movement, and the evolution of the African American tradition of music and dance, from the period of slavery to emancipation, culminated in the explosive rhythm and movement of the Jazz Age.

In her autobiography, Isadora Duncan recalls how she introduced herself at one of her first New York auditions.

I bring you the dance. I bring you the idea that is going to revolutionise our entire epoch. Where have I discovered it? By the Pacific Ocean, by the waving pine-forests of Sierra Nevada. I have seen the ideal figure of youthful America dancing over the top of the Rockies. The supreme poet of our country is Walt Whitman. I have discovered the dance that is worthy of the poem of Walt Whitman. I am indeed the spiritual daughter of Walt Whitman. For the children of America I will create a new dance that will express America.

Duncan, *My Life*, p. 31.

Dance signified transformations in class status and gender identity, and the form was a source of inspiration for writers during this period, which is evident in the influence of dance aesthetics on poetry and the significance of dance motifs in fiction.

The history of dance in America is comprised of many interwoven cultural strands. In the colonial period, figure dances, such as the minuet, waltz, quadrille, and English country dances, were imported from Europe. Each successive wave of immigration was accompanied by the music and dance of the respective Old World country—for example, the popular Irish jigs and the German schottische (polka). There was a social division among dancing styles that can be observed in the differences between the imported European figure dances performed at the society balls of the upper class, the folk dances of the immigrant class, and the intricate African American step dances. However, throughout the course of the nineteenth century, these boundaries began to dissolve. Square dancing, an amalgamation of various folk dances and European figure dances, evolved with the expansion to the West. Some of the square dances that developed in the South were accompanied by adaptations of African American slave songs; likewise, some Anglo-American fiddle chord variations were incorporated in African American music. Native American cultures are a notable exception to this hybridization. The indigenous populations of this country have a tradition of sacred dance and ritual that essentially remained separate and distinct.

CLASSICAL DANCE AND POETRY

There was not a tradition of classical dancing in America until the twentieth century; however, audiences were introduced to ballet in operatic productions and tours of European ballet companies. In 1840 Walt Whitman (1819–1892) saw Fanny Elsler (1810–1884), a British ballerina, when she toured the country. More than a half century later, in 1910, the next foreign ballerina crossed the shore. The prima ballerina Anna Pavlova (1881–1931) created a sensation because American audiences were finally able to view the virtuosity of a talented danseuse. Pavlova, whose dancing was a continuation of the aesthetics of the Romantic tradition, became the model for the ballerina. Serge Diaghilev's Russian company, Ballets Russe (with whom Pavlova occasionally performed) appeared in 1916 and 1917; the legendary Vaslav Nijinsky danced in the 1917 tour. The company's avant garde innovations in choreography, costume, and stage design influenced the modernist movement in literature in America and Europe.

American female dancers, however, had, for the most part, a more significant impact abroad than they did at home. In the syncretic interaction between dance and literature, two female dancers are significant: Loie Fuller (1862–1928) and Isadora Duncan (1877–1927). In fin de siècle Paris, Fuller created a fantastical effect onstage through her experimentations with lighting and her manipulation of yards of fabric. In fact, a special theater was constructed for her at the Paris World Fair in 1900. Auguste Rodin was one of her admirers, and she became a muse for several symbolist poets, including Stéphane Mallarmé and Anatole France. Duncan, a San Francisco native, revolutionized theatrical dance when she rejected the balletic tradition. She abandoned the restrictive costume, which consisted of corseted tutus and pointe shoes, and chose instead to dance barefoot in sheer flowing tunics that evoked ancient Greece. Enraptured by her northwestern homeland, the voluminous ocean and the massive pines, Duncan's movement embodied the expansive spirit of the country; indeed, her innovations ushered in the era of modern dance. She was also inspired by Whitman's poetry and, in fact, recited his poems to her American audiences during performances. For the poet, dance was an important metaphor that often provided the kinetic energy for his epic vision, most notably in *Song of Myself* (1881). Just as Whitman employed dance aesthetics in his poetry, so too did Emily Dickinson (1830–1886). In her poem,

Isadora Duncan performing "Omar," 1899. GETTY IMAGES

"I cannot dance upon my Toes—" (1862), balletic technique is a metaphor for the intellectual rigor of the poetic process. In one of Whitman's later poems, "Hands Round" (1876), dance aesthetics contribute to the overall structure of the poem.

At the outset of her career, Duncan exuberantly declared, "I am indeed the spiritual daughter of Walt Whitman. For the children of America I will create a new dance that will express America" (p. 31). European audiences responded enthusiastically to Duncan's performances; however, her dancing shocked the Puritan sensibility of American audiences, and she was coldly received in her 1909–1917 productions. Nonetheless, she enthralled many American artists who perceived her movement as emblematic of a new age. Duncan had a profound effect on Hart Crane, and she was an inspirational figure for his dance imagery in *The Bridge* (1927). Dance aesthetics continued to have a notable influence on modern poetry; in addition to Crane's poetry, the form is central to the works of T. S. Eliot,

H.D. (Hilda Doolittle), Wallace Stevens, and William Carlos Williams.

THEATRICAL DANCE AND NATURALISM

Because there was not a tradition of classical dance in the United States until the twentieth century, there was no distinction between high and low art in theatrical dance during the late eighteenth and nineteenth centuries. Stage dancing was a medley of tap dancing, toe dancing, acrobatics, pantomime, skirt dancing, and ballroom and interpretive dance performed in vaudeville acts, musical revues, minstrel shows, and saloon halls. This type of theatrical dance is depicted by the naturalist writer Stephen Crane (1871–1900) in *Maggie, A Girl of the Streets* (1893). Maggie is mesmerized by a dance hall production featuring a skirt dancer "attired in some half dozen skirts" (p. 26), a ventriloquist act, and an impromptu choral routine in which the performers mockingly imitate the movements of African slave dances.

During this period, female dancers and actresses were generally perceived as immoral; not only were they, for the most part, from the lower classes, but also the public display of the body smacked of impropriety. Nonetheless, the stage afforded many females from the lower classes, who were underpaid laborers in the factories and garment sweatshops in major cities, an opportunity to supplement their salaries in the hope of embarking on a new profession. However, these women often found themselves performing in dance halls and saloons, rather than in the theater. For example, in *Maggie,* a ballad singer, performing in a saloon in the Bowery district of New York, is finally able to rouse the enthusiasm of her male audience when, after each successive song, she reappears onstage wearing less clothing and her movements become increasingly more provocative. This precarious social positioning is also addressed by the naturalist writer Theodore Dreiser (1871–1945). In *Sister Carrie* (1900), the protagonist, Caroline Meeber, an impoverished young female from rural Illinois, relocates to Chicago where she is forced to contend with the perils of survival. She finds, albeit perhaps temporarily, an alternative to the street and her grueling factory job when she makes her way to the stage, where she struggles to gain a measure of independence and respectability.

SOCIAL DANCE AND REALISM/ REGIONALISM

Social dance was more respectable than theatrical dance because it was considered a mark of gentility; in this regard, the form was integral to the socialization process of the upper class. Dance was a necessary requisite for the marriage market because much of the courtship ritual centered on the formalities of elite society balls. Dances such as the waltz, polka, and mazurka were carefully orchestrated throughout the course of the evening. Partners were arranged in advance, and the gentlemens' names were notated on the ladies' dance cards. It was crucial for guests to observe social decorum at these balls, such as the correct arrangement of partners and whether or not it was appropriate to "sit out" a dance, in order not to risk tarnishing their reputation. This turn-of-the-century aristocratic world is meticulously described in the realist novels of Edith Wharton (1862–1937) and Henry James (1843–1916). These social galas often became routine by the end of the season, and, in an effort to break up the monotony, *tableaux vivants* were sometimes presented. A tradition dating to seventeenth-century England, the tableaux is a silent enactment of a scene or painting by one or more individuals. In Wharton's *The House of Mirth* (1905), Lily Bart, a socialite who has been on the circuit for several years, makes a stunning impression costumed as an artist's model in a famous painting of the day and, through this performance, is able to recapture her charm and allure.

In regionalist narratives, as in the works of realist writers, dance signifies issues of class; however, issues of race predominate. George Washington Cable (1844–1925) depicts the Creole culture of New Orleans in his works. The celebration of Carnival, which originated with the early French settlers in Louisiana, influenced the rituals of society balls. In addition to social dancing, masquerade and costume are customary. Cable's novel, *The Grandissimes* (1880), opens with a Creole *bal masque*, an elegant soiree attended by guests who are attired in popular costumes of the period, such as *commedia dell'arte* and religious figures. The definition of Creole is complex and has been variously interpreted as a European born in the West Indies or the Gulf States, a descendant of an original French or Spanish settler in the Gulf States, or an individual of mixed European and African descent. However, the Creole community that Cable describes distinguished itself by excluding individuals of African descent, an exclusion that elucidates the intricacy of race in the formation of regional identity in the Deep South. Dance is central to this identity because it reinforces local customs. Kate Chopin (1851–1904), focuses on both the Creole and Cajun (Acadian French immigrants) cultures of the Deep South in her works. The Acadian community, like the Creole community, distinguished itself by excluding Americans, who were referred to by the term "white." This exclusion is integral to the socialization process; for example, in "At the 'Cadian Ball" (1892), the narrator emphatically declares that "Anyone who is white may go to a Cadian ball, but he must pay for his lemonade, his coffee and chicken gumbo and he must behave himself like a Cadian" (p. 1599).

Free people of color and recently emancipated slaves were forced to negotiate "the color divide" when they chose to settle in the North. Individuals of biracial or multiracial lineage often found themselves in a quixotic social position because class status was dependent on skin color. This positioning is eloquently depicted in the "The Wife of His Youth" (1899) by the regionalist writer's Charles W. Chesnutt (1858–1932). In the narrative, set in the North, the protagonist, Mr. Ryder, a biracial former slave who becomes economically affluent, plans to host a ball that he has arduously planned to imitate the high society balls of the white upper class. The event will "mark an epoch in the social history" (p. 1641) of the city because he and the light-colored blacks who belong to the social group the "Blue Veins" will be able to set themselves apart through the prestige and grandeur of this ball. Ryder explains that "we people of mixed blood are ground between the upper and the nether millstone. Our fate lies between absorption by the white race and extinction in the black" (p. 1641). Ironically, the poignancy of this narrative is the omission of the ball; when the protagonist accidentally encounters his first wife, a former slave, on the day of the occasion, he chooses to introduce her to his guests rather than proceed with the planned event, thereby reclaiming his African heritage.

Issues of nationality and ethnicity, for the most part, elide issues of race in the establishment of the northern European immigrant communities in the North and the Midwest during this period; however, issues of race are a factor for some southern European immigrants in the Northeast and for Mexican immigrants in the Midwest and Southwest. For all of these various groups, cultural boundaries continue to be a source of anxiety, and the community dances that Willa Cather (1873–1947) intricately describes in her works elucidate the complexities of assimilation underlying this anxiety. In *Song of the Lark* (1915), the Scandinavian protagonist, Thea Kronenberg, becomes enthralled with the Mexican community in a small Colorado town when she attends a Mexican ball. Thea is impressed by the intimacy and refinement of the occasion, and she "could not help wondering whether the Mexicans had no jealousies or neighborly grudges as the people in Moonstone had" (p. 230). Cather captures the innocence and idealism that characterize the first generation of immigrants in the plains; nonetheless, she suggests that the inclusiveness of these

Scandinavian communities fostered discrimination, prejudice, and intolerance.

In *My Ántonia* (1918), Cather conveys the popularity of social dance during this period. As the protagonist, Jim Burden, recounts his childhood in Nebraska he fondly remembers one of the best summers of his youth, the summer that he and his friends spent dancing. A dance pavilion was constructed so that the dance instructors who were visiting the town would have a place to teach. Itinerant dancing masters created a sensation upon their arrival in small western towns because of the professional training they provided the community. However, lack of formal training did not discourage pioneers and cowboys from dancing; in fact, almost any occasion, for example, a barn raising or a quilting session, was reason to dance. On the frontier, dances were spontaneous and unstructured, and it was the role of the caller to impose order and to remember the steps. In *Song of the Lark*, when Thea compares the graceful Mexican dances to the rowdy county dances with which she is familiar, she notes "for the square dances there was always the bawling voice of the caller, who was also the country auctioneer" (p. 229).

AFRICAN AMERICAN AND NATIVE AMERICAN TRADITION

The African American tradition of rhythm and movement was instrumental to the music and dance of the Jazz Age. Aside from New Orleans, where slaves were allowed to observe tribal rituals on Sunday afternoons in a designated area of the city, Congo Square, slaves in the rest of the country were prohibited from beating drums, an important African cultural custom, by the Slave Laws of 1740 because the ritual signified the threat of insurrection to white masters. This prohibition resulted in the substitution of bone clappers, hand clapping, and footbeats for drumbeats. The rhythmic offbeat timing of the clapping and stamping, which mimicked the drumbeats, eventually developed into the syncopation that characterizes the jazz sound. The footbeats evolved into complex step dances and gradually the form of tap dance emerged.

In the nineteenth century, minstrel shows, a combination of jokes, songs, and dances that featured white performers in blackface, were wildly popular. Black performers, aware that whites were profiting from this exploitation, produced their own shows, in which, they too appeared in blackface in order to satisfy the white audiences' expectations. As minstrel shows began to wane in popularity, an exhibition dance called the cakewalk was performed at the conclusion of the show. In the 1890s the cakewalk created a national dance craze that was transported to Europe. The cakewalk originated on plantations in the 1850s by slaves who were parodying the ceremonial promenades of their white masters. The white owners, unaware of the mockery, began to imitate the cakewalk themselves. The popularity of this dance set the trend for the appropriation of other steps from African American dances into mainstream social dance; between 1907 and 1914, the "animal dances"—for example, the Turkey Trot and Grizzly Bear—incorporated movements such as thrusting the head forward, hopping, and flapping the elbows. The Charleston, the quintessential dance of the Jazz Age, which is distinguished by the characteristic gestures of crossing and uncrossing the knees, is a variant of the juba dance, an African step dance.

By the 1920s the African American tradition of rhythmic syncopation was the dominant force in music and dance, and social dance in America was no longer influenced by European styles. The jazz sound and the accompanying dance movements were the catalyst for the liberation of a generation, and the writer responsible for immortalizing this generation, beginning with his first novel, *This Side of Paradise* (1920), is F. Scott Fitzgerald (1896–1940), who coined the term "the Jazz Age." The wealthy ingénues who populate his narratives, the "flappers" with their shortened skirts and bobbed hair, symbolized the free spirit of the era. In the early decades of the twentieth century, this generation was introduced to jazz in the clubs in the inner cities of Harlem and Chicago, sites of innovation in the form. Although jazz originated in New Orleans, many musicians relocated to the North in an attempt to escape the oppression of racial prejudice and discrimination. The brutal fact of segregation became a reality for black performers, regardless of the venues in which they performed, from the theatrical stage to the cabarets and clubs. For the Harlem Renaissance writers, jazz music, and dance did not necessarily provide a libidinous release; instead the form increasingly signified the social inequity of racial injustice. Claude McKay (1889–1948), the writer credited with initiating the Harlem Renaissance movement with his publication of *Harlem Shadows* (1922), addresses these issues in his poetry. In "The Harlem Dancer" (1917), dance is a metaphor for the marginalization of the African American race; in the poem, the kinetic imagery conveying the movements of the black female performer evokes a sense of disembodiment and alienation. In "The Lynching" (1919), the dance motif eerily signifies the frenetic diabolic energy of white supremacy: "And little lads, lynchers that were to be, / Danced round the dreadful thing in fiendish glee" (p. 2085).

Just as African American dance engendered the fear of insurrection during the nineteenth century, so too did Native American dance. This fear was responsible for the massacre at Wounded Knee at the Pine Ridge reservation in South Dakota in 1890. Inspired by the visions of Wovoka, a Numa Indian (c. 1856–1932), many tribes in the region adopted the Ghost Dance religion. This religion, which had Christian overtones, espoused a new world order for Native Americans. Integral to the religion was the sacred ceremonial Ghost Dance, a communal round dance performed by tribal members through which they entered a trancelike state, thereby gaining access to the spirit world. Government Indian agents perceived the religion as a threat, and when the Native Americans refused to stop performing the Ghost Dance great violence ensued. In Native American orature, the Ghost Dance songs express the religious belief of a new world order in which, "A nation is coming, a nation is coming / The Eagle has brought the message to the tribe" (Mooney, p. 1789). Interestingly, there was a tradition of religious ecstatic dance in the colonization process of the United States. Like the Native Americans, a Protestant sect, the Shakers or Shaking Quakers, believed that dance was the medium for access to the spiritual world. This belief was antithetical to that of the Puritans, who denounced dance.

Sadly, during the course of the nineteenth century, the stage became the vehicle for the exploitation of both Native and African Americans because ritual dance was reinvented as spectacle in commercial venues, such as the aforementioned minstrel shows and Buffalo Bill's Wild West Show. The evolution of dance during the 1870–1920 period clearly signifies national tensions related to issues of race and ethnicity, as well as conflicted identifications across lines of class and race. During the 1920s, national dance was characterized by popular forms: the dances of the Jazz Age and the innovations in ballroom dances such as the foxtrot, waltz, and tango.

See also Music; Theater; Wounded Knee

BIBLIOGRAPHY

Primary Works

Cable, George Washington. *The Grandissimes; A Story of Creole Life.* 1880. New York: Sagamore Press, 1957.

Cather, Willa. *My Ántonia.* 1918. New York: Quality Paperback Book Club, 1932.

Cather, Willa. *The Song of The Lark.* 1915. Boston: Houghton Mifflin, 1932.

Chesnutt, Charles W. "The Wife of His Youth." 1899. In *The Norton Anthology of American Literature,* 6th ed., edited by Nina Baym. New York: Norton, 2003.

Chopin, Kate. "At the 'Cadian Ball." 1892. In *The Norton Anthology of American Literature,* 6th ed., edited by Nina Baym. New York: Norton, 2003.

Crane, Hart. "The Bridge." 1927. In *The Norton Anthology of American Literature,* 6th ed., edited by Nina Baym. New York: Norton, 2003.

Crane, Stephen. *Maggie, A Girl of the Streets, and Other New York Writings.* 1893. New York: Modern Library, 2001.

Dickinson, Emily. "I cannot dance upon my toes." 1862. In *The Norton Anthology of American Literature,* 6th ed., edited by Nina Baym. New York: Norton, 2003.

Drieser, Theodore. *Sister Carrie.* 1900. New York: Penguin, 1981.

Duncan, Isadora. *My Life.* New York: Horace Liveright, 1927.

Fitzgerald, F. Scott. *This Side of Paradise.* 1920. New York: Scribners, 1960.

McKay, Claude. "The Harlem Dancer." 1917. In *The Norton Anthology of American Literature,* 6th ed., edited by Nina Baym. New York: Norton, 2003.

McKay, Claude. "The Lynching." 1919. In *The Norton Anthology of American Literature,* 6th ed., edited by Nina Baym. New York: Norton, 2003.

Mooney, James. *The Ghost Dance Religion and the Sioux Outbreak of 1890.* 1896. In *The Norton Anthology of American Literature,* 6th ed., edited by Nina Baym. New York: Norton, 2003.

Twain, Mark. *The Adventures of Tom Sawyer.* 1876. Berkeley: University of California Press, 1982.

Wharton, Edith. *The House of Mirth.* 1905. New York: Macmillan, 1987.

Whitman, Walt. "Hands Round." 1876. In *The Norton Anthology of American Literature,* 6th ed., edited by Nina Baym. New York: Norton, 2003.

Whitman, Walt. *Song of Myself.* 1881. In *The Norton Anthology of American Literature,* 6th ed., edited by Nina Baym. New York: Norton, 2003.

Secondary Works

Doolittle, Lisa, and Heather Elton. "Medicine of the Brave: A Look at the Changing Role of Dance in Native Culture from the Buffalo Days to the Modern Powwow." In *Moving History / Dancing Cultures: A Dance History Reader,* edited by Ann Dils and Ann Cooper Albright, pp. 114–127. Middletown, Conn.: Wesleyan University Press, 2001.

Kraus, Richard. *History of the Dance in Art and Education.* Englewood Cliffs, N.J.: Prentice-Hall, 1969.

Lomax, M. A. *Cowboy Songs and Other Frontier Ballads.* New York: Macmillan, 1923.

Rodgers, Audrey T. *The Universal Drum: Dance Imagery in the Poetry of Eliot, Crane, Roethke, and Williams.* University Park: Pennsylvania State University Press, 1979.

Sommer, Sally. "Dance: II. Social Dance." In *The Reader's Companion to American History,* edited by Eric Foner and John A. Garraty. Boston: Houghton Mifflin, 1991.

Siegel, Marcia B. "Dance: I. Theatrical Dance." In *The Reader's Companion to American History,* edited by Eric Foner and John A. Garraty. Boston: Houghton Mifflin, 1991.

Elizabeth Miller Lewis

DARWINISM

Exploiting America's vast potential in the form of labor and resources, the Industrial Revolution epitomized the concept of cultural and technological evolution. Transforming America from the wild and sparsely populated agrarian society of the seventeenth and eighteenth centuries, technology brought the United States into the later nineteenth century with the promise of increasingly rapid growth, change, and progress. Increasing numbers of Americans and immigrants moved into city centers to work in the mills and factories that housed the new technologies. Urbanization, along with increased confidence in the use of machinery that streamlined mass production, was an important change in post–Civil War American society. This late-nineteenth-century America was prepared for new ideas, inventions, and theories that would benefit a nation on the rise as both a political and an economic power; scientific and technological advancement therefore became the philosophy of American life. This desire for progressive social, scientific, and economic advancement paved the way for America's interest in the work of the British naturalist Charles Darwin (1809–1882).

Darwin was not initially earmarked as one of the world's most influential and historically prominent figures; a self-proclaimed "naughty child," Darwin was an average student in many areas and was often disinclined to study. However naughty and inattentive Darwin was as a boy, he grew up curious about the world around him; this natural curiosity led him to the University of Edinburgh to study medicine. The practice of Victorian medicine was not suited to Darwin's gentle constitution, however, and he eventually attended Cambridge University as a student in theology and philosophy. Although he completed his degree at the university, Darwin's interests in science persisted and led him to the HMS *Beagle,* on which he would board as naturalist for five years while the *Beagle* traversed the globe. This journey proved instrumental in Darwin's discovery and cataloging of numerous ancient fossils he found in the Galapagos that were strikingly similar to contemporary species.

Determined to understand his findings, Darwin collected organic samples from around the world and studied them for many years; eventually this study resulted in several theories: first, that evolution did occur as a result of "natural selection" or the mutation and progression of an organism when the mutation or change was helpful to the survival of the species; second, that this process took hundreds of thousands to millions of years; and third, that all contemporary species of animate life were descendants of one ancient organism. Evolutionary theory effectively invalidated previous Victorian beliefs in a "clockmaker world" wherein God had placed all the species on earth for humans' pleasures and needs and replaced those beliefs with the knowledge that many species had come and gone over time. Further, evolutionary theory supported the fact that animals, including humans, could become extinct if their surroundings changed and they did not suitably change also.

Darwin's evolutionary ideas, published in 1859 as *On the Origin of Species by Means of Natural Selection,* rocked the religious foundations of Western society and thinking, altered the process of scientific discovery, and in fact colored every aspect of human life. Widely read in England immediately upon its publication, Darwin's text took nearly a decade to find its way into the American mainstream. However, it soon became the most popular and contentious book in the United States. It would perhaps have taken longer for Darwin's work to reach an American audience had it not been for the support of a leading American botanist, Asa Gray (1810–1888), whose own brand of "theological evolution" became a popular alternative to "pure evolution." Gray's ideas were shared by the likes of the American historian and philosopher John Fiske (1842–1901), whose works such as *Darwinism and Other Essays* (1879) and *Excursions of an Evolutionist* (1884) were curious blends of Spenserian Social Darwinism, Darwinism, and theology, and Joseph Le Conte (1823–1901), an American physiologist and geologist whose neo-Lamarckian version of evolution was, like Gray's and Fiske's, aimed at improved social conditions for all humanity.

At the heart of the heated debate surrounding Darwin's book was of course the premise that human beings, like all life on earth, had evolved over millions of years from first one, then a few, common, lower organisms and that the determining factor for any organism's ability to survive and evolve was its natural adaptability to its environment by means of innately "useful" characteristics. Unlike previous evolutionists such as Jean-Baptiste Lamarck (1744–1829), who had argued that organisms adapted to their surroundings by purposefully and often physically changing to suit them and that these changes forced by environment were passed on to subsequent offspring, Darwin's theory

The Darwin Club. Cartoon by Rea Irvin from the *Clubs We Do Not Care to Join* series in *Life* magazine, 18 March 1915. THE LIBRARY OF CONGRESS

instead implied that successful survival was a naturally occurring process of chance. While species whose chance mutations suited their environment survived, those whose changes did not eventually died out.

This relegating of survival to a sort of genetic serendipity was a bitter pill to swallow for many Europeans and Americans who had been taught to believe that their biological superiority was a gift from an all-knowing and powerful God. However, while many readers protested this secular explanation for human and indeed all organic development, others found in Darwin an explanation well-suited to contemporary modes of

progressive thought in late-nineteenth-century America. Seemingly, evolutionary theory supported current trends in technological and socioeconomic success, wherein many men who had previously been relatively unsuccessful, lower-middle-class laborers were now increasingly financially solvent men of business whose rise was due to chance or ingenuity.

DARWIN AND AMERICAN WOMEN

Darwin's later work, *The Descent of Man and Selection in Relation to Sex* (1871), asserted that, among other things, women rather than men were the ones in control of the sexual situation when in nature. Citing reproductivity as the major goal of humanity, Darwin placed women squarely in the center of life's most important undertaking. Although Darwin explained that socialization and domestication had altered the sexual situation by placing the male in the more controlling role, the idea of primeval woman selecting her mate was very exciting for women in the 1800s. Sexual selection lent itself to the idea of female equality and supported current trends in favor of women's civil and reproductive rights; it also opened a new door on the study of human behavior by becoming the foundation of psychology.

DARWIN AND THE "SEXOLOGISTS"

Sigmund Freud (1856–1939), the Austrian father of psychoanalysis, asserted the validity of the evolutionary premise and cited Darwin's work as integral to the foundations of psychological study. Freud's own theories were based on the evolutionary insistence of two primal drives: to kill and eat and to procreate. The fulfillment or repression of these needs, Freud argued, was at the nexus of human psychological health. By extension, so was Darwinism.

Like Freud, the British "sexologist" and psychologist Havelock Ellis (1859–1939) cataloged a series of mental and emotional disorders and conditions, and his seven-volume *Studies in the of Psychology of Sex,* compiled between 1897 and 1928, contained hundreds of case histories from all over the world. Ellis believed strongly in a form of Darwinism that agreed with the major premises of the great naturalist but which insisted that the sexual act itself transcended the physical; Ellis maintained that human sexual experiences could also be spiritually uplifting and psychologically healing. Ellis's ideas would eventually be eclipsed almost completely by those of Freud; however, in the 1900s, Ellis's explanations for human sexual behavior, based as they were primarily in Darwinian evolutionary thought, were hugely influential, and his works were widely read by intellectuals, artists, and philosophers as well as scientists. His coining of the term "sexual invert" gave many important figures of the late nineteenth century and early twentieth century, such as the writers Gertrude Stein, Natalie Barney, and Radclyffe Hall, a means of understanding their own sexual identities.

DARWINISM AND AMERICAN CULTURE

Because of Darwinism, social commentators began to make the connection between the idea of success and the idea of evolution. Offshoots of Darwinian thought arose in various forms and contended with both Darwin's work and that of Herbert Spencer (1820–1903), whose own version of evolution had been articulated in his essay "The Development Hypothesis" in 1852 and whose Spencerian "Social Darwinism" became extremely popular directly following the publication of Darwin's first book. More specifically, the notion that evolution could be tampered with in order to improve humanity was much discussed, fueled heavily by the unrest that an influx of "inferior" races in the form of eastern European immigrants had created among the upper middle class. Discussions of race and ethnicity were the cause of many debates in social and scientific circles; these debates were often caused by an increasing number of conflicting theories. Lester Ward (1841–1913), a geologist and paleontologist considered by many to be the father of American sociology, gave voice to one such theory, whose premise was that once any social law is identified, it can be modified and thereby controlled for the betterment of all involved. His work of 1883, *Dynamic Sociology,* identifies the effectiveness of this concept as a means for creating a more egalitarian society. Ward's desire for social equality included all races and both sexes and was often met with angry responses from other learned men of his day; however, his theories were of vital importance to contemporary schools of social thought and were founded on a "reformed" version of Darwinism.

The persistent habit of reforming Darwinism in the late nineteenth century and early twentieth century illustrates the common misinterpretation and misunderstanding of evolution's lengthy process; it also makes tracing the impact of both Darwinism and its competitor, Social Darwinism, difficult. Perhaps the most distinctive differences are Darwinism's focus on the biological impulse to procreate and its incorporation of chance.

DARWIN AND THE ARTS

While Darwinism's impact on American culture was certainly most keenly felt in science, socioeconomics, and philosophy, it was also a huge influence on late-nineteenth-century art, music, architecture, and literature. Because Darwin had aimed his narrative of evolution at both a scientific and a lay audience, it proved extremely readable and was therefore ingested by anyone interested in society and culture. The proof of Darwinism's impact on the arts lies in the radically different works created by individuals such as the architect Frank Lloyd Wright (1867–1959), whose "organic school" of architecture radically altered American living space, the American painter James Whistler (1834–1903), and the ragtime musician and composer Scott Joplin (1868–1917). However, as the visual and musical arts were evolving to reflect new and ever-changing tastes, so too was the literature of the day.

LITERARY DARWINISM

Like art, music, and architecture, literature was forced to evolve from its early-nineteenth-century romantic conventions into a more current reflection of nineteenth-century America's preoccupation with progress. Whereas readers of the mid-nineteenth century had devoured the gothic romance of Nathaniel Hawthorne and the transcendental and mystical qualities of Ralph Waldo Emerson, new audiences sought material in keeping with the changing times. Among the most notably Darwinian authors of the late 1800s was Kate Chopin (1851–1904), whose characters struggle to survive in a world controlled by their biology and their gendered roles of wife and mother, husband and father. Perhaps the most well known and well received of Chopin's works is her novel *The Awakening* (1899), in which the main character, Edna Pontellier, epitomizes a woman trapped by marriage and motherhood. Dissatisfied with both but unable to survive alone, Edna learns to swim only to drown herself in the ocean at the novel's conclusion.

The ocean is a constant symbol of Darwinism in the texts of American writers because it was in the ocean that primordial life began. Like Chopin, Jack London (1876–1916) employs the ocean as the suicidal end for his title character in *Martin Eden* (1913) and places his most Darwinian character, Wolf Larson, on the ocean in a ship in *The Sea-Wolf* (1904). Stephen Crane (1871–1900) likewise uses the ocean as a Darwinian image when the oiler, the best swimmer in "The Open Boat" (1897), drowns at sea. Many of Crane's works, like London's, have nature or the social environment—as in *Maggie, A Girl of the Streets* (1893)—pitted against the main character, and this seemingly inescapable enemy often gets the better of those characters ill equipped in the fight for survival.

Edith Wharton (1862–1937) also employed nature as the setting for much of her fiction, using it most often as an uncaring but undeniably violent entity; while many of her works are inspired by her acceptance of Darwinism, *Ethan Frome* (1911) is perhaps the best illustration of this idea. In the story, the title character gives in to his sexual and romantic attraction to a young relative; knowing that they cannot be together and thus be happy, the married Ethan climbs aboard a sled with the girl and attempts to kill them both. Ironically, nature and chance, in the form of a large tree, intervene with Ethan's plans, and the two characters end up miserable physical and emotional cripples as a result. Wharton demonstrates Darwin's awareness that even when characters are fit for survival, chance often wins out in the end.

Perhaps the most compelling example of Darwinism's element of sexual selection in American fiction is *Sister Carrie* (1900) by Theodore Dreiser (1871–1945). Explicit in its bleak portrayal of the darker side of the Darwinian reality, *Sister Carrie* is one of the most important novels of the early modern era. Theodore Dreiser's naturalist novel is an important bridge from the genteel works of the American realists to the gritty modernist prose that would come later.

Dreiser's *Sister Carrie* is among the first novels in American literature whose female protagonist breaks from culturally constructed codes of morality, puts her own interests ahead of others as well as any notions of right and wrong, and yet still comes out a winner. While initially an impoverished young woman from the country, Dreiser's youthful heroine makes it to the top of society's ladder by "selecting" first Drouet, a budding entrepreneur, and then Hurstwood, a successful married businessman, to assist her in making her social and financial ascent. When Hurstwood, her married lover, ceases to be of use to her, Carrie's complete abandonment of him results in his financial ruin and suicide. It would appear that Carrie is far more "naturally" suited to the harsh environment of the city than Hurstwood, for ultimately it is she who makes the ascent to artistic fame.

Dreiser's implementation of Darwinian language is unmistakable, and Carrie's selection, control, and ultimate rejection of Hurstwood exemplifies the principles of selection when applied to a "natural" (or naturalistic) woman. This natural characterization of Carrie is evidence of Dreiser's desire to present human behavior as a response to biological needs. While the text of *Sister Carrie* seems bleak indeed, it appears that Dreiser was merely replicating what he viewed as the harsh but natural reality around him, as were most American writers of the day.

As object of desire and subsequent catalyst for struggle between males, Carrie epitomizes the Darwinian female; she amorally chooses the male most likely to assist her in her struggle for success and survival. Dreiser's dark realism evinces the growing awareness of Darwin's theory regarding natural selection with its insistent "struggle for existence" as an important influence on human behavior.

See also Scientific Materialism; *Sister Carrie;* Social Darwinism

BIBLIOGRAPHY
Primary Works
Chopin, Kate. *The Awakening.* 1899. New York: Avon Books, 1994.

Crane, Stephen. *Maggie, A Girl of the Streets.* 1893. New York: Bantam, 1988.

Crane, Stephen. *The Open Boat and Other Stories*. 1897. Boston: Dover, 1993.

Darwin, Charles. *The Descent of Man and Selection in Relation to Sex*. 1871. Amherst, N.Y.: Prometheus Books, 1998.

Darwin, Charles. *On the Origin of Species by Means of Natural Selection*. 1859. Reprinted as *The Origin of Species*. Oxford: Oxford University Press, 1996.

Dreiser, Theodore. *Sister Carrie*. 1900. New York: Penguin, 1994.

Ellis, Havelock. *Studies in the Psychology of Sex*. 2 vols. New York: Random House, 1936.

London, Jack. *Martin Eden*. 1913. New York: Penguin, 1994.

London, Jack. *The Sea-Wolf*. 1904. New York: Bantam, 1992.

Wharton, Edith. *Ethan Frome*. 1911. New York: Signet, 2000.

Secondary Works

Gould, Stephen Jay. *The Structure of Evolutionary Theory*. Cambridge, Mass.: Belknap Press of Harvard University Press, 2002.

Gowaty, Patricia. *Feminism and Evolutionary Biology: Boundaries, Intersections, and Frontiers*. New York: Chapman and Hall, 1997.

Martin, Ronald E. *American Literature and the Universe of Force*. Durham, N.C.: Duke University Press, 1981.

Persons, Stow. *Evolutionary Thought in America*. New Haven, Conn.: Yale University Press, 1950.

Russett, Cynthia Eagle. *Darwin in America: The Intellectual Response, 1865–1912*. San Francisco: W. H. Freeman, 1976.

Young, Peyton. *Individual Strategy and Social Structure: An Evolutionary Theory of Institutions*. Princeton, N.J.: Princeton University Press, 2001.

Deirdre Ray

DIME NOVELS

The subject of scorn by moralists in the last quarter of the nineteenth century and the first quarter of the twentieth, "dime novel" was originally a brand name, but as has often been true of trademarks in America, it became a generic term and was soon applied to any work of sensational fiction despite the cover price. The publisher Irwin P. Beadle & Co. named its series of inexpensive storybooks Beadle's Dime Novels, and the name stuck. Beadle's first novel, *Malaeska: The Indian Wife of the White Hunter* (1860) by Ann Sophia Stephens (1813–1886), established early in the popular mind the western frontier of the United States as the paradigmatic theme of the dime novel despite the fact that the books covered a multitude of themes: mystery and detective stories, school and sports stories, comic stories, sea stories (including pirates), love stories

Advertising poster for Beadle's Dime and Half Dime Libraries. THE LIBRARY OF CONGRESS

(a very popular category), and science fiction (principally stories of boy inventors). There were also stories of the Revolutionary War, the Civil War, and of slaves as in Metta Victor's *Maum Guinea and Her Plantation "Children"* (1861), which sold more than 100,000 copies in short order and was translated into several languages. Abraham Lincoln pronounced it "as absorbing as Uncle Tom's Cabin" (Harvey, p. 39). For many readers the best of the dime novels were the first ones, those published by Beadle & Co. and its successor, Beadle & Adams, and they sold by the millions.

With such success competition is never far behind. A former employee at Beadle, George Munro, along with his brother Norman L. Munro, the sensational Frank Tousey, and Street & Smith, soon joined Beadle as major publishers of dime novels. The early books were small sextodecimo volumes of a hundred or so pages and emphasized recurring authors over continuing characters. In the 1870s the ten-cent and five-cent weeklies introduced the concept of continuing characters with the stories of Dick Talbot, Deadwood Dick, Buffalo Bill, and others. When mystery and detective stories became popular, the recurring heroes included Old Sleuth, Old Cap. Collier, Old King Brady, Joe Phenix, and the incomparable Nick Carter.

At first the readership consisted of adults, but by the 1870s publications designed to appeal to younger readers, primarily male, were common and story papers such as Frank Tousey's *Boys of New York* and Norman L. Munro's *Golden Hours* published serials and short stories specifically for the youth market. The five-cent weeklies were either anthologies of stories in various categories (travel and exploration, frontier and western, mystery and detective) or contained the continuing adventures of an individual hero as in the weekly *Diamond Dick Library*.

Public reaction to dime novels was mixed. Early critics welcomed the concept behind Beadle's "dollar book for a dime" (see Johannsen 1:31), which placed literature within the reach of the poorest reader and thus encouraged reading. Later critics might question the amount of violence but seldom the language; curses in the text were often represented by dashes. Some critics blamed the dime novel for leading boys astray, the same criticism that was leveled at movies, radio, and comic books during a later generation. When the dime novels and story papers ceased publication around 1915, nostalgia replaced criticism and collectors prized copies rescued from the trash. In 1922 the New York Public Library mounted an exhibit of dime novels, primarily Beadles from the collection given to the institution by Dr. Frank P. O'Brien. The dime novel has long been the subject of scholarly attention.

FRONTIER AND WESTERN STORIES

According to Daryl Jones in *The Dime Novel Western* (1978), there were six basic heroes: the backwoodsman, the miner, the outlaw, the plainsman, the cowboy, and the rancher. Many figures in the dime novel western belonged to more than one category. The backwoodsman served as guide to parties traveling through the new country in emulation of James Fenimore Cooper's Leatherstocking. Edward S. Ellis's Seth Jones (in the 1860 novel *Seth Jones; or, The Captives of the Frontier*) established the formula within the dime novel. Oll Coomes's Old Kit Bandy was a variant of the type, serving as both guide and comic relief. So popular was Deadwood Dick between 1877 and 1885, the year his creator Edward L. Wheeler died, that the publisher created a successor, Deadwood Dick Jr. (no blood relative). The writer of most of the new stories was Jesse C. Cowdrick, author of the Broadway Billy stories, who used Wheeler's name as a pseudonym. Deadwood Dick had no basis in fact, despite claims put forth to identify any number of individuals as the original of the character, while Calamity Jane, his companion in adventure, bore no resemblance to the historical figure either in appearance or in characteristics. They were creatures of the imagination.

Buffalo Bill, on the other hand, had a factual basis in William F. Cody (1846–1917), though the dime novel character was a romanticized version of the scout and showman of history. He was introduced to the public in 1869 by Edward Zane Carroll Judson (1823–1886, better known by his pen name Ned Buntline) in the serial *Buffalo Bill, the King of Border Men* in Street & Smith's *New York Weekly*. Despite writing two more Buffalo Bill serials for Street & Smith, inserting the character as a secondary figure in a third serial, and writing a stage play, *Scouts of the Prairies* (1872), Buntline wrote only one additional story about the scout, a serial for Beadle & Adams in 1885. Apparently not interested in maintaining the franchise, Buntline stepped aside and allowed Colonel Prentiss Ingraham (1843–1904) to continue the presentation of Cody's adventures to an eager public. When Ingraham died in 1904, having written eighty Buffalo Bill stories for Beadle & Adams and forty-eight for Street & Smith, other writers provided new stories until 1912. As portrayed by Buntline, Buffalo Bill was part backwoodsman, part prospector, and part plainsman with a bit of Native American as far as his skill at following a trail was concerned. Little in the dime novels was based on anything Buffalo Bill accomplished in real life; rather his exploits were what the public expected of such a legendary figure. When Buffalo Bill established his Wild West Show in the 1880s the blend of fact and fiction was complete. His costume in the arena and his costume in the cover illustrations became the same.

Albert W. Aiken's Dick Talbot preceded Deadwood Dick in print by six years and combined the abilities of the gambler, the road agent, and the miner with those of the rancher. In addition Talbot had the traditional mysterious past (which he had left behind him in the east) of many dime novel heroes. A recurring theme in the series was Talbot's wooing, winning, and losing (sometimes to death) many a young lady, a condition of which he is painfully aware. Richard Wade, frontier lawman, miner, and cowboy hero, was better known as Diamond Dick from the sparkling diamonds that decorated his clothes and the diamond sights on his revolvers. The identification with the miner came from the silver mine he inherited. He was based in part on the medicine show entertainer George McClellan, nicknamed "Diamond Dick." Wade was unique among dime novel heroes in having a son, Bertie, a blood relation, who traveled with him. Eventually the elder Wade retired and his son, known as Diamond Dick Jr., carried on the tradition of righting wrongs throughout the West. Other western heroes, such as Ted Strong and Young Wild West, fit the model of heroes as cowboys and ranchers and operated in the twentieth century driving vintage automobiles and riding horses. Young Wild West ended his adventurous career on the battlefields of Europe in the First World War.

MYSTERY AND DETECTIVE STORIES

Where the dime novel western borrowed characters and themes from Cooper, the detective story drew on the recorded exploits of the legendary Allan Pinkerton (1819–1884) and the men of his detective agency. The earliest detective serial in a story paper was probably the novelized version of Tom Taylor's play *The Ticket of Leave Man,* which appeared in the weekly *Flag of Our Union* in 1865. This was followed by Kenward Philp's "The Bowery Detective" in the *New York Fireside Companion* in 1870. But the first detective hero to appear in a series of stories was Old Sleuth, the creation of Harlan Page Halsey, in the same story paper two years later in 1872. In time the stories were signed by Old Sleuth as well, so there was an instant recognition that they were detective stories. In the first Old Sleuth story, the hero was a young man masquerading as an older one, a convention that was not maintained. A decade later the first publication specializing in detective fiction appeared, Norman Munro's *Old Cap. Collier Library* (1883), followed a few weeks later by Frank Tousey's *New York Detective Library.* Both were anthologies of stories about a variety of detectives. The first weekly publication to feature the continuing adventures of a single detective was the *Nick Carter Library,* which began in 1891.

The Pinkerton model for the detective was a man or woman who was the best in his or her profession, one to whom the official police could turn in time of crisis. He or she borrowed the skills of the hunter when tracking a suspect and thus was little different from the heroes of Cooper. Questioning the client and various suspects was accompanied by a visit to the scene of the crime. The detective was often layers deep in disguise and solved crimes as much by diligent eavesdropping incognito as by scientific deduction. The type of crime varied, though murder was prominent. While readers were allowed to observe the detective at work, there was little opportunity to match wits with the detective. The solution often depended on the detective gaining an understanding of the histories of the characters (victim and suspects), and in this the works of French novelist Émile Gaboriau (1832– 1873) served as models. After the Sherlock Holmes stories became popular in 1891, many writers emulated them.

Traditionally the dime novel detective was old and wise and the name sometimes reflected this, often with tongue in cheek: Old Search, Old Hawkeye, Old Neverfail, Old Bull's Eye, Old Spicer. In addition there were a number of women detectives, some of whom served as assistants to the hero (e.g., Ida Jones in the Nick Carter stories), others who worked on their own (e.g., Lady Kate Edwards in the *Old Sleuth Library*). The geriatric sleuth was eventually replaced by a series of younger men who were the equal of any predecessors. Nick Carter led the way as a youthful man in charge of an agency of sleuths with whom the boy readers could more readily identify and who solved mysteries for kings and presidents in a manner that was the envy of his readers. He competed with, but did not entirely replace, the western hero in the marketplace.

SCHOOL AND SPORTS STORIES

The boarding school story made famous in England by Thomas Hughes's *Tom Brown's School Days* (1857) was represented in the dime novels largely by stories reprinted from British sources. The Jack Harkaway series by Bracebridge Hemyng that began as stories set in a British boarding school continued as accounts of Harkaway's globetrotting adventures. The majority of the sports stories in dime novels were set in boarding schools or colleges and universities with the sport taking precedence over academic studies. The greatest and most popular school and sports hero was Frank Merriwell of Yale, the creation of Gilbert Patten writing as Burt L. Standish. With his skill at saving damsels in distress (one of whom he eventually married), winning at every sport he played, traveling to the far corners of the world, and gathering around him a coterie of friends who would die for him, he was indeed the idol of American youth. Beginning in 1896, Merriwell's regular adventures in Street & Smith's *Tip Top Weekly* were the staple of many a boy's library. The stories were kept in print for four decades. Merriwell had many imitators (Jack Lightfoot, Frank Manley, Fred Fearnot, Jack Standfast) but no equals.

SCIENCE FICTION

While a variety of stories could be called prototypes of science fiction, most involved some form of exotic travel by means of hot air balloon or fast land craft, in emulation of Jules Verne. Frank Tousey had a monopoly on these in the stories of the boy inventors Frank Reade Jr. and Jack Wright who filled the skies with imaginative airships and the seas with fantastic submersibles. The majority of the stories in both series was the work of one man, Luis Senarens (1865–1939), writing under the unimaginative pseudonym "Noname." The Frank Reade and Jack Wright stories began appearing in the 1870s in the story papers and were collected in the five-cent weeklies before disappearing from the newsstands in the onslaught of the new pulp magazines.

THE CRITICS AND THE END OF AN ERA

Dime novel publishers succeeded by utilizing the latest technology in papermaking, printing, and distribution to supply a newly literate market with inexpensive reading matter. Early criticism of dime novels usually came in the form of editorials that derided them as so much immoral sensationalism or blamed juvenile delinquency on the reading of cheap fiction. One famous case in 1874 involved Jesse Pomeroy, a fourteen-year-old who murdered two children. According to Edmund Pearson in *Dime Novels* (p. 93) the prosecution suggested he might have been led to his crimes by the reading of "cheap 'literature of the dime novel type.'" But Pomeroy denied ever having read a dime novel in his life. There were a number of rebuttals to these attacks. Beadle & Adams produced several editorials in defense of dime novels in the pages of their *Saturday Journal* and *Banner Weekly*. They even published a list of the guidelines they provided their authors in which (among other stipulations) they prohibited anything "offensive to good taste" (Pearson, p. 96). After an 1884 editorial in the *New York Tribune* which claimed boys were encouraged to run away to the Wild West by reading dime novels, Captain Frederick Whittaker, a dime novelist of long standing, wrote an extensive defense of the books. Prentiss Ingraham weighed in on two fronts, a letter to the *Mobile Sunday Times* in 1888 and a footnote in one of his "Dick Doom" stories for *Beadle's Half-Dime Library* in 1892

in which he denied the allegations that dime novel writers encouraged boys to leave home.

In the early twentieth century it was a combination of the pulp magazines and the movies that spelled the end of the dime novel. The same price once paid for the dime novel could buy more reading material in the pulp magazine or a vivid adventure on the silver screen. Readers in the 1920s looked back at the dime novels of their youth with nostalgia, remembering the way the slim books had fueled their imaginations, and they built collections of their childhood favorites. As Charles M. Harvey says in his essay for the *Atlantic Monthly*, "How those heroes and heroines and their allies, their enemies and their doings, cling to the memory across the gulf of years!" (p. 37) The value of the dime novels for later generations is as social history, collections of attitudes and beliefs from a period in American history when the hero always won and the villain received his comeuppance in the last chapter.

See also Book Publishing; Mystery and Detective Fiction

BIBLIOGRAPHY
Primary Works
Author of "Old Cap. Collier" [William I. James]. "The Seaside Detective; or, Ironclad in the Employ of the Government." *Old Cap. Collier Library* 4 (12 May 1883).

Buntline, Ned [Edward Zane Carroll Judson]. "Buffalo Bill's Best Shot." *Log Cabin Library* 127 (20 August 1891).

A Celebrated Author [Frederic Van Rensselaer Dey]. "Nick Carter, Detective. The Solution of a Remarkable Case." *Nick Carter Detective Library* 1 (8 August 1891).

Moore, Harry [Stephen Angus Douglas Cox]. "The Liberty Boys of '76'; or, Fighting for Freedom." *Liberty Boys of '76* 1 (4 January 1901).

A New York Detective [Francis W. Doughty]. "Old King Brady, the Sleuth-Hound." *New York Detective Library* 154 (14 November 1885).

"Noname" [Luis P. Senarens]. "Frank Reade, Jr., and His Queen Clipper of the Clouds. A Thrilling Story of a Wonderful Voyage in the Air." *Wide Awake Library* 993–994 (1–4 October 1890).

An Old Scout [Cornelius Shea]. "Young Wild West, the Prince of the Saddle." *Wild West Weekly* 1 (24 October 1902).

Old Sleuth [Harlan Page Halsey]. "Old Sleuth, the Detective; or, The Bay Ridge Mystery." *Old Sleuth Library* 1 (3 March 1885).

Standish, Burt L. [Gilbert Patten]. "Frank Merriwell at Yale; or, Freshman against Freshman." *Tip Top Weekly* 40 (16 January 1897).

Wheeler, Edward L. "Deadwood Dick, the Prince of the Road; or, The Black Rider of the Black Hills." *Beadle's Half-Dime Library* 1 (15 October 1877).

Secondary Works

Cox, J. Randolph. *The Dime Novel Companion: A Source Book.* Westport, Conn.: Greenwood Press, 2000.

Curti, Merle. "Dime Novels and the American Tradition." *Yale Review* 26 (1937): 761–778.

Denning, Michael. *Mechanic Accents: Dime Novels and Working-Class Culture in America.* New York: Verso, 1987. Revised edition, 1998.

Harvey, Charles M. "The Dime Novel in American Life." *Atlantic Monthly* 100 (July 1907): 37–45.

Johannsen, Albert. *The House of Beadle and Adams and Its Dime and Nickel Novels: The Story of a Vanished Literature.* 3 vols. Illustrated. Norman: University of Oklahoma Press, 1950–1962. The Multimedia Digitization Lab at the Northern Illinois University Libraries in DeKalb has much of Johannsen's text online at http://www.niulib.niu.edu/badndp/bibindex.html. The website includes additional material such as cover art and full texts of numerous dime novels.

Jones, Daryl. *The Dime Novel Western.* Bowling Green, Ohio: Popular Press, Bowling Green State University, 1978.

Noel, Mary. *Villains Galore: The Heyday of the Popular Story Weekly.* New York: Macmillan, 1954.

Pearson, Edmund. *Dime Novels; or, Following an Old Trail in Popular Literature.* Boston: Little, Brown, 1929.

Smith, Henry Nash. *Virgin Land: The American West as Symbol and Myth.* Cambridge, Mass.: Harvard University Press, 1950.

Stern, Madeleine B., ed. *Publishers for Mass Entertainment in Nineteenth Century America.* Boston: G. K. Hall, 1980.

Sullivan, Larry E., and Lydia Cushman Schurman, eds. *Pioneers, Passionate Ladies, and Private Eyes: Dime Novels, Series Books, and Paperbacks.* New York: Haworth Press, 1996.

Tebbel, John. *A History of Book Publishing in the United States.* 4 vols. New York: Bowker, 1972–1981. Volume 1, *The Creation of an Industry, 1630–1865,* and volume 2, *The Expansion of an Industry, 1865–1919,* are especially pertinent to the present essay.

J. Randolph Cox

DISASTERS

By the end of the nineteenth century in America, disasters occupied a prominent place in both mass media and the popular imagination, especially for those flocking to the cities. As Carl Smith notes in *Urban Disorder and the Shape of Belief,* "The increasing organization of human activity in cities was so repeatedly punctuated by major disruptions that disorder itself seemed to be one of the defining qualities of urban culture" (p. 1).

Newspaper publishers sought to increase circulation with huge banner headlines announcing the news of floods, fires, and volcanic eruptions all around the world. Quite simply, narratives of misfortune sold papers. Not only newspapers but also important periodicals like *Harper's* and *Atlantic Monthly* ran major feature articles following disasters, complete with eyewitness accounts and often with graphic illustrations and photographs. In the case of those major disasters that instantly caught public attention—like the San Francisco earthquake of 1906 or the 1912 sinking of the *Titanic*—publishers rushed whole books into print, often in a matter of months or even weeks, seeking to profit from the widespread and seemingly insatiable interest in these events.

Public curiosity about disasters eventually led to the development of new forms of mass entertainment. At New York's Coney Island amusement park, pleasure seekers eagerly experienced a variety of disaster reenactments, from the Johnstown (Pennsylvania) flood of 1889 to the Galveston (Texas) hurricane of 1900. Such "faux disasters" as those at Coney Island allowed people to escape the monotony of urban industrial life and at the same time subtly suggest that the effects of disaster could be minimized, managed, even mastered. In Ted Steinberg's words, "Perhaps no better way existed for coming to grips with the anxiety spawned by the spate of turn-of-the-century disasters than to schedule a trial run at apocalypse" (p. 3). And these spectacles were clearly big business. Andrea Stulman Dennett and Nina Warnke have called Coney Island "one of America's first permanent commitments to commercial leisure," noting that between 1897 and 1904 the amusement park was transformed from a "scandalous and unsavory place" to a "technologically sophisticated mass-entertainment center" (p. 101). Disaster attractions had wide appeal, drawing patrons from different social and economic classes and feeding the burgeoning amusements industry.

DEFINING DISASTER

Even as disasters were becoming the source of new forms of entertainment, they would soon become the subject of serious academic study, not only in the scientific and engineering communities but among those scholars developing the modern social sciences. The first attempt to derive a social theory explaining human response to disaster was a 1920 Columbia University sociology doctoral dissertation by Samuel Henry Prince, later published in several different editions

DISASTERS, 1870–1920

Chicago Fire: On Sunday evening, 8 October 1871, a fire began somewhere near the O'Leary barn in Chicago. Driven by strong winds, the fire soon burned out of control. The so-called Burnt District comprised an area four miles long and three-quarters of a mile wide, or about two thousand acres. More than 100,000 people were left homeless. On the same night, the deadliest forest fire ever, in Peshtigo, Wisconsin, killed nearly twenty-five hundred people and destroyed an area the size of Rhode Island.

Boston Fire: On 12 November 1872 a fire in the business district of Boston destroyed almost 800 buildings and caused $75 million in damage. Among those who suffered in the fire was James R. Osgood, publisher of the *Atlantic Monthly* and of many important American authors. Osgood's warehouse was destroyed, and a year later all of his remaining assets (including the original plates of famous books) were liquidated.

Johnstown Flood: On the afternoon of 31 May 1889 residents of Johnstown, Pennsylvania, were inundated by a wave of water when the poorly maintained South Fork Dam on the Little Conemaugh River failed due to overtopping, killing thousands.

Galveston Hurricane: On 8 September 1900 a hurricane with winds of 145 mph and a storm surge of almost 16 feet killed between 6,000 and 8,000 people in the Texas city of Galveston, whose population at the time was around 37,000.

San Francisco Earthquake: At 5:00 A.M. on 18 April 1906 San Francisco was jolted by an earthquake on the San Andreas Fault. The quake, which lasted a minute, is estimated to have been about 8.25 on the later-developed Richter scale. Although many poorly constructed buildings were destroyed in the quake, even greater destruction occurred from many fires that ignited after the earthquake. The earthquake and fires together left 250,000 people homeless and caused $350 million of property damage. The actual death toll remains unknown.

Cherry Mine Disaster: On 13 November 1909, 259 men died in one of the worst coal-mining disasters ever. At Cherry, just north of La Salle, Illinois, a fire started when hay used to feed mules was stored too close to an open torch inside the mine. The disaster eventually led to the adoption of workers' compensation laws.

Triangle Shirtwaist Fire: Near closing time on 25 March 1911, the Triangle Shirtwaist Factory in New York City caught fire, killing nearly 150 of the 500 workers, mostly young women. Many of the workers were immigrants. Workers were trapped, unable to reach safety, by locked doors and broken fire escapes. Unable to escape the burning building, many leapt to their deaths on the sidewalks below, to the horror of passersby.

Sinking of the *Titanic*: At almost midnight on 14 April 1912 the *Titanic,* the largest ship ever built, hit an iceberg on its maiden voyage. Because the ship was considered "unsinkable," there were lifeboats for only about half of the twenty-two hundred passengers and crew. Neither the crew nor the passengers had any training in how to use the lifeboats, and only about seven hundred survivors were rescued the next morning by a passing ship.

***Eastland* Disaster:** On 24 July 1915 the passenger ship *Eastland,* docked in downtown Chicago, rolled over, killing over eight hundred passengers within just a few feet of the shore. Most of the passengers were young employees of the Western Electric Company who had received tickets for a pleasure cruise on Lake Michigan. The passenger death toll on the *Eastland* actually exceeded the non-crew death toll of the *Titanic* disaster.

Halifax Explosion: On the morning of 6 December 1917 two warships, one of them a French ship carrying thousands of pounds of munitions, collided in fog in Halifax Harbor in Nova Scotia. The resulting explosions killed more than two thousand people and injured nine thousand. It destroyed 256 acres along the waterfront and left more than 750 families homeless.

Influenza Pandemic: In 1918 and 1919 influenza swept the world, killing more people than the Great War had killed. Sailors and soldiers returning home apparently brought the influenza with them to America, where approximately 675,000 died of the disease.

as *Catastrophe and Social Change* (Fischer, p. 9). Prince, who studied the 1917 Halifax (Nova Scotia) Harbor explosion, which he had witnessed, argued that disasters bring about both social and technological change. Prince was particularly concerned with how communities tried to recover from disasters and how disaster could exacerbate class differences. Thus the study of disasters begins with considerations of how such events change the communities that experience them.

Prince's work is generally seen as the beginning of a field of social science called "disaster studies" (or even "disastrology"), which emerged in full force in the late 1940s after World War II, the Holocaust, and the bombing of Hiroshima. Thus, much of what is known about the catastrophes of 1870–1920 has been filtered through the lens of later theories. But even long before Prince's work, it is clear that people understood catastrophic events in a number of ways—as failures of technology or of moral action or as the wrath of a vengeful God. Disasters often affected communities as a war would, leaving them in shock and highlighting vulnerabilities and weaknesses.

One can easily construct a timeline of American events between 1870 and 1920, all of which were widely viewed by contemporaries and later by historians as "disasters." Especially around the turn of the century, as the print media became a more powerful force in American life, these events amounted to just about one major news story a year. Coverage of these events not only sold newspapers but also provided inspiration for both serious literature and popular culture texts and performances.

DISASTER AND FICTION: *BARRIERS BURNED AWAY*

Popular writers used actual disasters as settings for novels and short stories, which often explored how ordinary people react in times of extraordinary trauma. Perhaps the most famous of these works was the Reverend Edward Payson Roe's 1872 melodramatic novel *Barriers Burned Away,* which became a best-seller for the fledgling publisher Dodd, Mead after two other publishers turned it down. Roe, who had served as an army chaplain during the Civil War, used the Chicago fire of 1871 as the backdrop for a novel that espoused Roe's own Christian democratic ideals. The plot follows an earnest, religious young man from the country, Dennis Fleet, who falls in love with Christine, the haughty, city-bred daughter of his wealthy and ambitious employer, the art dealer Baron Ludolph. As a result of the catastrophic events of the night of fire—in just one chapter, Dennis witnesses the death of Baron Ludolph, saves Christine from being ravished by a "ruffian" who had "planted his

big grimy hand in the delicate frill of her night-robe" (p. 398), and steals a pair of boots for "her tender little feet" from a deserted shoe shop (p. 400)—Dennis persuades Christine to renounce her life of materialism and to accept his Christian values. The message of the novel is unmistakably heavy-handed, and the style is somewhat overwrought and the plot improbable in places—for example, as the fire bears down upon them, Dennis tells Christine: "I give you just five minutes in which to make your toilet and gather a light bundle of your choicest valuables. Dress in woolen throughout and dress warmly" (p. 396). Still, Roe's narration often manages to capture well the chaos and frenzy of the disaster. The events are portrayed, quite simply, as both terrifying and disorienting. But more important than any attempts at a realistic rendering of the events is the way the fire serves the novelist as a metaphor for spiritual redemption and the source of new life. The fire has a cleansing effect. All the class and religious differences that had separated the two characters are swept away (or rather, "burned away") in the conflagration, and even as she loses everything she has prized before, Christine is transformed spiritually. The novel emphasizes the idea that catastrophe is both a collective and an individual experience, bringing out the best and worst in human nature. Roe also makes it clear that even as Dennis's piety triumphs over Christine's materialism, the city is still and perhaps inevitably a dangerous place, where different classes of people with different values and morals lived alongside each other—in short, a place that "could burst into uncontrollable flame at any moment" (Smith, p. 63). Strangely, the survivors' experience could be simultaneously ennobling and debasing.

THE EARLIEST DISASTER FILMS

If post–Civil War melodrama seemed an ideal literary medium to explore the consequences and effects of disaster, by the turn of the century the new medium of film proved ideally suited to portraying both actual disasters and the kinds of disaster re-creations popularized at Coney Island. In the history of films in this era one sees the evolution of both documentary and dramatic films based on disaster. Reality came first. The majority of the films released in the United States between 1897 and 1903 were of the "actuality genre" (Dennet and Warnke, p. 107). Film footage by Edison Company photographers of the Mount Pelée eruption in Martinique was released in 1902. Film also captured the effects of the 1900 Galveston hurricane, and footage from the 1906 San Francisco earthquake was edited into a short documentary called *San Francisco: Aftermath of Earthquake*. These early documentary films allowed people to see for themselves the devastation they

Currier & Ives print of the Chicago Fire, 1871. THE LIBRARY OF CONGRESS

had read about in the newspapers. While some films relied on footage taken of the actual disaster to create a sense of reality and immediacy, others used re-creations, like Biograph's 1905 film *Fighting the Flames*.

After about 1910, reality began to give way to fictional dramas, especially fictional stories of individuals caught up in either real or fictional calamities. Still, the lines between fact and fiction were often blurred. Dorothy Gibson, an actress with the Éclair Moving Picture Company in New Jersey, was a first-class passenger on the *Titanic* when it sank in April 1912. Just a month later Éclair released a fictionalized version of Gibson's survival called *Saved from the Titanic*. In the film, written by Gibson herself, the character uses flashbacks to tell her parents the story of her adventure. The parents' horror is heightened by the knowledge that their daughter's future husband is a seaman, and the threat of death at sea in some future disaster remains. While disaster survivors were showcased in some films, the heroes who tried to save the victims of disaster took center stage in others. In films made by both Biograph and Edison in the first two decades of the twentieth century, firefighters often emerged as

the heroes (Dennett and Warnke, p. 109). Already present in these early films are the basic plotlines of the classic Hollywood blockbuster disaster film: individuals tested by the challenge of a collective catastrophe; distinct lives about to be entangled in calamity; personal sacrifice that creates a sense of community. This narrative formula was just waiting for mid-twentieth-century technological advances to make realistic special effects possible. And perhaps because there were very real limits on the extent to which early filmmakers could re-create disaster—without sound, without color, without sophisticated film-editing techniques—they tended to focus even more than later filmmakers would on the human and individual dimensions of disaster.

EXPLAINING AND RESPONDING TO DISASTER

Why disasters occur and whether they can be prevented became important questions during this period and often shaped the disaster narratives that emerged from these events. Writers often responded to disasters initially with a range of emotions that reflected the various stages a community might go through as it coped with a disaster and attempted to recover from it over a longer period of time. A fifteen-line poem titled "Chicago," written by Bret Harte (1836–1902), who at the time of the fire in 1871 had already established a reputation based on his local color stories and sketches, illustrates some of these emotions. The reader is reminded of Chicago's former glory—"she who but yesterday stood alone" (l. 3)—and asked to consider what remains of this "shattered throne" (l. 2). The second stanza reflects both on how quickly Chicago had grown up out of the land and how quickly the fire had destroyed it:

Like her own prairies by some chance seed sown,
Like her own prairies in one brief day grown;
Like her own prairies in one fierce night mown.
(Ll. 7–9)

The imagery here forces the reader to see the disaster not as the result of human failure but of the whim of nature. Harte moves from this image to the idea that the world will respond to Chicago, to "the cry for help that makes her kin to all" (l. 12), and finally to the idea that this support from the wider world will be more than mere sustenance: "with wan finger she may feel / The silver cup hid in the proffered meal" (ll. 13–14). The poem represents the cycle that any community affected by disaster might encounter, from glory to desolation, to an outpouring from other communities, to help, and to the hope of rebuilding. By 1893 Chicago had rallied sufficiently to defeat Washington, D.C., New York, and St. Louis for the right to host the World's Columbian Exposition.

While there were not necessarily more or even deadlier natural disasters during this era than there had been at earlier periods in history (or would be later on), the effects of the disasters that did occur were compounded by several demographic changes. Not only was the nation's overall population continually increasing, there also were significant shifts to crowded urban centers. In general, people demonstrated a willingness to live and work in places where the risks of disaster were relatively high. The development of large-scale transportation systems and large mechanized factories similarly increased the chances that a disaster involving large numbers of people would occur. Then too, there was often little if any government intervention to prevent or minimize community risk before disasters occurred. Developments in mass communications, along with higher literacy rates, meant that more people were more likely to learn the details about disasters that occurred elsewhere, often far away. And the development of photographic processes and the ability to reprint photographs meant that people would be able to witness, albeit secondhand and two-dimensionally,

the aftermath of disaster. Even people not affected directly by disaster learned quickly and in detail about calamity in other communities. As both verbal and visual disaster narratives were told and retold, people began to see not only patterns of similarity but also the larger implications of these events.

Technological disasters like the Triangle Shirtwaist Factory fire in New York City in 1911 and the sinking of the *Titanic* resulted in extensive government inquiries, and narratives about these events often focused on assigning blame. But natural disasters posed a somewhat more difficult problem to analyze and explain. While certainly many of these disasters could have been mitigated, even just by recognizing the dangers and preparing more thoroughly for them, ultimately nature remains a force beyond human control, a fact that can paradoxically either reassure or terrify a community. Historians have noted that in many instances the business community worked hard to downplay the seriousness of natural disasters and to emphasize the "accidental" (and thus both unpredictable and unpreventable) aspect of the disaster. In one sense disaster was simply "normalized." The aftermath of disaster often involved creating a narrative of events that would elicit enough sympathy to secure much-needed outside aid while protecting the city's image as a good place to do business. As Steinberg points out, in the aftermath of the Charleston earthquake of 1886, both business and religious leaders sought to convince people not to see the disaster as "punishment for human wickedness" but simply as "the result of Charleston's particular location" (p. 14). Shifting the focus away from the possibility of divine retribution was especially urgent when large segments of the population there, especially the African American working class, had taken to the streets, crying and praying for God's mercy. Rather than engage in prayer, people were encouraged to return to work as soon as possible and to begin the rebuilding process. Receiving aid was often linked directly to how hard a person was willing to work. The inclination of the poor and the uneducated to see the hand of God in any disaster makes perfect sense, though, when in almost every major disaster, whether natural or technological, the poor were likely to suffer disproportionately.

In most disasters, stories of heroism received much attention in the media, but oral histories preserve some of the grimmer and more gruesome aspects of calamity. The survivors' accounts of the Galveston hurricane of 1900, where as many as eight thousand people may have died in a single night, make it clear that disaster survivors faced extraordinary and overwhelming circumstances. Establishing order was obviously a priority, and looting, sometimes out of necessity and sometimes for profit, was always a problem. One survivor noted

Photograph of San Francisco shortly after the earthquake of 1906. THE LIBRARY OF
CONGRESS

that "if you were caught stooping you might be shot,"
recounting a story about a man discovered with his
pockets full of fingers and ears, having clearly stolen
jewelry off the corpses in the most efficient manner.
"He would have been shot," the survivor observes,
"but his wife was pregnant and she begged for him. So
they didn't shoot him" (Greene and Kelly, p. 178).
What also emerges from the survivors is the sense of
shock that pervades a community after a major disaster.
As one observer noted, it was a month before "the
people came out of the daze in Galveston and they
started to rebuild" (Greene and Kelly, p. 161).

The business community often seized on disaster
as an opportunity to rebuild on a much grander scale.
Kevin Rozario has explored the "surprising relations
between disaster, capitalism, and urban development"
(p. 75), noting that the "rhythm of ruin and renewal"
(p. 79) was already part of American culture by the
late nineteenth century, when modern capitalism
seemed to thrive on "creative destruction." Rozario

notes that while individual owners rarely welcome
destruction, it "liberates and recycles capital that has
'ossified' in fixed structures, thus clearing space for
new development and opening up new investment
opportunities" (p. 81). In a strange twist, what might
hurt the individual capitalist in the short term actually
benefits the larger capitalist economy in the long term.
The rhetoric that emerged from calamitous events was
usually rife with glowing predictions of future greatness. As one writer noted after the Johnstown flood in
1889: "In ten years Johnstown will be one of the pret-
tiest and busiest cities in the world, and nothing can
prevent it. The streets will be widened and probably
made to start from a common centre, something after
the fashion of Washington City" (Johnson, p. 389).
At the same time, in the rebuilding frenzy the business
community often downplayed or ignored significant
problems that may have exacerbated the disaster. The
most important case study here would be the San
Francisco earthquake of 1906. Business leaders tended

to emphasize the fire rather than the earthquake, since fire seemed a much more manageable threat than earthquake. While admittedly the fire caused more actual property damage, this emphasis caused people to overlook some very real seismic dangers, in particular, the danger of building on landfill. Steinberg argues that the business community engaged in a "conspiracy of seismic silence" (p. 36) well into the 1920s, to the eventual detriment of communities all along the West Coast, most of which failed to take adequate precautions.

Finally, one of the most enduring legacies of this period may be the expectation that communities facing disaster can always expect help from the outside. As the Red Cross created a program of disaster response and relief, community leaders and even ordinary individuals began to expect consistent aid in times of disaster (Popkin, p. 104). Eventually the local, state, and federal governments began to assume responsibility for disaster relief. The overwhelming response of people outside the affected community may well have encouraged people to continue living and working in high-risk areas and to rebuild after disaster rather than relocate to someplace less risky. In short, the determination to rebuild in the face of disaster became both an integral part of the national character and a predictable element of disaster narratives.

See also Chicago; Diseases and Epidemics; San Francisco

BIBLIOGRAPHY
Primary Works
Harte, Bret. "Chicago." *Every Saturday,* 28 October 1871, p. 426.

Roe, Edward Payson. *Barriers Burned Away.* New York: Dodd, Mead, 1872.

Secondary Works
Biel, Stephen, ed. *American Disasters.* New York: New York University Press, 2001.

Dennett, Andrea Stulman, and Nina Warnke. "Disaster Spectacles at the Turn of the Century." *Film History* 4, no. 2 (1990): 101–111.

Fischer, Henry W., III. *Response to Disaster: Fact versus Fiction and Its Perpetuation; The Sociology of Disaster.* Lanham, Md.: University Press of America, 1994.

Gilbert, Claude. "Studying Disaster: Changes in the Main Conceptual Tools." In *What Is a Disaster? Perspectives on the Question,* edited by E. L. Quarantelli, pp. 11–18. New York: Routledge, 1998.

Greene, Casey Edward, and Shelly Henley Kelly. *Through a Night of Horrors: Voices from the 1900 Galveston Storm.* College Station: Texas A&M Press, 2000.

Johnson, Willis Fletcher. *History of the Johnstown Flood.* Philadelphia: Edgewood, 1889.

Kirby, Andrew, ed. *Nothing to Fear: Risk and Hazards in American Society.* Tucson: University of Arizona Press, 1990.

Popkin, Roy S. "The History and Politics of Disaster Management in the United States." In *Nothing to Fear: Risks and Hazards in American Society,* edited by Andrew Kirby, pp. 101–129. Tucson: University of Arizona, 1990.

Prince, Samuel. *Catastrophe and Social Change, Based upon a Sociological Study of the Halifax Disaster.* New York: Columbia University, 1920.

Quarantelli, E. L., ed. *What Is a Disaster? Perspectives on the Question.* New York: Routledge, 1998.

Rozario, Kevin. "What Comes down Must Go Up: Why Disasters Have Been Good for American Capitalism." In *American Disasters,* edited by Stephen Biel. New York: New York University Press, 2001.

Smith, Carl. *Urban Disorder and the Shape of Belief.* Chicago: University of Chicago Press, 1995.

Steinberg, Ted. *Acts of God: The Unnatural History of Natural Disaster in America.* New York: Oxford University Press, 2000.

Nancy Morrow

DISEASES AND EPIDEMICS

The nineteenth century was a time of dramatic change for American medicine. By the end of the century, the practice of medicine had acquired some of the characteristics of a science. Until then, medical care had been based on a belief system that did not recognize health and disease as separate and distinct entities; instead, the standard thinking was that each person possessed relative degrees of healthiness and sickliness, which coexisted in a treacherously shifting state of unsteady balance. The writings of the ancient Greek physician Claudius Galen (129–c. 199 C.E.) had been the dominant medical authority for two thousand years. Medical knowledge was stagnant, and medical practitioners of the early nineteenth century did not have any real appreciation of the nature or basis of any of the disease processes they encountered. They were not aware that specific diseases could be linked to defined biological processes such as bacterial infections. Instead, vague and generalized theories of total body dysfunction were employed to account for every type of illness. Therapeutic interventions were not based on research in physiology, pathology, and pharmacology but instead were derived from beliefs and expectations centered upon emotions, philosophies, hopes, desires, cultural considerations, and the individual idiosyncrasies of each person. The medical historian John Warner has cited a Cincinnati practitioner of 1848 who wrote that "disease is not an entity, or real existence, but is only the organic and functional forces, or powers of life, modified by perversion of activity" (p. 63). The medical condition of every person was considered to be nebulous, uncertain, and at risk for unexpected change for the worse due to the constant interactions between each person's own constitutional makeup and the antagonistic forces of each individual's environment.

The commonplace events in the life of the average human—teething, puberty, menstrual cycles, and even the change in weather with each new season—were considered to be among the potentially unsettling and destabilizing events leading to the unhealthy imbalance contained within each person. As Charles Rosenberg describes the prevailing understanding, the body was "a kind of stew pot, or chemico-vital reaction, proceeding calmly only if all its elements remained appropriately balanced. . . . the body was a city under constant threat of siege" (p. 13). In the absence of knowledge about specific diseases, there could be no targeted therapy for any specific ailment. Instead, the role of the physician was to readjust the imbalance by manipulating the intake and outgo of the disordered system. Typically this was accomplished through adjusting the balance of the body's fluids and secretions by removing blood, stimulating perspiration or urination, or purging the gastrointestinal tract through drugs that induced vomiting or diarrhea. In theory, diseases could be either "sthenic" (strong) or "asthenic" (weak), but in practice virtually all were sthenic and therefore required treatments that would decrease the patients' level of animation. "Draining off excess excitement from the body was not entirely metaphorical" (p. 92), Warner explains, but in fact was the basis for the use of bloodletting, cathartics, emetics, and counterirritants. Restoring the body's delicate balance was serious business, and huge ("heroic") doses were required so the patient would have no doubt about the gravity of the treatment.

After centuries without significant change in philosophy or methodology, however, medical practice began to acquire a more scientific perspective. The greatest advances during the nineteenth century occurred in Europe. The newer approaches caught the attention of medical practitioners in the United States, and many of the wealthier and better-educated American physicians flocked to Paris from the 1820s through the 1860s in search of better medical training than they could obtain in the United States. The emphasis of Parisian medicine was on the healing power of nature, an attitude that was an abrupt departure from the aggressive interventional approaches of traditional American medicine. The French approach to medical care was observational rather than interventional, and for the first time large amounts of information on the natural history of specific disease processes were being collected and evaluated. The Paris school initiated the use of simple statistics to assess the outcomes of patient management, and nothing was taken on faith—all therapies were open to doubt until proven to be effective by collection and thoughtful interpretation of numerical data. By the 1860s the primary destination for the European-bound American physician-in-training shifted from France to Germany and Austria. Vienna was the center of attention due to the large numbers of patients who were available for study in large hospitals. Opportunities abounded for intensive clinical experience and education in pathological anatomy. The German method, based in laboratory science, was more actively investigative and dynamic than the French approach; compared to the aggressive therapeutic orientation of American medicine, the German medical system was more intensely focused on pathophysiology (the study of the underlying basis of disease).

THE IMPACT AND UNDERSTANDING OF INFECTIOUS DISEASE

In the early nineteenth century, infections such as typhoid fever, cholera, and scarlet fever were commonplace causes of death, but the cause of these illnesses was not understood. (The impact of infection became evident during the Civil War; more deaths among the war's 620,000 casualties could be attributed to disease than to battle.) As the century progressed, important medical advances were made by the observations of individual physicians, and infectious diseases were among the earliest disorders to be understood as distinct disease processes. Even before the microbial basis of infection was understood, the Hungarian physician Ignaz Semmelweis (1818–1865) demonstrated the benefit of hand washing in prevention of the spread of disease; he observed that there was a 12 percent rate of fatal postpartum infection in the patients of his medical colleagues (who did not wash their hands between performing autopsies and delivering babies), compared to the 3 percent rate for midwives (who did not perform autopsies). Semmelweis's observations made it clear that doctors were obviously spreading diseases from cadavers to living patients. By the end of the nineteenth century, the germ theory had become well established due to

The influenza epidemic of 1918. Volunteers dispense food to the children of affected families. The influenza epidemic of 1918–1919 killed as many as forty million people worldwide and resulted in widespread social dislocation. © BETTMANN/CORBIS

the work of Louis Pasteur (1822–1895), Robert Koch (1843–1910), and others. With the advent of the twentieth century, medicine was becoming a scientific enterprise, and the basis of epidemics had become far better understood.

An epidemic is an outbreak of disease in which large numbers of people are affected at the same time. Epidemics have recurred throughout the history of mankind and have had a profound influence on life, civilization, and culture. The bubonic plague or "black plague" of the Middle Ages had a devastating effect on European civilization, killing about 60 million people. Fleas carried on infected rats were responsible for the spread of the plague, but in the final analysis it was the crowded conditions and poor sanitation of European cities that contributed to the widespread devastation of the disease. Populations with ongoing exposure to specific infections are able to develop an

immunity that promotes their survival, but the introduction of the same disease can be deadly to a population that has never been exposed before; when European explorers brought "new" infections such as smallpox to the New World, native populations were decimated. The influenza epidemic of 1918–1919 had worldwide repercussions due to its high mortality rate. Life in the late twentieth and early twenty-first centuries has been profoundly affected by the AIDS epidemic, not only in areas such as Africa, where the mortality has been overwhelming, but also in Western nations, where rate of infection is influenced by socio-economic status and where social stigma has been one of many factors creating challenges in controlling the infection.

For the American of the late 1800s, the infections to be feared the most included yellow fever, scarlet fever, cholera, typhoid fever, smallpox, and tuberculosis.

YELLOW FEVER

Yellow fever, one of the more frightful epidemic diseases of the nineteenth century, has striking features that led to its accurate description even before many other infectious illnesses could be characterized. Yellow fever is an acute viral illness that is transmitted by the bite of a mosquito. (Both the yellow fever virus and its *Aedes aegypti* mosquito vector were believed to have been imported from Africa as a side effect of the slave trade.) Within a few days of the insect bite, yellow fever victims develop fever, body aches, headache, nausea, and severe weakness. Liver damage causes the jaundice that gives the disease its name, and bleeding from the gastrointestinal tract commonly follows (at times associated with profuse vomiting of dark blood). The yellow fever death rate in the nineteenth century ranged from 15 to 50 percent. Because of its mosquito vector, yellow fever was predominantly a summertime disease. It was particularly prevalent in American coastal cities from Galveston, Texas, to Baltimore, Maryland; the virus and the vector and the victims all traveled together on the ships that traveled from port to port. Epidemics of yellow fever were recurrent throughout the nineteenth century. New Orleans was the epicenter of infection and always had at least a few cases in the best of years. In 1847 there were 2,259 yellow fever deaths in New Orleans, and 9,000 people (9 percent of the city's population) died from the disease in 1853. The Mississippi River was a conduit that permitted the infection to migrate from its coastal origins and travel upstream by steamship, and severe outbreaks occurred in Vicksburg, Mississippi, and Memphis, Tennessee. In *Life on the Mississippi* (1883), Mark Twain (Samuel Langhorne Clemens, 1835–1910) recalled "a desolating visitation of the yellow-fever" in Memphis, where "the people were swept off by hundreds, by thousands; and so great was the reduction caused by flight and by death together, that the population was diminished three-fourths, and so remained for a time" (p. 321). Memphis had been devastated by yellow fever epidemics in 1873 (when nearly 4,000 people died) and again in 1878 (when there were over 5,000 deaths, representing about 10 percent of the city's population).

MARK TWAIN: THE FEAR OF SCARLET FEVER

The severe apprehension associated with a scarlet fever infection is evident in *Tom Sawyer's Conspiracy*, an unfinished short novel that Mark Twain began to write in 1897. Tom Sawyer tries to catch measles from his friend Joe Harper, but Joe's diagnosis is incorrect, and Tom comes down with scarlet fever instead: "the doctor found it warn't measles at all, but scarlet fever. When aunt Polly heard it she turned that white she couldn't get her breath, and was that weak she couldn't see her hand before her face, and if they hadn't grabbed her she would have fell. And it just made a panic in the town, too, and there wasn't a woman that had children but was scared out of her life" (*Tom Sawyer's Conspiracy*, p. 186).

Twain considered scarlet fever to be one of the worst illnesses that could be transmitted from one person to another. In *Life on the Mississippi*, he used the disease as a metaphor for the injury that can be innocently and unknowingly inflicted by a well-intentioned but ultimately harmful ally, a person who "is like your family physician, who comes and cures the mumps, and leaves the scarlet fever behind" (p. 309). When the son of his friend William Dean Howells contracted scarlet fever, Clemens wrote a letter to Howells in January 1884 that empathized with Howells's plight: "The scarlet fever, once domesticated, is a permanent member of the family. Money may desert you, friends forsake you, enemies grow indifferent to you, but the scarlet fever will be true to you, through thick and thin, till you be all saved or damned, down to the last one. I say these things to cheer you. The bare suggestion of scarlet fever in the family makes me shudder" (*Mark Twain's Letters* 2:439).

SCARLET FEVER

Scarlet fever was another contagious illness that could be identified with reasonable accuracy by nineteenth century physicians and patients even before its causative bacterial agent was identified. Infection with scarlet fever gives rise to a unique rash that is the basis of the infection's name. The rash is the result of a specific toxin that is produced by an underlying bacterial infection with *Streptococcus* organisms. Bacteriology was in its infancy in the nineteenth century, but Americans lived in fear of scarlet fever epidemics long before its causative organism was isolated from human tissue in 1874. The *Streptococcus* is widely distributed in nature and is capable of causing infection in a variety of tissues. Although infections with the *Streptococcus* organism are now generally regarded as being relatively benign, with fairly innocuous skin infections and "strep throat" being among the more common illnesses that result from streptococcal infections, this was not the case prior to the development of effective antibiotics in the mid-twentieth century. Until, then, streptococcal infections could be devastating and life threatening (and it seemed as though the streptococcal infections associated with scarlet fever were particularly deadly). Parents were terrorized by the infection for good reason. The victims were commonly children; in the last half of the nineteenth century, two-thirds of deaths from scarlet fever occurred in children under the age of five years. For Americans in the 1800s, an outbreak of scarlet fever generated a fear that rivaled the dread associated with epidemics of cholera and plague.

CHOLERA

Cholera was another highly feared disease of the era. This very contagious bacterial infection of the intestinal tract caused severe diarrhea, dehydration, and, very often, death. Cholera was an annual visitor that traveled up the Mississippi River every spring, carrying with it a high risk of mortality for anyone afflicted with the disease. It was more common and far more deadly than any other infection. Nothing else created such a sense of panic as the arrival of cholera, and the risk of becoming infected with the cholera bacterium loomed as an overwhelming worry for anyone who lived near the river. Every year, the infection appeared to originate in New Orleans in the spring and then spread northward up the Mississippi through the summer months. The disease shared the same routes that were favored by yellow fever as it moved from one port to the next, carried by the steamboat traffic. The 1849 cholera death toll was devastating. In St. Louis there were 4,557 deaths from cholera during the year, compared to 4,046 deaths from all other diseases combined. In the month of July alone, there were 1,895 cholera deaths from the city's total population of 50,000.

The medical profession's first obstacle in dealing with cholera came from its ignorance of the disease's cause. As with the other serious infections of the nineteenth century, cholera epidemics created overwhelming health problems long before cholera's infectious nature was demonstrated. In the medical thinking of the era, disease in general was not attributable to specific causative factors but instead was believed to be the result of poorly defined interactions between the personal characteristics of each patient and vague environmental factors. A highly regarded nineteenth-century St. Louis physician and professor of therapeutics at the Missouri Medical College, Dr. William McPheeters, believed that the only real hope of eradicating cholera would be "the withdrawal of the peculiar unknown atmospheric poison which has always given rise to it" (McPheeters, p. 81). Because the disease seemed to be most rampant in the parts of St. Louis that were the dampest, dirtiest, and most crowded, hygienic approaches were initiated whenever cholera struck. In addition to the general cleaning of the city, "bonfires were nightly built in nearly every street and the whole city repeatedly fumigated with tar and sulphur" (p. 81), an approach that undoubtedly created a scene of ghastly smoky terror throughout the city and did nothing to reassure the minds of the fainthearted. When the 1849 outbreak finally subsided late in the year, McPheeters noted that the general level of health in St. Louis had become remarkably good, and in keeping with the concept of an environmental (rather that a bacteriological) basis for the epidemic, he suggested that "once the storm of disease had subsided the atmosphere seemed to be purified by its fury and rendered fitter for respiration" (pp. 83–84).

TYPHOID FEVER

Typhoid fever, also referred to as enteric fever, was another important contagious disease of the late nineteenth and early twentieth centuries. The disease is caused by an infection with *Salmonella* bacteria and transmitted through direct contact with an infected individual or through ingestion of contaminated food. Person-to-person spread is a particularly important mechanism of dissemination of the illness, as demonstrated by the case of "typhoid Mary," a cook in the early twentieth century who spread infection to approximately fifty other people. Typhoid fever is usually associated with high fever, abdominal pain, and enlargement of the liver and spleen. Other features can include diarrhea, a typical rash that is characterized by "rose spots," and neuropsychiatric features that can include confusion or delirium. As was the case with scarlet fever, the typical features of typhoid fever permitted accurate recognition of the disease even before its specific bacteriological cause was pinned down. Before the era of antibiotics, the death rate from typhoid fever was around 15 percent; the survivors commonly suffered a prolonged illness that lasted for weeks, with an interval of debilitation that could last for months.

Infectious diseases, especially those with a lingering course and significant mortality, became popular subjects for writers wishing to deal with topics of mortality, justice, suffering, anguish, and ethical dilemmas. For example, Samuel Clemens used his personal experiences with typhoid fever in a story first published in the December 1902 issue of *Harper's*. In "Was It Heaven? Or Hell?" Clemens addressed the ethical question of whether a physician should lie to a patient in order to give the patient hope. In order to write this story, Clemens needed a disease that was contagious, ran a prolonged course, and was associated with a fairly high death rate. Typhoid fever was the perfect disease for the story. Clemens first became familiar with the details of infection with typhoid fever when his wife Livy developed the illness in 1871. The Clemens household had initially been exposed to the disease in 1870 when Emma Nye, an old school friend of Livy's, came down with typhoid fever during a visit. Sam and Livy Clemens nursed Nye through her prolonged illness and thus observed every terrible feature of the infection firsthand. In a letter written in September 1870, Clemens lamented that "poor little Emma Nye lies in our bed-chamber fighting wordy battles with the phantoms of delirium. . . . The disease is a consuming fever—of a typhoid type. . . . the poor girl is dangerously ill" (*Mark Twain's Letters* 4:191). The Clemens family watched Nye's gradual and miserable death from the devastating illness, and there is no doubt that the anxiety in their household was extreme in February 1871 when Livy Clemens developed high fever and "rose spots" on her abdomen and was diagnosed with typhoid fever. She required around-the-clock nursing, and it was not until mid-March that she was even able to get out of bed and walk with assistance. Even as Livy appeared to be recovering from her own battle with typhoid, Clemens had guarded optimism about the likelihood of her recovery, and his worry was intense: "Livy is *very, very* slowly & slightly improving, but it is not possible to say whether she is out of danger or not—but we all consider that she is *not*" (4:334–335). The weariness created by the prolonged illness pushed Clemens to his emotional limits, and his writing productivity came to a standstill: "I am still nursing Livy night & day & *cannot* write anything. I am nearly worn out. . . . I have been through 30 days' terrific siege" (p. 341).

Clemens's memories of typhoid fever were clear in his mind thirty-one years later, when he wrote "Was It Heaven? Or Hell?" His fictional account is centered on a woman, Margaret Lester, who is restricted to her sickroom as she is dying of typhoid fever. When her sixteen-year-old daughter Helen tells an innocent lie, the woman's overly righteous aunts Hannah and Hester Gray force the girl to confess her moral transgression face-to-face to her contagious mother, in spite of the family physician's order that the mother must be kept in isolation. The doctor is angered when he finds out that the girl was unnecessarily exposed to the mother's infection for such a trifling reason, and he is further enraged when the aunts rationalize their action through their rigid advocacy of truth-telling at

all costs. Through the physician's retort to the aunts, Clemens makes clear his own position that a rigid commitment to the absolute truth is not always compatible with the role of the physician as healer:

> The doctor glowered upon the woman a moment, and seemed to be trying to work up in his mind an understanding of a wholly incomprehensible proposition; then he stormed out:
>
> "She told a lie! *Did* she? God bless my soul! I tell a million a day! And so does every doctor." ("Was It Heaven? or Hell?" p. 78)

The aunts initially remain steadfast in their belief that all lies are sinful, even as the physician argues that purposeful lying may be anything but a sin. As a result of the unnecessary exposure to her mother's typhoid fever, Helen herself contracts the illness and dies. At first the aunts feel compelled to maintain their commitment to the truth, and they fully intend to tell the dying woman that her daughter has preceded her in death. When they realize that this truth will bring profound despair to the dying woman, the aunts find themselves reversing their own strongly held moral position, and they proceed to invent a series of lies that spares the girl's mother from learning of the girl's death. As a result of their compassionate decision, the woman goes to her grave with the mistaken belief that her beloved daughter is still alive and well. Samuel Clemens ends the story with the rhetorical question posed in its title: "Was It Heaven? Or Hell?"

SMALLPOX

Smallpox was another contagious, deadly, and highly feared disease of the nineteenth century, as evidenced by a letter written by Samuel Clemens to his wife, Livy, in 1871. "Get vaccinated—right away—no matter if you were vaccinated 6 months ago. . . . Small pox is everywhere—doctors think it will become an epidemic" (*Mark Twain's Letters* 4:521). For Clemens, the disease apparently was everywhere, and smallpox appeared in *The Innocents Abroad* (1869), *Roughing It* (1872), *Adventures of Huckleberry Finn* (1885), *A Connecticut Yankee in King Arthur's Court* (1889), and *Following the Equator* (1897).

Advances in medicine such as vaccines against life-threatening diseases were among the benefits of the newly developing medical science of the era. However, medical advances often have political and social repercussions. In his role as a champion of the powerless and disenfranchised, Clemens was aware that the limitations in knowledge, sophistication, and financial resources of recent immigrants made them potential victims of a medical care system that could create obstacles as frustrating and baffling as those produced by any other bureaucratic structure. Physicians were taking advantage of immigrants by enforcing a requirement for universal vaccination while charging exorbitant fees. The year before he exhorted his wife to get vaccinated against smallpox, Clemens protested the vaccination policies of unscrupulous physicians and uninformed lawmakers in "Goldsmith's Friend Abroad Again" (1870), a series of fictional letters written by a recent Chinese immigrant:

> he said, wait a minute—I must be vaccinated to prevent my taking the small-pox. I smiled and said I had already had the small-pox, as he could see by the marks, and so I need not wait to be "vaccinated," as he called it. But he said it was the law, and I must be vaccinated anyhow. The doctor would never let me pass, for the law obliged him to vaccinate all Chinamen and charge them *ten dollars apiece* for it, and I might be sure that no doctor who would be the servant of that law would let a fee slip through his fingers to accommodate any absurd fool who had seen fit to have the disease in some other country. And presently the doctor came and did his work and took my last penny— my ten dollars which were the hard savings of nearly a year and a half of labor and privation. Ah, if the law-makers had only known there were plenty of doctors in the city glad of a chance to vaccinate people for a dollar or two, they would never have put the price up so high against a poor friendless Irish, or Italian, or Chinese pauper fleeing to the good land to escape hunger and hard times. (P. 135)

TUBERCULOSIS

As the nineteenth century gave way to the twentieth, the specters of scarlet fever, typhoid fever, yellow fever, and cholera were replaced by a different, but equally frightening, infection—tuberculosis. Tuberculosis, also referred to as "consumption" due to the slow wasting death of its victims, has historically been associated with increases in population density, and it became increasingly common with the spread of industrialization. Tuberculosis became the leading infectious cause of death in the United States between the 1860s and the 1940s, accounting for one out of seven deaths. The seventeenth-century religious writer John Bunyan (1628–1688) called it the "captain of all these men of death" in *The Life and Death of Mr. Badman* (1680). In 1861 Oliver Wendell Holmes (1809–1894) characterized tuberculosis as "the white plague." Tuberculosis has often been romanticized in literature—perhaps to a greater extent than any other infection—because of its prolonged, lingering, wasting course. Patients who are slowly dying of "consumption" have ample opportunities for moral reflec-

tion and inspirational suffering as they serve as emblems of human mortality. Tuberculosis has been associated with being the disease of the brilliant and the talented, and its victims included the Brontës, Frédéric Chopin, Anton Chekov, John Keats, and Niccoló Paganini. Before Robert Koch's identification of the causative bacterium in 1882 confirmed that tuberculosis was an infectious disease, social critics (in keeping with the medical concepts of the times) took a moralistic tone and associated the illness with the vices of an accelerated urban lifestyle; those who were most licentious in their use of alcohol or in their sexual conduct were thought to be at greatest risk for the disease. In the pre-antibiotic era, treatment by removal of the patient into a healthy environment was the preferred approach, and Thomas Mann's novel *The Magic Mountain* (begun in 1912 but not published until 1924) exemplifies the thinking of the times by linking social and emotional factors with the disease.

OTHER INFECTIONS AND EPIDEMICS AS LITERARY METAPHOR

Henry James's 1878 novella, *Daisy Miller: A Study,* employs a fatal infection with malaria (rather than tuberculosis) as a metaphor for the protagonist's loose moral standards. The scope of this type of metaphor, linking disease and behavior, is made even broader—encompassing not just the individual, but the entire social framework—in Jack London's novel *The Scarlet Plague* (1915). This science fiction story describes the aftermath of a new plague in the year 2013 which has killed most of the world's population. Social structures collapse and civilization is destroyed as a result of the plague, and society is set back to a primitive and nomadic existence. The novel demonstrated London's interest in the mysteries of microbiology, but its most important feature was the use of the epidemic to cause social disruption and give London an opportunity to criticize modern social structure.

Infections and epidemics are also major themes in Sinclair Lewis's 1925 novel *Arrowsmith*. The protagonist, Martin Arrowsmith, is a young physician who worships the pure science of his bacteriology professor but then makes the choice to pursue private practice. He is forced to leave his medical practice after misdiagnosing a case of smallpox. He then shifts to a career in public health and discovers a cure for bubonic plague. He hopes to test it scientifically, only to have his wife die of the infection. As a physician, Arrowsmith is torn between his desires of making money, treating illness, or pursuing scientific truth.

For Sinclair Lewis and Jack London, as with Samuel Clemens before them, infections and epidemics were metaphors for the catastrophes and injustices of life. The use of such diseases in literature creates an effective mechanism for exploring the behaviors of an individual or the values of a society.

See also Health and Medicine; Pseudoscience

BIBLIOGRAPHY
Primary Works
London, Jack. *The Scarlet Plague.* New York: Macmillan, 1915.

Twain, Mark. "Goldsmith's Friend Abroad Again." In *A Pen Warmed-Up in Hell: Mark Twain in Protest,* edited by Frederick Anderson, pp. 131–152. New York: Harper Colophon, 1972.

Twain, Mark. *Life on the Mississippi.* Boston: James R. Osgood and Company, 1883.

Twain, Mark. *Mark Twain's Letters.* Vol. 2, 1867–1868. Edited by Alfred Bigelow Paine. New York: Harper & Brothers, 1917.

Twain, Mark. *Mark Twain's Letters.* Vol. 4, 1870–1871, edited by Victor Fischer, Michael B. Frank, and Lin Salamo. Berkeley: University of California Press, 1995.

Twain, Mark. *Tom Sawyer's Conspiracy.* In *Mark Twain's Hannibal, Huck & Tom,* edited by Walter Blair. Berkeley: University of California Press, 1969.

Twain, Mark. "Was It Heaven? or Hell?" In his *The $30,000 Bequest and Other Stories.* New York: Harper & Brothers, 1906.

Secondary Works
Duncan, C. J., S. R. Duncan, and S. Scott, "The Dynamics of Scarlet Fever Epidemics in England and Wales in the Nineteenth Century." *Epidemiology and Infection* 117 (1996): 493–499.

Gray, Barry M. "Streptococcal Infections." In *Bacterial Infections of Humans: Epidemiology and Control,* 3rd ed., edited by Alfred S. Evans and Philip S. Brachman, pp. 673–711. New York: Plenum, 1998.

Greenwood, Ronald D. "An Account of a Scarlatina Epidemic, 1839." *Illinois Medical Journal* 150 (1976): 147–148.

Hornick, R. B., S. E. Greisman, T. E. Woodward, H. L. DuPont, A. T. Dawkins, and M. J. Snyder. "Typhoid Fever: Pathogenesis and Immunologic Control." *New England Journal of Medicine* 283 (1970): 686–691.

Keiger, Dale. "Why Metaphor Matters." *Johns Hopkins Magazine,* February 1998. Available at http://www.jhu.edu/∼jhumag/0298web/metaphor.html.

McPheeters, William M. "Epidemic of Cholera in St. Louis in 1849." In *A History of Medicine in Missouri,* edited by E. J. Goodwin, pp. 71–92. St. Louis: W. L. Smith, 1905.

Ober, K. Patrick. *Mark Twain and Medicine: "Any Mummery Will Cure."* Columbia: University of Missouri Press, 2003.

Patterson, K. David. "Yellow Fever Epidemics and Mortality in the United States, 1693–1905." *Social Science and Medicine* 34 (1992): 855–865.

Rosenberg, Charles E. "The Therapeutic Revolution: Medicine, Meaning, and Social Change in Nineteenth-Century America." In his *Explaining Epidemics: And Other Studies in the History of Medicine,* pp. 9–31. New York: Cambridge University Press, 1992.

Turco, Jenifer, and Melanie Byrd. "An Interdisciplinary Perspective: Infectious Diseases and History." *American Biology Teacher* 63, no. 5 (2001): 325–335.

Warner, John Harley. *The Therapeutic Perspective: Medical Practice, Knowledge, and Identity in America, 1820–1885.* Princeton, N.J.: Princeton University Press, 1997.

K. Patrick Ober

DIVORCE

See Courtship, Marriage, and Divorce

DOMESTIC AND SENTIMENTAL FICTION

Domestic and sentimental novels, most of them written by white, middle-class women, dominated the literary marketplace before the Civil War. These types of novels, purchased by millions of readers, most of them women, exerted tremendous cultural influence in the 1850s and 1860s. Although some men did write within the tradition, the domestic and sentimental forms became forever associated with female authors striving for popular acceptance with little interest in critical acclaim. Nineteenth-century and twentieth-century critics and scholars granted such works little respect, arguing they possessed predictable plots, happy endings, and stock characters; were concerned with a trivial "woman's sphere"; and were written in an often exaggerated style thick with melodramatic flourishes. However, feminist scholars of the 1970s and 1980s argued that these previously marginalized literary modes performed important "cultural work" (in Jane Tompkins's words), extending women's influence well beyond the domestic circle. As a result, a whole new field of scholarship formed in the late twentieth century and early twenty-first century to study the domestic and sentimental fiction written by women during the 1850s and 1860s and the culture that produced and was influenced by it.

But what happened to these extremely popular forms after the Civil War, as the domestic and religious ideology that sustained them began to lose cultural hegemony? Certainly, they did not just disappear. A few of the popular antebellum domestic and sentimental novelists continued to publish. Most important, however, the domestic and sentimental forms continued to exert their influence on a new generation of American women writers but with significant differences. While many women continued to write about what they knew, namely women's lives, they did so with an increasing focus on the restrictions rather than the empowering opportunities of domestic life. And as they continued to employ what Tompkins calls the "sentimental power" found in antebellum novels, they did so with a greater emphasis on realist techniques, such as unique characterization and the depiction of harsh realities previously deemed unfit for female writers and readers. The domestic and sentimental traditions in fiction, therefore, underwent important changes as women's lives were altered drastically by the Civil War and the social changes that followed it.

THE POSTBELLUM ERA

Most of the best-sellers of the 1850s and 1860s were domestic and sentimental novels written by women such as Susan Warner, E. D. E. N. Southworth, A. D. T. Whitney, and Augusta Jane Evans. These novels, in the words of Nina Baym, presupposed "that men as well as women find greatest happiness and fulfillment in domestic relations, by which are meant not simply spouse and parent, but the whole network of human attachments based on love, support, and mutual responsibility" (p. 27). The "cult of domesticity" that buttressed these novels posited the affectionate relationships that are sustained in the home as the model for how human beings should interact, as opposed to the competition and greed governing business and political relationships in the public sphere. The sentimental technique of eliciting sympathy from the reader for less-fortunate characters was tied to the idea of "separate spheres," particularly the idea that the domestic sphere of women was the haven of compassion and, ultimately, should provide a model for civic life. In addition, these novels promoted a kind of "domestic feminism" by making their heroines models of an idealized femininity with the power to overcome vice and immorality. Like Eva in Harriet Beecher Stowe's *Uncle Tom's Cabin* (1852), the female characters are closer to God and therefore are the

conduit for others to receive grace; or like Gerty in Maria Susanna Cummins's *The Lamplighter* (1854), they learn to rein in their unruly impulses and become the center of a re-created Eden in the home. What these heroines either model or learn, time and again, is that they can harness the power of "true womanhood"—that is, the power of womanly influence—only by subordinating their own wishes for self-fulfillment to the ideal of service to others. The reward for such sacrifice is most often the hand of a man who has proven himself to possess domestic values or who is to be reformed by the heroine's loving guidance. As a result, most of these novels follow a young woman through a series of trials as she learns to accept her role, culminating in her marriage to a man worthy of her sacrifice.

A few of the domestic writers continued to produce popular novels after the 1860s, including E. D. E. N. Southworth (1819–1899), who published until 1894. Susan Warner (1819–1885) published twenty novels between 1870 and her death. And Stowe (1811–1896), one of the nation's foremost promoters of the cult of domesticity—in her novels and articles and in the domestic manual she coauthored with her sister, Catherine Beecher—tried to adapt her valorization of domestic life to a modern, urban setting in her three New York novels, *Pink and White Tyranny: A Society Novel* (1871), *My Wife and I; or, Harry Henderson's History* (1871), and *We and Our Neighbors; or, The Records of an Unfashionable Street* (1873). Her last novel, *Poganuc People: Their Loves and Lives* (1878), returns to rural New England of the early nineteenth century and lovingly portrays quotidian rituals of the home and farm, leading up to the heroine's marriage and domestic bliss.

By the 1870s, however, it was clear that the heyday of domestic and sentimental fiction was waning. With the grim reality of war and its aftermath all around them and in the press, readers either sought escape in nostalgic local color fiction or demanded more realistic portrayals of increasingly complex ways of life in America. As a result, even the hugely popular E. D. E. N. Southworth, who through sheer productivity sustained a lucrative career as an author, did not match her earlier sales. In addition, as Richard Brodhead argues in *Cultures of Letters: Scenes of Reading and Writing in Nineteenth-Century America*, the literary marketplace of the 1860s and 1870s became increasingly divided between the literary magazines, such as the *Atlantic Monthly* and *Harper's New Monthly Magazine*, and the nonliterary or popular magazines, such as *Peterson's* and *Frank Leslie's Illustrated*. In its early years, the *Atlantic Monthly* (founded in 1857) had published many sentimental and domestic tales, but as Brodhead notes, during and after the war it experienced a "palpable stiffening of its selection criteria," resulting in the exclusion of many of its female contributors, who would find remunerative work to do for the more popular magazines. Many women writers pushed themselves in new literary directions, producing local color stories and realistic novels in line with changing literary tastes. However, the domestic and sentimental traditions continued to influence postbellum women writers, who often employed sentimental literary techniques but challenged the pieties of domestic ideology and plots. In essence, sentimentalism became more and more detached from the cult of domesticity, with which it had been intertwined during the antebellum years.

WOMEN'S CHANGING LIVES

The separation of male and female spheres that was the backbone of domestic ideology underwent significant challenges as the patterns of women's lives began to change during the Civil War (1861–1865). Women participated in all kinds of war work that took them out of the home, such as nursing, organizing fairs to raise money for the war effort, serving as clerks in governmental offices, and working in factories to produce ammunition and uniforms. In addition, women all over the North and South filled the voids left by their men in the field and in commerce. Although nearly all of them returned to more traditional domestic work after the war, the notion that women had no place outside the home had been dispelled. Perhaps more significant, marriage rates plummeted as over 600,000 men who went off to war did not return. Women left without the opportunity to fulfill their traditional roles as wives and mothers confronted new choices about how to live their lives. In Louisa May Alcott's (1832–1888) words, rather than be "sour, spiteful spinster[s], with nothing to do but brew tea, talk scandal and tend a pocket-handkerchief," many chose to "devote themselves to some earnest work" in fields such as "philanthropy, art, literature, music, [or] medicine" (p. 203). Many white, middle-class American women who had been raised to believe that their sole purpose in life was to create a happy home and devote themselves to the benefit of others began to assert their right to live for themselves. The social changes set in motion by the Civil War also began to erode the cultural hegemony of the domestic feminine ideal, the so-called angel in the house. Young women began to think of themselves as unique individuals rather than "true women," initiating the decades-long movement toward the independent "new woman," who would become a major cultural phenomenon at the turn of the twentieth century.

It is important to remember that the majority of nonwhite and lower-class women did not have the luxury of trying to live up to ideals of domestic femininity, nor did they participate in such ideological shifts about their roles. Other social upheavals of the postwar years, such as Reconstruction and the abolition of slavery, the Indian wars, urbanization, and industrialization tended to have a much greater influence on their lives. Works by women of color, which flourished in the 1890s, often took up issues of social injustice. While antebellum domestic and sentimental fiction confronted social issues from the vantage point of the home—as in *Uncle Tom's Cabin,* where Stowe attacked the institution of slavery for the way it wreaked havoc on the family—postbellum women's fiction tended to portray women leaving the home to confront the changing social landscape. Women's lives and the choices they made about how to live them were no longer confined to a private sphere of the hearth and the family but were increasingly the stuff of public discourse. Therefore, as women continued to engage the traditions of domestic and sentimental fiction, the cultural milieu in which they lived made it difficult, if not impossible, for those traditions to remain unchanged.

DOMESTICITY AND ITS DISCONTENTS

In the postwar years, idealized notions of hearth and home continued to appear in the works of Stowe and others but often with an elegiac tone, as if the simpler times and women's moral influence were waning. As with Stowe's *Poganuc People,* the novels of this period were often set in the prewar past, before the advent of factory towns, large-scale western migration, and the growth of eastern urban centers disrupted traditional, rural ways of life centered on everyday domestic rituals. A number of late-nineteenth-century women writers, influenced by Stowe, continued to focus on what Ann Romines calls the "home plot," but with a different perspective. Although Romines sees an even greater concern with domestic rituals in women's fiction in the postwar period, such rituals were "not always celebrated"; in fact, postwar women writers tended to tell more "complex truths about the satisfactions *and* dangers that domestic ritual has meant in female lives" (p. 9).

While previous domestic novels may have challenged the culture's basic assumptions about home life by exposing unfeeling family members who exploited young women, they nonetheless offered a reconstructed vision of home and family that could provide women with the security and power they desired. Late-nineteenth-century novels about domesticity, marriage, and motherhood rarely offered such alternatives. Instead, one sees a greater emphasis on the discontents of domesticity: the way it could

The Story of Avis, *more than any other novel of the postbellum period, sparked debate about women's discontent in marriage. Avis is an accomplished artist who has studied in Europe, and she has sworn she will never marry because she is not like other women. But she is ultimately won by the sweet promises of Philip Ostrander, who insists that he does not ask her to sacrifice her art and is not marrying her "to be my housekeeper!" In the scene below, the conflict between Avis's desire to continue her career as an artist and her duties as a new mother and wife reaches a crisis. Although she has believed that hiring help will solve the problem, it becomes increasingly clear that Avis must devote herself to housekeeping and caring for the baby while her studio collects dust. This realistic scene of domestic discontent is typical of late-nineteenth-century women's fiction, as opposed to the sentimental, idealized depictions of the home and family life in popular antebellum domestic novels.*

On this particular morning she [Avis] came down late and wan. The fierce, free fire of her superb eyes had given way to the *burnt-in* look of anxious patience, which marks a young mother out from all other young creatures in the world. Her husband sat with a disturbed face at a disorderly table.

"Avis," he began, without looking up to see how she was, "the cracked wheat is soggy again."

Avis for a moment made no reply: she could not for sheer surprise. The husband's tone, breaking in upon her exhaustion of mind and body, gave her something of the little shock that we feel on finding our paper give out in the middle of an absorbing sentence. When she spoke, she said gently, but with some dignity, —

"I am sorry, Philip: I will speak [to the cook] about it."

"And the cream," proceeded Philip, "is sour. The steak was cold; and the coffee will give me a bilious headache before night. I really don't see why we can't have things more comfortable."

"We certainly must, if they are so very uncomfortable," replied his wife with rather a pale smile, striving, she could hardly have told why, to turn the discussion into a jest. "But you remember you didn't marry me to be your housekeeper, Philip!" . . .

"Yes, I remember. I don't know what we were either of us thinking of!"

Phelps, *The Story of Avis*, chap. 15, p. 153.

imprison women, as in Kate Chopin's *The Awakening* (1899); stifle their ambitions, as in Elizabeth Stuart Phelps's *The Story of Avis* (1877); or expose them to brutal violence, as in Constance Fenimore Woolson's *Jupiter Lights* (1889). Marriage and motherhood are no longer the apex of a woman's life but the beginning of her ruin. In fact, these later novels focused on the unhappy aftermath of marriage rather than culminating in the marital bliss suggested but rarely described in earlier domestic novels. Domesticity is a burden rather than a reward for the heroines of these books, as illustrated when Phelps's (1844–1911) narrator explains Avis's downfall from accomplished artist to wife and mother:

> Women understand—only women altogether—what a dreary will-o-the-wisp is this old, common, I had almost said commonplace, experience, "When the fall sewing is done," "When the baby can walk," "When house-cleaning is over," "When the company has gone," "When we have got through with the whooping-cough," "When I am a little stronger,"

then I will write the poem, or learn the language, or study the great charity, or master the symphony; then I will act, dare, dream, become. (P. 149)

In the midst of such constant domestic demands, Phelps's novel asserts, there is no time or energy for a woman to do anything for herself. While the heroine of Stowe's *My Wife and I,* aptly named Eva, holds the accomplishment of domestic harmony as her highest ambition, the heroines of a younger generation of women writers long for something more. Such novels, therefore, although they focused on women's domestic lives, can be seen as signaling the death knell of the domestic literary tradition.

Scholars such as Romines and Josephine Donovan, however, cite another group of women as the most likely successors of Stowe's domestic realism and even domestic fiction generally: the New England regionalists, namely Rose Terry Cooke (1827–1892), Sarah Orne Jewett (1849–1909), and Mary Wilkins Freeman (1852–1930). Unlike the large, sprawling domestic novels of the antebellum period, the regional or local color sketch enabled writers of what one might consider late-nineteenth-century domestic fiction to focus on the realistic details of women's domestic lives. As Elizabeth Ammons writes, "The form permits women to offer ungrandiose, concrete art, shaped, more often than not, by the rhythms of domestic and feminine experience, which is cyclical, repetitive, and often inconclusive" (Cooke, p. xxii). Moreover, these writers often avoided the subjects of marriage and motherhood altogether, so that many of their stories celebrated domesticity but stripped it of the conflicts and entrapments many other women writers explored. Regional sketches often featured single women living alone by choice, as in most of Freeman's best stories, including "A Church Mouse" and "A New England Nun" (1891). Or they depict homosocial bonds between women who prefer the companionship of another woman over that of a man, as in Jewett's series of sketches in *Deephaven* (1877). Perhaps the most likely late-nineteenth-century candidate for a work that carried on the domestic tradition is Jewett's *The Country of the Pointed Firs* (1896), which portrays a single woman writer who discovers in the uncomplicated, rural life of a remote village a nurturing retreat from her busy, urban life. This quasi novel, comprising a series of related sketches, revels in the everyday details of men's and women's lives as well as in the traditional domestic rituals of the writer's landlady, Mrs. Todd. However, the book is peopled only by the elderly, nearly all of whom live alone. There are no children or traditional families because the town's young folk have left to find better economic opportunities in the cities or in the West. In the end, the writer returns to the city, leaving her friends and their domestic traditions behind. Domesticity is celebrated, but it is also a thing of the fading past.

SENTIMENTAL REALISM

In the words of Joyce W. Warren, late-nineteenth-century realists—meaning male writers such as William Dean Howells and Henry James —"established themselves in opposition to the feminine and asserted their realism by differentiating it from women's writing, which they characterized as sentimental and soft" (p. 5). Because of that stance, American literary realism, the dominant literary movement of the late nineteenth century, came to be deemed a masculine movement diametrically opposed to the domestic and sentimental writing of women, however much those male writers themselves were interested in the ways women's lives and the institution of marriage were changing. However, late-twentieth-century feminist critics, such as Warren, Sharon M. Harris, and Judith Fetterley,

stress the ways in which women writers anticipated the realist movement of the 1880s and 1890s by focusing on quotidian experiences as opposed to extraordinary events, using dialect for their characters' dialogue, and portraying the social reality of their time. Other critics point to the Civil War and women's participation in reform movements as influences on early realist texts by women, such as Louisa May Alcott's *Hospital Sketches* (1863) and Rebecca Harding Davis's "Life in the Iron Mills" (1861).

In the post–Civil War period, therefore, it is not surprising to see women writers such as Alcott, Davis (1831–1910), and Phelps producing works that clearly anticipate the tenets of masculine realism. However, their fiction does not set itself decidedly against the sentimental; rather, it suggests the ways in which, as Susan S. Williams argues, "we can see realism not simply as a reaction against the excesses of the sentimental and domestic novel, but in some ways as a logical continuation of it" (p. 167). For example, the realist's emphasis on exposing harsh truths is not so far afield from the sentimentalist's desire to uncover the pain and suffering of the oppressed. While male realists tended to emphasize the author's objectivity toward his characters, as a scientist would calmly and without moral judgment observe the specimen under his microscope, many women who wrote realistically tended to presume a moral universe or critique society from a decidedly Christian vantage point. Thus a belief in "the Hope to come," as in Davis's "Life in the Iron Mills," or the power of human sympathy to ameliorate harsh conditions here on Earth underpins their works, marking them as a hybrid of sentimentalism and realism.

Some good examples of sentimental realism include Alcott's *Work* (1872), Phelps's *The Silent Partner* (1871), Helen Hunt Jackson's *Ramona* (1884), S. Alice Callahan's *Wynema: A Child of the Forest* (1891), and Frances Harper's *Iola Leroy; or, Shadows Uplifted* (1892). Each of these novels combines important elements of the two traditions, reflecting the ways women writers strove to portray the transformation of women's lives in the post–Civil War era, to expose the mistreatment of masses of voiceless Americans, and to argue for a new social vision. *The Silent Partner,* for example, portrays a young woman, Perley Kelso, who undergoes a transformation from sheltered domestic woman to Christian reformer. Shut out of active management of her father's textile business after his death because of her gender, she takes it upon herself to become acquainted with the workers and the condition of the mills, which, she soon discovers, is appalling. A note from Phelps at the beginning of the novel declares that her "fiction" is grounded in "facts" she has compiled from the Reports of the

Massachusetts Bureau of Statistics of Labor and from firsthand testimony of friends. That realist base is then a catalyst for Perley's sentimental transformation as she is forced to see the effects of her class's decadence. When she is introduced to the crippled sister of a mill hand whom she befriends, she finds it difficult to look at her, but she does so, she says, "for love's sake" (p. 839). The realist gaze, therefore, is not merely voyeuristic but sympathetic and, in turn, motivated to change the circumstances that have created such pain and suffering. In the end, Perley rejects marriage so that she can devote herself to the work of reform, an outcome that shows how literary sentimentalism could be detached from the cult of domesticity.

Throughout the late nineteenth century, many women writers continued to compel readers to look at the injustices done to underprivileged groups (such as Native Americans for Jackson and Callahan or African Americans for Harper). But even as they insisted that their fictions were grounded in fact, they distanced themselves from the cold, scientific approach associated with male realists by carrying on the sentimentalist assertion of public feeling and sympathy as the goal of literature, continuing to place women at the center of such a project.

See also The Country of the Pointed Firs; Courtship, Marriage, and Divorce; Feminism; Iola Leroy; A New England Nun and Other Stories; Ramona; Realism; Regionalism and Local Color Fiction; Women's Suffrage

BIBLIOGRAPHY

Primary Works

Alcott, Louisa May. "Happy Women." 1868. In *Alternative Alcott,* edited by Elaine Showalter, pp. 203–206. New Brunswick, N.J.: Rutgers University Press, 1988.

Cooke, Rose Terry. *How Celia Changed Her Mind and Selected Stories.* Edited and introduced by Elizabeth Ammons. New Brunswick, N.J.: Rutgers University Press, 1986.

Davis, Rebecca Harding. "Life in the Iron Mills." 1861. In *Life in the Iron Mills, and Other Stories,* edited by Tillie Olsen. New York: Feminist Press, 1985.

Jewett, Sarah Orne. *The Country of the Pointed Firs and Other Stories.* Edited and introduced by Marjorie Pryse. New York: Norton, 1981.

Phelps, Elizabeth Stuart. *The Silent Partner.* 1871. In *Popular American Literature of the 19th Century,* edited by Paul C. Gutjahr, pp. 812–910. New York: Oxford University Press, 2001.

Phelps, Elizabeth Stuart. *The Story of Avis.* 1877. Edited by Carol Farley Kessler. New Brunswick, N.J.: Rutgers University Press, 1985.

Secondary Works

Baym, Nina. *Woman's Fiction: A Guide to Novels by and about Women in America, 1820–70.* 2nd ed. Urbana: University of Illinois Press, 1993.

Brodhead, Richard H. *Cultures of Letters: Scenes of Reading and Writing in Nineteenth-Century America.* Chicago: University of Chicago Press, 1993.

Donovan, Josephine. *New England Local Color Literature: A Women's Tradition.* New York: Frederick Ungar, 1983.

Fetterley, Judith, ed. *Provisions: A Reader from 19th-Century American Women.* Bloomington: Indiana University Press, 1985.

Harris, Sharon M. *Rebecca Harding Davis and American Realism.* Philadelphia: University of Pennsylvania Press, 1991.

Hendler, Glenn. *Public Sentiments: Structures of Feeling in Nineteenth-Century American Literature.* Chapel Hill: University of North Carolina Press, 2001.

Romines, Ann. *The Home Plot: Women, Writing, and Domestic Ritual.* Amherst: University of Massachusetts Press, 1992.

Showalter, Elaine. *Sister's Choice: Tradition and Change in American Women's Writing.* New York: Oxford University Press, 1991.

Tompkins, Jane. *Sensational Designs: The Cultural Work of American Fiction, 1790–1860.* New York: Oxford University Press, 1985.

Warren, Joyce W. "Performativity and the Repositioning of American Literary Realism." In *Challenging Boundaries: Gender and Periodization,* edited by Joyce W. Warren and Margaret Dickie, pp. 3–25. Athens: University of Georgia Press, 2000.

Williams, Susan S. "Writing with an Ethical Purpose: The Case of Elizabeth Stuart Phelps." In *Reciprocal Influences: Literary Production, Distribution, and Consumption in America,* edited by Steven Fink and Susan S. Williams, pp. 151–172. Columbus: Ohio State University Press, 1999.

Anne E. Boyd

EDITORS

Editors from 1870 to 1920 continued to mediate and walk a kind of balancing act between business interests and creative talent, but even though editors had charge of periodicals' contents, they often did not have the authority or autonomy this duty might suggest. Changing audiences and urban population growth also created problems in staffing and organization. Especially relevant at mass-circulation newspapers with multiple daily editions, concerns with urban growth created an impetus for modernized equipment, facilitating—even dictating—the development of technology that could quickly serve a rapidly growing number of readers. This, in turn, affected the need for additional reading matter and for identifying appropriate (and ideally, growing) audiences. At large publications, multiple editors with various duties were increasingly needed to handle the increased number of pages of reading matter, so staffing issues also caused changes for the increasing demands on editors.

The definition of work for editors was even less defined as one moves away from the larger cities like New York and Boston. In the case of small-town newspapers, a husband and wife often jointly fulfilled the role of editor in addition to other roles, such as paragrapher or advertising sales representative—whatever was needed. Typical of the small-town editor and publisher were Isaac Strouse and his wife, Juliet Strauss (who preferred the original German spelling of the family name), of Rockville, Indiana. To help fill their newspaper, the *Rockville Tribune,* Juliet Strauss (1863–1918) began a "Squibs and Sayings" column

in 1893 that caught the attention of Charles R. Williams, the editor of the *Indianapolis News,* wherein a Strauss column titled "Country Contributor" began appearing in 1903. That column in turn appealed to Edward Bok (1863–1930), the editor of the Philadelphia-based magazine *Ladies' Home Journal,* and by 1905 Juliet Strauss had a national audience, an achievement not so typical of the small-town husband and wife team. Sometimes other family members were called to the editor's role, as in the case of Frances Willard (1839–1898), who after her brother Oliver's death in 1878 joined her sister-in-law in taking editorial charge of a staff of sixty men, including a dozen editors and reporters, at the *Chicago Evening Post.*

As illustrated by Strauss's success, accompanying the population shift to cities was an increased interest in reading about small-town life. Clearly this appeal was important in the popularity of rural voices such as that of the poet James Whitcomb Riley (1849–1916), who like Strauss had been nurtured by the editor of the *Indianapolis News.* Newspaper editors such as Henry W. Grady (1850–1889) of the *Atlanta Constitution* and William Allen White (1868–1944) from Emporia, Kansas, were known for distinctive regional voices and, like many editors of mid-size cities' daily presses, promoted local poets and fiction writers. Readers of Bret Harte (1836–1902), who edited the San Francisco–based literary journal the *Overland Monthly,* could recognize the formula for success in writing that simply imitated a Dickensian blend of humor, sentiment, whimsy, and pathos. This formula can be seen plainly in the writing of Grady, as well as in that of the writers first encouraged by him and by other southern editors—George W. Cable, Joel Chandler Harris, James Lane Allen, and Mary Noailles Murfree, to mention a few.

Editors of association periodicals were also helpful to new writers. These publications arose through varying sources, from trade publications like the *Locomotive Firemen's Magazine,* published by the Brotherhood of Locomotive Firemen and edited by Eugene V. Debs (1855–1926), to the *Memphis Free Speech,* a weekly African American newspaper edited and part-owned by Ida Wells (later Ida Wells-Barnett, 1862–1931) through which she devotedly fought lynching. After her newspaper office was destroyed by a mob in 1892, she moved to New York and worked for the weekly *New York Age,* another African American newspaper. Every cause, every union, every association of the late 1800s seemed to have a periodical. Indeed some of the highest circulations were enjoyed by periodicals published by church organizations.

ENCOURAGEMENT OF YOUNG WRITERS

Many aspiring young writers sent their first verses to local editors and were frequently encouraged to continue writing. Sometimes—as in the familiar case of Louisa May Alcott (1832–1888)—the would-be writer was bold enough to send a story to an editor of what was then called a story paper. Alcott's foray into the world of gothic horror and thrillers brought her much needed freelance income. In addition to the sensational story papers, another kind of publication emerged—the predecessor of Sunday literary supplements, intended especially for weekend family reading. It was in one such publication that Florence Finch Kelly (1858–1939) was first published in the early 1870s when she was about fourteen. According to her autobiography, she submitted a story to an eight-page paper published "somewhere in Iowa" (Kelly, pp. 89–90) and discovered it printed with her name in the next issue. No local fame came from this first effort, and she was paid in copies of the paper, not money, although saving for college had been her goal.

Elizabeth Jordan (1865–1947), who worked at Joseph Pulitzer's *New York World* and was to become the editor of *Harper's Bazar* (as the name was then spelled), eventually played a part in the larger discovery of such authors as Sinclair Lewis, Zona Gale, and Dorothy Canfield. Her introduction to the writing world came, like Kelly's, when she was fourteen. Jordan was a little more fortunate, however, as she received the sum of two dollars for her first effort for Milwaukee's *Evening Wisconsin.* As an adult she described how at fourteen she read her story from the newspaper to the assembled family without telling who

had written it. Their reactions ranged from boredom to inappropriate amusement, and the wound was raw until twenty years later when she published the whole experience in *Harper's Monthly Magazine* as fiction.

Similarly, Elizabeth Meriwether Gilmer (1861–1951), who was to become known as Dorothy Dix, started her career with the publication of local color stories in newspapers in Nashville, Atlanta, and New Orleans. Comments by an editor in the *Nashville American* were typically solicitous, describing her as "a bright, witty, vivacious little woman" (Kane, p. 45) and expressing hope that she would write for them again. Indeed she did just that, and her article for the women's edition of the *Nashville American,* titled "A Woman's Experience as a Newspaper Editor," shows the wit for which she later became famous. Gilmer's first big opportunity had come in 1893 when she was staying at Bay St. Louis, Mississippi, in a house that was, by chance, adjacent to the home of Elizabeth "Eliza" Jane Poitevent Nicholson (1849–1896), the publisher of the *New Orleans Picayune.* Nicholson, who had assumed control of the newspaper upon her husband's death nearly two decades earlier, became Gilmer's mentor, and in addition to arranging for freelance income, she eventually arranged for Gilmer's employment in New Orleans.

The boost the women's edition article gave to Gilmer's career was typical of a phenomenon experienced by many would-be writers at the time. Throughout the country, special women's editions of newspapers were being published, and literary editors from Cincinnati, Danbury, Milwaukee, Memphis, Chicago, Louisville—even the small towns of New Castle, Indiana, and Gouverneur, New York—searched through their communities for women's literary talent with which to fill their papers.

OTHER OPPORTUNITIES FOR YOUNG PEOPLE

Sometimes the local editor arranged for a talented child (if male) to board with his family and work as a "printer's devil," where the first lessons in writing were accompanied by lessons in typesetting. Horace Greeley (1811–1872) spent his childhood as an apprentice and boarder in his editor's home. In the case of young women, the opportunity to work as a so-called printer's devil was closed, but biographies of Mary Abigail Dodge (1833–1896) show another path. Her opportunity came when Gamaliel Bailey, the editor of the *National Era,* asked her if she would like to live in Washington, D.C., with his family and work as governess. This arrangement gave her access to Washington's literary and political figures and helped her become the well-respected writer known as Gail Hamilton. A much-publicized legal battle between Hamilton and James T. Fields, her publisher, about remuneration led to widespread changes in publishing and has been identified as one of the important events leading to an end of an era dominated by the so-called "gentleman publisher."

William Dean Howells (1837–1920) was also introduced to the field of publishing at an early age. As a child he learned to set type for his father, William Cooper Howells, who worked variously as an editor, publisher, and printer in several different towns in Ohio. Moving from town to town in this manner was not unusual among journalists. In fact the itinerant printer was a common figure in the smaller villages that followed the progress of the railroads across the western half of the country.

One such nomadic journalist was Legh Freeman (1842–1915), whose newspaper operation historians have referred to as the "Press on Wheels." Actually further research has shown that the operation was somewhat more stationary than that title suggests, with Freeman's wife, Ada, editing the paper while her husband sent home accounts of his adventures as a frontier scout. Writing about herself, she said that she had come into Utah unacquainted with a single soul, and, within a period of six weeks, had organized, established, and published the *Ogden Freeman,* taken charge of two infant sons, and given birth to a third.

MARK TWAIN'S EARLY NEWSPAPER TROUBLES

As Ada Freeman would have known well, editors needed the support of their communities and sometimes needed to stifle views in order to keep their business solvent. One of the more lasting pictures of frontier life and journalism was made by one who was an editor only when his boss was gone. Samuel Langhorne Clemens (1835–1910), who had left Missouri with his brother Orion, an official for the territory of Nevada, wrote a few pieces for the *Territorial Enterprise,* a newspaper at Virginia City, Nevada, signing his submissions to the editor, Joseph T. Goodman, as simply "Josh." The *Enterprise,* unusual in that its staff included five printers and was large enough to accommodate a fluctuating full-time writing staff, welcomed "Josh," and later Clemens began using the pseudonym Mark Twain when he filled in as editor. In May 1864 he wrote a little piece suggesting that money raised locally for the national Sanitary Fund would actually go to a miscegenation society in the East. Though written as a joke and unintentionally printed, the comment angered many in Virginia City and stirred up

further criticism. Typical of Wild West newspaper editors, he traded insults and eventually challenged a rival editor, James Laird, to a duel. Shortly afterward he left for San Francisco to avoid prosecution under Nevada's antidueling law.

Twain continued to publish satiric tales exaggerating frontier life, and these writings, reprinted widely by exchange papers, have added to the tall-tale tradition. According to one biographer, Twain developed his style by imitating the writing of Charles Farrar Browne (1834–1867), an editor of the *Cleveland Plain Dealer* who created and wrote as the character Artemus Ward. As a dedicated fan of Ward, Twain borrowed phrasing and ideas from his Ohio literary contemporary. Another colleague of Twain also credited with aiding Clemens's professional development was William Wright, who wrote as Dan De Quille.

As seen in the careers of Mary Abigail Dodge (Gail Hamilton), Samuel Clemens (Mark Twain), Elizabeth Gilmer (Dorothy Dix), Juliet Strauss (the Country Contributor), and Charles Farrar Browne (Artemus Ward), the tradition of using a pen name was a common one. It was so common, in fact, that Henry Mills Alden (1846–1919), in his book *Magazine Writing and the New Literature* (1908), devotes a chapter to the historical practice of anonymity in journalism. Alden, a legendary editor for *Harper's,* was known for his helpful attitude toward new writers. His work was similar to that of his editor-colleagues from the major magazines issued from the eastern seaboard, namely William Dean Howells, George William Curtis, Thomas Bailey Aldrich, and James Russell Lowell.

HEARST AND PULITZER IN NEW YORK

The zenith of mass journalism appeared to have been reached in the form of the daily newspaper, and the rivalry of two editors of daily papers in New York City dominates most of the discussion of late nineteenth-century American journalism. For years the greatest of dailies was the *New York World* of Joseph Pulitzer (1847–1911), described by a biographer of Theodore Dreiser as a madhouse with a snarling savage for a city editor. But the madhouse was to get madder as the western shadow of William Randolph Hearst (1863–1951) came closer. Hearst, whose bid in the New York newspaper wars began with his purchase of the *New York Morning Journal* (which he promptly renamed the *New York Journal*), and Pulitzer were the biggest competitors in what was sometimes called "new journalism." Yet years before, the impetus for a different kind of journalism was being formed in the weekly press by editors like Frank Leslie (1821–1880), who used journalism to fight against social problems.

William Randolph Hearst. Caricature by Homer Davenport, 1896. Hearst brought Davenport from San Francisco to work for the *New York Journal,* where he became the highest paid editorial cartoonist in the country. THE LIBRARY OF CONGRESS

Spurred by the sensational approach of the New York City press in the 1890s, a different kind of "exposure" was beginning in the form of long investigative articles which appeared in *McClure's Magazine.* These muckrakers, as they were called, stand yet today as practitioners of journalism at its best and include Ida M. Tarbell, Ray Stannard Baker, and David Graham Phillips. Their work for the magazine's editor, S. S. McClure, was to rise above the more tawdry approaches popularized by the daily press, yet they had written for

newspapers and much of the crusading impetus was similar. Another exposure journalist was Jacob A. Riis, whose photography set the benchmark for documentary photography for decades.

GEORGE HORACE LORIMER OF THE *POST*

George Horace Lorimer (1867–1937), the longtime editor of the *Saturday Evening Post,* created a new model for magazine journalism in the early part of the twentieth century. Beginning as the *Post*'s literary editor in 1898, he arrived in Philadelphia at a relic of a magazine that claimed to trace its origins to Benjamin Franklin and the American Revolution. Within a few months Lorimer was promoted to editor in chief, a position he held through 1936. What Lorimer did—and in this he was a pathfinder like McClure and Frank Leslie—was bring timeliness and a national point of view to the *Post*. His publisher, Cyrus H. K. Curtis, had been successful with the *Ladies' Home Journal* and now wanted a magazine that would provide for male readers what the *Ladies' Home Journal* had provided for women. But Lorimer's vision was even bigger, and before the new century was fully underway, significant changes were materializing. Included in the earliest Lorimer issues were stories by Stephen Crane, Rudyard Kipling, Hamlin Garland, and one of Henry Grady's protégés, Joel Chandler Harris. As one critic put it, Lorimer wanted to create a magazine without class, clique, or sectional editing, and he meant to edit it for the whole United States.

Lorimer's genius at selecting talent was important, but paying writers upon acceptance was radical for the times. He also changed practices concerning copyrights and began to buy only North American serial rights, and magazines accustomed to acquiring all rights found themselves having to follow. The *Post* also has been credited with encouraging the short story form. It is true that Lorimer was uncanny in his judgments, and his skills at identifying and molding the elements of the short story deserve to be more highly appreciated. Certainly popularity was not Lorimer's only reward. He is remembered as an editor whose practices shook up the magazine empires at *Harper's* and the *Atlantic Monthly* and changed the practices of magazine journalism permanently.

See also The Atlantic Monthly; Book Publishing; Harper & Brothers; *Harpers New Monthly Magazine;* Houghton Mifflin; Journalism; Literary Marketplace; *McClure's Magazine; Overland Monthly;* Periodicals

BIBLIOGRAPHY

Primary Works

Baker, Ray Stannard. *American Chronicle: The Autobiography of Ray Stannard Baker.* New York: Scribners, 1945.

Jordan, Elizabeth Garver. *Three Rousing Cheers.* New York: D. Appleton-Century, 1938.

Kelly, Florence Finch. *Flowing Stream: The Story of Fifty-Six Years in American Newspaper Life.* New York: E. P. Dutton, 1939.

Riis, Jacob A. *The Making of an American.* New York: Macmillan, 1901.

Willard, Frances Elizabeth. *Writing Out My Heart: Selections from the Journal of Frances E. Willard, 1855–96.* Edited by Carolyn De Swarte Gifford. Urbana: University of Illinois Press, 1995.

Secondary Works

Beasley, Maurine Hoffman, and Sheila Jean Gibbons. *Taking Their Place: A Documentary History of Women and Journalism.* Washington, D.C.: American University Press, 1993.

Bennion, Sherilyn Cox. *Equal to the Occasion: Women Editors of the Nineteenth-Century West.* Reno: University of Nevada Press, 1990.

Boomhower, Ray E. *The Country Contributor: The Life and Times of Juliet V. Strauss.* Carmel: Guild Press of Indiana, 1998.

Bottorff, William K. *James Lane Allen.* New York: Twayne, 1964.

Coultrap-McQuin, Susan Margaret. *Doing Literary Business: American Women Writers in the Nineteenth Century.* Chapel Hill: University of North Carolina Press, 1990.

Coultrap-McQuin, Susan Margaret, ed. *Gail Hamilton: Selected Writings.* New Brunswick, N.J.: Rutgers University Press, 1992.

Cyganowski, Carol Klimick. *Magazine Editors and Professional Authors in Nineteenth-Century America: The Genteel Tradition and the American Dream.* New York: Garland, 1988.

Dary, David. *Entrepreneurs of the Old West.* New York: Knopf, 1986.

Filler, Louis. *The Muckrakers: Crusaders for American Liberalism.* Chicago: H. Regnery, 1968.

Gilmer, Elizabeth M. "A Woman's Experience as a Newspaper Editor." *Nashville American,* 9 May 1895, p. 35.

Ginger, Ray. *Eugene V. Debs: A Biography.* New York: Collier Books, 1962. Originally published as *The Bending Cross: A Biography of Eugene Victor Debs.* New Brunswick, N.J.: Rutgers University Press, 1949.

Huntzicker, William. *Frontier Press, 1800–1900.* In *The Media in America: A History,* edited by W. David Sloan. Northport, Ala.: Vision Press, 2002.

Kane, Harnett T. *Dear Dorothy Dix: The Story of a Compassionate Woman.* Garden City, N.Y.: Doubleday, 1952.

Kaplan, Fred. *The Singular Mark Twain: A Biography.* New York: Doubleday, 2003.

Milne, Gordon. *George William Curtis and the Genteel Tradition.* Bloomington: Indiana University Press, 1956.

Nixon, Raymond B. *Henry W. Grady: Spokesman of the New South*. New York: Knopf, 1943.

Okker, Patricia. *Our Sister Editors: Sarah J. Hale and the Tradition of Nineteenth-Century American Women Editors*. Athens: University of Georgia Press, 1995.

Putzel, Max. *The Man in the Mirror: William Marion Reedy and His Magazine*. Cambridge, Mass.: Harvard University Press, 1963.

Swanberg, W. A. *Dreiser*. New York: Scribners, 1965.

Tebbel, John William. *George Horace Lorimer and the Saturday Evening Post*. Garden City, N.Y.: Doubleday, 1948.

Tebbel, John William, and Mary Ellen Zuckerman. *The Magazine in America, 1741–1990*. New York: Oxford University Press, 1991.

Ann Mauger Colbert

EDUCATION

Herman Melville wrote in *Moby-Dick* (1851) that "a whale-ship was my Yale College and my Harvard" (p. 156), and W. D. Howells noted three generations later that "till journalism became my university, the printing-office was my school" (pp. 15–16). Melville and Howells were exceptions to the rule, however. Most major American writers after the Civil War were not autodidacts; rather, they received formal educations. In fact, American education at every level was profoundly transformed by the prosperity and pragmatism of the Gilded Age. As the period opened, the dominant philosophy in educational circles was deterministic, emphasizing strict discipline, rote memorization, repetitive exercises, and declamations or recitations. This pedagogical method is perhaps best illustrated in Mark Twain's *A Connecticut Yankee in King Arthur's Court* (1889), in which "the Boss" establishes "man factories" throughout Camelot to train the most gifted boys in the kingdom. "Training is everything," he believes (p. 114). In the end, only the young men educated in these "factories" from childhood remain loyal to the hero and the republic he declares against the interdict of the church. "Did you think you had educated the superstition out of the people?" his assistant asks (p. 299). Obviously so. Similarly, Charlotte Perkins Gilman, the author of "The Yellow Wall-Paper" (1892) and *Women and Economics* (1898), asserted in *Concerning Children* (1900) the Lamarckian and racially inflected belief that early education by a staff of professional teachers would enable children, once grown, to transmit acquired characteristics to their own progeny and subsequent generations. By 1920 more progressive educational practices, inspired by the pragmatism or functionalism of William James and John Dewey, had dramatically changed the American school system from kindergarten to the university.

KINDERGARTENS

"Child gardens," public nurseries or preschools on the German model, were introduced in St. Louis in 1873 at the direction of the local school superintendent, William T. Harris, later the U.S. commissioner of education, the author of *Psychologic Foundations of Education* (1898), and the editor of the *Journal of Speculative Philosophy*. The kindergarten movement grew slowly in the United States during its first twenty years and then blossomed. From about 30,000 kindergartens open in 1890, the number grew to over 200,000 in operation in 1900. Immediately upon founding Hull-House in Chicago in 1889, for example, Jane Addams established a kindergarten. Sarah B. Cooper, a suffragist, journalist, and president of the Golden Gate Kindergarten Association, was instrumental in founding kindergartens in the Bay Area around the turn of the century.

PUBLIC EDUCATION

During the era of the oft-sentimentalized one-room schoolhouse, few students continued their educations past the eighth grade. As late as 1918, barely half of all American children aged five to seventeen attended school. The hero of Mark Twain's *Adventures of Huckleberry Finn* (1885), son of the town drunk, goes to school only "three or four months" and learns the rudiments of reading, writing, and spelling. He "could say the multiplication table up to six times seven is thirty-five" (p. 18). And the students whose families could afford to keep them in school were often poorly instructed by teachers hired by the local school committee and before the standardization of curricula and teacher credentials. Twain's Tom Sawyer must suffer the punishments meted out by the sadistic schoolmaster Dobbins, whose rod and ferule "were seldom idle" (p. 150). In the end-of-school-year declamation scene in *The Adventures of Tom Sawyer* (1876), Tom and his classmates recite such sentimental chestnuts as Felicia Heman's poem "Casabianca" (or "The Boy Stood on the Burning Deck") and Patrick Henry's "Give Me Liberty, or Give Me Death" speech.

Few public high schools existed outside the major cities, though the number of high schools increased manifold between the Civil War and World War I as the result of court decisions that permitted communities to levy taxes to support them. From only a few hundred public high schools in 1870 (including the original Boston Latin School), their number swelled to over six thousand by the turn of the twentieth century. And while fewer than 7 percent of American teenagers attended public or private high schools in 1890, about 32 percent of them attended high schools in 1920. Still, public schools had their critics. The architect Richard Grant White scoffed in his essay "The Public-School Failure" (1880), "The mass of the pupils of these public schools are unable to read intelligently, to spell correctly, to write legibly, to describe understandingly the geography of their own country, or to do anything that reasonably well-educated children should do with ease" (p. 541). In his autobiography *Dawn* (1931), Theodore Dreiser remembered his parochial school education in Indiana in the early 1880s in remarkably similar terms: "No curriculum worthy of the name. A mixed gibberish of minor arithmetic, beginner's grammar, reading, Bible history, spelling, catechism, and then at about twelve years of age most of these spiritually afflicted underlings turned out to begin the work of making a living and planning their careers!" (p. 130).

Despite the many shortcomings in public education, teachers were often depicted in fiction of the period as agents of civilization and culture. The lineal descendants of the eastern teacher Miss Mary in Bret Harte's story "The Idyl of Red Gulch" (1869) include the hero of Edward Eggleston's *The Hoosier Schoolmaster* (1871), the heroine of Horatio Alger Jr.'s *The New Schoolma'am* (1877), and the eastern schoolmarm Molly Wood in Owen Wister's *The Virginian* (1902). Sherwood Anderson revised the type in *Winesburg, Ohio* (1919), in the character of Kate Swift, the most lonely and intellectually starved soul in the town.

The increased numbers of students attending public schools soon led to the professionalization of teaching. The National Bureau of Education, forerunner of the U.S. Department of Education, was established in 1867, and the National Educational Association, an organization of professional educators, was founded in 1898. Among the American authors who taught in public schools during this period were Willa Cather, Mary Austin, and Charles W. Chesnutt. The number of normal schools, forerunners of teachers' colleges, also dramatically increased from twenty-two in 1870 to about a hundred in 1900. Some of these normal schools (e.g., Illinois State Normal School, Indiana State Normal School, and Pittsburg Normal School) later became universities (Illinois State University, Ball State University, and Pittsburg State University in Kansas, respectively). Parallel to the standardization of the curriculum was the

***The Country School,* 1871.** Painting by Winslow Homer. Homer's naturalistic depiction captures the haphazard nature of early education during the period. © FRANCIS G. MAYER/CORBIS

emergence of standard textbooks in fields such as American literature. Henry Houghton, to repay the debt he assumed when he bought a Boston publishing house and renamed it Houghton, Mifflin and Company, urged the editor Horace Scudder to repackage the books on his list for every level of the market. For his part, Scudder believed that the textbook was a tool of social engineering. He edited perhaps the most influential literature anthologies in the history of American education, simply entitled *American Poems* (1879) and *American Prose* (1880). In 1891 he unveiled another textbook, *Masterpieces of American Literature.* Hundreds of thousands of cheap classroom editions in the Riverside Literature series, which included dozens of classic texts by American writers, virtually cornered the textbook market through the end of the century, and as late as 1917 they were still selling about a million copies a year. The same year, the first volume of the monumental *Columbia History of American Literature* also appeared.

PRIVATE EDUCATION

Among the alternatives to public education available to the children of privileged families were, of course, private tutors and preparatory schools. Their teachers were often improvident college graduates. Although he is best known in the early twenty-first century for his dozens of juvenile novels, Horatio Alger Jr., a Phi Beta Kappa graduate of Harvard, tutored such children as Edwin R. A. Seligman, later professor of economics at Columbia; Benjamin Cardozo, later associate justice of the U.S. Supreme Court; and Robert Grant, later a distinguished jurist and novelist. Similarly, George Herbert Mead, later a noted social theorist, tutored the children of William James, brother of the author Henry James. The younger James's tale "The Pupil" (1891) tells of an impecunious Yale graduate who tutors a precocious eleven-year-old boy, preparing him for admission to Oxford. As James's narrator caustically observes, the pupil "had the general quality of a child for whom life had not been simplified by school" (p. 418). (James, too, had largely been home-taught.) In "The Turn of the Screw" (1898), James depicted a much more peculiar relationship between a crazed governess and her charges. In addition, some seventy private academies or prep schools, still in existence in the early twenty-first century (e.g., the Groton School and Randolph-Macon), were founded between 1870 and 1920. But as Henry James famously lamented in his study of Nathaniel Hawthorne (1879), the United States had "no great Universities nor public schools—no Oxford, nor Eton" (p. 43). F. Scott Fitzgerald (1896–1940) similarly sneered in *This Side of Paradise* (1920) that "we have no Eton to create

the self-consciousness of a governing class; we have, instead, clean, flaccid, and innocuous preparatory schools" (p. 27).

TRADE SCHOOLS AND INDUSTRIAL EDUCATION

As for the children of the working class, they might choose among apprenticeships, vocational and trade schools, or business and commercial colleges. The scoundrel Bartley Hubbard studies law privately with Squire Gaylord in W. D. Howells's *A Modern Instance* (1882), for example. The title character of Frank Norris's *McTeague* (1899) is apprenticed to an itinerant dentist, earns the nickname "Doc," and practices dentistry in the Polk Street neighborhood of San Francisco, though he has no other professional training. Charlotte Perkins Gilman briefly attended the Rhode Island School of Design in Providence in 1878, and in her story "The Yellow Wall-Paper" (1892), the narrator remarks in passing that she knows "a little of the principle of design" (pp. 19–20). As Jane Addams details in *Twenty Years at Hull-House* (1910), moreover, the settlement house movement often went hand in glove with industrial education for immigrants and the underclasses. Some mission schools were also established by religious groups, such as the Presbyterian-sponsored Menaul School in Albuquerque, founded in 1881 to educate Spanish-speaking boys.

Other industrial or trade schools were race specific, particularly the Reservation Boarding School System in the United States. In 1870 Congress appropriated $100,000 to support industrial and other schools for Native American children. Unfortunately, the goal of these schools was forced assimilation of Native Americans ("kill the Indian, save the man"). No language except English was permitted in the classroom or elsewhere on campus. Indian schools were founded across the country in such towns as Albuquerque, Santa Fe, Phoenix, and Carlisle, Pennsylvania (the latter best known in the early twenty-first century for its student Jim Thorpe, one of the greatest athletes of the twentieth century). As early as August 1889, the American artist and novelist Frederic Remington criticized the system of Indian boarding schools:

> The present scheme of taking a few boys and girls away from the camps to put them in school where they are taught English, morals, and trades has nothing reprehensible about it, except that it is absolutely of no consequence. . . . The few boys return to the camps with their English, their school clothes, and their short hair. They know a trade also, but have no opportunity to be employed in it. . . . They go back to the camps, go back to the

blanket, let their hair grow, and forget their English. (P. 43)

In "An Indian Boy's Story" (1903), an example of a captivity narrative, Daniel La France chronicled his personal experience with Indian schools in the early- and mid-1890s, first on the Mohawk reservation. "There were four Indian day schools" there, "all taught by young white women" (p. 1781). But he learned "practically nothing" because "the teachers did not understand our language, and we knew nothing of theirs" (p. 1781). At the age of thirteen, La France was sent to a government-contract boarding school to learn to be a tailor but was soon disillusioned by the education there.

> There were endless rules for us to study and abide by, and hardest of all was the rule against speaking to each other in our own language. We must speak English or remain silent, and those who knew no English were forced to be dumb or else break the rules in secret. This last we did quite frequently, and were punished, when detected, by being made to stand in the 'public hall' for a long time or to march about the yard while the other boys were at play. (P. 1783)

Similarly, Charles Eastman, a native Sioux, reminisced in *From the Deep Woods to Civilization* (1916) about his experience as a student at the Indian school at Santee Agency, Nebraska, in the 1870s:

> How well I remember the first time we were called upon to recite! In the same primer class were Eagle-Crane, Kite, and their compatriot from up the river. For a whole week we youthful warriors were held up and harassed with words of three letters. Like raspberry bushes in the path, they tore, bled, and sweated us—those little words—*rat, cat,* and so forth, until not a semblance of our native dignity and self-respect was left. (P. 215)

Eventually, Eastman attended Dartmouth College Indian school and was educated as a physician.

Booker T. Washington, a graduate of the Hampton Institute, founded the most famous trade and industrial school for African American students, Tuskegee Institute, near Tuskegee, Alabama, in 1881. Only about thirty applicants were admitted to the first class, most of them public school teachers. As Washington reminisced in his autobiography *Up from Slavery* (1901), he tried to offer "such an education as would fit a large proportion of them to be teachers, and at the same time cause them to return to the plantation districts and show the people there how to put new energy and new ideas into farming, as well as into the intellectual and moral and religious life of the people" (p. 94). Black Americans, particularly in the South, suffered from Jim Crow laws and racial segregation of public facilities, including schools, a "separate but equal" doctrine sanctioned by the landmark Supreme Court decision *Plessy v. Ferguson* (1896). Within a few years of its founding, Tuskegee became a showpiece if not a model of industrial education, and Washington was hailed as one of the most important black leaders of his era. He was the first African American to dine at the White House, with Theodore Roosevelt in 1901. Yet Washington's policies, his acquiescence to segregation, and his insistence on industrial education as the sole means of racial uplift, were strongly criticized by such figures as the author and activist W. E. B. Du Bois and Charles W. Chesnutt. In the last novel he published during his lifetime, *The Colonel's Dream* (1905), Chesnutt excoriates the racial paternalism of whites who finance industrial schools for blacks modeled on Tuskegee.

COLLEGES AND UNIVERSITIES

What court decisions permitting taxation in support of local education were for high schools the Morrill Act of 1862 was for state colleges and universities. The legislation encouraged states to accept grants of land from the federal government to found vocational colleges for the working class. The curriculum of these colleges included courses in agriculture, veterinary science, and mechanics. Many of these land-grant colleges evolved into distinguished universities (e.g., Storrs Agricultural College, forerunner of the University of Connecticut; Iowa State Agricultural College and Model Farm, forerunner of Iowa State University; and Agricultural College of Pennsylvania, forerunner of Pennsylvania State University). Fred Lewis Pattee of Pennsylvania State College, the author of *A History of American Literature* (1896) and *A History of American Literature since 1870* (1915), was in fact the first professor of American literature at any college or university in the nation when he was awarded the title in 1920. Many of the land-grant institutions also pioneered the trend toward coeducation. The University of Illinois (originally the Illinois Industrial University), the University of Nebraska, the University of Maine (originally the Maine College of Agriculture and the Mechanic Arts), Iowa State, the University of Wisconsin, and Cornell University all admitted women shortly after the Civil War. Both Willa Cather (Nebraska) and Jessie Fauset (Cornell) graduated from land-grant schools around the turn of the twentieth century. In all, about a quarter-million undergraduate students were enrolled in schools in 1900, most of them in public universities.

With rare exceptions, most private colleges and professional schools (theological seminaries, law and medical schools) remained closed to women.

In response, several colleges that admitted only women opened during the 1870s and 1880s, among them Smith (1871), Wellesley (1875), the "Harvard Annex" subsequently renamed Radcliffe (1879), Bryn Mawr (1888), and Barnard (1889). Mount Holyoke Female Seminary, where Mary E. Wilkins studied in 1870–1871, also earned collegiate status in 1888. Gertrude Stein attended the Harvard Annex in 1893; H.D. (Hilda Doolittle) attended Bryn Mawr between 1904 and 1906; Marianne Moore graduated from Bryn Mawr in 1909; and both Adelaide Crapsey (1901) and Edna St. Vincent Millay (1917) graduated from Vassar. Not surprisingly, however, the education of women remained a contentious issue into the twentieth century. Gilman argued in "Does the Higher Education of Women Tend to Happiness in Marriage?" (1903) that career and family were not mutually exclusive. Still, women schoolteachers were not only paid less than men on the ground they were not "heads of households" but were also routinely dismissed when they married. And with rare exceptions (e.g., Harvard, which admitted Jews and African Americans), racial and ethnic minorities were denied higher education entirely.

The American critic and author Van Wyck Brooks claimed in 1908 that only at Harvard "are literary students so exclusively literary, for the Harvard man is left to himself" (p. 612). The claim would be difficult to deny on the basis of available evidence. Among the men of letters who graduated from Harvard between 1870 and 1920 were Du Bois, Owen Wister, Robert Herrick, e. e. cummings, John Dos Passos, Robert Grant, Witter Brynner, Hutchins Hapgood, Percy Mackay, and John Reed. The poets Edwin Arlington Robinson, T. S. Eliot, and Wallace Stevens also attended Harvard without taking a degree, and Henry James briefly studied at the Harvard Law School. Frank Norris was a student in Lewis E. Gates's creative writing course at Harvard in 1895–1896, and the playwrights Philip Barry and Sidney Howard were students in the famous 47 Workshop there directed by George Pierce Baker. The faculty included such luminaries as the historian Henry Adams, the philosopher and psychologist William James, and the philosopher and novelist George Santayana.

Adams reminisced about his years as a Harvard student between 1854 and 1858 in *The Education of Henry Adams* (1906), and he pulled no punches in his indictment. "No one took Harvard College seriously," Adams contended. "All went there because their friends went there, and the College was their ideal of social self-respect" (p. 54). Later, when offered a job there, he noted the irony: "Nothing in the vanity of life struck him as more humiliating than that Harvard College, which he had persistently criticized, abused, abandoned, and neglected, should alone have offered him a dollar, an office, an encouragement, or a kindness" (p. 305). The difference between the Harvard of Adams's undergraduate years and the Harvard whose faculty he joined was the curricular revision initiated by Charles W. Eliot, president of the university between 1869 and 1909 and editor of the "five-foot shelf" of *Harvard Classics*. Eliot introduced an elective system that effectively abolished the prescribed course of study at Harvard with its requirements in classical languages. Despite the reform, the social hierarchy at Harvard remained intact, as Howells illustrated in *The Landlord at Lion's Head* (1897), a precursor of the genre of academic novels, and many students still failed to exploit their opportunities, a point Wister made in his story "Philosophy 4" (1904).

Other distinguished universities also outgrew the tenets of orthodox Christianity on which they had been founded or reformed their curricula. Yale University finally inaugurated the first of its presidents not to be an ordained minister in 1899. Significantly, the villain of Mark Twain's *Pudd'nhead Wilson* (1894) is a Yalie, though in reality the graduates of Yale included the writers Stephen Vincent Benét, Waldo Frank, and Sinclair Lewis. The preceptorial system of teaching was introduced at Princeton University by Woodrow Wilson, who presided over the university between 1902 and 1910 before he was elected president of the United States in 1912. He was the only American president ever to earn a Ph.D. (Johns Hopkins, 1886). The playwright Eugene O'Neill studied briefly at Princeton (1908–1909). Much as Adams's *Education* ridiculed the respectability of Harvard students in the years before the Civil War, Fitzgerald's *This Side of Paradise* depicted the snobbery and shallow pretensions of Princeton students on the eve of World War I. Johns Hopkins University, primarily a graduate school on the German model and the first research university in the United States, was founded in Baltimore in 1876.

In addition to producing writers, universities were a boon to literary culture in other ways, particularly as sponsors of literary journals and presses. William P. Trent founded the *Sewanee Review* at the University of the South in 1892, and John Spencer Bassett established the *South Atlantic Quarterly* at Trinity College in 1901. By 1913 at least seven major university presses were in operation, including those at Cornell (1869), Chicago (1891), California (1893), Columbia (1893), Princeton (1905), Yale (1910), and Harvard (1913). In 1919 the Yale press inaugurated the Yale Younger Poets Prize, the first literary award to be granted annually in the United States.

Many other authors of the period were college graduates, among them Upton Sinclair (City College of New York), James Branch Cabell (William and Mary), Robinson Jeffers (Occidental), Charles Dudley Warner and Ezra Pound (Hamilton), Vachel Lindsay (Hiram), James Weldon Johnson (Atlanta University), Sidney Howard and Lincoln Steffens (California), Jean Toomer (New York University), Richard Harding Davis (Lehigh), and William Carlos Williams (University of Pennsylvania). Other writers attended college without taking a degree, including William Faulkner (University of Mississippi), Theodore Dreiser (Indiana), and Stephen Crane (Lafayette and Syracuse). Still other writers enjoyed sinecures as professors: Du Bois (Atlanta University), Robert Herrick (Chicago), Charles Warren Stoddard (Catholic University), Katharine Lee Bates (Wellesley). Pound taught for two years (1906–1908) at Wabash College in Indiana before he was fired for sequestering a woman in his room. Conversely, Bret Harte declined an invitation to become a professor of modern literature at the University of California soon after it opened, and Howells declined offers of professorships in literature at both Johns Hopkins and Harvard. Neither wanted academic commitments to interfere with his literary career.

Many of these colleges and universities had their critics. According to Laurence R. Veysey:

> Of the five hundred institutions of higher learning in the United States in 1903, a majority may not even have deserved the title of "college." It was estimated that only a hundred colleges held to standards that would permit their students to begin immediate study for the Doctorate after receiving the A.B., and only a dozen or so were clearly universities "of the first rank." (P. 359)

American literature as a discipline was also slow to enter the curriculum. Only fourteen colleges offered American literature courses in 1880, and only four Ph.D.s had been offered in the field by 1900. In a lament that has become increasingly familiar, the scholar and educator Irving Babbitt (1865–1933) insisted in *Literature and the American College* (1908) that "the humanities need to be defended to-day against the encroachments of physical science, as they once needed to be against the encroachments of theology" (p. 87). The economist Thorstein Veblen was even more blunt in *The Higher Learning in America* (1918). The American university, Veblen asserted, is merely a "corporation of learning" staffed by "captains of erudition" in departments that are headed by "chiefs of bureau" (pp. 88, 89, 112). In another lament that has become increasingly familiar, Veblen declared that "the intrusion of business principles in the universities goes to weaken and retard the pursuit of learning" (p. 224). As early as 1903, with only about six thousand graduate students enrolled in U.S. universities, William James indicted the trend toward credentialism in lieu of higher education in "The Ph.D. Octopus" (1903):

> The truth is that the Doctor-Monopoly in teaching, which is becoming so rooted an American custom, can show no serious grounds whatsoever for itself in reason. As it actually prevails and grows in vogue among us, it is due to childish motives exclusively. In reality it is but a sham, a bauble, a dodge, whereby to decorate the catalogues of schools and colleges. (P. 1115)

Such complaints continue to resonate in the early twenty-first century.

See also Adolescence; Indians; Lectures; Libraries; Reform; *Up from Slavery*

BIBLIOGRAPHY

Primary Works

Adams, Henry. *The Education of Henry Adams*. 1906. Boston: Houghton Mifflin, 1961.

Brooks, Van Wyck. "Harvard and American Life." *Contemporary Review* 94 (1908): 610–618.

Dreiser, Theodore. *Dawn*. New York: Liveright, 1931.

Eastman, Charles. *From the Deep Woods to Civilization*. 1916. Chicago: Lakeside Press, 2001.

Fitzgerald, F. Scott. *This Side of Paradise*. New York: Scribners, 1920.

Gilman, Charlotte Perkins. *The Yellow Wall-Paper*. 1892. New York: Feminist Press, 1973.

Howells, William Dean. *Years of My Youth*. 1916. Bloomington: Indiana University Press, 1975.

James, Henry. *Hawthorne*. New York: Harper & Brothers, 1879.

James, Henry. "The Pupil." 1891. In *The Complete Tales of Henry James, 1888–1891*, pp. 409–460. Philadelphia: Lippincott, 1963.

James, William. "The Ph.D. Octopus." 1903. In *Writings 1902–1910*. New York: Library of America, 1987.

La France, Daniel. "An Indian Boy's Story." *Independent*, 30 July 1903, pp. 1780–1787.

Melville, Herman. *Moby-Dick*. 1851. Indianapolis: Bobbs-Merrill, 1964.

Remington, Frederic. *Collected Writings of Frederic Remington*. New York: Doubleday, 1979.

Twain, Mark. *Adventures of Huckleberry Finn*. 1885. Berkeley: University of California Press, 1985.

Twain, Mark. *The Adventures of Tom Sawyer.* 1876. Berkeley: University of California Press, 1980.

Twain, Mark. *A Connecticut Yankee in King Arthur's Court.* 1889. New York: Signet, 1963.

Washington, Booker T. *Up from Slavery.* 1901. New York: Doubleday, 1998.

White, Richard Grant. "The Public-School Failure." *North American Review* 131, no. 289 (1880): 537–551.

Secondary Works

Babbitt, Irving. *Literature and the American College.* 1908. Washington, D.C.: National Humanities Institute, 1986.

Good, Harry. *A History of American Education.* New York: Macmillan, 1962.

Graff, Gerald. *Professing Literature: An Institutional History.* Chicago: University of Chicago Press, 1987.

Gross, Carl Henry, and Charles C. Chandler. *The History of American Education through Readings.* 2nd ed. Boston: Heath, 1964.

Vanderbilt, Kermit. *American Literature and the Academy: The Roots, Growth, and Maturity of a Profession.* Philadelphia: University of Pennsylvania Press, 1986.

Veblen, Thorstein. *The Higher Learning in America: A Memorandum on the Conduct of Universities by Business Men.* New York: Huebsch, 1918.

Veysey, Laurence R. *The Emergence of the American University.* Chicago: University of Chicago Press, 1965.

Gary Scharnhorst

THE EDUCATION OF HENRY ADAMS

Henry Adams's best-known work, *The Education of Henry Adams,* was first published privately and distributed to a select group of friends and acquaintances in 1907. This was a time of tremendous growth and dramatic change in the United States. The so-called captains of industry, men such as Andrew Carnegie and John D. Rockefeller, made American industry the envy of the world, and massive immigration swelled the population as millions made their way from the Old World to the New. A youthful and vigorous leader, Theodore Roosevelt, occupied the White House. Roosevelt seemed the perfect choice to lead a young and powerful nation into world prominence in what would become known as "the American Century." His presidency would mark the beginning of the aptly named Progressive Era in America. Despite all the excitement and hopefulness of this dynamic time, Henry Adams's classic work reflects a worldview that expresses not hope but rather confusion and a sense of despair at what he saw as the growing chaos of the modern age.

STRUCTURE

The Education has been seen as typical of fin de siècle (end of the nineteenth century) writing. This term describes the atmosphere of social and cultural fatigue that characterized for some the waning years of the 1800s (Contosta, p. 109). Many thoughtful people at this time believed, despite all the physical signs of progress, that modern civilization was, in fact, experiencing an exhaustion of values and was hurrying toward its own destruction. There was ample justification for such pessimism. A major economic depression in 1893 suggested to many that prosperity was a fragile thing. Despite the enormous wealth accumulated by the captains of industry, millions of Americans, especially immigrants, lived in poverty and squalor in America's cities. Working conditions for many men, women, and children were appalling due to the absence of effective labor laws, and social justice for women and African Americans was still a distant dream. Also, new scientific and technological discoveries in the period, especially those dealing with the development of electrical energy, radio waves, radium, and X-rays, suggested to some that the world was awash with mysterious and threatening forces that could not be controlled. Finally, Charles Darwin's theory of evolution, while confirming for some the inevitability of human progress, was seen by others as affirming that the human species was just another life-form, locked in a deterministic struggle for survival, ruled over by forces of nature that were inherently indifferent to individual existence. Indeed, "survival of the fittest" was a ruthless law that dominated all areas of human endeavor, according to Social Darwinists such as Herbert Spencer.

Henry Adams (1838–1918) was uniquely qualified to reflect on the dramatic developments that occurred in the nineteenth century. He was born at the beginning of the Industrial Revolution in America and died in the year after the United States entered World War I. He also came from an illustrious American political dynasty. His great-grandfather was John Adams, the second president of the United States; his grandfather was John Quincy Adams, the sixth president; and his father was Charles Francis Adams, the U.S. minister to Great Britain during the Civil War, a position of unparalleled diplomatic importance at the time. Henry Adams's historical memory encompassed the extraordinary evolution of American society from the revolutionary idealism of the early Republic to the gunboat diplomacy of the age of steel.

The Education is often considered to be an autobiography and was subtitled as such when it was issued by Houghton Mifflin in 1918, following Adams's death. While it is highly autobiographical in nature, it is clear

Henry Adams. Photograph by his wife, Marian Hooper Adams. THE MASSACHUSETTS HISTORICAL SOCIETY. REPRODUCED BY PERMISSION

that Adams intended it to be more than that. It is actually a reflection on the entire period, and Adams's protagonist, whom he refers to in the third person throughout, is intended to be representative. In fact, Adams calls him a "manikin," and some critics see him as "an ironic archetype for the protagonist of modern literature," an existential wanderer who is "defined by his *desire* for a coherent self" (Rowe, p. 123). Indeed, it is this representational quality that some insist is the basis for the work's status as great literature. Thus, in the words of one critic, the work is a classic "because it still has the capacity to enter into a relation with its present audience that generates a dynamic mirroring of one another's failings" (Thomas, p. 46).

The notion of writing an autobiography about a life that, by the author's admission, is a "failure" is one of the qualities that suggests the author's ironic intent throughout, and it tends to set *The Education* apart from other American autobiographies. Indeed, one critic suggests that "Adams is parodying the very genre of autobiography" (Horwitz, p. 122). Some

have held that, as autobiography, *The Education* has much in common with Saint Augustine's *Confessions,* the classic work of Christian theology that was written around the year A.D. 400. In addition to the confessional tone of *The Education,* Adams himself once declared, "St. Augustine alone has an idea of literary form—a notion of writing a story with an end and object, not for the sake of the object, but for the form, like a romance." His goal in *The Education* was, like Saint Augustine's, to "mix narrative and didactic purpose and style" (Samuels, p. 341) as a means of asserting meaning in a largely meaningless world. Indeed, one critic maintains that "the entire confessional mode from Augustine to Adams is dominated by a desire to order life, to make fragmentary experience meaningful in a larger context" (Rowe, p. 96).

THEMES
The search for meaning and coherence is most certainly the major theme in *The Education*. At the time he began writing the work, Adams saw it as

complementary to his earlier, privately published study *Mount-Saint-Michel and Chartres* (1904), which he subtitled *A Study of Thirteenth-Century Unity*. This work analyzed the unified sensibility of a period in European history that was characterized by a powerful Christian faith, a faith that found expression in the beautiful and imposing cathedrals built at the time. Many of these churches were dedicated to the Virgin Mary, and Adams found them irresistibly attractive. This would provide the starting point for *The Education,* which he envisioned as "a Study of Twentieth-Century Multiplicity" (Samuels, p. 312).

Adams had for some time become preoccupied with what he would later describe as the decay and disorder of modern civilization (Burich, p. 467). As a distinguished American historian, as well as a member of one of America's most distinguished families, Adams was particularly well equipped to write such a book. The tradition of service to God and country was a major component of the Adams family history, and all of Henry's progenitors were perfectly sure who God was and what the Republic stood for. Unfortunately, the certain faith and unifying truths that had been embraced by Henry's forefathers from the eighteenth century to the Civil War appeared increasingly irrelevant in the period following the war. The rise of corporations, laissez-faire economics, and the ruthless principles of Social Darwinism made the old notions of selfless service and high-minded idealism seem quaint and obsolete. Indeed, being born heir to such a legacy left Adams's protagonist a "branded" man who was "heavily handicapped in the races of the coming century" (Adams, p. 3). It soon became very clear to this "child of the seventeenth and eighteenth centuries" that he was not well equipped to deal with the reality of the twentieth (p. 4). Faced with an increasingly complex world, where new discoveries and new developments in virtually all fields of human endeavor leave him confused and anxious, Adams very soon discovers that his old way of thinking must give way to something new. The discovery of that new avenue becomes the goal of *The Education.* What this young man ultimately needs is a unifying truth that will give meaning and purpose to life and an answer to the primal question, "why do I exist"? He observes that "from cradle to grave this problem of running order through chaos, direction through space, discipline through freedom, unity through multiplicity, has always been, and must always be, the task of education" (p. 12).

The first half of *The Education* is more traditionally autobiographical. Adams describes the idyllic nature of his boyhood, his early memory of his grandfather, "the President," and the contrast he felt even then between the philosophical and patriotic ideals of his Adams paternity and the contrary pull of "State Street," the Boston business district where his mother's family established their fortune. Times clearly favored the latter, but Henry felt pulled more to the former, and he recounts his forefathers' heroism and idealism in war and peace, from the American Revolution to the antislavery movement.

If family traditions offered nothing to equip the young hero to deal with the modern world, Harvard College was little better. Its antiquated curriculum, which emphasized rote recitations based on classic works of the ancients, had changed little, if at all, since Ralph Waldo Emerson offered his searing criticism of the mind-numbing routine almost thirty years earlier. "If the student got little from his mates," Adams observes, "he got little more from his masters. The four years passed at college were, for his purposes, wasted" (p. 59).

Adams followed his graduation from Harvard with a tour of Europe, where he intended to undertake graduate study in Germany. While Europe offered the young man an exciting exposure to the great cultures of the past, especially Rome, the past was still no guide for the present, and the young student felt that he was, in Matthew Arnold's words, "wandering between two worlds, one dead, the other powerless to be born" (Adams, p. 108).

The outbreak of the Civil War in the spring of 1861 would be a defining event for Henry, as well as the rest of the nation. Adams served as his father's unofficial private secretary while Charles Francis Adams was minister to Great Britain. This allowed Henry to witness international power politics firsthand. While the young man took great satisfaction in the triumph of the antislavery movement, as represented in Abraham Lincoln's Emancipation Proclamation of 1863 and the eventual triumph of the Union cause in the war, the conduct of the British and the machinations associated with his father's sensitive position left him convinced that "truth in politics might be ignored as a delusion" (p. 159).

Upon returning to the United States in 1868, the Adamses discovered that their homeland bore little resemblance to the place that they had left behind. "Had they been Tyrian traders of the year 1000 B.C., landing from a galley fresh from Gibraltar," Adams observes, "they could hardly have been stranger on the shore of a world, so changed from what it had been ten years before" (p. 237). Great corporations had come into existence and, with them, elaborate systems of production, transportation, and finance. "The world," Adams observed, "after 1865, became a bankers' world" (p. 247), and he wanted no part of it.

Having given up the notion of public service because he was appalled at the blatant corruption that characterized the administration of President Ulysses S. Grant, Adams became for a time a political journalist in Washington, D.C. In 1870 he accepted a position as professor of history at Harvard and began in earnest his search for a principle of unity and meaning in an increasingly alien and fragmented world. Eventually, he would publish several books in his search for coherence, but the results were always unsatisfactory. "He had even published a dozen volumes of American history," he notes, "for no other purpose than to . . . fix for a familiar moment a necessary sequence of human movement" (p. 382). The effort ultimately failed because "where he saw sequence, other men saw something quite different, and no one saw the same unit of measure" (p. 382).

If history offered no principle of coherence, even at the level of cause and effect, science was even worse. The relentless and dramatic development of scientific knowledge in the late nineteenth century revealed a world of dynamic and even chaotic forces that previously were not even known to exist. He saw many of these at the World's Columbian Exposition in Chicago in 1893, where the latest technological innovations were on display. Such dramatic developments of arcane and complex forces represented for Adams yet another "breach of continuity—a rupture in historical sequence" (p. 340). The evolution of these apparently chaotic yet powerful forces led Adams and other thoughtful people to wonder where it was all going. "Blindly some very powerful energy was at work, doing something that nobody wanted done" (p. 338). It seemed that a new world was emerging, helter-skelter, and no one was sure just where it was leading.

In 1900 Adams visited yet another world's fair, the Great Exposition in Paris. What he found was both fascinating and disconcerting. Technology and science had made tremendous advances into the unknown. New energies and new devices such as electrical generators and internal combustion engines had emerged, and Adams wondered "how much of it could have been grasped by the best-informed man in the world" (p. 379). One scientific friend "seemed prepared for anything, even for an indeterminable number of universes interfused—physics stark mad in metaphysics" (p. 382).

When contrasting the unifying faith and force of the Middle Ages with the chaotic force of the present age in the chapter "The Dynamo and the Virgin (1900)," Adams found the differences between the two profound. While both ages possessed substantial energy, enough to build the great cathedrals then and the mighty electrical generators known as dynamos,

the contrast between these forces is stark. The force of faith in the Middle Ages brought harmony, meaning, and beauty to human existence, all symbolized by the Virgin and the magnificent cathedrals built in her honor. On the other hand, the electrical force of the dynamo, which Adams identifies as the symbol of the modern age, is arcane and, of itself, meaningless. It represents energy for energy's sake, and as such is worshipped because energy and those who control it rule the modern world. Adams notes of the mighty, forty-foot dynamo that before too long "one began to pray to it" as a symbol of "ultimate energy" (p. 380). Unfortunately, the dynamo's force can neither unify nor create and points to nothing beyond itself. Industrial might and scientific technology could not substitute for faith in the modern world. As an aging Adams sadly observes, "All the steam in the world could not, like the Virgin, build Chartres" (p. 388).

In his chapter "A Dynamic Theory of History (1904)," Adams attempts to find a unifying principle in the continued evolution of force itself. The appearance of force would change throughout the ages, he felt, but the underlying element would remain the same. "Whether the attractive energy has been called God or Nature, the mechanism has always been the same" (p. 487). For obvious reasons, such a theory, while possibly answering the need for some unifying principle in the evolution of human existence, could not be completely satisfying to one seeking faith and meaning as well.

In the final analysis, Adams's protagonist concludes that the modern world would simply have to learn to live with complexity, uncertainty, and even ambiguity. Unity, if it exists at all, will have to be self-generated by the individual since it appears that over the ages, "the universe that had formed him took shape in his mind as a reflection of his own unity" (p. 475). For Adams, this is the sum of knowledge and the concluding point of his lifelong pursuit of education. Quoting from Shakespeare's *Hamlet,* he observes, "The rest is silence" (p. 504).

RECEPTION

Despite its complexity, *The Education* was well received both by Adams's friends and acquaintances when distributed privately in 1907 and by the general public when it was published in 1918. Eventually, it became a best-seller and was awarded the Pulitzer Prize in 1919. That is not to say that opinions about the book were unanimous, then or now. Henry James loved it, Theodore Roosevelt called the work a "masterpiece," and the book received an enthusiastic response from the avant-garde of 1918 (Dusinberre, p. 210). However,

Charles W. Eliot, former president of Harvard, to whom Adams sent a private copy of the book, once made reference to Adams and his work as "an overrated man and a much overrated book" (Samuels, p. 334). Over the years, many readers have been both attracted to the book and "baffled" by it (Samuels, p. 336). It is partly because of this that Adams's biographer calls *The Education* "a consummately successful failure" (Samuels, p. 345). Also, many critics disagree as to the final tone of the work. One calls it "a long lamentation over the failure of a lifetime of 'education'" (Burich, p. 468). Another insists that "the apocalyptic vision of 'Chaos' reflects the entire tone of the work," and its final vision is characterized by "darkness" (Rowe, pp. 116, 130). Yet another critic insists that the final chapters of the work "form a triumphant conclusion" (Bishop, p. 116), while another refers to its "incongruous 'happy ending'" (Folsom, p. 162). Similarly, regarding the question as to whether Adams actually finds the unity that he seeks throughout the work, one critic observes that Adams found "the contradictions [of life] were unresolvable" (Samuels, p. 395), but another insists that, ultimately, Adams "rediscovers unity" (Horwitz, p. 137).

In the final analysis, *The Education of Henry Adams* is a work that a multitude of readers have continued to turn to again and again in the years since its publication. Its classic status is obviously and finally reflected in its enduring presence as an engaging, perplexing, and always fascinating example of the American consciousness examining itself.

See also Autobiography; Science and Technology; Wealth

BIBLIOGRAPHY

Primary Work

Adams, Henry. *The Education of Henry Adams.* 1918. Boston: Houghton Mifflin, 1973.

Secondary Works

Banta, Martha. "Being a 'Begonia' in a Man's World." In *New Essays on the Education of Henry Adams,* edited by John Carlos Rowe, pp. 49–86. Cambridge, U.K.: Cambridge University Press, 1996.

Bishop, Ferman. *Henry Adams.* Boston: Twayne, 1979.

Burich, Keith R. "Henry Adams, the Second Law of Thermodynamics, and the Course of History." *Journal of the History of Ideas* 48 (1987): 467–482.

Chalfant, Edward. *Improvement of the World, A Biography of Henry Adams: His Last Life, 1891–1918.* North Haven, Conn.: Archon Books, 2001.

Contosta, David R. *Henry Adams and the American Experiment.* Edited by Oscar Handlin. Boston: Little, Brown, 1980.

Dusinberre, William. *Henry Adams: The Myth of Failure.* Charlottesville: University Press of Virginia, 1980.

Folsom, James K. "Mutation as Metaphor in *The Education of Henry Adams.*" *ELH* 30 (1963): 162–174.

Horwitz, Howard. "*The Education* and the Salvation of History." In *New Essays on the Education of Henry Adams,* edited by John Carlos Rowe, pp. 115–156. Cambridge, U.K.: Cambridge University Press, 1996.

Rowe, John Carlos. *Henry Adams and Henry James: The Emergence of a Modern Consciousness.* Ithaca, N.Y.: Cornell University Press, 1976.

Samuels, Ernest. *Henry Adams: The Major Phase.* Cambridge, Mass.: Belknap Press of Harvard University Press, 1964.

Thomas, Brook. "The Education of an American Classic: The Survival of Failure." In *New Essays on the Education of Henry Adams,* edited by John Carlos Rowe, pp. 23–47. Cambridge, U.K.: Cambridge University Press, 1996.

Williams, William Appleman. "Thoughts on Rereading Henry Adams." *Journal of American History* 68 (1981): 7–15.

Len Gougeon

THE EMPEROR JONES

The Emperor Jones was written during the fall of 1920 in Provincetown, Massachusetts, and produced by the Provincetown Players, the amateur theatrical group that had discovered Eugene O'Neill (1888–1953) as a young playwright and given him the resources—in the form of a stage, actors, and very limited technical facilities—to develop into American's most promising young playwright. Indeed, in the spring of that year O'Neill had won the first of his eventual four Pulitzer Prizes. The play was first produced at the Provincetown Playhouse in New York's Greenwich Village on 1 November 1920. The production proved so successful that it was moved to Broadway, where it ran for 204 performances, the first modernist play by an American to be a box office hit. This was an unlikely outcome in 1920 for a play that not only was avant-garde theatrically but also featured an African American actor playing an African American tragic hero.

O'Neill said in an interview with Charles Sweeney in 1924 that the idea for *The Emperor Jones* was given to him by an old circus man who had traveled with a tent show through the West Indies in the early twentieth century. The man told O'Neill a story he had heard about the Haitian president Jean Vilbrun Guillaume Sam. Sam had taken office in March 1915 and in the face of violent opposition had executed 167 political prisoners by July. In the end a mob of

---

The Emperor Jones: Opening night in New York

Theater: Provincetown Playhouse
Opening night: 1 November 1920
Produced by: The Provincetown Players
Written by: Eugene O'Neill

Cast:

Jasper Deeter .... Harry Smithers, *a Cockney*
Christine Ell .... An Old Native Woman
Charles Ellis .... Lem, *a Native Chief*
Charles S. Gilpin .... Brutus Jones, *Emperor*

---

citizens literally tore him to pieces and bore his dismembered corpse through the streets of Port-au-Prince, the event that precipitated the U.S. invasion of Haiti and its subsequent nineteen-year occupation. O'Neill's friend said there was a story in Haiti that President Sam had claimed the people could never kill him with a lead bullet, that he would shoot himself with a silver bullet first.

In *The Emperor Jones,* Brutus Jones, an African American former Pullman car porter and escaped convict, has landed on a Caribbean island, which is, as O'Neill characterizes it in his description of the locale of the play, "as yet not self-determined by White Marines" (p. 1030). Working for the white English trader Henry Smithers, Jones has exploited the local black populace to get rich and then made himself into the "emperor" of the island. Through exorbitant taxation, he has made a fortune, which he has placed in an offshore bank account. The source of his power is a self-created myth that originated when an islander tried to shoot him. The gun misfired, and Jones shot the other man instead. Jones told the people that he survived because only a silver bullet could kill him. In the course of the play Jones flees on foot from the insurgents, who are preparing for attack with rituals involving a steadily beating drum.

Jones's well-planned escape is foiled when he gets to the night forest. He becomes exhausted, going around and around in circles, and begins to see hallucinations, which he calls "ha'nts." In six scenes O'Neill takes Brutus Jones from his present state of rising terror back through incidents from his own life and from the collective life of his ancestors. In scene 2 he hallucinates, seeing creatures that O'Neill calls "the Little Formless Fears" (p. 1045), a device that was suggested by an incident in Frank Norris's novel *McTeague* (1899). Jones relives killing a black man in a crap game (scene 3) and killing a white prison guard while on a chain gang (scene 4). Then he lives through a slave auction (scene 5) and a vision of being

imprisoned on a slave ship (scene 6). As he hallucinates he gradually fires each of the five lead bullets from his gun so that he is left with only the silver bullet with which he plans to shoot himself if need be. But this he shoots at a "Crocodile God" to whom he is about to be sacrificed by a Congolese "witch-doctor" (p. 1057) when he imagines being in Africa (scene 7). The play ends with a final scene in which gunfire is heard offstage while the insurgent leader Lem tells Smithers that he spent the night melting down coins to make silver bullets in order to kill Jones. As Smithers scornfully proclaims his doubt that the soldiers are capable of catching Jones, they emerge from the forest bearing the dead body (scene 8).

CULTURAL INFLUENCES

Besides the story about President Sam, there are several other immediate cultural influences on the play. O'Neill acknowledged that he had read about religious feasts in the Congo in which a drum began at a normal heart rate and then slowly accelerated and intensified, stimulating the heartbeats of the participants to do likewise. This was the source of the play's drum, which begins at seventy-two beats per minute and continues, slowly increasing in speed and intensity throughout the play and ceasing immediately when the gunfire is heard in the last scene. Like many other modernist artists in the late 1910s, O'Neill was deeply interested in the "primitive" and its possibilities for informing his drama. With his friend William Zorach, an artist, sculptor, and stage designer for the Provincetown Players, O'Neill shared a fascination with African art and particularly with masks, which were being introduced to New York at that time by the art critic Marius de Zayas, chiefly through Alfred Stieglitz's Photo-Secession gallery.

Travis Bogard has noted that *African Negro Sculpture*, a book of photographs by Charles Sheeler that appeared early in 1918, was of vital importance to O'Neill. A rare privately printed book, it includes twenty eight-by-ten-inch photographs of objects in Marius de Zayas's collection, most of which are sculptures from west and central Africa. Unfortunately de Zayas's attitude toward the art that he championed combined extraordinary racism with a passionate response to the beauty of the work. In a posthumously published article in *Arts Magazine,* de Zayas called African art the product of "a mentality of fear, . . . devoid of the faculties of observation and analysis" and the "pure expression of the emotion of a savage race" (p. 109). O'Neill certainly was aware of de Zayas's ideas about the African "mentality," and the play has been duly criticized for its suggestion of these ideas. However, as J. Michael Dash has noted, O'Neill's play is singular for its time in its attempt to treat a black protagonist in terms of a larger human tragedy. Rather than using Jones's journey into the forest and into his own psyche as a reinforcement of the myth of primitivism and a thus a justification for the occupation of Haiti by American marines, O'Neill uses it to explore the nature of human fear.

The conception of Africa as the "Land of Fright" (p. 109) fed into another of O'Neill's interests at this time, Jungian psychology. Like other modernists of his generation, he was intrigued by the new German psychology and read most of the books by Sigmund Freud, Carl Gustav Jung, and Alfred Adler that were translated into English during the second decade of the twentieth century. It was only Jung who interested him deeply, however, and the influence of Jungian thought is evident in *The Emperor Jones*. In the play, as Doris Falk was the first to note, Brutus Jones travels back through his own memory into a version of Jung's collective unconscious, where he confronts the unconscious ideas and symbols that O'Neill connects with the collective history of the African people. In the action of the play, Jones's journey takes place in his consciousness, but it is externally signified by his changing costume. When the play begins, Jones is clothed in an elaborate and colorful uniform of his own devising, meant to dazzle his "subjects" with his importance. As he makes his way through the forest and experiences his successive hallucinations, the accoutrements of civilization are gradually stripped away. In the series of scenes he removes his spurs, his sword, his jacket, and his boots. Gradually his clothes are torn away by the forest until he wears nothing but a fragment resembling a loincloth.

Finally Jones is brought back to Africa in his hallucination, where the last trace of his Western identity, his Baptist Christianity, is pitted against the pantheistic religion that O'Neill imagines for his ancestors. Jones's fear, the character trait that drives the action, is closely associated with his sense of guilt, a guilt that O'Neill suggests is grounded in his fundamental betrayal of his people, from the killing of his friend in the crap game to the subjugation of what he calls the "ign'rent bush niggers" (p. 1040) on the island. As Jones calls on Jesus to save him, the witch doctor mimes the demands of the African religion. Jones hallucinates being offered as a sacrifice to the Crocodile God for having betrayed the African people and their diasporic descendants, both in the United States and on the island. His final mistake, however, is shooting at the god, the ultimate betrayal of his ancestors and the rejection of his authentic self. This act results in his being discovered by the insurgents and killed.

Jung is not the only thinker in the background of Jones's journey into collective memory. Frederic Carpenter and Edwin Engel suggested several decades ago that Jack London might be a source for Jones's experience. Engel says that, using a concept London termed the "germplasm," he accounted for "the existence of racial memories in his 'atavistic brain,' 'memories of the whole evolution of the race'" (p. 53), a device that London uses in his science fiction novel *Before Adam* (1906). Noting the influence of O'Neill's favorite philosopher, Friedrich Nietzsche, Michael Hinden suggests that O'Neill is representing through Jones's psychological experience "the collective conscience of Americans" (p. 3) and uncovering Americans' national original sin, slavery. He contends that the crocodile is the "symbolic epiphany of the false god Mammon, upon whose altar Jones has sacrificed throughout his life" (p. 3), cheating, stealing, killing, and finally subjugating and exploiting the people on the island in pursuit of the "long green" (p. 1035), as Jones puts it.

O'Neill saw this self-betrayal as a national trait, a trait that he summed up in an interview with Hamilton Basso by quoting the biblical statement: "For what shall it profit a man if he shall gain the whole world and lose his own soul?" (p. 230). He said that the much-vaunted American Dream was nothing more than the selfish, greedy pursuit of material things and that the United States was a great failure as a nation because so much potential and such great ideals had been wasted on petty pursuits. Having risen from a passenger train porter to a wealthy "emperor," Brutus Jones is the epitome of the materialistic American Dream that O'Neill describes, and he has learned its rules directly from the "white quality" (p. 1035) on the Pullman cars. As he tells Smithers: "Dere's little stealin' like you does, and dere's big stealin' like I does. For de little stealin' dey gits you in jail soon or late. For de big stealin' dey makes you Emperor and puts you in de Hall o' Fame when you croaks" (p. 1035). In the course of the play Jones is proven wrong, at least in the context of the Caribbean. Like the imperial United States in the early twentieth century, Jones enters his Caribbean island with contempt for its inhabitants, and he quickly executes a plan to exploit them. In O'Neill's imaginative construction of history retribution is swift.

STAGING

In the staging of the play O'Neill received energetic and effective support from the Provincetown Players. In order to achieve the effect of infinite space that the director, George Cram Cook, thought was necessary for the play, the group constructed in its tiny theater a plaster dome modeled on the *Kuppelhorizont* (sky dome) that became common in German theaters after Max Reinhardt installed one in the Grosses Schauspielhaus in 1919. As Cook had hoped, with sets and lighting designed by Cleon Throckmorton, the dome proved extremely effective in creating the illusion of limitless space on the stage of the Provincetown Playhouse. The group also located in Charles Gilpin, and later in Paul Robeson, actors whose great talents had little opportunity to show themselves in the limited roles offered to African Americans in the commercial theater. It took a challenge like that of Brutus Jones for these actors to become known to the general American theatergoing public. After the breakthrough role of Brutus Jones, though, several plays with serious and demanding roles for African American actors were produced during the 1920s, including O'Neill's *All God's Chillun Got Wings* (1924).

See also Blacks; *McTeague;* Theater

BIBLIOGRAPHY
Primary Work
O'Neill, Eugene. *Complete Plays, 1913–1920.* Edited by Travis Bogard. New York: Library of America, 1988.

Secondary Works
Basso, Hamilton. "Profiles: The Tragic Sense." *New Yorker* (13 March 1948). Reprinted in *Conversations with Eugene O'Neill*, edited by Mark W. Estrin, pp. 224–236. Jackson: University Press of Mississippi, 1990.

Bogard, Travis. *Contour in Time: The Plays of Eugene O'Neill.* 1988. New York: Oxford University Press, 1988.

Carpenter, Frederic I. *Eugene O'Neill.* 1964. New York: Twayne, 1979.

Dash, J. Michael. *Haiti and the United States: National Stereotypes and the Literary Imagination.* 1988. New York: St. Martin's, 1997.

Engel, Edwin A. *The Haunted Heroes of Eugene O'Neill.* Cambridge, Mass.: Harvard University Press, 1953.

Falk, Doris V. *Eugene O'Neill and the Tragic Tension: An Interpretive Study of the Plays.* New Brunswick, N.J.: Rutgers University Press, 1958. New York: Gordian Press, 1982.

Hinden, Michael. "*The Emperor Jones:* O'Neill, Nietzsche, and the American Past." *Eugene O'Neill Newsletter* 3, no. 3 (1980): 2–4.

Murphy, Brenda. "*McTeague's* Dream and *The Emperor Jones:* O'Neill's Move from Naturalism to Modernism." *Eugene O'Neill Review* 17, nos. 1–2 (1993): 21–29.

Nolan, Patrick J. "*The Emperor Jones:* A Jungian View of the Origin of Fear in the Black Race." *Eugene O'Neill Newsletter* 4, nos. 1–2 (1980): 6–9.

Poole, Gabriele. "'Blarsted Niggers!': *The Emperor Jones* and Modernism's Encounter with Africa." *Eugene O'Neill Review* 18, nos. 1–2 (1994): 21–37.

Saiz, Peter R. "The Colonial Story in *The Emperor Jones.*" *Eugene O'Neill Review* 17, nos. 1–2 (1993): 31–38.

Sarlós, Robert Károly. *Jig Cook and the Provincetown Players: Theatre in Ferment.* Amherst: University of Massachusetts Press, 1982. Production of *The Emperor Jones* is discussed throughout the book, but of particular interest is the detailed description of the dome, pp. 204–206.

Sweeney, Charles P. "Back to the Source of Plays Written by Eugene O'Neill." *New York World,* 9 November 1924, p. 5.

Zayas, Marius de. "How, When, and Why Modern Art Came to New York." *Arts Magazine* 54, no. 8 (1980): 96–126.

Brenda Murphy

ETHNOLOGY

In 1888, while searching for lost cattle, Richard Wetherill and Charles Mason first caught sight of what is now called Cliff Palace in Mesa Verde, Colorado, the ancient cliff dwellings abandoned by Puebloan peoples centuries earlier. The Wetherill family's initial excavations soon turned into a family-owned cottage industry and a moneymaking venture as items yielded during their "digs" were sold to private collectors or museums. Wetherill would go on to excavate other well-known sites, including Chaco Canyon and Keet Seel. Ancient dwellings eventually received protection under the American Antiquities Act of 1906, which included legislation designed to thwart Wetherill's claims and to protect the U.S. prehistoric cultural heritage that was fast becoming prey to "pothunters" and others who wantonly destroyed these areas for sport. The act's language indicated that archaeologists and anthropologists had finally achieved scientific standing, because it limited the excavation of ruins to "institutions which [the secretaries of the interior, agriculture, and war] may deem properly qualified to conduct such examination, excavation, or gathering . . . [and provided that] the examinations, excavations, and gatherings are undertaken for the benefit of reputable museums, universities, colleges, or other recognized scientific or educational institutions."

BUILDING THE FOUNDATIONS FOR A NEW DISCIPLINE
Exploring and collecting became the distinguishing characteristics of the mid-1800s to early 1900s, a period that marked the emergence of research universities and major museums, some largely funded by the "robber

barons" Andrew Carnegie, John D. Rockefeller, and Russell Sage, men who adopted philanthropy as a way to polish their tarnished images. "The Age of Museums," as this period is often called, also grew out of the public's growing fascination with natural history. Amateur collectors and "scientists" assembled items and compared notes on everything they had gathered. There were also "gentlemen scholars" who employed collectors to accompany the U.S. Army Corps of Topographical Engineers (later called the Corps of Engineers) who were exploring and mapping the West and Southwest. These hired collectors brought back specimens for members of Albert Gallatin's American Ethnological Society to study, a group founded in 1842. In 1846, at the same time that natural history and other collections were being amassed and buildings were being created in which to house them, Congress established the Smithsonian Institution with funds bequeathed by the Englishman James Smithson.

When Spencer F. Baird (1823–1887) became the assistant secretary in charge of the National Museum in 1850, the Smithsonian began its first attempt at systematically collecting anthropological material. It received government collections containing items gathered by the U.S. Exploring Expedition, an international scientific voyage sponsored by the United States to travel the world and gather items for a natural history collection. It also received material from Matthew Perry's voyages to Africa and Japan and gifts to American presidents from foreign dignitaries, and in the late 1870s it would receive around five hundred paintings of North American Indians by George Catlin. Because the collections were growing so fast, Baird created a formal section of ethnology with curators who could care for them. The section's creation allowed Baird to institute a larger, more systematic method of anthropological collecting. It would also ease the efforts of John Wesley Powell (1834–1902) to establish a separate Bureau of Ethnology more than two decades later.

In 1866 the Illinois legislature granted Powell $25,000 to direct and curate a museum in Normal. To fund an expedition to the Rocky Mountains, Powell sought and received additional support and equipment from the Smithsonian and several Illinois public institutions. After a second successful trip, Powell received added funding from Congress to oversee the Geographical and Geological Survey of the Rocky Mountain Region. While on this survey, Powell spent two months at the Hopi mesas, studying Hopi culture, language, architecture, myths, and more, all of which he included in an 1875 *Scribner's Magazine* article. This trip set the stage for Powell's interest in the Southwest as a "laboratory" where various peoples living in the same environment could be studied.

Powell had become the noted expert on western Indians, and he used this image to garner congressional support for an ethnological classification of American Indians whose cultures he felt should be documented before they had disappeared, a prevalent belief held during this time period. In an 1879 letter to a longtime friend, J. D. C. Atkins, chairman of the House Appropriations Committee, Powell requested funding for the completion of *Contributions to North American Ethnology* under the Smithsonian Institution's direction. That same year Congress also implemented legislation that led to the Bureau of American Ethnology's establishment as a separate research unit of the Smithsonian, independent of the National Museum. The bureau's research focus was the ethnology, archaeology, and linguistics of North American Indians. The 1879 Civil Sundry Bill contained Powell's request to Atkins for a bureau, and by 1880 the Senate had confirmed Powell's position as director of the newly created Bureau of Ethnology. The bureau's projects helped found the field of anthropology at a time when universities offered no advanced degrees in the field and when no full-time anthropologists were employed.

While Powell was working toward the creation of the bureau, individuals from the Topographical Engineers were continuing their surveys of the Southwest. In this capacity Ferdinand Vandiveer Hayden (1829–1887) traveled to Colorado Territory in 1873 with a hired photographer, William Henry Jackson (1843–1942). While in Colorado, Jackson's photographic party observed and made note of numerous cliff dwellings, the same dwellings that Wetherill would soon "discover" and excavate. Additionally, in 1875 Jackson had also detected and photographed cliff dwellings in the Four Corners region, Mesa Verde, and Chaco Canyon. These photographs, along with the collections made by Powell's Rocky Mountain survey and three other surveys, would be consolidated to fashion the "Indian" displays at the Philadelphia Centennial Exposition. The exhibition's success is what prompted Congress to fund the U.S. National Museum building, which opened in 1878.

POWELL'S SOUTHWEST "LABORATORY"

As director of the new Bureau of Ethnology, Powell sent to the Southwest a team consisting of the bureau's administration officer and his wife, James and Matilda Stevenson; the photographer Jack Hillers; and the young curator of the ethnological department of the National Museum, Frank Hamilton Cushing. Their mission was to survey and collect items for the National Museum from Pueblo Indian villages and

Ruins at Canon del Muerte, Arizona. Photograph by Jack Hillers from a Bureau of American Ethnology expedition to the Southwest, c. 1880. THE LIBRARY OF CONGRESS

ruins in Arizona and New Mexico. They made their first stop in 1879 in Zuni Pueblo, New Mexico, "collecting," as Stevenson noted, "in the dead hours of night" (Fowler, p. 107), well over ten thousand pounds of cultural objects from the Zuni and Hopi Pueblos. Matilda Stevenson (1849–1915), the first woman to work in the Southwest, conducted her own studies with the Zuni. In particular, she was the first ethnologist to consider women and children worthy study subjects, and her gender allowed her access to areas generally unavailable to men. After spending a month at Zuni and Hopi, the Stevensons traveled to Fort Wingate, leaving Cushing behind, where he would remain for another 4.5 years.

During his tenure at Zuni, Cushing (1857–1900) was initiated into the Priesthood of the Bow, was made a Zuni war chief, and received the Zuni name Medicine Flower. He also learned the language and participated in all aspects of Zuni life. In 1881 Cushing met the *Boston Herald* journalist Sylvester Baxter, who had traveled to Zuni to do a story on Cushing. The two men became lifelong friends, and Cushing became the subject of many stories drawn from their correspondence, which Baxter included in the newspaper. The following year Cushing and several Zuni leaders headed east and became a media sensation with Boston's elite, which included Helen Hunt Jackson (1830–1885), author of *Ramona* (1884) and *A Century of Dishonor* (1881), an unconventional history that provided a searing indictment of federal Indian policy. Jackson had hoped that both of these publications would help redress Indian grievances.

Cushing wrote a series of articles about the years he spent trying to behave like a Zuni. Through the fall of 1882 *Century Illustrated Monthly Magazine* carried Cushing's highly romanticized articles under the title

"My Adventures in Zuni." "Zuni Fetishes," a paper describing myths and religious rituals, followed in 1883, and a series of eighteen articles collectively known as *Zuni Breadstuff* appeared in 1884–1885. Cushing was the first anthropologist who chose to live among the people he studied, transforming him from a detached observer to a community member. In speaking of cultures in the plural, his work foreshadowed the cultural relativism of Franz Boas. Indeed, Cushing's work became the impetus for generations of anthropologists to journey to the Southwest, thus making it the laboratory that Powell had imagined it was.

Conducting archaeological work near Cushing was Adolph Bandelier (1840–1914), who had arrived in the Southwest in 1880. Powell had recommended that Charles Eliot Norton's Archaeological Institute of America place Bandelier in the Southwest. Despite this endorsement, Bandelier remained distant from Powell and the Bureau of Ethnology, critiqued Powell's surveys, and disparaged the Stevensons' work methods. Four years after the Stevensons had raided Zuni, Bandelier visited and noted in his diary how their shameless plundering had destroyed the church there. Like Cushing, Bandelier pioneered many practices that have become foundational in modern archaeology, and he even authored a documentary novel called *The Delight Makers* (1890), a romantic tale about ancient Pueblo cliff dwellers that allowed him the opportunity to teach the public about Pueblo customs and beliefs. As the public's interest in anthropology and archaeology grew, efforts to preserve individual ruins from pothunters gathered momentum.

Anthropological work took the founder of modern anthropology, Franz Boas (1858–1942), beyond the Southwest from 1883 to 1884. In Baffinland, near the Arctic Circle, Boas studied the Eskimos and their perception of landscape as expressed through language. From 1886 to 1888 Boas studied the Kwakiutl of the Pacific Northwest, which became the group that formed the basis of his anthropological career. His language studies in the Arctic and Pacific Northwest led to his development of "cultural relativism," a theory that traced human difference based on culture rather than race or social evolution. At that time, accepted racial-scientific and cultural evolutionist theories claimed that race created difference, and this theory was used to demonstrate white superiority either through measurements of skull size in craniology or the perceived lack of culture in primitive or savage societies. But Boas believed that all groups had their own cultures; thus he promoted the idea of cultures as plural, not as something that groups had or did not have. White western European culture had become the norm by which all other peoples were measured, which was an

assumption that Boas understood and sought to discredit. Celebrated anthropologists who would study under Boas include Margaret Mead, Ruth Benedict, and Zora Neale Hurston, whom Boas aided in her publication of *Mules and Men* (1935), a book of African American folklore.

THE WETHERILLS AND THE AMERICAN ANTIQUITIES ACT

As anthropologists and archaeologists professionalized, the Wetherills remained a threat to their future. Between their first "discovery" of Cliff Palace in 1888 and their initial exhibition in 1889, the Wetherills located and named over 180 major and minor ruins in the Southwest. In addition to exhibiting and selling their collections, the Wetherills also guided tourists to the ruins for a fee. When the Swedish tourist Gustaf Nils Adolf Nordenskiöld (1868–1895) turned collector and attempted to ship several containers of artifacts gathered by the Wetherills back to Sweden, public sentiment against the commercial exploitation of archaeological sites grew. Although the second shipment was seized, no laws existed to stop excavations or shipment of materials out of the country, so the Wetherills continued their work unabated.

Between 1889 and 1899 the Wetherills worked their way, often multiple times, through Grand Gulch, Keet Seel in Tsegi Canyon, and Pueblo Bonito in Chaco Canyon. Their excavations ended in 1899, when Edgar Lee Hewett, president of New Mexico Normal University in Las Vegas, Santa Fe Archaeological Society members, and J. Bradford Prince, governor of New Mexico Territory, pressed for legislation to stop the looting and selling of artifacts. They also called for legislation designed to protect American antiquities, which resulted in the 1906 law. The Antiquities Act proved useful for the preservation of lands in the West and authorized the creation of national monuments, such as Chaco Canyon National Monument and Navajo National Monument. Publicity surrounding the Wetherills and the act's passage aroused the public's interest in archaeology.

Also rousing interest were three exhibitions—the 1892 Columbian Historical Exposition in Madrid; the 1893 World's Columbian Exposition in Chicago; and the 1904 World's Fair in St. Louis. In the Madrid exposition the United States occupied six rooms, and the American Southwest exhibit, occupying one large hall, received high praise. A young Franz Boas helped arrange displays for the Chicago exposition, a large portion of which eventually formed the Field Columbian Museum's foundation. This same period also saw the establishment of several archaeological and ethnological museums in major cities, such as the Museum of American

Archaeology in Philadelphia in 1889. In 1894 the American Museum of Natural History's anthropology program placed Frederic W. Putnam (1839–1915) in charge, and Putnam brought Franz Boas to work with him. Putnam played a major role in training future anthropologists at Harvard and Yale. He also helped organize anthropology departments at other universities. In particular he organized the University of California at Berkeley's Department of Anthropology in 1901. By 1906 the Yale University Museum, the Brooklyn Institute of Arts and Sciences, Phillips Academy, the Delaware County Institute of Science, the Ohio State Archaeological and Historical Society, the Minnesota Historical Society, the Milwaukee Public Museum, the University of California at Berkeley, and the Bishop Museum in Hawaii all included exhibits of anthropological collections.

WRITING THE SOUTHWEST

The 1880s and 1890s saw popular and scholarly writers transforming the Southwest into an exotic and foreign country within the United States. Indeed, the Southwest had become a "land of enchantment" created in work such as Bandelier's fictionalized story *The Delight Makers* and Frederick H. Chapin's *The Land of the Cliff-Dwellers* (1892). Powell's southwestern laboratory had created a yearning among tourists, artists, poets, novelists, and essayists for a different kind of life offered by romantic and noble visions of Indian and Hispanic lives. While anthropologists and archaeologists produced the first southwestern literature—Bandelier and Cushing, for example, told stories rather than science—many more writers wrote novels in an ethnographic framework that championed Indians' and Hispanos' rights as well as their cultures and arts. The lesser-known writers Charles Francis Saunders, author of *The Indians of the Terraced Houses* (1912), and Leo Crane, author of *Indians of the Enchanted Desert* (1925) and *Desert Drums* (1928), opposed attempts to assimilate Indians, and these men's romantic histories of the Pueblos provided a way for them to express their outrage over the Pueblos' mistreatment.

Another writer whose work echoed the ongoing activity of archaeologists and anthropologists such as Bandelier, Cushing, Jesse Walter Fewkes, Washington Matthews, and the Stevensons was Charles F. Lummis (1859–1928), a Harvard-educated easterner who had "tramped" his way across the country, traveling through Colorado, New Mexico, Arizona, and southern California. Lummis arrived in Los Angeles in 1885 and worked for the *Los Angeles Times* for three years until a severe stroke forced him to leave the city and recover in New Mexico, recuperating in the home of

Amado Chaves, former speaker of the New Mexico territorial government. Lummis's experience with the family cultivated a deep respect for old Spanish beliefs and practices and affection for the people. After recovering, Lummis spent three years at Isleta Pueblo recording and publishing his experiences. His work includes *A New Mexico David* (1891), *A Tramp across the Continent* (1892), *Some Strange Corners of Our Country* (1892), *The Land of Poco Tiempo* (1893), *The Spanish Pioneers* (1893), *The Man Who Married the Moon* (1894), *The Enchanted Burro* (1897), and *The King of the Broncos* (1897). Lummis mainly wrote for an eastern audience, promoting the region's unique landscape and population. Although he celebrated the more romantic elements of Pueblo Indian and Mexican American culture, he portrayed negatively the Indians' belief in witchcraft and the activities of the Mexican American *penitentes*. In addition to meeting the religious, educational, social aid, and political organizing needs of rural communities, the *penitentes* engaged in self-flagellation and crucifixion rituals.

Lummis's enthusiastic promotion of the Southwest continued during his tenure as editor and chief contributor of the influential magazine *Land of Sunshine*, launched in 1894. Lummis praised the culture, climate, "Spanish" heritage, and architecture of southern California and the Southwest. His new home became a meeting place for artists, intellectuals, and politicians, including Charlotte Perkins Gilman, author of "The Yellow Wall-Paper," Mary Austin, and John Muir. Lummis and Helen Hunt Jackson actively campaigned for the rights of southern California Indians. A negative outcome of Jackson's efforts to fictionalize the plight of Indians, however, was that individuals promoting investment and settlement in California had seized upon the romantic image of "Spanish" ranchos and missions that her novel *Ramona* had created, thus leading to Indians' further dispossession.

John Muir (1838–1914), founder of the Sierra Club, began a thousand-mile walk from Indiana to the Gulf of Mexico in 1867. He finally settled in California's Yosemite Vally and wrote well-received articles about the area that attracted writers like Ralph Waldo Emerson who eventually found their way to Muir's cabin. His articles in *Century Magazine* drew attention to the destruction caused by grazing and led to the creation of Yosemite National Park. His book *Our National Parks* (1901) caught the interest of President Theodore Roosevelt, who visited Muir in 1903. After this visit, Roosevelt signed legislation creating five national parks, and the Antiquities Act, passed during his term in office, allowed for the ongoing creation of historic landmarks.

Like Lummis and Jackson, Mary Austin (1868–1934) actively campaigned for Indian rights. Born and raised in Illinois, Austin moved with her family to California's San Joaquin Valley. Her journey toward Los Angeles led to her first publication in the *Overland Monthly*, "The Mother of Felipe" (1892). After her marriage, Austin and her new family settled in California's Owens Valley, where the Mojave Desert inspired her to write *The Land of Little Rain* (1903), a collection of nature essays that the *Atlantic Monthly* serialized. Austin was fascinated by indigenous peoples who regulated their lives according to the rhythms of the land and nature. Stories that dramatize the lives of these individuals include *The Basket Woman* (1904), *Lost Borders* (1909), *The Flock* (1906), and a play called *The Arrow-Maker* (1910). She remained in California until the late 1920s, when she settled in Santa Fe, New Mexico.

After moving to New Mexico, Austin was one of the group of artists who participated in the Taos "salon" of Mabel Dodge Luhan (1879–1962), a New York socialite and patron of the arts who had settled in the Southwest in 1917 and married the Pueblo Indian Antonio Luhan. Luhan's books, including her four-volume autobiography collectively titled *Intimate Memories* and *Winter in Taos* (1936) and *Edge of Taos Desert* (1935), contain stories about the artists who frequented her home, including the writers Willa Cather, D. H. Lawrence, and Oliver La Farge; the painter Georgia O'Keeffe; and the photographer Ansel Adams. Luhan's promotion of the arts put Taos on the map and popularized the Taos and Santa Fe artists colony of the 1920s and 1930s.

Like those before her, Willa Cather (1873–1947) was lured to the Southwest by romantic images of American Indians created in archaeological, anthropological, and fictional texts; her short story "The Enchanted Bluff" (1909), inspired by the mystery of ancient cliff dwellers, was written before she had ever been to the region. In 1912 Cather visited her brother in Winslow, Arizona, and took a trip to see the cliff dwellings in Walnut Canyon, not far from Flagstaff. That experience provided the basis for the chapter "The Ancient People" in *The Song of the Lark* (1915). She then visited Colorado's Cliff Palace in 1915, and her conversation there with Richard Wetherill's brother would motivate her to write "Tom Outland's Story" in *The Professor's House* (1925). The novel recounts Tom's archaeological "discovery" of ancient ruins as an almost reverential experience. After Colorado, Cather spent a month in Santa Fe, where she read the life story of Reverend Joseph P. Machelboeuf, the vicar to Archbishop Lamy of New Mexico. These individuals would become the characters Joseph Vaillant and Jean Marie Latour, respectively, in Cather's *Death Comes for the Archbishop* (1927). Unlike tourists who visited and remained awestruck by the ancient ruins, Latour's experience of the cliff dwellings is different. He is reluctant to enter a place he refers to as "terrible," and his discomfort is contrasted with Jacinto's experience of a place that his tribe regularly visited.

Oliver La Farge (1901–1963) was another eastern transplant. While studying archaeology at Harvard, he made field trips to Arizona in 1921, 1922, and 1924, which led to his fascination with Navajo peoples and a change in his studies. He decided to pursue anthropology and transferred to Tulane University, where Frans Blom recruited him for an expedition to various parts of Mexico. After his return, La Farge was fired as ethnology assistant in 1928 when he insulted the son and daughter of a Tulane trustee. His dismissal prompted him to pursue a writing career, and his *Laughing Boy* (1929) was released to critical acclaim, winning the Pulitzer Prize. The story presented La Farge's view that the dominant culture negatively affected American Indians.

Other writers who drew from anthropological sources were the friends Aldous Huxley (1894–1963) and D. H. Lawrence (1885–1930). Although Lawrence did not produce a Southwest novel, he was greatly influenced by the landscape and the Indians, which becomes clear in a posthumously published essay, "New Mexico." Anthropological writings on "primitive" religions, along with a trip he made to Mexico, influenced Lawrence's *The Plumed Serpent* (1926). Huxley had never visited the Southwest, but his novel *Brave New World* (1932) contains descriptions of New Mexico, the reservation, and American Indians' lives and cultures based on conversations with Lawrence, readings of Cushing, and examination of articles contained in ethnographic reports.

IN THE LABORATORY AND UNDER THE MICROSCOPE

A small number of Indian anthropologists have conducted their own fieldwork and published their own research. Francis La Flesche (Omaha) learned linguistics and research methodologies by working with Alice Fletcher and J. O. Dorsey in 1882. Arthur C. Parker (Seneca) directed New York State's Rochester Museum. He also published and was politically active in Indian affairs. Ella Deloria (Yankton Sioux) was another Franz Boas student. All three conducted anthropological research in their own communities and contributed to a better understanding of their peoples. Other Indian anthropologists include J. N. B. Hewitt (Iroquois), Jesse Cornplanter (Seneca),

Essie Parrish (Pomo), John Joseph Mathews (Osage), William Jones (Fox), James R. Murie (Pawnee), and George Hunt (Tlingit).

Increasingly since the 1960s, American Indian authors and scholars have read non-Indian anthropologists' work and have expressed outrage over the unequal power relations inherent in scholarly work. Chapter 4 in Vine Deloria's 1969 book *Custer Died for Your Sins* pointed to the way that power and the politics of representation have played out in participant-observer relations. Indians have furthered the careers of anthropologists, who have made Indians objects of study rather than perceiving them as communities with problems and concerns larger and greater than anthropological studies. In his book Deloria demanded a research agenda that focuses on the needs of Indian communities rather than anthropologists' careers. It can be said that Deloria's scathing yet humorous critique of anthropological methodology single-handedly changed the field's research methods.

The fiction writer Sherman Alexie also has poked fun at anthropologists' self-importance through the character of Dr. Mather, a university professor in *Indian Killer* (1996), as well as non-Indian "Indian experts" in the stories "Dear John Wayne" and "One Good Man" in *The Toughest Indian in the World* (2000). Alexie's critique mainly lies with scholars who consider themselves more knowledgeable about Indian cultures than Indians themselves. Alexie refuses to validate the notion that book knowledge or advanced degrees suddenly transform individuals into Indian experts. Critiques of non-Indian scholarly studies of American Indians also have been advanced by Craig Womack (Creek), Angela Cavender Wilson (Wahpetonwon Dakota), Duane Champagne (Chippewa), and Elizabeth Cook-Lynn (Crow Creek Sioux). They have called on "Indian experts" to consult and promote native peoples' scholarship and respect the different values and cultural perspectives that native scholars bring to their work.

American anthropology was founded on the study of American Indians, and over the decades thousands of Indians have worked as translators, cultural experts, or even anthropologists, helping to document Indian cultures. Anthropologists of Indian descent have increased over the years, and their work with early documents has helped tribes to recover cultural practices. However, anthropology's troubled history with native peoples means that researchers should continue to approach non-Indians' anthropological texts with caution.

See also American Indian Stories; Folklore and Oral Traditions; Indians

BIBLIOGRAPHY

Primary Works

Alexie, Sherman. *Indian Killer.* New York: Atlantic Monthly Press, 1996.

Alexie, Sherman. *The Toughest Indian in the World.* New York: Atlantic Monthly Press, 2000.

Austin, Mary. *The Arrow-Maker, A Drama in Three Acts.* 1910. Boston and New York: Houghton Mifflin, 1915.

Austin, Mary. *The Basket Woman: A Book of Indian Tales for Children.* 1904. Boston: Houghton Mifflin, 1932.

Austin, Mary. *The Flock.* 1906. Reno: University of Nevada Press, 2001.

Austin, Mary. *The Land of Little Rain.* 1903. New York: Modern Library, 2003.

Austin, Mary. *Lost Borders.* 1909. New Brunswick, N.J.: Rutgers University Press, 1987.

Austin, Mary. *Mother of Felipe, and Other Early Stories.* Edited by Franklin Walker. San Francisco: Book Club of California, 1950.

Bandelier, Adolph. *The Delight Makers.* 1890. New York: Dodd, Mead, 1960.

Cather, Willa. *Death Comes for the Archbishop.* 1927. Lincoln: University of Nebraska Press, 1999.

Cather, Willa. "The Enchanted Bluff." 1909. In *Willa Cather's Collected Short Fiction, 1892–1912.* Lincoln: University of Nebraska Press, 1965.

Cather, Willa. *The Professor's House.* 1925. New York: Vintage Books, 1990.

Cather, Willa. *The Song of the Lark.* 1915. Boston: Houghton Mifflin, 1988.

Cushing, Frank Hamilton. *My Adventures in Zuñi.* 1882. Palo Alto, Calif.: American West, 1970.

Cushing, Frank Hamilton. *Zuñi Breadstuff.* 1884–1885. New York: AMS Press, 1975.

Cushing, Frank Hamilton. *Zuñi Fetishes.* 1883. Flagstaff, Ariz.: K. C. Publications, 1966.

Deloria, Vine. *Custer Died for Your Sins.* 1969. Norman: University of Oklahoma Press, 1988.

Huxley, Aldous. *Brave New World.* 1932. New York: Harper Perennial, 1998.

Jackson, Helen Hunt. *A Century of Dishonor.* 1881. Norman: University of Oklahoma Press, 1995.

Jackson, Helen Hunt. *Ramona.* 1884. Madison, Wis.: Turtleback Books, 1988.

La Farge, Oliver. *Laughing Boy.* 1929. Boston: Mariner Books, 2004.

Lawrence, D. H. *The Plumed Serpent.* 1926. New York: Vintage Books, 1992.

Luhan, Mabel Dodge. *Edge of Taos Desert.* 1935. Albuquerque: University of New Mexico Press, 1987.

Luhan, Mabel Dodge. *Intimate Memories: The Autobiography of Mabel Dodge Luhan.* Edited by Lois Palken Rudnick. Albuquerque: University of New Mexico Press, 1999.

Luhan, Mabel Dodge. *Winter in Taos.* 1936. Denver: Sage Books, 1935.

Muir, John. *Our National Parks.* 1901. Washington, D.C.: Ross and Perry, 2001.

Secondary Works

Berkhofer, Robert F., Jr. *The White Man's Indian: Images of the American Indian from Columbus to the Present.* New York: Knopf, 1978.

Bieder, Robert E. *Science Encounters the Indian, 1820–1880: The Early Years of American Ethnology.* Norman: University of Oklahoma Press, 1986.

Dippie, Brian W. *The Vanishing American: White Attitudes and U.S. Indian Policy.* Middletown, Conn.: Wesleyan University Press, 1982.

Fowler, Don D. *A Laboratory for Anthropology: Science and Romanticism in the American Southwest, 1846–1930.* Albuquerque: University of New Mexico Press, 2000.

Hinsley, Curtis M., Jr. *Savages and Scientists: The Smithsonian Institution and the Development of American Anthropology.* Washington, D.C.: Smithsonian Press, 1981.

Jacobs, Margaret D. *Engendered Encounters: Feminism and Pueblo Cultures, 1879–1934.* Lincoln: University of Nebraska Press, 1999.

Morgan, Lewis Henry. *Ancient Society: Researches in the Lines of Human Progress from Savagery through Barbarism to Civilization.* Chicago: Charles H. Kerr, 1877.

Parezo, Nancy, ed. *Hidden Scholars: Women Anthropologists and the Native American Southwest.* Albuquerque: University of New Mexico Press, 1993.

Stocking, George, Jr. *Race, Culture, and Evolution: Essays in the History of Anthropology.* New York: Free Press, 1968.

Elizabeth Archuleta

EVOLUTION

See Darwinism

FARMERS AND RANCHERS

Unlike the westerns of dime novels and Hollywood cowboys, novels about farming and ranching do not romanticize rural life. Rather, they focus on the challenges encountered by people who transformed the continent's grasslands into consumable commodities: domesticated animals that ate the region's rich grasses or crops that thrived in the plowed prairie soil.

Farming and ranching stories focus on the land. Although there are stories of farming set in all parts of the continent, many of the novels that take place between 1870 and 1920 are set on the prairies and plains that extend from the Mississippi River west to the Rocky Mountain foothills. Conflicts center on the soil and climate that may or may not support the crops and animals needed to survive and also on the inevitable differences between husbands and wives and parents and children regarding the hard work farms and ranches demand.

Although their stories rarely overlap with the stories of white farming and ranching, there are Native American works that address the tribes' relationship with the land. For example, the autobiographical stories and legends published by the Sioux writer Zitkala-Ša (also known as Gertrude Simmons Bonnin, 1876–1938) focus on the American Indian's relation to place, with the land being an integral part of the narrative. The same is true of *The Soul of the Indian: An Interpretation* (1911) by another Sioux writer, Charles Alexander Eastman (also known by his family's Sioux name, Ohiyesa; 1858–1939).

As Richard White points out in *"It's Your Misfortune and None of My Own": A History of the American West* (1991), the first surveyors who were sent out by the U.S. government to map the western territories identified resources and hazards that later arrivals would find valuable or troublesome. John Wesley Powell focused on grazing lands, and Ferdinand Hayden believed, as many did, that rain would follow the plow; that is, when settlers plowed the apparently arid plains and released the soil's moisture into the atmosphere, it would return as rain. These surveyors were trying to shape a particular kind of society, however hazily envisioned. White points out that although nature left alone tends toward diversity, the Texas ranchers who drove the first cattle to the northern railroads and the settlers who plowed the first squares of land for corn or wheat preferred uniformity in crops and animals so that they could be managed and marketed in a cash-based society.

The central conflicts in most literature about farming and ranching reflect the efforts White identifies. Unlike the Native Americans who used the land lightly and moved often, ranchers and farmers identified a particular place as their own. They plowed the land for crops and introduced nonnative grasses and animals that would provide marketable goods. While history provides the broad background of this process, recounting the important mileposts in the nation's past, literature focuses on more dramatic situations: the challenges that a family or a community faces when the inevitable crises and conflicts arise.

Bronc to Breakfast. Watercolor by Charles M. Russell, 1908. Russell is renowned for his images documenting life in the American West. Here he captures the difficult task of breaking a horse to the saddle. MONTANA HISTORICAL SOCIETY, MACKAY COLLECTION

STORIES OF RANCHERS AND CATTLE RAISERS

There were cattle on the southern plains, principally in Mexico and Texas, long before the nineteenth century, but it was not until after the Civil War that their numbers and the land needed to support them increased, and ranchers began to establish operations in the central plains. The heyday of the open range, the source of many of the stories about cowboys and ranching, extended from the late 1870s into the 1890s. The classic account of life on the trail is *Log of a Cowboy: A Narrative of the Old Trail Days* (1903) by Andy Adams (1859–1935). Adams recalls an 1882 trail drive from the Mexican border to the Blackfoot Indian agency in Montana to deliver three thousand head of cattle. Published just a year after *The Virginian: A Horseman of the Plains* by Owen Wister (1860–1938), which was the first romantic portrait of the western cowboy,

Adams's account focuses on the grueling events of a cattle drive—stampedes, river crossings, boredom, and weather. Wister's *Virginian* became the model for the popular "cowboy" of movies, fashion, and parodies, but Adams's story remains one of the most vivid accounts of trail regimen.

Most of the novels about this period of the ranchers' ascendancy were written years later by men and women who remembered their own families' experiences or culled historical sources for a western adventure. Many of these works focus on the conflicts between ranchers, who depended on the cheap grass of the open, unregulated ranges to feed their cattle, and farmers, who were arriving, establishing homesteads, and erecting fences to protect their crops, thereby eliminating the open range. Mari Sandoz (1896–1966) wrote several accounts of the clashes between cattlemen and farmers

THE DIE-UP WINTERS

Horrific blizzards in the late 1880s were referred to as "the Great Die-Ups," or "the Big Die-Ups," or simply "the Ruin." Wet summers and mild winters in the 1870s encouraged ranchers to expand their herds, and investors from the East and England paid wildly inflated prices for a part of the anticipated windfall. The 1880s brought dry summers, but ranchers, eager to make a profit, overstocked their ranges, and cattle went into the winter weakened. During the winter of 1885–1886, many ranchers lost their entire herds, and in the spring, Texas ranchers skinned an average of 250 head to the mile along thirty-five miles of a Panhandle drift fence. The stench of rotting cattle could make life outside unbearable. During the storms, farmers who had thought nothing of living miles from town found themselves running out of food and fuel. People caught on the open prairie drifted like the cattle and were frozen or buried in drifts. An estimated three hundred people died in storms during the winter of 1885–1886 (Sandoz, Cattlemen, p. 261).

in her home territory, the Sandhills of northwestern Nebraska. *Old Jules*, published in 1935, is her account of her childhood and, more particularly, of her father's pioneering efforts from 1884 until his death in 1928 to settle farmers in the region, often on unclaimed land that cattle raisers regarded as their range. The clash with the cattlemen is tragically apparent in the murder of Jules's brother, who was "killed because . . . he knew too much" (p. 320).

Sandoz's *Slogum House* is an intense, violent account of the conflicts between ranchers and settlers. It was published in 1937, but the story is set in the years before President Theodore Roosevelt declared an end to the open range. The ruthless Gulla Slogum, who is determined to control an entire county, is fictional, but events in the novel are based on clashes that Sandoz witnessed between ranchers and farmers in the Sandhills at the turn of the twentieth century. Gulla's reign of violence does not end until the federal government declares the end of the open range and a moratorium on mortgage foreclosures. Sandoz is known for her exhaustive research and her ability to

tell a good story, a combination that leaves her works on a thin edge between history and literature.

Wallace Stegner's *Wolf Willow* reveals its multiple purposes in the subtitle: *A History, a Story, and a Memory of the Last Plains Frontier*. Published in 1962, it is Stegner's story of the summer of 1914, when he was a boy on the border between Saskatchewan and Montana, where his father fruitlessly pursued wheat farming. His own recollections of childhood adventures are mixed in with his impressions of the town on a return visit years later. Stegner's memory of the "gun-toting frontier" (p. 4) is embodied in a cowpuncher named Buck Murphy. "Genesis" is a vivid account of the efforts of cowhands to save their herd in the midst of a horrendous blizzard during the winter of 1906–1907. Stegner's writing style makes *Wolf Willow* concurrently a prose poem, an adventure tale, and a memoir. It is one of the most compelling accounts of both the ranching and farming frontiers in American and Canadian literature.

STORIES OF FARMERS

The Homestead Act, passed in 1862, is the most important piece of legislation in the history of farming in the United States. In the years following the Civil War, the myth of the safety valve evolved. Newly arrived immigrants from Europe and Americans displaced by the Civil War were crowding into the eastern cities. These unsettled people needed a place to go, so pundits and newspaper editors turned the "Great American Desert," a term coined by the explorer Stephen Long regarding the Great Plains, into the "Garden of the World" and encouraged western settlement as a solution for urban social ills. As the Native Americans were subdued and the land opened to settlement, thousands of eager would-be farmers took up land across the central Plains.

Hamlin Garland (1860–1940), William Allen White (1868–1944), and Willa Cather (1873–1947) addressed these myths and realities of western settlement. In "Among the Corn Rows," included in Hamlin Garland's 1891 edition of *Main-Travelled Roads: Six Mississippi Valley Stories*, Rob is a strong young homesteader in the Dakota Territory who believes in the realization of a democratic utopia on the level plains. He returns to Wisconsin to find himself a bride and hastily proposes to Julia Peterson, a Norwegian farm girl who is little more than an unpaid hired hand on her parents' farm. He knows that, unlike the more socially acceptable American girls, she will be a willing worker. When he proposes, he tells her "you needn't do anything but cook f'r me, and after harvest we can git a good layout o' furniture" (p. 117). He reminds her that if she stays on her family's farm, "they'll jest keep y' plowin' corn and milkin' cows til the day of judgment" (p. 118).

Most stories of the farmers' struggles to transform the prairie into orderly farms are not so benign. Other stories in Garland's collection are grim accounts of hard work that wore out the women and made the men sullen and silent. "A Day's Pleasure" tells the story of one farm wife's rare trip to town, where she wanders aimlessly until a sympathetic young town wife invites her and her baby in for tea and a brief respite from her dull existence. Butler, a sharp landlord, takes advantage of his renter Haskins in another story, "Under the Lion's Paw." Butler raises his price for the farm Haskins has rented from him to include improvements Haskins has made, forcing his tenant to pay twice for his work in exchange for a mortgage and the privilege of "owning" a farm that will barely support his family.

Boy Life on the Prairie, published in 1899, is Garland's chronicle of his boyhood on an Iowa farm in the years after the Civil War. Told from a boy's point of view, Garland's sketches present an idyllic view of farmwork, but the boy's adventures and the farm's routines are carefully recorded. The autobiographical *A Son of the Middle Border* (1917) is Garland's more complete autobiography that covers the same period. Farming is only one element in this story, however, which also includes accounts of Garland's moves from Wisconsin to Iowa, family routines, rural communities, small towns, and his increasingly successful literary career.

In his first collection of stories, *The Real Issue*, published in 1896, William Allen White includes two grim stories of newcomers who venture too far west onto the arid high plains. In "The Story of Aqua Pura" and "A Story of the Highlands," stubborn people, lured onto the plains by unusually wet years in the 1880s, hang on too long until they are too poor and too proud to admit defeat and return to points farther east. Willa Cather's story "El Dorado: A Kansas Recessional" (1901) is an account of land speculation and inevitable ruin. The story is manipulated to support a sentimental ending, but like White's stories, it reflects the blind enthusiasm of people who could be convinced on the slimmest evidence to settle far out on the high plains. The speculator's promises seem real in the wet years of the 1880s, but thousands abandon the failing community when the drought and nationwide economic depression of the 1890s collapses their dreams.

In addition to chronicling disputes between farmers and ranchers, Mari Sandoz's *Old Jules* presents the story of the homesteading era from the 1880s to the early twentieth century through her family's experiences on the high plains. The Swiss immigrant Jules is a stubborn, rough man who is determined to create a community of farmers. Sandoz does not gloss over the hardships created in part by her father's cruel indifference to his family and his habit of carrying on feuds with the area's ranchers and neighboring farmers. At the same time, Sandoz clearly admires her father's determination to settle on the land people who would be denied the American ideal of ownership and economic independence without his help. Jules also proves to be an astute judge of the land: his orchards were so successful that his farm became a horticulture experiment station for the University of Nebraska.

One of the most comprehensive accounts of the struggle to establish a homestead on the high plains is *Sod and Stubble: Story of a Kansas Homestead* (1936) by John Ise (1885–1960). The book recounts the experiences of Ise's parents, who were homesteaders near Downs, Kansas, in the 1870s and also addresses the author's childhood in western Kansas. Ise, an agricultural economist, tells the story of the efforts of Henry and Rosie to raise a large family (there were ten surviving children) on a small farm. Farming accidents, weather, neighborhood feuds, seasons of good crops and failures, Henry's declining health, and the always narrow gap between a successful year and failure result in an account that seems too dramatic until the reader realizes that this is a story based on very real experiences.

As Robert V. Hine and John Mack Faragher point out in *The American West: A New Interpretive History* (2000), 49 percent of all homesteaders failed to "prove up" their claims. In the late nineteenth century, thousands returned to the East. Many who stayed became tenant farmers like Garland's Haskins rather than landowners. Stories of loss and failure are familiar plot patterns in literature about farming.

The apparently empty landscape of the level grasslands often becomes a metaphor for the psychological trauma that results from the isolation and lack of community experienced by farmers and especially by farmers' wives. In *Giants in the Earth* (1927) by O. E. Rölvaag (1876–1931), Per Hansa and a small community of fellow Norwegian immigrants stake their claims on the western edge of the Dakota Territory in the early years of settlement. The wide horizon empowers Per Hansa to imagine his own kingdom with red barns and a neat house surrounded by abundant land, but the same scene terrifies his wife Beret, who responds to the uninhabited space with such fear that she retreats into depression and occasional fits of madness. The couple's contrasting approaches and the tragedy that arises inevitably from Beret's fears and

Per Hansa's confidence is one of the best accounts of the costs of immigration in American literature.

Willa Cather's novel *O Pioneers!* (1913) is an account of a successful farm managed by Alexandra Bergson, who shrewdly observes the land and adapts her own practices to take advantage of the rich soils and new agricultural practices. In Cather's words, the land "awakened" to her sense of its potential. In "Neighboring Fields," section two of the novel, Cather describes Alexandra's farm, a contrast to the "wild land" her father left his children on his death:

> On either side of the road, for a mile before you reached the foot of the hill, stood tall Osage orange hedges, their glossy green marking off the yellow fields. South of the hill, in a low, sheltered swale, surrounded by a mulberry hedge, was the orchard, its fruit trees knee-deep in timothy grass. Any one thereabouts would have told you that this was one of the richest farms on the Divide, and that the farmer was a woman, Alexandra Bergson. (P. 80)

But even in Cather's story of success and abundance, there is a price to pay: Emil, Alexandra's favorite brother, is murdered by Frank Shabata, a jealous neighbor (and failed farmer), after Shabata finds his wife, Marie, with Emil in the orchard. In many stories of the farming frontier, the death of a parent, a spouse, or a child signifies the hard life and sacrifices demanded of the people who established America's farms.

Cather's novel *My Ántonia* (1918) focuses on the particular difficulties of immigrant settlers. The story is based on the lives of Bohemian farm families Cather knew growing up in Red Cloud, Nebraska, particularly the life of Annie Pavelka. Cather balances the hard work and social isolation against the later success and independence of Ántonia and the other "hired girls" who go from their families' farms into Black Hawk to do domestic work. Lena Lingard avoids marriage to become a successful San Francisco dressmaker and manager of the money Tiny Soderball makes in Alaska. Ántonia's life does not take her so far from Black Hawk. Years later, when the narrator, Jim Burden, visits Ántonia, her husband, and her gaggle of irrepressible children, he discovers that he is a part of her world, a player in Ántonia's stories of her childhood. Ántonia has become the quintessential farm wife, nurturing children and carefully tending her garden, with her fruit cellar visible proof of her farm's fecundity.

Cather focuses on the immigrant children who adapt more easily than their parents to America's opportunities and limitations. Ántonia and the other immigrant girls do not miss the old country as their mothers and Rölvaag's Beret do. They resent the toll of relentless hard work on their parents, and their lives are carefully planned escapes from their parents' limited situations. Like thousands of other immigrants, they retain the strengths they acquired in their first hard years, but they soon become a part of American life and culture on their own terms.

Other writers have left records of similar experiences. Oscar Micheaux (1884–1951), a pioneer in black film, wrote two novels about black farmers in South Dakota, *The Conquest: The Story of a Negro Pioneer* (1913) and *The Homesteader* (1917). Although Micheaux uses different names in the novels, these are autobiographical stories that are interrelated. In the earlier novel, Oscar Devereaux saves enough money from his job as a Pullman porter to buy land in South Dakota. Like farmers before and after him, he works hard, overcomes setbacks, and increases the value of his farm.

CONCLUSION: PROSPERITY AND DEPRESSION

In the first decades of the twentieth century, farming increasingly became a business. Experience with various farming practices and growing sophistication in dealing with markets gave the farmer some success. World War I brought a boom in wheat production, but after a relative period of prosperity in the 1920s, the Dust Bowl and the Great Depression dealt a double blow to farmers and ranchers. Once again, out-migration left much of the land empty of people.

Stories written in the 1930s and in the decades since continue the story: despite improvements, farming and ranching remain dependent on the farmers' or ranchers' ability to survive inevitable economic downturns and destructive weather. At the turn of the twenty-first century, novels of farming and ranching were still being written. In history and literature, this cycle of failure and success is the story of America's farms and ranches.

See also Frontier; Labor; *Main-Travelled Roads;* Migration; *My Ántonia;* The Western

BIBLIOGRAPHY

Primary Works

Adams, Andy. *Log of a Cowboy.* 1903. New York: MJF Books, 1997.

Cather, Willa. "El Dorado: A Kansas Recessional." In *Willa Cather's Collected Short Fiction, 1892–1912.* Lincoln: University of Nebraska Press, 1965.

Cather, Willa. *My Ántonia.* 1918. Lincoln: University of Nebraska Press, 1997.

Cather, Willa. *O Pioneers!* 1913. Lincoln: University of Nebraska Press, 1992.

Eastman, Charles Alexander (Ohiyesa). *The Soul of the Indian: An Interpretation*. 1911. Lincoln: University of Nebraska Press, 1980.

Garland, Hamlin. *Boy Life on the Prairie*. 1899. Lincoln: University of Nebraska Press, 1961.

Garland, Hamlin. *Main-Travelled Roads*. 1891. New York: Signet, 1962.

Garland, Hamlin. *A Son of the Middle Border*. 1917. New York: Penguin, 1995.

Ise, John. *Sod and Stubble*. 1936. Lawrence: University Press of Kansas, 1996.

Micheaux, Oscar. *The Conquest: The Story of a Negro Pioneer*. 1913. New York: Washington Square Press, 2003.

Micheaux, Oscar. *The Homesteader*. 1917. Lincoln: University of Nebraska Press, 1994.

Rölvaag, O. E. *Giants in the Earth*. New York: Harper, 1927.

Sandoz, Mari. *Cattlemen from the Rio Grande across the Far Marias*. 1958. Lincoln: University of Nebraska Press, 1978.

Sandoz, Mari. *Old Jules*. 1935. Lincoln: University of Nebraska Press, 1962.

Sandoz, Mari. *Slogum House*. Boston: Little, Brown, 1937.

Stegner, Wallace. *Wolf Willow: A History, a Story, and a Memory of the Last Plains Frontier*. New York: Viking, 1962.

White, William Allen. *The Real Issue*. 1896. Freeport, N.Y.: Books for Libraries Press, 1969. All references in the text are to the original 1896 edition.

Wister, Owen. *The Virginian: A Horseman of the Plains*. 1902. New York: Pocket Books, 2002.

Secondary Works

Dary, David. *Cowboy Culture: A Saga of Five Centuries*. New York: Knopf, 1981.

Hine, Robert V., and John Mack Faragher. *The American West: A New Interpretive History*. New Haven, Conn.: Yale University Press, 2000.

Quantic, Diane Dufva. *The Nature of the Place: A Study of Great Plains Fiction*. Lincoln: University of Nebraska Press, 1995. This study includes extensive discussions of most of the works in this article and a bibliography of primary and secondary works relevant to study of farming in particular.

Quantic, Diane D., and P. Jane Hafen, eds. *A Great Plains Reader*. Lincoln: University of Nebraska Press, 2003.

Webb, Walter Prescott. *The Great Plains*. 1931. Lincoln: University of Nebraska Press, 1981.

White, Richard. *"It's Your Misfortune and None of My Own": A History of the American West*. Norman: University of Oklahoma Press, 1991.

Diane Dufva Quantic

FASHION

At the turn of the twentieth century, the United States witnessed great changes, including a shift in the phenomenon called "fashion," most particularly women's fashion. This shift had social, cultural, and political implications. In the 1870s a middle- or upper-class woman's daily garb consisted of ten to twelve pounds of flannel or muslin petticoats, stays, and a corset of whalebone. These underclothes were covered by a full-skirted woolen or muslin dress, a style that had prevailed since the 1840s. Confining, these clothes did not promote mobility; some women argued that such clothing impeded child rearing. Yet fashion—and for upper-class, white American women that meant dresses or dress patterns imported from France or styled after such—dictated, for the most part, a nipped waist, full breast, and flounce.

BLOOMERS AND DRESS REFORM

Indeed, until the first decade of the twentieth century American fashion was European; even jewelry was imported, not made and designed in America. But some American women argued that because "fashion" was a foreign import, it was un-American; women of the upper classes had a moral, even democratic duty to dress with less ostentation than French and European women; American women should begin a gradual shift toward a more healthful style befitting the natural shape of a woman's childbearing form—or what would eventually be termed "rational" dressing. And curiously, if asked, most women thought that trousers, when considered merely as an item of dress, were far more comfortable and hygienic than women's wear.

But trousers signified masculinity; when Amelia Jenks Bloomer (1818–1894), along with other abolitionist women, disseminated patterns for "harem-style" trousers—a design seen in European spas—in order to rid women of corset and skirts, the idea that women could wear trousers was deemed preposterous. (A hostile press would come to call these "bloomers.") This women's dress reform movement, mostly a political gesture aligned with abolitionist, child-labor, and temperance reforms, only lasted from about 1851 to 1854. Nevertheless, it had an impact: references to the bloomer can be found in diaries, novels, and newspapers; the bloomer craze even generated societies, music, and drama. No matter how much more comfortable or indeed "rational" bloomers were, by 1854 most women who had rallied around the cause of dress reform had returned to corset and petticoats because the costume had become a liability.

However, by 1873–1874, dress reform once again became an issue for public debate, first in Boston, then in other cities. Abba Louisa Goold Woolson (1838–1921), a teacher, popular literary essayist, and officer of the New England Women's Club, sponsored a series of lectures about dress. This is not to say that dress reform had died out in the intervening years; although Elizabeth Cady Stanton and Susan B. Anthony gave up on bloomers, Amelia Jenks Bloomer wore the costume until her death. But during the Civil War, the general public lost interest. In 1873, however, Woolson's lectures became so popular that they were collected and published. In addition to Woolson, four physicians also embraced the dress reform movement. Mary J. Safford-Blake, Caroline E. Hastings, Mercy B. Jackson, and Arvilla B. Haynes tried to convince people that "the whole structure and the essential features of our present apparel are undeniably opposed to the plainest requirements of health, beauty and convenience" (Woolson, p. vi). These women saw to it that an "accessible and attractive room, which is intended to serve for a bureau of information on all matters connected with dress reform," was set up in Boston at "25 Winter Street, over Chandler's dry-goods store, room 15." They also provided, at the lowest cost possible, garments and patterns for garments designed on "strict hygienic principles" (Woolson, p. 1).

Although she seldom said so in public, Woolson favored trousers; but in 1874 the memory of "bloomers" had yet to die, and trousers were still regarded as radical. Overly heavy skirts, corseting, flimsy materials: these might all prove to be physically dangerous, but bloomers were still deemed even worse. So Woolson and the doctors changed tactics. Rather than cite the rational politics of female emancipation and mobility, they chose to use moral patriotism and the science of hygiene to argue that fashion was a foreign import, that women of the upper classes had a moral duty to dress with less ostentation, and that American women should begin a gradual shift toward a more healthful style. They had, they said, a far more scientifically sound version of dress than that of the radical Bloomerites, and they offered a series of talks that presented what they saw as medical and historical evidence to prove that women's fashionable clothing was physiologically dangerous and morally repugnant, a threat to the life of the (white) woman, her child, and the future of the nation. "In presenting to you some thoughts upon the subject of dress," wrote Safford-Blake, "I do not desire you to accept my *ipse dixit* of right or wrong; but I hope you will probe the facts presented, and, if they appeal to your common sense and reason as truths, that you will heed them, not alone for your own good, but that your influence may go forth as a help and guide to others" (Woolson, p. 5). Jackson went even further: "I appeal to the moral sense of the

ladies present, and I ask them if they are willing, by their example and influence, longer to countenance a mode of dress which is so little fitted to answer the reasonable demands that should be made upon it, and so destructive of health and morals?" (Woolson, pp. 91–95).

Yet corset and hoop remained: a "lady," most people continued to believe, wore fashionable French frocks. The persistence of the corset and hoop shows that the women physicians ran into as much resistance as their forebears. It should be noted too that many of the physiological, hygienic, and antifashion arguments would continue to be made over and over again, as in, for example, Ada S. Ballin's *The Science of Dress in Theory and Practice* (1885). Ballin thought the bloomer had failed because it was too violent a change from tradition. She promoted the demure divided skirt. The author, socialist activist, and orator Charlotte Perkins Gilman (1860–1935) wrote a serial in 1915 for the *Forerunner*, now published in book form as *The Dress of Women*, that presented Gilman's sociological analysis of clothing in which she too concluded that the degrading, indeed slavish, aspects of women's dress need rational reform. In her speculative novel *Herland* (1915), she dressed her utopian young women in suits "of some light firm stuff, the closest of tunics and kneebreeches, met by trim gaiters" (p. 15).

During the 1870s and into the early twentieth century, most middle-class women continued to tightly lace and hoop, especially at the behest of the designer Charles Frederick Worth (1825–1895), whose "reign" over ladies' fashion became something of a dictatorship during the Gilded Age, when the United States saw an unprecedented economic boom. Worth, who had emigrated from Britain to France as a young man, made his salon in Paris at 7, rue de la Paix a mecca for wealthy American women, who between 1871 and 1920 would travel specifically to have their wardrobes made by Worth. It is no exaggeration to say that, at a time when upper-class American women had little to do other than attend society functions and wear clothes deemed suitable to that society, Worth's genius and arrogance made him the only absolute ruler left in Europe. Very few of his clients, even if persuaded that their health might be at risk, took heed of medical or scientific arguments against the corset or bustle, because a lady was not born, a lady was made (by Worth). Fashion signified gender, race, and class through the material means of silk, lace, and stays, and it held sway especially in the age of the robber baron. Both Henry James and Edith Wharton, writers who are seen as chroniclers of this "society," note at some length in many of their novels the degree to which dressing "fashionably"—in imitation of fading European royalty—was the epitome of an upper-class woman's life.

READY TO WEAR

By the 1890s, however, technological invention and changes in manufacturing, immigration, and labor practices began to put pressure on fashion in a number of significant ways. One of the most significant was the change in the manufacture of clothing. Invented as early as the 1830s but culminating in Isaac Merritt Singer's patent in February 1854, the sewing machine allowed what was soon to be the mass production of first men's then women's clothing—something that Worth capitalized upon, for he was the first dressmaker to streamline production through pattern design and the sewing machine. He was also the first dressmaker to use a label to guarantee the value or "worth" of his product. Indeed, as the twentieth century came into view, more and more clothes were being made for women "ready-to-wear," and by 1911 the most popular of these mass-market items was the shirtwaist—a stylish cotton blouse cheap enough for a working woman to buy and wear. The shirtwaist and skirt combination still allowed for a ladylike shape similar to the one produced by corset and stays, but this dress—the skirt was now raised to ankle height to allow more mobility—was more convenient and comfortable and was regarded as modern, stylish, sophisticated: all key issues for the increasing number of young women who worked, often as low-paid seamstresses who produced the same shirtwaists they wore. In New York City, which had rapidly become the center of the new mass-market ready-to-wear garment industry, the interrelation of women's labor and women's clothing became only too tragically clear when, in March 1911, a fire struck the Triangle Shirtwaist Company on the Lower East Side. In all, 146 workers died—most of them young, Jewish immigrant women, who either jumped from the ninth floor of the building or burned to death. The fire was a significant turning point for New York, for the garment industry, and for labor reform in general, because it underscored in blood the cause for which these same young women went on strike in the famous labor uprising of 1909. Both the 1909 strike—chronicled in Theresa Malkiel's *Diary of a Shirtwaist Striker*—and the horrific fire helped to bring upper-class women and working-class women together politically, an alliance that aided the suffragist movement.

Meanwhile, the first large-scale jewelry production in the United States began at the turn of the century, when corporations such as Gorham of Rhode Island and Krementz of New Jersey manufactured

Patience. Drawing by Charles Dana Gibson from *Collier's Weekly* magazine, 19 March 1910. THE LIBRARY OF CONGRESS

paste imitations of original French designs. Tiffany and Company, already established as the premier American jeweler, became involved in all branches of the decorative arts. In 1902 Louis Comfort Tiffany (1848–1933) opened an art jewelry department, which offered Byzantine and Oriental pieces, unusual at that time in America, where most jewelry designs were based on French art nouveau. Tiffany began to experiment with new combinations of colors and materials and was the first to make jewelry out of lava glass.

Indeed, young women in the late nineteenth century and the early twentieth century wanted innovation in clothing, in jewelry, in activity. They demanded more mobility than their mothers had enjoyed—thus the shirtwaist and shorter skirts. One invention that influenced their desires was the bicycle. Although the bicycle—also a French import—had been available as early as 1869, advances in design made it a popular and affordable vehicle only late in the century. As Elizabeth Ewing explains: "Women began riding bicycles and for this new sport, they wore bloomers. Soon after that bloomers became the name of a style of feminine drawers or knickers which had a great vogue in the early twentieth century, especially under sports clothes and schoolgirls' gym tunics" (p. 64). Sometimes called knickerbockers but more often and more generally once again named bloomers, the cycling costume spread with the bicycling craze. Like the bicycle itself, Betty Bloomer—also called the "New Woman" and sometimes the "Gibson Girl"— had arrived. Therefore, even if "Betty Bloomer was ahead of her time in pushing pants" (Green, p. 27), her ubiquity and familiarity, along with changes in manufacturing, labor practices, and technology, paved the way for the public's acceptance of changing standards of a woman's public costume. Thus many middle-class girls in the United States adopted the bike, the bloomer, and the shirtwaist, and the "New Woman" ushered in the twentieth century. Like Theodore Dreiser's infamous Carrie Meeber in his novel *Sister Carrie* (1900), women moved into the public sphere as industrialization and urbanization created the mass marketing of all household goods, and the department store was born.

This is not to say that changes in fashion were launched without controversy. Sharp battles were still being fought over woman's proper place as signified by her public appearance. If that bête noire of 1851 the bloomer saw acceptance, it was also understood that the bloomer was a specialized "costume" for the bicycle, for gymnastics, for bathing: not donned in lieu of a dress. For the upper class, opulent Worth gowns ruled; but the preeminence of the Worth name was severely shaken in the years before World War I, chiefly by another designer. Paul Poiret, a Worth employee who quit when his designs challenged tradition, revolutionized a woman's figure. Poiret's inventions—lithe and skimpy in comparison to a Worth gown—spurred the invention of the bra, originally designed to flatten the breast so that the Poiret shift could be worn properly; his "look" changed the fashionable woman's silhouette from the corseted hourglass to the more boyish flapper. Young women responded with enthusiasm; moreover, as previously noted, the growing participation of women in the workforce both before and during World War I required more functional clothing, especially during the day. After the war, women refused to return to anything like the restrictive formality of their mothers' corsets.

FLAPPERS AND ALL THAT JAZZ

By the 1920s the physical freedom and increasing athleticism of girls was generally considered natural and healthy. The New Woman and the Gibson Girl gave way

---

As the nineteenth century came to a close, changes in technology and marketing and the increase in industrial labor altered many aspects of daily life, including dress. Clothing once made in the home was now factory made, bought ready-to-wear. Women entered the workforce and became consumers in this new mass market. Fashion reflected these social changes, as young women abandoned the corset and adopted the less-restrictive shirtwaist, a jacket, and a shorter skirt, designed to allow a woman to walk city streets and to show off shoes. Ready-to-wear clothes became items of desire and emblems of mobility. Theodore Dreiser represented such a change in Sister Carrie. *In this excerpt Carrie Meeber, who has come from the county to the city to work, is seduced by such department store, ready-to-wear fashion.*

Fine clothes to her were a vast persuasion; they spoke tenderly and Jesuitically for themselves. When she came within earshot of their pleading, desire in her bent a willing ear. . . .

"My dear," said the lace collar she secured from Partridge's, "I fit you beautifully; don't give me up."

"Ah such little feet," said the leather of the soft new shoes.

Theodore Dreiser, *Sister Carrie* (New York: Modern Library, 1927), p. 111.

---

to F. Scott Fitzgerald's Jazz Age flappers featured in his short stories and novels, like "Bernice Bobs Her Hair" and *The Great Gatsby*. In fact, the economic and social pressures that immediately followed the First World War brought with them a new mood for a rigorous and clean-cut look. In the age of the flapper, function and sophistication were signified by a shift away from traditional fashion.

Influences on fashion also became more ethnic and varied. From dress to architecture, the styles inspired by such trends as pharaonic Egypt, Asia, tribal Africa, Cubism, and futurism all came and went. Hemlines rose; daring young women bobbed their hair, began to attend college in record numbers, smoked, and bought mass-marketed cosmetics. If trousers were yet to be seen as a form of women's wear, the burden of ten to twelve pounds of flannel or muslin petticoats, stays, and a corset of whalebone covered by a full-skirted woolen or muslin dress had been consigned to the past. The modern, fashionable woman—at least by 1920—looked nothing like the lady her mother had once been.

See also Domestic and Sentimental Fiction; Mass-Marketing

BIBLIOGRAPHY

Primary Works

Gilman, Charlotte Perkins. *Herland.* 1915. New York: Pantheon, 1979.

Stanton, Elizabeth Cady, Susan B. Anthony, and Matilda J. Gage. *History of Woman Suffrage.* 6 vols. New York: Fowler and Wells, 1881–1922.

Woolson, Abba Goold, ed. *Dress Reform: A Series of Lectures Delivered in Boston, on Dress as It Affects the Health of Women.* 1874. In *Women in America: From Colonial Times to the 20th Century,* edited by Leon Stein and Annette K. Baxter. New York: Arno Press, 1974.

Secondary Works

Brumberg, Joan Jacobs. *The Body Project: An Intimate History of American Girls.* New York: Vintage, 1997.

Ewing, Elizabeth. *Dress and Undress: A History of Women's Underwear.* London: Bibliophile, 1981.

Green, Nancy L. *Ready-to-Wear and Ready-to-Work: A Century of Industry and Immigrants in Paris and New York.* Durham, N.C.: Duke University Press, 1997.

Martin, Linda. *The Way We Wore: Fashion Illustrations of Children's Wear 1870–1970.* New York: Scribners, 1978.

Olien, JoAnne. *The Gilded Age: Charles Frederick Worth, the Founder of Haute Couture.* Available at http://www.mcny.org/Collections/costume/worth/worth.htm.

Peiss, Kathy. *Hope in a Jar: The Making of America's Beauty Culture.* New York: Henry Holt, 1998.

Smith, Stephanie. "Antebellum Politics and Women's Writing." In *The Cambridge Companion to Nineteenth-Century American Women's Writing,* edited by Dale Bauer and Philip Gould. New York and Cambridge, U.K.: Cambridge University Press, 2001.

Steele, Valerie. *Paris Fashion: A Cultural History.* New York and Oxford: Oxford University Press, 1988.

Von Drehle, David. *Triangle: The Fire That Changed America.* New York: Atlantic Monthly Press, 2003.

Whitehouse, Richard. *A History of 20th Century Jewelry.* Available at http://www.mschon.com/jewelryhistory.html.

Stephanie A. Smith

FEMINISM

The term "feminism," broadly defined as the advocacy of political, economic, and social equality between men and women, was not coined until the 1910s; however, though the word itself did not exist in the nineteenth century, the concept of "woman's rights" certainly did. The organized movement for female suffrage and gender equality began in the small upstate village of Seneca Falls, New York, where Elizabeth Cady Stanton (1815–1902) and Susan B. Anthony (1820–1906) organized the first women's rights convention in July 1848. This meeting, attended by some three hundred men and women, ratified the Declaration of Sentiments, a document written by Stanton based on the Declaration of Independence, outlining the key problems faced by nineteenth-century American women. As such the Declaration of Sentiments established the agenda of the women's rights movement for the next seventy-five years.

WOMEN'S ISSUES

In the Declaration of Sentiments, Stanton enumerated specific complaints concerning the oppressed status of women in American society: their inability to vote; exclusion from higher education and professional careers; subordination to male authority in both church and state; and legal victimization in terms of wages, property rights, and divorce. After identifying these injustices, the document proclaimed a series of resolutions, including the assertion that "woman is man's equal . . . and that all laws which prevent woman from occupying such a station in society as her conscience shall dictate, or which place her in a position inferior to that of man, are contrary to the great precept of nature, and therefore of no force or authority" (Kraditor, p. 187).

The right to vote became a pressing goal in the latter part of the nineteenth century; from 1870 to 1917 the American Woman's Suffrage Association sponsored the weekly *Woman's Journal,* edited over the years by Lucy Stone, Julia Ward Howe, Thomas Wentworth Higginson, Henry B. Blackwell, and others. Women would not formally be granted the right to vote until the passage of the Nineteenth Amendment in 1920, but significant progress was made in advancing their social, economic, and legal status during the latter half of the century. For example, in 1848, the same year as the Seneca Falls Convention, the state of New York passed the landmark Married Woman's Property Act, the first legislation of its kind in the United States, recognizing the right of women to own and retain property separate from their husbands.

This law was expanded in an 1860 omnibus Act concerning the Rights and Liabilities of Husband and Wife, which improved inheritance laws for women and acknowledged mothers as joint guardians of their children; however, this progressive legislation was partially rescinded in 1862.

The decades between 1850 and 1900 also saw unprecedented growth in the number of colleges founded for women. Many of the "Seven Sisters" were established during this time period—Vassar in 1861, Wellesley in 1870, Smith in 1871, Radcliffe in 1879, Bryn Mawr in 1880, and Barnard in 1893—joining the ranks of institutions like Oberlin and Mount Holyoke that had opened their doors to females in the 1830s. Yet even with improved access to higher education, admission into the professions remained elusive for women. An 1873 Supreme Court decision, *Bradwell v. Illinois,* epitomizes this difficulty. The case originated in 1869, when Mrs. Myra Bradwell passed the Illinois law exam but was denied admission to the state bar "by reason of the disability imposed by [her] married condition." Arguing that marriage is "neither a crime nor a disqualification" (Cullen-Dupont, p. 26), Bradwell claimed that the state of Illinois had violated her constitutional rights, specifically those guaranteed by the Fourteenth Amendment. She appealed her case to the U.S. Supreme Court, which ultimately decided against her. The opinion of Justice Joseph P. Bradley, in which he asserted his "repugnance" at the "idea of a woman adopting a distinct and independent career from that of her husband," is often cited as an example of the prevailing patriarchal attitudes toward women during this time period: "The paramount destiny and mission of woman are to fulfill the noble and benign offices of wife and mother. This is the law of the Creator. And the rules of civil society must be adapted to the general constitution of things" (Cullen-Dupont, p. 27).

As Bradley's statement suggests, women were not viewed as individuals in the nineteenth century. They were dependent beings confined to a domestic sphere who were completely defined by their social relationships to others—as daughter, spouse, mother, aunt, and sister. Female fulfillment was not to derive from the pursuit of personal ambition but rather from women's roles as "angels of the house," instilling moral values in their children and creating a tranquil domestic refuge for their husbands. Throughout the nineteenth century the notion of "true womanhood"—as illustrated in Louisa May Alcott's 1868 novel *Little Women*—dictated that females should be selfless, pious, submissive, and silent; women who deviated from these restrictive norms were ostracized and held in contempt.

Even in matters of dress, women were expected to conform to socially constructed standards of beauty and femininity, much to the detriment of their personal health. Traditional female attire featured long, heavy skirts with multiple layers of petticoats, often weighing as much as twenty pounds, and whalebone corsets so tight that broken ribs and organ damage were common ailments among middle- and upper-class women. Yet despite the obviously impractical and unsafe nature of these garments, Amelia Jenks Bloomer (1818–1894) was subjected to scathing attack in the early 1850s when she published a pattern for "rational dress"—nicknamed "bloomers"—in the *Lily* newspaper. Bloomers featured a knee-length skirt beneath which loose linen trousers, gathered at the ankle, were worn. No corsets, petticoats, or other confining undergarments were needed. Women who adopted the bloomer costume, like Elizabeth Cady Stanton, Lucretia Mott, and Susan B. Anthony, praised the physical freedom it afforded but endured both hostility and ridicule for appropriating traditional male attire. Fearing that the controversy over dress reform would eclipse critical issues like suffrage, these women eventually abandoned bloomers and returned to conventional apparel.

Dress reform resurfaced in the 1890s with the advent of the bicycle. In order to participate in the new recreational sport of cycling, women adopted "knickers" in increasingly large numbers. This manly garb was widely satirized in the popular press, just as bloomers had been four decades earlier; the cartoon "Life in the New Navy, circa 1900" which appeared in the 11 July 1896 issue of *Life* magazine, reflects a deeply rooted cultural anxiety about the subversive implications of women donning male clothes. As the image depicts, the navy of the future consisted primarily of women wearing uniforms of differently styled knickers—the unique details of each design apparently indicating distinctions in military rank. The cartoon humorously suggests that once females begin usurping traditionally male privileges, such as the wearing of pants, there is no limit to the potential power they might wield.

Beginning in the last two decades of the nineteenth century the "New Woman" emerged in both the United States and Europe as a reaction against the Victorian cult of domesticity. New Women were educated, were committed to the goals of personal autonomy and financial independence, and looked upon marriage and motherhood as a matter of individual choice rather than of economic necessity or biological destiny. The diverse ranks of New Women included writers, political thinkers, suffragettes, and social activists; through the medium of the popular press, they critiqued conventional views of female beauty

THE "NEW WOMAN" AND HER BICYCLE. — THERE WILL BE SEVERAL VARIETIES OF HER.

Illustration from *Puck*, 1895, by Frederick Burr Opper. Opper uses the bicycle as a means of lampooning the drawbacks of greater freedom for women. Both the bicycle and the more practical clothing required in its operation were widely viewed as a threat to traditional femininity. © CORBIS

(long hair and long skirts) and restrictive social protocols such as the need for women to be accompanied by chaperones. They also demanded an end to the sexual "double standard."

LITERARY REPRESENTATIONS OF WOMEN AND WOMEN'S RIGHTS

Many writers, both male and female, addressed the issue of women's social condition during this time period. For example, the 1879 novella *Daisy Miller* by Henry James (1843–1916), features a wealthy, attractive, but uncultured "American girl" touring Europe who openly rebels against the standards of female propriety. As the novella progresses, Daisy's behavior grows increasingly headstrong and reckless; dismissing the need for a chaperone as an absurd, infantiliz-

ing encumbrance, she walks unescorted in the Pincio Gardens and visits the Colosseum late at night with Mr. Giovanelli, her "third-rate" Italian suitor. James punishes Daisy for these infractions in etiquette not only by making her the target of malicious gossip but also by inflicting the most dire of consequences—death from malarial fever. In this respect *Daisy Miller* serves as a cautionary tale for young women, suggesting that their very survival depends on passive, unquestioning acceptance of restrictive gender roles. James's 1886 novel *The Bostonians* explicitly satirizes the "great sisterhood of women" committed to suffrage and social reform, lampooning their simplistic narrative of "how, during the long ages of history, they had been trampled under the iron heel of man" (p. 58). Some scholars believe that the romantic triangle James dramatizes in the novel, in which the feminist Olive Chancellor and the conservative southern attorney Basil Ransom vie for the affection and control of the beautiful "inspirational" speaker Verena Tarrant, is based on an actual incident involving the suffragist Susan B. Anthony, the abolitionist Wendell Phillips, and a popular young lecturer, Anna Dickinson.

Male aversion to women's entry into both the public sphere and professional careers is also reflected in James's characterization of the female physician Dr. Mary J. Prance in *The Bostonians.* Prance is unsexed by her profession, short-haired and boyish in her appearance, and forthright in her speech. James further undercuts Prance's legitimacy as a doctor by making her a proponent of homeopathy. Similarly, in William Dean Howells's 1881 novel, *Dr. Breen's Practice,* the anomalous figure of the female physician (who also happens to be a homeopath) is treated with overt contempt. Grace Breen enters the field of medicine not out of an altruistic desire to heal and to mitigate human suffering but because she has been disappointed in love. The inherent weakness of Grace's character is further symbolized by her inability to drive a carriage. Dependent upon a male driver for transportation to see her patients, Grace eventually falls in love with her chauffeur and forsakes her medical practice in order to marry him. Through his negative characterization of Grace, Howells insidiously questions the fitness and suitability of all women for the practice of medicine.

These negative attitudes toward female physicians are dramatically counterpointed in two contemporary novels by women—*Dr. Zay* (1882) by Elizabeth Stuart Phelps (1844–1911) and *A Country Doctor* (1884) by Sarah Orne Jewett (1849–1909); together these four works capture the tenor of the contentious public debate regarding women and medicine in the 1880s. In fact, Phelps's novel was largely inspired by the sense of outrage she experienced while reading *Dr. Breen's Practice* in serial installments in the *Atlantic Monthly.* In contrast to Grace Breen, Phelps's protagonist, Zaidee Atalanta Lloyd, is strong, competent, and highly successful in her chosen profession, ministering faithfully to her townspeople through epidemics of scarlet fever and diphtheria. Remarkably, Dr. Zay's proud, independent spirit and commitment to medicine do not preclude romantic involvement and marriage; by the novel's end she has accepted the hand of Waldo Yorke, a progressive-minded individual who understands that her duties will regularly take her away from home. As such, the Yorkes' marriage promises to be a true partnership predicated on mutual support and respect, unlike the pattern of domination and submission so common in nineteenth-century literature. Nan Prince, however, the heroine of Jewett's novel *A Country Doctor,* is not as fortunate. Believing that she must ultimately sacrifice personal happiness in order to pursue her medical career, Nan rejects the proposal of her devoted suitor, Mr. George Gerry, stating:

> I could not marry the whole of myself as most women can. . . . I know better and better that most women are made for another sort of existence, but by and by I must do my part in my own way to make many homes happy instead of one; to free them from pain, and teach grown people and little children to keep their bodies free from weakness and deformities. (P. 242)

Nan's statement reveals that she views the healing profession as all-consuming and therefore regards marriage as an unacceptable compromise for both spouses.

The complex issue of women, careers, and marriage is also examined in an 1874 novel called *Fettered for Life; or, Lord and Master* by the suffragist Lillie Devereux Blake (1833–1913). In many ways this melodramatic tale offers a compendium of the obstacles and injustices faced by nineteenth-century American women of various social classes. Blake's protagonist, Laura Stanley, is by all definitions a "New Woman," a recent graduate of Essex College (a thinly disguised version of Vassar) and a strong proponent of female suffrage, who has journeyed alone to New York City in order to establish a career as a teacher. There she encounters a former college acquaintance, a wealthy young woman named Flora Livingstone, who leads the glamorous but unfulfilling life of socialite—constantly dressing, dancing, and flitting from one superficial engagement to the next. Unhappily betrothed to the imperious Ferdinand Le Roy, Flora admires her friend's independence and professional ambition yet feels powerless to change her own situation. The misery of Flora's existence as Mrs. Le Roy is mitigated only by the private satisfaction of writing verse; yet when she dares to publish a poem in a literary magazine without her husband's knowledge or consent, he flies into a rage, burns her manuscripts, and forbids her to write again. Flora then attempts suicide by throwing herself into the sea; although rescued, she dies a few days later of a fever caused by exposure. On her deathbed, Flora pleads with her mother concerning the fate of her younger, unmarried sisters: "Mamma, don't let any of the other girls marry men they don't love. . . . You thought I should be happy in marriage, but it has killed me. . . . I want you to remember this. . . . that women as well as men need an occupation for their energies, and that marriage without love, is worse than death" (pp. 350–351).

Over the course of the novel Laura's life is also threatened by a man—the corrupt, licentious Judge Silas Swinton, whose avocation is the cavalier seduction, abandonment, and ruination of a series of attractive, independent women. When Laura resists Swinton's advances, he orders her kidnapped, chloroformed, and brought to his residence. Laura escapes sexual violation only through the intervention of two other women, Rhoda Dayton and the cross-dressing Frank Heywood, both of whom had been earlier objects of the judge's unsavory attention. With her virtue and reputation intact, Laura goes on to win first prize for one of her paintings at the New York Academy of Design and embarks on a career as an independent artist. And yet despite the successful trajectory of her professional aspirations, the novel ends on a conventional note with Laura's acceptance of a marriage proposal. As in Phelps's novel *Dr. Zay,* Laura's fiancé, Guy Bradford, offers a promising new model of marriage and manhood, assuring her: "Your obligations to me shall be no greater than mine to you. We will make life's journey hand in hand, equals in all things" (p. 379).

Perhaps the most intriguing character in *Fettered for Life,* however, is the mysterious Frank Heywood. Like Laura Stanley, Frank (whose female name is never revealed) arrives in New York City friendless and alone, eager to pursue her fortune. After enduring repeated insults, rejections, and sexual propositions, she pawns her last possession—her father's watch—and purchases a man's suit. The transformation, she states, is both instantaneous and remarkable: "My limbs were free; I could move untrammeled, and my actions were free; I could go about unquestioned. No man insulted me, and when I asked for work, I was not offered outrage" (p. 366). Disguised as a man, "Frank" secures a job as an investigative newspaper reporter and works his way up to the position of editor. His ultimate ambition is to become the owner and editor in chief of a prominent journal, which will be the vehicle for promulgating his own progressive social agenda. Yet because Frank's success depends entirely on maintaining a credible male identity, all intimate personal relationships must be forsaken; as he tells Laura, "I shall not marry; my work must be my father and mother, wife and children to me" (p. 302).

Fundamental questions about marriage, personal and professional independence, and the nature of female identity continued to preoccupy women writers throughout the 1890s. Two landmark works of fiction, the 1892 short story "The Yellow Wall-Paper" by Charlotte Perkins Gilman (1860–1935) and the 1899 novel *The Awakening* by Kate Chopin (1851–1904) reflect these concerns. The first-person narrator of Gilman's story, in the throes of postpartum depression, discovers she is imprisoned both literally in the upstairs bedroom of the home she and her physician husband have rented for the summer and figuratively by the rigid behavioral expectations of the Victorian cult of domesticity. Through her mounting obsession with the grotesque wallpaper decorating her room, she comes to realize that her husband's solicitous concern for her well-being is merely a way of infantilizing and controlling her. The narrator's descent into insanity at the story's end represents a desperate and extreme means of escape from these oppressive circumstances.

Similarly, Edna Pontellier, the protagonist of Chopin's novel, gradually "awakens" to her profound dissatisfaction with the roles imposed by marriage and motherhood. Though her husband, Léonce, provides generously for her outward existence, Edna feels empty and unfulfilled; looking inward she begins "to realize her position in the universe as a human being"—in other words, her identity as a separate, autonomous individual. Edna rebels against custom and convention, abandoning her Tuesday visits to other socially prominent New Orleans wives; she takes up sketching, learns to swim, and eventually becomes involved in an adulterous relationship. By the conclusion of *The Awakening,* Edna understands that while she can renounce the submissive, acquiescent role of wife, the role and responsibilities of motherhood cannot be ignored. Her sons appear in her imagination "like antagonists . . . who sought to drag her into the soul's slavery for the rest of her days" (p. 175). Edna eludes this entrapment by taking her own life; just as the narrator of "The Yellow Wall-Paper" finds freedom in madness, so Edna Pontellier discovers release in death.

The fiction of Edith Wharton (1862–1937) illustrates how the themes of female dependence and powerlessness persist in early-twentieth-century American literature. In her 1905 novel *The House of Mirth,* Wharton chronicles the tragic downfall of Lily Bart, a charming woman in her late twenties whose very survival depends upon marrying well. Born into an affluent family ruined by an unspecified financial reversal, Lily is orphaned as a young adult and minimally supported by her staid aunt, Mrs. Peniston. Because of her beauty, sophistication, and family lineage, Lily is welcomed in New York's elite social circles, yet she lacks the financial wherewithal to keep pace with her upper-class associates. Having incurred a significant debt from gambling at bridge, she naively allows Gus Trenor, the husband of a wealthy friend, to "invest" money in the stock market on her behalf. He agrees, hoping thereby to secure the young woman's sexual favors. Over time Trenor provides Lily with many thousands of dollars, which he falsely claims represent the dividends on her original investment. By the time Lily discovers Trenor's duplicity, she is more than $10,000 in debt, with no viable means of repayment.

As vague rumors circulate about the impropriety of her behavior, Lily's prospects of marriage evaporate; she is ostracized and eventually exiled from the privileged social set in which she previously circulated. Lily's downward spiral accelerates when she is disinherited by her conservative aunt and must actually work for a living for the first time in her life. She becomes an apprentice in a millinery shop, where she ineptly sews spangles and veils on ladies' hats and is soon dismissed. Musing on her failure, Lily realizes: "She had been fashioned to adorn and delight; to what other end does nature round the rose leaf and paint the hummingbird's breast? And was it her fault that the purely decorative mission is less easily and harmoniously fulfilled among social beings than in the world of nature?" (p. 311). Wharton's symbolism is clear—in a patriarchal society, women serve a merely "ornamental" function; they are passive, physically attractive commodities rather than active, purposeful agents. Just prior to Lily's "accidental" overdose from chloral at the end of the novel, she confides to Lawrence Selden, an acquaintance who has deliberately distanced himself from her like all the rest:

> I am a very useless person. I can hardly be said to have an independent existence. I was just a screw or a cog in the great machine called life, and when I dropped out of it I found I was of no use anywhere else. What can one do when one finds that one only fits into one hole? One must get back to it or be thrown out into the rubbish heap—and you don't know what it's like in the rubbish heap! (P. 320)

The "one hole"—or narrowly defined social niche—into which Lily is destined to fit is that of wife. Once she is deemed unmarriageable, however, Lily loses that foothold and becomes a pariah, concluding after a series of painful humiliations and rejections that her life as a single woman has neither purpose nor intrinsic worth. Like Edna Pontellier, Lily cannot be redeemed; as such, death offers her only means of escape.

These troubling representations of women's plight are echoed and reaffirmed in the work of other late-nineteenth- and early-twentieth-century female writers like Willa Cather, Susan Glaspell, and Mary Wilkins Freeman. While not overtly propagandistic, these literary texts played a crucial role in galvanizing the political movement for radical social change later known as feminism.

See also The Awakening; Cross-Dressing; *Daisy Miller; The House of Mirth; Woman's Journal; Women and Economics;* Women's Suffrage; "The Yellow Wall-Paper"

BIBLIOGRAPHY

Primary Works

Blake, Lillie Devereux. *Fettered for Life; or, Lord and Master.* 1874. New York: Feminist Press, 1996.

Chopin, Kate. *The Awakening and Selected Stories.* 1899. New York: Penguin Books, 1984.

James, Henry. *The Bostonians.* 1886. New York: Modern Library, 2003.

Jewett, Sarah Orne. *A Country Doctor.* 1884. New York: Penguin Books, 1986.

Wharton, Edith. *The House of Mirth.* 1905. New York: New American Library, 1964.

Secondary Works

Ammons, Elizabeth. *Conflicting Stories: American Women Writers at the Turn into the Twentieth Century.* New York: Oxford University Press, 1995.

Appleby, Joyce, Eileen Change, and Joanne Goodman, eds. *Encyclopedia of Women in American History.* 3 vols. New York: M. E. Sharpe, 2001.

Bardes, Barbara, and Suzanne Gossett. *Declarations of Independence: Women and Political Power in 19th Century American Fiction.* New Brunswick, N.J.: Rutgers University Press, 1990.

Coultrap-McQuin, Susan. *Doing Literary Business: American Women Writers in the Nineteenth Century.* Chapel Hill: University of North Carolina Press, 1990.

Cullen-Dupont, Kathryn, ed. *The Encyclopedia of Women's History in America.* New York: Facts on File, 2000.

Harris, Susan K. *19th Century American Women's Novels: Interpretive Strategies.* New York and London: Cambridge University Press, 1990.

Howard, Angela, and Frances Kavenik, eds. *Handbook of American Women's History.* Thousand Oaks, Calif.: Sage, 2000.

Kilcup, Karen, ed. *Soft Canons: American Women Writers and Masculine Tradition.* Iowa City: University of Iowa Press, 1999.

Kraditor, Aileen S., ed. *Up from the Pedestal: Selected Writings in the History of American Feminism.* New York: Quadrangle Books, 1968.

Langley, Winston, and Vivian Fox, eds. *Women's Rights in the United States: A Documentary History.* Westport, Conn.: Greenwood Press, 1994.

Marks, Patricia. *Bicycles, Bangs, and Bloomers: The New Woman in the Popular Press.* Lexington: University of Kentucky Press, 1990.

Norton, Mary Beth, and Ruth Alexander. *Major Problems in American Women's History: Documents and Essays.* 3rd ed. Boston: Heath, 2003.

Stanton, Elizabeth Cady, Susan B. Anthony, and M. J. Gage. *The History of Woman Suffrage*. 3 vols. New York: Ayer, 1979.

Kerry Driscoll

FOLKLORE AND ORAL TRADITIONS

Between 1870 and 1920, folklore studies in the United States blossomed. By the 1870s the analysis of Native American folklore already was in full swing, and serious interest in transplanted Old World traditions and American ethnic, regional, and occupational traditions was emerging.

NATIVE AMERICAN FOLKLORE

From the late 1870s through the first couple of years of the twentieth century, John Wesley Powell, head of the Bureau of American Ethnology, oversaw the publication of many of the important works on Native American folklore as annual reports of the bureau. These included *A Study of Siouan Cults* (1894) by James Owen Dorsey; *The Calendar History of the Kiowa Indians* (1898) and *Myths of the Cherokee* (1900) by James Mooney; *Outlines of Zuñi Creation Myths* (1896) by Frank Hamilton Cushing; and *The Mountain Chant: A Navaho Ceremony* (1887) by Washington Matthews.

Daniel Garrison Brinton, who published *The Lenâpé and Their Legends* (1885), tried to find a home for the study of Native American folklore in American museums beginning in the 1880s. This coincided with the early activities of Franz Boas (1858–1942), who launched his career as an anthropological folklorist in 1883 by conducting field research among the Eskimos of Baffin Island. Five years later he was serving on the faculty of Clark University in Massachusetts and producing his monumental collections of folklore from the tribes of northwestern North America—some, such as *Chinook Texts* (1894) and *Tsimshian Texts* (1902), were published as annual reports of the Bureau of American Ethnology. Eventually Boas established a base and a method for studying Native American folklore at Columbia University, where in 1899 he began his long career as professor of anthropology. His talented students continued to carry the torch in Native American folklore studies throughout the early part of the twentieth century. Among his students who became renowned for their work in Native American folklore were Alfred Louis Kroeber, author of *Indian Myths of South Central California* (1907); Robert H. Lowie, who wrote *Myths and Traditions of*

the *Crow Indians* (1918); and Paul Radin, author of *Literary Aspects of North American Mythology* (1915). It was an aim of Boas and some of his students to reconstruct Native American history and culture through oral traditions.

Though published in 1929, the classic collection *Tales of the North American Indians* by Stith Thompson is extremely useful for those interested in Native American oral literature between 1870 and 1920. Many of the tales in the anthology and many of the collections and studies cited in his thorough comparative notes and exhaustive bibliography fall into the period under review. Native American tales collected during this period include myths of the origin of the world and of humans; other etiological myths, including those explaining peculiarities of animals, birds, and plants; stories of tricksters and heroes; tales of journeys to other worlds, usually to the sky world; and stories of marriages between animals and humans. Native Americans also adapted folktales they borrowed from Europeans, as Thompson's eighth chapter of *Tales of the North American Indians* and his published dissertation, *European Tales among the North American Indians* (1919), show. Although Native Americans freely borrowed and adapted European tales, European settlers, save perhaps the French, did not borrow Native American oral tales.

AFRICAN AMERICAN FOLKLORE

Though much attention was paid to Native American folklore throughout the nineteenth century, little work was done on the folklore of other North American groups until after the Civil War, when some writers discovered African American folklore. The local color writer George Washington Cable, who published a couple of articles on Creole folksongs in *Century* magazine in 1886, was one of these writers. Joel Chandler Harris (1848–1908), another regional writer, published an article on "Folklore of the Southern Negroes" in *Lippincott's* magazine in 1877. It was Harris's book *Uncle Remus, His Songs and His Sayings* (1880), however, that produced the most interest in African American folklore. In all, Harris published six collections of Uncle Remus tales, including his highly regarded *Told by Uncle Remus: New Stories of the Old Plantation* (1905). Harris's animal tales inspired others to collect African American folklore in the United States.

The publication of William Francis Allen, Charles Pickard Ware, and Lucy McKim Garrison's *Slave Songs of the United States* (1867) stimulated an interested in another genre of African American folklore—folksongs—that has never abated. Many African American folksongs are functional. African work songs were fresh in the minds of newly arrived slaves, and on the plantations slaves created new work songs for picking cotton, plowing, husking corn, and other jobs in the field. When slavery was abolished, African American labor groups—often working on southern chain gangs, in prisons, and in construction camps—inherited the work song tradition. Their songs helped make the back-breaking work more bearable, and the rhythm of the songs kept the workers swinging their sledgehammers and picks more effectively than the whips of overseers. African Americans sang lyrical and narrative folksongs, too. In spirituals and blues, among the best of American lyrical folksongs, they sang their feelings. Though spirituals are religious and sung in groups and blues are secular and performed by individuals, both often express the same general feelings of bitterness and a desire to escape, sometimes employing the train as a symbol of getting away from unpleasant situations.

From the southern fields, African Americans moved to cities after the Civil War, hoping for freedom but often finding a different kind of servitude in city slums, where crime frequently provided the only means of making a living; consequently, many African American ballads deal with crime and often with murder. While white Americans sang of Jesse James, Sam Bass, and Billy the Kid, black Americans sang of Stagolee, Bill Brady, and John Hardy, with some of their ballads being historical. The ballad "John Hardy," for example, is based on a real event. On 19 January 1894, John Hardy was executed at Welch, West Virginia, for killing a fellow miner in a crap-game dispute over twenty-five cents. It was not a bad man, though, who inspired one of the great African American ballads but a hard-working, steel-driving man named John Henry, who died "with his hammer in his hand." The exact origin of "John Henry" will never be known, but it is thought that the John Henry legend got started around 1870 during the construction of the Big Bend Tunnel on the Chesapeake and Ohio Railroad in West Virginia. Whatever the origin, African Americans have largely been responsible for the preservation and diffusion of songs and stories about John Henry, and every state in the South claims him.

REGIONAL AMERICAN FOLKLORE

Between the Civil War and the end of the nineteenth century, regional folklore was best preserved by regional realists or local color writers. Representative of these authors was Rowland E. Robinson (1833–1900), a Vermont farmer, sports enthusiast, and illustrator who did not begin to write until after middle

John Henry. Undated lithograph. It is thought that the John Henry legend originated around 1870 during the construction of the Big Bend Tunnel on the Chesapeake and Ohio Railroad in West Virginia. THE CHESAPEAKE AND OHIO HISTORICAL SOCIETY, INC.

age, when his sight began failing. He wrote most of his stories and nature essays after he was blind. Robinson had a lifelong interest in the oral traditions of his region. While hiking, hunting, fishing, trapping, and sketching in the vicinity of his Ferrisburgh home, he encountered a wide variety of Vermont folk traditions. In realistic stories such as *Uncle Lisha's Shop: Life in a Corner of Yankeeland* (1887), *Sam Lovel's Camps: Uncle Lisha's Friends under Bark and Canvas* (1889), *Uncle Lisha's Outing* (1897), *A Hero of Ticonderoga* (1898), and *A Danvis Pioneer* (1900), Robinson drew upon nearly every form of folklife, including speech, proverbs, riddles, rhymes, games, beliefs, cures, songs, tales, customs, arts, crafts, and architecture. What is more, utilizing the frame device, he presents this lore in authentically reconstructed social and physical contexts. Because his main purpose for writing stories, as he points out in his author's note in *Danvis Folks* (1900), was to preserve folklore and

Rowland E. Robinson. Robinson is pictured here engaged in one of his favorite pastimes, etching a picture on a shelf lichen. COURTESY OF RONALD L. BAKER

because he was interested in context as well as in texts, his writings offer a literary ethnography of nineteenth-century Vermont folklife.

In the Midwest, the Hoosier poet James Whitcomb Riley (1849–1916) grew up at a time when the nation was making a transition from agrarianism to industrialism. Throughout his life he always looked back with nostalgia on his boyhood days in an Indiana village, as he suggests in one of his sentimental poems, "The Old Times Were the Best." Riley, like other regional writers, was selective in his use of folklore and altered and adapted the material to suit his purpose. But like Robinson, Riley consciously preserved folklore and believed that the creative writer who draws upon folklife should be faithful in his or her presentation. In "Dialect in Literature" (1892), for example, he says "the true interpreter" of common life should permit "his rustic characters to think, talk, act and live, just as nature designed them. He does

not make the pitiable error of either patronizing or making fun of them. He knows them and he loves them" (pp. 2682–2683). Although Riley is remembered for his poetry and not for his prose, his prose sketches, especially, indicate his thorough use of proverbs, superstitions, games, tales, songs, material culture, and customs. His work is also remarkable for its accurate transcription of regional speech. One value of his writings, as those of other regional authors of the period, is that they preserve a picture of folk practices from a time when no systematic field collections were made.

Many regional writers were inspired by tall tales—humorous narratives of lying and exaggeration—which were especially popular on the American frontier among hunters, fishermen, farmers, and river men, as the tales frequently deal with hunting, fishing, rough weather, fertile soil, big crops, and fabulous animals. Many tall tales deal with the legendary logger Paul Bunyan. As Daniel Hoffman shows in *Paul Bunyan: Last of the Frontier Demigods* (1952), this figure quickly passed from a folk hero of lumberjacks celebrated for his sexual prowess to a mass-culture hero found mainly in advertising and children's literature. Printed texts of Bunyan's exploits, however, fail to capture the tall tale's art, which, as Mark Twain suggests in "How to Tell a Story" (1897), lies in its manner of telling, not especially in its content. Twain (1835–1910) cites an old tale, "The Wounded Soldier," as told by James Whitcomb Riley in the character of an old farmer, to illustrate what he means. For his retelling of the tale, Riley, like Robinson, re-created a context of performance. This, according to Twain, is what makes Riley's treatment of the tale effective. In suggesting the importance of context and performance in oral storytelling, Twain predated the social scientists' interests in contextual folklore studies by at least forty years. Twain, himself, made good use of southwestern tall tales in his first book, *The Celebrated Jumping Frog of Calaveras County and Other Sketches* (1867), and also in *Roughing It* (1872). Some of his later works, such as *Adventures of Huckleberry Finn (Tom Sawyer's Comrade)* (1885), are storehouses of all kinds of regional American folklore.

THE AMERICAN FOLKLORE SOCIETY

Twain, in fact, along with his friends Joel Chandler Harris and the Indiana writer Edward Eggleston (1837–1902), were charter members of the American Folklore Society when it was founded in 1888. The goals of the society, enumerated in the first issue of the *Journal of American Folk-Lore*, involved collecting "the fast-vanishing remains of Folk-Lore in America."

This included English "ballads, tales, superstitions, dialect, etc."; folklore of "Negroes in the Southern States of the Union"; folklore of "the Indian Tribes of North America (myths, tales, etc.)"; and folklore of "French Canada, Mexico, etc." (*Journal of American Folk-Lore*, p. 3). Though the founders' notion of "fast-vanishing" traditions has proven false, their emphasis on English and other European folklore in the United States, African American folklore, and Native American folklore echoed the early research in American oral traditions and set the stage for folklore studies in the United States during the last part of the nineteenth century and the first part of the twentieth century. A prime mover among the founders of the society was William Wells Newell, who published *Games and Songs of American Children* (1883), the earliest annotated compilation of children's folklore in the United States. A forgotten founding member of the society, mainly because he wrote in German, was Karl Knortz, a prolific early collector of all kinds of folklore, including customs, beliefs, legends, games, riddles, rhymes, and proverbs.

Francis James Child, first president of the American Folklore Society, made British ballads his life's work but did not do any fieldwork in the United States; however, at Harvard he trained several notable American folklorists, including George Lyman Kittredge (1860–1941). While Kittredge continued Child's work on British ballads, he enlarged his range of folklore interests to include tales, beliefs, proverbs, European folklore in America, and folklore in ancient and medieval literature. What is more, he trained at least half of the American folklorists, including Stith Thompson, active in the first half of the twentieth century. Another of Kittredge's students was John Avery Lomax, who since childhood had been collecting cowboy songs in Texas. Kittredge recognized the importance of these songs and was instrumental in securing for Lomax three summer Sheldon Fellowships from Harvard to collect more cowboy songs in western states, resulting in the publication of *Cowboy Songs and Other Frontier Ballads* (1910), one of the early collections of cowboy songs. It had an enormous impact on the study of occupational folklore in the United States.

AMERICAN OCCUPATIONAL FOLKLORE

As a matter of fact, many American oral traditions from the late nineteenth century and early twentieth century were collected from occupational groups. In addition to cowboys, these included loggers, sailors, miners, railroaders, oil drillers, and steelworkers. The heyday of the cattle drive, documented in Andy Adams's *Log of a Cowboy: A Narrative of the Old Trail Days* (1903), occurred during the 1870s and 1880s. Adams

(1859–1935) spent twelve years in the saddle, mainly herding horses, not cows, though he did herd cattle at least once. The realistic *Log* accurately depicts the life of the cowboy on a drive of three thousand cows and four hundred horses from Texas to Montana in 1882, emphasizing the long hours, hard work, difficult terrain, inevitable stampedes, and predictable skirmishes with rustlers and Native Americans. Though Adams's book is fiction, his intimate knowledge of cowboy life equipped him to depict the cowboy as an occupational figure and present a more accurate picture of the cowboy than most plays, novels, and films dealing with the mythical or idealized cowboy. Adams is especially good at re-creating storytelling sessions around the campfire, even providing texts of some tales, but he also includes cowboy songs, beliefs, and sayings. Most early compilers of cowboy lore, however, focused only on songs. An early example is *Songs of the Cowboys* (1908) by N. Howard "Jack" Thorp (1867–1940), which includes versions of "Little Joe the Wrangler" and other familiar cowboy tunes. Cowboy songs tell a lot about the occupation. "The Buffalo Skinners" tells of hardships on the buffalo range, "Git Along, Little Dogies" deals with the cattle, "I Ride an Old Paint" celebrates the horse, "The Old Chisholm Trail" describes a trail drive, and other songs deal with branding, roping, and night herding.

The logging industry began in Maine and passed through Michigan, Wisconsin, and Minnesota on its way to Washington and Oregon, taking with it a body of oral traditions and place names. Historically, no other country experienced such an intensive and prolonged period of logging. Franz Rickaby, in *Ballads and Songs of the Shanty-Boy* (1926), called this era the "Golden Age of American Lumbering" (p. vii), and he sets its dates as 1870 to 1900. Rickaby—who collected songs from loggers who worked in the woods of Michigan, Wisconsin, and Minnesota during this period—claimed that no group celebrated itself in folksongs more than the lumberjack. Though many of the tunes of lumberjack songs were borrowed from Irish street ballads, the texts were unique. The songs celebrated cutting trees; hauling, rolling, and driving logs; breaking logjams; and the romance between a logger and a town girl, often ending in tragedy. Loggers preserved all kinds of songs, though, including some not dealing with their occupation. This resulted from the fact that they came from a variety of ethnic and occupational backgrounds and did not have much else to do to while away their time in the lumber camps except play checkers, tell tales, and sing songs like "Lost Jimmie Whalen," "The Banks of Gaspereaux," "The Jam on Gerry's Rock," "The Little Brown Bulls," and "Canada I. O."

In parts of the United States mining was an important occupation that produced a body of folklore, especially stories and songs but also speech, beliefs, naming, and other traditions. Coal miners generated most of the mining lore since more Americans worked in coal mining than in lead, gold, silver, or copper mining. Coal miners' songs are especially important for historical and sociological interests, for unlike the songs of cowboys and lumberjacks, coal-mining songs represent mass protest. In their songs there is a growing passion for unionism that does not appear in the songs of most other early occupational groups. Miners' songs tell of greedy bosses, long hours, dangerous work, poor working conditions, and disasters. In addition, miners lived with their families close to the shafts, so miners' songs reveal a domestic life that does not appear in the songs of lumberjacks and cowboys. George Korson published two important books—*Minstrels of the Mine Patch: Songs and Stories of the Anthracite Industry* (1938) and *Coal Dust on the Fiddle: Songs and Stories of the Bituminous Industry* (1943)—on mining folklore. Although published after 1920, many of the traditions Korson reports date from the late nineteenth century and early twentieth century.

Ore boats on the Great Lakes and steamboats on the big rivers generated all kinds of folklore, too, including tall tales. Along the big rivers comic legends were told of steamboat and keelboat pilots, especially Mike Fink, hero of the boatmen. *A Treasury of Mississippi River Folklore: Stories, Ballads, Traditions, and Folkways of the Mid-American River Country* (1955) by B. A. Botkin provides broad coverage of Mississippi River folklore. What Korson did for mining folklore, the Texas folklorist Mody C. Boatright did for oil field workers in a couple of books, including an excellent one on Gib Morgan, an oil-driller hero who told fabulous tales about himself that other drillers later retold. Following the Civil War, the fast-developing railroad industry produced another body of occupational lore, including a ballad about a brave engineer, John Luther "Casey" Jones, who in 1900 "died with the throttle in his right hand." Such tales follow a familiar pattern in American occupational folklore, for countless cowboys, loggers, miners, and railroaders get killed performing their jobs in American ballads. Another example comes from the steel industry, where there is a legend about a worker who fell into a furnace and came out in an ingot.

BRITISH BALLADS IN THE UNITED STATES

After World War I, there was renewed interest in regional folklore, especially ballads and folksongs, largely because of Cecil Sharp's fieldwork in Appalachia between 1916 and 1918. At the encouragement of Olive Dame Campbell, who began collecting folksongs in the Southern Highlands in 1908, Sharp, a native of England who was an experienced collector of folksongs, spent forty-six weeks collecting surviving British ballads and other folksongs in North Carolina, Virginia, West Virginia, Tennessee, and Kentucky. Accompanied by an assistant, Maud Karpeles, he found a rich folksong tradition—collecting about 35 songs a week, a total of 1,612 songs with tunes, one of the largest and best collections of folk music from the United States. The efforts of Campbell, Sharp, and Karpeles not only inspired other folklorists to collect ballads and songs in other regions of the United States, they forever identified Appalachia as the region most closely linked with American folklore.

See also Blacks; Ethnology; Indians; Regionalism and Local Color Fiction

BIBLIOGRAPHY

Primary Works

Adams, Andy. *The Log of a Cowboy: A Narrative of Old Trail Days*. Boston: Houghton, Mifflin, 1903.

Journal of American Folk-Lore 1, no. 1 (April–June 1888).

Rickaby, Franz. *Ballads and Songs of the Shanty-Boy*. Cambridge, Mass.: Harvard University Press, 1926.

Riley, James Whitcomb. *The Complete Works of James Whitcomb Riley*. Vol. 10. New York: Harper & Brothers, 1916.

Robinson, Rowland E. *Works of Rowland E. Robinson*. 7 vols. Edited by Llewellyn R. Perkins. Rutland, Vt.: Tuttle, 1934–1938.

Thompson, Stith. *European Tales among the North American Indians: A Study in the Migration of Folk-tales*. Colorado Springs, Colo.: Board of Trustees of Colorado College, [1919?].

Thompson, Stith. *Tales of the North American Indians*. 1929. Bloomington: Indiana University Press, 1966.

Twain, Mark. *Selected Shorter Writings of Mark Twain*. Boston: Houghton Mifflin, 1962.

Secondary Works

Baker, Ronald L. *Folklore in the Writings of Rowland E. Robinson*. Bowling Green, Ohio: Bowling Green University Popular Press, 1973.

Dorson, Richard M. *America in Legend: Folklore from the Colonial Period to the Present*. New York: Pantheon Books, 1973.

Dorson, Richard M. *American Folklore*. Chicago: University of Chicago Press, 1959.

Johnson, Guy B. *John Henry: Tracking Down a Negro Legend.* Chapel Hill: University of North Carolina Press, 1929.

Korson, George, ed. *Pennsylvania Songs and Legends.* Philadelphia: University of Pennsylvania Press, 1949.

Laws, G. Malcolm, Jr. *Native American Balladry: A Descriptive Study and a Bibliographical Syllabus.* Philadelphia: American Folklore Society, 1964.

Leach, MacEdward. "Folklore in American Regional Literature." *Journal of the Folklore Institute* 3 (December 1966): 378–397.

Lomax, John. "Self-Pity in Negro Folk-Songs." *The Nation,* 9 August 1917, pp. 141–145.

Ronald L. Baker

FOOD AND DRINK

During the first half of the nineteenth century, American food was a local affair. Apart from certain imports such as tea, coffee, and spices, Americans tended to eat what was at hand: Marylanders ate their oysters, Hoosiers enjoyed their corn, Plains Indians continued to live off dwindling buffalo herds, southern slaves were kept to a diet of hog and hominy, and western settlers as memorialized in Owen Wister's *The Virginian* (1902), ate the local dust right along with the victuals: "Colonel Cyrus Jones's eating palace . . . opened up on the world as a stage upon the audience. You sat in Omaha's whole sight and dined, while Omaha's dust came and settled upon the refreshments" (p. 148). Until reliable refrigeration and transportation became widely available, Americans grew, raised, hunted, cooked, preserved, and ate food that was indigenous to their particular region, while food making was a daily, full-time occupation for many.

After the civil war, however, with the completion of railway lines to western territories—and the development of the icebox car—regional food gained a national market: the territories shipped grain to the east; Florida shipped fruit to the north; and Chicago received its first fresh lobster from Boston. Meat, milk, fish, fruits, and vegetables could now be transported from the country to the city, from one state to another, and by 1869, when Chinese laborers drove home the last spike of the transcontinental railroad stretching from New England to California, the very first boxcar of fresh fruit made its way from the West Coast to the East. Thus, an American gastronome could count on variety. In Mark Twain's fictional account of a European tour, *A Tramp Abroad* (1880), his narrator expresses a distaste for what he deems the "monotonous variety of UNSTRIKING dishes" characteristic of European cookery and yearns for the diverse foodstuff of his native country: soft-shell crabs from the Chesapeake, turtle soup from Philadelphia, broiled Virginia bacon, Baltimore duck, San Francisco mussels, Connecticut shad, Southern-style fried chicken, and all-American (i.e., salted) butter. "A man accustomed to American food and American domestic cookery would not starve to death suddenly in Europe," observes Twain, "but I think he would gradually waste away, and eventually die."

With the advent of a national market and consumer interest in diverse fare, the American food economy shifted from subsistence and local production to profit-driven, mechanical production—from the homemade to the industrial. Although canned fish and vegetables had appeared as early as 1825 (when the first patent was granted for the tin can), the expanding railroad networks made the tinning of salmon, tomatoes, strawberries, and corn a lucrative business. "Canned foods now became status symbols," notes Leslie Brenner in *American Appetite,* "since they meant one could eat things out of season or locale, a luxury previously reserved only for the very wealthy" (p. 16). Condensed milk and baking powder first appeared in 1856, and packaged yeast was introduced in 1868, inaugurating an era of commercially made bread. In essence, then, "American" cuisine quickly became commercial.

"AMERICAN" CUISINE

American cuisine assumed its modern form as Civil War soldiers came home and asked their mothers and spouses to make them the foods they had become accustomed to on the front lines—that is, canned foods. The war had spurred the industrialized North to produce grains, vegetables, fruits, and meat in ever more efficient ways, which led to such technological developments as the mechanical harvester, condensed liquids such as blackberry juice, and tin cans fused not by hand but by machines. "By 1870," explain Waverley Root and Richard de Rochemont, "the nation was consuming thirty million cans of food annually. During the decade which followed, the product of the canneries increased, in terms of value, by 200 percent" (p. 190).

In other words, "American" cuisine became synonymous with mass-produced food that was prepackaged, often precooked, and entirely uniform. Hence the many commercial success stories during the last two decades of the nineteenth century and the first decade of the twentieth: John T. Dorrance, a chemist, concentrated canned soups under his partner's name, at the Joseph Campbell Preserve Company; Henry J. Heinz, a salesman, eventually developed fifty-seven varieties of bottled condiments; Gail Borden sold condensed milk to the federal government for consumption by the military; Philip Danforth Armour pushed for refrigerator cars to ship his Chicago beef; and J. H. Kraft packaged cheese wedges in identical foil packets and sold them door-to-door.

Even the kitchen became a site of mass-produced wonder. The wood-burning stove was replaced by gas and then electric ranges; the apple parer became a universal kitchen implement; and, in large part thanks to Fannie Farmer's 1896 *Boston Cooking-School Cook Book,* which published cookbook measurement standards for the first time, measuring cups and bowls became regular kitchen tools. In other words, both food and its preparation became professionalized, with "amateur" homemakers and servants turning to the expertise of cooking schools and the national food industry. As a result, mass-produced food became a symbol of purity, health, consistency, ease, and economy to a consumer group of largely middle- and working-class Americans.

Yet despite Americans' reliance on consistent, commercialized food, homemade fare continued to have appeal, especially if it was feminized and racialized. Even during World War I, when industrialized, sanitized edibles and the high-tech kitchen were marks of America's economic and social progress, Willa Cather romanticized "real" down-home Nebraska meals in her novel *My Ántonia* (1918): "On Sundays [grandmother] gave us as much chicken as we could eat, and on other days we had ham or bacon or sausage meat. She baked either pies or cake for us every day, unless, for a change, she made my favourite pudding, striped with currants and boiled in a bag" (p. 45). The emphasis here on maternal abundance, especially in meats and the extravagance of sweets baked every day, marks a fundamental contradiction in the American food culture of the period—between nostalgia for the homemade food of the past and a glorification of the standardized, nutritious, and hygienic food of the present. This contradiction became part of the mythos of modern-day American food as well, where food preparation by women and nonprofessionals is often attributed to industrialized foods to make them appear "authentic."

In turn, after the Civil War, as more white, upper- and middle-class households employed servants, the black female domestic, known as the "Mammy," was increasingly exalted for her cooking—a cookery that was depicted as handed down from generation to generation, improvised, never written down, and almost mythic. As the nation moved from Reconstruction to the Jim Crow era, the figure of the Mammy served to bridge the cultural gap between the plantation South and the highly industrialized North, especially as American consumerism became molded by national advertising. "Advertisers of certain processed foods engaged in commodity fetishism," writes Alice A. Deck, "whereby the black cook's face appeared on the box of pancake flour to suggest that she would be going home with the consumer as a spiritual guide during the cooking process" (p. 70). Thus companies that made processed foods such as Aunt Jemima Pancake Flour for consumption by middle-class housewives appropriated femininity and blackness to sell their products—qualities antithetical to an industry modeled on white, masculine entrepreneurship and professionalism.

FOOD REFORMERS

Thanks to the proliferation of new food technologies and food availability in the second half of the nineteenth century, gastronomic reformers abounded. After Louis Pasteur's discovery of disease-causing bacteria in cows and chickens in the mid-1870s, America experienced its first nationwide "health craze." Of course, food reformers had been preaching their doctrines in antebellum America as well, but with the discovery of food-borne bacteria in tandem with new mass media that enabled writers and orators access to a wider audience, health food enthusiasts such as Dr. John Harvey Kellogg (1852–1943) gained a national following. At Kellogg's Battle Creek Sanatorium for the dyspeptic in Michigan, Kellogg touted the restorative qualities of natural foods, particularly bran, believing that if people chewed tough, dry cereal, they would keep their teeth strong, their bowels healthy, and their systems free from the bacteria that, Kellogg believed, lived in the colon of anyone who consumed meat. His 1877 grain mix called Granose was in essence the first Kellogg cereal, and a patient of his, Charles Post (1854–1914), soon after developed Grape-Nuts (first called "Elijah's Manna"). Post went on to invent Post Toasties, Kellogg his famous Toasted Corn Flakes, and the notion of selling good health via commercialized foods was born.

In the two decades following the initial successes of Kellogg and Post, the Department of Agriculture published specific data gathered by the chemist Wilbur Olin Atwater (1844–1907) on the nutritive value of food, thereby originating terms now taken for granted, such as "calories," "dietary fat," and "carbohydrates." Food historian Harvey Levenstein explains

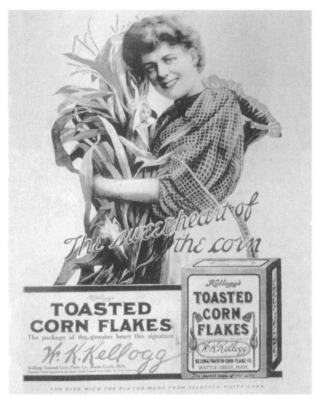

Advertisement for Kellogg's Corn Flakes, 1907. GETTY IMAGES

that from 1880 to 1930, the American middle class turned to such scientists as Atwater who first created and then propagated the principles of what came to be called the "New Nutrition." "These taught that all foods could be broken down into proteins, carbohydrates, and fats, and that one should eat only as much of each of them as the body required. The idea that the body's energy needs could be measured in calories took hold, along with the notion that one would gain weight if one ingested more of these than the body burned" (p. 9). This development, in conjunction with the vegetable diet and temperance movements, led to the establishment of domestic science at the turn of the century. (The modern-day legacy of this movement is the home economics class.) Self-made nutritionists such as Sarah Rorer (1849–1937), the 1890s "Queen of the Kitchen," jumped on the domestic science bandwagon and founded a century-long obsession with weight. Rorer, for instance, believed each unnecessary pound was a pound of disease and argued that a person's stomach mucus accumulated each night, leading to obesity if combined with a breakfast of eggs, cheese, and bacon; thus, Rorer insisted that fruit and cereal were the only digestible morning fare. Thus, the regulation of food and the body converged with pseudoscientific

discourse, which led to a widespread reformist impulse to manage lower-class bodies, diseased bodies, sexualized bodies, raced bodies, women's bodies, infants' bodies, and soldiers' bodies via the "scientific" control of food in industry, cookbooks, schools, and welfare programs.

Throughout this period, high on the list of those in need of reform were citizens who imbibed too much alcohol—who were "intemperate." With the formation in 1895 of the Anti-Saloon League and similar organizations, particularly the Woman's Christian Temperance Union (1874), the campaign to prohibit alcohol went national. Popular authors and religious advocates linked alcohol to the working class and moral laxity. For instance, the novelist Elizabeth Stuart Phelps (1844–1911), interviewed for *Our Famous Women* in 1884, adopted the temperance movement as one of her pet reforms, part and parcel with her overall interest in "uplifting" her readers, especially young women who might persuade their husbands to stop drinking. "[Phelps] saw how intemperance on Eastern Point added a cruel weight to the hard lot of fishermen's families," explains the interviewer, Elizabeth Spring, "and through her efforts a Reform Club of sixty-five members was sustained there. A club-room had been otherwise secured; it was brightened with pictures and music; addresses were delivered and sermons preached to the men; but her personal work was of a deeper and more wearing sort. . . . They came to her house with their hopes and despair, their temptations and troubles" (pp. 576–577). Thus, "improving" the body came with the promise that, if certain populations could control their desire for alcohol, they could acquire the "deeper" and "more wearing" morality of a reader, of someone (like Phelps) who had already learned how to improve the mind and heart via reading. In this way, the culture of letters was directly linked to the cult of the American body.

EATING OUT AND EATING IN

Charles Dickens, in his 1842 travelogue *American Notes,* writes that he "never could find out any difference between a [dinner] party at Boston and a party in London, saving that at the former place all assemblies are held at more rational hours; that the conversation may possibly be a little louder and more cheerful; and a guest is usually expected to ascend to the very top of the house to take his cloak off; that he is certain to see, at every dinner, an unusual amount of poultry on the table; and at every supper, at least two mighty bowls of hot stewed oysters, in any one of which a half-grown Duke of Clarence might be smothered easily" (p. 60). Indeed, from mid-century on, abundant oysters were not only swallowed at posh oyster parties, they were sold by street peddlers, carried by oyster express wagons, and served in oyster houses in Baltimore, New York, and Boston. Thus oysters crossed class boundaries: one could down them with the lawyer and legislator Abraham Lincoln in Illinois, yet one could also buy and eat them right off the street.

There were foods specifically attached to haute cuisine, however, especially as upscale restaurants became fashionable after the Civil War. The two gastronomic centers on the East Coast were Boston and New York. Boston was touted for upscale New England cooking, New York for its enduring dedication to French cuisine. During the rise of rampant restaurantism, certain hotels were known for their divine (if expensive) fare. In Boston, the Parker House was extolled for its rolls and filet mignon, while the Winter Place Hotel (which eventually became the Locke-Ober) developed a "cross" menu that was both French and thoroughly Bostonian (including a dressed-up clam chowder). In New York, one needed a top hat and tails to eat at the Ritz-Carlton, but the finest restaurant—and the one that became a fixture of New York cuisine for 150 years—was the French Delmonico's, which opened in 1832. Delmonico's made pretension fashionable by printing its menus in French, listing the names of diners in newspaper society columns, providing live music and fresh flowers, and serving such exotic vegetables as eggplant. Even Dickens was moved to sing America's praises in 1868 after eating Delmonico's *petites timbales à la Dickens*.

Haute cuisine was not limited to restaurants, however. Famous literati, from Harriet Beecher Stowe to John Greenleaf Whittier, were feted at swank birthday dinners (Mark Twain himself gave Whittier a famous birthday dinner in 1877). In turn, depictions of domestic food within the pages of American literature ranged from the countrified nostalgic (as in *My Ántonia*) to middle-class lunches (the title dentist in the novel *McTeague* (1899), by Frank Norris, is served "sausages, . . . with mashed potatoes . . .; chocolate, which Trina adored; and a side dish or two—a salted herring or a couple of artichokes or a salad" [p. 142]) to the private tables of the urban elite, often representative of Americans' apparent need to simulate British foodways to gain cultural credibility. *The Age of Innocence* (1920), by Edith Wharton, is replete with lavish gastronomic descriptions that reveal the aridness of New York society throughout the 1870s:

> A big dinner, with a hired *chef* and two borrowed footmen, with Roman punch, roses from Henderson's, and *menus* on gilt-edged cards, was . . .

not to be lightly undertaken. . . . The Roman punch made all the difference; not in itself but by its manifold implications—since it signified either canvas-backs or terrapin, two soups, a hot and a cold sweet, full *décolletage* with short sleeves, and guests of a proportionate importance. (P. 327)

This paradox of spiritual famine within somatic plenty is perhaps best rendered by William Dean Howells in his novel *The Rise of Silas Lapham* (1885), in which Lapham, a new city professional from the Vermont countryside, must negotiate the rituals of a Boston dinner party.

> It was not an elaborate dinner; but Lapham was used to having everything on the table at once, and this succession of dishes bewildered him; he was afraid perhaps he was eating too much. He now no longer made any pretense of not drinking his wine, for he was thirsty, and there was no more water, and he hated to ask for any. (P. 199)

Thus food, especially as presented in the home, was a potent symbol for American writers: simultaneously, it bespoke an ethos of plenty—a nation with grandmothers who could make more chicken than children could eat—as well as a contradiction between the pastoral values inherent in amber waves of grain and the "bankrupt" values of Roman punch and wine for water.

Anglo-American cuisine had carried the symbolic weight of class, race, gender, religion, and region ever since 1630, when William Bradford and his Puritan settlers arrived at Plymouth and began appropriating Native American foodways. But the extensive industrialization and rise of mass transportation and advertising that occurred between 1870 and 1920 meant that North American food came to symbolize national values, not just regional identity. In essence, then, what is now called "American" cuisine originated with the technological, industrial, and economic shifts that occurred just after the outbreak of the Civil War—and that continue today in the forms of fast food, chain restaurants, the microwave, the frozen dinner, the boxed cake mix, and—paradoxically—Julia Child, Martha Stewart, Emeril Lagasse, and the Frugal Gourmet.

See also Domestic and Sentimental Fiction; Health and Medicine; Temperance

BIBLIOGRAPHY

Primary Works

Cather, Willa. *My Ántonia.* 1918. Boston: Houghton Mifflin, 1949.

Dickens, Charles. *American Notes.* 1842. The Oxford Illustrated Dickens. Oxford and New York: Oxford University Press, 1997.

Farmer, Fannie. *The Original Boston Cooking-School Cook Book, 1896: A Facsimile.* New York: H. L. Levin Associates, 1973.

Howells, William Dean. *The Rise of Silas Lapham.* 1885. New York: Penguin Books, 1983.

Norris, Frank. *McTeague: A Story of San Francisco.* 1899. New York: Holt, Rinehart and Winston, 1966.

Spring, Elizabeth T. "Elizabeth Stuart Phelps." *Our Famous Women: Comprising the Lives and Deeds of American Women Who Have Distinguished Themselves in Literature, Science, Art, Music, and the Drama, or Are Famous as Heroines, Patriots, Orators, Educators, Physicians, Philanthropists, Etc.,* pp. 560–580. Hartford, Conn.: A. D. Worthington and Company, 1884.

Twain, Mark. *A Tramp Abroad.* London: Chatto & Windus, 1880.

Wharton, Edith. *The Age of Innocence.* 1920. New York: Collier Books, Macmillan, 1968, 1993.

Wister, Owen. *The Virginian, a Horseman of the Plains.* 1902. New York: Grosset & Dunlap, 1911.

Secondary Works

Brenner, Leslie. *American Appetite: The Coming of Age of a Cuisine.* New York: Bard, 1999.

Deck, Alice A. "'Now Then—Who Said Biscuits?': The Black Woman Cook as Fetish in American Advertising, 1905–1953." In *Kitchen Culture in America: Popular Representations of Food, Gender, and Race,* edited by Sherrie A. Inness, pp. 69–93. Philadelphia: University of Pennsylvania Press, 2001.

Fernández-Armesto, Felipe. *Near a Thousand Tables: A History of Food.* New York: Free Press, 2002.

Levenstein, Harvey. *Paradox of Plenty: A Social History of Eating in Modern America.* New York: Oxford University Press, 1993.

Levenstein, Harvey. *Revolution at the Table: The Transformation of the American Diet.* New York: Oxford University Press, 1988.

Root, Waverley, and Richard de Rochemont. *Eating in America: A History.* Hopewell, N.J.: Ecco Press, 1995.

Jennifer Cognard-Black

FOREIGN VISITORS

When Americans of the late nineteenth and early twentieth centuries traveled abroad, their reason was painfully self-evident: as citizens of a somewhat provincial and isolated nation, they wished to broaden their limited perspective. Typically, a wealthy young American of the period toured "the continent" (there was only one, really, to see) or sometimes traveled around the globe to seek greater sophistication and variety. But what could motivate travelers from foreign cultures to visit the United States, when it was still an emerging nation?

Some visitors, such as Oscar Wilde (1854–1900) in 1882 and Matthew Arnold (1822–1888) the same year, came to the United States as cultural ambassadors, seeking to bring the secret of life (which secret, Wilde finally revealed, was beauty) or sweetness and light (which, Arnold felt, embodied culture) to their English-speaking but otherwise benighted cousins across the Atlantic. Of course, Wilde and Arnold, and other such ambassadors, were also drawn by money—each of their lecture tours spanned months, many dozens of speaking engagements, and thousands of miles of travel, for which they had arranged to be very handsomely compensated, a prerequisite for either gentleman even to consider the arduous trip to the United States, much less the more arduous task of touring it from end to end.

Other visitors came to study America's ongoing political experiment: the practice of running a postcolonial democratic republic. A typical visitor of this stripe might be Domingo Sarmiento (1811–1888), the young Argentinean who would soon serve as president of his country, or Georges Clemenceau (1841–1929), who first visited the United States as a young man, returning to his native France in 1870. After serving as his nation's prime minister during World War I, Clemenceau paid a final visit fifty-two years after leaving the United States. Similarly, James Bryce (1838–1922) visited America close to the beginning and ending points of the 1870 to 1920 period. A student of American political economy who arrived in New York in 1870 at the age of thirty-two, Bryce wrote the classic *American Commonwealth* in 1888, and in his later years served as Britain's Ambassador to the United States from 1907 through 1913. All such observers could return home with a wealth of firsthand experience with the ways American government functioned.

Not all such observers, however, felt that the American government functioned very well at all. Even those who were impressed with American ideals saw the sordidness and the casual disregard for dignity in electoral politics. Both Bryce and Clemenceau noted that political life in Europe was far more professional and decorous than in the United States. Clemenceau was fascinated and appalled by the holiday-like atmosphere of political rallies, writing that campaigns that "should be a serious and considered act" (Pachter and Wein, p. 173) were anything but sober. Bryce contrasted America's easy mixing of its social classes with the stiffer distinctions made in Victorian England and generally approved of the informality but disapproved of Americans' lack of reverence for its government: for Americans, he wrote in *American Commonwealth*, the government is not some "ideal moral power, charged with the duty of forming the characters and guiding the lives of its subjects. It is more like a commercial company or perhaps a huge municipality created for the management of certain business" (Pachter and Wein, p. 213). On a national level, such a purely functional role for the government was disturbing, but Bryce felt a far greater cynicism prevailed on the local level, where American state and city governments were notoriously corruptible. "The government of cities is the one conspicuous failure of the United States," he wrote, noting the "extravagance, corruption and mismanagement which mark the administrations of most of the great cities" (Pachter and Wein, p. 216). Because Americans did not look to their government to protect them from economic danger any more than they expected it to protect them from natural disasters, they suffered needlessly when disaster struck: Bryce wrote that the government stood in the face of economic forces as helpless as "the farmer, who sees approaching the tornado which will uproot his crop" (Pachter and Wein, p. 213).

PERCEPTIONS OF RACIAL AND CLASS DISCREPANCIES

Shortly after the end of the Civil War, Clemenceau noted that it was still permissible, even common, for politicians, particularly Democrats, to insinuate aloud "that a negro is a degenerate gorilla" and resist giving power "to a savage race which can never be civilized, whose intelligence level is barely above that of a beast . . . This is the theme of all the democrats' speeches" (Pachter and Wein, p. 171). The racial divisions present in U.S. culture after the Civil War dismayed many who admired the principles of a class-free society that the United States found impossible to put into practice. White-skinned visitors could plainly see that high-toned phrases like "All men are created equal" were merely phrases, but darker-skinned visitors, such as Edward Blyden (1832–1912) of the West Indies, could do far more than just see the inequalities being practiced. After arriving in New York at the age of seventeen in 1850, Blyden was denied entrance to theological study, as he put it, because of "deep seated prejudice against my race" (Pachter and Wein, p. 159). Discouraged, he soon traveled to the newly independent country of Liberia where he found that blacks could fill "the most dignified stations that white men can fill in" the United States (Pachter and Wein, p. 160). Over the next forty-five years, as Blyden made repeated trips

into and out of the United States, he expressed his firm belief that assimilating into a culture so steeped in racism was an impossible goal for American blacks. In 1889 and 1890, after the publication of his 1887 book, *Christianity, Islam, and the Negro Race*, Blyden toured the United States, advocating the mass migration of African Americans to their ancestral continent, where they might achieve genuine political equality. Criticized and misperceived as a Muslim proselytizer (Blyden never formally converted to Islam), he called on blacks to free themselves from the shackles of recent history, when they had been enslaved in a Christian country, and become citizens of the modern world.

Radical criticism of American principles and practices was the avowed purpose of many visits by foreign ideologues. The Bolshevist writer Maxim Gorky (1868–1936) came to the United States in 1906 to raise funds for the revolutionary movement in Russia, and he was welcomed by Americans opposed to the autocratic tsarist rule that Gorky wanted to remove. Mark Twain (1835–1910) had written an effusive letter, praising Gorky's ideals: "My sympathies are with the Russian revolution, of course. It goes without saying. I hope it will succeed . . . and it is to be hoped that the roused nation, now rising in its strength, will presently put an end to [tsarism] and set up the republic in its place" (Paine, p. 1283). But the plans of Twain, and of William Dean Howells (1837–1920), who had planned to take part in a dinner celebrating Gorky's cause, were derailed when Gorky ran afoul of an American posture even firmer than the one opposing Bolshevism: just before the dinner, a newspaper reported that the woman sharing Gorky's living quarters during his tour of the United States was not his wife, but his mistress. Madame Maria Andreieva, with whom Gorky had cohabited openly in Russia, was far more newsworthy than Gorky's political beliefs, and the coverage splashed all over the front pages concerning the respectable hotels turning away the Russian couple all but obliterated Gorky's cause with scandal. According to Howells's memoir *My Mark Twain* (1910), acknowledging that there could no resistance to the public's demonizing of Gorky's morals, Twain sarcastically observed "there can be but one wise thing for a visiting stranger to do—find out what the country's customs are and refrain from offending against them" (Paine, p. 1285).

Gorky's plans changed: instead of raising funds by lecturing on the Russian political scene, the playwright and novelist tried to work on essays and fiction in the Adirondack mountains. Before the year was out, however, he and his mistress were deported, resettling finally on the isle of Capri.

Other visitors found American moralizing to be provincial, puritanical, self-serving, and oppressive. H. G. Wells (1866–1946), already well known as the author of *The Time Machine* (1895) and *The War of the Worlds* (1898), witnessed firsthand the shabby treatment received by Gorky. Touring the United States himself at the time, Wells interpreted the Gorky incident as a sign of America's small-mindedness and, worse, as a sign of the low esteem in which women were held in the United States. A socialist as well as an advocate of women's rights, Wells wrote that American independence ran roughshod over opposing points of view in general: "America can be hasty, can be obstinately thoughtless and unjust" (*The Future in America*, p. 169). He had met Booker T. Washington and W. E. B. Du Bois in 1906 and was deeply concerned about their ability to overcome the "Tragedy of Color" (as he entitled one chapter of his 1908 account *The Future in America*). The spectacle of a nation calling itself classless and free while systematically oppressing whole classes of its citizens troubled Wells, who described "the noblest thing in life and the least noble, that is to say, Liberty on the one hand, and on the other the base jealousy the individual self-seeker feels towards the common purpose of the State" (*The War in the Air*, p. 135).

A far more conservative British author, Rudyard Kipling (1865–1936), who lived in Brattleboro, Vermont, from 1892 to 1896, shared with Wells a sense of outrage over America's lingering racial problem: "What will the American do with the negro?" Kipling asked. "The South will not consort with him. . . . The North is every year less and less in need of his services. And he will not disappear. He will continue as a problem. . . . It is not good to be a negro in the land of the free and the home of the brave" (p. 40). Race was the most obvious manifestation of the disjunction of American rhetoric and realities but far from the only one. When Kipling arrived from India in San Francisco in 1889, he bristled at the Americans' ceaseless assertions of equality where deference was called for, noting that

> money will not buy you service in the West. When the hotel clerk . . . stoops to attend to your wants he does so whistling or humming or picking his teeth, or pauses to converse with some one he knows. These performances, I gather, are to impress upon you that he is a free man and your equal. (P. 9)

MANNERS, CULTURE, AND AESTHETIC STYLE

It was not only visitors from Britain who took exception to American manners. True, the rude American style masquerading as an assertion of equality had been noted by Englishmen throughout the century, most notably Charles Dickens (1812–1870), who had lampooned oafish Americans since his first visit in 1842 and in the novel *Martin Chuzzlewit* (1844). But Wells and Kipling joined not only Dickens but also visitors from around the globe in their dismay at American manners; the future Nobel Prize–winning novelist Henryk Sienkiewicz (1846–1916) observed that American men of the 1870s "do not take off their hats even in private homes, and yet they remove their coats everywhere, even in the presence of ladies or in places where dignity would require otherwise" (Pachter and Wein, p. 182). Like Dickens three decades earlier, Sienkiewicz deplored the "disgusting" and omnipresent chewing tobacco in American mouths: "If you glance at any group of people," he wrote, "you will notice that the majority of men are moving their jaws rhythmically, as though they were some species of ruminating animals" (Pachter and Wein, p. 183). The Argentine statesman Domingo Sarmiento had noticed a few years before Sienkiewicz that "while conversing with you, the Yankee of careful breeding lifts one foot high [and] takes off his shoe in order to caress the foot. . . . Four individuals seated around a marble table will infallibly have their eight feet upon it" (Pachter and Wein, p. 111). Visitors often regaled their readers with accounts of American social barbarities: Sarmiento describes a man, seeing an American smoking a cigar, pluck the cigar from the stranger's mouth, light his own cigar with it, and replace the stranger's cigar "without the good fellow. . . . making any movement other than opening his mouth to receive back the borrowed cigar" (Pachter and Wein, p. 109).

This casual familiarity with one's fellow citizens had a virtue, too, that even these shocked visitors could appreciate. If Americans lacked cultural refinement, they also lacked the rigorous class distinctions measured by that refinement. To Sienkiewicz, manners and knowledge were available only to the European upper classes, whereas in the America he visited "both are certainly more widely diffused" (Pachter and Wein, p. 183). Overfamiliarity was a cheap price to pay for reducing class barriers, and it was this awkward plunge toward classlessness that was striking to many foreign visitors. Compared to the elaborate European rituals in which "gentlemen . . . presented to each other . . . prance about like two monkeys in ardent courtship," Siemkiewicz applauded the informality with which Americans greet each other (Pachter and Wein, p. 177).

Perhaps the least approving of American lapses in upholding cultured traditions was Matthew Arnold, who had compared Americans to philistines badly in need of "cultivation." (To be sure, Arnold had noted that Britain was not by any means free of philistines, though they were far more numerous in the United States.) Writing in "Civilization in The United States" some five years after leaving the United States in 1883, Arnold observed that "Americans . . . deceive themselves, to persuade themselves that they have what they have not, to cover the defects in their civilisation by boasting" (p. 492). Arnold was particularly annoyed by the American assumption that solutions ratified by a majority vote may then dispense with any fine moral or ethical issues, and he warned against the danger of an overly democratic society in which the "glorification of 'the average man,'" prevents the achievement of true distinction.

Arnold also noted much that was ugly in the United States. Kipling felt that the awful pronunciation of English was Americans' well-deserved punishment for having ignored international copyright laws. Having cursed them for "piracy," Kipling wryly regretted, in his 1891 *American Notes,* the "horror" of now having to hear Americans speak: "They stole books from across the water without paying for 'em, and the snort of delight was fixed in their nostrils forever by a just Providence. That is why they talk a foreign tongue to-day" (pp. 13–14). But Arnold's aesthetic was offended on a more profound level:

> Let us take the beautiful first, and consider how far it is present in American civilisation. Evidently this is that civilisation's weak side. There is little to nourish and delight the sense of beauty there. In the long-settled States east of the Alleghanies the landscape in general is not interesting, the climate harsh and in extremes. (Arnold, p. 173)

The subject of Beauty had, of course, already been covered extensively by Oscar Wilde, who toured the United States in 1882. Wilde toured the United States for almost the entire year, arriving on 2 January and leaving on 27 December. Wilde was welcomed to America to speak on the subject of "The Beautiful." Unlike Arnold, who found American newspapers vulgar and sensational, Wilde encouraged them to cooperate with him in inventing a fantastic persona for himself, and both he and the press prospered by this invention. Remarking merely that his trip was uneventful and the ocean "not so majestic as I had expected" (Ellmann, p. 158), he found himself quoted as pronouncing his disdainful disappointment with the ocean in newspaper headlines on both sides of the Atlantic. Also unlike Arnold, Wilde seemed to want to share his aesthetic with America, rather than to impose one on it.

When a reporter challenged Wilde, for example, by pointing to an unsightly grain elevator in New Jersey, asking if something so ugly and purely func-

tional could have aesthetic value, Wilde evaded a direct answer, rather than haranguing the reporter with aesthetic pronouncements from on high. The endless searching after beauty, he explained, had gone on in all previous cultures and would continue in all new ones, an inclusive concept designed to please American ears. "Man is hungry for beauty," he told that reporter, and spent the next year saying much the same to Americans across the continent (Ellmann, p. 159). Wilde's message to a practical country in a great hurry was that its breakneck progress must halt so that Americans might stop to smell the roses—or, in his chosen examples, the lilies and sunflowers. In a technology-mad country, Wilde extolled the virtues of handmade artifacts, explaining through paradox how embracing machine-made objects would retard and not advance the progress of civilization. Like Robert Louis Stevenson, the Scots-born peripatetic writer whose *The Silverado Squatters* (1883), *Across the Plains* (1892), and *The Amateur Emigrant* (1894) closely detailed his affinities with American westerners, Wilde seemed remarkably comfortable out West. He took pleasure in lecturing in places that might seem the most resolute against his cultural mission. In the frontier mining town of Leadville, Colorado, Wilde lectured on Florentine art and the paintings of James Whistler, drank whiskey at the bottom of a silver mine, and regaled the miners with writings of the Renaissance silversmith and autobiographer Benvenuto Cellini. Leadville was America writ small—once Wilde had spoken there on aestheticism "there was no challenge that he failed to take up," noted Wilde's biographer Richard Ellman. "He boasted smilingly to Whistler, 'I have already civilized America—il reste seulement le ciel'" (there remains only heaven) (Ellmann, p. 205). What he proposed, finally, according to Ellman, was a doctrine that was "the most determined and sustained attack upon materialistic vulgarity that America had seen. . . . Wilde presented a theory not only of art but of being, not only a distinguished personality but an antithesis to getting on without regard for the quality of life" that America had never heard before and certainly had not heard from so colorful an advocate of impractical beauty (p. 205).

Criticized by Ambrose Bierce, warmly embraced by Walt Whitman, Wilde's aestheticism aligned with American values most neatly when he met Henry James (1843–1916). Confessing his nostalgia for London, James no doubt expected Wilde's sympathy, but Wilde instead superciliously expressed his astonishment: "You care for places? The world is my home" (Ellmann, p. 179). This approval of rootlessness perhaps explains what Wilde enjoyed about America, and what

Oscar the Apostle. Illustration by Frederick Burr Opper from the satirical journal *Puck*, 11 January 1882. Wilde's view of the aesthetic potential of the United States is lampooned.

James enjoyed least about it: the mutability of the American work-in-progress, which offended and puzzled some visitors, also held its most paradoxical appeal for others.

See also Americans Abroad

BIBLIOGRAPHY

Primary Works

Arnold, Matthew. "Civilization in the United States." *The Nineteenth Century* 21, no. 134 (April 1888): 486–496

Arnold, Matthew. *Discourses in America*. London: Macmillan, 1885.

Belloc, Hilaire. *The Contrast.* 1924. New York: Arno Press, 1974.

Bennett, Arnold. *Your United States: Impressions of a First Visit.* New York: Harper & Brothers, 1912.

Brooke, Rupert. *Letters from America.* 1916. With a preface by Henry James. New York: Beaufort Books, 1988.

Bryce, James. *The American Commonwealth.* New York: Macmillan, 1888.

Kipling, Rudyard. *American Notes.* 1899. New York: Arno Press, 1974.

Paine, Albert Bigelow, ed. *Mark Twain's Letters.* New York: Harper & Brothers, 1917.

Pender, Rose. *A Lady's Experiences in the Wild West in 1883.* With a foreword by A. B. Guthrie Jr. Lincoln: University of Nebraska Press, 1978.

Russell, William Howard. *Hesperothen: Notes from the West.* London: S. Low, Marston, Searle & Rivington, 1882.

Santayana, George. *Character & Opinion in the United States: With Reminiscences of William James and Josiah Royce and Academic Life in America.* New York: Scribners, 1920.

Sienkiewicz, Henryk. *Portrait of America: Letters.* Edited and translated by Charles Morley. New York: Columbia University Press, 1959.

Stevenson, Robert Louis. *Across the Plains: With Other Memories and Essays.* London: Chatto & Windus, 1892.

Stevenson, Robert Louis. *The Amateur Emigrant.* 1894. With a preface by Fanny Stevenson. New York: Carroll & Graf, 2002.

Stevenson, Robert Louis. *From Scotland to Silverado.* Edited by James D. Hart Cambridge: Belknap Press of Harvard University Press, 1966.

Stevenson, Robert Louis. *The Silverado Squatters: Six Selected Chapters.* 1883. Delray Beach, Fla.: Levenger Press, 2001.

Webb, Beatrice Potter. *American Diary, 1898.* 1898. Edited by David A. Shannon. Madison: University of Wisconsin Press, 1963.

Wells, H. G. *The Future in America: A Search after Realities.* London: Chapman & Hall, 1906.

Wells, H. G. *The War in the Air.* London: G. Bell and Sons, 1908.

Secondary Works

Athearn, Robert G. *Westward the Briton.* New York: Scribners, 1953.

Ellmann, Richard. *Oscar Wilde.* New York: Knopf, 1988.

Gorky, Maxim. *The City of the Yellow Devil: Pamphlets, Articles and Letters about America.* Moscow: Progress Publishers, 1972.

Hasty, Olga Peters, and Susanne Fusso, eds. and trans. *America through Russian Eyes, 1874–1926.* New Haven, Conn.: Yale University Press, 1988.

Joseph, Franz M., ed. *As Others See Us: The United States through Foreign Eyes.* Princeton, N.J.: Princeton University Press, 1959.

Mulvey, Christopher. *Transatlantic Manners: Social Patterns in Nineteenth-Century Anglo-American Travel Literature.* Cambridge, U.K.: Cambridge University Press, 1990.

Nevins, Allan. *American Social History, as Recorded by British Travellers.* New York: A. M. Kelley, 1969.

Pachter, Marc, and Frances Wein. *Abroad in America: Visitors to the New Nation, 1776–1914.* Reading, Mass.: Addison-Wesley, 1976.

Steven Goldleaf

THE FOUR MILLION

The Four Million, a collection of twenty-five short stories by O. Henry (William Sydney Porter, 1862–1910), appeared in 1906 to largely laudatory reviews in the *Atlantic Monthly,* the *Critic,* the *New York Times,* and the *Independent,* among other publications. It contains three of O. Henry's most famous stories, "The Gift of the Magi," "The Cop and the Anthem," and "The Furnished Room." The Canadian humorist Stephen Leacock concluded that O. Henry was one of the first true literary artists to achieve commercial success. O. Henry was called a "born storyteller" and was praised as "the American Maupassant." In addition to the famous French short story writer Guy de Maupassant, reviewers frequently compared him to Bret Harte, Mark Twain, and Charles Dickens. In addition, he also enjoyed some vogue in Europe. The French and Russians, in particular, admired his plots' tightness, crisp proportions, and neutral moral stance. This collection launched O. Henry's serious career as a writer and, some say, his reputation as a true American literary artist. Either way, nearly five million books were sold by the 1920s.

The stories in *The Four Million* were set in New York City. This caused reviewers and critics alike to label O. Henry a "regionalist" or " local colorist." In East Side tenements, in Wall Street offices, or along Fifth Avenue, his readers recognized their city and loved the stories. The novelist Frank Norris once told him that "there are just three big cities in the United States that are 'story cities'—New York, of course, New Orleans, and best of the lot, San Francisco." But in his well-known story "A Municipal Report," from *Strictly Business* (1910), O. Henry replied: "It is a rash one who will lay his finger on the map and say: 'in this town there can be no romance—what could happen here?' Yes, it is a bold and rash deed to challenge in one sentence history, romance, and Rand and McNally" (p. 148).

The title of the book refers to the 1900 census, which counted four million residents in New York City. O. Henry writes, "Not very long ago some one invented the assertion that there were only 'Four Hundred' people in New York City who were worth noticing. But a wiser man has arisen—the census taker" (p. 149). The "four hundred" was the group of New York socialites, membership to which was limited by old money and the size of Mrs. Astor's ballroom.

Two major questions about O. Henry and his work have never been settled to anyone's satisfaction, and opinion seems to be almost evenly balanced. One question is whether he is a true American artist or merely a literary populist. The second question is whether he was guilty of the embezzlement that purportedly occurred while he was working at the First National Bank of Austin in Texas. O. Henry consistently claimed innocence, although he was convicted and served three of five years in prison. Shame about this episode caused him to create his pseudonym and to keep the incident a deep secret, but his imprisonment probably did more than anything else to create O. Henry the writer. Upon his arrival at the federal penitentiary in Ohio, he was asked his occupation and at first answered "newspaper reporter," then added as an afterthought that he was also a registered pharmacist. Consequently, he found himself assigned to the night shift in the pharmacy, which provided ample quiet writing time. While he was in prison, he met a few of the scoundrels and scalawags featured in his tales.

COMPOSITION AND STYLE

O. Henry deliberately wrote for an audience of the "subway-riding masse" (O'Connor, p. 164). He wanted to appeal to a solid democratic public that enjoyed recognizing itself in its stories, and critics have been divided about whether he set out to satirize capitalism or whether he accepted it dispassionately. In marked contrast to Edith Wharton's conception of "Old New York" society, O. Henry wrote about the "little people" living in a colorful urban world, and he felt he could type the entire population of lower class immigrants, especially the Irish, which would account

for his underdeveloped, cartoonlike characterizations. Yet he treated his characters with sympathy, wit, irony, and humanity.

WORKING METHODS

O. Henry wrote fast, once producing more than one hundred short stories in two years. He was prone to using long words and long sentences but was most exceptionally observant of detail. For example, one of his most famous stories from *The Four Million,* "The Furnished Room," includes a description that uses a sailing metaphor:

> The mantel's chastely severe outline was ingloriously veiled behind some pert drapery drawn rakishly askew like the sashes of the Amazonian ballet. Upon it was some desolate flotsam cast aside by the room's marooned when a lucky sail had borne them to a fresh port—a trifling vase or two, pictures of actresses, a medicine bottle, some stray cards out of a deck. (P. 243)

O. Henry's somewhat leisurely style wasted no words, yet he claimed never to edit or rewrite. He took a distant narrative stance from his main characters, who are cleverly but not deeply drawn—usually shopgirls, derelicts, vagabonds, and the working poor. He exposes the cruel, rough side of the social fabric while at the same time giving readers a quaint, romantic glimpse of the more golden side of human nature. One secret of his popularity was that his stories were fun and people looked forward to his famous surprise endings—the "O. Henry twist"—motivation for which might be found in the text, albeit well hidden. Those who find such conclusions cheating call them "trick endings," complaining of empty puns, paradoxes, and abuse of coincidence. Fully aware of the controversy over his conclusions, O. Henry remarks in *Cabbages and Kings* that "the art of narrative consists in concealing from your audience everything it wants to know until after you expose your favorite opinions on topics foreign to the subject" (p. 92).

Karen Charmaine Blansfield calls his plot structure a "cross pattern" having three subpatterns: cross-purposes, crossed paths, and cross-identities. The plot's central problem—often financial—demands actions by both characters, who will reunite at the close of the story. The two characters work simultaneously to solve some problem, each one unaware of the other's efforts. When they unite at the end and each discovers the other's strategy, it turns out that one person's efforts have affected the other's, with the result often being that they cancel each other out. Unwittingly, the characters have been working at cross-purposes. For example, in the most famous short story from *The Four Million,* "The Gift of the Magi," the newlyweds Della and Jim sell what little they have to buy each other Christmas presents. The twist is that Jim has sold his treasured pocket watch to buy Della a tortoiseshell comb for her hair, and Della has sold her long hair to buy Jim a chain for his pocket watch.

O. Henry's genre borders on the tall tale; his plots include mistaken identity, coincidence, fate, and separated lovers and feature colloquial New York dialect and slang that has been comically distorted for effect. However, the slang is sometimes obscure for readers not of O. Henry's time. He enjoyed displaying his extensive literary facility through parodies, irony, and twists on authorial quotations. In addition, he had a strong appreciation for the absurd and apparently learned the inverted axiom from Mark Twain. There is some debate about whether he had a sense of the naturalism that was being employed at the time by writers such as Edith Wharton and Theodore Dreiser. Morality was a social concern at the turn of the twentieth century, and some critics faulted O. Henry's stories as immoral because they sympathized with scamps and rogues, safecrackers, confidence men, and other outlaws—yet they never included anything the least bit risqué. People also criticized him for crude philosophies and lack of high ideals, trite and dated plots, and complacent approval of the status quo. In much of his work he editorializes, making the audience aware of his presence as author-raconteur by apparently randomly discussing, for instance, how to write or by alluding to various literary works.

O. Henry was known as a hard-drinking night owl who rattled off stories in an easy manner. According to one of his biographers, Richard O'Connor, O. Henry found it easier to procrastinate than to write, and his working methods were eccentric at best. Under self-imposed pressure, he was said to invent a title and then write a story for it overnight. "The Gift of the Magi" was overdue for the center section of the *World*'s Christmas issue, which was to be in color—a difficult process that required the illustrations to be drawn in advance. The frantic illustrator, Dan Smith, not having heard from O. Henry, finally tracked him down at his apartment to find that not only had O. Henry not written the story but he had no glimmer of an idea for it. Smith protested again that he must turn in an illustration immediately. Finally, O. Henry told him to draw a room,

> the kind you find in a boarding house or rooming house over on the West Side. In the room there is only a chair or two, a chest of drawers, a bed, and a trunk. On the bed, a man and a girl are sitting side by side. They are talking about Christmas. The man has a watch fob in his hand. He is playing with it while thinking. The girl's principal feature is the long beautiful hair that is hanging down her back.

That's all I can think of now. But the story is coming. (Bloom, p. 23)

Altogether, O. Henry's stories have elicited contradictory opinions. They were trite and dated with trick endings, or they were clever and contemporary with surprise endings. He had a sentimental love of the little people, or he had a detached democratic attitude. Grim or lovely, either way, his stories were tightly written with linear plots, observant of detail, with an ear for dialogue. Whatever the verdict, people find them fun, and at the turn of the twentieth century O. Henry did more to popularize the short story as a form than anyone since Edgar Allan Poe.

See also New York; Short Story

BIBLIOGRAPHY

Primary Works

Henry, O. *Cabbages and Kings*. New York: Doubleday Page, 1904.

Henry, O. *The Four Million*. New York: Doubleday Page, 1904; A. L. Burt, 1906.

Henry, O. *Strictly Business*. New York: Doubleday Page, 1915.

Secondary Works

Bates, H. E. "American Writers after Poe." In *The Modern Short Story*. 1941. Boston: Writers, 1956.

Blansfield, Karen Charmaine. *Cheap Rooms and Restless Hearts: A Study of Formula in the Urban Tales of William Sydney Porter*. Bowling Green, Ohio: Bowling Green State University Popular Press, 1988.

Bloom, Harold, ed. *O. Henry*. Bloom's Major Short Story Writers. Edited and with an introduction by Harold Bloom. Broomall, Pa.: Chelsea House, 1999.

Boyd, David. "O. Henry's Road of Destiny." *Americana* 31 (1953): 579–608.

Brooks, Cleanth, and Robert Penn Warren. "An Interpretation of 'A Furnished Room.'" In their *Understanding Fiction*. New York: F. S. Crofts, 1943.

Current-García, Eugene. *O. Henry (William Sydney Porter)*. New York: Twayne, 1965.

Éjxenbaum, B. M. *O. Henry and the Theory of the Short Story*. Translated by I. R. Titunik. Ann Arbor: University of Michigan Press, 1968.

Hicks, Granville. "A Sleight-of-Hand Master." *New York Times Book Review* 12, no. 2 (1956): 6.

Leacock, Stephen. "O. Henry and His Critics." *New Republic* 9 (1916): 120–122.

Long, E. Hudson. *O. Henry: The Man and His Work.* Philadelphia: University of Pennsylvania Press, 1949.

Moyle, Seth. *My Friend O. Henry.* New York: H. K. Flag, 1914.

Narcy, Raoul. "O. Henry through French Eyes." *Living Age* 303 (1919): 86–88.

O'Connor, Richard. *O. Henry: The Legendary Life of William S. Porter.* Garden City, N.Y.: Doubleday, 1970.

Ostrosky, Martin B. "O. Henry's Use of Stereotypes. New York City Stories: An Example of the Utilization of Folklore in Literature." *New York Folklore* 7 (1981): 41–64.

Patee, Fred Lewis. "The Journalization of American Literature." *Unpopular Review* 7 (1917): 374–394.

Pavese, Cesare. *O. Henry; or, The Literary.* Translated by Edwin Fussell. Berkeley: University of California Press, 1970.

Peel, Donald F. *A Critical Study of the Short Stories of O. Henry.* Maryville: Northwest Missouri State College, 25, no. 4 (1961): 3–24.

Prichart, V. S. "O. Henry." *New Statesman* 54, no. 1393 (1957): 97–98.

Quinn, Arthur Hobson. "The Journalists." In his *American Fiction: American History and Critical Survey.* New York: Appleton-Century-Crofts, 1956.

Review of *The Four Million. The Independent.* Quoted in *Book Review Digest* 65, no. 552 (1908): 3.

Review of *The Four Million. Public Opinion.* Quoted in *Book Review Digest* II (1907): 152.

Smith, C. Alphonso. *O. Henry Biography.* Garden City, N.Y.: Doubleday, Page, 1916.

Steger, Harry Payton. "O. Henry: New Facts about the Great Author." *Cosmopolitan* 53 (1912): 655–663.

Steger, Harry Payton. "O. Henry: Who He Is and How He Works." *World's Work* 18, no. 2 (1909): 11724–11726.

Stuart, David. *O. Henry.* Chelsea, Mich.: Scarborough House, 1990.

Van Doren, Carl. "O. Henry." *Texas Review* 2 (1917): 248–259.

Van Doren, Carl, and Mark Van Doren. "Prose Fiction." In their *American British Fiction since 1890.* New York: D. Appleton–Century, 1939.

Voss, Arthur. "The Rise of the Journalistic Short Story: O. Henry and His Predecessors." In *The American Short Story: A Critical Survey.* Norman: University of Oklahoma Press, 1973.

Williams, William Wash. *The Quiet Lodger of Irving Place.* New York: Dutton, 1936.

Helen Killoran

FREE LOVE

Free love became a polarizing political issue around the time of the presidential election of 1872. Before then it was just one of many utopian ideas in the air, although arguably the most radical. The utopian impulse was very strong in the nineteenth century. The majority who dreamed of a perfect society saw economic reform as the key. Free lovers, on the other hand, focused their desire for change on the personal matters of love and sex.

The prime tenet of free love held that love was sacred, and as such it must not be regulated by law. Since marriage was the institution that imposed rules upon the divine bond between a man and a woman, free lovers took aim against it, proposing that a woman and man were free to share love without either one expecting marriage to be the outcome. Free love relationships were called "elective affinities," a phrase implying that the partners were equals who freely chose to pursue a strong mutual attraction to see if love could be at its root. Although love could grow into a marriage in the spiritual sense, it was under no pressure to become marriage in the conventional sense, which was viewed as exploitative or even as a form of enslavement or prostitution. Indeed, neither party was obligated to stay in a relationship that no longer proved fulfilling.

In addition to their rejection of marriage, free lovers scoffed at certain attitudes toward sexuality held dear by the nineteenth-century middle class. Women of this era were idealized as pure and passionless, meaning that they were believed to have no sexual desire. Free lovers, however, celebrated the erotic side of human experience. They acknowledged that women, like men, were sexual by nature. Further, they maintained that the goal of sexual intercourse was mutual gratification. This idea clashed with the belief that sex was a duty that married couples undertook for the purpose of procreation. This is what the church taught, and what most middle-class couples practiced.

Although dismissed harshly by its critics as a justification for promiscuity, free love was at heart an issue of civil liberty that questioned the state's authority to regulate the individual. The first writings on the subject are usually credited to the Frenchmen Charles Fourier in the 1840s. Men such as John Humphrey Noyes, John Murray Spear, and Stephen Pearl Andrews were instrumental in introducing free love to America. Putting theory into practice, several utopian communities were formed where free love was encouraged. The so-called Perfectionists of Oneida in upstate New York considered each member of one sex to be married

> *Controversy over free love divided members of the nineteenth-century woman's movement. The abhorrence with which some women regarded free love was explicit in this resolution passed at the American Equal Rights Convention in 1869.*
>
> While we recognize the disabilities which the legal marriage imposes upon woman as wife and mother, and while we pledge ourselves to seek their removal by putting her on equal terms with man, we abhorrently repudiate Free Loveism as horrible and mischievous to society, and disown any sympathy with it.
>
> Goldsmith, *Other Powers*, p. 185.

to all members of the other sex. In 1869 Noyes, the founder of Oneida, wrote, "Sexual intercourse should be no more restrained by law than eating and drinking" (Goldsmith, p. 53). Clearly this was a view too radical for the American mainstream.

FREE LOVE AND WOMEN'S RIGHTS

Only for a brief moment in the history of the United States did the theories of free love filter into that mainstream. Without embracing free love ideas on sexuality, leaders of the woman's rights movement, namely Susan B. Anthony and Elizabeth Cady Stanton, agreed with many things that the free lovers believed, particularly the argument for equality between the sexes. The idea of a relationship as an equal partnership was a far cry from the reality of most marriages at the time. Indeed, the advantages granted to men in marriage were considerable. Through the laws of property rights, a husband in effect owned his wife. Further, she swore in her marriage vows to obey him. So completely did she subsume her identity to him that she became, for example, "Mrs. Henry Parker." She was expected to follow the teachings of the church and the norms of society by being sexually submissive, complying with her husband's requests for intercourse. She had little recourse if her husband should commit adultery or become abusive. Divorce laws differed from state to state, but they invariably favored the husband. Moreover, few unhappy couples chose to pursue divorce because of the scandal it would cause.

Evidence that marriage was not all bliss can be found in popular nineteenth-century fiction aimed at women readers, where bad marriages were a staple. In September of 1871, in a review of an anonymous novel called *Won—Not Wooed*, a writer in *Harper's New Monthly Magazine* complained that he was bored "by the most approved pattern of the modern novel, which pretty invariably marries the heroine to the wrong lover, by way of pleasant preparation for marriage to the right one" (p. 623). Another novel reviewed in the same column remains faithful to "the approved pattern," featuring a "true and loving wife" who suffers miseries "at the hands of a husband who intends to be neither unjust nor cruel, but is simply insufferably vain." The husband's death "leaves the wife to marry the one who truly loved her, and whom she truly loved" (p. 623). Fiction of this ilk continued to appear through to the end of the century, novels with titles such as *Wedded Unwooed* (by Julia Howard Gatewood, 1892), *Married the Wrong Man* (Benoni Mendenhall, 1890), and *Wed to a Lunatic* (Frank W. Hastings, 1896). The lesson these novels taught was that if a wife were patient and toughed it out, she would be rewarded. Her husband would eventually change his behavior—or he might conveniently die.

Two important novels of the realist period in American literature, William Dean Howells's *A Modern Instance* (1882) and Henry James's *The Portrait of a Lady* (1881) offered no such neat endings for marriages in crisis. In the former Marcia Hubbard suffers the irony of being sued for divorce by a self-centered husband who abandoned her, while in the latter Isabel Osmond returns home to her disastrous marriage after her cousin Ralph's funeral. As early as 1848 James's father, Henry Sr., had ostensibly advocated free love in his essay "Love and Marriage" (which he would later renounce), but the younger James was no radical. Isabel refuses to comply with her husband's chauvinistic code of obedience, yet she does not walk out on her marriage.

With women on the short end of so many marriages, Susan B. Anthony and Elizabeth Cady Stanton believed that it was within their role as leaders for social reform to raise questions about marriage and to welcome anyone into their National Woman Suffrage Association (NWSA) who wished to do the same. But not everyone who cared about improving the status of women agreed. Members of the Boston-based American Woman Suffrage Association (AWSA) were frequently at odds with their New York counterparts over what direction the women's movement should take. The more conservative AWSA felt that the struggle should not get sidetracked but should stay focused on the main issue of gaining the right to vote. It did allow for advocating on behalf of working-class women, who were grossly underpaid, but it refused to play host to the disparate group of suffragists, anarchists, and Marxists who were welcomed into the ranks of the NWSA. To the AWSA, the NWSA's interest in reforming the laws of marriage and divorce smacked of "Free Loveism," and a resolution denouncing free love was passed at the American Equal Rights Association convention in 1869.

The controversy moved beyond the immediate circle of the women's movement, providing fodder for columns that began to appear in middle-class magazines. For example, in the October 1873 issue of *Scribner's Magazine*, Lulu Gray Noble applauds "the many superior and excellent women who are advocating woman's right to the ballot . . . unmixed with loose social theories." Noble notes with regret that these "loose social theories" are gaining currency "with the movement of our day known as the woman movement." In "respectable journals" no less, one finds essays voicing "their denunciation of legal marriage, and endorsement of the whole new theory of what is called marriage" (p. 658). Although Noble does not explicitly mention free love, the title of her article, "Free Marriage," leaves little doubt as to the cause of her anxiety. Thus the predicament that the progressive wing of the women's movement faced was clear: however enlightening a public debate on marriage might prove to be, anyone who pressed the issue ran the immediate risk of being branded a proponent of free love. And such people simply had no place in respectable society.

It must be made clear that the women's movement at no time included free love notions of sexual freedom in its official platform. Yet it remained the perception of many Americans that the movement "stood for" free love. Intensifying this perception was the fact that a bold woman had become a prominent lecturer for the movement. Her name was Victoria Woodhull.

VICTORIA WOODHULL

Susan B. Anthony's and Elizabeth Cady Stanton's places in history are secure. Controversial in their own time, if not often widely denounced, they are now considered American heroes who devoted their lives to battling inequality and injustice. The Nineteenth Amendment to the Constitution granting women the right to vote—passed in 1920, fourteen years after Anthony's death—was even named after her. For a short time in the 1870s Victoria Woodhull (1838–1927) was arguably as famous as Stanton and Anthony, although she has now been reduced to a curious footnote in American history. In 1871 she was invited to speak to Congress on the topic of woman's rights. Anthony and Stanton, who had been involved in the

---

It was not until 20 November 1872 that Victoria Woodhull openly declared that she was a practicing free lover. Yet even before then, she was enlivening her lectures with remarks that could have been taken from the pages of a free love manifesto.

On female sexuality: "Some women seem to glory over the fact that they never had any sexual desire and to think that desire is vulgar. What! Vulgar! The instinct that creates immortal souls vulgar? Who dares stand up amid Nature, all prolific and beautiful, where pulses are ever bounding with creative desire, and utter such sacrilege."

On marriage: "There may be prostitution in marriage and proper commerce in the bawdy house. It depends upon the specific conditions attending [sexual intercourse] itself and not where or how it is obtained."

On law and love: "People may be married by law . . . and they may also be married by love and lack all sanction of law. . . . Law cannot compel two to love. . . . Where there is no love as a basis of marriage there should be no marriage!"

Goldsmith, *Other Powers*, pp. 149, 152, 301.

---

struggle for many years, had never been granted this access to political power. In fact, Woodhull was the first woman ever to address a joint session of Congress, that is, the House of Representatives and the Senate (Goldsmith, pp. 5, 248).

The biography of the beautiful, charismatic upstart who spoke so passionately that day (11 January 1871) is certainly one of the most extraordinary of her era. Born in Ohio as Victoria Claflin, Woodhull was a clairvoyant whose powers would bring her great wealth after she moved to New York in 1868. There, she and her sister, Tennessee, befriended the famous capitalist Commodore Cornelius Vanderbilt, with Victoria becoming his financial adviser. Woodhull received her directions on how Vanderbilt should manage his stocks from the spirits. Following her advice, Vanderbilt scored a profit of $1.3 million on "Black Friday," 24 September 1869, an infamous day in Wall Street history that ruined many other investors. Vanderbilt gave half his profit to Woodhull, who, with Tennessee, opened a brokerage firm, thus becoming the first women in America to do so. The Claflin sisters were rich enough to start a journal: *Woodhull and Claflin's Weekly,* which they envisioned as a forum for progressive thought, especially in regard to issues affecting the sexes. Stephen Pearl Andrews, the founder of the free love community Modern Times, was a frequent contributor. A month before the first issue appeared on 14 May 1870, Woodhull had placed notice in the *New York Herald* that she was running for president of the United States.

Although Woodhull associated with free lovers, her address to Congress, the so-called Woodhull Memorial, revealed no links to those people. As her popularity as a lecturer grew, however, her words became bolder. Her rhetoric was that of a free lover, as in this attack on marriage from her keynote speech to the NWSA convention, 11 May 1871: "Why do I war upon marriage. . . . because it is, I verily believe, the most terrible curse from which humanity now suffers, entailing more misery, sickness, and premature death than all other causes combined. . . . Sanctioned and defended by marriage, night after night there are thousands of rapes committed, under cover of this accursed license" (Goldsmith, p. 274).

Neither major candidate for president in 1872, Ulysses S. Grant or Horace Greeley, made women's rights a part of his campaign. Although Woodhull's candidacy was quixotic at best, her electrifying presence on the lecture circuit brought attention to the issues that progressive women considered important. The fact that she was chosen as the NWSA keynote speaker underscores her quick rise to a position of honor within the women's movement. But even many members of the NWSA were uncomfortable with her views and the outspoken way in which she asserted them. By Election Day 1872 she had fallen completely from favor.

THE FREE LOVE SCANDAL

On 20 November 1871, before a crowd of three thousand people, Woodhull was angered in the middle of a lecture by a heckler demanding to know if she were a free lover. "Yes, I am a Free Lover!" Woodhull recklessly declared. Rumors about her personal life had been rampant, and now she was standing in public and proclaiming: "I have an inalienable, constitutional, and natural right to love whom I may, to love for as long or as short a period as I can, to change that love every day if I please! And with that right neither you nor any law have any right to interfere" (Goldsmith, p. 303).

The price that Woodhull paid for this public assertion of her sexual freedom was enormous. Already demonized in the media (the famous cartoonist Thomas Nast depicted Woodhull as Satan, and Harriet Beecher Stowe caricatured her as Audacia Dangereyes

in her 1871 novel *My Wife and I*), Woodhull suddenly found her very livelihood threatened. Her attempts to rent halls for her lectures were denied. The landlord who owned the building that housed the operations for *Woodhull and Claflin's Weekly* raised the rent, thus forcing Woodhull to leave. Individuals and organizations with public images to uphold dissociated themselves from her. In a desperate attempt to explain herself to an outraged public, Woodhull garnered the resources to publish another issue of the *Weekly,* dated 2 November 1872. In it, she revealed that Henry Ward Beecher, a New York preacher of celebrity status (and Harriet Beecher Stowe's brother), had initiated a number of extramarital affairs with women of his parish. Rather than condemn Beecher for committing adultery, Woodhull meant to point out that the only difference between him and her was that she was forthright about her desire to love freely while he was secretive. Soon after the *Weekly* hit the streets, Woodhull and Tennessee were arrested and charged with distributing obscene material through the mail. They would spend Election Day in jail.

Victims of a fanatical campaign by Anthony Comstock, head of the New York Society for the Suppression of Vice, to rid the country of obscenity, the sisters would be jailed on two other occasions. Meanwhile Beecher was exonerated by a church committee more intent upon clearing his name than asking hard questions about his private life; a lawsuit brought against him in 1874 by one of his parishioners, Theodore Tilden, husband of one of his purported lovers and former editor of the New York *Independent,* a weekly Congregationalist paper, ended with a hung jury. Woodhull eventually moved to England where she rebuilt her life, becoming the wife of a titled British gentleman.

Whether the woman's movement would have sputtered even without the free love scandal to compromise it is a question for historians to debate. The fact is that the movement found itself in disarray after the 1872 election. A writer in the March 1875 issue of *Scribner's Magazine* pointed to the defeat of the Woman Suffrage Amendment in Michigan and gloated: "That that movement is waning in power must be painfully evident to its friends; and we trust the time may come when they will rejoice in the fact as heartily as we do" (p. 628).

The example of Victoria Woodhull serves to show the lengths to which nineteenth-century American society went to punish a woman who was openly and shamelessly sexual. The country's most vocal proponent of free love was silenced and cast out. Curiously enough, her persecution did not stop others from publishing their frank views on sexual matters. Ezra Heywood, author of the tract *Cupid's Yokes* (1876), and Moses Harmon, who published the radical journal *Lucifer* from 1883 to 1907, were other advocates of free love worth noting. Like Woodhull, both were imprisoned by Comstock, who was incessant in his crusade to silence sexual radicals until his death in 1915.

See also Feminism; Prostitution; Reform; Sex Education

BIBLIOGRAPHY

Primary Works

Andrews, Stephen Pearl, Henry James Sr., and Horace Greeley. *Love, Marriage, and Divorce, and the Sovereignty of the Individual.* 1853. Boston: Tucker, 1889.

James, Henry, Sr. "Is Marriage Holy?" *Atlantic Monthly,* March 1870, pp. 360–368.

James, Henry, Sr. "Love and Marriage." *Harbinger,* 23 October 1848, pp. 202–203.

Noble, Lulu Gray. "Free Marriage." *Scribner's Magazine,* October 1873, pp. 658–664.

Noyes, John Humphrey. *Dixon and His Copyists: A Criticism of the Accounts of the Oneida Community in "New America," "Spiritual Wives," and Kindred Publications.* Wallingford, Conn.: Oneida Community, 1871.

Secondary Works

Blatt, Martin Henry. *Free Love and Anarchism: The Biography of Ezra Heywood.* Urbana: University of Illinois Press, 1989.

D'Emilio, John, and Estelle B. Freedman. *Intimate Matters: A History of Sexuality in America.* New York: Harper and Row, 1988.

Gabriel, Mary. *Notorious Victoria: The Life of Victoria Woodhull, Uncensored.* Chapel Hill, N.C.: Algonquin, 1998.

Goldsmith, Barbara. *Other Powers: The Age of Suffrage, Spiritualism, and the Scandalous Victoria Woodhull.* New York: Knopf, 1998.

Habegger, Alfred. *Henry James and the "Woman Business."* New York: Cambridge University Press, 1989.

Johnston, Johanna. *Mrs. Satan: The Incredible Saga of Victoria C. Woodhull.* New York: Putnam, 1967.

Meade, Marion. *Free Woman: The Life and Times of Victoria Woodhull.* New York: Knopf, 1976.

Sachs, Emanie. *The Terrible Siren: Victoria Woodhull, 1838–1927.* New York: Harper & Brothers, 1928.

Stoehr, Taylor. *Free Love in America: A Documentary History.* New York: AMS Press, 1979.

Paul Hadella

FRONTIER

The concept of a frontier—some kind of dividing line between nature and civilization—was present in some form or other in the minds of European discoverers and explorers of North America almost from the beginning, and early on it became a defining phenomenon in American history. As settlers confronted the interior of a vast continent full of exotic people, animals, and plants as well as geographic and geologic wonders, they came to realize that although they intended to transplant and perpetuate European institutions and to exploit the new continent for European purposes, indigenous circumstances were inevitably going to make life in America significantly different from that in the Old World.

Images of the frontier in early American literature vary greatly, from a place of darkness and dread, the domain of the devil, to a happy, peaceful realm of opportunity for the human spirit to recover a presumed primeval innocence cleansed of civilization's corruption and indeed even a place to achieve union with God. It was violent and perilous, but it was also a land of opportunity, where an enterprising person with a sharp ax could become the master of his own destiny. The frontier was thus fraught with ambiguous meaning, but it was a place few Americans could ignore. The novels of James Fenimore Cooper, the histories of Washington Irving and Francis Parkman, and the government reports of John C. Frémont all found enthusiastic audiences among Americans who felt themselves drawn to the frontier or who only dreamed of going there.

However the frontier might have been defined, it was a transitional phenomenon, a passing phase on the road to civilization. Civilization of course contains its own problems, and as Americans found themselves confronted increasingly by those new problems, their concept of the frontier acquired a nostalgic component. In that view America's best days lay in the past, in a time when life's essentials were laid bare and challenges brought out the best in human nature. This nostalgic view became more and more prominent in American literature and history during the years after the Civil War, when a country newly reunited and invigorated by the Industrial Revolution rushed to vanquish the remaining Indians, settle the open spaces, and exploit the continent's natural resources.

When the University of Wisconsin historian Frederick Jackson Turner (1861–1932) read his path-breaking paper "The Significance of the Frontier in American History" before the American Historical Association in Chicago on 12 July 1893, he both represented contemporary interest in the frontier and foreshadowed the fascination with the subject that lasted well into the twentieth century. Like the ancient Roman god Janus, Turner looked both ways, reacting to previous views as well as preparing the way for other viewpoints that dominated writing about the frontier in the next decades. The "frontier" or "Turner" thesis, although much challenged in the late twentieth century and early twenty-first century, nonetheless remains the beginning place for understanding the central concept of the frontier in American history and literature. In addition, because novelists, historians, and moviemakers are not immune from their own times, their interpretations of the frontier often reflect their present-day experiences as much as the events of the past. Over time the frontier has become as much a metaphor for presenting one's views as a series of historical events.

THE FRONTIER BEFORE FREDERICK JACKSON TURNER

Turner built on an enduring interest in borders and frontiers. In Europe well before Turner spoke of the idea, the frontier referred to set boundaries between nations. In the United States in the nineteenth century, frontiers were often points of contact between colonial empires or of division between white and Indian societies. Travelers and writers of the nineteenth century provided varied depictions of the frontier. The journals of the explorers Meriwether Lewis and William Clark, Zebulon Pike, and Stephen H. Long, for example, spoke of the vast spaces, the giant mountains and rivers, and numerous Indian tribes. They also warned of dangers from natural disasters and native opponents. If explorers in the early nineteenth century furnished close approximations of what they saw and experienced, more imaginative tourists, authors the likes of Washington Irving and James Fenimore Cooper, the historian Francis Parkman, and artists such as Albert Bierstadt and Thomas Moran provided more romantic depictions.

Toward the end of the century, other writers and publicists further wilded up the West. From 1860 into the early twentieth century, dime novelists utilized the frontier repeatedly for sensational and lurid tales of historical and quasi-historical figures like Billy the Kid, Buffalo Bill Cody, Wild Bill Hickok, and Calamity Jane as well as wholly fictional characters like Deadwood Dick, Rattlesnake Ned, and Sagebrush Sal. Dime novels depicted a West much more of fantasy than of reality. The most influential of all such promulgators of the romanticized West was William F. Cody, "Buffalo Bill" (1846–1917), who in 1883 organized his Wild West show and took it throughout the United States

***Under Attack*, c. 1880.** Painting by Frederic Remington of a stagecoach being attacked by Indians. Through his paintings and sculpture Remington helped create the myth of the American West. GETTY IMAGES

and western Europe. Cody's circus-like exhibition provided a mix of cowboys, Indians, shootists, and fancy riders, but most of all Buffalo Bill portrayed the frontier as a setting of nonstop vigorous competitions.

The local color movement in American literature, which lasted from the end of the Civil War until the 1890s and provided the southern animal fabliaux of Joel Chandler Harris and the Hoosier dialect stories of James Whitcomb Riley, also manifested itself in the stories of Mark Twain, Bret Harte, Joaquin Miller, and Alfred Henry Lewis, who utilized historical and imagined characters to depict mysterious, adventurous, and faraway frontiers peopled with exotic miners, courageous explorers, and exuberant cowboys. "Local color" denotes a literary tradition based on folklore and character types that are charming representations of life in a particular time and place but which do not transcend their roots to achieve a timeless universal significance.

The most influential interpreter of the frontier before Turner was the Boston Brahmin Francis

Parkman (1788–1852). A horticulturist by training, Parkman was one of the first in a long line of talented researchers and writers who have made immense contributions to American history as hobbyists rather than as professionally trained scholars. Parkman's most celebrated work is *The Oregon Trail* (1872; first published as *The California and Oregon Trail* in 1849), a now-classic memoir of Parkman's direct experience of the frontier during a trip across the Great Plains on the overland trail in 1846. Parkman has been accused, most notably by the historian Bernard DeVoto, of missing the larger significance of the historic moment he witnessed because of his aristocratic disdain for the unwashed mountain men and the Indians, whom he typically referred to as savages, who shared the trail and were effecting the continental expansion that DeVoto considered the basic theme in American history. Be that as it may, the experience aroused Parkman's literary instincts and set a great career in motion.

Parkman's voluminous histories, which continued to flow from his inkwell until the early 1890s, were deeply grounded in the grand Romantic vision that inspired his fellow historians George Bancroft and William H. Prescott as well as writers like Irving and Cooper. His pages are filled with such epic themes as the clash of empires in the Seven Years' War (*The History of the Conspiracy of Pontiac and the Indian War after the Conquest of Canada* [1851] and *Montcalm and Wolfe* [1884]) and the heroic deeds of great explorers and missionaries like La Salle and the French Jesuits.

Modern western historians owe a great deal to Parkman, both for his tireless exploitation of archival resources and for his literary style, which, while no one would write in that mode in the early twenty-first century, reminds one that history is a literary art as well as a science. Interpretively his contribution is much thinner. Parkman was certainly aware of the existence of a frontier as a line separating the primitive from the civilized, but he saw little utility in it or any other sociological phenomenon in his literary purposes. He was much less interested in explaining than in simply narrating. Issues of causation and significance—the interpretive elements in which modern historians believe history achieves its explanatory force and intellectual height—were less important to Parkman than exploring the literary potential of his epic themes and characters.

Another pre-Turner historian of the West, who was much more read in his day than in later years, is Theodore Roosevelt (1858–1919). Only a little psychoanalysis is required to understand that Roosevelt's interest in what he imagined to be the robust masculinity of western life grew out of his personal determination to triumph over the limitations of the weak body with which he was born, a determination that made him a horseman, hunter, boxer, cowboy, and lifelong advocate of what he came to call "the strenuous life." Born into a wealthy New York aristocratic family, Roosevelt was a voracious reader who early became aware of the frontier and the outsize adventures of the colorful characters who populated it. No armchair adventurer himself, Roosevelt's passion for the West led him to ownership of two cattle ranches in the Dakota Territory in the 1880s. Although the rough-edged cowboys in his employ sometimes found themselves snickering at his Harvard accent, they had to applaud his toughness and energy, and Roosevelt vindicated his authentic western-ness by knocking out a bully in a Dakota saloon.

The long shelf of Roosevelt's writings includes several titles recounting his experiences and travels in the West, but his multivolume history of the frontier, *The Winning of the West: An Account of the Exploration and Settlement of Our Country from the Alleghanies to the Pacific,* which appeared during 1889–1896, was most influential in promoting a particular view of the frontier that remains vital in popular culture even to this day. Driven by an unabashed racism that underlay most of the European and American imperialism of that day, *The Winning of the West* was the story of the triumph of the Anglo-Saxon pioneers in supplanting indigenous "savagery" with civilization. Filled with dramatic battles, desperate struggles, and similar vindications of "the strenuous life," Roosevelt's history was an implicit rebuke to the effete easterners of his native society whose vision failed to embrace the great challenge of redeeming the earth through Anglo-Saxon conquest.

THE "WATERSHED" OF THE 1890s

The frontier began to take on increased importance in the American mind as a result of what various historians have called the "watershed," the "psychic crisis," and the "reorientation of American culture" during the 1890s. Although twentieth-century western historiography, with its focus on ethnic and cultural minorities and on women, has tended to minimize some of the traumatic aspects of that decade as a tempest only within the teapot of elite white Americans, the fact that those Americans were the dominant power in politics, society, and culture gives the thesis some force.

In broad terms, the thesis focuses on a widespread failure of confidence in the basic soundness of American culture in the face of the end of the frontier, the great economic depression of the decade, the resulting revolt of farmers, labor unrest and violence in the Homestead and Pullman strikes of 1892 and 1894, respectively, ostensibly unassimilable waves of immigrants and the resulting ghettos and slums, widespread civic corruption, and the death of free enterprise and competition by the domination of big business conglomerates. The West played a major role in the attempt of Americans to revert to and reassert virtues and attributes that they imagined had defined America's strength in the simpler years before the Industrial Revolution. A new focus on the outdoors as opposed to the city was manifested by the creation of national parks such as Yosemite and Sequoia, in the nature writings of Ernest Thompson Seton and John Muir, by the founding of organizations like the Boone and Crockett Club (1887) and the Sierra Club (1892), and a general emphasis on Roosevelt's "strenuous life." Those emphases came to the surface of public life perhaps most tellingly in the jingoistic patriotism that led to imperialistic ventures in the Caribbean and the Philippines during the Spanish-American War (1898), to the Open Door Policy (1899), and to the building of the Great White Fleet (1907–1909).

FREDERICK JACKSON TURNER AND THE FRONTIER

Before Turner could give the frontier its rightful place in the American past, he had to clear away what he considered three major impediments. For one, after the Civil War, American historians had placed too much stress, Turner was convinced, on the controversies that led to that fratricidal conflict. True, slavery and the attendant political and economic embroilments were important, but they must be viewed in larger contexts, alongside other powerful forces that shaped what became the United States. Second, Turner urged his fellow historians to avoid their nearly exclusive emphases on the molding influences of Europe on American history. In this urging, Turner was separating himself from his teacher Herbert Baxter Adams. As Turner's doctoral mentor at Johns Hopkins University, Adams preached the doctrine of the "germ theory," which asserted that the "germs" of European history and culture were the primary shaping forces of the American past. Third, Turner wanted to put distance between himself and historians and popularizers who wanted to turn the frontier into a Wild West replete with gigantic heroes and villains. Without naming names Turner implied that his analytical approaches to the study of the frontier were miles distant from the kinds of Wests that Buffalo Bill, Theodore Roosevelt, and others were portraying in their arena shows and romantic narrative histories. Turner was con-

vinced that if the underbrush of slavery, the "germ theory," and a Wild West could be cleared away, his ideas about the significance of the frontier as the most important force in influencing American history could gain the attention they merited.

In the opening paragraph of Turner's notable presentation in 1893, he sounded the tocsin for the importance of the frontier in American history. Out on the frontier, he argued, "the existence of an area of free land, its continuous recession, and the advance of American settlement westward, explain American development" (*Frontier in History,* p. 1). The frontier experience did not help explain, partially explain, or largely "explain American development"; it did the explaining by itself. This is the boldest statement in an iconoclastic essay. Once one accepts the proposition encapsulated in that sentence, it is not difficult to understand the central significance of the frontier to American history.

Turner pointed to several results of the American frontier experience. The outcome of demanding wilderness contact, Turner asserted, encouraged individualism and a democracy derived from individual effort and from the necessity of working together to survive and to form political and social institutions. On the frontier a social and economic leveling took place when all families, without servants or slaves, had to do their own work. Here were Thomas Jefferson's yeoman farmers laboring in a setting where class divisions could not be sustained. Besides individualism and democracy, the frontier spawned a new, corporate nationality, a real melting pot in which ethnic differences dissolved in the light of common experience. Turner was equally convinced that the frontier had encouraged another of kind of nationalism in which frontier residents forged links with the federal government through their need for banks, tariffs, and internal improvements such as canals and roads.

A new kind of culture had also emerged on the frontier and influenced the remainder of the nation. Turner notes elsewhere that historical figures such as Daniel Boone, Andrew Jackson, Abraham Lincoln, and Mark Twain prove that the frontier produced, in the words of the transcendentalists, men of reason (homespun, grassroots, intuitive democrats) rather than men of understanding (rational intellectuals and philosophers). The "intellectual traits" of the frontier, Turner opined, were a "coarseness and strength combined with acuteness and inquisitiveness." These traits also included a "practical, inventive turn of mind, quick to find expedients." Finally, the frontier mind demonstrated a "masterful grasp of material things, lacking in the artistic but powerful to effect great ends . . .

restless, nervous energy . . . a dominant individualism, working for good and for evil, and withal that buoyancy and exuberance which comes with freedom" (*Frontier in American History*, p. 37).

Reflecting the nationalistic, reforming, and positive spirit of his time and personal temperament, Turner produced a generally optimistic essay. True, the frontier had closed, but its powerful, shaping legacies would sustain Americans in the future. The individualism, democracy, nationalism, and social mobility that the frontier fostered were beacons for Americans facing an uncertain horizon. Turner's forward-looking vision, based on a valuable past, comes into focus in the rhetorical flourishes appearing at the end of his remarkable essay. Turner, the historian and poet, wrote: "What the Mediterranean Sea was to the Greeks, breaking the bond of custom, offering new experiences, calling out new institutions and activities, that, and more, the ever retreating frontier has been to the United States directly, and to the nations of Europe more remotely" (*Frontier in American History*, p. 38).

REACTIONS TO TURNER'S FRONTIER THESIS

Although a few years passed before Turner's frontier thesis became irrevocable doctrine, most American historians had converted to the Turner camp by 1910. In that year Turner was elected president of the American Historical Association and was named to a chair of history at Harvard, two signs that he was among the most influential historians in the United States. Turner's students and other disciples carried the frontier message throughout the country. Hardly a major college or university was without its Turner man. Indeed, when Turner's replacement at the University of Wisconsin, Frederic Logan Paxson (1877–1948), wrote a book-length frontier history that Turner often promised but never completed, Paxson seemed a Turner look-alike in arguing in his preface "that the frontier with its continuous influence is the most American thing in all America." For that book, *History of the American Frontier, 1763–1893* (1924), with its clear Turnerian stamp, Paxson won a coveted Pulitzer Prize. Soon after Turner died in 1932, Paxson wrote an overview of frontier historiography, declaring that Turner's frontier thesis "stands today as easily to be accepted as it was when launched" ("A Generation of the Frontier Hypothesis," p. 51).

ZANE GREY

One of the most widely read fictional proponents of the significance of the frontier in American history is an Ohio dentist turned novelist, Zane Grey (1875–1939). Grey's fictional portrayal of life on the frontier owes a good deal more to the hairy-chested imperialism of Theodore Roosevelt than to the social analysis of Turner, but Grey, by becoming one of America's best-selling authors, demonstrates the depth and persistence of interest in the frontier within the reading public.

Frustrated with dentistry, Grey in 1903 began trying his hand at fiction in the form of a trilogy based on the historical exploits of his ancestors on the Ohio River frontier. *Betty Zane* (1903), *The Spirit of the Border* (1906), and *The Last Trail* (1909) were melodramas featuring lurid prose and violence similar to the dime novels. Although they sold poorly, they provided Grey with practice plotting frontier action stories and convinced him that a literary career was possible. A trip in 1907 to the ranch of the former buffalo hunter Colonel C. J. "Buffalo" Jones in northern Arizona gave Grey his first actual experience with frontier-like conditions and began to incubate the themes that became the framework of his most popular books. Jones's Mormon cowboys, the colorful Indians of the Grand Canyon region, the dramatic scenery, and the challenges of life in the desert all found prominent places in Grey's interpretation of the frontier.

Those elements coalesce in *The Heritage of the Desert* (1910), the first of Grey's "Mormon" novels and the first to develop his idea of the frontier as a theater of Darwinian natural selection, in which an ill and exhausted easterner, symbolizing the cultural bankruptcy of industrialized urban civilization, comes west and, responding to the moral and physical challenges of a harsh frontier life, finds rejuvenation and, of course, love. Grey further develops that theme in his other two "Mormon" novels, *Riders of the Purple Sage* (1912) and *The Rainbow Trail* (1915), perhaps the most famous westerns ever written. In those books Grey also introduced the character of Lassiter, the mysterious avenging gunman almost as lacking in antecedents as Owen Wister's Virginian, whose guns impose justice where vestigial frontier institutions cannot.

Grey's frontier Darwinism reached its apogee during the 1920s. Two character types appearing in his novels of that decade find physical and moral healing in the West: broken and unappreciated veterans of World War I and superficial flappers of the Jazz Age. The books featuring those themes—*The Man of the Forest* (1920), *The Call of the Canyon* (1924), and *30,000 on the Hoof* (1940)—are arguably his most philosophical and culturally significant works. During the 1930s Grey's literary output continued unabated, but with his audience now assured, his stories were less imaginative. Other novelists and historians—Willa Cather, Walter Prescott Webb, and Herbert E. Bolton among them—by that time had also rushed out onto the literary frontier, and an abiding interest in the significance of the frontier in American history had become a fundamental element in American culture.

See also Annexation and Expansion; Dime Novels; Farmers and Ranchers; History; Parks and Wilderness Areas; The Western; Wild West Shows

BIBLIOGRAPHY

Primary Works

Parkman, Francis. *The Oregon Trail*. Boston: Little, Brown, 1872. A revised version of *The California and Oregon Trail*. New York: Putnam, 1849.

Paxson, Frederic Logan. "A Generation of the Frontier Hypothesis: 1893–1932." *Pacific Historical Review* 2 (March 1933): 34–51.

Paxson, Frederic Logan. *History of the American Frontier, 1763–1893*. Boston: Houghton Mifflin, 1924.

Roosevelt, Theodore. *The Winning of the West: An Account of the Exploration and Settlement of Our Country from the Alleghanies to the Pacific*. 4 vols. New York: Putnam, 1889–1896.

Turner, Frederick Jackson. *The Frontier in American History*. 1920. Tucson: University of Arizona Press, 1986. Contains "The Significance of the Frontier in American History." The quotations in the present article are taken from the 1986 edition.

Turner, Frederick Jackson. *The Significance of Sections in American History*. New York: Henry Holt, 1932.

Secondary Works

Bogue, Allan G. *Frederick Jackson Turner: Strange Roads Going Down*. Norman: University of Oklahoma Press, 1998.

Commager, Henry Steele. *The American Mind: An Interpretation of American Thought and Character since the 1880s*. New Haven, Conn.: Yale University Press, 1950.

Cronon, William. "Revisiting the Vanishing Frontier: The Legacy of Frederick Jackson Turner." *Western Historical Quarterly* 18 (April 1987): 157–176.

Etulain, Richard W. *Re-Imagining the Modern American West: A Century of Fiction, History, and Art*. Tucson: University of Arizona Press, 1996.

Etulain, Richard W. *Telling Western Stories: From Buffalo Bill to Larry McMurtry*. Albuquerque: University of New Mexico Press, 1999.

Gruber, Frank. *Zane Grey: A Biography*. New York: World, 1970.

Higham, John. "The Reorientation of American Culture in the 1890s." In his *Writing American History: Essays on Modern Scholarship*. Bloomington: Indiana University Press, 1970.

Hofstadter, Richard. "Cuba, the Philippines, and Manifest Destiny." In his *The Paranoid Style in American Politics, and Other Essays*. New York: Knopf, 1965.

Klein, Kerwin Lee. *Frontiers of Historical Imagination: Narrating the European Conquest of Native America, 1890–1990*. Berkeley: University of California Press, 1997.

Limerick, Patricia Nelson. *The Legacy of Conquest: The Unbroken Past of the American West*. New York: Norton, 1987.

Morris, Edmund. *The Rise of Theodore Roosevelt*. New York: Coward, McCann, and Geoghegan, 1979.

Nash, Gerald D. *Creating the West: Historical Interpretations, 1890–1990*. Albuquerque: University of New Mexico Press, 1991.

Ridge, Martin. "The Life of an Idea: The Significance of Frederick Jackson Turner's Frontier Thesis." *Montana: The Magazine of Western History* 40 (winter 1991): 3–13.

Smith, Henry Nash. *Virgin Land: The American West as Symbol and Myth*. Cambridge, Mass.: Harvard University Press, 1950.

Steiner, Michael C. "Frederick Jackson Turner and Western Regionalism." In *Writing Western History: Essays on Major Western Historians*, edited by Richard W. Etulain. Albuquerque: University of New Mexico Press, 1991.

Topping, Gary. "Zane Grey: A Literary Reassessment." *Western American Literature* 13 (spring 1978): 51–64.

Richard W. Etulain
Gary Topping

GENTEEL TRADITION

The term "genteel tradition" was coined by George Santayana (1863–1952) in 1911 in reference to an attempt by a group of refined New England intellectuals—poets, academics, editors, critics, and publishers—to control literary and moral standards, maintain social hierarchies, and encourage conservative political reform. These well-bred, educated, and decorous Anglo-Saxon men asserted their cultural authority soon after the Civil War, claiming that they were the only ones capable of defining and maintaining American high culture. They criticized popular culture and censored what they considered "bad" literature, particularly literary realism. Rigidly conforming to Victorian standards of taste, they argued that "good" literature had only two functions: to transport readers from the real world to one of ideal truth and beauty and to teach "proper" manners to members of the middle and upper classes. Because the defenders of the genteel could control most of the literature written, edited, reviewed, and published at this time, they were often the only authoritative secular voice America heard on the subjects of personal conduct, intellectual thought, and artistic taste.

As noted by John Tomsich in *A Genteel Endeavor: American Culture and Politics in the Gilded Age* (1971), prior to the beginning of the twentieth century, most Americans admired the genteel elite and aspired to join their ranks. Many conformed to cultural conventions because they had not yet escaped their Old-World dependence on an aristocratic class, which they expected would provide the young nation social stability and cultural nobility. However, the pretentious proponents of the genteel tradition soon lost their influence because they were out of touch with American democratic individualism and cultural diversity. They were idealists and elitists who refused to adapt to a changing society or address the realities of America's industrialization, urbanization, immigration, and democratic frontier spirit. "Genteel" became a derogatory word, used to criticize the smug elite's Old-World social hierarchies and intellectually stale literature. An increased awareness of the nobility of the individual and the inherent instability of the modern world resulted in a new, anti-genteel era of innovative and realistic fiction.

THE HARVARD SCHOOL

The driving force behind America's genteel tradition from 1870 to 1910 consisted of the most influential and popular figures in intellectual and literary circles. The most important magazines, publishing houses, social clubs, literary academies, and eastern universities subscribed to, or at least did not dare contradict, the standards of taste and manners propounded by the defenders of the genteel tradition. The most significant genteel poets included George Henry Boker (1823–1890), Richard Henry Stoddard (1825–1903), Bayard Taylor (1825–1878), Edmund Clarence Stedman (1833–1908), and the Harvard School of George Cabot Lodge (1873–1909), William Vaughn Moody (1869–1910), George Santayana, and Trumbull Stickney (1874–1904). Other genteel intellectuals included Thomas Bailey Aldrich (1836–1907), novelist and editor of the *Atlantic Monthly* from 1881 to 1890;

George William Curtis (1824–1892), political editor of *Harper's Weekly* from 1863 to 1892; Richard Watson Gilder (1844–1909), editor of *Century Magazine* between 1881 and 1909; and Charles Eliot Norton (1827–1908), a Harvard professor from 1875 to 1898 and co-founder of *The Nation* in 1865.

The Harvard poets and New England academics worried about protecting high culture from the materialism and democratizing effects of industrialization and urbanization. They recognized that the rash of depressions and strikes in the 1880s and 1890s, as well as the rapid increase in immigration and urban slums, made social and cultural evolution, if not revolution, an immediate threat to the social hierarchy and the elite's cultural authority. These fears made the genteel intellectuals extremely conservative, causing them to advocate paternalistic, centralized government and anti-union legislation. They assumed the middle and upper classes needed their intellectual and moral direction, and they considered the masses irrelevant. According to F. Brett Cox in the essay "'What Need, Then, for Poetry?': The Genteel Tradition and the Continuity of American Literature" (1994), Boker, Taylor, and Stoddard "argued for a literature of pure and noble thoughts produced by a clerisy of artists who were apart from and above the common horde" (p. 215). As the self-proclaimed custodians of high culture and proper behavior, these poets, academics, and editors relied upon their own European roots of Calvinist hierarchical authority and Romantic metaphysical idealism to lift American literature and its reader out of the "ugly," practical world of commercial and political affairs.

The genteel poets despised American provincialism and looked to their European forefathers and contemporaries for sophistication, elegance, and "proper" behavior. Like the English Romantic and Victorian poets, the erudite Harvard poets chose a "pure and noble" language so they could sing sentimentally about high-minded ideals. They produced well-crafted lyrics that followed conventional forms, and they emphasized subject matter that was polite, abstract, earnest, morally uplifting, and uncontroversial. Aldrich defended this position in his "Ponkapog Papers" (1907): "A man is known by the company his mind keeps. To live continually with noble books, with 'high-erected thoughts seated in the heart of courtesy,' teaches the soul good manners" (Aldrich, p. 31). An example of these high-erected thoughts is Santayana's polished, sentimental "Sonnet III (O World, thou choosest not the better part!)" (1894), which employs traditional meter and rhyme and relies on hackneyed Romantic images and ideals. It concludes:

Our knowledge is a torch of smoky pine
That lights the pathway but one step ahead
Across a void of mystery and dread.
Bid, then, the tender light of faith to shine
By which alone the mortal heart is lead
Unto the thinking of the thoughts divine.
(*Complete Poems, p. 92*)

Santayana also emulated the Victorian style in his earnest, elegiac, formal "Ode II." Although the poem begins by addressing a contemporary socioeconomic issue: "My heart rebels against my generation, / That talks of freedom and is slave to riches" (*Complete Poems*, p. 140), it quickly turns to abstract idealism and sentimentalism. Santayana acts as a "philosopher-poet," who asks his muse, Mother Nature, to help his readers escape the material world and find Beauty and Truth in the eternal realm.

The genteel intellectuals suppressed any literature they deemed inappropriate for the refinement and uplift of American readers. Stedman criticized literary realism, stating in *Victorian Poets* (1876) that it was "not well that repulsive or petty facts should always be recorded; only the high, essential truths demand a poet's illumination" (pp. 304–305). Stedman privileged authors of the genteel tradition in *Poets of America* (1885), a book of literary criticism, and *A Library of American Literature from the Earliest Settlement to the Present Time* (1888–1890), a popular and critically acclaimed eleven-volume anthology that he edited with E. M. Hutchinson. The latter book completely ignored the work of Herman Melville (1819–1891) and only superficially considered the work of Walt Whitman (1819–1892), Edgar Allan Poe (1809–1849), and Nathaniel Hawthorne (1804–1864). In the opinion of Richard Ruland and Malcolm Bradbury in *From Puritanism to Postmodernism*, Stedman and Hutchinson's anthology presented a version of American letters that could be interpreted as "a branch of English literature" (Ruland, p. xii).

Naturalist authors also had trouble publishing their manuscripts. Many editors and publishers, adhering to genteel values, rejected the work of Stephen Crane (1871–1900), including *Maggie, A Girl of the Streets (A Story of New York)* (1893) and *The Red Badge of Courage: An Episode of the American Civil War* (1895). Richard Watson Gilder rejected both manuscripts on behalf of *Century Magazine*, telling Crane that *Maggie* was "cruel" and "too honest" (Crane, p. 60). Theodore Dreiser (1871–1945) also had trouble publishing *Sister Carrie* (1900) because it challenged genteel politeness and delicacy and forced readers to face and deal with the pain and ugliness of real life.

The Harvard School of genteel poets followed the conventions of past European and American masters,

George Santayana, 1930s. © THE LIBRARY OF CONGRESS

but their poetry lacked those authors' originality, imagination, and philosophical depth. Therefore, popular authors like Aldrich and Curtis quickly disappeared from the canon. Their subject, message, and style quickly became obsolete, especially after Ezra Pound (1885–1972) and H. D. (the penname of Hilda Doolittle, 1886–1961) introduced imagism to American poetics.

SANTAYANA

Jorge Agustin Nicolas de (George) Santayana was of Spanish American ancestry and was educated at Harvard; he joined the faculty in 1889, teaching philosophy alongside William James (1842–1910). Santayana was an important member of the Harvard School of genteel poets, but he blamed his failure as a poet on the oppressive, uniform, and monotonous intellectual atmosphere of the genteel tradition. Therefore, when he decided to leave Harvard and the United States in 1911, he publicly criticized America's genteel tradition in a lecture he gave at the University of California at Berkeley entitled "The Genteel Tradition in American

Philosophy." According to F. O. Matthiessen in *Theodore Dreiser* (1951), "Santayana coined the phrase 'the genteel tradition' to describe what he considered the most dangerous defect in American thought" (p. 62). This defect was an inability of the American intellect, symbolized in Santayana's lecture by the colonial mansion, to escape from the social hierarchies and cultural conventions of America's European heritage. Santayana warned that a continued reliance on Victorian ideals and standards would emasculate the American will, symbolized by the skyscraper. Santayana stated that the genteel tradition had already split the American psyche, causing a dual mentality: "one a survival of the beliefs and standards of the fathers, the other an expression of the instincts, practice, and discoveries of the younger generations" (*Genteel Tradition*, p. 39). Santayana argued that American intellect and American will had become alienated from each other, resulting in a disconnection between the nation's passive, backward-looking academic and cultural self-identity and its aggressive, forward-looking commercial and political self-identity.

Santayana posited that "the mediocrity of the genteel tradition" (*Genteel Tradition*, p. 44) had corrupted American literature and intellectual thought, stating, "what has happened is that the heredity philosophy has grown stale, and that the academic philosophy afterwards developed has caught the stale odor from it" (*Genteel Tradition*, p. 39). He argued that American thought and literature must reject the obsolete Calvinist and transcendental attitudes and embrace the practical, commercial, empirical, and modern nature of American life. Otherwise, Santayana complained, the idealism of the genteel tradition would prevent Americans from writing serious poetry and fully understanding themselves because it "forbids people to confess that they are unhappy" (*Genteel Tradition*, p. 51). He asserted that if Americans did not escape the genteel tradition, they could not grow as individuals or develop a national literature and culture.

Unlike others of the Harvard School, Santayana had not become completely pessimistic about the future of American taste and manners. He encouraged the young nation to challenge the cultural elite and its reliance on European tradition. Santayana applauded Whitman's vital, modern, native verse, stating that he was perhaps the only "American writer who has left the genteel tradition entirely behind" (*Genteel Tradition*, p. 52). However, Santayana explained that contemporary intellectual circles would not allow Whitman's democratic, Bohemian, and original poetry to represent American culture because "the genteel Anglo-Saxon convention" (*Genteel Tradition*, p. 52) was too deeply ingrained. For this same reason, Santayana claimed that Mark Twain

(1835–1910) and other regional humorists could only half escape from the genteel tradition. Their successful parodies of the tradition proved its pervasiveness in the American consciousness, as did their inability to replace it with anything concrete.

Santayana recognized, however, that the next generation of realist and naturalist authors and philosophers had begun to destroy the authority and influence of the genteel tradition. Santayana stated that Henry James (1843–1916) "has overcome the genteel tradition in the classic way, by understanding it" (*Genteel Tradition*, p. 54). *Daisy Miller* (1878), *The Bostonians* (1886), and *The Ambassadors* (1903) exposed the rigid, absolutist rules and its stale idealism of the old order. Furthermore, William James overpowered the genteel tradition and "enticed faith in a new direction" (*Genteel Tradition*, p. 60) through his pragmatic, empiricist philosophy and his uniquely American spontaneity and vitality. Santayana praised his colleague's open mind and sympathetic attitude to the wisdom of the non-elite:

> William James became the friend and helper of those groping, nervous, half-educated, spiritually disinherited, emotionally hungry individuals of which America is full. He became, at the same time, their spokesman and representative before the learned world; and he made it a chief part of his vocation to recast what the learned world has to offer, so that as far as possible it might serve the needs and interests of these people. (*Genteel Tradition*, p. 55)

For all of Santayana's criticism of the genteel tradition, he concluded his lecture by defending its motto: "Let us be content to live in the mind" (*Genteel Tradition*, p. 64), and then he expatriated to Victorian Europe. He did, however, inspire Van Wyck Brooks (1886–1963) to follow up his critical analysis of American culture. Brooks analyzed the divide between "Highbrow" and "Lowbrow" in *America's Coming-of-Age* (1915), and he sharply criticized the genteel mind in America. He called for a cultural awakening and the development of a new literature that was natural, realistic, energetic, and nationalistic.

REALIST REBELLION

Even before Santayana's lecture and Brooks's book, a number of authors and critics had already suggested that the genteel tradition and its powerful supporters were stifling literary innovation and disrupting the establishment of a truly American literary voice and cultural identity. Whitman, Twain, William Dean Howells (1837–1920), and Edwin Arlington Robinson (1869–1935) challenged convention and injected vitality and the American spirit into literature. They rejected the

idealism of the genteel tradition and created an innovative new genre, literary realism, in order to connect readers directly to contemporary American experiences and America's oral tradition. Realism represented and celebrated everything that the genteel poets and editors resisted: democratic values, commercial activities, the immigrant and poor urbanite experience, the commonplace and the physical, raw human emotions, psychological pain and frustration, use of the vernacular, and original and non-formal modes of writing.

Whitman, who broke nearly every stylistic and thematic convention the genteel poets held dear, stated derisively in his essay "Democratic Vistas" (1871): "Do you call those genteel little creatures American poets? Do you term that perpetual, pistareen, paste-pot work, American art, American drama, taste, verse? I think I hear, echoed as from some mountain-top afar in the west, the scornful laugh of the Genius of these States" (pp. 388–389). Whitman argued that in order to find a truly American poetic voice and cultural presence authors must reject the elegant, complacent "parcel of dandies and ennuyees [*sic*]" (p. 408) as their models. Robinson satirized the genteel poets in "Sonnet" (1897), calling them "little sonnet men" who write "Songs without souls, that flicker for a day / To vanish in irrevocable night" (p. 93). Robinson's poem "Richard Cory" (1897) uses realism and the search for psychological truth to directly challenge the hypocrisy of the genteel tradition in modern American life. Richard is a wealthy and genteel gentleman, but his loneliness and spiritual emptiness cause him to "put a bullet through his head" (p. 82).

Howells, Twain, and Henry James presented common, American characters living normal, everyday life in their novels. Although some modernist authors and critics linked the realists, particularly Howells, with the genteel tradition, the realists were never popular with the genteel authors and editors. Hamilton Wright Mabie (1845–1916), an apologist for the genteel tradition, was extremely critical of Howells's *The Rise of Silas Lapham* (1885). According to John Tomsich in *A Genteel Endeavor: American Culture and Politics in the Gilded Age* (1971), Mabie and other intellectual elites considered Howells too commonplace, Twain too colloquial and racy, and James too depressing. Thomas Bailey Aldrich often criticized literary realism and stated in his "Ponkapog Papers" that "in nine cases out of ten an exact reproduction of real life would prove tedious. Facts are not necessarily valuable, and frequently they add nothing to fiction" (Aldrich, p. 32). He refused to accept realism as art, arguing: "Art should create nothing but what is beautiful . . . and leave real life to do the rest" (Tomsich, p. 145).

However, the realists would not be deterred. Twain, as Santayana indicated, wrote about and for the masses, challenging genteel social and literary values directly. He compared idealism and respectability to individualism, practical competence, and common sense in *The Adventures of Tom Sawyer* (1876) and *Adventures of Huckleberry Finn* (1885). In these novels, Tom learns to be a responsible member of middle-class society, whereas Huck challenges society's genteel norms and adopts a personal sense of morality and manners. Huck's individualism and frontier spirit shows that America need not define itself or its tastes by the standards of the educated, refined elite of New England. Twain's *A Connecticut Yankee in King Arthur's Court* (1889) also satirizes the battle between the genteel tradition and the vernacular tradition, arguing that Americans must fight the cultural dictatorship of the genteel intellectuals.

The naturalists stepped even farther away from the genteel tradition. In the opinion of F. O. Matthiessen, the raw, harsh reality presented by authors like Crane, Frank Norris, Jack London, and Theodore Dreiser exploded the genteel tradition's "idealized picture of civilized refinement" (Matthiessen, p. 62). These authors refused to obey the genteel elite's belief in social hierarchy and standards of literary taste. Instead they alerted readers to the effects environment and heredity have on a human being's life, especially the sordid life of someone living in the slums.

Turn-of-the-century realist, naturalist, and modernist authors, as well as a forward-thinking new group of critics and publishers, effectively challenged the narrow standards of the genteel tradition and soon broke its authoritative stranglehold. Santayana proclaimed in 1911: "No one need be brow-beaten any longer into accepting it" (*Genteel Tradition*, p. 60). Unable to change the direction the country was headed, the genteel poets and academics became pessimistic and alienated, withdrawing to their ivory towers and eventually disappearing from the canon of American literature.

See also Aestheticism; Art and Architecture; Philosophy

BIBLIOGRAPHY
Primary Works
Aldrich, Thomas Bailey. "Ponkapog Papers." In *The Writings of Thomas Bailey Aldrich*, vol. 9, *Ponkapog Papers, A Sea Turn, and Other Papers*. Boston: Houghton Mifflin, 1907.

Brooks, Van Wyck. *America's Coming-of-Age*. 1915. New York: Octagon Books, 1975.

Crane, Stephen. *Stephen Crane: Letters*. Edited by R. W. Stallman and Lillian Gilkes. New York: New York University Press, 1960.

Hollander, John, ed. *American Poetry: The Nineteenth Century*. Vol. 2. New York: Library of America, 1993.

Robinson, Edwin Arlington. *Collected Poems of Edwin Arlington Robinson*. New York: Macmillan, 1954.

Santayana, George. *The Complete Poems of George Santayana: A Critical Edition*. Edited by William G. Holzberger. Lewisburg, Pa.: Bucknell University Press, 1979.

Santayana, George. "The Genteel Tradition in American Philosophy." 1911. In *The Genteel Tradition: Nine Essays*, edited by Douglas L. Wilson. Cambridge, Mass.: Harvard University Press, 1967.

Stedman, Edmund Clarence. *Victorian Poets*. Boston: Houghton Mifflin, 1896.

Whitman, Walt. "Democratic Vistas." 1871. In *Prose Works 1892*, vol. 2, *Collect and Other Prose*. New York: New York University Press, 1964.

Secondary Works
Cox, F. Brett. "'What Need, Then, for Poetry?': The Genteel Tradition and the Continuity of American Literature." *The New England Quarterly* 67, no. 2 (1994): 212–233.

Dawidoff, Robert. *The Genteel Tradition and the Sacred Rage: High Culture vs. Democracy in Adams, James, and Santayana*. Chapel Hill: University of North Carolina Press, 1992.

Matthiessen, F. O. *Theodore Dreiser*. New York: Dell, 1951.

Ruland, Richard, and Malcolm Bradbury. *From Puritanism to Postmodernism: A History of American Literature*. New York: Viking, 1991.

Tomsich, John. *A Genteel Endeavor: American Culture and Politics in the Gilded Age*. Stanford: Stanford University Press, 1971.

Tuttleton, James W. "William Dean Howells & the Practice of Criticism." *The New Criterion* 10, no. 10 (1992): 28–37.

Matthew Teorey

GHOST STORIES

The term "ghost story" has been widely employed to denote an entire range of literary works that suggest the existence of supernatural entities, whether they be actual ghosts or other creatures such as vampires, werewolves, witches, or revenants (the dead revived to a semblance of life); the term has even been used, over the objections of some theorists, to denote works embodying supernatural scenarios of a broader kind, such as haunted houses, fantastic voyages, or speculative tales of the future. In recent years the terms "supernatural fiction" or "weird fiction" have been proposed as more representative of the wide range of conceptions exhibited by such literature, but whatever genre designation one uses, the works to be studied here have in common the suggestion of at least a single departure from mimetic realism, whether that suggestion is ultimately explained away naturalistically or is made for symbolic, metaphorical, or allegorical purposes.

In the United States, the shadow of Edgar Allan Poe (1809–1849) loomed large in this domain for a century after his death. Although relatively few of Poe's works could be considered ghost stories or even supernatural tales in the strictest sense, he effected a radical revolution of the conventions of gothic literature that had already become stale in the two generations after their initiation in Horace Walpole's *The Castle of Otranto* (1764). The gothic novels of that period were almost entirely a British phenomenon, and the lone American representative of any consequence, Charles Brockden Brown, did not attain widespread recognition. American writers were faced with a curious historical dilemma in translating British gothic fiction to their shores: since most of that fiction was set in the medieval age (in order to render the exhibition of supernatural phenomena more plausible by a patina of remoteness and primitive superstition), how does one write gothic fiction in a land that had no medieval period? Poe solved the problem by transferring the locus of terror to the baffling workings of the human mind ("The Tell-Tale Heart"; "Ligeia") or by setting his tales in a nebulous never-never-land ("The Fall of the House of Usher") or by transferring his characters to remote settings (*The Narrative of Arthur Gordon Pym*). But what Poe established for a century and a half by his meticulous example was the radical superiority of the short story as a conveyer of fear, so that the novel of the supernatural became a rare exception.

Poe—and to a lesser degree his younger contemporary Fitz-James O'Brien, whose promising career as a supernaturalist ("What Was It?"; "The Diamond Lens") was cut short by his death in the Civil War—did not garner disciples immediately. It took a generation or two for successors to emerge, but when they did so they not merely developed his intense investigation of aberrant psychology but, curiously, adapted the ghost story to the purposes of regionalism. Accordingly two distinct schools, one on the West Coast and the other on the East Coast, emerged as inheritors of Poe's legacy.

THE WEST COAST SCHOOL

The most distinguished of the West Coast school was Ambrose Bierce (1842–1914?). His taste for the supernatural developed early in his career, if the satirical squib "The Discomfited Demon," a dialogue between a devil and a ghoul included in *The Fiend's Delight* (1873), is

any indication. But the bulk of Bierce's tales of psychological and supernatural horror were produced when he became William Randolph Hearst's chief editorial writer for the *San Francisco Examiner* in 1887. During the next six years he generated one of the most impressive bodies of short fiction in all American literature, most of it collected in two landmark volumes, *Tales of Soldiers and Civilians* (1891, but actually issued in February 1892) and *Can Such Things Be?* (1893). The former volume, of course, also contained his gripping tales of the Civil War, many of which can themselves be considered works of psychological horror by the grim, at times bitterly cynical investigation of their characters' emotional traumas as they face the horrors of war. But the latter volume—especially as Bierce revised it for the third volume of his *Collected Works* (1909–1912)—is exclusively devoted to stories of the supernatural, ranging from the spectacular supernatural-revenge tale "The Middle Toe of the Right Foot" (*Examiner*, 17 August 1890) to the ambiguous "The Death of Halpin Frayser" (*Wave*, 19 December 1891), perhaps the pinnacle of his supernatural output in its appalling suggestions of mother-son incest and the death of that son by the "lich" (soulless revenant) that his mother has become. A later tale, "The Moonlit Road" (*Cosmopolitan*, January 1907), displays a trilogy of narratives—by Joel Hetman Jr.; his father, Joel Hetman Sr. (now going by the name Caspar Grattan); and his mother, the late Julia Hetman, "through the medium Bayrolles." Each of these figures is missing a vital piece of information that could have averted tragedy; instead, the misunderstandings cause Julia's death at the hands of her own husband.

It is difficult to deny that Bierce's tales of the Civil War and of psychological horror are considerably superior to his supernatural tales. The latter are almost always ghost stories, such as the lackluster and unimaginative "Beyond the Wall" (*Cosmopolitan*, December 1907), and in many cases the climax of the tale is merely the confirmation that something supernatural has actually occurred. The satire that is at the very heart of Bierce's work finds its most piquant expression in those non-supernatural tales, whether of soldiers or civilians, that display human beings psychologically crushed by the weight of fear—whether it be the fear of death as embodied by a corpse ("A Tough Tussle," *Examiner*, 30 September 1888; "A Watcher by the Dead," *Examiner*, 29 December 1889), or the fear of being thought a coward in battle ("George Thurston," *Wasp*, 29 September 1883; "Killed at Resaca," *Examiner*, 5 June 1887).

Bierce's achievement, in such tales as "The Middle Toe of the Right Foot" and "The Boarded Window" (*Examiner*, 12 April 1891), was to convey the latent horror to be found in the deserted mining camps and boomtowns of the West, where spectacular wealth, decadence, and lawlessness could be followed by the sudden departure of its generally crude and ill-educated denizens for greener pastures. This was the dark side of the settlement of the West whose more wholesome facets had been presented by Bierce's early colleague Bret Harte. These ghost towns could then serve as potently as the focus of supernaturalism as the hoariest castle of old Europe.

Almost by accident Bierce produced a few pioneering tales that looked forward to future developments of the form. "Moxon's Master" (*Examiner*, 16 April 1899), although possibly derived in some degree from Poe's "Maelzel's Chess-Player" (1836) effectively exhibits a robot gradually developing quasi-human emotions and can be thought of as a work of proto–science fiction. Even more significant is "The Damned Thing" (*Town Topics*, 7 December 1893), although it may owe something to Fitz-James O'Brien's "What Was It?" In this account of an invisible monster, Bierce probes the notion of "colors that we cannot see" (i.e., infrared and ultraviolet rays); as his protagonist proclaims melodramatically at the end: "And, God help me! the Damned Thing is of such a color!" The influence of this tale on such later stories of invisible monsters as Algernon Blackwood's "The Wendigo" and H. P. Lovecraft's "The Colour out of Space" and "The Dunwich Horror" is patent.

Bierce gradually gathered around him a band of like-minded colleagues and disciples who both vaunted his own work and strove to capture something of his psychological insight and sense of place. Perhaps the most distinguished of these is W. C. Morrow (1854–1923), son of slave-owning parents in Selma, Alabama, who came to California in 1879. For the next twenty years he wrote voluminously for the *Argonaut* and other San Francisco papers, publishing dozens of short stories as well as the acclaimed novel *Blood-Money* (1882), a scathing exposé of the ruthlessness of the railroad industry in the state. The piquantly titled *The Ape, the Idiot, and Other People* (1897) contains only fourteen stories, and not necessarily his best ones. The great majority are tales of psychological suspense, but his most famous story, "The Monster-Maker" (*Argonaut*, 15 October 1887), is a gripping account of a crazed surgeon who, when a despairing man wishes to be euthanized, uses the body for an experiment in creating a headless but animate entity. It may perhaps be misleading to refer to Morrow as merely a disciple of Bierce, for the chronology of his tales suggests that he himself may have influenced Bierce or that they mutually influenced each other. Another colleague, Emma Frances Dawson (1851–1926), included some ghost stories in *The Itinerant House and Other Stories* (1897).

THE EAST COAST SCHOOL

The East Coast school of supernatural writing might itself be said to have split into two branches, one centering around the New England regionalists and the other coalescing around the imposing figure of Henry James. A quartet of women writers—Mary Eleanor Wilkins Freeman (1852–1930), Sarah Orne Jewett (1849–1909), Charlotte Perkins Gilman (1860–1935), and Olivia Howard Dunbar (1873–1953)—emphatically drew upon the craggy landscape and history of New England as a means of simulating the hoary medievalism that in Europe facilitated the introduction of the supernatural. Freeman's volume of ghost stories *The Wind in the Rose-Bush* (1903) does not necessarily represent her at her best; the tales, all written for *Everybody's Magazine* in the year prior to their book publication, focus almost claustrophobically upon the pinched lives of New Englanders trapped by archaic notions of decorum and propriety, leading to cruelty, neglect, and outright savagery that entail inevitable supernatural vengeance. The title story of this collection, for example, features the ghost of a neglected child, while "The Southwest Chamber" features a malevolent old woman whose hatred survives her death.

If Freeman's supernatural tales are set in an increasingly urbanized milieu, Jewett's tales draw poignantly upon the wild and unforgiving landscape of the untenanted Maine woods to evoke fear. Although she produced no single volume of ghost stories, Jewett throughout her career employed the supernatural as a means of adding depth to her portrayal of character and landscape. Her most celebrated work, *The Country of the Pointed Firs* (1896), contains only one incidental supernatural episode, but several short stories tread the borderline between psychological and supernatural horror. Perhaps her most successful tale in this regard is "In Dark New England Days" (*Century Magazine*, October 1890; in *Strangers and Wayfarers*, 1890), in which two sisters, Betsey and Hannah Knowles, after a long, hard life, lose a fortune in silver coins and curse the right hand of the man they suspect of the crime, Enoch Holt; subsequently three members of the Holt family, including Enoch, lose their right hands. Ambiguity is maintained to the end as to the perpetrator of the crime and whether the supernatural has genuinely come into play, but the story is an unforgettable depiction of the cheerless poverty of an aging New England family. "The Foreigner" (*Atlantic Monthly*, August 1900) is a powerful portrayal of a French-born woman who marries a New England sea captain but is never accepted by the community; on her deathbed she and her one friend see the ghost of her mother, who comes to bear her spirit away.

Charlotte Perkins Gilman wrote relatively little fiction in the midst of a busy career as magazine editor and crusader for women's rights, but she did produce several ghostly tales. "The Giant Wistaria" (*New England Magazine*, June 1891), is a seemingly light-hearted but ultimately grim story of a ghost of a woman who had had a child out of wedlock—and who, it is suggested, was murdered along with her baby by her own shame-stricken family. Gilman's signature piece, however, is "The Yellow Wall-Paper" (*New England Magazine*, January 1892), which has become emblematic as a feminist tract; its central scenario is reflected in the title of Sandra Gilbert and Susan Gubar's pioneering study of literary feminism, *The Madwoman in the Attic* (1979). And yet it has not been widely observed that this tale of a woman who, suffering from postpartum depression, is all but imprisoned in the attic of an old house in New England to which her husband has taken her for a "rest cure," is in fact a tale of the supernatural, and not merely one of progressive madness. The tale provides numerous clues that the attic was not a place where, as the protagonist initially believes, children were housed but where a madwoman, or perhaps even a succession of madwomen, has been confined, and that the protagonist is insidiously possessed by the spirit of one of these until at the end she identifies herself with one of the previous occupants. This supernatural interpretation need not in any way contradict the feminist message of the text, where the infantilization of women and the condescension of male physicians in regard to women's ailments are emphasized; in many ways the reinterpretation of "The Yellow Wall-Paper" as an authentic ghost story enhances the feminist message by hinting at generations of psychological abuse of women.

Another feminist, Olivia Howard Dunbar, wrote a handful of ghost stories that similarly underscored her sociopolitical concerns. "The Shell of Sense" (*Harper's*, December 1908) is a remarkable ghost story narrated in the first person by the ghost of a woman whose husband has married her sister, and whose fluctuating emotions—love, jealousy, resentment, pity—are effectively captured by Dunbar's elegant prose. Perhaps Dunbar's greatest weird tale is "The Long Chamber" (*Harper's*, September 1914), in which a woman who had subordinated her life to that of her husband sees a ghost who inspires her to achieve independence and emotional fulfillment. Dunbar's ghost stories are marked by exquisitely orchestrated prose, delicate character portrayal, and skill at employing the supernatural as a symbol for profound thematic concerns.

From the cramped quarters of the New England regionalists to the social expanse of Henry James's Europe and America would seem a significant shift, but

James too could invoke the claustrophobia of ghosts and haunted houses almost in spite of the flaccid orotundity of his prose. Of *The Turn of the Screw* (1898) it is difficult to speak in small compass, and many scholars have accepted Edmund Wilson's thesis that the tale is by design irresolvable: there is an insufficiency of clues as to whether the events depicted—a governess tending to a man's two small children believes herself haunted by the ghosts of Peter Quint, the man's former valet, and Miss Jessel, the governess's predecessor—are supernatural or psychological in origin. The supernatural interpretation appears to dominate at the start, but as the narrative proceeds the reader's increasing suspicions about the reliability of the governess's account throw the matter into doubt—a doubt that is maintained to the end. Some scholars of the genre, most notably Tzvetan Todorov in *The Fantastic* (1970), have found this tale so compelling as to vaunt it as the prototypical fantastic narrative, although this kind of ambiguous weird tale is in fact quite rare: the great majority of horror tales resolve fairly clearly into the supernatural or the psychological mode. James of course wrote an abundance of other weird tales—collected by Leon Edel in *The Ghostly Tales of Henry James* (1949)—but his most innovative venture might have been his final work, the unfinished novel *The Sense of the Past*, depicting a man who falls into the past and fears that he will remain there.

James's fellow expatriate F. Marion Crawford (1854–1909) was considerably less subtle in his horror tales, and it is of some significance that, although immensely prolific and popular, he himself never bothered to collect his scattered tales of the supernatural; they were assembled only posthumously in *Wandering Ghosts* (1911). It certainly cannot be said that Crawford showed any inclination to follow James in the meticulous dissection of the shifting psychological states of his characters; nevertheless, his most celebrated weird tale, the much-reprinted "The Upper Berth" (1886), is a triumph of cumulative horror. This account of a cold, wet, oozy entity that haunts the upper berth of a passenger ship is made the more effective by its narration by a bluff, no-nonsense protagonist named Brisbane. Of "The Dead Smile" (*Ainslee's*, August 1899) it is impossible to speak without a smile: this venture into unrestrained, "oh my god" horror is nonetheless effective in its very excess of lurid prose and its suggestions of incest.

More in line with James's style and methodology was the work of his friend Edith Wharton (1862–1937), the final representative of the conventional ghost story. Wharton collected her earlier supernatural tales in *Tales of Men and Ghosts* (1910) and more definitively in her last volume, *Ghosts* (1937), which includes an

Frontispiece illustration from Robert W. Chambers's ***Maker of Moons.*** © COURTESY OF S. T. JOSHI

illuminating essay on the ghost story. And yet even her most artfully crafted weird tale, "Afterward" (*Century Magazine,* January 1910), is nothing more than a skillful portrayal of supernatural revenge. Another, more distant colleague of James's, the Californian Gertrude Atherton (1857–1948), could be said to have effected a union between the East Coast and West Coast schools of ghostly writing. Her principal collection of supernatural tales, *The Bell in the Fog* (1905), is dedicated to James, and its title story (*Smart Set,* August 1903) features a lonely writer, clearly based on James, who believes that a little girl he encounters near his ancestral estate in England is the revenant of a girl whose portrait hangs in his home.

What is surprising is the degree to which, during this period, the most unlikely writers made forays into the weird, either for the space of a single story or per-

haps an entire volume. The architect Ralph Adams Cram produced a slim body of ghost stories, *Black Spirits & White* (1895), including the masterful tale of a haunted locale "The Dead Valley." Julian Hawthorne, although laboring under the shadow of his celebrated father, Nathaniel (himself a highly skilled manipulator of supernatural imagery in novel and tale alike), regularly included at least one token ghost story in nearly every one of his story collections of the last two decades of the nineteenth century, although his greatest contribution was the ten-volume *Lock and Key Library* (1909), a still-valuable anthology of mystery and supernatural tales from world literature. Perhaps most surprisingly of all, William Dean Howells, the reigning dean of American letters, filled two entire volumes, *Questionable Shapes* (1903) and *Between the Dark and the Daylight* (1907), with a series of somewhat attenuated supernatural tales. At the turn of the twentieth century several popular magazines, such as *Collier's, Saturday Evening Post,* and *Ainslee's,* opened their pages to the weird, and leading short-story writers of the period did not fail to supply them. Although O. Henry skirted the supernatural in several tales, only one, the much-reprinted "The Furnished Room" (1904), can be considered an authentic ghost story.

LOOKING FORWARD

A scattered array of novelists and short-story writers around the turn of the twentieth century produced, almost by accident, a body of work that carried the supernatural tale into new directions, directly influencing the generations that followed them. These writers either abandoned or so radically modified the conventional ghost and haunted house that they became pioneers in spite of themselves. Indeed, by the end of the nineteenth century the standard literary ghost had in some quarters become an object of derision and mockery. The advance of scientific knowledge rendered increasingly unlikely the reality of ghostly manifestations, and such writers as John Kendrick Bangs and Frank R. Stockton had no compunction in poking fun at the form. Bangs's much-reprinted "The Water Ghost of Harrowby Hall" (in *The Water Ghost and Others,* 1894) is prototypical: a female ghost who creates a nuisance by dousing the phlegmatic owner of a decrepit old house with water is finally dispatched by being led out into the bitter cold of a Christmas Eve and being frozen. In Stockton's best-known supernatural tale, "The Transferred Ghost" (*Century Magazine,* May 1882), a ghost is assigned to haunt a house even though the ghost's body is still living.

A highly surprising contributor to the new trend in supernatural writing was Robert W. Chambers (1865–1933)—surprising because, although he wrote some

> *In Robert W. Chambers's* In Search of the Unknown *(1904), the narrator, an employee of the Bronx Zoo, travels to a place in Canada known as Black Harbor and, in the company of Burton Halyard (a local resident) and his nurse, encounters the hybrid amphibian entity known locally as the harbor-master.*
>
> ---
>
> "What's that soft thumping?" I asked. "Have we run afoul of a barrel or log?"
>
> It was almost too dark to see, but I leaned over the rail and swept the water with my hand.
>
> Instantly something smooth glided under it, like the back of a great fish, and I jerked my hand back to the tiller. At the same moment the whole surface of the water seemed to begin to purr, with a sound like the breaking of froth in a champagne-glass.
>
> "What's the matter with you?" asked Halyard, sharply.
>
> "A fish came up under my hand," I said; "a porpoise or something—"
>
> With a low cry, the pretty nurse clasped my arm in both her hands.
>
> "Listen!" she whispered. "It's purring around the boat."
>
> "What the devil's purring?" shouted Halyard. "I won't have anything purring around me!"
>
> At that moment, to my amazement, I saw that the boat had stopped entirely, although the sail was full and the small pennant fluttered from the masthead. Something, too, was tugging at the rudder, twisting and jerking it until the tiller strained and creaked in my hand. All at once it snapped; the tiller swung useless and the boat whirled around, heeling in the stiffening wind, and drove shoreward.
>
> It was then that I, ducking to escape the boom, caught a glimpse of something ahead—something that a sudden wave seemed to toss on deck and leave there, wet and flapping—a man with round, fixed, fishy eyes, and soft, slaty skin.
>
> But the horror of the thing were the two gills that swelled and relaxed spasmodically, emitting a rasping, purring sound—two gasping, blood-red gills, all fluted and scolloped and distended.
>
> Frozen with amazement and repugnance, I stared at the creature; I felt the hair stirring on my head and the icy sweat on my forehead.
>
> "It's the harbor-master!" screamed Halyard.
>
> Robert W. Chambers, *In Search of the Unknown* (New York: Harper & Brothers, 1904), pp. 32–33.

scintillating weird tales early in his career, he later prostituted himself with an unending succession of shopgirl romances that ensured his material comfort but spelled his aesthetic undoing and ultimate oblivion in the Gehenna of outdated bestsellerdom. And yet *The King in Yellow* (1895), his second volume, drawing a bit affectedly upon his early experiences as an art student in Paris, is nonetheless remarkable in the nightmarish intensity of some of its tales. "The Repairer of Reputations" depicts a New York of the 1920s that has arisen white and austere from the horrors of Victorian architecture and in which euthanasia chambers are available to assist those who wish to slough off the burden of a tiresome existence. "The Yellow Sign" potently describes an artist pursued by a hideous hearse driver who himself seems to be not merely dead but rotting. Later works by Chambers mingle humor and horror in increasingly ineffective ways, the nadir being reached in *Police!!!* (1915), whose interesting conceptions—mammoths in the glaciers of Canada, a group of "cave-ladies" in the Everglades, a school of minnows the size of railroad cars—are spoiled by flippancy and a meretricious love interest.

Chambers's *In Search of the Unknown* (1904), however, introduces the notion of hybridity that a number of other writers also developed. Its opening chapters—originally published as a story, "The Harbor-Master" (*Ainslee's,* August 1899)—terrifyingly depicts a creature that appears to be half-human and half-fish, with the suggestion that an entire colony of such entities dwells under the sea. The popular Irvin S. Cobb (1876–1944), chiefly known as a humorist, utilized this same conception in "Fishhead" (*All-Story Cavalier,* 11 January 1913), about a rustic mixed-blood fisherman who has an anomalous affinity to the enormous catfish that populate the Kentucky lake near which he dwells. Gouverneur Morris (1876–1953) also enjoyed tremendous popularity as a short-story writer, and in

"Back There in the Grass" (*Collier's*, 16 December 1911) he continues the theme of hybridity in presenting a colony of foot-high half-human, half-snake entities on a Polynesian island. The early work of Edward Lucas White (1866–1934) can also be cited in this context, for many of the horror tales in *The Song of the Sirens* (1919) and *Lukundoo* (1927) were written in the first decade of the twentieth century but not published until their book appearance. "The Snout" (written in 1909) concerns a band of thieves who come upon a half-man, half-pig in the rich mansion they seek to rob.

There is considerable evidence to suggest that this theme of hybridity was a response both to concerns regarding the biological integrity of the human species in light of Darwinian evolution and to fears of miscegenation in the wake of the immense influx of immigrants in the period 1890–1920. Another horror story by Cobb, "The Unbroken Chain" (*Cosmopolitan*, September 1923), is openly racist in its premise. A Frenchman whose ancestry can be traced back to an African slave experiences an access of "hereditary memory" when he cries out in an obscure African language as he is run over by a train—an echo of his ancestor's death by a rhinoceros. Robert W. Chambers's later novel *The Slayer of Souls* (1920) clumsily mingles supernaturalism with the "yellow peril" topos, depicting a band of Asians, descended from the "devil-worshipping" Yezidis of central Asia, threatening to overthrow the U.S. government.

Cobb's "Fishhead" was published in one of the numerous magazines of Frank A. Munsey's publishing empire. Munsey, whose first magazine, the *Golden Argosy*, began issuance in 1882, was very accommodating to stories of fantasy, terror, and proto–science fiction (notably the work of Edgar Rice Burroughs, whose stories of Tarzan began appearing in 1912), but these forerunners of the pulp magazines tended to cater to the poorly educated by purveying contrived, shoddily written tales generated by a cadre of hack writers who could write stories of any given genre almost at will. They—along with such other early magazines as the *Black Cat* (1895–1923) and the *Popular Magazine* (1903–1927), issued by Street & Smith—may have had a role in the eventual banishing of weird material from the standard "slick" magazines, a tendency radically augmented by the full-fledged emergence of the pulps in the 1920s.

The horror fiction of this period, diverse as it is, is united by its demonstration that the use of the supernatural, whether it be a ghost, a haunted house, or some less classifiable phenomenon, need not result in mere shudder-coining. The supernatural was shown to enhance the portrayal of character, the probing of aberrant psychology, and the depiction of landscape in all its historic and cultural richness. That some of the leading writers of the period chose this venue to express their literary concerns confirms the viability of the ghost story as art form no less worthy of critical attention than its congeners in mimetic realism.

See also Pseudoscience; "The Yellow Wall-Paper"

BIBLIOGRAPHY
Primary Works

Bierce, Ambrose. *Can Such Things Be?* New York: Cassell, 1893.

Bierce, Ambrose. *Tales of Soldiers and Civilians*. San Francisco: E. L. G. Steele, 1891 [1892].

Chambers, Robert W. *The King in Yellow*. New York: F. Tennyson Neely, 1895.

Cram, Ralph Adams. *Black Spirits and White*. Chicago: Stone & Kimball, 1895.

Crawford, F. Marion. *Wandering Ghosts*. New York: Macmillan, 1911.

Freeman, Mary E. Wilkins. *The Wind in the Rose-Bush and Other Stories of the Supernatural*. New York: Doubleday, Page, 1903.

James, Henry. *The Two Magics: The Turn of the Screw, Covering End*. New York: Macmillan, 1898.

Morrow, W. C. *The Ape, the Idiot and Other People*. Philadelphia: J. B. Lippincott, 1897.

Wharton, Edith. *Ghosts*. New York: Appleton-Century, 1937.

White, Edward Lucas. *Lukundoo and Other Stories*. New York: George H. Doran, 1927.

Secondary Works

Daniels, Les. *Living in Fear: A History of Horror in the Mass Media*. New York: Scribners, 1975.

Grenander, M. E. *Ambrose Bierce*. New York: Twayne, 1971.

Heller, Terry. *The Delights of Terror: An Aesthetics of the Tale of Terror*. Urbana: University of Illinois Press, 1987.

Joshi, S. T. *The Weird Tale*. Austin: University of Texas Press, 1990.

Lovecraft, H. P. *The Annotated Supernatural Horror in Literature*. 1927. Edited by S. T. Joshi. New York: Hippocampus Press, 2000.

Moskowitz, Sam. *Under the Moons of Mars: A History and Anthology of "The Scientific Romance" in the Munsey Magazines, 1912–1920*. New York: Holt, Rinehart and Winston, 1970.

Moskowitz, Sam. "W. C. Morrow: Forgotten Master of Horror—First Phase." In *Discovering Classic Horror Fiction I,* edited by Darrell Schweitzer, pp. 127–173. Mercer Island, Wash.: Starmont House, 1992.

Penzoldt, Peter. *The Supernatural in Fiction.* London: Peter Nevill, 1952.

Ringel, Faye. *New England's Gothic Literature: History and Folklore of the Supernatural from the Seventeenth through the Twentieth Centuries.* Lewiston, N.Y.: Edwin Mellen Press, 1995.

Robillard, Douglas, ed. *American Supernatural Fiction: From Edith Wharton to the Weird Tales Writers.* New York: Garland, 1996.

Todorov, Tzvetan. *The Fantastic: A Structural Approach to a Literary Genre.* Translated by Richard Howard. Cleveland: Press of Case Western Reserve University, 1973. Translation of *Introduction à la littérature fantastique* (1970).

Weinstein, Lee. "'The Yellow Wallpaper': A Supernatural Interpretation." *Studies in Weird Fiction* 4 (fall 1988): 23–25.

Wilson, Edmund. "The Ambiguity of Henry James." *Hound and Horn* 7 (1934): 385–406. Reprinted in Wilson's *The Triple Thinkers.* New York: Oxford University Press, 1938.

S. T. Joshi